MANTEGNA

Frontispiece. Bronze head of Andrea Mantegna. Mantua, Sant'Andrea (Cat. no. 62)

MANTEGNA

WITH A COMPLETE CATALOGUE OF
THE PAINTINGS, DRAWINGS
AND PRINTS

RONALD LIGHTBOWN

PHAIDON · CHRISTIE'S
OXFORD

Phaidon · Christie's Limited, Littlegate House, St Ebbe's Street, Oxford OX1 1SQ

First published 1986
© Phaidon · Christie's Limited 1986

British Library Cataloguing in Publication Data

Lightbown, R. W.
Mantegna: with a complete catalogue of the paintings, drawings and prints.
1. Mantegna, Andrea
I. Title   II. Mantegna, Andrea
759.5   ND623.M3

ISBN 0-7148-8031-7 ✓

Typeset in Bembo (270) and
printed in Great Britain by BAS Printers Limited, Over Wallop, Hampshire

PUBLISHED WITH THE ASSISTANCE OF

THE J. PAUL GETTY TRUST

Contents

Acknowledgements

The Publishers have endeavoured to credit all known persons holding copyright or reproduction rights for this book, and wish to thank all the public, private and commercial owners and institutions concerned, and the photographers and photographic archives, especially Gordon Roberton of A. C. Cooper Ltd, London, Alinari (Florence), Giovetti (Mantua) and the Soprintendenze per i Beni Artistici e Storici of Bologna, Ferrara, Forlì and Ravenna; Brescia, Cremona and Mantua; Milan; Modena and Reggio Emilia; Naples; Piemonte; Venice; and the Soprintendenze alle Gallerie of Florence and Pistoia.

(References are to Plate numbers.) IV, 46, 100, 191, 250 (Gemäldegalerie), 221, 226 (Kupferstichkabinett): Staatliche Museen Preussischer Kulturbesitz, Berlin (West); 188: Courtesy, Museum of Fine Arts, Boston. Purchased, George Nixon Black Fund; 213: Courtesy of the Fogg Art Museum, Harvard University, Gift – Mrs Jesse I. Straus in memory of her husband; 219: The Trustees of the Chatsworth Settlement; 225: The Art Institute of Chicago, Ryerson Collection; 140: The Cincinnati Art Museum, Bequest of Mrs Mary M. Emery; 184: Photo courtesy Rheinisches Bildarchiv, Cologne; Fig. 14 and Plate 132: Staatliche Kunstsammlungen Dresden, Gemäldegalerie Alte Meister; 141: Courtesy of the National Gallery of Ireland; Frontispiece, Figs. 1, 2, 3, 6, 10, 15, 17, and Plates 4, 5, 6, 9–20, 22–6, 28, 30–2, 36, 37, 39, 40, 51, 55–62, 75, 87, 88, 91–5, 98, 121, 134, 156a, 175, 198, 248: Archivi Alinari, Florence; I, V, VI, VII, X, XII, XIII, XIV, XV: Scala, Florence; 253a and b: Photos Christian Jungwirth; 205, 208, 215, 216, 217 (Photo courtesy Sotheby's), 218, 222–4, 227b, 228b, 230–6a, 237, 238a–47: Reproduced by Courtesy of the Trustees of the British Museum; XVI, 206, 207: Photos courtesy Christie's; 125: Photo courtesy Colnaghi; 209a and b (Princes Gate Collection), 254 (Seilern Collection); Courtauld Institute Galleries; 109, 118: Photos courtesy Harvey Miller Publishers (from Andrew Martindale,

Mantegna's Triumphs of Caesar, 1979); Front of jacket, II, Fig. 13 and Plates 122, 137, 139, 144–6, 179–81: Reproduced by courtesy of the Trustees, The National Gallery, London; Figs. 9, 12, and Plates 34, 101–18: Reproduced by gracious permission of Her Majesty The Queen; 165: reproduced by permission of the Trustees of the Wallace Collection; 66, 76–84b, 86, 89, 90, 149–54, 158, 160–4: Studio Fotografico Giovetti; Mantua; 142, 143: The Montreal Museum of Fine Arts, Purchase, John W. Tempest bequest; Fig. 4, and Plates 33 (Anonymous Gift, 1932), 174, 183, 195, 228a (Rogers Fund, 1921), 229 (Harry Brisbane Dick Fund, 1929): (c) 1986 by The Metropolitan Museum of Art; 255: Photo courtesy Jacob M. Heimann Gallery, New York; 176: The Governing Body, Christ Church, Oxford; 257: Photo courtesy the Ashmolean Museum, Oxford; 136, 138, 194: Photos courtesy Bulloz, Paris; III, VIII, 38, 41: Photo Lauros-Giraudon, Paris; XI, 167: Cliché des Musées Nationaux, Paris; 200: Photo courtesy of San Diego Museum of Art; 192: Samuel H. Kress Collection, Philbrook Art Center, Tulsa; 190, 249: Photos courtesy Osvaldo Böhm, Venezia; Fig. 16 (Aus dem Bildarchiv d. Öst. National-bibliothek), 119, 227a: Graphische Sammlung Albertina, Wien; 99, 186, 197 and 204 (all Samuel H. Kress Collection), 120 and 182 (Widener Collection), 193 (Mellon Collection): National Gallery of Art, Washington.

DEDICATION

TO †FATHER, TO †GEOFFREY
AND
TO MOTHER, TO MARY AND TO MARK

Preface

THAT this book has been eleven years in the making is a testimony not merely to the limited amount of time at the author's disposal but to the difficulty and complexity of the subject. Mantegna, though one of the most powerful artists of the Italian Renaissance, has suffered from the bias among art historians of the last eighty years towards Florence, the great powerhouse of stylistic and technical innovations of the fifteenth century. His world, whose artistic capital was Venice, and whose leading patrons were great patricians and territorial princes, has been far less thoroughly explored, perhaps because its partial dependence on influences from Florence has made it seem secondary, perhaps too because the sixteenth century, the great age of Venetian painting, has overshadowed its predecessor, less magnificent certainly but more various and surprising, as being a century of endings and beginnings. In the fifteenth century humanism in the Veneto and the surrounding principalities was still a personal culture, the possession of a minority of great lawyers, great nobles, great ecclesiastics and great princes, whose interest in antiquity and humanistic studies, indeed in studies and arts of all kinds, found one of its most important manifestations in collecting. Such men made their collections, however, not solely for the sake of accumulating fine or rare works of art and antiquities. Their desire was to enter into physical possession of the relics of the classical past in order to restore its atmosphere and to penetrate into its spirit and into its life.

During the same years the new modern style of Florence, at once scientific and humanistic, was eagerly adapted by certain artists in Padua and Venice to their own tastes and preferences. Such artists, like humanist men of letters, tended to be drawn into the orbit of the great humanist patrons and collectors. Yet the art of Giotto and his followers and of International Gothic, which had produced works of such power and refinement in fourteenth-century Verona and Padua, though now in decline, still underlay the new humanistic style, suffusing it with its plastic strength, its richness and vivacity of pictorial invention and detail, its mastery of colour and its interest in naturalistic illusion. The art into which these old and new traditions fused was not so intellectual an art as that of Florence, and was therefore not so much interested in closeness of narrative or iconographical exposition, as in vividness, immediacy and magnificence of illusion. The florid decorative forms of late Gothic long continued to find acceptance, and influenced the richer, more fantastic taste in architectural and ornamental forms which prevailed in Northern Italy during the early Renaissance. And in Venice itself there is sometimes perceptible a lingering Byzantine influence, difficult to demonstrate stylistically but none the less subtly present.

The present book attempts to set Mantegna in the context of this world and to explore the nature of the potent art that he evolved under the stimulus of its influences. Because of the relative liberty of fancy artists allowed themselves in Venice and North Italy, the interplay of patron's instructions and artist's independence is more than usually complex and fascinating in Mantegna's art, ebbing and flowing between the poles of exact exposition as demanded by Isabella d'Este and by those patrons who supplied him with a drawing, and of relative freedom of illustration and anecdote as permitted by others who were less preoccupied with the precise representation of a favourite ideal or of a favourite devotional image. The attempt to penetrate behind the powerful and assured surface of Mantegna's art in order to understand those shifting constraints and freedoms has always been taxing, but always stimulating to the author.

Besides these tasks the book endeavours to provide a *mise au point* of the literature of Mantegna. The three fundamental books on the artist are those of Kristeller (1901, 1902), Fiocco (1937) and E. Tietze-Conrat (1955). Only the last contains a catalogue. Many documents concerning Mantegna – more perhaps than for almost all his contemporaries – were already known by 1902, and others have been discovered since. In addition, special monographs have been published on certain of Mantegna's works, notably Puppi's book on the altarpiece of San Zeno (1977) and Martindale's book on the *Triumphs* (1979), while the inexorable flow of studies in the form of periodical articles threatens to overwhelm the student in the near future. Among more recent scholars I would like to single out the names of Erice Rigoni, Clifford M. Brown, Andrew Martindale, Giovanni Paccagnini, Lionello Puppi and Rodolfo Signorini in recognition of the help I have received from their researches. Of long-dead scholars it would ill become me not to pay tribute to Alessandro Luzio and Rodolfo Renier, who documented and studied the whole cultural world of late fifteenth- and early sixteenth-century Mantua with unequalled precision and intelligence. Their work is far from having exhausted its suggestiveness. Other scholarly studies are acknowledged in the text, catalogue and bibliography.

I am deeply grateful also to all those who have given me actual assistance during the compilation of this book. I wish in particular to thank Allan Braham and Alistair Smith of the National Gallery, London, for many kindnesses. Alistair Smith allowed me to profit from his observations concerning the *Cybele*, and gave me special opportunities for studying it, as well as arranging for tests to be carried out on three other paintings. In Berlin I was given help and information by Dr Erich Schleier, who was all that was kind and helpful. In Mantua I wish to acknowledge with much gratitude the help and courtesy of Professoressa Ilaria Toesca, until recently Sopraintendente for the city, and the cordial assistance of Professore Rodolfo Signorini, who not only allowed

me to profit in discussion from his long study of the Camera Picta, but kindly revised with me *in situ* my description of that marvellous but far from uncomplicated work. We did not find ourselves in entire agreement over certain questions, but this in no way affected the spontaneous generosity of Dr Signorini's communications. In Padua I would like to thank our old friends Professoressa Rachel Toulmin-Meoli and her husband Professore Umberto Meoli. In Florence I received as always much kind help from other dear friends, notably Dr Marco and Signora Françoise Chiarini. In Paris I was assisted by M. Pierre Rosenberg of the Louvre and allowed full access to the Louvre's records. I would also like to thank the staff of the Musée de Tours, of the Musée Jacquemart-André and of the Statens Museum for Kunst, Copenhagen, Natalie Rothstein of the Victoria and Albert Museum and Peter James of the Natural History Museum (Botany) for help in connection with my research. In America I would like to thank my friend Millard Rogers, Director of the Cincinnati Art Museum. I would also like to thank Professor Peter Corbett, Claude Blair FSA, and Dr D. Chambers of the Warburg Institute for help and information.

On the editorial side my first thanks must go to Diana Davies, for her patience, critical insight and vigilance, and for the enthusiasm with which she worked on the book. I would also like to thank Margaret Fraser, its designer, Peg Katritzky, Phaidon's picture researcher, and Marie Leahy, editor at Phaidon. The book was first commissioned by the late Keith Roberts, and after his premature death was taken over by Simon Haviland. I wish to thank Phaidon for their support, and to thank also the University of California Press for associating itself with the project. The two readers who so warmly endorsed it for the University Press deserve my best thanks for their comprehension of the book and its aims. Barbara Cole typed the manuscript with unfailing care and interest and I would like to express my very true gratitude to her for her patience and efficiency. My final thanks must take the form of an expression of great gratitude to the Trustees of the Getty Foundation, who made a most generous grant towards the costs of publication.

MANTEGNA

I

Mantegna and Squarcione

ANDREA Mantegna was born late in 1430 or in 1431. Most probably his birthplace was Isola di Cartura, a village a few miles north of Padua, in the *contado* of Vicenza.[1] Here his father Maestro Biagio had his family home and Andrea's elder brother Tommaso was born. By trade Maestro Biagio, who died late in 1449 or early in 1450, when Andrea was 18 or 19, was a master-carpenter (*marangone*). The family, said by Vasari to have been of 'very humble stock', belonged to the class of small craftsmen, of little means and less social standing, which occupied a precarious position above the lowest class of all, that of journeymen and peasant labourers. As a little boy Mantegna herded cattle in the flat fields around the village, and Vasari cites the story of his life as a proof that genius, if it is to succeed, requires both recognition and reward. These Mantegna was to win while still in earliest youth, and his art was to raise him from poverty and obscurity to fame, nobility and riches.

Andrea may have owed the first change in his fortunes to his elder brother. By 1446 Maestro Tommaso had been settled for some years in nearby Padua in his trade as a tailor, and was doing well enough to make investments in cattle and land, to which in 1449 and 1452 he added leases of property in his native village. He had a house in the contrada di Santa Lucia, a quarter in the heart of Padua, north of the Piazza della Frutta, where some years later Andrea himself was also to have a house.[2] Accordingly it was perhaps Tommaso who in 1441 or early in 1442 arranged for his brother to be apprenticed[3] to the painter Francesco Squarcione (1394 or 1397–1468), who had himself begun life as a tailor and embroiderer.[4] There is however another possibility about the origin of this apprenticeship.

Among Squarcione's steadiest patrons were the De Lazara family of Padua. In 1437 the Bishop of Vicenza, who was the feudal lord of Isola di Cartura, invested Leone di Francesco de Lazara with the fief of the village.[5] It was Leone, in his day an eminent jurisconsult, for whom Squarcione painted the altarpiece which is one of the two surviving pictures that are securely associated with his workshop. Perhaps then it was through Leone that the boy Andrea was brought into Squarcione's shop. Squarcione not only took him as an apprentice, he adopted him as a son. The practice of adoption, despite what is sometimes alleged to the contrary, was far from being unique to Squarcione, for it is found among both earlier and contemporary painters in Padua. The statutes of the Paduan *fraglia* or guild of painters, which Squarcione himself had helped to reframe in 1441, perhaps explain it, for they excused the son of a master in the guild from payment of its full dues.[6]

Ambiguity and controversy have long involved the figure of Francesco Squarcione. But the problem of the part he and his famous school played in the development of the Renaissance style in painting in the Veneto has to be affronted if we are to understand Mantegna's formative years as an artist. Essentially the scholarly dispute over Squarcione proceeds from the discrepancy between the eminent position he assigned to himself as a teacher and founder of a school of painters and the very moderate accomplishment of the two documented works associable with his shop, one already mentioned, the Lazara altarpiece, painted between January 1449 and May 1452, the other, a signed *Madonna*, also with a provenance from the Lazara family.[7] The problem is perhaps an artificial one, because it moves from the false assumption that only an excellent artist can be an excellent teacher of art. In fact there have been artists, like Giles Hussey in eighteenth-century England, whose importance as the institutors of a new generation of artists was lauded by their contemporaries far beyond any significance that posterity can attach either to the bulk or to the quality of their work.

Nevertheless, the problem is not so easily resolved as this first analysis might suggest, for Squarcione's pretensions as a teacher were called seriously into question by one at least of his pupils, and his motives in taking pupils at all were attacked as crooked and self-interested by more than one. He was accused of deceit in the very last transaction in which we know him to have been engaged: the extraction of a promise from the painter Pietro Calzetta to pay him a cut of three ducats in return for an undertaking to hand over to Pietro, or else get for him, the commission to paint two marriage coffers for the wedding of the daughter of the Paduan nobleman Arcoano Buzzacarini. The money was never paid, and was claimed by Squarcione's heirs after his death: the dispute was taken to court and from the conflicting statements of the witnesses it would appear that Buzzacarini had indeed wanted to order the coffers from Squarcione, but that his intended son-in-law would have none of him, preferring the work of Calzetta. Accordingly Calzetta obtained the commission directly from Buzzacarini, and refused to pay Squarcione any commission on the price of the coffers when asked for it, claiming that Squarcione had deceived him.[8] A real difficulty is that all our information of this kind comes from documents arising from disputes taken to legal arbitration or judgement, and these are justly open to suspicion as partisan statements or exaggerations. Nevertheless, there are grounds for looking on Squarcione as in some respects sly and dubious and not scrupling to overreach if tempted by his own interest or pressed for money.

Such a judgement, even so, is not a ground for concluding that in his profession as a teacher Squarcione was nothing but a confidence trickster, as Giuseppe Fiocco was inclined to proclaim him. The question is whether his own claims, as recorded in a *libellus* or little book of *ricordi* in which according to a contemporary custom he apparently noted the salient events in his own life, ought to be accepted at face value, or abated. The *libellus* itself has long been lost, but fortunately it was used by Bernardino Scardeone (c.1478–1574) for the biography of Squarcione he wrote in his great Latin history of Padua, the *Historiae de urbis patavinae antiquitate et claris civibus patavinis*, published in 1560.[9] Scardeone transfused passages from Squarcione's *libellus* into his biography, and in the view of critics of Squarcione, also transfused that artist's own too favourable image of himself. A dispassionate reading of Scardeone's text suggests that this is unjust to him, since he manifestly shows some detachment towards Squarcione. For his account of him, moreover, he drew on at least one other important Paduan source, which he also used for his biography of Mantegna. It can be shown that this was another lost document, a Latin letter on the arts and artists of Padua written by Girolamo Campagnola (1433/5–1522) to the philosopher Niccolò Leonico Tomeo (d. 1531), probably at some date after 1497, when Leonico began teaching at the university of Padua.[10] Campagnola must be regarded as a primary witness. He knew both Squarcione and Mantegna in Padua, and maintained his youthful friendship with Mantegna long after Andrea had removed to Mantua, for in 1497 Mantegna was urgent in persuading Girolamo to allow his son Giulio, then a brilliant and gifted youth of 15, to enter the household of the Marquis of Mantua.[11]

Campagnola's letter was also used by Vasari in the revised life of Mantegna he published in the second edition of his *Vite* in 1568. Comparison of Vasari's text with Scardeone's establishes what is common to both and therefore derived from Campagnola. According to Campagnola, as rendered by Vasari, Squarcione was certainly not the best painter in the world.[12] Scardeone, less eager to dim the glory of a fellow-citizen, cautiously describes him as 'a man assuredly of the greatest judgement in his art, but, so it is said, of not much exercise in it (*exercitii*)'. For this reason, Scardeone implies, he devoted himself to teaching his art: 'He was not content to be alone in knowing it, but being full of humanity, he delighted in teaching the art in which he was skilled to a future generation and in teaching as many pupils as possible, so much so, that as he asserts of himself in a certain little book (*libellus*), he had in all from different cities one hundred and thirty-seven pupils.'

Before making any assessment of the worth of the titles *pictorum pater* (father of painters) and 'singular prime schoolmaster [*gymnasiarcha*] of all the painters of his time' which Squarcione earned from Scardeone by these activities as a teacher, let us consider what other literary and documentary evidence has to tell us about his life and his school. The son of Giovanni, a notary formerly in the service of the Da Carrara lords of Padua, he first worked as a tailor and embroiderer, probably because the uncle who became his guardian on his father's death in 1414 was a tailor. In 1418 he married and went to live with his wife in her parents' house in the contrada di Pontecorvo, a street near the great pilgrimage church of the Santo, which for this reason was also known as the bersaglio di Sant'Antonio. Here he had his home and *bottega* for the rest of his life, though from time to time he also leased a house in Venice. He was still making embroideries in 1423, and our first known record of him as a painter dates from 6 April

Fig. 1. Self-portrait head. Detail from *The Trial of St James* (Plate 13)

1426, when he contracted to paint an altarpiece for the new chapel of St John Baptist in the church of the Olivetan monastery of San Giovanni Battista at Venda, south of Padua.[13] By his own account, transmitted through Scardeone,

> from boyhood he had taken the greatest delight in the study of painting, and shortly (as he writes of himself), on emerging from adolescence and being able from his age to live for himself after his own fashion, he determined to see the world and travel to distant cities and through different peoples and nations. Wherefore he sailed to Greece and wandered all over that country, whence he brought home with him, both in his mind and in drawings, many things worthy of note that seemed likely to promote skill in his art. He journeyed in similar fashion all over Italy and won the friendship of many noblemen by his affability and virtuous disposition.

The likeliest date for these journeys falls between the summer of 1426 and August 1428, when there is a gap in the known documents concerning his activities in Padua: indeed 1427 is perhaps the most probable date of all. By Greece of course neither Squarcione nor Scardeone necessarily meant exclusively the country we know as Greece, for Greece in the fifteenth century could also mean the empire of Byzantium, and Squarcione may well have visited Constantinople, where Venice and its merchants were so powerful.

On his return to Padua he discovered a vocation to teach the art of painting. He was already taking pupils early in 1431, when he contracted to take a certain Michele di Bartolommeo da Vicenza into his workshop. Significantly the contract stipulates that he is to allow Michele 'opportunity to study his *exempla*', by which were surely meant drawings collected to serve as models.[14] The collecting of drawings by various hands, including those of his pupils, is one of Squarcione's few securely documented activities. From very early days he must have set about accumulating a stock of them, not only for his own benefit, but in order to attract pupils to his workshop. Some may have been the drawings that he had made on his travels in Greece and Italy; others he procured, if not in the 1430s, then certainly at a later date, from Florence and no doubt elsewhere. Vasari tells us that to drawings he added, now or in the years following, sculptures, either originals or plaster casts, and paintings, likewise by other hands than his own. Scardeone lays stress on the importance of this collection for his pupils, among them Mantegna. He taught 'from the statues and very many paintings he had, by whose mastery and art he instructed Andrea and the rest of his fellow-pupils, rather than from originals (*archetypae*) he had

executed himself or worked up or from new models (*exempla*) provided for copying.' Although Squarcione's practice of taking plaster casts has been doubted, it is confirmed beyond doubt by documents of 1455 concerning the apprenticeship of Marco Zoppo. These declare categorically that Zoppo brought from Bologna and handed over to Squarcione as part of the price of his tuition in the art of painting a quantity of plaster 'for shaping to figures and images'.[15] We can therefore believe what Vasari reports, no doubt on the authority of Campagnola, that Squarcione had plaster casts 'formed from ancient statues'.

The search for drawings by other artists to serve as models and aids to invention is a well-attested practice among late fifteenth-century artists and in this respect Squarcione's collection was not remarkable. It is only the general lack of early records about collecting among artists that has caused some scholars to marvel at what appears, but only appears, to be an exceptional case. What seems to have been truly unique to Squarcione, at any rate in North Italy, was the systematic use of this material for instruction in painting, for '*pictorie studium*' to use the expression of the physician and humanist Michele Savonarola in his *Libellus de magnificis ornamentis regie civitatis Padue*, a panegyrical description of his native Padua which he wrote during the later 1440s.[16] This expression pays to painting, though not to its representative Squarcione, about whom Savonarola is silent, the compliment of ranking it not too far below the liberal arts and the studies of law and medicine.

Squarcione was at first content to retain the old name of *bottega* for his workshop, but by 1455 he was dignifying the rooms in which his collections and 'things pertaining to painting' were housed with the title of *studium*, or place for study, a name that clearly indicates a change of emphasis from workshop to school. By 1440 his first *studium*, though large, was no longer big enough for his purpose, and he bought the adjoining house, made it into one with his own and formed a second small *studium* in it. This extension cannot have been forced on him by pressure of commissions and must have been the consequence of his success as a teacher. That he made it to accommodate an expansion of his teaching collection seems to be confirmed by the inventory of the contents of his house taken on 24 May 1455. This tells us that it contained a large *studium* 'with reliefs, drawings and other things within it', and a second small one 'in the house called the house of reliefs'.

The inventory also speaks of 'all the things' within the two *studia* 'pertaining to the art of painting and the paintings within them that are not described here'.[17] The reference to paintings supports the testimony of Vasari, undoubtedly derived from

Campagnola, that Squarcione obtained paintings on canvas 'from different places, and especially from Tuscany and Rome'. There was also a taste in quattrocento Italy for collecting Byzantine icons, in none more eager than in Squarcione's contemporary, the Venetian Cardinal Pietro Barbo, later Pope Paul II, who sought for 'Greek' icons with especial avidity. Squarcione seems to have shared this taste, for an icon signed by Emanuel Zarfenari, now in the Vatican, was believed in the early eighteenth century to have belonged to Squarcione.[18]

His collection of drawings and paintings bulked large in the eyes of Squarcione's pupils. The stipulation of 1431 that Squarcione should 'show his drawings' reappears in the contract he made with Dario da Treviso on 25 August 1440 and in ever more detailed form in two other contracts of 1455 and 1467.[19] That of 1467 stipulates that the pupil shall be allowed to copy figures from Squarcione's stock of drawings, touching them in *biacca* (white lead) on a copy sheet (*carta d'esempio*). We have a little information about some of these drawings. In 1466 Pietro Calzetta agreed to paint an altarpiece for a chapel founded by Bernardo de Lazara in the Santo; its subject was 'to be like the sketch on this leaf which is copied from a drawing belonging to Maestro Francesco Squarzon which was done by the hand of Niccolò Pizzolo.' Again in 1474 Squarcione's son Bernardino reclaimed by process of law along with eighteen other drawings 'a cartoon with certain nudes by Pollaiuolo'.[20] The value of Squarcione's collection in the eyes of his pupils is attested not only by their contracts of apprenticeship, but by that form of practical admiration which made some of them carry off or borrow drawings from his house, so that steps had later to be taken to compel them to restore them.

Squarcione then was the master of the earliest known private art-school, a form of instruction which as academy or artist's studio was to have a long and flourishing life into modern times. Possibly he had a natural bent for education, but if so, it was reinforced by the lack of customers for his pictures. In spite of the claims of Paduan local patriotism, it is plain from the history of painting in fourteenth- and fifteenth-century Padua, as indeed of sculpture also, that there had long been a deficiency of local talent in the arts. From the days of Giotto almost every commission of more than ordinary size and importance had been awarded to an artist from outside Padua. When Michele Savonarola came to extol the glorious achievements of the Paduan school of painting, four of the six artists he lauds were confessedly from outside the city. For him the modern style and with it the greatness of the art in Padua began with Giotto, 'the first who departed from figures in the ancient style and in mosaic and shaped modern figures in marvellous wise.' Second to Giotto he puts Jacopo Avanzo of Bologna (working *c*.1380), awarding third place to Altichiero of Verona (working *c*.1369–84) and fourth to Stefano da Ferrara (working *c*.1349–70). As native glories of Padua he cites Guariento (working *c*.1338–68), who does indeed seem to have been born there, and Giusto de' Menabuoi (working *c*.1349–97), who as a Florentine was a Paduan only by adoption.[21] With the exception then of Guariento all the painters who executed major works in trecento Padua came from elsewhere.

The story is no different in the early quattrocento, except that as knowledge of the new Renaissance style spread from Florence, the painters summoned to Padua were for some two decades Florentine. They were usually called to the city from Venice. One of the most important of Early Renaissance Florentine painters, Paolo Uccello, was in Venice from 1425 to 1431, and later, so Vasari says, was brought by Donatello to Padua. Here he painted a fresco of gigantic figures in chiaroscuro in the entrance of the Casa de' Vitaliani, a work long lost but which according to Campagnola was greatly admired by Mantegna. This visit of Uccello to Padua is usually dated to 1445.[22] It is often suggested that the influence of the Casa de' Vitaliani giants can be seen in the gigantic head, generally identified as a self-portrait, that Mantegna frescoed on the entrance of the arch opening on to the tribune of the Ovetari Chapel, opposite a similar head by his partner and fellow-disciple of Squarcione, Niccolò Pizzolo (Plates 7 and 8). Filippo Lippi was in Padua by July 1434, when he was busy decorating the *tabernacolo delle reliquie* in the Santo. On 15 October 1434 he acted with Squarcione as arbitrator in an agreement concerning an altarpiece painted for the cathedral. He also painted a fresco of the *Coronation of the Virgin* on a pier of the nave of the Santo and other paintings in the Cappella del Podestà. Lippi's influence is clearly perceptible in Squarcione's Berlin *Madonna* in the suppleness of form and pose in the Child, and it seems fair to assume that the Paduan teacher admired and imitated him.[23]

What is known of the *fraglia* or guild of painters in Padua *c*.1440 and even later leaves an impression of a body as modest in its ambitions as in its membership. From its resuscitation of 1441, in which Squarcione played a part, we have statutes and lists of admissions which give some picture of its activities over the next two decades, and the evidence besides of disputes brought to law. These documents show that the standard domestic commission to Paduan painters of all ranks was for the pair of coffers and a picture (*ancona*), surely a Madonna, which formed part of the customary baggage of a bride on her marriage and were paid for by her father. The members of the *fraglia* included a certain number of painters of such coffers and of the sort of decorative work that was scornfully dismissed by the youthful Niccolò Pizzolo in 1449 as *laboreria grossa*.[24] Part of the custom of masters of standing was also made up of orders to paint coffers, woodwork and rooms: this was a matter of course in the fifteenth century. The difference was that such masters could also execute fine work as well. In Padua business was slack in winter: 'it is true', testified Andrea di Natale in 1449, 'that masters of painting get only a little profit in winter over and above their expenses, indeed almost nothing on account of the adverse season.'[25]

Squarcione's school must have stood out in this sluggish, provincial milieu. It was the first studio to develop away from the old tradition of workshop instruction in that its master professed to offer his pupils more than practical tuition in his own techniques and manner. It has been suggested that he was following the practice of Gasperino Barzizza (*c.* 1360–1431), whose private school in Padua, opened from the years 1407 to 1421, was the first in which boys and instructors were assembled in the house of their master and lived as part of his household, giving an example that was to be copied by all the great humanist educators of fifteenth-century Italy.[26] Naturally enough Squarcione's school, which was probably not founded on any system other than that of attracting pupils, retained many of the characteristics of the old *bottega*, both in the custom of formal apprenticeship and in the relations obtaining between master and apprentice-pupil. In these matters Squarcione was bound by the statutes of the *fraglia*. Indeed to Squarcione his pupils were in some respects always a *bottega*, for in 1443, having enlarged his premises by the addition of the adjoining house, he declared to the authorities that he lived in these dwellings 'with my family and *botega*'.

Naturally too he made varying conventions with prospective pupils according to their age, knowledge, skill and usefulness. Thus some were to be maintained by him, but paid no salary; some paid him for their maintenance and instruction, while to others he gave both maintenance and a salary. When his pupils became skilled, or if they were already skilled, he recompensed himself for the expenses of their keep and instruction by selling the paintings they executed for him in his workshop. In judging the ethics of this practice two things have to be remembered: first that Squarcione, though a teacher, made his living as a working painter, and second that in the economy of the fifteenth century, which was not a fully developed money economy, payments in kind or by labour were customary, indeed they were the underlying assumption of the system of apprenticeship. On the other hand such an arrangement might well lead to abuse; it left much to desire from its vagueness and looseness, and the different valuations that could be set by master and pupil on work done by the pupil and on the master's tuition easily gave rise to disputes and quarrels. Undoubtedly a number of Squarcione's pupils, among them Mantegna, felt that they had flagrantly overpaid their master by their paintings for their keep and tuition.

This resentfulness at what they considered unjust exploitation was no doubt strongest among the young men of talent and those who were already trained artists and had only entered Squarcione's workshop in order to learn his much-vaunted new 'foundation and technique' in the art. Some of his pupils had recourse to law to recover what they felt was due to them, and in some of these cases, among them those brought by Mantegna and Marco Zoppo, the court found in their favour, confirming the charges of unscrupulousness and fraud they had levelled against their master. In itself Squarcione's practice was not out of keeping with fifteenth-century workshop custom, in which the work of the apprentice passed for that of the master or at least for that of his shop. But it does singularly complicate the question of attributions to his hand and probably explains, for example, the discrepancies of style so often pointed out between the Lazara altarpiece and the Berlin *Madonna*. Moreover, as we have seen, and will see again in the case of the Ovetari Chapel, on occasions Squarcione seems to have acted as an agent, receiving a commission from a patron and then sharing it out or handing it over entirely in return for a cut on the price.

At least one of his pupils, Maestro Agnolo di Maestro Silvestro, after spending, it must be said, only three or four months in Squarcione's workshop, claimed in 1465 that Squarcione was not even qualified to teach his pupils the lessons of which he made such a vaunt.

> It is ever his custom that he ever seeks to delude them with his promises, boasting about things he does not have and about knowledge he does not have and he promises people to do things for them until such time as he has worn them out and squeezed all the juice out of them and then picks a quarrel with them . . . This is what he is now trying to do with Maestro Agnolo: he gave him to understand that he would teach him the true method of perspective and of all other things pertaining to the painter's craft, telling the said Agnolo: 'It was I who made a man of Andrea Mantegna, who worked for me and I will do the same with you.' Agnolo, knowing Mantegna's great fame and believing the said Francesco's words, was content to agree with him and has been with him for some time and with his own

hands has made many things which the said Francesco has converted to his own profit and never has taught or showed him anything, indeed he knows not how, either by his own work or by any words of explanation to do the things he promised the said Agnolo.[27]

By 1465 Squarcione was approaching seventy, and from other documents of that year we know that he was hard pressed for money, had lost much of his custom to Pietro Calzetta and could no longer paint because of failing sight. Without justifying his enticement of Maestro Agnolo into his shop when he was probably no longer able to teach him much, it seems fair to set against these complaints of a disappointed pupil the undoubted reputation of Squarcione and his school in its heyday. He was summoned to the presence of the Emperor Frederick III during his visit to Padua in 1452, an honour he would hardly have received if his school had not been something of a show-place and an object of civic pride in Padua. Among his friends he numbered both a Patriarch of Aquileia, perhaps the very Cardinal Lodovico Trevisan whose portrait was to be painted by Mantegna in 1459 and who was an ardent collector of ancient gems and medals, and San Bernardino of Siena, the most venerated popular preacher of the day, who gave him spiritual counsel during his sojourn in Padua in April 1443. And a singular testimony to his reputation outside Padua is the fact that among the very few paintings by North Italian artists owned by Lorenzo de' Medici was a painting by Squarcione of 'the head of St Sebastian and other figures'. Framed in a tabernacle, it bore the Medici arms and so may have been a direct commission from Piero or Cosimo de' Medici. Lorenzo thought well enough of it to hang it in his principal ground-floor chamber, decorated with rich paintings by Uccello, Pesellino, Fra Angelico and Piero del Pollaiuolo.[28]

Yet more eloquent of Squarcione's reputation as a teacher is the emphasis with which some of his most successful students proclaimed that they had been his pupils. This is true of Giorgio Schiavone, and also of Marco Zoppo and Mantegna, in spite of their quarrels and lawsuits with him. But even if we exclude his ambiguous financial dealings with his pupils, there were other complexities in his behaviour towards them. For many years, until c.1457, he was childless, and from time to time he would take a pupil and adopt him, as happened with Mantegna, and even make him his heir, as happened with Marco Zoppo. Although frustrated paternity and pedagogic pride may have been powerful motives in these acts of adoption, Squarcione has also been suspected of resorting to them in order to avoid paying his pupils their just dues. Yet we perhaps attach an over-great significance to the legal forms in which

the impulsive and litigious fifteenth century liked to embody its disputes. Mantegna himself after falling out with Squarcione in 1447 and quitting his house could still be called Andrea Squarcione in Paduan notarial documents of 9 January 1454, even though other documents show that he had reverted to his own name. More significantly he called himself Andrea Squarcione in Mantua in 1459 and in 1466 in Tuscany, and he was known by this name to the Florentine architect Filarete.[29] In other words, he used the name Squarcione in places and at times when neither custom nor compulsion could oblige him to use his master's name rather than his own. Indeed some eight years after parting from Squarcione, and much litigation, they were still on good enough terms for Mantegna to introduce his portrait into the *Martyrdom of St Christopher* in the Ovetari Chapel.

A real difficulty about Squarcione's school and one invariably evaded is that although we know pupils were always attracted to it because he taught the modern fashion in painting,[30] that is, what we know as the Renaissance style, all our information about the things he actually professed to teach dates from the 1460s, at a late stage in the history of his tuition. The sophisticated instruction in linear perspective and foreshortening that he undertook to give in 1467 was certainly not what he was already professing to teach in the 1430s and early 1440s. As Fiocco has emphasized, the work of his early pupil Dario da Treviso is in a Gothic manner of the most rustic kind,[31] and indeed in many of the Squarcionesques there is a contrast between the treatment of the figure, often slender and twisted with true Gothic incorporeality, and the solid robustness of the architectural setting. And the exclusive admiration that Michele Savonarola, an avowed dilettante of painting, expresses for the Giottesque and International Gothic traditions suggests that by the later 1440s Squarcione's school had as yet made no great impression stylistically. It may even have been Mantegna's precocious genius that brought to it much of its subsequent fame.

If we look at the Lazara altarpiece (Plate 248), painted as it was when Mantegna had already embarked on his own independent career, we can see that for all its International Gothic figure-style and unreal colour, it contains elements that may have influenced Mantegna, that is, if we accept those elements as original to Squarcione. These are the use of foreshortening in depth, as in St Jerome's simple rustic table, the tree used to mark a plane in the picture, the introduction of ruined classical architecture, with simulated real cracks, a wattle fence marking the foreground and the marking of the background by architecture, the pebble-strewn rocks which form the ground and the single plants growing from them, the simulated wooden shoe marking a plane before the fence, the illusionistic rings from which two classical swags depend that are used to decorate the bases on which the saints stand, the employment of contrasting poses – pure profile, three-quarter profile – to suggest movement. However, these devices are present in the Squarcione picture in embryonic form, and not in the full and majestic deployment that Mantegna will achieve.

Linear perspective, so far as is known, was discovered in Florence about 1425 by Filippo Brunelleschi.[32] He taught its principles to Masaccio, Masolino and Donatello, who began putting them into practice more or less immediately. If Squarcione made his journey to Greece and through Italy c.1427, as seems most likely, then it is always possible that he visited Florence on his travels and somehow gained an early knowledge of Brunelleschi's perspective. But the contract of 1431, with its specification of *exempla* to be shown to his pupil, suggests that what he then had to offer as an attraction were drawings by other artists and the drawings after the antique he is said to have brought back from his travels. The principles of linear perspective were first put into writing, at any rate in a formal treatise, in Leone Battista Alberti's *De pictura*, which he compiled in 1435 and 1436, both in Latin and in Italian (*Della pittura*). For all their novelty and importance they take up only a limited part of Alberti's text. It is all the more remarkable then that Michele Savonarola, writing in the later 1440s, should single out perspective as painting's principal claim to hold primacy among the mechanical arts. Painting, he says, is 'the practice of the mathematical arts', and he explains, 'To painters it is given to know the outlines of figures and the projections of lines, so that these things, in which the science of perspective [i.e. optics] glories, are demonstrated in their practice.' Elsewhere he writes, 'I hold in no small account our school (*studium*) of pictorial art, which is a singular ornament to our city, for it is connected with the study of letters and the liberal arts more than any of the other (mechanic) arts, as it is a branch of perspective, which discourses of the projection of lines, and perspective is a branch of philosophy.'[33]

So strong an emphasis on perspective is difficult to explain without a lively interest among certain Paduan artists and dilettanti in the mathematical foundations of painting. By the later 1440s the interpenetration of linear perspective and painting was already a fundamental premise of Squarcione's school, as can be seen from the roundels painted on the ceiling of the Ovetari Chapel by Niccolò Pizzolo, the young artist who was the most advanced and modern-minded of all his pupils, with the exception of Mantegna. Yet in praising the glories of the Paduan school Savonarola seems to have had in mind

not so much his own contemporaries, whom he barely mentions, as painters of the recent past. And certain devices used by the Squarcionesques as aids to perspective illusionism are not Florentine, but appear to be developments of the older illusionistic tradition of the trecento. That tradition has left few traces now visible in Padua, but one of them is the much restored fresco of Petrarch, recently attributed to Altichiero, in the Sala dei Giganti of the Palazzo Carrarese.[34] Here the poet is shown seated at his desk in his study, a room seen through a frame as if with a wall removed. The receding lines of the desk and of the book coffer set before it, drawn in the rising perspective of the trecento, lead the eye into the study with an evident attempt at full spatial illusionism in depth. In the later fourteenth and early fifteenth centuries Paduan painters were already attempting *tours-de-force* of representational illusionism in the purely decorative parts of their works, sometimes with considerable ambitiousness. In the Oratorio di San Giorgio in the Santo, frescoed by Altichiero (1377–84), we find figurations of a friar kneeling in a niche, of an arch with a wooden frame set with a grille and resting on a panel of stone inset with porphry, of a Gothic window, of an altar projecting beneath an arch. This taste for virtuosity of illusionism extended to ornament. Among the decorative motifs of Pietro Storlato's frescoes of 1436 in the chapel of St Luke in Santa Giustina, for which Mantegna was later to paint an altarpiece, are simulated panels of grey stone in moulded frames decorated in grey with Late Gothic foliage and flowers.

Florentine perspective, although it too assumes that the spectator will see the picture as through a window, assumes as well that the wooden frame enclosing the picture will define that window space. By contrast the Squarcionesques, most notably Mantegna, make heavy use of a painted architectural framework to represent an actual window space. The painted framework of the frescoes in the Ovetari Chapel, as we shall see, is all important to the definition of the pictorial space of the scenes it encloses; and it was surely for this reason that in 1449 Mantegna reserved its execution to himself.

For the Florentines perspective was a means to a unitary illusion, harmonizing all the elements of the picture, figures and setting into a natural relation. The Squarcionesques, by contrast, became so intoxicated with their newly acquired skills in perspective and foreshortening and the freedom these gave them to represent objects and figures in three-dimensional space that an ostentation of illusionism, particularly in the rendering of still-life motifs, became with them something of an end in itself. Here again can be sensed an attachment to an older tradition of trecento illusionism. That tradition was certainly well known in Padua, as can be seen from the same fresco of Petrarch in the Sala de' Giganti, where the objects that surround the scholar – books, a little desk for reading and writing, an ink-well and a coffer for books – are figured in the same spirit of precise fidelity, if with much less refinement of technique, as in the frescoes of Niccolò Pizzolo and the panel of St Luke in Mantegna's Santa Giustina altarpiece. In a miniature that copies this much-damaged fresco of Petrarch and may reproduce some of its original features we even find an open cupboard door, such as the perspective illusionists of the quattrocento still delighted to simulate in proof of their skill in trompe-l'œil.[35]

In consequence the Squarcionesques give a very different stylistic expression from the Florentines to the common aim of creating an illusion of real space.[36] Even in those of their pictures that lack a painted architectural frame, architecture and still-life motifs are used as devices to define the picture plane and the middle ground, in a manner quite uncharacteristic of Florence. Most of the paintings of the Squarcionesques that survive are Madonnas, as might be expected of a workshop of young artists, who must certainly have been called on to paint this kind of picture more than any other, given the very general demand for Madonnas. Paradoxically, Madonnas allowed the young artist of the 1440s and 1450s greater independence than more ambitious works such as altarpieces, where the patrons of Padua and Venice usually expected a work to a traditional pattern and the artist was as often as not the prisoner of an already prepared framework in the loud and florid Late Gothic style, commissioned independently from the woodworker.

In Squarcionesque Madonnas the foreground is generally a parapet, behind which the Virgin sits or stands before a throne or niche, which serves to mark off the middle ground. The background is of little importance and the figure itself, as already noted, has often a Gothic frailty that contrasts with the robust architectural forms – in a rich and sometimes fantastic Renaissance style – enclosing it. The threefold division of the planes is emphasized by certain other standard devices. Much favoured was the suspended classical swag of leaves and fruit which hangs by rings from the architectural framework, marking its relative position in space and simultaneously, by swinging forwards of it, breaking down the barrier between the real space in which the spectator stands and the artificial space of the picture and so establishing a continuum between the two. Another trick is the placing of still-life motifs so as to contribute to the illusion of naturalistic recession from the spectator – fruit is set on a parapet in the foreground: to the front of the parapet is attached a crumpled cartellino, books are shown edgeways, so that they

appear to protrude into space. Some at least of these visual sleights were known in the Veneto by 1448, for in Jacopo Bellini's Madonna in the Louvre, painted in that year, the Virgin stands behind a classical parapet with a cartellino attached to its front and a book laid upon it. It will be obvious that such devices all express a single aesthetic, that of art as an imitation of nature. And this indeed is the fundamental concept of Mantegna's art from his early youth: the imitation of the antique was shortly to be superimposed on it, but never until the last years of his life to challenge its primacy.

Three at least of the devices of the Squarcionesques are known to have made an earlier appearance elsewhere.[37] The classical parapet is first found in a portrait by Jan van Eyck which bears the date 10 October 1432.[38] In another portrait a classical moulded frame, bearing the date 21 October 1433, encloses the head and shoulders of a man in a red turban, giving the effect of looking through a window at the figure. The earliest known cartellino to survive occurs on a painting by a Florentine, the Tarquinia Madonna, painted in 1437 by Fra Filippo Lippi, an artist, as we have seen, known and admired by Squarcione. As for the classical swags which are so prominent a motif in Squarcionesque paintings, their prime source was undoubtedly antique sarcophagi. In the seventeenth century an antique sarcophagus carved with a swag of bulging fruit and suspended from ribbons and rings in just the fashion copied by the Squarcionesques was in the collection of Andrea Vendramin of Venice. The motif also appears on other monuments. A pedestal carved with heavy ribboned laurel swags, the ribbons curling with much the same decorative scrolling as in Squarcionesque paintings, was drawn in the fifteenth century for some antiquary or by some artist while it was still at Este, and copied by Jacopo Bellini into one of his books of drawings: clearly it was well known in Padua, to which place it was eventually removed.[39]

These are all motifs which, if they became standard in Venice and the Veneto, are found elsewhere in Italy. More exclusively characteristic of Squarcione and his school is the preference for strong, brilliant, at times almost metallic colour – gay and bright hues, yellows, reds, olive-greens, are their favourites. That this was a conscious preference in Squarcione is revealed by his criticism made some years later, about 1455–6, of Mantegna's Ovetari frescoes of St James, that their colours were not bright and strong enough. A liking for warm and glowing colour was a Venetian heritage from Byzantium, and the tonality of the Vivarini, the most prominent of the younger Venetian masters of Mantegna's youth, maintains this tradition. And Mantegna's own early panels, notably the altarpiece of St Luke, will show this strong metallic brightness of colour.

Besides Pollaiuolo's study of nudes, Squarcione's drawings probably included other studies from the nude, as well as essays in perspective and foreshortening and copies after the antique.[40] Some of these last no doubt were faithful, but many were surely already embellished by the artist's fancy, like those made by Jacopo Bellini in his sketchbook. It must never be forgotten that to fifteenth-century artists the evocation of antiquity was far more important than rigid archaeological accuracy. An antique motif was as often as not a stimulant to the imagination rather than a model to be copied literally, and if quoted, was quoted so as to harmonize with a larger setting. This is true even of Mantegna, for if he became a serious antiquary in his admiration for the antique, his primary artistic motive was that search for verisimilitude of effect and detail which as we shall see was also a governing canon of his landscape settings. Drawing the nude or draped figure was evidently important, whether from life, from a specially prepared model, from the antique or from other works of art, for in certain of their works the Squarcionesques made a display of their skill by showing closely similar figures in contrasted views from the front or from behind. Thus in Marco Zoppo's Wimborne *Madonna* a naked putto seen from the front is contrasted with one seen from the rear, and in Mantegna's Ovetari fresco of the *The Preaching of St James* a figure with hands raised in astounded fear is seen from behind in the left foreground in contrast with a similar figure seen from the front in the centre.

Unfortunately we do not know if Squarcione encouraged anatomical studies, though it is evident from the works of Marco Zoppo as well as of Mantegna that some were made, by certain at any rate of his pupils. In many ideal figures, such as Christ of the Pietà or child angels, the Squarcionesque conception of the human figure was from the first heavily influenced and at times overwhelmed by the classical nude, so that there is always a tension in the school between a naturalism that tempers the imitation of figures from classical art and a classicism tempering that naturalism. In a famous criticism of Mantegna's Ovetari frescoes of St James Squarcione gave the preference to nature and life, but Mantegna was to give it to classical statues. Gothic traditions of the figure also retained an influence, as we have already seen; these were more thoroughly shaken off by Mantegna than by any of the other artists trained by Squarcione or who felt his influence. The revival of the antique was such a distinguishing feature of the '*pingere in recenti*' and antique motifs are introduced with such flourishing exuberance and fantasy into the works of the

Squarcionesques that it seems foolish to question the great significance to his pupils of Squarcione's casts and drawings. Without them they would have been compelled to the great expense of time and money, which none of them could afford, required to scour the vestiges of antiquity that still survived in the countryside around Padua, at Brescia and above all at Verona, with its great amphitheatre, its triumphal arch, its Roman gateways, its sarcophagi and its sepulchral slabs.

Ancient painting was known to the Renaissance only from literary sources, first and foremost from the Elder Pliny, who alone had left a connected history of it, then from scattered descriptions and remarks in Lucian and other ancient authors. These were attentively studied, for it was assumed that ancient painting had reached the same perfection as ancient sculpture, and conscious attempts were made by Renaissance painters to realize certain effects of ancient painters that were much praised in classical authors. And Squarcione and his pupils must have found every encouragement to their own variety of illusionism in the stories recorded by Pliny of Zeuxis, whose pictures of a bunch of grapes and of a boy carrying grapes deceived the birds themselves, and of Parrhasius, whose picture of a curtain deceived Zeuxis.[41] Certainly a tradition retailed by Lomazzo in 1584 suggests that these stories were current in Squarcione's studio. He writes that 'Andrea Mantegna deceived his master with a fly painted above the eyebrow of a lion.'[42] Similarly, the effect of protrusion from the picture plane, which is found in Andrea del Castagno, Antonio Vivarini and the Squarcionesques, is lauded again and again by Pliny, notably in his accounts of Timanthes and of Apelles, that most perfect of all the painters of antiquity to the Renaissance imagination.

In Venice and Padua there was possibly an exception to the general feeling that nothing had survived of the realities of ancient painting, for it is difficult to understand why humanists such as Pietro Barbo were so eager to collect Byzantine icons unless they felt that in them there was some survival, however faint, of a lost tradition. And in the tall, slender figures favoured by Jacopo Bellini and Mantegna, there perhaps shows through the naturalistic suppleness a consciousness of Byzantine art, sprung from the same motive.

Nevertheless it remains true that the realities of antique art were familiar to the quattrocento only from the relics of classical architecture and sculpture. Sculpture was perhaps the better known, not from large-scale figures in the round but from gems, medals and sarcophagi and other sepulchral monuments, in other words, from reliefs. Squarcione had quite a number of such reliefs, largely as we saw in the form of casts, so that by 1455 one of his two houses could be called the 'domus cum relevis'. Scardeone indeed describes Squarcione's sculptures as *signa* and Vasari as *statue*, meaning figures in the round, and perhaps Squarcione also possessed some antique bronze statuettes, again either originals or casts,[43] and some lamps, perhaps too a few small marble heads and fragments. But original antique sculptures were usually too costly not to be the preserve of the great and wealthy, and there can be little doubt that in the 1440s and 1450s it was casts from sarcophagi that were most familiar to Squarcione and his pupils, if only from their constant repetition of the motifs of putti and swags. It was of course sarcophagi carved with winged geniuses and swags that had first been copied in Florence itself.

Squarcione and his pupils may also have had access to other collections in Padua made by the learned antiquaries of the city. Thus the Venetian nobleman Francesco Contarini, who settled in Padua after receiving his doctorate in laws in 1442, is known to have decorated his house there during the next ten years with antiquities and inscriptions.[44] Certainly Squarcione's own collection of medals, mentioned in 1455, would have drawn to his house men like Contarini and his friend Giovanni Marcanova, another antiquary whom we shall shortly meet in connection with the Ovetari frescoes.[45] At his death in 1467 Marcanova had a great collection of medals, 180 of silver, 21 of gold or silver-gilt, 18 in 'white metal', 20 in bronze and some others in lead. The collecting of antique medals had long been a well-established activity in Verona, Padua and Venice. Both Padua and Verona had witnessed humanist revivals at the end of the thirteenth century, and the Veronese humanist Giovanni Mansionario (d.1337) seems to have had a collection of medals assembled as illustrations of Roman history, long the *raison d'être* of such collections.[46]

Ancient medals were already influencing art in Verona as early as *c*.1364 when Altichiero decorated the *sala grande* of the Scaliger palace at Verona with a frieze of forty-four portraits of the Caesars evidently taken from antique medals.[47] The traditions of humanism were revived in Padua by Petrarch, who held a canonry there from 1350 and lived in nearby Arquà under the protection of the Da Carrara from 1369 until his death in 1374. The first known modern medals in the antique fashion were struck in Padua under the lordship of the Da Carrara: thus two were made to commemorate the recovery of Padua by Francesco II da Carrara in 1390. In Venice the Sesto family were making medals in imitation of imperial medals from 1393.[48] And indeed in Venice, always intimately linked with Padua, the collecting of antique sculptures and medals is attested from as early as the 1330s. Oliviero Forzatè, a notary and moneylender of Treviso, was

collecting medals, bronzes and antique marbles in 1335, while the inventory of the collection of Marino Falier, taken in April of the same year, includes two ancient swords, a box 'with fifty coins of marvellous antiquity' and three antique inscriptions found at Treviso. By 1433 the Florentine Ambrogio Traversari, friar and Christian humanist, was noting that many ancient medals and coins were to be found in the hands of Venetian noblemen.[49]

The Squarcionesque style ought then to be regarded as the expression of a consciousness among the young artists of north-eastern Italy that there was now a modern or, as we should say, a Renaissance style in painting. Those who were eager to learn it made their way to the school of Squarcione or to the workshop of one of Squarcione's pupils, such as Niccolò Pizzolo. In their eyes the modern manner was founded partly on perspective, partly on the antique. As regards the first, complete obscurity surrounds Squarcione's teachings on perspective in the 1440s: in particular we do not know if the principles of the new Brunelleschian perspective as codified by Alberti had come to his knowledge during the years of Mantegna's apprenticeship. It is a fact that Mantegna's first two Ovetari frescoes, painted in 1450, do not make use of Alberti's perspective, whereas the two that followed show him in full possession of its principles. As regards the influence of the antique, it should always be borne in mind that the quattrocento made no rigid distinction between the aesthetic of painting and that of sculpture, but saw the two arts as competing with each other in the simulation of nature. It was from the copying of antique sculptures that the Squarcionesques came to give their figures that firmness of volume, that clarity of contour, that smoothness of planes which were to remain constants of Mantegna's art. For Mantegna ancient sculpture, and in particular the classical relief style he had first learnt to admire in his youth, were to remain perennial ideals. To the end of his life he was to imitate or emulate in paint reliefs in marble or bronze, designing compositions of figures silhouetted against a background of neutral black or simulated marble.

Other influences also bore on Mantegna's youth, not least that of the great pictorial exemplars of the trecento in Padua – Giotto, Altichiero, and Avanzi. But their study is fraught with problems, such as those of time and place and sequence. Thus the presence of a Flemish influence is distinctly felt in his art, but can be defined only indistinctly, because we have no record of any works by Netherlandish masters that he certainly saw, and can only conjecture what he may have seen. Precedents and parallels from surviving Flemish pictures – and those that survive, it must always be recalled, are merely a small proportion of what was painted – can easily be cited for certain significant features in Mantegna's art, such as *di sotto in sù* perspective, relief sculpture simulated in monochrome, bust-length portraits painted in three-quarter profile, and a certain literalness in portraiture that does not suppress the occasional unattractive detail in the aspect of the sitter. What is not so easily demonstrated is the immediate source of such features. Even in those instances where Flemish influence is conspicuous, it is impossible to do more than make surmises about the intermediate works that transmitted it, so scanty are our records of Flemish pictures that were known in North Italy during the early Renaissance.

Accordingly it has seemed best to cite Flemish parallels strictly in connection with the works to which they are relevant. Here we can only summarize what is known of Netherlandish art and its reputation in the regions where Mantegna can reasonably be expected to have encountered them. Recently some evidence has been collected for Flemish pictures in the Veneto in the fifteenth and sixteenth centuries. Unfortunately, since they were admired and collected in Italy well into the sixteenth century, the presence of fifteenth-century Flemish paintings in sixteenth-century Venetian collections or churches is not in itself a reliable proof that these paintings reached the Veneto at a much earlier date, although this may well have been the case. Adhering to records strictly contemporary with Mantegna's youth in Venice itself we know that Santa Maria della Carità bought an altarpiece by Pietro di Fiandra in 1451, evidently a costly work, for its price was 78 ducats. The future Doge Marco Barbarigo had himself painted in London while living there in 1449 by a follower of Van Eyck: this portrait, now in the National Gallery, returned with him to Venice. So many Venetian merchants and agents went to the Netherlands that some of them at least must have brought back at an even earlier date small portable pictures, such as the diptych by Memlinc dated 1470 which by 1502 was in the collection of the Bembo family in Venice.

As early as 1457 Northern pictures were also being imported into Venice as a commercial speculation, for in that year 'a picture or altarpiece worked and gilded' was seized from a German merchant as contraband, though eventually released to him again. Unfortunately we have no securely dated provenance for an Eyckian *Crucifixion*, now in the Ca' d'Oro, which is known to have been in Padua in the late fifteenth century when it was copied by a Paduan artist.[50] That we cannot be sure of its earlier presence in Padua is regrettable, since the claim has been made that its influence can be seen in Mantegna's predella panel of the *Crucifixion* from the San Zeno altarpiece (*c.*1456–9). We ought too to allow for a possible transmission of influences

through Flemish manuscripts, though the detailed studies that would allow us to speak more definitely are still wanting. However this may be, in the 1450s and 1460s the influence of Flemish art was limited to forms, and in particular to forms expressive of pathos and realism.

The only certain testimonies we have of Flemish works of art within Mantegna's near range concern Ferrara. In the private apartments of Leonello d'Este, Marquis of Ferrara, there was a *Deposition from the Cross* by Rogier van der Weyden with figures of Adam and Eve expelled from paradise painted on one wing and a praying donor, presumably Leonello, on the other. This painting was already in Ferrara by 8 July 1449, when Leonello showed it to the antiquary Ciriaco d'Ancona. Ciriaco praises it for the 'divine rather than human art' with which it represented the grief and piety of the spectators.

> You seem to be seeing living faces breathing in those whom he wished to show as alive, and the semblance of death in the dead man [i.e. Jesus] and assuredly you might well say that so many draperies, so many cloaks of such various colours, so many dresses beautifully worked in crimson and gold, such living meadows, flowers, trees and leafy and shady hills and also richly ornamented porticoes and gateways, such gold like unto gold, such pearls, gems and all the other things in the picture were not produced by the hand of a human artificer, but were born within it of nature herself, the universal parent.[51]

This picture was also much admired by another humanist, Bartolommeo Fazio, who mentions it in 1456 in the chapter on painters of his *De viris illustribus*, laying stress on its realistic representation of tears and grief.[52]

Rogier came as a pilgrim to Rome in the Jubilee year of 1450, apparently during its first months, for he was back in Bruges by June, and probably before. During his sojourn in Italy he is known to have painted at Belfiore for Leonello,[53] and on 15 August 1450 the Ferrarese accounts record a payment of 20 ducats made before that date to Rogier in Bruges 'as an earnest and part-payment' for several pictures Leonello had asked him to paint, presumably on his return to the North.[54] Mantegna may therefore have seen paintings by Rogier during his documented visit to the court of Ferrara in May 1449. He may also have visited Ferrara on later occasions, for his next-door-neighbour and landlord in the contrada di Santa Lucia, Michele Savonarola, author of the *Libellus de magnificis ornamentis* and an enthusiastic *amateur* of painting, was established there as court physician from 1440.[55]

A disputed question is the influence of Donatello on Mantegna's art.[56] Certainly an overwhelming vision of the modern style at its most vital and expressive was revealed to Padua during the years from 1443 to 1454 when Donatello and his workmen were living there, making first the bronze equestrian monument of Gattamelata (d. 1443) to the commission of his widow, Giacoma, later to be a patron of Mantegna, and then the high altar of the Santo, with its rich decoration of reliefs and figures in bronze and stone. Accordingly Giuseppe Fiocco, that grand proponent of Tuscan influences as the fertilizing fount of the Paduan Renaissance, attributed to Donatello's example the bias of Paduan painting towards the sculptural. As proof that Donatello cast a powerful spell over Mantegna the claim is often advanced that in the San Zeno altarpiece, painted during the later 1450s, he copied Donatello's altar for the Santo, a long-destroyed work whose original design and appearance have not yet been convincingly reconstructed on a sound documentary foundation. Yet although Donatello's art did not leave Mantegna indifferent, it is certain that Erica Tietze-Conrat sensed the relationship between them more truly when she argued that Mantegna resisted his influence rather than succumbed to it.

In Donatello's Santo reliefs the relationship between setting and figures differs profoundly from that in any composition by Mantegna. The figures, all taken in poses of gesture or feeling, are not truly ordered in harmony with the often audacious and dizzying lines of the perspective of the setting. This is because Donatello is primarily interested in compositions of figures as crowds, swayed by powerful feeling and movement, deeply engaged in what is going forward, though with an inner diversity of motifs and incident for variety of interest. Outside these self-absorbed groups the setting extends itself in independence, differing from Mantegna's settings not only in its multiplicity of perspective lines, but in the care Donatello has taken to break up the architectural forms into many units of structure or decoration, so that the eye finds no smooth unbroken surface on which to rest. By contrast even in the earliest of Mantegna's works to offer analogies of subject-matter with the Santo relief, the fresco of *The Preaching of St James* in the Ovetari Chapel, a few figures serve to represent the crowd to whom St James preaches. Their responses under the impression of violent fear offer a limited sequence of paired yet contrasted reactions, expressed by each figure in its own space, with little care for group effects and none for crowd effects. The figures are contained within the architecture, on a perspective pavement that has dictated their placing, and figures and setting are accordingly more finely balanced and integrated than in Donatello's reliefs, where the vertiginous movement of the action proceeds without real reference to the vertiginous architecture of the setting.

Not only are Mantegna's figures far more self-contained and statuesque than Donatello's, they are conceived in terms of a different relationship between drapery and body. Donatello, with that same artful disconnection of things which leads him to treat crowds and setting as separate entities, gives his draperies an independent vitality that is accentuated by a multiplicity of long rhythmic lines and folds. As in nature the forms of the body mould the pull and fall and shape of the drapery, but always as in nature there is a sense that these forms act beneath a material which has an existence of its own. In Mantegna's early frescoes the drapery rises sharply, it is true, into his typical acute ridged folds, but between these it models the body closely, and indeed the figures by their action are made to pull and draw their drapery about them so as to accentuate the shape of the underlying limbs.

All this is not to deny that Mantegna may have taken from Donatello certain gestures and other dramatic devices for directing the eye through the action of his histories. But none of those cited seems so close as to preclude the inspiration of the Giottesque and International Gothic tradition of the Veneto. The influence of Altichiero's fresco of the *Crucifixion* in the Santo seems for example to be more perceptible in the *Crucifixion* panel of the predella of the San Zeno altarpiece than Donatello's reliefs in the Old Sacristy of San Lorenzo, for which an influence has recently been claimed. Similarly, though no formal disproof is possible of the claim that Mantegna learnt from Donatello the device of introducing figures into his compositions simply as spectators, that device was already a common one in trecento painting. Thus the motif of a woman holding a child by the hand found in the Florence *Circumcision* is related to a similar motif in Altichiero's *Crucifixion*. Mantegna employs this means of adding dramatic variety and naturalistic verisimilitude to his compositions with an austere economy that is in the strongest contrast with Donatello's crowded displays of the richness of his passionately human invention. More plausible perhaps are the suggestions occasionally advanced that Mantegna imitated or developed motifs from Donatello. Thus Donatello's *St George* may have suggested the figure of the guard with grounded shield in the Ovetari fresco of *St James on the way to Execution*, while the cut-off figures of the soldiers on the steps to Golgotha in the panel of the *Crucifixion* from the San Zeno altarpiece find a parallel in the cut-off figure of a soldier mounting the steps in Donatello's tondo of *St John boiled in oil* in the Old Sacristy. Yet it must also be said that the trend of Mantegna's art was such that both these figures may well be independent inventions.

Because Filippo Lippi's frescoes in the chapel of

the Palazzo del Podestà and Uccello's frescoes in the Casa de' Vitaliani are lost, it can never be known what Mantegna learnt from them. One of Lippi's assistants in the Cappella is said to have been the Ansuino da Forlì who was subsequently called in to paint two of the frescoes of St Christopher in the Ovetari Chapel, and certainly the influence of Lippi is clearly felt in his style. The influence of Andrea del Castagno's frescoes on the ceiling of the apse of the chapel of San Tarasio in the great Venetian Benedictine nunnery of San Tarasio, completed in August 1442, can however still be seen distinctly in the frescoes painted on the ceiling of the tribune of the Ovetari Chapel by Niccolò Pizzolo and Mantegna, who began work on them in partnership in 1448.[57] Almost all Pizzolo's work was lost in the air-raid which destroyed the Ovetari Chapel in 1944, but something of his art is known from photographs. Pizzolo, unlike Ansuino, was a painter of sharp talent. The fresco of God the Father painted on the ceiling of the tribune of the chapel shows a clear grasp of how to depict a figure in foreshortening and movement and as if floating freely in space. The arrangement of the drapery, moreover, makes use of the same principle of narrow ridged folds alternating with flat surfaces modelling the body that is so characteristic of Mantegna's drapery. Furthermore, the framework of the ceiling shows the same taste as Mantegna's own framework on the wall: it differs in its classicism from the rich Late Gothic foliated scrollwork preferred by Antonio Vivarini and Giovanni d'Alemagna, the Venetian partners of the two Paduan artists in the decoration of the chapel. However, these borders seem to have been Mantegna's work, at any rate in execution, and probably also in design.

In Pizzolo's four roundels of the Doctors of the Church there is a new sureness and audacity of perspective. The medallion frames are foreshortened, so that the lower section sinks into invisibility, and the point of view of the spectator is fixed by the artist as a result of this ingenious and innovatory device of *di sotto in sù* perspective. Within, the figures are seen by us as if looking up through a window. Even in photographs we can still admire the precise, confident skill with which geometrical perspective and strong still-life forms are used to suggest depth in recession while closing the composition effectively within the circle of the framework. Although the medallion frames are Renaissance in general conception and in much of their ornament, enough Late Gothic motifs persist on those of St Augustine and St Jerome to show that Pizzolo was rather behind Mantegna in his evolution, and indeed the types of his figures are vulgar in their animation, with far less of Mantegna's ideal beauty.

Pizzolo's art, then, so far as it is known to us, discloses a vigorous talent travelling the same road as Mantegna, but not necessarily escorting him along it, as Fiocco thought. What his Ovetari frescoes principally reveal is that at least one other artist in Padua shared some of the same artistic ambitions — virtuosity of perspective and of illusionism — as Mantegna. That Niccolò was recognized as a master of the 'modern' manner in painting appears from the record concerning an Apulian painter Luca de Mola, who was anxious to enter his shop in November 1448 in order to learn how to *'pingere in recenti'*.

The part of the ceiling of the Ovetari Chapel painted by Antonio Vivarini and Giovanni d'Alemagna, for all its differences of exuberant decorative emphasis, discloses that this modernity was contagious, for the four roundels of the Evangelists are imitations, even though rather superficial imitations, of those of Pizzolo, even to the adoption of a *sotto in sù* perspective. The medallions enclosing them, the elegant antique nudes of the young angels in the spandrels below, the ornaments of medallions and framework — festoons of fruit, scallops tied with fantastical ribbons, scrollwork of leaves and fruit — testify to a well-developed vocabulary of Renaissance ornamental forms, even if the nudes retain something of stiffness, and the scrollwork a certain Late Gothic intricacy of naturalism that is still transitional rather than fully Renaissance in spirit.

Mantegna's acquaintance with Jacopo Bellini must have gone back some time before Bellini decided in 1452 to give him his daughter Nicolosia in marriage. The two probably met in Venice, where Squarcione leased a house from time to time and where he and Mantegna were living together in 1447. Jacopo was then the leading master of Venice, saluted by the poet Ulisse degli Aleotti, later to be Mantegna's admirer and friend, in a sonnet written *c*.1441 as a 'new Phidias' who showed others how to follow the road of 'divine Apelles and noble Polycletus'.[58] Bellini must have known Mantegna for long enough to satisfy himself as to his character, talents and prospects, before offering him his daughter, all the more because Mantegna had no money or property of his own. Their association had considerable effect on certain elements of Mantegna's style which had not already received a firm formation in Squarcione's *studium*. Bellini's art is principally known to us from two surviving books of drawings, handed down as heirlooms in his family, and now preserved in London and Paris.[59] They are generally dated to the 1440s, but Bellini plainly continued to use them into later years as can be seen by the pronounced influence of Donatello which appears in a number of the drawings, not least in a copy of the Gattamelata horse, which must date from 1453 or later.

From these two books we can see that Bellini influenced Mantegna's conception of landscape settings as essentially picturesque constructions of layered rocks, a conception not original to Bellini, since it derived from trecento tradition, but applied by him in a manner that precedes Mantegna's in its sense of compartmented structure, though not in Mantegna's meticulous naturalism of treatment. In Bellini too we find the first of those tall slender small-scale figures, at times rather sketchy in treatment, who people Mantegna's works until the early 1460s. Some of them wear Roman armour of a kind that Mantegna will attempt to represent with greater variety and greater archaeological exactitude in the Ovetari frescoes. Among the drawings are a number of compositions and details that Mantegna seems to have studied with special care, or that suggested ideas to him: these will be noted in connection with the works to which they relate.

Finally, Bellini's drawings contain a number of studies in perspective, drawings of the nude and copies after antique monuments that are of especial interest because they show an artist of International Gothic formation evolving into a Renaissance artist under the influence of the new vogue for geometrical perspective and for the antique. As such they are precious evidence for the artistic milieu in which Mantegna's genius began to evolve. Paduan art historians tend on the whole to overstress the purely Paduan influences in Mantegna's formation. Without depreciating the unique nature of his education under Squarcione, he surely learnt much from his early experience of Venice, observing carefully not only the art of Jacopo Bellini, but that of Antonio Vivarini and Giovanni d'Alemagna, and learning the traditions of Venetian religious iconography. As with the art of Donatello, he certainly rejected much, and indeed the florid Late Gothic manner still current in Venetian workshops had little interest for a young artist already intent on reviving the ideal perfection of antique painting. Nevertheless it would be a mistake to discount these other influences and their effect on Mantegna's art: within the finished perfection of his paintings their influence is often perceptible, since his allegiances, like those of all fifteenth-century artists and patrons, were multiple, for all the grandeur of his bias towards the modern and the antique.

II

The Ovetari Frescoes

WE have seen that in the early 1440s, when Mantegna entered Squarcione's *bottega*, it was the only workshop in Northern Italy which professedly taught how to paint in the modern manner (*pingere in recenti*). Whatever its master's failings, a number of his pupils, Mantegna himself, Niccolò Pizzolo, Matteo Pozzo, Marco Zoppo, Dario da Treviso, Giorgio Schiavone, won lasting reputations. With Dario da Treviso and Marco Zoppo, Mantegna was to remain friends long after all three had left Squarcione. As already related his formal break with Squarcione in 1448 followed the set pattern of a quarrel about wages. That in 1447 he had already won some sort of emancipation as well as the fame of a prodigy appears from the documents concerning his earliest known commission, an altarpiece for the high altar of the church of Santa Sofia.

His patron was a wealthy master-baker, Bartolommeo di Gregorio, who had already commissioned in 1429 a Pietà for another altar in the same church from the sculptor Egidio of Wiener Neustadt.[1] Although Mantegna was only 16 and legally still the apprentice and adopted son of Squarcione, the earnest for the picture, some forty ducats, was paid to him and not to Squarcione and he is described in the documents concerning it as *Magister*, that is, as a fully fledged master. The altarpiece is now lost, but Vasari, who saw it, declared that 'it seemed painted, not by a youth, but by an old man of long practice.'[2] Its disappearance is to be lamented, for it would have told us much about the origins of Mantegna's art. On completing it in 1448, he signed it with great pride as his own handiwork, executed at the age of 17. The inscription was in Latin, but followed a simple conventional formula, with none of the humanist

pretensions to classical Latinity of some of the later inscriptions on his paintings.

The altarpiece must have made a great impression, for it at once brought Mantegna a share in the most important commission Padua then had to offer, the decoration of the funeral chapel of Antonio degli Ovetari in the church of the Eremitani. Before considering the complex history of the Ovetari frescoes, it is as well to review what the legal documents record of Mantegna's years under Squarcione's tutelage. According to a petition submitted on his behalf on 28 November 1455, Mantegna had served Squarcione continually for six years 'both in the necessary business of his household . . . and also in making pictures of great price and of other conditions as necessity and chance demanded',[3] all to the great advantage and profit of his master. The mention of the price of pictures is interesting, for one of the necessities from which Mantegna was quickly to escape on leaving Squarcione was that of painting humble works of art, either in the form of decorative ornaments on woodwork or modest religious pictures, such as Madonnas. Unfortunately, none of the Madonnas attributed to his early years in various collections seems certainly to be his, though he must of course have painted a number in Squarcione's shop, like his fellow-pupils.[4] The profit Mantegna had earned for Squarcione, so he now claimed, had mounted up to the great sum of more than 400 ducats, Squarcione having had the exclusive benefit of his labours, and having in consequence become rich. But Mantegna had remained poor, not having received any portion of the 400 ducats, contrary to all law and decency.

This was the main grievance that led Mantegna to separate himself from Squarcione. They quarrelled in Venice, where Squarcione had a house, at

Fig. 2. Spectators on a balcony. Detail from *The Baptism of Hermogenes* (Plate 12)

some date before the end of 1447, for on 26 January 1448 they took their difference to two arbitrators, one of whom was Ulisse degli Aleotti (c.1400–88), a Venetian notary then living in Padua in the service of one of the Venetian Rettori of the city. Aleotti was a humanist and poet, and, as we have seen, a friend of Jacopo Bellini, Mantegna's future father-in-law, in whose praise he had already written at least two sonnets; now or later he was to write a sonnet in praise of a portrait painted in Venice by Mantegna of a girl who was about to become a nun.[5] The arbitrators gave their award that same day.[6] It was a decision that could not satisfy Mantegna for it gave him much less than the half which he claimed as his share of the 400 ducats.

Presumably Mantegna once more began demanding his fair share from Squarcione as soon as he came of age, more or less about 1455,[7] when he claimed that he had asked him privately for it more than once and only now, after Squarcione's obstinate refusals, was appealing to the Paduan courts. Squarcione succeeded in having the case transferred to a Venetian court, only to have sentence given against him. On 2 January 1456 the Venetian Consiglio dei Quaranta ordered the award of 1448 to be quashed on the grounds that it had been made while Andrea was still a minor, and that his father's consent had not been given. It was, moreover, the opinion of one of the judges that Mantegna had been made the victim of a deception. The verdict was in some ways superfluous, for Squarcione and Mantegna had already amicably agreed to the cancellation of the award – so little did such legal disputes in that age of constant litigation and formalization of business before notaries necessarily imply irreconcilable quarrels. And indeed on 5 September 1448, only a few months after their separation, Squarcione and Mantegna are found acting together to assess the value of frescoes executed by Pietro da Milano, one of the leading masters of Padua, in a chapel in the church of San Jacopo.

For all that Mantegna had left Squarcione's house, then, and gone to live in the contrada di Santa Lucia in Padua, almost certainly in the house of his brother Tommaso, there may be some truth in Campagnola's story that the commission for the Ovetari frescoes was originally offered to Squarcione and that he passed it on to Mantegna and to his other former pupil Pizzolo. And throughout the vicissitudes of the frescoes he was repeatedly invoked as assessor, critic and judge in a manner which argues against any permanent breach with Mantegna.[8]

The patrons who commissioned the Ovetari frescoes belonged to the patriciate of Padua. All were members or kinsfolk of the great and wealthy family of Capodilista, who were descended from the ancient territorial nobility of the region and claimed for themselves a legendary origin from German knights who had fought with Charlemagne in Italy. By the fifteenth century they had become one of the legal dynasties so characteristic of Renaissance Padua. In Mantegna's youth the head of the family was Giovan Francesco (c.1380–c.1450), a distinguished jurist and lecturer in law at the University who had been one of the Venetian representatives at the Council of Basle in 1433–5. He recounted the history of the family in a splendid illuminated chronicle, which has recently been published.[9] The arms of Ovetari are impaled in the frescoes with the arms of Capodilista, indicating that Madonna Imperatrice, the widow of Antonio Ovetari, and the patron in whose name they were commissioned, was a daughter of the Capodilista family.[10] It seems in fact that her husband had named old Giovan Francesco as one of the five executors of his will: while the two brothers Antonio and Francesco Forzatè, who were also named as executors, belonged to a cognate house of the Capodilista. Most probably Imperatrice was Giovan Francesco's sister, given that her name is not listed among his daughters.

As Giovan Francesco was now too old to act, his son Francesco acted in his stead. Francesco Capodilista (1405–28 March 1460) was an interesting figure; like his father he became a jurist and lecturer in the University, and from 1430 he occupied various public offices in Padua, serving among other things as one of the deputies charged by the Comune with the care of the fabric of the churches and monasteries of Padua, including the Eremitani. Francesco's younger brother Gabriele (c.1420–77) made in 1458 a pilgrimage to the Holy Land, of which he wrote an account which was published in 1475.[11] Gabriele's wife, Romea, was a daughter of Antonio Borromeo, who was a friend of Mantegna and was portrayed by him in the St Christopher frescoes of the Ovetari Chapel. The family palace of Giovan Francesco Capodilista was in the contrada di Santa Lucia, where Mantegna's brother already had a house and where Mantegna himself was later to have one too. The family had also some association with Giacoma della Leonessa, the wife of Gattamelata, for in April 1444 Francesco acted as the promoter of the doctorate of Jacopo della Leonessa. Without being professed humanists, Francesco and Gabriele were certainly in sympathy with humanism, while their father had associations with the humanistic circle which gravitated around Pietro Donato (1380–1447), who was bishop of Padua from 1428 until his death, earning a life from Vespasiano da Bisticci for his activity as a book-collector.[12]

The Ovetari frescoes were destroyed in 1944. Only *The Martyrdom of St Christopher* and *The*

Assumption survive complete, because they had long been detached and removed from the chapel by reason of their extreme deterioration. All discussion of the frescoes has therefore to be founded largely on photographs, and for this reason it is impossible to say much of their colouring and technique. Kristeller, who examined them *c.*1900 perhaps more intelligently and thoroughly than any other student, records of the two upper ranges of the St James frescoes and of the *St James on the way to Execution*, the first fresco in the bottom range, that Mantegna's technique showed

> no relation to the refined and highly developed manner of the Veronese painters, Altichiero, Avanzo and others, who worked in Padua . . . In this department Mantegna is quite independent of old Paduan art; he has more points of similarity with the Florentine technique, which he might actually have studied at Padua in the works of Uccello and Filippo Lippi. The effect of the first frescoes is light and hard, and, notwithstanding the dullness of the colours, diversified. The colouring forms a homogeneous surface, and is only toned off by darker or brighter hatching. The very first painting of the lower course shows a transition between the hard technique, consisting of thick closely packed brushstrokes, applied rapidly, though with great certainty, with harsh contrasts of light and shade . . . and a finer technique with more delicate lines and softer transitions of light and shade.[13]

The history of the frescoes as related in contemporary documents is far from plain. For clarity of exposition they are considered here largely from the point of view of the evolution of Mantegna's art, which they show, not at a single stage of its development, but in four successive stages. All the other questions involved in their creation are reserved for the catalogue. In order to throw the necessary emphasis on the astonishing innovations Mantegna made in his art, especially during the years from *c.*1448 to *c.*1456, each fresco is considered in strict chronological sequence, making due insertion of the other works that Mantegna is documented as painting during the time that elapsed between the initiation and the completion of the Ovetari Chapel. The imperative advantage of this approach is that the frescoes are presented not in an artificially smooth succession, but as they were executed, with halts and intervals and resumptions of work, so that the advances made at each stage become clear.

From the first, work seems to have gone on slowly and irregularly. Although Mantegna had contracted on 16 May 1448 together with his partner Niccolò Pizzolo to paint the frescoes of the tribune and the histories of St James on the left wall of the chapel,

it was only on 16 July 1449 that he received his first payment.[14] Two months before, in late May, he was at the court of Ferrara, where he painted for the Marchese Leonello a portrait intended as a 'leal souvenir', a tender record of romantic friendship in the chivalric mode. On one side was the portrait of Leonello himself, and on the other that of his loyal companion and chamberlain, Folco da Villafora. The document recording the commission states that the panel on which it was to be painted had been ordered by Leonello and was delivered to Mantegna already framed and prepared for painting. From the description it would seem to have been a narrow upright panel rather like that on which Pisanello's famous portrait of Leonello at Bergamo is painted. Mantegna's portrait is lost, though that it once existed is another proof of the early recognition of Mantegna's genius by patrons of a refined taste.[15] With it has disappeared all evidence of Mantegna's early portrait style: indeed very few portraits survive from the Venice and Padua of Mantegna's youth, although a good number must have been painted. A little profile portrait of the Emperor Frederick III, now in Florence, dates from Frederick's Italian journey of 1452, and is sometimes attributed to Squarcione, perhaps because of his known encounter with the Emperor during his visit to Padua.[16] Jacopo Bellini seems to have had a reputation as a portraitist: he painted at least two portraits of Leonello d'Este, one in 1440 in competition with Pisanello, and another which was in profile – probably at this date a more usual pose than three-quarter face.[17]

By 27 September 1449 Mantegna had finished only three small works in the Ovetari Chapel, the figures of St Peter, St Paul and St Christopher flanking Niccolò Pizzolo's God the Father on the vault of the tribune (Plates 4, 5, 6). The saints were represented as floating in space on clouds, against a blue background. As already noted, they show a knowledge of Andrea del Castagno's San Tarasio frescoes, but it is typical of Mantegna's temperament that his figures already have a sculptural quiescence of pose, with none of the dynamic vigour seeking to compel the spectator through eyes and gesture of the Tuscan artist. Simply posed, with left or right leg flexed, they wear robes and cloaks classically draped. The draperies themselves are cast on a system that Mantegna was to follow throughout his career. His long adherence to it, as to other constants in his art, was compelled not by conservatism, but because he had derived it from antique sculpture, though it is impossible now to say from what particular model he learnt it. That it could be studied in Squarcione's school, at any rate from drawings, is indicated by the appearance of the same drapery style in the paintings of Pizzolo. This classical cast of drapery was softened naturalistically, partly in order to suit the unclassical garments to which it was applied, but its underlying pattern always remains perceptible. In some places the draperies are made to cling close and flat to the body, so as to reveal the form of its limbs, while in others they are pushed up into narrow, ridged folds that create decorative patterns independent of the shaping forms below.

This play of ornamental forms, strictly controlled, yet developed for their own sake with their own elegant rhythmical elaboration, continues in Mantegna's art to the very last, attaining, if anything, ever greater decorative autonomy. It has been suggested that Mantegna obtained this disposition by modelling wettened draperies on to lay figures, and certainly the Lombard painter and art theorist Gian Paolo Lomazzo (1538–1600), writing in 1584, says that Mantegna painted his draperies 'from models dressed in paper and cloth glued on to them'. Lomazzo believed that this practice was not Mantegna's own invention, but had been followed by 'the old painters' and then laboriously perfected by Mantegna and others.[18] It was certainly used by Pizzolo, in all probability prior to Mantegna. This so-called 'chartaceous' drapery is rightly associated by Meder with an attempt to revive antique drapery folds, and with the Paduan, Ferrarese, Lombard and Venetian schools, and it is not impossible therefore that Lomazzo was recording an authentic tradition concerning Mantegna's working methods.[19] Certainly the technique of drawing from figures modelled in wax or clay and then clothed in draperies of wettened cloth or paper may have been suggested to Mantegna by his early training in copying after antique sculptures. Such a technique might well have accentuated the natural or acquired direction of his art towards strongly sculptural figures. And if it was his ordinary practice to model small figures for his pictorial compositions, this in turn would explain the extreme perfection of his technique as a modeller in the only work of sculpture certainly by his hand to survive – the bronze bust of himself now in his funerary chapel in Mantua.

Mantegna and Pizzolo soon disagreed, and in July 1449 the two were already invoking the arbitration first of one mutual friend, the distinguished Paduan jurist Giacomo Alvarotti (c.1385–1453), and then after Alvarotti's attempt at reconciliation had failed that of a second, the Venetian patrician Francesco Morosini. By Morosini's award of 27 September 1449, made after an inspection of the chapel 'with experts and more especially with Maestro Francesco Squarcione and after a conference with him', it was agreed that Mantegna should paint all the histories of St James except that on the bottom left, Pizzolo no doubt insisting on at least this one opportunity to display his powers as a painter of histories, which otherwise would have been denied him. The award

also stipulated expressly that Mantegna was to paint the framework enclosing the histories.[20] This was all-important to his illusionistic scheme for them, and it was surely for this reason that he reserved it exclusively to himself.

The framework of the Ovetari histories is one of the most remarkable and neglected features of the frescoes. In themselves, bold ornamental borders dividing histories into compartments were by no means an innovation: indeed they were a cardinal principle of Gothic design. Thus Altichiero's frescoes on the walls of the Oratorio di San Giorgio are enclosed within a strongly marked framework, richly ornamented with geometrical motifs. On the walls of the Ovetari Chapel Mantegna translates the form and ornament of such Late Gothic frameworks into Renaissance guise. His framework is adjusted to the pointed Gothic vault by the customary device of indentations in the upper part of the second tier, used among others by Storlato, in his frescoes in the chapel of St Luke in Santa Giustina for which Mantegna was later to paint an altarpiece. With Mantegna's usual resourcefulness the necessity for an adaptation of this kind is artfully exploited so as to enhance the extension of the scenes within beyond the visual field demarcated by the framework, a trick which he could already see used in Jacopo Avanzi's frescoes of the history of St James in the Cappella di San Giacomo in the Santo.

Mantegna has conceived his framework of vertical and horizontal partitions as creating tiers of scenes that are seen through their openings as through windows; they appear indeed like so many stage tableaux. Perhaps the closest comparable work is Ghiberti's Porta del Paradiso, made from 1425 to 1452 for the Florentine Baptistery. But on Ghiberti's doors the moulded frames simply enclose the reliefs – indeed it is known that they were cast later than the reliefs – whereas in the Ovetari Chapel the framework, at least on the St James wall, where alone it was executed as originally designed, forms a true architectural frontispiece or proscenium for the scenes enacted within, and Mantegna's compositions are plainly adjusted so as to sustain this illusion. The unity of space this device imposed on the wall is further enhanced by other illusionistic devices – the swags that hang across the front of the framework, the shield quartering the arms of Ovetari and Capodilista that appears to be suspended from its upper crossing. The sophistication of the framework's conception as a *tour de force* of illusionism is maintained in the simplicity of its ornament, a stem linking classical bunches of fruit and foliage. This simplicity is broken only on the central part of the vertical bar, where a rather motley assemblage of motifs appears, including a classical vase and a quatrefoil clipeus with the bust of a boy in quattrocento costume, shown in three-quarter profile to the right – motifs that faintly, and no doubt through coincidence, echo similar motifs on Ghiberti's doors. But the putti who clamber about the swags surely owe something of their inspiration to the ornamental border of putti sustaining roundels of the prophets painted by Andrea del Castagno on the underside of the tribune arch of the San Tarasio chapel. Certainly the putto supporting the shield is directly imitated from one of these.

Mantegna began work on the histories of St James from the top of the wall, as was customary. The uppermost frescoes, *The Calling of James and John* (Plate 10) and *The Preaching of St James* (Plate 11), were painted in 1450. They have been rather neglected in the literature since they do not present the astounding developments of the two frescoes immediately below. Yet they have their real interest for the origins of Mantegna's art. *The Calling* on the left is his first landscape composition; it is also the first of those characteristically high settings which rise up two-thirds of the picture and are at the same time 'deep' backgrounds in that they compass what in actuality would be an immense view. Rising up the lower slope of the mountain on the left is the prototype of those steep, narrow, winding roads that reappear again and again in Mantegna's paintings as devices to lead the eye through the picture, to aid perspective effects with their converging lines, and to form yet another means of division in the settings of an artist who always orders his backgrounds into rigid compartments. The road is ascended by tiny figures, another feature that will constantly recur in Mantegna's paintings. A similar contrast between large-scale foreground figures and such tiny background figures appears elsewhere in fifteenth-century art: an early example is Jan van Eyck's *St Barbara* (*c*.1437). It is in describing Van Eyck's lost painting of *Women emerging from the bath* that the Italian humanist Bartolommeo Fazio mentions the device in 1456, in words which reveal that what the fifteenth century admired in such landscape settings and their figures was a form of aerial perspective: 'And also horses and men of tiny stature, mountains, woods, villages, castles contrived with such artifice that you would think them fifty miles apart from each other.'[21] This diminution of background features and figures was to remain Mantegna's standard form of aerial perspective until the end of his long life, when it was already becoming antiquated. Only occasionally does he use the change of colour by which hills are made blue in the distance that was the great Flemish contribution to aerial perspective in his century.

The standing figures of Jesus and the Apostles Matthew and Peter are about a third of the maximum height of the fresco, but are placed towards the bottom, so as to be more clearly visible from below. The kneeling figure of James is set in the foreground, before John. Throughout the frescoes he wears the same dress, a white robe and deep green cloak: here he is also distinguished by his beard and by the praying hands he extends in answer to Jesus. Behind, on the lake of Galilee, Zebedee hauls a draught of fish into his boat. The landscape setting, still rather abrupt and crude, is the first in which Mantegna uses his towering mountains of rock piled on rock, often appearing about to topple over at the summit and broken into pinnacles and blocks and endless facets of plane surfaces.

These rocks continue the tradition of the artificial rock settings of trecento painting as they can be seen in the paintings of Altichiero and Avanzi and, in more evolved form, in the drawings of Jacopo Bellini. That rocks and platforms of rock were also favoured as settings in the *bottega* of Squarcione can be seen from the works of the Squarcionesques. They seem to have been a characteristic of the school in the 1440s and 1450s and still appear in the predella panels of Marco Zoppo's triptych painted in Bologna *c*.1461–8 for the Collegio di Spagna. Their appeal then as now lay in their fantastic nature, using fantastic in its fifteenth-century sense to mean an invention of the fancy, stranger and more extraordinary than reality. To this power of improving on ordinary nature, when found in nature herself, the eighteenth century was to give the name of the picturesque. In Mantegna, while the general forms retain a contrived picturesqueness, the whole is imagined and figured so as to produce a semblance of overall plausibility within the limits of the convention. To this romantic naturalness is added a meticulous and minute naturalism of detail, even here, in this early work, where the scenery is especially wild and dramatic. Accordingly, in the foreground we find the first of those rocky surfaces sparsely scattered with plants and tufts of grass, with pebbles and small stones, each rendered with sharp precision, but never allowed to blur the general effect, that will be a feature of Mantegna's paintings until the very end. The little leafless bushes that grow here and there out of the slopes are another ever-recurrent motif of the same kind. Both are devices found in Squarcione's Lazara altarpiece, and we have seen that Mantegna may have learnt them from his master.

Imaginary rock formations were not only picturesque in themselves, they had the advantage of allowing the fifteenth-century artist to contrive his settings to suit his composition and fill and open his background to make a pleasing variety of views. Thus on the left of *The Calling* the rocks close the scene which behind the palm-tree balancing the figures of Christ and the Apostles opens on to the lake, then beyond to the towering, battlemented walls of Caphernaum, with its great castle rising against the cloudy sky. Caphernaum is represented as a picturesque medieval town, according to established convention, with none of the monuments of classical antiquity such as Mantegna was soon to introduce into his paintings in a spirit of archaeological verisimilitude. Around it wheels a flight of birds, a motif found also in contemporary miniature painting and typical of the descriptive International Gothic sensibility to nature.

Soaring, rugged mountains formed of great rocks must have had especial power over the fancy of dwellers in the flat plains of Lombardy and the Veneto. Rocks and platforms of rock will always form the evident structure of Mantegna's landscapes, however relieved by green slopes, by the ruins of antiquity, or by walled cities. With him even in nature we inhabit a universe of stone, where verdure is an accident drawn over the substance of rock. Indeed it might almost be said that for Mantegna mountains were rude monuments and that he saw in their irregular heaps of rock, which sometimes he echoes in irregular piles of man-shaped stones, heaped up from the ruins of antiquity, a sort of natural architecture, interpreting literally the Renaissance concept of 'fabrica mundi'.

The figure of Zebedee, shown bending into the composition, artfully suggests not only depth of space behind the picture plane, but also that space continues beyond the frame laterally. And on looking again at Caphernaum and the rocks on the left it will be seen that they too are cut off in order to produce the same effect. Here then for the first time Mantegna displays his unrivalled power of suggesting to the imagination that his pictorial scene is not finite, but extends beyond our visual rays, as it would in nature. Plainly he had already taken to heart Pliny's words about the ancient Greek artist Timanthes that 'in the works of this man alone more is always understood than is depicted.'[22] As we have already seen, it is sometimes held that Mantegna learnt this form of composition from the example of Donatello, in particular the device of cut-off figures as stimulants to the imagination to conceive a wider reality. But there are imposing instances of it in earlier painting in Padua, as for instance in Altichiero's frescoes of St George, and in Avanzi's frescoes of the history of St James, in which the action moves in space through and among the openings of a complex and fantastic Gothic architecture with a freedom whose lesson was evidently not lost on Mantegna. At this stage his figures of this kind are cut off vertically at the side: only some eight years later, in the Crucifixion of the San Zeno predella, will Mantegna attempt figures cut off horizontally across the body.

The skill with which the swag and putto at the top of the fresco are illusionistically contrived to seem in free movement in front of the frame has already been noted. In Mantegna the effect is intended not purely for ostentation, but to suggest a continuum between the real space in which the spectator finds himself, and the pictorial space, so transposing the painted history into an apparent extension of reality. In such a transposition, whose underlying aesthetic is that of naturalism, there is always a danger that imitation in itself may become the end of art. Mantegna was possibly the first artist consciously to counter this danger with the doctrine later to become classical, that the end of art is not simply to reproduce nature, but to reproduce her in forms of ideal perfection. As we shall see, he could find authority both for virtuosity of illusionism and for the improvement of nature from the majestic tradition of ancient painting, as recorded by Pliny the Elder and other ancient authors. And it will become ever plainer that for him the antique was the model from which he hoped to learn how to give ideal perfection to his own forms.

Indeed the companion fresco of The Preaching of St James contains Mantegna's first architectural setting all'antica. It is deliberately contrasted in its smooth elegance with the rugged mountains of Galilee. The scene takes place in a courtyard, with its pavement tiles and the cut stones of its enclosing wall meticulously indicated. At the back of the courtyard is a building partly concealed from view, pierced by a doorway whose door is ajar, giving entrance into the room beyond and presumably access to the arched niche which flanks it on the left. This arched niche is an attempt to give classical form to one of the external pulpits of Mantegna's own day. Architecturally it is rather implausible, for it has rather the air of an arched window that has lost its surrounding wall. Like the open door, it is a triumph of foreshortening and perspective, but of that traditional kind whose pride lay in effects such as doors that appear to protrude or swing forwards or backwards. The pulpit proper has legs formed of laurel leaves, terminating in feet carved as rolls of laurel leaves bound with ribbons, an adaptation of antique ornamental forms rather naïve and grotesque in its effect. A medallion encircling an antique mask, strangely wild with its open eyes and mouth, and probably inspired by a medallion-wreathed Roman funerary portrait, is set on the face of the wall above the doorway, whose pediment is formed of two scrolled dolphins. This last motif was perhaps suggested by the two dolphins on the funerary stele of M. Gavius Severus, copied at Verona in its perfect state by or for the Paduan antiquary Giovanni Marcanova (c.1418–67) in the mid-fifteenth century.[23] All these ornaments are in that rather fantastic and exuberant antique taste which was to become characteristic of North Italian Renaissance art, and which contrasts so strikingly with the severer taste of Florence.

The various effects of terror and stupefaction among the spectators as the demons appear, conjured up by the magician Hermogenes, who is not seen in Mantegna's fresco, but who appears in Avanzi's earlier fresco of the theme in the Santo, are invented with lively dramatic power. The personages of Mantegna's scene are much fewer than those of Avanzi's, for Mantegna is already shunning the richly peopled histories so greatly beloved of International Gothic art, and so well exemplified in the frescoes of Altichiero and Avanzi. Instead, a few figures are skilfully arranged on a curve in the foreground and thickened on the right into a group by the addition of two heads behind. The curve is not arbitrarily imposed on the composition, but appears to be the natural consequence of the starting and sheltering and running movements of the three figures on the left, and of the flight and amazement of those on the right. Mantegna already seems to be of the opinion of Alberti in his *De pictura* 'that no history should be stuffed with such a variety of things that nine or ten men cannot worthily enact it.'[24] In designing such a scene, Donatello would have been absorbed in representing a surge of fear through a great concourse: Mantegna prefers a few effects expressed with concise vigour in a setting where figures and architecture are perfectly balanced. That his avoidance of violent action dramatically interlaced through a multitude of figures was a deeply held stylistic preference is proved by another consideration: he never copies tumultuous scenes from Roman sarcophagi, though examples must have been known to him as they were known to Jacopo Bellini. Bellini copied a *Centauromachia* in one of his drawings, retaining its turbulence;[25] the *Centauromachia* set in the wall of a house in the fresco of *St James on the way to Execution* is stilled into solemnity. Mantegna was drawn then to those same aspects of antique art that were to appeal to Poussin and later to the Neo-classical movement: its calm grandeur, expressed through idealization of the human figure, its sense of harmonious interval and proportion, its austere eloquence, sparing of all unnecessary ornament or enrichment of expression.

Yet although the figures wear tunics and cloaks of classical dignity, their types and poses are human and natural enough – though they do not necessarily all proceed from direct observation, for the figure bending over and stopping his ears with his cloak was certainly inspired by a very similar figure on the right of Avanzi's fresco of the *St James disputing*.[26] Mantegna is far from eschewing the familiar: his is not the exclusive classicism of the Franco-Roman Baroque or of the eighteenth century, deliberately foregoing all humble motifs as incompatible with nobility of style. In his fresco a youth dives in such terror among the group of terrified spectators on the right that only his left leg and back are visible. Such a leavening of the action in solemn histories with a light intermingling of diverting or familiar anecdote was greatly admired in the fourteenth and fifteenth centuries. As a taste it was given an early literary expression by Fazio, who cites in 1456 for especial praise in Pisanello's lost fresco of the Emperor Frederick Barbarossa, painted in the Sala del Consiglio of the Palazzo Ducale, Venice, the figure of a priest distorting his mouth with his fingers.[27] In the minor interludes they introduced into great histories, motifs of such a homely naturalism anticipate the English and Spanish drama of the Renaissance, rather than the aulic tragedies in the manner of Seneca which became the taste of the Renaissance in Italy. In Mantegna such motifs are never a discord in the harmony of the total effect, but gently humanize either with their vivacity, as here, or with a certain tenderness, as in the *Circumcision* painted in Mantua. Indeed the sedulous grace and sculptural dignity of his figure style are often warmed inwardly with a lively, even smiling humanity, though this inner warmth is so carefully restrained in its expression that sometimes a second look is needed before we remark the affectionate impishness that lurks beneath apparent gravity.

The orthogonals of the pavement, when prolonged, are found to converge roughly in the same area, a spot on the left near the right end of the second side of the hexagonal base of the Apostle's pulpit. They do not, however, converge on a single vanishing-point, and it is this feature which suggests that only after painting this fresco did Mantegna master Alberti's perspective, in which the convergence of the orthogonals on a single vanishing-point is a fundamental principle. Pisanello and Jacopo Bellini both learnt to make use of Alberti's perspective in the 1440s, possibly even making its acquaintance as early as 1441, when they were in Ferrara at the court of Leonello d'Este. Alberti was a friend of Leonello, who took a profound interest in painting, sculpture and architecture, in their theory as well as their practice; indeed it was at Leonello's request that Alberti wrote his *De re aedificatoria*. Critics have been inclined to make much of the influence on Mantegna of Piero della Francesco's lost frescoes painted *c.*1449–50 to the commission of Leonello d'Este for the Castello of Ferrara and of other frescoes he painted during his sojourn in Ferrara for the church of San Agostino. But any resemblances between the two artists are more probably due to similarities of temperament and exposure to the same cultural imperatives. On the evidence of the two uppermost frescoes in the Ovetari Chapel, it is most unlikely that Mantegna acquired any knowledge of Alberti's perspective during his visit to Ferrara in May 1449. An alternative possibility is that he learnt it from Donatello, who used it with great virtuosity in his bronze reliefs for the altar of the Santo. Yet as these were designed and executed in the years 1447 to 1449, it is surprising that Mantegna had not mastered the principles of Alberti's perspective from them before 1450.

Altogether it seems more plausible to suppose that a copy of Alberti's treatise on painting or some other means of instruction fell in Mantegna's way in 1450. For in the two frescoes of the second tier, *The Baptism of Hermogenes* and *The Trial of St James*, Alberti's perspective is applied with astonishing virtuosity. The orthogonals in both scenes are made to converge at the same vanishing-point, on the rim of the lower half of the vase in the framework, so binding them together into what becomes almost a unified composition. This unity is skilfully heightened by the architectural setting, in both a courtyard framed by stately classical buildings, and by the disposition of the principal figures, set on the left in the *Baptism* so as to balance the figures of James and Herod Agrippa in the *Trial*. The books and scrolls lying in the foreground of the left fresco and the helmet on the pavement in the right are Mantegna's tribute to his Squarcionesque training. But he has already learnt to use a silent skill of art and these still-life objects are rendered with a quiet naturalness that conceals the artist's real virtuosity of illusionism. That he was conscious of the brilliance of his achievement in these two frescoes appears from his self-portrait in the person of the Roman guard who stands, a conspicuous figure, in the left foreground of the *Trial*, gazing fixedly at the spectator. This is one of the first of a number of self-portraits that appear in Mantegna's work (Fig. 1).

Apart from a new mastery of perspective, the frescoes reveal an increasing attention to verisimilitude of setting and costume. Because of Mantegna's enthusiasm for the antique, scholars have tended to concentrate almost exclusively on his studies of classical art and architecture – with which the quattrocento of course classed monuments that would now be described as Early Christian or Byzantine. Although the most prominent element in Mantegna's art is certainly a classical antiquarianism at once romantic and archaeological in its inspiration, there are plain testimonies, beginning with *The Baptism of Hermogenes*, to a parallel care for verisimilitude in his depiction of oriental costume. This interest was not original to Mantegna, but is found as early as the later fourteenth century among the painters of north-eastern Italy. In Padua figures wearing oriental turbans and pigtails already appear in Altichiero's frescoes of the Chapel of San Giacomo in the Santo (c.1374–9),[28] and in those of the Oratorio di San Giorgio (1377–c.1384) where the fresco of *The Beheading of St George* includes a particularly fine study of a Turk holding an arrow.[29] His frescoes of the martyrdom of St Catherine of Alexandria in the Oratorio contain quite a number of figures, of both men and women, dressed in oriental costume in an evident attempt to give Moorish local colour to the scene.[30] This tradition continued, for there are a number of figures in oriental costume in the drawings of Jacopo Bellini.[31]

In such histories, oriental costume was used for the representation of paynims, who during the fourteenth and fifteenth centuries were synonymous in the general imagination with Moors and Turks and Mongols. In Venice and the Veneto some knowledge of the costumes of the Levant must have been fairly widespread, since figures in oriental costume were introduced by painters there into histories set in the East for vivid suggestiveness of local colour. Mantegna must have been well aware that the early scenes of the life of James were passed among the Jews, not among paynims properly so-called, but plainly he brought to the invention of this scene a historical and topographical vagueness in keeping with the general vagueness of the Middle Ages and Renaissance about the lands beyond the pale of Christendom. Although both race and costume were anachronistic, for Mantegna as for his predecessors Moorish figures in Moorish costume sufficed to set the scene in the East and to distance it in time as well as place.

The scene of the *Baptism* (Plate 12) is a marketplace in Jerusalem, and prominent among the spectators is a reverend white-bearded man, costumed as a Moor in a large white turban, a long-sleeved brown robe and a white scarf (*fazzuolo*, really serving as a handkerchief). The aged figure behind him is to be understood as wearing the same dress. Their plain brown robes indicate that they are ordinary citizens, but otherwise the costume corresponds exactly to that of an Egyptian Mameluke nobleman or a North African Moor as represented in Venice by Cesare Vecellio in the 1590s.[32] Its model was doubtless an Egyptian or North African 'Moor' either as observed on the quays of Venice or as pictured in drawings. Of the two spectators on the right, one wears a hat with a white scarf tied round it, the other a cap of dyed wool or lambskin that may be a variation of an oriental cap. Except for the children, who wear contemporary dress, the rest of the costuming is either classical or semi-classical, though the buttoned robe of the man gesturing towards the scene from the front opening of the portico is again anachronistic.

The static poses of those isolated figures, varied by an elegant classical *contrapposto* in the aged oriental figure and in the man reading a book, help to explain Squarcione's famous criticism of the St James frescoes, that in them Mantegna had created a world of statues. Nevertheless, they are enlivened by naturalism of anecdote; the aged oriental clutches his scarf, the boy leaning against a pier holds a gourd and restrains his baby brother, the man reading a book has picked it up from the pile of Hermogenes' magic books and scrolls, two boys watch the scene leaning over the railing of an outer staircase. The introduction of such motifs was an established pictorial tradition in Padua: in Altichiero's fresco of *The Miracle of the Dragon and the Untamed Bulls* in the Cappella di S. Giacomo a little boy in the left foreground pulls at another to look at the scene: in the right foreground a mother puts up two little boys so that they can see better, and women look down on the scene from balconies above.[33]

In the pose of the man reading a book Mantegna adopts for the first time a dramatic device which reconciled the need to draw such accessory figures on the same scale as the principal figures with the need to subordinate their importance in the composition. This was all the more necessary because if not duly subordinated they might easily acquire a spurious prominence in pictorial actions with so few figures. The solution Mantegna adopts is to make the figure turn its back to the viewer, a device which also has the advantage of suggesting spatial depth, for which purpose it had already been used in Padua by Giotto in the Arena chapel and by Altichiero.

Mantegna plainly designed his unitary treatment of this pair of scenes in alternation with the deliberately contrasted settings of the two frescoes above them, for in the two frescoes below the contrast between an architectural and a landscape setting is repeated, but in reverse order from the two uppermost frescoes. In some ways the *Baptism* and *Trial* represent an imposition of Alberti's perspective on compositions whose conception still makes heavy use of the more traditional devices for creating spatial illusionism that Mantegna had already learnt. Figures turning or cut off by the frame continue to suggest the lateral extension of space. More important, in both scenes the principal action takes place in the middle ground, so as to emphasize the space before it, through which we look. And Squarcionesque illusionistic swags and scrambling putti dominate the upper part, once more cunningly prompting the eye to believe that the picture space continues in front of the plane marked by the framework. Some of the putti indeed peer down at the scenes below. If Mantegna's compositions are compared with those drawings of Jacopo Bellini[34] in which the figures are scaled according to the prin-

ciples of Alberti's perspective, it will be seen that he avoids a prime failing of Bellini, who often sets his principal figures in the middle ground, in obedience to well-established narrative convention, but reduces them accordingly. The result is that in scale they appear of lesser significance than the figures in the foreground, who are usually ancillary or accessory figures, and present largely to give pleasing variety. Some sharp contrasts of scale among the actors do nevertheless occur in Mantegna's histories of the 1450s, as in the figures looking down from a loggia in *The Baptism of Hermogenes*, and more remarkably, in the later histories of St Christopher, where the tyrant and his courtiers in the upper windows of the palace are considerably reduced in an attempt to reconcile the laws of aerial and geometrical perspective with clarity of exposition and with the limitations of the setting. The high vanishing-point of the second row of frescoes also has a further motive, for it is calculated with the spectator's height in mind. On looking up at the frescoes, the pavement of the courtyard and the base lines of the architecture appear to rise in a gentle slope, but at a rather less sharp angle than the foreground in the two uppermost frescoes. The consequence is an easy relationship between the spectator's space and the pictorial space.

The frescoes are likewise expressions of an aesthetic of dramatic verisimilitude to which Mantegna's search for illusionism also belongs. Certainly, as with the rocks and mountains of his landscape, Mantegna's purpose in his exotic costumes and vividly naturalistic motifs and actions is to add to already established pictorial traditions naturalistic plausibility of detail. The *Baptism*'s setting of a market-place, one of the focal centres of everyday activity in city life, is contrasted with the official grandeur of the tribunal in the *Trial*. In the *Baptism* we find ourselves in a paved piazza. On the left is a stately porticoed building, enriched with sculptured classical ornament; at the rear a line of houses rests on arches that make a porticoed side of the square. The arches are filled with the booths of shopkeepers: the booth that we see is that of a vendor of pottery. It may fairly be suspected that this is a classicized version of one of the great market piazzas of Mantegna's Padua. According to Savonarola, the Piazza of the Coopers was ringed with no less than 130 shops, set in pairs, one above the other, with the craftsmen seated on wooden platforms inside the doorway, and a sample of their goods set out for display before it, under a narrow portico running round the piazza.[35] The architecture confirms this impression, for the upper storey, with its steps leading up to a grilled lobby and its small round-headed windows, is a very medieval-looking superstructure, and the buildings owe their classical aspect solely to the inset medallion and the piers richly decorated with stems of acanthus.

The change in the companion fresco of the *Trial* (Plate 13) from the superficial classicism of the *Baptism* to the detailed evocation of a Roman provincial king enthroned in all the majesty of ancient justice is generally explained by the assumption that in devising this scene Mantegna sought and obtained advice from a humanist antiquary.[36] The inscription on the triumphal arch is known to have been taken from an antique slab, now lost, but formerly at Monte Buso, near Este, about twenty miles to the south-west of Padua. Since this inscription was also copied by Giovanni Marcanova, who though by profession a doctor of arts and of medicine, was by inclination an antiquary, humanist and poet, it is usually assumed that it was he who was Mantegna's early adviser. This slab and its inscription, however, together with a drawing of a funerary monument formerly in the church of San Salvatore, near Brescia, of which Marcanova also had a drawing, were both copied by Jacopo Bellini into his book of drawings, along with other antique monuments and medals.[37] The question of Mantegna's sources is therefore more complex than so simple a solution allows, especially as Marcanova is known to have drawn amply for his collections of monuments and inscriptions on the records of Ciriaco d'Ancona (*c.*1391–*c.*1455), merchant, traveller and indefatigable antiquarian, whose collection of Italian inscriptions was in its day the largest ever assembled. Ciriaco visited Padua in 1443 and made a collection of inscriptions for its humanist bishop Pietro Donato.[38] In the 1450s, and certainly by 1457, the scribe Felice Feliciano of Verona (1433–80), a friend of Mantegna and also of Giovanni Bellini and Marco Zoppo, was already engaged in the transcription of parts of Ciriaco's collections for various patrons, including Giovanni Marcanova. In addition, Feliciano himself drew monuments, if rather fantastically, and collected inscriptions, occasionally adding his own falsifications. About 1464 he made a copy of a collection for Mantegna and another for Mantegna's friend, the painter Samuele da Tradate.

It is usually assumed that the Giovanni Antenoreo with whom Mantegna and Feliciano and Samuele da Tradate made a famous visit to Lake Garda in 1464 was Marcanova. But for many reasons, not least from the want of any special title of respect, such as appertained to a dignified physician like Marcanova, in Feliciano's account of this holiday outing, we can be certain that this Giovanni was Giovanni da Padova, an engineer in the service of the Marquis of Mantua, and a friend of Mantegna. The only proven link, therefore, between Mantegna and Marcanova is their common acquaintance Feliciano, who was certainly working in Bologna in 1465 as a scribe for Marcanova.[39] However, Marcanova is also known to have been an intimate friend of the Veronese monk Matteo Bosso (*c.*1427–*c.*1502), who was certainly a close friend of Mantegna and who probably met them both *c.*1451, when he went to Padua to study.[40] It was Marcanova, moreover, who composed the inscription for the base of Donatello's statue of Gattamelata, so that he must also have been on terms of friendship with Gattamelata's widow, Giacoma della Leonessa, who some years later was to commission from Mantegna an important series of frescoes for a chamber in her palace.[41] And among the witnesses present at his death-bed in Bologna in 1467 was Ulisse degli Aliotti, Mantegna's early friend and admirer. Bosso describes Marcanova as delighting 'after philosophy and the ornaments of learning in painting and the portraits of illustrious men' and as relaxing his mind from the study of letters in contemplating 'such excellent monuments of antiquity as medals'.[42] Like his contemporary Michele Savonarola, he was a learned man who was also a dilettante of painting. It may be suspected that such men were not unique, and that in the Padua of the 1440s there was a circle of humanist antiquaries who were also amateurs of painting; their existence may help to explain so original an institution as Squarcione's school. It might also account for the patronage and admiration accorded to the youthful Mantegna, whose antiquarian studies the antiquaries of Padua probably encouraged, though perhaps rather more patronizingly than we should now expect, to judge from the tone in which Feliciano, a man of much less status than Marcanova, could address Mantegna in the 1460s.

To such men, preoccupied as they were with finding moral justifications for human activities, art and antiquities were means of instruction as well as of pleasure. On the one hand ancient medals taught men of noble disposition and good education about the famous men of classical antiquity, inciting them to emulation of their achievements, while the representation of saints in churches and on altars moved reverent beholders 'more than history itself or sermons, so strong and vehement a spur and good is there in painting that urges to the emulation of their worth.' So wrote Bosso, the learned Christian humanist. Marcanova's own collection of the inscriptions and antiquities of Italy survives in two recensions, one begun at Padua in 1457, completed at Cesena and transcribed at Bologna in 1460, and a second, also begun in Padua, completed in 1465. One recension, now at Modena, was intended for presentation to Marcanova's patron, Malatesta Novello, lord of Cesena, and was largely written by Felice Feliciano. It is notable for a series of eighteen drawings, now also sometimes attributed to Feliciano, in which the monuments of ancient Rome are re-created in a rich and fantastic manner very different from the restraint of Mantegna, whose simplicity reflects a truer archaeological vision of antiquity as well as his native lucidity of style.[43]

As Marcanova did not leave Padua to teach philosophy at Bologna until the late summer of 1452, there is no ostensible reason why he should not have given his counsel about *The Trial of St James* to Mantegna. Yet the depth of Mantegna's antiquarian knowledge at this early age should not be exaggerated, nor the extent of the antiquarian advice he received. Like so many classicizing works of art produced in the quattrocento, the *Trial* is a compound of motifs, disparate and anachronistic in their nature, which have been fused into a harmonious composition by the imagination of the artist. It is set in an evening light, for the sky is dark above the great triumphal arch which closes the open paved courtyard in which the trial takes place. The arch itself is a plausible recreation of an antique arch, modelled perhaps on medals and on the now destroyed Arco de' Gavi at Verona. But its use as a rear wall to the courtyard, indeed as a sort of architectural curtain cutting off the middle ground from the background, suggests that Mantegna had as yet no real sense of the Roman triumphal arch as something that bestrode a way, and is employing it with characteristic economy of invention as a decorative compositional device which at one and the same time was an appropriate symbol of Roman Imperial majesty. In the background, too, with its varying prospect of crags and valleys, of hills topped by castles and spired and towered towns, the picturesque is still that of contemporary Flemish and earlier Italian art, treated with Mantegna's inimitable naturalism. It is not one of those prospects of an antique city that crown so many of his landscapes from about 1454 onwards.

The real disparateness underlying a superficial unity of effect appears in the symbols of majesty attending Herod Agrippa. The throne, with its sphinx-shaped arms, and the fluted columns and red marble panels of its back, is an assemblage of authentic and fanciful motifs. As in paintings by nineteenth-century artists striving for historical colour, it has of course to be accepted that in quattrocento attempts at the re-creation of antiquity considerable unevenness of success was inevitable. For example, it was far easier for Mantegna to design an authentic Roman triumphal arch, either from representations on ancient medals or from surviving examples of which drawings were already in circulation, than an ancient throne, of which no specimen was known in his day. He was therefore forced into supplementing archaeological reality with plausible inventions, achieved as often as not by using buildings and objects belonging to his own times and introducing into them classical forms and ornaments. Plainly he

was unable to imagine, for instance, any ruler enthroned without the canopy of estate which was one of the major symbols of princely rank in his own age, and naïvely attached to his antique throne by means of a brass gadget is just such a fifteenth-century canopy. Decorum of time and place is restored on top of the canopy, however, by the figure holding an orb and standing on a globe. Inspired by some antique bronze, it is an emblem of Rome's universal rule.

The *Trial* also contains Mantegna's first essays in the representation of ancient costume and armour. Here again he was not so much an innovator as the developer of a tradition: his real originality lies in his substitution of a uniformity of Roman dress and armour for the motley variety of costumes that had pleased his predecessors. In this, however, as in his introduction of antique architecture, sculpture and ornaments into his paintings, he deserved his reputation as a restorer of antiquity, in spite of the elements of fantasy which his inventions necessarily contained. From the time of Giotto artists had been introducing features copied from ancient armour as represented in ancient sculpture into the armour with which they costumed their figures. *Antiquisant* armour and costume appear for example in Guariento's painting of *The Angelic Host* executed for the chapel of the Palazzo Carrarese and in Altichiero's figure of *Fortitude* in the Cappella di San Giacomo.[44]

With the advent of a sharper archaeological sense in the Early Renaissance came greater thoroughness and accuracy of classicization. Thus Donatello's *St George* (c.1417) is clad in an antique breastplate (*lorica*) with a tunic of *laminae* (lappets) and shoulder-pieces also of *laminae*. Mantegna's soldiers wear breastplates of plate armour, shaped to the chest, with short *laminae* pendent from them. Under this they wear a short tunic of leather *laminae* over a longer tunic. Their shoulder-pieces are of pleated stuff, and they wear arm-pieces, military boots and sometimes helms as well. Some have military cloaks and swords suspended from a baldric. It has been shown that the general type derives from armours depicted in late Imperial works of art.[45]

Yet in spite of the care Mantegna has taken to produce plausible versions of antique armour, anachronistic details occur, such as the winged cherub-head on the breastplate of the guard behind the Apostle. Perhaps these crept in because Mantegna was at pains to introduce small variations into the form of the armour. On some figures in the *Trial* the breastplates are tinted grey, indicating that they are of metal; on others they are coloured in a variety of hues, pinkish-brown, greenish-yellow, yellowish-brown, continuing a trecento tradition of unreal colour chosen for decorative effect. It has been suggested that these coloured armours should be

understood as painted leather, but their tints obey
the artist's fancy, rather than any reality of antique
or later times. All these features of Mantegna's classical armour recur in his art even as late as the *Triumphs*
(c.1485–92), a sure sign that much of his knowledge
and vision of antiquity was acquired during his formative years in Padua with its circles of learned antiquaries. Mantegna was always to remain the darling
painter of such men, as well as of the great humanist
nobles, princes and ecclesiastics whose taste for antiquity led them to form collections of gems, medals
and small sculptures, and libraries of classical authors.

Late in 1451 Mantegna stopped work on the
Ovetari frescoes, seemingly because his patroness
Imperatrice Ovetari had temporarily run short of
money, and took up other commissions. On 22 July
1452 he completed a fresco of *The Sacred Monogram
held by St Anthony of Padua and San Bernardino* (Plate
30) for the lunette of the central doorway of the
Santo, signing it in elegant humanist Latin. The
Franciscan St Anthony was the tutelary saint of
Padua and his church of the Santo one of the great
pilgrimage shrines of Christendom, and the association of Bernardino on a footing of equality with him
is a striking proof of the enthusiastic reverence felt
for this latest Franciscan saint.

Bernardino's canonization on 24 May 1450 was
undoubtedly the inspiration of the fresco. It
legitimized the ardent devotion felt for the great
revivalist preacher, and his cult was immediately
instituted in many places throughout Italy. We shall
encounter it again in Mantua, for Bernardino had
been a revered spiritual counseller of Mantegna's
future patrons, the Gonzaga. In Padua, where the
saint had preached in April 1443, arousing passionate
demonstrations of fervour, the Comune erected a
church to him in 1451 and decreed that his memory
should receive solemn honours every year.[46]
Although St Anthony is placed in the dexter place
of honour, the centrepiece of Mantegna's fresco is
the Name of Jesus, recalling Bernardino's custom of
holding up a tablet inscribed IHS during his
sermons. The Holy Name was executed in gilt metal
by the Paduan goldsmith Niccolò del Papa, a friend
of Mantegna and later to be portrayed by him in
the fresco of *The Martyrdom of St Christopher* in the
Ovetari Chapel.

In the Santo fresco, now detached and heavily
restored, Mantegna adapts the principles of
Squarcionesque spatial composition to the semi-
circular form of the lunette. As always, the framework is clearly articulated and strongly emphasized.
The medallion inscribed with the Holy Name is
encircled by a classical wreath and suspended from
the middle of the underside of the arch. The two
saints kneel on the ledge, holding the medallion,
with their attributes laid before them, two books and

a jar with a plant (?) for Bernardino, for Anthony
a lily and books. Their kneeling poses cleverly
reconcile the constraint imposed by the arch with
the theme of the verse from Philippians inscribed on
the medallion: 'In the name of Jesus, every knee
should bow of those that are in heaven, on earth and
in hell.' But the importance of the fresco in the
development of Mantegna's art is that in it, for the
first time, as far as we know, he deploys a device
of *di sotto in sù* perspective, which he was to make
peculiarly his own and which was to win him
repeated tributes of admiration from sixteenth-
century artists and virtuosi. Where, as here, the plane
on which the scene is set is above eye-level and
consequently the horizon is below, not above the
base-line of the picture plane, Mantegna suppresses
all floor and diminishes the feet and legs of the figures
by foreshortening and by omission of their forms,
the degree of suppression being calculated according
to distance from the base-line. Still-life objects are
similarly treated.

On this system, the lower limbs to the front of
the pose are more visible than those to the rear,
which are treated as becoming progressively more
invisible, just as they would in reality. The parts
principally subjected to this modification are usually
the feet and ankles, but in the Santo fresco it is
already applied with great mastery to the massive
lower forms of the kneeling body as united by the
robes worn by the two saints. Only the front profile
of the ledge is represented: the rear feet and legs of
the saints, the further side of the attributes and the
bottom of the medallion frame are all suppressed and
the illusion is created of a real arched space, receding
deeply behind the architectural frame. The only
incongruity is that the point from which the medallion frame hangs is forward of the line where it passes
behind the ledge below, so that there is a discrepancy
between the depth figured and the depth that is really
required. But such minor arbitrarinesses of spatial
construction, sacrificing mathematical exactness to
a general pictorial effect, recur more than once in
Mantegna's paintings during his Paduan years: they
indicate to us that for him geometry and perspective
were in the last resort instruments of his art, not a
pedantic passion. So much said, his employment of
this fresh device marks a further step in Mantegna's
search for verisimilitude of space, for a means to
make his simulations appear like extensions of
reality. Yet for all the speculation and experiment
it must have cost him, he never allows it either to
escape beyond his controlling search for an ostensibly easy naturalness of illusion over a whole design,
or to serve merely for surprising displays of
virtuosity.

Mantegna's use of the device raises a historical
problem. Its first appearance in Italian art is in Masac-

cio's fresco of the *Trinity* of *c*.1426–8 in Santa Maria Novella, Florence, where it is used, not so much because of the height at which the fresco is set, but to suggest the recession of the floor of the feigned chapel.[47] On the other hand, at about the same time the device had been used for the same effect as in Mantegna's fresco in Flanders. At the summit of the Van Eyck *Adoration of the Lamb* (completed 1432) Adam is shown in perspective from below standing in a niche, his right foot resting on the frame and his other foot cut off at the sole, while in the panel of Eve only her left foot is shown. Jan van Eyck was of course as celebrated in Italy as in the Netherlands: indeed we owe our earliest literary mention of him to Ciriaco d'Ancona, who speaks of him *c*.1450 as 'Johannes of Bruges, the ornament of painting'. Ciriaco had travelled in the Netherlands and his close relations with the antiquaries of Padua and the Veneto have already been noticed. Andrea may have heard an admiring account of the altarpiece, in the fifteenth century as now the boast of Ghent, and therefore of this particular refinement of perspective. But it is virtually certain that he can never have seen a large altarpiece by Van Eyck or one of his followers and only in a work set above eye-level does the device as he uses it have any justification. The truth is that too many works of art are lost, too many verbal reports and instructions and exchanges have left no echo for us to be sure of the history of the transmission and development of perspective devices in the Early Renaissance. And there is always the possibility that Mantegna developed this particular device independently, for its elements were, so to speak, in the air of the times. Yet it may also be that Mantegna learnt it from a lost work by Andrea del Castagno, who was in Venice in 1442, and who, as Vasari says, observed this perspective device 'with great diligence' in his *Cenacolo* in the refectory of Santa Maria Nuova in Florence, painted from July to October 1447.[48] Here the device is used for foreshortening the vessels on the table.

Of Mantegna's next securely dated work,[49] the altarpiece he painted between August 1453 and November 1454 for the chapel of St Luke in the monastery church of Santa Giustina in Padua (Plate 1), the claim is sometimes made that it was rather antiquated in taste by 1453, and that it was its patron, the abbot Mauro dei Folperti, rather than Mantegna, who was responsible for its old-fashioned Gothic richness, with a florid frame (now lost), pointed panels and gold ground. And indeed it may reasonably be supposed that left to himself Mantegna would have designed the altarpiece and its frame in Renaissance form. Yet it has to be remembered too that gold ground altarpieces on panels and in frames of Gothic design were still the settled preference of patrons in the Padua and Venice of the late 1440s

and early 1450s, as can be seen from Squarcione's Lazara altarpiece of 1449–52 among others. Indeed the Vivarini were to continue to paint such altarpieces into the last decades of the century. Accordingly Mauro dei Folperti and the Fra Antonino to whom he delegated the ordering of the frame from the woodcarver Maestro Guglielmo were not themselves behind their times in desiring an altarpiece of traditional form and splendour, its saints glowing against a ground of refulgent gold, in a framework of Gothic colonnettes, crockets and pinnacles. The chapel itself is so wholly Gothic in architecture and frescoes that the Gothic design of its framework was in complete harmony with the setting.

Santa Giustina was the greatest and most venerable of Padua's Benedictine monasteries,[50] but the importance of the chapel for which the altarpiece was intended also justified such magnificence. Like all medieval cities, Padua trusted for protection against the perils of this life, war, the plague, sickness, drought and famine, to the treasury of bodies and relics of the saints enshrined within its walls. By the fifteenth century it had a richly furnished spiritual arsenal. In general esteem the most powerful and efficacious of all its holy relics were those of St Anthony, housed in the Santo. Savonarola describes the sumptuous cult attending the shrine of the saint, the vestments of cloth of gold and silk, and the reliquaries of gold and silver, among them one for the saint's tongue commissioned by Antonio degli Ovetari.[51] The bodies of other saints lay in other churches and convents within and without the city. Santa Giustina possessed those of two of the Apostles, St Luke the Evangelist and St Matthew, St Luke being even more especially venerated because he was believed to have been the companion and guardian of the Virgin. The church also held the bodies of San Prosdocimo, a disciple of St Peter and first bishop of Padua, of St Maximus, second bishop of Padua, of St Julian and St Felicitas, and of the virgin martyr Santa Giustina herself. The body of the martyred St Daniel of Padua, discovered in the church in the twelfth century, had been translated to the cathedral; in popular belief to drink holy water in which a fragment of his shrine had been mixed was a sovereign cure for fever. All or almost all these saints are figured, no doubt at the behest of the abbot and monks of Santa Giustina, in Mantegna's altarpiece.

Tradition held that the body of St Luke had been brought from Constantinople during the great Iconoclastic controversy of the eighth and ninth centuries. Later it was concealed, along with the bodies of Prosdocimo, Giustina, Julian, Daniel, Maximus and Felicitas, and only in 1177 was it rediscovered. By the 1430s the early fourteenth-century shrine and chapel which housed it were in sore need of repair.

After the usual campaign for pious legacies, redecoration of the chapel began in 1436 when the Venetian painter Filippo Storlato was commissioned to fresco its walls with scenes depicting the body's translation to Padua and its invention in 1177. Storlato had completed his frescoes, which are wholly Gothic in conception and naïveté, by August 1441, but another twelve years were to pass before sufficient moneys had been accumulated for an altarpiece. The commission was formally given to Mantegna on 10 August 1453.

In his iconographical scheme and general design, Mantegna followed a standard pattern which is also found in a number of earlier polyptych altarpieces painted by Antonio Vivarini and Giovanni d'Alemagna in partnership during the 1440s, such as that of Parenzo (dated 1440) and that of the abbey of Praglia, near Padua, painted c.1448. It was used again by Antonio and Bartolommeo Vivarini in their altarpiece painted at Venice in 1450 to the commission of Pope Nicholas V for the Certosa of Bologna.[52] The altarpiece of Praglia may well have been the model for Mantegna's altarpiece, may indeed have been imposed on him as such by Mauro dei Folperti, for Praglia joined the congregation of Santa Giustina on 17 May 1448 and its altarpiece, which alludes to this union, was probably well known to Mauro as the congregation's head.

In altarpieces of this kind, the central division has two compartments, the upper one being smaller than the lower and containing a Pietà, the lower one an image of the principal figure. The narrow vertical section formed by these two compartments is flanked on its lower part by a range of full-length standing saints, figured on single panels not quite so tall as the central panel, and by a corresponding upper row of half-length figures of saints, whose panels again are not so tall as that of the central Pietà. In Mantegna's altarpiece the full-standing figures of the major saints, Scolastica and Prosdocimo, Benedict and Giustina, flank St Luke to left and right. Above, to the left of three small panels figuring the Pietà flanked by the mourning Virgin and St John the Evangelist, shown in three-quarter length, are three-quarter-length figures of St Daniel and St Jerome, while to the right are similar figures of St Maximus and St Julian. With his left hand St Jerome points to his repentant heart, while clasping in his right the stone with which he strikes his bared breast. His dark brown body and shadowed eyes impress the image of a profoundly penitential spirit as he contemplates the figure of Christ. In the Pietà seamed brown faces and parted mouths express the inner movements of anguish: their emotional realism is for once something that Mantegna may have learnt from Donatello. The noble sculptural torso of Christ rises in a pose of *déhanchement* from the sarcophagus of brown marble veined with red and green; his arms, with their starting sinews, have something of the thin, fleshless boniness of Northern Gothic art as he shows his wounded hands, and blood streams from his side.

There can be no doubt that the group of Jerome and the Pietà are intended to move the spectator to contrition, and the same penitential theme is urged again in the scourge of thorns held by St Benedict. This gentle severity of admonition expresses the ascetic spirit of Santa Giustina during these years. In 1408 the lax monastic life of the black Benedictines of Santa Giustina had been reformed by Cardinal Antonio Correr, nephew of Pope Gregory XII and uncle of the Gregorio Correr who was shortly to commission Mantegna to paint an altarpiece for another Benedictine monastery in Verona, the abbey of San Zeno. With Lodovico Barbo, who ruled as abbot from 1409 to 1443, a new spirit of simplicity and fervour entered the monastery and the full observance of the primitive Benedictine rule was introduced. It was Barbo who began the rebuilding and redecoration of the monastery, which had fallen into a ruinous state. So successful was his reform that Santa Giustina ceased to be large enough for its monks. Barbo sent out groups of them to other decayed monasteries and at the same time accepted the affiliation of other religious houses which were anxious to reform themselves. In this way Santa Giustina became the head of a new reformed congregation of Benedictines, known as the congregation of Santa Giustina, which was formally established by Pope Martin V in 1419 and confirmed by Eugenius IV in 1432. In the late 1440s Savonarola wrote of its monks: 'They do not run up and down through the city, but enclosed within their walls sing most devoutly the canonical hours in such silence and with such sweetness that the minds of the listeners feel themselves to be rapt into a divine repose.'[53]

The altarpiece sustains this spirit of austere, enclosed, penitential devotion in the dark, penitential colours worn by several of its saints, black, dark blue, olive-green. These are relieved by the gold background, by the light that falls on them from the left, and by the whites, coral red, scarlet and crimson of the other saints. Yet even the gold ground seems muted by austerity of spiritual feeling, as if there for decorum, rather than for splendour. The figures are posed with all that strength and drawn with all that firm and exquisite clarity of outline for which Mantegna was unequalled in his lifetime. The gold is treated as if it were in all reality heavenly light. The stately, solidly conceived figures seem to turn and move in it as if it were terrestrial space, posed in profile, three-quarter profile and full-face, in a smooth lustrousness of refulgent colour whose strength of contrast approaches the effect of translucent enamel on gold. In further defiance of the flat brilliance of gold Mantegna has set the four principal saints on a continuous platform paved with coloured marbles, green and red and purple, whose orthogonals converge on a vanishing-point a little above the gilt base of St Luke's columned table, a low viewpoint carefully chosen in relation to the spectator. He has also developed an initiative of Antonio Vivarini and Giovanni d'Alemagna in breaking with the hieratic symmetry traditional in altarpieces of this kind. If the saints on the left all look inwards, nevertheless their heads are at different angles; and those on the right look outwards, instead of inwards, except for St Daniel. It must be said in favour of Squarcione that he too in his slightly earlier Lazara altarpiece had already abandoned rigid formal symmetry.

The poses of Scholastica, Prosdocimo, Benedict and Giustina recall sculptural formulae of distributing weight in figure poses in the prominence given to the flexed knee. And if Mantegna's figures are compared with those of Antonio Vivarini and Giovanni d'Alemagna it at once becomes plain that he does not allow the robes to impose a cylindrical form of their own on the figure, like Antonio and Giovanni, but uses the device of the flexed knee to suggest the body posed within the ample draperies. St Luke is emphasized not only by the greater size of his panel, but by the larger scale of his figure, and by the stepped platform on which he sits at his table. For reasons of dignity this is raised above the level of the platform of the flanking saints and made discontinuous with it. The notions of relative scale governing this relationship are hieratic and medieval, and it is Mantegna's skill to have avoided the appearance of incongruity among his figures.

Learned Padua was partial to representations of saints and learned men writing at their desks. As we know Altichiero had painted a fresco of Petrarch in his study in the Palazzo Carrarese;[54] in the apse of the Ovetari Chapel Pizzolo depicted the Four Doctors of the Church, each in his study, surrounded with books and papers, and absorbed in composition, writing, looking up a reference, meditating or mending a pen. Similarly Mantegna shows the figure of Luke not as an image posed to receive the adoration of the faithful, but in a naturalistic attitude, seated with legs apart at a great marble table, one foot resting on a lower step of the platform, wholly taken up in writing. As so often with monastic commissions, particularly in reformed monasteries, this pose may be due to the instructions of the abbot and be a figured admonition to the monks to occupy themselves with *lectio spiritualis*, the study of sacred scripture and theology. About the Apostle Mantegna makes a display of all the illusionistic devices that he had now learnt or mastered for himself. The knobs of fruit surmounting the pilasters framing the semicircular back of the saint's throne are treated in his new perspective; because they appeared above eye-level, their lower part is suppressed. The throne and the circular top of the marble table and its column are marvels of foreshortening – again Mantegna treats the gold background as space, not as a plane. The book, the lamp, the coral jar with a wick, the inkwells, one with red ink for rubrication, one with black for text, are further small essays in virtuosity, as are the figs which lie on the steps to mark the first plane of illusionism, in true Squarcionesque fashion.

The altarpiece is the first surviving work in which Mantegna reveals his love of marble and particularly of coloured and variegated marbles, to him and to his age the noblest of stones, whose richness was admired perhaps even more in Lombardy and Venice than elsewhere in Italy. Mantegna's astonishing skill in imitating the colours and markings of marbles has never been equalled, though the taste for such simulations was well established in the trecento. The throne is inlaid with panels of a veined red marble and raised on two low steps of a mottled marble, predominantly green above and red below, which are set on a floor paved with grey stone and porphyry. The tall column of the marble table is veined with red and blue and green: its top is red and pale yellow. This sensibility to the natural variegation of spots and veins and mottlings of colour in marble is accompanied by a hard precision and minuteness of style in the rendering of other still-life objects. The veining of the light unpolished wood and the rough edges of Luke's plain writing-desk are rendered in meticulous detail and at the same time with great variety of outline. The broad clear flow of light to the right, modified only by some local cast shadows, serves to enhance the sharp clarity with which each motif is rendered – a clarity which makes the painting a construction of single objects, in a sort of additive illusionism. The fenestration of the chapel has been altered, but Mantegna implies that the light falls from the left. A close attentiveness to the actual source of light is a constant in Mantegna's art from first to last. Plainly it was always one of his first considerations in the invention of his paintings, and a prime element in the aesthetic of his naturalism, so intent on concord with reality.

Luke's red robe and Giustina's pink cloak have white highlighting – Mantegna's first surviving use (it was also employed in the Ovetari frescoes, so we are told) of what was to become a favourite means of modelling draperies and of softening areas too strong in colour. Giustina is, in addition, his earliest known type of a beautiful maiden. She has uplifted eyes, and her chin is foreshortened in a manner characteristic of Mantegna, who uses this pose again in the more or less contemporary Ovetari *Assumption*. A difficult motif, it taxed and displayed his power of rendering volume in space with accurate refinements of recession and foreshortening. Giustina has a head of squarish form: not therefore of the elongated type dear to Gothic taste such as we find in the St Catharine of Squarcione's Lazara altarpiece. The forehead is high and smooth, the eyebrows are thinly pencilled and the mouth is a small Cupid's bow – all points of beauty in the fifteenth century. The features are strongly outlined and modelled in a few smoothly sculptural planes. The head rests on a long, gracefully inclined neck, set off by the curling brown tresses that fall luxuriantly from the centre parting. The body itself is tall and slender, with a high waist clasped by a belt: typically, Mantegna has disguised its pose of elegant *déhanchement*, with the weight resting on the right leg, in the heavy draperies of the cloak, without losing the feeling of truly sculptural flexion.

Giustina's pose and costume were both to remain favourites with Mantegna until the end of his career. They are found reversed in the Naples *St Euphemia*,[55] which is signed and dated 1454 on a *cartello*, Mantegna's earliest known use of this device, soon to become a favourite Venetian motif. In format the *St Euphemia* (Plate 31), now much damaged, is a tall vertical oblong, and it was perhaps intended to be hung on a pier, above an altar. The saint's figure is silhouetted within an arched window frame of variegated marble, hung with brightly coloured swags suspended from the front of the arch. Traces are still visible of two other swags that once hung from the rear of the arch to define its depth in space. In spite of this care to mark the planes of recession, Euphemia's tawny lion, with white whiskers and glaring orange eyes, is set beside and behind her feet on the ledge, where by the definition of the swags there cannot be place enough for him, even though the saint's body is inclined in a strong *déhanchement* to right of centre in order to give him room. Mantegna has disguised the difficulty by making him stand on his left front paw and lift his right in a pose that helps to conceal this irrationality. But the picture is yet another proof, like the later Venice *St George*, that whenever there is a conflict between spatial logic and pictorial effect, he resolves it in favour of pictorial effect.

Euphemia's long golden tresses are a first tribute to that admiration for crisply curling luxuriant blond beauty which is still found in Mantegna's latest pictures and was to be celebrated with such sensuality in Venetian cinquecento art.[56] She is richly costumed in a robe of red patterned damask and a dark mantle, both edged with vair. The ends of her sleeves are clasped by gold bracelets set with rubies and pearls: also of gold set with rubies and pearls is her martyr's crown. Mantegna is restrained in his use of such ornaments so as not to give idle distraction to the eye, yet he renders these and the other still-life motifs, lily, palm and sword, the fruit of the swag, with precise and delicate sensibility to glistening surface and the change of light and shade. Even in the picture's ruined state it is still possible to appreciate the glow of its colour and the intense compact dignity of the saint's figure, as of a statue, confronting the faithful with a vision of supernatural beauty in corporeal form. She has, it is true, the impassive, closed expression typical of Mantegna, whose figures so often seem severely contained within their own perfection of form, yet her eyes hold the worshipper without aloofness or disdain.

III

The Ovetari Frescoes

IN 1452, at the age of 22, Mantegna was betrothed to Nicolosia, the daughter of Jacopo Bellini. The exact date of their marriage has not been discovered, but most probably it took place a little before or after 25 February 1453, when Jacopo received twenty ducats from the Scuola Grande di San Giovanni Evangelista as a subvention towards his daughter's marriage.[1] According to Vasari, almost certainly repeating gossip he found in Campagnola, Jacopo arranged the marriage because he was a rival of Squarcione and because he foresaw Andrea's future fame from the pictures he had already painted.

The marriage certainly emancipated Andrea from Squarcione and transferred him to the protection of the leading master of Venice, giving him a father-in-law to replace his own dead father and a family of artists with whom he could learn and study. Mantegna's art was to affect profoundly the art of his brother-in-law Giovanni, the greatest of the Bellini, but in his youth, as we have already seen, Andrea profited from his association with Jacopo. Perhaps it should be emphasized again that the quarrel with Squarcione which ensued was not permanent, for Mantegna continued to call himself Andrea Squarcione, and in 1465 Squarcione was enticing a new pupil to enter his workshop by the resounding claim that it was he who had made a man of Mantegna.

At the earliest in 1454, but more probably in 1455 and 1456, Mantegna completed the last two histories of St James on the left wall of the Ovetari chapel. The first of these, *St James on the way to Execution*, was the history that originally had been reserved for Niccolò Pizzolo, but it had not been begun before Pizzolo's death in the middle of 1453. Once again, Mantegna's resourceful invention met a new chal-lenge with a new solution, for these two frescoes, although the lowest, were still set a little above the spectator's eye-level, with a base-line about two metres from the floor.[2] In *St James on the way to Execution* (Plate 14), Mantegna again employs the perspective device, first found as we saw in the Santo fresco of *The Sacred Monogram*, of taking a point of sight below eye-level, so that the rear limbs of all the figures in the foreground and both limbs of all the figures in the plane behind are cut short. As a result the spectator, who is envisaged as standing on the floor of the chapel, not, as in the two frescoes above, on the base-line of the painting itself, has the sensation of watching actual figures enacting a scene on a platform just above his eye-level. This illusion is reinforced by the shoes of some of the front figures, which appear to protrude into space beyond the edge of the platform. This device also appears in Andrea del Castagno's fresco of Pippo Spano, probably painted in the later 1440s, and for this reason its appearance in this St James fresco has been attributed to Tuscan influence on Mantegna. In reality, by 1454 it had already been known for twelve years or more in Venice, for it was used by Antonio Vivarini and Giovanni d'Alemagna on the rear side of the San Tarasio altarpiece. Here four figures among the lower ranks of saints are shown with one foot apparently protruding over the pedestals on which they stand. The device is one that is attractive and plausible only at or near eye-level, and this must be why it appears in *St James on the way to Execution* for the first time in Mantegna's Ovetari frescoes.[3]

These were not Mantegna's only audacities of perspective and illusionism in the fresco. The tower in the right background is represented at an angle to the picture plane in order to suggest to the spec-

tator the curve of the street. This presented a problem in that the horizontal lines of the palace had to
be drawn parallel with the line of the ground level,
and therefore at an angle to the base-line visible in
them, but not visible at the base-line of the picture,
since the perspective adopted by Mantegna involved
suppression of any view of the ground level.
Mantegna has solved the problem correctly, and has
given the solution to a second problem of the same
sort in the palace in the right foreground. A diagram
of the fresco shows in fact that all the lines in flight
meet on a single horizon below the sight-line, as
demanded by the perspective. His solutions must
have involved him in much geometrical and mathematical speculation: his reward was the rigorous perfection of his design, with its extreme precision of
intervals and solids according to a mathematically
calculated scale. The resulting work of art might
well have been rather rigid, but in fact the looming
architectural background, with its plunging lines,
the turning movement of the street, and the exceptional perspective with its swift recession, give even
in a photograph a sensation of dizzying movement.[4]

St James on the way to Execution is the most powerful and dramatic work of the entire sequence, and
of all Mantegna's Ovetari frescoes the one that most
nearly approaches the spirit of Masaccio's Carmine
frescoes. It is also the only one for which a drawing
(Plate 205) is preserved, and from this we can discover something of the evolution of the composition. From its sketchy indications it seems that
originally the background was to have been a curving street, its curve running across the fresco. A
building abuts on it at right angles on the left, leaving
only a narrow way between. A projecting house in
the centre divides the scene into two halves. In the
left half St James blesses a kneeling cripple, dressed
in a tunic, who implores him for a cure, while a
Roman centurion lifts his hands in amazement, and
a half-naked man, perhaps a beggar, seated on a stone
behind rests his hands on his knees and gazes with
bold curiosity at the Apostle. Behind the centurion
stands a file of Roman guards, lining the left side
of a narrow street, while in the right half of the composition a naked soldier presses back with his staff
a naked spectator, first of a row of spectators who
stand closely fronting the guards. The motif of this
invention is anecdotal: it does not seem that the spectator has started forward to see the miracle. The
drawing also reveals that the perspective scheme was
intended from the first, for the feet of the figures
are cut off at the bottom in recession, and a line runs
across to mark the base-line.

The fresco retains the separation of the scene into
two halves, but now the division is marked in the
architectural background, not by a projecting block,
but by a great triumphal arch whose summit soars
beyond the frame. It appears to be modelled on the
Arco dei Gavi at Verona, destroyed by the French
in 1805, but before that greatly celebrated for its
beauty. To the arch itself Mantegna has added an
attic storey in the form of an arched gallery copied
from the upper gallery of the Roman gate of Verona
known as the Porta dei Borsari. The reason for this
curious amalgamation can only be caprice or archaeological ignorance. If not caprice, and certainly
Mantegna was always careful not to make slavish
copies of known antique monuments, but to use
them simply as models, sometimes, as in the arch
of the Trial, inserting inscriptions and motifs from
one kind of monument into another, then it raises
the question of whether as yet Mantegna knew the
monuments of Verona only from drawings.[5] The
plunging lines of its architecture and of the caissons
of the arch, correctly divided into an uneven number
according to the practice of antiquity, lead the eye
through the arch to the line of houses on the left
and to the opening on the right between the arch
and the serpentine line of palaces, towers and houses
closing the composition on the right. That the arch
is at the top of a rise, and that the two lines of buildings unite to form a single street that curves away
downwards to the right is suggested with consummate skill and an audacious reversal of usual pictorial
practice. Mantegna was again to display the same
virtuosity in sinking an inner part of the picture in
relation to the foreground in the Crucifixion panel
of the predella of the San Zeno altarpiece and in the
Vienna St Sebastian, where it is the middle ground
that is sunk, not, as here, the background.

The subject of the fresco has also been slightly
changed. In view of the difficulties that were later
to arise over the fresco of the Assumption, it would
be interesting to know whether this was from
Mantegna's own preference or at the behest of his
patrons. It now represents, not the miracle of the
cripple, but the conversion of the scribe Josias, who
is dressed in a scribe's long robes and has an inkhorn
hanging from his belt. According to the Legenda
Aurea, Josias was escorting James to execution, and
on witnessing the cure of the cripple threw himself
on his knees and asked to become a Christian. The
action is still pivoted on three foreground motifs,
with the figure of the marvelling centurion continuing to serve as a vertical division between the
principal action in the left half of the fresco and the
guard pressing back a spectator on the right. But in
order to accentuate his effects of perspective and of
illusion, Mantegna has brought the centurion and
guard forward to the edge of the scene. Here he has
also positioned the scribe, turning his figure inwards
at an angle so that only the outline of his profile is
visible. Accordingly, James no longer faces him in
near profile; he stands with his right foot projecting

Fig. 3. Heads of two Roman soldiers. Detail from *St James on the way to Execution* (Plate 14)

slightly into space, but with the rest of his body and head in near three-quarter profile fronting Josias. By this change Mantegna not only encloses the dialogue between the two, but wonderfully suggests the Apostle pausing on his way to execution to give his blessing. Simultaneously the responding hands of James and the centurion, with their contrasted gestures, are silhouetted with sharp eloquence against the opening of the arch.

Mantegna compensates for the loss of weight these alterations entailed on the left of the composition by introducing another soldier, who stands watching on the extreme left of the foreground in a pose cunningly aligned with that of James. In the interests of a subtler and more dramatic naturalism the curious beggar, originally introduced to close the group of the miracle at the rear, has been removed, an alteration allowing Mantegna to open the background still further. The soldiers behind the centurion are no longer lined up in a file, but the significance of the principal action is intensified by adding a second guard immediately behind the centurion. This figure is made at one and the same time to deepen and seal off further the space within which the conversion is enacted, and to serve as a link between the two halves of the composition. In the right half the rank of spectators has been removed from the foreground, where they would have been too prominent for their significance in the scene and obstructed the second opening into the background. Instead the guard is made to force back with an angry shout a young Jewish nobleman. Two Roman standards rise behind, one with a flapping banner whose scrolling, decorative folds introduce between the rigid lines of the architecture an animated movement echoing the movement on the ground below. The soldiers and spectators lining the way are set on both sides against the architecture and diminished in scale, so that they enliven the background without preoccupying the eye, a purpose also attained by the small half figures of women spectators who look out of the windows.

For a composition which offered little contrast in depth between its two halves these adjustments substitute one in which the main block of figures is on the left, while on the right the scene sinks away down the street up which James and his escort have come on their way to his execution. The quarrel between the guard and the youth is of no importance to the story, but is an anecdote introduced in order to provide the right half of the composition with a motif whose weight and action balance those of the left without distracting from them. Although this was certainly Mantegna's intention, the naturalism that led him to distribute an equal emphasis in his crowd scenes over all the figures in the foreground leads here, as perhaps also in *The Baptism of Hermogenes*, to an undue prominence of figures and actions that are ancillary, and are present merely for the sake of narrative illusion or to add variety and colour. Yet the turbulence of this invention is in profound accord with the dark shadows about the limbs of the figures, with the pale evening light below an angry dark blue sky, with the dizzying height of the arch and the lofty prospects through and beside it plunging on to the curving irregular lines of the street behind.

Finally, it should be noticed that the medieval tower-houses fronting both sides of the street make a cunning contrast with the severely noble antique architecture and rich sculptural ornament of the great triumphal arch, attributed in its inscription to the great architect Vitruvius, whose work on architecture was already being eagerly studied by humanists and artists, and with the classically designed palace in the right foreground. These two, arch and palace, unite to form a proscenium of antique magnificence on which the principal action is performed. With subtle verisimilitude the re-created glories of Roman imperial architecture are profiled against a background of the tall brown houses of everyday.

Unlike the *Trial* above, the composition of *The Execution of St James* (Plate 15) is not orientated to the right to match its companion, nor does Mantegna place the same emphasis on a low point of sight: only in one or two of the foreground figures are the ends of the rear feet cut off. One reason for this change was iconographical: the martyrdom of St James is figured as taking place below the walls of Jerusalem. But a more powerful intention was to affront the spectator with the brutality of the scene. He is hardly separated from the head of the prostrate saint fixed under the *mannaia*, a crude medieval prototype of the guillotine which was in general use in Italy in the late Middle Ages and is figured in the drawing of the Capitol in Marcanova's Modena manuscript, where a criminal is being executed with it under a guard of Roman soldiers.[6] To enhance the immediacy of the scene, Mantegna sets before it only the light barrier of a rustic fence of trees and tree-trunks; if this parts the spectator from the scene by its railing, it is only to suggest that he looks over and through it, so putting real and pictorial space into continuity. The centre foreground, demarcated by the bars of the fence, is occupied by the foreshortened body of the saint and the frightening figure of his executioner, an incarnation of coarse and cruel plebeian strength, with strongly marked features, bald head, black hair and beard, wearing a ragged grey coat that parts to show a short tunic and powerful legs. His figure is said by Campagnola to have been taken from a real model, a certain Marsilio Pazzo (perhaps to be interpreted as Marsilio the madman). In deliberate contrast is the refined cruelty of the gauntleted officer who stoops down over the fence to watch the blow fall with coldly eager interest. The horror of the scene is a little mitigated by the rich accoutrements of the soldier on the left, which include a cylindrical quiver patterned with classical laurel leaves, and by his handsome white horse, shown foreshortened in rear view, a motif already dear to International Gothic art.

It is softened too by the contrasting figure of the white armoured soldier on a bay horse, shown prancing on the right, like an equestrian statue come to life, and by two spectators, Negroes dressed in Moorish costume. The suggestion that the picture-space extends laterally beyond the frame, present in all the frescoes, is here even more strongly felt, and not merely because much of the ruined classical building and half of the bay horse are cut off on the right, but because of the rising slope of the high mountain, which divides the picture diagonally, throwing up the fierce red sky and evening blue. With uncompromising naturalism only one bare leg appears behind the bay horse, probably that of a youthful soldier; we are presumably to figure him as dressed like the small group of three young Roman soldiers standing a little way off up the road. In the same way, only one of the two 'Moorish' spectators is shown reasonably fully. This use of partly concealed figures, found already in *The Baptism of Hermogenes*, is here used with greater daring and confidence, rousing our curiosity and stimulating our imagination, in accordance with Pliny's eulogy of Timanthes 'that more is suggested than is depicted.'

The diminished scale of the background is emphasized by the lopped tree. With characteristic compositional economy this serves as one of the vertical bars of the fence, and by rising the full height of the fresco it simultaneously unites top and bottom and relieves with its leaves and branches the great triangle of sky. The mountain is the first of its kind in Mantegna's art and the first of many similar landscape inventions. It rises high up the picture, in deepening recession, so that all its features and the figures walking upon it diminish dramatically in scale as it rises. A winding road relates it to the foreground. The line of the slope is smooth, broken only by a few widely spaced small trees and bushes; not so the face that confronts the eye, whose surface is compartmented by curving roads cut deep into the rock, and further divided into horizontal parallels by the lines of its fields and rows of bushes and by the great wall that runs below the summit of the mountain. On the upper slopes appear for the first time the little classical ruins that will become characteristic of Mantegna's landscapes, *vestigia antiquitatis* introduced for their romantic evocation of fallen grandeur, that is with a motive not so much histori-

cal as poetical and pictorial. Above are the white walls and towers and pink and white citadel of Jerusalem, not yet, it should be noted, the city part oriental, part classical of the London *Agony in the Garden* and of the predella panels of the San Zeno altarpiece.

The fresco, in comparison with its predecessors, is said by competent nineteenth- and early twentieth-century scholars to have shown a striking stylistic and technical change in the direction of softer form and warmer colour. In the words of Kristeller,

In contrast to the earlier frescoes, which derive a cold and slightly unnatural colour from the harshly juxtaposed, earthy, grey, blue and violet tones with white lights, large white surfaces, and sharp reddish-brown or heavy grey shadows, the tone in this part of the work is like the modelling, much softer and warmer, and is mellowed to a general reddish-brown.[7]

Kristeller was inclined to attribute this change to the influence of the Bellini, and we shall shortly see that Squarcione was to criticize the histories of St James for their pale colours, perhaps voicing criticisms that had already been made by others and prompting Mantegna to modify his style. The destruction of the fresco makes it impossible now to reach any conclusion about the origins of the change: but another observation made by Kristeller should be recorded because it suggests that Mantegna may already have been making the experiments in techniques of wall-painting which were to result in the entirely original technique used on a wall of the Camera Picta in Mantua. He notes that the head of St James in the *Execution* was painted on a piece of stucco that seemed 'to have been submitted to a different process; the surface is smooth and shining, and the colour is put on liquid with a light brush.' However, we must repeat his caution that this effect may have been due to restoration.[8]

Dramatic invention, tensed action, brutal violence set these two scenes on the lowest register of the wall in powerful contrast with the pair above, whose figures seem arrested in poses of calm dignity. The same passionate grandeur of conception animates *The Assumption of the Virgin* (Plate 21) which after the death of Pizzolo in 1453 it fell to Mantegna's lot to paint on the tall narrow panel of wall in the centre of the apse of the tribune. Such evidence as we have indicates that he designed and painted it after completing the histories of St James, probably late in 1456. The scene is enclosed in a simulated framework, a tall and narrow Renaissance arch richly decorated with acanthus stem. With daring invention Mantegna has shown the Virgin rising through the blackness of night into heaven. She is already high in the space framed by the arch, but about to pass from our sight: the upper edge of her blue almond-shaped mandorla is already beyond the arch. Here then his illusionism, always so preoccupied with solid forms in three-dimensional space, finds a triumphant physical expression for a mystical apotheosis. The Virgin's eyes are uplifted, her lips parted and her hands outspread in the ancient *orans* posture of Early Christian and Byzantine art as she utters a prayer to her Son, whom we are to imagine as already manifest in heaven. On the underside of the arch glitter golden stars: her red robe is lit with gold, and golden rays emanate from her head and body as she is borne upwards by six child angels, their forms self-evidently modelled on the genii of ancient sarcophagi. Beneath her feet is a bank of pale blue cloud supported by golden cherubim; other cherubim, fiery red with the flames of love, form a second mandorla about the first; yet others, pale blue and gold, attend her on small clouds, the forms of all moving freely in the depths of space. Some play pipes and trumpets, clash cymbals, shake tambourines, making a music of rejoicing in accordance with the introit of the first Mass of the Assumption: 'The holy mother of God is raised above the choirs of angels to the kingdom of Heaven' (*Exaltata est sancta Dei genetrix super choros angelorum ad coelestia regna*).

Four more child angels under the bank of cloud extend the motif of the actual *Assumption* so that it fills the entire upper part of the fresco and the topmost section of its middle band. The lower section of this middle band, with great audacity, is left as empty sky, so reinforcing the effect of upward movement in a great height of space. Below are eight amazed Apostles, tall, slender figures crowded together in a circle on one of Mantegna's too narrow platforms at the base of the arch, gazing upwards at the confounding miracle. In reality the arch is merely a spatial device, marking a pictorial plane rather than a pictorial fact. Mantegna has one of the Apostles clasp its left pilaster with an arm, so suggesting that we, the spectators, are witnesses standing behind the actual figures of the Apostles. This beautiful fresco, now much deteriorated, is perhaps the only early work of Mantegna that can be called visionary: the strong sculptural head and limbs, boldly foreshortened, of the Virgin, her long slender body in a simply draped robe, whose narrow vertical folds are contrasted with the broad folds of her blue cloak, executed in the costly *azzurro ultramarino*, make a figure of transcendent majesty and beauty.

The *Assumption* is the most conspicuous example of Mantegna's disregard of narrative and iconographical accuracy in the interests of purely pictorial effect. In February 1457 his indignant patroness, Imperatrice Ovetari, brought a suit against him on the issue of the plain question, whether the Apostles had been only eight in number, as Mantegna had shown them in the fresco, or whether they had been twelve. The dispute involved not only devotional and historical proprieties, but also the price of the fresco, for in valuing a work of painting or sculpture for payment it was customary to take into account the number of figures it contained. On Mantegna's behalf the painter Pietro da Milano testified that given the smallness of the space, Mantegna could not have included all twelve Apostles and that the eight he had represented were painted 'with great art'. He was entitled therefore to be paid as much for the eight as for all twelve. Giovanni Storlato, who had been appointed to act with Squarcione and Pietro da Milano as an arbitrator, was of a different opinion; all twelve Apostles could have been included, but the figures would have had to be smaller. Squarcione's opinion is unfortunately not recorded.[9] Imperatrice had already had a dispute with Pizzolo over the Apostles, and some compression was forced on Mantegna by the narrowness of the wall. He has in fact used 'great art' by composing the group in a circle so as to suggest that the missing figures are there, but hidden by their companions.

Again it would be a mistake to deduce that bitter personal antagonisms necessarily arose from such legal disputes over payments. The matter must have been settled to the satisfaction of all parties, for Madonna Imperatrice now commissioned Mantegna to complete the histories of St Christopher on the right wall of the chapel. These had been finished up to and including the middle band in 1451, before financial difficulties brought work more or less to a standstill for two or three years. From the beginning of this century it has been hotly argued by one party of scholars that Mantegna must have painted the lowest pair of St Christopher frescoes before completing the St James frescoes. Their reason is that the St Christopher frescoes do not take into account the spectator's eye-level in the same fashion as the lowest register of the St James frescoes, so that there is neither illusionistic protrusion of feet over the edge of the base-line nor cutting short of limbs in recession. However, their argument rests on shaky historical foundations.

The two upper registers of the St Christopher frescoes were painted by Bono da Ferrara and Ansuino da Forlì, and Ansuino is known to have received a payment on 30 October 1451. Mantegna cannot therefore have begun work on the lowest register of the St Christopher frescoes before that date. As we have seen, his first surviving work whose perspective takes account of the spectator's eye-level by diminishing or omitting the lower parts of limbs and other features is not the lowest register of the

St James frescoes, as the proponents of an early date for the St Christopher frescoes often carelessly assume, but the Santo fresco of *The Sacred Monogram*, which Mantegna himself signed and dated as finished on 21 July 1452. Such a revolutionary innovation must have required much optical and geometrical calculation and many trial sketches, and it is most improbable that Mantegna would have omitted all exhibition of his newly acquired skill in the lowest register of the St Christopher frescoes, situated as they were in an ideal position for its display a little above the spectator's eye-level, had he been designing and painting them during these same months of 1452. He does indeed make such a display in *St James on the way to Execution*, but it has already been noted that he lays comparatively little stress on it in *The Execution of St James*, which was certainly the last of the sequence to be painted, if only because it heralds his subsequent manner in landscape. The truth is that in the Ovetari frescoes Mantegna attempts to give versatile proofs of his skill, and we mistake his genius if we suppose that he was interested in the mechanical repetition of previous triumphs. He seems indeed to have recognized that the choice of a low point of sight or systematic shortening of limbs had its disadvantages. When the device recurs significantly in his work, it is in the processional compositions of the *Triumphs*, where he uses it not merely because his canvases were set slightly above eye-level, but in order to avoid an endless repetition of marching feet and legs.

In the vain hope of getting the frescoes finished quickly, the histories of St Christopher had from the first been allotted to other painters and for this reason alone a new agreement would always have had to be made with Mantegna for their completion. In this the case was different from that of the work he undertook on account of Pizzolo's death, such as the painting of the frescoes of *St James on the way to Execution* and of the *Assumption*, for although Pizzolo and he later quarrelled, they did begin work on their allotted share of the chapel as partners. That the frescoes of St Christopher were painted after those of St James is also confirmed, at least by implication, by the surviving documents and by a famous story which certainly originated with Girolamo Campagnola, Mantegna's friend and contemporary, and is recorded independently by Scardeone and Vasari. 'First', according to Scardeone,

> he painted the history of St James the Apostle in not very bright colours. But when Squarcione, his master and father by adoption, though giving it commendation enough, yet condemned these colours, Mantegna, angered by his words, painted under it afterwards the history of St Christopher which still remained to be painted there. In this

he no longer took his figures as before from Roman statues, which could be counterfeited only in outline, but from living men. Such figures from the life are much more highly approved by the vulgar, who greatly prefer them to the former, but their author himself approved more of pictures taken from Roman sculptures than from living bodies, and principally for this reason, because the statuaries and sculptors of antiquity were wont to choose from many bodies the parts that were perfect so as to form those parts without fault. But as for the artist who imitates only the natural appearance of one single living being, given that there is hardly a body that is without fault, it needs must be that those who desire to be imitators of that appearance will fall with nature herself into error.[10]

Vasari reproduced substantially the same passage, undoubtedly from Campagnola, but adding from the original that Mantegna was also of the opinion that 'statues displayed the muscles, veins, sinews and other small parts of the body more clearly than nature, which often covers such roughnesses with the sinews of flesh, except in men of old or extenuated bodies, which artists avoid for other reasons.' Vasari also gives Squarcione's criticism more fully, saying that he complained of Mantegna's frescoes

> because he had copied antique marbles, which do not teach how to paint perfectly, for they always have something of hardness in them, and nothing of the tenderness or softness of flesh and natural things, which bend and move. Andrea would have done better if he had painted them the colour of marble and not in such lively colours, inasmuch as his paintings had no semblance of living things, but only of antique statues and such-like things.[11]

Here then is what appears to be the earliest statement of an antithesis that was to divide European painters, theorists and connoisseurs for centuries. It was an antithesis founded on the opposition between a conception of art as the imitation of nature in its individuality and a conception of art as the creation of an ideal nature. Mantegna's inspiration was the famous anecdote of the ancient painter Zeuxis, who is said by Pliny to have held a review of the naked maidens of Croton on being commissioned by the city to paint a picture for the temple of Lacinian Juno, making choice of five of them so as to reproduce in his picture whatever was most beautiful in each. The story was well known to Alberti, who took the side of Zeuxis, citing as a warning the example of the ancient painter Demetrius, who according to Quintilian was censured 'as being too close to nature, and fonder of making a likeness than of beauty'.[12]

It should be remembered that this theory of ideal art does not commend an unnatural beauty, but the addition of beauty to the human figure by a choice of the finest parts discoverable in nature, which the artist then combines into a whole more perfect than can be found in nature. For Mantegna as for many later generations of artists, ancient sculptors had already produced figures which were patterns of nature perfected, and he therefore took them as his models. That he did not feel himself obliged by this choice to exclude all individuality of type, all spontaneity of motif, and all roughness and brutality of feature and action is plain from his paintings. While the theory provided a canon of beauty, the painter was also expected to observe nature in her differences and to be able to reproduce these with expressive verisimilitude according to the different characters, actions and passions he had to represent. Thus a history like *The Execution of St James* contains figures which depict a variety of motives, from crude violence to idle curiosity.

There were indeed grave authorities for an aesthetic of propriety of imitation even if the thing represented were ugly. In his essay on the study of poetry, Plutarch, comparing poetry to painting as an imitative art, declared:

> when we see a lizard or an ape or the face of Thersites in a picture, we are pleased with it and admire it, not as a beautiful thing, but as a likeness. For by its essential nature the ugly cannot become beautiful; but the imitation, be it concerned with what is base or with what is good, if only it attain to the likeness, is commended. If on the other hand it produces a beautiful picture of an ugly body, it fails to give what propriety and probability require.

Alberti himself recommends the painter to study individuality in nature:

> you will see that one man has a nose that is turned-up and crooked, another will have nostrils like a monkey's or turned backwards, another will thrust out lips that hang down, yet others will have the ornament of thin lips, and so let the painter examine everything that makes each member, by being larger or smaller, different and let him also note how we see that our limbs as children are round, as if turned by the lathe, and delicate, whereas in more advanced age they are rough and sharp-cornered. So will the studious painter learn all these things from nature and will ponder within himself most assiduously how each is formed. And he will continually be about this investigation and labour with eyes and mind wide-awake: he will note how the lap forms when someone sits, how pleasantly the legs hang in a

seated man; he will note the body of one standing up and there will be no part of it whose office and measurements he does not know. And of all these parts it will be his pleasure not only to render the likeness, but more still to add beauty to them, for in painting delightfulness is both pleasing and desired.[13]

For Alberti, as for Mantegna, that delightfulness was produced not by designing figures of a smoothly empty beauty, but by giving to each figure, according to its individual nature, a superior concinnity of parts. By this canon the ferocity of the executioner in *The Execution of St James* is not an intrusion of crude naturalism but as perfect an expression of his individual nature as the mild dignity of the Apostle is of his. That the theory of ideal beauty was an aesthetic superimposed on the bias of Mantegna's early training is evident from his paintings. Rather than attributing this development to influences from another artist, we ought perhaps to reckon that Mantegna moved from a purely external study of the forms and ornaments of antique sculpture, begun in Squarcione's workshop, to a perception of the principles of ideal art in antiquity, as recorded in Pliny and Quintilian and in such ancient sculptures as were known to him. No doubt he was helped to this perception by one or more of the humanists of Padua and Venice, but the affinity he felt with the lucidity, grace and serenity of antique art, and with its ennoblement of form was certainly a natural one, as it was certainly exclusive to him in his own time and place, for no other artist of Padua, Venice or Mantua appears to have shared it.

That Mantegna was stung by Squarcione's criticism into proving in the St Christopher frescoes (Plates 26 and 28) how perfectly able he was to draw lively similitudes from nature if he so chose explains why he has made such a display in them of figures in contemporary costume. These never reappear so prominently or in such numbers in any of his earlier or later histories – the figures of the Camera Picta in Mantua belong to portraiture, not to history. The anachronistic mingling of figures in contemporary dress with figures in antique or exotic or fanciful costume was an inheritance from trecento art that fifteenth-century artists in general accepted uncritically and transmitted into the sixteenth century. According to a tradition dating back to Campagnola, Mantegna took a number of his friends as models for some of the figures or else inserted their portraits as spectators. Squarcione himself is said to be figured in the short stout guard of the first fresco. He holds, like his fellow-guards, a weapon which was a combination of axe and spear. The names of the others give an interesting picture of Mantegna's circle in Padua: the Florentine Nofri di Palla Strozzi, banker, humanist, friend of Donatello and of Mantegna's patron, the great Venetian nobleman Jacopo Antonio Marcello; the physician and Latin poet Messer Girolamo della Valle, author of *Iesuida* (*c*.1430), a little Virgilian poem on Christ's Passion; Messer Bonifacio Frigimelica, a jurist and one of the friends or kinsmen Madonna Imperatrice appointed to oversee the frescoes; a certain Baldassare da Leccio of whom nothing is known; and the goldsmith Niccolò del Papa, who had collaborated with Mantegna in the Santo fresco. According to Vasari, copying Campagnola with some misunderstanding of his Latin, these five are shown clothed in white armour, burnished and glittering like real armour, by which he must mean the white dress of the archers. Also portrayed are Antonio Borromeo, who belonged to a great Paduan banking family, and the Hungarian humanist, poet and ecclesiastic Janus Pannonius (29 August 1434–72), who did not come to Padua to study canon law before the autumn of 1454, a further confirmation of a late date for the St Christopher frescoes. He too moved in the circle of Marcello and will be encountered again, for in 1458 Mantegna was to paint his portrait.[14]

Identification of these personages shows unsuspected or unrealized connections between some of them and Mantegna, so lending support to Campagnola's account of the St Christopher frescoes. Three of them are introduced as spectators on the extreme right in the first history of St Christopher. The two nearest to the palace wear red robes, the third black. They stand in left profile, gazing impassively before them with hands composed in courtly repose, to indicate their detachment from the action, as was usual in the quattrocento when for some reason portraits of personages were introduced without associating them with the action. The heads of the other figures are figured with animated variety of pose, some full-face or in near three-quarter view, while of others we see only the slanting edge of their profile as they look upwards. In the second history the passivity of pure profile is avoided in the long line of figures strung out along the right: they turn to each other in conversation, or else look downwards or outwards, either absorbed in the general action or, like the guard at the front, in a local one that provides a momentary distraction. Perhaps Mantegna was consciously emulating the ancient Greek painter Cimon, who, according to Pliny, was 'the first inventor of oblique portraits and of the art of varying the features so as to look backwards, upwards or downwards'.[15] And since all the figures in the fresco are sharply individualized, whether they are ostensibly portaits or disguised as actors in the scene, Campagnola's story receives yet further confirmation.

Mantegna himself has signalled that these frescoes, the last of all, announce yet another new departure in this extraordinary sequence through which he invites the spectator to follow him step by step in his discovery of even more sophisticated means of simulating three-dimensional space on a plane surface, that is, in his own terms, the illusion of natural space. His signal is the fluted Ionic column which he has substituted for the vertical bar of the framework on the other wall and drawn so that it projects in part in front of the picture plane. This violent innovation in the design, for certainly both walls were from the first intended to have the same framework, is a further indication that the St Christopher frescoes are late in date. It was surely only because the uniform correspondence of the St Christopher frame with the St James frame, carefully preserved by Ansuino, had been spoiled by Bono, who introduced ornaments of his own, that Mantegna allowed himself to deviate from the original scheme.

He now made it his purpose to realize a new effect of illusionism. In *The Execution of St James* he had brought the spectator face to face with the horror of the Apostle's execution, but the bars of the framework still marked the plane at which reality ended and simulation began, however much Mantegna made play here and in the companion fresco with forms that appear to protrude beyond the picture plane into real space. At the same time the central vertical bar of the framework defined a border that was also a boundary between the separate histories of the St James cycle. The themes of the two St Christopher frescoes were sufficiently connected, being two successive acts in a single history, that of the saint's martyrdom, for Mantegna to develop the unitary scheme of the second register of the St James frescoes into a real space. This is obtained by giving both scenes a common setting, a paved piazza before a side wall of the royal palace of Samos, one half of the wall appearing in the left fresco, the other half in the right. The orthogonals of the pavement and the lines of the trellised roof of the vine-hung pergola converge on to a single point of sight, set low on the bottom part of the column to suit the lower vantage-point of the spectator. The unity of setting is maintained not only by the sharp thrust of the converging lines of the perspective, but by the projecting column, which asserts a lateral continuity of space, abolishing any implication that the scenes are divided by an inward projection of the bar, such as the eye assumes in the other registers. Meanwhile there is no real break between the spectator and the narrow platform running between the two pilasters at either end, which opens the setting, and allows the action to take place as it were before his eyes.

The foreground is framed in the centre and on the right by stately Renaissance buildings of stone and marble. The palace is a curiously capricious architectural invention, with its narrow white wall of two bays, its pilasters richly carved with acanthus scrolls, its heavy entablature between the first and second storeys sculptured with fantastical antique figures, perhaps copied from drawings of the ornaments of the Temple of Hadrian at Ephesus, its lower storey recessed into two blind panels decorated with copies of two antique sepulchral slabs and inlaid with roundels of verd-antique and *rosso antico* marble. Together with the stately arches of the *cavalcavia* and the porticoed building on the right it is conceived in deliberate contrast with the pink, 'white and brown tower-like houses, some with washing hanging out from them on poles, of the very medieval-looking street on the right and the dusty red-brick of a building – the palace guard-house perhaps – on the left and of the tower and adjacent building beyond. The whole is animated by tiny spectators who fill the *cavalcavia* and the windows of the building overlooking it with their vivid costume and various poses. Over all lowers a lurid sky, dark red on the left, dark blue on the right, a change of hue that might be found in a single sky, yet at the same time an unobtrusive indication, made without disjoining the setting, that the two episodes are enacted on successive days.

The actors on this stately scene are posed with a dramatic skill remarkable even in Mantegna. In the first composition an arrow miraculously blinds King Dagnus of Lycia. Mantegna seems to have considered the scene as a challenge to represent with dramatic immediacy complicatedly interwoven contrasts of action and reaction. On the extreme left we are confronted by the figure of the saint fastened to a pier. To the right is an escort of guards dressed in a livery of red and white and a detachment of archers largely in white and black. In the left middle ground two of the guards shoot round their heads to stare in astonishment as an arrow falls harmlessly away from the saint. Simultaneously, the central figure, a guard whose back is turned to us, so summoning our attention to what absorbs his eyes, points up in amazement to the sinister black window where the King, who has been watching the execution, staggers back with a cry as one of the arrows flies back and blinds him, while a horrified courtier puts up a hand to catch him in his fall. The sill, with Mantegna's sure sense of propriety in local colour, is hung with an oriental carpet.[16] Before the central guard, a man in a rich long red robe, presumably an official deputed to oversee the execution, also turns his head to look up aghast at the window. On the right, the archer who has just shot his arrow at the saint watches astounded its harmless fall. Behind, a young archer in front of the palace who stoops after letting fly his arrow at Sebastian turns up his

face wonderingly as it strikes the King. A motif of anecdotal naturalism is introduced for variety in the shape of two archers, one seated on the ground, the other standing over him, in apparent ignorance of what is happening. The tunic in the foreground also adds realism to the scene, serving at the same time as a counterpoise to the balancing motif of the head in the companion fresco.

In the second composition two guards haul away with a rope the huge decapitated blue-clad corpse of Christopher before the curious or indifferent eyes of spectators. The guard on the right still wears his breastplate, while the other has sensibly doffed his. The history of the saint's martyrdom is bloody, and Mantegna has not spared us brutal realism. The head is laid on the extreme margin of the foreground to the left of the body, resting on its foreshortened halo as on a platter, and the ground to either side of the neck, according to old copies, was bespattered with blood. The figures in both scenes are strongly diminished from the front plane, so that the King and his courtier are smaller in scale than the figures in the courtyard, where those in the foreground are conspicuously taller than those in the rear.

In designing the frescoes a problem of scaling was also posed by the giant stature of St Christopher. Mantegna has dexterously resolved it in the first fresco by placing him in the extreme left foreground, against the even loftier architecture, so that his figure serves as a measure for the other figures, and in the second by showing the decapitated corpse in foreshortening. The first of these solutions had perhaps been anticipated by Jacopo Bellini, one of whose drawings represents the saint almost like a giant St Sebastian, set against a post on the extreme right of the composition, taller by a massive head and bust than the figures of the archers in front.[17] In Mantegna's scene, the conception is far more imaginatively dramatic: the saint stands meditatively, bound to a pier, while the turned backs of the guards and archers draw our eyes instinctively to look inwards at the staggering figure of Dagnus. Mantegna was to develop this device in his composition of *Christ in Limbo*, known now only from copies and an engraving, where this time it is Christ himself who is seen only in rear view. Both inventions are an eloquent testimony to the dramatic naturalism which circulates through compositions that at first sight can sometimes seem like studies in arrested motion. In rising to the second challenge of depicting the corpse Mantegna perhaps had in mind the celebrated picture by Timanthes, cited by Pliny in antiquity and by Alberti in his *Della pittura*, in which a sleeping Cyclops was represented on a small panel, his vast bulk being suggested by the device of showing satyrs measuring his thumb. In a drawing of Christopher carrying Christ Jacopo Bellini shows naked putti playing on the river bank for contrast with his height.[18]

To study the Ovetari frescoes is to experience a sense of dazzlement as Mantegna, through eight years of a prodigious youth, produces a succession of masterpieces in which illusionism, perspective and foreshortening are used with ever-increasing sophistication and virtuosity. What is the nature of the world of landscape, architecture and figures that we see on the stage of that simulated extension of our actual world? We know already that the landscape is a romantic world of rocky mountains, hills and valleys, cast into capriciously picturesque forms that are nevertheless composed of geometrical shapes and planes – rocks that are oblong, striations that are parallel lines and curves. Over them Mantegna throws a deceptive plausibility by his meticulous verisimilitude of detail. In colouring they range from that dull volcanic red which exercised so lasting a fascination over Mantegna's fancy to the light yellows and ochres which he was always to use in contrast with its suppressed fiery glow. In his architectural settings we have noticed his use of the everyday buildings of Italian city streets as a foil to the magnificence of antique architecture. His image of antiquity is a romantic one, conveying in the massive assurance of its recessed and projecting forms, in its balance of decorated and undecorated members, of moulded frame and plain surface, his own nostalgia for a lost world of conscious art, whose buildings were designed with a noble vocabulary of forms and ornaments according to harmonious rules of symmetry, proportion and rationality and reared in white stone and sumptuous marble, finely cut and wrought.

According to the decorum of each personage the figures who inhabit this solidly imagined world may be types of brutal roughness or of gentle grace, and their dress vary from a coarse tattered coat to oriental costume, from the robes of antique dignity to the glittering panoply of Roman military might. Their poses are as often as not statuesque; even when an attitude expresses a movement or a familiar observation it frequently seems suspended and self-enclosed. When action is sharply reported, therefore, as in the guard pushing back the spectator, the executioner about to strike, the guards and archers amazed by the death-dealing arrow, the contrast of violence is all the more disturbing. But generally the artist appears like an enchanter who has transfixed by some spell of immobility a tableau of living figures. And in the Ovetari frescoes Mantegna is above all an inventor of tableaux. Although some contain passages of great dramatic power, perhaps only in *The Execution of St James* is there a perfect fusion of narrative and pictorial emphasis. Judged as histories the other scenes do not concentrate the eyes and judgement sufficiently on the principal figures and their interaction. In reality, Mantegna was essentially an unliterary artist, to use a not very happy term of twentieth-century criticism, in that his concern is with a total pictorial effect. Figures and setting are conjured into being not so much for their narrative significance, but as features in a world where illusionism has possessed itself not only of the painter's art but of his imagination as well, so that his purpose is to embody a vision in space and then in time with telling verisimilitude. In the Ovetari frescoes, for all their economy of figures, the costuming of the story at times surpasses in interest and vividness the story itself, as so often in the historical novels which in some ways they resemble. Accordingly we must judge them not as narratives, in spite of their great passages of narrative eloquence, but as evocations conjured up before the eye by a master of setting and atmosphere.

Fig. 4. St Joseph. Detail from *The Adoration of the Shepherds* (Plate 33)

IV

Mantegna in Padua

WHILE Mantegna was working on the major commissions just described, he was also engaged on some smaller works, painted in all probability during the early or middle 1450s. We have no documentary information for them, and their dating and sequence have therefore to be assessed on grounds of style, aided by such indications as can be drawn from their subject-matter. It must be said at once that Mantegna's style is unusually stable and therefore an uncertain criterion of date, and it is applied in his art to conceptions of setting, figure and costume and of the relationships which ought to exist between the various parts of a picture that varied singularly little for three decades. Accordingly, any concrete or external indication of date is more than usually valuable in fixing the chronology of his works. All the evidence we have tends to prove that he worked in general slowly, rather than expeditiously, and so may have been even more prone than other painters to take up or suspend work on a single picture as his *fantasia* and humour moved him or, perhaps more justly, as he slowly and deliberately resolved the problems of each composition.

The earliest of Mantegna's surviving history paintings is *The Adoration of the Shepherds* (Plate 33), now in New York.[1] The Virgin kneels in the centre middle ground, dressed in the pale crimson robe and blue cloak of convention, both heightened with the gold of divine light as cherubs hover around her, to the bottom right and above her head flaming red with the fire of heavenly love, gold with the gold of heaven to either side. She is raised above the foreground by a diagonal road of rock running across the picture from left to right. The foreground itself is broken into two gullies by ridges of rock; down the left-hand gully flows a stream of green water.

With characteristic economy these gullies not only diversify the foreground picturesquely, but direct the eye inwards to the Holy Family, while the raised road enables Mantegna to set St Joseph and the adoring shepherds in the foreground, to either end of a triangular composition of figures, so subordinating them to the Virgin, who forms its apex. In turn Joseph, in pale crimson robe and yellow cloak, with a halo of powdery gold, is given greater prominence than the shepherds by his seat on the road of rock, with his feet, shod in classical sandals, resting on the ridge below. He rests his right hand familiarly on his knee as he slumbers, supporting his head on his left hand, itself supported by the crook of a lopped bush (Fig. 4).

In contrast with the still attitudes of the Virgin and Joseph, the two shepherds are shown in movement: having uncovered their heads on espying the Holy Family, they make to kneel in adoration. The action is cleverly chosen so as to maintain the symmetry of the composition, and their impulse of devotion breaks into the solemn scene without troubling its serenity. One is clad in a shirt of pale brownish-green cloth over blue hose, rent at the knees, while the other wears a blue tunic over a red shirt that with his red hat catches up and balances the crimsons and reds of the Holy Family and the cherubs. His hose of bluish-white are ragged and torn. Their coarse-cropped hair and plain, worn faces, one simple, one stupid, enhance the touching reverence of their demeanour. In type and dress the pair are treated with a naturalism that has no earlier or later parallel in Mantegna's art, where ugliness and ragged clothes are marks of plebian brutality and cruelty. Here, on the contrary, they represent an objective observation of the realities of peasant life in a spirit of pastoral decorum. Mantegna, after all, if Vasari and through him Campagnola are to be believed, had himself been a herd-boy in the fields. Shepherds in the fifteenth century, as before and later, were the humblest and simplest of rustics, not only in literature, in which the poor shepherd was a type, but in life.

To rectify the imbalance created by the bending pose of the two shepherds, and to lead the eye into the right background Mantegna has added two small figures of a peasant and his wife bringing a basket of eggs to the market of Bethlehem, a motif that would irresistibly have suggested early morning to a fifteenth-century eye. They are costumed with the same realism: the man wears red torn hose, a repetition of colour that again adds necessary balancing weight of red to this side of the picture, a pale greenish-brown cloak of poncho type over a brown tunic and a blue hat. His wife wears a gown of greyish-white. This interest in the realistic representation of peasants was not unique to Mantegna: the drawings of Jacopo Bellini include a number of realistic studies of rustics and rustic labours.[2]

From the two peasants the eye passes up the steeply slanting narrow slope that forms a ledge along the brown rocky mountain which closes off the middle ground on the right. On it tiny angels make the announcement of joy to shepherds grazing their sheep. The mountain is balanced on the other side by the manger, formed by a wattle fence enclosing a stall of light brown wood and a ruined temple whose line runs diagonally inwards, accentuating the sharply angled bias already created by the line of the road in this half of the composition. It is planted with orange-trees, the earliest examples in Mantegna's art of a motif that will remain a favourite with him until the end of his life. A true son of his age, he seems to have loved in such trees the union of bright green leaves with glowing fruit and scented blossom, and also the feeling they gave of the warm pleasantnesses of the orchard. To the ruined stable he has given only an austere architecture; if for no other reason, an early date for the picture is probable because Mantegna has not taken the opportunity to trick this building out in ruined antique magnificence. Beyond it a conical mountain of rock further screens off the middle ground: between this and the opposing mountain opens a landscape of green and pale brown, with a winding valley along which the eye travels by a winding road, with a bare tree, a rounded hillock and the conical mountain marking the planes of recession. In the distance is a city; above is a pale dawn sky, darkening at the top with grey shadows on its white clouds.

The influence of Jacopo Bellini is strongly felt in Mantegna's other surviving early *istoria*, *The Agony in the Garden* (Plate II) in the National Gallery, London, evidently painted as a private devotional picture, since it is signed on one of the rocks above the Apostles. In a drawing by Jacopo Bellini of the same subject Christ is on the extreme left, kneeling on Gethsemane, a steep mount of striated rocks, below whose sides the Apostles slumber. The composition is divided into two halves by the brook Kedron, flowing through a flat plain at the foot of hills between low banks of smooth rock. On the plain to the right stands Jerusalem, a walled city overtopped by medieval palaces and towers, against which the domed temple and a stately column stand out by reason of their classical architecture. Down a winding road widening towards the foreground advances the troop of soldiers, led by Judas. The design illustrates Bellini's tendency to fill the left-hand side of his compositions with towering features, leaving a deeply recessed void on the right in which the action takes place.[3]

By contrast with this loose disposition all the elements of Mantegna's design are tightly and expressively compacted so that even the setting contributes to the eloquence and pathos of the narrative. The mountains and rocks, though of a conception ultimately pictorial, are treated with a delicate naturalism that describes their forms with minute detailing and precise brushwork, recording the change to shade on every surface that is concealed from the light and depicting the many little stones and pebbles and the few thin plants that are scattered here and there with painstaking care. Once again this rocky setting is contrived so as to divide up the scene into sharply defined planes and compartments. The Rock of Gethsemane, rising into a cubical summit on the left and then extended into a long descending spur three-quarters of the way across the picture, separates the foreground from the background. Set at a slight angle to the picture plane, it turns the kneeling figure of Christ away from the beholder, so that his face is fully visible only to the angels who appear with the Instruments of the Passion. This dramatic device of *profil perdu*, found also in the Ovetari Josias, will recur again and again in Mantegna's histories. Iconographically justified here by the need to convey Christ's isolation in his Agony, it is a subtly meditated expression of Mantegna's preference in dramatic invention for compositional devices that suggest to the imagination more than is actually painted, and that at the same time lead the eye naturally from one incident to another.

With the same sure pictorial economy, the Rock, itself the middle ground, not only provides a raised stage on which the manifestation of his Father's will is made to Christ, but marks off the foreground, on which the Apostles lie, sunk in stertorous sleep, and the background, with Jerusalem, overtopped by the conical peaks of Mount Zion, and Judas guiding the Roman soldiers towards Christ. In addition, its curving slope defines on the right the valley of Jehoshaphat, through which flows the brook Kedron. Across these divisions the eye is led to the three groups that compose the whole history by a series of visual bridges. On the left the flight of rocky steps draws the eye up sharply to the scene of the kneeling Christ and the five angels, while on the right the perspective curves of road and stream direct it to Judas and his companions. In the right foreground a tree-trunk laid over Kedron leads the eye inwards to the sleeping Apostles. Jacopo Bellini's Kedron is also crossed by a low, humped bridge. According to one of the legends with which piety regaled pilgrims to Jerusalem, over the brook Kedron was set for a bridge a tree-trunk that was later made into the Tree of the Cross, and so it may be that Mantegna's tree-trunk has not simply a visual function, but makes a historical and symbolic allusion to the Crucifixion.[4] As a purely pictorial motif, it is perhaps not Mantegna's own invention, for in another drawing by Jacopo Bellini of Christ being nailed to the Cross a tree-trunk with a hand-rail fixed to it serves as a bridge across a stream in the right foreground.[5]

The Agony in the Garden is also a concentrated expression of Mantegna's power to suggest atmosphere by expressive colour. A chilling mood of despair and grief is imposed by the dark green-blue of the evening sky, the cold golden light of the sinking sun and the streak of whitish light on the dark blue mountains in the western horizon on the upper right. Against the sunset the sombre green branches and brown trunk of a palm are silhouetted darkly, and the falling shades of evening are powerfully simulated by two other patches of shadow, one on the front of the slope of Gethsemane, the other, the dark inner face of the rock before which Christ prays. The shadows are thrown up by their contrast with the sunset light, which falls on the road and on the slopes immediately below Jerusalem, coloured a bright ochre, and on two of the sides of the western mountain, which are coloured green and yellow except where the mountain obstructs the sun's last rays. The darkness in the depths and hollows and on the surfaces against the light chequers the picture with a marvellous effect of fading day.

The source of light in the picture comes from the west: it is met by a divine light emanating in a gentle glow from the five child angels who come to Christ on a cloud of deepest blue, the foremost proferring the brown cross which is the answer to his prayer. Originally their red wings were shot with gold, and the fall of divine light on the figure of Christ is represented by delicate strokes of gold on the edges of Christ's dark blue cloak and along its front and the folds of its sleeve, in continuance of a trecento tradition. The ochre and green of the setting throw up the deep and vibrant colour of the figures. Of the three Apostles, Peter wears a cloak of crimson lit with white, wound over an azure robe, James a yellow robe under a dark purplish cloak, and John a scarlet robe and cloak of olive-green. John's scarlet, verging on coral-red, is repeated in Christ's robe and again in the line of togaed men and soldiers who follow Judas, and the yellow of James's robe recurs on the corslet of one of the soldiers.

Mantegna's interest in expressive light derives ultimately from International Gothic art, and in the taste of International Gothic art are the hares and white egrets, depicted with lively delight in their beauty and grace, which he introduces to relieve the austerity of setting and mood. The sinister black vulture perched on the topmost bough of the old olive-tree on the right, with eyes fixed on Christ, is there as an augury of his approaching death. The bird's reputation for snuffing out its prey was already well established in trecento Italy. There seems to be no pictorial precedent for this imaginative use of the vulture, a bird rare in Italy, but certainly well known to Venetian merchants journeying in the East. In itself the motif of a bird perched on a naked tree was no innovation: it appears in drawings by Jacopo Bellini and on the reverse of Pisanello's medal of Leonello d'Este, dated 1444, where the bird is an eagle, a heraldic emblem of the Este.[6] The suggestiveness of Mantegna's invention was so admired by Giovanni Bellini that he imitated it in *The Madonna of the Meadow*, where a vulture foretells the sufferings of the Passion that await the infant Christ.

Especially interesting is the great view of Jerusalem, whose pink walls extend in a mighty curve across two-thirds of the landscape, above the Valley of Jehoshaphat and below Mount Sion. This is Mantegna's first known attempt at a plausible representation of the city as it stood in ancient times. The pink walls derive from trecento convention, but are represented with Mantegna's minute naturalism, that details even their bricks, and also with his own peculiar historical sense, for some parts of them are shown as built on earlier foundations, while patches of red and purple figure the stains of time and a partly ruined tower surmounts the main gateway. In style most of the buildings are purely medieval; there are battlemented palaces and tower-houses and a campanile, all of true North Italian character. Among these everyday buildings are set two of Renaissance form, one with a classical cornice and pillared or pilastered façade, and one divided into three tiers by a rusticated base and a string-course. Above rise three towers, one with a domed summit, the others spired and surmounted by a crescent, traditionally a symbol of paynim rule, and here attributed to the Jews and Romans according to current convention because it suggested the East. Before them is an amphitheatre, probably copied from the Arena of Verona, and to the right of this a Roman imperial column, with spiral reliefs winding up it as on Trajan's column, and a gilt equestrian statue modelled on that of Marcus Aurelius set on its top. A similar column topped by a cone surmounted by a ball, together with two other classical columns surmounted by statues, appear in Jacopo Bellini's view of Jerusalem in his drawing of the Funeral of the Virgin, where there is the same mingling of medieval and classical architecture.[7] The probability is therefore that Mantegna knew Trajan's column and the statue of Marcus Aurelius from drawings that circulated in Venice and Padua. The omission of the domed Temple, a traditional feature of views of Jerusalem, is surprising, and since it is carefully included in the two views of Jerusalem which appear in the predella of the San Zeno altarpiece, its absence can perhaps be taken as another proof that the picture is an early work.

Two other paintings from the middle 1450s, *The Presentation in the Temple* (Plate IV), now in Berlin, and the *St George* (Plate 32), in Venice, are the last works for many years in which Mantegna uses a marble window-frame as a formal boundary between our real space and his pictorial space in order to pretend that there is no barrier between the two. There is no need to interpret over-subtly the conceptions underlying such tricks of illusionism: they range from the aesthetic of simulating nature to that of a *lusus* of the fantasy, making a sophisticated play with forms. In the *Presentation*[8] the figures, all half-length, are enclosed in a frame of pinkish-white and greenish-white marble, opening on to a background of deep black. The Virgin and Simeon, as befits their principal roles in the action, are set in the front plane: Mantegna uses the frame to give the greater prominence to the Virgin, for Simeon stands behind it, whereas she rests her elbow on it as she clasps the swaddled Child. Simeon prepares to lift him with tender care from the dark blue cushion, its tassel of gold set with pearls, that protrudes beyond the frame in a *lusus* of illusionism. The Virgin and Simeon face each other, posed in pure profile. It is a characteristic of Mantegna's art, acquired from ancient sculpture, but certainly an expression also of an innate stylistic tendency, that his figures remain enclosed in themselves, with little contact of gesture or expression beyond that strictly required for the action. Even here the eyes of the Virgin and of Simeon seem to avoid fixing each other, partly no doubt to express the maidenly reserve of the Virgin, but partly also from this instinctive avoidance of contacts that might dissolve the self-contained perfection of the figures. In this way Mantegna gives to his compositions the relief and immobile marble calm of antique sculpture.

The Virgin's head, of touchingly youthful grace, is of a rather Gothic cast of beauty, with its long neck, and high, smooth forehead. Her cheeks and lips are lightly flushed with pink; indeed almost all the flesh tints are delicate and pale. The light is from the traditional left, so throwing the Child, one of Mantegna's earliest and finest studies of a human figure in terms of pure volume, a little into shadow, but falling on Simeon's brown face heightened with crimson-red in the cheeks, the white of eyebrows, beard and moustache painted over a grey undercoat in a sequence of falling serpentine hairs.

The importance of the Virgin and Simeon is emphasized by their costume, whose richness of material and patterning is in keeping with their significance in the eyes of the artist. In draping it Mantegna avoids all but a few simple folds, so that the elaborate patterns of the stuffs appear with bold formality and splendour. Over a close-fitting robe of light crimson the Virgin wears a rich gown, whose stuff has a heavy and magnificent Late Gothic ornamentation in black of foliage and other designs on a cream-coloured ground – both ornament and colours being of a type fashionable in the 1450s. The black has the effect of subduing the gown and attuning it to the background. Simeon wears a blue close-fitting cap and a mantle of lustrous brown, richly decorated with a pink damask pattern and a border of pink diaper. The picture also contains in the Child's swaddling clothes the first passages known to us executed in Mantegna's incomparable whites, so delicately pure in their opaqueness, so tenderly modulated into grey in the shadows. But it should be noticed that the white, which would otherwise be too prominent, is harmonized with the background by the running lines of the crinkling folds and a pattern of blue stripes.

In the middle plane, between the Virgin and Simeon, but set slightly lower, both for due subordination and for recession, is the grey-bearded St Joseph, wearing a robe of coral-red shadowed with grey. Set full-face in a frontal pose, he recalls a portrait on a Roman tomb-slab. To either side, made smaller and placed at a reverent interval behind the Holy Family, are the figures of Mantegna and his wife Nicolosia. She wears a dress and hood of yellow, softened by shadows and by the dark ground, over the pleated white-grey head-dress and cap of a matron. Her face, a long pure oval, dark-complexioned with dark red lips and cheeks, is turned to the left with an expression of pensive modesty. Mantegna, in a dark-coloured gown, with dark brown curls, not the blond locks of the self-portrait in *The Trial of St James*, has strongly marked cheeks and deep pouches below the eyes. He has drawn himself in three-quarter profile, using a mirror.

The figures of the Holy Family are united not only by their action and proximity, but by the strong pattern formed by the simple circles of their gold haloes, which stand out boldly on the black ground. The divinity of the Child is discreetly emphasized by the golden rays that dart from his dark red cap, around which runs a golden border of imitation Cufic letters. In its severity of design the picture is a formal and hierarchical arrangement of figures, warmed by an austere humanity expressed in the grave tenderness of their aspect and the soft delicacy of their flesh tints, and vivified by the refined splendour of the costume. The sculptural clarity of their contours is accentuated by the black field, which throws up the boldness and simplicity of their forms and planes. As in relief sculpture they seem like rounded figures on a flat ground, though Mantegna has once again exploited the ambiguity of painting to treat the ground as both space and plane. The contours are accentuated by outlining the figures strongly in black, a device Mantegna was to use again and again as a means of giving his figures that clarity and strength of contour which other painters, even in Mantegna's old age, were to envy.

By a technical device found among Mantegna's other surviving pictures only in the nearly contemporary portrait of Cardinal Trevisan the black background is worked up into relief so that it encircles all the heads with a raised edge, outlining them with a sculptural sharpness of definition. In itself the use of a black background for contrast was not an innovation: as a stylistic invention it belongs to International Gothic art and is found in earlier Veronese painting, for example in the *Pala della Levata* sometimes attributed to Giovanni Badile. It seems to have enjoyed a certain vogue in portraiture during the 1440s and 1450s. Mantegna continued to use it, especially in small religious paintings, until the end of his life, no doubt because it detaches the figure with more of sculptural relief than any other colour.

The presence of Andrea and Nicolosia indicates that this is a votive picture, painted to commemorate the birth of a child. It is on canvas, not on panel like *The Agony in the Garden* and Mantegna's other Paduan pictures. Accordingly, it may have been painted in Venice, for Vasari records that unlike the Tuscans, who preferred panel, the Venetians favoured canvas because it did not split or worm, could be used for pictures of the very largest size and was easily transported from place to place.[9] Another intimation that the picture was painted in Venice is the existence of a version of it by Giovanni Bellini. In this picture figures of Giovanni and his brother take Mantegna's place while their mother Anna stands by her daughter. Plainly it too was a thank-offering from Nicolosia's family for the safe

birth of her child. We do not know the date of birth of any of Mantegna's children, but the picture cannot have been painted before 1454, if Mantegna was married, as he almost certainly was, early in 1453, or later than 1459, given his own youthful appearance and that of Nicolosia.

The *Presentation* is Mantegna's earliest attempt at a painting conceived compositionally as a relief sculpture. It differs radically from the feigned reliefs of his later works in paint, which are close in conception to the simulated sculptures of Flemish art. Legitimately we can wonder if here Mantegna was not painting for himself a personal picture in what he supposed to be the style of antique painting, as deduced from an admiring study of ancient sculpture and from the references in Pliny and other classical authors to such *tours de force* of illusionism as Zeuxis' grapes, Parrhasius' curtain, and Apelles' horse that caused other horses to whinny. It is important to bear in mind what has already been noted in another context, that there was no cleavage in the quattrocento between the aesthetic of sculpture and that of painting. The two arts were considered as companions and rivals and their practitioners sought to outvie each other in the challenge of simulating nature. Thus Vasari records a dispute between Giorgione and certain unnamed sculptors who claimed that sculpture was superior as an art to painting because a sculptured figure shows different aspects and views as we move around it, whereas painting can show only one single aspect of a figure. To prove that a picture was better able to do this than a statue, Giorgione painted a picture showing the front, the back and two profile views of a single figure. He achieved this effect by juxtaposing a nude with a pond, a corslet and a mirror in which other views appeared as reflections.[10] The great Renaissance debates between the partisans of painting and sculpture, of which this is one of the earliest recorded, turned then not on any differences of aesthetic aims, but on which of the two arts could produce the fuller simulacrum of nature. Most quattrocento reliefs are overtly what we might call pictorial, especially those of Ghiberti and Donatello. Even the Florentine neo-classical reliefs of the 1430s, such as those of the two Cantorias by Luca della Robbia and Donatello, are literal revivals of the antique rather than a reaction against this pictorial style. Mantegna, it may be suspected, easily assumed that there had been no great difference except in medium between antique sculpture, of which examples were known to him, and antique painting, of which nothing was then known to survive, and concluded that antique painting could be revived from the study of antique relief sculpture, with its emphasis on the isolated figure, its plain ground, and essentially two-plane composition.

Like the earlier *St Euphemia* the Venice *St George*[11] shows how purely conventional for Mantegna were his marble window-frames. Here again he uses one arbitrarily as a convenient device with small regard for logical plausibility of illusion. The saint stands on the frame as if it were a ledge, a mountain landscape rising in the distance behind him to a blue, cloud-flecked sky. The transition from ledge to landscape, which might have posed an awkward problem, is masked by the corpse of the slain dragon, laid triumphantly over the ledge, with the rear end out of sight, the chest resting in a pictorially effective but physically insecure position on the further edge of the ledge and the neck and head lying aslant the right corner and protruding beyond the frame into space. On the opposite side the saint's right hand, grasping his broken lance, is also thrust forward beyond the picture plane, a motif that may have been inspired by Pliny's description of Apelles' painting of Alexander holding a thunderbolt, in which 'the fingers seem to protrude and the thunderbolt to be outside the picture.'[12] These projections are justified above by the customary swag suspended from the front of the frame.

The saint is set in a typical sculptor's pose of victorious calm after action. The weight rests on the right foot, throwing the body in a gentle curve to the left, an imbalance corrected by turning the head in three-quarter profile to the right, by the crook of the left arm as the saint sets his left hand proudly on his hip, and by the landscape, whose mass is to the right. The saint's halo is conceived as turning with the head it ornaments and is therefore drawn at a sharp angle to the front plane in correct foreshortening and with a darker patch of shadow upon it from the head to indicate where the rays of light falling obliquely from the right upon the figure do not illuminate it. This naturalistic treatment of the halo in perspective as a physical attribute of the figure, rather than as a flat aureole around its head, first appears in the fresco of *The Calling of St James*, but has become a striking feature of the San Zeno altarpiece (*c*.1456–9). It supports a rather later date, *c*.1456–7, for the *St George* in preference to the earlier date advocated by some scholars, while stylistic reasons preclude the later date in the 1460s preferred by others. There is already an attempt at foreshortening haloes in Altichiero's *Crucifixion* in the Oratorio di San Giorgio, in the figure of the kneeling Magdalen and in the angel to the left of the cross, and Andrea del Castagno had also shown in Venice, in the Cappella di San Tarasio, other haloes foreshortened according to the new perspective. The device is employed with great skill in the terracotta altarpiece of the Ovetari Chapel but only as Mantegna's art advances through the 1450s does he come to practise it with almost ostentatious virtuosity.

The pose and angle of the halo, as well as the direction of the light, suggest that the picture was designed to be seen by a spectator approaching from the right. It evidently hung a little above its source of light, for the lighting is *di sotto in sù*. Unfortunately, the name of the patron who commissioned it is unknown, but there is a possibility that he was Jacopo Antonio Marcello (1398–after 1461), the Venetian general who was one of Mantegna's patrons in his later Paduan years. Marcello lived at Monselice, south of Padua, where according to an apocryphal tradition, but one generally believed in fifteenth-century Padua, the body of St George was preserved in the church of San Giorgio.[13]

The landscape setting of a hill crowned by the Libyan city of Selene divides the background into two. On the left is a pale blue sky striated with long fleecy white clouds against which the saint's head is silhouetted; on the right is the hill, with a plain lying at its foot from which a road winds up to the summit in diminishing perspective. Neither the city nor the landscape below, it should be noted, contains any of the nostalgic picturesque of antique monuments or ruins. The green and tawny colours of the dragon's body are wonderfully harmonized with the saint's armour of black and grey, heightened with white to suggest the lustrous sheen of the metal where the light falls upon it. In contrast with these cool colours are the bright scarlet of his short military cloak and the coral-red of the St George's crosses on his broken lance, of the straps that tie his armour, of the sword-belt and of the sheath of the long sword hanging down behind his legs. The armour itself is a very faithful representation of a mid-fifteenth-century Italian armour: for some reason Mantegna has not given his St George the classicizing armour in which Donatello costumed his earlier St George. It is tempting to wonder whether such a piece of modernity, which gave more immediate vividness to the figure by not distancing it in time, was the result of Squarcione's criticisms and should be taken as yet another indication of a date for the picture *c*.1456–7. The forms of the armour are finished with especial sharpness and minuteness; in the shirt of mail, the links are figured by means of white dots on grey, while its two borders are executed in yellow to simulate gilding.

St George with his firm, rounded features, ruddy complexion and dark golden locks is an ideal type of youthful male beauty, transfigured by the inner purity of a saint. He is often compared with the youthful St Laurence in the great altarpiece (Plate 36)[14] Mantegna painted for the 'most eloquent and grave' Gregorio Correr (*c*.1411–64), abbot of the ancient Benedictine monastery of San Zeno in Verona.[15] This commission is one of two evidences that Mantegna's reputation had now extended beyond the walls of Padua, the other being an invitation from Lodovico Gonzaga, Marquis of Mantua, to enter his service.[16]

Mantegna had accepted this invitation by 5 January 1457, but in his letter of reply told the Marchese that he was bound by his previous undertaking to Correr, and was about to set out to see him in Verona. The paternal Lodovico encouraged him to go, as an outbreak of the plague was expected in Padua and he seems to have formed the impression that Mantegna intended to paint the altarpiece in Verona. In fact it is certain that he painted it in Padua. This is all we know of the early history of the picture, except that Vasari, probably recording the testimony of some Veronese informant, declares in 1550 that Mantegna 'executed as a sample a very beautiful figure, having a great desire to undertake the work.'[17] We can surmise that he received the commission because there was no artist of the first rank left in Verona after the death of Pisanello in 1451, and Correr had to look for a painter elsewhere.

The monastery of San Zeno had been given *in commendam* to Gregorio Correr in 1443, the date written on the oriental carpet set beneath the Virgin's feet in the altarpiece. The Correr were one of the greatest patrician families of Venice. They had attained to great power and influence in the Roman Curia with the election to the Papacy in 1406 of Angelo Correr, who took the name of Gregory XII. Gregorio was the great-nephew of the Pope, and the nephew of Cardinal Antonio Correr, who had held San Zeno before him. These two great churchmen had both had close links with the ascetic movement for monastic reform whose fountain-head was the Venetian monastery of San Giorgio in Alga, a movement that strongly influenced their nephew. It is important to know something of Gregorio's life and mentality for these are reflected in the altarpiece. As a boy in Venice his tutor had been Vittorino da Feltre, the great humanist educator. When Vittorino removed in 1423 to Mantua at the invitation of the Marchese Giovanfrancesco Gonzaga to teach his children and there founded his celebrated school known as the Ca' Gioiosa, Gregorio followed him and spent two years in close intimacy with the Gonzaga household, including Giovanfrancesco's son Lodovico, Mantegna's future patron. At the age of 18 he wrote the earliest Renaissance humanist tragedy, *Progne*, in Latin verse. But in 1429 he entered the household of his uncle Cardinal Antonio Correr in Rome and under Antonio's influence was converted from the cult of secular letters to the study of the Scriptures.

As a result of this spiritual crisis, to which like so many learned ecclesiastics he was moved by the example of St Augustine and St Jerome, Correr became one of the leaders in the movement known to modern scholars as Christian Humanism. This sought to turn profane letters to religious ends by reviving the study of the Fathers, both Greek and Latin. The Christian humanists, like the secular humanists, were eager in the quest for new texts and it was Correr who during his attendance at the Council of Basle discovered in Switzerland and brought back to Italy a copy of Salvian's *De gubernatione Dei*. And as we have just noted, he was also touched by that same movement of penitential devotion, stemming ultimately from the Venetian monastery of San Giorgio in Alga, which had inspired Ludovico Barbo and the reform of Santa Giustina in Padua.

Correr was persuaded by Pope Martin V first to become a cleric and then shortly afterwards, in 1431, to take ordination as a priest. The Venetian Gabriele Condulmer, who succeeded Martin as Eugenius IV, was Gregorio's cousin. Shortly after his accession in March 1431 he appointed Gregorio, still only 22 or so, a Protonotary Apostolic, the highest dignity of the Curia after that of bishop, and an office which when conferred on a young man was intended to single him out for even higher preferment to come. It seemed that Correr was safely on the highroad to the Cardinalate, but at the Council of Basle, to which he was sent in 1433, he wrecked his chances of promotion by delivering on 10 October a famous speech in which he proclaimed an idealistic vision of universal peace through a union of Church and Empire, which was to be brought about by the Emperor. To the Curia this indiscretion was a rank betrayal of the cause of Papal supremacy over the Church and he was now kept apart from great affairs. By 1439 Gregorio had rejoined his uncle's household, and he followed Cardinal Correr first to Florence and then in 1443 to Padua, where the Cardinal had decided to spend his last years in retreat. Here Gregorio became one of the circle of humanists which gravitated around Bishop Pietro Donato.

On his uncle's death in January 1445 he moved to Verona to assume the governance of San Zeno. He introduced strict observance of the rule into the monastery, taking only a portion of its revenues for himself, and leaving the rest to his monks, contrary to the usual practice of abbots *in commendam*, for whom their monasteries were primarily sources of income. For himself he built a set of apartments apart from those of the monks, in order to spend his time there in religious occupations. His connections with Padua remained close, for in 1447, after Pietro Donato's death, the canons of the cathedral elected him as their candidate for the bishopric. In spite of his exemplary life of piety and learning advancement to a bishopric was blocked for him by the long struggle between the Venetian Senate and the Popes over the right to nominate to bishoprics in the Venetian dominions. Traditionally the Senate had made nominations to all the sees in its territory: moreover, it was bent on having resident bishops. The Popes by contrast were eager to assert their direct jurisdiction over the Venetian sees, and were prone to appoint dignitaries of their own Curia as non-resident bishops. Correr was passed over for Padua, and his promotion to the see of Verona on the nomination of the local chapter in 1453 was superseded by a direct Papal nomination. And in 1459, when the humanist Pope Pius II attempted to arrange an exchange by which Cardinal Pietro Barbo would be appointed to the newly vacant see of Padua, resigning his own see of Vicenza to Correr, who in turn would surrender San Zeno to the Pope's nephew, the scheme foundered on the steady opposition of the Venetian Senate. Finally, on 11 August 1464, the Senate nominated Correr to the vacant Patriarchate of Venice, only to meet with an obstinate refusal from the former Cardinal Barbo, now Pope Paul II, who insisted on his own nominee. The impression left by these disputes is that Correr's reputation for austerity and sanctity of life was used as a pawn by both sides in a game of ecclesiastical politics. Argument over the Patriarchate was still dragging on when Correr died on 19 November 1464.

The altarpiece that he commissioned from Mantegna is one of the great turning-points in the history of painting in the Veneto. It was to be admired and imitated in whole or in part, in general design and in its individual figures, until the end of the century, especially in Verona and Venice. In Correr Mantegna had found a true humanist patron, who did not demand of him a Gothic triptych or polyptych altarpiece, with its separate panels for each saint, its formal gold background, its floridly pinnacled framework, such as he had executed for the abbot of Santa Giustina. Instead he was encouraged to deploy the canons and graces of the new art.

Nevertheless, it is important not to exaggerate the originality of Mantegna's conception. His real innovation lay in his transformation of a Gothic scheme and iconography into Renaissance form. He was not an innovator in imposing a unitary composition on the three panels, so that the Virgin and her attendant saints are no longer isolated figures, but grouped together in a single scene. He had been anticipated in this some ten years before by Giovanni d'Alemagna and Antonio Vivarini in the triptych they completed in 1446 for the Scuola Grande della Carità in Venice (now in the Accademia),[18] a picture Mantegna must have known, for its great size brought it great reputation. Almost all the premises of Mantegna's composition are already present in this painting, the single unitary scene in three divisions, with the framework serving as a portico, the enclosed architectural setting, here a *hortus conclusus* in the more conventional form of a walled garden with openings on to an encircling garden, the enthroned Virgin flanked by angels, who are shown holding a canopy, the saints to either side on the same pavement, ranked obliquely so as to direct the eye, along with the horizontal lines of the architecture, inwards to the Virgin.

Yet Giovanni and Antonio made a picture which is still essentially Late Gothic in its conception of space and perspective, and whose decorative language is that of Late Gothic, rich in multi-membered pointed motifs and flourished with gilded ornament. In Mantegna's picture a modern invention has shaped the enclosing architecture into classical forms, adorned with panels of coloured marble and with classical medallions and friezes, the effulgence of gilding being reserved for the framework. Its three panels are bound together by two devices. The perspective scheme imposes a rigorous geometrical unity, while the enclosing garden and the architraves and piers in the foreground add unifying elements of architecture and setting. Both devices serve to correct the disjunction of the panels that would otherwise be created by the vertical columns of the frame.

The principal architectural feature of Mantegna's unitary setting is a covered open-sided pavilion of horizontal oblong plan. In the richest classical style, it is composed of a coved ceiling resting on piers that rise from a pavement or raised dais of chequered black and white marble set in a border of coloured marble. At once an enclosure and a canopy, it combines in itself two motifs that were features of Giovanni and Antonio's painting. For all its restraint and monumentality the architecture of this pavilion still has something very Squarcionesque in the fantasy of certain forms and decorations. At the sides and rear its piers are topped by cushion capitals that are not true capitals, but designed in the fashion of an entablature, with cornice, frieze and architrave. The front piers have capitals that approach more nearly to true capitals, and their strange proportions were perhaps adapted from crude pilasters seen on some provincial antique relief, but their design is not really that of a true ancient capital; rather it is a composition of two volute brackets conjoined. In spite of the dignity of the pavilion, and Mantegna's exquisite sensibility to antique mouldings and ornament, it is plain that his knowledge of classical architecture was still imperfect. And even if we allow for the imaginative need for a pavilion of heaven to exceed in splendour any earthly pavilion, its decoration is influenced by considerations of richness of ornament and symbolism rather than by regard for historical and archaeological plausibility. The front piers are comparatively plain, even in their mouldings, and not inset with panels of red Veronese marble and carved with medallion reliefs like those at the sides and rear. These medallion reliefs have no prototypes in classical art, and were evidently inspired by the miniature sculpture of ancient medals and gems, rather than by true antique relief sculpture. The broad leaves that fill their spandrels are by contrast distinctly Late Gothic, not antique in inspiration.

Above the piers runs a coved entablature, on whose frieze of red Veronese marble are set reliefs in grey stone of classical putti holding swags between palm-trees. The palm-trees allude to a verse from Ecclesiasticus (xxiv, 18) in which wisdom is compared to a palm-tree: 'I was exalted like a palm-tree in Cades.' As on the base of the Virgin's throne, the extremities of the putti and of the other motifs are shown as carved in one with the mouldings of plain stone running along the top and bottom of the frieze for the sake of an effect of illusionism. No fifteenth-century sculptor would have cut out figures and motifs from a block of stone and applied them to a ground of coloured marble in this fashion, and the complexity of carved and pierced work implied in Mantegna's scheme is for this reason alone implausible as a simulation of sculpture. For all their conception as bold sculptural relief, these lively motifs are, in essential aspects of their conception, pictorial, and we shall find that this intrusion of a pictorial dimension into what purport to be carved reliefs remains a constant feature in Mantegna's representations of sculpture.

The caissons of the ceiling are carved with rosettes and have gilt bosses. Through the openings of the piers can be seen a blue sky, in which float thin white clouds, and below it a garden of red and white roses. These last are symbolical not merely ornamental in their beauty and allude to the continuation of the same verse in Ecclesiasticus: '(I was exalted) as a rose-plant in Jericho.' Set in a garden, the pavilion had its prototypes in reality, even if in the 1450s princely garden pavilions were almost certainly far less rich in style. The garden of the Castello at Ferrara had just such a pavilion, according to a description of it written by Sabadino degli Arienti in the late 1490s. Set in the centre of the garden, it was of 'appropriate height, with a ceiling of strong timbers, beautifully covered with lead'. It rested on sixteen columns or piers of white marble, with a marble bench for sitting whose back, a cubit high, was carved with foliage and naked boy angels 'who sing, gazing on a book they hold in their hands and with other angels sculptured in different actions'. The floor was paved 'with marvellous mastery with subtle inlays of various colours of marble'.[19]

The symbolism of a *hortus conclusus* is illustrated in the picture only by implication. This may be because the pavilion probably figures a tabernacle, in allusion to Ecclesiasticus xxiv in which Sapientia (Wisdom) utters her own praises. As we have seen, the palm-trees and the roses allude to verses from this chapter, which was interpreted mystically by the Church as figuring both the Virgin Mary, who was identified with Sapientia, and the incarnation of Christ, whose coming its verses prophesy. The absence of the garden walls of a *hortus conclusus* might be explained by the wish to figure verse 12, 'he that made me, resteth in my tabernacle'. Again the throne can be linked to verse 7, 'my throne is in a pillar of a cloud' and to verse 34, 'He appointed to David, his servant, to raise up of him a most mighty king, and sitting on the throne of glory for ever.' Correr would have been attracted to the chapter, not only by its traditional association with the Virgin, hallowed by inclusion in her daily Hours, but by its last verses (44–7) in which Sapientia, by interpretation the Virgin, declares that she will 'make doctrine to shine forth to all as the morning light' and will 'enlighten all that hope in the Lord', pouring out doctrine for those that seek wisdom and instructing their offspring. This lesson of the pursuit of divine wisdom through study is enforced as we shall see by the saints of the altarpiece.

Worshippers beheld the scene as if through an open portico, for the frame is designed as a composition of four fluted classical columns, which in separating the three panels form a columned front. That this columned front is divided from the front of the pavilion behind is clearly indicated in each panel by the pairs of swags depending from the middle of the cornice. These pass between the columns and piers and define the pictorial space as beginning behind the columns. There is certainly no deep significance in the relationship of frame and picture, which characteristically is directed to enhancing the illusion of successive planes of space, with no regard to the simulation of a plausible architectural construction. Although the columns recall the visual conceit of the St Christopher frescoes, they fulfil no primary role in the illusionistic scheme, but are ancillary to the majestic front piers of the pavilion. If they do not conflict with the illusionistic scheme, neither do they form an integral extension of it. The passages in which Mantegna makes a slight use of the illusion of features protruding into our space – the Baptist's feet, the tunics of the music-making angels – support this interpretation, for they all assume the picture-plane to be the front of the pavement.

If not the earliest, then certainly one of the earliest large picture-frames in the full Renaissance style in the Veneto, this massive structure of gilded wood was surely designed by Mantegna. It is now usual to assert as a proven fact that its design was borrowed from Donatello's altar in the Santo. But our ignorance of the original aspect of that long-destroyed masterpiece is at present complete, and as all reconstructions of it are conjectural prudence recommends that we content ourselves with noting that there still survives a prototype for the San Zeno frame in another work of sculpture which was exceptionally well known to Mantegna, since he had himself tried to meddle in the making of it. This is the altarpiece designed by Niccolò Pizzolo and executed by Giovanni da Pisa in 1448 for the Ovetari Chapel. Mantegna probably took this design as his model and modified it to suit his painting. Originally the frame was surmounted by a finial, which may have been purely decorative, or, less probably, symbolic or heraldic. The importance of the framework in early Renaissance perspective design and ignorance of the new style among woodworkers must have prompted a number of painters to design Renaissance frames in the years when Gothic still kept its hold in many carpenters' workshops. The drawings of Jacopo Bellini include a design for a frame for an altarpiece in a pure Renaissance style, perhaps recording a moment when he was obliged to furnish a model for a patron or a carpenter.[20]

Most unlikely, if only from the nature of the relationship between frame and picture, is the suggestion of some scholars that the perspective of the altarpiece was devised as part of a unified perspective that included the whole of the monks' choir. The viewpoint chosen is low, in the centre bottom of the carpet below the Virgin's feet, that is at eye-level when the picture was raised on its predella above an altar. This low viewpoint implies an expectation of fairly close inspection and an awareness in Mantegna that the altarpiece was to be viewed in a contracted setting. The scene is beheld as if enacted on a platform at the spectator's eye-level, as a stage-tableau, in fact, provided we always remember that this is a modern critical metaphor, and not necessarily in correspondence with the realities of the fifteenth-century stage. The vision of heaven opens upon us in a continuity of space, but fronted and confined by gilded columns that bar familiarity and distance it into the divine.

All that is known of the picture's original setting, which was much altered in the sixteenth century, bears out this interpretation. Before Correr became abbot, the monks had held their services in the crypt of the church, where San Zeno, bishop and patron of Verona and their titular saint, lay entombed. The crypt had only a small apse, and was wholly occupied by the monks' presbytery and choir, to the no small inconvenience of pilgrims and the faithful. The *cappella maggiore* of the upper church had already been enlarged in the fourteenth century, and Correr now determined to enlarge the apse of the crypt, so easing access to the saint's tomb, and to move the monks' choir to the *cappella maggiore*.

Work in the crypt began in January 1446 and had probably been more or less completed by 26 September 1451, when the new altar was consecrated. The enlargement of the apse had entailed raising the floor of the *cappella maggiore*. To meet this change of level, four steps were placed between the first pilasters of the entrance to the *cappella*: these led to a lightly sloping pavement terminating in another step which preceded a second set of pilasters. Between these second pilasters, on a floor paved with marble, rose a new altar, also consecrated in 1451, probably on 18 July: it was for this altar that Mantegna's altarpiece was commissioned. Constructed of a core of brick and *tufo*, it was dressed with panels of red Veronese marble, with which the simulated panelling in red marble of the pavilion in Mantegna's painting must have harmonized in richness and colouring. This marble dressing was applied only to the front and sides, and since the altar-table of *broccatello* (speckled yellow marble) was again decorated solely on the front and sides it appears that originally the altar stood against a transverse wall. The presbytery choir so formed was concealed from the nave by Correr's new choir-stalls and the high *pontile* separating it from the nave. In the usual monastic fashion the monks were shut off from the nave inside their choir: within it the light must have been darkened by the stained glass that Correr placed in the four windows he opened in the *cappella maggiore*. From the first, the altarpiece must have been one of the most invisible of great works of art, except when the darkness that still shrouds it was illuminated by candlelight.

The theme of the altarpiece and the saints who appear in it were chosen by Correr and reflect his own especial devotions as well as those of the monastery and of the Veronese. The Virgin appears enthroned in glory attended by the court of heaven triumphant: it was to the Virgin and to the *universa caelestis curia triumphans* that Correr commended his soul on his death-bed.[21] In his figuration of heaven as well as of pictorial space Mantegna has now removed to the opposite pole from the Santa Giustina altarpiece, whose heaven was a simple depth of gold above a pavement of rich marbles. Correr was a great humanist ecclesiastic for whom the magnificence of the courts of heaven could be blazoned in the vocabulary of antique architecture and antique ornament, relieved by the blue of sky and white of clouds, and by the green and pink and white of a garden of roses.

In the central panel is the Virgin, seated on a great marble throne whose elaborate design *all'antica* is the most consummate and rational expression of that richly fantastic invention which all the Squarcionesques seem to have lavished on the thrones of heaven in the hope of suggesting a celestial magnificence. Two of the most prominent antique motifs of Mantegna's throne, the form of its seat and the relief of putti holding a laurel-wreathed medallion on its base, are inspired by Roman sarcophagi. The tracery which fills the medallion is echoed in the great wheel-shaped circle of pierced marble resting on volutes which surmounts the dossal of the throne. The volutes are repeated in the ends of the arms, so imposing further unity on the design. For all the fantastic classicism of its invention, the decoration of the throne makes one last appeal to an earlier style, for the motif of pierced trefoils whose interlinked gadroons fill the laurel-wreathed medallion are markedly Gothic in feeling. We shall find this call on styles external to the antique for additional decorative richness repeated in the orientalizing ornaments Mantegna introduces into the picture. The yellow marble with which the face of the throne is set must have been chosen to echo the *broccatello* of the altar-table beneath, while the porphyry of the base accentuated in a deeper and more imperial red the dominant pinkish-red of the Veronese marble below.

The Virgin's head is a smooth oval, of singularly perfect outline, but a little broader than the narrow oval of Gothic art, in keeping with that sense of solid volumetric form already in the 1450s so typical of Mantegna's heads. The appearance of greater breadth is enhanced by the pleated veil, concealing a high smooth forehead which completes the oval according to a fifteenth-century canon of beauty in women. The slender eyebrows accent the pure line of the double arch of the forehead above the smooth sockets of the eyes and the smooth straight nose, the only sharply modelled features on the single volume of the head. Mantegna has carried its approximation to sculptural simplicity and unity of form as far as the nature of painting allowed. The white flesh, yet another point of beauty, is only lightly flushed with pink in the cheeks and with red on the lips. Absorbed in meditation, the Virgin looks outwards to her left, and by the direction of her gaze attracted the eyes of the monks seated in the choir-stalls on the right. Head and neck are united in a serpentine curve which produces a graceful fusion of their forms. According to Mantegna's customary practice at this date, breadth and weight are added to the body, which in itself is tall and slender, by massing drapery about it. The blue cloak adds breadth on the left to her shoulders and upper chest, and to both sides of the lower part of her body, so giving a hieratic squared solidity to a figure of underlying slenderness and flexibility. The solid blue mass so created is relieved by disposing the folds to make displays of its green lining at the side, and balanced by the vivid scarlet of the robe across the bosom and over the right leg.

In a further show of virtuosity Mantegna has pain-

ted a scarf of light transparent stuff falling from the Virgin's head on to her bosom: through it we see the blue of her hood, the white of her flesh and the gold and scarlet of her robe lightly changed by the white of the scarf. Such effects of transparency were greatly admired in fifteenth-century art as an ultimate in illusionistic skill. The Virgin holds up one end of the scarf under her right arm as she clasps the Child: by this device Mantegna, perhaps in response to a request from Correr, brings the scarf in a graceful curve across the Child's genitals and so softens their form under a light and apparently unaffected veil. In contrast with the firm perfection of the Virgin's features, he has attempted to give the Child's flesh something of a child's soft and yielding suppleness. The broad snub-nosed little face, the plump little arms and legs are constructed in dimpled forms creating a succession of small curves: the fat little belly sticks out with a swelling uncertainty of shape that imitates reality. Nevertheless, these observations of nature are tempered into a figure of ideal beauty. The golden hair is crisped into a formal pattern of smooth and narrow, lightly undulating locks, parted to either side, with one or two short curls escaping in a carefully ordered disorder. The figure itself is constructed on a classical curve, with a marked *déhanchement* to the left. The pose is chosen to complete that of the Virgin: the Child gazes tenderly downwards in the opposite direction to draw the eyes of the monks seated in the stalls on the left.

The garlands which hang from the entablature were as we know a favourite motif of Squarcione and his pupils, attracting them both as a spatial device and as an ornamental motif with classical authority. Hanging swags decorate the pedestals of the saints in the Lazara altarpiece, and in one of the frescoes Squarcione painted for the church of San Francesco in Padua, *St Francis presenting roses to Pope Honorius*, ribboned swags of laurel decorate the panels between the pilasters of the room, rather irrationally in fact, and for ornamental enrichment solely, not for spatial effect.[22] The garlands of his pupils are highly distinctive. Essentially bunches of various kinds of dark green foliage and brightly coloured fruit, they are so arranged as to give prominence to the single fruits and to the still-life naturalism of their simulation. As garlands or swags they are suspended from hoops or nails by ribbons, which in Mantegna are usually executed in strong colours, such as coral-red, to contrast with the green of the foliage. Mantegna's earliest garlands are those on the ceiling of the tribune of the Ovetari Chapel, and are composed of branches of foliage and fruit threaded on a cable and expanding from a thin stem into fat heavy swags. The garlands of the uppermost tier of the St James frescoes are lighter. Those on the second tier are arranged in bands of foliage alternating with bands of fruit or flowers. In the *St Euphemia* of 1454 and the Venice *St George* there is a freer, less patterned disposition and a richer assortment of fruits, including oranges, yellow figs and grapes. A more rigid disposition returns in the San Zeno altarpiece. Here diversity is obtained by the great variety of the foliage and of the fruit, nut and vegetable forms introduced, each simulated with careful naturalism, and by Mantegna's favourite contrast of deep reds and brilliant yellows. The leaves are of oak and bay-laurel, while the fruit, vegetables and nuts comprise cob-nuts, acorns, strawberries, raspberries, cherries, lemons, apricots, peaches, pineapples, oranges, beans, grapes, figs, gherkins, gourds, nectarines and apples. The diligence of imagination Mantegna lavished on the altarpiece is plain from this very variety. Above the Virgin's head, for extra richness, are suspended two strings of oval beads of coral, an ornament that will recur even in Mantegna's late works.

From the ring that holds the pair of swags, hangs that precious medieval rarity, an ostrich egg, suspended over a glass lamp in a mount of gold set with sapphires, rubies and pearls and decorated with sunk rosettes or sexfoils. A candle-flame appears above its edge: in a characteristic display of refinement of virtuosity even in details, the flame is cut off in perspective. The lamp proper is an oil-lamp, of a type invented by Venetian glass-makers which survives only in later versions.[23] This combination of glass oil-lamp and ostrich egg existed in reality in churches. It can be seen in the Venetian church of Sant'Antonio di Castello as depicted in Carpaccio's *Apparition of the martyrs of Ararat in the church of Sant'Antonio*, painted c.1512. Here it hangs from a cross-beam: again there is a cap to protect the egg from the flame. The lamp itself has a curved base, with a projecting finial, but its mount is very similar to that of Mantegna's lamp. The same combination is repeated in a set of five hanging lamps worked by a winch which Carpaccio shows suspended from the same beam. Another is shown on Marco Marziale's *Circumcision* in the National Gallery, London, painted for San Silvestro, Cremona. Ostrich eggs were also hung up by themselves in churches: a number are shown hanging from the nave screen in Carpaccio's painting.[24] The thirteenth-century author Durandus explains in his *Rationale Divinorum Officiorum*, a work much read well into the sixteenth century, that they were used to attract the people by their rarity. Lamp and ostrich egg may therefore appear in Mantegna's painting simply as the richest and rarest sort of earthly lamp, glorified yet further by a mount of gold and gems to fit it to be a heavenly lamp.

Yet a symbolic meaning is probable. A similar lamp with an ostrich egg is suspended from an architrave above San Bernardino's head in the altarpiece Mantegna painted in 1469 for the saint's chapel in San Francesco, Mantua. Its appearance in this different context suggests that too much should not be made of the ostrich egg in terms of purely Marian symbolism. Passages in Durandus suggest that its symbolic meaning is essentially an exhortation to follow the example of Christ and his saints, who are the lights of mankind and of the church. His words certainly indicate the sort of meditations Correr intended to encourage in his monks. Explaining why ostrich eggs are hung up in churches, he writes:

> Again some say that the ostrich, being a forgetful bird, leaves its eggs in the sand: at last, on seeing a certain star, it recollects them, and returns to them, fostering them with its gaze. Accordingly its eggs are hung up in churches to signify that should a man be abandoned by God on account of his sins, if at length he be illumined by the divine light and recollect himself and repent of his sins and return to him, he is fostered by the aspect of his light, as it is said in Luke, that the Lord turned and looked on Peter after he denied Christ. They are also hung up in order that every man may contemplate therein how man easily forgets God, unless being illuminated by a star, that is, by the influence of the Holy Spirit, he is reminded to return to him through good works.[25]

Lamps to Durandus are a symbol for Christ, who is the Light that shineth in darkness, the true Light which enlighteneth every man that cometh into this world. He explains that the lights of the Church may also signify the Apostles and the other doctors with whose light the Church shines, 'of whom Our Lord sayeth, you are the light of the world, that is, exemplars of good works'. Wherefore he admonished them, 'Let your light so shine before men that they may see your good works.'[26] This must be the meaning of the lamp in the San Bernardino altarpiece. In the San Zeno altarpiece the burning lamp also indicates that the hour is evening, when lamps were lit and vespers sung in churches. Durandus associates lamps with vespers and the Virgin, and in particular with her canticle of the *Magnificat*. According to Bede, he says, the *Magnificat* is sung at vespers, in preference to the other offices of the church, first because it was during the evening of the world that the Virgin consented to the Divine will and so saved the world from destruction, secondly because it is sweet for this reason to remember that the Incarnation took place in the evening of the world, thirdly because she is the star of the sea (*stella maris*), whose light rescued us in the evening of the world, fourthly because our minds, wearied by the thoughts of the day are cleansed at the approach of night by the recollection of the Virgin, and fifthly because the Virgin bore the Child in the evening of the world. In order to represent the rejoicing of the *Magnificat* lamps are lit at vespers: alternatively they are lit because this canticle is part of the Gospel, 'or again so that we like the wise virgins may run with the lamps of good works in the odour of the unguents of the Blessed Virgin, entering with her into the joy of Our Lord. And inasmuch as our works do not shine in their lamps unless they be informed with charity, so the canticle is ended with an antiphony by which charity is inculcated.'[27] This didactic symbolism, as we shall see, is only one of the lessons enforced on the monks of San Zeno by the altarpiece.

The Virgin's feet rest on a costly oriental carpet of red and green: so much was this motif admired that Veronese masters imitated it in painting their thrones of the Virgin until the end of the century. In type it is a Turkish Anatolian carpet of the sort conventionally known as a 'Holbein' carpet. The colours are convincingly simulated; faithfully reproduced too is the general form of the border and centre. The Cufic letters of the border, by contrast, are a trifle too regularized and over-elaborate for this type of carpet, and may have been taken from some other Islamic source, such as a manuscript. The selvage too is wrongly shown, without any contrast of texture with the main carpet. Together with the perfunctory nature of the fringe, these details suggest that Mantegna had seen many Turkish carpets, but did not actually have one before him as a model.

To enhance the figures of the Virgin and Child with a discreet richness of ornament Mantegna has again used Islamic motifs. The Cufic letters which fill the gold border of the Virgin's cloak had long been imitated in Europe from oriental textiles; so too the Cufic letters filling the border of the Virgin's halo and the haloes of the attendant saints were a conventional ornament of haloes. Indeed Mantegna had already used similar letters to enrich the borders of robes in the Santa Giustina altarpiece. He has designed them here with something of a Late Gothic feeling for florid calligraphic decorativeness. Much more unusual are the Islamic-style panels with pointed ends containing Cufic letters which make a cruciform pattern on the Child's halo. And more singular still are the books held by St John the Evangelist and by San Zeno: that held by St John is only influenced by oriental bindings, but that held by San Zeno appears to figure a binding in true Islamic style. They are of exceptional interest, for the earliest known Western bindings to use oriental designs and techniques of gilding were executed in Padua and Venice *c.*1457 for a known patron of Mantegna, the Venetian patrician Jacopo Antonio Marcello.[28]

All these motifs suggest that Mantegna had recently seen and studied precious Islamic artefacts, perhaps in Marcello's palace at Monselice, perhaps in the studies of the learned men of Padua and Venice. This openness of taste in Mantegna and his patrons deserves some stress, for all it is expressed only in subordinate motifs, as here. In Mantegna, as in other artists of his century, a predominant enthusiasm for the antique did not suppress a lively pleasure in the intricate pattern and bold colour of the rich and strange artefacts, the textiles, the Syrian glass, the Chinese porcelain, that were brought through Venice from the lands of the Moors and the Turks and, more rarely, from the vaguer Indies that lay beyond the Levant. The unifying aesthetic that could allow the combination of objects in classical style and exotic style, so disparate to modern eyes, was one of virtuosity in the imitation of all that was held rich and delightful to the eye.[29]

Clustered on the steps of the Virgin's throne are child angels, four singing *laudi* in her praise to the accompaniment of two others gazing out of the altarpiece and playing lutes that are represented in contrasted perspective views with easy and masterly skill. The iconographical invention, a Renaissance translation of an old medieval motif, is probably Squarcionesque. It appears in the *Wimborne Madonna*, signed by Marco Zoppo as '*opera del Zoppo di Squarcione*' and probably painted *c.*1455, where four angels on a parapet before the Virgin laud her on trumpets, a lute and a zither, while in the niche behind her two others play a bag-pipe and a pan-pipe.

Attending the Virgin is a court of saints, who stand in two files to either side of her throne in the two side panels. In the left panel, San Zeno stands on the Virgin's right hand, as the titular saint of the monastery. Next to him is St John the Evangelist, earnestly reading his gospel. In front of the Evangelist is St Paul, his back turned to St John as he converses with St Peter, who stands on the edge of the marble platform, his head turned to look out at us. By contrast the right panel makes no use of such a device to draw the spectator's eyes into the pictorial space. Paired with San Zeno in the second place of honour on the Virgin's left is St Benedict, the founder of the order to which the monastery belonged. Looking downwards he opens his book and prepares to read his rule – a motif of subtle naturalism in its apparent casualness. Next to him are St Laurence, St Gregory Nazianzen, and St John the Baptist, whose pose of strong *déhanchement* contributes to our impression of the intentness with which he studies in his book. The visible emphasis in the altarpiece on sacred learning – six out of the eight saints hold or read books – culminates in this figure of the Baptist. Not only is he one of the two most prominent saints in the altarpiece, but instead of being given his traditional pose as the forerunner of Christ, pointing to him with extended finger, he is shown quite exceptionally as buried in a book, with his cross-stave leaning against his shoulder, not grasped in his hand, to express his absorption.

This insistence on the reading of the Gospels, of the Benedictine Rule, of books of theology and devotion can only have been introduced into the altarpiece at the desire of Correr, whose spiritual crisis had moved him to forsake the world for the church, the study of profane letters for that of sacred letters. He certainly intended it as an admonition and example to his monks, whom their rule ordered to give up a third of their time to the *lectio divina* (scriptural, devotional and theological reading). In this sense the altarpiece is closely linked with Correr's introduction of strict observance of the rule into San Zeno. For him its didactic reinforcement of a prime duty of monastic life may have justified all superfluity of expense on so splendid and costly a picture – not that there is any reason to suppose he viewed its making as anything other than an act of piety in itself. The altarpiece is a monument therefore not only to Mantegna's art and to the introduction of the Renaissance style into Verona, but to Christian Humanism and the movement of austerity and reform associated with it.

All the saints who figure with San Zeno and St Benedict belong to the early centuries of the Church, and in this their choice is again characteristic of a Christian humanist. With one exception they were the objects of a cult in Verona or in the monastery itself. The exception is St Gregory Nazianzen (*c.*330– 90), who is clad in a richly apparelled cope and dalmatic of cloth of gold patterned with scarlet foliage and stems, and so is singled out from his fellow saints, who are attired plainly or with modest ornament. At the head of the apparel of his cope is an oval laurel-wreathed medallion with a saint on a blue ground with a Greek inscription. A similar medallion appears below. These two medallions are copied from Byzantine embroidered silks to indicate the saint's origin in the Eastern Empire and his association with the Eastern Church.[30]

Gregory Nazianzen is so rarely represented in Western art between the twelfth and seventeenth centuries that he must appear as Gregorio Correr's personal choice. Correr himself was surely given the saint's name of St Gregory the Great, who as a Benedictine monk, a student of sacred letters and a Latin doctor of the Church might have figured more than appropriately in his altarpiece, or so it might be thought. The reasons for his choice of Gregory Nazianzen instead lie in the correspondence of ideals and conflicts that he found between Gregory's life and his own. A theologian, whose writings – ora-

tions, letters, poems – are in the classical rhetorical tradition, Gregory too had loved secular letters and had had a tormented vocation. And although he had been compelled to assume high ecclesiastical offices, like Correr, he had abandoned the world for a life of studious retreat and retired to his native province, dedicating himself to his writings and to the direction of a monastic community. Neither man himself became a monk. To Correr Gregory's life must have seemed a justification of his own resolution of the conflict between aspiration to forsake the world and reluctant involvement in its turmoil. Gregory and his works had exercised great influence in the Byzantine East, but had been little known in the medieval West. The discovery and translation of his writings was begun by the Christian humanists, more especially by Correr's friend Ambrogio Traversari (1386–1439), the Camaldolese monk who was their leader. Traversari obtained a number of Gregory's works from various sources, and in 1431 procured from the library of the Basilian monks of Grottaferrata a Greek life of the saint which he translated into Latin 'on account of its novelty'. It was surely this translation which introduced Correr to the vicissitudes of Gregory's life.[31]

To compare Mantegna's attendant saints with those of the Vivarini triptych of 1446 is to understand at once what his humanist eulogists had in mind when they exclaimed in their eloquent Latin that his figures seemed to move and breathe and have life. Far from standing with stately immobility, encased in rich, stiff draperies, his saints have bodies that curve and inflect under their own weight; their draperies model the limbs and forms beneath. They themselves turn and look and contemplate and study and hold attributes that are not merely symbols of their identity, but motives of activity or absorption.

The altarpiece glows with Mantegna's intense effulgent colour, yellow, coral-red, pink, scarlet, dark blue, green. The strong hues are largely in the draperies, which on the whole are austerely plain in material, and quietly cast in Mantegna's usual alternation of ridged folds with body-clinging forms. The bold, apostolic simplicity of the draperies is contrasted with the sumptuousness of the architecture, so profusely adorned with panels of coloured marble, with ornamental figures in relief and with ornamental medallions. Mantegna is now evolving towards what may be called his second manner. The brilliantly coloured swags and careful isolation of each panel within a painted architectural frame are lingering mannerisms, but the painted framework has ceased to be an arbitrary window and become an articulate member of a structure that has an expressive as well as a technical function in the picture. Foreshortening, too, is no longer ostentatiously paraded.

It is often said that for these changes Mantegna was indebted to Donatello's altar in the Santo; it is even argued that the tripartite form of the altarpiece was inspired by two of the bronze reliefs from the Santo altar, *The Miracle of the Ass* and *The Miracle of the New-Born Child*, both of which use architecture to break up the narrative into tripartite form. But this is to attribute to Donatello what belongs to the triptych of Giovanni d'Alemagna and Antonio Vivarini. In reality nothing could be more different from Donatello's figures, instinct with eager life and feeling and anecdotal movement, always in a relationship of gesture and expression with others, than the stately figures of Mantegna, each enclosed within its own perfection, drawing no vitality from the presence of their fellows. Mantegna represents a patrician humanism which is far from excluding all naturalness and warmth and play, but does not set on the expression of emotion and on the participation of action and feeling from one human being to another the value that the more democratic Donatello set. The figures of Peter and Paul in the San Zeno altarpiece are turned to each other, yet neither their hands nor their eyes engage in any dialogue. The inspiration of this effect, certainly intended, was antique relief sculpture: its stylistic consequence is a very Roman *gravitas*.

In the ideal figures of the Virgin and Child and their attendant angels Mantegna is moving to an ever severer conception of figures as pure volumes, approaching them as much as the counter-force of naturalism and the medium of paint allowed him to the smooth and simple planes of sculptured marble. In the attendant saints, where pictorial variety required a variety of types, there is more of human irregularity. Yet if Mantegna has abandoned Gothic stiffness, we feel that he has advanced towards the future without crossing its threshold. In a sense he was always to remain an artist of transition. The figures of the saints are tall and slender, though this is sometimes disguised by amplitude in their robes, for Mantegna strictly observes the canon of proportion by which the body and legs are six times the length of the head. The ultimate debts of Venetian art to Byzantium are recalled, if only faintly, not only by this preference for tallness and slenderness but by the long, narrow faces and dark beards of St Paul and San Zeno. The Baptist is a study of a semi-nude figure in *contrapposto*, and is surely one of the figures on which the sixteenth century founded its praise of Mantegna for having introduced 'softer curves' into representations of the human body, in place of the earlier rigidity.[32] Characteristically the smoothly rounded limbs are naturalistically wrinkled by lines and veins in the wrist and hands, informing their perfection with a just sufficient hint of living flesh.

The predella of the altarpiece, now dismembered, figures scenes from Christ's Passion and the Resurrection, and as the Virgin and Child symbolize the Incarnation, so in its entirety the altarpiece offered the whole mystery of man's redemption to the meditation of Correr's monks. *The Agony in the Garden* (Plate 38), now in Tours, reverses the composition of Mantegna's earlier painting of the same subject, no doubt because it was to the left of the predella. The light is from the right, and the darkness of evening is again suggested by painting the faces of the rock of Gethsemane in shadow, and shadowing what is beneath them. Against a pink ridge, which rises into the dark crimson-pink of a conical mountain, Christ's face is lifted in prayer, as a cloud-borne angel, robed in sad grey, stoops from the air in shadow above the dark foliage and bright fruit of a tree to offer him the golden chalice. Even the colour of his face, hands and feet seems to express his agony – it is a burning tender pink-brown. His robe is whitish-pink, his cloak dark green, heightened with delicate strokes of gold in the passages that are lit. The attitudes of the Apostles are conceived with the same naturalism as in the earlier *Agony*: if anything, their realism is sharper and our awareness of the living model greater, as in the figure of James, who lies flat on his face, with his feet protruding towards us. The reproach of apathy implied in their poses is here more directly expressed, though as always the figures are fused by the beauty of colour of their draperies – brilliant yellow in Peter's cloak, pinkish-white in James's robe, white in his cloak, blue in John's robe, dark olive-green in his cloak – into the intensely poetical realization of the scene.

This part of the picture is separated from the rest of the composition by the broad, steeply plunging valley of Jehoshaphat, and by a tall dead tree in the foreground. The vine trained up its withered trunk and the two apple-trees, one to either side of the rock, tell us that Gethsemane is a garden, not indeed of the green northern kind, but of a stony, desolate eastern sort. So too do the two beehives, made of grey cylindrical trunks hollowed out, pierced by a door and window and covered by flat lids of wood. These features suggest what the view of Jerusalem confirms, that Mantegna has progressed in topographical and historical knowledge and therefore in exactitude, for in the earlier *Agony* there was nothing to indicate that Gethsemane was a garden. A grey city with a few dark pink roofs, Jerusalem now rises up its mountain slope above a dark chasm, through which flows the brook Kedron, crossed by rustic bridges. At its lower end is a suburb, enclosed by a ruined wall continued by a palisade: a winding street leads up through it to the principal wall, which encloses the Temple, represented as an arcaded circular building with a domed roof surmounted by a pineapple finial. Its form is roughly modelled on the Mosque of Omar, which during the Middle Ages was often believed to be Solomon's Temple. Above rises a third wall encircling towers and the citadel of Antonia.

This division of Jerusalem corresponds to the description which Josephus gives of the city in *The Jewish War* (v, c.4). Josephus was an author very familiar to scholars and ecclesiastics and to the lay public in the fifteenth century: *The Jewish War* had already been translated into Italian in the trecento. That there was an interest among such men in the topography of the Holy Land appears from the inventory of Giovanni Marcanova, who owned in 1465 a 'mappemondo, sive descriptio Judeae in membranis', that is, a map of Palestine on parchment.[33] Topographical views of famous cities were much sought after by fifteenth-century princes, and no doubt by others too: Lorenzo de' Medici had one of Rome in 1492, while Francesco Gonzaga in the 1490s had Mantegna's son Francesco decorate a chamber in his country palace at Marmirolo with a *mappamondo*, or figurations of the world.[34] Hence Mantegna was satisfying a general taste in his increasing attempts at topographical exactitude. As usual he has enlivened his antiquarian reconstruction of the city with realism of detail – broken walls and towers, water that falls from a drainpipe and splashes on to a heap of rocks on the further side of Kedron. His particularizing imagination adds in this way verisimilitude and suggestive power to settings whose general conception often owes much to established pictorial convention.

The Crucifixion (Plate III), now in the Louvre, shows the same graphic care for topographical exactitude and far greater visual cunning. Mantegna has set himself the problem of representing the scene as the worshipper would see it if standing just below the hither slope of the summit of Mount Calvary. Immediately before his eyes is the Crucifixion itself on the paved top of the Mount, while beyond is the fall of its further slope and the panorama of Sion and Jerusalem. The pavement of Calvary is already pitted with holes that have served for other crosses and thus is evidently 'a place of execution'. The crosses of the thieves are wedged into two of these old holes, while Christ's cross is propped up by stones. Our viewpoint is marked in the foreground by two steps, the last of the eighteen by which the Mount was ascended,[35] and by the cut-off figures of two conversing soldiers, whom we are to imagine as standing on the steps below. Having prompted the eye by these ingenious devices to figure to the inner fancy the front slope of the Mount, Mantegna amazes it with others that suggest its farther slope. The orthogonals of the paved summit are made to recede to a point of sight which is in the centre of the rear edge of the platform. That rear edge is curved, and the curve, aided by the converging lines of the orthogonals and the decreasing size of the paving stones as they diminish in recession, produces the illusion of the rounded top of a farther slope. Below the edge the limbs of the figures ascending or descending the slope are cut off and those descending are shown in diminishing scale, beginning with the Roman halberdier who walks away from the spectator. The extraordinary sensation of movement this device creates in the middle ground is prolonged into the background by the procession of figures riding or walking up the road that winds towards Jerusalem around a cliff below the steep vertical face of Sion. The dark volcanic rock of this cliff, the dark rocks in the left background and the dark spur of rough rocks running into the right foreground encircle the platform with a frame of gloom, hardly relieved by the delicate grey of the sepulchre on the left. About the sepulchre the ground is littered with skulls and bones to show that it is Golgotha, the place of skulls; following established iconographical tradition, the skull of Adam, the first man, which according to legend was found near the rift in Calvary hard by Golgotha and was still being shown to pilgrims in 1495, is set beneath the cross.[36]

The light is concentrated in the central band of the picture, on the cross of Christ: the crosses of the thieves are largely seen against shadow. As in his earlier *Agony*, Mantegna manages the light for expressive purposes – features are in shadow or lightly lit so as to darken or to silhouette more sharply. Thus Christ's face is shadowed in agony: on the left the good thief is symbolically in the light, while the bad thief on the right is in shadowed gloom. Below, the figures on the further side are in shadow or wear dark garments, while those on the nearer side are in lighter colours for prominence.

Unlike Christ, the thieves are not nailed to their crosses: in obedience to North Italian, and more especially Venetian, iconographical tradition they are bound to them with a rope around the feet and have their arms twisted back and tied behind their bodies on the rear side of the crosses. The contorted poses of both show the agony they suffer. The bad thief has his left foot free and lifts it in an attempt to relieve his pain; blood runs down his legs; he seems nearer to death than the good thief, who lifts his eyes heavenwards. Mantegna has also sought other expressive contradictions of emotion and action. The grief-stricken figures of St John, the Virgin and the three Maries on the left are contrasted with the group of idling, gambling Roman soldiers on the right. Both groups are turned away from the Cross, leaving it in a yet more emphatic isolation, with Christ's blood trickling down its shaft. Only St John gazes at it, hands clasped and head inclined in a bitter agony of grief as he contemplates the Passion, a contemplation in which his pose invites the spectator to join. His olive-green cloak makes a passage of dark colour which is continued in the cloak of darkest green that muffles the pink robe of the Virgin. Her fainting figure is thrown up by the two Maries who support it, the one on the left in white robe and coral mantle, the other in a cloak of light purplish-grey over her dark olive robe, and by the upturned face of the Mary behind. The faces of these four mourning women are perhaps Mantegna's most poignant studies of emotion: their haloes, not sharply outlined disks, but narrow circles of golden radiance, transfigure without softening the bitterness of their sorrow. The golden light that plays on their draperies also helps to transmute the harshness of expression, and with one of Mantegna's most poetical transitions these anguished figures are modulated into the gentle serving-woman in bright azure cloak and yellow robe who stands modestly behind, her arms folded, her eyes downcast. Her tall slender grace and deportment are conceived according to an ideal of serene beauty that will recur in Mantegna's Mantuan paintings of the 1460s.

The three gambling private soldiers are figures of plebeian coarseness, expressing in their aspect and attitude a brutal indifference to the suffering behind them, and an eager absorption in the lots they are throwing on the circular board – a triumph of foreshortening – for the seamless tunic. One end of this is held by a tall standard-bearer, wearing a coral-crested helm, a bright yellow cloak and olive-green armour spotted with gold. The other end is held by a bearded, barefoot man in dark robe and blue cloak: although the standard-bearer speaks to him, apparently in anger, he gazes with characteristic Mantegnesque aloofness straight before him. From behind a man in violet eyes the dispute with lively interest, while a young officer looks on from a stately dark brown horse whose colour blends with the shadow that falls from the rock and with the rock itself. In front, balancing the figure of St John, is another officer on a dapple-grey horse seen for contrast from the rear, a motif that serves to lead the eye into the picture, making it follow his raised head to gaze at the crucified thief above. The types of these figures are more refined than those of the common soldiers, Mantegna evidently thinking this proper to their rank, and moreover being unable to sever all idea of dignity and grace from his representations of Romans. In this little scene of the casting of lots, however, there is also an inspiration from the recent past, from Altichiero's fresco of the *Crucifixion* in the Oratorio di San Giorgio.

It would be difficult to find another Renaissance picture in which the setting and accessory figures are invented with greater dramatic skill to suggest the streaming movement of a crowd, while the principal figures are either static, absorbed in or stunned by their own grief, or caught either at a pause in their action, like the gambling soldiers, or in suspended motion. Yet the naturalism of the observation is fused into ideal beauty by Mantegna's solemn, isolated figures and by the pure and glowing colour, the rich and strange inventions of antique military costume, and a landscape at once fantastic and expressive in the bright pink slopes of its rocks and their faces of gloomy shadow.

The tunics, cloaks and armour of the legionaries mingle in Mantegna's usual fashion antiquarian verisimilitude with richly fanciful colour – the armour is gold, green, blue, pink with studs of gold, the tunics and cloaks are red, blue, pink, coral and yellow. The same variety appears in the armour of the guards who are wakened in the dawn light of *The Resurrection* (Plate 41), the last panel of the three. Dominating the scene is the sepulchre itself, a great brown rock set on a platform of rock. It is hollowed out inside, and the principal effect is the contrast between the pale dawn without and the fiery light that shines within, becoming a red glow behind the sarcophagus and illumining the rough-hewn walls with coral colour. Its burning splendour is diffused by the golden rays that shoot from a great mandorla of cherubs, of red lit with gold, encircling the tall figure of Christ. A type now of human perfection, his muscular body and slender limbs no longer attenuated by the expressive emaciation of Gothic art, he steps up from the tomb, his right hand raised in blessing, his left holding a coral-coloured standard topped by a cross which is designed, interestingly enough, in the Late Gothic style that still prevailed in contemporary Italian goldsmith's work.

The light comes from the right, so that the right side of the rock is in contrast with the shadowed left, which is relieved against a brighter sky. This direction of light also produces an opposing contrast within the sepulchre, where the right side is in deep shadow. Christ's white-clothed body forms the central vertical axis of the picture, and the lines of the platform of rocks and of the sarcophagus converge sharply on the rising figure in the tomb chamber. The sleeping guards about the tomb are placed with careful regard to the need to mark the planes of the picture. The guards seem always to have interested artists who represented this theme for the possibilities they offered of anecdote and variety of attitude. Jacopo Bellini's drawings include two of *The Resurrection* which are a series of naturalistic studies of men sleeping.[37] As always, Mantegna links his figures much more dramatically to the scene and to the setting than Bellini, and searches out action for them with far greater subtlety of invention. Again, these common soldiers are plebeian in type:

each is so posed that he constitutes a separate study in the varied positioning of legs as well as of physical reactions that range from the torpid stupor of half-awakeness to horrified amazement.

Internal stylistic evidence suggests that Mantegna painted the altarpiece proper first and the predella panels last, *The Crucifixion* probably last of all, given its subtlety of conception and masterly execution. The entire work took Mantegna some two and a half years to complete, so putting the patience of his prospective lord, Lodovico Gonzaga, to serious trial. Lodovico wrote to Gregorio Correr on 27 November 1457 to say that he had had no news of Mantegna for a good while and to enquire whether he had finished the altarpiece. About or in March 1458 the Marchese even sent Luca Fancelli, his court architect, to visit Mantegna in Padua and settle the terms on which Andrea would agree to remove to Mantua and enter his service. In a letter of 16 April, written after Fancelli's return, Lodovico expressed his pleasure at hearing that Mantegna still intended to enter his service and renewed and improved the terms he had previously offered him by letter. He was prepared to grant him a provision of fifteen ducats a month, a dwelling for himself and his family, enough corn for the consumption of six mouths and all the wood he needed. He was also prepared to meet the expenses of Mantegna's removal to Mantua, which was to be by boat. Fancelli had reported to him that Mantegna would be grateful for a delay of six months in order to finish his work for Correr and to despatch all his other business, and Lodovico would be pleased to grant him this respite and even to allow him one or two months more if necessary. Indeed, provided Mantegna undertook to come to Mantua next January without fail, he could have leave to delay until then.

Although Mantegna did not remove to Mantua at once in answer to this invitation, he must have gone there in January 1459 and formally entered the Marchese's service. By a diploma of 30 January 1459 Lodovico granted to 'Andrea Mantegna, painter of Padua, a very dear member of our household (*familiarem*), whom we have lately taken into our service', the right of using the Gonzaga coat of arms. The grant was made at Andrea's petition, and the diploma recited that 'as it would be very pleasing to him and meet his desire . . . we have judged it worth our while not to let the said Andrea depart from us without this gift.'[38] The coat was to be slightly differenced from that borne by Lodovico, and in chief above the Gonzaga arms was to display a sun in splendour encircled with a scroll bearing the motto *par un désir* in Gothic letters on a white field.

Both device and motto had been adopted by Lodovico at the end of 1448, after the disastrous battle of Caravaggio in which he had lost all his baggage, including his seals.[39] Mantegna was to have the right to bear these arms in private and in public: by granting them Lodovico conferred on him a feudal badge that proclaimed the painter's allegiance to the house of Gonzaga and to himself. At one and the same time as he gratified the young artist's vanity by this stamp of nobility, he also gave him a formal assurance of the footing on which he would be received at the Gonzaga court. Mantegna used the coat of arms as his seal until at least 1468, though from 1472 to 1492 he replaced it with a seal of Julius Caesar's head and by 1505–6 he was employing the simple initial M.[40] The Marchese also signalled that Mantegna had become a member of his household by giving him three and a half *braccia* (something more than two yards) of crimson damask brocaded with silver to make a *giuppone* or doublet.[41] He was making him a grant of livery, for crimson and silver were the Gonzaga colours, and the doublet was to be part of his court dress. Doublets and tunics of gold brocade edged with white appear in the fireplace fresco of the Camera Picta of the Castello of Mantua.

Mantegna returned to Padua at once. Correr's altarpiece was still not finished, and in response to a request from Gregorio, Lodovico wrote to Mantegna on 2 February granting him a further stay of two months but asking him at the same time to ensure the despatch of all his other business in Padua within that time and then come to Mantua without further delay. He enclosed this letter in one to Correr thanking him for having used every persuasion and encouragement to Mantegna to come and settle in Mantua. On 14 March, in a letter of much courtesy and graciousness, he consented to a further delay of eight or ten days beyond the two months already granted, this time at the urgent request of Jacopo Antonio Marcello, so that Mantegna might finish 'a certain small work . . . that formerly you began for him'. To Mantegna himself he wrote that he looked on Marcello as a brother, and desired Mantegna therefore to serve him as well as if he were already really and truly in Lodovico's service. After finishing Marcello's picture, however, he was to put all else aside, take on no more work, and come to Mantua. But on 4 May he was obliged to write again, telling Mantegna that by this time he ought to have done everything and as the chapel was now nearly completed, he, Lodovico, was eager for him to come to Mantua at once. This chapel was the new chapel of the Castello di San Giorgio, the great late fourteenth-century brick fortress which Lodovico had lately elected to make his residence in Mantua and whose decoration was one of his principal reasons for taking Mantegna into his service.

Mantegna, Lodovico added, was sure to be pleased with the chapel, for it had been built 'according to the fashion you gave' (*facta secondo il modo vostro*), and Lodovico did not want to finish it entirely 'except in the form and fashion you shall ordain'. Accordingly he was sending twenty ducats by the bearer and Mantegna was to hire a boat, load all his goods and family on to it and come away to Mantua.

Still Correr's altarpiece, it now transpired, was unfinished and on 29 June the ever-patient Lodovico wrote to Mantegna that he was pleased to hear it would be ready shortly. Correr, whom he calls Monsignor Protonotario, would prefer the picture to be taken straight to Verona: although Lodovico was sorry not to see it, he hoped in the future to see many other works from Mantegna's hand. He had obtained a promise from Correr that when Mantegna took the picture to Verona he was to spare a day to come over to Mantua and see and advise about the chapel before any further work was done.

Mantegna, so we learn from documents, brought the altarpiece to Verona at the end of July, stabling his horses in the monastery of San Zeno. He received payments of 25 ducats for it from 24 July 1459 to 24 January 1460; with an earnest of 15 ducats formerly paid to him in Padua these made up a total price of 40 ducats. From all the evidence we have it would seem that Mantegna did not finally remove to Mantua until shortly before 13 April 1460, the date from which he leased his house in Padua to his nephew-in-law.[42] We now know from a recently discovered document that he was certainly settled there by 21 June 1460, for a letter of Lodovico written on that day asks one of his servants to warn that scatterbrain Giovan Filippo da Correggio not to invite Mantegna and his wife out to his country villa to dine, as he was on bad terms with his villeins and Andrea's life might be at risk as well as his own.[43]

Among the reasons for this long delay were Mantegna's own hesitations as to whether he was well advised to listen to Lodovico's offer. Many years later he declared that there were those in Padua who had strongly dissuaded him from going to Mantua.[44] Reluctance to put himself entirely at the mercy of the vicissitudes of court favour as well as a natural wish to have a retreat if things turned out badly may explain why on 13 November 1458 he bought the sub-lease of a house in Padua in the quarter of Santa Lucia, on the corner of the ancient *androne* di Santa Lucia. He bought it from Niccolò Savonarola, acting as agent for his father Michele, who had been living since 1440 in Ferrara, as court physician to the Marchese. It was not the house in which Tommaso Mantegna had once lived, for in 1443 Savonarola declared that it was in a ruinous state and by 7 January 1452 Tommaso was living in the contrada di San Fermo.[45]

By the end of 1456 Tommaso had died, leaving Andrea as sole guardian of his daughter Caterina and of another daughter named Elisabetta, who is not mentioned again in the published documents. He had had the two girls by a wife named Vendramina (or of a family named Vendramin). His brother's inheritance involved Andrea in financial difficulties: it was in order to meet them that on 2 June 1457 a certain Domenico, known as Giudeo or the Jew, compelled him to pawn one of Nicolosia's rings.[46] Most pressing of all was the need to find a dowry for Caterina, who was now married to a certain Gianfrancesco, son of a Giuliano da Rimini who made his living by the hire of beds. The amount of the dowry, 500 *lire piccole* (about 83 gold ducats), Mantegna paid to Gianfrancesco the very next day.[47] If 200 of the *lire piccole* were due to Caterina from her father's estate as her mother's dowry, the other 300 were found by Mantegna from his own resources. On 11 March 1458 he was able to recover the pawned ring, having paid his debt to Domenico. When Mantegna finally removed to Mantua in 1460 it was to Gianfrancesco that he let his house in the contrada di Santa Lucia: the lease, as we now know from a recently discovered document, was to run for ten years from Easter, which fell that year on 13 April.[48] As a result Mantegna was to revisit Padua every ten years, in order to renew the lease and collect his rent, until he sold the house in 1492. One of Gianfrancesco's acknowledgements of liability for this rent, dated 15 June 1470, reveals that he had been successful in collecting some of the money owed by Squarcione to Mantegna.[49] Later, in 1472, about four years after Caterina's death, Mantegna was sued by her husband and by her son Giuliano for payment of her dowry, and for not having rendered accounts of his guardianship. Mantegna was obliged to resist their claims, which perhaps were only terminated on 23 May 1480 with a formal acknowledgement by Gianfrancesco that he had been paid the dowry.[50]

Another cause for Mantegna's hesitation over Ludovico's offer must have been that he had no lack of commissions in Padua, and from illustrious patrons. If his first order for a picture in 1447 had been from a master-baker, his next, for the Ovetari frescoes, had come from Paduan patricians. Now he was working for great nobles and ecclesiastics who were among the most prominent and influential figures in Padua, Venice and the Veneto. From this time onwards Mantegna's patrons were always to be personages of similar standing. No doubt it was his familiarity with men like Gregorio Correr and Jacopo Antonio Marcello that recommended him to the notice of Lodovico and fostered in Mantegna himself an inclination to a career in court service.

It was probably about this time that he was commissioned by Giacoma della Leonessa, widow of the famous *condottiere* Erasmo da Narni, better known as Gattamelata, to fresco a chamber in her palace with scenes from the life of her husband[51] and of her only son, Giannantonio, also a *condottiere*, who died in 1456. Mantegna was certainly well known to Giacoma, if not as a painter, then certainly as a near neighbour, for her palace was the Romanesque house now known as the Casa di Ezzelino, which abutted on to the contrada di Santa Lucia only a few yards away from the house Mantegna bought in 1458. In 1560 Scardeone singled out these frescoes for special mention, and their destruction by a fire in 1760 is a serious loss. Had they survived we should know how Mantegna responded to the challenge of decorating a state-chamber in the 1450s, several years before the Camera Picta in Mantua. We should also know something of his early style in secular *istorie*, and in *istorie* moreover where the clash of combatants may have been figured, perhaps making it necessary for Mantegna to adjust the statuesque dignity of his style to the representation of violent action. One of the frescoes seems to have been a Lamentation over the dead body of Giannantonio da Narni: only a fifteenth-century drawing by an unknown hand of mourners grieving around the naked corpse, placed on a table for laying out, survives to give some impression of its appearance (Plate 165). The theme of mourners lamenting around a corpse on a table, at any rate in a secular context, seems to be peculiar to the Veneto: certainly the only contemporary parallels occur in drawings by Jacopo Bellini.[52]

Giacoma's widowhood was devoted to the worthy commemoration of her husband and son, whose rapid rise from humble birth to military fame and high estate had ended bitterly and abruptly in Giannantonio's early death. Gattamelata had already been commemorated in Donatello's famous bronze equestrian statue. Had Mantegna not departed for Mantua, quite possibly Giacoma might have commissioned from him the altarpiece for the funerary chapel she founded in the Santo; instead it was painted, surely on his recommendation, by Jacopo, Gentile and Giovanni Bellini in 1460.[53] The epitaph on Giannantonio's tomb in this chapel was composed by the young humanist Galeotto Marzio da Narni (*c.*1428–*c.*1497), who was a fellow-townsman of Gattamelata and for this reason had been taken under the patronage of his family in Padua. Galeotto in turn was the intimate friend of the young Hungarian poet and humanist Janus Pannonius whose portrait Mantegna had included in the St Christopher frescoes. So intimate a friend indeed that during the first half of 1458, when Janus was preparing to leave Padua and return to Hungary, he commissioned a joint portrait showing 'Galeotto breathing in one picture with Janus', as Janus himself wrote in an enthusiastic panegyric of the painting. This portrait,[54] as a memorial of friendship, Janus took back with him to Hungary. All trace of it has long since been lost, and it now survives only in Janus's poetical eulogy, which lauds it for its truthfulness of proportion and lifelikeness of colour and celebrates Mantegna as the prime glory of the art of painting, one who is able to simulate all that nature produces, whether it be a foaming mouth or the Venus of Cos. Besides its interest as a record of a lost work, the poem testifies to a concord of aesthetic ideals between Mantegna and his humanist patrons.

As the widow of an old fellow-campaigner Giacoma della Leonessa was befriended by the Venetian nobleman Jacopo Antonio Marcello, who like Gattamelata had distinguished himself as a general during the long and hard-fought war between Venice and Filippo Maria Visconti, Duke of Milan. Marcello was also the friend and patron in Padua of Janus Pannonius, who celebrated his life and achievements in the war in a long *Panegyris*, written in elegant Latin hexameters. Pannonius also addressed a eulogy to Lodovico Gonzaga, the *Carmen ad Gonzagam*, and thus provides a further link between the circle of Marcello, which now included Mantegna, and Ludovico.[55]

The little work that Mantegna painted for Jacopo Antonio Marcello is often identified as the *St Sebastian* (Plate 43) now in Vienna.[56] If so, this little picture was evidently begun, then set aside, then completed fairly quickly. It is signed in Greek, which indicates a particular pride in the picture and in the reputation Mantegna had now made for himself, for in signing it as an ancient Greek master would have signed it, he was surely making a claim to be the modern Apelles. The promotion of a knowledge of Greek culture in Padua and Venice owed its first serious impulse to the Florentine Palla Strozzi. In spite of its close commercial and political ties with Byzantium, Venice for many years took little formal humanist interest in Greek, valuing it mainly as a practical accomplishment. Strozzi came to Padua in 1434 as an exile from Florence, long the principal centre of Greek studies in Italy. He was an avid student of Greek, taking Byzantine scholars into his own house as tutors. Although some Venetian noblemen and scholars had a private interest in Greek, Palla's son Nofri is known to have been a close friend of Mantegna, as well as of Marcello, and it is perhaps not fanciful to attribute the presence of this Greek inscription on Mantegna's painting to influences emanating from the Strozzi circle in Padua. Certainly no Greek inscriptions recur again in his art until the 1490s and then strangely enough they seem to be simulated rather than true Greek inscriptions.[57]

St Sebastian was universally venerated in the fifteenth century as a protector against the plague, and Mantegna's picture may have been painted for a studio or a state-chamber in a palace. The viewpoint is low, suggesting that it was intended to be seen more or less at eye-level. Once more the setting is contrived so as to include both antique ruins and romantic views of landscape. The foreground is a courtyard paved with a diaper of white stone and moss agate and bounded at the back by a low wall of masonry, now broken and fallen. From the floor of the courtyard rises a pier belonging to a great triumphal arch; its right side is only a little cracked and damaged; its spandrel, carved with the figure of a Victory poised in the air holding a trophy of a cuirass, is intact. The left side in contrast is shattered and decayed, its fragments littering the courtyard, its front pilaster broken away, its brick core revealed in the spandrel of the arch, where only the feet of another Victory remain to testify to the sculptured decoration that has fallen from it. This setting of a triumphal arch in an enclosed courtyard is so artificial and argues such persisting ignorance in Mantegna of the true function of an ancient triumphal arch that it is a strong argument for dating the picture in the 1450s, rather than in the 1460s or even the 1470s as some scholars have suggested. Leaning against the enclosure wall is a fragment of a Bacchic relief, with the head of a statue laid on top; in the foreground, mingled with the stones of the arch, are another head, a left foot wearing a Roman military sandal, and a torso. There may be some allusion to the fall of paganism and the victory of the Christian faith in these ruined monuments[58] but more probably Mantegna is imaging a monument of military triumph standing broken and neglected 'in the middle of the countryside', in other words the Campagna of Rome where legend places Sebastian's martyrdom.[59]

Mantegna makes no use of a painted architectural frame to enclose the composition. Its absence is significant, for in the *St Euphemia* and *St George*, also vertical pictures showing a single saint silhouetted full-length against a background, this device was a fundamental premise of the composition. Foreshortening is not obtruded, and there is no attempt to use emphatically projecting forms as a means of linking real and pictorial space. In place of these is a preoccupation with suggesting a lateral continuum of space. The pier is set to the right of the picture, as the four rows of diaper paving to the left and the single row to the right help to make plain, so that the arch entering on the right and the broken arch on the left imply a continuity of architecture to either side. The asymmetry thus created is corrected by the column of variegated brown marble to which the saint is bound 'like a mark', in the words of his

legend. Set against the pier, it stands out by reason of its colour, forming a strong central vertical axis. With naturalistic cunning, the feet of the saint are set on one of the blocks of broken masonry lying below the pier. The pose is subtly exaggerated from the usual graceful classical serpentine curve of a body at rest into a forced *contrapposto* of suffering. The upper part of the torso is thrust forwards, at an angle, with the right shoulder retracted; the head, with eyes devoutly upturned to heaven, bends to the left in a straining contrast.

The torso, with belly and stomach designed as conjoined U-shaped forms, a strongly pronounced rib-cage encircling the stomach, swelling thoracic muscles tipped by pronounced nipples, and at the neck V-shaped, is drawn according to a formula found also in the *Crucifixion* panel of the San Zeno altarpiece. Mantegna was to follow it unvaryingly in his representations of the male nude. The reason for its lasting authority over him was its derivation from the antique. It is taken from the torsos of the celebrated antique statues of the Dioscuri, on the Piazza del Quirinale in Rome. Drawings of these statues were already in circulation in North Italy. One now in the Ambrosiana, Milan, is a copy from one of the Dioscuri attributed to the workshop of Pisanello, and may date from Pisanello's sojourn in Rome in 1431–2.[60] It shows almost the same system of forms, except that the belly is not defined by an inverted U-form as in Mantegna. Since we have no early nudes by Mantegna we cannot say when he first saw pictures of the Dioscuri, but it seems likely that drawings of such very celebrated statues were already available to him in Squarcione's collection or at any rate in Padua or Venice.

The arrows pierce Sebastian's body at angles indicating that they have been shot by archers standing to the right and left. By this device, while the saint remains the fixed image required by piety, our imaginations are prompted to figure the scene of his martyrdom. It is found at least once earlier, though in a much more summary form, in the grisaille figure of St Sebastian painted as a simulated sculpture on one of the panels of Rogier van der Weyden's altarpiece of the Last Judgement at Beaune (c.1443–6). The light, falling from the left, leaves a cold and melancholy penumbra of shadow to the right, along the saint's body and on the pier. The streaks of crimson blood on the pale flesh colour add a further controlled suggestion of suffering. But neither the pathos of strained head and contorted pose, nor the sharp lines of the arrows, nor the creeping trickles of blood are allowed to suggest a violence of hurt or pain that distorts ideal beauty into agonized expressiveness.

Through the two uneven divisions of the background made by the pier there appears a characteristic landscape of a rising slope, with a sunken road winding up it under banks of rock. White hares play on the road and on the green slope to the left, perhaps to suggest the peace and innocence of the fields. Just as the contorted pose of Sebastian recalls the thieves of the San Zeno *Crucifixion*, so too the visual sleight by which Mantegna has diversified the usual even rise of his slopes recalls his use of a similar device in the setting of the same picture. Taking the eye up the road to where two of the archers stride towards its top, he then indicates that the road sinks down to the river beyond by showing only the upper half of the descending figure of a third archer. Across the level band of water, traversed by boats going to the further shore, rises a hill with lines of red buildings and towered fortifications to the right at its base and on the left ruined classical structures, including an aqueduct, one of the typical monuments of the Campagna.

In the top left corner of the sky, Mantegna has figured part of one of the cloud forms as a naked bearded horseman. It has been suggested by H. W. Janson that Mantegna is here illustrating the classical notion that Nature is herself on occasion an artist and likes to form images in her own works.[61] Revived by Alberti, this fancy long haunted the imaginations of Renaissance and Baroque scholars. Recognizable shapes also appear in clouds in much later paintings by Mantegna. In the *Triumphs of Caesar*, painted *c*.1485–92, a gigantic head is figured on Canvas III as forming the left edge of a cloud. In another great cloud, that which billows over the mountain in *Pallas expelling the Vices from the Garden of Virtue*, painted for the Studiolo of Isabella d'Este in 1502, two great profile male heads are figured. Other forms in clouds may also have appeared in paintings that are now lost, but their appearance in three pictures of different subjects, painted at three different dates for three different patrons, is a strong argument that they have no symbolic significance,

but are capricious ornaments that Mantegna thought appropriate to the nature of clouds.

Janson is surely correct in seeing them as figurations of the chance shapes that are formed by clouds. Such shapes attracted a certain amount of attention in antiquity: they are mentioned by Aristotle and Pliny, and are described by Lucretius in a passage of the *De Rerum Natura* (iv, 132 ff. 735 ff.) which may have influenced the literary-minded Mantegna in his later representations of cloud-borne heads:

> There are likenesses of things that are born spontaneously and come into existence in this lower heaven, that is called the air. So we behold at times clouds collect without difficulty on high and violate the serene aspect of the sky. As they are borne aloft formed in many fashions, sweeping through the air, often the faces of great giants are seen flying and spreading their shadow afar. At times great mountains and rocks torn from mountains are seen to go before and rise up to the sun: then a beast draws and leads forward other clouds: nor do they cease to melt and change their aspect and turn themselves into the outlines of forms of every kind.[62]

The forms in Mantegna's clouds are adumbrated, rather than sharply defined, no doubt because he shared Cicero's opinion of chance as an artist, that it may be able to create an accidental likeness 'but has never imitated the truth to perfection.'[63] Cloud-borne forms appear in no other Renaissance paintings, and in Mantegna's art they testify to a curious, day-dreaming aspect of his *fantasia*, ordinarily so concerned with a sculptural definiteness of form. This awareness of natural forms assuming transient shape as images of things is perhaps to be linked with that sense of nature as herself a rude architect which seems to be present from his earliest works. Art, to such a philosophy, becomes a perfecting of nature.

V

Mantegna and the Gonzaga

MANTEGNA'S earliest surviving portrait, small like all fifteenth-century portraits, is that of the Venetian Cardinal Lodovico Trevisan (Plate 46). The drawing for it was certainly made in Mantua, during the Council convoked there by Pope Pius II to unite Europe in a crusade against the Turks. The Cardinal entered Mantua on 27 May 1459 and left it on 8 February 1460, and Mantegna almost certainly drew his likeness in January, when he visited Mantua to make his formal entry into Lodovico's service.

The portrait itself he must have painted after his return to Padua. The drawing probably bore notations of dress and colour; notes of colour are found on Jan van Eyck's drawing, now in Dresden, for the portrait in Vienna usually identified as that of Cardinal Albergati. In 1451 Cardinal Trevisan had bought the palace of the Arena in Padua and after rebuilding it gave it in December 1462 to his nephew Francesco Trevisan, intending in this way to establish the lasting greatness in Padua of his family, of whose rise he himself had been the sole architect. Mantegna was almost certainly commissioned by Francesco to paint this portrait of his uncle, to whom he owed everything he had. Trevisan was a forceful prince of the Church of a type not uncommon in later medieval times: such men saw their particular vocation as the defence of the Church's temporalities both against the encroaching lay rulers of Christendom and against the advancing Turks. They did not shrink from leading armies in the field, and Trevisan had fought in the Papal service at the battle of Anghiari in 1440 and as general of the fleet sent by Calixtus III to Rhodes to fight the Turks after the fall of Constantinople. His tastes were those of a humanist collector: at Florence in the 1430s he had been a friend of the archetypal humanist collector Niccolò Niccoli; he received copies of ancient inscriptions from Ciriaco of Ancona, and he assembled a notable collection of antique medals and gems, as well as amassing plate, jewels, tapestries and a large fortune.[1] The contemporary Mantuan chronicler Andrea Schivenoglia describes him in 1459–60 as he must have appeared to Mantegna, 'a small, dark, old, hairy man, aged 60, very proud and grim', and says that he moved about with a great escort of splendidly mounted horsemen.[2]

Mantegna's portrait does full justice to the Cardinal's stern and resolute character. He is shown bust length in three-quarter profile, a pose first found in Flemish art in the portraits painted by Jan van Eyck in the 1430s. The three-quarter portrait had for Mantegna the sanction of antiquity, for Pliny records the Greek painter Cimon with approval as the inventor of 'oblique portraits'.[3] The ground is dark green, a ground colour which seems to have been Mantegna's preference in portraits of this kind during the 1450s and 1460s. Green was to remain a favourite background colour in Venetian portraits into the sixteenth century. A strong light falls from the left, leaving the right side of the face in shadow, but not modifying the ground. The Cardinal is shown wearing a white stole over a vermilion gown and a white shirt whose edges are just visible under the collar of the stole. The white is lightly painted, and there is a little pink in the centre and in the bottom of the folds to suggest the red beneath. Over this is a mantle of vermilion watered silk, whose pattern is executed in lines of red. The sumptuousness of this stuff, exceptional in fifteenth-century representations of a Cardinal's red robes, bears out Schivenoglia's account of the splendour of Trevisan's train of life. Watered silk appears here for the second time, so far as we know, in Mantegna's paintings. The young Jew repelled by the centurion in the fresco of *St James on the way to Execution* appears to be dressed in it, and evidently its richness appealed to Mantegna. In the later 1480s and 1490s he was to make much use of watered silk, more especially of blue watered silk, in costuming his figures.

The red-framed white of the bust throws up the Cardinal's head, with its strongly marked features, reminiscent of a Roman bust, its ironical compression of the mouth, its beetling black eyebrows, its short, wiry, grizzled locks of hair. The incisive drawing of the face is enhanced by the background, which here as in the *Presentation* is executed in slight relief in relation to the figure. Rather lower along the shoulders, this relieved edge of ground follows the outlines of the hair, except that the light strokes of the outermost hairs are painted over it, for greater verisimilitude. This is only one of the subtler observations of treatment in this remarkable portrait. The curls of the hair – each hair being executed with a fine, separate stroke – bend downwards on the left of the forehead: over its centre they curl up, down and sideways with an effect of bristling vigour, then on the shadowed right fall in smoother curls over rough-cut ends of hair. The upper hairs are white or grey lit with white; because the dark green of the ground absorbs the white, the hair is at once a lively frame for the head and a transition to the ground. This free naturalistic treatment of the hair has a parallel in one of the few surviving Paduan portraits of the mid-fifteenth century, a much damaged work thought to represent Francesco da Carrara the Elder.[4] The area below the nostrils and on the chin is modelled in thin strokes of white over flesh-colour, as is the middle of the forehead: this throws up the pale pink of the temples, the stronger reddish-pink of the cheeks and the light carmine of the lips. The bushy eyebrows cast a shadow over the eyelids and upper eye that makes the brown eyes stand out with great power, a white highlight to the left of the pupil and a sharp stroke of brilliant white along the left edge enhancing their forcefulness of impact. With a realism of Flemish inspiration the eyelids are touched with a strong pink that is in contrast with the carnations of lips and cheeks. In accordance with fifteenth-century convention, the portrait is objective, in that there is no attempt to render mood or expression, yet Mantegna's image does more than record the Cardinal's features, for it suggests the strength of will, the severe habit of command, the disillusioned experience of affairs that had stamped the countenance of this exceptional sitter.

Cardinal Trevisan was either a crony or *compatre* (co-godfather) of Lodovico Gonzaga, this last being a very close tie in the quattrocento, and no doubt the Marchese gladly gave Mantegna leave to paint his portrait.[5] For now that Mantegna was in Lodovico's service, he was no longer free to accept commissions from any patron he chose, and all who wanted a picture from his hand had first to solicit the Marchese's licence. This was the counterweight to his greatly privileged position as court artist. As in so many of the smaller princely states of Italy, the Gonzaga court was the centre of all magnificence and animation in Mantua.[6] Without its lords the city might well have fallen a prey to the Visconti of Milan or to Venice, the two large and predatory neighbouring powers whom the Gonzaga became adept at exploiting and playing off against each other. Alternatively the Mantuans might have wasted their energies in the factions and struggles for lordship among rival families that were endemic in Italian city life.

The Gonzaga themselves had first seized power in just such a struggle with the Bonacolsi in 1328.[7] To legitimize their rule they anxiously sought for Imperial confirmation of their lordship, for Mantua, like the rest of Lombardy, was legally an Imperial fief, and its proximity to the Imperial lands north of the Alps made the Emperor and his suzerainty something more than a mere fiction. At first they received it as Imperial Vicars, a title they carefully buttressed with the office of Capitano of Mantua, to which each Gonzaga was duly elected on succession by the Comune. The consecration of their power came in September 1432, when the Emperor Sigismund in person, in return for a donation of 12,000 florins, made Mantua and its territory a marquisate and bestowed it upon Gianfrancesco Gonzaga, Lodovico's father, and his descendants. To this Imperial legitimization of their rule the Gonzaga always attached the highest importance, as also to the title of marquis, the second highest in the hierarchy of Imperial titles. However, it was for reasons of social prestige as well as to establish a right to Imperial favour that they concealed their upstart origins by claiming a Germanic origin for their family.

The Gonzaga reinforced their pretensions to belong to the original Teutonic aristocracy of the Empire by marrying for preference German princesses, a policy also followed by the Visconti of Milan. They had already connected themselves with the Hapsburgs in the fourteenth century, and so anxious was Lodovico's father Gianfrancesco to ally the Gonzaga with the house of Brandenburg that in 1433 he waived in her marriage-contract all claims to a dowry with the hand of Barbara of Brandenburg (b. 30 September 1422–d. 7 November 1481), daughter of the Markgraf Johann. Instead the Gonzaga themselves gave her a dowry of 25,000 florins, guaranteed from the revenues of the two *castelli* of Peschiera and Ostiglia, and in addition made a donation of 25,000 florins to the Markgraf Friedrich when he brought the child Barbara to Mantua in 1432. Lodovico continued this tradition. In 1463 he married his eldest son and heir Federico to Margaret, daughter of Albert, Duke of Bavaria, while of his daughters Barberina was married to Eberhard, Count of Wurtemburg, in 1474 and Paola to Count Leonhard of Görz in 1476.[8] Even in the seventeenth century two Eleonora Gonzagas were to marry two Hapsburg emperors.

Although Imperial authority was light, its prestige in the eyes of the Gonzaga ought never to be discounted. Their allegiance to the Emperor as their suzerain is figured in the Camera Picta or statechamber of the Castello di San Giorgio. On its ceiling Mantegna painted for Lodovico Gonzaga the first eight Caesars, the founders of the Empire, and one of the scenes on its walls includes a portrait of the Emperor Frederick III (reigned 1440–93).

The territories of Mantua were not large enough to support the Gonzaga and their court in the state their rank demanded, especially as the family was prolific and followed the feudal custom of forming appanages for younger sons from the family lands, so surrounding Mantua with a ring of small, secondary courts. They added to their income by the noble profession of war, hiring out their services as *condottieri*. Lodovico was a typical fifteenth-century Italian prince in his shrewd pursuit of profit from war and this in spite of his physical disabilities, for he was small and hunchbacked as a result of the hereditary family complaint of rickets.[9] Because of his position between Milan and Venice he was obliged to offer his services as *condottiere* to both, and he is found alternating between one and the other, sometimes in the same war. But any change of side he made was honourable by the notions of the age, and unlike other *condottieri* Lodovico was never reproached with shifting loyalties and bought treachery. Indeed he set great store by his knightly word and maintenance of knightly faith.

Lodovico's amusements were those of a great nobleman: he had a passion for hunting and falconry, for horses and dogs.[10] But he had also received one of the best humanist educations of the day from his tutor, the famous Vittorino da Feltre, who saw with equal care to his physical and intellectual development. Under Vittorino he studied first Virgil, Homer, Cicero and Demosthenes, learning the rules of Latin and Greek grammar from these authors, and then went on to the study of dialectic and rhetoric. Afterwards came mathematics, arithmetic, geometry, astrology and music. For music Vittorino had a special enthusiasm, and Lodovico's lasting taste for it is reflected in the Camera Picta. The course was crowned with the philosophy of Plato and Aristotle. The imprint of this humanist education appears in the care which Lodovico took to build up the family library he had inherited, adding principally texts of the classics, but also works of natural science, and poems and romances in Italian and French.

Among the few documents to survive that throw some light on the interest taken by Lodovico and his circle of artists in classical antiquities is a letter of 24 October 1476 to Lodovico Gonzaga from Angelo Del Tovaglia, a member of a Florentine merchant family closely linked with the Medici. Angelo's reason for writing to Lodovico was to ask him to find a book of drawings 'of certain antique sculptures, which for the most part are battles of centaurs, of fauns and of satyrs, and also of men and women on horseback and on foot and other similar things. And especially I should like to have those of the centaurs, for of the others there is some knowledge here.' On searching for the book in Florence he learnt that it was now in the hands of Lodovico and 'his servants': accordingly, 'because I know these things are prized and the originals are not sent about', he asks if copies could be made for him at his expense. A month later, on 22 November 1476, Lodovico replied saying that he had asked Luca Fancelli for the book, and that Luca said he had given it to Mantegna some time ago. Mantegna had forgotten what had happened to it, and thought it had passed on from him into the hands of an unnamed painter of Mantua. Lodovico was continuing the search.[11]

Lodovico extended the usual princely patronage to humanists, receiving in return the customary tributes of an epic poem and a history, both celebrating his family. The epic poem was the *Gonzagidos* of Giovanni Pietro Arrivabene (*c*.1460–70), while the history was Bartolommeo Platina's *Historia inclyte urbis Mantuae et serenissimae familiae Gonzagae* (*c*.1460–4), of dubious value as a chronicle, even in Lodovico's eyes, but nevertheless a solemn glorification in stately Latin of Mantua and its Gonzaga lords. After narrating the history of the wars between Filippo Maria Visconti and Venice in which Lodovico had served both sides as a general, Platina describes how he 'turned to the works of peace, and set about adorning the city with buildings public and private and the countryside with agriculture for both pleasantness and delight.'[12]

This was not merely the rhetoric of humanist eulogy, for Lodovico devoted himself in reality to the adornment and improvement of Mantua and its territory. His policies, for all their benevolence, were centralizing and despotic: under him all the life of the *stato*, always concentrated on the city, became concentrated on the *corte*. He was fortunate in being able to unite the appanages of his brothers Carlo (d.1456), Gianlucido (d.1448) and Alessandro (d.1466) with his own and he determinedly obtained for members of his family all the important ecclesiastical preferments and wealthy abbeys within the confines of his territory. He strengthened the city's fortifications and embanked the Mincio to prevent it from flooding; he paved many of the streets and piazzas, began in 1450 the great new hospital of San Leonardo, erected in 1470–3 a clock-tower with an ingenious mechanical clock by Bartolommeo Manfredi, and between 1462 and his death nearly completed a new market-house. The poor were helped by the foundation in 1462 of the Camera dei Pegni, a public pawnshop, and for a time usury was officially forbidden. In the territory around Mantua he drained marshes, dug irrigation canals and built aqueducts. Under his rule, in spite of the almost annual ravages of the plague, the city's population increased from about 26,000 in 1463 to about 40,000 in 1478, the year of his death.[13]

Lodovico also began that ambitious programme of building churches, palaces and castles in Mantua and its territory which was continued by his descendants and which was to stamp the impress of the princely grandeur of the Gonzaga on the city and its surroundings. Outside Mantua he built partly to fortify his state, partly for pleasure and utility. Like all medieval and Renaissance princes he liked a change of residence from town to country and accordingly surrounded Mantua with summer palaces, a tradition in which he was followed by his successors. But because the borders of his territories were exposed to incursions from bandits and soldiers, these country residences were part villa, part castle in their nature.

Lodovico was not a passive patron, content to take advice from his architects about the design of his churches and palaces, but a conscious partisan of the new 'antique' manner, which we know as the Renaissance style, in opposition to the 'modern' manner, or Gothic style. In his *Trattato di Architettura*, whose composition seems to date from *c.*1460 to late 1464, the Florentine architect Filarete champions the antique manner, praising Brunelleschi as the man who had first revived it in Florence, where today 'no other manner is used both in churches and private buildings . . . and it would not be used there were it not handsomer and more useful.' As a persuasive example in North Italy, where Filarete was living at the court of Milan, he cites 'the Lord of Mantua, who has a most excellent understanding of the art, and would not use the antique manner, if it were not what I say. And that I say truth, is witnessed by a house he has had built in one of his castles on the Po.' Filarete is also a witness to Mantegna's reputation in Lombardy, for to decorate a loggia in his own imaginary ideal palace Filarete declared he would call among other 'suf-

ficient' masters of painting 'an Andrea da Padova called Squarcione'.[14] In the choice of architects, engineers and artists to carry out the schemes he meditated 'for our honour and the honour of the city', Lodovico showed a laudable resolve to call into his service the best and most modern masters that he could procure. We have already seen the patience with which he wooed Mantegna, and it was not from any failure in persistence that he was unable after eight years' endeavour to obtain from Donatello more than a few carvings and models, including one for a shrine to contain the relics of St Anselm of Lucca, the patron saint of Mantua, which had been translated in 1392 to the right of the high altar of the cathedral.[15]

The church of San Sebastiano, begun in 1460, and that of Sant'Andrea, begun in 1472, were built to designs by Leon Battista Alberti. The church of Sant' Andrea was the most important in Mantua because it housed the city's most wondrous relics, those of the Precious Blood of Christ. According to tradition, these had been brought to Mantua and concealed there by Longinus, the Roman centurion who had pierced Christ's side with his lance. Twice had their place of concealment been disclosed by St Andrew, appearing in a vision. The importance of Sant'Andrea as a shrine dates from 1401, when Francesco Gonzaga ordered the relics to be exhibited every year on Ascension Day.[16] This annual festival attracted vast numbers of pilgrims to the church, and the sanctity of the relics was confirmed in 1459 by a learned debate concerning their authenticity and by a miraculous cure from gout experienced by Pope Pius II after praying before them.[17]

San Sebastiano and Sant'Andrea were erected under the supervision of Lodovico's court architect-engineer, the Florentine Luca Fancelli (*c.*1430–after 1494), who figured as an emissary in the negotiations between Mantegna and Lodovico.[18] For Lodovico Fancelli built the country palace of Revere (1451–8), the fortified castle-palace of Cavriana, constructed at intervals from 1458 to 1478, and a new palace in the *rocca* of Gonzaga, the original seat of the family, which was begun in August 1458, almost completed in 1462, and extended from 1467 to 1472. He also completed from 1470 to 1477 a palace at Saviola, on the Po.[19]

Mantegna was to be closely involved with Fancelli in the decoration of the palace at Gonzaga, and was concerned through a subordinate master, Samuele da Tradate, with that of Cavriana. The typical plan of these palaces, all except Revere now ruined or destroyed, was a square of four wings around an internal courtyard with towers at the corners. All contained an apartment for the Marchese: that at Gonzaga, which was probably typical, is known to have comprised a single *sala* or great room for receptions and festivals, a large *camera* or privy chamber, with an *anticamera* (antechamber), a chapel adjoining the *camera*, and other *camere* named from their particular decorations. It was with the painting and adornment of these state rooms that Mantegna was usually concerned; in 1464, for example, he was busy at Goito as well as at Cavriana.

Fancelli also supervised the alterations to the Castello di San Giorgio, which the Marchese elected to make his principal residence in Mantua some two or three years before 1459. The Castello had been built *c*.1390–1406 to defend the approach to the Gonzaga Corte and to the centre of the city across the Ponte di San Giorgio. Lodovico's decision to move into this strong brick fortress led to drastic alterations of its interior: on 6 September 1459 he writes to a country *vicario* whose pretensions to astrology were heartily despised by his lord: 'We have no need of astrologers at the moment, and if you are the man who predicted to our late illustrious father that the Castello of Mantua would fall down, you have not been able to divine that we would have it half pulled down, as we have done.'[20] Among his changes was the construction of a chapel which from the first he intended to have decorated by Mantegna, who accordingly was consulted about its design.

The work of alteration was carried out over many years and the state-chamber was not ready for decoration by Mantegna until 1465. In 1472 Luca Fancelli was deep in discussion with the Marchese about the exact form that certain features of the courtyard were to assume. Lodovico took a close and active part in all the work, at times designing himself, as in the case of a chapel intended for Gonzaga, or else dictating to his architect, as occurred in 1472, when he told Fancelli not only what to do, but sent him 'a drawing done by the hand of Andrea Mantegna which we believe will give occasion for the master to understand the pupil.'[21] The allusion here is to Lodovico's own knowledge of architecture, which he is known to have acquired under Fancelli's tuition, not to Mantegna's.

Much has been made of this letter as proving that Mantegna had a hand in many buildings in quattrocento Mantua, but it shows only that he had a sound enough knowledge of architecture to embody Lodovico's instructions in a drawing. Indeed this ought to have been plain from the designs he is known to have given for the Gonzaga chapel and from the house he later built for himself in Mantua. Other architects such as Luciano Laurana also worked for Lodovico,[22] sometimes essentially as supervisors of buildings designed by others and as what we should now call engineers. Giovanni da Padua, a fellow townsman of Andrea, who also took part in Lodovico's negotiations with him, had a great reputation as a military architect and engineer but

also built civil buildings. He will appear again as a crony of Mantegna. Lodovico, though patient when necessary, was well able to drive work forward if he so willed, and there is no doubt that he kept Mantegna, like everyone else in his service, fully occupied. Andrea Schivenoglia records of the work begun at Gonzaga in 1468: 'Now I will say nothing of the troubles it brought on the men of the place and how hard they had to work, for the Duke of Milan wanted to come and see it and take his pleasure in that place: all the masons, carpenters and painters of Mantua had to go out and work at Gonzaga.'[23] Men can be seen toiling on palaces and castles in the background to the open-air scene in Mantegna's Camera Picta.

Possibly the earliest painting Mantegna executed for Lodovico is the little panel portrait (*tavoletta*) of his second son Francesco Gonzaga[24] (1444–83) wearing the curial dress of a Protonotary Apostolic (Plate 47). This rank and honorary office in the Papal Curia had been conferred on him in 1459, while still a boy, as an earnest of greater honours to come. The portrait was painted in 1460. It established a first link between Mantegna and Franceso, who shortly afterwards was to be made a Cardinal and to leave Mantua for a career in the Roman Curia. Francesco, whom Schivenoglia described early in 1462 as 'handsome and courteous',[25] had a community of interests with Mantegna: like a number of other Cardinals of the 1450s and 1460s he was a collector of antique medals, gems, bronzes and sculptures. With Mantegna he formed a steady friendship. Already on 26 April 1464 Mantegna 'for the love I bear to my Reverend Monsignor' was soliciting Lodovico for a donation of three ducats in order to respond worthily to an invitation from the Cardinal to figure in his suite during the celebration of a *trigesima*.[26]

In the portrait Francesco is represented in all the serious innocence of boyhood. He is shown in pure profile to the left, not in three-quarter profile, like Trevisan and like Carlo de' Medici, the sitters in Mantegna's other surviving early portraits. In using pure profile Mantegna was following earlier precedent rather than more recent Flemish example, for the first painted portraits known to us are all in pure profile. Profile portraits were popular throughout most of the quattrocento, and Mantegna was to continue to paint them, certainly into the 1480s. Francesco is shown bust-length on the same dark green ground that Mantegna uses in the Trevisan and Medici portraits, above a narrow ledge of white, in a slightly angled pose that animates the figure with a suggestion of freedom in space. His face is delicately painted, with only light shadows, and with a flush of pink in the carnations of the brown flesh. He wears the *berretta* of a curial prelate, dimpled in the centre top and pink in colour, a pink *mantello* edged with white fur, a pink *cappuccio* which hangs down to the right of his chest, and a white stole over a pink gown and white shirt. In fact the whole costume is a study in pink, relieved by whites. By a skilful invention the swing of the *mantello* covers the left arm, concealing what would otherwise be an awkward projection beneath a single unitary form.

One of a court painter's ordinary duties was the painting of portraits, portraits of his lord and lady for other princes, for relations, friends and courtiers, portraits of their children, for use in the marriage negotiations of daughters or as remembrances after daughters were married and sons had left home. The Gonzaga, from Lodovico to Isabella d'Este, seem to have found Mantegna not so successful in portraiture as in other forms of his art, perhaps because of the very strength and sternness which make his portraits so triumphant to modern taste. Nevertheless, they constantly employed him to produce portraits, no doubt from motives of economy. In 1466 when negotiations were once more on foot to marry the sickly Dorotea Gonzaga (b. 7 December 1449–d.1467) to the youthful Galeazzo Maria Sforza,[27] the Mantuan envoy in Milan sent the portrait of a rival candidate for Galeazzo's hand to Lodovico, who hurriedly advised his wife Barbara on 1 March to have a copy made of it at once: 'You may give this charge to Andrea Mantegna ... Our Dorotea seems no less handsome than this girl.' Again in August 1471 we hear that Mantegna was anxious to bring out to Gonzaga two portraits he had just finished in order to show them to the Marchese. A letter he wrote on 6 July 1477 to Lodovico illuminates some of the difficulties encountered by painters in meeting demands for portraits that were often sudden and pressing: 'I advise your Excellency that if you wish to have those portraits, since Your Lordship wants them so quickly, I do not understand how I am to make them, whether just as drawings or else coloured on panel or on canvas and of what size. If Your Lordship desires to send them a long distance they can be done on thin canvas so as to allow them to be wrapped round a thin stick.' And he adds a complaint which painters and sculptors often found themselves making to princely patrons: 'Moreover as Your Excellency knows, nothing can be well done from life if there is no opportunity of seeing it.' Evidently he was being expected to produce lifelike portraits without sittings, in this instance, it would seem, of Lodovico and Barbara, for he adds: 'Your Excellencies are out of Mantua, I will guide myself according to what you approve, I will wait to hear and to receive either small panels (*tavolete*) or small canvases (*telereti*), so that I may make a beginning on the said portraits.'[28] There do exist two small portraits[29] of Lodovico and Barbara which may be copies after originals by Mantegna, executed in

obedience to this commission. One reproduces Barbara as she was represented in the Camera Picta *c.*1469–70, the other is a portrait of Lodovico as a general. The letter also tells us that Mantegna was evidently well accustomed to making portrait drawings as well as painted portraits.

During much of the 1460s Mantegna's principal single task, often enough interrupted by other tasks, was to paint a cycle of pictures for the new chapel of the Castello. The cycle was long proudly exhibited to visitors[30] and in the honorific diploma by which the Marchese Francesco Gonzaga, Lodovico's grandson, conferred on Mantegna in February 1492 a grant of land it was singled out as one of three works by which he had deserved especial favour of the Gonzaga. During a remodelling of the Castello in the 1560s and 1570s, however, its paintings were dismantled and the chapel itself was destroyed. Nothing is known of its situation except that it was close enough to the Camera Picta for Lodovico, when ill in that chamber, to hear mass through the doorway. Of its appearance we know only that it was small, as might be expected of a chapel that was really only a large-scale oratory, and that it had a dome resting on four arches, two of which were engaged in the walls to either side. Most probably, as Paccagnini suggests, it resembled the more or less contemporary Cappella del Perdono in the ducal palace of Urbino, with a curved niche rising above the altar.

The usual assumption is that Mantegna ended his work on the chapel in 1464. This is because of a letter to Lodovico on 26 April of that year in which he says of some paintings that 'these are the last according to me that should be put up in the little chapel.' But this letter was written from the Marchese's new palace at Goito, where Mantegna had already been working at least as early as the previous October, and from the context it is plain that the 'little chapel' was that of Goito. Thus Mantegna complains that the frames of the paintings are not yet gilt, and says that he does not think it proper to add varnish and anyway does not have the necessary materials to hand.

Nothing is known from documents or descriptions of the subjects that Lodovico chose to have represented in the chapel of the Castello. But certain surviving paintings and copies of paintings and certain engravings by Mantegna or after him have been associated with the decorations executed for it. These suggest that Mantegna executed one, if not two cycles of religious paintings that were clearly much admired in North Italy. The paintings usually associated with the chapel are *The Adoration of the Magi, The Circumcision* and *The Ascension*, all three in Florence, and *The Death of the Virgin* in Madrid. The engravings are *The Flagellation, The Deposition from the Cross, The Entombment* and *The Descent into Limbo*. Not only is the style seen in these engravings that of the paintings, but resemblances such as that between the Virgin of the *Circumcision* and the Virgin of the *Deposition* seem to indicate that the original of the *Deposition* formed part of the same cycle as the *Circumcision*. In addition, two miniatures painted in 1492 by Michele da Genova in an antiphonary belonging to San Giovanni Evangelista of Parma copy the *Adoration* and the *Circumcision*, thus making it virtually certain that his miniature of the *Resurrection* in a second antiphonary of the same date, which is clearly after Mantegna, records yet another picture from the same ensemble.[31] If the cycle included an *Entombment*, then Mantegna's original composition is probably most faithfully reflected in two miniatures, one in the Seilern collection attributed to Butinone (Plate 254), and one in the British Museum in grisaille. These are so close that they must copy, with small variants, a painting by Mantegna of this subject which was plainly related in style to the Florence panels and at the same time cannot be much later than the San Zeno predella panel of the *Resurrection*. Finally, an inventory taken in 1665 on the death of Duke Carlo II of Mantua lists as an 'original of Andrea Mantegna' a small painting of *The Flight into Egypt* on panel, now lost, which may well have originated from the chapel.[32]

However, the problem of the paintings that were executed for the chapel is singularly complicated by the fact that in April 1464 Mantegna had also completed, in his own eyes at any rate, his cycle of paintings for the *cappelletta* at Goito. Any panels he executed for this second chapel must have been very like in style to those he painted for the chapel of the Castello. The difficulty is compounded by the existence of three vertical oblong panels, now in the National Gallery, London, representing *The Resurrection, The Maries at the Sepulchre* and *Noli me tangere* (Plates 179–181).[33] The status of these has fluctuated. Their old attribution to Mantegna's hand is untenable but a recent technical examination has shown that they must have been painted at some date between the late fifteenth and mid-sixteenth centuries. They are in fact flat but faithful later copies of originals by Mantegna which were plainly of very great beauty. The style reflected in all three is close to that of the predella panels of the San Zeno altarpiece and of the London *Agony in the Garden*, which they recall in the structure of their rocky settings, in their use of violent contrasts of light and shadow on opposing surfaces of rock, in their atmospheric light and in certain motifs – the depiction of birds and animals for picturesque effect, the types and poses of the sleeping soldiers in the *Resurrection*, and the beehive of the *Noli me tangere*, introduced as in the San Zeno *Agony* to indicate that the scene

is a garden. The figures too have the characteristic elongation of other works of this period, while the fence that divides the spectator from the *Noli me tangere* recalls the fence used even more dramatically in the Ovetari *Execution of St James*.

This adaptation of motifs from slightly earlier works suggests an artist working under pressure from a patron anxious to have several commissions completed more or less at once. And the delicate use of gold to edge or light foliage and other motifs in all three pictures points to a patron of rank and opulence. These are features that would certainly suit Lodovico Gonzaga in the early 1460s. The format of the panels suggests that their originals were set into a framework on a wall, and together they represent a cycle of the Resurrection of Christ that was perhaps complemented by a Crucifixion, perhaps too by other subjects, for example an Ascension. It must be a moot point whether the original paintings adorned the walls of the chapel of one of Lodovico's country palaces such as Goito or that of the Castello itself. The repetition of earlier motifs, and the invention and style, which are less refined than those of the Florence and Madrid pictures, seem on the whole to favour the surmise that the originals were painted for a country palace.

Accepting then, but only as a hypothesis, that the paintings usually associated with the chapel of the Castello were in fact executed for it, its decoration would seem to have followed a simple programme of the principal events in the life of Christ and the Virgin, beginning with the Nativity and ending with the Death of the Virgin, with the Adoration of the Magi as the main subject because the chapel was that of a prince. In this way the principal feasts of the liturgical year, including the mysteries of Christ's Birth, Passion and Glorification, were represented in a chapel where the Marchese and his family daily heard mass. There is reason then to associate with these paintings that 'history of Limbo', in other words, of Christ's descent into hell, which in a letter of 28 June 1468 Mantegna tells Lodovico he has just begun in obedience to his commands.[34] If the *Death of the Virgin* closed the cycle, this 'Descent' would have been the last picture but two of the series, assuming, as seems logical, that it was followed by an Ascension, which would have completed the cycle of the Resurrection. In favour of this reconstruction is an iconographical argument: it seems that at this date the Descent into Hell almost always formed part of a larger scheme. Indeed Mantegna's lost painting and the engraving after it were the inspiration of the only other known Italian fifteenth-century paintings of the subject, one by Mantegna himself, dating from the 1490s, one a copy of a lost work, and one attributed to Giovanni Bellini, which is in fact a miniature on vellum after the

engraving. However, it must be said that Jacopo Bellini's drawings include two for this subject.[35] In support of a date later than 1464 for the completion of
the chapel is Platina's gift to Lodovico in 1466 of
a marble basin for holy water, indicating that the
chapel was not completely ready and furnished by
that date. We cannot entirely exclude then that
Mantegna's work on the chapel may have continued
well after 1464, with true quattrocento desultoriness.

If the chapel resembled the Urbino Cappella del
Perdono, this would explain why the largest picture
which appears to originate from it, *The Adoration
of the Magi* (Plate 50), has a concave surface. It was
this highly original feature, without a known parallel in quattrocento art, which inspired Paccagnini to
suggest that originally the *Adoration* was the
altarpiece of the chapel and was shaped to fit a curved
niche above the altar. Kristeller pointed out long ago
that the light in the *Adoration* comes from the front
and diffuses itself to right and left, implying that it
was set in a small space facing a window. On this
hypothesis, it would appear that Mantegna
deliberately created for himself the difficulty of the
niche above the altar in order to resolve it by a triumphant optical *tour de force*, calculated to impress his
new patron during his early days of service. The
curved surface of the painting, for all it displays his
ingenuity and science, has not been to its advantage,
as a large cigar-shaped area has flaked from its upper
centre left. His theme also imposed a careful regard
to the source of light, in order that the composition
should be entirely legible in its original setting. Pictorial tradition dictated that in depicting this favourite subject painters should exert themselves to array
a bright pageant of richly costumed figures, pressing
forward as a motley throng. Accordingly the *Adoration* is the most crowded and variously picturesque
of Mantegna's smaller paintings.

It is also the last of his autograph works in which
the influence of Jacopo Bellini is prominent. Among
Bellini's drawings are three that are varyingly similar
to Mantegna's picture.[36] In all the scene is set at the
bottom of a valley, beneath high mountains, and a
train of laden horses or camels descends a steep and
narrow road down the mountainside, exactly as in
Mantegna's *Adoration*. But once more Mantegna has
condensed Bellini's loose compositions and articulated them with a far finer sense of balance
between setting and figures. Even in the closest of
the three drawings, one which seems almost a sketch
in reverse for Mantegna's picture, with the road and
its procession leading the eye across the scene to the
principal group, the figures are dwarfed by great
rocks and by the huge wooden framework of a stable
carefully drawn in perspective. Mantegna has also
dispensed with the deep foreground of the other two
compositions, curving the processional descent of

the Magi into his own foreground so that their
arrival before the grotto of the Nativity on the right
is the action most immediately before the eye. And
if he has not decorated the front of his scene with
the scattered picturesque and exotic motifs which
amuse the beholder in one of the Bellini drawings
– a grazing horse, a leaping dog, a dwarf holding
a falcon, two chained leopards – he has studied to
give the Magi and their train a true verisimilitude
of picturesqueness. For the same reasons of local and
historical exactitude, he has replaced the lofty stables
of Bellini, with their dizzying lines of timber
rendered in perspective, by a cave.

Mantegna has set his scene in a dawn light, with
the sun rising in yellow behind the hills and a light
blue sky darkening towards the top. The very high
horizon allows the Magi to be shown descending a
road of natural rock, painted light green and grey,
which winds steeply downwards in perspective
through a cleft of rocks on the upper left and bends
through the middle ground, past the grotto of the
Nativity on the lower right. On the lower left the
road is sharply raised above ground level, so
emphasizing its function as the ever-widening
serpentine way on which the procession traverses the
picture. At bottom right it is abruptly cut off, so as
to suggest to the eye that it continues onwards; providing yet another illustration of Mantegna's conception of a picture as a field of vision plausibly
isolated from a larger reality, rather than as a field
of vision wholly enclosed within a frame.

The bright colours of the costumes and the gold
profusely scattered on the principal figures stand out
against the shadowed background, still darkened by
the gloom of night, with sharper splendour. The
grotto is set at an angle to the picture plane, fronting
the road and the adoring Magi rather than the spectator, and so bringing the Virgin and Child and the
three Magi into an intimately dramatic relation. The
rock into which it is cut fills the right half of the
picture, forming with the rocks on the upper left
a natural frame for the principal action. The grotto
itself is represented as a great black cavern, to accord
with what the age knew of the realities of the
Nativity. In ancient Palestine natural or artificial
caverns were often used as stables, with a manger
cut out of the living rock. In the fifteenth century
pilgrims to the church at Bethlehem were shown,
to the right of the altar in the crypt, which had a
golden star against the arch above it, 'an altar below
a hewn-out rock. Here the Three Holy Kings offered
to the new-born Child, and in front of this same altar
the rock is also hewn out . . . This was the manger
of the asses and oxen, in which Christ was laid wrapped in swaddling clothes.'[37]

The blackness of the cavern throws up the figure
of the Virgin by a device already present in Byzan-

tine and trecento art. As imagined by Mantegna she was sitting sideways to the road on a seat of rock, holding the Child and conversing with St Joseph, but has now turned her body forwards to greet the Magi and proffer the Child for their adoration. The naturalness of the motif and its transmutation into a statuesque pose of serene dignity are quintessentially Mantegnesque. She is clothed in sober colours that contrast with the great mandorla of adoring cherubs, of fiery red lit with gold on the left, of flesh-colour lit with gold on the right, who float behind her on light blue clouds. Her own halo is the conventional circle of gold, but from the Child emanates only a mystical radiance like that of the Holy Women in the San Zeno altarpiece. On the left the Virgin's dark blue cloak is heightened by a close network of finely hatched gilding, figuring the golden light that falls from the star, which has halted just over the rock and sends down a long ray of gold to point out the Virgin and Child. The same light simultaneously diffuses itself over Melchior, the eldest of the Magi, the mandorla of cherubs, and St Joseph, whose red robe is subdued by the thick hatching of gold on his yellow cloak. Around the star float four adoring seraphim, habited in red and olive-green, also hatched with gold, their bright colours echoing those of the figures below and illuminating what would otherwise be the too sombre upper half of the picture.

All this gold is not real gold, but a pigment that simulates its effect. Vasari claims that it was Domenico Ghirlandaio in Florence who at some date during the second half of the fifteenth century 'became the first to counterfeit certain trimmings and ornaments of gold with colours . . . and largely did away with those borders that were made of gold with mordant or with bolus.'[38] This cannot be correct, for in his *Della pittura* (1435–6) Alberti had already condemned the profuse employment of gold in pictures, recommending instead the use of colours simulating gold. 'I would have no use of gold at all, forasmuch as in colours imitating the radiance of gold there stands more room for admiration and praise of the artist.'[39] The tendency to treat gold so as to blend it with the other colours of a painting rather than make it stand out against them with an emphasis of costly splendour was already present in Mantegna's art during the 1450s. By using simulated gold in the *Adoration* and its companion pictures Mantegna is able to obtain delicate effects of highlighting and glow that are in perfect modulation with the other colours, yet provide a mystical richness of heightening. In this way gold illuminates with points and passages of climax, while fusing naturalistically with the rest of the picture.

The difference between this expressive emphasis and the more formal and decorative treatment of gold customary in Gothic art appears when Mantegna's *Adoration* is compared with Antonio Vivarini's *Adoration* in Berlin, in which gold laid on raised mandorlas breaks the unity of the picture. No theoretical arguments by critics like Alberti could dislodge gold from the high estimation in which it was held by patrons for its conspicuous magnificence. It was still to play an important part in Mantegna's decoration of the Camera Picta at Mantua and of the now destroyed chapel of Pope Innocent VIII in Rome. But so far as our evidence allows us to tell, after the early St Luke altarpiece Mantegna always employed it in just such skilfully integrated effects of splendour. A similar restraint appears in the *Adoration* when Mantegna resorts to the technique of working certain features such as the star and some of the plants on the rock in slight relief in order to give them greater boldness. In the *Circumcision* and the portrait of Cardinal Trevisan the technique of relief was used to make the outlines stand out within a raised ground: after the *Adoration* it appears no more in any form in Mantegna's surviving works. Like so much else in the *Adoration*, it is a refinement of elaboration tending to confirm that this was the first history he painted for the Marchese Lodovico.

Such details do not distract from the overall unity of the picture, rewarding only a closer inspection. Mantegna's larger power is evident in the skill with which the principal group of the Virgin, Melchior and St Joseph is disposed, so that the faces of the two old men, turned in profile, direct our eyes to the tiny blessing Child. The poses of the Magi belong to the conventional iconography of the *Adoration*, but Mantegna, within the stately calm of his figure-style, has contrived to express their different movements of devotion – the grave reverence of Melchior, who has doffed his turban on coming within sight of the Holy Family and laid it on the ground, then drawn near and sunk in courtly fashion on to bended knee and humbly crossed his hands on his breast; the eager gesture of Balthasar, who holds his turban in his right hand and steps forward, proffering his gift with his left hand as he too prepares to sink on to bended knee; the humility of Caspar, who has dropped on to both knees and holds out his gift from a distance.

The three are costumed with all the richness at Mantegna's command but only their turbans and Balthasar's hood are oriental. Not so with their retinues, where Mantegna has sought for more exactitude of oriental colour than any of his predecessors, even than Bellini, who had already given his Magi trains of laden camels and the occasional servitor with a turban, but had not gone beyond these superficial touches of local colour in his attempts to suggest the East. Mantegna's oriental world, as we have already noted, is that of fifteenth-century Italy, an

Fig. 5. Landscape with camels. Detail from *The Adoration of the Magi* (Plate 50)

Orient of Turks, Moors, Negroes and Tartars, in other words of Turkey, Persia, the Levant and North Africa. Unlike his predecessors with their motley troops, he has Negroes attend the Negro king Caspar, Moors the Moorish king Balthasar, and Persians and Tartars the Persian Melchior, though all are mixed together on the road for picturesque effect. Mantegna would have had many opportunities to study and draw types of these races from the life: Negro and Moorish and Tartar slaves were common in the fifteenth century – there is a very faithful image of a laughing Moorish woman on the ceiling of the Camera Picta, evidently a portrait of a household slave of the Gonzaga – and Venice was the great slave-market of Italy.[40]

To his Persians Mantegna gives tall conical dervish hats, to his Moors and Negroes turbans and white hoods. Especially notable is the figure of a Tartar groom holding a camel in the left middle ground: he wears a white tunic with hanging sleeves, yellow boots and a round fur-edged hat striped with blue, white and red. From a girdle round his haunches is slung a quiver of red oriental leather, tooled in gold and blue with an Islamic design, and with a Tartar bow and arrows protruding from it. However, Mantegna's exoticism is largely an exoticism of accessories, such as turbans, dervish hats and quivers, for the escort mostly wear tunics of standard fifteenth-century type. Mantegna's Magi have journeyed like Bellini's on camels, and he has figured these with the same observant fidelity (Fig. 5). Thus the camel behind Caspar is correctly given tufts of hair on the thighs and the stiff curls of its fur are skilfully rendered with short delicate strokes. In the quattrocento menageries of rare and exotic animals were the prerogative of princes and of the ruling magistracies of the great Italian republics, who alone could afford to maintain them. Mantegna had perhaps seen camels and dromedaries sent as a present to the Venetian Senate by a Levantine sultan or prince; alternatively he may have used drawings and descriptions made in the Levant. From the early trecento artists and their patrons had taken an eager pleasure in the representation of animals and of man, and especially of the types and costumes of exotic man.[41] That pleasure was the expression of a new delight in the spectacle of the world and in its variety and strangeness, a delight that was felt equally in response to beauty and to curiosity in the natural world, to beauty and to grotesqueness in the human world. Alberti recommends artists to introduce into their pictures 'copiousness and variety . . . I shall call that history most copious in which are mingled old men, young men, boys, women, girls, little children, hens, puppies, little birds, horses, sheep, buildings, landscapes of provinces, and all other similar things, each in their proper place.'[42] The love of exotic

variety that lies behind this precept appears in Mantegna's contemporaries, in Jacopo Bellini, for example, and in Pisanello, with his drawings of exotic animals, of a Cufic inscription, of a Tartar, which are surely only the scant survivors of many more such studies.

Mantegna's self-discipline is apparent in the due subordination of all these picturesque features to the exposition of the theme. The figures are grouped so that the most important are in the foreground, the principal group of attendants closes the middle ground behind them on the left, and the rear of the train, consisting of its baggage, straggles down the hill behind. To aid in this distribution of emphasis he has recourse to sharp distinctions of scaling; this device, anti-naturalistic in effect, even when deployed with Mantegna's artful naturalism, he was to retain until the 1490s, so indispensable did he find it as an aid to clarity of composition.

In the panel generally known as the *Circumcision* (Plate VI), three scriptural events are conflated, the Circumcision of Christ, his Presentation in the Temple and the Purification of the Virgin. The moment figured is that when Simeon picks up the knife with his right hand from a basin held by an acolyte and takes the Child from the Virgin with his left, which is covered by a white handkerchief in the form of a scarf, in preparation for the act of circumcision. The light comes from the left; it is a divine light that falls in gold on the Virgin's red robe and dark olive-green cloak and on the dark olive-green robe of the woman, a friend or attendant, who stands on the right, and rests her hand on the head of a little child wearing a coral tunic. The figures are arranged in a gentle curve which is emphasized by the line of their shadows as they fall on the chequered pavement of porphyry and variegated white marble. The composition is closed on the right by the two women and the child and on the left by St Joseph as he stands in a dark red robe and a cloak of yellow, holding a basket of pigeons, his grey hair and beard arranged in crisp, classical curls. The strong verticals of these figures frame the principal group of Simeon and the Virgin, skilfully disposed so that neither is quite central to the picture, yet both share its centre, linked by the Child, whose active, semi-frontal pose emphasizes his primary significance in the scene. The whole group of tall slender figures, clad in draperies that partly model, partly decorate their graceful limbs, recalls a classical relief in its disposition on two planes, in its closed, statuesque poses and in the use of profile views for three of the actors.

However, as so often in Mantegna, the inspiration of marble does not repress human warmth of observation, any more than it precludes bright warmth of colour. Our first impression is of a tranquil scene, in which figures of ideal dignity are posed in attitudes of quiet absorption in the action. Yet this predominant aspect of serenity gracefully throws up the sharpness and spontaneity of certain gestures and movements: Simeon taking up the knife, the frightened Child turning away from him and clutching at his mother's cloak with a cry for help. In the tradition of varying the solemn mood of a history with anecdote, the child on the right sucks his finger and holds a circle of bread from which he has taken a bite: his restlessness is curbed by the gentle pressure of his mother's hand. So too the ideal forms of the figures are varied with a delicate naturalism. The three women are studies of different ages, the bloom of the young mother being contrasted with the sunken face of the old woman standing behind her, and both in turn with the Virgin's sorrowful countenance, which is that of a woman in early middle age. It should be noted that the old woman's narrow face, with its pinched features, sharp nose and sharp chin is the first known appearance in Mantegna's art of his standard type for aged women, one that is found even in his latest works.

The impression of holiness, purity and innocence that emanates from all these figures is enhanced by the white robes of Simeon and the acolyte and the white hoods of the women. Their simplicity of dress is set off by the magnificence of the setting. The background figures a section of the altar wall of the Temple, whose solemn grandeur is suggested by making it rise to almost twice the height of the figures and by cutting off the cornice above the arches, leaving our imaginations to surmise the rest. The whole wall, of which we see only part, is imagined as decorated with rich stones and marbles, with an altar of grey stone in the centre and two sets of doors, one to either side of the altar, giving access to the Holy of Holies. Here Mantegna makes the same artful use of asymmetry as in the Vienna *St Sebastian*. The figures are placed before a section of the wall that includes on the left a part of the altar and on the right part of one of the sets of doors. Once more a column gives a central vertical axis to an asymmetrical design: this time a column of variegated marble rising behind Simeon. Symmetry is re-established by the two arches of grey stone that spring from the column, forming part of a blind arcade of three arches which runs along the whole wall, as Mantegna has indicated by truncating the arches and the lunettes beneath them to either side of the laurel-garlanded medallions of inlaid serpentine. A continuity of extending space is suggested from which our scene is isolated.

Certain variations emphasize this effect. Within both arches is a second framework of pilasters supporting an architrave and lunette, all of porphyry decorated with gilded classical ornaments of acanthus and palmettes in relief. But the ornament on the left pilaster and on the lunette above differs from that on the right in order to indicate that they frame the altar, the central feature of the wall. In keeping with the Jewish prohibition of idolatry, the reredos above the altar is a plain composition of four contrasting panels of two sorts of red variegated marble recessed within a plain grey framework of variegated stone. The fiery red of the panels and their richer variegation, as of watered silk, make them stand out even against the ornate splendour of the rest of the wall. Between the two arches is a gilded six-winged cherub; figured, like the gilded ornaments of the doors and marbles and the gilded reliefs of the lunettes, in an attempt to represent the decorations of the Temple as described in the sixth chapter of the First (Third) Book of Kings. For the subjects of the reliefs decorating the lunettes there was of course no Biblical authority. But the scene of Moses showing the tablets of the law to the Jews was an obvious choice for the decoration of the Temple, since it recalls the divine origin of its ritual and sacrifices, and embodies the authority of the Old Law whose commandments are so scrupulously fulfilled by the protagonists of the scene below. Nevertheless, the greater prominence is allotted to the Sacrifice of Isaac, which is figured over the altar. This was surely because the Temple was built on Mount Sion, and Mount Sion, according to a generally received interpretation of the commentators was the Mons Moria of the Bible on which Abraham offered up Isaac to the Lord. The Sacrifice proclaims the first consecration of Mount Sion, forming a decoration historically appropriate for the Temple. For Christians it also contained an allusion to Christ, of whom Isaac was a type and an ancestor. Indeed the Sacrifice of Isaac was not only that sacrifice acceptable to God which was the foundation of Israel, but an antetype prefiguring the Passion of Christ. In turn this symbolism may explain why the Virgin is shown with careworn, melancholy features, as if foreseeing the suffering and death that her Son must endure in his sacrifice.

The two scenes are figured as reliefs in gilded stone applied to a ground of serpentine marble: they are the earliest examples of a type of simulated relief that Mantegna was shortly to use on a much ampler scale in the Camera Picta. Although Mantegna's simulated relief sculptures are much more strictly classical in feeling than those of his predecessors, there were precedents for them in Flemish art, as for example in the relief of Cain and Abel on the Van Eyck *Adoration of the Lamb*. In their stylistic conception they derive from ancient relief sculpture, and in particular from ancient gems, but are elaborated with a Renaissance sense of detail and spatial effect. To accommodate Abraham and Isaac in the truncated lunette Mantegna has had to move them into its right half and find balancing features on the left: it will be seen that he has contrived to turn this difficulty into an eloquent enrichment of the composition. In all this decoration Mantegna has assumed that the classical antique represented the Jewish antique, and on this assumption he has overlaid a classical structure with imagery drawn from Biblical sources and enriched by motifs that united historical plausibility with iconographical significance. Yet this imaginary architecture and sculpture, for all the sedulousness of its evocation of the antique, expresses in its richness of ornament, its glow of colour and gilding, its contrast of polychrome variegated marbles with elegant grey stone those sumptuous preferences of Lombardy and Venice that were later to be realized in the architecture and sculpture of the Lombardi.

The orthogonals of the pavement converge on a point just above a third of the way down from the top of the column shaft, indicating that the picture was set a little above eye-level, a supposition confirmed by the gentle rise of the pavement. Such a placing must have added to the effect of the *Ascension* (Plate 51), in which Mantegna has used a compositional device similar to that of the Ovetari *Assumption*, setting the figure of Christ high above the awestruck group of the Virgin and Apostles to convey the physical fact of his ascent into heaven. The light is from the right, so that originally the panel must have been set on the opposite wall to the *Circumcision*, as must the other surviving panel from the sequence, *The Death of the Virgin*, where the light is also from the right. This care to make the pictorial fall of light correspond with the real fall of light is of a piece with Mantegna's conception of a painting as a projected illusion and, as we already know, is one of the fundamental premises of his art.

The floor of the *Ascension* is a low shelf of rock, again shown gently rising; on the right and in the foreground it curves gently downwards to indicate that we are on the summit of Mount Olivet, from which Christ ascended into heaven. On the left is a steep sharp slope of rock, fringed with bushes and rocks; in the background a flat-topped rock, perhaps that of Gethsemane. Before this mount are low trees, of a stylized kind, one of which frames in its dark green leaves the brightly clad figure of the Virgin, her red robe and blue cloak lit on the right by the same divine gold that falls on the garments of her son. Her figure is the central vertical axis of the middle plane, but is set to the rear and raised on a low natural pedestal of stone so as to form the key figure of the inward-turned circle of companions from whose midst Christ has just ascended. That she is a being set apart is emphasized not only by the pedestal but by the intervals that separate her to

either side from the two groups of Apostles. She lifts her hands in an *orans* posture of prayerful wonder, while they stand or kneel in various attitudes of reverence and amazement, one on the left shielding his eyes as he gazes upwards at the resplendent figure of his departing master.

The time is dawn: the sky rises from a pale blue on the horizon to a dark blue at the top of the picture. Against this dark blue Christ is silhouetted, framed in a fiery mandorla of cherubim resting on pale blue clouds. He wears a crimson robe and a dark blue cloak which fuses with the blues of clouds and sky in a marvellous unity. His figure forms the upper part of the central vertical axis begun by the figure of the Virgin below: the half-turned pose of the body is aptly chosen to manifest at one and the same time his triumphant ascension into heaven and his benignant care to signal to his mother and to his followers that he must now quit this earth. The colouring, deep, rich and lustrous, glowing rather than glittering, confirms that Mantegna's preference for strong and pale hues was innate: he had no great taste for middle hues, which did not meet his liking for sharpness of definition and clarity of contrast. For this picture he must have made a number of studies of figures seen from the rear in various postures, given that he again uses the device of figures turned inwards which he had used in the St Christopher frescoes, and for the same reason: accentuation of the dramatic interest and its concentration in the rear of the middle ground. Accordingly their draperies are broken into particularly sharp decorative patterns. So many upturned heads must have been a welcome challenge to his favourite technique of foreshortening. Once more their haloes are formed as a soft radiance of gold like those of the holy women in the San Zeno *Crucifixion*, perhaps because a sequence of boldly defined circles would have interfered with the unity of effect. As with all his haloes of this period, they turn in perspective with the heads to which they belong, so much so that the halo of the kneeling Apostle in the left foreground is rendered perpendicular to the front plane.

The Death of the Virgin has come down to us in two fragments, one in the Prado (Plate 53), showing the Apostles celebrating her exequies, the other in the Pinacoteca Nazionale at Ferrara, showing Christ receiving her soul (Plate 52). The iconography is Venetian, and resemblances have long been noted between the composition and the mosaic of the same subject in the Cappella della Madonna (later dei Mascoli) of San Marco in Venice, a work whose design is variously attributed to Andrea del Castagno, Michele Giambono and Mantegna himself. The ascription to Mantegna can be rejected: the latest solution to the difficulty, which attributes the design to Andrea del Castagno and the execution to

Michele Giambono, at least recognizes the necessity of reconciling the style of the figures and of some of the architecture with the Venetian iconography and certain Venetian features such as the frieze and the railing that surmounts the arch. The resemblances between Mantegna's painting and the mosaic have perhaps been exaggerated: both scenes show a perspective view through an opening at the rear, but this is their most salient resemblance, for the theme itself imposed the grouping of the Apostles about the Virgin's catafalque. And until a firm date is found for the mosaic it is unwise to deduce conclusions about the one work from the other.[43]

The mosaic sets the scene in the open, with the Virgin's catafalque placed prominently in the foreground on the pavement before a great triumphal arch leading into a street. Mantegna lays his scene in the intimacy of a long narrow chamber, and for greater dramatic naturalism withdraws the catafalque towards its further end, so that it stands at the rear of the middle ground, the area where the interest was likewise focused in the *Ascension*. The Apostles, eleven in all, line the sides and the back of the chamber, conducting the exequies about the simple wooden frame of the catafalque, covered with a red cloth and red pillows, on which the Virgin lies composed in death. Their grouping is at once formal and natural: nine of them are mourners and are aligned in groups of three, one to either side, one at the rear. The poses, actions and expressions of grief of these nine are carefully varied; the three Apostles on the right intone a response, while the others gravely listen, or gaze at the Virgin. Nor are they placed in rigid symmetry: the furthest Apostle on the left stands behind the catafalque, unlike his counterpart on the right. In the centre St Peter, richly vested as a bishop in cope and dalmatic, conducts the service from an office-book, while another Apostle, bending over the catafalque from the other side, censes the Virgin, his body screening her lower limbs and throwing up her waxen features and crossed hands. To the left of Peter a pitying Apostle holds a holy-water stoup: his counterpart to the right of Peter appears to be drawn from the same model as Balthasar in *The Adoration of the Magi*. Golden light again falls on the Virgin from above, where her soul is received by her son.

The open space before the catafalque leads the eye inwards to the dead Virgin, then with the orthogonals of its floor to a high point of sight in the background at the further end of the bridge crossing the water, so directing it into the view that is seen through the arched window of the chamber. In the seventeenth century this view was identified as a view of Mantua seen across one of the lakes formed by the Mincio, with a bridge running towards it. But far more probably the bridge is the Ponte San Giorgio which linked the Castello di Corte with the Castello di San Giorgio. Before it was rebuilt after the damage it received during the siege of 1630, the Ponte San Giorgio was regarded by the Mantuans as one of the great works of the world. It rose 28 *braccia* from the bottom of the lake to its surface, then rose another 12 *braccia* above it, and ran in length for about 2000 *braccia*. The bridge itself was covered with a roof, and had a tower in the middle to defend the passage against enemies, exactly as in Mantegna's painting.[44]

The censer, the stoup and the two candlesticks standing at either corner are in Renaissance, not Gothic style, a sign that Mantegna was beginning to apply classical forms and ornaments to the design of ideal objects, where once he had been content to simulate the real objects of his own day. Nothing survives to illustrate his significance as an innovator in the design of objects in the Renaissance style, but just as his knowledge of architecture can be surmised from the consultations that were held with him, so, as we shall see, there are signs in documents that he was the first to introduce the antique style into tapestries and goldsmith's work made for the Mantuan court.

We know something of Mantegna's movements during his first years in Mantua. In the summer of 1461 he went back to Padua to attend to some business, most probably the collection of debts. To assist him in bringing his journey to a successful issue Lodovico gave him a letter of recommendation, dated 14 July 1461, to Jacopo Zeno, Bishop of Padua. 'Andrea Mantegna, bearer of these presents,' it begins, 'is going to Padua, and as we believe your Reverend Lordship knows, has been with us for a good time now and is making some works of his art, in which, as you may have heard, he is a great master (*solemne magistro*) and on this account we hold him most dear.' Lodovico requests the Bishop's aid and counsel to Mantegna in his business 'in which, so he tells me, your Reverend Lordship can do him much favour', in order that he may despatch it successfully and return speedily to Lodovico's service.[45] Zeno (*c*.1417–81) was a learned humanist and a friend and admirer of Ciriaco of Ancona, with an interest in the study of antiquities. He was also a friend and admirer of Cardinal Lodovico Trevisan, and so on many counts was likely to be sympathetic to Mantegna.[46]

Our first record of the friendship that linked Mantegna with the fantastical humanist and scribe Felice Feliciano dates from 13 January 1463.[47] It is a letter from Feliciano dedicating to Mantegna a *Liber epigrammaton* or collection of ancient inscriptions which Feliciano had compiled. In it Feliciano salutes Andrea admiringly as 'prince of painters, and their only light and comet and man of great genius' and affectionately as 'incomparable friend' and 'the glory of all his friends', and calls him 'ever most prompt and partial to the investigation of antiquities of this sort'. But his other words are more protective, not to say patronizing. He assumes the tone of a tutor to a pupil:

> there is no desire in me that is dearer or more ancient than that thou shouldst become as learned as may be, and be a man of consummate knowledge in all worthy subjects which I have little fear shall come to pass if thou wilt but study to unite to the goods of the body and of fortune those of the mind, by which thou shalt prepare for thyself beyond all peradventure an illustrious name and one that will be immortal, for their nature is such that they seem in a fashion to overcome death itself and slay it.[48]

Here then is a glimpse of Mantegna at the age of 32 as seen by an intimate friend who was also a humanist. The relationship is one of affection, but also one in which the man of letters assumes the right to instruct the artist, as a man who aspires to learning but has yet to acquire it, at any rate in full measure. Feliciano's words imply a consciousness of the distinction separating scholars and humanists from the practitioners of a mechanical art. A distinction founded on the primacy of humane letters, it entailed on artists an inferiority which until the end of the eighteenth century they were often quite content to acknowledge.

Feliciano was born in Verona, the son of an excise official, and from the first seems to have followed the profession of a scribe. He first met Mantegna in Padua during the 1450s, for a manuscript he made for him contains a copy of an ancient inscription in Mantegna's house at Padua. He became one of the same circle of friends in Padua and Venice, for he has left poems addressed to Giovanni Bellini, Marco Zoppo and the sculptor Cristoforo di Geremia. He was a lively, witty, whimsical and inconstant character, a poet, an alchemist passionately addicted to antiquarian studies, and with that taste for collecting drawings so characteristic of the humanists of Verona, Padua and Venice—in a will of 1466 he makes a bequest not only of his antique medals but also of his 'drawings and pictures on paper by many excellent masters of design'. In 1465 Feliciano went to Bologna and entered the service of Giovanni Marcanova as a scribe, perhaps on the recommendation of Mantegna. The two had had a 'parliament' together about getting Feliciano an entry into the household of Cardinal Franceso Gonzaga, whom Feliciano calls Mantegna's *compatre* and crony, perhaps as his secretary, perhaps as a scribe. Feliciano encouraged his friend's goodwill with a sonnet. In a distinctly humble tone, he turns to Mantegna, saluting him as a new Polygnotus and Apelles and as 'his lord', and invokes his aid to enable him to pass the rest of his days with some prop of support, for life is painful for one bitten by that stinging nettle poverty.[49]

A gay holiday interlude during these years was the famous excursion to the Lago di Garda (the ancient Benacus), which Feliciano made in company with Mantegna, Samuele da Tradate and Giovanni da Padova on 22 September 1464.[50] In Mantua, Verona and Brescia an excursion to Lake Garda and especially to Toscolano and its gardens on the western shores of the lake was considered one of the pleasantest of holiday jaunts. It had been Vittorino da Feltre's custom to take his pupils to the lake in the summer, out of the heat of Mantua, and at the end of the century Isabella d'Este often made expeditions there in company with other great ladies or simply with her own waiting-women.[51] Feliciano's companions were all artists. Samuele da Tradate, for whom he made and wrote out another collection of ancient inscriptions, was a painter, and the son of the better-known sculptor Jacopino.[52] From 1462 he was working on the decorations of the principal rooms of the new Gonzaga palace at Cavriana, for which Mantegna had given the designs, and early in 1464 was busy painting its *camera*. Giovanni da Padova we have already encountered as architect, engineer and intermediary between the Marchese Lodovico and Mantegna: it would be fascinating to know if he was the young 'lapicida' Zuane da Padova who is recorded in 1448 as a pupil of Donatello (*so desipolo*) and as working with him on the altar of the Santo.[53] Perhaps he too was employed at Cavriana, and the jaunt to Lake Garda was taken by all three as a holiday interval in the work or at its conclusion.

Samuele was appointed *imperator* or leader of the expedition, no doubt in his capacity as a 'facetious man'; the *viri primarii* Mantegna and Giovanni serving under him as consuls. Feliciano made all the arrangements, and later wrote an account of their experiences in a manuscript executed for Samuele da Tradate. They went on an excursion by boat from Toscolano, and came to a place on the shore of the lake where there were paradisaical orchards, veritable gardens of the Muses, studded with pink and purple flowers and with sweet-smelling orange and lemon-trees, spreading wide their shady boughs. They also visited the islands on the lake, rejoicing in the springs that flowed through their meadows and in the ancient laurel and palm-trees that adorned them. On Isola di Garda they found an antique inscription, which Feliciano copied.

They began next day by exploring Toscolano.

Feliciano, crowned with a garland of myrtle, periwinkle, ivy and other leaves led the company together with Samuele through shady groves of laurel. They entered the church of San Domenico, where they found an inscription of the Emperor Marcus Aurelius Antoninus, then went on to the nearby church of Santo Stefano, under whose porch they found an inscription of the Emperor Antoninus Pius. Near the house of the Arciprete of Santa Maria they found a second inscription of the Emperor Marcus. All these Feliciano copied.[54] Then they found a monument which they identified as a shrine of Diana and her nymphs. After examining all these relics of antiquity, they got into a boat strewn with carpets and other coverings, having first garlanded it with laurel leaves and leaves from other noble trees. They flew swiftly over the waters of Lake Garda, Samuele singing to them continually and accompanying himself on the lute. They landed at Garda on the opposite shore and went into the church of Santa Maria Maggiore, where they returned hearty thanks to God Almighty and his Mother for having illumined their hearts to join in company together, for having opened their minds to the design of visiting and investigating these mighty sites, for having caused them to see so many delightful things, including several antiquities, and for having given them a fine day, bright weather, a prosperous sail and a safe landing.

The sensibility to nature Feliciano reveals in his account of this excursion is also that of Mantegna, who ornaments his pictures with trees that evoke the tranquil haunts of the Muses and the gardens of the Hesperides, lemon- and orange-trees, with their brightly glowing fruits and sweet-scented white blossom, laurels, the tree of antique nobility and victory, and also of poetry and the arts, olives, the tree of Pallas and of learning. He has little interest in any great variety of trees and plants, preferring these few as belonging to man and to his orchards and fields and gardens, and as redolent with literary associations of idyllic or paradisaical beauty. The pursuit of antique remains and inscriptions has its parallel in the antiquities with which Mantegna so often enriches his backgrounds to give them a romantic association with the classical past.

In May or June 1466 Mantegna was despatched by Lodovico to Florence for a sojourn that was to last for some time, as appears from a letter of 5 July 1466 to Lodovico from Giovanni Aldobrandini (1422–81), one of his Florentine agents, commending Andrea and his companion Girolamo as 'persons of great worth',[55] and Andrea especially as having 'perfect gifts and excellent insight not only in painting but in many other things as well'. This judgement implies that Aldobrandini had shown Mantegna the principal paintings in Florence, but in spite of claims made by Fiocco and some other modern scholars and critics, there is no real evidence of any change in Mantegna's style as a result of this visit, and no sign of fresh Tuscan influences in his work. The vivid, romantic Florentine manner, with its interest in the expressive representation of action and feeling had little to contribute to the furtherance of Mantegna's art: indeed to him it may have seemed wanting in weight and dignity. There is no record of his business for the Marchese, who had close connections with Florence going back to his appointment in 1447 as Captain-General of the Comune.[56] In addition, like many fifteenth-century princes and magnates he found it expedient to be on terms of friendship with the Medici, who lent him money with which to finance his ambitious building projects. Possibly Mantegna's visit was connected with schemes for the tribune of the Annunziata, for whose construction the Marchese Lodovico had set aside 2000 gold florins of his Florentine stipend in 1451 and which the architect Michelozzo was building at his expense. Certainly Giovanni Aldobrandini was in vigorous correspondence with Lodovico in the first months of 1471 over the form the tribune ought to take.[57]

Whatever it was, Andrea's business left him time to entertain offers of commissions. On 3 July 1466 the accounts of the Opera of the Campo Santo in Pisa record a payment for a dinner given to Andrea Squarcione 'to do him honour . . . because he is to undertake to finish painting the Camposanto'.[58] The negotiations evidently came to nothing, for the Operai agreed with Benozzo Gozzoli, who began his famous series of frescoes in 1467. Nevertheless the portrait of Carlo de' Medici (Plate v), illegitimate son of Cosimo, and provost of Santo Stefano in Prato, was most probably painted during this visit to Florence, where the need for Lodovico's licence could be conveniently overlooked. This cultivated prelate was an eager collector of classical gems and medals: his taste for antiquity may have prompted him to commission this portrait from his fellow-enthusiast Mantegna.

So similar in style is the portrait of Carlo[59] to the portrait of Cardinal Trevisan that in itself it disproves the thesis of any significant Florentine influence on Mantegna. Again there is robust strength of conception; again the sitter is shown in three-quarter profile on a dark green ground. He wears a white shirt under a prelate's robe of a pinkest-red obtained by hatching pinkish-white over red. The *cappuccio* is brought over the shoulder in a decorative bow-shaped curve: from beneath the gown emerge the coral-red sleeves of an under-robe. His prelate's *berretto* is likewise pinkish-red: the thickness of the material is wonderfully suggested by the broad border. The pinkish-whites of hatching and highlights deepen and soften the shadowed coral-red beneath; framed by the glowing pinks of *berretto* and gown the dark brown face stands out strongly. As the picture is lit from the left, the side of the face in shadow blends with a skilful transition into the dark ground, while the right cheek, the eyes, the nose and the red lips are thrown up in contrast. The bone structure and features are boldly defined in the manner of a Roman bust; with typical accessory realism, the face is seamed across the forehead and round the eyes with horizontal wrinkles. The reflective, almost pensive gaze of the eyes out of the canvas, past the spectator, suggests with the same shrewd strength of perception as the Trevisan portrait the inner character of the sitter, transmuting the image from a simple record into a lively simulacrum.

Fig. 6. Marchese Lodovico Gonzaga. Detail from the outdoor scene of the Camera Picta (Plate IX)

VI

The Camera Picta

WITH the destruction of the Ovetari frescoes, the paintings of the Camera Picta, or Camera degli Sposi as it is popularly known, in Mantua are left as the only major decorative works by Mantegna to have survived in their original setting and in reasonable fullness, though not without damage and restoration over the centuries.[1] Although many palace chambers in the fourteenth and fifteenth centuries were splendidly ornamented with frescoes, few have come down to us and still fewer from the hand of a major artist. The Camera itself is a small room on the first floor or *piano nobile* of the north-east tower of the Castello di San Giorgio: it has two windows, one on the north side looking out over the Lago di Mezzo, and one on the east side. The name Camera degli Sposi was not its original designation, indeed is first attested only in the middle of the seventeenth century. No doubt it came to be given to the room because of the portraits it contains of Lodovico Gonzaga and Barbara of Brandenburg as man and wife sitting among their family and household. Its earliest name was the *camera picta* or *camera depinta*, meaning painted chamber. A painted chamber was a universal feature of every fourteenth- and fifteenth-century residence of the great, not only in Italy, but throughout Western Europe – there was one, for instance, in the Palace of Westminster. The Camera was described with pride in an official act transacted there on 1 July 1475, about a year after its completion, 'as the great painted audience-chamber of our illustrious lord'.[2]

Originally a *camera* had been strictly a bedroom, and a state bed was long to remain a feature of European state-chambers.[3] In the Camera Picta the iron hooks for supporting the canopy of the bed, which stood in the south-east corner, can still be seen on the south wall and in the ceiling above.[4] And certainly Lodovico on occasions slept there.[5] On 25 May 1475, for instance, he asked Barbara to have the *camera depinta* made ready for him on his return to Mantua, and to have the other chamber at the other end of the great *sala* which preceded the Camera got ready too, so that he could go from one to the other when he wished.[6]

A ruler like Lodovico, daily absorbed in managing the internal and external affairs of his state, might resort to his painted chamber for leisure, but would have to attend there to urgent matters of business as well. In more modern terms a painted chamber was at once a bedroom, a sitting-room where the family met together with its privy courtiers, waiting-women and attendants, and entertained itself or was entertained by others, and an audience-chamber, where the head of the household could transact business both formal and informal. To the notions of the age, the presence of a state bed and use as a bedroom in no way precluded these functions. Unlike the *studio*, a small room where personal interests and studies could be pursued alone and undisturbed, the *camera* was a room intended for some privacy, but not for exclusive intimacy or solitude.

The paintings of the Camera Picta are executed in fresco, except on the fireplace wall, which was painted *a secco* in a technique that appears to have been peculiar to Mantegna and is still in some respects a mystery. The surface of the wall was first covered with a hard plaster, which was then rubbed and smoothed down until it had lost almost all its porousness. Into this dry surface the colours did not sink as in true fresco, where the wet plaster absorbs and fixes the paint: on the contrary, although the paint adheres closely to the plaster, it adheres as a separate layer. The ultimate consequence was disastrous, for the layer of paint has scaled and flaked in many areas where the plaster itself remains intact. But the immediate effect was no doubt unusually warm and splendid, since the white of the plaster did not add a chalky tone to the pigments, whose pallidness in the Ovetari frescoes Squarcione, it will be remembered, had censured so sharply. Mantegna, it seems, used for the *tempera* of his pigments a special preparation of his own, which rendered them thick and lustrous. Paccagnini has suggested that his purpose in these innovations was to imitate the technique of ancient Roman painting, which at this date can have been known to him only from the descriptions of Pliny and Vitruvius. In spite of the impression of breadth and bold definition the frescoes give, they are executed in a refined miniaturistic style which must go some way to explain the length of time it took Mantegna to finish the Camera. The strokes are carefully and delicately graduated, and the effect of largeness which the finished works most certainly have is due to the skill with which the colours are balanced and subdued against each other and the skilful transitions from light to shade.

In shape the room is a cube whose sides measure 8.2 metres. Its present form dates from between 1458 and 1465, when Lodovico was remodelling the interior of the Castello. To adorn it Mantegna conceived an illusionistic decoration which from the first must have been the fundamental premise of his scheme, for the ceiling has been painted with feigned ribs to effect a transition from the famous painted oculus, simulating a circular railed opening in its centre, to the square form of the room below. Only a few details of this decoration, for example some edges of the ribbons on the ceiling grounds of feigned gold mosaic, are executed in stucco in true relief, and that very lightly. Plainly Mantegna intended the Camera as a dazzling display of virtuosity. He sustains the minutest attention to simulation in all the motifs he designed for its decoration, prominent or subordinate, decorative or significant, in form, colour, recession and projection, and some of his tricks have continued to deceive the eye until the present day. The general scheme of this decoration must have been conceived as early as 1464 or the first half of 1465. But in the long period between 16 June 1465, the date painted by Mantegna himself, probably on commencement of work, as a simulated graffito on the simulated marble panelling of the window embrasure of the north wall, and the Camera's final completion in 1474, some alterations of the original scheme, if only to introduce new figures, were certainly made.

Looking up at the painted oculus we see through it the sky overhead, with laughing figures and classical putti looking down at us from the balustrade.

The oculus is encircled by a beribboned Squarcionesque garland of flowers and fruit within the larger frame of a great lozenge formed by the intersection of the ribs. These rise from carved stone corbels shaped as classical capitals set on the four walls, one in each corner and two on the wall itself, where they appear to be supported by painted pilasters. Crossing the ceiling diagonally, they form eight lozenge-shaped caissons disposed about the central lozenge, a diaper pattern essentially Gothic in its ornamental conception for all its Renaissance expression. The ribs are moulded and decorated with antique ornaments, all in the same illusionistic technique. Each of the eight caissons contains a medallion with a portrait bust of one of the first eight Caesars on a ground of simulated gold mosaic (Plates 55–62) – medallions on a gold ground already appear on the ceiling of Altichiero's Oratorio di San Giacomo (1377–84). The heads of the Caesars are shown turned to the right or to the left in pairs so as to animate the composition; and the pose of each is slightly varied to add further liveliness to images necessarily rather formal. Each medallion is enclosed in a beribboned garland of laurel, the ribbons twisting into a fanciful pattern of curling scrolls. Supporting each one is a caryatid putto of the kind Mantegna had first used on the framework of the Ovetari Chapel, having copied the motif, it will be remembered, from the San Tarasio frescoes of Andrea del Castagno. Here the motif is put to secular use. Mantegna, like Castagno, gives his putti a variety of attitudes, and sets four of them on carved pedestals of different sorts and four on foliated ornaments. As always, there is a tension between their sculptural form and pictorial treatment.

The intervals of the diaper of caissons form twelve triangular spandrels, decorated, again on a ground of simulated gold mosaic, with mythological scenes, six representing episodes from the life of Hercules, six figuring the power of music in three scenes from the life of Orpheus and three from the life of Arion. Mantegna had certainly made the acquaintance of mosaic as a living art in Venice. Here on the ceiling of the Camera he has simulated its gold backgrounds to create an antique effect – early in the Renaissance, both in Florence and Venice, it was known that mosaic had been a favourite technique of antiquity. The scenes have been accused of some inequalities of execution, but these are more apparent than real and probably attributable to their condition. Executed in simulated relief in grey monochrome lit with white, they show great virtuosity in the adaptation of the compositions to the triangular frame. This Mantegna treats sometimes as a rigid border, at other times as a device for three-dimensional illusionism, in that feet and arms are made to protrude beyond it or rest upon its outer mouldings. Although the ground is treated in places as a depth rather than as a plane when it suits Mantegna's convenience, there is a conscious effort in the disposition of the figures and in the use of interval to reproduce the effects of relief sculpture. It is sometimes said that the scenes of violent action, such as the *Hercules and Antaeus*, show the influence of Pollaiuolo, but comparison with works by Pollaiuolo, for example the *Battle of the Nudes*, only reveals the difference between his nervous straining active figures and the weighty stability of Mantegna's. In fact the *Hercules and Antaeus* appears to be closely copied from an antique medal.

The pendentives formed by the ribs of the ceiling leave twelve lunettes on the flat wall surface between them. Each of the twelve is enclosed in an illusionistic architectural frame, one of Mantegna's last tributes, so far as we know, to his Squarcionesque youth. From a hook in the top centre of each frame hang two swags of fruit and foliage, which are attached to the bottom corners, the whole against a background of sky. In the eight corner lunettes a medallion is suspended between the swags, bearing a device of the Gonzaga, either a family device or one of those assumed by Lodovico (Plates 75–82). These devices are complemented by the family coat of arms which is painted over the doorway in the south wall.

All the walls of the chamber are painted with wall-hangings of gold damask, lined with crimson or blue and some certainly once decorated with patterning on the lining. They are just such hangings as generally decorated the walls of the chambers of the great in the fifteenth century: thus in 1494 in getting ready Francesco Gonzaga's new *camerino* at Gonzaga Teofilo Collenuccio had its walls hung with crimson velvet.[7] They are suspended from rails running from corbel to corbel. It may be that they are intended to emulate Parrhasius' famous painting of a curtain, which was so lifelike that the painter Zeuxis was himself deceived and asked for it to be pulled back.[8] They offer two patterns. One is of rosettes on a groundwork of thistle stems and foliage, the other of medallions interlaced with curling straps set with an acanthus, the medallions being linked by octofoils of interlace in a style reminiscent of some of the interlaced ornaments which are found in Felice Feliciano's manuscripts and elsewhere. On the east wall the left hanging is of the thistle design, while the right two are of the interlaced design: on the south wall this arrangement is reversed. Unfortunately the hangings on these walls have had to be particularly heavily restored.

On the south and east walls the hangings fall undisturbed: on the north and west walls they are pulled back on their runners to reveal an architectural framework of two central piers and two pilasters at the sides. These rise to the corbels and divide each wall into three compartments, forming a sort of loggia through which we behold, as in the St Christopher frescoes and the San Zeno altarpiece, a single tableau. Space is figured as continuous behind the piers and pilasters, and indeed on the north wall as continuous before them as well. Both piers and pilasters are decorated with rinceaux of acanthus on a gilt ground: they rest on a moulded dado of grey stone, carved with linked oval medallions. These medallions and the spandrels between them are inlaid with pink and green marble, both colours being heraldic colours of the Gonzaga. The regularity of this scheme is broken by certain functional features of the room: in the north wall by a fireplace to right of centre and a window in an embrasure on the left, in the west wall by a doorway a little to right of centre, on the east wall by a window to the left of the centre, and on the south wall by a second doorway on the right, with a small shuttered recess, in a rich moulded stone frame, immediately to its left. As we shall see, the design of the two great compositions that fill the three compartments of the west and north walls has been cleverly adjusted so as to take these features into account. But it is nevertheless true to say that Mantegna's illusionistic scheme is imposed on the room rather than integrated with its architectural features. Indeed it seems that the original windows may have been moved in order to make room for his frescoes and to give them light from the direction Mantegna preferred.

To understand this decorative scheme we must dismiss all notion of it as intended to be a naturalistic representation of something else, for example a pavilion, as Kristeller suggested.[9] The simulated hangings and the heavy vaulted ceiling alone would have prevented any such confusion with a pavilion in quattrocento eyes. Mantegna's contemporaries no doubt understood at once that the decoration was conceived in terms of the state-chamber which the room in reality was. By a decorative device as arbitrary as the simulated architectural frame in which he had so often enclosed the paintings of his Paduan years, Mantegna lifts the veil of the hangings on two walls and pierces the veil of the ceiling to simulate the framework of an open loggia on the north and west walls and a balustraded circular opening on to a terrace in the ceiling. If there was a guiding principle of overall simulation in the conception, it was the transformation of a square chamber in a frowning tower into one that was in part a rich tapestried chamber, in part a bright garden room, where the eyes were delighted on one wall by a romantic mountain landscape, on another by a garden terrace, and overhead by another garden walk of delicious trees and exotic birds. But if such a guiding principle existed at all in the clarity of formulation that modern art history sometimes too willingly lends to the Renaissance, with its more permissive approach to the fancy, it can have maintained only the loosest governance. The logic of Mantegna's design is that of a decorative illusionism which exercises itself in single compositions employing all the cunning devices of his art – perspective, foreshortening, the simulation of architecture and textiles – to open or close pictorial space before the spectator. Artistically, the Camera, with its walls concealed by hangings or revealed by the running back of hangings, figures a double illusion, that of a curtained chamber, and then that of a chamber whose walls, by a feat of transformation, are abolished when their curtains are withdrawn to disclose an interior prospect and an exterior prospect. If we knew more of fifteenth-century stage-craft, we could perhaps say with greater certainty whether the drawn-back curtain as a device for enhancing the illusion of a scene in three-dimensional space is theatrical in its inspiration or not. All we can be sure of is that Mantegna's invention appears to be the ancestor of the draped curtain, which from the sixteenth century was to become one of the great conventional props of European state portraiture.

Stylistically, in its play on the continuum between illusion and reality, in its use of such arbitrary spatial devices as the architectural framework and the pendant swag, the Camera is the culmination of Mantegna's Paduan style. It carries that style's artful combination of naturalism and geometrical perspective with the picturesque of landscape and of antiquity to a yet greater extreme of virtuosity. In the oculus of the ceiling, Mantegna sets himself the problem of representing the illusion of figures and objects in three-dimensional space to an eye that looks upwards. The methods he employs are partly geometrical, partly naturalistic. The framework essential to Mantegna's perspective is ingeniously provided by the medallion form of the ornamental moulded circle that encloses the oculus. This acts as a circular window frame. Within it he has conceived a design capable of treatment as a sequence of concentric circles, with radii converging through them to the centre point, so forming a cone of perspective lines up into which the spectator looks (Plate VII).

The peg of Mantegna's conception, then, is the double role of the medallion frame, which serves him both as an ornamental form and as an architectural form, in that its inner border forms the lower moulding of a dado, which in terms of the room below is also the entablature. From this dado a balustrade forms a sequence of diminishing concentric circles, those of major architectural significance being sharply defined, while those between them are more lightly adumbrated. Radii are already marked on the frieze of the dado by its decoration of two rows of alternating blocks of red and white marble, which unite to form a chequer pattern. The blocks are parallelograms, and those of the upper row are smaller than those of the lower, so beginning a convergence that is continued by the verticals of the balustrade above. To further this convergence the balustrade is figured as a sequence of twenty-four panels of hollow double oval frames of white stone. These ovals are flattened, and are arranged in columns of four, diminishing in recession. To left and right they are linked by banded clamps, whose interrupted horizontals form a minor sequence of concentric circles; in the centre they are conjoined by clamps formed as vertical rolls framing a flat band. The interrupted vertical lines of these central clamps do not continue the radii of the frieze below, which would create too obvious and rigid a pattern, but project their own radii, increasing the fineness of the network of converging and concentric lines. Mantegna has also made the projecting cornice of the dado conceal the lower part of the bottom row of ovals, so showing the balustrade in recession from its dado frame below, an ultimate refinement of that perspective illusionism he had first applied in the lunette fresco of the Santo. The care with which the design was set out can be seen now that the paint has worn, revealing the verticals carefully drawn to establish the bounds of the panels and the lines of the vertical rolls.

On this geometrical simulation of a dado and balustrade Mantegna has superimposed features and figures that complete and ornament the illusion. First of course is the sky, in which float a large puffy light grey cloud, white along the edge where the sun falls on it, and several little pale white clouds.[10] Then there are the figures, consisting of a lesser group of winged putti and a principal group of five women. One of these, judging by her elaborate coiffure and gauzy headdress, is a court lady of high rank. Next to her is the famous Moorish slave, one of the many to be found in the palaces and houses of Renaissance Italy. She wears a striped Moorish head-dress formed as a cap in front and a veil behind over a white matron's hood.[11] On the other side of the rustic garden tub containing a lemon-tree are three waiting-women, two wearing white bandeaux over their carefully flattened and coiled hair, and one with a maiden's long loose tresses, which she is about to smooth with the humble wooden comb she holds in her right hand, a motif that adds to the lively informality of the group.

Only the heads of the women appear over the balustrade. That they are the principal group Mantegna has indicated in various ways, by their downward-looking eyes, by grouping them together, in opposition to the scattered putti, by the contrast in scale between their larger figures and the small figures of the putti, and by allotting to them a full third of the balustrade, the nine panels that are left in shadow by the light, which is figured as a morning light proceeding from the south-east and falling obliquely from above the tub. To see them full-face the spectator must be placed in the centre of the room or on the northern or fireplace side. This positioning must have been chosen so that the practical joke they are about to perpetrate is visible only to someone sitting to the right of the fireplace in a chair facing the door. That someone, as we shall see, there is every reason to believe was the Marchese Lodovico himself. Laughingly two of them prepare to let fall the tub which they have balanced on a pole.

The remainder of the balustrade is tenanted by the playful winged putti. Three are shown full length, standing on the cornice of the dado, two in front view and one in rear view, in deliberately contrasted poses. They are strongly foreshortened; that this was a first trial of rigorous *di sotto in sù* foreshortening is betrayed by its imperfect artistic success, for the division of the folds of flesh of thighs and arms for the sake of recession into so many sharply defined curved parallel rolls, as if they were concentric geometrical rings, can hardly be said to make a happy effect. The foreshortening seems to have had as its foundation studies from the life of a baby boy or boys lying down flat, drawn from a point behind the feet, probably from some distance away. These studies were then adjusted to fit the vertical poses required by the composition. Of the other putti some put their heads through the ovals of the balustrade, further projecting that illusion of free movement in space whose creation is so fundamental a premise of Mantegna's art. Three are seen half-length looking over the balustrade in various attitudes. One of these holds a stick with which he is trying to chase back a peacock, aided by another putto, whose hand alone is visible as he thrusts up a stick through an oval of the balustrade to poke the bird.

In all probability this peacock was drawn from life. We know that Lodovico's garden at Mantua contained exotic birds, for on 11 July 1469 he commanded Mantegna in a letter from Goito to make drawings from the life of a male and a female 'galina de India', adding, 'you will be able to see ours which are in the garden there at Mantua.'[12] It is not certain whether by 'galine de India' Lodovico meant peacocks: the term is vague, but there does survive a tapestry made for the Gonzaga court after a design by Mantegna in which a peacock figures prominently. This makes it virtually certain that peacocks, rather than turkeys, which were not represented in European art until the sixteenth century, were Lodovico's Indian birds.[13] In any case we can be sure

that just as the five women portrayed are members of the Gonzaga household, so the peacock was a prized inhabitant of the Gonzaga gardens. The introduction of its bizarre form is a striking invention that redeems the elegant motifs of the putti from conventionality, while the lucent green of its plumage balances the green of the foliage on the opposite side.

The oculus thus introduces us to the theme which is the real unity of the Camera, its depiction of the Gonzaga family, using the word in the extended sense of the Middle Ages and Renaissance, that is to mean not only the family proper but its intimate household of courtiers, officers, retainers and servants. On the north or fireplace wall we see the Marchese Lodovico at home, wearing the long robes of domestic life, surrounded by his wife and family of sons and daughters (Plate 87). On the west wall he is out of doors, wearing outdoor dress, attended by his sons and grandsons (Plate 86). In both paintings the composition and colouring are adjusted to the direction of the light. On the west wall, there is frontal illumination from the window in the east wall, and some illumination from the western corner of the north wall. Accordingly here Mantegna has avoided as much as possible the device of contrasting the light and dark sides of a face for relief, of which he makes great use on the fireplace wall, with its lateral light. Instead of showing his figures full-face or in three-quarter profile, he shows most of them instead in pure profile, so largely dispensing with the need for more than local shadows for modelling. In further observation of the logic of the fall of the light, there is strikingly little contrast of illumination elsewhere in this painting, where again the shadows are local, and the tonality of colour is noticeably lighter than on the fireplace wall, where more modulation and deeper contrast were possible.

The interpretation of these two paintings offers problems, though not because they envelop complex thoughts or deliberate obscurities of allusion. Unlike the paintings which Mantegna was to paint some twenty-five years later for another room in the Castello, the Studiolo of Isabella d'Este, which were intentionally recondite, holding a private meaning fully intelligible only to Isabella herself and the few she favoured, these great wall-paintings, once immediately comprehensible, now contain puzzles only because they assume a familiarity with the Gonzaga family and court, with costume and precedence as expressions of rank, with the identity of individual personages, that is hard to recover after the lapse of five centuries.

Both paintings are unitary scenes, beheld, as we already know, through a feigned architecture that divides them into compartments. In both, the compartment with the principal figures is not in the centre, but at one end of the composition, with the result that the Marchese and his family are grouped together in sections adjacent to each other, to either side of the window in the north-west corner of the room. This asymmetrical emphasis cannot be accidental: but only on the west wall was it forced on Mantegna by the central position of the doorway. Perhaps it was this difficulty that first stimulated his invention: whether so or not, he has turned it with incomparable virtuosity by deploying both compositions with a view to setting the principal group of each in the position most easily visible from the place where the most important persons habitually sat.

In confirmation of this explanation, it should be noted that in the fresco over the doorway the tablet bearing Mantegna's dedication (Plate 84a) of the Camera to Lodovico and Barbara is orientated by the putti who hold it towards persons sitting by the far side of the fireplace, facing the doorway. Anyone seated in this position would have in full view the principal group on the right of the west wall, and a view of the principal group on the fireplace wall. Thus the natural conclusion is that the two scenes were designed to be most fully within the range of view of the Marchese Lodovico, whose habitual seat in the room was presumably that indicated by the orientation of the tablet, on the further side of the fireplace, facing the doorway so as to see at once all who entered. Quite possibly he sat on just such a richly covered, fringed and tasselled faldstool as he occupies in the fresco above the fireplace. From such a position, moreover, on looking up at the ceiling to his left, he would have had before his eye the laughing women who are the principal group of the oculus.

The Marchesa must have sat facing the fireplace, again much as in the fresco above it. From here she would have a full view of this fresco, seeing herself a little to left of centre, and a view of the other group of the male members of her family on the west wall. Such an interpretation also explains why the other compartments of the frescoes are filled only with lesser members of the household and servants and why the other two walls are decorated with simulated hangings, since the backs of the two chief personages in the room were always turned to them. In the pulling back of the hangings on the other two walls to reveal the frescoes there is, then, besides the formal illusionism, an aspect of courtly entertainment, as of a retainer, such as Mantegna was, who has drawn them back to reveal to his lords the scenes that image themselves before them. Such a conception goes far to explain the mingled solemnity and intimacy of the words of Mantegna's dedication of the Camera: 'For the most illustrious Lodovico, second Marquis of Mantua, a prince most excellent and of a faith most unbroken, and for the most illustrious Barbara,

his spouse, glory beyond compare of women, their Andrea Mantegna of Padua completed this poor work to do them honour in the year 1474.' And it also explains why Mantegna has inserted in the grisaille foliage on the feigned pilaster to the right of the doorway, just below the inscription, a tiny self-portrait in grisaille, as if parting its stems to watch in his turn what will happen when the tub falls into the room.[14]

The playful threat of the waiting-women from the oculus above of toppling a tub on to those in the room below illustrates an aspect of fifteenth-century court life that to twentieth-century notions seems incompatible with its ceremoniousness, and often real refinement. This is its taste for *burle*, that is, for horseplay and practical joking. The age's mingling of splendour and homely familiarity is also nicely illustrated in the fresco above the fireplace. The scene is a composite and artificial one, for its left half is a terrace enclosed by a garden wall of white stone, topped by a fanciful parapet of swags and acanthus crockets, above a moulded cornice decorated with scale-work and billets. The wall itself is composed of linked medallion frames of white stone; both the medallions and their interstices are inlaid with panels of richly coloured marble. On the floor of the terrace is a row of citrus trees in tubs: before these are laid two oriental carpets, which Mantegna figures as falling over the edge of the terrace on to the wall of the room, as if the terrace were a real space. The terrace ends behind the central pier; and the right half of the scene is a flight of steps leading up from a landing or corridor against a background of a rich hanging of brocaded cloth of gold, drawn back at the end to reveal an aperture through which the Castello is seen. On the left of the painting, the post of honour, because it is the dexter side in heraldry, sits Lodovico. His figure is parallel to the picture plane, but Mantegna avoids a profile view and at the same time gives him additional emphasis by having him turn sideways on his faldstool to give instructions concerning a letter delivered to him by a messenger, wearing a plum-coloured *gonnella* edged with white, who listens deferentially, holding his vermilion bonnet in his hand. The motif also gives prominence to Lodovico by showing him in a moment of action, while the spiral of his turning body not only accentuates this impression of movement and occupation, but distinguishes him in a composition of static figures.

Beneath Lodovico's faldstool crouches a favourite dog. Recently, in a charming article, Rodolfo Signorini has produced evidence that Lodovico had a great affection for dogs,[15] and especially for a large dog named Rubino, who was as attached to his master as his master was to him. When Rubino died in August 1467, Lodovico ordered him to be buried behind the Castello 'so that just as he gladly used to stay in our chamber (*camera*) so we shall see from our chamber his burial-place.' And he had a little tomb made for him and inscribed with an epitaph. Since the dog portrayed beneath the chair is a large dog with a russet coat, Signorini very plausibly suggests that he is to be identified as Rubino, whose name means russet. If he is correct, then Rubino's appearance is posthumous, and gives us an early warning of the artificial composition of the scene.

Lodovico is dressed in a long loose red gown trimmed with bands of yellow and with an edging and collar of white fur. This is a *veste togata* of the kind worn in the quattrocento by older men: under it he wears a yellow tunic or under-robe, probably cloth of gold, with close-fitting white-edged sleeves. On his head is a vermilion *berretta capitanesca*, a broad flat-topped hat with flaring brim which seems to have had military associations – Lodovico was still active as a princely *condottiere*. He wears no hose, only grey shoes. The heraldic colours of the Gonzaga were *gules* (red), *argent* (silver or white) and *or* (gold or yellow) and the red, white and yellow of this costume are thus the Marchese's family colours. They are also worn in one form or another by most of the figures in the painting, including the messengers: it must be remembered that the materials for clothing of this sort were usually issued by the prince to his family and household, hence the term livery.[16] The Marchese's livery hose, white on the right leg, red on the left, are worn by almost all those males of his family, nobles and servitors who lead the active or semi-military life. In addition all the members of his family, men and women, and the nobles, wear cloth of gold, trimmed with a white edging. The colour-scheme of the scene was therefore not a matter for Mantegna's free choice, but was partly dictated by the heraldic and livery colours of the Gonzaga.

The Marchesa Barbara (Plate 88) is shown in a three-quarter profile that is near full-face, attending closely to what is passing between her husband and the messenger. Her pose of attention is not simply a device for making a pictorial link, but expresses the reality of her life, for during the Marchese's frequent absences on his campaigns, the governance of the city and state of Mantua was left to Barbara, who managed actively the administration of their day-to-day affairs, and attended as well to their security from outside attack. Like Isabella d'Este some twenty years later, she was her husband's chief partner and deputy in the task of ruling and preserving the Gonzaga territories.[17] Barbara's stately figure is set a little back from her husband's, by the depth of his chair in fact, though this subordination is tactfully softened by the spreading fall of her ample robes before and around her knees. As a result of this recession, her head is set a little lower than Lodovico's. She is clad in a *camorra* or robe of stiff-brocaded cloth of gold, trimmed with white edging, which she pulls up over her knees with a white-gloved left hand, revealing an under-robe also of cloth of gold. Gold brocade was the richest stuff of the day: in 1473 Eleonora of Aragon made her entry into Ferrara as its new Duchess wearing a dress of gold brocade, and her wedding present from Barbara was a piece of gold brocade.[18] On Barbara's head is a plain white matron's head-dress, indicating that within the splendid accoutrements befitting her rank is housed a character of dignified simplicity, conscious of the sobriety and restraint proper to a mature and pious lady.

Between Lodovico and Barbara, gazing outwards to the right and so directing our eyes to the other half of the group, stands a figure who is probably Gianfrancesco, their second son. He wears a tunic or gown of brocaded cloth of gold, trimmed with white edging. If a gown, it is the costume of maturity and dignity.[19] He rests his hands with protective affection on the frail figure of his youngest brother Lodovico. At the age of nine Lodovico had been ordained a cleric and appointed a Papal protonotary and Bishop Elect of Mantua, offices of which he entered into formal possession on 5 February 1468;[20] he is shown here wearing the red *berretta* and white stole of a prelate. Before Gianfrancesco and Lodovico their young sister Paola leans on her mother's knee, within the sheltering embrace of Barbara's right arm. The little girl is shown in pure profile to the right: she wears her best chaplet of gold and pearls on her loose maiden tresses, but with childish simplicity holds an apple which she is about to bite.

The poses of Lodovico and Paola, like the more emphatic pose of Gianfrancesco, gently direct us to the right half of the group, which is divided from the left half by the strong central axis created by the figure of Barbara and continued above her head by the figure of her third son Rodolfo (Plate 94), who stands behind her, resting his hands on the back of her chair and inclining his head to watch his father and the messenger. Over a red doublet he wears a garment of brocaded cloth of gold in front and grey behind, in his case a *giornea*, or short tunic split at the sides. The *giornea* was much affected by soldiers for its lightness, and Rodolfo was in fact a professional soldier or soon to become one. A pace behind him, as was proper for a girl, stands Barbara, the only adult daughter of Lodovico and Barbara living in their household at the time the scene was painted, her hands modestly composed before her in a manner that seems to appertain at once to the etiquette of court deportment and to the reserve of her sex and maidenhood.[21] Over her rich *camorra* of brocaded cloth of gold she wears a white *mantellino*, a short white cloak held by straps across the front of her dress and apparently of the fashion later called in Ferrara a *bernia*.[22] She gazes along the terrace to the right, not confronting us or intruding into the rest of the group with unbecoming boldness. There is a glimpse of how she appeared in reality in a letter of 10 April 1470, in which two Milanese ambassadors describe how Madonna Barbara was sent for by Lodovico as he was showing them the portraits in the painting. To them she seemed 'a fair and courteous lady, with a good air and good manners'. Some four years later Schivenoglia describes her as 'handsome and very stout'.[23]

Along with the family stands the stocky figure of the Marchesa's woman dwarf, in a pose obviously studied from the life.[24] Dressed in a robe of red edged with white and a short cloak of red trimmed with white, a white matron's head-dress framing her square, middle-aged features, at once curious and detached, she gazes out full-face at us with beady eyes, the only personage of the scene to do so, crumpling a narrow white handkerchief in her right hand as in childish imitation of the decorum of composed hands she inserts a forefinger into her clenched left hand. Behind stand other intimate members of the household. In attendance on Lodovico and Gianfrancesco are three men, one, a hidden figure wearing a vermilion *berretta capitanesca*, probably not intended as a portrait or to signify more than the presence of a noble courtier. The other two are shown as elderly men with strongly characterized features in three-quarter profile: their black hats and robes suggest that they are trusted officials of the household. Quite possibly they represent the Marchese's two confidential secretaries, Zaccaria Saggi and Marsilio Andreasi, who are described as being in attendance on him when he gave informal audience in the Camera de l'Oro of the Castello in April 1470 to the two Milanese ambassadors. Behind the young Barbara stand two women. One is a young lady in waiting, the other is a matronly figure, from her black dress and modestly downcast eyes, probably an old nurse or a widow serving as a duenna. The instructions given by Galeazzo Maria Sforza in 1472 for the decoration of a *saletta* in the Castello of Milan support this interpretation, for they order his little daughter Bianca Sforza to be shown beside her mother the Duchess with her nurse and Nanneta, probably a waiting maid, standing by in attendance.[25]

The family group is linked to the scene on the right by a youth standing in the foreground before the pier at the head of the stairs, with one foot set before the end of the Marchesa's gown. He wears a short tunic of brocaded cloth of gold edged with white, held by a narrow girdle from which his dagger and a handkerchief hang on the left. This tunic was known as a *gonnella* and is the garment worn by all the remaining figures in tunics, with the exception of the messenger mounting the stairs, who wears a *giornea*. Like the tunic of the man behind the pier, it is edged with the white of the Gonzaga colours. That such tunics in household colours were a feature of court dress is proved by a specification for a fresco given in 1469 by Galeazzo Maria Sforza, which stipulates that one of his servants named Spagnolo was to be portrayed life-size wearing a '*giornea alla Sforcesca*'.[26] And as we have seen, on entering Lodovico's household, Mantegna was issued with sufficient cloth to make a court dress for himself of crimson and silver, the Gonzaga colours. With left hand set on his hip, right hand clasping one end of his girdle, he may be so prominently shown because he is more than a courtier of the Gonzaga, perhaps a young kinsman. His head is turned in three-quarter profile to the right away from Lodovico and Barbara, so gently pointing the spectator towards the further section of the composition.

Behind, his left side concealed by the pier, stands a tall man in early middle age, wearing a tunic of brocaded cloth of gold edged with white and hose of the Gonzaga livery. Clasping gloves – in the quattrocento gloves were a symbol of standing – he turns with extended left arm towards the visitor from another court who waits behind the pier. The presumption must be that he is Lodovico's principal chamberlain.[27] At the audience given to the Milanese ambassadors in 1470 three noblemen are described as attending Lodovico, Messer Raymondo di Lupi, Messer Jacomo da Palazzo and Messer Francesco Secco: it may be that one of these three is portrayed in the figure of the chamberlain. From his rich dress and the position assigned to him, at once a little detached from the family and yet as it were within its circle, we can deduce that he occupied a place of special confidence in the household, and again may even have been a kinsman of some kind. Mantegna cuts off his long and slender legs to suggest the recession of the terrace, but discreetly softens the effect of this perspective device by setting the pier and the youth's right foot before them. Elsewhere in the frescoes it is avoided.

The figures of Lodovico, Barbara and their elder children are arranged so as to form a shallow half-circle across the foreground. They are also arranged hierarchically in due order of precedence from the Marchese, a ceremonial disposition, but not one of rigidly stiff formality, for they are linked by gestures of natural warmth and homeliness, and the two smaller children, the dog and the dwarf mingle unconcernedly in the group. The dog appears as the Marchese's favourite pet, the dwarf as the Marchesa's, employed to amuse the court with her tricks and deformities; probably little distinction was made between the two. At a respectful pace behind, in the interstices left by the figures of the family, stand their intimate counsellors, attendants and servants.

The pier and the rich curtain beyond it mask the abrupt transition from the garden terrace on which the family are grouped to the indoor stairway leading up to the terrace. At the head of the stairway stands another middle-aged nobleman of high rank, his hands decorously composed before him and clasping white gloves. From his dress, a crimson tunic edged with blue, and his red hose, he is evidently not a member of the Gonzaga court. Blue and red were the heraldic colours of the D'Este and he is perhaps an emissary from the neighbouring court of Ferrara, with which the Mantuan court was always on close terms of friendship and alliance. His position behind the pier suggests that he waits to be introduced into Lodovico's presence, and his pose that the Gonzaga chamberlain to the other side of the pier bids him wait for a moment with his extended left arm until Lodovico has finished giving his instructions to the messenger. He cannot be a visitor or emissary of the greatest distinction, for had he been so the Marchese would have risen and come forward to the head of the stairs beyond the loggia to greet him. Thus Federico in person was sent to greet the two Milanese ambassadors at the gate of the Castello, and Lodovico himself 'came nearly to the bottom of the staircase' to meet them. Instead he is introduced by a nobleman, indicating that he is not an emissary of Pope, Emperor or King, but more the sort of ambassador who if of dignity, so the court of Milan decided in 1468, was not to be received by the Duke himself, but by two of his brothers, the council and some gentlemen, and if of less worth, by some gentlemen alone.[28]

The two oriental carpets laid on the floor, one specially for the Marchese, it should be noticed, and set transversely to the other beneath his faldstool, end just beyond this figure, at the head of the flight of steps. On the first of these stand two other richly dressed noblemen, one in brocaded cloth of gold, one in green, another Gonzaga colour, and both in Gonzaga hose. Again these are obviously intimate courtiers of the Marchese, most probably chamberlains; it may be that they portray the other two of the three noblemen who attended Lodovico at the audience of April 1470. The nearer of them lifts his hand towards another personage – probably a nobleman – clad in a green tunic and plum jerkin who mounts the steps, as if bidding him too to wait for a moment before entering the presence of the Marchese. At the foot of the stairs are a fourth courtier, in a complex pose, half frontal, half turned, and a page in a blue tunic edged with white and red. On the extreme right the curtain of cloth of gold is lifted to give a glimpse of a background of the Castello buildings and the legs of another Gonzaga servant before the closing pilaster.

There can be no doubt that the purpose of these figures on the stairs is to fill out the composition with a lively action that contributes to its vivacity of naturalism without bearing directly on what is going forward in the principal compartment. Mantegna has here used the device of filling the scene with accessory figures that he had already employed in the Ovetari fresco of *St James on the way to Execution*. It is one that can confuse the modern iconographer in his earnest search for narrative or symbolic significance in Renaissance painting, but its anecdotal licence of embellishment was to remain a constant feature of Venetian art.

The whole composition is skilfully adjusted to fit awkward features of the room, in this case the fireplace, with apparent naturalness. The flight of steps is a marvellously ingenious device to suggest that the terrace on the left where the Marchese sits, which had to be depicted above the fireplace, is on a floor above the vulgar level, on the first floor, in fact, or *piano nobile* of the Castello. As we have just seen, it corresponds to the reality of life in the Castello: Lodovico, we remember, 'came nearly to the bottom of the staircase' to meet the two Milanese ambassadors. At the same time it allowed Mantegna to bring the right half of the composition down below the level of the fireplace, the inevitable disproportion between the two compartments being partly corrected by the Marchese's oriental carpet, which falls illusionistically over the edge on the left. This solution to the compositional problem miraculously reconciles the need to lead up to the principal group on the left with an appearance of artful naturalness, while preserving as much of formality and symmetry as possible. There is a deliberate contrast between the shallow space of the left-hand compartment, where the figures fill all the space defined by the loggia wall, with its rich panelling of oval medallions and inlaid coloured marbles, and the inward curve of space in the right-hand compartment, with its suggestion of courts and corridors beyond. And there is yet another contrast between the animation of the movement on the stair and the stately decorum of posture observed among the immediate attendants on the Gonzaga.

Various interpretations have been advanced of the scene, but there can be no doubt that it portrays the everyday life that flowed through the Marchese's chamber. The letters that were continually brought to him in the Castello are mentioned in May 1478, when Lodovico took refuge at Goito from an outbreak of plague in Mantua and ordered his wife and family to leave the city as well. In reply Barbara wrote to him on 29 May: 'I remind your Lordship that since I and Federico are to go out of Mantua, someone ought to be deputed to stay here in the Castello in order to receive and forward the letters that may be brought and to make any other provision that may be necessary for the Castello.'[29] This was in distinction from some other person who ought to be deputed to stay in the Corte Nuova to look after the needs of the city. And indeed the archives of the Gonzaga still contain the innumerable letters that flowed in to Lodovico and in his absence to Barbara from the *vicari* and *castellani* of the Mantuan state and from other informants about the most various matters, disturbances on the borders, a case of abduction, the planting of almond trees, news of the passage of boats on the Po, the movements of soldiers and *banditi*, the smuggling of flour, repairs under way, taxes, dues, works in progress, permission to cut wood in the Marchese's woodlands, the regulation of the irrigation canals so important to the agriculture of the state.[30]

The arrival and despatch of messengers on the business of Mantua and its territory was an ordinary event in the Camera Picta as the Marchese sat there with his wife and family, his chamberlains and trusted officials. But in it the Marchese also received visitors of dignity and rank, expected and unexpected. A very similar scene was prescribed by Galeazzo Maria Sforza in 1469 for the decoration of a wall in the Camera Rossa of the Castello of Pavia. He gave commands that he was to be shown seated attended by his brothers and Don Cecco, who were to be shown standing, giving audience to ambassadors and 'in the act of consulting and despatching business'.[31]

The scene on the west wall is set in open countryside, and accordingly none of the female Gonzaga appears in it. Again the grouping in the principal compartment is hierarchical in that the three senior male members of the Gonzaga family are arranged in strict order of precedence in a shallow semicircle in the foreground. On the left, the post of honour, it should be recalled, because it is the dexter side in heraldry, stands Lodovico dressed in a short grey *giornea* over an arming doublet – the links of mail sewn to the shirt are carefully depicted – and a cloak, white hose and spurred shoes. At his side hang a long and a short sword with gilt handles, that of the short sword being also jewelled. He raises his right hand and speaks – his lips are shown parted – to Cardinal Francesco, giving his paternal advice or instructions about the matter contained in the letter or document that the Cardinal holds. The gesture, half one of precept, half one of counsel, is in keeping with the Marchese's speech at Bozzolo on 1 January 1462, made on meeting Francesco as a new cardinal for the first time, 'as regards the world I desire to be your father, but as regards God, your son.'[32] As the Marchese's second son, Francesco would ordinarily have ranked behind Federico, his elder brother, who stands on the right, but as a Cardinal he was a prince of the Church, the equal of all secular princes, and so is allotted a post of honour, though naturally in a family picture the invention preserves the relationship of father and son. Because of the family's pride in his exalted dignity, and perhaps too because he was not figured in the adjacent scene, he is shown in near full-face (Plate 93), while Lodovico and Federico are shown in profile, although their lofty secular rank is duly recognized by their position in the front foreground.

Francesco wears ecclesiastical dress, a red *cappa* lined with white, a white *rocchetta* and blue stole with close-fitting sleeves and a red *berretta*. Federico, in outdoor dress, has a short yellow tunic, a cloak of yellow lined with green and parti-coloured hose of red and white, the family colours, and blue and white, his own personal colours. He wears no spurs, and so like his brothers has no intention of riding. In the hollow of the semicircle are grouped three of the younger members of the family. Francesco was the administrator of the diocese of Mantua of which Lodovico was bishop-coadjutor, and for this reason he clasps the right hand of Lodovico, who wears the costume of a protonotary, as we can see on comparing his dress with that worn by Francesco Gonzaga in Mantegna's little portrait of 1460–1. Clutching Lodovico's left hand is Federico's younger son Sigismondo. Probably he is shown so because already the family designed him for the career in the church in which he was to follow his two uncles, becoming first a protonotary and then in 1505 a cardinal. Federico's elder son Gianfrancesco, as the eventual heir of his father and grandfather, is placed beside Lodovico. Sigismondo wears white, Gianfrancesco green and white and a grey cloak. Both have parti-coloured hose like those of their father.

Once more a suite of courtiers and retainers of the family is arranged in the middle ground behind them, in the intervals left by their figures. Those on the left are shown in profile, those on the right are turned to right or left in poses that further the illusion that what we see through the piers is a continuous field of space. At the same time some indications are given as to which of the three Gonzaga princes each has particular allegiance. The livery colours of blue, white, red and yellow of the dress worn by the man standing in right profile immediately to Federico's left indicate that he belongs to Federico's household: the composition, which sets him behind and out of the semicircle formed in the foreground by the Gonzaga princes, makes it clear that he does not belong to the family. The youth in right profile a little to the fore of Lodovico is another prominent portrait, evidently of a personage of noble birth. From the green colour of their hats the two men behind him are, as we shall see, grooms of the Marchese. Behind these figures, formally posed and clearly portrayed, is a line of others of whom we see only the hats and hair: they are introduced to swell and animate the retinue. The solemn gravity of the scene is enlivened by a small white dog, who lifts a front paw impatiently behind Lodovico's legs.

About the identity of two personages in the back row new evidence has recently come to light. The custom in such frescoes of the prince was to represent him with his friends and allies as well as his courtiers,[33] and Lodovico chose to have his suzerain the Emperor Frederick III and his most exalted relation, Christian I, King of Denmark, who had married his sister-in-law Dorotea of Brandenburg, portrayed in this scene. Frederick never visited Mantua, but on his return from his second journey to Rome, while he was sojourning in Ferrara, a company of princes and dignitaries of the Gonzaga court, including Rodolfo Gonzaga and Francesco, arrived there on 28 January 1469 in order to obtain the honour of knighthood from the Emperor in person.[34] Mantegna himself is known to have gone with the company, for in a letter from Ferrara of 2 February Marsilio Andreasi reported to the Marchesa Barbara that 'Andrea Mantegna says that he too had himself made a count and hopes to get the privilege.'[35] Frederick was a lavish dispenser of such honours, for the privileges which embodied them in legal form were a lucrative fount of revenues. In fact many of those who obtained honours at Ferrara were unable to afford the exorbitant fees which the Imperial chancery demanded for making out their privileges and Andrea in all probability made one of this disappointed majority. It is not known if he went especially to take the Emperor's portrait, but it is very likely that he did so, for late in March or early in April 1469 the Marchese Lodovico sent Galeazzo Maria Sforza a portrait of the Emperor which it seems Galeazzo then wished to keep, so that Lodovico was obliged to ask for the return of it for a few days so as to have a copy made.[36]

The portrait of Christian (1426–81) must have been taken much later, on the occasion of his visits to Mantua during the pilgrimage he made to Rome in 1474. Christian reached Mantua on 22 March and stayed there until the 24th. The chronicler Andrea Schivenoglia has left us an impression of his aspect: 'a man of fifty-six years, tall, stout, with a lordly air, dressed in black and so were all his train'.[37] The black dress, of course, was the sober dress of a pilgrim: when he reached Bologna, however, he is said to have been wearing a red *berretta*, not the black hat which was its proper complement. Christian came back to Mantua on his way home to Denmark, and stayed there from 10 to 16 May. Other Italians who saw him during his pilgrimage describe him as being tall, full in the face, with hair that was red and turning white. We know that both King and Emperor were included among the personages portrayed in the Camera from an exchange of letters in 1475 between Lodovico and his ambassador in Milan. They are self-evidently not portrayed in the fireplace fresco, and the problem remains of identifying them in the outdoor scene.

This is no easy task, for the two have been introduced without any of the insignia appropriate to their rank and like the portraits of friends Mantegna painted in the St Christopher frescoes have plainly been blended into the scene as actors or spectators. Accordingly they can only be tentatively identified by comparison with other portraits. Signorini regards the man in a tunic of yellow and blue standing to the left of Federico as the Emperor. He is the only figure shown with a protruding Hapsburg lip, but on the other hand he wears a livery, and is too young to represent an Emperor who was already 54 when Mantegna saw him in 1469. But the difficulty of reaching a firm conclusion from such arguments and from the evidence of other portraits appears when we consider the question of the colour of the Emperor's hair. In an anonymous Italian portrait of *c.*1452 in the Uffizi this is correctly shown as a very fair yellow, but in a second portrait of Frederick as Archduke of Styria in the Joanneum, Graz, his hair is shown as dark brown, which is the colour of the hair of the figure Signorini identifies as the Emperor.[38]

On grounds of age, dignity and costume the only figure who might seem qualified to be Frederick is the stately figure in red gown and *berretta capitanesca* who stands behind Federico and the man in yellow and blue. This figure Signorini would like to identify as Christian, but Christian could be the tall man dressed in black, with reddish hair, who appears between the two groups. This figure has the long hair Christian wears in the commemorative medal made by Bartolommeo Melioli, the Gonzaga court medallist, in 1474 to commemorate the King's visit, while the figure in a red gown has short hair, like Lodovico. Signorini has also found evidence that when Christian came to Mantua he was in all probability wearing a long beard. Since no bearded figure appears in the fresco his likeness must have been taken by Mantegna during his stay in Mantua on his journey home, by which time Christian, having completed his pilgrimage, had presumably shaved his beard, and indeed he is shown without one in Melioli's medal.[39] But the convention of disguise by which the two portraits have been introduced as part of the scene makes it impossible to attain conviction about any of these identifications.

Galeazzo Maria Sforza had the lowest opinion of both King and Emperor, and in November 1475 treated Lodovico's ambassador Zaccaria Saggi to a long lecture on the failings of the King, who had tried to borrow the huge sum of 100,000 Rhenish florins from him and then accepted a gift of 4000 ducats. The lecture wound up with the tart observation that 'Your Lordship, in memory of two of the worst men in the world, has had the Emperor's Majesty and that of the aforesaid King portrayed in your *camera*!' Zaccaria understood that Galeazzo, who regularly hired Lodovico's services as a *condottiere* and was besides a friend and ally, was piqued because Lodovico, 'having had made such a beautiful *camera* as that, of which everyone here is talking and all who have seen it without exception say it is the most beautiful *camera* in the world, yet Your Lordship has not had His Excellency portrayed in it, and something has been muttered to me about it on the side.' Three days later, on 30 November, Lodovico replied that the Emperor was his suzerain and the King his brother-in-law, and they had been seen by so many persons it would be shaming to remove them: let them be what they may, they gave no trouble to anyone by staying on the wall. Then he went on to say that he had thought of allotting the post of honour in the fresco to Galeazzo, but that when Mantegna had drawn his portrait before, the Duke had been very dissatisfied and had had the sheets on which it was drawn burnt. And Lodovico added: 'It is true that Andrea is a good master in everything else, but in making portraits he could have more grace and he does not do so well.' Accordingly Lodovico had refrained from having Galeazzo portrayed by Mantegna, not wishing to annoy him by a portrait he might dislike. The Duke's distaste for a style of portraiture that was too direct and severely naturalistic, not graceful and complimentary, was to be shared in later years by Mantegna's future patron, Isabella d'Este.[40]

The pose of the two grooms behind Lodovico is repeated in that of the men who stand to the left of the doorway in the second compartment, one in a red tunic and green doublet holding a letter and waiting to give it to the Marchese, the other in green tunic and doublet with letters stuck in his red hat. Beside them are three bloodhounds, whose leash is held by a man hidden by the pier. This is a device, like the pose of the two men, to give continuity to the scene, interrupted as it is in this compartment by the doorway. Again Mantegna has neatly turned to good use the awkwardness presented by an architectural feature of the room, for above the doorway he has simulated a painted lintel on which stand

winged putti supporting with the assistance of others from the air the gilded tablet that bears his dedicatory inscription. In the last compartment a man wearing a green tunic edged with white, a white shirt and red hose, all Gonzaga colours, holds on a leash with both hands a brace of powerful hunting-dogs, in all likelihood boar-hounds. These, like all the other dogs, are probably portraits of real dogs belonging to Lodovico.

We know that Lodovico was passionately fond of his dogs and a keen appreciator of their points. Thus in September 1458 he ordered Giacomo Bellanti, a miniature painter in his service, to make a drawing of one of his two favourite mastiffs (*alani*) for use as a design for wall-hangings. Bellanti was to draw the dog 'from the life in its true proportion and measure', and Lodovico suggested he should take as his model the smaller of the two, 'which to us seems handsome, and has a good head and is in better condition than the bigger one.'[41] Another man stands behind the hounds, his left arm akimbo, gazing impatiently towards the princely group in the direction indicated by a pointing hand just visible on the left of the fresco, all that now remains of a figure which once stood there. He wears particoloured hose of green and white, as do two other men, presumably grooms, whose heads and bodies are hidden by the stately white horse which paws the ground impatiently with its left leg. The gazing man wears a belt studded with Lodovico's personal *impresa* of a radiant sun — that same device, it will be remembered, which he granted Mantegna in chief when giving him a coat of arms in January 1460. The lappets of the horse's saddle and its trappings are splendidly ornamented with pendants in gilt metal bearing the same device, indicating that he is Lodovico's own steed. Horse and dogs are rendered with masterly observation and draughtsmanship and a true feeling for animal strength and beauty expressed in smoothly massive volumetric forms. The left side of the compartment is now missing but fragments remaining show that it was originally framed by a pilaster.

Here then we have Lodovico's horse and dogs. But this train of attendants and animals does not figure a hunt or even the return from a hunt, as so often believed. Lodovico has no companions in riding, and none of the men carries hunting-spears, as do the huntsmen in Uccello's famous *Hunt by Night* (Oxford) who are otherwise dressed very similarly to the Marchese's attendants. Then too the saddle on the horse is not a light hunting-saddle, like those in the Uccello hunt, but a heavy riding or war-saddle. Lodovico is indeed known to have delighted like all fifteenth-century princes and noblemen of a knightly persuasion in the chase, which was considered the proper sport of nobility, training and maintaining the mind and body in the valour and endurance so necessary in war.[42] Here, however, we merely see him in riding dress with a train of attendants, accompanied by his dogs in case any game is started or to give them a run. Yet quite probably the mastiffs and hounds are not portrayed as they were used in reality – the mastiffs are for hunting boars, the greyhounds for hunting animals like deer – so that here too we may well be confronted by an ideal portrait grouping retainers, serving men and beasts together solely because they are Lodovico's favourites.

Some scholars, among them Signorini, link this fresco with a known historical occasion, the encounter between Lodovico and Francesco at Bozzolo on 1 January 1462. Schivenoglia tells us that on 27 December 1461, when news was brought to Mantua that Francesco had been made a cardinal, there was great rejoicing and his brother Federico at once took horse to go to Pavia, where Francesco was studying, in order to congratulate him. Together the two of them rode off to Milan to thank Francesco Sforza, who had played a great part in securing Francesco's promotion. Sforza, though seriously ill, welcomed them heartily and immediately sent for the Marchese Lodovico to come and join them. The courier covered the distance between Milan and Mantua in only nineteen hours, and Lodovico set off at once and on his way encountered the Cardinal coming on to Mantua at Bozzolo. To show his respect for Francesco's new dignity, Lodovico dismounted a bow-shot away from his son, and the Cardinal did likewise, and then they both advanced to meet each other on foot. On drawing close, each did the other 'great reverence', and the Marchese spoke to the Cardinal the words we have already quoted. Then they separated, and the Marchese continued on his way to Milan.[43]

Signorini believes that the scene on the opposite wall represents the arrival of the news in Mantua, so linking the entire programme of the two walls with Francesco's promotion. In favour of this interpretation it can be argued that the Marchese is shown dressed for riding and that his horse and attendants are grouped behind. He and the Cardinal, moreover, are certainly the principal figures in the outdoor scene, and are shown in discourse together. And as we have seen, at one moment Lodovico had intended to give Galeazzo Maria the post of honour, and this could fairly be interpreted as a wish to recognize the important role the Sforza had played in securing a cardinal's hat for Francesco.

There are, however, serious difficulties in the way of accepting the outdoor scene as a portrayal of the encounter at Bozzolo. In the first place, there is nothing in either of the two scenes to suggest an atmosphere of special jubilation, even when due allowance is made for courtly decorum. Although too much stress should not be laid on the anachronistic presence in the outdoor scene of younger members of the Gonzaga family who were not yet born in 1462 – anachronism was not so disturbing to the quattrocento as to us – yet their presence is disconcerting when we see that the Cardinal himself is not attired for riding, as he was at Bozzolo, but forms a natural group with his brothers. It is by no means clear why the Marchese, if riding post-haste towards Milan, should be accompanied by a train of dogs, one of them a small domestic pet, not a hunting-dog. More important still, has he dismounted from the horse or is he about to mount it, and go for a ride with his dogs? Since the little dog and the horse are both shown pawing the ground impatiently behind him, it would seem that he is about to go for a ride, rather than just returning from one. And this seems to be confirmed by the men waiting with the letters – a motif quite out of keeping with the thesis that Lodovico is interrupting his ride at Bozzolo on unexpectedly encountering his son. Surely they are waiting for the Marchese to turn round and read the letters and despatch the business in them before going off on his ride.

All these difficulties disappear if the scene is treated as an ideal composition, which figures the Marchese with the heirs to his secular dignities, Federico and Gianfrancesco, and with the son to whose exalted dignity in the church he hoped his son Lodovico and his grandson Sigismondo would in turn succeed. Indeed this is surely the most plausible explanation of why Lodovico is the only son of the family to appear in both frescoes. The emphasis in both scenes is on the Marchese attended by his family, and family relationships, achievements, and hopes are surely what is portrayed in them, with a little action to animate what would otherwise be statuesque groups.

The likeliest interpretation of the outdoor scene is that Lodovico is giving his counsel about some affair to his Cardinal son before setting off for a ride on which he is going alone, for only he wears spurs. In fact, the two scenes are family portraits of the sort later to be known as family or conversation pieces in eighteenth-century England, and no more than with these group portraits is it justifiable to imagine that the figures portrayed in them were once all gathered together on some actual occasion precisely as depicted. Rather Mantegna's task was to invent scenes that showed them grouped in relationships corresponding to reality, even though not figuring it literally, and engaged according to themes given him by his patron Lodovico. Above all else we must not assume that the Gonzaga posed for him in groups as for a photographer. The presence of the Emperor and of the King of Denmark in the outdoor scene stamps it at once as an ideal scene, not as a reproduction of some historical encounter. And if this is doubted we should remember that Lodovico had thought of giving Galeazzo Maria Sforza 'the worthiest place' in it. As regards the other scene, it is equally improbable that the Gonzaga were all once gathered together sitting informally at ease on a terrace. The two settings share the same duality of fiction and truth idealized.

Lodovico's life in the frescoes is one of constant preoccupation, and the same message is delivered by the mythological subjects figured in the spandrels of the ceiling. Half of them represent episodes in the life of Hercules (Plates 63–68), including three of his Labours, emblems in the Renaissance of the struggles that the virtuous man must undergo to vanquish life's difficulties. Hercules clearly had a special significance for Lodovico, perhaps because his tutor Vittorino had given him the name Ercole as a boy. One of the chambers at Cavriana painted by Samuele da Tradate in the early 1460s was called the chamber of Hercules, evidently from the scenes represented in it.[44] Probably Lodovico chose him as a symbol of his active life for much the same reasons as the Bolognese humanist Giovanni Sabadino degli Arienti gave in the 1490s for the hero's appearance in frescoes commissioned by Duke Ercole d'Este to decorate his country palace of Belriguardo. Two ways, he explains, were proposed to Hercules as a young man – the allusion is to the famous myth of the Choice of Hercules. 'Through prudence he left the way of pleasure and chose that of difficulty and labour, as is right and proper for valiant youth, for rest and quiet are right and proper only for old age. By this the Hercules of antiquity won for himself felicity and very great glory.'[45]

In the other spandrels Arion and Orpheus figure the power of music to soften life's asperities and charm away its cares (Plates 69–74). Music, as we already know, had been a favourite art of Vittorino. In 1433 Ambrogio Traversari found two ancient works on music in Vittorino's library at Mantua, and later Sassolo da Prato, one of his masters, defended Vittorino's love of music and the instruction he gave in it to his pupils, calling it an art given by the gods to be 'the guardian and guide of men's mind'. In a short didactic poem on the education of children Gregorio Correr, Vittorino's pupil and Mantegna's patron, writes:

> While Greece, the great nurse of studies, flourished, the sound of strings and the song of voices were richly rewarded and in great esteem. Thus honour accrued to divine poets, and Amphion was believed to move rocks and Orpheus to soften fierce lions with the lyre. Do we not see how men soothe their long labours

with song, whether ditchers or harvesters of the grape? Fierce Aeacides too touched the strings of the lyre in Chiron's cave and struck the air with his rude voice, laughing at the tail of his centaur tutor. Music then is not to be despised . . .[46]

All this symbolism is lightly adumbrated, hinting at Lodovico's own moral consciousness of the nature and purpose of his life rather than transposing it into a heavily allegorical mode. The figure of Hercules recurs in the mountainous landscape setting in the outdoor fresco where a marble statue of him stands on a great circular pedestal. Again the motif is discreetly subordinated, but it confirms that in Hercules Lodovico saw a figure emblematical of his own life. The first eight Caesars are represented on the ceiling for a different reason: they appear as the founders of the Empire and so as the ultimate source of the Marchese's right to rule the Imperial fief of Mantua. The devices of the Gonzaga in their turn complement the large family coat of arms as granted by the Emperor Sigismund in 1433 to Lodovico's father Gianfrancesco which is painted over the south doorway. Together they blazon in the symbolic languages of chivalry the heraldic achievements of the house and its fortunes, aspirations and resolves, both those hereditary to it and those personal to Lodovico. Such a use of devices and heraldry was a commonplace of decoration in princely and noble palaces.

The landscape of the outdoor fresco and the buildings scattered over it fuse a love of romantic scenery and an equally romantic love of the antique with allusions to Lodovico's tireless activities as a builder. Nothing could be more unlike the flat marshy plains that surround Mantua than the towering precipices, pierced by a great natural arch, that fill the left half of the painting, rising into rocky summits crowned with castles and fortresses, or than the smoother slopes of the right half of the composition. This is one of Mantegna's few landscapes, it should be noted in passing, to make use of aerial perspective: the prospect ends in a blue distance of hills and a town. The conservatism of Mantegna's approach to landscape and his conception of it as an artificially picturesque setting, to be opened or closed before the eye by surprising natural forms, appears in the arch of rock and its prospect of a swell of ground and a city-crowned hill beyond. Some twenty-five years later these devices reappear in the *Parnassus* painted for the Studiolo of Isabella d'Este.

On the right is a great walled city, whose houses and palaces are in the style of architecture that we call medieval and that Mantegna uses to figure the everyday townscape of his own times. But in addition the city has an antique gateway surmounted by a medieval gate-tower, an antique amphitheatre just within the gateway, and an antique pyramid, modelled on some drawing of the Pyramid of Cestius in Rome, and scattered ruins of antiquity just without it. This city most probably symbolizes Mantua, for on the gate-tower is a panel blazoned with the Gonzaga arms. A panel with the same arms is set on the gateway to the village below the city walls where the statue of Hercules stands as the cornerstone of a wall enclosing a great palace being erected in antique style. The two poles of washing sticking out from the same gateway indicate that even in such dignified compositions Mantegna still prized small touches of homely naturalism. Along the steep road cut in the precipitous rocks directly above Lodovico's head, tunnelled through them and bridging the chasm below the gateway, little figures of masons bring up stones for the palace.

In all probability the aspect and situation Mantegna has given to his city are simply romantic licences, taken so that it may form part of a picturesque prospect of hills, rocks and mountains, whose abrupt summits and sheer rock faces, relieved by some fertile slopes and by the orchard of trees, were certainly pleasing in their fantastic variety and union of the associations of wildness and cultivation to a fifteenth-century eye.

A curious exotic motif is provided in the left compartment by the line of three men riding camels, with four attendants on foot, that descends the slope under the arch of rock (see Plate 89). Their presence warns us against too literal an interpretation of the setting as the figuration of an actual scene: rather they are a signal that in devising it Mantegna's principal guide was his *fantasia*. Once again, then, his aim is to charm the eye; neither he nor his patron seems to have sought for more than the lightest symbolic allusions. Thus the vestiges of antiquity, and especially the classical gateway crowned by a medieval tower, perhaps recall the Roman origins of Mantua through a choice of monuments inspired in part by the surviving Roman gateway and amphitheatre of neighbouring Verona. Mantegna shows one country palace and one fortress (*rocca*) as under construction. These could figure the country residences finished for Lodovico in the 1460s, such as Goito or Cavriana, in whose decoration Mantegna was closely involved in 1463 and 1464.[47] Alternatively, the palace may be that within the Rocca of Gonzaga on which work had recently begun in 1468, and was still in progress when the scene was painted. But it is always possible that the country palace and fortress simply figure the nature of Lodovico's building enterprises in general.

The themes of the Camera Picta were certainly given to Mantegna, at least in their general nature, by Lodovico, who also chose the personages who were to be portrayed. For the mythological subjects he may have sought the counsel of his court humanists. We can imagine what the specifications he gave Mantegna were like from the sets of written instructions given by Duke Galeazzo Maria Sforza of Milan for the decoration of rooms in the Castello at Pavia in 1471 and the Castello of Milan in 1472, which still survive.[48] They specify the subject-matter, whether hunt or portrait-group, the figures who were to be portrayed, and in certain cases give indications of attributes, pose and motif. Thus in the hunting fresco in the great *sala* of Milan a certain Alexio was to be shown knocked off his horse by a stag and with his legs in the air, while the Duke was to be on horseback with sword in hand and about to strike a stag. At Pavia even the colours of the purely decorative work were carefully specified for each room: some were to be painted in white and murrey, one was to be 'all gilded', while others were to be green.

From these specifications for the two great Sforza castles and from what we know of the secular decorations in the Este palaces at Ferrara it is plain that the subjects of the two main scenes of the Camera Picta derived from well-established traditions.[49] Group portraits of the princely family and of their friends, courtiers, officials and servants were common, at any rate in the second half of the fifteenth century. In 1472 Galeazzo Maria Sforza ordered a *saletta* in the Castello of Milan to be painted with a complete dynastic family piece. It was to show his great-grandfather Duke Giovanni Galeazzo Visconti and his wife Caterina, and their son Duke Filippo Maria, attended by their servitors. Filippo was to stand with his hands resting on the shoulders of two of his chamberlains, a gesture of affection that recurs in Gianfrancesco Gonzaga's pose in the fireplace scene in the Camera Picta, and around him were to be 'likewise some of those dearest to him'. Beside these portraits the scene was to include Galeazzo Maria's father, Francesco Sforza, and his wife Bianca, the daughter of Duke Filippo, together with portraits of some of their councillors and chamberlains, whose names were specified. Finally Galeazzo Maria himself was to be figured, holding his little son Giovanni Galeazzo by the hand, together with his duchess, the Marchese Lodovico Gonzaga and other princes and lords who were friends and allies of Galeazzo, and members of the family and the court, including the sword-bearer. The regard paid to hierarchy in the composition of such paintings appears in another instruction for the same fresco, which orders that the Marquis of Montferrat is to be included as well as Lodovico: 'both on a par, in such form and attitude that it cannot be understood that one of them is superior to the other or greater.' The expense of this fresco was estimated at the great sum of 1000 ducats, while the hunting fresco in the Sala Grande was estimated at 2300 ducats, more than twice as much.[50]

Similar group portraits were painted in the palaces of Ferrara. The scene at Schifanoia of Duke Borso surrounded by his courtiers giving money to his court-fool Scocola is the only one that survives, but there are descriptions of many others. In Belriguardo Ercole d'Este, so Sabadino degli Arienti reports, was figured in a *salotto* 'breathing and lively as life, with all his courtiers whom I recognized by their portraits and their names.' He was portrayed again in a *camera* on horseback, attended by his brothers, by prominent courtiers and his court physician, and in another *camera* wearing a knight's collar and the order of the Garter, and attended by others of his courtiers who were knights.[51] Given the terms of the dedicatory inscription of the Camera Picta, some motifs were probably introduced into it by Mantegna himself in compliment to his patrons, but these are now impossible to detect.

One of the worst difficulties Mantegna had to encounter in designing his scenes must have been that of obtaining sittings for the individual portraits that were to be included in them. In some cases, like that of the Emperor Frederick, he may have used existing small portraits, but in others if his experience was at all like that of other painters then and in later centuries, he will have found this a task calling for all his tact and patience. The poses of a number of the figures, for instance those of the youth before the pier and the dwarf in the indoor fresco, indicate that they have been transferred to the wall more or less directly from single portrait sketches. These were surely made from formal sittings, at least for the head. That Mantegna could also sketch portraits from observation without a formal sitting we know from his letter of 14 June 1489 written from Rome to Lodovico's grandson, the Marchese Francesco. In this he describes how he is watching for an opportunity to memorize the features of the captive Turkish prince Djem in order to make a drawing of him.[52] In 1502 moreover the physician Camillo Leonardo declares that Mantegna 'can seize a pen or piece of charcoal and figure in the twinkling of an eye the image and portraiture of the various ages of man and of different animals, and the dresses, manners and gestures of different nations, so that they almost seem to move.'[53]

The impression of single portrait studies grouped together is perhaps inherent in the genre of the group portrait. So much said, we can only admire the skill with which Mantegna has achieved unity among his two groups while preserving for each sitter a strong and individual presence. To some extent this is achieved by his portrait style. Rarely has the human head been treated in painting with so solid a sense of pure volume. The features are pronounced as in a Roman bust on a ground of a few strongly defined planes, while the characteristics proper to each age and character are represented either with naturalistic fidelity, as in the seams and wrinkles of the middle-aged messenger's face and the red rims of the old duenna's eyelids, or with a tactful adjustment to the demands of ideal beauty, as in the smooth cheeks, golden hair and carmine lips of Barbara, or the flowing golden locks of the youth before the pier. We know that the Gonzaga suffered from physical deformities: Lodovico was small and hump-backed, and by 1462 Federico was also a hunchback. It is sometimes said that Mantegna has represented these defects unsparingly: in fact, they are concealed as tactfully as truth of likeness allowed. As against this he has caught family resemblances to admiration.

The skill with which costume and accessories are rendered is evident despite all the damage and restoration the Camera has suffered. Especially admirable in the terrace scene is the mastery with which the cloth of gold is subdued by the reds and blacks of its brocaded patterns and by a constant counter-change with strong pinks and reds and whites, so that its splendour never becomes a monotonous glow. The sense of dignity impressed on the spectator by the costume of the Gonzaga and their courtiers is strengthened by the impassivity of the single figures. That this impassivity was deliberate, and not the result of any limitations of Mantegna's portrait style, appears from the extreme skill with which he renders the deferential attention of the humble messenger as he prepares to receive Lodovico's commands. Its courtly reserve was in keeping with the ideal propriety of deportment that he has given to his princely and noble sitters in whom the expression of vulgar emotion or curiosity would have been a derogation from their high rank.

Naïveté of feeling is found in the frescoes, but only in the impatience of the plebeian attendant waiting for Lodovico and in the Moorish slave and waiting-women of the oculus. Mantegna, for all that his principal sitters are linked by family ties or ties of service, does not establish complete communication among them, and this is another secret of their strength of individuality. Courtly propriety and Mantegna's own art combine to produce the calm of those antique reliefs in which there is no haste or abruptness of action or feeling. Yet the complete aloofness that would deprive his compositions of all animation is also avoided. Thus Barbara and Rodolfo turn their heads to watch Lodovico and the messenger, but without betraying any undignified interest. Once again then Mantegna has solved the problem of reconciling his conception of the painted figure as having the rounded volume and the self-containment of a statue with the demands of naturalism and of human warmth.

Mantegna's evident need to assemble portrait-studies of his sitters raises the problem of the chronology of the Camera, no simple question in spite of recent important discoveries. It is now known that the first mention of it occurs on 26 April 1465, when Lodovico ordered two cartloads of lime for plastering its walls. The date 16 July 1465 is painted in the window of the north wall: in Latin and in a humanist hand, this is almost certainly Mantegna's own record of the date of inception of his work. After no more than a year that work was interrupted by his journey to Florence. Mantegna's activities during 1467 are not known, but he was certainly in Mantua in the summer of 1468, for in June or July of that year he had already begun his picture of *The Descent into Limbo* for the Marchese. Moreover he was certainly at work on the Camera, for on 10 July Lodovico ordered linseed oil for Mantegna to mix with the colours he was using to paint it. The work was delayed, according to Lodovico, by Mantegna's dilatoriness, but if there was some justification for his patron's impatience, no doubt Mantegna felt equally impatient at the constant interruption of a major task by continual demands for portraits, designs and other pictures made of him as their court painter by the Gonzaga. We now know, however, that the compartments with portraits were under way by 10 April 1470, for the two Milanese ambassadors specifically say that Lodovico showed them 'a chamber he is having painted, in which his Lordship, the lady Barbara his consort, Messer Federico and all his other sons and daughters are portrayed after the life.'

In May and June 1470 Mantegna obtained leave of absence to go to Padua in order to see about his affairs. His presence there is recorded in a document of 3 June in which his niece's husband Giovanni Francesco da Rimini acknowledges himself debtor to Mantegna for the sum of thirty ducats, partly due for his ten years' lease of Mantegna's house, which had terminated that Easter, and partly for money he had collected from the now deceased Squarcione on Mantegna's behalf.[54] On 22 October 1470 we find Lodovico regretting that he cannot allow Mantegna to paint a Crucifixion for Alessandro Sforza (1409–73), lord of Pesaro, because 'it is years now since he began painting our Camera and the half of it is not yet finished.' Any interruption, complained the Marchese, gives him an excuse for prolonging the work: indeed Lodovico never expects to see it finished. If this letter is taken literally, it would seem that by October 1470 Mantegna had completed only the ceiling of the Camera. To begin with the ceiling would have been the natural order of work, and indeed it was only after finishing the ceiling of the *camera* at Cavriana that Samuele da Tradate asked for Mantegna's designs for its walls. Yet, in spite of

these complaints, Lodovico again interrupted Mantegna's work on the Camera in the following year, in order to have him at Gonzaga, where the Marchese was hastening on the completion of his new buildings and their decorations. He was certainly at Gonzaga in June, and probably a number of times before and after.[55]

If the Marchese's letter of July 1469 asking Mantegna to draw two '*galine de India*' refers to peacocks, it implies that Mantegna had not yet seen and drawn these birds, and so the fresco of the oculus must have been designed and begun after this date, since it includes a peacock. Presumably Mantegna had occupied himself before with the decoration of the rest of the ceiling. It may be in fact that Mantegna first drew the scenes on the walls of the Camera, before colouring them in. This would explain why it was possible for the Milanese ambassadors to see the portraits of all his sons and daughters in 1470, even though the outdoor scene was certainly not completed until 1474. We know that this was the method of working in the decoration of rooms practised by Francesco, Mantegna's son, for in letters of 1494 we are told that he had drawn the decorations of the Camera del Mappamondo on the walls in charcoal 'but as yet they have received no colouring.' Such a method would also explain why Lodovico and Mantegna were able to alter the figures, as we know they did, or introduce new ones.[56] The internal evidence of the two scenes on the walls does not conflict with this interpretation. In both scenes the younger Lodovico wears the dress of a prelate, but on the fireplace wall he is still only a boy, whereas in the outdoor scene he is in early youth. The inference must be that the fresco on the fireplace wall was completed before that on the west wall, and at an interval of some years. As Lodovico only became a Protonotary Apostolic and Bishop Elect of Mantua on 5 February 1468, the fireplace wall was clearly not finished until after that date. Other relevant dates emerge from what we know of the movements of some of the other sitters. Rodolfo Gonzaga, who had received the honour of knighthood from the Emperor Frederick III at Ferrara on 22 February 1469, left Mantua on 13 July of the same year to complete his chivalric education at the court of Burgundy and was still there early in 1470.[57] Since both he and Gianfrancesco are represented in the fresco, it must have been painted while they were in Mantua, and the most probable date for it is therefore 1469. What Mantegna had already done in the Camera by August 1471 was enough to make Zanetto Bugatti, the court painter of Galeazzo Sforza, who had accompanied the Duke on a visit that month to Gonzaga, anxious to come in to Mantua to see 'those things of yours', so Lodovico wrote to Andrea.[58]

The dating of the other fresco depends on the ages and movements of the Gonzaga who are represented in it. The little Francesco was born in 1466: it is difficult to be certain of his age in the fresco, but as his even smaller brother Sigismondo was only born in 1469, and is about three years of age, he must be about six. However, the real limits within which the fresco was painted are fixed by the movements of Cardinal Francesco Gonzaga. After he was made a cardinal in December 1461, he resided at the Roman Curia, as was expected of all cardinals unless delegated to missions or offices elsewhere, and visited his family in Mantua only at infrequent intervals. The dates of these visits are known, and from them it would appear that Mantegna's first opportunity of taking his portrait fell in the summer of 1472. In July of that year Francesco journeyed northwards to take up residence as Papal Legate of Bologna, to which great office he had been appointed the year before. On 18 July he wrote from Foligno to his father, advising Lodovico that he expected to reach Bologna on 5 or 6 August, but would only stay there for two days, and then to go on to the baths at Porretta. In order to have some entertainment that would keep him awake while at the baths, he asked his father to send him Mantegna and the musician Malagise. 'With Andrea I shall take pleasure in showing him my cameos and my figures of bronze and other fine antique things, and we will study and discuss them in company with one another.' One of the gems Mantegna was being summoned to see was perhaps the Felix Gem, now in the Ashmolean Museum, which belonged, it has recently been shown, to Cardinal Francesco Gonzaga. Afterwards the Cardinal would return to Bologna for eight or ten days, and then come on to Mantua. Lodovico at once granted these requests, and on 27 July summoned Andrea to Gonzaga, where he was then entertaining Galeazzo Maria Sforza, to tell him what he was to do during his excursion to Porretta to amuse the Cardinal.[59]

In the Cardinal's train were Leone Battista Alberti, Angelo Poliziano and Pico della Mirandola, and some scholars have been rashly tempted to find their portraits among the figures attendant on the Gonzaga. In August Francesco left Bologna and on the 22nd was met by his father at Sichia and escorted to Gonzaga. On 24 August he entered Mantua in state and remained there for almost two months, leaving for Bologna on 12 October. Mantegna decided to entertain both him and his suite to an open-air dinner outside the bastion, and on 21 September appealed to Lodovico to order quails and pheasants to be caught by his falconers for the feast so that it might do Mantegna honour. Twenty quails were hunted down at once and handed over to him. Francesco came again to Mantua from 9 to 23 May 1473 to convalesce in his native air, and 'passed every day in pleasure and rejoicing', and again from 26 June for some days, but the sojourn at Porretta followed by the long residence in Mantua of 1472 seems the likelier occasion for Mantegna to have drawn his portrait from the life.[60] Accordingly the most plausible date for the inception of the fresco is after the summer of 1472 or that of 1473. The portrait of King Christian cannot have been added before May 1474 and the scene as we have it can only have been completed in that year, though there is always the possibility that other heads were scraped out to include those of the King and Emperor. The especial friendship and attachment that Mantegna felt for Francesco are reflected in the inscription *Andrea me pinxit* which appears on the document that the Cardinal holds.

The dedicatory inscription declares that the work of painting was finished in 1474, and this is also known from documents. In March 1474 Lodovico was writing to Venice for azurite and beaten gold in order to hasten its completion, for he was anxious to show off the Camera to King Christian, whose arrival on his way to Rome was now imminent. We do not know if Andrea had largely ended his work by early May when Christian came back to Mantua, especially as the portrait of Christian was plainly added after that date: perhaps too that of the Emperor. If Christian's portrait signified family pride and Frederick's feudal allegiance, both were also tokens of those ties with the world of Northern princedom that the Gonzaga so eagerly maintained. Our last documents concerning the Camera date from June 1474, when Lodovico was giving instructions to Luca Fancelli about the pavement that was to go under the settle in the Camera, and from August that same year, when on his return from a pilgrimage to Loreto he gave yet further instructions about the stone corbels, which still had to be installed.

From the first the Gonzaga recognized that the Camera was an exceptional achievement. This was acknowledged by all Lombardy. We have already heard of the admiration of the Court of Milan: in 1486 the chronicler Antonio Crema speaks of 'the archetypal Camera of the Castello of Mantua, painted by Messer Andrea Mantinea, the first man in all the whole machine of the world for drawings or paintings'.[61] It was shown to all visitors of rank or importance and as late as the autumn of 1506, when Pope Julius II seemed about to come on a visit to Mantua, Isabella d'Este busied herself with having it repaired so that it should be fit for his reception. In the same year she hung up in it a *St Sebastian* painted by Pietro del Fajna, to invoke the saint's protection against the plague then raging in Mantua. Such details of its history confirm that it long continued in use as a great state-chamber and intimate family-chamber,[62] and was long held in reverence as a masterwork of Mantegna's art.

We have seen that the Camera Picta is merely the supreme representative of a well-established genre. Yet this should not blind us to the mastery with which Mantegna attempted and solved the problems of the family picture – the need to create a linking action while maintaining naturalness of effect, the need to subordinate some figures to others without depriving them of all interest, the need to reconcile fidelity of portraiture with tact, the need to represent the hierarchy of external and internal rank without sacrificing all domestic feeling. The importance of the ceiling fresco as the progenitor of a peculiarly Italian technique, *di sotto in sù* perspective, and of a peculiarly Italian genre, the ceiling treated as a dome of sky, has long been recognized. Its winged putti, its clouds, its gaiety of theme were to inspire Correggio and through Correggio exercise a shaping influence on Baroque and Rococo ceiling decoration in Italy and beyond the Alps.

Fig. 7. Fig tree and sculptured foot. Detail from *St Sebastian* (Plate XI)

VII

Mantegna in Mantua

THERE is only one surviving large picture by Mantegna part of whose execution can safely be attributed to assistants, almost certainly because it was painted in 1469, when Mantegna was busy with the Camera Picta. This is the huge altarpiece representing San Bernardino (Plate 96), painted for his chapel in the conventual church of San Francesco. The chapel had been dedicated to the saint, with whom in his life the Gonzaga had had close spiritual ties, by the Marchese Lodovico, and it was to be his burying-place. The walls had already been frescoed in a late Gothic style with four scenes from the life of another saint,[1] and the altarpiece signalized its rededication. Another reason for the use of assistants may be that the chapel was not a work of absolutely primary importance in the eyes of Lodovico compared to Mantegna's other tasks, rather as he was content to have Samuele da Tradate execute Mantegna's designs at Cavriana. It is Mantegna's earliest surviving large painting on canvas, which was perhaps chosen as a medium because of the picture's great size and vertical shape. The great architectural framework, and the oriental carpet laid on a pedestal of veined red marbles standing in a garden of plants and flowers closed by a balustrade of linked roundels, inset with coloured marbles, and with golden cherub heads in their interstices, are related in invention to the fireplace fresco of the Camera Picta.

The tall, emaciated saint, dressed in the ash-grey robe of a Franciscan Friar Minor, stands on the pedestal, his weight resting on his right foot. He holds up the tablet inscribed IHS or the Name of Jesus that he always carried when preaching his sermons. This motif and the finely lettered inscription above, HVIVS LINGVA SALVS HOMINVM, are chosen to emphasize his fame as a preacher to repent-

ance. Behind, two golden-haired angels, robed in pink and blue, hold up a cloth of state of scarlet damask lined with gold. In type they resemble the *St Euphemia* of 1454: the wings of the left-hand angel change in colour from coral to pale blue to white, the first instance in Mantegna's art of *colori cangianti*. Other motifs recall the San Zeno altarpiece: the candlestick-vase held by putti in the lunette, the lamp suspended from the cornice. The taste for beautiful and exotic animals and birds appears again in the white hare that peeps round the corner and in the two parakeets, one pink, one blue. As far as the poor state of the picture allows a judgement, it seems that Mantegna designed it, devised its colour scheme, and painted most of the central part, leaving the sides and some details to be finished by assistants.

From the decade 1470 to 1480 we have many documents concerning Mantegna's properties and financial affairs. The terms Lodovico had offered him were generous. The Gonzaga paid the officers of their household by *bocche* (mouths). On this system salaries were given half in money, half in kind from the corn and foodstuffs and other goods which the Gonzaga received as dues and rents. Mantegna received a salary of fifteen ducats monthly, a house large enough for himself and his family, enough corn every year to meet amply the consumption of six *bocche* and all the wood he needed for his own use. This was his *provisione* or regular provision, and Lodovico had encouraged him in 1458 to expect that it would be the least part of his recompense. The fifteen ducats monthly (900 lire annually) long remained his allowance, but at the end of his life in 1505 his salary was raised slightly to 930 lire. In 1470 Lodovico Gonzaga, complaining to Alessandro Sforza of Mantegna's delays in finishing the Camera Picta, declared: 'he has from 15 ducats a month, a house and other prerogatives, which is a great expense.'[2]

Mantegna must soon have become aware that his would be the usual lot of all who served a prince for a salary, whatever their rank. Like all revenues in the days before a full money economy, the Marchese's own revenues were paid to him partly in money, partly in kind. As his receipts were often in arrears so were his salaries.[3] Mantegna quickly found that he would have to solicit and even importune for payment, but as Kristeller pointed out long ago, it is wrong to suppose either that he was grasping or that Lodovico and his successors were mean because of the many letters and petitions in which Mantegna presses for payment of the whole or part of his arrears of salary and other dues. The patience and courtesy with which they almost invariably answered him and the pains they took to satisfy him or to give him some good reason for delay indicate the justice of his demands as well as the value they set on his services. Mantegna's solicitations began at least as early as 28 December 1463, when he complained to Lodovico that he had not been paid for four months and asked for something to be given on account, in view of his entire dependence on the Marchese for his subsistence. The very next day a messenger was sent with an apology and thirty ducats, but in March and April 1464 Mantegna was compelled to renew his suit for money and to solicit delivery of his agreed allowance of wood.[4] The general attitude of the Gonzaga is perhaps best summed up in a letter of 21 May 1479 from the Marchese Federico, then campaigning in Tuscany, to his wife. Telling her that some of the court are paid every month, including Mantegna, he remarks that it will not matter greatly if they are paid every thirty-five days instead of punctually at the end of the month: 'considering our need they will have no cause for complaint.'[5]

Such temporary financial straits were no impediment to Mantegna's social ambitions. As we have seen, when Frederick III came to Ferrara in January 1469 Mantegna was among those who hurried over from Mantua in order to obtain a title from him. Marsilio Andreasi, one of the Gonzaga secretaries, reported to his masters on 2 February 1469, 'Andrea Mantegna says that he too had himself made a count, and hopes to get the privilege.' But to have the necessary privilege of a count palatine in due form cost money, and it seems that Mantegna failed to get it from the Emperor's itinerant chancery, for there is no record then or for many years later, in any document drawn up in Mantua or Padua, of his using the title of count. When he eventually did become a knight, probably in 1484, it was from the Gonzaga that he received the title. In fifteenth-century Italy such honours no longer necessarily entailed any reality of feudal service as in the past, but still carried a notion of dignity. Even the purely formal title of count palatine had prestige in the eyes of an Italian prince, for in answer to Gianfrancesco Gonzaga's request for it, the Emperor Sigismund explained in 1432 that it was an honour more proper for 'ordinary citizens than for princes'.[6] That Andrea sought such distinctions, and sought them without ridicule, proves not only his consciousness of his own genius, but also its flattering recognition by all whose opinion counted in the Italy of his day, princes, great ecclesiastics, noblemen, humanists and poets. His aspirations were shared by his brother-in-law, for on 13 February 1469, Frederick created Gentile Bellini a knight and a count palatine, dignities proudly commemorated by Gentile on his medal of Sultan Mohammed the Conqueror, made in the 1480s.[7]

It is true that such titles of a lesser degree had, according to the usual wont, lost much of their real value. 'We have granted more than a hundred titles of count palatine since we have been here in Italy,' said Sigismund in 1432.[8] Nevertheless, Mantegna and Gentile Bellini were the first artists to push themselves forward to high formal rank in their own society. That they used their energies to do so, one in the aristocratic republic of Venice and the other in the princely state of Mantua, while fifteenth-century Florentine artists took no such trouble, is a testimony to the rather different value set on nobility in mercantile Florence and in north-eastern Italy. Indeed in their aspiration Bellini and Mantegna overshot some of the greatest of their successors for more than three centuries, since Rubens, Bernini, Vandyck and Reynolds were all content with the title of knight. Mantegna also seems to have received more poetical honours than any other contemporary artist: eulogies were addressed to him in both Latin and Italian verse from poets of all kinds and ranks, ranging from notaries and fellow-artists to noblemen and bishops, from men for whom poetry was a vocation to men for whom it was an amusement. These tributes began as early as c.1450, when Andrea was still a youth, and were to continue until his death.

Mantegna's sense of his own standing as a courtier of the Gonzaga, perhaps too his ambitious hopes for future advancement in dignity, are expressed in the fine house that he eventually built for himself in Mantua (Plate 149). His first house there was probably a villa on land at Pradella, outside Porta Aquadruccio, that the Marchese had granted him. It was much less imposing, and its construction merely signified the resolution that he had taken to fix himself permanently in the service of the Gonzaga. He seems to have reached this decision only after a long trial of six years, for it was not until 2 December 1466 that he announced to Lodovico a desire to improve his *logeto* or 'little lodging' by erecting a 'little house'. Accordingly he asked the Marchese to lend him a hundred ducats with which to buy bricks and lime, to be repaid by monthly deductions of three to four ducats from his provision. In September and November 1473 he was pressing Lodovico through Giovanni da Padova, who appears to have been his builder, for wood for the roof of this house.[9] But by 1476, having now become something of a landed proprietor, he embarked on the construction of a great house in Mantua itself, on a site given to him by Lodovico in 1476, near the church of San Sebastiano in the contrada dell'Unicorno, where there were great empty meadows known as the *prati di Redevallo*. This site, by successive acquisitions, he eventually enlarged into a property of some two and a half acres.[10] Its foundation stone (Plate 151) was laid on 18 October 1476; it bears the inscription SVPER/ FUNDO/A DI. L. PRIN./OP. DONO/DATO AN/G. MCCCC/LXXVI. AND./MANTINIA/HAEC IECIT/ FONDA MEN/TA XV KL./NOVEMBRIS // IN FR. B. LII/ RETRO/B.CL. (On ground given by Divus Lodovicus most excellent prince, in the year of grace 1476 Andrea Mantegna laid these foundations on 18 October: in front *braccia* 52 behind *braccia* 150.)

Laid out with austere gravity to resemble a Roman inscription and lettered in perfectly proportioned Roman capitals, it was certainly designed by Mantegna and cut under his supervision. Great care was taken by Mantegna in such matters. From the Camera Picta onwards the wording of his inscriptions has an assured humanist ring in its lapidary union of Ciceronian phrase with the formulae of Roman epigraphy, and as here an antique dignity is matched by antique beauty of lettering. Mantegna indeed wished to stamp a Roman dignity and elegance even on his handwriting, for his letters, of which a number survive from 1463 onwards, are written in a refined humanist cursive hand, sometimes delightfully ornamented with a flourishingly fanciful formality of layout (Fig. 8).[11]

The construction of the new house was protracted over many years for want of money, and until it was completed Mantegna rented various other houses in Mantua. He had already incurred debts for it by June 1479, when he begged the new Marchese Federico for payment of his arrears of salary, partly in order to meet them. After Federico's death in 1484, and while still uncertain of the favour of his son and successor Francesco, he turned to Lorenzo de' Medici for financial help. They were already known to each other, since Mantegna had taken steps to bring himself and his work to Lorenzo's notice by sending him a letter and a painting, for which Lorenzo thanked him in a letter of 2 March 1481. The painting may have been the little picture of Judith by Mantegna which was listed in the inventory taken of Palazzo Medici after Lorenzo's death in 1492. Lorenzo visited him at his lodging in Mantua on 23 February 1483, 'where he saw with great pleasure some paintings by Andrea and certain heads in relief [i.e. busts] with many other antique things, in which, it sccms, he greatly delights.' Mantegna not only thought Lorenzo a congenial spirit, but likely to prove a liberal patron, for his letter of 26 August 1484 seems confident of Lorenzo's generosity and sympathetic assistance. Mantegna explains that he has begun his new house relying on the favour first of Lodovico and then of Federico for the means to finish it, 'not having means myself'. Now Federico is dead, and not knowing as yet the disposition towards him of his new lord, he appeals to Lorenzo, and promises, if help is given, 'to make such commemoration of it that no reproach or stain of ingratitude shall ever be laid upon me.' We do not know if Lorenzo responded.[12]

The house is built of the brick and terracotta which were the characteristic building materials of Lombardy. Originally it faced on to the piazza in front of San Sebastiano, not as now, on to the street.[13] A cube in form, it has three storeys, of which the uppermost contains attics and is topped by a noble projecting cornice. The garden side was painted in fresco with ornamental motifs, of which some traces still remain, and the severe plainness of the exterior was relieved by a stately cornice decorated with a classical frieze of palmettes alternating with a fan-shaped plant. Attached to its corners, just below the cornice, are two shields, superimposed on each other saltire-wise, the upper one projecting boldly beyond the line of the building. The armorial bearings represented on them have disappeared, but the device AB OLYMPO (from Olympus) is still inscribed in beautifully proportioned Roman letters on the lintels above the four doorways of the circular central courtyard, which is the principal interior feature of the house. The full form of this device, which also appears in Mantegna's funerary chapel in Sant' Andrea, was an eagle, the bird of Jove, perched on a stone inscribed AB OLYMPO. Originally a device of the Gonzaga, it was used here by Mantegna perhaps to blazon his allegiance, but perhaps too in graceful allusion to the gift of the ground by the Gonzaga and their contributions to the cost of the house.[14]

The architectural design of the circular courtyard (Plate 150) is of an elegance at once dignified and severe; at each of the four apexes of the circle is a pair of pilasters supporting a stately entablature whose heavy cornice is decorated with antique ornaments, ovolos, dentils, and water-leaves. Each pair of pilasters frames a doorway, whose decoration repeats the motifs of the cornice: to either side the pilasters are flanked by recessed blind panels, divided by a moulded dado into upper and lower sections, and pierced in the upper section by a simple window resting on the dado. The second storey is plain, and is pierced all round with windows corresponding to the windows and doorways below. On this storey there are still some remains of gaily frescoed plaster to the right of the present entrance. The original appearance of this courtyard is difficult to gauge, as most of its decoration and all except one of the inscriptions has disappeared, but probably it was rather brighter than its present elegant sobriety suggests. The second storey ends in a plain moulded frieze: above rises a square third storey, so that the effect is that of a square courtyard into which a cylinder has been fitted.

The probable use of some of the fifteen rooms of this house, which provided ample accommodation for Mantegna and his household, has been ingeniously worked out by Rosenthal. The rooms on the right side of the ground floor have no decoration, and since they contain a well and are above the storage room in the basement, this must surely have been the service part of the house containing the kitchen and servants' quarters. On the opposite side is a long first room which has a rich wooden ceiling with painted caissons, an illusionistic entablature simulating grey stone, a painted frieze, and traces of frescoed decoration below. The long central room was most probably Mantegna's painting-room. The wedding-contract of his daughter Laura was signed on 31 August 1486 in 'the lower *studio* or chamber' of the house Mantegna was then occupying, though here the term *studio* may well mean a study in a dignified sense, rather than a painting-room.[15] And it may be that the ground-floor room adjoining this long central room on the garden side was a *studio* of this kind, for it has a painted cornice of palmettes and interlaced tendrils, and consoles decorated with acanthus. Here Mantegna may have housed his collection of busts and other antique works of art, which it was customary in the fifteenth century to keep in a *studio*.

The handsomely decorated rooms on the first floor were certainly for the domestic use of the family. The three on the left side have cornices and ceilings richly ornamented with various motifs, scrolling acanthus surmounted by a classical banded swag of laurel, interlaced straps linked by scroll-work, and interlinked circles. Among the decorations on their walls are the device AB OLYMPO and a large stemma of Mantegna's arms complete with comital crown, while the corner room on the garden side has a wall still displaying the remains of a dado of interlinked medallions, as in the Camera Picta, painted in the Gonzaga colours of blue and yellow, with a central medallion bearing the Gonzaga device

of the radiant sun with the motto *per mon desir* in Gothic letters. All this decoration must date from the late 1490s, given the shape of the shield of arms, and was plainly designed by Mantegna. Indeed, Vasari says he painted it. In all probability these three rooms were the principal reception rooms – a dining-room, a *sala* or main reception room, and a *camera* or principal bed-chamber. The rooms on the right side would have accommodated Mantegna's children.

According to two nineteenth-century scholars, Braghirolli and Bertolotti, this house was built for Mantegna by Giovanni da Padova, but no contemporary document has yet appeared to support their claim. Rosenthal has shown that both in its size and in its plan, a circle inscribed in a square, it aspired to be what was known in the fifteenth century as a *casa di signori*, that is, a nobleman's house. He has found precedents for the plan itself among the designs for smaller palaces conceived by the Sienese architect and artist Francesco di Giorgio after his visit to Rome in 1463. These were inspired by Roman monuments, notably by the Pantheon, and for the open inner rectangular court of large Renaissance palaces they substitute a round or octagonal atrium covered by a dome and lit by an oculus in the dome or by clerestory windows below a ceiling.

Although Francesco di Giorgio was working in 1477 and probably before then on the ducal palace of Urbino, a building of great interest to the Gonzaga, it seems unlikely that Mantegna derived the form of his house from a knowledge of Francesco's designs. It might be argued that his inspiration came from Vitruvius and from Leone Battista Alberti, Lodovico's close and honoured friend and principal adviser in matters architectural, whom Mantegna certainly met in 1472 at the baths of Porretta, but must surely have encountered before during Alberti's visits to Mantua in 1461, 1463, 1465 and 1470, one of which, that of 1463, was a prolonged sojourn of about a year. But it must be said that if in his *De Architectura* Alberti regards the antique atrium as having almost always been circular, he also envisages his atrium as a sort of outer vestibule, preceding the true *sinus* or heart of the house, the chief room on which the others converge. For Vitruvius, the atrium is a quadrangular room. Accordingly Mantegna's courtyard corresponds neither to Vitruvius, for it is circular, nor to Alberti, for it is not a vestibule, but the main internal space of the house.[16]

All this is relevant to the much-debated question of whether he originally intended the courtyard to be roofed over with a dome, so converting it into the domed room of Francesco di Giorgio's designs. If so, his house would be the first in which the Renaissance conception of the Roman house as

Magnifico s(igno)re et benefactore mio singullare: do poi le debite Recommandacione; La V. M(ag)cia E oprima
mente informata de lo amore mesera portato da li doi miei s(igno)ri: la gracia de li quali più
pareua hauere in tal forma uendicato: ch mi persuadeuo de loro ogni bene in ogni mia oppor
tunita: per la qual cosa presi animo in uolere fabricare una casa: la quale speraua medi
ante le loro S(igno)rie no hauendo facultà da me: consequire lo opimo mio desiderio de
fornirla: M(anca)ronmi la prima speranza no senza mia grã iactura. M(anca) e mon
cata la seconda: La quale mi augumentaua lanimo amazor cosa: tanto erano le dis
mostracione de la sua felice memoria uerso di me: il perche no dico chel mi para
essere destructo per la perdita facta: ho dcmesso alquanto de animo: No obstante che la
indole di questo nouello signore mi fa pilgiare qualche restauracione uedendolo
curo in dinaro ale uirtu: pur mi bisogna far qualche pratica: la quale si tanto no se
peruiene al fine: fa stare sempre lhomo dubioso. e e causa che io pilgi rassugio doue
so certo no mi ha essere denegato subsidio: el quale reputo per el più uero quello de
la V. M(ag)cia benche io habia facto perdita di molti s(igno)ri: to li quali teneuo seruitu
et da loro no uulgare mente amato, mediante le sue humanita, et lo admiciculo
di qualche mea operetta: onde hauendo in dubitata speranza i la M(ag)cia uostra ricorro
a quella si uolgia dignare per sua liberalita darmi qualche adiuto; et acontentarsi
uolere participare in essa casa promerendoli farne tal memoria che in me no sera mai
imposto macula de ingratitudine: et questo mio fiduciale scriuere no lo impurt
me ma ala V. M(ag)cia La quale per sua benignita e sempre solita far bene: no
tanto a quelli che sonno suoi dediti: ma achi ella no uide mai: et se ella ro
gnosce: ch sia in me bo che io habia cosa li sia grata prego ura magnificentia,
no cu manchia promtezza uolgia fare prova di me: che sia la fiducia che ho
presa in lei: per questa mia litera: il che reputero ad cosa gratissima: Recom(m)an
domi in finite uolte ala V. M(ag)cia la quale idio felice mente conserui. mantue
die 20 augusti · 1484

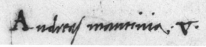
Andreas mantinia · V.

Fig. 8. A page of Mantegna's handwriting. Florence, Uffizi

centring round a central hall was realized in bricks and mortar. In reality, as nothing about the house, with its rich ceilings and painted decorations, suggests that it is unfinished, so nothing about the courtyard suggests that it was ever intended to be anything else, least of all an ambitious internal hall rising two storeys high and more. On the contrary its large size, its architectural features and its painted decoration all fit best with the notion that it was always designed to be an open courtyard. Nor do such contemporary or near-contemporary documents as there are support the theory that Mantegna's intention was to vault over such a large space with the very expensive feature of a dome. In a document of 10 January 1502 the house is described as *'cupata et solerata'* (having a roof and upper storey), the standard phrase in contracts of sale for houses which were properly roofed.[17] And in his poem *Monumentum Gonzagium*, completed in 1526, the humanist Giovanni Bonavoglia wrote: 'Mantegna, that true imitator of antiquity, that second Apelles, the honour of our times, founded this house and gave it the form of a little amphitheatre.'[18] As ancient amphitheatres were circular, but unroofed, his words show that in early sixteenth-century Mantua there was no notion that Mantegna had ever intended to roof his circular courtyard. Vasari tells us that Mantegna took great delight in architecture, and probably we should see the design as his own attempt to build a house on what he himself believed to be a Roman plan. In this it is certainly one of the most original expressions of his romantic fascination with antiquity. But we are probably wrong in looking on it as the prototype of such buildings as Palladio's Villa Rotonda near Vicenza, built three-quarters of a century later, which does have a domed central hall. Bonavoglia's poem reveals that it was considered something exceptional, and it may be that many of Mantegna's own contemporaries looked on it as something of a caprice, rather as Cardinal Francesco Gonzaga in 1473 scornfully dismissed the church of San Sebastiano in Mantua as 'being built in the antique fashion, not very dissimilar from that fantastic design of Messer Battista Alberti, so that I could never yet make out what it was to turn out, a church, a mosque or a synagogue.'[19]

The house when begun was described by Schivenoglia as *'una bella stancia'*, but Mantegna occupied it for only a few years towards the end of his life. From 1473 to 1481 he lodged in the contrada dell'Aquila near the cathedral and close to the court; then in 1482 he moved to a house in the contrada del Cavallo (the modern Via Mazzoni 16), which he rented from the Malatesta family.[20] There still exists a letter of 3 January 1487 in which Gian Galeazzo Visconti, Duke of Milan, asks the Marchese Francesco Gonzaga on behalf of Gian Francesco

Malatesta 'our most beloved counsellor' to take means to compel Mantegna to disgorge his arrears of rent for this house, as 'he is showing himself obstinately behindhand in making payment.'[21] In fact the Gonzaga took all responsibility in the matter of Mantegna's lodging, even to paying his rent: on 15 February 1482 one of Federico's secretaries, Matteo Antimaco, wrote pressingly to Gabriele da Fogliano, of a great noble family of Reggio, asking if he would be willing to let his house in Mantua to Mantegna 'our most dear painter and familiar for his dwelling-place as we have to make provision for him at this present either of a house or its rent. We shall willingly pay the rent, for so the most illustrious lord our father of happy memory ever did and so we ourselves have done until now.'[22] From the standing of Mantegna's landlords, clearly the Gonzaga expected to lodge him in houses of dignity. At the request of the Malatesta he moved from their house in 1494, or shortly afterwards, and went into his own stately house, which he had been so long in building. Indeed it was still unfinished, for in a letter of 3 September 1494 he complained to the Marchese Francesco that 'ever since I began my house by San Sebastiano, I have continually been robbed', but not knowing the culprit, he had been obliged to keep silence.[23] Now his son Lodovico has discovered the thief, a man named Il Rovida in the service of the Marchese, who has been carrying away bricks from the pile assembled for building.[24] Il Rovida could hardly have been stealing bricks for eighteen years, so the beginning to which Mantegna refers must be that of a last campaign to finish the house. Mantegna was not to remain in it for long: in 1501 he was obliged to agree to an exchange with the Marchese Francesco, who wanted it in order to enlarge his new Palazzo di San Sebastiano (also known as Palazzo della Pusterla), where in 1506 he was to instal Mantegna's *Triumphs of Caesar*.[25] In return Mantegna received a house, known as the *domus Mercati*, in what is now the Via Fortunato Calvi. In this house he appears never to have lived, continuing instead to lodge in the contrada dell'Unicorno. He was still living there in 1504, but not long before his death, perhaps in 1505, he bought yet another house 'to avoid going about wandering here, there and everywhere'.[26]

The Gonzaga lodged Mantegna, paid his rent, gave him a monthly salary in money and made him allowances of wood and other necessaries, but, as we have seen, Lodovico had promised Mantegna in 1458 that his 'provision' would be the least part of his recompense. His first known benefaction to Mantegna dates, however, from 1472, when he obtained from the Spedale Nuovo of Santa Maria della Corneta in Mantua the lease of some 110 acres at Buscoldo, a few miles to the south-west of the city. With this property Mantegna was formally invested on 13 November 1472.[27] The price of the lease was 1401½ gold ducats: the Marchese was to help Mantegna with the down-payment of 600 ducats, and to pay the remainder himself. Both payments were to be made within the next four years. Until the purchase money was cleared, interest on it was to be paid annually every Christmas in the disguised form of a rent-charge of 70 gold ducats, 7 soldi, and Lodovico also undertook to pay this annual rent-charge during the four years allowed for payment.[28]

Mantegna completed the payment of his own share of the purchase price in May 1476, some months within the term, when he advanced 200 gold ducats to the Spedale Nuovo for a purchase of land.[29] Not so the Marchese, to the great dissatisfaction of his servant, who complained to him in a letter of 19 May 1478 that after nearly nineteen years' service, begun 'with the mind so to do that Your Excellency might boast of having what no other lord in Italy has, as indeed I have so done', his promise of 1458 remained unfulfilled. Mantegna's querulous complaint drew from Lodovico the feeling reproof that 'it was a letter which truly it seems to us there was no necessity for you to write to us', inasmuch as he had kept well in mind the promises made to Mantegna on entering his service and had not failed of keeping them. He admitted nevertheless that Mantegna's claim was just: the times had brought reverses and his own revenues and dues were so much in arrears that he had been forced to pledge his plate and jewels. Mantegna was not to doubt that his property would be paid for cheerfully and soon.[30] Three years later the debt was still unpaid, and in a decree of 21 August 1481 Lodovico's son and successor Federico formally assumed liability for it and for the yearly interest of forty ducats arising from it, of which only four years had been paid. But even in 1506 the 800 ducats were still outstanding, and as Mantegna lay on his death-bed that September almost his last words were to ask for the Marchese Francesco in order to make a final supplication to him for the discharge of the debt. In the end the Gonzaga were able to escape the obligation, for one of the conditions on which the property sequestrated from Mantegna's son Francesco by the Mantuan treasury in 1512 or 1513 was restored to him was that he should take on himself payment of the 800 ducats and of the annual interest. Unable to pay even the interest, Francesco formally renounced all his rights to the Buscoldo lands on 10 October 1513, whereupon the Spedale sold them to Niccolò Aliprandi.[31]

The property at Buscoldo consisted of the usual scattered *poderi*, with a house on one of them at Frasanello, with a well, oven, threshing-ground and outhouses.[32] On entering into possession Mantegna found that land brought its problems, not least in the form of disputes over boundaries. In 1473 he brought a lawsuit against his neighbours Franceschino and Giacomo Galini over the boundaries of two of their properties. The law found for Mantegna and on 18 December the Galini were ordered to rectify their boundaries in Mantegna's favour. In fact they preferred to sell him the two pieces of land for fifty ducats by a transaction of 11 January 1475.[33] In June 1474 he asked for an audience with the Marchese in order to lay another complaint. His principal quarrel appears in fact to have been with the Aliprandi, who belonged to the old nobility of Mantua and presumably looked askance on an upstart. In September 1475 he complained again to Lodovico that Francesco degli Aliprandi was trying to usurp a common way between their properties and had instigated a theft of some 500 apples and quinces from his orchards, not so light a loss in those days as might appear now. Francesco retorted that Mantegna was so difficult and disagreeable that he was at law with all his neighbours, to which Mantegna replied that the great hatred Francesco entertained for him was manifest to all. Lodovico wisely committed the dispute to his council, with an admonition to the two litigants to try to come to an amicable agreement. The quarrel was finally settled by an exchange of lands, effected at the persuasion of Lodovico, but only finally ratified under Federico, by Aliprandi rather grudgingly, for he stipulated that he was not to pay the customary legal dues on the transaction.[34]

Much has been made of this fierce exchange of complaints, and especially of Aliprandi's sharp censure of Mantegna's character, but tempers were evidently roused by questions of disputed ownership between a new landlord and his neighbours, conjuring up a hail of charges and counter-charges. And indeed on 15 February 1499, while Aliprandi was in office as Rector of the Spedale Nuovo, Mantegna and he appeared amicably together before its Presidents, who included the Marchese Francesco himself, to have their original agreement formally set down in a document, which had not yet been done, though it had been made some nineteen years before. Plainly the two had lived on good terms ever since and the Marchese Francesco, declaring that both deserved the remission of all dues promised to Aliprandi and 'even greater things', gave his consent to this and to the whole transaction.[35]

Like many landlords before and since Mantegna was eager to enlarge and round off his property and free it of charges. At Buscoldo the distresses of his poorer neighbours gave him the opportunity to purchase some of their land. In 1475 he was able to buy a piece of land at Buscoldo itself for 7½ ducats, and in 1484 he bought another at Sorgentia, close by, for 11 ducats. On 24 April 1488 his son Francesco took possession on his behalf of another piece of land at Sorgentia acquired in payment of a debt of some 26 ducats incurred by the Bazano family for money and fodder lent them by Mantegna 'during the late war'. All these pieces of land adjoined his own properties and in 1496 he was still adding another small *podere* at Sorgentia to his own for 6½ ducats.[36] Earlier, in October 1483, he had obtained a feudal investiture of some lands belonging to the bishopric of Mantua at Scorzarolo and in the vicariate of Borgoforte, to the south of Mantua, on the Po. Although part of the estate leased to him by the Spedale Nuovo, legally these were among the fiefs of the bishopric.[37]

The Marchese Lodovico also made Mantegna grants of other small *poderi* in the territory of Mantua. One, with two houses, was at Bonmercato, near Goito, another was close to Ponte di Revellino and Naviglio and included an island in the Mincio. For none of these grants had deeds been drawn up or registered and the Marchese Federico therefore confirmed them on 8 June 1481 at Mantegna's petition by a special decree.[38] On his land at Pradella, a suburb just outside the Porta Aquadruccio of Mantua, he had soon been at dispute with his neighbours, a gardener and his wife, who stole from his *orto* (vegetable garden) and used bullying and insulting words to him and to his wife. Lodovico immediately enquired into the affair and on 1 August 1468 ordered one of his servants to warn the gardener 'that the tip of Andrea's foot is dearer to us than a thousand poltroons like him.' The dispute ended at once, for the gardener was dismissed.[39] To this property at Pradella Mantegna added in 1473 a meadow, bought for 67 ducats, and in 1476 a piece of ground acquired from two young brothers in settlement of a debt of 61 ducats for woollen cloths they had bought of Mantegna.[40] Like the previous money-lending transaction, this one raises the question of whether Mantegna did not act at times as a sort of small merchant-capitalist in the rural districts where he held property, perhaps too in Mantua itself.

In spite of modern claims these acquisitions did not make Mantegna into a great landed proprietor. Before 1492 his country properties cannot have amounted in all to more than 160 acres. In a decree of February of that year they were greatly augmented when the Marchese Francesco granted him some 120 acres at Bosco della Caccia in Scorzarolo. This grant was made at Mantegna's importunate petition and after pressing reminders of his long and honourable service, but partly, it must be said in fairness to him, in satisfaction of his arrears of salary. It seems, too, to have been made from the confiscated property of a faithless cook; evidently Mantegna was well versed in the courtly art of begging for juicy morsels snatched from others. Altogether his properties constituted an estate suitable for a small nobleman.[41]

Mantegna's dealings in land reveal a hard-headedness and tenacity in the acquisition of property and maintenance of his rights that may have sprung from his early experiences as a poor boy. They perhaps explain why the life of a fifteenth-century courtier suited him so well. Yet he certainly entertained a lofty opinion of his own art and a proud consciousness of his own genius in it, and there is no sign that he ever sought to quit it or to put his sons to pursuits that were generally considered nobler or more lucrative. His own attitudes were expressed by the words of the decree of 1492, which declare that it is the duty of princes to study how they may best 'turn their subjects to worthy pursuits, be useful to all the studious, ennoble the good with honours worthy of them and exalt those endowed with excellence and enrich them with gifts and favours.' This is the way to true praise and greatest glory, a glory that is a kind of immortality and that will defend Francesco's name from the death of oblivion and obscurity. So his familiar consort with Archimedes, the mighty architect, illuminated with no mediocre brightness the fame of Hiero king of Syracuse; so the most celebrated of Alexander's edicts is that in which he forbade himself to be painted by anyone save Apelles or sculpted by anyone save Lysippus. And it was greatly to the honour and glory of Augustus that he treated his architect Vitruvius of Verona so liberally 'that from a poor man he made him a rich one and from an obscure man one of great renown'. No fourteenth-century prince had thought himself obliged to exercise his patronage in this style or on such a scale, and we are certainly confronted in these words with a new conception of the status of the great artist and of an enlightened patron's obligations, framed on the pattern of antiquity.

These grants gave Mantegna *poderi* of ploughland and vineyards, producing corn, wine, oil and fruit, and stretches of woodland, producing firewood. He exploited them through *contadini*, partly, it would seem, on a crop-sharing basis. Their produce, however, was subject to all the usual hazards of farming, and was not always sufficient to meet the charges, including ground-rent, that they imposed on him. Besides these properties, as Mantegna often complained, he had no other resource than his provision from the Gonzaga. As a salaried retainer, he could accept no commissions from others without licence from his lord: to have a painting from the hand of Mantegna even such great personages as Giuliano della Rovere, Prefect of Rome and nephew of the reigning Pope Sixtus IV, Bona Duchess of Milan and

Pope Innocent VIII had to have recourse for permission in the first instance to the reigning Marquis of Mantua. Mantegna would probably be allowed to accept nothing as a recompense or payment from patrons of such high rank, and his work would become a princely present, for the Gonzaga were always anxious to oblige their equals and superiors with gifts that pleased them. The most Mantegna could hope for was a *mancia* or gratification, either from his own lord or from his patrons, which was sometimes forthcoming as a gift of money, plate or jewels.[42] This state of affairs may explain in part his interest in engraving, which he may well have seen as a means of augmenting his income, allowing him as it did to reproduce his compositions for sale to artists and dilettanti – it is a modern illusion that early Renaissance prints like Mantegna's were cheap works intended for a popular market – without encroaching on the exclusive right of the Gonzaga to his paintings. If this is so, it would explain as we shall see why as early as 1475 Mantegna was interested in hiring the services of an engraver.

Nothing is more difficult than to form a true impression of a man like Mantegna, who died fifty years before the biography of artists was created as a genre by Vasari. We might know more of him if Campagnola's letter to Leonico, which was used by Scardeone and Vasari, had not been lost at an early date. Yet even if we had contemporary biographies it might still be difficult to penetrate the veils of discretion and rhetorical eulogy which so often disguise the truth about individuals in the formal writings of the fifteenth century. Many early biographies show little interest in their subjects beyond the achievements that brought them notability and so give little insight into personality, whatever their value for reconstructing the events of a life and its activities. Mantegna's surviving letters are all addressed to great personages and so present him on his guard or as a suitor and always in the posture of a courtier who has to ingratiate himself or importune. The evidence about his character that we owe to his disputes has to be treated with reserve, as already noted, given the hot-tempered exaggeration that was characteristic of the age both in informal quarrels and in formal litigation.

Yet when all the unfavourable evidence is considered with due allowance made for its context, it does appear that Mantegna had a difficult side to his nature. Towards the end of his life he had come to see himself as a man of genius continually assailed and thwarted by the detraction, envy and incomprehension of foolish and stupid little men. This consciousness of his own greatness was present with him from his early days in Mantua, and certainly did not endear him to all his fellow-artists, although there is no doubt that he was deeply admired and even revered by many of them.[43] Accordingly it may be true that he dominated the little artistic world of Mantua like a tyrant, holding it under 'his pride and dominion', as the engraver Simone Ardizone claimed in 1475, in his certainty of the favour of his Gonzaga patrons.[44] He was aware that there were no serious rivals to his eminence in Mantua itself, or indeed in the rest of Lombardy, Emilia, the Veneto and the Marches. That Lodovico early came to use him as an intermediary in his commissions to other artists appears from a letter of 10 November 1461 to his son Francesco in which Lodovico tells him that he has arranged to have the illumination of a missal completed by 'a young man of this place, who illuminates very well' rather than by Belbello of Pavia and has asked Mantegna to make the necessary agreement with the new miniaturist.[45]

At the same time Mantegna plainly felt an insecurity that perhaps stemmed partly from the poverty of his youth, followed by his dependence on court favour, partly from the endemic insecurity that was a trait of the mentality of the age. If on the one hand this insecurity urged him to pursue wealth, property and honours, on the other hand it encouraged a suspicious and irritable sensibility that expressed itself in quick resentments of injuries and slights, real and fancied, perhaps too in an overready vengefulness, which may lie behind some of the litigation in which he was involved over his properties. But it is doubtful whether he went quite so far as meditating assassination as he was once accused of doing. He also had his share of caprice and wilfulness, though the tension between obstinate artists procrastinating over a piece of work and exasperated patrons pressing for its prompt completion was a commonplace in the artistic relationships of the time. In Mantegna's case the most frequent burden of complaint was undoubtedly caused by his extreme perfectionism. It is greatly to the credit of all the Gonzaga princes whom he served that for all their complaints and occasional attempts to hurry him, they understood and made allowances for his nature in this respect, certain that in the end his works would bring glory and fame to themselves as his lords.

So much said, there are witnesses to testify to a courteous, affable and kindly side to Mantegna's character. The Mantuan nobleman and poet Filippo Nuvoloni (1441–78) speaks in a laudatory sonnet of 1469 addressed from Ferrara to Mantegna of 'the gentle sweetness that ever appeared in thee while we were together', and of the affection he ever feels for 'thy courteous person'. Filippo is perhaps a surprising friend of Mantegna, for he was a tall, handsome figure, fond of dancing and gambling, with an eloquent tongue and a libertine disposition that often got him into trouble. But whatever his love of dissipation, his admiration for Mantegna breaks out in a second sonnet addressed to Andrea accompanying a gift of a book containing his *frottole* and other poems. In this he praises him as greater than any of the ancient Roman painters, and exclaims that he can show with his colours all that God and nature have made, portraying 'every noble figure so that it seems to enclose in itself a soul and hills and valleys and every river and stream.' The extension of high praise to Mantegna's landscapes is exceptional among the many laudations of his art by literary men. Both sonnets were transcribed by Feliciano into his own personal anthology of poems.[46]

Again the humanist Battista Guarino writes to Isabella d'Este in October 1490 that 'besides the excellence of his art, in which he has no equal', Mantegna 'is all courtesy' (*tutto gentile*).[47] In his Latin dictionary of 1502 (ready by 1498) the Augustinian friar Ambrogio Calepino (*c.*1435–1509) of Bergamo, who spent two years in Mantua in 1461–2, commends him as second to none in honourability as well as in the art of painting and as a 'man excellent in every kind of virtue.'[48] And in 1506, even when writing a letter of complaint about Mantegna to Isabella d'Este, Pietro Bembo exclaims: 'I put my hope likewise in the courtesy and civility of Messer Andrea, from which two virtues he is never wont to be far astray.'[49] Vasari too was surely recording testimony heard from artists in Lombardy when he writes in 1550: 'His honourable way of life is still held in very present recollection, as is the praiseworthy civility that he had and the lovingness with which he taught the art to other painters.'[50]

Lodovico Gonzaga died of the plague on 11 June 1478. He was succeeded by his son Federico, who took Mantegna into the same favour and treated him with a gentle courtesy which suggests how anxious he was not to lose the services of so famous an artist. As early as 16 October 1478 he summoned him by letter to come out to Gonzaga, 'if you are not too busy otherwise, in order to make some designs'. These may have been for the new palace which he intended to build at Marmirolo, of which he had obtained possession from his brothers Rodolfo and Lodovico on 28 June 1478. Mantegna was ill of a quartan ague – fever was an endemic complaint of marshy Mantua – and had gone out into the country to recover. He professed himself ready to move nearer to Federico by boat, since he was not in a fit state to ride, but Federico replied by return of messenger urging him to get better first. Yet on 6 June 1479 Mantegna had to petition Federico, then in Tuscany fighting on behalf of Florence and Milan against the Pope and the King of Naples, for payment of his arrears of salary, of which he had

received only six instalments in the year since Lodovico's death.[51]

In 1480 Mantegna's son fell ill, and Mantegna took him to Venice to consult the physician Gerardo da Verona, for whom on 11 May Federico gave him a flattering commendatory letter which calls Mantegna 'his noble and most dear familiar . . . one whose gifts are such that they make him known to the whole world and consequently commend him to all persons of worth'.[52] On his way to Venice Mantegna halted in Padua, where on 23 May he reached a legal settlement with Giovanni Francesco, the husband of his late niece Caterina.[53] It seems that there was no cure for Mantegna's son, if it is to this son's death that a letter from his old friend Matteo Bosso refers.[54] In the late 1470s and 1480s Bosso was moving through North Italy, holding office as prior of various convents of his order. From 1475 to 1479 he was prior at Mantua, moving for a year to Padua before returning there again in 1480–1. From 1484 to 1492, though engaged at times on special missions for his order, he was Prior of the Badia Fiesolana, to which he gave a Madonna by Mantegna, now lost, that was seen by Vasari above the door of the library.[55] Bosso relates that the death of this son was a heavy blow to Mantegna, partly because he promised to be his father's equal as a painter.[56] Bosso asks his correspondent, Aloisio dell'Antella, a jurist of Florentine descent then living in Mantua, to beg Andrea to bear up under his misfortune with all courage; 'I will not say, let him show understanding, for he has a most lofty understanding, and one that foresees all and embraces all.' Like Aldobrandini's letter of 1466, this is another testimony that Andrea possessed a power of mind in matters outside his profession which struck those who associated with him: it perhaps helps to explain why his company was so sought after by the great and learned.

Nothing certainly survives of Mantegna's work for Federico, who like his father made great use of his services. Mantegna decorated some rooms in the Castello for him, and played an important part in the design and decoration of Marmirolo, which was begun in 1480 under the supervision of Giovanni da Padova. On 24 April 1481 Federico wrote to Giovanni that he would send him instructions about the work he was to undertake there through Mantegna, who was also at Marmirolo, presumably in connection with its decoration.[57] Mantegna was also kept busy in Mantua. On 25 February 1484 the Protonotary Lodovico was obliged to tell Giovanni della Rovere that Mantegna could not make a painting for him because he was working on a *camera* for Federico, apparently in the Castello, which would occupy him throughout the summer and had to be finished quickly because Federico wanted to move into it.[58]

The same letter makes interesting mention of how long Mantegna expected smaller paintings to take him: 'did it not need more time than eight or ten days to make the picture you request, he would have made it willingly. But as he sees it would take him at least a month, to him it seems an enterprise that would do him no honour.' The letter also implies what appears even more clearly in a slightly earlier correspondence with the Duchess of Milan, that patrons sent specifications and even drawings of the subjects they wanted to have painted. Mantegna's art, rather than his invention, was what they sought, all the more so because such commissions were often for religious pictures, of the Madonna, of the Crucifixion, and the like, in which some particular model or expression was wanted in order to satisfy a personal devotion. Mantegna was always more than willing to execute paintings of subjects that were given to him: as we have seen, in 1464 he sought Lodovico's commands before making his designs for the *camera* at Cavriana, and there is no reason to suppose that he felt any sense of slight when a subject was specified to him in detail. His task was to give pictorial expression to the theme and to invent its ornaments of costume, accessory figures and background. When in June 1481, Bona, Duchess of Milan, sent Federico, who was then in her employ as her general, 'certain designs of paintings which we pray you to be pleased to have portrayed by your Messer Andrea Mantegna, the famous painter', Federico found that Mantegna could not be persuaded 'to reduce them to elegant form'. This was not because the subject was another's invention, but because 'the work is better suited to a miniaturist than to him, for he is not used to painting little figures, and would make a better work of a Madonna or some other subject of the length of a *braccio* [about 2 ft (61 cm)] or a *braccio* and a half, did it please your Highness.' And he adds a famous, rather rueful observation, which speaks worlds for the value that refined patrons set on works of art: 'Most Illustrious Lady, if I knew how to do what Your Ladyship requests, I would endeavour with all speed of time to satisfy your wish, but commonly these masters of great excellence have their fancies and one has to take from them what one can get.'[59]

Although Mantegna was before all else a painter, he took a lively interest in others of the arts as well, architecture, as we have seen, and also sculpture and engraving. In addition he was occasionally employed by the Gonzaga as a designer of goldsmith's work, tapestries and embroideries, for in the fifteenth century as later a court artist was expected to provide inventions and designs for all the furnishings and occasions where his fancy was necessary for embellishment. In 1489 Francesco Gonzaga is found urging Mantegna's return from Rome because he required his services in organizing the festivities that were to greet his bride Isabella d'Este.[60] Mantegna was also one of the earliest artists, if indeed he was not the first, to make 'presentation' drawings, drawings, that is, which were not simply sketches or designs or executed as part of an artist's private repertory of studies and inventions, but were highly finished works intended as independent inventions to be given or sold to patrons or friends. Unfortunately it is hard to document his activity in any one of these other arts in continuous detail, largely perhaps because they were an occasional rather than a regular preoccupation, and what exactly he did in them is therefore a subject of scholarly contention.

As regards architecture, probably Vasari best sums up the true state of affairs: 'he also took delight in architecture and obliged many of his friends by furnishing them with his knowledge.'[61] That knowledge was already considerable enough by the late 1450s for him to give a design for the new chapel in the Castello and for Lodovico, himself an amateur architect, to order it to be carried into execution. From the little that we know it appears to have been a design of a very modern Renaissance kind, with a central dome, and as it was designed c.1458, before Mantegna can have met Alberti, the question of the possible influence of Brunelleschi's Pazzi chapel, begun in 1442 and completed 1459–61, remains an open one, as does that of the intermediaries through which that influence might have been transmitted. Indeed, as we have already seen, Mantegna designed his own house in a form which reveals him as a true Renaissance architect-designer in the daring archaeological romanticism with which he sought to make it a house of antique Roman fashion. He was certainly much involved with Lodovico's many building projects. Certainly too he must have been called in for consultation about the architectural forms of the many state-chambers in Lodovico's palaces whose decoration he executed or designed.

Under Federico, we find him for the first time designing elements of an exterior rather than of an interior. The building was an exceptionally important one, Federico's Domus Nova, intended to replace the Castello with a residence that would be more palace than fortress. Begun by Luca Fancelli in the summer of 1480, it was left uncompleted after Federico's sudden death in 1484.[62] The original design of the whole seems to have been Fancelli's and consisted in all probability of four wings around a central courtyard. In May 1481, before the Domus Nova had risen much above its foundations, Federico wrote to Urbino for drawings of the Palazzo Ducale, 'whose design we are informed is of singular excellence', receiving in return two plans and a drawing. Probably as a result in August 1481 Fancelli submitted new designs to Federico.

Mantegna now enters on the scene. The secretary, Lancillotto Andreasi, who was charged with keeping an eye on the progress of the works in Federico's absence, reported to him on 10 September 1481 that Pietro da Torlezza, the mason who was making the stone frames for the windows, had been told to make a moulding on the inside into which the windows themselves, of wood or oiled paper, were to be fitted. Andreasi thought that the moulding was too large and took away much of the beauty of the stone, and had the mason say something about it to Mantegna, 'who says he wants it to be thus.' But as 'the said Andrea, ever since this master was given the work on these windows, has always been vexed with me' Andreasi thought it best not to say anything about it to him so as not to vex him even more. Instead he tried to get Luca Fancelli and other masters to intervene with Mantegna, but Luca refused on the ground that 'it could be Andrea was having the windows done in this way with the knowledge of your Excellency.' Only about two windows had so far been made, and unfortunately Federico's reply to Andreasi's question has not been found. But the incident reveals that the windows of the Domus Nova were designed by Mantegna for Federico independently of Fancelli. It also shows that as with Lodovico's palaces so with Federico's we must not underestimate the role played by the Marchese himself in the conception, disposition, execution and embellishment of his buildings. Unlike Lodovico, who mastered something of the theory and practice of architecture under Fancelli's tuition, Federico, though a student of Vitruvius, needed Fancelli to explain the plans of Urbino to him, but there can be no doubt that in rearing the new palace his was a coordinating and modifying will.[63]

One of the fuller records to survive of Mantegna's role as a designer concerns the tomb of Barbara of Brandenburg, who died on 7 November 1481. Her executors were her two ecclesiastic sons, the Cardinal Francesco and the Protonotary Lodovico, who were instructed in her will to make her tomb in the Duomo, in the chapel and close to the shrine (archa) of San Anselmo, the patron saint of Mantua, for whom Barbara felt an especially deep devotion as the protector of her family and of its rule over the city. Mantegna was asked to submit a design for the approval of the commissaries entrusted by her two sons with the actual execution of the will, and by 25 January 1482 he had produced one that incorporated the shrine of San Anselmo, and is described as 'most beautiful'. Mantegna had already shown this design to Federico, who did not accept it, preferring a scheme already proposed in private discussions to set up the shrine of San Anselmo on four columns in the centre of the chapel. Federico felt that his mother's tomb could then be placed beneath the

shrine, on the ground, but that to wait for the moving of the shrine would protract the whole business. Cardinal Francesco was consulted by letter, but sent no reply, and on 30 April the commissaries decided to obtain another design. On 5 July Mantegna's design was sent privately to Cardinal Francesco at his own request, but again he returned no answer, and on 31 July the commissaries met to decide first of all whether they should inter Barbara under the archa of San Anselmo, as had been her wish in life, and secondly which of the two designs they were to choose and who was then to execute the work. They did not dare, however, to come to a decision without the Cardinal's approval and agreed to write to him once more.

Still nothing was heard from the Cardinal and on 12 December the commissaries met and resolved to advise him that Federico was pressing for work on the tomb to begin and that unless they heard to the contrary, they would assume that he was pleased with the design that had been sent and proceed with the work. By their next meeting on 1 February 1483 the Cardinal had written to say that he liked Mantegna's design and that the commissaries should consult his brothers and having obtained their opinion consider who was to execute the work. They resolved to speak with Federico and to have a meeting with Andrea and adjust the matter as seemed best.[64] Probably because of Cardinal Francesco's death on 21 October 1483 nothing more was done, and when the tomb is mentioned again, it is in a letter of 20 November 1484 from the Protonotary Lodovico asking the painter Giovanni Luigi de' Medici to make a design for a bronze tomb, evidently a slab, to be set before the shrine of San Anselmo.[65] Bronze must have proved too expensive, for on 26 December 1489 Lodovico says the tomb is complete in all save the epitaph, whose letters still have to be cut on it, suggesting that in the end only a stone slab was provided.[66] From all this it would seem that Mantegna evidently produced a design which obtained the greatest effect possible under the rather restrictive conditions imposed by Barbara's wish to have a humble tomb by or under San Anselmo's shrine.

In the 1490s Mantegna was asked to make a design for a statue Isabella d'Este proposed to erect to Virgil, Mantua's most illustrious son. But there are also literary records and a single surviving work, the famous bronze self-portrait in his chapel at Mantua, to testify that Mantegna worked as a sculptor, or rather as a modeller, for Mantua has no marble quarries, and marble for sculpture had always to be brought from Venice or elsewhere. Hence he was obliged to model in clay, the usual medium of sculptors in south-eastern Lombardy and Emilia. In the title of his verse epitaph on Mantegna, written on

Andrea's death in 1506, the poet, critic and scholar Julius Caesar Scaliger (1484–1558), son of the Paduan painter, miniaturist and publisher Benedetto Bordon (c.1450–1530), describes him as 'pictor et plastes', that is, as 'painter and modeller'.[67] The only contemporary to mention his works of sculpture in unequivocal terms is the painter Giovanni Santi of Urbino, the father of Raphael, who came to Mantua in 1493 to paint a portrait of Isabella d'Este and has left a long and admiring tribute to Mantegna's universal genius as an artist in his verse chronicle of Duke Federigo da Montefeltro. Santi records that Mantegna 'has not omitted to work in relief in pleasing and graceful fashion, so as to show sculpture how much heaven and the sweet fates have bestowed upon him.'[68] These lines allow us to interpret as literally referring to works of sculpture part of another poetical tribute to Mantegna's greatness from a second contemporary, the Mantuan poet Fra Battista Spagnoli. In a silva written between c.1486 and c.1497 Spagnoli, like Santi, extols Mantegna as having equalled and surpassed not only the greatest painters of Greece but also her sculptors. 'Why gaze on the statues of Myron and Lysippus? Why do the breathing marbles of Praxiteles and the statues of Euphranor delay your step? All the ivory of Phidias is overmatched. The genius (virtus) of Polycletus is tarnished and loses all lustre when compared to the genius of Andrea.'[69]

Two panels of the Justice of Trajan (Plates 251a and b) from two marriage-chests which Paola Gonzaga took with her on her marriage in 1476 to Leonhard, Count of Görz, have figures in painted stucco modelled on a painted background. Though strikingly interesting in their classicism and in their anticipation of the processional movement and even of some of the antiquarian features of Mantegna's Triumphs, they cannot be by Mantegna's own hand. Nevertheless their architectural elements recall the St Christopher frescoes of the Ovetari Chapel, while the sophisticated narrative style and some of the figures are very close to Mantegna. They appear to have been modelled and painted after Mantegna's designs, perhaps even under his supervision, but by a craftsman modeller and a professional painter of coffers, both of independent training and personality.[70] Spagnoli's mention of the ivory sculptures of Phidias may induce the eye to look speculatively at two other marriage-chests belonging to Paola, now in Graz, which are inset with ivory plaques of the Triumphs of Petrarch (Plates 253a and b), a subject Mantegna is known to have painted, only to recognize that there is nothing Mantegnesque in their conception or style.[71] Of late attempts have been made to attribute a variety of other sculptures to Mantegna,[72] but only the bronze head (Frontispiece), installed since 1516 in his funer-ary chapel in Sant'Andrea, can safely be considered an autograph work.[73] The casting in bronze of the clay model has been attributed to the medallist Sperandio and to the goldsmith Marc' Antonio Cavalli among others, but the testimony in 1560 of Scardeone, probably transmitting that of Campagnola, is unqualified: 'he [Mantegna] fused it for himself with his own hands' (quod sibi suis con-flaverat manibus). Almost certainly this was in the foundry which the Gonzaga maintained for their cannon; it was the only large one in Mantua at this date. In 1498 when resisting the importunity of the Duchess of Milan, who wanted an antique marble bust he owned, Mantegna offered to have it cast in bronze.[74]

The head shows him as a mature man, rather older than in the small self-portrait of the Camera Picta. The making of so proud an image in the immortalizing medium of bronze must have had some cause besides Andrea's awareness of his own genius, and of its nature we might be surer if we had a certain date for it. The hair-style might be thought to indicate a date, but the medallic portraits of Mantegna's contemporaries hint that from c.1485 to 1510 its loose cap-less freedom belongs, like the laurel-wreath and bared chest, to a heroic or idealizing genre of portraiture, signifying genius in poetry or the arts.[75] Since nothing is more perilous than to date a portrait too precisely from the apparent age of the sitter, the head must be left as dating most probably from the 1480s, Mantegna's middle age.

In reality, though often called a bust the head is not a bust in the true sense of the word, but imitates another form of antique sculpture, the imago clipeata, in which a bust was set on a shield which was then hung up for display either in the house or in temples. The imago clipeata appears in other guises in Roman art, and was a popular motif in early Renaissance art for heads of Roman emperors, being found in jewellery as well as in sculpture. Mantegna was almost certainly familiar with the long passage in Pliny the Elder in which Pliny records that in his day the fashion for painted portraits was obsolete and that they had been replaced by shields of silvered bronze, with the portrait figure or figures represented in low relief.[76] And he mentions as a novel invention the setting up of bronze portraits of famous men in libraries, dedicated to the immortal souls which speak within their walls. Some such desire for immortal commemoration surely inspired Mantegna, who may also have been encouraged by the severity with which Pliny speaks of the modern neglect of the Romans to leave likenesses of them-selves to their descendants, according to the good old custom.

His imago clipeata is formed of a bronze head and shoulders set on a ground of porphyry, which is framed in an angled border of white Istrian stone. The bronze and porphyry, both costly materials, were chosen to evoke antiquity, following a taste characteristic of humanism in the Veneto, which favoured bronze and inlays of coloured marbles. Even the Istrian stone, the characteristic medium of Venetian decorative sculpture, must have been procured at some expense from Venice. The conception and design of the whole are plainly the work of Mantegna, whose taste can be recognized in the contrast between the white stone of the frame and the porphyry, and in the perfect foil which the full rich red of the porphyry makes for the sombre brown of the bronze. But frame and roundel must have been cut, carved and polished in the studio of a professional sculptor, by a hand highly trained in decorative work. The frame is delicately carved with a bobbin ornament round its inner rim and with classical foliated scroll-work on its sloping central frieze, setting off the smooth glow of the porphyry. The bronze is conceived as a head to be applied to frame and roundel, and in a sense it ought to be seen as a work in high relief, rather than as a bust proper. This treatment is a characteristic expression of Mantegna's interest in the effect of relief for its own sake, and betrays, more perhaps than the want of a structural sense of volume, for which the bust has been criticized, something of the essentially pictorial spirit in which Mantegna approached sculpture.

The inward-sinking of the frame is calculated to set back the chest and shoulders, so throwing up the head, on which the interest is concentrated. The head is life-size, and turned to the left so that as set up in Mantegna's chapel it greets every entrant. On top of the head the hair is treated as a pattern of flat formal curls, parting to either side over the forehead and lying smoothly, single hairs being indicated by sharply incised rhythmic lines. To either side of the face it falls in longer, serpentine locks, in a rich arrangement that is balanced, yet not perfectly symmetrical, so as to suggest an unartificial looseness. The face itself is modelled with a naturalism that is formalized into a severe Roman strength of bone and line and feature, tempered by the lively rendering of such details as the crow's feet at the corners of the eyes and the scar across the brow. The surface is worked into the hard perfection proper to eternal bronze by the finish of its chasing, which must be the work of an experienced bronze-chaser even though the actual modelling and casting were done by Mantegna himself, as Scardeone reports.

As a whole the portrait is one of the finest and most sensitive that the quattrocento has left us, yet in the powerfully marked features it is true that there is a sense of something additively rather than organically conceived. The pupils of the eyes are left hollow. According to a legend recorded by the eighteenth-century chronicler of Mantua, Federigo Amadei, they were once filled with two diamonds set there by command of the Marchese Francesco when the medallion was placed in the chapel in Sant' Andrea.[77] More probably Mantegna intended to have them silvered, rather as the eyes of some of the bronze statuettes of the late fifteenth-century Mantuan bronze sculptor Antico are silvered in imitation of the antique. The laurels he wears on his head are copied from some Imperial Roman bust. Laurel crowns were used in antiquity to honour heroes, victorious generals, athletes and poets. The practice of crowning poets with a laurel wreath was revived in Italy during the Middle Ages: a famous instance was the laureation of Petrarch on the Campidoglio in Rome in 1341. Accordingly fifteenth-century portraits of poets often show them wearing a wreath of laurel. But is it quite exceptional to find an image of a painter wearing a wreath. In this self-coronation Mantegna may have been recalling the example of Parrhasius who, according to Aelian, was in the habit of wearing a robe of the royal colour of purple and a golden crown, 'as the inscriptions of his portraits testify'. And Pliny records that he used to call himself 'the prince of painters and the perfecter of the art'. Some such idea of himself was certainly in Mantegna's mind in laurelling his own brow.[78]

As with an antique *imago clipeata* the arms and part of the shoulders are cut off and the body is finished as a rough curve. The chest is not a smooth formalized plane but is naturalistically modelled *all'antica*, more so perhaps than a professional sculptor might have wished. The two small stone volutes attached to the bottom of the frame to either side of the chest seem designed to link the medallion with a laudatory tablet below, as is their function now. And even though the present inscription dates only from 1516, ten years after Mantegna's death, it would seem from this feature of the design that the image's original purpose was funerary, and that Mantegna, who expected, as we know from his wills of 1504 and 1506, to be interred under a slab in the floor of his chapel rather than in a raised tomb, designed it from the first to be his own commemorative monument. Such an intention would explain the choice of costly and durable materials, which were both necessary and appropriate to tombs and monuments, and the presence of laurels, with their symbolism of triumphant achievement and immortality of fame. Moreover, in an *imago clipeata* of this kind Mantegna would have found a truly antique form of commemoration, for Pliny also records that it was Roman practice to dedicate such *clipei* in temples and public places.

Mantegna's work as an engraver has been left for a later chapter, together with his drawings, on account of the very complex problems raised by his works in these two media, not least by the scarcity of contemporary records. Slightly better documented is his role as a designer of tapestries, embroideries and plate for the Gonzaga court. Already on 5 December 1465 one of his retainers was reminding Lodovico to send Maffeo the tapestry-maker with Giovanni Strigii to Venice to buy silk 'for that set of tapestries for which Andrea Mantegna has made the design.'[79] And indeed for so many new palaces Lodovico must have needed many new tapestries.[80] It was in fact quite customary to invite painters to make designs for them, and the Corradi, a family of Mantuan painters, had been supplying the Gonzaga with designs for their tapestries from at least as early as 1427. In July 1469, it will be remembered, Lodovico ordered Mantegna to make drawings of a male and female 'galina de India' (peacock) 'because we would like to have them put on our tapestries.' There still survives in Chicago a Gonzaga tapestry of the Annunciation (Plate 225) woven after a cartoon by Mantegna, with a peacock standing on the pavement, almost certainly the male galina de India of Lodovico's letter. The oblong frame is of simulated marble, and is designed in perspective, with the light falling from the left and casting the left and upper inside surfaces into shadow, an effect of contrast exactly paralleled in the simulated marble frame of the Berlin Presentation. The pattern of the garden pavement, with its inlays of marble in lozenges enclosed by squares, is typical of Mantegna, as is the steep hill in the background with a road winding in perspective up its slope and its city-crowned summit. These features might indicate a date of c.1460 for the original design, but the garden wall of linked medallions inset with marble is a motif found only in two works of c.1468–71, the fireplace fresco of the Camera Picta and the altarpiece of San Bernardino. The presence of the male peacock, together with the design of the garden wall, associate the cartoon of this tapestry with the drawings Mantegna was commissioned to make for a tapestry in 1469. As so often, the weaver has interpreted Mantegna's design and transformed it from an organic pictorial whole into an assemblage of decorative motifs perhaps more truly suited to his medium than Mantegna's intransigent original. But even through his translations Mantegna's characteristic drapery style can easily be recognized.

Little or nothing more is known of Mantegna as a designer of tapestries, but one set he designed for the Gonzaga was described by the Venetian connoisseur and collector Marc' Antonio Michiel in a letter of 1519 as among the most famous sets of the age, though now surpassed by the Raphael tapestries woven for Pope Leo X.[81] As a designer of embroidery he appears only in one document, a letter of 6 March 1469 from Barbara of Brandenburg to Giulia della Mirandola acknowledging receipt of a paper pattern for a purse Giulia wanted to have made, and saying that she has given it to Mantegna 'so that he may adjust it as it ought to be: but we are not sure of getting it all that quickly because he is wont to take a little long over these works of his.'[82] Mantegna had an exceptional eye and feeling for the rich stuffs of his age, for its gold brocades and watered silks, for the bold black patterns that unrolled their foliage and flowers over women's robes and men's tunics alike, and for the more subtle and subdued ripple of gold in irregular waves over a surface of deepest blue and red. Already manifest in the Presentation, this sensibility to magnificence of costume naturally became more intense after his introduction to the splendours of court life at Mantua.

Designs for secular goldsmith's work figure among the drawings of Jacopo Bellini, and even in Padua Mantegna may well have made designs both for domestic plate and for church silver. As far as church plate is concerned, five Mantegnesque drawings still survive in Frankfurt for part of a series of motifs to be executed, probably in niello, on the front and back of a processional cross (Plate 214).[83] Following invariable precedent, these motifs were intended to decorate the ends, and possibly also the central knop of the cross. In form the cross itself was evidently of typical North Italian Late Gothic design, for each motif is enclosed in an octagonal moulded frame. Into these frames the designs are fitted with Mantegna's customary care to suggest space; thus each is set on a protruding pedestal, while the wings of the pelican protrude before the frame and the finger-tips of the Virgin of the Assumption rest on the moulding. Such effects would never have been reproduced in niello or in any other decorative technique of the goldsmith, and are a sufficient indication that the designer was not himself a goldsmith or much aware of the limitations or conventions of the goldsmith's art in this respect. In themselves the motifs belong to the conventional iconography of crosses: the Virgin and St John were to be set in their usual position to the left and right respectively of the transverse bar on the front of the cross: the pelican was to be on the front of the lower bar, under the feet of the crucifix figure, while the Pietà and the Virgin of the Assumption were intended for the rear of the cross, the Virgin undoubtedly on the top bar, the Pietà in the central knop. Four or five other designs can therefore be presumed to be missing from the set. Although the Virgin of the Assumption reproduces in miniature the fresco of the Ovetari Chapel, the style of the other designs seems later, and all should probably be dated to the late 1480s, and the Virgin explained as Mantegna or someone in his studio economizing on his invention by using an earlier design. To this late dating the Gothic frames provide no objection, since the Gothic style persisted in the most sophisticated Italian goldsmiths' work until late in the fifteenth century.

As regards secular plate Mantegna may well have had a prime importance in north-eastern Italy as the introducer of an antique style into the design of the vessels of silver and silver-gilt used on the tables and dressers of the great. So very little remains either of designs for plate or of domestic plate itself from the quattrocento that the assertion cannot be made with any confidence, but designs by Giovanni Antonio da Brescia (*fl.*1510–20) and one from late fifteenth-century Padua show classical forms and ornament such as Mantegna may have used.[84] Probably he was invited to design plate because of his mastery of the vocabulary of the antique, though it is also true that it was now becoming customary to ask painters to make designs for works of decorative or sumptuary art when exceptional inventiveness of fancy or novelty of form was required. But this was usually without stylistic prescription. Nevertheless, it was probably the antique style that was sought by Federico Gonzaga. Ordinarily even into the last decades of the fifteenth century the Late Gothic or 'German' style as it came to be called in the 1490s was still highly admired in goldsmiths' work by many patrons in Lombardy and north-eastern Italy.[85] But when late in 1482 or early in 1483 Mantegna made designs for *olle* (pots) and *bocalli* (jugs) and a *fiasco* (flask) for Federico, the marquis's secretary Lancillotto Andreasi describes the '*olle*' as '*vecchie*' in a letter of 12 February 1483, and from the context this must mean that they were designed in the antique style. Andreasi tried first to make a bargain for the execution of these pieces with the goldsmith Gian Marco Cavalli (*c.*1454–after 1508), who was one of the witnesses to Mantegna's will on 1 March 1504 and later in the same year, on 11 August, a witness to the concession of his chapel in Sant'Andrea. Cavalli's price for the work was too high, and the commission was given instead to a young goldsmith, Gian Francesco Roberti, Federico being indifferent as to who did the work, and anxious only that the goldsmith should be given silver enough to make it 'beautiful and honourable'.[86]

Only one painting still survives that may have been commissioned by Federico, though it is equally possible that it was a commission from his son and successor Francesco. This is the great altarpiece of *St Sebastian* (Plate XI), now in the Louvre, but formerly in the Sainte-Chapelle at Aigueperse, in the Auvergne, where the dukes of Bourbon-Montpensier, a junior branch of the blood royal of France, had their chief castle. Through the marriage in February 1481 of Chiara Gonzaga with Gilbert de Bourbon-Montpensier the château of Aigueperse and the adjoining Sainte-Chapelle acquired a number of Italian works of art. Chiara shared the passion of her family for the collecting of antiquities. On 21 January 1485 her cousin Lodovico wrote to her:

> It displeases me and grieves me greatly that I have no cameos with which to satisfy your ladyship's request: those of the late Reverend Cardinal [Francesco] of happy memory now belong to Giovanni Francesco, his nephew and my brother. I have none, and none are to be found for sale. Of the medals I have, which are few, I will send you your share on the return of the Count your consort, and I will act like a good brother and give you half.[87]

The style of the *St Sebastian*, still so close in its landscape to the landscape of the outdoor fresco of the Camera Picta, and still so naturalistic in the realism of its figures, argues for a date shortly after Chiara's marriage. Because the painting is evidently an altarpiece for a church rather than for a domestic chapel, for which a very much smaller picture would have been painted, it was probably commissioned for the Sainte-Chapelle and therefore after Chiara had reached Aigueperse. Certainly it was intended as an invocation of the saint's protection against the plague and some votive impulse may lie behind its creation. It must have made an impression on contemporaries, for it was copied by the Paduan painter Bernardo Parentino, who is now known to have been at Mantua in the service of Francesco Gonzaga late in 1484 and 1485. Indeed we could safely date the Aigueperse *St Sebastian* c.1484–5 and suppose it to have been a commission given by the young Francesco to Mantegna for his favourite sister Chiara, were it not for the possibility that it took Mantegna a long time to complete such a huge painting.

The altarpiece is painted on canvas, not solely because of its great size, which meant that it had to be rolled up on rods for despatch to France, or because Mantegna had now, as we shall see, come to think canvas a more durable medium than wood. There were besides aesthetic reasons for the choice: in certain areas the canvas is used to suggest texture and so is thinly painted, a technique that is found a number of times in Mantegna's later works. In general the picture is grey. Its light chalky tonality is carefully maintained in the white loin-cloth, draped in Mantegna's customary sharp folds, in the light boxwood of the arrows and in the light green lichen stains on the stones. The light falls downwards from the upper right, throwing up the saint's torso as a strongly lit area of pale flesh colour on which shadows do no more than model the outlines of the forms. Elsewhere there is a strong contrast between the parts in shadow and those on which the light falls. The saint's pose is devised with this effect in mind, for his head and torso are turned to the right, in contrast with the violent *déhanchement* of the Vienna *St Sebastian*, where the torso is turned to the left, in *contrapposto* with the head, which is turned to the right. Mantegna must have thought this gentler classical curve more suitable for a large-scale altarpiece. Iconographically the pose is effective, for Sebastian's eyes appear to be lifted up beyond the pale of the picture in contemplation of the heavenly vision to which his lips are opened in prayer. One of the strongest contrasts in Mantegna's treatment of the figure is that between the brown, lined features framed by dark brown curling locks and the ideal chalky-white forms lit with pink of the torso: a contrast that knits a harsh intensity of experience and suffering in the face to a classical nobility of body. In general the type, representing a man of some thirty to forty years, is historically better suited than the youth of the Vienna picture to the centurion pious history in the *Legenda Aurea* declared Sebastian to have been.[88]

Sebastian has been set by his executioners on a flat block, part of a moulded cornice that lies in fragments before a fluted Corinthian column and broken arch resting on a pier, all that remains of the façade of an antique monument. The block is set obliquely to the picture plane, and the pier and arch also run obliquely to it, as can be seen from the line of the ruined entablature supported by an open portico that forms the adjoining right wall of the enclosure. With great art, the cylindrical form of the column is used to arrest the flight of these oblique lines into the right half of the picture and to give a just sufficient impression of frontality to that part of the architecture which is immediately behind the saint. Sebastian is bound to the column by cords round his ankles and wrists, so allowing him to stand before the vertical axis of the picture, which runs between the pier and the column. It will be noticed that the ruined and broken forms of the entablature, while crowning the architecture with a suitably picturesque feature, allow Mantegna to avoid any awkwardly dominant lines of direction which might over-emphasize his carefully modulated optical effects. There is a similar calculated subtlety in Sebastian's pose: only the line between the thorax muscles of the chest is on the central axis, and only the legs are shown frontally, so that the slanting pose of head and torso, while it repeats the oblique lines of the architecture, is arrested at the thighs, and frontality is restored.

The saint's feet, powerfully foreshortened, are shown beside a life-size sculptured foot, a fragment of an antique statue (Fig. 7). The foot is shod in a *crepida* or Roman military sandal, with fragmentary indications of a long robe above. In the ruins grows a fig-tree, as it might well do in reality. But it has been suggested that the tree makes allusion to verses of Martial and Juvenal in which fig-trees are described as splitting the marbles of ancient tombs and bringing them to desolation. So too ivy winds itself over the arch and entablature, bringing inevitable destruction on them. It is difficult to decide whether these two trees are introduced naturalistically, or whether they are charged with the symbolic figuration of the vanity of human magnificence. Any interpretation depends on establishing whether the monuments are introduced simply as picturesque ruins or figure the fall of paganism. Historically Mantegna must have known that paganism was far from having fallen when Sebastian was martyred, and the appearance of other partly ruined antique buildings in unison with a well-preserved antique fountain in the background suggests that no more was intended to be conveyed than a vision of antiquity in decay, even, as it were, in antiquity itself.[89] Again, as in the earlier *St Sebastian*, what we see is perhaps a romantic evocation of the Roman Campagna as a scene of mouldering grandeur.

Compositionally the diagonal bias of the figure and façade permits Mantegna to suggest that there is a lateral recession in space both behind and before them, a suggestion carefully reinforced, once more as in the earlier *St Sebastian*, by the positioning of the arrows in the body. This device leaves room for Mantegna to detach two of Sebastian's executioners, an archer and his companion, in the bottom right, with a natural-seeming emphasis aided by the use of strong colours, browns and blacks and purple, yellow and red. The two are figured as walking callously away along the road that behind them sinks into the middle distance. Their poses are typically Mantegnesque examples of figures that are in movement, yet suspended so to speak within a statuesque pose. St Sebastian is raised to the level of their necks, while they are shown cut off bust-length. From this we deduce that the monument is raised on a podium, while they, so it is implied, stand at ground-level, which in turn is made to correspond with reality, given that fifteenth-century altars rose to a height of about three feet. By this same device, moreover, we are made to raise our eyes to contemplate the saint.

In contrast with the nobility of Sebastian, though with the same sharpness of realism in the features, is the plebeian grossness of the archer and his companion, remarkable studies in two types of brutality set off against the saint's face of lined and careworn piety. The archer, his features darkened by stubble, his hair a rough dark grey, his lips parted to reveal gums that are largely toothless, figures a rough beastliness of cruelty such as Mantegna may well have seen in the plundering mercenary soldiery of the fifteenth century. His face is turned in three-quarter profile to the right, so that the light falls on the blood-shot whites of his eyes and the pouches beneath. His companion, in red, allies sensuality and cunning with cruelty. His broad strong features are shown in shadow, to darken their expression, his ugliness is pointed up by the light that falls on his bald head, by the scar through his left eyebrow, by the wart on his face, by his reddish nose and by the rolls of flesh on his neck. On the whole these two figures are treated with a suggestive sobriety of realism; comparison with the figures of grotesque brutality who fill contemporary German representations of the Passion and of martyrdoms marks out at once the greater dramatic objectivity of Mantegna in his figurations of stolid ferocity.

To either side of the column and pier open oblique views of a landscape background. With one of Mantegna's favourite effects, this sinks behind the foreground to rise again into a mountain of picturesque asymmetry and abruptness, sloped so as to carry up the eye from the left to its castle-crowned summit. Mantegna has added expressiveness to the scene by an atmospheric effect: he has made the sky on the left grey and stormy, with a layer of clouds of white hanging above the dark grey rock. On the lower slopes to the right is a little medieval hill city with ruined antique buildings of a mighty magnificence. Some of the medieval buildings are also majestic, like the frowning citadel on the upper crags, while some are homely, like the buildings behind the town wall and gateway. The great antique arched base of rusticated masonry carries a podium panelled with reliefs from which rise the truncated stumps of six fluted columns, and the gateway into the town is really an antique triumphal arch topped by a ruined attic storey or tower and with a central relief of a victor in his triumphal car. In contrast with these massive monuments, whose ruin had so powerful a sentiment for Mantegna and his age, laying on them the same spell as Gothic ruins on the eighteenth century, are little figures going about their business on the great lichen-stained platform. A woman holding a cauldron walks to the stately antique fountain and conduit on the right; two men ride towards the gateway; a man stands in the doorway of a shop selling copper bowls established in one of the bricked-up arches of the town wall, while another sits on a bench before it.

These observations of daily life were intended by Mantegna to give realism to his resurrections of antiquity. They belong to the aesthetic he had first formulated in his youth, an aesthetic that informed ideal figures and landscapes with minuteness of naturalistic detail in order to communicate to them a deceptive verisimilitude. The St Sebastian, so far as we know, is the last of his large-scale paintings in which Mantegna uses this stylistic formula with all his old thoroughness. In the early to mid-1480s there appears in his work a tendency to soften minuter naturalism into a larger, more generalized observation, and from the middle to the end of this decade ideal forms, based ever more closely on classical models, assert a new predominance. This is not to say that the earlier balance disappears entirely from his art: it is found for example in the Madonna delle Cave, a small late work of c.1490. What happens is that idealization, always either latent or fully formulated in Mantegna's earlier works, attains to an importance that subordinates, though to a varying scale, the significance of naturalistic detail in Mantegna's art. That art, in some respects deeply conservative, was never to move entirely into a world of ideal forms or to lose touch with the living world for the sake of the classical model. It is rather that the proportion between ideal and real alters, so that what is observed from life still enlivens what is figured with pictorial perfection, but in subordination. In this as in other ways Mantegna's art moves towards forms that presage the High Renaissance.

A number of works can be assigned to the earlier stage of this softening, more generalized realism, though Mantegna's tendency to preserve or revive earlier stylistic formulae makes it a hazardous undertaking to risk a close dating for these as for others of his undocumented works. The first of the group is the celebrated painting usually known as the Dead Christ (Plate x), now in the Brera. Its tonality of chalky grey resembles the tonality of the Aigueperse St Sebastian, and it may have been painted not too long afterwards. Really a Lamentation over the Dead Christ, it seems to have been painted by Mantegna as a private devotional picture, but such is its virtuosity of foreshortening that many critics have regarded it as a pure exercise in technique, for all its evident power and sincerity of feeling. And certainly Mantegna has sought from the technical point of view to image to the eye on what is really a medium-sized canvas a life-size figure seen from the front lying flat on a table in an interior setting. This naturally entailed an extreme of foreshortening, and indeed in its early days the picture was known as the Cristo in scurto, the foreshortened Christ. The degree of foreshortening in the legs and body, which occupy about two-thirds of the height of the canvas, can be seen from their dimensions, which are about four times the length of the head, instead of the usual six. As in the putti of the Camera Picta, the foreshortening is partly obtained by dividing the body into a sequence of horizontal divisions, which are figured as curves sinking behind each other as the eye looks upwards.

Recently Robert Smith has shown that the figure of Christ corresponds in its proportions to a live model similarly posed as seen from a distance of 25 metres (about 92 feet).[90] The figure itself has not been distorted to match the demands of strict mathematical perspective: thus the head, the part of the body furthest from the eye, is shown without diminution. In reality perspective imposes such a diminution only when the figure is drawn from a much nearer viewpoint. A photograph of the same live model taken from a distance of about $1\frac{1}{2}$ metres (4ft 8in) illustrates the consequent distortion, for it shows the feet greatly exaggerated in contrast to the head. However Mantegna set his model for the Christ in actuality his purpose must have been to obtain a plausibly foreshortened figure in which the natural proportions threw a pathetic emphasis on Christ's wounds and sufferings by contracting the intermediate forms of the body. He cannot have calculated that his medium-sized picture was to be viewed from such a distance as 92 feet in reality. And indeed we know this was not so, for the perspective scheme of the slab of marble on which the body is laid implies a viewpoint about twice the width of the picture away from the picture plane, in other words about 4ft 8in.

Presumably Mantegna superimposed a figure drawn from a greater distance on a perspective calculated from a near distance because it created the illusion that he sought of an expressively foreshortened life-size figure within a medium-size canvas. The incompatibility of the two does not seem to have troubled him. Smith suggests a reason. We do not apply the laws of perspective rigidly to the human body, but accept unreal relationships of scale in a foreshortened figure because they portray an image proportioned to our knowledge of the real proportions of the figure and the relative importance of its parts. In other words, the eye perceives not what it sees, but what it knows. Smith shows that in practice such rectifications were made, albeit unconsciously, by fifteenth- and early sixteenth-century artists. And indeed it is obvious that any diminution of the head of Christ in submission to strict perspective would seriously impair the picture's emotional force.

It is Mantegna's use of this formal invention to obtain expressiveness of emphasis that makes the true eloquence of the *Lamentation*. The spectator is placed on the hither side of the table, directly in front of the body and at eye-level. Because the picture was devised to be hung at eye-level Mantegna was able to use the flat soles of the feet, as they protrude with all his old illusionism beyond the edge of the table, to arrest the spectator's attention with their powerful

forms as it were even before the line of the picture plane. His horrified sight falls first on their wounds, then moves above to the wounds in the hands, then upwards again, directed by the axial line of folds in the loin-cloth and by the central line of the thorax, to the head which has rolled limply to one side. By its diminution of all other realities, the foreshortening thus intensifies the emotional impact of the wounds of Christ: that the effect is obtained by means essentially intellectual does not lessen the dramatic power with which it forces us to the contemplation of Christ's sufferings and death.

The lines of the perspective converge well above the picture, so deepening its space to produce the illusion that the body is lying in a horizontal plane perpendicular to the picture plane and enhancing our impression that we see a section isolated from the larger reality of a room, an impression which is essential to the verisimilitude of the picture and at the same time preserves its austerity of concentration on the body of Christ. Because of the steep angle chosen for the body and the pose of the head, the wounds of feet and hands and the livid features of the face appear in significant prominence from whatever side the picture is viewed, again according to a conception that transmutes the intellectual devices of foreshortening and geometrical perspective into a constant reminder of the sorrows of the Passion. Because the apex of the perspective triangle is well above the picture, the head of Christ is made the apex of a compositional triangle, formed by the lines of the arms and drapery to right and left of the torso. The rigour of its formal and emotional conception lends all the thrust of surprise to a painting of a theme which by Mantegna's day was well worn in art: here foreshortening, perspective and illusionism are used to express that deep devotion to the wounds of Christ characteristic of the fourteenth and fifteenth centuries. The livid grey of the passive body, the closed eyes, the sharp angle of the mouth, the flare of the nostrils, the limply hanging hands, all reinforce the image of a cold and lifeless corpse. As in the Aigueperse *St Sebastian*, in type the figure is conceived as a whole of ideal beauty, but Christ's humanity is made to transpierce the majestic forms of head, torso and hands by means of their pallor and by the brutal directness of the pose, which confronts us with the soles of the feet, the humblest of man's limbs, their wounds and crinkled seams detailed with a literal unsparing realism.

The austerity of the *Lamentation* is strengthened by its setting, which is severe to bareness, brown and dark, except for the pale pink stone of the table, which stands out in gentle contrast. The light falls downwards from the upper right, as from a window in the right wall of the room, leaving the left side of the picture in shadow. Light thus becomes an expressive device, and indeed is used for telling local contrasts, as where it falls on Christ's eyes and nose and on the dark hair on his chin, relieving them against the flesh tones of the mourning Virgin and St John. The moment represented is that when the body was laid out on a table top, before being washed, anointed and wrapped in a shroud, according to an ancient custom which still prevailed in fifteenth-century Italy. Mantegna has figured Christ's body as laid on a sheet that is folded over beneath the right leg and brought over the belly and left leg to lie in crumpled folds on the table, whose pink shows through the stuff, so thinly painted is the canvas. A second sheet lies under the thighs and emerges above from beneath the upper arms and shoulders. The artful naturalness of this arrangement is modified, characteristically, by the elegant pattern of the folds. The stone in the ground on which Christ's body was laid for washing, anointing and shrouding is described by fifteenth-century pilgrims to Jerusalem as being of white marble 'where the Mother of God sat lamenting with the body of our Lord Jesus'.[91] For reasons of pictorial composition or, it may be, misunderstanding his authorities, Mantegna has transformed it into a stone table, in conformance with the custom of his own day.

For the traditional *Imago Pietatis* so dear to fourteenth- and fifteenth-century piety, with the Virgin holding the lifeless body of her son before the Sepulchre or the Cross, attended by the three Maries, St John and Nicodemus, Mantegna has substituted a scene of dramatic verisimilitude in a setting of intimate realism. He shows us a modest room with brick-paved floor, its rear wall pierced on the right by a doorway leading into a dark interior. In all probability Mantegna worked up this setting from the *donnée* of the stone table. There is the same attention to plain and touching realism in the figures of the Virgin and St John, who stand with the Magdalen at the head of the bed, lamenting in passionate grief. John, clad in a dark tunic, is represented as a figure of humble and worn simplicity, not as the handsome young man of traditional iconography. His brown features are marked by a few strong lines, with touches of red for modelling. He is taken in a foreshortened profile view, balancing the half-discerned head of the Magdalen to the further side of the Virgin. Mantegna has cut off their three figures so as to leave only their heads and hands in expressive juxtaposition with the head of Christ, their pale flesh colours emerging from a shadowed background. John's pose is conceived with the same marvellous economy of form that gives such emotional starkness to the picture; only those parts of the figure that express anguish are seen, the face, with its muscles contracted about the eye, a falling tear,

the tightly locked hands. As befits her importance, the Virgin is shown in full profile. She is represented not as a type of ideal dignity but as a plain ordinary woman in late middle age. Her face is taut with grief, as we see from the muscular distortion of the mouth. A coarse light-brown robe and head-dress throw up the white wimple and white kerchief encircling her face. Her right hand is raised, wiping away the tears as they fall from her eyes. A motif of great poignancy in its sure observation of the physical signs of deep grief, it is rendered with a restraint exceptional in an artistic culture that was too prone to consider extreme facial distortion and violent gesticulation as the only eloquent demonstrations of suffering. Its ultimate inspiration may well have been some Flemish picture, for the representation of tears seems to have been first mastered in the Netherlands. But although Flemish pictures of the Lamentation were popular in fifteenth-century Italy because of their pathos, in none of them do we find as in Mantegna's great picture virtuosity of design and ideality of form blended with sobriety of realism to make an invention of such startling expressiveness. It was almost certainly of these figures that Lomazzo was thinking when in his *Idea del Tempio della Pittura* (1590) he writes: 'He was no less great in the representation of the affections, as may be seen in the Virgin Mary he has painted weeping over her son and in the other Virgins and in St John, in all which figures he has expressed grief and tears so naturally that it is impossible for others to do better.'

In the Virgin, as in the St John, a dry truth of history and emotion replaces the ennobling style of quattrocento art. This reappears in the Magdalen, traditionally a type of beauty, who stands behind the Virgin, lips parted in a cry of sorrow. There are, however, two touches of quietly refined splendour, the pillow of pale pink watered silk on which Christ's head rests, and the dark goblet of hardstone or marbled glass which contains unguent for his anointing. Only Christ of all these holy figures has a halo, and that is a delicate and transparent radiance.

The *Lamentation* was greatly admired in North Italy throughout the Renaissance and there still exist quite a number of copies and versions. Its transfigured realism is also found in three small Madonnas, now in Berlin, Bergamo and Milan, that date from the later 1480s and early 1490s.[92] All have the black background of the early *Presentation*, perhaps an indication that Mantegna was reverting to the influences of his Paduan youth, especially as the Berlin and Milan Madonnas recall Donatellesque Madonna compositions in their passionate vitality of feeling. The figures of Virgin and Child are interlocked in compositions of equal skill in all three. In the Milan picture (Plate 98) it is implied by means of clever drawing and foreshortening that the Virgin is seated and the Child is set between her upthrust knee and the cheek she lovingly presses against his head. In the Bergamo Madonna (Plate xv), more formal in its conception, the Virgin stands at an angle, clasping the Child, whose head is detached against the background and alone is parallel to the picture plane. In the Berlin Madonna (Plate 100), the latest of the three, the Virgin supports the swaddled Child in a fold of her cloak, a motif that unites them into a single oval form. The Milan Child is surely drawn from a very small baby, so natural is his attitude as he sleeps on his mother's knee, his mouth open, with tongue and upper gum showing in its tender coral pink. The Bergamo Child is a little older, with a baby's light fine hair: he is getting his first two teeth in his upper gum. All three Madonnas have in common a type of child whose soft limbs are observed with great tenderness from the living model.

This tender sympathy for babies and for the relationship between mother and child, though expressed with all his customary objectivity of observation and reserve of feeling, is an unexpected source of human warmth in Mantegna's marmoreal art. In all these small pictures he also searches for delicately graduated effects and contrasts, preferring a low fall of light on one side of the face that leaves the other in gentle shadow. Comparison with Giovanni Bellini shows how much more closely interested Mantegna was in the modulation of light and shade on surfaces. In the Bergamo Madonna, the most beautiful of all, shadow falls on the Virgin's face with a mysteriousness that adds the necessary dimension of awe to an invention so tenderly naturalistic within its sculptural severity of contour. The colour too is low in these pictures, playing on quiet contrasts between delicate whites and sober blacks and a refined richness and elegance of pattern and colour in the costume, as in the orange-red robe of gold-figured watered silk of the Milan Virgin, or the beautiful mantle of the Bergamo Virgin, a watered silk of pale azure with the waves executed in gold and the edges hatched in gold, so that the overall effect is of light golden ripples in the surface of blue. In these pictures Mantegna begins to move towards that style of his old age in which his paintings simulate a coloured or monochrome relief, with all background suppressed or else supplanted by a panel of coloured marble and the figures treated as isolated sculptural forms.

The Washington *Christ Child Blessing (Imperator Mundi)* (Plate 99) is almost certainly intended to be a pictorial equivalent of a small statuette of the Bambino Gesù.[93] Such small statuettes were the favourite images of this particular cult of the Christ Child, originally a Franciscan and then later a feminine devotion which was now coming into the perennial vogue it has ever since enjoyed in the Catholic world. In 1510 Isabella d'Este ordered an ivory statuette of a Bambino holding an orb (*balla*) which was evidently of the same type as Mantegna's Child.[94] In Mantegna's painting the Child is shown standing on a cross-foot in a niche of variegated marble, against an inset cross of green serpentine. His weight resting on his left leg, he gazes outwards with solemn childish tenderness, his lips parted and his right hand raised in blessing, his left hand holding the cross, at once a sceptre and an emblem of his future passion. With exquisite skill Mantegna has united in the little figure grave tenderness, childish dignity and a pathetic adumbration of future sufferings. He has clothed him in a short white chemise, with a broad band of cloth wrapped round his waist: the sharp narrow horizontal folds of the band, contrasted with the similar vertical folds of the chemise, produce an intricate surface pattern which is set off by the stiff smooth fall of the blue cloak with its gold-embroidered borders and blue clasp. His pose, intended to be seen from below, suggests that the painting was to be set above a doorway, so that the Christ Child would stand in continual blessing over the occupants of the chamber.

VIII

The Triumphs of Caesar

ON 14 July 1484 Federico Gonzaga died suddenly. He was succeeded by his son, the eighteen-year-old Gianfrancesco, usually known as Francesco. Mantegna now once again found himself labouring under all an old courtier's uncertainty of favour under a new lord, for although Francesco was '*tutto inclinato ale uirtù*', he had as yet vouchsafed no sign of interest in Mantegna.[1] Like his father and grandfather, Francesco depended on what he could earn as a *condottiere* to maintain himself and his court in due state, but he was far more exclusively interested than they in warfare and in knightly exercises, such as jousts and tournaments, and in improving his famous stud of horses. He made no pretension to be a collector of works of art. When the Bolognese goldsmith and littérateur Girolamo Casio, anxious to obtain a grant of nobility from Francesco, sent him from Bologna on 4 November 1513 a present of an intaglio of the Holy Ghost in a stone 'which shows the rays of fire naturally', Francesco returned it three days later with the brusque message that 'we deem it would be better in your hands, as a person who understands its value better than we, for we have a better understanding of horses and arms than of intaglios.'[2]

Yet it would be unjust to conclude from such rough answers as this or from any reluctance in Francesco to apply himself to his books as a boy that he was hostile to art in the fashion of a late Victorian Philistine hearty. On the contrary in the family tradition he was a builder and a decorator of buildings. In an affectionate letter of 20 June 1491 to his sister Chiara in France he writes proudly of showing off to his father-in-law Ercole d'Este 'a certain addition of building we have designed and almost finished at one end of the *palazzetto*' at Gonzaga, 'which we are certain is in no way inferior in the

quality of its rooms to those the happy memory of that late Illustrious Lord our grandfather had made. Then we came on the road to Marmirolo, where likewise we have made a *palazzetto* of great convenience and ornament to that place.'[3] He also built a new palace in Mantua, that of San Sebastiano, or alla Pusterla,[4] begun *c.*1505, and a new country palace at Poggio Reale. And in the honorific decree of 13 June 1494 by which he granted Francesco Bonsigori a goodly piece of land he declares 'painting delights us not a little and by its pleasures we often relax and console our mind from the various occupations, anxieties and cares in which it is involved.'[5]

For all these new buildings Francesco naturally commissioned decorations, just as his father and grandfather had done. The difference between his patronage and theirs sprang from Francesco's enthusiasm for war and military prowess and from the ambition which he nursed to become a great and successful general. War was still the proper pursuit of a knight, and still more that of a prince for whom it was the only means of enlarging his state, increasing his revenues and augmenting his glory. As a young man Francesco's aspirations to future military greatness were naively eager and hopeful. In the later 1490s when his secretary Jacopo d'Atri dedicated his chronicle of Francesco's successful campaigns at Fornovo and in South Italy to his master, he did so 'as to one who by his virtue and fatal predisposition art alone destined to triumphs and the acquisition of most ample kingdoms.'[6] And in his *Manto* the Ferrarese poet Ercole Strozzi saluted Francesco as a 'novo Cesare'.[7] Accordingly, wherever decorations were executed for him in the *sala* or principal room of one of his palaces, at Gonzaga, at Marmirolo, in the Castello at Mantua or the Palazzo di San Sebastiano, their theme was always that of victory

Fig. 9. Corselet-bearer. Detail from *The Triumphs of Caesar*. Canvas VI (Plate 106)

or triumph. For the Castello Mantegna was commissioned to paint *The Triumphs of Caesar*, seven of whose canvases were later transferred to the Palazzo di San Sebastiano and completed by the addition of canvases by Costa celebrating the Triumph of Francesco. For Marmirolo Mantegna's son Francesco painted from 1491 the Triumphs of Alexander, while at Gonzaga in 1496 the theme was 'the victories of the most Illustrious and Excellent Lord', Francesco's grandfather Lodovico, probably chosen in emulation of the victories of Francesco Sforza which Lodovico il Moro had had painted on great canvases in the Castello of Milan.[8]

Caesar and Alexander were the greatest captains of classical antiquity. To the knights and nobles of the fourteenth and fifteenth centuries they were heroes, and this was as true of the International Gothic age, with its romantic cult of chivalry, as of the Renaissance, when that cult was infused or overlaid with humanism. It is not surprising then if the two were frequently made the theme of paintings, more especially Caesar, who was not only a hero of war, but the first of the Roman emperors. Thus the Corte Vecchia, the first palace of the Gonzaga, built during the second half of the trecento, had a loggia painted 'with the history of Caesar and Pompey'.[9] Leonello d'Este had a special admiration for Caesar, whom as a humanistic prince he must have revered for his combination of greatness as a general with literary gifts. Guarino translated the *De Bello Gallico* for Leonello, and to the controversy started by Poggio Bracciolini in the 1430s over the respective claims of Caesar and Scipio Africanus to be the greatest general and hero of antiquity he also contributed a treatise taking the side of Caesar, which he dedicated to Leonello. In 1441 a room in the Castello of Ferrara was called the *stanza di Cesare*, probably because it contained paintings of histories from his life. These may well have been commissioned by Leonello. And on the occasion of Leonello's marriage in 1435 to Margherita Gonzaga, Pisanello presented him with a portrait of Caesar.[10]

Among the first books Isabella d'Este bought in Venice in 1491 was a *Vita di Giulio Cesare*, probably a translation of Plutarch, and in 1496 she was searching for an Italian translation of Caesar's *Commentaries*.[11] The spell which the triumphs of ancient Rome cast on a Renaissance imagination, conjoined in Mantegna's *Triumphs* with the spell cast by Caesar, appears in a letter of 7 July 1507 from Isabella to her sister-in-law Elisabetta Gonzaga, Duchess of Urbino. In this she confesses that she has the greatest longing to visit Rome, 'not to see the court and the different nations . . . but to see the antiquities of the famous ruins of Rome and contemplate what it must have been like when a victorious general was celebrating his triumph.'[12]

Most probably Mantegna's *Triumphs of Caesar* (Plates 101–118) were commissioned by Francesco in 1485 or thereabouts. There is every reason to think that originally they were intended to decorate the great *sala* preceding the Camera Picta on the second floor of the Castello. We shall see that in all probability this scheme was never carried out, but there can be no serious doubt of Francesco's original intention, which was to complete in this way the decoration of all the principal rooms of the *appartamento marchionale* of the Castello that Mantegna had begun under his grandfather Lodovico and had already completed as far as the chapel and Camera Picta or state-chamber. The great size of the canvases made it impossible for Mantegna to paint them in his own house, and it seems that he was given a room in the Corte Vecchia, the old Gonzaga palace, in which to work. Here on 26 August 1486 'the Triumphs of Caesar which Mantegna is painting' were shown to Ercole d'Este, Duke of Ferrara. 'They pleased him greatly', and after viewing them he returned to the Castello by the covered way that linked it with the Corte. The work, as always with Mantegna, was prolonged, and when it was interrupted by his sojourn in Rome from the summer of 1488 to September 1490 to paint a chapel for Pope Innocent VIII, he wrote to Francesco asking him that if repairs were made to the windows of the room in which the *Triumphs* were kept, to take care that the canvases were not spoiled, 'for in sooth I am not ashamed of having painted them.'[13] And on 23 February 1489 Francesco reassured him that 'good order has been taken to keep them safe, for although they are the work of your hands and genius, we glory none the less in having them in our house, where they shall be a monument of your loyalty and talents.'[14]

The notion of executing these great wall-decorations on separate canvases rather than as frescoes or wall-paintings was not original to Mantegna. There can be little doubt that it was suggested to him by the example of his brother-in-law Gentile Bellini. Commissioned in September 1474 to restore the historic decorations of the greatest state-room of the Venetian Republic, the Sala del Maggior Consiglio in the Palazzo Ducale, Gentile had substituted paintings on canvas (*teleri*) for the earlier frescoes, which had gravely deteriorated. The disadvantage of painting directly on to a wall was of course the risk of damage from damp or salts in the wall and from flaking plaster, all of which were even greater hazards in the climate of Venice than elsewhere. Hence the ingenious remedy proposed by Bellini.[15] In part too his reasons were certainly the same as those which Mantegna's son Francesco and the painter Tondo Tondi gave in July 1491 for preferring to paint the Triumphs of Alexander at Marmirolo on canvases 'as Messer Andrea has done'.

They urged that 'they will work more quickly and they [the paintings] will be more beautiful and more lasting and so says everyone who is expert in this craft.'[16] That Mantegna and other fifteenth-century painters felt they could work more expeditiously on canvas than directly on to the wall is a consideration that has not received due emphasis. From the time of the *Triumphs* canvas will be Mantegna's preferred medium: so much so that Morelli in the nineteenth century assumed that any work on canvas must be a late work, thus imposing on Mantegna a consistency which distorts the history of his art.

The Triumphs of Caesar depict the triumphal procession through Rome of the victorious Caesar and his army. They brought Mantegna a celebrity that was to last throughout the sixteenth century, being admired as one of the greatest achievements of Italian painting since its modern revival not only by Venetian and Lombard artists and dilettanti, but by such advocates of Tuscan purism as Michelangelo and Vasari. Yet for all their fame in Mantegna's own lifetime and during the century that followed, serious problems attend the study of them. Here we shall consider first their pictorial conception and their iconography, and then in the light of these the vexed questions of their destination and chronology. As we have them, the *Triumphs* are painted on nine canvases, and the woodcuts which the Mantuan wood-engraver Andrea Andreani made of them from 1598 onwards show that this was their number at the end of the sixteenth century. They have no true single titles, since they are a processional sequence, not a series of independent compositions, and here they are named and numbered as in Andrew Martindale's recent study and catalogue, though for convenience the traditional titles acquired by some of them are also used.[17]

The canvases were designed to be seen a little above eye-level, and Mantegna has used his customary perspective device with works intended to be seen at such a height, posing the figures at the front, in the admiring words of Sebastiano Serlio in 1537, 'on a line, with no flat plane visible'.[18] The general composition also takes account of this intended height. Whole-length figures appear only on the foreground plane: the ranks of figures behind are largely concealed, and because of the perspective are sunk in relation to the front rank, with the result that the eye is drawn not to them but to the panoply of standards, weapons and other objects that they escort or carry. This panoply animates the upper half of the canvas, creating a second tier of forms of marvellous variety above the lower tier of figures. The sole exception is Canvas VII, the *Captives*, where Mantegna has modified this formula, filling half the background with a palace from whose grated windows tiny spectators watch the triumphal

procession, a change made to concentrate our attention on the solemn pathos of the action. By this construction in two tiers Mantegna has avoided great uninteresting expanses of sky or lengths of overdominant architecture and has gained effects of daring imaginative grandeur, such as the tremendous looming siege-engines of Canvas II.

Mantegna's originality in the *Triumphs* lies in his attempt to recreate an image at once splendid and yet historically, archaeologically and humanly plausible of a great Roman triumph. He wanted to show how Caesar and his army might in reality have appeared as they paraded through the city with their array of weapons, spoils and captives. Naturally he could not sacrifice considerations of pictorial effect entirely to considerations of historical accuracy. The settings, for example, contain much pure landscape in the form of swelling green hills, with cattle grazing on some of their slopes, a fall of woodland on others, and even, on Canvases IV and V, a crown of Mantegna's favourite classical ruins. Yet Mantegna was certainly aware that triumphs followed a hallowed processional way through the streets of Rome, and this feature of the *Triumphs* can only be explained as a decorative solution to a major problem of composition, the imperious need not to diminish the impact of the procession by filling the entire length of the canvases with a continuous background of distracting buildings. In order to relieve more effectively his rich and motley diversity of instruments of war, trophies, insignia and spoils Mantegna omits all background in Canvases I and II, silhouetting them instead against the sky. The light seems intended to be an evening light, to match the words of one of his most important ancient literary sources, Suetonius, the biographer of the Caesars, who says that Caesar's Gallic triumph was held by night.[19] It is of course difficult to be certain of this in the ruined state of the *Triumphs*, but an evening light would also explain the burning torches which appear in five of the canvases, and the burning candelabra carried by the elephants.

With an art that conceals art, the pageant of the victorious army unrolls with an apparent naturalness that deliberately avoids symmetrical patterning, relying instead on a few strong rhythms of line and movement to order and balance the composition of each canvas. Another danger in making designs for a procession intended to be seen above eye-level is that the lower parts may become simply arrangements of moving legs. Mantegna has found a variety of solutions to this problem: difference of pose, as in Canvas I, where figures are seen in profile, semifrontally, and from the rear, and differences of costume, military tunics being contrasted with long robes, cloaks and togas. In Canvases II, III, IV and V the front plane is shared by figures and by animals or non-figural motifs, in II by a car bearing the image of a captive god and a horse, in III by a car laden with trophies, in IV by the sacrificial oxen, in V by the elephants. The monotony of an unbroken processional line is avoided with the same skill: not content with all the diverse shapes of musical instruments, standards, banners, candelabra, images and weapons, Mantegna breaks the forward advance with anecdotal moments, a soldier looking back, an infantry man speaking to a mounted officer, a crippled beggar, buffoons, a child complaining to its mother, this last a motif greatly admired by Vasari.

The principal visual inspiration of Mantegna's invention was beyond all doubt the relief of the spoils of Jerusalem on the Arch of Titus in Rome, with its advancing figures, its composition in two tiers, its spoils and standards raised as in the *Triumphs* into the upper tier, and its compositional device of backward-turning heads. It was also the source for certain antique motifs proper to a Roman triumph, the litters (*ferculae*), the trumpets, the *tabulae ansatae*. But Mantegna has enriched his scheme with motifs and hints taken from other Roman monuments, such as the Arch of Constantine, the Arch of Septimius Severus, Trajan's Column, the Column of Marcus Aurelius, three reliefs of the Triumph of Marcus Aurelius, then in the church of Santa Martina, and now in the Palazzo dei Conservatori, and the Arco di Portogallo. Before 1488 these can have been known to him solely from drawings. But drawings of antiquities by antiquaries and artists were in Mantegna's hands from his Paduan days, and he certainly added to his knowledge in Mantua, as for instance with the book of drawings of antiquities that Lodovico Gonzaga bought in Florence and lent to him in 1476.

More complex is the problem of interpreting the historical and antiquarian learning deployed in the *Triumphs* with such majestic grace. In his letter of 23 February 1489, Francesco Gonzaga, as we have seen, speaks of the *Triumphs* as 'the work of your hands and genius (*ingegno*)'. There can be little doubt then that the invention of the *Triumphs* was Mantegna's own. A first difficulty appears, however, when we try to establish what they actually represent. According to Suetonius, as dictator in 45 BC Caesar celebrated five triumphs, 'the first and most magnificent' commemorating his conquest of Gaul, the second his victory over Ptolemy, Pompey's murderer, in Egypt, the third his recovery of Pontus, the fourth his victory over Metellus, Scipio and Cato in Africa, the fifth his victory over the younger Pompey in Spain. Of these five triumphs only two, the Gallic triumph and the Pontic triumph, were free from the taint of civil war, and celebrated the subjugation or recovery of territories occupied by external enemies of Rome. Mantegna or his patron

Francesco most probably decided that their great processional canvases should represent only these two triumphs, the Gallic and the Pontic triumph. It may be indeed that there were allusions in the inscriptions to the other triumphs, but such is the uncertainty attending their true reading that there can be no sure proof of this. If the *Triumphs* figure all five triumphs, they are conflated into one, with the civil wars deliberately subordinated because they were triumphs over fellow-Romans.

In reality Caesar held each of his five triumphs on five separate days, but Mantegna figures his theme as a single triumph, using a licence that finds a later parallel in the *Introduction of the Cult of Cybele* of 1506. It has recently been argued that the *Triumphs* represent only the Gallic triumph. But Suetonius, who was certainly Mantegna's authority for introducing elephants bearing candelabra into the Gallic *Triumph*, also says that in the Pontic triumph Caesar paraded a *titulus* inscribed VENI. VIDI. VICI. A *titulus* bearing this inscription is carried in Canvas IX, and there is evidence that the motif was already present in the sixteenth century, before the heavy restorations of the seventeenth, so confirming technical analysis, which shows that the passage is largely autograph. Since the point of these three famous words is that Caesar came, saw and conquered in a trice, they cannot by any stretch of imagination be applied to the ten-year struggle in Gaul, with all its long drawn-out vicissitudes, but must refer to the three-day campaign in Pontus.

In keeping with Suetonius, who says that the Gallic triumph was held first and excelled the others in splendour, whereas the inscription VENI. VIDI. VICI 'signified not so much the actions of the war, like the others, but its swift completion', Mantegna has given greatest prominence to motifs illustrating the Gallic triumph. It occupies the lion's share of the nine canvases, and even so Mantegna implies that not quite all of it is shown, for with his usual suggestiveness of narrative Canvas I opens *in medias res*, with figures already passing off the canvas. It is important to notice that figures and spoils from the two triumphs, Gallic and Pontic, are blended into a single procession. An Ethiopian figures in Canvas I, and in Canvas IV, among the spoils, is a huge vase whose inscription in Cufic letters indicates its oriental provenance. In Canvas VII the captives are Greeks, not barbarian Gauls, while Canvas VIII exhibits a Phrygian musician – Phrygia, like Pontus, was in northern Asia Minor – wearing an oriental turban. To many of the emblems of captive towns Mantegna has given the form of a bust of Cybele, perhaps intending to associate then with the Pontic campaign, for Cybele was a deity from Asia Minor. The crowns and diadems carried as spoils in Canvas VI belong to the Hellenistic rulers of the east: so too the diadem and *armilla* worn by the most prominent male captive in Canvas VII proclaim him an effeminate oriental monarch, not a rough chieftain of Gaul.[20] Indeed he may be King Pharnace of Pontus himself.

Analysis of the literary and visual sources used by Mantegna reveals not only how complex they are, but also discloses the process by which motifs for which there was literary or visual evidence have been blended with motifs invented or supplied to fill lacunae in that evidence. Thus if the head of Caesar we now see faithfully reproduces Mantegna's original, he had obviously substituted for his earlier image of Caesar in the Camera Picta another type, one still derived from ancient coins, but influenced by literary descriptions such as those in Suetonius and Plutarch of Caesar's baldness and of his habit of combing his hair forwards.[21] Other motifs are designed for purely pictorial effect or intended simply to distance the scene in time. For Mantegna has not lost sight in antiquarian researches of his ultimate purpose, which was to devise a rich and animated procession that would wind around the walls of a room along great canvases filled with lifelike figures and ornamented with splendour of colour and variety of invention.

Much effort has gone into the identification of Mantegna's visual sources, and it is therefore a surprise to discover in the *Triumphs* singularly few straightforward reproductions of surviving antique buildings, sculptures and medals. The most conspicuous example is the representation of the horse-tamers on the Quirinal in Canvas IX, figures that had of course been known to Mantegna from his Paduan days. But even these he has mounted on a triumphal arch, which for all that it may recall the arch at Pola, has nevertheless been varied to become his own invention. In the *Triumphs*, then, as in his earlier and later works, Mantegna devises classical monuments and sculptures in the style of antiquity using drawings of surviving *vestigia antiquitatis* as an inspiration and a guide, but not as models to be copied in any sedulous and servile spirit. He seems to have wished to penetrate beyond the actual remains of the classical past to a fullness of lost magnificence that they still suggested to his eye, but no longer represented. Like all humanist imaginations, his sometimes surpassed in its creations the reality of the classical world. Especially is this so in the *Triumphs*, which have none of that careful mingling of everyday buildings with great monuments that is found in his paintings as late as the Aigueperse *St Sebastian*. Rome exalted his fancy and he evidently shared the general Renaissance belief that the ancient city had been a scene of unrivalled architectural grandeur, a succession of palaces, triumphal arches, columns, statues and amphitheatres.

The imaginative transformation which Mantegna has wrought on his visual sources does not mean that he did not seek antiquarian authority from ancient monuments for the dress, weapons, standards and spoils that he figures in the *Triumphs*. Thus the medallions worn by the horses derive from those worn by the famous bronze horses of San Marco, Venice. His vocabulary of armour and weapons is mixed, in that fifteenth-century weapons unknown in antiquity, such as the pole-axe, figure among the panoply of his soldiers, and fifteenth-century models influence the design of his helmets. The rich colouring of his cuirasses, too, belongs to fifteenth-century taste, not to antiquity. But there seems to be evidence that he knew and used for his representations of trophies and of men carrying weapons two piers, now in Florence, but then in the church of Santa Sabina at Rome, which are carved with trophies of arms, and other sculptures of trophies from the Nymphaeum Aquae Juliae, then in Sant'Eusebio, Rome, and now on the Capitol.

Yet as we study the sources of the *Triumphs*, the conclusion forms itself that Mantegna drew a primary part of his inspiration from literary descriptions of Roman triumphs. Here again we find a mosaic of authorities. The laconic Suetonius gives only the scantiest details of Caesar's triumphs, and in devising his procession Mantegna or his advisers turned to other historians, and principally to Plutarch's description of the triumph of Aemilius Paulus in 168 BC after his victorious campaign in Greece,[22] and to Appian's account in his *Romaica* (VIII, 34–6) of the triumph of the younger Scipio Africanus in 146 BC. Appian in particular must have seemed an excellent authority, for he declares that the form of triumph he describes was that customary in Rome. By conflating Plutarch and Appian Mantegna devised the general order of his procession. It is opened by trumpeters, who are followed by standards and banners depicting the glorious deeds of the army, then by colossal figures, by wooden models and busts surmounted by mural crowns symbolizing captured cities, by trophies of arms and by spoils of gold and silver plate and crowns. Next come white sacrificial oxen led by youths bearing the vessels of sacrifice, then more trumpeters, then more oxen, then elephants, then more bearers of spoils of plate and of trophies of royal arms and royal crowns and diadems. Next come the captives, men, women and children and their attendants and after them buffoons who mock the captives. Then follow soldiers bearing boughs of laurel and a standard, a musician playing the cithara, the Phrygian musician, who dances as he plays his trumpet and bag-pipes, a youth playing the tympanum, and more trumpeters and standard-bearers. Last comes the victorious general on his triumphal car, drawn by white horses and attended by boys, youths and bearers of trophies and *tituli*.

This cortege omits Appian's lictors who precede the musicians and also his bearers of incense who precede the general. We shall return to this problem: more immediately significant is the fact that the sequence as we have it ends with Caesar in his triumphal car. At one time Mantegna certainly intended to add the part of the procession that according to both Plutarch and Appian followed the general's car. In Appian, this tail is composed of secretaries, servants and shield-bearers, in Plutarch, of soldiers bearing laurels. We know that such was Mantegna's intention from the existence of a drawing in Vienna and of a related engraving, both copies of a lost tenth composition for which Appian and Plutarch conflated provided the principal motifs. It is true that the subject of this composition is traditionally identified as the 'Senators' (Plate 119), and senators may indeed be figured in the two front ranks, but after these come scribes and soldiers carrying laurels and shield-bearers. An interesting feature of the composition is that it matches the *Captives* closely in design, even to the division of the background into a palace with spectators on the left and an opening on to monumental buildings on the right. Mantegna never transferred his design to canvas. Mario Equicola, the historian of Mantua, who from 1508 as secretary of Isabella d'Este was a member of the Gonzaga household, records that the omission of the procession which followed the triumphal car was much criticized and that at one time Francesco Gonzaga announced his intention of remedying this defect. We can still see that Canvas IX was designed to be followed by at least one more canvas since two of its larger figures look backwards at what comes after them.

Although Mantegna follows Plutarch and Appian, the triumphs he was depicting were not those that they described. Accordingly he takes motifs from other sources. From Suetonius, as we have seen, came the elephants bearing candelabra and the flaming torches of the Gallic triumph and the *titulus* of the Pontic triumph. These had to be included, since they were the features of Caesar's triumphal processions for which there was authentic historical evidence. The candelabra are given the form of ancient incense-burners, and it may be that here Mantegna took a hint from a description of a triumph in Ovid, as Cecil Gould has suggested, and that the youth standing on the back of one of the elephants and holding his head above the flames is adding incense to them. Besides ancient authors Mantegna perhaps consulted modern antiquaries. The antiquarian investigation of Roman triumphs had already begun in the middle of the century with the collection of monuments and literary references.

Flavio Biondo had included an account of triumphs in his *Roma triumphans* (1457–9, printed 1472), as had Roberto Valturio in his *De re militari* (1460, printed at Verona in 1472, and in an Italian version in 1473), while at some date before 1465 Giovanni Marcanova had composed a treatise, now lost, entitled *De dignitatibus Romanorum triumpho et rebus bellicis*.

However, Mantegna at times departs from the texts he can be shown to have used. The figure of Caesar, for instance, by no means corresponds entirely with what Appian and Plutarch say of their triumphing generals: if he wears their gold fillet set with jewels, his dress is of gold, not of purple interwoven with gold, as in their descriptions, and he holds a golden, not an ivory sceptre. And in his left hand he bears not a laurel, but a palm. Perhaps Mantegna chose this alternative symbol of victory in preference to what his ancient authorities indicated in order to distinguish him from the common soldiers, who do bear laurels. The wreath of laurel held above his head is a detail from the Elder Pliny, who says it was held by a slave.[23] Accordingly Mantegna or his advisers cannot have derived their information from him directly, but must have taken it instead from Flavio Biondo, who after citing Pliny's text observes: 'but in the marble figures of triumphing generals that still survive it is winged Fortune, not a slave, who holds up the crown.' Presumably Biondo was thinking of the Arch of Titus, where a winged figure stands behind the triumphing Emperor. In fact Mantegna's wreath-holding figure is not a winged Fortuna but a youthful winged genius, perhaps intended to be seen as a boy in the costume of a genius, in keeping with the conventions of Renaissance pageantry, rather than as an allegorical figure proper.

In other instances Mantegna appears to have been guided unconsciously by his own preconceptions of the meaning of his authorities. The Latin term *signum* he seems to have rendered or found rendered in Valturio as statue rather than as standard, and this is why small statues are borne on poles or carried in Canvases I and II. More amusing is his transposition, again in Canvas I, of the Latin *tabula*, meaning a painting on panel, to mean a painting on canvas, suggesting that this is what the Italian *tavola* now meant for him.[24] In designing the spoils of plate he was largely thrown back on his own invention, for no classical gold or silver plate was known to the Renaissance. The forms he devised seem partly to be derived from antique vessels as shown on medals, like the ewer in Canvas III, and partly from contemporary plate, with the form slightly classicized, like the great bowl and jug in the same canvas and the basins in Canvas IV. In fact, as we know, the task of designing plate in a classical style was not a new one for him.

If the pervading inspiration of the *Triumphs* is a picturesque neo-classicism, Mantegna's characteristic care for plausibility leads him to introduce exotic motifs where decorum demanded them. The trappings of the elephants, like the vase in Canvas IV, bear Cufic letters intended to indicate their oriental origin, though their saddle-cloths are of purest Renaissance design. Mantegna has preserved some of the traditional features of the conventional elephant of medieval art, but we know that a real elephant was brought to Mantua in 1479, and in a letter from Rome on 15 June 1489 he says of the Turkish prince Djem that 'his walk is that of an elephant'. However, the representation without a howdah, which had assumed the form of a tower in medieval art, and with an elaborate cloth flung over the backs of the animals may well owe something to representations on ancient medals, like that on a medal of the Emperor Philip which was certainly known to sixteenth-century antiquaries.[25] In other cases he has had to use modern motifs in his ignorance of the appearance of the antique equivalent; in Canvas IX the torques of the young man holding a garlanded *titulus* who looks back at Caesar is indicated by a fifteenth-century knight's collar, figuring this ancient Roman military award for bravery. Nor has he attempted to represent the gesticulating figure wearing a fringed ankle-length robe and gold armlets who mocks the captives in Appian's triumph: perhaps for greater clarity of narrative effect he has introduced instead two figures, a dwarf buffoon and a sneering jester in a pointed cap, who may well have been inspired by the buffoons of the Gonzaga court.

The canvases of the *Triumphs* are designed so as to take account, by changes of background and breaks in single motifs, of the vertical pilasters that were to frame them at the sides. Once again, Mantegna evidently treated these as if they were the pilasters of a loggia beyond which the procession passes continuously in the open air. There are nevertheless significant breaks and continuities in the canvases which divide them into groups, interconnection being in general carefully maintained within each single group by motifs linking canvas to canvas. Canvases I, II and III are linked as a whole by a continuous background of sky and individually by the black horse in I and II and the sacrificial bull and two chests in II and III. There is no direct connecting link between III and IV, although the movement of the procession is continued by the motif of litters bearing booty, with a slight effect as of outward motion in IV, perhaps to imply a turn. Canvases IV, V and VI form a coherent group, linked by a common landscape background and by the trumpets in IV and V and the elephants and sacrificial goats in V and VI. Canvas VII marks a break, but

is not linked to Canvas VIII, though there is evidence, to which we shall return, that originally the design contained *citharoedi* (players of the cithara) who linked it to the *citharoedus* of VIII.

Canvases VIII and IX are linked by their landscape background: although the triumphal arch of IX ends its composition with a monumental structure, this forms only a vague link with the palace of the putative Canvas X or 'Senators', which seems nevertheless to have been conceived in some sort of balance with Canvas VII, as we have already noticed. In general the designs illustrate once again Mantegna's unique power to devise a narrative with a continuity prolonged beyond the field of each canvas, so stimulating the imagination to fill the gaps between them. There are certain local inconsistencies: thus there is no evident means by which the car bearing the colossal statue in the left foreground of Canvas II is drawn forwards, and the landscape that is wooded in Canvas IV is rocky and barren in Canvas V. As a sequence, nevertheless, the *Triumphs* are a logical development of the concept of the pictorial field as a section isolated from a larger space whose existence must always be suggested to the eye.

Clearly Mantegna made this division into groups because of the nature of the interior for which the *Triumphs* were intended. If, as is probable, this was the *sala* or great public room of the Castello, the division we now have implies that they were mounted in three groups on three of the walls of the *sala*. In the *sala* as it was in the late fifteenth century a distribution into three groups would find a natural explanation, for its fourth wall would have been unsuitable for such great canvases, since it was pierced by three windows overlooking the courtyard of the Castello.[26] It has been argued that the *Triumphs* cannot have been set round a room, but must have hung instead in a row on a long wall on account of the light, which falls throughout the nine canvases in the same direction, near frontal, with a slight bias to the left. But a wall of the required length would have to have been the wall of a corridor, and it is inconceivable that in the fifteenth century a set of decorations of this size, expense and importance would have been commissioned to ornament a corridor, a very subsidiary part of a dwelling in the notions of the age. And indeed all the earlier instances known to us of *Triumphs* as a monumental wall-decoration, a *Triumph of Marius* by Jacopo Avanzi and the *Triumphs of Roman Emperors* by Altichiero and Ottaviano Prandino in the Sala dei Giganti of the Palazzo del Capitano at Padua, and two *Triumphs* by Avanzi in the Sala Grande of the Scaliger palace at Verona, were painted for the great *sale*, which were the most important rooms of these two palaces. Mantegna knew all these works, and indeed is said to have admired the Avanzi *Triumphs* in Verona.[27] The *Triumphs of Alexander* decorated the *sala* at Marmirolo, and when Francesco Gonzaga removed seven of the *Triumphs of Caesar* to his new palace of San Sebastiano *c*.1507, it was for installation in the *sala*.

As we have them, Canvases I to VI of the *Triumphs* form two groups, whose differing backgrounds can only be explained on the supposition that each of these two groups was set up on a wall to form a single prospect. Canvas VII is an odd man out, but VIII and IX are a pair. Hung up together in one continuous line, as now, the backgrounds of the nine canvases appear incoherent. The near frontal fall of the light must therefore have some other explanation. In all probability it is merely a device to emphasize that all nine canvases, though displayed around three walls of a room, are isolated from a single procession advancing along a triumphal way. Clearly Mantegna expected the beholder to move in orderly progression from the first canvas to the last. The unity of the sequence is enhanced by repetitions of colour: figures and banners in vermilion occur in all the canvases, as do passages in azure, green, blue, golden-yellow and white. Because the canvases have undergone drastic restoration and repainting, much of the subtlety of the colouring has been lost and many of the contrasts now seem harsh, all the more so from the heroic scale of the *Triumphs*. Yet the loss of the gold that heightened and the glazes that softened still leaves their essential splendour unimpaired.

Nevertheless, the series as we have it raises serious problems. Canvas VII, the *Captives*, is an anomaly in the scheme. We know from the Chantilly drawing, which copies an earlier state of this composition, that at one time it was to have been linked with Canvas VIII by figures of *citharoedi*, but in the end these were omitted. Even in the drawing, however, the background signals a strong break from Canvas VI and it might be that at some stage two other canvases were to have been inserted to either side of Canvas VII. Certainly there is evidence in the omission of the lictors preceding the musicians of Canvas VIII and of the incense-bearers preceding Caesar of a departure from the texts of Appian and Plutarch and therefore of some reason for compression at this point. But if Canvas VII was originally intended to be set at the end of a wall, the break that it forms would be sufficiently explained. This solution is supported by the testimony of Equicola, who assumes that only one subject, the procession that followed the triumphal car, was wanting. Canvas VIII would then have been designed at one stage to open a final group of three canvases, in which the 'Senators' would have formed the last. Certainly a sequence of ten canvases would have been better adapted to a *sala* that was oblong in form. Accordingly we may

wonder if the original scheme was not for just such a sequence, forming two groups of three canvases to decorate the short walls and four for the long wall, which if Paccagnini is correct in his reconstruction of the *sala* faced the windows. In such a scheme Canvas IX, with Caesar on his triumphal car, would have hung in a central position at the end of the room. Certainly the head of the room was the position later allotted in the *sala* of the Palazzo di San Sebastiano to a huge canvas by Costa of the Marchese Francesco and his sons sacrificing to Hercules, which was the climax of the new installation of the *Triumphs*.

The uncertainties and changes which evidently affected the scheme of the *Triumphs* towards its end acquire a new significance from evidence that some of the canvases never received Mantegna's final touches.[28] Canvases VI and IX in particular were said in the sixteenth century to be unfinished by visitors who were presumably told as much by those who showed them round the Palazzo di San Sebastiano, where the *Triumphs* had become a regular sight for travellers. Canvas VII is apparently incomplete in the upper left-hand corner. What all this suggests is that Mantegna had been working with his usual notorious slowness, and that the series was hastily brought to an end after his return from Rome in September 1490, under pressure from Francesco Gonzaga, who was already impatient for their completion in February 1489,[29] and no doubt became even more so after another year and a half's delay. Francesco was certainly more than capable of insisting on a delivery date, as we know from a correspondence late in 1485 concerning a Madonna 'with some other figures' which Mantegna had begun for Eleanora d'Este, Duchess of Ferrara, but had not yet finished.[30] To satisfy Francesco's urgings then, perhaps even commands, Mantegna may have been persuaded to cut short the sequence and join the *Captives* and the last two canvases to form the final group. If it is asked how this can have been satisfactory to Francesco, the answer may be that he needed the *Triumphs* urgently for display on some great occasion and was not prepared to wait.

Such a reconstruction of events squares well with what is known from documents of their history. They had not been begun, or even thought of by 26 August 1484, when Mantegna wrote to Lorenzo de' Medici in terms implying that as yet he had received no commission from the new Marchese. But probably it was not very long afterwards that he was ordered to paint them because enough had been done by 26 August 1486 for the work to be shown to the Duke of Ferrara. Some of the canvases had been finished by the time of Mantegna's departure for Rome in June 1488, but in the letter to Francesco which speaks about their safekeeping Mantegna adds that 'I am in hopes of painting others, if it please God and Your Lordship.' And the completion of the *Triumphs* was the principal reason why Francesco was anxious to get Mantegna back to Mantua. Strictly interpreted, Mantegna's words about 'others' that were to be painted could even be taken to mean that he still had designs to make.

The backgrounds of the *Captives* and the 'Senators', as already noted, differ completely from those of the other compositions in that they represent street settings showing the Via Sacra along which triumphal processions paraded through Rome. Accordingly, Martindale's argument that this change of background may be due to Mantegna's direct experience of Rome could well be sound. Mantegna's letter of 1464 from Goito advising Lodovico Gonzaga that the paintings he is working on ought in his opinion to be the last to go into the chapel proves that his patrons did not always embark on decorative schemes with a clear idea of exactly how many pictures they wanted or were needed, so that there is nothing implausible in the suggestion that the scheme for the *Triumphs* was evolved, altered, and perhaps both enlarged and truncated over the eight years or so that Mantegna was engaged on them. Moreover, although it may be of course that Mantegna finished the canvases in regular and orderly succession, one after the other, the probability is that he did not, but worked on them partly in groups and partly as his caprice dictated. It is at least possible that while he was working on Canvas VII, the *Captives*, Francesco ordered him to abridge the series. In fact the background in the last two canvases resembles that in Canvases IV, V and VI, which may indicate that he had already designed their compositions before his departure for Rome. Whether or not this was so, in January 1492, four months after his return, he was once again hard at work on them. The honorific decree of 4 February of that year granting him more land specifies among its motives 'those works which he is now painting for us, the triumph of Julius Caesar with figures that are almost alive and breathing, so much so that the thing seems not so much to be represented as happening.' He had certainly handed over nine canvases before 2 March 1494, when the 'camera and Triumphs' were shown to Giovanni de' Medici as part of the decorations of the Castello.[31] Indeed he may even have completed them by 10 December 1492, when a Venetian ambassador was shown 'all that is beautiful in the town, and he has already seen the *spalliera*, the Camera Picta, the little chapel and the things of Messer Andrea Mantegna, viz. the Triumphs and his other pretty devices.'[32]

However, it remains an open question whether the *Triumphs* were ever permanently installed in the *sala* of the Castello. That such a permanent installation was envisaged appears from their design, which

as we saw assumes that they will be separated from each other by a framework. And indeed an engraving by Zoan Andrea reproduces a drawing for Canvas VI with a design for a pilaster added on the right. In this we can perhaps see Mantegna trying the effect of cutting off the forms at the end of a canvas in relation to the framework and even designing a suitable pilaster. Yet the mere fact of the removal of only seven of the canvases to decorate the *sala* of Palazzo San Sebastiano towards the end of 1507 in itself raises the question whether they were ever mounted in a fixed framework on the walls of the *sala* or indeed elsewhere in the Castello. It seems strangely wanton to strip a great public room in the principal family residence of a major part of a celebrated set of decorations, leaving two canvases behind, if they had already been set up in an expensive architectural framework, richly carved and gilded. And the mere fact of the removal of seven alone of the canvases suggests that the *Triumphs* were not housed in the Castello in a manner that was thought worthy of them or within the sort of framework that had originally been intended.[33]

The explanation of all these problems may be the very simple one that the *Triumphs* were originally to be hung in an altered and enlarged *sala*, but that the designed changes were never made and so the whole scheme was first postponed and then abandoned. Certainly Equicola, writing in 1521, emphasizes that when the *Triumphs* were moved to the Palazzo di San Sebastiano, it was for their safe housing, 'per sicuramente collocare in una salla ad solo questo effecto fabricata lo triumpho di C. Iulio Cesare, fatiga de molti anni di misser Andrea Mantegna.' The implication is that prior to their installation in this new *sala*, they had not been suitably displayed or safely housed in their old home.

Other references to the *Triumphs* between their completion *c.*1492–4 and the removal of seven of them in the latter part of 1507 put it beyond doubt that they remained movable decorations during these years. On 14 January 1497 Fedele da Forlì, a courtier of the Marchese Francesco, wrote to him anxiously about the temporary theatre that was being set up in the courtyard of the Castello under the supervision of Bishop Lodovico Gonzaga for the usual carnival festivities of the court of Mantua. It was to be roofed over only with canvas and Fedele feared 'that as Your Excellency wishes to put among the decorations both the Triumphs and many other precious adornments (*ornamenti*)', if rain fell, they would be damaged 'to our small honour and profit'.[34] Again on 13 February 1501, Sigismondo Cantelmo, a Ferrarese envoy, reported of another temporary theatre in the courtyard of the Castello that 'one of the sides was adorned with the six paintings of the Triumphs of Caesar by the hand of the singular Mantegna.'[35] On 11 January 1505, again in connection with decorations for theatrical festivities, Il Milanese, a courtier of Francesco, reported that a temporary roof was now up over the courtyard, and asked if he should send now while the weather was good for 'the canvases that are at Gonzaga and ask Mantegna for his, and have them brought to the palace'. In reply Francesco agreed and ordered both the canvases at Gonzaga and 'those that Messer Andrea Mantegna has' to be taken 'to their places'. If Mantegna's canvases were *The Triumphs of Caesar*, then these letters are another indication that they were not permanently mounted, but left under the care of Mantegna to be hung up like tapestries when they were wanted. If this is so, it would seem that Mantegna had removed them temporarily in this instance to his own house, perhaps for restoration.[36] The *Triumphs* were again set up for the decoration of a temporary theatre early in 1507,[37] but after their installation in the *sala* of the Palazzo di San Sebastiano we hear no more of their being used as temporary decorations. Instead, as we have said, they became a much-admired attraction for visitors of the city.

The manner in which they are mentioned in the 1490s together with the other sights of the Mantuan palace also suggests that they were never given a permanent installation there, but were put out on special occasions, such as the visits of personages of rank or importance. It should be remembered that the *sala* immediately preceded the Camera Picta. As we have just seen, in December 1492 a Venetian ambassador saw 'the *spalliera*, the Camera Picta, the little chapel and . . . the *Triumphs*', and in March 1494 Giovanni de' Medici saw 'the Camera and the *Triumphs*'. On neither of these occasions are we told that the visitor was shown a room decorated with the *Triumphs*: he was shown the *Triumphs* themselves, just as the ambassador saw the *spalliera*, not the room decorated with the *spalliera*. This *spalliera* was in itself a celebrated possession of the Gonzaga, which visitors to the court asked to be allowed to see or else were shown with pride.[38] It had been acquired by August 1486, probably only shortly before, for on his visit to Mantua that month Ercole d'Este asked especially to see it. Another implication of the Duke's request is that the *spalliera* was not permanently hung up, but was put out for visitors on special occasions. That this was in fact so is confirmed by orders given on 1 September 1492 that it was to be shown '*distesa*', that is, unfolded and hung up, to Bernardo de' Rossi, the youthful Bishop of Belluno, who was anxious to see it. Again in July 1493, when a Turkish ambassador was to be lodged in the Castello, the *sala* was to be 'adorned with the beautiful *spalliera* in the usual manner'.[39] If the *spalliera* was, as seems likely, a textile dado, it may have ben intended to run round

the room below the *Triumphs*, just as in the Sistine Chapel decorations of the 1480s a simulated textile dado runs below the frescoes. Such a scheme might in turn explain the vantage-point assumed by Mantegna in devising the perspective of the *Triumphs*.

An advantage of canvas over panel as a medium was that it made large paintings movable, so that if necessary they could be rolled up and transported from room to room or from place to place like tapestries. Such removals were simplified on occasions by a system of mounting pictures in simple gilded frames, apparently of rods, that were easily dismounted. Just such a frame enclosed a painting by Mantegna which was brought from Mantua and hung up in the *camerino* of Francesco Gonzaga's new palace at Marmirolo in April 1494 in a place where two *trionfi* were missing, either temporarily or because they had not yet been completed. The picture came first, followed by the architect Bernardino Ghisolfo with its frame, and was put back into it and hung up in a few hours.[40] There was nothing extraordinary then in the decision of Francesco Gonzaga not to mount the *Triumphs* permanently in the *sala*, according to the first intention, but to treat them as movable decorations. Other large canvases and *Triumphs* were brought to Mantua from his country palaces to decorate theatrical performances: those of Gonzaga[41] were brought in 1503 and again in 1505 and 1507, while in this last year it was mooted that those at Marmirolo should be brought as well.[42] Indeed *trionfi* were highly suitable in Renaissance eyes as decorations of a festival, for the word mingled notions of joy and celebration with those of triumph.

That some of the *Triumphs* were completed before Mantegna went to Rome is a fact of the greatest importance in the history of his art, for it proves that certain major changes in his style took place before he had any opportunity of studying antiquity among the ruins of Rome. Indeed it is open to question whether his Roman sojourn had that profoundly modifying effect on his art with which it is sometimes credited. For example, given Mantegna's long interest in antique ornament, which he had observed and reproduced with admiring carefulness from his early days in Padua, it is surprising that he ignores the grotesques of Nero's Domus Aurea, already known to artists as early as the middle and later 1480s.[43] He certainly bought antique sculptures in Rome to add to his collection for as we shall see in 1498 he was forced to part with an antique bust of a woman he had brought from there.[44] But a classicism that is already tending to neo-classicism is apparent in all the canvases of the *Triumphs*. As its inspiration is patently drawn from classical sculpture, it seems that its sources should be sought in

Mantegna's own collection and in other collections that he saw in Mantua and elsewhere in North Italy, in Verona, Padua and Venice.

Antique sculptures were rare and costly in the quattrocento, so much so that even princely collectors were reduced to having plaster casts made of them. One such collector whom Mantegna certainly knew well was the Protonotary Lodovico Gonzaga, Bishop-Elect of Mantua. They seem to have been on excellent terms, though Lodovico was at odds with his nephew Francesco, who appears to have suspected him of plotting against him.

Easy-going and generous, fond of wine, food and women, Lodovico was a typical cultivated prelate of the day, a humanist, a collector of books and manuscripts, a student of astrology and a patron of theatrical performances, whether of *rappresentazioni sacre* or classical comedies in Italian versions. He was a friend of many of the prominent literary figures of Mantua, Bologna and Ferrara, including the poets Battista Spagnoli and Niccolò da Correggio and the humanist Paride da Ceresara, all personages who gravitated around the Mantuan court or were in close relations with it. He had the family taste for art, and the medallist Ermes Flavio de Bonis and the sculptor in bronze Pier Jacopo Alari Bonacolsi (Antico) were in his service. Lodovico was not rich enough to buy many antique marbles, though he certainly owned originals and in 1489 had a collection of busts in his house in Rome, some apparently on a part-share basis with certain Romans. But his interest in the antique was that of an antiquary as well as a collector and at least as early as 1489 Ermes was employed by him to make plaster casts of antique sculptures acquired by friends and relations. He also bought casts ready made: thus in November 1501 he sent three ducats to Florence in order to buy casts of four antique busts, three of emperors, and one of a beardless and nameless young man.[45]

Originally Antico had been in the service of Lodovico's brother Gianfrancesco and his wife Antonia del Balzo at Gazzuolo, apparently from *c.*1480, and for them he made a number of casts from antique bronzes and small copies in bronze of ancient sculptures, of a kind which are known to have been circulating among Renaissance collectors by the 1450s. An inventory taken in 1496 after Gianfrancesco's death includes bronze figures of Hercules, a bust of Caesar 'in metal', statuettes of the horses of the Quirinal and of the equestrian statue of Marcus Aurelius, both copies in bronze of famous antique sculptures in Rome, a head of Pompey in bronze, 'a woman with a cornucopia', a small Minerva and a Cupid 'of metal'. Most of these were certainly modern copies, and perhaps by Antico, but the collection also included a number of bronzes whose broken condition suggests that they were

antique or believed to be antique. From 1498 Antico was certainly busy making bronze copies of the antique or bronzes in the antique style for Lodovico Gonzaga at Bozzolo, where he had a *studiolo*: one of these was a small version of the *Spinario* which was presented in 1501 to Isabella d'Este.

This enthusiastic collecting of originals, plaster casts and bronze versions among his circle of princely, noble and ecclesiastical patrons and friends must always be remembered in considering Mantegna's familiarity with the antique.[46] Artists in the quattrocento had already come to be regarded as the best connoisseurs of the quality and genuineness of antique sculptures, and Mantegna, we saw, was in sufficient esteem as an antiquary and connoisseur of the antique by 1472 for Cardinal Francesco Gonzaga, coming from Rome itself, to ask for his company at the baths of Porretta in order to study and discuss his gems and bronzes with him. If Antico (b. *c.*1460) could form a classical style for himself in the atmosphere of the Gonzaga courts by copying bronze copies and versions of classical marbles – it seems that he only visited Rome and saw its 'bele antichaglie' in 1497 – there is all the more reason not to attribute the classicism that pervades Mantegna's later art to his Roman sojourn. In fact, its ascendancy can be dated from *c.*1485, when Mantegna began painting the *Triumphs*. He was already well equipped by years of studying the antique from surviving remains in North Italy, from marbles, bronzes and medals in learned and princely collections, from his own collection, which by 1484 included quite a number of antique originals,[47] as well as drawings of monuments and copies of inscriptions, and from the pieces that constantly circulated on approval among collectors and were shown to him for his opinion.

When the scenes of the Camera Picta, painted ten years earlier, are compared with those of the *Triumphs*, it is obvious that Mantegna's style has undergone another great change. The figures in the *Triumphs* are far more easy and natural in their movement, their robes no longer have the stiff and heavy self-containment of the 1460s and 1470s, but float freely and lightly. Even the sharp incisiveness of Mantegna's definition of form seems to have relaxed a little in the interests of more spontaneous modelling, although in the dire condition of the canvases it would be dangerous to make too much of this. As we have seen, traces of a certain human softening appear in other works of the mid-1480s, but the metamorphosis in his art which appears in the *Triumphs* ought perhaps to be attributed largely to the *Triumphs* themselves. In them for the first time as far as we know a vital classicism rather than a classicism of antiquarian ornament was demanded, inasmuch as Mantegna made it his purpose to recreate 'al naturale', that is, as if from life, the pageantry of Rome in all the fullness of authentic costuming and all the splendour of its panoply.

Mantegna was challenged then by a theme in which his art had to equip itself to embody in lifelike form the ideal world of antiquity, and in which the representation of movement was not simply a means of animating sufficiently a static scene, but a prime essential of composition. These twin challenges he met triumphantly. Though his figures are still conceived in sculptural isolation – in all nine canvases there is only one dialogue, that between the mounted officer and the foot-soldier – each is a separate study of a different active pose, drawn with graceful naturalness. Of most of the figures it can be said that they are framed on one of three conceptions: either they are absorbed in their own part in the procession – music-making or standard-bearing or carrying spoils – or they are sunk in pensive meditation, or they express some curiosity about the procession that follows behind. From time to time they are arranged in the files proper to a procession, but Mantegna has been at great pains to avoid any rigid alignment, and has taken the same care with the animals. He also avoids sequences of heads in strict profile: the only canvas in which they appear is the *Captives*, where they are introduced to express a sense of melancholy subjugation in the prisoners. For a sense of movement along each canvas Mantegna relies on juxtaposed individual movements. These create rhythmic patterns of advancing legs, varied naturalistically here and there and especially in Canvases II and III by figures and animals who walk at a different pace or are shown with a leg uplifted, rather than with both feet on the ground. In shaping these rhythms and dissonances Mantegna has skilfully prevented any domination of his compositions by inexorably advancing legs.

So great was his sense of the need for the richest variety of motif in compositions where there was no history to link the figures into a dramatic or emotional interaction, that he has made great use of other devices as well. The spoils themselves and the cars on which they are borne share the interest with the figures, and are alternated with them, as are the powerful forms of the animals. Indeed only three of the canvases, Canvases I, VII and VIII are predominantly figure-compositions. Backward-looking or backward-turning figures are introduced: not only do they vary the movement of the procession, but they serve to link the canvases as a whole into a continuous sequence. There is no attempt to draw the spectator into the procession; although one or two of the figures do glance outwards or downwards in a manner which suggests that the spectator shares the scene with them, the parade in general moves onwards engrossed in its own march.

For Mantegna only figures of ideal severity of beauty could fitly represent Roman soldiers, and the majority of his figures are therefore ideal in type, but according to new canons of ideality. In the *Triumphs* we meet for the first time the smooth-faced youths, with richly curling blond tresses, who appear in his works of the 1490s and 1500s, and also the older and sterner figures in whom Mantegna expresses a vision of Roman character and virility derived from the portraiture of ancient busts and medals. Again it must be emphasized that damage and restoration may have increased the deceptive smoothness of the figure-style: in some of the poses and faces glimpses are visible of the old solid naturalism. And indeed Mantegna has not sought for a monotonous nobility of style, but instead has obeyed tradition and maintained the canon of variety and contrast. In Canvas I he has introduced a Negro and in Canvas II, with a trace of the impish humour that always lurks within his gravity, a dog marching along and gazing up hopefully at the jug held by the statue which is carried by the figure on the right. The beggar in Canvas VI is in dramatic contrast with the wealth that passes him by, while in Canvas VII the child clinging to its mother and soothed by an old woman introduces an anecdote of human liveliness, even though the group of mother and children is modelled on an antique *Caritas*. The little dog, the monkey, and the buffoons and jester in the same canvas and the Phrygian musician who breaks with his stamping dance the smooth rhythms of Canvas VIII are other motifs that serve to counterpoint with their realism and grotesquerie the strong and graceful figures of the rest of the procession.

The heroic scale and grandeur of the *Triumphs* are an expression of Francesco's ambitious enthusiasm for military greatness and glory and also of Mantegna's own ambitious genius. Yet through their celebration of triumph there sound one or two notes of that deep bitterness which Mantegna seems to have felt in the last decades of his life. It was a bitterness inspired by his sense of the life of the man of superior virtue as a constant struggle against the envy of the ignorant and small-minded. In his letter of 31 January 1489 to Francesco Gonzaga he expresses in the bitter Latin apothegm 'virtuti semper aduersatur ignorantia' his own personal sense of resentment at the ease with which the presumptuous and coarse win the rewards of life while men of retiring nature like himself are left in discomfort.[48] He repeats the apothegm again in another letter to Francesco of 28 November 1491 and observes that 'it is most true that envy ever reigns in little men and they are enemies of virtue and of men of worth.'[49] That he became to some extent obsessed by this grim vision of worth ever neglected, and ever exposed to the assaults of ignorance, folly and avarice, also appears from a design and an engraving of the 1490s, which illustrate the theme in a visual allegory and introduce the same Latin adage in abbreviated form. It is even introduced into Canvas II of the *Triumphs*, where an inscription declares that Caesar's Gallic triumph has been decreed 'envy scorned and overcome'. It was adumbrated still more forcibly in yet another inscription which is now lost, but was recorded in the sixteenth century. Probably inscribed on Canvas IX, it celebrated 'the twofold victory of Divus Iulius Caesar, in his constant overcoming of envy and his bold overcoming of the enemy'.

For the great Paduan antiquary Lorenzo Pignoria (1571–1631) Mantegna was second only to Giovanni Marcanova as a reviver of the study of antiquity. Pignoria's judgement is an eloquent expression of Mantegna's achievement in the eyes of the learned Renaissance:

Next to Giovanni Marcanova I place Andrea Mantegna, a painter of great renown, who commanded painting to aspire to its ancient beauties. In order to win painting from a thin, dry, juiceless manner to that lively, animated and flourishing manner he used himself, he called Antiquity to his assistance. And indeed everything that he found in her, provided only it was of some beauty, he converted to his own use. His paintings are filled with vases, arms, costumes and ornaments sought from the richest repositories of the ancients.[50]

IX

Mantegna in Rome

IN 1487 Pope Innocent VIII, having built his new villa of Belvedere, summoned Pinturicchio to decorate its apartments and Mantegna to decorate its chapel.[1] In such matters Mantegna, as has been seen, was subject to his lord, and Innocent wrote, not to him, but to the Marchese Francesco, probably early in 1488. Mantegna seems to have left Mantua about 10 June, for this is the date of the letter of commendation from Francesco which Mantegna was given, according to the usual custom, to take with him for presentation to the Pope.[2] Quite a number of letters concerning the enterprise survive, including some written from Rome by Mantegna himself. From these it emerges that Francesco lent Mantegna's services in order to ingratiate himself with the Pope, and that Mantegna received strict instructions not to accept any payment or reward from Innocent, but only his expenses. This inhibition did not prevent Mantegna from seeking to turn his residence at the Curia to his family's advantage by asking Francesco's consent for his son Lodovico to hold benefices in the territory of Mantua to the value of 200 ducats if the Pope could be persuaded to confer them on him, a request to which Francesco readily agreed. On Francesco's part there was a natural anxiety that this 'excellent painter, whose equal our age has not seen' should not be enticed from his service by the Pope. Mantegna's letters, protesting loyalty to the house he had now served for thirty years, constantly reassure him, directly or indirectly, on this point. No doubt the strictly limited expenses Innocent saw fit to allow Mantegna helped to guard him against any temptation, but he was at pains nevertheless to make himself agreeable to the Pope and to all the other personages of the Papal palace.

Mantegna's mentality as revealed in these letters to Francesco is that of a dexterous old courtier, in some ways easy and familiar with his lord, as became a privileged old retainer, yet conscious too of bounds that might not be overstepped, of good graces that could be lost as well as won, adroitly balancing protestations of devotion and affection with requests for favours. Again there is no escaping the conclusion that court life suited Mantegna, offering as it did rank, friendship with princes and among its benefits, if properly solicited, the solid reward of lands and houses and the establishment of his sons. To him, born so poor, it must have appeared, not as a servile dependence, but as the surest means of advancing himself and his family to standing and fortune. That he valued standing and fortune more than the free life of an independent master may be unpalatable to our notions, but was perfectly in accord with those of his own society, which assigned to ambition different forms from ours, and saw in the exchange of services and rewards between princes and their courtiers a dignified road to worldly honours and wealth. To dismiss Mantegna as no more than a self-seeking courtier is to misunderstand an age when the choice between the worldly and the unworldly was that between full participation and absolute renunciation.

The chapel of the Belvedere was destroyed under Pope Pius VI in 1780, a sign of the comparatively low estimation into which Mantegna's art had fallen in the eighteenth century outside North Italy, and also of the poor state of preservation of its frescoes. It was dedicated to St John the Baptist, the patron saint of the Pope, who had been born Giovanni Battista Cibo. Entrance to it was through the end wall of the *sala* of the villa. This wall was pierced by a window of the chapel proper, whose gilded grating allowed those in the *sala* to hear mass, and by a door

Fig. 10. Haymakers and shepherds. Detail from *The Madonna delle Cave* (Plate 121)

giving entrance to the little sacristy which preceded the chapel. Above the window was a painted lunette with a half-figure of St John the Baptist, while above the door was a similar lunette with a half-figure of St John the Evangelist, both, according to Taja, writing *c.*1712, by the hand of Mantegna.[3] The chapel, really a private oratory, was only eleven palms (about 6½ feet) square, and the sacristy preceding it was even smaller. The carved ceiling of the sacristy was composed of square, round and octagonal compartments, decorated with classical ornaments in gold on a blue ground, with a compartment formed as a Greek cross in the centre bearing the Pope's arms. Its walls were divided by feigned pilasters decorated with classical ornaments, one in each corner and two marking off the middle of the two longer walls. Each of the three spaces formed by the pilasters on the longer walls was enclosed by a feigned frame, in which was painted a small cupboard containing chalices, pyxes, crosses, candlesticks, patens, censers, mitres, everything in fact required for the celebration of the liturgy. There is an evident resemblance in conception between this *trompe l'oeil* decoration, simulating in paint what would really be found in a sacristy, and the *trompe l'oeil* decorations in intarsia of such rooms as Federigo da Montefeltro's studio in the palace at Urbino.[4] The ornament in the frame around the cupboards was painted on a gold ground in counterchange to the ornament of pilasters, frieze and cornice, which was in gold on a blue ground. On each of the two shorter walls was a console feigned as of stucco supporting a cornice, also feigned as of stucco. In the wall opposite the entrance door was a window looking out over the countryside and closed by a grating and decorated on its arch and sides with gold ornaments on a blue ground.

A door in the left wall of the sacristy gave entrance into the chapel proper. Here the general decorative framework was again an illusionistic scheme of four pilasters, one in each corner, supporting a cornice from which rose four arches forming lunettes. Between the lunettes were four pendentives supporting a gilt cornice: on each of these was figured the full-length figure of an Evangelist against a background of sky, reading, writing or meditating. From the gilt cornice rose a cupola decorated with a framework of interlaced circles interrupted by fifteen putti holding garlands. Above this was a second cornice, feigned as of stucco, from which rose an ornamental framework terminating in a central motif of Innocent's arms and with cherub heads appearing here and there in it. In its general outlines and in many details this scheme, clearly a development from the Camera Picta, was closely related to that which was later carried out in Mantegna's funerary chapel, also dedicated to St John the Baptist, in Sant' Andrea at Mantua. This late scheme, posthumously executed,

therefore gives us the best idea we can now form of the probable appearance of the Belvedere chapel, at any rate in its general aspect.

The altar wall was that to the right of the entrance. The wall above the altar of white marble was entirely painted with *The Baptism of Christ*, serving as an altarpiece: an arrangement perhaps suggested by that in the lately completed Sistine chapel, where the altar was surmounted by Perugino's fresco of *The Assumption of the Virgin*. Presumably it was adopted because of the tiny scale of the chapel, which would have made an altarpiece in panel or canvas proportioned to the altar too small for Italian taste. The scene in all likelihood followed the traditional iconography, such as we find in the large painting of the *Baptism* designed by Mantegna *c.*1504 for his own chapel, but largely executed by his son Francesco. Angels held Christ's clothes and in the background was a delightful landscape with a city in the distance. Vasari's eye, always interested in incidentals, was caught by the figures of people undressing in preparation for baptism, and especially by a man trying to peel off one of his hose, which was stuck to his leg with sweat, by crossing it over his other shin, 'making such effort and strain that the one and the other are seen in his face, a thing which in those days was held a matter for wonder and awe.' This figure is yet another proof that the introduction for contrast and variety of motifs of homely realism was still a fundamental principle of Mantegna's invention in history. In the sky was the Holy Ghost, together with 'two festoons of fruit of superior delineation' and a gold *cartello* suspended between them, a motif that recalls the Ovetari frescoes of forty years before. By *c.*1712 the *Baptism* had been damaged by nitrous salts exuding from the wall and by poor restoration.

On the wall facing the entrance wall was *The Decollation of the Baptist*, who was shown attended by a crowd of soldiers and patiently awaiting the fall of the sword brandished by his executioner. These figures were life-size. In the background was the banquet of Herod, with tiny figures busy about a long table richly spread for a feast in a stately garden, 'with many ornaments of greenery',[5] and in the middle of the garden a credence set out with dishes of gold. Salome was dancing before the table. Half of this picture had perished by *c.*1712 and a door and oblong compartments had been painted over the damaged section. On the entrance wall, above the door, was a large painting of the Virgin enthroned with the Child on her lap, attended on her right hand by St Peter, St Andrew and behind them by female saints and on her left by St Paul, St John the Baptist and St Catherine of Alexandria. The Pope was shown kneeling in profile before St Peter, who laid his hand upon his shoulder to commend him to the protection of the Virgin. These figures too were apparently life-size, and the composition must have been a conventional donor composition of the same kind as Pintoricchio's later fresco in the Appartamento Borgia.

Below this painting, to either side of the doorway, was a band of figured decoration. At the head of one band was *The Nativity*, at the head of the other was *The Adoration of the Magi*. Below, on one side, under *The Nativity*, in a space only three palms high and one wide (approx. 1¾ feet by 7 inches) were half-figures of St Anthony Abbot and St Paul the Hermit, habited as hermits. On the corresponding side were St Stephen and St Lawrence, habited as deacons. The sides and arch of the doorway were painted with ornaments in chiaroscuro on a gold ground. The fourth wall was pierced by the window with the gilded grating that gave on to the *sala*. The sides of the window frame were painted with a very Mantegnesque decoration of compartments inlaid with marble: on the arch were putti on a blue ground holding an oval laurel-wreathed medallion bearing an inscription recording Innocent's dedication of the chapel to the Baptist in 1490. To either side of the window on a band or frieze of some sort was Mantegna's own inscription: ANDREAS MANTINIA COMES PALATINVS EQVES AVRATAE MILITIAE PINXIT. Above this, occupying the rest of the wall below the lower cornice, was *The Annunciation*, with the Virgin, Gabriel and the Holy Spirit in the form of a dove figured on a gold ground.

Three of the lunettes made by the four arches rising above the lower cornice were pierced with round glazed windows, but only that on the altar wall admitted the light. In the fourth lunette, above the left or window wall, was a roundel in which *The Sacrifice of Abraham*, a type, as we have already seen of Christ's Passion, was figured in chiaroscuro on a gold ground. To either side of these four roundels was a full-length standing female figure of a Virtue. Seven of these figured the three theological Virtues, Faith, Hope and Charity, and the four moral or cardinal Virtues, Prudence, Justice, Temperance and Fortitude. Mantegna had to find an eighth Virtue to depict opposite the figure of Prudence on the window wall. He figured a Virtue as an old woman, which by some sources is identified as Patience, by others as Discretion, but the invention gave rise to an exchange with the Pope which became a celebrated story. Discussion of this, however, must be for the moment reserved.

Beyond the fact that the window wall must have been painted last, since it bears Mantegna's signature and the date 1490, we have no clue to the internal chronology of the chapel. Though the decorative part of the work was probably left to Mantegna's fancy, the themes he depicted in the histories and the figure subjects were certainly given him by the Pope. But Mantegna apparently consulted the humanists and learned men of Rome about the form and attributes he ought to give to at least one of the Virtues. A pithy little Latin dialogue, *De Ivsticia pingenda*, written on the model of a Lucianic dialogue by the young Mantuan physician, humanist and poet, Battista Fiera, who was in Rome *c*.1490, purports to describe Mantegna's various visits to the city's philosophers, some mentioned under disguised, some under their real names, in order to find a suitably expressive invention for the figure of Justice.[6] The interlocutors are Mantegna and Momus, the son of Night and Sleep, and the personification of mockery and critical censure. Mantegna tells Momus the different suggestions he has received, that he should paint Justice with only one large eye, or seated holding a balance, or standing with eyes all round her head and holding a sword, or seated on a square throne and measuring with a leaden ruler, as in ancient Lesbos. Fiera, he says, favours this last suggestion, but thinks that she should have large ears. But the Carmelite Fra Battista Spagnoli, also of Mantua, but then living in Rome, as a theologian and a man of great reverence and a devout follower of Christ, had declared that it is impossible to depict Justice because it is the will of God.

The glimpse *De Ivsticia pingenda* gives us of Mantegna consulting philosophers and theologians about the invention of an allegorical figure he had been commanded to paint is precious, for it is our sole glimpse of the consultations to which he must often have resorted in cases of doubt or where pregnancy of invention required a wittier learning than he himself possessed. No doubt such consultations took place even over questions concerning classical antiquities in which he himself had a considerable competence. The dialogue also contains a few biographical touches: Mantegna declares himself a Christian, but refuses to be drawn into the exposition of theology, showing himself absorbed in his art and reluctant to leave his brushes. It contains too a significant sentence which well expresses the conscientiousness of an art in which every stroke was the result of meditation, and consequently slow and painstaking in invention and execution. 'Since I am that sort of painter', Fiera makes Mantegna say, 'who takes exceptional care even of the least lines, and since I had always heard varying accounts of Justice herself, I thought I ought to consult philosophers about her.'[7] And indeed the Papal chapel excited the wonder of Rome for 'its marvellous minuteness of workmanship'. The dialogue also reveals something of the circle of Mantuan learned men and of other humanists with which Mantegna consorted while in Rome. Spagnoli and Fiera were both close friends and both wrote poems in praise of Mantegna and his works.

Our impressions of the chapel beyond what can be deduced from comparison with Mantegna's own chapel in Mantua are of a lively splendour of blue and gold, the costliest of colours and in the eyes of fifteenth-century patrons the most beautiful, and of a decorative illusionism that drew the maximum of architectural and ornamental effect possible from a very confined space. Mantegna painted it without assistance, for in a letter to Francesco of 15 June 1489 he laments, 'The work is great for a single man who desires to have honour from it, above all in Rome where there are so many worthy men of good judgement.' Clearly he was anxious to surpass himself before eyes that understood his art – his words are another of the few but significant testimonies to the existence in the quattrocento of a public of *intendenti*, whose opinion could challenge an effort to excel from artists of reputation. Since Mantegna put out all his powers so as to impress the *intendenti* of Rome, taking even more than his usual pains to finish it to perfection, the chapel's loss is a disaster. The tireless precision of Mantegna's style, with its meticulous rendering of every least pebble, must have come as a surprise and a marvel to Roman eyes, accustomed as they were to the pictorial styles of Tuscany and Umbria, so much broader and less minutely laborious.

By the end of 1489 the most important parts of the work were completed, and Francesco was anxiously requesting the Pope for the temporary despatch of Mantegna to Mantua, where his help and genius were indispensable if his approaching marriage with Isabella d'Este was to be celebrated with due magnificence. But Mantegna, it seems, had had a bout of severe sickness, and as his legs were still too swollen and painful for a journey on horseback, Innocent declined to release him, fearing his life might be at risk. The chapel was dedicated only in 1490, so that Mantegna must have completed his work about the end of summer that year. In September he returned to Mantua. With him came a brief from Innocent warmly thanking Francesco for satisfying his desire to possess some work of Mantegna's art in his palace and declaring that to what Mantegna had accomplished nothing could be added. Whatever therefore of advantage or honour Francesco could confer on Mantegna as a reward would be most grateful and acceptable.

We have already seen that Mantegna had to find an eighth Virtue in addition to the seven cardinal and theological Virtues in order to round out symmetrically the decoration of his lunettes. According to a story related by Paolo Cortese, a well-informed contemporary, Mantegna, irked by Innocent's failure to make him any present throughout the two

years he had spent on the chapel, at first sketched out the figure of a woman on the chapel wall.[8] When the Pope asked him what it represented, Mantegna replied 'Ingratitude', whereupon Innocent slyly remarked that the figure of Patience would go well beside it. Other versions alter the Virtue to Discretion, and one associates the story with a long delay in obtaining the desired gift of benefices for his son. Certainly Mantegna himself told Francesco Gonzaga in January 1489 that Innocent was giving him no more than '*spese cossi da tinello*', literally, 'expenses about enough for the common-hall', in other words, what more or less it would have cost to feed him in the common-hall where his courtiers dined. 'I would be better off at home', he complained, but either his pride or strict instructions prevented him from asking the Pope for more money.

Yet if the Pope gave Mantegna no reward in money or benefices, he may at least have given him a title, for Mantegna signed the chapel as *Comes Palatinus* (count of the palace) and *Eques auratus* (knight of the golden spur). The knighthood was certainly a Mantuan rather than a Papal title, since it is in a Mantuan document of 11 March 1484 that he is first given the title of *eques*. And in his brief of 6 September 1490 commending Mantegna Innocent speaks of him as '*eques mantuanus*', implying that he already held the title. Again Vasari records in 1550 that it was the Marquis of Mantua who made him a '*cavaliere a spron d'oro*'.[9] The title of *eques auratus* arose because new knights generally wore gilt spurs at the ceremony of knighthood: its other insignia were a ring, a collar and a sword.[10] Technically any knight could make another knight, but the title of *Comes Palatinus* was granted by Emperor and Pope alone, the Popes having begun to confer it in imitation of the Emperors. If Mantegna was not simply reviving his old claim of 1469 to have been made a count palatine by the Emperor Frederick III in order to impress the Papal court, he must have received his title from the Pope. If so, it is strange that no mention of it is made in Innocent's commendatory brief of 6 September 1490. Mantegna is known to have used it for a little while after his return from Rome. He also added a comital crown to his arms, impaling it in chief or with the Gonzaga sun in splendour. But he seems to have dropped the title itself some three or four years later. Mantuan documents indeed only give him the title of knight, and the sole known document to call him a count palatine is a Paduan one of June 1492.[11]

The history of his use of this title has its importance in the history of his work, for it suggests that the one undated work he signed as *Comes Palatinus*, the altarpiece of *The Virgin and Child with the Baptist and the Magdalen* in the National Gallery, London, was painted for a very important patron and was executed c.1490–3. Both his titles were in fact personal distinctions, bestowed as a special mark of favour or to reward a signal service, and carried no special privileges. Indeed Mantegna's contemporaries themselves largely disregarded them in favour of honorific references to his primacy as a painter. These abound even in dry legal documents: 'pictore omnium famossisimo', 'pictorum omnium re et fama facile princeps' (1484), 'pictorum etatis nostre principe' (1486), 'omnium antiquitatis et temporum nostrorum pictorum excellentissimus et princeps' (1492), 'archipictor' (1499), 'pictor eximius' (1503).[12]

According to Vasari, writing in 1568, Mantegna painted the most famous of his small Madonnas, *The Madonna delle Cave* (The Virgin of the Quarries) (Plate 121) during his sojourn in Rome.[13] The only difficulty in accepting his testimony is geological, for it has been claimed that the fantastic brownish-red rocks of the mountain in the background represent a volcanic basalt rare in Italy, but found at Monte Bolca, between Verona and Vicenza.[14] The grape-purplish lining of the Virgin's cloak is a sign that it must have been painted c.1488–92, while the volcanic mountain in its asymmetry, its suggestion of threatening instability and in its pictorial treatment is closer to the rocks of the *Parnassus* and *Pallas expelling the Vices*, painted for the Studiolo of Isabella d'Este, than to even the wildest of Mantegna's earlier mountains. The painting figures a symbolic theme of true fifteenth-century pathos. The Virgin and Child are seated on the summit of Mount Calvary, the Virgin, her eyes downcast in pensive meditation, gently restraining the lively Child, whose action is a motif of restlessness unusual in Mantegna. In the right background stonemasons shape a column and a sarcophagus before the grotto of the Holy Sepulchre for a tomb that is to be Christ's own tomb.

The subject entwines the themes of Christ's Incarnation and Passion to remind us that he was born and suffered for our redemption. The treatment is suitably subdued: the light, falling downwards from the left, leaves the right side of the picture in a pale gloom appropriate to the sombre work of making the tomb. Nevertheless, Mantegna skilfully throws a shaft of it behind the Virgin to fall on the lower part of the rough plateau where the men are working so as to draw our eyes to them. In the composition he has resorted to devices first evolved for his works of the later 1450s, but that for him had lost none of their effectiveness with the passage of the years. That the small lozenge-shaped platform of rock on which the Virgin is seated is the summit of a hill is adroitly indicated by the trees beneath it on the left, by the deep winding valley below, with the three white lanes of its country road

peopled by small figures of Orientals in turbans and of shepherds with their flock, and finally by the massive plinth and soaring rocks of the mountain of the Sepulchre behind. The field of the picture is isolated from the continuity of setting it so skilfully implies with unusual abruptness: the volcanic mountain is cut off below its summit, a device that also makes its curious form more of a foil for the sturdy figure of the Virgin, and three of the corners of the lozenge-shaped platform are also cut off, as is the last fold of the Virgin's cloak on the right.

Beyond the Virgin open Mantegna's usual two contrasting views of a single prospect: for the first time he introduces an effect of sunlight on the left, with men making hay (Fig. 10) and a ploughed field and clumps of trees as darker passages to balance the darkened right. All is rendered with Mantegna's customary painstaking minuteness: yet a different naturalism suffuses the rocks and stones. They are still conceived on Mantegna's old additive principle, as if they were rough structures built by nature block by single block, but now they are an igneous colour overlaid with patches of ochre that gives them as it were a larger geological unity. As always this profusion of small single details is a means of adding naturalistic plausibility and ornament to a composition that solves by bold manipulation of setting and clever handling of light the problem of isolating the Virgin and Child with all due prominence, while hinting expressively at the future Passion.

The altarpiece of the *Virgin and Child with St John the Baptist and the Magdalen* (Plate 122) in London is one of the late pictures by Mantegna to be enclosed in a painted window-frame, simulating a marble window-frame in perspective.[15] The others are the more or less contemporary *Redeemer* at Correggio (Plate 123) and the Castle Ashby *Adoration of the Magi* (Plate xvi), where its use approaches that of the early *Presentation* (Plate iv). Here the loss of much of the framework has destroyed some of the perspective effects: thus the canopy was originally intended to be seen as cut off by the framework, behind which it was figured as rising. Some of the characteristics of Mantegna's last great altarpieces appear in it: the comparative homeliness of the Virgin and her cheeks flushed with the bright apple-red he gives to women's cheeks in his late pictures, the waving wantoning looseness of hair of the two saints. The cloaks of the Baptist and the Magdalen are painted respectively light blue and dark blue over red to give a *chatoyant* effect, the red showing through the folds in a marvellous changing glow, softened by white highlighting. It is interesting to compare the Magdalen with the Santa Giustina and the St Euphemia of the early 1450s: the type of beauty is still the same, blond and broad-featured, but the drapery now emphasizes the slenderness of the tall figure, instead of thickening it, and its folds have that stiff patterned regularity which Vasari criticized as harsh and dry. The robe she wears, in keeping with the evolution of Mantegna's art, is more truly classical in its fall beneath the girdle.

This is perhaps the earliest known picture in which we can see the change to brighter and gayer colouring which is so characteristic of Mantegna's last years. The tonality is now light, and often chalky, and there is less of the intensity and depth of colour that Mantegna had inherited from Venetian tradition. Among favourite colours, besides the apple-red already mentioned, are a light apple-green and also a delicate warm pink, which is used to animate flesh-tones that are pale and subdued. The resulting matt brightness of effect is enhanced by a technique that uses notably thin painting in tempera on canvas. The change becomes even more noticeable in the altarpiece of 1496–7 painted for Santa Maria in Organo and in later works, though the *Parnassus* and *Pallas* show that Mantegna could still achieve effects of a lustrous richness of colour against grounds of brown, yellow and dark green when required to do so for expressive reasons. In his very latest works, such as *The Holy Family* of his chapel, his colour will assume a prevalently orangey tone in its brightness.

Mantegna used his title of *Comes Palatinus* not only on this picture but on the much restored *Redeemer* in Correggio, which bears an inscription recording that it was a gift from Mantegna made in 1493, on 5 January, the day before the Feast of the Epiphany when it was and is the custom in Italy to give presents.[16] This image of Christ as Redeemer is a version of a famous and much copied Flemish image whose original appears to be a painting by Jan van Eyck. The image was already well known in the Veneto, and was copied, for example, in Verona;[17] we must allow for its diffusion through Flemish illuminated Books of Hours, as well as through Flemish paintings. Mantegna probably painted it to satisfy a private devotion. In the early seventeenth century the picture was in the collection of the princes of Correggio, and it is virtually certain therefore that it was painted either for Francesca da Brandenburgo, Barbara's niece, who in 1477 married Borso da Correggio (d.1504), or for Borso's cousin Niccolò II (1450–1508), joint lord with Borso of Correggio. Although their links were principally with Ferrara and the court of the Estensi, both Borso and Niccolò were also friends of the Gonzaga, Niccolò especially being an intimate of Isabella d'Este, who admired him both as a poet and as a pattern of knighthood.[18]

Mantegna has translated the Flemish prototype into his own grave classicism of form, emphasizing the structure of the neck and articulating the forms of the chest in the antique manner. Yet he has preserved the sense of Christ as a Man of Sorrows, which was one of the secrets of the appeal of the original image: the sombre black background, lit only with the thin pale golden radiance of the nimbus, which outlines the upper hair and sends out cruciform gleams of light, the dark tresses, and the almond-shaped eyes, typical of the late Mantegna, all contribute to an effect of contemplative pathos. A vertical inscription in gold letters on the left emphasizes the penitential devotion which is the inspiration of the picture, by bidding the beholder reproach himself before this image of Christ's face. The picture is enclosed in a window-frame, crimson in colour, on which Mantegna has placed both the inscription inviting to repentance and the inscription recording his gift of the picture. The frame and the dark background it encloses are perhaps intended to suggest an interior, for on the book which Christ holds is an inscription bidding us have no fear, taken from St Luke's account of Christ's words when he appeared in a chamber at Jerusalem to his disciples after his Resurrection. If Christ's sorrows ought to prick us to repentance, the book, which must be the New Testament, and its inscription proffer a message of Christian hope and faith. They are additions to the established image of Christ the Redeemer made by Mantegna or his patron to counterbalance the purely affective piety of the Flemish original.

To emphasize the window effect and to obtain an effect of spatial depth Christ is shown half-length, with his head turned at a slight angle to the picture plane, while his hands and book set his chest and head a little to the rear. The picture is now greatly worn and restored, but in its pristine state its sombreness must have been delicately relieved by the crimson watered silk of the robe, the vermilion of the book and the gold of the inscriptions, as well as by the light pinks of the carnations, all adding not only warmth but a discreet richness, which is characteristic of Mantegna's religious art even in its moods of austerest gravity. The inscription relating to repentance is written out in a fanciful style, some letters being inverted to read horizontally not vertically. The same fancy appears in the inscription recording the date and authorship of the work on the drawing of *Judith* (Fig. 15) in the Uffizi (1491). It is also found on the engravings of *Hercules and Antaeus* made by North Italian engravers after what must have been a very similar presentation drawing of about the same date. The effect is to give the eye the intriguing pleasure of a moment's puzzle.

1. *The Polyptych of St Luke*. Milan, Brera (Cat. no. 3)

II. *The Agony in the Garden*. London, National Gallery (Cat. no. 6)

III. *The Crucifixion*. Paris, Louvre (Cat. no. 9)

IV. *The Presentation in the Temple*. Berlin–Dahlem, Staatliche Museen (Cat. no. 7)

v. *Portrait of Carlo de' Medici*. Florence, Uffizi (Cat. no. 19)

VI. *The Circumcision*. Florence, Uffizi (Cat. no. 15)

VII. The Oculus of the Camera Picta. Mantua, Palazzo Ducale (Cat. no. 20)

VIII. The indoor scene of the Camera Picta. Detail of Plate 87 (Cat. no. 20)

IX. The outdoor scene, right-hand compartment, of the Camera Picta.
Detail of Plate 86 (Cat. no. 21)

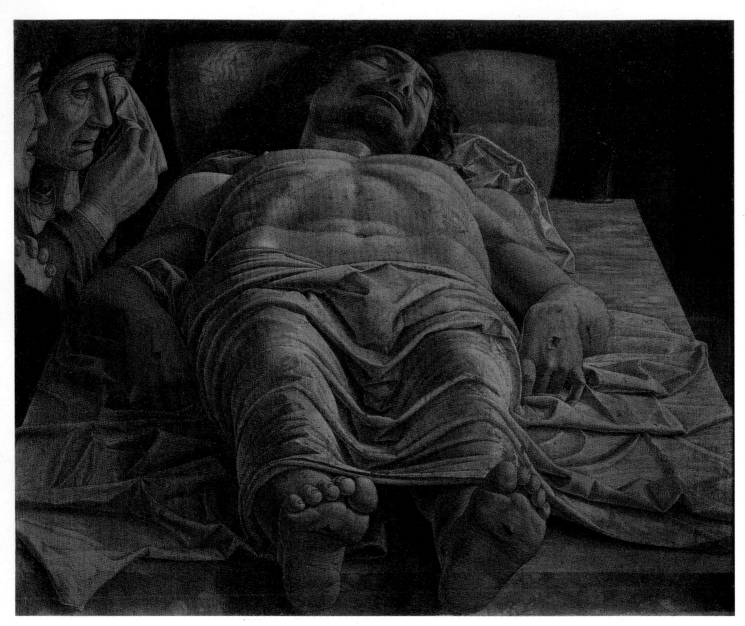

x. *The Lamentation over the Dead Christ*. Milan, Brera (Cat. no. 23)

XI. *St Sebastian*. Paris, Louvre (Cat. no. 22)

XII. *The Parnassus*. Paris, Louvre (Cat. no. 39)

XIII. *Pallas expelling the Vices*. Paris, Louvre (Cat. no. 40)

xiv. *The Madonna della Vittoria*. Paris, Louvre (Cat. no. 36)

xv. *Virgin and Child*. Bergamo, Accademia Carrara (Cat. no. 25)

XVI. *The Adoration of the Magi.* Malibu, J. Paul Getty Museum (Cat. no. 43)

X

The Great Altarpieces

THE conception of the figure as an ideal being, whose proportions, colouring and hair correspond to an aesthetic of beauty that is found also in Renaissance literary imagery, appears in accentuated form in the two great altarpieces painted by Mantegna in the middle of the decade for Santa Maria della Vittoria in Mantua (Plate XIV) and for Santa Maria in Organo in Verona (Plate 127). That for Santa Maria della Vittoria was a votive painting, commemorating Francesco Gonzaga's delivery from death and his victory in the bloody battle of Fornovo, fought on 6 July 1495 between an Italian army of which he was general and the retreating French army of King Charles VIII. In the eyes of Francesco and his allies the battle was a resounding defeat for the French, even though it failed in its object of destroying their army or even to obstruct their retreat.[1] Francesco saw himself as the liberator of Italy and had a medal struck with the motto OB RESTITVTAM ITALIAE LIBERTATEM.[2] All contemporaries agree that he fought like a lion, forcing his way almost to the King's person and taking such great risks that, as he wrote to Isabella next day, 'we found ourselves in a strait where it may be said that only God freed us from it, and if the others had followed us the victory was entire and none of the enemy would have survived.'[3] Later, in a decree of 1 December 1499, he himself described

> how we were fighting among the thickest of the enemy, with danger on every side and there seemed no way of escape. We therefore sought refuge with our whole mind in the most certain protection of Mary, spotless Mother of God. As soon as we had implored it, our courage was raised, our strength was renewed, and thereupon our enemies, who were pursuing us in troops, with levelled spears and drawn swords, began to flee, as if terrified by God, so much so that we cut them down in their tracks.[4]

Francesco was especially devoted to the Virgin, and had recourse to her in all his perils. Already in 1490 he had vowed to erect a votive church to her at Gonzaga, to be called the Madonna dei Miracoli, on a spot where his horse had fallen and almost flattened him in its fall. When the church was completed he hung up in it a horseshoe that had become detached from the horse's hoof in the fall, as later he was to hang up in the votive church of Madonna della Vittoria the armour in which he had fought at Fornovo.[5] He shortly found means to express his gratitude to the Virgin in a fatal error of judgement made by a prominent Jewish banker and moneylender of Mantua, Daniele di Leone da Norsa (d.1504). The Gonzaga protected the Jews and encouraged them to settle in Mantua, but made them pay dearly for their immunities.[6] After due payment Daniele had obtained licence from the Vicario of the Bishop of Mantua to destroy an old fresco of the Virgin attended by saints painted above the doorway of a house which he had bought in 1493, being afraid that 'if these figures were damaged by other persons', he would be blamed.[7] In the early morning of the Tuesday before Ascension Day 1495, while he was out of the city, some person or persons unknown daubed figures of saints with inflammatory verses beneath them on the walls of the house. Later that day, when the Rogation procession passed by, the crowd was incited by the sight of these to throw stones at the house, and if the *bargello* (constable) of Mantua had not had the figures effaced it would have been sacked by the populace. By a petition of 29 May Daniele implored Francesco's protection. Ordinarily he would have received it, but his petition went unheard for two months in the tumult of the continuing campaign, and when Francesco at last recalled the matter, it was at the end of July, some three weeks after the Virgin's intercession at Fornovo, while he was still naturally inflamed by an especial desire to repair any dishonour done to his heavenly patroness.

Accordingly on 31 July Francesco wrote to his brother Sigismondo, then governing Mantua during his absence, commanding him to cause Daniele to have the figure of the Virgin repainted without delay, 'as richly and handsomely as possible'.[8] Sigismondo, already a Protonotary and afire with ambition to obtain a cardinal's hat, received the order with enthusiasm and at once imparted it to two clerics, Padre Marco Antonio da Porto and Fra Girolamo Redini, whose austerity of life and fanatical devotion had gained them great influence at the Gonzaga court. Of the two Redini, a former court official turned priest, hermit and visionary, but still employed by the Gonzaga in their diplomatic affairs, had the greater ascendancy.[9] He at once became a prime mover in the business, perhaps because he was already deeply involved in the building and decoration of the votive church of the Madonna dei Miracoli at Gonzaga and was fired by the pious ambition to have Francesco adorn his city and territories with more and more churches commemorating the Virgin's glorious protection.[10]

On 8 August he wrote to Francesco that he was urgently soliciting the restoration 'in lovely and exceeding rich fashion' of the image of the Virgin whose destruction by the Jews her sweetest son Jesus had taken in very ill part. Concerning this restoration he had been favoured with especial signs from God, to be revealed to Francesco when they met. Among other advices two friends of God, unbeknownst to each other, had come to him, though he had no acquaintance with them, and told him separately of two wondrous visions they had received of this blessed image. Padre Marco Antonio da Porto, he continued, was sure that Francesco would now raze the Jew's house to the ground and build a church to be named Santa Maria della Vittoria on its site, for he and Redini had discovered that a church dedicated to Our Lady had once stood there. 'Meanwhile M. Andrea Mantinia, at the great suasion of the most Reverend Monsignor your brother, is to make the picture of this image. Under the mantle on one side shall be you, fully armed as a victorious captain with your brothers, and on the other your most illustrious consort &c. which will be a most noble work.'[11]

At this stage then what was contemplated, or so it would seem, was a simple image of the Madonna della Misericordia type, without any attendant saints. Evidently this first invention was devised in a state of mystical inflammation by Francesco's clerical brother Sigismondo, aided by Redini and Marco da Porto, at a time when it was still intended to be no more than a fresco. Its general conception was to remain unchanged even after it became an altarpiece, though certain figures were added and others were altered. At first Francesco was reluctant to demolish Daniele's house, and in a letter of 18 August he told Sigismondo to order the Jew to set up an image of the Virgin in the same place as the old one. It was to cost the great sum of 110 ducats, to be by Mantegna's hand and 'in such fashion as to be worthy of the price'. Should Daniele fail to disburse the money within three days he was to be hung up before his own house in the place where the Virgin's image had been painted and the house itself was to be confiscated.[12] Sigismondo sent for Daniele, and notified him of the Marchese's will and of the penalty he would incur if he disobeyed it. Daniele produced the money that very same day 'and now' wrote Sigismondo on 26 August, 'we shall attend to the fulfilment of your Excellency's will in this matter by means of Mastro [sic] Andrea Mantegna, so that you will need make no more demonstration against this Jew by reason of his error.'[13] This seems to be the sole occasion on which any Gonzaga gave Mantegna the craftsman's title of master rather than the dignified title of Messer; although he reverts to Messer in later letters, its use here perhaps indicates Mantegna's real status in Sigismondo's eyes.[14]

On 30 August Sigismondo reported that he had already disbursed part of the 110 ducats to Mantegna, 'who desires to make a work of excellence'.[15] He would pay over the remainder of the money the moment Mantegna began it, and for all else remitted himself to a letter Francesco would receive from Redini. That letter had already been written the day before. In it Redini lauds Sigismondo's warm zeal in the business and renews his solicitations for Francesco to build a church dedicated to Santa Maria della Vittoria on the site of Daniele's house, according to Don Marco da Porto's inspiration, instead of contenting himself with having the fresco renewed. The plan, he urged, was greatly favoured by Sigismondo, who had already given his orders in council concerning the design of the picture, subject to the Marchese's approval. Sigismondo had now decided that two saints were to be added to the picture, in attendance on the Virgin, for reasons Redini proceeded to explain:

M. Andrea Mantinia is to make two saints, one to either side of the Madonna, who are to hold up her mantle, under which is to be Your Lordship, fully armed &c.[16] These saints are to be St

George and St Michael, which pleased everyone greatly, and me more than all, on account of the words that he added, sagely, and as I believe, inspired by God, saying that these two saints were bringers of victory, one to the body, the other to the soul, and that together with the Most Holy Mother of Christ, your most devout advocate and only hope, they would grant victory to your Most Illustrious Lordship.

Francesco was of course still in the field against the French, which explains why Sigismondo placed such emphasis on future divine protection. Redini added that as a gift to this new devotion of Santa Maria della Vittoria Sigismondo had vowed the first *palio* to be won by Francesco's sick horse, whose cure he was superintending.[17]

Francesco was now won over to this scheme of a votive church with a votive altarpiece, principally moved no doubt by the incitements of the visionary Don Marco da Porto. During his absence from February to September 1496 on a long campaign against the French garrisons in South Italy the church was completed by his architect Bernardino Ghisolfo, who worked with such a will that it was ready by the anniversary of Fornovo (6 July 1496). According to Vasari it was built to a design by Mantegna: the structure is in any case a simple one.[18] In the scheme for the picture as proposed by Sigismondo alterations were certainly made, for in it as painted St Andrew and St Longinus, patron saints of Mantua, are added to St Michael and St George. And in place of Isabella d'Este, who was to have been figured kneeling under the other side of the Virgin's mantle opposite to her husband, we find her patron saint, St Elizabeth, and the young Baptist, raised above his mother and pointing triumphantly to Christ. There has been speculation about this particular change. It might be taken as an expression of Isabella's veneration for her patroness, to whom she may well have commended her husband's safety during his dangerous campaigns. But there is evidence to suggest that little or no allusion is made to Isabella in these figures, at any rate in their primary role, and that they are intended to symbolize Christian victory over Jewish presumption and impiety.

Elizabeth and the young Baptist reappear on the Virgin's left in a picture painted by a follower of Mantegna either *c*.1498–9 for Redini, into whose charge Francesco gave Santa Maria della Vittoria on 9 March 1498, or else *c*.1500 for the refectory of the Hieronymite friars whom Francesco appointed on 1 December 1499 to serve the church in Redini's place.[19] Beyond all doubt it celebrates the votive church of Santa Maria as a triumph over Jewish temerity, for on the Virgin's right stands St Jerome, the name saint of Redini and patron saint of the Hieronymites, holding up a model of the church for the spectator's edification. Four despondent Jews, two men and two women, depart from before the Virgin's throne, their humbling proclaimed by the tablet inscribed DEBELLATA/HEBRAEORVM/ TEMERITATE held by two angels above her head.

In this picture, which can have no connection with Isabella d'Este, St Elizabeth and the Baptist appear because they figure baptism, the rite that above all others separates Christians from Jews. While not excluding all secondary allusion to Isabella, it would seem that in Mantegna's austere old matron and in the graceful child who is given such especial prominence, we ought to see figured, decorously and discreetly, without the triumphant crudity of the lesser picture, that fanatical hatred of the Jews which was so deeply interwoven with the foundation of Santa Maria della Vittoria and the painting of the altarpiece. Plainly Francesco himself attached great importance to the association of St Elizabeth with devotion to the church. The day he appointed for an annual procession of thanksgiving to Santa Maria della Vittoria, which continued to be held without interruption well into the eighteenth century, was the Feast of the Visitation (2 July) when Mary and Elizabeth are honoured together.[20]

These figures are important changes in the design of the altarpiece, and probably it was modified by Francesco himself after his return to Mantua on 1 November 1495.[21] It can only have been by his will that his brothers Sigismondo and Giovanni, who originally were to have been represented beside him, were excluded from the painting, and likewise, if the interpretation advanced above is correct, it must also have been he who forbade any representation of Isabella. These exclusions altered the nature of the picture from a family into a personal act of thanksgiving, a votive offering made by the Marchese alone for the victory he had won at Fornovo. The two decrees of 9 March 1496 and 1 December 1499 by which Francesco assigned Santa Maria first to Redini and then to the Hieronymites support this interpretation, for they associate its foundation exclusively with the battle and with Francesco's escape from death by special interposition of the Virgin. For all these reasons the final design of the picture was probably not settled before November 1495 at the earliest, although it must have been fixed by 26 February 1496 at the latest, because on that day Francesco left for his campaign in Naples against the French garrisons. Clearly Mantegna made his portrait sketch for the head of Francesco in the painting during this winter residence in Mantua. All these considerations tend to a date in the first six months of 1496 for the actual initiation and completion of the picture and this date finds support in a letter of 7 July 1496 from the Marchese's secretary Antimaco describing it as '*de recenti picta*' (recently painted).[22]

In its ultimate form, then, the altarpiece images the double motives intertwined in its creation: the Marchese's gratitude to the Virgin for his victory and its expression in the exemplary punishment meted out on those rancorous enemies of Christ and his Mother, the Jews, in expiation of an insult they had dared to offer to her image. On 6 July 1496, the anniversary of Fornovo, the painting was exhibited on a richly decorated stand before San Sebastiano, the church opposite Mantegna's house. Here it figured as the centrepiece of one of those tableaux of living figures so dear to the later Middle Ages and Renaissance. Above it was God the Father, represented by a youth in costume: to left and right of this figure were two prophets, and at either side of the picture three child angels sang the pious songs of praise known as *laudi*. In front were gathered the twelve Apostles. This show had been devised by Sigismondo Gonzaga and Isabella d'Este, who had also arranged the procession which was to escort it to Santa Maria della Vittoria. At the proper moment twenty *facchini* (porters) raised the whole machine and bore it in a solemn procession formed by Sigismondo, the clergy, monks and friars of Mantua and great numbers of the citizens to the corner of the new church. Here Isabella's confessor Fra Pietro da Canneto preached 'a beautiful oration in the vulgar tongue to the people in praise of the glorious Virgin', who had delivered Francesco in his hour of peril and to whom they should pray for his future preservation. Mass was then celebrated at a stately altar which had been erected at the corner of the church, and 'after dinner the image was set up in the place appointed for it', in other words the high altar. It had not been there three hours before some wax images and candles and other votive gifts were offered to it, 'from which cause', so Sigismondo declared with proud satisfaction, 'I do believe there will shortly grow up a very great devotion towards it, and of all this good Your Excellency will have been the cause.'[23]

Francesco testified his own devotion by various acts. He had the words VICTORIAE MEMOR inscribed above the altar, probably on the frame of the picture. This frame is now lost, but we know it to have been rich and carved with his initials FSC and with a device of two hands uplifted between two wings, which seems to have been compounded of the family device of two falcon wings with two praying hands in order to figure Francesco's vows to the Virgin.[24] In addition he hung up the armour he had worn at Fornovo as a votive offering beside the picture, in which it is represented, and ordained, as we have seen, that every Feast of the Visitation in perpetuity there should be a procession of thanksgiving from the cathedral to the church of all the clergy and monks of Mantua and of all the *arti* with their banners, followed by a sung Mass in honour of the Virgin.[25]

Such were the circumstances, known to us in exceptional fullness, which led to the painting of this celebrated picture and such the religious passions, crude, superstitious and violent, that underlie its imagery, veiled in the sweetness and elegance of form with which Mantegna has clothed them. 'It pleased all who saw it', declares Vasari 'and still pleases.' This *dolcezza* exactly suited the idealizing taste of the incipient High Renaissance; it tricks out in forms of sweetened classical nobility that extreme notion of heavenly beauty which was the concomitant of those poignantly literal figurations of Christ's sufferings so dear to fifteenth-century piety. Hence the picture made an equal appeal to a similar taste for idealizing sentiment in the eighteenth and nineteenth centuries: indeed the *Madonna della Vittoria* is the only work by Mantegna ever to have achieved anything like wide popularity. Modern eyes are more disturbed by its edulcoration of the rapt figures of earlier visions of heaven into figures that seem bland in their golden corporeality. To us its relaxation of the tenser sentiment of earlier art into a kind of celestial pageantry may seem to approach dangerously to emptiness and insincerity. Yet the change merely reflects the historical evolution of Renaissance humanist taste. The picture is recognizably the counterpart of the Christian Latin epics of the High Renaissance, the *De Partu Virginis* (*c.*1506–26) of Jacopo Sannazaro, the *Christiados* (*c.*1515–35) of Marco Girolamo Vida, with their Virgilian hexameters, their imitation of the structure and machinery of ancient epic, their descriptions and speeches generalized in colour and sentiment according to the most approved precept and practice of ancient rhetoric. In Mantegna's expression of an earlier Christian humanism in the San Zeno altarpiece there was a harsher austerity of conviction, a sharper realism of enforcement. In the *Madonna della Vittoria* these are dissolved into a courtly vision, where humanity ennobled according to a classical ideal expresses a spirituality that now requires of art suavity and sweetness, majestic amplitude of form and harmony, rather than poignancy of feeling. This change in the cultivated religious sensibility of the High Renaissance was put into words by Michelangelo when he told the Portuguese artist Francisco da Holanda that Flemish painting was cherished by devout old women and girls, by monks and nuns and by gentlemen lacking in any true sense of harmony, because it moved them to tears. Italian painting, he declared, would not bring a single tear to the eye of a devout man, and yet there was nothing nobler or more devout than the true manner of Italian painting, which was that of ancient Greece, since in enlightened spirits nothing excited devotion more than the imitation in art of the perfections of God.[26]

Nevertheless the *Madonna della Vittoria* has its own originality and beauty. The composition, as we already know, images the Virgin's protection of Francesco, to whom she leans down from her throne, her right hand lowered in blessing close to his head, while the Child also lifts his hand to bless the kneeling Marchese, whose hands are joined in prayer. St Michael and St George hold out the sides of her mantle, sheltering the figure of Francesco, on whom they look down with benignant eyes. The mantle also shelters the young Baptist, here, as we have seen, an emblem of the Christian faith, and also, though less completely, the kneeling figure of his mother Elizabeth. Behind appear the heads of St Andrew and St Longinus, Andrew looking up to catch the spectator's eye according to approved pictorial precept, Longinus gazing contemplatively to the right. Both saints were closely associated with the cult of the Holy Blood, the most precious relics of the city, for it was Longinus who had brought them to Mantua and St Andrew in whose church they were housed. No doubt Francesco had invoked them in the fray as saints to whom his family had done peculiar honour and as especial guardians of his city and himself. For Longinus, as a military saint and owner of the Holy Lance, which the Sultan of Turkey had presented to the Pope in 1491, only a few years before, Francesco may have felt especial reverence. As a whole the composition, for all its inner complexities of allusion and symbol, is of a monumental simplicity: the figures of Francesco and St Michael, St Elizabeth and St George form two verticals surmounted by the triangle of the Virgin and Child and united by the sheltering spread of the Virgin's cloak. The light comes from the upper right, illuminating the Virgin and Child, and falling eloquently on the saints and on the figure of Francesco, in a picture that is generally dark in tone, with its highest accents the yellow head-dress of St Elizabeth and the Virgin's robe.

The Virgin is figured as the Queen of Heaven, as the words REGINA/CELI LET/ALLELVIA inscribed in letters of gold on a medallion in the centre of her footstool declare. These are the opening words of the antiphon *Regina celi letare alleluia* sung in the Office of the Virgin as celebrated from the vespers of Holy Saturday until Ascension Day: they are found on other quattrocento pictures, for example Matteo di Giovanni's altarpiece of *The Assumption of the Virgin* in the National Gallery, London.[27] She is seated on a throne of panelled stone with baluster legs of red variegated marble, and with a dossal of panelled wood whose border is inlaid with flowers and foliage in ivory and lighter woods. The dossal appears to be unique of its kind in quattrocento art and must reproduce the richest contemporary style of Lombard woodwork. Like the stone dossal of the San Zeno throne it is surmounted by a jewelled medallion, decorated with a band of coral red and with one of interlacing strapwork resembling that used in the simulated hangings of the Camera Picta and recalling the similar interlaced ornaments in the manuscripts of Felice Feliciano. The red stone set on a star of gilt rays in its centre and the crockets of precious stones topped with pearls that radiate like spokes from its edges are symbolic, the pearls of purity, the red stone, most probably a carbuncle, of the fire of love.

The throne stands on a pedestal, a circular drum of grey stone set with three panels decorated with simulated reliefs on a ground of dark porphyry. With Mantegna's usual licence these reliefs ignore the bounds of the moulded frames that contain them: indeed although they have the form of reliefs, their figures and other motifs are rendered three-dimensionally, so that feet and shoulders protrude beyond the plane of the relief and the porphyry ground is treated as if it were space. The central panel (Fig. 11) represents the Fall: the left figures Eve, now fully clothed, listening to God's rebuke after the Fall: 'I will greatly multiply thy sorrow and thy conception; in sorrow thou shalt bring forth children.'[28] In the right panel is the flying figure of Michael, the angel of the expulsion, driving Adam and Eve out of Paradise. The purpose of these reliefs is to figure the Virgin as a second Eve, according to an established iconographical theme: Eve, Man's first mother, brought about his fall, Mary, the Mother of God, his Redemption.[29]

The throne stands in a bower of Paradise, the heavenly garden which Man, who has forfeited Eden, may hope to enter through the mediation and the merits of the Virgin's Son. The bower (*pergola*) is one of Mantegna's loveliest inventions. Its framework is an arch of wood surmounted with a crocketing of Renaissance ornament. From the rear of the top centre a wooden scallop curves inwards and so is drawn in foreshortening. From behind it descend the vertical bands of the framework, which are crossed by transverse bars to form two rows of openings on to the pale and cloudy sky. Trained on to this framework, intertwisted round its bars, and hanging through its crockets are branches of citrus trees, their dark green foliage lit up by white blossom and by the orange, red and yellow of their fruit, which is bright or shadowed as the light falls on it, and arranged so that oranges and lemons contrast their warm and cold colours in close juxtaposition. The bottom of the bower is dark, so throwing up the bright oval and vertical openings above, on which the fruit and flowers glow with a Hesperidean beauty, to which the birds perched in them – a white oriole, parakeets, a red parrot – add animating motifs of exotic colour and grace.

From the scallop two loops of beads, composed of six sections of oval coral beads separated by larger crystal beads, curve across the top of the bower to the framework. Between them depends a string of pearls, divided after every six by a ball of crystal – in the lower crystal is a marvellous effect of red fruit seen through its transparency – from which hangs a great stem of red coral, a wondrous branchage of intertwisted stems. These strings of coral and pearl and crystal have the form of paternosters, the corals and pearls marking the Aves, the crystals the Paters. A simpler paternoster (*corona*) of round coral beads, without the marker beads, is held by Elizabeth, to express her devotion to Mary: it is of a contemporary type, for on 14 February 1501 Bishop Lodovico Gonzaga writes that he does not possess the '*corona di corali*' which a certain Francesco Binasco wants to borrow.[30] On such paternosters the Virgin's aid was and still is besought by the faithful: here their symbolism intertwines invocation of her assistance with celebration of her virginity through those symbols of stainless purity and virginity, crystal and pearls. Because coral was believed to have prophylactic powers of warding off demons and the illusions and fears with which they deceive man it is in general a symbol of the Virgin's interposition in favour of those who commend themselves to her protection. Its appearance in the *Madonna della Vittoria* has also a particular application. Coral in the Middle Ages and Renaissance was believed to be especially efficacious as a protection in battle and as a bringer of victory to the wearer.[31]

The Virgin's feet rest on a footstool richly carved and gilt: shown in perspective with its feet partly concealed by the pedestal, it is an indication that in its original setting the painting was slightly above eye-level. The footstool is pushed slightly to the right of the central axis of the picture, marked by the tree of Eden below and the Child above. The purpose of this asymmetry is naturalistic, to emphasize the energy of the movement with which Mary inclines downwards to the left to bless the Marchese. Francesco is figured as having mounted a low flight of steps to the marble platform, which is shown in perspective at an angle to the picture plane in order that we should realize this. He kneels with hands joined in prayer in the conventional profile pose of a donor, but with none of the pious compunction or solemn respectfulness usual in donors: his lips are parted and his eyes lit in a smile of gratitude for the favours he has received from the Virgin and her Son. Care has nevertheless been taken not to give undue prominence to Francesco in this celestial company. Over his armour of black steel he wears a rich surcoat patterned with bands of dark green and crimson, embroidered in gold, with a cross of St George on its lapel. The light falling from above from the right lights up the lapel and its device and the whites of teeth and eyes in a face that is olive-pink, and framed by dark brown hair and beard, while the kneeling pose throws up the gilt spurs he wears in sign of knighthood. The same light falls in gold on the Virgin's dress of pinkish-red watered silk, detaching her figure even more brightly against the deep green lining of her cloak. She is figured as a modest maiden, with narrow oval face and flattened brown hair.

St Michael and St George, both slightly larger than life, have long, flowing golden locks, pale flesh tints, and soft and delicate features, to suggest youth and virginity. Michael is garbed in the long white robe of an angel under his golden classical breastplate and tunic. Iconographically this exceptional, not to say singular, combination of dress must be designed to signify the archangel's dual role as the angel who escorts the souls of the dead to judgement and as the heavenly warrior who triumphs over Satan. It would seem in fact to have been evolved to match Sigismondo's conception of the saint as the bringer of victory to the soul triumphant over death. Michael rests his hand on a great two-handed sword which he bears as the standard-bearer of heaven (*signifer coeli*): its hilt of polished onyx is topped by a pommel of crystal. Michael was venerated by Francesco as well as by Sigismondo as an especial protector; in a fresco, long destroyed, but seen by Bettinelli in the eighteenth century and attributed by him to Mantegna, Francesco was depicted kneeling before St Michael, who was riding on the Marchese's horse, which had brought him safely out of a melée, though it had lost a leg from a cannon shot. Said to have been one of Mantegna's finest works in fresco, it was painted above the eighth arch of the Piazza dell' Erbe in Mantua, facing the clock tower, and according to Bettinelli commemorated the Marchese's escape from death at Fornovo. By 1774 it had already largely vanished.[32]

St George stands in a flexed pose matching that of Michael: he is placed on the Virgin's left hand, as befits his lesser degree in heaven. In Sigismondo's conception he was the bringer of victory to the body, and indeed he was the favourite patron saint of medieval and Renaissance soldiers. Here he bears an attribute that symbolizes an especial act of protection accorded to Francesco by Heaven, a broken lance. There is no slaughtered dragon to explain this broken lance, as in Mantegna's early *St George*, neither is it a usual attribute of the saint, indeed it appears to be unique to this picture.[33] Accordingly it may be identified as either the lance which was broken in Francesco's hand by the stone cannon-ball that also carried away his horse's leg,[34] or else as a

Fig. 11. Adam and Eve. Detail from *The Madonna della Vittoria* (Plate xiv)

lance that he broke on the field of Fornovo. Certainly he despatched a truncated lance as a gift to Isabella d'Este along with some of the booty from the French king's tent shortly after the battle. This '*tronchono di lanza*', and the Marchese's *apparamento*, by which seems to be meant the armour he wore in the battle, were given to Isabella as chivalric presents from a knight to his lady: 'my mistress has had great pleasure that you should have sent them to her', wrote her secretary, 'and likewise thanks you very much.'[35]

In the fifteenth century great vertical altarpieces such as the Aigueperse *St Sebastian* and the *Madonna della Vittoria* are a genre especially characteristic of Lombardy and the Veneto. Uncommon before the second half of the century, they tend to grow ever larger towards its end, culminating in the next century in the mighty canvases of Titian and Veronese. Mantegna's most ambitious essay in the genre, the gigantic altarpiece of the *Virgin and Child in glory, attended by angels and by St John the Baptist, St Gregory the Great, St Benedict and St Jerome* (Plate 127) was painted in 1496–7.[36] His patrons were the Olivetan monks of Santa Maria in Organo in Verona. Originally a Benedictine monastery of black monks, Santa Maria had been turned over to the Olivetans, a reforming congregation of white Benedictines founded in 1319, by Cardinal Antonio Correr, Gregorio's uncle, who held it as abbot in *commendam*. In 1481, under the rule of the abbot Fra Girolamo de' Bendadei or Tea of Ferrara, the Olivetans began the renovation and redecoration of the church, and it is probably for this reason that St Jerome is represented in the altarpiece as holding a model of the church. By the 1490s they were ready to turn their attention to the choir. From 1493 to 1499 Fra Giovanni da Verona, one of a number of talented woodcarvers and *intarsia* workers who brought the Olivetans a great reputation in this craft, made the celebrated choir-stalls which are still the greatest ornament of the church. The Olivetans had been founded to revive the strict observance of the Benedictine rule and of its precept *ora et labora* (prayer and labour), and this emphasis on manual toil explains why they produced so many woodworkers and also miniaturists and painters like Fra Girolamo dai Libri.

Mantegna's altarpiece, like his much earlier Veronese altarpiece of San Zeno, was designed as the crowning feature of a new monks' choir. It is first mentioned in the account books of the monastery on 8 October 1496, when the Olivetans disbursed two lire and two soldi on a brace of pheasants, a brace of partridges and a brace of thrushes as a present to Mantegna. This date can be taken as marking more or less the beginning of the work. On 26 October the monastery spent eleven ducats on the expensive pigment of *azzurro ultramarino*, the costliest of all blues, and two ducats on gold 'for Messer Andrea Mantegna for our picture'. The monks were determined to keep Mantegna's goodwill through the presents of food which were considered so graceful and appropriate in those times. On 10 November they paid for a hare and more thrushes, which Fra Giovanni took to Mantua, and on 22 December they gave money to Fra Giovanni to buy pots in which to carry olives and conserves to Mantegna.

The interest of these documents is more than anecdotal, for they reveal that the intermediary between the monastery and Mantegna was Fra Giovanni da Verona, who besides being a woodcarver was also an architect, illuminator and sculptor in marble and bronze. In all probability it was he who gave the invention of the altarpiece to Mantegna, the abbot having delegated this task and all the business connected with its execution to him, rather as Fra Mauro de'Folperti of Santa Giustina had long ago delegated the business of the frame for the altarpiece of St Luke to Fra Antonino. There may be some allusion to him in the figure of St John the Baptist, but it is known that this saint, who also appears in the San Zeno altarpiece, was greatly venerated in Verona and the name of Giovanni was often assumed by Veronese who took the Olivetan habit in Santa Maria in Organo. A more certain token of his presence is the model of Santa Maria held by St Jerome, for it was Fra Giovanni who designed the new sacristy and campanile of the church. The sacristy was begun on 2 July 1495 and the campanile a month later on 7 August, but as the sacristy was not completed until 1505 and the campanile until 1533, Mantegna must have followed a design provided by Fra Giovanni. Of the other two saints, St Benedict appears as the founder of the order: he is shown wearing the white Olivetan habit. St Gregory appears as one of its glories: with St Jerome, he is an example to the monks of the need to study the scriptures and other branches of sacred learning, a lesson enforced by the books they hold.

The Virgin, holding a pink rose and dressed in a robe of red watered silk and mantle of blue and green, is shown floating in heaven in a mandorla of cherubs, with the Child seated on her right knee, his hand raised in blessing. This motif was deliberately chosen to recall her Assumption, and with good reason, for the church of Santa Maria is dedicated to the Assumption of the Virgin. Indeed the date of Mantegna's signature, 15 August 1497, is the date of the festival of the Assumption and Mantegna must have deliberately completed the picture on that day to honour the Virgin and testify his devotion. Below, an angel plays an organ while two others sing the Virgin's praises. The motif is a graceful invention taken from the organ which the monks had adopted as their device in the belief that their church had got its name from an organ, though in reality it derived from the gateway known as the Porta Organa which stood close by.

The invention of this great altarpiece thus assembles devotional motifs and saints of very especial significance to the monastery. It was embodied by Mantegna in a composition of great mystical beauty. To either side of the picture are orange- and lemon-trees whose glowing fruit and white blossom and sweet scent made them to Mantegna and his contemporaries fit trees for Paradise. White doves, symbols of peace and purity, fly among them. The trees form a broken natural arch beside the mandorla, so that the Virgin appears between them as an ultimate vision of heavenly glory in a depth of blue. Of the four saints Gregory and Benedict are at the rear and closer together and to the Virgin, a placing that befits their rank and at the same time narrows into diagonals the corridor of space before the middle ground in which the Virgin floats, so that our eyes are directed principally towards her and her Son, aided by the pointing finger of the Baptist.

In the monks' choir the altarpiece was raised above eye-level, in a great frame of carved and gilded woodwork. Here it must have seemed truly an apparition of the court of heaven, especially during the midnight services of the order. Mantegna has set the saints simply on a line, according to his old perspective device for simulating recession in depth above eye-level, with no indication of a pavement or other footing, and cutting off the figures of the two rear saints at the base. Although they are impressive in weight of form and drapery and colour, and although their poses, that of the Baptist in particular, leave no doubt of a level on which they stand, and indeed the trees of the garden of Paradise rise behind them in confirmation, nevertheless it is difficult to conceive that level's exact form and nature. We may be intended to conceive it as the summit of a holy mountain, for the three angels at the centre bottom of the middle ground are cut off below waist and neck, and so must be standing below the saints. As a result of this deliberate suppression of all physical support, the altarpiece is more ethereal in conception that any of Mantegna's earlier paintings. Its visionary effect of supra-reality is heightened by the haloes, soft arches of golden radiance with a cross of deeper gold in that of the Child, by the cherub-heads emerging from clouds, some flesh-coloured, it is true, but most of the same ghostly grey-blue as the clouds themselves. The light falls from the top right, presumably reflecting the natural sources of light in an Italian church, but creating gentler, rather local contrasts, as so often in Mantegna's late pictures. It is heightened too by the mandorla, whose burning red and gold reduce in value the pale blue and white sky. The tonality of the picture is light and chalky, as in many late Mantegnas, with deeper chords struck by the warm orange rippled with gold of Gregory's dalmatic of watered silk, by the cardinal scarlet of Jerome's cloak and skull-cap, by the crimson gold of the Virgin's robe and the red wings of the organ-playing angel.

The poor condition of the picture and its removal from its original frame and setting have deprived it of much of its mystical intensity and of its power to summon up awe and devotion in the worshipper. Nevertheless, to a modern age there does appear a want of vitality in parts of it, as in the face of the Baptist, where a cold conventionality of feeling seems to have betrayed Mantegna into vapidity of form and expression. This vapidity recurs in a number of Mantegna's later religious pictures: that its real origin stems from a confusion of ideal beauty with empty softness of design and sentiment rather than from failing powers is evident from the sharpness of characterization in the other saints in this very picture, above all in the tremendous figure of St Jerome.

XI

Isabella d'Este and her Studiolo

ON 15 February 1490 the sixteen-year-old Isabella d'Este entered Mantua as the bride of Francesco Gonzaga. She had received a humanist education at the court of Ferrara, where she had been taught the fables and histories of antiquity and had learnt to read Terence and Cicero and to read and scan Virgil, whose *Eclogues* she had by heart. Although these scholarly accomplishments were rather elementary and at times became distinctly rusty, throughout her life Isabella was to aspire to be a pattern of the cultivated lady of the High Renaissance, distinguished above all others by the great collection of works of art, antique and modern, that she assembled around herself with a persistence equalled only by her taste. With admirable dedication she sought to maintain or improve her knowledge of letters, of Latin, of poetry and music, undeterred by pregnancies and by the cares of state that early overwhelmed her.[1] During Francesco's military expeditions it was she who was left to govern Mantua and spin the diplomatic webs that helped to preserve the Gonzaga from the many greedy enemies who threatened their state during the turbulent years of foreign invasion and internal warfare which began in 1494. She bought books, usually in Venice, 'of battles, histories and fables, both of the moderns and of the ancients' and from 1492 appointed a series of preceptors whose duty was to improve her Latin and her knowledge of letters. Already in February 1493 her old tutor Battista Guarino was congratulating her on her will to learn, 'for in these times few ladies are your equals, and in Italy there is perhaps none who is a lettered lady.'[2]

Almost at once Isabella set about making a small suite of private apartments for herself in the Castello. The fashion for creating an intimate chamber to which a great man could withdraw from the stage of court or household life to pursue private interests and studies unobserved and unhindered set in during the fifteenth century. The most important of these rooms was always a *studio* (study) or *studiolo* (little study).[3] Originally it was what its English name still implies, a study, where scholars or those of a scholarly turn read, studied or wrote and kept their books and papers. At Vincennes a royal apartment consisting of an *estude*, a small chapel, an oratory and a chamber was built as early as 1373 for King Charles V of France, who had such an *estude* in all his principal palaces. In early fifteenth-century Florence the *studio* of merchants and notaries was not only a study, or place where books were kept, but also a *scrittoio* or writing-room, where intimate family papers and the private family archive were preserved. And in the *studio* of Cosimo de' Medici we find not only books, but small paintings, precious objects in gold and silver and a collection of ancient medals. By the mid-fifteenth century the *studio* was becoming a small room reserved as a private retreat for the master of the household, and used to house his books, his papers and his personal collections of objects of price and antiquity. The ideals it embodied then were those of quiet study and contemplation, in a retreat undisturbed by the world.

The first Italian prince known to have had a *studio* was Leonello d'Este, Isabella's great-uncle; it was in his suburban palace of Belfiore, outside Ferrara. Later Federigo da Montefeltro had a *studio* in his palaces at Urbino and Gubbio, and in 1478 Federico Gonzaga, an admirer of the Duke of Urbino as a domestic architect, had Luca Fancelli create one for his use in the Castello di San Giorgio.[4] The princely *studio* was richly decorated, usually with subjects reflecting the ideals or the interests of the owner and with portraits recording his friendships. It was

Fig. 12. Lorenzo Costa: *Portrait of Isabella d'Este*. Windsor, Royal Coll.

unprecedented for a woman to have a *studio*, and in making one for herself Isabella was setting up as a learned and lettered lady, who preferred the pleasures of the mind to frivolous amusements. Being Isabella, she was no doubt conscious of her own uniqueness and anxious to put all other feminine rivals into the shade.

The public rooms allotted to Isabella, at any rate in June 1498, were Lodovico's old state apartments. They comprised Mantegna's Camera Picta, the large room described as a *salotto* adjoining the Camera, a small chamber known as the *camerino del sole* or *dei soli*, no doubt from its decoration with the Gonzaga device of the sun, the chamber called the *camera del cassone*, a small chamber or *camerino*, and a chamber which in previous years had been used as a dining-room. All these rooms formed an apartment on the second floor and occupied the side of the Castello running from the Camera Picta in the north-west tower to the *Sala delle Armi* in the corresponding tower on the south-west. Below them, on the first or ground floor, were the apartments of Francesco. In order to make private apartments for herself Isabella remodelled a small tower projecting from the wall beside the south-west tower, forming the *camerino* (little chamber), better known as the Studiolo, on the level of the *piano nobile* and under it a room called the *grotta*, perhaps because it was a secluded retreat below the rest of her apartments, with access by a narrow staircase within the walls, either from the Studiolo or the *Sala delle Armi*.[5]

One of the few things that is quite clear about the history of the furnishing and decoration of the Studiolo is that they took a long time to reach finality. Isabella naturally made changes in her scheme of ornamentation, which became more ambitious as the years passed, and in addition there were the usual difficulties attendant on all such enterprises, shortages of money and the delays of artists. In her attitude to the delays of artists Isabella varied from weary patience to peremptory impatience, depending largely on the standing of the artist and whether he was under her thumb in Mantua or enjoyed the irresponsibility of independence in Venice, Bologna or Florence. It is customary to censure her imperious commands to artists as betraying a want of finer sensibilities, but there can be no doubt that she was much tried – Perugino kept her waiting for two and a half years and Bellini broke his word to her twice over, and never produced a painting for the Studiolo at all.

In its first state the Studiolo was furnished with cupboards whose doors were decorated on the inside by the painter Gianluca Liombeni, who also painted the 'frieze' on the upper part of the wall. Liombeni was allowed to paint what he liked on the cupboards, but the ornament of the 'frieze' was composed of five devices furnished by Isabella, two on each of the long walls and one on the short wall by the entrance. After Isabella had threatened him with a spell in the dungeons of the Castello, Liombeni finished this decoration by March 1492. In this first state the Studiolo was as simply furnished and decorated as might be expected of a room got ready for use in a comparatively short time.

Mantegna had taken early steps to have himself recommended to Isabella's notice and good graces. Experience warned him that it was imprudent in an old courtier to expect favour from a new lord or lady without influential recommendation. Accordingly on his return from Rome in September 1490 he approached Isabella's tutor Guarino, to whom she was much attached.[6] On 22 October Guarino wrote to her from Verona warmly commending Mantegna to her notice.

> Messer Andrea Mantegna prayed me much to commend him to your Excellency, having persuaded himself that my words have some weight with you. To whom I answered that gifted and virtuous men (*uomini virtuosi*) like him have no need of recommendation to Your Excellency, for of yourself you are exceedingly inclined to love and favour those who are deserving, but yet that I would do so, and thus I pray you to entertain him lovingly and hold him in good esteem, for in truth besides his excellence in his art, wherein he has no equal, he is all courtesy and kindness, and Your Ladyship will get from him a thousand good conceits in designs and other things that will befall; he is fitted to do honour to that illustrious Lord and city.[7]

It has been claimed that Isabella did not admire Mantegna, but on 11 August 1492 we find her writing to her husband Francesco of the daughters of Antonia del Balzo, wife of his uncle Gianfrancesco Gonzaga, that 'they are so beautiful that Messer Andrea Mantegna could paint them no finer.'[8] Late in 1492 or early in 1493 she commissioned from him a portrait of herself to send as a present to her friend Isabella del Balzo (1465–1533), Countess of Acerra and wife of Isabella's cousin Federico d'Aragona, later to be King of Naples.[9] Isabella was the sister of Antonia del Balzo and was later to be praised by Castiglione in the *Cortegiano* for the fortitude and resignation with which she endured the misfortunes of her family. This portrait was not successful, at any rate not in the eyes of the sitter, perhaps because she judged a portrait entirely by her opinion as to its likeness, and on 20 April she wrote to Isabella: 'We are extremely sorry that we cannot send you our portrait at present, for the painter has done it so ill that it has no resemblance to us.' Accordingly she sent to Urbino for Giovanni Santi, Raphael's father, who accomplished the portrait to Isabella's satisfaction and as we have seen left in his verse chronicle of Federigo da Montefeltro a long tribute to Mantegna as the first of painters ancient and modern and as a universal master in all branches of the art.[10]

This mishap did not seriously affect relations between Mantegna and Isabella, who employed him not only in the Studiolo but on other tasks besides. One project was to design a statue of Virgil to replace that which according to tradition had been thrown down by Carlo Malatesta in 1397.[11] Early in 1499 she sought the advice of Giovanni Pontano, the leading figure in that brilliant circle of humanists which brought a crepuscular glory to the Aragonese court in late fifteenth-century Naples, and perhaps the finest of all Neo-Latin poets. Pontano's opinion is of interest as it illustrates the sort of consultation with a learned humanist over the invention of an important work of art that so often preceded its physical embodiment in an artist's design. From it we can see something of what was dictated to the artist, and what was left to his fancy. As regards the medium of the statue, although Pontano thought bronze the nobler material, it was always in danger of being melted down to make bells or cannon, better then to have the statue made in fine marble, with a handsome marble base beneath, by a sculptor of worth. Battista Fiera had discovered an authentic likeness of Virgil, and Pontano advised that this should be copied. Otherwise, it would be best to follow the style of the ancients, by which he meant simplicity and reticence, as opposed to emphasis of attribute and laudatory inscription. The poet should wear only a simple laurel wreath on his head, and be shod in antique sandals. He should have a mantle in the antique fashion, over a toga, with the usual knot on the shoulder, or else wear a senatorial dress of a robe and a mantle slung over the shoulder. Mantegna, he thought, would easily be able to find out about these forms of dress. Finally, the figure was not to hold a book or any other attribute, and was to be figured in whatever action best approved itself to Mantegna. He also suggested inscriptions for the base of suitably lapidary brevity.[12] A drawing of a statue of Virgil, now in Paris, though only a copy after Mantegna, reveals that Pontano's suggestions were accepted by him almost literally; of the alternatives of costume, however, he preferred the toga and antique mantle with a knot on the shoulder.[13] In the end the scheme came to nothing, but it gave Isabella a lasting reputation as a lady of lofty mind among the Neapolitan humanists.

Mantegna was already being urged by her before 4 March 1492 to paint something for the Studiolo as soon as its decoration was finished. Whether he did so is uncertain. In 1494 rats made it necessary to take up the old wooden floor and replace it with a floor of maiolica tiles decorated with Gonzaga devices which Isabella ordered from the potters of Pesaro. Only in the following year does she seem to have determined on redecorating the Studiolo in a more ambitious manner. On 1 May 1495 she sent from Ferrara to Mantua for a drawing with measurements of her 'camerino', perhaps in order to have the advice of humanists and painters at her father's court.[14] Work did not begin on the new scheme till the spring of the following year, when she ordered white marble for 'a door and window for our Studiolo', and hired Bernardino, a master from Padua, as a painter. It is a reasonable supposition that the first picture Mantegna executed for the Studiolo, the so-called Parnassus, was conceived and commissioned as part of this redecoration. If so, it may have been begun in 1496; it was certainly installed in the Studiolo by 3 July 1497, when Alberto da Bologna told Isabella that on her return from Ferrara she would find the framework of her picture by Mantegna carved and set up on the wall and perhaps already gilded.[15]

Plainly Isabella had now conceived her celebrated scheme for decorating her Studiolo with 'paintings of histories by the most excellent painters at present living in Italy'.[16] Mantegna's Parnassus was her initial success in this project. In November 1496 she made the first of her abortive attempts to obtain a painting from Giovanni Bellini and in April 1497 she took the first step in what was to prove an infinitely protracted negotiation with Perugino. As nothing was forthcoming from either, she turned in December 1497 to ordering a spalliera or hanging of verdura from Venice. She then allowed her scheme to lapse for some years, only resurrecting it in September 1500 with a new approach to Perugino, followed in March 1501 by another to Bellini. It was almost certainly in connection with this revival of her project that she commissioned from Mantegna the picture of Pallas expelling the Vices from the Garden of Virtue. This was probably finished in July 1502 and mounted on a wall of the Studiolo by November of that year. Perugino and Bellini had still produced nothing by the beginning of 1504 when Isabella had already altered or begun altering the arrangement (ordine) of the Studiolo. As a result of these alterations Perugino was asked to change the size of the picture he was to paint for her. Verheyen points out that since his picture is 147 cm high, some 12 cm less than the two Mantegnas, it must have been at this time that the upper edge of Mantegna's canvas was bent over and hidden under its frame while the Parnassus was shortened in its width, apparently to fit a new framework on the walls.[17]

There can be no doubt that Mantegna's two paintings set the pattern for the paintings by other masters, not only in their crowd of figures occupying a romantic landscape, but in the actual proportions of those figures. Late in 1503 Perugino anxiously enquired about the size of the figures he was to put into his painting, as from the drawing he had been given for his guidance the figures seemed to him too small. He asked if he could be told the size of the 'figures that are in the other histories which are or will be set beside this one, for if the desire is that all should turn out well, it is needful for them to be made to concord in their measurements, or that the difference should be small.'[18] In reply Isabella sent him on 12 January 1504 the measurements of the height of the figures, with an apology for the delay 'because we have not been able to get them before from Messer Andrea Mantegna.'[19] There can be no doubt too that Mantegna was regarded as having set a standard of excellence for the paintings as a whole. Isabella congratulated herself that Perugino would feel obliged to do his best for her 'especially as his work . . . will be in comparison with the paintings of Mantegna',[20] while Bellini was more than half afraid to undertake a painting for the Studiolo because it would have to suffer the test of hanging beside his brother-in-law's work. And indeed when Lorenzo da Pavia, the musician and maker of musical instruments who acted as her agent and factotum in Venice, went to see in July 1504 the picture of a *Nativity* which Bellini eventually did paint for Isabella, he found it 'truly a beautiful thing, better than I thought it would be . . . in this picture he has made a great effort to do himself honour, most of all in respect of Messer Andrea Mantegna. True it is that for invention he cannot approach Messer Andrea, who in this is excellent beyond compare.' And again in a second letter, written ten days later, he says that Bellini is excellent in colouring, and the things in his picture are well finished and deserve close inspection, but that no one can rival Mantegna for invention.[21] Similarly when Isabella received Perugino's picture in June 1505 her first reaction was to compare it, not wholly favourably, with Mantegna's paintings. 'It pleases us from being well drawn and well coloured, but had it been finished with greater diligence, having as it does to hang beside those of Mantegna, which are supremely neat, it would have been to your greater honour and more to our satisfaction.'[22]

It is often claimed that Isabella sought to bind her painters too tightly to a literary programme, on the strength of the famous objection, made by Giovanni Bellini when she invited Pietro Bembo to devise an invention for the picture he was to paint for the Studiolo, that 'it would have to be accommodated to his fancy, given that it is he who has to execute it, and his pleasure is not to have very fixed bounds given to his brush, being used, as he says, to wander at his own will in his pictures, so that they may satisfy those who look at them so far as in him lies.'[23] Plainly Bellini disliked being given more than the principal subject of the picture – and indeed a distaste for precision and a liking for errant freedom of fancy remained a persistent characteristic of Venetian artists.

With the sole exception of those for Perugino's *Triumph over Chastity* we do not know the actual instructions that Isabella gave her painters. The invention she gave to Perugino, which very exceptionally was transcribed into the contract by her agent,[24] is quite reasonable in its specifications, stipulating only that the four principal figures and their actions and attributes were to be represented without alteration, but leaving the artist a certain latitude over the accessories, in that he could reduce these, though he might not augment them. The details on which she insisted were those necessary for the representation of the allegory embodied in the scene and for its illustration in secondary figures, actions and symbols. And as we have seen, the 'reduction to elegant form' of such specifications was a task that had long been customarily expected of all artists, even the greatest, like Mantegna himself. But at least once Isabella was content not to impose a subject on an artist, for in 1501 she told Leonardo that if only he would paint a picture for her she would leave both the *invenzione* and the time to his own choice.[25]

Although Isabella wished to have pictures from the most famous hands, all were to be of subjects that were suitable as exemplary ornaments of a great lady's private *studio*. Accordingly they figured the virtues proper to woman, and more especially that held in the highest estimation of all, chastity. But far from leading a contemplative life in the cloister, Isabella led an active life in the world and the pictures of the Studiolo all contain some representation of a combat between virtue and vice in which virtue is triumphant. As she also spent her hours of leisure in this room a second theme of its pictorial decoration is virtuous leisure and the occupations that are proper to it. The subjects of each of the pictures were devised at intervals, but Isabella must have determined from the first on these two principal themes, for each successive picture illustrates them in new guises.

The invention she gave to Perugino is described in the contract as 'our poetical invention' (*la poetica nostra invenzione*), but it later transpires that it had been contrived with the aid of her adviser Paride da Ceresara (1466–1532), a Mantuan noble and humanist, and most probably it was largely his work. In fact she seems almost always to have asked a friend, usually a nobleman with literary and humanist interests, rather than a professional poet or humanist, to devise an *invenzione*, which the artist then had to figure in his picture. Once or twice she may have asked such persons for an invention without specifying any subject, but this seems to have happened only when the personage was of especial eminence, like Bembo, just as she was prepared to accept a subject of his own choice from an exceptional artist like Leonardo. But usually she must have asked her ordinary advisers to body out an agreed theme into the figures and images of a history. Certainly both she and Francesco Gonzaga, when asking their friend Niccolò da Correggio, count and poet in *volgare*, to invent devices and mottoes for them, specify the mood and sentiment. And when in 1505 she heard that Perugino had altered a Venus that was to be clothed into a naked Venus 'to make a better display of the excellence of his art', she was not only very annoyed, but wrote off at once to a correspondent in Florence asking him to look at the drawing and written instructions Perugino had been given and make him keep to them, 'for by altering a figure the sense of the fable would be perverted.'[26]

For most of the inventions of her Studiolo Isabella seems indeed to have employed Paride. He was a remarkable figure. Tall, handsome and well proportioned, with red hair, face and beard, he was a wealthy jurisconsult, descended from the feudal counts of Ceresara, and in 1527 built himself a splendid palace in Mantua. He had a true Renaissance appetite for every kind of learning, including cosmography and poetry as well as the graver sciences, and gratified it regardless of expense. Not so unusually for his age, he was steeped in Greek and Latin literature; more exceptionally he had some knowledge of the sacred languages of the East, Hebrew, Syriac and Chaldean. On 30 September 1498 Isabella wrote to thank him for the gift of a Hebrew or Syriac alphabet:

> We have received the greatest pleasure from the sacred letters, or are they Syriac or Babylonian, as you write ... that you have sent us, and we thank you for them. But for our clearer understanding, we should be grateful if you would advise us if certain foliage [*sic*: flourishes] which these letters have are significant, or else solely for ornament, in which case we would pray you to send us another copy of the same letters, pure and simple, as they were usually written in their own time.

Paride's Hebrew learning, to which there are other testimonies, and this letter from Isabella are interesting in view of the Hebrew inscriptions which figure in Mantegna's picture of *Pallas expelling the Vices*, and in at least two of his late religious paintings. Paride had an inclination to recondite and hidden studies which must have suited Isabella, who had a strong dislike of all that was clapper-clawed by the vulgar. Congenial to her too was his learning in astrology, in which she was a devout believer. Later he was to addict himself wholly to the study of astrology, chiromancy and magic, but he was to remain always a popular and highly esteemed figure, a steady favourite of the Gonzaga and the friend of many of the literary luminaries who gravitated around their court, Battista Spagnoli, Matteo Bandello, Battista Fiera and the like.[27]

In making inventions for paintings it was the inventor's task to devise the history, or fable as Isabella called it, in Horatian term, and set it out in words, specifying the figures that were to be represented, together with such of their attributes as were necessary for the signification of the allegory, and specifying too something of the landscape background in general and even in detail where the symbolism of nature was required to enrich or extend the allegory. After Isabella had approved the invention she would send a painter 'to make a sketch of the fable after your fashion', to use her own words to Paride in 1504. As she explained in a letter of 27 November 1504 to the Protonotario Bentivoglio, who was acting as her intermediary in Bologna: 'our slowness in sending Your Lordship the fancy (*fantasia*) of the picture we would like ... has proceeded from our wish to have it put into the shape of a drawing, so that the painter may better understand what he has to do, for many times the conceit cannot be so well expressed in words.' Invention and drawing would then be despatched to the artist who was to paint the history, the written invention in its turn being intended to prevent any misunderstanding of the subject by the painter. This was an ordinary practice: as we have seen the Duchess of Milan sent instructions and drawings for the painting she wished to have Mantegna make for her in 1481.

Such was the course that Isabella followed in 1502 with Perugino in Florence and again in 1504 with Lorenzo Costa in Bologna.[28] Mantegna of course was at hand to receive her guidance, and no doubt made his designs purely from the literary invention, taxing his learning and fancy to embody its conceits in graceful and appropriate form. We have no proof that it was Paride who devised or elaborated the inventions of the *Parnassus* and *Pallas expelling the Vices*, but it is possible that he did so as Isabella excuses herself on 10 November 1504 for perpetually having to ask him for fresh inventions for the Studiolo because of the tergiversations and delays of her painters.[29]

The figure of Anteros in the *Parnassus* gives a clue to one of the books that was used by the contriver of its invention.[30] The few appearances Anteros makes in classical antiquity he makes as a deity who presides over reciprocal love or alternatively as a deity who avenges slighted love. He maintained this character, so far as he was thought of at all, until the early 1490s. Then he was suddenly transformed into an enemy of carnal love and an advocate of celestial love in opposition to his brother Cupid. The transformation was effected by a provincial humanist of the Veneto, Pietro Hedo (Petrus Haedus) of Pordenone,[31] in his Latin dialogue *De amorum generibus*, also known as the *Antierotica*, printed at Treviso in October 1492. Hedo (1427–1504), whose real name was Capretto, was prompted to his invention by the passage in Ovid's *Metamorphoses* (1,466ff.) which describes how Cupid on the summit of Parnassus took from his quiver two arrows, one with a sharp golden tip, which causes love, the other with a blunt tip of lead, which puts love to flight. To Hedo it seemed contrary to reason that one god should produce opposing effects: 'fire can apply heat, but cannot remove it.' Accordingly there must be one Cupid who causes love, and a second Cupid who removes it. They are twins, alike in name and in their birth from Venus, though not from the same Venus, alike in their power to shoot and strike with arrows and alike in their wings. Hedo derived his authority for the existence of two Cupids from Cicero, who explains in his *De Natura Deorum* that there are three Venuses.[32] Of the first and second Venus two Cupids were born, while the third Venus, though married to Vulcan, bore Anteros to Mars. But Hedo reduces Cicero's three Cupids to two on the authority of Seneca – who speaks of twin Cupids, '*geminus Cupido*' – and claims that the Cupid who inflames our desires works in accordance with our nature, while the other is his perpetual adversary, and therefore is called in Greek Anteros, which in Latin means *contrarius amori* (contrary to love).

Hedo reared this unhistorical interpretation of the nature of Anteros on his interpretation of the Greek *anti* as meaning contrary. Any prominence that Anteros obtained in the Renaissance as love's adversary owed its original inspiration to his book. Since Anteros figures in the *Parnassus* in the role that Hedo attributed to him, plainly the *Antierotica* was the source of one of the principal concepts of the picture. *Anteros* was adopted almost immediately as the title of a second assault on carnal love printed at Milan in 1496.[33] The work of the deposed Genoese Doge Battista da Campo Fregoso, better known to his contemporaries as Fulgosius,[34] this *Anteros* is a dialogue in *volgare* setting out why carnal love ought to be considered a vice. Neither as deity nor as personification does Anteros figure in the text, his name being given to the book on the mistaken interpretation of it as meaning contrary to love for which Hedo was responsible. Fregoso's book was certainly used by the deviser of the invention of *Pallas expelling the Vices*, but there is no trace of its influence in the *Parnassus*, which is yet another reason for believing that the *Parnassus* was painted earlier and that its invention was contrived before the publication of Campo Fregoso's *Anteros*. Accordingly the document of 1497 which mentions a painting by Mantegna for Isabella's Studiolo must refer to the *Parnassus*.

It has been argued that the South Italian courtier and littérateur Mario Equicola (c.1470–1525) should be credited with the inventions of Mantegna's two pictures.[35] Equicola is known to have suggested subjects in 1511 for paintings to decorate a *camera* of Alfonso d'Este, Duke of Ferrara, and in 1522 for the Palazzo del Te in Mantua, but any claim for his association with the Studiolo is disproved by the chronology of his career and by what he actually says of Anteros in his book *Libro di natura d'amore*, so often cited as the source for the figure in the *Parnassus*. Equicola, who was born at Alvito, in Terra di Lavoro, entered courtly life in the service of the great Neapolitan family of the Cantelmi, and gravitated into the circle of Neapolitan humanists, known as the Accademia Pontaniana from its leading figure Pontano. It was in Naples that he wrote as a young man in 1494–6 the original Latin version of the *Libro*. Equicola was still in the Regno in 1497, but the death of Pietro Giampaolo Cantelmo, Duke of Sora, in February 1497 and the confiscation of the feudal estates of the family ruined the fortunes of the Cantelmi. Equicola therefore migrated to Ferrara, where Sigismondo Cantelmo (c.1455–1519) had long been established at court, and became the secretary of his wife, Margherita.[36] In Ferrara he presented a copy of the Latin original of his *Libro* to Cardinal Ippolito d'Este, but for the Cardinal's private pleasure, without any wish to have it published or even circulated.

Equicola may have come to the notice of Isabella during one of her frequent visits to her father's court, but correspondence between them only began in May 1503. Five years more were to pass before Equicola finally moved to Mantua in the autumn of 1508 to enter Isabella's service, first as her preceptor in letters and later from 1519 as her secretary. Shortly before his removal to Mantua he made a present of the Latin version of the *Libro* to his nephew, who was so impressed by it that he arranged for its translation into the vulgar tongue. The surviving manuscript of this translation was transcribed in Mantua between January and October 1509, and dedicated to a member of the Ferrarese court, probably Sigismondo Cantelmo. In 1510 or 1511, when Equicola made a thorough revision of his book, the dedication was transferred to Isabella. Her manuscript copy of the translation was presumably presented to her after this revision had been completed. The printed version, published at Venice in 1525, shows signs of further change.

Plainly from these dates and from the known history of the Studiolo neither Equicola nor his book can have influenced the inventions of any of the pictures painted for the Studiolo before 1508. And indeed if we examine Equicola's conception of Anteros, as expressed in the *Libro di natura d'amore*, we find it totally opposed to that figured in the *Parnassus*. Rejecting Hedo's interpretation of Anteros as the enemy of carnal love and advocate of celestial love, he restores the god to his classical role of protector of reciprocal love. With obvious tilts at Hedo and at Fregoso, he writes: 'In some authors I find it related that the ancients called Anteros a god averse from love: the opinion of these men I deem totally false, and its signification to be mutual, equal and reciprocal love. We say that although *anti* may mean contrary, it also denotes equal; so Homer calls Polyphemus *Antideo*.' He continues by citing Suidas, Pausanias and other ancient authorities to prove his point.[37] What all this demonstrates is that of the three books on love by Hedo, Fregoso and Equicola the deviser of the *invenzione* of the *Parnassus* used only Hedo's *Antierotica*, the deviser of the *invenzione* of the *Pallas* used in addition Fregoso's *Anteros*, while Equicola's *Libro* had no influence at all.

Isabella was wholly a child of her times and there was nothing innovatory or recondite in the dominant themes of the paintings of the Studiolo, the praise of virtue and of virtuous occupations, or in much of the imagery in which it is embodied. In a letter of 10 May 1497 Lodovico, Mantegna's son, describes with something of the disdainful scorn of Shakespeare's courtiers in *Midsummer Night's Dream* for the rustics' 'Pyramus and Thisbe', an entertainment (*rappresentazione*) which the rustic inhabitants of the Val Camonica intended to put on for the reception of Caterina Cornaro, Queen of Cyprus. Its subject and imagery were much the same as those of the Studiolo.

> The Comunità awaits the Queen of Cyprus with great expectation, and to do her honour everyone is going a-fishing for new fancies, so that I am in doubt whether the onlookers will not laugh at the silly wits, for a goddess Diana will go to meet the Queen by reason of chastity and there will be a Cupid despoiled by certain nymphs, whereupon Venus, having heard the insult done to her son will make a stew so that even Bacchus shall burst with laughter.[38]

In the Studiolo, however, there is this significant difference: the figures and motifs borrowed from classical mythology are sometimes elaborately obscure, either in themselves or in the relations created by their juxtaposition. This obscurity was pleasing to Isabella, who in her characteristic Renaissance disdain for the vulgar, no doubt wished to reserve for herself and a favoured few the plenary significance of the pictures that decorated her intimate retreat.

Her wish to have only what was novel and to keep it for her own exclusive use appears in her attitude to the poems by living poets that she so eagerly collected. On 25 April 1498 she writes to Bishop Lodovico Gonzaga that she is making an exception for him and allowing him to have a copy of Serafino dell'Aquila's *Capitolo del Sogno*, 'although I had thought not to give it out to great circulation . . . the enclosed copy is taken from the original itself, of which I deprived Serafino so as to be the only person to have it . . . I pray you to have a care . . . not to give it to any one, for I should like to have it by me for some time without its being circulated abroad.'[39] Her intimate friend and equal in rank, the poet Niccolò da Correggio, shared the same sense that his poetry was for circulation among his friends, and that its more intimate meanings were for their private ear. Writing to Isabella on 7 July 1493, he sends her a pastoral eclogue which he has composed in which the shepherd Mopsus complains of fortune and the shepherd Daphnis boasts of it. 'The allegorical meaning I shall tell Your Exellency by word of mouth when I speak to her.'[40] And he sympathized with Isabella's desire to have things that were novel and invented for her exclusive use. In 1498, when she complained that a motto he had sent her for her medal had been used before, he wrote: 'I am in accord with you that you ought not to do anything that has been done by others before.'[41] We have here that same anxiety to distinguish herself in competition with other great ladies which also expressed itself in the invention of new fashions to wear and in the creation of the Studiolo.

We have seen that Isabella called the invention she gave to Perugino 'our poetical invention'. The close alliance between poetry and painting had been explicitly acknowledged in the Renaissance from the time of Alberti, who had advised artists in his *Della pittura* to read poets and orators in order to learn how to paint histories 'whose sole praise consists in the invention' and declares that they 'have many ornaments in common with the painter'.[42] The links between poetry and painting were felt to be exceptionally close in allegorical histories since the physical traits and attributes in which poets clothed their allegorical figures to show their nature could also be represented with the same suggestiveness in painting. In the absence of all except one of the written inventions Isabella gave to her painters, we can find illuminating parallels to the allegories and imagery of the pictures and their figures in contemporary poetry, notably that of one of Isabella's favourite poets, the Carmelite friar Battista Spagnoli (*c*.1447–1516).

Spagnoli was born in Mantua, the son of a Gonzaga courtier, and entered the Carmelite order in 1463. He led the usual itinerant life of a friar in those days, being sent from convent to convent, and rose to high office in his order. But he always retained close connections with the Mantuan court, addressing poems to the Gonzaga and celebrating Francesco's victories over the French in an epic poem *Trophaeum Gonzagae*, which also sings the praises of Isabella. To Mantegna himself Spagnoli addressed a laudatory *silva*, in which he celebrates him as the greatest of painters, who imitates nature to perfection. As an eulogy it expresses perfectly what a pious humanist friar found to admire in Mantegna; striking too is its sense of the vitality of the times and their achievement in the *bonae artes*, and its Ovidian praise for those liberal arts that require knowledge and understanding for their practice, and have utility and delight not sordid profit as their object. It opens with a celebration of the age as a true renaissance, a new spring whose flourishing geniuses do not allow the arts to grow torpid. Painting owes as much lustre to Mantegna's works as poetry to those of Virgil and Homer. To him nature has shown herself in all her variety, and taught him how she herself fashions men and things.

> Thou canst feign living faces with colours, and the shadowed countenance deceives the eyes of men. One might well believe they could speak; their limbs are thought to be living; warm blood fills their veins and spirits. Their feet do not seem to adhere to the panels, but seem to move with alternate step, leaving real traces. The face, eyes and arms make living gestures, so well does the image show the various movements of the mind, so well has your graceful hand imitated the hidden affections and feigned the truth of beauty.

From the summit of his art, where he now stands, Andrea can go no further, unless he usurp the rights of Jove and infuse life into his paintings. But since virtue cannot dissolve itself in sloth, he must exercise his hand and increase his fame, not by his art, but by the number of his works. He can do what nature cannot, figure the king of heaven before our eyes, and if virtue has no rewards equal to his deserts, let him reck it as naught: virtue, rising above mortal things, seeks its true reward among the stars. May the deities therefore grant Andrea a life as long as Nestor and Methuselah, and after death a place in heaven.[43]

The *Parnassus* (Plate XII) and the *Pallas* (Plate XIII) were companion pictures, set facing each other on opposite walls, to either side of a window. At least this is what is usually deduced from the fact that in the *Parnassus* the light is from the left, whereas in the *Pallas* it is from the right. And the care Mantegna has taken to balance the masses and forms of the two compositions so that they match or are in contrast confirms that they were intended to be seen in relationship with each other. Thus in both pictures the background peaks on the left in fantastic rocks of carefully parallel shape, while in one a natural and in the other an artificial garden wall separates the background from the middle ground. And on the right the rocks of the *Parnassus* and those of the *Pallas* are given the same bulk and a certain similarity of shape.

In the *Parnassus*, an inaccurate title first given to the picture in the seventeenth century, Mantegna searches for atmospheric unity.[44] The hour is evening, and the lower sky is pink and white, rising to pale green above; the golden light is united with the rich colours in a mellow harmony suited to the divine beauty of the actors. The scene is the mountain range of Mount Helicon and Mount Parnassus, chosen for their dwelling-place by Apollo and the Muses as a secluded retreat in which to pursue their arts and sciences undisturbed by the vulgar herd and by popular commotions, and therefore an apt emblem of Isabella's Studiolo. However, the picture is not simply an evocation of Apollo and the Muses, but an illustration of an allegory of larger import, and for allegorical reasons other features of landscape, which have no association with Parnassus or Helicon, are introduced. Only the lower part of the painting, showing Apollo and the dancing Muses, Pegasus and Mercury posed on a platform of rock in front of the garden of the Muses, and the fount of Hippocrene welling up in the platform, is a representation of the haunts of the Muses.

In ancient myth the fount of Hippocrene sprang up on Helicon when Pegasus struck the ground with his hoof, and for this reason alone it is plain that the scene before us takes place on Helicon, not on Parnassus. The left foreground of the platform is strewn with curious rocks which are studded with fossil shells; on the right is a low formation of jagged rocks in which are embedded fragments of pink marble. Shells and marble betoken Mantegna's interest in the wonders of nature, and especially in the problem, long to exercise the pre-Darwinian learned, of why fossil shells are found on mountain summits. For many they were a visible proof of the Biblical account of the Flood, and indeed Mantegna may be making some allusion to the classical myth of the Deluge, from which Deucalion and Pyrrha took refuge, according to Ovid, on the twin peaks of Parnassus.[45] These appear on the right, behind Pegasus and Mercury, where a steep slope of rock rises into two summits, between which a stream issues in an ever-broadening waterfall. The twin summits identify the mountain as Parnassus. The stream is Castalia, another celebrated spring of the Muses, correctly shown by Mantegna as issuing from a fissure between two cliffs.[46]

Above the platform, in the centre of the picture, rises a natural arch of rock, through which is seen a distant landscape, almost certainly intended to represent the Vale of Tempe, for it figures a valley whose meadows are dotted with farms and towered buildings. The valley runs between light green hills, and then fades into a deep blue-green and light blue range of hills with an effect of aerial perspective long familiar in Flemish painting and in Italian landscapes painted under Flemish influence, but rare in Mantegna's art of sharp horizons. Unfortunately this area has been heavily repainted. X-ray analysis has revealed that originally the rock and the hedge of the garden ran continuously across the middle ground, and that the arch with its plunging view was an afterthought. On the artificially levelled summit of the arch stand Mars and Venus. She is naked, save for her yellow scarf – the zone of Venus – winding about her limbs in floating, decorative loops and for a pair of armlets. Her pose is adapted from the antique, but she is given a blond and shapely beauty, with compact, voluptuous forms and white, smooth limbs in the taste of the late fifteenth century. Her figure is in reversed *contrapposto* to that of Mars, who is depicted according to canons of ideal beauty as a tall, slender, handsome youth, with flowing locks of golden hair. He wears a coral-crested helm of grey steel, a golden breastplate of antique form encircled by a girdle of twisted red cloth, an antique military *tunica* with lappets of deep azure over a tunic of coral red, and golden greaves and sandals. In his right hand he grasps the coral-red shaft of his spear; looped over his right shoulder, and falling in serpentine folds, varied by Mantegna's ridgy crumplings, is his long crimson military cloak.

The two stand before the end of a bed richly draped in white, scarlet and blue, a piece of furniture for which, it must be said, there hardly seems to be room on the rock. In the antique Roman style, it resembles the bed in the ancient painting known as the *Aldobrandini Wedding*, but must follow some other classical representation, perhaps a *lectisternium* on an ancient medal, since the *Wedding* was discovered only in 1605. Above is an arbour of citrus trees, darkly hung with glowing fruit, and sheltering the bed with its boughs from any rudely errant breeze, aided by an azure cloth attached to its trunks. Mars gently clasps Venus's wrist, turning his head to gaze ardently into her eyes, while she, with feminine modesty of sentiment, inclines her head tenderly towards him, her eyes looking upwards and outwards. It must be stressed that compositionally she is the more important of the two: although they

are figured as an amorous pair, Mars is placed a little to the right, while Venus is set on the vertical axis of the picture, above the natural arch and a gap in the linked forms of the dancing Muses below. And her whiteness and nakedness contribute to the assertion of her presidency.

Venus, like Mars, holds a weapon, an arrow tipped with gold. It is an arrow much celebrated in literature and a favourite symbol in the amorous Petrarchan poetry of the Renaissance. It owes its fame to Ovid. In the story of Apollo and Daphne, in the first book of his *Metamorphoses*, he relates how Cupid, angered by Apollo's boasting, flew to the summit of Mount Parnassus, and took from his quiver two arrows, one with a sharp golden tip, which causes love, the other with a blunt tip of lead, which puts love to flight. With the gold-tipped arrow he transfixed Apollo, with the lead-tipped arrow Daphne.[47] It should be noticed that here Venus holds the gold-tipped arrow point downwards, so that it can do no harm by accidentally piercing a heart. In ancient poetry Venus is often angry with Cupid and takes his arrows from him to hinder him from wantonly kindling the mischievous passion of love. We are intended to divine then that she has confiscated this golden-tipped arrow from her son Cupid, who was born to her of her husband Vulcan. According to a Platonic allegory much canvassed in the later fifteenth century by those philosophers and writers on love who sought to clothe in classical guise the tenets of courtly love, there are two Venuses. One is a pure and celestial Venus who inspires man with pure and heavenly love, the other, an earthly Venus, is the goddess of the vulgar herd and inspires human lust. Cupid was born of this earthly Venus: accordingly the Venus of the picture, who has confiscated the arrow of lust, is the heavenly Venus, the adversary of lust.[48] This is why she can be represented presiding over the chaste Muses, and their celestial dance.

Towards the top of the natural steps leading up the left side of the rock is Anteros, the son of Venus by Mars, and, as we already know, an enemy of the sensual love inspired by his half-brother, Cupid. With his left hand he holds a bow, with his right a coral-red blow-pipe which he aims mockingly at the genitals of Vulcan, on the left. As the god of fire, Vulcan is an apt father for a son who kindles the flames of lust, and whose arrows of desire he forges in his cave on Mount Etna in Sicily, here for the purposes of allegory transported to Greece and set beside Mount Helicon. A line, once golden, runs from the blow-pipe to the genitals of Vulcan, signifying the extinction of sensual love by the higher love. To express the baseness of lust Mantegna has represented Vulcan as the '*faber deformis*' of Albericus, that is, as a base mechanic.[49] Small, rough and ignoble, with burnt face and shaggy hair and beard, he is ignored by the courtly lovers standing exalted in serene beauty on the rock above. Absurdly furious, he is that classic butt of Renaissance mockery, the betrayed husband. Raising himself from his forge, his coral cloak billowing in angry yet decoratively crimped folds behind him, he shakes his left hand in rage and threatened vengeance at the adulterous couple, his uplifted forefinger and thumb figuring a pair of cuckold's horns. With his right hand he seizes the instrument of his vengeance, a bunch of steel wires hanging from the roots of a bush behind him. With these he will forge the net of steel in which he will enmesh the sleeping Venus and Mars and exhibit their shame to the other gods. To one side of him is his forge, while to the other are his anvil, a hammer, two rods, a compass and a coil of wire, the tools of his base craft.[50] The self-agitated movement of his cloak perhaps derives, as Michael Vickers has suggested, from some classical source, such as the Felix Gem, now in the Ashmolean Museum, Oxford. On this Diomedes holds a fluttering cloak over his arm. Indeed, the decoratively scrolling bands of drapery which are such a feature of Mantegna's art in its last two decades are probably to be seen as a development of such classical motifs.

It may seem strange that the extinction of carnal lust should be figured by a little god born of an adulterous couple. The difficulty had already occurred to one of the interlocutors in Hedo's Anti-erotica. 'If', says Emilia, 'this Anteros be born as you say in adultery and be contrary to nature, I do not see why he should not be spurned and rejected by all mankind, as being stained with so conspicuous and singular a spot and so inhuman and savage.' To which Antonius gives the answer which is the key to the motif in the picture. 'We did not say either that Anteros is illegitimate or contrary to nature; only that he seems so.' And in a later passage he explains that the mystery is resolved by the ancestry of Anteros, whom Cicero says was born of the third Venus. This Venus was the daughter of Jove and the female Titan, Dione, and he interprets her as signifying man's nature. For man is composed of soul and body, the soul having its origin from Jove, who signifies the ether, or upper air, and the body from Dione. So Venus as their daughter figures the two elements of body and spirit that compose man's nature and for this reason is said to have married Vulcan, who signifies the spirit. Anteros is born of her and Mars, because he is an image of those men who being procreated as it were by the conjunction of the mind and of reason, rather than of the mind and of the senses, continually wage war on carnal pleasures. Such men, writes the evangelist St John, are born not of the blood or will of man but of a god. This god is Mars whom the Psalmist calls a strong lord and mighty in battle. Anteros may therefore be called a movement of the mind originating in the understanding and obedient to reason, and having no fulfilment except in frugality, a quality embracing all the virtues – for all the virtues are interconnected among themselves – and one, moreover, that is especially opposed, in Cicero's view, to lust.[51]

Hedo's interpretation explains the figures of Mars, Venus and Anteros. But the deviser of the invention has discarded his interpretation of Vulcan as spirit, associating him instead with fire, and therefore by a transition natural to a Renaissance mind, with the fire of carnal lust. Again neither he nor Mantegna adopted Hedo's personification of Anteros as a chaste youth, resembling the chaste Hippolitus of antiquity. Hedo in fact was careful to point out that this image of Anteros was wholly his own invention. He was uncertain, he says, what the likeness of Anteros ought to be or even if a likeness of him had ever been made. For as poets and painters try to please the generality they may have thought the likeness of such a figure as Anteros, so austerely contrary to love, unlikely to please the vulgar. Or else they may have thought that as Cupid's image was well known, it would be easy to deduce from it a counter-image of Anteros. Mantegna and his adviser evidently thought Anteros better represented as a twin of Cupid, following the indication of Seneca's geminus Cupido (twin Cupids) which is cited by Hedo as his authority for reducing the three Cupids of Cicero's De Natura Deorum to two.[52]

In the form of a bright company of mythological figures, then, the upper half of the painting figures the extinction of sensual lust and the primacy of celestial love. That its lofty meaning is partly expressed through the figures of a licentious myth ought not to surprise. Isabella was no prude, and for the Renaissance the sanction of antiquity and of poetry removed the fable from the domain of obscenity to that of art. And in a society which took nature naturally, even so literal a visual rendering of the numbing of Vulcan's genital fire stirred no sense of false shame. Indeed it certainly amused Isabella and her ladies, who were not averse to broad jokes, rather unfortunately for their reputation with modern historians.[53] The serenity of mind and the freedom to pursue the higher occupations and studies to which this extinction of earthly lust gives room are figured in the lower part of the painting, where the Muses dance on Helicon to the cithara of Apollo, in the presence of Mercury and Pegasus. Evidently key figures, Mercury and Pegasus are made larger in scale than the other personages and placed in the foreground, though well to the right so as not to impede the view of the music-making Apollo and the carolling Muses, who fill the middle ground, before their garden, planted with quinces on the left and laurels on the right.

The attitude of Mercury is contemplative: he stands in a statuesque pose of calm *contrapposto*, resting his elbow on the back of Pegasus, and listening to the music. His pink cloak, changing to yellow in the lights, is partly wound about his loins, partly curves up behind his shoulder into a decorative scallop form and then falls to the left in flying ridgy folds. In type he is the young and graceful deity of antique art, with golden hair falling in ringlets about his head. His winged *petasos* is coral-red, heightened with gold: his feet are shod in winged buskins of dark green, patterned with gold. Lightly with both hands he holds his caduceus, its coral shaft topped by a pair of black and yellow serpents and grey wings, while from his left hand is suspended the syrinx or pipe of seven reeds with which he lulled the many-eyed Argus to slumber.

The caduceus is a symbol of peace and concord, to which the higher arts incline the mind of man. Here it also alludes to music. In ancient myth it was Mercury who invented the lyre, which he gave to Apollo, receiving in return the gift of the caduceus. Mercury was the god of eloquence, in antiquity and in the Renaissance a rhetorical art; eloquence indeed was symbolized by his syrinx. In the tenth *Ode* of his first book Horace salutes him as 'Eloquent Mercury, thou who hast skilfully reformed the savage ways of later men by thy voice.' Mantegna seems also to have regarded him as man's guide in the pursuit of knowledge and the arts of '*virtù*' in the Renaissance sense. It is he who in the engraving of *Virtus deserta* stoops to draw the blind victims of Ignorance out of the pit into which they have fallen. Poetry and rhetoric were still regarded in the Renaissance as inseparable arts, and for this reason Mercury is conjoined with Pegasus, a symbol of poetry because he is the winged horse on whom poets mount to Helicon and Parnassus to drink of their inspiring founts.

Pegasus stands with left leg raised and head turned to nuzzle Mercury, who rests his arm on his back. The motif probably expresses its inventor's opinion that eloquence is the friendly master of poetry and guides it to the heights of Helicon. With graceful skill Mantegna conveys that Pegasus is a divine horse. In colour he is dapple-grey, with a thick tufted coat and a beard, but the line of hairs running down his chest is heightened with gold and his mane is groomed into ringlets. His housings are of light golden wire, strung with ruby, sapphire and crystal beads, sixteen in all, one hanging as a horse pendant below his chest, one set on his forehead. They are Mantegna's figuration of the golden bridle Pallas gave to Bellerophon in order to help him capture and tame Pegasus for his fight against the Chimaera.

The crystal beads, if not simply a rich ornament, were perhaps suggested by a misunderstanding of a line in the *Sixth Eclogue* of the ancient pastoral poet Calpurnius. This speaks of a harness strap set with '*vitreae bullae*'. The beads have recently been identified as symbols of the stars that compose the constellation of Pegasus; perhaps then it should be emphasized that they are not placed in the fixed positions on his limbs which literary and pictorial tradition assigned to the stars of Pegasus.[54] At his feet is the fountain of Hippocrene, the falling water forming a circle in the dark green surface of the pool. From Hippocrene poets drank inspiration for their verse: indeed the Pegasean fount was a literary commonplace of Renaissance poetry. Thus in punning allusion to the poet Marco Cavallo (*c.*1475–1524) the poet Cariteo called him 'a new Pegasus, at whose foot a flowing fount rises in arid ground', while Ariosto says of the same Marco that he will create such a fount of poetry in his native city of Ancona 'as the winged horse made issue from the mount, I am not sure whether of Parnassus or Helicon'.[55]

In the middle ground are the smaller figures of Apollo playing the cithara[56] and the Muses. They are the divinities of music and poetry and history and the arts. However, in the inventory of Isabella's Studiolo taken in 1542, after her death, these same figures are described as 'Orpheus playing with nine nymphs dancing'. Now it is true that in another ancient myth Mercury and Orpheus were closely associated; after inventing the lyre, Mercury according to this myth gave it to Orpheus. The same myth also associates Orpheus and the Muses, for it relates that after the Bacchantes had rent him asunder the Muses collected his limbs and gave them sepulture. And another myth makes Orpheus the son of the Muse Calliope.[57] It is also true that the youthful figure playing the cithara has no wreath of laurel, nor any other attribute of Apollo.[58] On the other hand the dancing nymphs are nine, the number of the Muses, while Pegasus and Hippocrene indicate that we are on Mount Helicon, the haunt of Apollo and the Muses, whereas Orpheus is associated with Mount Olympus or Mount Pangasus. There was ancient authority for representing the Muses as nymphs: in his *Seventh Eclogue* Virgil invokes them as 'Nymphae, noster amor', and Servius, his ancient commentator, explains that Varro, the great Roman lexicographer, had identified the Muses as nymphs because the movement of water makes music, an explanation to which the ripple of water in Mantegna's Hippocrene may make allusion.[59] Decisive for the identification of the nine nymphs as the Muses is Battista Fiera's poem on the picture, apparently written shortly after it was set up in the Studiolo, for in it the dancing goddesses are called the Muses.[60] Finally, in May 1512 the Marchese

Francesco paid for a picture by Matteo Costa which seems to have been his own version of his wife's painting and was hung up in one of the chambers in his new palace of San Sebastiano, where in 1506 Isabella had laughingly told him he had copied her own chambers in the Castello. This huge painting represented 'Nine muses that are singing, Apollo who is playing, our lord (Francesco) who is listening and furthermore landscapes with clouds'.[61] Accordingly it seems certain that the compiler of the inventory made one of those confusions of subject not uncommon in inventories of this kind, taken by court servants *viva voce* and in haste, and as physical, not interpretative descriptions. Here then we have Apollo as Apollo Musagetes, singing and making music for the dance of the Muses.

Three of the Muses, as is shown by their parted lips, sing the carol of the dance; but it seems that originally all the others were shown singing too, with open mouths, and that some later owner had their lips closed by a skilful restorer. There was already a tradition in Ferrara and elsewhere of decorating a *studio* with paintings of Muses. In 1447 Leonello d'Este decided to decorate his *studio* at Belfiore with pictures of the Muses and consulted the court humanist Guarino on how they should be represented. Two at least were finished before Leonello's death and the set was completed between 1459 and 1463 by Cosimo Tura. Whether or not these pictures were destroyed in the disastrous fire of 1483, as is sometimes thought, it is certain that they were much admired and must still have been well known in the Ferrara of Isabella's youth.[62] About 1460 Cosimo de' Medici had the doorway of the library he had built for the Badia at Fiesole decorated with a carving of Apollo playing the lyre and the dance of the Muses. The theme found its most elaborate known expression before Isabella's day in a small *studio* in the Palazzo Ducale of Urbino, which perhaps dates from the 1480s. In this series as in the Studiolo Pallas figured as a companion of Apollo, and as such she still appears on the *intarsia* doors of the Sala degli Angeli, giving access to the throne-room of Federico, where both she and Apollo tread down emblems of vice.[63]

To understand the full significance of the scene, it should be remembered that poetry, music and dancing were not the dissociated arts they have since become, and that much lyric verse in *volgare*, not merely the poems called *canzoni* but also many of the sonnets and *strambotti* which were among the age's favourite genres of courtly verse, were written to be set and sung to music. Thus Pietro Bembo, writing on 1 July 1505 to Isabella after his first visit to the Mantuan court, sent her some sonnets and *strambotti* 'desiring that some verses of mine may be recited and sung by Your Ladyship'.[64] And Isabella is known to have commissioned settings for poems written for her by members of her literary circle from the musicians who were in the service of the Mantuan court and were already one of its glories.[65]

Apollo sits on a broad tree trunk, resting his leg on a smaller one in the manner of a mortal musician in order to support his wooden cithara, whose strings he plucks with both hands, inclining his head to listen to the sound and at the same time watching the dance of the Muses. His great crimson cloak, delicately lit with white and gold, is held across his chest by a band which also supports his cithara. A youth divinely beautiful, his curling locks are of dark gold, his body dark brown, flushed with pink. None of the Muses has an identifying attribute, so they must be understood as symbolizing in general the nobler arts, in the words of Guarino 'as certain conceptions and intelligences, which have thought up various actions and works for human studies and ingenuity'.[66] A rhythm of dancing legs, their round fills the middle ground with a zone of rich colour, olive-greens, reds, blues, yellows, to which Apollo, seated and in shadow, is subordinated. They are posed in carefully varied poses, full-face, three-quarter profile, profile and rear views, their classical draperies parting to show the beauty of their naked forms and swung into sharp-edged, decorative swirls and lappets by the agitation of the dance. Moving in a long sinuous line that turns on itself to the left in the round of the dance, they are linked by scarves and hands. The faces of some express contemplative absorption, but the two in the rear at either end watch their companions. Since the Muse on the extreme right lifts her left hand in a gesture of instruction, she may be Terpsichore, the Muse of dancing; perhaps her gesture is provoked by the wandering eyes of the two Muses before her. Curiously enough, fifty years before, Guarino had advised Leonello d'Este that Terpsichore should be represented with the 'gesture of one commanding the dance'.[67]

Some antique relief may well have been the inspiration of this dance of the Muses. According to Vincenzo Cartari, writing some sixty years later, and perhaps describing an antique sculpture seen in Rome,

> the ancients, to show that the liberal arts and sciences all follow on one another and are as if linked to one another, used to depict the Muses, who were the discoverers of the arts ... holding each other by the hand and leading a beautiful dance in a round, and Apollo either leading them, as the superior light which illuminates the understanding, or in the midst of them.

Some such conception may underly Mantegna's representation of the Muses circling to Apollo's cithara, but in antiquity and the Renaissance the Muses were first and foremost the goddesses of poetry and music. Since they are undifferentiated, we should see them not only as a round of the liberal arts and sciences, but especially as that choir of the Muses invoked by poets and musicians as they sing and dance in their mountain haunts to the cithara and song of Apollo, god of music and poetry, and the author of harmony in those two arts.[68] Indeed harmony may be another underlying concept that links the figures of Venus and Mars with the Muses and Apollo, for according to Hesiod Harmonia was the daughter of Venus and Mars.

Poetry and music were regarded in antiquity and in the Renaissance as noble and virtuous occupations for the mind, banishing all the persuasions to vice, and especially to wanton love, that are so apt to invade it. 'There is no medecine, be it potion or unguent, that repels the flames of love more than the power of the Muses', wrote Theocritus in the *Cyclops*. Lucian in his *Dialogues of the Gods* makes Venus ask Cupid why he has never dared to pierce the Muses with his arrows: because, he replies, they are ever deep in meditation and song.[69] Mantegna's painting thus figures the honourable occupations of Isabella in her own retreat of the Muses, occupations proper to that chastity which was the chief jewel of virtue in every Renaissance as in every mediaeval lady. Indeed her friend and admirer, the poet Galeotto del Carretto, a nobleman of the court of Monferrat, speaks of his visits to Mantua as visits to 'all the academy of Parnassus'.[70] Of the arts of the Muses Isabella best loved poetry. She collected it, and was in correspondence with the most admired poets of her day, Antonio Tebaldeo, Vincenzo Calmeta, Niccolò da Correggio, Pietro Bembo, all of whom wrote verses for her. She herself began to write verses in *volgare* under the tuition of Tebaldeo during his residence in Mantua from late in 1495 to 1500 as salaried court poet, the very years during which the *Parnassus* was conceived and painted. In his fourteenth *Capitolo* Tebaldeo celebrates his role as Isabella's preceptor and guide in the writing of verse with an invocation to the Muses:

> Sacre leggiadre honeste immortal dive
> Senza il favor di cui smarrito resta
> Come Icaro qualunche in versi scrive
> Se mai dentro di Cirrha si fa festa
> Hoggi si faccia che anchor mai novella
> In Parnaso non fu simil a questa.
> La magnanima, saggia, alma Isabella
>
> Da ogni altra cura se aliena e parte
> Per prender contra morte il vostro scudo
> Che si guadagna con inchiostro e arte
>
> Me per sua guida a questa impresa chiede

(Sacred, fair, virtuous, immortal goddesses, without whose favour whosoever writes in verse loses like Icarus the true way, if ever within Cirrha rejoicing is made let it be made today, for ne'er was there news like this on Parnassus. The noble-minded, wise and gracious Isabella . . . estranges herself and departs from all other cares to take against death your shield, which is earned by ink and art . . . Me she asks to be her guide in this emprise.)[71] And in a later Latin elegy the poet Giangiorgio Trissino of Vicenza lists among Isabella's praises 'that Apollo has not enviously refused thee genius, nor is learned Pallas unkind to thy elegies: thou dost not despise the arts that are common to thee with me, and thou delightest in poetry because thine own poems are of such worth.'[72] It would seem that the contriver of the invention was making a particular allusion in the figures of the Muses to Isabella's new preoccupation in the mid-1490s with acquiring the art of poetry, the art of the Muses above all other arts.

She also sang: if her admirers are to be credited, delightfully. In 1505 Bembo recalled 'how sweetly and smoothly you sang that happy evening', while Trissino declared 'that when she moves her lips in song, such sweetness rains from heaven that the air rejoices and the wind pauses, intent on such sweet harmony'.[73] Like all singers in that age, she accompanied herself on various instruments, the *manocordo*, the lute, the *clavicordo* and perhaps also the *citara* and the lyre. Many letters survive in which she asks the celebrated instrumentalist Lorenzo da Pavia to obtain for her instruments of elegant form and ornament and perfect sound. One of her *imprese* or devices was a composition of musical keys, *tempi* and rests, which later she used in the decoration of her new *camerini* in the Corte Nuova, but which she had already invented by 1502 when she appeared at one of the fêtes given in Ferrara for the marriage of Lucrezia Borgia to Alfonso d'Este in a beautiful *camora* (gown) embroidered 'with that invention of *tempi e pause*' (times and rests).[74]

As a great lady, Isabella was reluctant to sing in public, reserving her performances for a few favoured friends and courtiers. This desire for exclusiveness is surely a key to the spirit of the Studiolo. It explains why one of the themes of its decoration is the serene retreat of the Muses on a mountain-top far above the vulgar turmoil below. There was every reason why the deviser of the invention should choose these images to praise Isabella. Her love of the Muses was proverbial among her literary contemporaries. Francesco Roello, an author and 'poor fallen gentleman', wrote to Isabella from Rimini as early as 3 August 1490 asking for assistance, and promising in return to make her immortal throughout the world in prose and verse. He is sure she will become his patroness because 'she is most learned, and has been to the mount of Parnassus and to the Pegasean fount', and is 'wholly given up to the Muses'.[75] After a dinner held at Christmas 1517 the humanist wits of Rome amused themselves by playing the strange Renaissance game of *Sortes Virgilianae*, in which a Virgil was opened at random and the verses pitched on were taken as oracular. The verses applied to Isabella spoke of her in highly complimentary terms. In answer to the question, 'What is your opinion of the Marchioness of Mantua', the oracle answered: 'To me first and foremost the Muses are sweeter than all else; I maintain their sacred cult, smitten by great love for them. Let them receive me, and show me the paths of heaven and the stars, the various eclipses of the sun and the labours of the moon.'[76]

Two other motifs in the foreground point up the themes of the picture. On the left are two scourges of green rushes, their handles bound with two bands of cord.[77] These are sometimes identified as brooms, as if the Muses were excellent housewives. But any Renaissance eye would at once have perceived that they are instruments of chastisement and would have understood that they allude to the scourging of Cupid by Venus, who has also removed his arrow. Lastly, about the spring are three white hares and a grey squirrel. The squirrel has baffled all attempts at interpretation, since it figures scarcely at all in the emblematic vocabulary of the Renaissance. With some appearance of plausibility, however, it has been argued that the hares are emblems of Venus. But they are emblems of Venus because of their fecundity, an association that would be a discord in the picture. What squirrels and hares have in common is their timidity: that the hares appear from their burrows and the squirrel pauses on the platform signifies the celestial peace and innocent tranquillity that prevail in the retreat of the Muses,[78] and are produced by the caduceus of Mercury.

Sources for the individual figures of the painting have been earnestly sought among the antique sculptures known to the late fifteenth century. But as so often in Renaissance art, here too the worn and fragmentary indications of ancient marble have been clothed in all the smoothing fullness of flesh, and it is now difficult, if not impossible, to adduce their certain origins. Within a constant canon of ideal beauty Mantegna's treatment of the nude varies from the delicate sensuousness of Venus to the virgin grace of the Muses, from the ardent boldness of Mars to the pensive nobility of Mercury, but always adding warmth of colour and feeling to the inspiration of the antique.

Although the painting's principal theme is the exaltation of the arts and the abasement of sensual love, within it there may also be secondary allusions. Thus Phyllis Lehmann has linked the blue and red

and white and gold of Venus and Mars and their couch with the heraldic colours of the Gonzaga (*gules* and *argent* and *or*) and of the Este (*azure* and *or* and *argent*).[79] There are probably other courtly compliments to Francesco and Isabella in these two figures. Plutarch, addressing his famous essay *Coniugialia Praecepta* to the newly married Pollianus and Eurydice, prays that

> the Muses may assist and accompany the goddess Venus in your regard, for it is no less their office to bring good accord and consonance to a marriage, by means of the discourse of reason and the harmony of philosophy than to accord a cithara or a lyre. This is why the ancients desired the image of Venus to be placed adjoining that of Mercury, as wishing by this means to give men to understand that the pleasure of marriage must needs be maintained by good and wise words.[80]

The imagery of Mars and Venus gave rise to literary contests at the Mantuan court, in which compliments to Isabella were intermixed with teasing sallies and graceful vindications. One poet slyly insinuated that Venus was Isabella herself: in an answering epigram Mantegna's friend Battista Fiera declared:

> For thee Isabella, our Apelles painted a beautiful Venus, and painted no more than thy beauty. He painted likewise that it is thy pleasure to draw nigh unto the Muses when a sweet measure is set and join them in the circling dance. Because of this a poet, addressing thee as Venus in a witty poem, asserted that Mars' own bed is thine. The rest he suppressed from reverence for the honour of the picture, deeming perhaps that the work itself was about to speak. All incautious, he had not seen the smith's rage urging on avenging hands against Mars. Steropes sweats at the flames. Etna bellows with the noise of Brontes, Pyracmon's right hand revolves the meshes. Thus most ridiculously do the quarrels of a dispute arise, nor is there aught that makes pleasanter noise throughout the whole city. One man complains that thou, white Isabella, art called Venus, but it was thy image with which the poet played. Art thou then Venus because thou art joined to the chaste bed of Mars? Art thou then Venus because he makes of thee a Venus?

The epigram turns on accepting the compliment to Isabella's beauty, while laughingly defending her against the offence to decorum implied in supposing that she was lending countenance in the picture to unchastity and adultery or that she could have allowed herself to be portrayed naked.[81]

We know of another poetical contest in which Isabella's literary friends vied with each other in teasingly amorous interpretations of a picture of her, apparently after some accident to it, perhaps even its theft and return. Again there is a play on the theme of Venus and Mars; the picture which gave rise to the poems was perhaps a portrait of Isabella, perhaps even the *Parnassus* itself. Isabella had sent her friend Niccolò da Correggio a sonnet by Tebaldeo, which in turn incited him 'to speak my own sentiment upon the case' in an answering sonnet. 'I do not believe,' wrote Niccolò in a letter of 10 August 1500,

> that Venus was ever jealous of this super-excellent lady [Isabella] for fear that she might steal her own Mars from her, for even supposing the beloved god to burn with love for her, he would not be bold enough to discover himself, either perforce or because he believed himself to excel her own Mars [Francesco] in anything. Rather would I believe that the painter himself or some other desired this image for his own self, even though there has befallen her and perhaps overtaken him that which befell with the young man of Cnidos who became enamoured of the Venus sculptured by Praxiteles and had himself shut up for the night in the temple where the statue was, leaving it with a stain ever afterward. If this painter has made her beautiful, he has done it in order that on beholding herself she may soften her divine mind into consenting to be loved; just as by the contrary a tigress should take fright on seeing its own horrid aspect, so she, seeing her own sweet and naturally benign and pleasing aspect may use humanity. This is my own belief. Nevertheless I laud Messer Antonio's belief.[82]

That Mantegna in his paintings for the Studiolo was 'reducing to elegant form' the inventions of a literary allegory appears even more plainly in *Pallas expelling the Vices from the Garden of Virtue*, in which we see the armed and angry goddess driving out a wanton train of vices. Here Mantegna was unable to embody his subject in intelligible inventions without the aid of inscriptions, some to identify certain of the figures, some to conduct part of the action, and some to point a moral lesson. Such inscriptions were not of course an innovation: inscribed scrolls are often found in quattrocento religious pictures, and in secular art they must have been much commoner than now appears. The allegorical figures in the woodcut frontispiece to the 1496 edition of Battista da Campo Fregoso's *Anteros*, for example, are carefully labelled INOPIA, ZELOTYPIA, DERRISIO, LVCTVS, [MORS] INMATVRA and MORS AETERNA, while the remedies of love, MATRIMONIVM, ORATIO, NEGOTIA and ABSTINENTIA, are inscribed on scrolls wound round the branches of a tree, just as Daphne's cry is inscribed on a scroll in the *Pallas*. It may be suspected that in the *Pallas* we have the subject which Isabella originally desired Giovanni Bellini to paint for her as a companion-piece to Mantegna's *Parnassus*, but which he refused to execute, daunted by its difficulty and reluctant that an inferior work of his own should be placed where it could be compared to its disadvantage with a work by Mantegna. Isabella could not compel Bellini to execute her commands but with Mantegna the case was different.[83]

In the *Pallas* the light is from the right, so that the picture is in darker shadow on the left. The setting is a closed garden, which represents, as will become plain, the garden of the mind, open to habitation by the Virtues or Vices according to the virtuous or vicious inclinations of the individual. On the left is a portico of dark green trees, cut and shaped to form seven tall, narrow arches, topped by a cornice. Their openings are dark, and there is nothing to reveal if they bound a covered walk, lead into another part of the garden, or give entrance to the mountain that soars behind. The portico runs obliquely into the picture to meet a pergola of Mantegna's favourite citrus trees, whose oranges and lemons he uses as lamps of colour in the dark evening light that prevails. Its four open arches close the garden across the middle ground, giving on to a landscape of fields closed by low hills. Before the pergola is a garden of white roses enclosed by a low trellis hedge. Both pergola and hedge abut to the right on a wall of rock, whose rugged inner face, built up of strata of natural rock masonry, is in deep shadow, while its front face is brightly lit. The contrast is deliberate, for as we shall see, the gloomy inner face is the wall of a prison cell.

This walling of sombre green rises three-quarters of the way up the picture and effectively darkens it. The garden itself is one of Mantegna's typical shelves of rock, covered with fine grasses, painted in sharp single strokes of dark green. It slopes down to a scummy green pool filled with tall grasses, algae, white-flowered water plants and lilies. These delicate growths, like the bed of white roses, indicate that there is nothing sinister in the pool and garden in themselves: rather they represent an innocence and beauty that has been foully invaded. Behind, pierced in the sheer side of the great mountain of rock, is an arched opening, artfully drawn so as to appear a heavily rusticated arch designed by nature. Along a horizontal line over this arch the brown of the rock terminates sharply: above, the mountain summit burns with a fiery orange-red, and has split at the top, so that the rocks on the right appear to be toppling forwards at a dizzy angle, an effect of the dramatic picturesque to which Mantegna was plainly partial during these years, for it occurs in both the *Madonna delle Cave* and in the *Parnassus*. Here Mantegna has perhaps attempted to figure a volcano, for the summit opens into what appears to be a black crater.

In front of the toppling slope is a great dark grey cloud, billowing in a sky that rises from white to pale blue and then into a darker blue. In the cloud appear two great profile heads, themselves of cloud-colour. To the right an oval mandorla of cloud descends towards the garden, bearing three of the four cardinal or moral Virtues, Temperance, Justice and Fortitude, back to its pleasaunces, which they have quitted in indignation, as we learn from the inscription attached to the tall tree of Daphne rising in the left foreground. The invention here is founded on the myth of Astraea, goddess of Justice, the last divine being to inhabit the earth, who left it after the iron age of blood and violence had succeeded the ages of gold and silver and brass.[84] Justice, wrapped in an azure cloak, and Temperance, in a robe of green shaded with brown, stand serenely aloof from all that is passing, as befits their nature, while Fortitude, a virtue that can be made manifest only in the trials of life, gazes eagerly down at the scene enacting in the garden.

The tree of Daphne Mantegna has figured as an olive, the tree of Pallas, not as a laurel, the tree of Apollo, but he has figured it according to a convention well-established for representations of Daphne, as a tree with a human head.[85] Mantegna perhaps devised the motif to symbolize the intimate union between the pursuit of learning and arts, of which the olive of Pallas is the symbol, and chastity, of which Daphne, changed to a laurel to escape Apollo, is the symbol. He has developed it with ingeniously realistic allegorical invention. Two tall and narrow leg-shaped roots rise from the ground to form a single trunk shaped as a female torso, from which two arms emerge to become tufted branches lifted in a desperate appeal. The head and face retain their human form and features, but olive leaves form the hair and sprout from the neck, shoulders and arms, while branches of olive sprout from nipples, trunk and legs. The brown of the body is brushed over with green to simulate moss, and though the foliage reaches high up the picture and is dark in colour, yet it is most artfully silhouetted against as well as blended with the dark foliage of the portico. The meaning of the invention is that the active virtue personified in Pallas and in the arts of Pallas expels the vices which are a threat to the chaste life.

The appeal of the olive's branched arms is voiced by a scroll that winds about her trunk bearing inscriptions in Latin and in Greek letters and in the sacred letters of Hebrew.[86] The choice of the alphabets of these three learned languages deliberately emphasizes the association of learning and chastity. And in this visual expression of the intrinsic alliance of learning and chastity there is cer-

tainly intended a compliment to Isabella, who was so eager to collect all ancient and modern authors for her *studio*, could read and write Latin, bought and commissioned translations from the Greek and was interested in Jewish learning. The olive's cry is addressed to unnamed goddesses, who are the companions of the returning Virtues, and reads AGITE PELLITE SEDIBVS NOSTRIS FOEDA HAEC VICIORVM MONSTRA VIRTVTVM COELITVS AD NOS REDEVNTIVM DIVAE COMITES (Come, divine companions of the Virtues who are returning to us from Heaven, expel these foul monsters of Vices from our seats). It rises as it were in a diagonal from the left to the upper right of the picture. Another urgent appeal is addressed in a counter-diagonal from a hollow within the rock on the right. It is inscribed in Latin on a white banderole fluttering above a natural aperture in the rocks, which is closed up by bricks of orange-red. The prisoner immured within describes herself as MATER VIRTVTVM (Mother of the Virtues). Her cry continues the appeal of the olive and implores the help of unnamed gods, who are not shown, but left to be imagined, like the goddesses. We are to suppose both gods and goddesses are still in heaven or following in the steps of Pallas. The inscription reads ET MIHI VIRTVTVM MATRI SVCCVRRITE DIVI (and you, o gods, succour me, the Mother of the Virtues). The invention, if on the one hand it throws up the 'literary' nature of the narrative, illustrates Mantegna's constant preference for suggesting more than is seen.

There is a difficulty, invariably evaded, in deciding who is meant by the Mother of the Virtues. Philostratus, whose works were printed in Venice in 1503, and who was certainly already known to the literary circle of Mantua, since Comus, the last of the Studiolo paintings in which Mantegna had a hand, is a figure found only in his *Imagines*, calls Truth the Mother of Virtue.[87] Truth is certainly a possible identification, for the discovery of truth is one of the ends of wisdom and learning, and Pallas, the chaste goddess of wisdom and learning, is the principal figure in the picture. But Philostratus speaks of Virtue in the singular, whereas the invisible prisoner speaks of herself as the Mother of the Virtues. Almost certainly then she is Prudentia, the fourth moral Virtue, figuring prudence and reason, which were considered indispensable to the acquisition of the other virtues. Accordingly Prudentia was also often depicted as the queen of the Liberal Arts. Her figuration as *Mater Virtutum* has a classical sanction in Cicero's observations in the *De Legibus* that wisdom is the mother of all good things (*mater enim omnium bonarum rerum sapientia est*), while voluptuousness is the mother of all evils (*voluptas malorum autem mater omnium*).[88] The epithet may also have been chosen in conscious opposition to the title of

Mater saeva Cupidinum (fierce mother of desires) which Horace bestows on Venus in the opening invocation of the famous Nineteenth Ode of his First Book, an allusion which Renaissance literati, brought up from boyhood on this favourite poet, would have recognized at once. In his *Anteros* Battista da Campo Fregoso expounds the moral thinking that links Prudentia with the allegory.[89] He explains that carnal love does many injuries to body and mind, not least in that lovers lose the use of their prudence and reason. To prove his claim that 'love is contrary to the peace of mind needful to prudence' he cites the authority of Aristotle that 'carnal delights are an impediment to wisdom (*prudentia*)',[90] of the Elder Seneca that 'nothing is so deadly to man's wits as lust',[91] of Cicero that love is 'a bitterest perturbation of mind',[92] of St Augustine that 'lust overwhelms almost all keenness and as it were wakefulness of mind'.[93] The imprisonment of Prudentia in a dark cell where she can neither see nor be seen, but only make herself known by a desperate cry for divine aid, is a visual image of the imprisonment of man's rational mind where the appetite of love rules. The motif perhaps incorporates another standard concept of the debate on love, in which love is condemned as an enslaver. In Fregoso's words, 'love deprives lovers of liberty, and reduces them to vilest servitude.'[94] And for the metaphor of the prisoner's cell we may cite Petrarch's references in his *Trionfo dell'Amore* to prisoners of love as being *in carcere*, and the title *Cárcel de Amor* (Prisoner of Love) of Diego de San Pedro's popular fifteenth-century Spanish novel, which was a great favourite with Isabella.[95]

The allegory is that the Vices of wantonness have invaded the garden of the mind, the 'seats' of the olive's cry, imprisoned Prudence, imperilled Chastity and driven Justice, Fortitude and Temperance away. Prudence and Chastity implore the gods and goddesses who favour them for aid, and are already receiving the all-powerful assistance of Pallas. A Renaissance imagination could instantly supply likely names for the divine figures so invoked – Diana, Juno, Apollo, Jove. But as in the *Parnassus*, so here too the complexity of his subject has forced Mantegna to resort to devices that prompt the imagination towards significant motifs for whose representation there was no room in the picture. Thus in the *Parnassus* two scourges and a golden-headed arrow imply the chastizing of Cupid, while in the *Pallas*, so much more crowded with figures, a plural noun has to do duty for pictorial symbols. And Mantegna himself may have preferred yet once again to stimulate rather than satisfy our fancy.

Pallas is represented because she is the most complete embodiment of Virtue: indeed in the 1542 inventory of the Studiolo she is described as 'Virtue

chasing away the Vices'. The goddess of wisdom and learning and poetry, she taught the arts to mankind, and especially the arts of women – tapestry, weaving and embroidery – so that she not only symbolizes the multiple themes of the picture as no other classical deity could but had an especial aptness for the decoration of Isabella's *camera*. She was chaste and therefore proper to defend not only Prudence, but also the terrified Chastity. Hers finally was an active and martial virtue, able to repel the assaults of vice, whether in the form of sloth, ignorance, avarice, or most perilous of all, lust.

In her figure there may well be a compliment to Isabella's own chastity: Battista Spagnoli, in his *Trophaeum Gonzagae*, speaks of the 'Palladius pudor' of Isabella, which guards her marriage bed with inviolable chastity. And in his *De calamitate temporum*, composed *c*.1484, he introduces Virtue as Pallas, using conceits and images that illumine the conception of Pallas in Mantegna's painting. 'I am the tamer of Fortune, the scourge of crimes: ever I bear my weapons in my hand, ever against crime', he makes her exclaim. It is she who protects man and guides him on the path to heaven. Because she is ignorant of all soft delights, insidious pleasure can strike no treaty with her, rather the vices have a quarrel with her over the limits of their empire, and she fights amid much opposition, for her kingdom has fallen to her among these her enemies. As often as need may be, she gives battle, unafraid of any weapons: she knows not what it is to be defeated and succumb. Besides this, she teaches man to understand both the wondrous machine of the world that God has created and the wondrous nature of the Trinity. She has taught him laws, so softening his savage ways, and taught him how to gain victory in war, and how to build boats and sail the seas.

> By my strength Hercules overcame so many hideous monsters, and whatever antiquity ascribed to Phoebus and the Muses is ours: I endue poets and the sacred breasts of poets with copious draughts of the divine shower of mellifluous nectar and I purify them with a sprinkling of sweet water: I am the Castalian spring: I am Pallas, the same under many names: I am not withered by disease or by the years: I have remained ever incorruptible, flourishing and immortal.[96]

A stern, heroic figure, she emerges from the portico in swift pursuit of the retreating Venus and her wanton train, poised on her left foot, about to take the next step, an active pose suiting her active virtue. Her aspect is severe, almost masculine: her lips are parted in angry bidding to the fleeing Vices. Her tresses are golden, not only because golden hair was esteemed the most beautiful, but because Ovid describes her as '*flava Minerva*'. She wears a golden helmet, surmounted by a triple crest of coral, partly fringed with gold.[97] Her golden breastplate bears a winged Medusa head above the breasts: beneath she wears a bright yellow tunic, girded up for the combat, and a loose-sleeved pink robe, delicately heightened with gold and lined with pale green. As she resolutely advances the robe swirls and flares in sharp triangular folds revealing her white under-robe, buttoned down the side. Those parts of the robe and under-robe that are in shadow are pale brown, with the green lining showing only as highlighting – yet another instance of Mantegna's delight in shot colours during these years. With a pointed oval buckler strapped to her left arm she wards off the arrows darted at her by the Amores, while with her right hand she brandishes a broken lance, broken in the fury of her assault, for its bladed upper end lies on the ground in front of her. Strangely some scholars suppose the broken lance to mean that she has been defeated. But in the vocabulary of the chivalric battle of the tournament the breaking of a lance on one's opponent was an *attaint* that signified a score because to shiver one's lance was a sign that one had touched one's enemy. The broken lance is therefore an emblem of victory, as in the *Madonna della Vittoria*, not of defeat.

The Vices flee before her, some with sluggish reluctance, some in quick terror, their varying attitudes suggesting their various nature with great subtlety and richness of allegorical invention. Their queen is Venus Impudica, who is borne on the back of a centaur to the right of centre, standing in a pose of immodest languor. She forms one side of a triangle of figures of which Pallas is the opposite side and the swarm of flying Amores the apex. In contrast with Pallas, whose flowing tresses are the plain and unadorned tresses of virginity, she has blond hair that is carefully crimped and curled round her head, then partly plaited and wound into a circle as a bun, partly left to wanton down her back. On her right arm she wears a golden armlet, from which rubies and sapphires dangle on wires: over her shoulders is hung the golden bow with which she deals love's wounds. Mantegna has shorn her provocative serpentine nudity of appeal by making her stand boldly astride the centaur's back with a look of brazen impudence on her downcast face. She shelters her body with a cloak of dark olive green, wound about her loins and held aloft behind her back like a sail by her upraised left arm. The motif of a sail, usually associated with her birth from the sea, here more probably alludes to her inconstancy, in deliberate reminiscence of the sail which signifies Fortune's caprice and inconstancy. Fortune with a sail was an image so familiar in the fifteenth century that Mantegna's contemporaries would instantly have seized the allusion.[98]

Again Spagnoli's *De calamitate temporum* supplies an enlightening parallel for the allegorical invention. In Book I he describes the uprising from hell of seven dreadful monsters which afflict the earth. They are the Seven Deadly Sins, personified in Renaissance guise, with a wealth of classical allusion. The sixth, Luxuria, or Lust, is figured as Venus. She rises with a train bearing her standards, arrows, quivers, the bows that wound the hearts of men, the torch that lights the flames of lust. Cupid hangs on her lap, bearing a standard on a long stem, and meditates his ambushes and merry jests and all his various arts. Venus is portrayed as outwardly beautiful, inwardly spotted, deceiving the unwary with her powerful wiles and cheats, pretending all the while peace with a friendly countenance. Incomparable beauty shines in her face, and she sets off her beauty by her adornments. A flame-coloured band encircles her golden hair, and falls over her shoulders to end in gently waving coils – a description that aptly fits the many elegantly waving bands of drapery that unwind themselves in decorative coils in Mantegna's later pictures. Her forehead is broad and white, her bright eyes are veiled by black eyebrows: beneath her shapely nose are lips that imitate crimson. Around her tall and slender neck hangs a golden necklace enwreathed with myrtle in which perch two kissing doves, while its pendant is engraved by the hand of Pyrgoteles with the figure of the handsome shepherd Adonis. From it hangs a golden ball which beats against her breast as she moves; an ivory brooch clasps her thin robe of scarlet silk interwoven with gold, beneath which her body gleams white and rose-colour. A transparent cloak encircles her bosom, allowing the white skin to show through and the swelling breasts. Many jewels glitter on her shoulders and fingers. Such was the fashion in which she met Anchises or Mars while her husband sweated at the furnace in his cave under Etna.

As the monster Venus advances, she wounds man by the apt motion of her eyes and her beauteous gestures, shaking her flowing hair and dress with graceful movements and diffusing a heavenly perfume. She simulates modesty and chaste blushes on her face, for beauty moves man more if joined to modesty, and beauty when sauced with grave affability kindles flames that are blown into fires by the Furies. Provident Nature intends love for the continuation of the race, and God, who has given to man largely of divine light and also reason, ordered love's fury to be contained within the fixed bounds of marriage between one man and one woman, whence children and the sacred faith of marriage. 'But Venus cannot endure . . . these bonds added to nature, and cannot be tamed by any chain.' In Mantegna's picture too she represents unbridled lust, who is expelled by reason from the garden of the mind.

One end of Venus's cloak is clasped by her centaur mount, figured as a combination of faun and horse. He begins to wade through the pool, his head turned back in fear towards Pallas. A traditional symbol of beastly lust, he has a body of spotted grey, the spots figuring the maculations of vice. His hair, beard and moustache are green and his ears end in foliage. In an elegy *Contra amorem* addressed to Sigismondo Gonzaga while still a youthful Protonotary, Spagnoli warns of the dangers of love in images that illustrate the symbolism of the centaur. 'Every lover becomes a beast while lust rules all his judgements with its nod in place of reason.' Hence poets have not uttered lying fictions when they have given new shapes to men: 'if you look only at the face of sirens, satyrs, Pans and sea-nymphs, you would think them men, but if you look at their bodies you will see they are beasts.' Those men who are guided partly by reason, partly by the senses are 'two-formed Centaurs and Minotaurs, monsters of a double and ambiguous race, which signify that minds sunk in love continually degenerate into the nature of dumb beasts.'[99] By giving the human part of his centaur the form of a lustful 'Pan' or Faun, Mantegna has emphasized this symbolism of lustfulness.

The flight of the Vices is opened on the right by Avarice, a sharp-breasted woman with a vigilant face and black hair. The association of avarice and wantonness is a classical one: in his *De Oratore* (II,40,171) Cicero observes: 'If you wish to get rid of avarice, you must get rid of its mother, lasciviousness.' (*Avaritiam tollere si vultis, mater eius tollenda est luxuries.*) And in classical times, as in the Middle Ages and in the Renaissance, avarice was considered peculiarly a female vice in love. In *Anteros* Fregoso declares that 'women being by nature for the most part avaricious or prodigal, spending much on adornments and their other disordered appetites, they ever keep their mouths to the ears of their lovers and their hands in his purse.' And he cites Juvenal, Ovid, Propertius and Sappho, together with several examples of rich and greedy ladies, in justification of his claim that it is as natural for women to suck money to themselves as for leeches to suck blood.[100]

Assisted by Ingratitude, a fat, mean-faced female figure, Avarice wades through the water bearing the gross, slothful figure of Ignorance, slumped in a pose of lethargic indifference, with dangling arms and vacant gaze, to signify the inertness proper to ignorance. Mantegna shows her crowned to signify that she rules the world, and indeed in *Virtus combusta*, a drawing of this period intended to illustrate the evils and dangers of ignorance, he shows her not only crowned but enthroned upon a globe. We have already seen that for Mantegna ignorance is always the enemy of virtue, by which he understood not so much moral virtue, as man's active powers and talents, developed by cultivation of the understanding. He expressed this thought in his letter of 31 January 1489 to the Marchese Francesco in the pithy Latin phrase '*Virtuti semper adversatur ignorantia*' and the initials of these words are inscribed on a stone in the engraving, attributed to Zoan Andrea, of *Virtus deserta*, made after the lower half of the composition of which *Virtus combusta* is the upper half.[101] Avarice and Ingratitude are associated with Ignorance because they are the vices of sordid minds, and towards them Mantegna entertained the characteristic disdain of the Renaissance gentleman for all that is mean and ignoble. In the engraving of *Virtus deserta* Virtue, meaning the arts or 'virtues' of Apollo, is figured as a bay laurel in human form, rather on the same pattern as the tree of Daphne in the *Pallas*, and the inscription VIRTUS DESERTA is slung from her shoulder.

Avarice, Ingratitude and Ignorance are three vices that give rein to lust and folly, a lesson also illustrated in the engraving, and for this reason they open the train of Venus fittingly. Behind them comes a personification of lust, a grotesque satyr, with brutish flat-nosed face and a wolf or fox-skin over his left arm to signify the vulpine nature of lust. In his arms he clasps a golden-haired Amor, who will no longer be able to flutter wantonly in the air, discharging his arrows at the hearts of men, for his azure wings have been cut off in the combat before the flight, and he now holds them in his left hand.[102] Perched on the satyr's shoulder is a second Amor, brandishing two flaming torches with which to ignite the fires of love. In his *Contra amorem* Spagnoli warns that love sinks man's heart and breaks all generous enterprise, concerning himself only with women's work. 'He praises soft delights, unguents, merriment and slothful ease (*inertia ocia*).' Because he is naked he studies to make men denude themselves of their patrimony, because he is a boy, he loves the consolations of trivial things, soft speeches, kisses, songs. Because he is winged, he is speedily inconstant; because he is blind, he is quick to rush into every crime, and because he carries a bow and an arrow-bearing quiver and a torch, he has an evil mind and a fierce nature. 'His wicked fury begins in laughter, waxes amid bitter cares, and ends in tears.' Mantegna has pointed the theme of the contrast between the fair outward nature of love and its true inner beastliness by picturing the golden-haired Cupids as borne by the brutish figure of a lustful satyr.

On the bank, in the interval between the centaur and the satyr, are two attendant nymphs of Venus, garlanded as for a feast. One holds a bow, perhaps to simulate a chaste nymph of Diana, the other has folded hands and downcast eyes and may therefore be False Modesty. They are diminished in scale, too much so, but Mantegna has sacrificed plausibility to his composition, which requires a falling diagonal of figures from Venus to the Vices. Behind Venus come others of her attendants, no longer moving with insolent sluggishness, but hasting away before the wrath of Pallas. First come two nymphs, crying out in fear. The first, in a pose which reverses that of the Muse on the extreme right of the circling dance of *Parnassus*, wears a robe of azure lined with purple-shaded yellow over an under-robe also of azure. Her aspect is lovely, but a bow is slung from her purple girdle and a crimson quiver full of arrows from her shoulder, signifying that she shoots the darts of love. Her companion holds a torch of wood and an end of wax wrapped round with smouldering tow, in allusion to the deceptive slowness with which the flames of love can be ignited. The beauty of the two nymphs symbolizes then the deceitfully pleasing disguise under which love can present itself.[103]

Behind runs an affrighted female satyr, again fair haired and beautiful in the smooth nudity of her body, only her goat's legs, white with delicately marked brown stripes, betraying her animal nature. If the skin she wears is a bear-skin, as Förster suggests, it too may be an illustration of her lustful nature, for in some authors Luxuria, or lust, is said to ride upon a bear. Leading an infant satyr by the hand and clasping three others to her breast in the folds of her coral-red cloak, she turns and with a cry of apprehension sees that the goddess is still in pursuit. Above flies a band of terrified Amores, their butter-fly wings of blue, white and red, with markings of blue and yellow eyes, signifying their inconstancy. Two bear bows, one holds the yellow girdle of Venus (the *cestus Veneris*), a fourth arrows and a coral-red quiver, a fifth a broken net of gold (*retia Veneris*). Before them fly four more tiny Amores, one with a bird's head, one with an owl's head, one with a monkey's head, and one with a grotesque moustachioed human head, as of a man in his forties. The symbolism of the first and last is obscure, but a moustachioed faun carries a Cupid in Perugino's *Combat of Love and Chastity*.[104] The owl of the second Amor is probably an allusion to the sloth caused by love, for the owl was the emblem of Somnus, the classical god of sleep. And Ulisse Aldrovandi (1522–1605), the great sixteenth-century naturalist, finds the owl an apt emblem of adultery, incest, and homosexuality because it is a night-loving bird, and those who commit such sins seek the night to cover their turpitude.[105] So too the monkey is a well-known symbol of lust. In these little Amores lust, it will be noticed, is once again represented as a combination of fair and foul, figured in forms that like the centaur are part human and part animal. The bird-headed Amor holds a sword and a grotesque basin-shaped shield, while the other

three hold the broken wires of another of Venus's golden nets. Again Spagnoli illustrates the underlying concepts in his *Contra amorem*: Sigismondo Gonzaga must study to avoid 'those places where Cupid sets his nets (*retia*) and lurks in ambush. His nets are the aspect of youth and its attractiveness, which captivate and entangle the fresh senses of a young man.'

In the centre-left foreground, cut off at eye-level, three other figures of Vices wade away in flight. First comes the black-brown figure of a hermaphrodite, with a monkey's head and a torso whose left breast is male and whose right breast is female. The monkey is a symbol of malice as well as of lust, and a white scroll inscribed Immortal Hatred, Fraud and Malice identifies the figure as a personification of these vices. The ills it scatters abroad hang about its person, for suspended from cords tied round its body are three bags whose labels indicate they contain respectively evils, worse evils, and the worst evils, while a fourth contains the seeds of discord. And one of the banderoles is labelled Suspicion. The moral inspiration of the invention is perhaps in part derived from a passage in St Jerome's *Contra Jovinianum* cited by Fregoso in his *Anteros*, 'Love', says the saint, 'wastes much time in suspicions . . . it breeds hatred of its own self and finally itself is hatred (*ipse novissime odium est*).'[106] To the left of this repulsive figure move a last unlovely pair. Idleness is a gross female figure, with unkempt white hair, a double chin, and stumps of arms, signifying her reluctance to toil. She does not even move of her own volition, but is led forward by a rope looped round her waist and held by Inertia, whose ragged white robe and unkempt dark hair sufficiently indicate her slatternliness. Inertia turns her thin slut's face in fear towards her active persecutor, Pallas.

Beside Idleness is inscribed a line from Ovid's *Remedia Amoris* (139), a didactic poem on the cure of love: OTIA SI TOLLAS PERIERE CVPIDINIS ARCVS (if you do away with idle hours, Cupid's bows have already perished). We find the same line cited in *Anteros* in the definition of love with which Fregoso opens his disputation. This definition, borrowed from Plato's *Phaedrus*, makes love 'a desire or unbridled appetite conjoined with lust (*luxuria*), incited by idleness (*otio*) and lasciviousness (*lascivia*).' In justification of it he cites verses from Petrarch, from Ovid and from Seneca, among them this very line from the *Remedia Amoris*.[107] The coincidence of thought between this passage and the picture is too striking to be accidental. The lesson is that *otium* or idle leisure is the mother of all vice, but more especially of wantonness. It is one common in High Renaissance moralists: in his *Ricordo LXXX: Cerca fuggir l'otio*, Isabella's friend Fra Saba da Castiglione[108] advises his great-nephew that idle leisure is the evil and vice most to be feared in this mortal life, as being the principle, origin, root and fomentation of every fault and that its only cure is occupation of body and mind. The exercise that best suits an honourable gentleman, he continues, is found in reading and writing, but only in the reading of authors who have written things worth reading and in the writing of things worthy of being written.[109] Our leisure should be filled with the arts and pursuits of Pallas, which will bring us wisdom, learning, sobriety, justice, constancy, chastity and nobility of mind and expel all the vices, lust, sloth, hatred, suspicion, malice, fraud, discord, avarice, ignorance and ingratitude that spring up like weeds in the idle mind.

As in the *Parnassus*, then, so in the *Pallas* the emphasis is on virtuous occupation as the proper tenant of our empty hours. The passage in the *Remedia Amoris* from which the inscription is taken enforces the importance of activity as a means of resisting love: 'Venus loves idle hours as the plane-tree wine or the poplar water . . . You who seek an end to love, do something, for love gives place to active things . . . That boy [Cupid] follows sloth: he hates those who are active.'[110] Battista Spagnoli's Pallas says, 'I know no delights: insidious pleasure has no treaty of peace with me; I have a dispute with the vices about the limits of my kingdom, and I fight against much opposition, for my kingdom has fallen to me among my enemies. Assiduous toil makes me strong: idleness weakens me. So often as need be I give battle, terrified by no arms, however powerful, for I know not how to admit defeat and yield.'[111]

The condemnation of idleness as the mother of vice and lasciviousness goes back to classical antiquity. Battista Guarino was able to cite antique example in commending Isabella's zeal for study in a letter of 17 July 1492:

> I know not how it has flown to my ears that Your Excellency has returned to the study of letters, a thing from which I have received such great pleasure that I could not express it either with tongue or pen. And so I exhort and pray you to persevere, for in truth there is nothing that can acquire greater honour and fame for Your Lady-ship than learning, which hath ever been rare in the female sex and in these days is like unto a phoenix. And when Your Excellency hath no other exercise, this is the most delightful that man can speak or think of, according to that saying of Cicero's, *nil ocio litterato dulcius* (nothing is sweeter than literary leisure), and that other of Seneca, *ocium sine litteris vivi est hominis sepultura* (leisure without letters is the entombment of a living man).[112]

Again we should recall that Isabella had a deep and lifelong love of letters, classical and modern. Writing on 10 July 1501 to Alfonso Trotti, she declared: 'To adorn our study we are taking pains to have the works of all modern authors, both in Latin and in the vulgar tongue', and we have many letters in which she eagerly solicits poets for a sight of their verses, the newer and more private, the better.[113]

Idleness and Inertia move in parallel with the three other Vices of Ignorance, Avarice and Sloth, who lead the flight on the other side of the pool: they make the same diagonal movement out of the picture. In this way the special emphasis on *otium* demanded by the theme of the picture is expressed in the two allegorical groups, one of Ignorance and Avarice carrying Sloth, the other of Inertia leading Idleness, who open and close the front plane of the composition. In the right background we see through the last arch of the pergola three tiny naked figures of women in flight, one pausing to catch breath, the others climbing up and moving away from the garden. They are the only disturbing element in the tranquil beauty of the landscape, in which Mantegna has again imitated Flemish aerial perspective, so that a serpentine river leads the eye through a green valley that fades into blue hills and a white sky.

The picture as a whole is Mantegna's one surviving painted history in which the action is expressed through allegorical personifications, a form of invention which Alberti especially commended to painters, citing as an example the *Calumny* of Apelles, a subject of which Mantegna made a drawing (Plate 224), again during these last years, when his interest in personification seems to have been prompted by an urge to moralize on life and to illustrate from his experience of it the bitter lessons of human envy and ignorance. Alberti envisaged allegory as a branch of painting which partakes of the same kind of invention as poetry and eloquence. 'Force of invention', he writes, 'is evident when we see that a fine invention is pleasing in itself, without the aid of painting, so that the mere reading of it pleases, as we see in the case of Lucian's witty device of the *Calumny* of Apelles.' The painter should therefore learn from poets, as Phidias confessed that he had learnt from Homer.[114] Such was the theory of the relationship between literary invention and painting as perceived by Isabella and practised by Mantegna. Andrea was praised in 1506 by Lorenzo da Pavia as an incomparable inventor for just these late pictures,[115] in which the simpler art of the quattrocento is evolving into the elaborately complex symbolic art of the sixteenth century. By invention Lorenzo meant the power to embody concepts in expressive figures and compositions; no easy task if the figure was to be significant not only of a general idea, but also pregnant with associated or subordinate concepts. We find indeed that Mantegna had second or third thoughts even on canvas: thus the monkey originally had a satyr's ear, while the face of the satyr carrying Cupid has been much changed.

In the *Pallas* Mantegna embodies with equal skill the severe ideality of Pallas, the various nature of vice, sometimes presenting itself as wholly fair, sometimes as part fair, part foul, sometimes in its true brutishness and sometimes in its grossness. The means he employs to construct his personifications are diverse. Sometimes he makes use of a visual language of symbolic attributes – the golden nets of Venus, the arrows of Cupid – which was even more familiar then than now because the metaphors it uses were conventional in classical literature and in the poetry and more especially the love poetry of the day. At other times he is obliged to resort to the literary language of inscriptions, in itself a confession that the powers of pictorial invention were perhaps being tested beyond their limits by a literary invention. Yet the deftness and naturalness with which these inscriptions are introduced, on bandeaux and fluttering bands, subordinate them to the action of the figures and allow the eloquence of the composition to remain primarily a pictorial eloquence. The distortions of the human figure are of two kinds: either animal and human forms are married, when the personification is understood to have the characteristics of the animal, or the human figure is shaped to match a conventional typology of physical forms and features as expressions of aspects of man's moral nature. The figures from classical mythology, literature and art, Pallas, Venus Impudica, the centaur, the satyrs, the Amores, already had a fixed symbolic value. Finally, the allegorical significance of the figures is cleverly pointed up by colour, as in the black-brown flesh of the hermaphrodite, and by expression.

Among the many passages from Spagnoli's poems that illuminate the imagery of the Studiolo is one from the elegy *Contra poetas impudice loquentes* which denounces erotic poetry and lauds chastity in words that parallel the pictorial encomium of chastity and chaste pursuits of Mantegna's two paintings.[116]

Expel the bow of quiver-bearing Cupid with his mother and withdraw your neck from the Dionean yoke ... Venus is the mother of adultery and seduction: she favours the brothel and haunts of ill-fame. The mother of God is chaste: chaste too is the ruler of Olympus ... chaste are the Muses, chaste the waters of the fount of Libethrus.[117] All true poetry loves chastity. Helicon is a virgin: a virgin too is Peneian Daphne, and they say the daughters of the Castalian fount were sprung of a virgin mother. Depart, ye poets of

Venus, from the river of Helicon: your mouth pollutes the virgin waters. Not ivy nor the laurel tree of Apollo are meet for you: a chaste garland loves not impure tresses.

Here, summed up in Spagnoli's flowing elegiacs, is the meaning of the *Parnassus* and of the *Pallas expelling the Vices*.

One of the last works on which Mantegna was engaged just before his death was yet another painting for Isabella's Studiolo, a picture of *Comus*.[118] Isabella had ordered it by the summer of 1506, and on 13 July that year Mantegna wrote to her: 'I have almost finished designing Your Excellency's history of *Comus*, which I shall go on pursuing as greatly as my fancy shall aid me.' On 15 July what he had already done was inspected by Isabella's courtier Gian Giacomo Calandra while negotiating for his mistress over the purchase of Mantegna's antique head of Faustina, which Mantegna was selling because he was in desperate straits for money. Isabella had not yet paid him an earnest for the picture and Mantegna was clearly hoping that the pathetic narrative of his plight would move her to come to his aid. The prudent Calandra asked to be shown the picture, no doubt in order to see for himself what had been done. 'I desired to see the painting (*tabula*), in which are drawn out these figures, the god Comus, two Venuses, one habited, the other naked, two Amores, Janus grasping Envy (*Invidia*) with his arm and pushing her outside, Mercury and three other figures put to flight by Mercury. Some other figures are still wanting, but the design of these is very beautiful.' Work on the picture was stopped by Mantegna's death in September, and the commission was revived only in 1509, when it was handed over to the new court painter Lorenzo Costa (*c*.1460–1535), who had entered the Gonzaga's service by November 1506.

Costa completed his work in 1510. The status of this *Comus* (Plate 128) is uncertain. On the one hand, it certainly reproduces Mantegna's work, for it contains all the figures in all the actions mentioned by Calandra. Moreover, these are the principal figures: clearly Mantegna had begun by putting them in across the middle ground. Accordingly he may well already have worked out these parts of the composition in preliminary drawings: since Calandra was aware that some figures were still missing, he and Mantegna must have known what these were to be. It might be then that Costa used some drawings by Mantegna and a literary invention rather than Mantegna's canvas. On the other hand the canvas itself would normally have been paid for by Isabella, and given by her to Mantegna, and would therefore have been returned to her on his death. Furthermore, we might expect that she would hand it over to Costa. It is at this point that a real difficulty arises. X-ray analysis of the picture has failed to reveal any sign of the underdrawing which Calandra's description would lead us to expect, and Mantegna's underdrawing, it should be added, is likely to have been in strong and sharp black outlines. The technique in fact reveals only one hand, that of Costa. All in all then the probability is that Costa's *Comus* is a new picture, which follows Mantegna's original canvas so far as it supplied a model. It would have served Costa in fact rather as the drawing which it was Isabella's practice to have made as an exemplar to accompany the literary text of the inventions she desired to have painted.

XII

The Paintings in Monochrome

THE *Parnassus* and the *Pallas* are the first great triumphs of neo-classicism in painting: in them Mantegna is a forerunner of Poussin. Like so many of Mantegna's late works, they raise the complex question of his relationship with contemporary classicizing trends in Venice. A similar elegant neo-classicism shapes the sculptures of the Lombardi, while on 7 February 1506 Dürer could write to Pirckheimer that a number of Venetian artists disliked his painting 'because it is not antique and therefore is not good.'[1] The Mantuan court was in close and constant touch with Venice, with Venetian fashions and Venetian humanism, with Venetian artists, craftsmen and musicians, and Mantegna must always have been aware of what was happening in the artistic world of the great city, all the more because of his own ties with the Bellini. His own works were well known there, to some by report, to others from engravings: that their fame was great appears from Dürer's eager acceptance of Mantegna's invitation to visit him in Mantua, though their meeting was frustrated by Mantegna's death.[2] Certainly the *Triumphs* and the two altarpieces of the 1490s, though from one point of view they represent the stylistic premises of the quattrocento developed to unprecedented scale and grandeur, from another herald the monumental style of the Venetian High Renaissance, rather as the late works of Signorelli herald the monumental style of the Florentine High Renaissance. And Mantegna's smaller histories of the years from *c.*1491 to 1506 show a refined ideal of antique figure style which may well have influenced the formation of a similar style in late quattrocento and early cinquecento Venice.

From the early 1490s onwards dates a group of pictures simulating sculptured reliefs in marble or bronze.[3] All are painted on canvas, except for one, the *Occasio* (Plate 173) in Mantua, which is a fresco. Although four of the pictures on canvas correspond closely in size, the *Samson and Delilah*, the *David and Goliath*, *The Sacrifice of Isaac* and *The Judgement of Solomon* (Plates 139, 171, 170, 169), this is not a reason for believing them to originate from a single series, since there are differences in their conception and in the colour of their background. In these paintings of simulated sculptures the motifs in relief are executed in monochrome, or chiaroscuro, as the technique was known in the Italian Renaissance, generally, though by no means invariably, on a ground of richly variegated marble, either green or pink or red. Isabella's Studiolo was decorated with two paintings by Mantegna of this kind, according to the inventory taken after her death; both are described as '*finto di bronzo*' (feigned as of bronze) and therefore perhaps of a deeper brown colour, rather than the light amber we find in Mantegna's surviving monochromes. They are now lost, but one of them seems to have figured Arion being cast into the sea and so to have emblematized in yet another form that theme of music which sounds through the decoration of the Studiolo.[4]

The illusionistic simulation of sculpture in paint is found as early as Giotto's frescoes in the Arena, but in the fifteenth century perhaps received a new impulse in Italy from Flemish example. In both Giottesque and Flemish form such painted sculptures are always represented in an architectural framework. And a century and a half later, in Italy, Vasari still associates the technique of simulating sculpture in chiaroscuro with the decoration of palace façades, of theatrical scenery, and of triumphal and other temporary structures erected for festivals and *trionfi*. In Padua there was a well-established tradition of

Fig. 13. Devotee. Detail from *The Cult of Cybele* (Plate 146)

figures and histories executed in *terra verde*. According to Vasari, no doubt repeating Campagnola, this was the technique in which Uccello's figures of giants were executed in Casa Vitaliani.[5] Pizzolo painted some figures in the house of the butcher Paolo Grasseto '*in viridi*' and Squarcione's scenes from the life of St Francis on the portico of San Francesco were also in *terra verde*. The technique of other fifteenth-century wall-decorations in *terra verde* in the Scuola della Carità is analysed by Muraro. The outlines were drawn in black; the lights were executed in white lead and yellow earth.[6]

At first Mantegna appears to have used chiaroscuro as a means of simulating sculpture in association with architecture. Thus in the *Circumcision* of the early 1460s monochrome reliefs are figured as applied to the lunettes of the altar wall of the Temple. The chiaroscuro mythological scenes and imperial busts of the Camera Picta, firmly enclosed within a simulated framework, and set on a ground of simulated gold mosaic, essentially are conceived as decorations of a vaulted ceiling. Again the chiaroscuro reliefs and figures of the Belvedere Chapel seem to have been subordinated to an architectural framework; this is certainly the case with those of Mantegna's funerary chapel, executed after his death, but probably to his design.

Mantegna appears to have conceived the notion of simulating small independent relief sculptures in paint in the 1490s, three decades or so after the first independent reliefs in stone or bronze representing religious and secular histories had appeared in Italy. This emancipation of relief sculpture from its traditional role as a decoration of architecture or of architectural forms, such as altar, altarpiece, and tomb sarcophagus, seems to have been effected quite late, in the 1460s and 1470s. It was certainly prompted by the influence of antiquity, or rather by the collecting of antique sculptures, and is perhaps to be associated with Pollaiuolo in Florence and with Francesco di Giorgio, who worked in Siena, the Marches and Venice. By it was created a new genre of relief sculptures which had much the same decorative purpose as paintings.[7] They were indeed collected by dilettanti. Saba da Castiglione (1480–1554), the first Renaissance writer to give advice on the collecting of modern sculptures, speaks of great lords who liked to adorn their chambers (*camere*) and studies (*studii*) with sculptures in marble and terracotta by Donatello, Gian Cristoforo Romano, Alfonso Lombardi and others, and casts in bronze, including reliefs, by Verrocchio and Pollaiuolo.[8] He explains that these are a substitute for antiquities, and the reason he gives for the substitution probably has something to do with the invention of painted reliefs. 'Because good antiques, as they are rare, so they cannot be had without the greatest difficulty and expense.' The vogue for such ornamental relief sculptures – 'histories' or pictures in sculpture as we may call them – appears to have flourished less in Florence than in the Marches and north-eastern Italy, and more especially Venice, where antique sculptures figured in the studios of many late fifteenth-century collectors.

In late fifteenth-century Mantua there was no sculptor of the first rank readily available to carve or cast reliefs of this kind, which were essentially refined works of art executed in costly materials and intended for patrons of wealth and learning. Gian Cristoforo Romano seems to have come to work in Mantua only in 1497, while Antico (Pier Iacopo Alari Bonacolsi) was kept busily employed first at the court of Gianfrancesco Gonzaga at Bozzolo and from *c.*1496 at that of the Protonotary Lodovico Gonzaga, also at Bozzolo and then later at Gazzuolo, and was only occasionally at the disposal of Francesco and Isabella. Even when what the Gonzaga wanted was only fine decorative sculpture, during the late fifteenth and early sixteenth centuries they generally sent out of Mantua for the work. On 14 August 1484, when there was question of a tomb that Francesco Gonzaga desired to have made, Antonio Scazzano declared, 'there is no master in Mantua who knows how to make such a work: when we went to Venice we wanted to discover the master who made Torelli's tomb, but he could not be found ... I have spoken with Maestro Luca [Fancelli] who says there is no master here or in Verona: if Your Excellency agrees, we will write either to Venice or to Florence.' Again in 1495 when Francesco wanted carved marbles for a chapel, he ordered them from Pietro Lombardo in Venice. And as late as the early 1520s Isabella gave the commission for a doorway for her new Studiolo in the Corte Nuova to Tullio, Pietro's son. It was from Venice or Verona that Francesco and Isabella and the Protonotary Lodovico had to procure unworked marbles, there being none available locally, a fact which explains the scarcity of decorative sculptures in marble in late fifteenth-century Mantua. Thus in 1489, when Lodovico set about fulfilling his vow to build a chapel dedicated to the Precious Blood in the cathedral of Mantua, he obtained fine stone and marbles from Verona and Venice.[9]

Accordingly it may well have been cheaper and less troublesome for the court to obtain painted reliefs from Mantegna. This might explain why he invented this genre and why it remained peculiar to him and to Mantua, for almost all the surviving examples are by him or by his pupils. Evidently it became associated with him and, as we shall see, in 1505 a commission for four paintings of this kind came to him from Venice. For its effects of relief monochrome depends on a few bold forms, with strongly outlined contours and light but firm model-ling in white, grey or yellow, with some use of black in the deeper shadows. Mantegna's simulated reliefs tend to be in umber, with strong black contours, lights in yellow or white, and shadows in black or grey. The general effect that he seeks in them is of a setting and figures in high relief applied to a plane surface, generally of coloured marble, though in some instances, as in the Cincinnati *Sibyl and Prophet*, an architectural setting forms the background. When this is so, however, it too is rendered as a flat plane, any openings required for reasons of contrast or narrative being dark-coloured so as not to draw the eye beyond the plane.

Mantegna's works of this kind have all the ambi-guity of a mixed genre, for if the two-plane con-struction and the silhouetting of the figures and setting against the ground simulate effects of classical relief sculpture, the conception of the figures and their action often seems to imply the three-dimensional depth of space proper to painting. This contradiction emerges most notably in the reliefs on grounds of coloured marble, where the eye perceives the figures as applied to the ground, not emerging from it, as in sculptures of white marble. And the settings and draperies are detailed with a minuteness and naturalism that are pictorial rather than sculptural.

We have no real knowledge of how these small independent histories in monochrome were dis-played in their original settings. The two in Isabella's Studiolo, which must in any case have been reinstal-led when she moved to the Corte Nuova in 1522, were both set above a door as *sopraporte* and this is certainly one position in which real sculptures are known to have been placed in the quattrocento. Unfortunately we know nothing of how the com-parable small marble reliefs by the Lombardi, such as those executed in 1508 for the Camerini d'Alabastro of Alfonso d'Este, were displayed.[10] By their nature marble reliefs must have been set in or on a wall, but many of the Lombardi reliefs have protruding bases and architecturally shaped grounds, which makes it even more difficult to visu-alize their original placing. For only one Mantegnesque monochrome do we have precise information about its original position: this is the *Occasio*, which was painted for the canopy of a chimney-piece in the Palazzo Biondi in Mantua. The canopy clearly had the usual inward sloping sides, for to this shape the format of the *Occasio* is adapted. There are two records of such monochromes as sets of four – one set representing *Esther*, *The Sacrifice of Isaac*, *Tobias* and *Moses*, the other *Judith* and presumably three other heroines, suggesting a fairly elaborate scheme of decoration as their origin. Again a number of monochromes seem to have been

conceived for viewing at the same level as a sculp-tured frieze. *Tuccia* (Plate 144) and *Sophonisba* (Plate 145) and *The Introduction of the Cult of Cybele* (Plate 146), all now in London, and the Cincinnati *Sybil and a Prophet* (Plate 140) have the familiar perspective of works Mantegna knew were to be set above eye-level: others, like *The Sacrifice of Isaac* (Plate 170) and *David* (Plate 171) in Vienna, are intended to be viewed more or less at eye-level. For paintings of the former kind we must suppose some sort of archi-tectural framework above a high dado or a cornice, while the latter were perhaps inset in wainscoting or mounted in a framework above a low dado. Since all are substitutes for decorative sculptures, it can be assumed that the sort of room for which they were most often intended was a *camera* or *studio*, evoking as they do in their refined classical style the small antique sculptures in marble or bronze with which collectors liked to decorate such rooms.

The *Occasio* is the only known painting from Mantegna's circle which is directly modelled on a literary description, in this case a sculpture of *Occasio et Penitentia* attributed to Phidias and described in an epigram by the fourth-century poet Ausonius. But the composition has been modified to introduce the figure of *Vera Eruditio* from the *Tabula Cebetis*, so that the fresco is not a faithful reproduction of the original sculpture as described. Otherwise the subjects of these simulated reliefs range from figures like Dido, Tuccia and Sophonisba, who were depic-ted on the walls of chambers in the fourteenth and fifteenth centuries as an expression of the chivalric cult of heroines, to mythological and Biblical sub-jects containing some exemplary lesson. Thus *Sam-son and Delilah* (Plate 139), one of Mantegna's finest works in this style, is a warning in the best medieval tradition against the wiles of women and lascivious love, probably commissioned by some ecclesiastic, perhaps indeed by Sigismondo Gonzaga himself, to whom Spagnoli addressed his poem *Contra amorem*. Delilah with smooth, youthful face, shaped as a long oval, with incurving cheeks and chiselled lips, her robe slipping off her shoulder in imitation of an antique motif found in ancient sculptures of Venus, her hair dressed in antique fashion, looks down on the recumbent Samson as she prepares to cut off a second lock of his hair. In a drunken slumber, sym-bolized by the vine that twists itself around the olive-trunk behind the pair, he lies sprawling on a cloak in a pose copied from some ancient sarcophagus decorated with Bacchus and Ariadne. Although the picture admonishes the spectator of woman's wick-edness, Mantegna also emphasizes the sensuality and folly that have made Samson fall a prey to her: his face is coarse, almost negroid in type, with thick lips, and his shorn hair gives him a foolish look.

Mantegna's most ambitious composition in

monochrome is *The Introduction of the Cult of Cybele at Rome*.[11] The picture is one of a set of four commissioned from him early in 1505 by Messer Francesco Cornaro (1481–1546), the eldest son of Giorgio (d.1527), one of the greatest and probably the wealthiest of the Venetian patricians of his day. Indeed Giorgio's branch of the Cornaro had become semi-royal, for his sister was Caterina Cornaro, Queen of Cyprus. The family had close links with Gentile and Giovanni Bellini; as early as 1471 we find Elisabetta Morosini, Giorgio's wife, asking them to take a pupil into their shop.[12] To obtain permission for Mantegna to paint his pictures Francesco had resort to his younger brother Marco (d.1524), who was the equal in dignity of Francesco Gonzaga, having been made a cardinal in 1500 by Alexander VI and in November 1503 Bishop of Verona by Julius II. Marco sent Niccolò Bellini, a member of his household and Mantegna's brother-in-law, from Verona on 15 March 1505 with a letter putting forward his brother's request.[13] The letter makes it clear that the long-standing etiquette by which licence had to be solicited of the Gonzaga before Mantegna could execute a painting for any other patron still prevailed. Francesco Cornaro, it explains, 'knowing he [Mantegna] is dependent in such matters on the will of Your Most Illustrious Lordship, as dedicated and bound to your service, and being unwilling to contract for any work from him without your goodwill and commands' has asked his brother to desire Francesco's leave. Presumably this was granted at once, the Marchese being no doubt anxious to gratify one of the great patrician families of Venice, in whose service he was so often engaged as a *condottiere*, and Bellini went on from the court to persuade Mantegna to paint the pictures.

In becoming a cardinal Marco Cornaro had pre-empted Francesco's own ambition, for already in January 1500 Francesco, then on a mission as Venetian envoy in Rome, was in treaty along with other competitors for a cardinal's hat, and like them was said to be willing to spend more than 20,000 ducats to obtain it. He was unsuccessful, and passed through the regular *cursus honorum* of a Venetian patrician, serving as a castellan and as a captain of a galley. In 1509 he fought in the defence of Padua against the Imperial troops, and later became a Consigliere at an early enough age to excite comment. In 1516 he was made a Savio, and in 1517 went as Venetian ambassador to the Catholic king. Finally in 1528 Clement VII made him a cardinal.

In some ways his career was not dissimilar from that of the learned and gifted Pietro Bembo (1470–1547), his near kinsman and intimate friend. Bembo indeed looked on Francesco as a brother and on Giorgio as a second father. By 1506 he had become one of the patterns of the age. Although Isabella had had some correspondence with him in 1503 and 1504, and had invited him repeatedly and pressingly to Mantua, they had never met, and she was highly flattered when this established favourite of the courts of Ferrara and Urbino and admirer of her sister-in-law, Lucrezia Borgia, Duchess of Ferrara, turned aside in a journey from Urbino to Venice in the late June of 1505 expressly to visit her in Mantua. Bembo's presence brought no disappointment: on 4 July, after he had left, Isabella wrote to the poet Tebaldeo that he had surpassed all her expectations, great as these had been. Soon, as we have already seen, she was making use of him in her negotiations with Giovanni Bellini and inviting him to be the 'inventor' of the picture Bellini was to paint for her Studiolo.[14] Bembo was a typical *gentiluomo* of the Venetian Renaissance in the delight he took in art, both in that of classical antiquity and in that of his own time. Later his collection in Padua was to include two of Mantegna's most personal works, the early votive *Presentation* (Plate IV) and the late *St Sebastian* (Plate 130).

Francesco Cornaro was likewise 'greatly enamoured of rare things, as is the wont of almost all lofty and gentle spirits'[15] and had a certain influence with Giovanni Bellini, whose studio, like Bembo, he frequented. The prestige of Mantegna as the 'supreme designer and inventor of his age' is demonstrated not only by Bellini's reluctance to compete with him by executing a painting to hang beside his in Isabella's Studiolo, but by the eagerness of this great Venetian gentleman, who could command works from the best Venetian painters, to have a set of pictures from his hand. The four pictures he commissioned, no doubt for his own personal chamber or *studio* in the family palace, for his father Giorgio did not die till many years later, were intended to celebrate the imaginary glories of his family in antiquity. Although the Cornaro had a long and distinguished ancestry, it was neither long enough nor distinguished enough for their Renaissance representatives, who were satisfied with nothing less than a descent from ancient Rome. Accordingly they attached their line to one of the greatest of all Roman patrician families, the *gens Cornelia*, which had produced in the Scipios a succession of illustrious men celebrated for their civic virtue and military prowess, appropriate ancestors and models therefore for Venetian patricians, who were also called on to exercise civic and military virtue in the service of their republic.[16] Saluting Marco at his formal entry into Verona on 4 November 1504 to take possession of the see, Hieronimo Avanzi exclaims in his oration of welcome,

Neither shall we celebrate in a fashion worthy of its dignity the Cornelian line, which as Sextus

Pompeius Festus asserts, is ancient and noble above all the other families of Europe and is rich in splendid deeds performed in every age. Famous for ever is he who, as Cicero writes, compelled Hannibal, till then unconquered, to depart from Italy and return to Africa [i.e. Scipio Africanus] ... Another of your race is adorned with extraordinary glory because he razed two cities utterly hostile to the Roman power, Carthage and Numantia [P. Cornelius Scipio the Younger]. L. Cornelius Nasica [the subject of Mantegna's picture] was adjudged the best of all men known from the beginning of time.

Francesco and Marco, who signed themselves Cornelius, were certainly very conscious of this august ancestry. But there is reason to doubt whether Francesco himself had the needful learning in Roman history and literature to choose appropriate subjects from the history of the Scipios, or to devise the learned inventions and inscriptions that figure in *The Cult of Cybele*, the only one of the four pictures that Mantegna finished. According to his funeral panegyrist, Hieronimo Negri, who had been a member of the Cornaro household, Francesco had not been taught letters sufficiently as a boy, and when at the mature age of 47 he became a cardinal he was obliged to apply himself to the study of Latin and the acquisition of learning.[17] Accordingly there is a real possibility that he was advised by the lettered Bembo in his choice of inventions. Alternatively it may have been Francesco's brother Marco, a patron of learning and letters, or one of the literati of Marco's household who devised the subjects of the four pictures.

'From your tender age you have been seen to aspire to the pursuit of letters and religion,' Avanzi declares to Marco Cornaro in the same oration of November 1504.

In your years of puberty you met with a tutor of the greatest probity for your morals, who was also a most learned teacher of eloquence. He set before you the virtues of the Cornelian house, he held up your father to you as a model for a hero's instruction ... Soon you burned so greatly with desire for knowledge of the sciences that as you approached the flower of your age, though a cynosure from the amplitude of your fortune and overflowing with wealth and delights, yet were you not content with your ancestral dignity or your father's happy state, but preferred to a palace resplendent with a royal luxury and to all the pleasures permitted to youth golden virtues and ingenuous arts, and went to Padua, that second Athens. You did not tarry long there, but attained to a knowledge of all the more abstruse sciences under a most eminent and famous professor of our times, winning to yourself the eyes and affections

of all ... We have ever admired your affection and liberality towards literary men and your erudition in all the disciplines of learning. Though you are eminent in the methods of the dialecticians, the dogmas of the philosophers and the deepest mysteries of our religion, yet you are never long on holiday from politer studies. Moreover, keeping your knowledge of these things to yourself, you explore the genius of the philosophers and also of the orators and poets with whom your house ever abounds, and by the native sweetness of your speech you gently insinuate it, as if on some other purpose intent, into the arena of disputation when questions arise ... Hence the sacred choir of poets sings of you as their Maecenas and acknowledges you as the one protector of studies and the studious and as it were an Aesculapius of the Muses.

Evidently Mantegna did not get enough guidance, for late in 1505 he decided that the task was too great for the price of 150 ducats originally agreed, 'although,' complained Bembo, 'he was first sent the measurements and had well seen the work that was to go into them.' Early in January 1506, therefore, Bembo invoked the intervention of Isabella d'Este. To Isabella Francesco Cornaro seems to have been well known, at least by reputation, for in her reply of 31 January she promised that Mantegna, who was only then recovering from a mortal sickness, would complete the task as soon as he was better, and this so that Isabella might oblige Bembo and also Francesco 'since he is a second Messer Pietro'.[18] Mantegna sketched out all four canvases, at least so much appears to be implied in a letter written after his death by his son Francesco Mantegna, but only the *Cult of Cybele* had been fully finished before his death on 13 September 1506. Francesco Cornaro may then have had the other three completed in Venice, for in all probability a rather longer canvas of *The Continence of Scipio* by Giovanni Bellini, now in Washington, is another painting from the series. In it Bellini has made an evident effort to match Mantegna's technique and style as seen in the *Cybele*, if indeed he was not simply completing Mantegna's design, for the *Continence* is executed in monochrome on a background of simulated red variegated marble. As in the *Cybele*, the perspective implies that the painting was meant to be seen slightly above eye-level. Indeed the four paintings were clearly to have been set with a frieze-like effect on the walls of the room for which they were intended.

The *Cybele* is inscribed *S hospes numinis Idaei C.* The main part of this inscription is taken from the lines in the third satire of Juvenal (138–9) which praise the reverence of old republican Rome for the gods, and instance the reception of the cult of Cybele. The larger letters SC may stand for Scipio, but more probably are an abbreviation for *Senatus Consulto* (by decree of the Senate) and refer to the official decree by which the Senate in 204 BC ordered Publius Scipio, as the most virtuous of all the Romans, to receive the goddess. The scene depicted by Mantegna was taken from Valerius Maximus, an ancient author of *exempla*, or stories of memorable deeds and words, which are arranged according to the virtues they illustrate. His *Memorabilia* was much read in the fifteenth century. The inscription *hospes numinis Idaei* stresses that Scipio was host to the goddess, and it is Valerius Maximus who records that Scipio took her into his own house until such time as a temple could be built for her. And the ancient scholiast on the verse of Juvenal from which the inscription is taken expressly glosses *hospes* as meaning 'that he should keep the image in his own house until a temple was made ready for her'. If we look carefully at the building on the right of the picture, we see that it is indeed a private house and not a temple, as it is so often taken to be. For Valerius Maximus, that Publius Scipio should be chosen while yet a youth for the privilege of being host to a deity was an honour beyond compare. 'Unfold the whole calendar of history, set before yourself every triumphal car, yet you will find nothing of more glorious preeminence in moral worth.'[19] It is this theme of heroic moral virtue that is celebrated in the painting, as it is celebrated in Bellini's *Continence of Scipio*, suggesting that the programme of the four canvases was the glorification of the exemplary private virtues of the Cornelian house as expressed in their public actions.

For the background of the story we must turn to another ancient historian, Livy, who gives a long account of how the cult of Cybele, also known as the Magna Mater, goddess of Mount Ida in the Troad, came to be introduced into Rome. He relates that in 205 BC, towards the end of the Second Punic War, the Romans discovered from the Sibylline Oracles that their victory would be hastened if they brought the goddess of Ida to Rome. Goddess of Ida was an epithet often given to Cybele in ancient literature because Mount Ida, above Troy, was the most celebrated centre of her cult: an instance is Juvenal's use of it in the inscription on the painting. The ambassadors sent by the Senate to the temple of Pessinus in Phrygia to obtain the goddess consulted the Oracle at Delphi on the way and were told that their mission would be successful and that when the goddess reached Rome she was to be received by the best of all the Romans. King Attalus of Pergamum himself conducted the envoys to Pessinus and gave them the small sacred stone, reputed to have fallen from heaven, which in the eyes of the Phrygians was the goddess herself. In 204 BC, when the arrival of the goddess was imminent, the Senate decided that Publius Scipio, a youth who had not yet reached the rank of quaestor, was the best of all the Romans, and commanded him to go down to Ostia, accompanied by all the matrons of the city, to receive her. According to Ovid's version of the story in his *Fasti*, Cybele entered Rome through the Porta Capena.

Mantegna has figured a processional scene in which the interest is concentrated on the approach of the goddess. On the left is the goddess on the road just outside the city, passing the tombs of two of the Scipios, Publius and Gaius, the uncle and father respectively of the young Publius, who had fallen together in Spain in 211 BC fighting the Carthaginians. Their tombs are imaginary creations, exemplifying the filial and family piety of the young Publius, who brought their bodies back from Spain. Besides illustrating additional glories of the line of the Scipios and of their descendants, the Cornaro, they indicate that the procession is advancing along the Via Appia towards the Porta Capena, for it was known from Livy that the tombs of the Scipios stood on this most famous of Roman roads, which ran from the Porta Capena to Capua.[20]

Livy says that the goddess was carried into Rome from Ostia by Roman matrons. But plainly Mantegna was unwilling to sacrifice to cold historical fact the picturesqueness of the Phrgyian cult, notorious in antiquity for its eunuch priesthood and for its orgiastic ceremonies of worship. Accordingly he has taken a hint from Ovid, who says that the goddess, after halting for a night on the Tiber, was brought further up the river and then carried to land for a ceremony in which a white-haired priest, clad in crimson, washed her effigy and her sacred emblems, while her attendants ululated, blowing their flutes and beating on their drums of bull-skin. The picture assigns an even more prominent role to the Galli, as the priests of Cybele were called. Four of them carry a bust of the goddess on a platform supported by two poles and covered by a rich carpet decorated with a dodecagonal rosette and fringed with tasselled strings hanging from pearls. Beside the bust of Cybele is a small stone sphere, certainly intended to represent the stone that fell from heaven; to the left is a smoking classical incense-burner (*turibulum*). Another Gallus walks behind, his head concealed by the bust, while a youthful acolyte kneels on the rear edge of the litter, to the further side of the bust, and in so doing helps to define the litter's depth to the eye. He is clad in female dress to suggest the self-castration by which men sacrificed their virility to the goddess and became her servants. This device of female or semi-female costume is used by Mantegna to identify other eunuch attendants of the goddess and to suggest their effeminacy.

Before the litter walks a young chief priest with flowing locks, clad in *anaxyrides*, the long loose trousers worn by Scythians and other Eastern peoples, a long-sleeved tunic and a cloak. The procession is awaited before Scipio's house by Scipio himself, attended by a mingled group of Romans and Phrygian attendants of the goddess, the latter recognizable by their costume and their feminine or near-feminine countenances. The chief priest motions to calm a youthful devotee of the goddess, who has been expecting her arrival with the group of Romans and Phrygians and has flung himself down on his knees at her approach with hands outstretched and eyes uplifted in longing adoration. His round-cheeked female face, flowing female locks and prominent Adam's apple mark him as a self-castrated votary of the goddess, who has assumed female dress and become her servant. The mood of this motif of a youth in ecstatic adoration of Cybele was perhaps suggested by Catullus' famous poem *Attis*, which describes the frenzied self-devotion of a young man who makes a pilgrimage to her shrine on Mount Ida, only to repent and then be inspired anew with *furor mentis* by the mighty goddess. The figure is certainly one of Mantegna's finest and most original inventions.

Scipio, who stands behind, makes no move to receive the goddess himself, but simply gestures towards the young votary as he addresses the stout elderly Roman at his side. With the chief priest and the young votary he forms the central culminating group of the picture. Their three figures are linked in a curve: Scipio, who is otherwise rather subordinated by his portrayal in *profil perdu*, being emphasized by his height, by the accentuated white highlighting on his costume, and by the line of division between the two marble panels of the background, which descends to his head. Recent cleaning has shown that these two panels are intended to suggest the difference in time and setting of the two parts of the action. On the left, behind the advancing procession of the goddess and the young votary, the marble is a variegated fiery red; on the right, where the approach to Scipio's house is represented, the marble is a variegated pale yellow. The two figures of priest and youthful votary, their costume executed in a yellowish grey that sets them off against the whitish grey of the other figures, form the pivot of the composition. The priest turns his head backwards to speak to those who follow him: the youthful priest kneeling on the litter points to the young votary, so linking the advancing cortège of the goddess with the waiting company of Romans and Phrygians.

The left-hand group is closed by a Roman standard-bearer, his banner inscribed SPQR, in token that this is an official reception by the Roman people. On the right, before Scipio's house, a caesura is made and a third, contrasting group begun by a Roman soldier standing guard. He is shown frontally, listening as an old Phrygian, dressed in robe and turban to indicate that he is an Oriental, bearded to indicate that he is not an eunuch, tells him of the new goddess. Behind, on the steps, a eunuch priest in *anaxyrides* attends closely: in his figure Mantegna has indicated a *semivir*, or self-castrated effeminate, with especial skill. Last of all is a musician dressed as a priest of Cybele, wearing a pointed fur cap (*koros*) into which are stuck two plumes, and a girdled chiton with dangling sleeves. The plumes are not a fanciful adornment, but a detail borrowed from Lucretius' famous description of Cybele and the Curetes who accompanied her image in processions, 'shaking terror-striking plumes on their heads under the influence of the goddess'.[21] With his right hand he beats a drum, the tympanum of Cybele, with his left he plays a flute, the *tibia* of Cybele. His music celebrating the advent of the goddess is accompanied by the trumpet of another musician, which protrudes from the door of the house, in what is perhaps the final example of that desire always 'to suggest more than is represented' which Mantegna had nursed from his early youth. The inscription SPQR on a band shaped as a tablet *all'antica* which is sewn to the tippet of the Curete bespeaks the official adoption by Rome of the cult of Cybele: the Romans themselves were forbidden to wear the costume or practise the rites of the Phrygians.

The motif of four Galli bearing the image and attributes of the goddess on a litter is inspired by an antique relief. Some idea of what it was like can be gained from a relief on a Roman marble monument of Cybele (Plate 148), now in the Fitzwilliam Museum, Cambridge,[22] whose early provenance is unfortunately untraced. In this four Galli carry a sacred bier slung on two poles. On it are set the throne of the goddess, with a mystic basket on its seat, and her footstool; to either end of the bier is attached a tall stem of laurel. The four Galli who carry the bier wear *anaxyrides*, sleeved chitons and Phrygian caps. The differences in the costume of Mantegna's Galli and in the emblems on his litter make it unlikely that the Cambridge relief was his source, but he evidently knew a similar relief or reliefs in the original or from drawings. There are perhaps indications in the costume that Mantegna may have drawn some of its details from other classical sculptures, from literary sources and from his own invention. The trousers worn by the priest carrying the front forward pole, by the chief priest and by the priest on the steps of Scipio's house must have their source in some processional relief of Galli wearing *anaxyrides* – there are ancient parallels for the short *anaxyrides* worn by the priest carrying the front pole. In a relief in San Lorenzo, Rome, where Galli bear a litter with a statue of the goddess, they wear short, lightly girdled chitons of the type worn by the old bearded priest on the extreme left and the musician on the extreme right.[23] The young beardless priest also wears a hat of semi-turban form of a kind commonly used for oriental costuming in quattrocento painting. The old bearded priest wears a head-dress modelled on an ecclesiastical mitre, but split from front to back, not from side to side, into two pointed wings. This is Mantegna's visual rendering of the *mitra* mentioned by ancient authors, and specifically by Juvenal, as a head-dress of effeminate Asiatics. Again the hat worn by the Gallus who holds the rear back pole is a mitre of the type known as a *tiara*, another oriental head-dress that figures in ancient literature.[24]

To his image of the goddess Mantegna has given the form of a classical bust, wearing a *corona turrita* in conformity with ancient representations of Cybele, some of which were certainly known to him. In this guise the goddess closely resembles the busts symbolizing captured cities which are figured in the *Triumphs*. Five of the six Galli bear boughs of laurel, perhaps in misunderstanding of their antique prototype; on the Cambridge relief the boughs of laurel are attached to the sacred bier itself. Alternatively, Mantegna may have known some ancient representation of Galli bearing laurel boughs, or again the motif may have been suggested to him by the laurel bough which Cybele often holds on Roman medals.[25] From such a complex interweaving of visual and verbal sources, Mantegna has created an unforgettably vivid and original work of art; it is not perhaps surprising that he felt he was owed a greater reward for so toilsome a task.

The *Cult of Cybele* is an essay in the manner of the *Triumphs*, but reduced in scale and format to serve as a frieze. The figures are grander in conception than in Mantegna's other surviving monochromes, and their draperies more broadly handled. They are disposed essentially in two planes, along a road seen in section as a grey platform. The suppression of all save the barest essentials of setting approaches the composition even more nearly to an antique relief. In spite of the rigid red and yellow marble ground, the careful gradation of light and shade and the perspective device of vanishing feet give the illusion of movement and depth. The main compositional problem, how to unite the parts of a strung-out horizontal action by reconciling the conflicting claims of distribution and concentration of interest, is skilfully answered. The forward motion of the cortège of the goddess from the left meets the urgent opposing movement of the young ecstatic devotee, and is resolved in the serpentine curve of his figure. The waiting group behind stands in calm contrast, linked to the scene as interested spectators, while the discoursing priest and the music-making Curete on the right introduce necessary motifs of action and sound to balance the animated approach of Cybele on the left. Lesser links are established by turned heads and gesturing hands. The classical serpentine curve on which the principal figures are constructed adds to the rhythmic pattern, while emphasis on the foreground figures and narrative clarity are secured by the bold use of white highlighting. The evocative picturesqueness of contrast between the dignified gravity of the Romans and the flutes and drums, the flowing robes and exotic head-dresses of the Phrygians, while ensuring a continual attraction of the eye as it moves along the picture, is not permitted to disturb the passionate ecstasy that is the culminating passage of Mantegna's invention.

XIII

Devotional Pictures

URING these last years, from *c.*1491 to 1506, Mantegna also painted a number of devotional pictures in which the general compositional scheme is adapted from antique portrait reliefs on funerary monuments and the whole is treated in the manner of an antique relief. The adult figures are shown half or three-quarter length, often in full-face or near full-face. Most of these pictures have a plain background, and where this is the case, the figures are usually arranged in two shallow planes. In one or two instances, such as the London *Imperator Mundi* (Plate 137), in which a well is figured for iconographical reasons, Mantegna has introduced a background hedge of his usual citrus fruit, but even of the *Imperator Mundi* a version exists in which the well serves merely as a pedestal and all background is suppressed, reducing the design to a severely sculptural conception. That Mantegna was now tending in his religious as well as in his secular style to conceive of smaller pictures as coloured reliefs, with an ever more austere concentration on the bust-length figure and on the naked eloquence of juxtaposed heads for all interest of narrative and feeling, appears in the Castle Ashby *Adoration of the Magi* of *c.*1500 (Plate XVI). Here a theme on which painters customarily lavished an elaborate opulence of attendant figures and accessory ornaments is stripped to a simple composition of four bust-length figures encircling the Child, with the head of St Joseph in the left background. As in a classical drama, there results an exclusive emphasis on the essentials of the action and the emotions that prompt it: the Virgin, with the downcast eyes of modesty, proffers the Child, while the Kings, kneeling or standing, proffer their gifts in reverent attitudes, skilfully varied, of ardent devotion.

Compositions of this kind, it will already be evident, revive and develop the style first found in that early masterpiece, the *Presentation*, with more fluency of accomplishment, though perhaps with a less touching simplicity and seriousness of sentiment. As in the *Presentation*, the figures are carefully arranged according to their rank. Thus Christ and the Virgin and Child are always set in the foreground, the Virgin usually seated, while the ancillary figures stand immediately behind, forming a closed group. When Mantegna figures the Holy Family, a devotion that had become very popular in the late fifteenth century, and one to which this type of composition is well suited, deriving as it does from family portraiture on Roman reliefs, the effect is of a dignified intimacy. Some of these representations of the Holy Family anticipate the *Sacra Conversazione* in that they juxtapose in a new, affective relationship with the Holy Family saints whose only real association with them is the devotion of the patron. In general Mantegna avoids that too rigid solemnity of symmetry which can be found in Roman art and especially in Late Roman art; by varying the poses of the heads of the figures to either side of the principal figure, he retains the effect of ideal beauty or gravity vitally quickened by human personality and warmth that was always an innermost secret of his art.

So much has Mantegna concentrated on sculptural severity in his works in this style that in some of them the ancillary saints cannot now be identified, as he has given them no decisive attributes. With pictures of this private devotional sort, it was evidently enough if the patrons themselves knew which saints were represented. Thus the badly ruined Verona *Madonna* (Plate 134) groups a young female saint with the Holy Family, but gives no clue to her identity. A number of letters from the 1480s testify, as we have seen, to the great importance attached by fifteenth-century patrons to pictures embodying their personal devotions. In these late paintings, for all their apparent hierarchical dignity, there are traces of this link of feeling, binding patron to image. In the beautiful Dresden *Holy Family* (Plate 132), whose refined splendour makes it perhaps Mantegna's most perfect work in this style, the composition gracefully emphasizes the ties of tender family affection uniting St Elizabeth and the young Baptist (Fig. 14) with the Virgin and Child. By contrast St Joseph simply stands to the left with his usual patriarchal aloofness, but here with double propriety, for he is represented according to a not uncommon custom with the features of the patron who commissioned the picture.

From *c.*1490 onwards the type of the Christ Child and of the youthful Baptist changes in Mantegna's pictures in keeping with the evolution of his late art. The face becomes a broad square terminating in a pointed chin, emphasis being given to the point by a curved cleft below. Putti of this sort already have that artificial winsomeness so characteristic of sixteenth-century art: their appearance in Mantegna's paintings is another sign of his final rejection of naturalism as a mainspring of inspiration in favour of a courtly ideality styled on the antique in its severer and lighter moments alike. The peril of this change was its tendency to substitute generalized stereotypes for those earlier figures whose perfection was animated by some vitality of reference to nature. Nevertheless, it was this late figure-style that was to influence Correggio and his followers and through them the course of painting in North Italy. In Mantegna, if it sometimes results in an empty elegance, it never deadens entirely the grave mysterious humanity of his art.

In one religious picture of these last years, the Copenhagen *Pietà* (Plate 124), painted in the mid 1490s, this style's suave superficiality is present only in the face of Christ, conformed by Mantegna to an ideal type of classical oval, in which the very perfection of the drawing serves only to emphasize his failure to achieve pathos of expression. Otherwise this picture, one of the most remarkable of Mantegna's late paintings – significantly he has signed it prominently in letters of gold – demonstrates that even in his old age he could still captivate with well-tried effects and at the same time enrich them with new. In format a small oblong, the *Pietà* is a devotional painting for a private chamber. Its light falls downwards from the left, throwing the right side of the picture into cool grey shadow. With eyes intent and lips parted, showing his white teeth, the Resurrected Christ displays his wounds and calls the beholder to contemplate them and be moved by them to remembrance of what he suffered on the Cross for our redemption. His tall chalk-white body is still reminiscent of Late Gothic art in its elongation and in the starting sinews of the arms, but in accordance with Renaissance notions of perfect beauty, his hair and beard are golden brown. He is seated on a sarcophagus whose sides plunge inwards in a sharp perspective, withdrawing its opposite end from the visual consciousness. In itself the sarcophagus is a most beautiful invention, painted with all Mantegna's customary delicacy and precision in the rendering of stone. Its material is a grey marble, delicately flecked with white and changing to purplish-grey: the moulded lid is set with a panel of darker marble; the carved semi-circular front, decorated with acanthus, is framed by legs in the form of scroll-shaped volutes, with a gilt rosette in the roll of the volute.

Two angels kneel behind Christ on the sarcophagus, in attitudes skilfully chosen to express differing affections of grief. One, on the right, holds up an end of the shroud and lifts his eyes upwards and outwards in wonder and grief. The other, on the left, supports Christ's body and looks down on him with tender sorrow. This left-hand angel wears a crimson peplos, and has wings of dark crimson, feathered with deep black-blue. His companion has a blue robe, bordered with gold round the neck, and wings that are dark green, edged and lit with gold and a patch of brilliant kingfisher blue. All four wings are disposed so as to form a wonderful near-symmetrical pattern, whose formality sets off the contrasted attitudes of the angels' heads. The sombreness of the theme is gently emphasized in this group of heads and wings, designed by Mantegna so as to form two inverted triangles. The dark-coloured wings are set against dark grey clouds and a deep blue sky: the faces of the angels are partly in shadow, and that of Christ wholly in shadow. His eyes hold those of the spectator, their compelling power enhanced by the tilted head and the skilful placing of the white in the pupil.

The foreground is Mantegna's customary platform of natural rock, here ochre-yellow and light brown, and carpeted with light green moss or spotted with single rocks and a scattering of pebbles. Inlets of rock indent it at the front and sides, a familiar device to raise the central motif. As ever Mantegna uses a sharp contrast of scaling to distinguish the principal figures and motifs from the background. In that background the lines of the sarcophagus converge on the horizon, set half-way up the picture, in a landscape painted in the same technique of aerial perspective as the *Parnassus*, with blue-green hills fading into the yellow light of dawn. The sky rises from light yellow on the left, indicating the east, and pale yellow on the right, behind the rocky hill of Golgotha, through layers of dark grey

Fig. 14. The Infant Baptist. Detail from *The Holy Family with the Infant Baptist* (Plate 132)

clouds from pale blue to deep blue at the top of the picture. On the left is the grey-purple slanting mass of Mount Sion: darkening at the rear, it rises above Jerusalem, whose buildings lie in shadow before it, but are touched with the yellow of the rising sun where they stretch beyond it. The view of the city is summary; Mantegna is above all interested in the flecks of light. This new interest in the dramatic use of light finds its most remarkable expression on the right below the bare, pale purple rock of Golgotha. Here a cleft divides Golgotha from a rock pierced by a natural arch, and Mantegna has introduced a marvellous effect as of a narrow band of light beyond the darkness of the archway. On its edge stands a man, his dark figure lit up by light from behind, again an exceptional effect. Before the archway is a quarry where masons shape stones and cut columns for a temple and a sculptor in a red cap chisels the base of a roughed-out marble statue propped up against a wall of natural masonry. This little scene makes a symbolic allusion to the paganism that the religion of Christ will overthrow. On the left, the two Maries, one in a yellow, the other in a blue cloak, walk along the road to the tomb in the cold dawn, while three shepherds, one piping, herd their sheep in the fields below Jerusalem.

The tonality of the picture is in keeping with the tendency of Mantegna's late art to brighten in colour. The overall effect is of a delicate grey sadness tinging the perfection of the forms, so precisely drawn and finished, and so light and brilliant in their cool tones. Mantegna has achieved one of his usual deliberate contrasts between the smooth planes of Christ's torso, delicately modelled in its noble classical musculature to suggest the firm softness of flesh on a perfect body, and the rich complication of the folds of the drapery, as always sharply ridged in their overlapping fall and arranged into rhythmic patterns, varied by bunching and pinching the drapery, and gathered into tumbled forms of stylized naturalistic complexity between his legs, where the two ends of the shroud meet. The colour balance is particularly beautiful in the upper half of the picture, where the blues of the angels fuse with the blue of the sky and the grey shadows of the shroud with the greys of the clouds and of Sion. That the whole is executed in a refined humanistic style, with no violent appeal to the emotions, is self-evident, but it ought nevertheless to be noted that the wounds of Christ, the theme of the picture, are indicated with the quietest of emphasis, as can be seen by comparing them with the forceful naturalism of the wounds of the Brera *Dead Christ*. There could be no stronger proof that in these later years Mantegna was moving more and more in a world of perfect ideal forms and among patrons for whom these were more truly expressive of beauty than lively imitations of the natural world. The transition is that from an antiquarian humanism, admiring the ideal forms of antiquity as the perfection of nature, to a Neo-platonic humanism, in which ideal forms mirror the perfection of God.

Yet in the Ca' d'Oro *St Sebastian* (Plate 130) the divine serenity of those forms is distorted by undisguised movements of imploring appeal and sombre despair. In this huge picture Mantegna's late figure-style, with its smoother, more idealized forms and its preference for pinks in the flesh tones and for loose aureoles of golden hair, is strangely combined with a reversion to the painted frame and to the sharp foreshortening of his Paduan youth, to the old play on real and pictorial space artfully conceived as a continuum. Such is the agonized expressiveness of the saint's uplifted face that the critic's judgement is sentimentally tempted to look on the picture as one of Mantegna's latest works, owing something of its torment to an anguished sense of the transience of life and of the perils that transpierce it. To succumb to this temptation is not wholly unjustified. During the first six months of 1506 Mantua was dreadfully ravaged by the plague, so that food, money and work became scarce or unobtainable and Isabella d'Este took refuge with her court at the country palace of Sacchetta. The inference has been made that this picture was painted by Mantegna, who had already been at death's door in January 1506, to invoke Sebastian's aid.[1] All that can certainly be said of its early history, however, is that it is probably the painting of St Sebastian which was in his house at his death and which he had ordered his sons to give to the Bishop Lodovico Gonzaga, apparently in satisfaction of some debt or obligation.[2]

It is true that the decorative treatment of the loincloth, though stylistically a late feature, is found as early as the first canvas of the *Triumphs*, painted c.1485, and the Uffizi drawing of *Judith*, which is signed and dated February 1491. But the device of a burning candle and its hexameter motto NIL NISI DIVINVM STABILE EST: COETERA FVMVS (nothing stands firm, except the divine: the rest is smoke)[3] with their allegory of the inconstancy of fortune and of earthly things, which are consumed and vanish away like a burning candle into its own smoke, figure a disillusionment with this world which Mantegna may well have felt most sharply during his last years of illness and debt. Iconographically the prayer for aid and protection against the perils of sickness is reinforced by the *corone* (paternosters) of coral and crystal beads suspended across the framework behind the saint's head; like those in the *Madonna della Vittoria* they substitute for decorative garlands of fruit and foliage an invocation, here an invocation for health, for coral, besides its other prophylactic powers, was thought good for complaints of the stomach and heart.[4]

The invention of this last *St Sebastian* breaks with the traditional iconography of this favourite theme of the plague-haunted quattrocento. Mantegna has retained only the uplifted eyes, the bound hands, the body-piercing arrows. His saint has his arms fastened, not to a stake or column, but behind his back, and is set up for execution in a niche, where his hair and loin-cloth are blown to the left by a breeze. The outer painted framework of red marble, with its protruding ledge on which the saint's left foot and the burning candle are placed, is conceived for a secular setting,[5] and in some ways it invites us to view this great nude figure in its arched niche of grey-green marble as a feigned sculpture. Yet as always, Mantegna can never bring himself to sacrifice pictorial freedom for the sake of simulating a sculpture, and the pose is too active, too independent of the niche for us to look on the figure as a classical nude sculpture imitated in paint. The painted frame, then, is an unreal, decorative frame within which the figure moves freely in space. Mantegna uses the strings of beads in the old Squarcionesque way to define a plane and so emphasize the outward thrust into our space of the saint's body and legs. These strings of beads have no attachments and their ends were evidently intended to be concealed by a wooden frame, like the front of the ledge, which is left unpainted.

The figure of Sebastian is Mantegna's nearest approach to the heroic nude of the High Renaissance, and yet another conception from his last years in which the past appears in a form pregnant with the future. Its mass is thrown to the right, for the pose is one of classical *déhanchement*, with the weight resting on the left leg. The left ankle alone is on the central axis of the picture, but to counteract any undue subordination of the head by its expressive displacement to the right, its importance is emphasized by the halo. The serpentine line enforces the contrast between the shoulder out-thrust to the right and the foot outthrust to the left; simultaneously it creates an equipoise between the two sides of the body and a balance of masses, which is assisted by the floating ends of the loin-cloth, falling and curling in whorls of complex, sharp-edged folds.

Ordinarily the serpentine line promotes an easy, graceful interflow of forms. Here the sharply poised right foot and the head uncomfortably upturned at the edge of the framework tauten the pose and give to the figure a necessary tension of suffering. That Mantegna deliberately sought to enhance the rightward curve of the body away from the centre for the sake of augmenting this effect of tension is revealed by a *pentimento*, which shows that originally the figure was set a little more to the left. To the agonized head, with its forced pathos of ideal beauty furrowed and distorted in pain, and to the strained body Mantegna has added the expressiveness of shadow; by making the light fall obliquely downwards from the right, he leaves the right side of the niche in deep black, so that the curve of its arch is visible only on the left and the left side of Sebastian's face is darkened. The arrows are shown piercing the body from various angles, as in Mantegna's two earlier versions of the theme, and for the same reason: to prompt the imagination to figure the archers standing in a curve around the figure in the viewer's space. Their arrangement forms almost a trellis-work pattern on the legs, where they are shown lengthwise at a shallow angle to the front plane, broadening the composition to either side of the figure to fill the niche. Above they pierce the body more deeply in a counterchange of contrasted angles. They are painted with all Mantegna's customary meticulousness: heads of grey steel, shafts of pale brown, and ends coloured red, pale blue, black, to which the feathers are attached. He has even marked the division in the lip of the ends for fitting to the bowstring.

Various incidents in Mantegna's life are recorded from the years between 1498 and his death in 1506. That he had other valuables besides his collection of antiques emerges from an irate letter of 8 May 1499, in which he complains to Francesco Gonzaga that he has been robbed first of some coins and then of a ruby ring valued at sixteen ducats by a barber called Saviola, who had stolen them on two Saturdays when he had been to shave Mantegna. It should not be thought that Mantegna had a rich ring simply for ostentation: jewels set in rings were a favourite form of investment in the Middle Ages and Renaissance; they were a hedge against inflation and in times of financial stress could always be pledged for money. Mantegna had Saviola arrested, and a witness examined, and 'the evidence was so strong that he could have been put to the cord.' But Saviola had a friend who interceded for him with the Podestà, and he was released from the claws of justice, only to be arrested again at the instance of Mantegna, who now had even stronger evidence against him, so he claimed in his letter to Francesco. He demanded summary justice on the culprit, 'in which you will do a good and holy work and sweep all the city clean of such a pestilence, and I make no doubt of finding my ring and money.'[6]

Other documents concern his collection of antiques and his reputation as a connoisseur of antiquity. In both capacities he was involved with that insatiable collector Isabella d'Este. Early in 1498

Isabella Sforza, Duchess of Milan, took a fancy to possess an antique female marble head belonging to Mantegna, having heard that it resembled her.[7] Accordingly she asked Isabella d'Este through the preacher Fra Pietro da Nuvolara to obtain it for her. Mantegna had brought the bust from Rome and Isabella found it no easy task to persuade him to part with it, 'because it is of supreme excellence and he is an enthusiast (*professore*)[8] for antiquity'. At first he tried to circumvent the importunate request by offering to have the bust cast in bronze and give the Duchess the cast, keeping the original for himself. As already noted, this passage is important for his bronze bust of himself because it proves his familiarity with the process of bronze-casting. But Isabella was not to be put off and herself pressed Mantegna so pertinaciously to give her the marble that finally he surrendered it. Apart from the bust of Faustina, to be mentioned in a moment, this is the only precise record we have of an antique belonging to Mantegna.

Isabella often took Mantegna's opinion about new acquisitions for her *studio*, or collection of works of art and antiquities. Early in 1505 she was considering an ivory head which her brother-in-law Giovanni Gonzaga had obtained on approval with a view to making her a present of it. On 28 March she sent it back to Giovanni with a letter of thanks, saying it was fortunate that he had only had it on approval, for Messer Andrea Mantegna and the sculptor Gian Cristoforo Romano had seen it 'and judged it neither antique nor good'. And when Saba da Castiglione began sending her antiquities from Rhodes, he wrote in a letter of 16 April 1507 accompanying a small marble torso of a woman from Naxos, that in his opinion 'although mutilated and truncated, it will not displease Messer Andrea Mantegna or my own Giovanni Cristoforo Romano.'[9] By this date Mantegna of course was dead, but Saba had not yet had news of this in Rhodes.

Late in 1505 Mantegna fell seriously ill, and for some days was at the point of death. In 1506, after his recovery, he addressed himself to Isabella on 13 July asking her to come to his aid with a subvention of money. Not having received any of his salary for months, contrary to his expectation, he was entangled in serious difficulties, having bought a house from Hieronimo Boso to replace the one he had exchanged with Francesco and so stop wandering from lodging to lodging in Mantua. The price was 340 ducats, to be paid in three instalments. The term for one of the payments was now past, and Boso was harassing him, and since all work was suspended in Mantua where the plague was raging 'as your Excellency knows, nothing can be sold or pledged at the moment and also I have other debts enough.'[10] Accordingly,

I am minded to help myself as well as I can with the things that are dearest to me, wherefore having oft been requested both at diverse times and by sundry persons to part with my dear antique Faustina of marble, from necessity which makes a man do many things, I have desired to write to Your Excellency since if I am to deprive myself of it, I would like you to have it more than any other lord or lady in the world.

His price for the bust was 100 ducats, 'which I could have had several times from great masters', that is, artists. From Sacchetta, where she had sought refuge from the plague and other evils afflicting Mantua, Isabella sent instructions to her young courtier Gian Giacomo Calandra to negotiate with Mantegna. He was to find out Mantegna's best price, but her determination, which Calandra was to disclose to no one else, was to give him no more than 25 gold ducats. As soon as the plague was over she would give him all he could wish as an earnest for the *Comus*. Calandra went at once to see Mantegna, but all his efforts to reduce the price from 100 ducats, which seemed to Isabella *ingordo* (exorbitant), to the 25 she thought a just price, were vain. Mantegna was querulous about his necessities and debts, for which he had pledged goods to the value of more than sixty ducats, and offended besides that Isabella had not written in reply to his letter. With an ironic sneer he told Calandra 'that perhaps she had kept silence from shame, seeing she could give him no help in his present necessities.' Calandra answered that a visit from her servant was equivalent to a letter, and that 'she feels no shame at all, for the state of times is her excuse, if she uses not towards him that courtesy and liberality his virtues deserve.' And indeed the Gonzaga in these months were in dire straits for ready money, like their subjects, and for the same reason, the suspension of all business on account of the plague and the previous year's famine. Calandra thought that Mantegna had no other chance of selling the bust at his own price, except to Bishop Lodovico Gonzaga 'whom he says delights in such things, and is a spender'.[11]

Isabella was eager to buy the Faustina, but prudently thought it best to consult a sculptor about its value. Accordingly that same 15 July she sent a messenger with a letter to Antico at Gazzuolo asking him for his opinion about how much 'to the last copper (*quadrante*) we can spend on it', and pledging her faith to say not a word about his answer to anyone. Antico, who was evidently thoroughly familiar with Mantegna's collection, replied in a note brought back that same day 'that if Messer Andrea's head had not been worn in many places by time, I would value it at even more than 100 ducats.' He advised Isabella to try to find some other bust in Rome 'as this one will not fail to fall to you', and she could continue negotiations for it.[12] The upshot was that Mantegna agreed to let Isabella have the Faustina on approval for six days, handing it over on 1 August, 'without security' wrote Calandra, 'and very willingly to gratify Your Ladyship, but giving it to me with great ceremony and commending it with the greatest earnestness, not without great manifestation of jealous care, so much so, that were the six days to pass without his having it back again, I am almost certain he would die of it.' Calandra again tried to reduce the price, but Mantegna would have none of it, declaring that if necessity did not compel, he would not let it go for much more.

It took Isabella only two or three days to make up her mind, and on 4 August she offered to buy the bust for the price Mantegna had named. She took on herself the payment of what he owed Boso to the amount of 100 ducats, explaining that even if the Faustina was not worth this sum she was pleased to make him a gift of it 'to do you a pleasure and a service'. But she was unable to find a further 27 ducats which Mantegna owed Boso 'on account of the extreme want of money in which we find ourselves at present'. She would have liked to give him this sum as earnest for the *Comus*, but he would have to excuse her because of the times. In spite of the criticisms that have been levelled at her part in this transaction, Isabella seems to have acted very fairly by Mantegna and not to have taken advantage of his distress. She was jubilant about her acquisition: on 5 August she wrote to Gian Cristoforo Romano about her latest additions: 'We shall also have Mantegna's Faustina and so little by little we shall make a *studio*.'[13] Mantegna's bust was once confidently identified with a rather poor bust of Faustina in the Palazzo Ducale at Mantua, but this has no known history earlier than the seventeenth century and the identification has recently been questioned.[14] From Antico's letter and from the slight reserve about its value expressed by Isabella, the bust, it would seem, was worn and broken in several places.

Prospective patrons anxious to obtain a painting by Mantegna still had to resort in the first instance either to Francesco or to Isabella. Thus on 6 March 1498 Isabella replied to Maestro Francesco da Castello, who had written to her from Ferrara of his desire 'to have something from the hand of Messer Andrea Mantinea' for his *studio* 'that she would speak to Andrea herself and even more efficaciously than in her own behalf'. Francesco da Castello, who gives himself the artist's title of Maestro, was either the Veronese miniaturist of this name or his Milanese namesake, also a miniaturist, who had worked for Matthias Corvinus of Hungary. Presumably his wish was to have an exemplar by a supreme artist hanging

before his eyes, rather than just to add to a collection of pictures or drawings. Such commissions for paintings or drawings to decorate a *studio*, whether painting-room or study proper, or a chamber may explain, as we have seen, why Mantegna painted a number of versions of the same subject, most notably of Judith, in the technique of simulated relief, for paintings in this technique are most likely to have been intended for rooms of this kind.[15]

Mantegna's reputation now extended far beyond the borders of Italy itself. He was greatly admired by the French governors who ruled Milan after Louis XII had taken it from Lodovico Sforza in 1499. Rather than paintings of secular subjects they seem to have wanted religious pictures from him for their private chapels: in late fifteenth-century France secular chambers were still hung with tapestries rather than decorated with paintings. In 1499 Cardinal Georges d'Amboise asked Isabella for a picture by Mantegna for the chapel he was building in the archbishop's palace at Rouen; even before this was painted Francesco despatched an altarpiece by Mantegna to him on 19 November[16] as an independent gift. It seems likely too that it was for the chapel of his château of Thouars that the great general Louis II de La Trémoille (d.1525) wanted a painting from Mantegna's hand. It was ready by August 1502 and was described by Franceso Gonzaga as 'one of the most beautiful things Messer Andrea Mantinea has ever done'. Such commissions were valuable diplomatic gifts in the dangerous politics of these years, when the mighty power of France had replaced the Sforza as Francesco's Lombard neighbour. Even after Mantegna's death in 1506 his prestige among the great men of France was still so great that Florimond Robertet (1457–1532), the art-loving treasurer of Charles VIII, Louis XII and Francis I, was anxious to obtain a picture by him. On 11 April 1508 Francesco wrote to his agent in France that in spite of every effort he had been unable to find a suitable picture. But Mantegna's severe, strong outlines, if they still pleased Isabella, lacked the *dolcezza* of style that Perugino and Leonardo had made fashionable, and Francesco added that if Robertet would say what sort of picture he wanted and what saint he wished depicted in it he would see that he was 'well served and perhaps by a hand softer and sweeter than Mantegna's was'.[17]

Mantegna's fame had also spread to Germany, and not merely among admiring artists like Dürer. In December 1507 the Elector Frederick of Saxony wrote to the Marchese Francesco that he had heard 'from your servant the bearer that Your Grace takes great delight in the beautiful and excellent painting of that worthy master Andrea of Mantua'. He asked Francesco for some fair 'piece' from his hand, offering in exchange some fine Geman picture.[18]

Mantegna was equally celebrated in Spain. In 1499 the youthful Gonzalo Fernández de Oviedo, later a *conquistador*, was showing off before Isabella d'Este his skill in cutting figures in paper:

> I cut some things which those lords doubted it were possible to do, until they saw me cut other pretty devices in their presence. And much more greatly did they cause wonder to that most excellent painter who was then dwelling there, called Andrea Mantegna, who was another Leonardo da Vinci, and indeed in the art of painting some held him for the chiefest master of all those then living at that time in the whole of Italy.[19]

XIV

Mantegna's Technique

THERE has been little scientific investigation of the technical aspects of Mantegna's paintings, and what has been done has been done mostly in France, on pictures dating from *c*.1496 to 1502, a very short stretch in an exceptionally long working life. The aristocratic nature of his art is emphasized by his insistence on using only the finest pigments and gold, an insistence that explains of course in part the extraordinary depth and beauty of his colours. In Padua, as an independent master, Mantegna seems to have found himself in colours: thus in the contract for the altarpiece of Santa Giustina he agrees to 'paint all the figures at my expense and with my colours', but to use the cheaper azurite (*azzurro tedesco*) rather than the expensive *azzurro ultramarino* on the flat ground of the frame. On the other hand the gold for the gilding of the frame, which he later agreed to undertake, was found for him, as it was too costly for a craftsman like himself to purchase.[1] In Mantua by contrast the Gonzaga bought his colours and gold, which they obtained from Venice. On 4 March 1470 for instance Giovanni de Striggi sent from Venice 52 ducats' worth bought so that 'Andrea Mantegna may not stand idle'.[2] The fuss that Mantegna made in 1471 about the quality of some azure that was to be used for painting carved woodwork at Gonzaga indicates that even for purely decorative work he was not eager to abate his standards of excellence of finish.[3]

By 1493 the Marchese Francesco Gonzaga had so much work in hand for his painters that he took a colourman into his service. On 2 September of that year Antonio Salimbene sent by boat from Venice 'the master who makes *azzurro ultramarino* and other perfect colours', and 'by his hand I send the colours requested by Andrea Mantegna, as contained in the enclosed list.'[4] Late in 1496 the monastery of Santa

Maria in Organo in Verona bought two ounces of *azzurro ultramarino* and two ducats' worth of *oro macinato* (powdered gold) for Mantegna to use in painting their altarpiece.[5] Technical examination has shown that the colours of the *Parnassus* and of *Pallas expelling the Vices* are of the finest quality, though in passages Mantegna economized with the expensive blue: in the *Pallas* the sky is of azurite and the blue of a robe is put on in two layers, of which the lower is the cheaper azurite, while the layer above is of *azzurro ultramarino*, whose basis is *lapis lazuli*, and is laid on more thinly.[6] This already seems to have been his practice in 1471, for the better blue he wanted in that year was to be used for laying over the less good blue which had already been bought in Venice.

Generally Mantegna painted in tempera, a preference that had become old-fashioned by 1505, when Isabella d'Este expressed her disappointment that Perugino had used tempera in his painting for her Studiolo because tempera was the medium used by Mantegna. Oil, she thought, was Perugino's medium and would have been more delightful, no doubt as the softer and more fusing medium.[7] Nevertheless, there are references as early as 1471 to Mantegna's use of oil. Indeed as we have seen, he was an artist keenly interested in techniques, and it is perhaps significant that the oil he needed in 1471 was for his work in the Camera Picta, where his use of an exceptional and experimental technique has already been discussed. It is mentioned in an order of 5 October 1471 from the Marchese Lodovico to his factor telling him to let Mantegna have '3 *pesi* (weights) of oil of nuts to work on that *camera* of ours'.[8] Mantegna also used the mixed techniques so characteristic of his century: in the *Pallas* the blues are mixed with a little oil of nuts, no doubt to prevent their alteration, but over some of them a layer of egg tempera has been laid to modify the effect.

In general his earlier pictures are painted on panel, but that this was not his invariable practice appears from the votive *Presentation*, which is on canvas, perhaps because it was painted in Venice. Moreover in 1458 the Marchese Lodovico sent him by the hand of Giovanni da Padova three canvases on which he was to execute 'certain designs', though in the event Mantegna failed to paint them. Nevertheless his smaller paintings executed for the Mantuan court in the 1460s still usually seem to have been on panel: on 28 June 1468 he speaks in a letter to Lodovico of receiving the panel on which he has just begun the 'history of Limbo'. But in 1477 he announced to Lodovico that before beginning two portraits he waits for instructions as to whether he is to paint them on small panels or small canvases.[9] After this date there is no further reference to panels. Already in 1469 the altarpiece of San Bernardino for his chapel in San Francesco was painted on canvas, and Mantegna seems to have come to prefer it as a medium, probably for some such reasons as his son Francesco gave for preferring canvas to fresco in 1491. The execution was quicker, he said, the work appeared more beautiful and the canvas itself lasted longer. And as Eastlake points out, the advantage of tempera in painting on cloth is that when delicate modelling is required too rapid drying can be prevented by wetting the back of the canvas. To Mantegna's obsessively perfectionist temperament the appeal of this is obvious. Mantegna seems to have been the first artist to use the texture of the canvas to suggest the texture of drapery by painting thinly over it, though thin painting was in any case necessary in tempera, as the size colours tend to crack if used thickly, unless a layer of oil is applied above.[10] At other times, as in the *Pallas*, where great smoothness of finish was sought, he laid down a ground of thin gesso.

From Calandra's account of his inspection of the *Comus* we can see that Mantegna sometimes sketched the rough outlines of a composition on to his canvas, and then worked up the drawing of individual figures. More usually, perhaps, he followed customary practice and transferred a finished drawing to canvas. The contours of the preliminary underdrawing were strongly outlined in black, so accentuating the sculptural bias of the forms and aiding in that sharp definition, or *nettezza*, so greatly admired in Mantegna by Isabella d'Este.[11] In the *Madonna della Vittoria* and in the two pictures for the Studiolo the under-modelling of the flesh is boldly laid in; by contrast Francesco's armour in the *Madonna* is very fully and smoothly painted. In Mantegna's calculation of the final effect of his pic-

tures the use of varnish played an important part from at least as early as the 1460s and probably well before. Varnish no doubt attracted him for the luminous glow it gives to colours and for its smooth harmonization of the overall surface of a picture. Its transparent lustre, moreover, adding as it were a lucent aerial depth to the painter's simulated depth, surely possessed strong additional charm for Mantegna. He added his varnish at the very last stage of all, so it seems, apparently even after the picture's frame had been gilded, for in April 1464 he wrote to Lodovico: 'it does not seem right to me to varnish the pictures (*tavole*) yet, because their frames are not yet gilded . . . but whenever it please Your Excellency, the work on them can be finished in a few days.'[12] On 16 December 1484 Francesco Gonzaga admonished him to order the varnish he needed for the picture he was painting for Eleonora d'Aragona, Duchess of Ferrara, in good time from Venice, so as to have it ready for Christmas. Early in July 1497 Lorenzo da Pavia sent Isabella d'Este from Venice 'an *ampolla* (cruse) of marvellous varnish' for a painting which was probably the *Parnassus*: it was not enough and on 14 July he was asked to send twice as much again. Another request was made for varnish on 13 July 1502, this time for the *Pallas*.[13]

Yet in using a varnish on canvas Mantegna rather surprised some of his professional contemporaries. Antonio Galeazzo Bentivoglio, writing from Bologna to Isabella on 1 December 1501 about a painting Lorenzo Costa was to execute for the Studiolo and which was to be set next to one of Mantegna's paintings, questioned her on this very point. 'Messer Andrea's picture seemed to me to have a lustre, or else to be varnished, which he [Costa] marvelled at as it is on canvas. It is needful that Your Excellency advise me if Messer Andrea's work is lustred, and with what lustre, or else whether it is varnished or not.' Three years later Isabella explained to him that Mantegna's pictures 'are not coloured in oil, but just in tempera and then varnished over after all the figures have been finished.' Almost a century later Lomazzo remarks: 'I have had two paintings, one by Mantegna, the other by Bramante, so coloured that above them was spread a certain viscous liquid.'[14] Traces of a thin varnish still remain in the landscape under the rock in the *Parnassus*, with blue overpainted, suggesting that Mantegna in fact built up his effects with a complex technique of layers of paint and glazing, then completing them with a lustrous surface of varnish.

From Mantegna's techniques in painting it is natural to turn to his drawings.[15] Mantegna's drawings offer problems that perhaps would not exist if more of them survived. He was an admired designer; after his death Lorenzo di Pavia called him 'the most beautiful inventor there ever was' and many of his drawings must have been worn out from sheer use in the sixteenth century. The earliest drawings related to his works are a celebrated crux of connoisseurship; they are executed in a rough, sketchy style in which the figures are swiftly modelled by vibrant line and bold hatching so as to acquire three-dimensional form, but without the sharp exactitude of definition and classical line of the later drawings. Because of this they have also been attributed to Giovanni Bellini. Drawings in this style survive for the Ovetari fresco of *St James on the way to Execution* of *c*.1451, for the San Zeno altarpiece of *c*.1456–9, and for a lost *Flagellation*, presumably painted in the early 1460s for the chapel of the Castello di San Giorgio (Plates 205, 206, 209a and b). But two other drawings for the *Circumcision* and the *Ascension* (Plates 212 and 213), also executed for the chapel, are in a completely different style. These are *modelli* drawn on blue-green paper, with every line and fold of the features and drapery indicated with sharp precision, exactly corresponding to the finished work, with the fall of the light as it will be in the painting indicated by white heightening. The two groups could be reconciled on the assumption that the first group are simply first sketches, in which the whole or parts of composition were set down rapidly as Mantegna began or adjusted his scheme. Certainly the second group represent final drawings made in preparation for the translation of a figure or figures into paint. They are a confirmation therefore of the care with which Mantegna prepared the paintings for the chapel of the Castello, deploying every resource of his art with concentrated richness to compensate for the small format of the single panels.

After *c*.1464 no drawings survive in the sketchy style, perhaps because Mantegna now made a regular practice of producing highly finished *modelli*, and it was these that were sought after by his pupils and other artists. Certainly the other early drawing, a *Hercules and Antaeus* in Florence (Plate 211), which is a *modello* for the monochrome of this subject painted in the Camera Picta *c*.1465–9, is a carefully finished drawing executed in brown watercolour with white highlighting on paper tinted in brown wash to obtain something approaching the effect of the final monochrome. Here again the figures are fully and precisely detailed and carefully modelled. The white highlighting indicates the fall of the light in the finished work, and outlining in shadow deepens the effect of relief and of spatial depth. Even the rocky setting is painstakingly described. The evolution of Mantegna's designs from putative first sketches to those carefully elaborated final designs, in which nothing is left for the invention in the ultimate stage of execution on wall, panel, or canvas, explains the slowness which at times so exasperated the Gonzaga.

No securely dated drawings survive from the 1470s. Perhaps from the 1480s is the study in the British Museum of a naked young man, covered only with a shroud, raising himself up from a stone slab (Plate 215). Stylistically, though not thematically, this belongs to the same period as the *Dead Christ* in the Brera. The drawing is a sketch rather than a finished design. From the 1490s and early 1500s, on the other hand, there survives quite a number of drawings that are highly elaborate and carefully finished. The earliest of these, the Florence *Judith* (Fig. 15), signed and dated February 1491 in an inscription composed of ingeniously patterned and flourished letters, introduces us to the question of Mantegna's presentation drawings. Although Renaissance drawings have been so eagerly collected and studied since the nineteenth century, this esteem was not theirs in earlier days. Drawings by quattrocento artists were not usually produced with an eye to their sale to collectors. Yet then as now the power of invention was a precious faculty, separating the masters who possessed it from less gifted compeers and the world of humbler craftsmen, who often depended on the pictorial inventions of others. Drawings were therefore a valuable stock in trade both for masters who were capable of invention and for those who were not. We have seen that the reputation of Squarcione's school was partly founded on his collection of drawings, which all the evidence suggests were by other hands. There must in fact have been quite a brisk circulation of drawings by or after masters of reputation among artists, as well as of the drawings of antiquities to which so much reference has already been made: borrowing, theft, surreptitious and legitimate copying were no doubt used to obtain them as well as outright purchase.

At the same time there also existed, at any rate in the Veneto, a tradition among art-loving dilettanti of collecting drawings by artists. As early as 1335 we find Oliviero Forzetta of Treviso making a note to remind himself that when he went to Venice he must try to buy certain books of drawings there, largely it would seem from painters or their heirs. Although Felice Feliciano, as a scribe, might almost be considered a professional artist, in many respects he was a dilettante, and he too makes mention in a will of 1466 of his collection of drawings by 'several excellent masters' along with his collection of coins and medals.[16] He had probably been able to put these drawings together because of his friendships with artists, Giovanni Bellini and Marco Zoppo as well as Mantegna. It is this tradition of collecting drawings in the Veneto that must explain, at least in part, why Mantegna came to make highly finished drawings for presentation to his friends or for sale to patrons. Perhaps a contributory reason is to be found in the popularity of highly finished portrait drawings, which were often needed urgently for matrimonial and diplomatic negotiations to which their portability made them eminently suitable. Already in July 1477 we find Mantegna enquiring of Lodovico whether he is to make some portraits the Marchese wanted in a hurry 'simply as drawings'. And we have just seen that by the 1460s, if not earlier, he was making drawings which are so close to the finished work that almost the only absent feature is colour. It is easy to understand that the step from these to drawings which were finished works of art in themselves was not a great one.

The great size of the Uffizi *Judith* is one indication that it was intended to be viewed as a *quadretto*, but Mantegna leaves us in no ambiguity as to its nature by his use of various devices to suggest the three-dimension spatial effects proper to a finished work rather than to a drawing. Judith stands to the right in the front plane, at an angle and in a pose that show her figure half-turned and largely from the rear, with only her left hand and her head shown to the spectator, both in profile to the left and in harmonious alignment with each other. This use of the back view to excite the spectator's curiosity and suggest dramatic verisimilitude dates back, it will be remembered, to the Ovetari frescoes of Mantegna's youth. Here it is contrived to emphasize the figure of Judith and still more her action. The maid too is shown at an angle, stooping in the middle ground to hold the bag; this gives a deeper recession to the composition and allows Mantegna an additional effect, for while we see the maid in nearly full profile, she attends only to her mistress's bidding. These compositional means of suggesting two figures in a dialogue of action in three-dimensional space are enhanced by technical devices. Both figures are bordered on the right by a band of darker brown wash suggesting an indefiniteness of shadowed space around them, while the right side of the maid's face and the right side of Judith's left arm and the edges of some other contours are heavily outlined for accentuation of definition and relief. Both these devices must have been used more than once in his later years by Mantegna. They appear in the engraving of the *Madonna and Child*, which plainly reproduces another highly finished drawing. In other engravings after late drawings, such as the *Risen Christ with St Andrew and St Longinus*, the *Bacchanals*, the *Battle of the Sea-Gods* and the *Triumphs*, the dark band is extended to form a more or less continuous background, in some cases forming a penumbra, in others an almost full ground of shadow, or of hatching, but everywhere manipulated with great freedom. Thus at times it is skilfully intermitted or darkened or lightened to enhance or relieve the figures and other motifs. Always, however, its primary intention is to suggest three-dimensional space and so prevent these late compositions from becoming too much like friezes of relief sculpture.

The figure of Judith is yet another of Mantegna's inimitable transfusions of a strong action into a statuesque pose. Tall and slender, a type of heroic beauty, she stands still clenching her sword in her right hand, disdainfully depositing the head of Holofernes into a bag held out by her maid, and bidding her take it. Her weight rests on her left foot, while her right foot is half raised, so communicating a tension as a desinence to the serpentine curve of her body, whose pronounced thrust to the left gives an unusually mannered exaggeration to this classical line of construction. Mantegna has set off the calm dignity of her figure by the restless curves of the ends of her bandeau, as they twist on themselves again and again in their decoratively crumpled fall. This stylistic mannerism of a crumpling scroll used to off-set the repose of figure and other drapery is first surely dated in this drawing: it reappears constantly as a decorative convention in Mantegna's late works and presumably derives from antique gems. The dramatic tableau is completed by the contrasting and subordinate figure of the maid Abra, who is figured as a coarse, thick-lipped Moorish servant-girl, wearing a Moorish head-dress and double-earring, her cloak wound rudely, apron-fashion, round her waist, her hood fallen on to her shoulders, her stockings all wrinkled, as she stoops to obey her mistress.

The drawing is executed with pen and brush, in brown wash, with some highlighting in white on the left sleeve and left shoulder. It is difficult to be certain whether it is the drawing of *Judith* which Vasari owned and with which it is often identified. This was on a half folio sheet, and was 'done in a chiaroscuro not now in use, for he has left the white of the sheet to serve for the heightening of the white lead so sharply, that the wantoning hairs and other subtleties are seen as clearly as if they had been done very carefully with the brush. Hence this sheet may be called rather a coloured work than a drawing on paper.' Vasari's words imply that his drawing was in a wash where the highlighting was obtained by leaving parts of the paper uncoloured, which is certainly not true of the *Judith*. The same decorative lettering as on the Uffizi *Judith* is also found in engravings after a design by Mantegna of *Hercules and Antaeus*, which suggests that the original of these was perhaps a presentation drawing of more or less the same date.

Two at least of Mantegna's surviving late drawings are quite elaborately coloured, though in neither is the colouring fully finished. The surviving upper half of the drawing *Virtus combusta et deserta* (Plate 222) has a background coloured black over red: the figures are the colour of the ground proper,

Fig. 15. *Judith*. Drawing. Florence, Uffizi (Cat. no. 188)

brown heightened with white, while the rubies in the crown of Ignorance, the fire on the right and the scarf of the blindfolded woman are coloured red. In the allegorical drawing of a hero seated between two naked goddesses or nymphs (Plate 223), the body of the hero is shaded in crimson, and the goddess to the right in blue. It is impossible now to say whether this was in trial for a picture, or whether these drawings were to be coloured works in their own right.

Drawings also survive to show that Mantegna continued to make highly finished *modelli*. They are either copies of Mantegna's *modelli* or perhaps more dubiously his *modelli* themselves: they have one extension in a number of engravings which record lost drawings. Thus the evolution of the *Triumphs* is partly documented by seven drawings, all, with one possible exception, copies rather than originals, and by three engravings after compositions recorded in three of these drawings. These ten versions are related to six canvases only, Canvas I, Canvas III, Canvas V, Canvas VI, Canvas VII, Canvas IX and the composition of the 'Senators'. Students have been puzzled by this apparently random choice, but it either reflects the availability of copies of compositions that became celebrated as soon as they were painted, or else that other factor so often forgotten, loss. What survives in the museums and collections of the world of the drawings and engravings of the quattrocento is the merest fraction of what was produced. A complete enough series of copies of Mantegna's *Triumphs*, whether drawings or engravings, was available in France by *c.*1502–10 for them to be copied in sculptured reliefs on a courtyard wall of the Château of Gaillon, while seven at least of the compositions were known to Jacopo da Strasbourg, who published a set of woodcuts of the *Triumphs of Caesar* at Venice in 1503. In 1504 the miniaturist, painter, designer and publisher Benedetto Bordone (*c.*1450–1530) of Padua, father of Mantegna's eulogist Scaliger, issued at Venice a *Triumpho di Cesaro*, now lost, which was probably derived from Mantegna's designs.

The *Triumphs* were conceived as a continuous procession passing over a number of canvases separated by pilasters behind which it is imagined as continuing to emerge on the other side. Such a conception must have required the whole sequence of compositions to be invented in some detail and worked out in drawings so that the distribution of the various features of the procession could be arranged and their effect gauged not only within each single composition, but in relation to the adjoining canvases and also within the groups into which they are divided. Their assemblage of processing figures and of a rich and complex variety of objects demanded careful patterning so as to main-

tain lucidity, balance and rhythm. Martindale has pointed out that some such set of drawings must have existed in Mantegna's studio, given the close correspondence in dimensions of all the drawings and engravings. The existence of such a set can also be argued for yet another reason. None of the drawings or engravings reproduces Mantegna's first inspirations or studies: what they record are the elaborate and detailed drawings which it was Mantegna's practice to make during the later stages of his designs. On any other assumption it is impossible to explain their careful and finished detail of inscription and ornament. Not all of them, however, represent the same moment in the evolution of the final composition. In the case of the Rothschild drawing for Canvas I, the only drawing related to the *Triumphs* with claims to be by Mantegna's own hand, we are perhaps confronted with an intermediate stage in that final evolution. In the Vienna drawing for Canvas III and the Chantilly drawing for Canvas VII, we may even see a first stage, for important changes were later made in the arrangement and balance of the motifs in Canvas III and in the individual figures of Canvas VII, especially in the right half. The changes in the drawings for Canvases III, V and VI affect only a single figure, or else details such as the omission of heads and modifications in the nature and the arrangement of the trophies.

The changes recorded in the actual canvases were not necessarily all made at the same time: very probably too the infinitely painstaking Mantegna made for some or indeed all of the single compositions other drawings in which they attained their final form. The complexity of the *Triumphs*, the vicissitudes of the scheme and its protraction over at least seven years sufficiently explain the differences between these drawings and engravings and the canvases as executed. Mantegna's designs for single compositions were sometimes developed in *modelli* of individual groups and figures. This is what appears to have happened in the case of the *Parnassus*, where two engravings record drawings of two groups of four of the dancing Muses, again representing a late stage in the evolution of the design, while two drawings are *modelli* for two of the Muses as painted. Martindale rightly points out that the absence of significant *pentimenti* in the canvases of the *Triumphs* is virtual proof of the existence of designs brought to a last finality of conception and realization.

Of another kind of drawing by Mantegna we have only a notice in Lomazzo's *Idea del tempio della pittura*, published in 1590. Lomazzo records that 'Andrea Mantegna made some drawings in perspective, in which he has delineated the figures posed as they appeared to his eye. Of these I have seen some by his own hand, with his notes in writing, in the hands of Andrea Gallarato, a great imitator of this art.' These seem to have been drawings made to try out perspective effects, rather than notes for a formal treatise on perspective, as is sometimes surmised. It is perhaps not too fanciful to link them with such paintings as the Brera *Dead Christ*, for which drawings of the figure posed as it 'appeared to his eye' were certainly made by Mantegna. If this interpretation of Lomazzo is correct, it does away with any aspiration in Mantegna to compose a treatise on perspective or on his art, such as were written by Piero della Francesca and by Leonardo.[17] Yet unlike many artists he could write fluently, for if Bettinelli was correct in attributing to him a sonnet which he found in the Archivio Gonzaga then Mantegna could turn a set of Petrarchan verses to a mistress when he wished, like any other polished courtier of the age.[18]

XV

The Engravings

MANTEGNA'S engravings are intimately linked with his drawings. Simone Fornari says in 1550 that 'the art of engraving on copper impressions of figures was his invention.' Also in 1550, seemingly independently, Vasari records that 'he bequeathed to the art of painting . . . the method of engraving on copper the shapes of figures, truly a most singular convenience, by which the world has been able to see . . . the Bacchanal, the Battle of the Sea-Monsters, the Deposition from the Cross, the Entombment of Christ, the Resurrection with Longinus and with St Andrew, works of this Mantegna . . .' In 1568, however, he corrected this passage, no longer attributing the invention of engraving to Mantegna, but simply saying that 'he took delight in making engravings on copper' and adding to the list of his engravings that 'among other things he did the *Triumphs* and in those days they were reckoned something, because nothing better had been seen.' The addition of the *Triumphs* was presumably due to the fact that in the interval between his two editions Vasari had seen Campagnola's letter to Leonico about art in Padua. In his life of Marc' Antonio, he says of Baccio Baldini, the Florentine goldsmith and engraver, that 'not having much gift for drawing, all he did was from the invention and design of Sandro Botticelli. This came to the knowledge of Andrea Mantegna in Rome and was the cause of his beginning to engrave many of his own works.'[1] In 1560 Scardeone, who also used Campagnola, writes: 'he painted [sic] small brazen pictures, engraved with shapes so as to make the Roman triumphs, and the feasts of Bacchus and the sea gods. Also the deposition of Christ from the cross, and his entombment in the sepulchre, and very many other things. Now these pictures are all held in the highest estimation,

and only a few have them: we however have nine of them in our house, all different.' Cellini comments tartly in the 1560s: 'Before [Dürer] Andrea Mantegna, a great Italian painter, had made engravings but did not succeed . . .'. On the other hand Lomazzo in 1590 found Mantegna's engravings admirable:

> He was no less great in representing the affections . . . in the Tritons that go through the sea, he has feigned them with shells in their mouths and blowing into them with such force of art that the great effort they make in blowing cannot be shown in more lively fashion with the swelling of the jaws and the littleness of the eyes. He has done likewise in his Bacchanals and in the satyrs blowing into their pipes.[2]

The first known mention of engraving in connection with Mantegna during his lifetime dates from a famous episode in 1475. On 15 September of that year Simone Ardizzoni of Reggio, who describes himself as a '*pictore e taliatore di bolino*' (painter and engraver with the burin), sent in a petition of complaint to the Marchese Lodovico about the treatment he had met with in Mantua.

> When I came to Mantua, Andrea Mantegna made me many offers, making show of being my friend. Now I have been a friend for a very long time of Zoan Andrea, painter in Mantua, and when in conversing with him he told me that he had been robbed of his engraved plates, drawings and medals, it moved me to compassion that he should be so badly treated and I told him I would remake the said engraved plates for him and I worked for him for about four months. When that devil Andrea Mantegna learnt that I was remaking the

Fig. 16. *The Virgin of Humility*. Engraving. Vienna, Albertina (Cat. no. 207)

said plates he sent to threaten me by means of a Florentine, swearing he would pay me for it. And in addition to this, Zoan Andrea and I were assaulted one evening by the nephew of Carlo de Moltone and over ten armed men so as to kill us, and I can give proof of this. And again Andrea Mantegna to prevent the said work from continuing has found certain knaves who to serve him have accused me of sodomy to the *Maleficio*, and he who has accused me is called Zoano Luca de Novara. The notary who has the accusation is kin to Carlo Moltone. Being a stranger perforce I had to flee and at present I am in Verona so as to finish the said plates.

In order to maintain his honour he demanded the arrest of his accuser:

you will see then if ever I did such evil knavery and you will discover who it is who had me accused. Wherefore, my lord, I pray your lordship to make such demonstration of justice that neither I nor my kin may be tempted to take vengeance on him for I believe I have been in about forty cities without ever a word said in despite of my good name, save now at last from Andrea Mantegna with his pride and dominion over Mantua and if your lordship does not restrain him, great scandals will come about on his account.[3]

Lodovico determined to inquire into the affair and on 20 September he gave Simone a safe-conduct for fifteen days, so that he could come to Mantua and state his grievance. Presumably Simone did not come at once, for on 6 October the safe-conduct was extended for a further fifteen days. Meanwhile on 1 October Lodovico ordered Niccolò Cattabeno 'to see about having a word with Zoan Andrea, the painter who had that difference formerly with Andrea Mantegna, and tell him to find that man from Reggio he knows of, the one who was accused of sodomy and tell him to come and see us next Thursday at Borgoforte and neither you nor he are to say anything about it.' On 3 October Cattabeno replied that Zoan Andrea had promised that Simone would present himself without fail at Borgoforte on the day named. No more is known of what transpired: plainly Lodovico sought to keep matters as quiet as possible.[4]

It is possible to contribute some new facts to this story. First Simone does not seem to have returned to work in Mantua, for in 1476 he is found in Reggio, his birthplace, claiming a final payment from the Anziani for a painting of the ducal arms of the Este which he had executed on the façade of the Palazzo del Comune.[5] The painter Zoan Andrea was surely the Zohanne Andrea, son of the late Maestro Billano de' Bugatti, and 'our beloved citizen and painter' whom Lodovico recommended to the magistrates of Vicenza on 29 March 1469, in order to obtain expeditious justice for his lawsuits so that 'he may return quickly to our service.' Zoan Andrea was evidently unsatisfactory, for on 28 April 1471 Lodovico wrote to one of his officers that he was to pay Zoan Andrea his demand, telling Andrea Mantegna of the business, 'and then the quicker he is allowed to take himself off the better it will be.' Clearly there had been some dispute between Zoan Andrea and Mantegna, perhaps even the 'difference' of which Lodovico spoke in 1475. The identification seems certain, for Simone's Zoan Andrea was from Mantua and Lodovico speaks of his Zoan Andrea in 1469 as '*il nostro citadino*'. During these years Zanetto Bugatti was a court painter to the Sforza of Milan: quite possibly Zoan Andrea was a member of the same family.[6]

Simone, if not the son, was certainly a relation of the goldsmith Gaspare Ardizzoni of Reggio, who is recorded in the city archives in 1444.[7] The connection is of interest, given the intimate association between the art of engraving and that of the goldsmith. Indeed engraving was originally a goldsmith's technique and the art of engraving prints seems to have begun in goldsmiths' shops. He must be the same as the Simone da Lolio whom Malaguzzi-Valeri records as a different artist, since the only document to which he refers for this Simone da Lolio concerns the same ducal coat of arms painted in 1476 on the Palazzo del Comune.[8] As a vast superstructure of attributions to Simone and to Zoan Andrea of engravings after Mantegna has been raised on these documents of 1475, it is as well to be quite clear about what they tell us. First they make it more than plain that Simone made no engravings after Mantegna, though we may deduce that he was invited to do so. Instead he made engravings after Zoan Andrea, who was perhaps not able to make them himself, since he employed Simone for at least four or five months to re-engrave the plates of which he had been robbed. All that is certain about the stolen plates is that they were his property, like those re-engraved for him by Simone, and they may well have been made for him by some such an engraver as Simone. Whether it is prudent therefore to identify the Mantuan Zoan Andrea with the engraver Zoan Andrea who subsequently engraved some of Mantegna's designs must be strongly open to doubt.

The causes of the quarrel between Mantegna and Zoan Andrea must also remain open to doubt. Plainly Zoan Andrea was sufficiently in the wrong in 1471 for Lodovico to dismiss him; moreover as a painter in Lodovico's employ he was under Mantegna's general superintendence. There may be a hint in Simone's petition that Mantegna was responsible for the theft of Zoan Andrea's engravings, drawings and medals, but it is no more than a hint, and had there been grounds strong enough to sustain an open accusation, it would surely have been made by the angry and threatening Simone. Kristeller suggested that Zoan Andrea had come by some of Mantegna's designs and was seeking to pirate them, and that for this reason Mantegna had Simone driven from Mantua, but this seems to be a gratuitous attempt to palliate Mantegna's conduct.[9] Simone's statements cannot be taken at their face value, but what can legitimately be deduced from them is that Mantegna was anxious to recruit him to engrave his own designs and that he was furious when an enemy succeeded in capturing his services. We can perhaps conclude too from all the fuss that engravers were not common birds in places like Mantua. Reggio in the fifteenth century was a very provincial centre in matters of art, and Simone seems to have been no more than a modest craftsman, executing decorative paintings like most of his fellow painters in the city. Only his experience of engraving on copper can have made him a desirable acquisition to Mantegna's studio.

One of the keys to the history of engraving is the ordinary divorce between the artist who makes the design and the engraver who reproduces it. The rise of the art of copper-plate engraving must be connected with the discovery by artists that their drawings could be reproduced and sold to a wider clientele, if not for as much as a painting, then certainly for enough money to make it worth their while to have their drawings engraved. It cannot be emphasized too strongly that at this date there was no question of engraving after completed paintings or even, so it would seem, from drawings made from completed paintings. Thus the engravings after *The Triumphs of Caesar* reproduce Mantegna's drawings for the series, not the finished canvases. Drawings for paintings that had already been executed could be used in this way, allowing artists to put their accumulated stock of designs to profitable use. Mantegna certainly kept even early drawings till the end of his life: thus his pupil Francesco Bonsignori copied the composition of Mantegna's lunette fresco of *Sant'Antonio and San Bernardino* on the Santo in Padua for a lunette-shaped parapet on a pulpit in San Francesco, Mantua (Brera), which shows St Louis of Toulouse and San Bernardino kneeling to either side of a medallion of the Holy Name. Naturally inventive artists, like Botticelli and Mantegna, could also make new drawings in a fraction of the time required to make a painting. Botticelli seems to have sold many of his designs to the goldsmith Baldini, but other, more provident artists preferred to pay an engraver to make engraved plates which they kept as their own property. To engrave copper plates is a laborious task, demanding in time as well as on the eyesight, and Mantegna, busied on tasks for the Gonzaga, may have been anxious to spare himself such labours. A court painter of great reputation, as often as not busy with court commissions, could in this way meet the demand for his designs without breaking his understanding with his lords. The making of engravings, then, at least in Mantegna's case, must have been linked in some ways with the collecting of drawings by artists and craftsmen, and in others with the wish among his patrons to possess images by so excellent a hand.

In 1475 Mantegna was anxious to recruit an engraver to reproduce his designs, and the question therefore arises, when did he begin to make engravings himself? According to Vasari, as we have seen, he began during his sojourn in Rome from the summer of 1488 until the autumn of 1490. Curiously enough the only other strictly contemporary documents concerning Mantegna and his engravings lend some support to this statement.[10] In November 1491 Andrea presented the Marchese Francesco with a '*quadretino*' (little picture), which from subsequent documents it transpires was an engraving. Francesco decided to make a present of it to someone in Milan, presumably a personage about the Sforza court, and by 6 December it had been safely packed up in a case with a ring for suspension so that the courier would not damage it in transit. On 21 December Mantegna wrote to Francesco that having heard the Marchese had given it away, he was sending him another: 'however there still remain with me the plates to make others of them, by the grace of the glorious Virgin Mary from whom I have ever obtained many more graces than I have ever deserved.' Mantegna was pressing Francesco at just this moment to fulfil his promise of the grant of land at Borgoforte, which he finally received in February 1492, and this overwhelming preoccupation largely fills the two letters in which he mentions these two gifts of his engraving. Clearly then the 'little picture' was something in which he took enough pride to present it to his lord and which also was fine enough for Francesco, child of an age that set great store by fine presents, to look on it as a fitting gift for him to make to another great lord. The documents do not unequivocally prove that it was an engraving by Mantegna's own hand, since the plates of which he speaks could perfectly well have been engraved by an engraver in his service. But they do suggest there was something unusually excellent about the engraving, and that therefore it may have been from Mantegna's own hand.

Engravings after designs by Mantegna fall into three classes, those after his drawings, but executed by an engraver working under his superintendence, those that were engraved as well as designed by him, and those that are after his drawings, but executed by engravers not under his control.[11] It is obvious that the date of engraving is not necessarily an indication of the date of the drawing, and that Mantegna may have had engraved or himself engraved drawings he had made ten or fifteen years before, or even more. This is the case with the engravings of *The Flagellation* (Plate 233), *The Descent into Limbo* (Plate 236a), *The Descent from the Cross* (Plate 234) and *The Entombment with three birds* (Plate 235b) and the unfinished engraving of *The Adoration of the Magi* (Plate 237), where the original drawings in all probability are designs executed in the early 1460s for the *cappella* of the Castello di San Giorgio or some other Gonzaga chapel. Mantegna's practice of making highly finished sketches for his compositions must have been one of the reasons that prompted him to have them engraved, since such drawings were ready for reproduction on an engraved plate. It is an interesting fact that this series of engravings is attributed now, not to Mantegna himself, but to engravers working from his designs. As a group they correspond therefore to the state of things when Mantegna was looking out for an engraver to reproduce his drawings. He is known to have been anxious to recruit Simone in 1475, but may of course have recruited other engravers at other times. An examination of the watermarks on their paper, if this ever becomes possible, may settle finally the question of the date of these engravings. But they seem to be earlier than the other engravings after or by Mantegna. The *Adoration*, by a particularly gifted engraver, is unfinished as is the *Flagellation*: it is an open question whether the plates themselves were ever completed, or whether Mantegna's drawings were simply reproduced as they were found, to serve as inventions for use by other artists.

The seven engravings attributed to Mantegna himself are *The Entombment* (Plates 227a and b), *The Virgin of Humility* (Fig. 16), *The Risen Christ between St Andrew and St Longinus* (Plates 228a and b), the two *Bacchanals* (Plates 229 and 231) and the two *Battles of the Sea-Gods* (Plates 230 and 232). They are a battleground of conflicting datings. In part the conflict arises because of the uncertainty that surrounds the early history of engraving in Italy, for there is no doubt that in its origins it was an art largely practised by humble artists and craftsmen like Simone degli Ardizzoni, whose activities are naturally far less well documented than those of major painters and sculptors. After Antonio del Pollaiuolo Mantegna seems to have been the first great artist to use the technique himself, and there has been much argument as to whether he learnt it by copying the Florentines or even during his visit of 1466 to Florence itself. A Florentine was evidently in his service or entourage in 1475, for he was sent to threaten Simone degli Ardizzoni. On the other hand we know nothing of the spread and practice of engraving outside Florence, and especially in Venice and Ferrara. Simone degli Ardizzoni after all claimed to have worked in some 'forty cities' of Italy. There are even disputes as to the exact technique Mantegna used. Investigation of these problems must be left to specialist historians of engraving, but it does seem that he was influenced by the Florentine 'broad manner', which is perhaps not surprising, given that Italian engraving, so far as we know, seems to have first become a craft in Florence. In general Mantegna uses for shading parallel hatching with 'return strokes', but in some passages, as J. L. Sheehan points out, this technique is varied by zig-zag lines, also used by Pollaiuolo, and short hook lines accenting the beginning of longer strokes. In larger areas of hatching the narrow ends of one set of lines emerge from the broader sections of another, giving an effect of lines with return strokes. On rare occasions, too, Mantegna makes use of cross-hatching.

The problems of Mantegna's engravings are compounded by the extreme rarity of early impressions of his prints: most of the impressions that survive were taken after the plates had lost their first freshness and in certain cases had been reworked. In my own opinion, the history of Mantegna's style as we know it from his paintings makes a date earlier than the mid-1480s difficult to sustain for six of the seven prints generally accepted as autograph. The one chronological crux is the *Entombment*. It has recently been asserted that this print must date from the 1460s, rather than from the 1490s, which has been the usual dating. The chief argument put forward is a stylistic one: Mantegna's forms in the *Entombment* are created by outlines and by areas of shading in which the lines are cut so close together that they assume almost the value of a tone. This is the method of early Florentine engravers and contrasts with the strong, incisive outlines and bolder hatching of Mantegna's later engravings. The lightly outlined, delicately modelled figures of the *Entombment* must then on this view precede the more powerfully outlined and plastic figures of the later engravings. There exists a drawing which is an early copy of the group of three Holy Women: if the attribution of this drawing to Marco Zoppo, Mantegna's old friend, advanced by some authorities, is accepted, then it must date from before his death in 1478. It is not so clear that it consequently dates the engraving to the earlier 1470s or before, since Marco may have copied a drawing by Mantegna. It is also claimed that the St John reproduces the St John of the San Zeno *Crucifixion* in reverse, and that motifs from the engraving reappear in sculptures executed by Agostino dei Fonduli.[12] On the other hand the emphasis on movement, action and gesture in the poses of the figures, the free fluttering of the decoratively crumpled drapery, the violently rhythmic forms of the jagged rocks which form the right side of the tomb are all difficult to parallel in Mantegna's paintings before the 1490s. Comparison between the San Zeno St John and the St John of the engraving reveals close similarities, but also the contrast between a statically posed figure, whose draperies statically encase and model his body, and one whose draperies have a semi-autonomous life of their own. All in all it is best to regard the *Entombment*, the *Virgin of Humility* and the *Risen Christ*, all of which have features of the engraving style in common, as Mantegna's earliest engravings, executed in the late 1480s or early 1490s.

The beautiful *Virgin of Humility* is associable stylistically with the Brera *Dead Christ* and the *Madonnas* of the later 1480s and early 1490s. A point of reference for *The Risen Christ between St Andrew and St Longinus* is the fresco, now detached, of *St Andrew and St Longinus* from the façade of Sant'Andrea, which is dated 1488. The iconography of the engraving, linking a Risen Christ with two saints venerated in Sant'Andrea, shows that it must reproduce a design made in connection with the church. As the figures are posed on a platform in Mantegna's *di sotto in sù* perspective, which he uses for figures that were to be seen above the line of vision, it seems a fair conclusion that the engraving represents a rejected design for the façade. In the event separate frescoes in tondo form of the *Ascension* and *St Andrew and St Longinus* were painted on the pediment of the portico and its atrium. Since the date 1488 is painted below the fresco of the two saints, the drawing reproduced in the engraving must have been made in the 1480s, when work on the church was sufficiently advanced for the decoration of the façade to be considered.[13]

For the celebrated engravings of the *Bacchanals* and *The Battle of the Sea-Gods* there fortunately exists a *terminus ante quem* in the copies of the *Bacchanal with Silenus* and of the right half of the *Battle* made by Dürer, which were inscribed by him with the date 1494. Stylistically they cannot be much earlier and again both are by Mantegna himself. The engravings of *The Triumphs of Caesar*, even though they follow Mantegna's drawings and not the completed canvases, were surely executed in the 1490s, but in them the hand of subordinate engravers rather than Mantegna's own hand appears. This is also the case with other engravings whose designs date from the 1490s, the *Virtus deserta*, the *Risen Christ*, the engravings of *Hercules and Antaeus*, *Hercules and the Hydra* (Plates 238, 244, 247) and *Hercules and the Nemean Lion*, which reproduce presentation drawings of c.1492, the *Holy Family* (Plate 245), the engravings of two sets of four of the dancing muses

from the *Parnassus* (Plate 240), and the two engravings of *Silenus with children* (Plate 241). With some of these engravings we perhaps move out of Mantegna's own studio into the hands of pirate engravers copying prints made under Mantegna's auspices for their own benefit, or working from surreptitious copies of Mantegna's drawings. To sum up, then, the surviving evidence seems to support the tradition recorded by Vasari that much of Mantegna's own personal activity as an engraver falls around the time of his Roman sojourn, in the years from c.1485 to c.1493.

Some of these engravings of the 1490s, whether made by Mantegna himself or by engravers in his employ, seem to reproduce drawings made by Mantegna especially for engraving rather than studies for paintings. This is certainly the case with the *Bacchanals*, the *Battles of the Sea-Gods* and the *Virtus combusta et deserta* (Plates 239a and b). In the case of the *Virtus deserta*, as we have seen, the upper half of the original drawing still survives and proves it to have been a carefully finished and coloured design. These are all works in the bitter and contemptuous allegorical style most fully exemplified in the painting of *Pallas expelling the Vices* and corresponding to that mood of disillusioned and embittered frustration documented from 1489 onwards. The *Bacchanals* satirize intemperance, the *Battle* depicts the grotesque jousts excited by envy between two sets of marine deities. The *Virtus combusta et deserta* is a particularly sharp allegory of a world ruled by ignorance, lust, sloth, avarice and folly. The moral vision imaged in these works is deeply rooted in scorn of man's lower nature and in reverence for his higher or rational and intellectual nature and for the arts which are practised by the virtuous part of mankind. In the world as experienced by Mantegna, men of *virtù* have to endure at the hands of the ignorant and foolish all the consequences of the envy with which they are distracted. The pungent satire of human folly was a preoccupation of late fifteenth- and early sixteenth-century humanism: in 1494 for instance Sebastian Brandt published his *Stultifera Navis* (*Ship of Fools*), and in 1513 Erasmus his *Encomium Moriae* (*Praise of Folly*).

The two *Bacchanals* are generally regarded as pendants. The setting of the *Bacchanal with a wine vat* is a shallow platform of earth with depth of space indicated by the diagonal hatching of the ground which presumably renders the wash of the original drawing. As in a classical frieze the figures are distributed in two planes, but with Mantegna's usual elegant articulation of interval. They are posed as three sculptural groups, in a tripartite composition which avoids interrelationships between the groups, linking them instead by secondary figures set in the intervals. The first group on the left consists of a tall man wearing a goat-skin and bearing on his shoulders a man with satyr-like face holding a wreath of vines and grapes. Below, the youthful god Bacchus looks up with typically foreshortened head, and makes to take the wreath with his left hand, resting his right hand on an upturned cornucopia of vines and grapes. The motif of this group is the crowning of Bacchus, victor of man's senses, by a drunken follower. The two other groups illustrate the effects of wine in scenes of drunken revelry and stupor. In the centre is a great wooden vat, set beneath a vine trained in Italian fashion along a tree. To the left of it a satyr holding a jug and bowl walks towards the vine. Overcome by wine and sleep, a youth, his cloak wound in disorderly fashion about his middle, leans back over the vat, held in his fall by another satyr. On the ground before the vat a bowl to the left and a jug to the right explain why two putti slumber between them. On the right wine pours from a pipe in the vat into the pool, in which stands a satyr drinking greedily from a bowl and pulling down a horn which his companion satyr, seated on the vat, is blowing in order to fill the bowl again. The seated satyr holds the spike with which he has opened the vat: perhaps he is blowing his horn in signal to revellers. Both satyrs wear armlets set with little bells whose jingle is intended to enhance the raucous jollity of their music and dance.

In the *Bacchanal with Silenus* the background is a rough vine hedge, with on the left a sedgy pool rather like that of *Pallas expelling the Vices*. Once again the composition is tripartite, but here the division into three is imposed on a processional movement. The subject is a rustic triumph, that of Silenus, the old and drunken tutor of Bacchus. The procession opens with two musicians, one holding the syrinx of Pan, the deity on whom the satyrs attend, the other dancing in the *tripudium* of the ancients and playing the double tibia. The dancer looks back at Silenus, who is carried on a goat-skin by a satyr and two Fauns. He places a wreath of grapes and vine-leaves on his own head with one hand, drunkenly allowing wine to fall to the ground from the jug he holds in the other. Behind, a man, unable to move his limbs from drunkenness, is borne on the shoulders of another. Both of them have just emerged from the pool and turn to watch a gross, obese woman mounting a man's back using a tree-trunk in the water as a mounting-block. She is presumably the sloth that follows intemperance, and figures the fate of those who abandon themselves to Bacchus.

Mantegna was obviously inspired in these compositions by Bacchic sarcophagi, but the motifs these suggested, of satyrs, of Silenus being carried on a goat-skin, of the musical revelry and the double tibias, have been interwoven, as always, into inde-

pendent compositions. Indeed Bacchic sarcophagi had already been used to form a vocabulary of decoration in Renaissance book-illumination in the Veneto, but with lively freedom of invention.[14] In Mantegna's art, while losing nothing of their gracefulness, they are transmuted into a symbolic vocabulary, yet without slavish imitation of the antique. Similarly, the leaf-shaped hair and ears of the satyrs is taken from the antique. In these latest works as in Mantegna's earliest, antiquity is renewed as well as revived: its vestiges studied as a stimulus, not as a block to the artist's invention. The world of classical art, myth, literature was so intimately fused with Mantegna's imagination that its language to him becomes the vocabulary of fresh compositions in the antique style.

The completeness of this fusion, in which the artifice of classical allusion is melted into a neo-antique sensibility, belongs to a golden moment of humanism in the Veneto, of which the short poems and epigrams of the *Lusus* of Andrea Navagero (1483–1529) are perhaps the most perfect expression in poetry. Mantegna then enforces his lesson against intemperance in a visual language elegantly suggestive rather than explicit. Natale Conti, in his *Mythologia* of 1560, expresses in words what Mantegna's visual exhortations were intended to convey. Speaking of Silenus, he says:

> The ancients said of him that he was the companion of Bacchus, an old man, pot-bellied, and unsteady, because wine and drunkenness make men obese and pot-bellied. Then in general those two things make the head heavy, and make men unsteady and bring them more swiftly to old age. For this reason they feigned all these inconveniences and turpitudes of the body as the accompaniments of Bacchus. Some have thought the old man Silenus was a pupil of Bacchus because aged wines increase all the aforesaid turpitudes.[15]

The *Battle of the Sea-Gods* takes up the themes of envy and lust and gives them yet another allegorical expression. The invention is figured on two engravings, obviously intended to be placed together and read as a continuous composition. Mantegna has taken as his actors sea-deities, copying the two Tritons and the Nereids who ride on their backs from an antique source which has been plausibly identified as a relief of a sea-thiasos or procession of Neptune now in the Villa Medici. This relief seems to have been already well known and much copied in the quattrocento, and a similar relief was probably the source of the hippocamps, or sea-horses. More puzzling is the origin of the two figures astride the hippocamps: they have the leaf-shaped hair and ears, and in the case of the older man the leaf-shaped beard, of two of the satyrs in the *Bacchanals*, and the leaf motif recurs in the acanthus that springs from the knee of the youth blowing the horn, itself an ensign of the Tritons. Ordinarily in classical art and literature Tritons are figured as half-man, half-dolphin; possibly Mantegna conceived his three men as marine satyrs, giving them the generic name of Triton. It is certain that he would have called the two combatants who are half-men, half sea-horse, Tritons, rather than by the technically correct, but rare term of Ichthyocentaurs, which is found only in the Byzantine commentator of Lycophron, Joannes Tzetzes, an author first printed in 1546, who uses it only as an epithet applied to Triton.[16] In ancient art Tritons are figures of lust, marine satyrs and marine centaurs, but they are not so described in ancient literature, and Mantegna must have taken them as types of lust and other vices because of their half-human, half-bestial nature. Spagnoli, it will be remembered, declared that

> poets have not uttered lying fictions when they have given new shapes to men: if you look only at the faces of sirens, of satyrs, of Pans and sea-nymphs, you would think them men, but if you look at their bodies you will see they are beasts. Those men who are guided partly by reason, partly by the senses are two-formed Centaurs and Minotaurs, monsters of a double and ambiguous race, which signify that minds sunk in love continually degenerate into the nature of dumb beasts.

Mantegna was not the first Renaissance artist to figure sea-gods, or even sea-gods fighting. These were already part of the vocabulary of ornament of book-illuminators: thus two battling Tritons are used by the Putti Master of Venice to decorate the lower margin of the illuminated frontispiece of a Livy printed at Venice in 1470. But Mantegna has transmuted such incidental ornaments, whose ancestry lies in the long medieval tradition of droleries, into deeply felt allegorical exemplifications of man's bestial nature. In the left-hand scene two men, one older than the other, fight each other mounted on hippocamps. The older man grasps a bunch of three fish that have been skewered on hooks and straps, and makes ready to strike his opponent, who brings down a rough stick on the head of his enemy's hippocamp, while the hippocamps themselves fight ferociously: one rearing its front hoofs against the body of the other, which bares its teeth in a savage bite. The pointed invention of these rustic weapons wielded by the combatants ought to have been a warning to students that the mood of the composition is one of angry and contemptuous burlesque, for although part of a conventional imagery – the Tritons of the Putti Master

wield rough knotted staves – Mantegna has sharpened their significance. It seems not to have been realized that the entire scene is a parody of a tourney. In the left foreground, with his head turned away from the two knights of the sea and their chargers, is the marshal of the lists, a young man mounted on a scaly monster which is probably Mantegna's conception of a *ceto* or whale. He holds the marshal's wand with which he should in theory control the combat. Behind him, on the monster's back, stands this strange tourney's hideous Queen of Beauty, the naked figure of Envy, thin and sharp-featured as ever, with dangling breasts and unkempt hair streaming in the wind. As she eggs on the combatants with her cries, she holds out a tablet inscribed with her abbreviated name INVID and with four mysterious letters over whose interpretation much ink has been spilt. On the shore a statue of Neptune, flanked by a libation jug, stands on a pedestal, its back derisively turned to the grotesque battle: from reeds on the right hangs the oval targe garlanded with laurel which is the challenge of the tourney.

The theme of a burlesque formal combat is repeated in the right-hand scene in the guise of a sword and buckler combat. A youth, apparently a faun, gives the signal for fighting to begin by sounding a horn, though the solemnity of the rite is disturbed by a man who is swinging a bunch of fish round his neck previous to striking an unceremonious blow which the youth makes ready to ward off with his left hand. Again the combat pits an older Triton armed with bow and quiver against a younger one. They are perhaps at discord over the rival merits of their Nereid mistresses, who are seated on their backs in poses which are close copies of the antique. Again the combat is burlesqued by the grotesque weapons with which it is fought. The younger Triton wields a split and pointed stick as his lance and lifts a buckler which is nothing more than an ass's skull to ward off his opponent who is about to bring down a blow with the leg-bone of an animal, probably the thigh-bone of an ass or sheep. Instead of swords, both hold rough sharpened stakes; a bow is slung round the body of the older man.

The *historia* then of these two engravings images envy, jealousy and lust as the causes of discord. It is impossible now to read the undertones of the mock chivalric burlesque as Mantegna intended: but given his essentially aristocratic mentality, more probably what is being mocked in these engravings is the rusticity and rudeness of the combatants rather than the chivalric rites of the tournament and the realities those rites conceal. Mantegna's style was now so heroic that even in the ironic mode of the *Bacchanals* and of these two engravings the satire is expressed through figures which are either classical or else distortions of a classical form.

XVI

Mantegna's Last Years

EVEN at the end of his life Mantegna was still kept busy with commissions from the Gonzaga, and as usual continued to make them impatient with his delays. On 7 April 1500 Isabella asked the Prior of Santa Maria in Vado to tell a certain Suora Theophila, who wanted either a St Jerome or a Madonna by Mantegna to adorn her cell, that if she would say which of the two she wanted more Isabella would take steps to provide it at once. 'But from the hand of Mantegna it will not be possible, for we ourselves cannot get out of his hands certain things that he began in our name a good while ago already.'

As Mantegna's years drew further into the seventies, he began to be visited by severe illnesses, and it was no doubt under the threat of one of them that on 1 March 1504 he drew up a will. Its witnesses were the Mantuan painters Francesco de' Corradi and his brother Girolamo, the goldsmith Gian Marco Cavalli, the weaver Domenico di Martino de Corona and the hatter Jacopo Antonio del Cornello, these last two humbler craftsmen probably called in as neighbours living in the same street, and Battista Fiera, socially the most elevated of all, being 'a worthy doctor of arts and medicine'.[1]

Besides the bequests establishing and providing for the endowment and decoration of his funerary chapel in Sant'Andrea, the will concerns itself with the division of Mantegna's property between his two sons Lodovico and Francesco, and with provision for a natural son, Giovanni Andrea. Lodovico was to have the land and buildings at Pradella, called Il Dosso, just outside the Porta Aquadruccio of Mantua, and 200 ducats as a dowry for his daughter, but on condition that he gave food and lodging in his own house to Giovanni Andrea for the term of his life. To Giovanni Andrea Mantegna left 300 *lire*

piccole of Mantua, which were to be invested in some kind of property to be bought by him or in his name, this last a clause which suggests that Giovanni Andrea, though not officially of age, was already a youth able to act for himself. If Giovanni died while still a ward or even after coming of age at 25 then the bequest was to revert to Lodovico. In addition Lodovico was to give 50 ducats as a dowry for Anna, the natural daughter of Francesco and to pay her a further legacy of 50 ducats. Having provided impartially in this way for his other two closest dependents, Mantegna left all his remaining property to be divided equally between Lodovico and Francesco, with careful provision for its substitution in case of the death of one or both of them or of their children.

This will he modified by a codicil of 24 January 1506, made during or shortly after an illness that brought him to death's door. Giovanni Andrea was now to have suitable maintenance till coming of age, and could live where he liked provided it was in Mantua, and from the age of 25 onwards was to receive an allowance of 8 ducats yearly. The clause certainly suggests that Giovanni Andrea and Lodovico had not found the scheme of their living together a harmonious arrangement, and plainly Giovanni Andrea wished to be at liberty to live under another roof. But it does not allow of any of the sinister imputations against the character of Mantegna's two legitimate sons that have been drawn from it in modern times. Accordingly the bequest to Lodovico of the property at Il Dosso was also revoked and it was now to be divided equally between Lodovico and Francesco. Only a few months later death claimed Mantegna, at eighteen hours of the clock on Sunday 13 September.

Mantegna, like other very great artists, seems to

Fig. 17. The cupola of Mantegna's Funerary Chapel. Mantua, Sant'Andrea (Cat. no. 58)

have had a numbing effect on his immediate pupils, although he was fondly remembered after his death, as Vasari records, for his kindness to his assistants. He was unlike his master Squarcione, whose very mediocrity as an artist was an advantage to him as a teacher, partly because there was no question of his appearing inimitable to his pupils and partly because he was more anxious to encourage their talents than impose his own. Yet from quite early days Mantegna took pupils into his shop, just as he continued from youth into age to appear as a professional assessor of the quality and price of works executed by other painters. The first record we have of his taking a pupil dates from 14 October 1458, when Martino da San Clemente, a crier, bound his little brother Giovanni Battista, then aged 13, to Mantegna as an apprentice for six years. Giovanni Battista was to pay Mantegna 13 lire a year and be good and obedient and stay with him for the agreed term, and Mantegna was to find him in food and clothes. No doubt this contract was typical of a number of arrangements of the kind into which Mantegna must have entered throughout his working life as a master.[2]

In Mantua, as we have seen, Mantegna superintended for the Gonzaga much of the work of painting that was executed in their palaces, sometimes providing designs and perhaps overseeing the work. Painters who worked under his superintendence or to the designs he furnished were not necessarily in the strict sense his assistants, forming rather temporary teams enlisted to carry out special tasks of decoration. Of the assistants who must have aided Mantegna in his own work, and particularly larger decorative tasks like the Camera Picta, we know nothing, except that with a master so insistent on perfection to the last detail their tasks are likely to have been limited to the more practical forms of service, such as grinding colours. It is significant that he painted the Pope's chapel unaided, obviously preferring to work by himself. And indeed of all the painters who have been linked with him, there is none before the 1480s, when he was already in late middle age, who was of any talent or distinction, or indeed is more than a ghost in documents, with a career open to conjecture. Two names which may be those of *garzoni* (apprentices) occur in the published records: one is a Corradino del Mantegna, mentioned on 29 September 1475 as involved in a dispute with a Jew named Moses,[3] and the other is Carlo Braccesco, known as Carlo del Mantegna, a Milanese who worked in Genoa from *c*.1478.[4]

Two artists of real importance who were pupils of Mantegna were both from Verona, where the local school of painting was undistinguished and much under awe of Mantegna. Probably it was from their families, with which he was acquainted, that

Vasari learnt of Mantegna as a careful and affectionate teacher of his pupils. The first was Francesco Bonsignori (*c*.1460–1519), who is said to have been Mantegna's pupil in early youth. He then went on to Venice, where he is recorded shortly after 1480, only settling in Mantua in 1490 to become a favourite artist of the Marchese Francesco. Bonsignori excelled as a portraitist, and among other portraits painted one of Mantegna, keeping as was his custom a drawing of it, which Vasari saw in the possession of his heirs.[5] The other painter of note was Giovanni Francesco Caroto (*c*.1480–1555), who began as a pupil of Liberale da Verona, but seems to have been inspired by Mantegna's *Santa Maria in Organo* altarpiece to complete his training, with leave from Liberale, under Mantegna.[6] Caroto probably entered Mantegna's studio *c*.1498, and finished his apprenticeship *c*.1500, for by 1500 he is known to have been established in Verona. His first signed work, a *Madonna* of 1501, shows the influence of Mantegna in both style and iconography, and Vasari declares that 'he made such improvement in so short a time that Andrea used to send out works by him as works from his own hand.' It is amusing to find Mantegna apparently reviving the practices of his old master Squarcione, if Vasari is recording what really happened. This practice was justified, as we saw, by workshop custom, but it may mean no more than that Caroto's promising performance as a youth was exaggerated in family tradition, and that Mantegna, on discovering Caroto's gifts, allowed him a greater role than usual in the execution of his own pictures. On the other hand these were years of sickness and increasing age for Mantegna and of unrelenting demands on his brush, when he may have found himself in need of help from pupils.

Mantegna's pupils lead on by a natural transition to his family, for he brought up at least two of his sons to be painters. When he moved to Mantua his household was only a *brigatela* (a little troop).[7] But at least two sons, Lodovico and Francesco, and perhaps his two daughters, Taddea and Laura, seem to have been born to him there. Probably after the death of Nicolosia, his wife, and certainly after 1480, he had a natural son, Giovanni Andrea, who was as we have seen still a youth in March 1504. Of his legitimate sons, one who had made a very promising beginning as a painter died in youth, at some date between May 1480 and 1493, and a son said to have been named Bernardino, who may or may not be the same, is said to have died in 1493.[8] Of his daughters, Laura was married in 1487 to Pietro Luca de' Marini de' Raffi of Mantua, with a dowry valued at the considerable sum of 400 gold ducats, which included a trousseau partly consisting of *jocalia*, that is, of jewellery and plate. Pietro Luca was already or became through this marriage a courtier and officer of the Gonzaga, and there is still extant an agitated letter from Mantegna of 6 August 1494 asking for him to be transferred from the vicariate of Vilimpenta, to which he had just been appointed, because he would be exposed there to a family vendetta in which one of his cousins had already been killed.[9] Taddea must have been much younger than Laura, for she was married only in 1499, to Viano Viani, again with a dowry of 400 gold ducats, of which 260 had been paid by 4 July of that year.[10]

At the end of his life Mantegna was left with only two legitimate sons, Lodovico and Francesco. Lodovico was surely named after the Marchese Lodovico, who was in all probability his godfather. Lodovico's son Andrea was born in 1499, and if we assume that Lodovico probably married more or less when he came of age at 25, it is a reasonable conjecture that he was born c.1470–5. That he was younger than Francesco, even though his name sometimes precedes his brother's in documents, is suggested by his father's hopeful scheme, mentioned by Mantegna himself in a letter from Rome of January 1489 and by Scardeone, of making him a priest and obtaining benefices for him in the territory of Mantua.[11] For the Church then and later was a career for younger sons. From the eighteenth century it has been asserted that Lodovico was a painter,[12] but this is almost certainly untrue, for the holding of ecclesiastical benefices was incompatible with the profession of a painter. In reality Lodovico was already in the service of the Marchese Francesco in 1488, and after the failure c.1492 of his father's hopes for him of preferment in the Church, he seems to have aspired to a career as a courtier of the Gonzaga.[13] We find him ingratiating himself in order to advance in their service: thus on 20 December 1494 he sent Isabella a medal 'because I know you delight in them extremely'. By 12 July 1498, when Francesco Gonzaga made him a grant of full rights over a piece of land in the contrada della Pusterla, close to his father's house, he was a *cameriere* or chamberlain of the Marchese, a gentleman's post. And when Mantegna agreed to surrender his house to Francesco in 1501, Lodovico proposed that in exchange some honourable office, such as the vicariate of one of the Gonzaga possessions, should be conferred on him for life.[14]

Probably this proposal was accepted, for in January 1502 he is found holding the vicariate of Cavriana. But Lodovico had his full share of the impulsive violence which was such a feature of Renaissance psychology. Already in 1494 he had intercepted a thief who was stealing bricks Mantegna had acquired for building his house, and assaulted him with his half-sword. He also had an evil tongue, and was vengeful and unscrupulous. Early in 1505 he fell into deep disgrace and was deprived of his vicariate. In vain Isabella wrote pleadingly to Francesco Gonzaga on 1 April that

> Messer Andrea Mantinea has come to me to recommend his son, and seeing him all tearful and anguished and so fallen in the face that he appeared to me more dead than alive moved me to such compassion that I knew not how to deny him my favour with Your Excellency, whom I pray to use your accustomed mercy and grant him his son, for though he has erred gravely against you, the long service, incomparable gifts and excellent deserts of Messer Andrea entreat that he be privileged with Your Excellency's grace in the person of a contumacious son. If we want him to live and finish our works, Your Excellency must needs content him, otherwise we shall never more have the service of his person, which will fail not so much on account of his age as from this sorrow.

There also survives a pathetic letter from Mantegna to Francesco written on 31 March in which he says that his daughter-in-law Libera is still at Cavriana, pregnant and about to give birth, and in deep depression at the absence of her husband. He asks if he is to remove her, and pleads for Lodovico to be restored to favour. But Francesco was obdurate. On 3 April he answered Isabella that in spite of all Andrea's great and long services, they were not enough to overshadow the crimes of his son, who had not only persecuted and shamed with his calumnies 'the most ancient servant of the household', but under cover of religion 'though the most irreligious man in the world' had invented fresh calumnies against 'others of our gentlemen', and finally had even dared to utter false charges against the Marchese himself. Accordingly he would remain deprived of office and of favour.[15]

Nevertheless, Lodovico was a man of cultivation. He wrote a fine Italic hand and a lively sketch of himself under the signature of a letter he wrote to the Gonzaga suggests that he may have had some talent as an amateur artist.[16] He also inherited his father's antiquarian tastes and during his attendance on Francesco in the expedition to Naples of 1496 he consoled himself in his troubles by studying the ruins of antiquity at Benevento.[17] Later, in 1502, he was busying himself at Cavriana writing a comedy, seemingly for performance at court. He was also a friend or at least an acquaintance of Baldassare Castiglione. By 1506 he had been restored to favour, and from 1508 dates a decree of Francesco granting him full exemption from tax on all the crops grown on his property at Pradella, partly 'in consideration of the innumerable services to us and to our most illustrious progenitors of the late magnificent and noble knight and painter, the most excellent Messer Andrea'.[18]

If Lodovico was only a mediocre success as a courtier, equally his brother Francesco was only a mediocre success as a painter. It must be borne in mind that in all his social aspirations Mantegna intended no reflection on the painter's art, which plainly he saw as noble and lofty since he destined two of his sons to follow his own profession. Like Lodovico, Francesco began life at the Gonzaga court under favourable auspices on account of his father's great services: indeed the Gonzaga for understandable reasons liked to surround themselves with hereditary servitors. That no documented work by him survives is a misfortune, for he certainly worked under his father's eye, either to his designs or else in consultation with him. He is first mentioned in published documents in April 1488, when he was already old enough to act as his father's proctor. Since minors came of legal age in Mantua only when they were 25, this opens the intriguing possibility that he was named Francesco after Mantegna's adoptive father Squarcione, unless Mantegna gave his sons the names Francesco and Bernardino in the same spirit of devotion to the Franciscans that is known to have animated Squarcione and his real son, Bernardino. However Francesco, like Lodovico, seems to have been born in Mantua, for in a letter of 2 October 1506 to the Marchese Francesco he calls Lodovico and himself 'born servants of Your Excellency and all the glorious house of Gonzaga'.[19]

As a painter Francesco is first recorded in 1491, working in Francesco Gonzaga's new palace of Marmirolo. His earliest work there, executed in company with Tondo Tondi, was the decoration of the great *sala* with the *Triumphs of Alexander*, a commission which suggests that he was already a practised artist. The *Triumphs* had been completed by 1494, when Francesco is found painting the Sala or Camera del Mappamondo, which sixteenth-century descriptions of Marmirolo describe as 'entirely frescoed' and as 'representing very beautifully the geography of the world, with the names of the peoples, lands and seas diligently noted and the painter's device QUOD HVIC DEEST ME CRUCIAT (what here is wanting torments me)'. On 10 May 1494 Francesco wrote to the Marchese appealing to him to come out and see what had been done and to command that the painters working with him should be guided by his counsel, 'for I shall tell them not a single thing but what I have previously conferred about with my father.' He was still engaged on the Camera in October, when he begged the Marchese to give him money for his own expenses and those of his assistants.[20]

Like his brother, Francesco had a turn for literary composition: in a letter of 15 April 1494 from Marmirolo he sent the Marchese a sonnet of his own composition, slyly pleading the hot weather as an excuse for demanding a fresh suit of clothes,[21] apparently promised him by the Marchese. As with Lodovico too, there was something bizarre and capricious, even violent in his nature. Teofilo Collenuccio, one of the Gonzaga courtiers, commented sourly in May 1494 on some of the masters working at Marmirolo, who had suspended their tasks in order to purge themselves: 'and I marvel at it not at all, for the painter, the musician and the poet have need by their nature of a long purgation, especially of the head, since there is something of the madman in most of them.'[22] Francesco Mantegna certainly seems to have been hotheaded; about 1500, after one of the officers of the Marchese's household had persisted in refusing to give him some lengths of damask cloth in spite of an order from the Marchese, he vowed not to touch his brushes again and stopped painting for six years. When he took them up again, in the spring of 1506, on receiving a commission for a painting from the Marchese, he was living on his father's property at Pradella just outside the Porta Aquadruccio, under sentence of confinement to the *contado* for some quarrel or offence.

On 3 June 1506 he wrote to Francesco asking for leave to enter Mantua in order to visit his father and receive Francesco's instructions through the keeper of the Porta Aquadruccio about the colours of the picture he was to paint and particularly about the sky, for whose uppermost coat of blue he was in hopes of getting some of the costly *azzurro ultramarino*. Not long after he was restored to favour. In a letter of 15 September announcing his father's death to Francesco, he says he has not yet completed more than half the picture he is painting for him, 'but as soon as the offices for the dead are finished I will set myself to complete the work, although I have lost my master.' The picture was delayed yet again when in late September Isabella d'Este set him to repairing the Camera Picta in readiness for the projected visit to Mantua of Pope Julius II. For Francesco Gonzaga, unaware of Mantegna's death, had written to her with commands 'to arrange for Messer Andrea Mantinea or his son to mend it wherever the paintings are spoiled, and if they cannot or will not, let Maestro Francesco Bonsignori fill their room.'[23]

After this we lose sight of Francesco as an artist, except perhaps in his father's chapel in Sant'Andrea. He strove anxiously to keep the Cornaro *Cybele* for himself 'in memory of my father and so as to have something to study . . . having no other picture left by my father', but was unceremoniously deprived of it in November 1506 in favour of the original patron.[24] In the first half of 1510 Lodovico Mantegna died,[25] and Francesco was soon involved in ugly squabbles with his sister-in-law, Libera. On 16 January 1507 Mantegna's property had been legally divided between his two sons, Francesco receiving the house in Mantua known as the Casa del Mercato and the lands at Buscoldo, Lodovico the lands at Borgoforte. By 19 October 1510 Libera had been deprived by the Marchese of the Bosco della Caccia at Borgoforte, granted to Mantegna in the altisonant decree of 1492, and had been assigned instead the property of Francesco Mantegna, who seems to have fallen into serious disgrace. But the Marchese subsequently reversed his original decision, so that Libera found herself summarily deprived of both properties. Borgoforte was however restored to her, for Francesco was compelled by the Marchese to make formal renunciation of the rights he had fraudulently acquired over the Bosco to the disadvantage of his nephew Andrea, Lodovico's eldest son, who was not yet of age. Knowing the Bosco della Caccia to be a fief of the bishopric of Mantua, he had gone to Bishop Lodovico Gonzaga, his father's old friend and patron, and obtained the investiture of it for himself. He was now obliged to transfer his rights to the Marchese, who had admonished him to behave like a good brother to his sister-in-law and family and not to seek to deprive them of their inheritance. The Marchese then confirmed on 24 April 1511 his original donation of 1492 in favour of the boy Andrea.[26]

Francesco now had recourse to the Marchese's sister, Elisabetta Gonzaga, Duchess of Urbino (1471–1526), claiming that the adjudicators in the original division had acted corruptly and iniquitously towards him and that he had been unjustly deprived of his fair share. Elisabetta took up his cause in a letter to her brother of 1 August 1511: 'Having loved uncommonly Messer Andrea Mantegna . . . the love I bore him in life has not ended with his death, but extends to his former son Francesco, to whom I am the more inclined to bear the greater affection in that I know he is now his father's only son.' By 1512 Libera was married again, to a certain Aurelio Mussano, but by some means Francesco was able to excite the suspicions of her new husband against her, and early in July he was arrested as an accomplice in an attempt on her life made by Aurelio, in which she had been beaten and wounded. The terrified Libera implored the protection of the Marchese, and it was only at the special petition of Matthias Lang, Bishop of Gurk, and a favourite minister of Emperor Maximilian, who visited Mantua from 27 July to 21 August 1512 for a congress of the Holy League, that the Marchese consented to pardon Francesco for his part in the business. He also agreed to restore him his lands, but not his house, both of which had become forfeit to the Marchese's treasury. By a further decree of 20 February 1513 he ordered the cessation and abolition of all process of law mounted against Libera, and once more confirmed the Bosco della Caccia to her son Andrea.[27] On 29 April 1513 Francesco[28] addressed a cringing supplication to Federico Gonzaga, Francesco's little son, beseeching him to obtain confirmation of his pardon. When Buscoldo was restored to him, however, it was with the penalty, as we already know, of paying the rest of the original purchase price and its annual interest, a condition which compelled him to renounce it on 10 October that same year.[29]

The last known records of Francesco date from 1517. In a letter of 4 September he wrote from Milan to the Marchese Francesco complaining of the many evil blows Fortune had dealt him and praying for some assistance in his sore necessities and poverty, perhaps in the shape of the vicariate of Marmirolo, where he would keep the paintings (many of course his own work) and other decorations of the palace in good repair. In the same year he reached an accord with Libera and sold the Casa del Mercato, which had evidently been restored to him. By 1517 he was married and with children, but they seem not to have lived long. Only one is known by name, and she was the natural daughter called Anna, who is mentioned in Mantegna's will of 1504.[30] The direct male line of the family ended therefore with Francesco's nephew Andrea (d.1564). It was this Andrea who in 1560 made a new sepulture in the family chapel and in it laid the bones of his grandfather, his father, and his uncle.[31]

From this account of his career it is plain that Francesco Mantegna was busy at Marmirolo from 1491 to 1494, that he ceased painting from c.1500 to 1506, and that he worked again from that year, initially for the Gonzaga. It can be assumed that he worked in Mantegna's last technique of simulated relief, if only because the *Cybele*, which he wanted to keep as a model to study, is executed in this style. One or two religious paintings that copy Mantegna's late style of semi-relief, but with a pinched, dry facture, can perhaps be attributed to Francesco, notably the *Christ carrying the Cross* in Verona.

It was probably Francesco who completed in 1516 the pictorial decoration of Mantegna's family chapel in Sant'Andrea (Plates 154–164) and set up the bust of his father at its entrance. The chief evidence for this is a letter, now apparently lost, but which was seen in the late eighteenth century by Coddé and is summarized in Zani. Its date is not given, but it was written by Francesco Mantegna to Isabella d'Este to apologize for not being able to serve her in certain commissions she had given him because he had already promised the priests of Sant'Andrea not only to finish the decoration of the family chapel, which his father had left unfinished, but also the portico of the church, whose decoration had been begun in 1488.[32] The disappearance of this letter is regrettable, for it might have clarified the difficult problems of attribution which vex the study of Mantegna's chapel.

Our first knowledge of the chapel dates from 1504.[33] Like a true son of his age, Mantegna as he felt the ever nearer approach of death turned his thoughts to the foundation of a funeral chapel, where a priest would sing Masses for his soul and for the souls of his dead wife Nicolosia and of his parents, and where he and his descendants could be interred. Although his purpose was pious, the worldly ambitions that had haunted him from his youth found a last expression in this chapel, for such special foundations, with altar, priest and at times as here enclosing walls, were the prerogative of the noble and rich, and commemorated not merely the piety of the founder, but also his standing in the world. The great church of Sant'Andrea probably attracted Mantegna because it was dedicated to his name-saint, because it contained the holy relics of the Precious Blood, and because in it he would lie in death as in life he had desired to live, in a building of Roman grandeur. The chapels in Sant'Andrea had been given their dedications in 1481 by Cardinal Francesco Gonzaga, who also set a limit on the number of sepultures that each was to be allowed to contain.[34] However, some twenty years passed before Mantegna opened negotiations with Sigismondo Gonzaga, who as Primicerio of Sant'Andrea was the head of the collegiate foundation. He had fixed his eye on the chapel of St John the Baptist, the first on the left of the nave, and as yet unbespoken and undecorated.

The affair had come to a successful issue by 1 March 1504, when Mantegna made his first will. Among other provisions he ordered his body to be buried 'in the church of Sant'Andrea within or before the chapel built and founded under the title of St John Baptist and there he ordered a tomb to be dug and covered with a marble stone engraved with the name and surname of the testator.' And he bequeathed to the chapel among other sums 50 ducats for 'adorning the said chapel with paintings and other decorations as they [his executors] shall think proper' and all this within a year after his death. The grant of the chapel was solemnly ratified by the assembled college of Sant'Andrea on 11 August 1504, Mantegna appearing in person, the goldsmith and bronze founder Gian Marco Cavalli and Zaccaria di San Columbano, a sculptor or more probably a stonemason, attending him as his witnesses. Mantegna here declared his intention to endow the chapel with a foundation of not less than 100 ducats, and to decorate it and raise a family tomb within its walls. In addition the clergy conceded to Mantegna and his descendants in perpetuity a piece of ground behind the chapel. This Mantegna requested for the characteristic reason 'that no one

may build on it and the light of the chapel may remain forever unobstructed'. He himself proposed to wall in this plot, make a little garden in it, and build a little cell below the level of the chapel window, so as to have a pleasant retreat now that he was worn with age where he could warm himself with a fire in winter.

What followed is not entirely clear. By August 1504 the chapel's walls of plain brick were still unadorned and unpainted. Mantegna certainly began two paintings intended for the chapel, for they are mentioned on 2 October 1506, shortly after his death, by Lodovico Mantegna, as being still in his house. But Mantegna had died deeply in debt, to the tune of 200 ducats, and Lodovico was anxious to sell the *Dead Christ* and the *Cybele* to Sigismondo Gonzaga in order to raise money with which to pay these debts and also to finish the chapel within the prescribed year and then endow it. Mantegna had now ordered 100 ducats to be spent on its decoration and 100 on its endowment, 'things which seem to us right and honourable'. Sigismondo took the *Dead Christ* and the *Cybele*, but on 12 November 1507 Lodovico complained to Isabella d'Este that he had received only 75 ducats, and that the whole sum was needed to pay the expenses of his father's exequies and of mourning dress, as well as other debts. He now found himself daily bothered by workmen and bailiffs and therefore had recourse to her for payment as a special grace.[35] According to Yriarte, who cites no source and is often unreliable, but who did work in the archives of Mantua, the Primicerio of Sant' Andrea had a seizure laid on the dead Mantegna's property because the endowment of 100 ducats had not been paid and 100 ducats had not been spent on the decoration of the chapel.[36] The death of Lodovico in 1510 and the subsequent quarrels between his widow and Francesco over the family property must also have delayed or halted work. It was not finally completed, perhaps not even begun, until 1516, the date inscribed beneath the frescoed figure of *Judith showing the head of Holofernes to the Jews*. If the testimony of the letter seen by Coddé is accepted, then the work was carried out by Francesco, as indeed seems most likely on general grounds.[37]

The two paintings which Mantegna had begun for the chapel were a large picture of the *Baptism of Christ* (Plate 154), a subject chosen because of the dedication of the chapel to St John the Baptist, and an altarpiece of the *Family of Christ with the Family of St John the Baptist* (Plate 155), again in tribute to the chapel's patron saint. There is general agreement that the latter is at least in part an autograph work, though probably completed by Francesco Mantegna, while the *Baptism* must have been largely executed by Francesco. The two were still in

Mantegna's house at the time of his death, but they prove that he had already given thought to the decorations of his chapel and the subjects they were to depict. His will of March 1504 envisages that it was to be decorated by others, presumably because Mantegna was already in poor health and did not seriously expect to live to paint it himself. And his final augmentation of his bequest for its decoration to the large sum of 100 ducats, perhaps in deathbed confirmation of his earlier promise to the chapter of Sant'Andrea to spend this sum, proves that he did little or nothing before his death for its actual adornment beyond work on the two paintings.[38]

The real question is whether it was Mantegna or his son who designed the decoration that was subsequently painted on the walls of the chapel. This is no straightforward question, for, as we have already seen, the architectural conception of the chapel itself and part of its painted decoration appear to have been directly modelled on the chapel of the Belvedere, also dedicated to St John the Baptist, which Mantegna had painted fifteen years before for the Pope. For these sections of the decoration either Mantegna, old and tired, must have brought out his Belvedere designs and taken them as models or else Francesco took them and reworked them. In either case new designs must have been added. The iconographical coherence of the decoration perhaps supports the attribution to Mantegna himself of the original inventions for the whole scheme. The architectural transformation of the chapel's rude brick walls into an elegant composition of engaged arches, decorated with an egg-moulding and pearl-beading, supporting a little dome must certainly follow his design, if indeed it was not executed during his lifetime. His too must be the conception of the illusionistic painted decoration, with its characteristic union of simulated openings to the sky in the dome and its spandrels and of simulated reliefs and revetments of coloured marbles on the walls.

Mantegna seems to have envisaged a single large painting on either side wall. He was only able to begin the *Baptism*, which now hangs on the right wall. A crude *Entombment* which hangs on the opposite wall was plainly intruded after his death, perhaps even after Francesco's death, as an inadequate completion of the original scheme, which presumably envisaged another subject from the life of the Baptist. Originally these two paintings were enclosed in a painted arched framework, composed of three oval panels, one at the top, two at the sides, set between oblong panels with incurved ends. Of these panels the oval one at the top is painted with a history, while the two oval panels at the sides contain illusionistic sculptures of Virtues on a pink ground. The upper oblongs are painted with histories: each of the lower ones contains a winged

putto naturalistically and brightly coloured holding a shield. Above the painting the head of the arch is filled with a great lunette containing a pink scallop-shell: below the painting the socle was originally decorated to simulate variegated marble, but much of this decoration is lost. The frame of the lunette and of the oval above interlace in a fashion that anticipates the ornamental intricacies of Mannerism.

The pink scallop-shell motif is repeated over the entrance, within a painted framework of the same design as those on the side walls. The decoration of the window wall is almost entirely lost, but included, like the side walls, a simulated revetment of oval panels of pink variegated marble on the inner side of the arch and an arched frame above the altar. The architectural ornament of the walls is therefore a scheme of four simulated arches, decorated with simulated sculptures and reliefs. On the window wall were angels painted in grisaille holding up a shield with the arms of Mantegna. On the altar, now dismantled, was the altarpiece of the *Holy Family*, certainly designed by Mantegna as a low oblong in order not to interfere with the light from the window. To the altar was attached an altar frontal, or *paliotto*, bearing, as usual, heraldic charges: the imperial eagle of the Gonzaga in the centre on the dexter side (spectator's left), and on the sinister side, a shield bearing Mantegna's ordinary arms impaling six hills surmounted by three stars and an eagle on a red pedestal inscribed with the Gonzaga device, AB OLYMPO, that was so prominently displayed on his house. If this heraldry blazons him a courtier and servant of the Gonzaga, elsewhere the decoration insists with assertive variety on Mantegna's own coat of arms. Thus the shields held by the winged putti in the oblong panels at the bottom of the side walls are blazoned on the left wall with Mantegna's full arms (Plate 160), surmounted in chief by a comital crown containing two palms and by a sun in splendour: on the right, only one still has a legible charge, a lion's paw rampant on a red field (Plate 162), perhaps the arms of Nicolosia Bellini, for whose soul the chapel was also founded. The climax of the composition of the dome is again a shield of Mantegna's full arms set on a scalloped rosette of gadroons and encircled by a medallion frame. The eye is led inwards and upwards to it from the bold mouldings of the low drum by the eight bands of trellis-work that rise in a perspective, in alternance with bowers of foliage and fruit. This composition has its importance, for it evidently influenced the scheme of Correggio's ceiling of the Camera di San Paolo in Parma, painted in 1518–19. And indeed tradition from the late sixteenth century persistently associated Correggio's name with some of the decoration of the chapel.[39]

The four pendentives of the dome are frescoed with the Four Evangelists, seen in illusionistic perspective as if through apertures in the wall (Plates 156a and b). Each Evangelist sits behind a curved balustrade apparently projecting into space before him; indeed St Mark's foot is made to protrude into the same space, recalling Mantegna's early feats of this kind. Behind grows one of those low green hedges bearing red or golden fruit that appears so often in Mantegna's late works and in the chapel's altarpiece of the *Holy Family* itself. The Evangelists are present because they symbolize the Gospels, which narrate the life of Christ, of whom the Baptist was the forerunner. St Luke, significantly, is shown painting, rather than reading a book like the other three, in allusion to Mantegna's own art.

More complex is the programme of the simulated reliefs and sculptured figures on the walls below. That it is not without its subtleties again suggests Mantegna's hand in the invention of the decoration. With the exception of the *Judgement of Solomon* over the doorway, the Biblical themes are chosen to illustrate typologically the role of the Baptist as prophet of Christ's coming and of the New Dispensation and also his relationship with the Holy Family, which is of course the theme of the altarpiece. To either side of the *Judgement of Solomon* on the entrance doorway are scenes of the *Angel with Tobias* (left) and the *Sacrifice of Manoah* (right) executed in terracotta-coloured figures on a dark ground. Both are Biblical histories in which angels appear to men and were therefore regarded as prefigurations of the Annunciation to the Virgin and also of the Annunciation to Zacharias, father of the Baptist. The oval scene on the right wall represents the *Annunciation to Zacharias* with the angel appearing to Zacharias in the Temple to announce that his aged wife Elizabeth will bear a son who will be called John. To either side are scenes from the life of David, the type of Christ and his ancestor, also executed in terracotta colour on a dark ground. On the left is *David with the head of Goliath*, on the right *Samuel anointing David*. The first of these scenes prefigures Christ's triumph over Satan, the second his Baptism.

The oval scene on the left wall represents the *Decollation of the Baptist* (Plate 163), thus opposing on the right and left walls the first and last scenes in the cycle of the life of the Baptist. To either side are scenes, again in terracotta colour, from the history of Judith, the type of the Virgin in the Old Testament. On the left is *Judith giving the head of Holofernes to her maid*, a scene paired with the scene of *David and Goliath* because it typifies the Virgin's triumph over Satan, as the *David and Goliath* typifies her Son's. On the right is *Judith showing the head of Holofernes*, a scene linked in the Bible narrative with the praises of her cousin Ozias: 'Blessed art thou o

daughter, by the Lord, the most high God, above all the women upon the earth.'[40] These words in turn were taken as a prefiguration of Elizabeth's words to the Virgin at the Visitation, when the Infant John leapt in the womb and saluted the Virgin as blessed among women. Accordingly, the scene of *Judith showing the head of Holofernes* became a type of the Visitation.

Taken together these scenes and personages and those of the Evangelists figure the annunciation of Christ's coming by his prophet John, and the New Testament, in which Christ's life and teaching are revealed to mankind. The *Judgement of Solomon* is outside this scheme, as are the Virtues. Two of these, Temperance and Charity, are represented in the oval simulated panels underneath the scenes of *Tobias* and *Manoah*, and four in the oval panels on the two side walls, Fortitude and Prudence on the right wall, Faith and an illegible figure on the left. This illegible Virtue presumably figured Hope, for the figure holding a compass on the entrance wall, facing the bust of Mantegna, must represent Justice.[41] They are to be associated instead with the funerary purpose of the chapel. The *Judgement of Solomon* is a type of the Last Judgement, at which the good will be finally separated from the wicked, while the Virtues figure the hope of the deceased commemorated in the chapel of finding mercy when presented after death for judgement before Christ.

Some of the scenes and figures in simulated relief are very delicately executed, in a style clearly learnt from Mantegna and it is probable that all these are by the hand of Francesco. The figural decoration makes use of three techniques: monochrome, terracotta colour, and naturalistic colouring, against a background which must have been predominantly of pink marble. We may wonder whether these terracotta-coloured paintings are not Francesco's own invention; they are certainly not in the technique described in the 1542 inventory of Isabella's Studiolo as '*finto di bronzo*'. If the Four Evangelists, which have greatly suffered, are by Francesco Mantegna, yet the frescoes of the *Holy Family* and *Deposition* (Plates 164b and c), formerly in the atrium of Sant'Andrea may not be by him, whatever his lost letter to Isabella would seem to suggest. Their style is a High Renaissance style, more advanced, more expressive, and not dependent like the Evangelists on Mantegna.

Fashions in art are never stationary, and the admiration felt for Mantegna in the early sixteenth century, though great, was not great enough to inspire imitation. He left scholars, but no school. His strength was already coming to seem harshness to his last Gonzaga patron, the Marchese Francesco, in the early 1500s, and Vasari was later to condemn his sharp, thin drapery and general dryness of manner. Only the *Triumphs* continued to be generally admired and copied, largely for their embodiment of great antiquarian learning in forms that seemed to awaken Roman magnificence to vivid and noble life. For all his conventional fame he was neglected for three centuries, except in north-eastern Italy where he had lived and worked. Even in the nineteenth century the Pre-Raphaelites were condemned for their preciosity in preferring Mantegna and Botticelli to Raphael, but with Burne-Jones Mantegna's severe, mysterious art begins once more to haunt painters as it had haunted so many artists who were his contemporaries. Yet only in our own century has he been rescued from a dignified neglect, and restored to his true degree as a prince of painters in his own age.

Notes

I Mantegna and Squarcione

1. Now known as Isola Mantegna. For Mantegna's family see Lazzarini & Moschetti, 1908, pp. 62–7, and Sartori, 1976, pp.144b, 145a.
2. For the site of Mantegna's house see Fabris, in *Emporium*, lxviii, p.324; Lazzarini & Moschetti, 1908, pp.65–7, and note 45 to Chap.IV. The statement that he was a herd boy goes back to Simone Fornari da Reggio's brief biography of Mantegna in his commentary on Ariosto (*La Spositione sopra l'Orlando Furioso*, ii, Florence, 1550, p.509).
3. For Mantegna's apprenticeship see Rigoni, 1970, pp.1,11. The documents mentioning an 'Andrea depentor' working with a Mastro Francesco in the Santo in 1441–2 and again in 1447 (published by Puppi, 1975, p.3) are unlikely to refer to Mantegna.
4. For Squarcione's dates see Lazzarini & Moschetti, 1908, pp.14–61, and especially for his death, p.30, to be taken with Sartori, 1976, pp.220,223, where Squarcione is mentioned as dead in a document of 13 July 1468.
5. G. Rassino, *Albero overo genealogia de' signori Lazara*, Padua, 1650, pp.62, 72–3. Leone was a friend of Giacomo Alvarotti and Francesco Capodilista, respectively a friend and a patron of Mantegna. For earlier associations of Squarcione with Leone's family see Lazzarini & Moschetti, 1908, pp.16,19,20–3.
6. For the statutes of the Paduan *fraglia* see M. Urzi, 'I pittori registrati negli statuti della fraglia padovana dell'anno 1441', in *Archivio veneto*, s.5, xii, 1932, pp.209–37. See also the comments of Lazzarini & Moschetti, 1908, p.62.
7. Moschini, 1826, p.30 (with earlier references).
8. Sartori, 1976, pp.223–6.
9. Scardeone, 1560, pp.370–1.
10. For Campagnola and his dates see the article by E. Safarik, in *Dizionario biografico degli italiani*, xvii, 1974, pp.317–18. For a discussion of Campagnola as a source of Vasari and Scardeone see pp.16,393.
11. Kristeller, 1902, pp.563–4, doc.148.
12. Vasari, 1878, p.85.
13. Sartori, 1976, p.200.
14. Lazzarini & Moschetti, 1908, pp.37–8, 132, doc. XVII.
15. Published by Lazzarini & Moschetti, 1908, pp.52,149, doc. XXXVIII.
16. Savonarola, *op. cit.*, ed. A. Segarizzi, 1902 (*R.I.S.*, xxiv,

pt.4), p.55. The reference to *pictorie Studium* comes in connection with a eulogy of the *Studium* or university of Padua. For his placing of painting in the hierarchy of the arts see p.44.
17. For this crucial document see Lazzarini & Moschetti, 1908, pp.149–52.
18. For this see Moschini, 1826, p.26: for Barbo's collection see E. Müntz, *L'art à la cour des Papes*, ii, 1879, pp.203–5.
19. Lazzarini & Moschetti, 1908, pp.137–9, doc.XXIII; pp.44–5, 166–7, doc.LVIII.
20. Moschini, 1826, pp.66–7, n.1. Lazzarini & Moschetti, 1908, p.169, doc.LXI. See also Sartori, 1976, p.223, *sub* 1464.
21. Savonarola, *op. cit.*, p.44.
22. Vasari, ii, 1878, pp.214–15; cf. also the Anonimo Morelliano (Marc'Antonio Michiel), 1884, p.66.
23. For Lippi in Padua see M. Pittaluga, *Filippo Lippi*, 1949, p.159.
24. Sartori, 1976, p.222; Rigoni, 1970, pp.28,39–40.
25. Rigoni, 1970, p.28. For the *fraglia* see Urzi, *art. cit.* in Note 6.
26. By Muraro, in *Da Giotto al Mantegna*, exh. cat., Padua, 1974, pp.70–2.
27. Rigoni, 1970, pp.15–17; Lazzarini & Moschetti, 1908, *passim*.
28. The literature of Squarcione and of Squarcionismo is extensive. The fundamental documentation of his career was published by V. Lazzarini & A. Moschetti, *Documenti relativi alla pittura padovana*, Venice, 1908 (also in *Archivio Veneto*, n.s., xv, 1908, pp.72–190, 249–321; xvi, 1908, pp.68–102), reprinted with new pagination by Forni, ed. Muraro, 1974). Other documents are published by Lazzarini (in *Bull. Mus. Civ. Pad.*, i, 1898, pp.1–4), by Rigoni (1970, *passim*), by Sartori (1976, pp.219–26) and Sambin (1979, see below). The first independent study of Squarcione was written by Pietro Selvatico (*Francesco Squarcione, studi storico-critici*, Padua, 1839). Three recent essays (with ample citation of earlier literature) are Muraro, 'Francesco Squarcione pittore "umanista" in *Da Giotto al Mantegna*, exh.cat., *op. cit.*, pp.68–74; M. Boskovits, 'Una ricerca su Francesco Squarcione' in *Paragone*, xxviii (pt.I) 1977, no.325, pp.40–70; P. Sambin, 'Per la biografia di Francesco Squarcione: briciole documentarie', *Medioevo e rinascimento Veneto . . . studi in onore di Lino Lazzarini* (*Medioevo e umanesimo*, 34), 1979, pp.443–65. For the controversy about Squarcione's character and collections and a strong advocacy of the case against him see Fiocco,

'Il museo imaginario di Francesco Squarcione' in *Memorie dell'Accademia Patavina di Scienze, Lettere ed Arti*, lxxi, 1958–9, pp.1–16. For a general comment on the cultural background see M. Salmi, 'Aspetti del primo rinascimento: Firenze, Venezia e Padova' in *Rinascimento*, ser.2, ii, 1962, pp.77–87. The closest analysis yet published of Squarcionismo is by L. Armstrong, *The paintings and drawings of Marco Zoppo* (a revised doctoral dissertation), 1976, pp.11–28.

29. For these references to Mantegna as Andrea Squarcione see Rigoni, 1970, p.43, doc.XII (January 1454); Brown in *Mitt. des Kunsthistorischen Institutes in Florenz*, xvii, 1973, p.158, n.13, a Mantuan document of 23 January 1459; Filarete, *Trattato*, ed. L. Grassi, i, 1972, p.227 (references of *c*.1460–4); Supino, *Il Camposanto di Pisa*, 1896, p.28, Pisan doc. of 1466; Müntz, *Les collections des Médicis*, 1888, p.78 (ref. in Lorenzo de' Medici's inventory of 1492 to a *Judith* by Andrea Squarcione).

30. Rigoni, 1970, p.39, doc.V.

31. Fiocco, 1937, p.18.

32. For the origin and early development of linear perspective see S.Y. Edgerton, *The Renaissance rediscovery of linear perspective*, N.Y., 1975. Mantegna's perspective is usually neglected in studies of the subject, which tend to have an exclusively Florentine bias.

33. Savonarola, *op. cit.*, pp.44,55.

34. Reproduced by G.L. Mellini, *Altichiero e Jacopo Avanzi*, 1965, pl.281.

35. Reproduced by Mellini, *op. cit.*, pl.280.

36. For some notes on trecento illusionism see Maginnis, 'Assisi revisited', in *B.M.*, cvii, 1975, pp.516–17.

37. For a good discussion of the early Squarcionesque style see L. Armstrong (Anderson), *The paintings and drawings of Marco Zoppo*, 1976, pp.11–28.

38. Panofsky, *Early Netherlandish Paintings*, 1953, i, p.196, ii, figs.261,262.

39. Goloubew, ii, no.XLIII.

40. For Pollaiuolo's nudes see L. Armstrong (Anderson), 'Copies of Pollaiuolo's *Battling Nudes*' in *Art Quarterly*, xxxi, 1968, pp.155–67; *id.*, 'Aspects of the influence of Pollaiuolo on Northern Italian Artists' in *The paintings and drawings of Marco Zoppo*, 1976, pp.268–87.

41. Pliny, xxxv, 36.

42. G.P. Lomazzo, *Trattato dell'arte della pittura scultura ed architettura*, ed. of Rome, 1844, i, p.320.

43. See Müntz, *L'art à la cour des Papes*, ii, 1879, p.200, for a cast made for Pietro Barbo of an antique bronze of a seated boy holding a dog to his face and laughing.

44. For Contarini see A. Zeno, *Dissertazioni Vossiane*, i, 1752, cols.189–96.

45. For Marcanova and his collection see Zeno, *op. cit.*, pp.140–6; L. Sighinolfi, 'La biblioteca di Giovanni Marcanova' in *Collectanea variae doctrinae Leoni S. Olschki...*, 1921, pp.187–222.

46. For Mansionario see R. Weiss, *The Renaissance discovery of classical antiquity*, Oxford, 1969, p.23. This book should be consulted for the humanist rediscovery of antiquity in general. For reproductions of drawings of Mansionario's medals see Mellini, *op. cit.*, figs.28–42.

47. Mellini, *op. cit.*, pp.25–32, figs.1–17.

48. Hill, Nos.1–9. See F. Cessi, 'Monetazione e medaglistica Carraresi' in *Da Giotto al Mantegna*, 1974, pp.86–9.

49. C.A. Levi, *Le collezioni veneziane d'arte e d'antichità*, i, 1900, pp.xxxvi–vii; Weiss, *op. cit.*, pp.28–9.

50. For Flemish art in Italy and more especially the Veneto see R. Weiss, 'Jan van Eyck and the Italians' in *Italian Studies*, xi, 1956, pp.1–15; xii 1957, pp.7–21, and the recent study by L. Campbell, 'Notes on Netherlandish pictures in the Veneto in the fifteenth and sixteenth centuries' in *B.M.*,

cxxiii, 1981, pp.467–73. For the Eyckian *Crucifixion* see A. Chatelet, 'Un collaborateur de Van Eyck en Italie' in Institut Historique Belge de Rome, *Relations artistiques entre les Pays-Bas et l'Italie à la Renaissance: études dédiées à Suzanne Salzberger*, 1980, pp.43–60; S. Osano, 'Rogier van der Weyden e l'Italia' in *Antichità viva*, xx, 1981, no.4, pp.14–21, n.5, pp.5–14, with an endeavour to trace a specific relationship between arches in the art of Rogier and the arch in a drawing by Jacopo Bellini and the arch in Mantegna's *Assumption*.

51. Quoted by A. von Wurzbach, *Niederlandisches Künstlerlexikon*, ii, 1910, p.875.

52. Fazio, 'De pictoribus' from *De viris illustribus*, ed. M. Baxandall, in *J.W.C.I*, xxvii, 1964, p.105.

53. A. Venturi, in *Rivista storica italiana*, i, 1884, p.608.

54. Kantorowicz, 'The Este portrait by Rogier van der Weyden' in *J.W.C.I*, iii, 1939–40, pp.179–80.

55. For Savonarola see Segarizzi's introduction to the *ed. cit.* of *Libellus de magnificis ornamentis*, and *id.*, *Della vita e delle opere di Michele Savonarola*, 1900. Cyriac, *loc. cit.*; Fazio, *op. cit.*, pp.103,101; Kantorowicz, *loc. cit.*

56. A recent discussion of the problem is M.L. Dunkelman, 'Donatello's influence on Mantegna's early narrative scenes' in *A.B.*, lxii, 1980, pp.226–35.

57. For Niccolò Pizzolo see Rigoni, 1970, pp.25–46, and G.M. Canova in *Da Giotto al Mantegna*, 1974, pp.75–80.

58. Aleotti's sonnet is printed by A. Venturi, 'Jacopo Bellini, Pisanello und Mantegna in der Sonetten des Dichters Ulisse' in *Der Kunstfreund*, i, 1885, cols.259–62.

59. The two sketchbooks of Jacopo Bellini in the Louvre were published by C. Ricci, *Iacopo Bellini e i suoi libri di disegni*, Florence, 1908, and V. Goloubew, *Les dessins de Jacopo Bellini au Louvre et au British Museum*, 1908–12. For Jacopo see also M. Röthlisberger, 'Nuovi aspetti dei disegni di Jacopo Bellini' in *Critica d'Arte*, xiii–xiv, 1956, pp.84–8; *id.* 'Notes on the drawing books of Jacopo Bellini' in *B.M.*, xcviii, 1956, pp.358–64; *id.* 'Studi su Jacopo Bellini' in Fondazione Giorgio Cini, *Saggi e memorie di storia dell'arte*, ii, 1958–9, pp.43–89 (important for the physical make-up and condition of the two books of drawings). A.M. Tamassia, 'Jacopo Bellini e Francesco Squarcione: due cultori dell'antichità classica' in *Il mondo antico nel rinascimento (Atti del V Congresso Internazionale di Studi sul Rinascimento)*, Florence, 1958, pp.159–66; G. Mariani Canova, 'Riflessioni su Jacopo Bellini e sul libro dei disegni del Louvre' in *Arte Veneta*, xxvi, 1972, pp.13–30; C.L. Joost Gaugier, 'The Tuscanization of Jacopo Bellini. Part I. The relation of Jacopo to problems of the 1420s. Part II. The relation of Jacopo to problems of the 1430s and 1440s' in *Acta Historiæ Artium Academiæ Scientiarum Hungaricæ*, xxiii, 1977, pp.95–112, 291–313; *id.* 'Some considerations regarding the Tuscanization of Jacopo Bellini' in M. Dalai Emiliani, ed., *La prospettiva rinascimentale: codificazioni e transgressioni: atti del convegno (1977)*, Florence & Milan, 1980, pp.165–76; *id.* 'Jacopo Bellini and the theatre of his time' in *Paragone*, xx, pt.I, no.325, pp.70–80; *id.*, *Jacopo Bellini: selected drawings*, London, 1980; H.F. Collins, 'The Cyclopean vision of Jacopo Bellini' in *Pantheon*, xl, 1982, pp.500–4; *id.*, 'Major narrative paintings by Jacopo Bellini' in *A.B.*, lxiv, 1982, pp.466–72; *id.*, 'Note on Jacopo Bellini's lost St Michael...' in *Zeitschrift für Kunstgeschichte*, xlv, 1982, pp.283–6; Osano, *art. cit.* in n.50 above.

II The Ovetari Frescoes

1. Rigoni, 1970, p.58. See also Cat.no.63.

2. Vasari, 1568, i, p.488.

3. Rigoni, 1970, pp.10–11, doc.1.

4. See e.g. Cat.nos.161–2, 165.

5. For Aleotti see the article by P. Rizzi in *Dizionario biografico degli italiani*, ii, 1960, p.155 (with bibliography). See also Cat.no.65.

6. For the documents relating to the case see F. Stefani, 'Andrea di Biagio Mantegna di Vicenza' in *Archivio Veneto*, xxix, 1885, pp.191–2; Lazzarini & Moschetti, 1908, p.50; Rigoni, 1970, p.1.

7. Young men came of age in Padua at 25 (cf. Lazzarini & Moschetti, 1908, pp.16,125).

8. Rigoni, 1970, pp.1–23.

9. M. Blason Berton, ed., *De viris illustribus familiae Transelgardorum Forzatè et Capitis Listae*, Rome, 1972, and the articles for Giovan Francesco, and Francesco and Gabriele Capodilista in *Dizionario biografico degli italiani*, xviii, 1975, pp.633–40. See also R.J. Mitchell, *The Spring Voyage*, 1966.

10. This has escaped previous notice.

11. G. Capodilista, *Itinerario*, in Santo Brasca, *Viaggio in Terrasanta 1480*, ed. A.L. Momigliano Lepschy, 1966.

12. Vespasiano da Bisticci, *Le vite*, ed. A. Greco, i, 1976, pp.263–66, with previous lit.

13. Kristeller, 1901, pp.105–8.

14. For this and all subsequent documents connected with the Ovetari frescoes see Cat.no.1.

15. Cat.no.64.

16. For this portrait see the exh.cat. Wiener Neustadt, *Friedrich III. Kaiserresidenz Wiener Neustadt*, 1966, no.12; it must date from before his coronation in March 1452. For Frederick's Italian itinerary see Pastor, *History of the Popes*, ii, 1899, pp.138–62.

17. Venturi, in *Der Kunstfreund*, i, 1885, cols.259–62.

18. Lomazzo, *Trattato*, ed. of 1844, i, p.312, ii, p.413.

19. Meder, *Handzeichnung*, 1919, p.443.

20. Rigoni, pp.17–20, doc.VI; p.42, doc.X.

21. Fazio, *ed. cit.*, p.103.

22. Pliny, xxxv, 36,74 (Loeb ed., p.317).

23. For this see Huelsen, *La Roma antica di Ciriaco d'Ancona*, 1907, p.10.

24. Alberti, *De pictura*, ed. Grayson, 1972, p.78 (c.40), compare *Della pittura*, ed. Mallé, p.92.

25. Goloubew, i, iv.

26. Mellini, pl. facing p.18.

27. Fazio, *ed. cit.*, p.105.

28. Mellini, fig.62.

29. Mellini, fig.178.

30. Mellini, figs.180–2.

31. e.g. Goloubew, i, XXVII, ii, LXXIII.

32. Compare C. Vecellio, *De gli habiti antichi, et moderni*, Venice, 1590, ff.480v–481,484v–485.

33. Mellini, fig.102.

34. For the back view in earlier art see M. Koch, *Die Rückenfigur im Bild vom der Antike bis zu Giotto*, 1965. For Bellini drawings scaled according to Alberti's perspective see e.g. Goloubew, ii, X, XII, XXXIV, LXXIII.

35. Savonarola, *op. cit.*, p.54.

36. See Cat.no.1.

37. For Marcanova see pp.25,254, n.45. Goloubew, ii, XLIIIb.

38. For Ciriaco d'Ancona see M.E. Cosenza, *Biographical and bibliographical dictionary of the Italian humanists*, ii, 1962, pp.1169–71; to this can be added E.W. Bodnar, *Cyriacus of Ancona and Athens*, Brussels, 1960; E.W. Bodnar and C. Mitchell, *Cyriacus of Ancona's journeys in the Propontis and the Northern Aegean 1444–1445* (*Memoirs of the American Philosophical Society*, Vol.112), 1976; and P. Lehmann, *Cyriacus of Ancona's Egyptian visit and its reflections in Gentile Bellini and Hieronymus Bosch*, 1979.

39. For Feliciano see pp.94–6.

40. For Bosso see G. Soranzo, *L'umanista canonico regolare lateranense Matteo Bosso di Verona (1427–1502)*, 1965, and C. Mutini in *Dizionario biografico degli italiani*, xiii, 1971, pp.341–4.

41. Sighinolfi, pp.189,192.

42. Sighinolfi, pp.188,196.

43. Published by C. Huelsen, *La Roma antica di Ciriaco d'Ancona*, Rome, 1907.

44. Mellini, fig.138.

45. See the article by Knabenshue cit. in Cat.no.1.

46. Cat.no.2. For Paduan devotion to San Bernardino see Lazzarini & Moschetti, 1908, p.28.

47. A. Parronchi, *Studi su la dolce prospettiva*, 1964, p.282.

48. Vasari, iii, 1878, pp.399–400; Horsten, *Andrea del Castagno*, 1980, pp.24–5, 175–6.

49. See Cat.no.3.

50. For Santa Giustina and its reformed congregation see L. Barbo, *De initiis Congregationis S. Iustinae de Padua*, 1908; G.C. Coulton, *Five centuries of religion*, iv, 1950, pp.215–24; L. Pesce, *Ludovico Barbo, vescovo di Treviso*, 1969; R. Pepi, *L'abbazia di Santa Giustina in Padova: storia e arte*, 1966; Padua, Banca Antoniana, *La basilica di Santa Giustina: arte e storia*, 1970.

51. Savonarola, *op. cit.*, pp.13,15–16,18–19.

52. Pallucchini, *I Vivarini*, 1962, pp.3,77,90,107.

53. Savonarola, *op. cit.*, p.10.

54. Mellini, pl.281.

55. See Cat.no.4.

56. For a study of blond beauty in the Venetian Renaissance see A. Baschet & F.S. Feuillet de Conches, *Les femmes blondes selon les peintres de l'Ecole de Venise*, 1865.

III The Ovetari Frescoes

1. The original document was published by P. Paoletti, *Raccolta di documenti inediti per servire alla storia della pittura veneta*, fasc. I, 1894, p.9. For a vindication of the date as 1453, not 1454, see L. Testi, *La storia della pittura veneziana*, i, 1909, pp.454–5, who points out that the Venetian style of the original date of the document (25 February 1452 m.v.) is correctly given by Paoletti in modern style as 25 February 1453. Kristeller (1901, p.38) mistakenly supposed that Paoletti's 1453 ought to be altered to 1454: he has been followed by others even in modern times. The 20 ducats were given 'per sovinzion del maridar di Nicholoxa'.

2. Kristeller, 1901, p.98.

3. Pallucchini, *op. cit.*, pp.17,99–100, pls.32,33,34.

4. For an analysis and discussion of the perspective in this scene see also L. Testi, *Storia della pittura veneziana*, i, 1909, pp.478–83.

5. See the pertinent observations of Testi (*op. cit.*, i, p.460; ii, p.641) on Bellini's knowledge of antique remains, which he surmises was largely from drawings, rather than from originals. Compare also Röthlisberger, *op. cit.*, in note 59 to chapter I, pp.69–71 (of *Studi*).

6. Huelsen, *La Roma antica di Ciriaco d'Ancona*, Rome, 1907, pl.IV. This source is noted by Edgerton, cit. Hartt, *A history of Italian Renaissance art*, 1980, p.392.

7. Kristeller, 1901, p.106.

8. Kristeller, 1901, p.107.

9. Rigoni, 1970, pp.21–3, docs.VIII,IX.

10. Scardeone, 1560, p.372 (reprinted in Cat.no.1).

11. Vasari, 1568, i, pp.488–9. Paintings in *chiaroscuro verde* were in fact executed in Padua, not least by Squarcione himself, who decorated the cloister of San Francesco with paintings in this technique.

12. Pliny, xxxv, 62–5; Alberti, *Della pittura*, ed. Mallé, 1950, pp.107–8; Quintilian, xii, 10.

13. Plutarch, 'Quomodo adolescens poetas audire debeat', 17–18, in *Moralia*, trans. F.C. Babbitt (Loeb edition), i, 1927,

pp.92–3. Alberti, *ed. cit.*, pp.106–7.

14. For all these personages see Cat.no.1.

15. Pliny, xxxv, 34(56).

16. This carpet, compared with the oriental carpet in the San Zeno altarpiece, is surprisingly crudely painted, but this may be due to poor restoration.

17. Goloubew, i, xx.

18. Pliny, xxxv, 36(74); Alberti, *ed. cit.*, p.70; Goloubew, i, xlv.

IV Mantegna in Padua

1. See Cat.no.5.

2. Goloubew, i, xxxviii,xli,xliii,ii,lvi. For earlier representations of ragged clothes in trecento Ferrara see R. Varese, *Trecento ferrarese*, 1976, col. pl.ix, fig.42.

3. See Cat.no.6. Goloubew, i, l.

4. See for instance Arnold von Harff, *Pilgrimage*, ed. M. Letts, 1946 (Hakluyt Society), pp.212–13; G. Capodilista, *Itinerario* of 1458 in Santo Brasca, *Viaggio in Terrasanta*, ed. of 1966, p.191.

5. Goloubew, ii, i.

6. Goloubew, i, cxxxi. For a close parallel to the motif of the watching bird in a tree as a funereal motif see Jacopo Bellini's drawing of the funeral procession of the Virgin (Goloubew, ii, vi); Pisanello's medal is Hill, 32.

7. Goloubew, ii, vi.

8. See Cat.no.7.

9. Vasari, iii, 1878, pp.152–3, i, 1878, pp.188–9.

10. Vasari, iv, 1879, p.98. His date is chronologically impossible.

11. See Cat.no.8.

12. Pliny, xxxv, 36(92).

13. Savonarola, *op. cit.*, p.17 & n.; A. Gloria, *Il territorio padovano illustrato*, iii, s.d., p.145.

14. See Cat.no.9.

15. For Correr see above all F.G. Degli Agostini, *Notizie istorico-critiche intorno la vita, e le opere degli scrittori viniziani*, i, 1752, pp.108–34; and a well-researched study by L. Puppi, in *Il trittico di Andrea Mantegna per la Basilica di San Zeno Maggiore in Verona*, 1972, pp.35–49.

16. The expression *solemnis magister* is used of Mantegna by Pietro da Milano in his testimony of 14 February 1457 (Rigoni, 1970, p.22).

17. Vasari, 1550, p.511.

18. As noted by Kristeller, 1901, pp.149–52.

19. W.L. Gundersheimer, *Art and life at the court of Ercole I d'Este: the 'De triumphis religionis' of Giovanni Sabadino degli Arienti*, 1972, pp.52–3.

20. Goloubew, ii, ii.

21. Puppi, *Il trittico*, 1972, p.74.

22. Reproduced from an engraving by F. Novelli in *Boll. Mus. Civ. Pad.*, l, pt.2, 1961, p.22.

23. G. Mariacher, *Illuminazione in Italia dal quattrocento all'ottocento*, 1965, p.18, col. pl. facing p.40, pp.43,44.

24. See M. Meiss, 'Ovum Struthionis, Symbol and Allusion in Piero della Francesca's Montefeltro Altarpiece' in *Studies in Art and Literature for Bella da Costa Greene*, ed. D. Miner, 1954, pp.92–101. Cf. also C. Gilbert, in *A.B.*, xxxiv, 1952, pp.208–11; Meiss, 'Addendum ovologicum' in *A.B.*, xxxvi, 1954, pp.221–2 (useful for concrete illustrations and documents), and a correspondence in *A.B.*, xxxv, 1955, pp.329–30, in which Gilbert has been misled by a misprint in the text of Durandus. Ostrich eggs were still commonly used in church lamps in the early seventeenth century (cf. Lobo, *The Itinerário of Jerónimo Lobo*, ed. and trans. D.M. Lockhart & C.F. Beckingham, 1984 (Hakluyt Society), p.97: 'their famous eggs, so familiar in the decoration of church lamps'.

25. Durandus, i, iii, 43; Job, 39,14; Luke, 22,61.

26. John, 1:5,9; Durandus, i, i, 40.

27. Matthew, 25; Durandus, v, ix, 9.

28. See A.R.A. Hobson, 'Two Renaissance bindings' in *The Book Collector*, vii, 1958, pp.265–6.

29. For exoticism in quattrocento Italy perhaps I may be allowed to refer to R.W. Lightbown, 'L'esotismo' in Einaudi, *Storia dell'arte italiana*, x, 1981, pp.445–55.

30. In type Mantegna's Gregory does not correspond to any known Byzantine prototype. See G. Galavaris, *The illustrations of the liturgical homilies of Gregory Nazianzenus*, 1969, pp.23–5, figs.451–3.

31. So much emerges from Traversari's letters (these can be consulted in Martène & Durand, *Veterum scriptorum et monumentorum ... amplissima collectio*, iii, Paris, 1724, or in the ed. of Mehus). In Book xii, ep.3, Traversari says that he has received the volumes of Gregory Nazianzen and enquires for a volume of his sermons. In ep.21 he records that Francesco Barbaro in Venice has given him a Greek volume of twenty short works by Gregory Nazianzen. In Book xv, ep.11, he says of his translation of the saint's life: '*Gregorii Nazianzeni vitam ut Graecam haberem, cardinalis sancti Angeli fecit diligentia. Erat enim in illo Cincitii volumine, quod ex Cryta ferrata acceperat. Post opera ipsius Gregorii duosque quaterniones ad me misit solutos ex volumine, in quibus ipsa vita habebatur, quam Latinam facere ipsa novitas persuasit: ipsique Cardinali dedicare idcirco visum est, quia amantissimus erat, & suo studio ad nos potissimum venerat.*' This took place in 1431, about the time of the death of Pope Martin V and the election of his successor Eugenius.

32. Anonymous sixteenth-century author, quoted by Donnesmondi, *Dell'istoria ecclesiastica di Mantova*, ii, 1616, p.48.

33. Sighinolfi, p.199. For other Paduan 'descriptiones', probably maps, of the Holy Land, sent by Jacopo Antonio Marcello to René of Anjou in 1457 see Martin in Soc. Nat. des Antiquaires de France, *Mémoires*, s.6, ix, 1900, pp.265–6.

34. Müntz, *Les collections des Médicis*, 1888, p.64: D'Arco, ii, p.32; Luzio, in *Archivio storico dell'arte*, i, 1882, pp.276–8.

35. Harff, *ed. cit.*, p.198; Gabriele Capodilista, *Itinerario* in Santo Brasca, *Viaggio in Terrasanta*, ed. A.L. Momigliano Lepschy, 1966, p.203.

36. Harff, *ed. cit.*, p.200.

37. Goloubew, i, xxv; ii, xxv.

38. This document was first published by Davari, in *Archivio storico dell'arte*, i, 1888, pp.81–2.

39. A. Portioli, *La Zecca di Mantova*, pt.I, 1879, p.84.

40. C. Elam, in *Splendours of the Gonzaga*, exh.cat., V. & A. Museum, 1981–2, p.25, n.9.

41. See C. Brown in *Mitteilungen des Kunsthistorischen Institutes in Florenz*, xvii, 1973, p.158, n.13, doc. of 23 January 1459.

42. For the lease see Puppi, 1975, pp.6–7,11.

43. Published by M. Dell'Acqua, 'Mecenatismo e collezionismo dei Gonzaga da Ludovico a Isabella d'Este ...' in *La Corte e il 'Cortegiano'*, ii, *Un modello europeo*, ed. A. Prosperi, 1980, p.310, n.

44. Kristeller, 1902, p.535, doc.70.

45. For Mantegna's house in Padua the fundamental study is G. Fabris, 'Le case di Pietro d'Abano, di Andrea Mantegna e dei Savonarola in Padova' in *Atti e memorie della R. Accademia di Scienze Lettere ed Arti di Padova*, n.s., xlv, 1929, pp.49–80. The house was demolished in the 1920s. It was in the contrada di S. Lucia, on the corner of Via P. d'Abano (formerly the *androna di S. Lucia*). In quattrocento documents it is described as having a courtyard, well and garden and an upper loggia of wood: traces of frescoes of quattrocento date were still visible in the 1920s between the windows of the upper floors. The house belonged to the canons of the cathedral, who leased it to Michele Savonarola, by whom it was described in 1443 as '*ruinosa*'. Mantegna bought the *dominio utile* of part of it on 13 November 1458, and paid rent to the

cathedral chapter (docs. of 1462 and 1488) jointly with Savonarola's sons. He ceded this *dominio utile* on 22 June 1492 to Bernardino Giorgi, *rigattiere*, in return for 113 gold ducats and a pair of *spallacci*.

46. Fiocco, 1937, p.155, citing an unpublished document in the Paduan archives.

47. Sartori, 1976, pp.144b,145.

48. Puppi, *loc. cit.*

49. Sartori, 1976, p.145.

50. Fiocco, 1937, pp.161,166, citing unpublished documents in the Paduan archives.

51. See Cat.no.67.

52. Goloubew, i, p.63.

53. For this chapel see Gonzati, *La basilica di S. Antonio di Padova*, i, 1852, pp.52–3, ii, 1853, pp.134–5; for the Bellini altarpiece see i, pp.56,59, pp.xlii–xliii; Anonimo Morelliano, 1884, pp.8–9, with correction of Gonzati's reading of the date in the inscription; Robertson, *Giovanni Bellini*, 1968, p.12.

54. See Cat.no.68.

55. For these poems see Janus Pannonius, *Poemata*, i, Utrecht, 1784, pp.62–210. (Panegyric on Jacopo Antonio Marcello); pp.238–51 (*Carmen ad Ludovicum Gonzagam, Principem Mantuanum*). The poem to Ludovico, addressed to him after he had sent a gift to Janus's tutor Guarino, was not offered to him in person by Janus, but by Calcagnini (*Carmen*, 245–8). For Jacopo Antonio Marcello see pp.494–5.

56. See Cat.no.10.

57. See Geanakoplos, *Greek Scholars in Venice*, 1962, pp.13.40.

58. For a further discussion of this problem see the Aigueperse *St Sebastian*, p.135.

59. Jacobus a Voragine, *Legenda Aurea*, ed. Graesse, 3rd edn., 1890, p.112.

60. See M. Fossi Todorow, in M. Salmi, *Scritti di storia dell'arte in onore di Mario Salmi*, ii, 1962, pp.144,146, with previous literature.

61. H.W. Janson, 'The "Image by Chance" in Renaissance Thought' in *Sixteen Studies*, s.d., pp.65–6.

62. Lucretius, cited from the Aldine edition, January 1515, f.60r. Later editors altered the order of the lines in the text reducing the emphasis on clouds. The text of Lucretius was first printed at Brescia in 1479.

63. Cicero, *De divinatione*, i, 13.

V Mantegna and the Gonzaga

1. See Cat.no.11. Müntz, *Les arts à la cour des papes*, ii, 1879, pp.178–9; *Kyriaci Anconitani Itinerarium*, ed. Mehus, 1742, pp.77–80.

2. Schivenoglia, p.137.

3. Pliny, xxxv, 34(56).

4. Padua, Museo Civico 408. See *Da Giotto al Mantegna*, ed. L. Grossato, exh.cat. Padua, 1974, no.73.

5. See the Cardinal's letter of 2 September 1462 to Lodovico in Bertolotti, *Le arti minori alla corte di Mantova*, 1889, p.14.

6. For the Gonzaga see the Bibliography, p.502.

7. For the rise of the Gonzaga see above all Luzio, *I Corradi di Gonzaga*, 1913.

8. Luzio, *Galleria*, 1913, p.5.

9. See Coletti & Camesasca, p.27, n.4, for detailed notes on the hereditary deformity of the Gonzaga; cf. also Luzio-Renier, in *G.S.L.I.*, xvi, 1890, pp.134–5.

10. Schivenoglia, p.165.

11. Published by Brown in *Mitteilungen des Kunsthistorischen Institutes in Florenz*, xvii, 1973, pp.158–9, For the Del Tovaglia and their relations with the Gonzaga see F. Rodolico, 'Ricerca ed acquisto di "pietre antiche" alla corte dei Gonzaga' in *Archivio storico italiano*, cxiv, 1956, pp.749–53. For Lodovico's interest in Ciriaco d'Ancona's collections

of inscriptions see Luzio-Renier in *G.S.L.I.*, xvi, 1890, p.159.

12. Platina, *Historia*, cit. in Grævius, *Thesaurus Antiquitatum et Historiarum Italiæ*, iv, pt.2, 1722, col.201.

13. D'Arco, *Studii statistici della popolazione di Mantova*, 1839.

14. Filarete, *Trattato*, ed. L. Grassi, i, 1972, pp.227–8, 258.

15. For the relationship between Lodovico and Donatello see now also M. Dall' Acqua, *op. cit.*, pp.303–5. His article should be consulted for its discussion of aspects of Lodovico's taste as a patron.

16. E.J. Johnson, *S. Andrea in Mantua: the building history*, 1975, p.7.

17. For the relics of the Precious Blood see G.B. Cremonesi, *Frammenti storici del Sangue Preziosissimo di Gesù che con somma venerazione si conserva nel celebratissimo Tempio di S. Andrea*, 1741. See also Donnesmondi, *Istoria ecclesiastica di Mantova*, i, 1612, pp.1–5,138.

18. For Fancelli see above all C. Vasić Vatoveć, *Luca Fancelli, architetto. Epistolario gonzaghesco*, 1979.

19. For the dates of all these buildings see C. Vasić Vatoveć, chap.III, pp.249–400; for Revere see also P. Carpeggiano, *Il palazzo gonzaghesco di Revere*, 1974.

20. Luzio, *Galleria*, 1913, pp.20–1; Vasić Vatoveć, pp.174–88.

21. Vasić Vatoveć, pp.325,182–3.

22. Luzio, *Galleria*, p.21n.

23. Schivenoglia, p.161.

24. See Cat.no.12.

25. Schivenoglia, p.149.

26. Kristeller, 1902, p.523. A *trigesima* is a Mass said thirty days after a death.

27. For the background to these see Coniglio, pp.66–71, 74–5.

28. Luzio, *Galleria*, p.24; Kristeller, 1902, pp.527,534.

29. See Cat.no.153.

30. See Cat.nos. 13–18. Luzio, *Galleria*, 1913, p.25, n.1.

31. For these see L. Testi, 'I corali miniati della chiesa di S. Giovanni Evangelista in Parma' in *La Bibliofilia*, xx, 1918–19, pp.21–3,26–7.

32. The *Entombment* miniatures are published in *Seilern Catalogue, Addenda*, 1969, pp.42–4 (No.346: 17.1 × 12cm., executed in grisaille). For the *Flight into Egypt* see *Fonti per la storia della pittura*: iv, *Serie documentaria. Raccolte di quadri a Mantova nel sei-settecento*, 1976, p.44.

33. See Cat.nos.149–51.

34. Kristeller, 1902, p.525. The unconvincing reading as 'libro' sometimes advanced for this word can be dismissed: see the reproduction of the original in Luzio, *Galleria*, 1913, pl. facing p.56.

35. Goloubew, i, XXXIX; ii, XIX.

36. Goloubew, i, LXX; ii, XXIX, XXX.

37. Arnold von Harff, *Pilgrimage*, ed. M. Letts, 1946, pp.187–8.

38. Vasari, iii, 1878, p.257.

39. Alberti, *Della pittura*, ed. Mallé, 1950, p.102.

40. L. Olschki, *L'Asia di Marco Polo*, Venice and Rome, 1957.

41. Cf. the drawings and model-book of the Venetian painter Prenzolo di Maestro Angelo, including drawings of lions, horses, oxen, birds, indeed 'of all animals and all beautiful things', which Oliverio Forzetta of Treviso wanted to purchase in 1335 (Levi, *Le collezioni veneziane d'arte e d'antichità*, i, 1900, pp.xxxv–vi).

42. Alberti, *Della pittura, ed. cit.* pp.91–2.

43. For the controversy about this mosaic see the article by F. Hartt, 'The earliest works of Andrea del Castagno' in *A.B.*, xli, 1959, pp.159–81,227–36, and Horsten, *Andrea del Castagno*, 1980, p.173.

44. Kristeller, 1901, p.220.

45. Luzio, *Galleria*, 1913, p.23, n.1.

46. For Zeno see Vespasiano da Bisticci, *Le Vite*, ed. A. Greco, i, 1970, pp.267–8; L. Bertalot & A. Campana in *La Bibliofilia*, xli, 1939, pp.356–76.

47. For Feliciano see Sabadino degli Arienti, *Le Porretane*, ed. Gambarin, 1914, pp.17,71; G. Fiocco, 'Felice Feliciano amico degli artisti' in *Archivio Veneto-Tridentino*, ix, 1926, pp.188–99; L. Pratilli, 'Felice Feliciano alla luce dei suoi codici' in *Atti del Reale Istituto Veneto di Scienze, Lettere ed Arti*, xcix, 1939–40, pp.33–105; H. Mardersteig, 'Nuovi documenti su Felice Feliciano da Verona' in *La Bibliofilia*, xli, 1939, pp.102–10; Feliciano, *Alphabetum Romanum*, ed. Mardersteig, 1960; C. Mitchell, 'Felice Feliciano Antiquarius' in *Proceedings of the British Academy*, xlvii, 1961, pp.197–221; G. Gianella, 'Il Feliciano' in *Storia della cultura veneta. Dal primo Quattrocento al Concilio di Trento*, i, 1980, pp.460–77.

48. The dedication figures in two copies of one of Feliciano's collections of inscriptions. One dated Idibus Januarii 1463 (n.s. 1464?) is in the Biblioteca Capitolare, Verona (Cod.269), the other, dated 1464, is in the Biblioteca Marciana, Venice (Cod.Lat.x, 196.3766). The dedication page of the Venice MS is reproduced by G. Romano, in Einaudi, *Storia dell'Arte*, II, ii–i, 1981, p.9, pl.1. Printed by Kristeller (1902, pp.523–4, doc.22) and Rastrilli (pp.49–50) from the Verona manuscript. A third manuscript collection of inscriptions dedicated by Feliciano to Mantegna with the simple words 'Ad Andream celeberrimum pictorem nec non amicum incomparabilem' is in the Biblioteca dell' Archiginnasio, Bologna (Cod.A.186): for this see Mardersteig, in *Italia medioevale e umanistica*, ii, 1959, p.296n.

49. The manuscript (Modena, Cod.Est.*a* N.7,28) containing the sonnet has an inscription by Feliciano on its first leaf saying that it was written in July 1460. But the sonnet must be of later date, since in its title Francesco Gonzaga is called a cardinal, and he only received news of his promotion to the cardinalate late in December 1461. A possible date for it might be the months of January–March 1462, when Francesco was in Mantua putting together the 'bella famiglia' with which he left it on 4 March 1462 for the Curia (Schivenoglia, p.149). Moreover the sonnet addressed to Mantegna by the Mantuan poet Nuvoloni (see p.260) that follows it can only have been written after Mantegna had moved to Mantua in May 1460, and is dated 1469 by Faccioli (see p.260). The text of the sonnets is printed by Kristeller (1902, p.489): that of Feliciano's also by Rastrilli (p.74). See also p.127 for Nuvoloni.

50. The account of the expedition occurs on ff.201v–205v of a handsome manuscript executed by Feliciano for Samuele da Tradate and now in the Biblioteca Capitolare, Treviso (Cod I,138). It is a copy of a collection of inscriptions preceded by Scalamonti's life of Ciriaco d'Ancona. The section concerning the expedition is printed by Kristeller (1902, pp.523–4) and by Rastrilli (pp.53–4).

51. See Ateneo di Salò, *Il lago di Garda*, 2 vols., 1969; A. Pedrazzoli, 'La Marchesa Isabella d'Este Gonzaga a diporto sul lago di Garda colla sua Corte' in *A.S.L.*, ser.2, vii, 1890, pp.866–78; Luzio, *Mantova e Urbino*, 1893, p.55; Platina's life of Vittorino da Feltre, in Garin, ed., *Il pensiero pedagogico dell'umanesimo*, 1958, p.692.

52. For Samuele da Tradate (d.1466 in Rome), who worked under Mantegna's direction at Cavriana, see Kristeller, 1902, pp.522–3, docs. of 1464; Luzio, *Galleria*, 1913, p.22; Volta, *Compendio cronologico-critico della storia di Mantova*, iii, 1827, p.120, for the very elegant humanist inscription (now lost) with which he adorned the tomb of his father, the sculptor Jacopino, in the cloister of Sant'Agnese; C. Perina in Istituto Carlo d'Arco, *Mantova*; ii, *Le arti*, 1961, pp.265,271,315. No works by Samuele have been identified.

53. Sartori, 1976, p.92. For Giovanni da Padova see also Vasić Vatoveč, 1979, p.256 and *passim*.

54. For these inscriptions at Toscolano see besides the classic collections of ancient inscriptions, such as Mommsen, Ottavio Rossi (Rubeus), *Monumenti Bresciani* (trans. as *Monumenta Brixiana* in Graevius, *Thesaurus Antiquitatum et Historiarum Italiae*, iv, pt.2, 1722, cols.79–81).

55. Printed in Kristeller (1902, p.524, doc.36). For Aldobrandini see Litta, *Famiglie celebri italiane*, iv, 1837, Aldobrandini di Firenze, tav.1.

56. Coniglio, pp.52–3.

57. Gaye, i, 1839, pp.225–42. Work had halted *c*.1460 because of Manetti's death and because the Signoria had not released the 2000 florins to the Servite friars of the Annunziata (Paatz, i, p.62).

58. Document printed by I.B. Supino, *Il Camposanto di Pisa*, 1896, p.28. It is invariably misdated to 1467, with a consequent doubling of Mantegna's visits to Tuscany, because it has not been realized that the date 1467 is Pisan style i.e. 1466. Compare Supino, p.194.

59. See Cat.no.19.

VI The Camera Picta

1. See Cat.no.20.

2. Luzio, *Galleria*, 1913, p.25, n.2.

3. Compare e.g. Kristeller, 1902, p.124, where the 'camera dalli cavalli' at Gonzaga is described in 1494 as containing 'el suo lecto con un paramento de broccato doro azurro con un bellissimo pavaglione de renso lavorato doro e de seta'. Similarly other *camere*, including Francesco's own, had their splendid beds. Such beds were often show-pieces in themselves: compare M. Mallett, *The Borgias*, 1969, p.88 for tributes of admiration paid to the state-beds belonging to Cardinal Rodrigo Borgia in 1484.

4. As noted by Kristeller, 1901, p.237.

5. For Lodovico Sforza's stay see Luzio-Renier, 'Delle relazioni di Isabella d'Este Gonzaga con Ludovico e Beatrice Sforza' in *A.S.L.*, ser.2, vii, 1890, p.656. The *camera* was allotted to Lodovico as part of Isabella's suite of apartments, comprising 'il salotto de la camera depinta, essa camera depinta, il camerino dali Soli, la camera dal cassone, il nostro [i.e. Isabella's] camerino, e la camera dove mangiamo adesso'. Lodovico himself was to have the *camera del cassone* (letter from Isabella d'Este of 8 June 1498).

6. Cited by R. Signorini, in *J.W.C.I.*, xli, 1978, p.319, n.21. See also Luzio, *loc. cit.*, n.3.

7. Kristeller, 1902, p.555, nos.124,125.

8. Pliny, xxxv, 36.

9. Kristeller, 1901, p.237.

10. For the time of day see Gould, 'On the direction of light in Italian Renaissance frescoes and altarpieces' in *G.B.A.*, ser.6, xcvii, 1981, p.22.

11. Compare Cesare Vecellio, *Gli habiti antichi et moderni*, 1590, 'Africana', pl. facing p.489. For oriental and Moorish slaves in Italy see Bongi, 'Le schiave orientali in Italia' in *Nuova antologia*, June, 1866; Verga, 'Per la storia degli schiavi orientali in Milano' in *A.S.L.*, ser.4, iv, 1905, pp.188–95.

12. Kristeller, 1902, p.526, no.42.

13. For the representation of turkeys in European art see L. Müller, 'Der Indianische Hahn in Europa' in *Art the Ape of nature: Studies in honour of H.W. Janson*, 1981, pp.313–40. For Lodovico's interest in exotic birds and animals and in pictures of them, see Luzio-Renier in *G.S.L.I.*, xvi, 1890, p.148.

14. Discovered by R. Signorini: published by him in *Mitteilungen des Kunsthistorischen Institutes in Florenz*, xx, 1976, pp.205–12.

15. Signorini, in *J.W.C.I.*, xli, 1978, pp.317–20; on dogs and cats at the Gonzaga court see C. Cottafavi in *Il Ceppo*, Milan, 1934.

16. Compare Lodovico's making Mantegna on taking him into

his service an issue of cloth to make a tunic of his livery colours (see p.76).

17. Coniglio, pp.86–8.

18. Luzio, *Isabella d'Este e Francesco Gonzaga promessi sposi*, Milan, 1908, p.4.

19. This figure is sometimes identified as Federico: I now share Signorini's opinion that it is more probably Gianfrancesco.

20. Amadei, ii, p.153. Lodovico was formally made Francesco's coadjutor as Bishop of Mantua by an act of 5 February 1468.

21. See the painting of a procession, probably a fragment of a cassone panel, attributed by Longhi to the circle of Bonifacio Bembo in the Accademia Carrara, Bergamo (no.1095, Rossi, *Catalogo*, 1979, p.87, as *c*.1460, by a painter of Milan or Pavia).

22. R. Levi-Pisetzky, *Storia del costume in Italia*, ii, 1964, pp.254–5.

23. Schivenoglia, p.179. The presence of Paola and Barbara in the scene is confirmed by a recently discovered letter of 10 April 1470 in which the painting is described by two Milanese ambassadors (published by A. Tissoni Benvenuti 'Un nuovo documento sulla "Camera degli Sposi" del Mantegna' in *Italia medioevale e umanistica*, xxi, 1982, pp.557–60). This letter is crucial as proving that Lodovico, his wife, his sons and his two daughters are portrayed in the Camera and as providing a firm date in the chronology of the work. Unfortunately I cannot accept Dr Tissoni Benvenuti's interpretation of the iconography of the painting.

24. Her name has not been identified. The standard study of dwarfs and buffoons at the Gonzaga court is Luzio-Renier, 'Buffoni, nani e schiavi dei Gonzaga ai tempi d'Isabella d'Este' in *Nuova Antologia*, cxviii, 1891, pp.618–50, and cxix, 1891, pp.112–46, especially p.130.

25. L. Beltrami, *Il Castello di Milano*, 1894, p.281.

26. Sacchi, *Notizie pittoriche cremonesi*, 1872, p.218; Baroni & Samek-Ludovici, *La pittura lombarda del quattrocento*, 1952, p.111. Sacchi seems to date this document to 1471.

27. Schivenoglia, p.162, gives the name of Lodovico's chamberlain in 1469 as Niccolò Terzo, of Parma.

28. For this ceremonial of the court of Milan see A. Maspes, 'Prammatica nel ricevimento degli ambasciatori inviati alla Corte di Galeazzo Maria Sforza, Duca di Milano (1468–10 dicembre)' in *A.S.L.*, ser.2, vii, 1890, pp.146–51.

29. Mantua, Istituto Carlo d'Arco, *Mantova: La storia*, ii, 1961, pp.34–5.

30. Coniglio, pp.84–9.

31. Sacchi, *op. cit.*, p.218; Baroni & Samek-Ludovici, *op. cit.*, p.111, 'Camera rossa dal raso . . . la fazata de verso la torre ove se pinza el Signore con li ambasciatori a sedere e li fratelli e d. Cicho in pede in atto di consultare et expedire facende'.

32. Schivenoglia, cit. Signorini, in *Mitteilungen des Kunsthistorischen Institutes in Florenz*, xviii, 1974, p.245.

33. Compare the instructions given by Galeazzo Maria Sforza for the decoration of the Castello of Pavia in 1469 (Sacchi, *loc. cit.*; Baroni & Samek-Ludovici, *loc. cit.*) and for that of the Castello of Milano in 1472 (Beltrami, *op. cit.*, pp.280–3).

34. Schivenoglia, p.166; 'Diario Ferrarese' in *R.I.S.*, xxiv, 1933, pp.44–5; Signorini, in *Mitteilungen des Kunsthistorischen Institutes in Florenz*, xviii, 1974, pp.229–30.

35. Kristeller, 1902, p.526, no.42.

36. For attempts to identify historical events in the frescoes see Cat.no.20.

37. Schivenoglia, pp.177–8; Signorini, *art. cit.*, p.233. For the existence of these two portraits and a study of them see Signorini's excellently documented article (cit. note 32).

38. For portraits of the Emperor and his effigy by Niklas Gerhaert van Leyden, see Wiener-Neustadt, *Austellung Friedrich III*, 1966, fig.37, cat.204; E. Buchner, *Das Deutsche Bildnis der Spätgotik . . .*, 1953, pp.133–4, no.122.

39. Repr. by Signorini, *art. cit.*, p.247, fig.15.

40. Signorini, *art. cit.*, pp.230–2. For Isabella and Mantegna's failure to please her as a portraitist see p.172.

41. Dell'Acqua, 'Mecenatismo e collezionismo dei Gonzaga da Lodovico . . .' in A. Prosperi, ed., *La Corte e il 'Cortegiano'*, ii, 1980, pp.299–301. Dell'Acqua identifies the dogs as *alani* and would like to give them a heraldic significance.

42. Schivenoglia, pp.164–5; Coniglio, p.63. See also A. Magnaguti, *Cacce gonzaghesche*, 1933.

43. For this see Schivenoglia, pp.147–8.

44. Luzio, *Galleria*, 1913, p.22.

45. W.L. Gundersheimer, ed., *Art and life at the court of Ercole I D'Este: the 'De triumphis religionis' of Giovanni Sabadino degli Arienti*, 1972, p.31.

46. For the quotations from Traversari, Sassolo and Correr see E. Garin, ed., *Il pensiero pedagogico dell'umanesimo*, 1958, pp.526–30,704,710.

47. Kristeller, 1902, pp.522–3, docs.28,29,31–3.

48. Luzio, *Galleria*, 1913, p.22. For these see Beltrami (*loc.cit.*) and Baroni & Samek-Ludovici (*loc. cit.*).

49. For decorations of outdoor scenes of hunting see Luzio, *Galleria*, 1913, p.20; Beltrami (*loc. cit.*) and Baroni & Samek-Ludovici (*loc. cit.*); Gundersheimer, *op. cit.*, p.68.

50. Beltrami, *op. cit.*, pp.281–2.

51. Beltrami, *loc. cit.* Sacchi, *loc. cit.*; Baroni & Samek-Ludovici, *loc. cit.*; Gundersheimer, *op. cit.*, pp.61–2.

52. Kristeller, 1902, p.547.

53. Leonardo, *Speculum Lapidum*, 1502, p.xlviii *v* (from the dedication to Cesare Borgia dated 13 September).

54. Published by Puppi, 1975, pp.6–7; Sartori, 1976, p.145.

55. Vasić Vatoveć, pp.302–3, letters between Lodovico and Fancelli of 17 June 1471.

56. Kristeller, 1902, pp.555–6, docs.126,127.

57. Schivenoglia, pp.161,167; Kantorowicz, in *J.W.C.I.*, iii, 1939–40, pp.172–3.

58. Schivenoglia, p.149; Kristeller, 1902, p.527, doc.44, letter of 2 August 1471.

59. Kristeller, 1902, pp.527–8, docs.45–7.

60. Kristeller, 1902, p.528, doc.47; Resti-Ferrari, pp.263–4; Schivenoglia, pp.170–3.

61. Cit. Kristeller, 1902, p.491, from D'Arco, ii, p.27.

62. Luzio, *Mantova e Urbino*, 1893, p.173; Kristeller, 1901, p.240, n; Luzio, *Galleria*, 1913, p.25, n.3; Luzio, *Rivista d'Italia*, xii, pt.2, 1909.

VII Mantegna in Mantua

1. See Cat.no.21. D'Arco, i, pp.54–5. For the earlier frescoes, now dated to *c*.1360, see Istituto Carlo d'Arco, *Mantova: Le Arti*, i, *Il medioevo*, 1960, pp.268–79. For Lodovico's burial in the chapel of San Bernardino see Signorini, 'Ludovico muore', in Mantua, Accademia Nazionale Virgiliana, *Atti e memorie*, n.s., l, 1982, pp.95,112, n.58.

2. Luzio, *Galleria*, 1913, pp.12–13; Kristeller, 1902, p.516, doc.11; C. Elam, in *Splendours of the Gonzaga*, 1981–2, pp.15,25; Brown, in *B.M.*, cxiv, 1972, p.862.

3. Coniglio, pp.54–7.

4. Kristeller, 1902, p.522, docs.29,30, pp.522–3, docs.31,33.

5. Luzio, *Galleria*, 1913, p.23, n.2.

6. A. Luzio, *I Corradi di Gonzaga signori di Mantova: nuovi documenti*, Milan, 1913, p.83.

7. Hill, 432 (cf. also his p.314).

8. Luzio, *op. cit.*

9. Kristeller, 1902, p.525, doc.37; pp.528–9, docs.50,51. It is Gerola (p.911, n.1) who suggests that these documents refer to a villa, rather than to a house in Mantua.

10. See Gerola, nos.8,9,10,14,15,18.

11. For a photograph of the foundation stone see Plate 151.

Kristeller (1901, p.204) misreads the inscriptions as *anno Christi* and XVI KAL: for its correct interpretation see Marani, in Istituto Carlo d'Arco, *Mantova: le arti*, ii, 1961, p.154, n.22. For photographs of autograph letters by Mantegna see Luzio, in *Emporium*, x, 1899, p.372; Luzio, *Galleria*, pl. facing p.56; Tietze-Conrat, 1955, p.250, and Garavaglia, p.84. For a study of the so-called 'littera Mantiniana' see Meiss, 1957, pp.52–78. For the *Prade di Redevallo* see Schivenoglia, p.145n. Mantegna's stone was imitated a few years later by Giovanni and Gianpietro Arrivabene, who in 1481 set a very similar one surmounted by carvings of a serpent encircling a wreath and a caduceus on the corner of their palace in the Via Fratelli Bandiera, Mantua.

12. Kristeller, 1902, pp.536–7, doc.75; p.542, doc.88; p.541, doc.86. Cat.no.78.
13. For Mantegna's house see E.E. Rosenthal, 'The house of Andrea Mantegna in Mantua' in *G.B.A.*, ser.6, lx, 1962, pp.327–48, and E. Marani, in *Mantova: Le Arti*, ii, 1961, pp.147–57. Although they supersede the earlier reconstructions of Yriarte, 'La maison de Mantegna . . .' in *Cosmopolis*, March, 1897, pp.738–61: *id.*, 1901, pp.100–14, these should still be consulted. There is an unsatisfactory article on the inscription AB OLYMPO by A. Dorez, in Paris, Académie des Inscriptions et Belles-Lettres, *Comptes-rendus*, 1918, pp.370–2. For the decorations of the house see R. Niccoli, in *Le Arti*, iii, 1940–1, pp.390–4. See also Marani, in *Civiltà Mantovana*, i, 1966, no.2, pp.53–6, 58–60 (with further literature).
14. A. Portioli, *La zecca di Mantova*, i, 1879, p.87, incorrectly attributes this device to Lodovico's great-grandson, Federico.
15. Kristeller, 1902, p.544, doc.97.
16. Alberti, *De Architectura*, ed. Bonelli & Portoghesi, 1966, Bk. vi, 33. For a study of when Mantegna and Alberti may first have met see Muraro, 'Mantegna e Alberti' in *Arte, pensiero e cultura a Mantova*, 1965, pp.103–32.
17. Gerola, no.18. This document, previously overlooked, may be thought to settle the vexed question as to whether Mantegna roofed the house.
18. Cited by Kristeller, 1902, p.497, doc.23 (with earlier lit.) and by E. Faccioli, in Mantua, Istituto Carlo d'Arco, *Mantova: le lettere*, ii, 1962, pp.382–3.
19. Marani, *op. cit.*, p.134, n.15.
20. Cited by Marani, 'L'Architettura' in Mantua, Istituto Carlo d'Arco, *Mantova: le arti*, ii, 1961, pp.148,155, n.31, from a MS version of Schivenoglia's chronicle in the Biblioteca Comunale, Mantua, Cod.I.1.2.
21. Marani in *Civiltà Mantovana', loc. cit.*; Gerola, p.911, n.12; Kristeller, 1902, p.545.
22. Resti-Ferrari, p.265.
23. Kristeller, 1902, p.557, doc.131.
24. For the interpretation of *pietre* as bricks see Coniglio (p.32) for a letter of 24 October 1461 which refers to a promise by Lodovico of 'pietre de la sua fornace qui di Revere'. Compare a similar letter of 10 September 1481 in Vasić Vatovec, p.241.
25. Gerola, pp.914, doc.18,915 n.
26. Kristeller, 1902, p.577, doc.174 (wrongly dated January for July).
27. Resti-Ferrari, pp.266–8, with documents describing the property and its boundaries, and recording Mantegna's payments until 1476.
28. Kristeller, 1902, p.528, doc.49, p.540, doc.80. These set out Lodovico's part in the transaction.
29. Resti-Ferrari, p.267.
30. Kristeller, 1902, pp.535–6, docs.70,71.
31. Kristeller, 1902, pp.582, doc.186, p.587, doc.203.
32. Resti-Ferrari, pp.266–7.
33. Gerola, no.5.

34. Kristeller, 1902, p.529, doc.52, pp.531–4, docs. 59–63,65,66.
35. Resti-Ferrari, pp.269–71.
36. Gerola, nos.6,12,13,16.
37. Gerola, no.11; Resti-Ferrari, p.271.
38. Kristeller, 1902, pp.539–40, doc.82.
39. Kristeller, 1902, pp.525–6, doc.40; Luzio, *Galleria*, 1913, p.23.
40. Gerola, nos.2,7.
41. For the text of this decree see Kristeller, 1902, pp.551–2, doc.115. For Sigismondo Golfo, the humanist who drew it up, see Luzio-Renier, 'La coltura' in *G.S.L.I.*, xxxiv, 1899, pp.22–4.
42. For an offer of a *mancia* from the Marchese Francesco see Kristeller, 1902, p.544, no.94.
43. See the letter from Marco Zoppo to Barbara of Brandenburg of 16 September 1462 (Kristeller, 1902, p.521, doc.26); the letter of 29 March 1481 in which Francesco de'Corradi and his brothers are reported as saying that they will serve Barbara as well as any painter in Mantua, excepting always Mantegna (Resti-Ferrari, pp.274–5).
44. Kristeller, p.530, no.55.
45. Kristeller, p.521, doc.24. The missal is usually identified as that of Barbara of Brandenburg, now belonging to the cathedral chapter, Mantua (cf. C. Perina, in Istituto Carlo d'Arco, *Mantova: le arti*, ii, 1961, pp.253–4).
46. For Filippo Nuvoloni see E. Faccioli, in Istituto Carlo d'Arco, *Mantova: le lettere*, ii, 1961, pp.85–112, cf. especially p.90 for the poem to Andrea (also in Kristeller, 1902, p.488), and Signorini, 'Due sonetti di Filipppo Nuvoloni ad Andrea Mantegna' in *Studi in onore di Raffaello Spongano*, 1980, pp.165–72, who publishes a second one.
47. Kristeller, 1902, p.549, doc.110.
48. Calepino's entry is cited by Kristeller, 1902, p.495, no.14. For Calepino see also G. Soldi Rondinini & T. de Mauro in *Dizionario biografico degli italiani*, xvi, 1973, pp.669–70, s.v.
49. Kristeller, 1902, pp.576–7, doc.173.
50. Vasari, 1550, pp.511–12.
51. Kristeller, 1902, pp.536–7, docs. 72–5. One or two of Mantegna's letters (e.g. Kristeller, 1902, pp.538–9, doc.80) seem to show a sense of the value Federico set on him in their veiled threats of quitting the Marchese's service.
52. Kristeller, 1902, pp.537–8, docs.76,77.
53. By this settlement Giovanni Francesco acknowledged that Caterina's dowry had been paid to him and that he still owed Mantegna 30 gold ducats for the rent of his house. These he now undertook to pay in small instalments.
54. The letter was published in Bosso's *Recuperationes Faesulanae*, Bologna, 1493, f.L2ᵇ–L3ᵃ. It can conveniently be consulted in Kristeller, 1902, p.491, no.4. See pp.40,128, for Bosso.
55. See Cat.no.74.
56. See also p.228 for the question of which son it was who died.
57. Kristeller, 1902, p.534, doc.81: Vasić Vatovec, p.376.
58. Kristeller, 1902, pp.541–2, doc.87.
59. Kristeller, 1902, p.538, docs.78,79. See Cat.no.73.
60. Kristeller, 1902, p.548, docs.105,106.
61. Vasari, *Vite*, 1550, p.512. Simone Fornari da Reggio also records in 1550 that 'he took delight in architecture' (*La Spositione*, ii, 1550, p.509).
62. For the history and documentation of the Domus Nova see Vasić Vatovec, pp.224–6.
63. Vasić Vatovec, p.241.
64. Resti-Ferrari, pp.275–6.
65. D'Arco, ii, p.18, no.20.
66. Rossi, 'I medaglisti del Rinascimento alla corte di Mantova' in *Rivista italiana di numismatica*, i, 1888, p.31. Cited by Kristeller, 1902, p.508, from Scaliger, *Poemata*, ed. of 1591, i, p.127.
67. For Bordon, who applied in 1504 for a privilege to publish

woodcuts of a *Triumpho de Cesare* that may have been Mantegna's, see M. Billanovich in *Dizionario biografico degli italiani*, xii, 1970, pp.511–13. Kristeller, 1902, p.494.

68. Reprinted by Kristeller (1902, pp.493–5, no.12) from Santi, *Cronaca*, ed. H. Holtzinger, 1893, pp.187–8.

69. Reprinted by Kristeller (1902, pp.491–2, no.10) from Baptista (Spagnoli) Mantuanus, *Sylvarum libri*, II, vi, as printed in *Opera omnia*, c.1499, ff.48c–49v.

70. Essentially the opinion of R. Milesi, *Mantegna und die Reliefs der Brautrühen Paola Gonzagas*, 1975, who attributes the figures to Melioli and the background to a painter of coffers. For these Klagenfurt marriage-chests, first published by R. Eisler, 'Die Hochzeitstruhen der letzten Gräfin von Görz' in *Jahrb. der K.K. Zentral Komission für Erforschung und Erhaltung der Kunst- und Historischen Denkmäle*, n.s., iii, 1905, pp.64–175, see also Fiocco, 1937, pp.61, 99–101 (as autograph) and Martindale (1979, pp.46, 53–4).

71. For the *Triumphs of Petrarch* see Cat.no.88. For the Graz chests see I. Graus, *Die zwei Reliquienschreine im Dome zu Graz*, in *Der Kirchenschmuck*, xii, 1881; J. Wastler, 'Mantegna's Triumphe des Petrarca' in *Z.B.K.*, xv, 1880, pp.61–72; Eisler (*op. cit.*); E. Coudenhove-Erthal, *Die Reliquienschreine des Grazer Doms*, 1931; Fiocco, 1937, pp.61–98, and Tietze-Conrat, 1955, p.270. In 1459 a MS of Petrarch's *Trionfi* was being prepared for Lodovico Gonzaga cf. Luzio-Renier, in *G.S.L.I.*, xvi, 1890, p.145.

72. Notably in the exh.cat. *Andrea Mantegna*, Mantua, 1961, pp.148–50.

73. See Cat.no.62.

74. Bertolotti, *Figuli, fonditori e scultori in relazione con la Corte di Mantova*, 1890, p.46. See Cat.no.62.

75. See Hill, 406,435,658,998A,1034,1035.

76. Pliny, xxxv, 2–5. For the *imago clipeata* in antiquity see J. Bolten, *Die Imago Clipeata: ein Beitrag zur Portrait- und Typengeschichte*, 1937.

77. Amadei, ii, p.440.

78. For the laureation of poets see V. Lancetti, *Memorie intorno ai poeti laureati d'ogni tempo e d'ogni nazione*, 1839. Examples of fifteenth-century portraits of poets wearing a laurel are the relief portrait of Francesco Cinthio Benincasa and the painted portrait of a poet ascribed to Filippo Mazzola in the V. & A. Museum. Aelian, *De varia historia*, ix, c.2; Pliny, xxxv, 36,71.

79. Kristeller, 1902, p.524, doc.35.

80. For the making of tapestries in Mantua see Braghirolli, 'Sulla manifattura di arazzi in Mantova' in *Atti e Memorie della R. Accademia Virgiliana*, 1879–80, *Memorie*, pp.1–66.

81. Published by Cigogna in *Archivio Veneto*, ix, 1860, pp.405–6.

82. Discovered by R. Signorini: published by Brown, in *B.M.*, cxvi, 1974, p.102.

83. See Cat.no.184.

84. cf. J.F. Hayward, *Virtuoso goldsmiths and the triumph of Mannerism*, 1976, pls.8,9.

85. cf. references in the Este inventory of 1494 to jewels 'ala todescha' (published by Campori, *Raccolta di cataloghi ed inventarii inediti*, 1870, pp.4–5).

86. Rossi, 'Gian Marco Cavalli' in *Rivista italiana di numismatica*, i, 1888, pp.441–2, for the letter of 12 February 1483 and Federico's reply on 14 February. See Kristeller, 1902, p.541, doc.85, for Andreasi's reply to this on 17 February.

87. See Cat.no.21. D'Arco, ii, p.198, n.4, where Chiara's name is wrongly given as Lucrezia.

88. Jacobus a Voragine, *Legenda Aurea*, ed. Graesse, 1891, p.110.

89. By J. Caldwell in *J.W.C.I.*, xxxvi, 1973, p.376. See Martial, ii, 9; Juvenal, x, 144. Martial and Juvenal allude to the destructiveness of the fig in relation to the decay of mighty tombs, and it is by no means certain that the monument to which Sebastian is bound is a tomb, rather than a temple.

90. Smith, 'Natural versus scientific vision: the foreshortened figure in the Renaissance' in *G.B.A.*, ser.6, lxxxiv, 1974, pp.239–48.

91. See Gabriele Capodilista, *Itinerario* of 1458 in Santo Brasca, *Viaggio in Terrasanta*, edn. of 1966, p.206; Harff, *Pilgrimage*, ed. M. Letts, 1946, p.201.

92. See Cat.nos.24, 25 and 27.

93. See Cat.no.26.

94. Cited by Luzio-Renier, 'Il lusso' in *Nuova Antologia*, cxlix, 1896, p.275.

VIII *The Triumphs of Caesar*

1. cf. Kristeller, 1902, p.542, doc.88.

2. Cited by Luzio-Renier in *G.S.L.I.*, xxxviii, p.57, n.1.

3. Coniglio, pp.122–4.

4. For Palazzo San Sebastiano see D'Arco, ii, pp.78–9, docs.100–1; Marani, in Istituto Carlo d'Arco, *Mantova: Le Arti*, ii, 1961, pp.184–5; Martindale, 1979, pp.92–6.

5. Luzio, *Galleria*, 1913, p.191.

6. Jacopo d'Atri's chronicle was published by C.E. Visconti, in *A.S.L.*, xi, 1879, pp.38–68, 331–56, 500–13. For the quotation see p.40.

7. Cited by Luzio-Renier in *G.S.L.I.*, xxxviii, 1901, p.57, n.1.

8. D.D. Franchini and others, *La scienza a corte: collezionismo eclettico natura e immagine a Mantova fra Rinascimento e Manierismo*, 1979, pp.194–200; D'Arco, ii, p.38; Beltrami, *Il castello di Milano*, 1894, p.455. There was nothing in fact exceptional in such subjects of great generals of antiquity as wall-decoration: in 1488 the Mantuan court lent the Ferrarese court six large tapestries of Hannibal and Scipio (Luzio, *Isabella d'Este e Francesco Gonzaga promessi sposi*, 1908, pp.27–8). For the marriage of Lodovico Sforza and Beatrice d'Este and of Alfonso d'Este with Anna Sforza in January 1491 Lodovico had the walls of the *salla grande della balla* 'covered with paintings on canvas on which we for this feast had put all the victories and memorable deeds of our illustrious grandfather, with his effigy at the head over against the door, on horseback under a triumphal arch' (Beltrami, *op. cit.*, p.455).

9. Paccagnini, *Il Palazzo Ducale di Mantova*, 1969, p.18.

10. Pez & Hueber, *Thesaurus anecdotorum novissimus*, vi, pt.3, pp.156–8; Vasari, *Le Vite: I. Gentile da Fabriano e il Pisanello*, ed. A. Venturi, 1896, pp.38–9, no.xxiv; E.G. Gardner, *Dukes and poets in Ferrara*, 1904, p.51.

11. Luzio, *I Precettori*, pp.18,28.

12. See Luzio, in *A.S.L.*, xv, 1901, pp.157–9.

13. See Cat.no.28. Martindale, 1979, p.181, doc.1 (also in Kristeller, 1902, p.544, doc.96). For the topography of the Corte and Castello and a discussion of this document see Martindale, *op. cit.*, pp.34–42.

14. Kristeller, 1902, p.546, docs.102,103. The deduction that they were kept in a special painting-room is based on the first of these documents (Mantegna's letter of 31 January 1489), and on the report that they were seen by Ercole d'Este in August 1486 in the Palazzo della Corte.

15. For the Bellini canvases see Robertson, *Giovanni Bellini*, 1968, pp.81–3, with references.

16. Kristeller, p.102, p.550, doc.111; Martindale, 1979, p.182, doc.5.

17. A. Martindale, *The Triumphs of Caesar by Andrea Mantegna*, 1979, cit. as Martindale, 1979.

18. Serlio, *Libro Quarto di Architettura*, 1537, c.10 (cit. Kristeller, 1902, p.498, doc.24, and Martindale, 1979, p.185, doc.27); see p.150.

19. Suetonius, *C. Iulius Caesar*, c.37.

20. For *armillae* see Daremberg and Saglio, s.v.

21. This observation is made by A. Allison, 'Four new busts by

Antico' in *Mitteilungen des Kunsthistorischen Institutes in Florenz*, xx, 1976, pp.219–21. She suggests that the type was influenced by literary descriptions (Suetonius, c.45, Plutarch, *Julius Caesar*, iv, 7) but was unaware that the head of Caesar in the original canvas is now largely a reconstruction from the Vienna copy (Martindale, 1979, pp.157,159).

22. Plutarch, *Aemilius Paulus*, 32–4. The triumph was celebrated in November 167 BC (Loeb ed. of Plutarch, vi, 1918, p.441 ff).
23. Pliny, xxxiii, 4.
24. cf. Martindale, 1979, p.136, for a discussion of the *tabulae*.
25. Martindale, 1979, p.147 n.1; Kristeller, 1902, p.547. For the elephant on Philip's medal see Du Choul, *Discours de la Religion des anciens Romains*, ed. of 1567, p.142.
26. For the *sala*, whose existence in the fifteenth-century is well documented, but which has now disappeared, see Paccagnini, 1969, pp.88–9.
27. Vasari, iii, p.634, citing the testimony of Girolamo Campagnola as his source for Mantegna's admiration of Avanzi's frescoes.
28. Martindale, 1979, pp.85–6.
29. Kristeller, 1902, p.546, doc.103.
30. Kristeller, 1902, pp.543–4, docs.90–5. See Cat.no.76.
31. Kristeller, 1902, p.554, doc.123; Martindale, 1979, p.182, doc.9.
32. Martindale, 1979, p.182, doc.6, letter from Antimaco to Isabella d'Este.
33. This argument would apply even if they were installed in a corridor.
34. Luzio, *Galleria*, 1913, p.105; Martindale, 1979, p.183, doc.12.
35. Kristeller, 1902, p.568, doc.156; original repr. in Luzio-Paribeni, 1940, pl. facing p.12.
36. Martindale, 1979, p.184, docs.17 and 18.
37. Letter of 20 May 1507 from Fra Mariano da Gonzaga to the Marchese Francesco, cit. Luzio, *Galleria*, 1913, p.105; Martindale, 1979, p.184, doc.22.
38. Martindale, 1979, p.95, n.2.
39. Luzio, *Galleria*, 1913, p.25, n.1, n.3; Martindale, 1979, p.34, n.2, p.95, n.2.
40. Kristeller, 1902, p.555, docs.124–5; Martindale, p.182, docs.10,11. See Cat.no.73.
41. The term *telari* of the documents implies that they were of some size.
42. Martindale, p.179, p.183, docs.15–16,18,20,21.
43. For these see N. Dacos, *La découverte de la Domus Aurea et la formation des grotesques à la Renaissance*, 1969.
44. Kristeller, 1902, pp.564–5, doc.149.
45. For Lodovico and the artists he employed see D'Arco, ii, p.197 (letter of Affò of 2 April 1775 concerning him); U. Rossi, in *Rivista italiana di numismatica*, i, 1888, pp.25–40 (for Ermes Flavio de Bonis), pp.161–94 (for Antico) and *id.*, 'Commedie classiche in Gazzuolo nel 1501–1507' in *G.S.L.I.*, xiii, 1889, pp.305–15. For Antico's letter from Rome see Gaye, i, 1839, pp.337–8, and D'Arco, ii, p.40 (wrongly supposed to be written from Cosenza), and Rossi, *art. cit.*, pp.169–70.
46. See the inventory taken in 1457 of the collections of Cardinal Pietro Barbo, in Müntz, *Les arts à la cour des papes*, ii, pp.196–200 (cf. pp.158–9 for Müntz's comments).
47. That Mantegna owned quite a collection of original antique sculptures as early as 1484 is proved by Lorenzo de'Medici's visit to him in February of that year in order to see them (Kristeller, 1902, p.541, doc.86).
48. Kristeller, 1902, p.546, doc.102.
49. Kristeller, 1902, p.550.
50. Pignoria, *Symbolicarum epistolarum liber*, Padua, 1628, p.18.

IX Mantegna in Rome

1. See Cat.no.29.
2. Kristeller, 1902, p.545, doc.101. For the remaining correspondence see pp.545–9, docs.100–9.
3. Taja, *Descrizione del Palazzo Apostolico Vaticano*, 1750 (written c.1712) p.402.
4. For these intarsia decorations see M.J. Thornton, 'Tarsie: design and designers' in *J.W.C.I.*, xxxvi, 1973, pp.377–9.
5. Here I follow Taja (*op. cit.*, p.404), whose description makes better sense than that of Chattard (*Nuova descrizione del Vaticano*, iii, 1767, p.141), who says this scene was painted on a cornice.
6. Fiera, *De Ivsticia pingenda*, ed. J. Wardrop, 1957, pp.18–24. For Battista Fiera see C. Dionisotti, 'Battista Fiera' in *Italia medioevale e umanistica*, i, 1958, pp.401–18; E. Faccioli, in Istituto Carlo d'Arco, *Mantova: le lettere*, ii, 1962, pp.366–73; R. Jones, 'What Venus did with Mars: Battista Fiera and Mantegna's *Parnassus*' in *J.W.C.I.*, xliv, 1981, pp.193–8.
7. Fiera, *op. cit.*, p.18.
8. Cortese, cit. in Cat.no.29.
9. Gerola, p.911, no.2: cf. also C. Elam in *Splendours of the Gonzaga*, 1981–2, p.25 n.11; Kristeller, 1902, p.549, doc.109; Vasari, 1550, i, p.511.
10. For *equites aurati* and for papal knighthoods and papal grants of the title of count palatine see H.C. Zeininger, 'Essai sur l'ordre de l'éperon d'or' in *Rivista araldica*, xxxiii, 1935, pp.52–61; *id.*, 'Contribution à l'histoire des comtes palatins du Latran', *ibid.*, xxxv, 1937, pp.390–7; *id.*, 'Contribution à l'histoire des ordres de chevalerie pontificaux' and 'Nouvelle contribution . . .', *ibid.*, xxxvii, 1939, pp.168–84, xxxviii, 1940, pp.170–83; *id.*, 'L'Ordre de l'Eperon d'Or' in *Archives*, liii, 1939, pp.91–5; G. Bascapé, 'Gli ordini di Cavalleria Pontifici . . . ii, Ordine dello Speron d'Oro a Milizia Aurata', in *Rivista araldica.*, xxxvi, 1938, pp.558–6; D.L. Galbreath, 'La Militia Aurata' in *Archives héraldiques suisses*, xxvii, 1927, pp.25–8. See also Moroni, *Dizionario di erudizione storico ecclesiastica*, xvii, pp.56–60. There appear to have been no papal orders of knighthood before 1520, but papal knighthoods were already being conferred in the fourteenth century.
11. Kristeller, 1902, p.553, doc.116 (*spectabilis miles et comes magnificus*). For Mantegna's claim of 1469 see pp.120. For G. Bellini's grant see Hill, i, p.173. For the Emperor's visit to Venice see Ghinzoni, in *Archivio Veneto*, xxxvii, 1889, pp.133–44.
12. Gerola, p.913, no.16; Kristeller, p.542, doc.9, p.544, doc.544; Gerola, p.913, no.15; Resti-Ferrari, p.270; Gerola, p.915, nos.19–20.
13. See Cat.no.31.
14. According to Kristeller, 1901, p.228.
15. See Cat.no.32.
16. See Cat.no.33.
17. C. del Bravo, *Liberale da Verona*, 1967, fig. cxcvi, for a version in the Museo Correr.
18. For Niccolò see Tiraboschi, *Biblioteca modenese*, ii, 1782, pp.103–35, and Luzio-Renier, 'La coltura e le relazioni letterarie di Isabella d'Este Gonzaga' in *G.S.L.I.*, xxi, 1893, p.205 ff.; xxii, 1893, pp.65 ff.; xxxv, 1900, pp.233–5.

X The Great Altarpieces

1. See Cat.no.36. For Francesco at Fornovo see Luzio-Renier, 'Francesco Gonzaga alla battaglia di Fornovo (1495) secondo i documenti mantovani' in *A.S.I.*, ser.5, vi, 1890, pp.205–46, and L. Mazzoldi, in Istituto Carlo d'Arco, *Mantova: la storia*, ii, 1961, pp.100–8. For the *Madonna della Vittoria* see Cat.no.36.

2. Hill, 400 (by Sperandio), cf. also 205.

3. Luzio-Renier, *op. cit.*, p.221, letter to Isabella of 7 July 1495.

4. Portioli, 'La chiesa e la Madonna della Vittoria di A. Mantegna in Mantova' in *Atti e memorie della R. Accademia Virgiliana*, 1884, p.77.

5. Donnesmondi, *Dell'istoria ecclesiastica di Mantova*, ii, 1616, pp.74–5, 85; Portioli, *op. cit.*, p.64, n.2; Bertolotti, *I comuni e le parrocchie della provincia mantovana*, 1893, p.93, says the church was built in 1494: its building and decoration were going forward in 1495 (Portioli, *loc. cit.*).

6. For the Gonzaga and the Jews, who were primarily a community of bankers, see Coniglio, p.57 (for Leone da Norsa, Daniele's father, who settled at Castel Goffredo in 1468), Luzio, *Galleria*, 1913, pp.14–15; L. Mazzoldi, in Istituto Carlo d'Arco, *Mantova: la storia*, ii, 1961, pp.437–43, and above all Castelli, 'I banchi feneratizi ebraici nel mantovano' in Mantua, Accademia Virgiliana, *Atti e Memorie*, n.s.xxxi, 1959. Leone da Norsa built the first synagogue in Mantua (Castelli, p.35): later (pp.36–7) it appears that Daniele and his brothers Simone and Moisé were one of three Jewish banking houses in Mantua. Daniele was succeeded by his son Isaac on 17 June 1504 (p.39).

7. Portioli, *op. cit.*, pp.59–61.

8. Luzio, 'La "Madonna della Vittoria" del Mantegna' in *Emporium*, x, 1899, p.360.

9. For Redini see Portioli, pp.65 ff; Luzio, *art. cit.* in *Emporium*, id., 'Isabella d'Este e i Borgia' in *A.S.L.*, ser.5, xli, 1912, pp.498,500–2; Amadei, ii, p.353; Donnesmondi, *op. cit.*, p.85.

10. Portioli, *op. cit.*, pp.64–5.

11. Luzio, *op. cit.*, p.360. According to Donnesmondi (*op. cit.*, pp.123–4), Don Marco da Porto, a priest, had little learning, but was endowed with spiritual insight and the gift of prophecy. He was a visionary and a friend of the Beata Osanna Andreasi.

12. Luzio, *op. cit.*, p.360.

13. Luzio, *loc. cit.*, wrongly dated by Portioli.

14. On the assumption, that is, that the document was correctly transcribed by Luzio.

15. Luzio, *op. cit.*, p.365. Daniele was only absolved from the accusation of having profaned sacred images (though not proved) by a decree of Francesco issued on 19 August 1497 (Castelli, *op. cit.*, p.39).

16. The *&c.* must include the other figures mentioned in the letter of 8 August (see above) to which it seems to refer.

17. Luzio, *op. cit.*, pp.365–6.

18. Vasari, iii, 1878, p.403.

19. See Luzio, *op. cit.*, p.365, where the picture is reproduced, and pp.373–4. See also Amadei, ii, p.318, 353 (compare Donnesmondi, *vol. cit.*, p.89). The picture was originally in the refectory of the convent built by the Hieronymite friars: the Jews wear the yellow disc which Isabella d'Este had reimposed by an edict of April 1496, in deference to the fiery preachings of a friar (see Mazzoldi, *op. cit.*, p.439 and refs.). For anti-Jewish sentiment in late fifteenth-century Mantua see also Luzio, *op. cit.*, p.374.

20. Donnesmondi, *vol. cit.*, pp.85–6; Amadei, ii, p.319.

21. For his return and subsequent campaigns see the chronicle of Jacopo d'Atri, in *A.S.L.*, vi, 1879, pp.352–4, 500 ff. For his especial devotion to the Virgin see p.64.

22. Kristeller, 1902, pp.561–2, no.141.

23. Luzio, *op. cit.*, pp.367–8.

24. Portioli, *La Zecca di Mantova*, i, 1879, p.85.

25. See note 20.

26. Vasari, *loc. cit.* Francisco da Holanda, *Dialogos de Roma. Da Pintura Antiga*, ed. M. Mendes, 1955, pp.18–20.

27. For this picture see Davies, 1961, pp.370–71.

28. Genesis, 3, 16.

29. For the Virgin as a second Eve see E. Guldan, *Eva und Maria: eine Antitese als Bild motiv*, 1966 (for Mantegna's picture see pp.87,123,201, no.101).

30. D'Arco, ii, p.197.

31. For the symbolism of coral see in the first instance Tescione, *Il corallo nella storia e nell' arte*, 1965, with ample bibliography. Tescione (pp.243–4) interprets the coral as a child's coral. See also Leonardus, *Speculum lapidum* 1502, f.xlviii,v.

32. For this fresco see Bettinelli, *Delle lettere e delle arti mantovane*, ed. L. Pescasio (first printed 1774), p.61; and Amadei, ii, pp.318–19. Its last traces disappeared with the destruction in 1944 of the building on which it was painted. Donnesmondi (*vol. cit.*, pp.84,86) describes another fresco on another arch facing the Salaio, which he attributes to Correggio, and which he says represented Francesco kneeling before the Madonna with his horse by his side.

33. Its uniqueness is noted by S. Braunfels in the article on St George in W. Braunfels, ed., *Lexikon der Christlichen Iconographie*, vi, 1974, col.377.

34. cf. the verses in Battista Spagnoli's poem *Trophaeum Gonzagae* in *Poemata*, ii, ed. of 1512 by Ascensius, f.95v.

35. For this broken lance see the letter of 11 July from B. Capilupi to Francesco, cit. Coniglio, p.147; cf. also Luzio-Renier, in *A.S.I.*, ser.5, vi, 1890, p.234.

36. See Cat.no.37.

XI Isabella d'Este and her Studiolo

1. Luzio, *I Precettori*, 1887, p.18.

2. Luzio, *I Precettori*, pp.21–8.

3. For the history of the *studio* and *studiolo* see W. Liebenwein, *Studiolo: die Enstehung eines Raumtyps and seine Entwicklung bis um 1600*, 1977.

4. Vasić Vatoveć, 1979, pp.177,186.

5. Davari, in *A.S.L.*, ser.3, iii, 1895, pp.434–9. For Isabella's Studiolo in general see E. Verheyen, *The Paintings in the Studiolo of Isabella d'Este at Mantua*, 1971, here especially pp.6–9. See also Cat.no.38.

6. For Guarino and Isabella see Luzio, *I Precettori*, 1887, pp.12–26; Luzio-Renier, 'La coltura', in *G.S.L.I.*, xxxiii, 1899, pp.3–4, and *G.S.L.I.*, xxxv, 1900, pp.212–18.

7. Kristeller, 1902, p.549, doc.110.

8. Kristeller, 1902, p.553, doc.117.

9. For Isabella del Balzo (b.1465) see Ricca, *La nobiltà delle due Sicilie*, i, 1859, p.447, iv, 1879, pp.69,72; Cian, 'Di Giovanni Muzzarelli e d'una sua operetta inedita' in *G.S.L.I.*, xxi, 1893, pp.366–7n; B. Croce, 'Isabella del Balzo regina di Napoli in un inedito poema sincrono' in *Archivio storico per le province napoletane*, xxii, 1897, pp.632–701.

10. See for this correspondence Luzio, in *Emporium*, xi, 1900, pp.347–8. Kristeller, 1902, pp.553–4, docs.118,119,120,122. The extract from Santi's chronicle, published by Holtzinger, ed., *Cronaca di Giovanni Santi*, 1893, pp.187–8, can be conveniently consulted in Kristeller, 1902, pp.493–5, no.12.

11. See for this statue D.J.B. Robey, 'Virgil's statue at Mantua . . .' in *Rinascimento*, ser.2, ix, 1969, pp.183–203.

12. See Luzio-Renier, 'La coltura' in *G.S.L.I.*, xl, 1902, pp.298–300,304; letter reprinted in Kristeller, 1902, pp.566–7, doc.152.

13. See Cat.no.85.

14. Verheyen, pp.10,11.

15. Verheyen, p.12, n.25; Kristeller, 1902, p.563, doc.146; Verheyen, p.13, n.27. The *piedestalli* of Alberto's letter are to be interpreted as the pilasters of the framework or the framework, cf. Florio, s.v.

16. F. Canuti, *Il Perugino*, ii, 1931, p.209, no.308, letter from Isabella to Francesco Malatesta of 15 September 1502.

17. Verheyen, 1971, p.13, n.28; p.14, n.29.

18. Canuti, ii, p.217, no.327, letter of 10 December 1503.

19. Canuti, ii, p.217, no.328. Similarly she wrote to Bentivoglio on 14 November 1504 when giving instructions about a painting to be executed for her in Bologna: 'Inclusa li mando la longheza de le magior figure che sono in li quadri del Mantigna, qual è da uno groppo a l'altro del filo: le altre figure che vanno minore se hanno a fare a beneplacito del pictore, secundo la rasone di la stantia et sorte di esse.' (Published by Luzio, in *Rivista d'Italia*, xii (pt.2), 1909, pp.864–5.)

20. Canuti, ii, p.210, no.312, letter from Isabella of 22 November 1502 (or 18 October, see Verheyen, p.14, n.30).

21. Kristeller, 1902, p.572, doc.164; repeated in a letter of 16 July 1504, p.573, doc.165.

22. Canuti, ii, p.236, no.376, letter from Isabella to Perugino of 30 June 1505.

23. For this letter see Luzio-Renier, 'La coltura', in *G.S.L.I.*, xxvi, 1901, p.205. But see Luzio, 'Disegni topografici e pitture dei Bellini' in *Arch. stor. dell'arte*, i, 1888, p.277, for a letter in which Bellini expresses a preference for hearing his patron's fancy before beginning a picture.

24. For this see Canuti, ii, pp.212–13, doc.316.

25. Luzio, *I. Precettori*, 1887, p.35.

26. See Luzio-Renier, 'Niccolò da Correggio' in *G.S.L.I.*, xxi, 1893, pp.227,230–1, 252–4; cf. also *id.*, 'La coltura', in *G.S.L.I.*, xxxviii, 1901, p.62, for a letter to Casio of 2 April 1505 in which Isabella asks for the return of 'la lettera contenente la historia che dovea fare quel frate suso uno quadro per mettere nel camerino nostro … perchè voressimo mutare el sentimento.'

27. For Paride da Ceresara see Amadei, ii, pp.556–9 (for palace); Tiraboschi, *Storia della letteratura italiana*, vii, pt.i, 1784, pp.428–9 (for physical description); Rossi, in *G.S.L.I.*, xiii, 1889, pp.310–11 (especially for Hebrew learning); Luzio-Renier, 'La coltura', in *G.S.L.I.*, xxxiv, 1899, pp.86–90 (for Isabella's letter); F. De Angelis, in *Dizionario biografico degli italiani*, xxiii, pp.720–1 (poorly informed). For contemporary references see Luca Gaurico, *Opera*, ii, p.1634; Niccolò d'Arco, *Carmina* in Fracastoro, *Carmina*, ii, 1739, pp.215–16 (Book 2, carm. xviii, a funeral elegy, xix–xx). Paride was part of Mantegna's circle in Mantua: a letter of 17 June 1500 from Matteo Bosso in Padua to Agostino Strozzi, a fellow Canon Regular in Mantua, reports that he has welcomed Paride to Padua and ends: 'Reverendo Stefanino, Antillae atque Mantineae me si commiseris, facies rem mihi pergratam' (Bosso, *Epistolarum tertia pars*, pp. Dviii *v*-E(i)*v*). D'Arco (see above) praises him for his profound and arcane learning in the secrets of nature, and adds: 'at quicquid Apollo/fila movens citharae docuit, dum sacra canentum/Ora aperit vatum, & divinum concitat oestrum.'

28. Luzio-Renier, 'La coltura' in *G.S.L.I.*, xxiv, 1899, p.89. Luzio, 'Isabella d'Este e Giulio II' in *Rivista d'Italia*, xii (pt.2), 1909, pp.863–4. For a calendar of documents concerning the commissioning of pictures from Costa and Francia see Brown, in *Mitteilungen des Kunsthistorischen Institutes in Florenz*, xiii, 1967–8, pp.321–24. Costa's *invenzione* was devised by Paride da Ceresara.

29. Canuti, ii, p.223, doc.346.

30. The standard study of Anteros in the Renaissance is R. V. Merrill, 'Eros and Anteros' in *Speculum*, xii, 1944, pp.265–84 (but see note 33 below).

31. For Hedo (Capretto) and his book see V. Zabughin, 'Petri Haedi Sacerdotis Portusnaensis "Anterotica"' in *G.S.L.I.*, lxxviii, 1919, pp.313–17; M. Miglio, in *Dizionario biografico degli italiani*, xix, 1976, pp.186–89, s.v. Capretto.

32. Cicero, *De Natura Deorum*, III, c.23.

33. The date of this edition, all important for the chronology of the Studiolo, is wrongly given by Merrill (*op. cit.*, p.273) as 1493, misquoting Brunet, *Manuel*, ii, 1861, 1421.

34. For Battista da Campo Fregoso (1453–1504) also known as Fulgosius, see Apostolo Zeno, *Dissertazioni Vossiane*, ii, 1753, p.215; Litta, *Famiglie celebri d'Italia*, iii, s.v. Fregoso, tav. x; Flamini, *Il cinquecento*, s.d., p.378; Levati, *I dogi perpetui di Genova (1339–1528)*, 1930.

35. The argument for Equicola as inventor is urged by Verheyen, *op. cit.*, pp.28–39. For Equicola see Luzio, *I Precettori*, 1887; Renier, 'Per la cronologia e la composizione del Libro de natura de Amore' in *G.S.L.I.*, xiv, 1889, pp.212–33; Luzio-Renier, *La coltura* in *G.S.L.I.*, xxxiv, 1899, pp.8–20; D. Santoro, *Della vita e delle opere di Mario Equicola*, 1906; G. Bertoni, 'Nota su Mario Equicola bibliofilo e cortigiano' in *G.S.L.I.*, lxvi, 1915, pp.281–3; P. Rajna, 'Per chi studia l'Equicola' in *G.S.L.I.*, lxvii, 1916, pp.360–75.

36. For his early service in Ferrara see T. Ascori, in *Dizionario biografico degli italiani*, xviii, 1975, pp.277–9, s.v. Cantelmo, Sigismondo.

37. Equicola, *Libro di natura d'amore*, ed. of Venice, 1526, f.63r.

38. For Lodovico's letter see Luzio, *Archivio Gonzaga*, ii, 1922, p.239.

39. Cited by Luzio, *Mantova e Urbino*, 1893, p.93.

40. Luzio-Renier, in *G.S.L.I.*, xxi, 1893, pp.247–8, letter from Niccolò to Isabella of 8 July 1493.

41. Luzio-Renier, *op. cit.*, pp.253–4.

42. Alberti, *op. cit.*, ed. Mallé, 1950, p.104.

43. *Silva*. First printed *c*.1499 in *Opera omnia*, p.48b–49b. It can be read in Kristeller, 1902, pp.491–3, no.10.

44. See Cat.no.39. For the iconography of Parnassus in general see E. Schröter, *Die Ikonographie des Themas Parnass vor Raffael: die Schrift und Bildtraditionen von der Spätantike bis zum 15. Jahrhundert*, 1977. See pp.280–300 for her discussion of Mantegna's picture.

45. Ovid, *Metamorphoses*, I, 313–19.

46. See the descriptions by Pausanias, X, c.6.32, and Strabo, IX, 2, but the twin peaks of Parnassus were a well-established feature of poetic scenery. For Helicon see Pausanias and Strabo, *loc. cit.* The pierced rock is surely not the Corycian cave of Parnassus as sometimes claimed, nor that of the Libethrides on Helicon. To begin with it is not a cave, and the motif of a rock pierced by a passage is found in the outdoor fresco of the Camera Picta and in the *Madonna delle Cave*. It is simply a picturesque invention.

47. For a representation of a lectisternium of the kind that may have influenced Mantegna see a medal of Faustina with lectisternium dedicated to Juno reproduced in Du Choul, *Discours de la Religion des anciens Romains*, ed. of 1567, p.52. Ovid, *Metamorphoses*, I, 466 ff.

48. For the doctrine of the two Venuses see Plato, *Symposium* (trans. by Ficino as *Convivium*), II, 7. For a discussion of the Neo-Platonic interpretation of these ideas see Panofsky, *Studies in Iconology*, 1959, pp.141 ff.

49. Albericus Philosophus, *De deorum imaginibus libellus*, xv.

50. The identification of these wires and tools, though quite unambiguous, is denied by Verheyen (p.37, n.67).

51. Hedo, 1492, ff.vi–vii (Bk. I, c.2), ff.xxxi–ii (Bk.II, c.36).

52. Hedo, f.xxvi (Bk.I, c.33), ff.vi–vii (Bk.I, c.2).

53. For an example of Isabella's liking for broad jokes see Luzio-Renier, 'La coltura', in *G.S.L.I.*, xxxv, 1900, p.243 and n.2. (cit. also by Coniglio, p.148). However, these things should not be exaggerated: the letter of 20 February 1511 from her lady-in-waiting Brognina (Luzio-Renier, *Mantova e Urbino*, 1893, p.203) to Isabella's son Federico, so often cited as a proof of the shamelessness of Isabella and her entourage (e.g. by Coniglio, pp.148–9), was written to Federico when he was only 11 and does not bear the

prurient interpretation usually put on it.

54. T. Calpurnius Siculus, *Bucolicon*, VI, 39–41. For the identification as the stars of the constellation Pegasus see P. Lehmann, *Samothracian Reflections*, 1973, pp.70,132–9.

55. For Cavallo and these quotations see Luzio-Renier, 'La coltura', in *G.S.L.I.*, xxxix, 1902, pp.247–9; Balestrieri, in *Dizionario biografico degli italiani*, xxii, 1979, pp.789–92.

56. I term it a cithara rather than a lyre, as this is probably what Mantegna and the Mantuan circle called it. In design it is a cithara stylized. (Blum, *Mantegna und die Antike*, 1936, p.102; Lehmann, *op. cit.*, pp.89–90; Schröter, p.287, n.1033; Martindale, 1979, p.155.)

57. Hyginus, *Fabulae*, c.14; *Poeticon Astronomicon*, c.vii.

58. Although this is so, the identification of the figure as Linus, son of Apollo, favoured in the Louvre exh.cat. *Le Studiolo d'Isabella d'Este*, ed. S. Béguin, 1975, pp.33,73, n.133, seems implausible.

59. Virgil, *Ecloga VII*, 21, and Servius' commentary on the line.

60. Attention was first drawn to this poem by E. Battisti, 'Il Mantegna e la letteratura classica' in Florence, Istituto Nazionale di Studi sul Rinascimento, *Arte pensiero e cultura a Mantova nel primo rinascimento*, 1965, pp.42–3; cf. also R. Jones, '"What Venus did with Mars": Battista Fiera and Mantegna's *Parnassus*' in *J.W.C.I.*, xliv, 1981, pp.193–8.

61. D'Arco, ii, p.79, no.101.

62. See Baxandall in *J.W.C.I.*, xxviii, 1965, pp.186–8, 201–2.

63. For these and other fifteenth-century representations of the Muses see Schröter, *op. cit.*, pp.238–306; Chastel, *Art et humanisme à Florence*, 1959, p.257, where the verses on the Badia relief are wrongly interpreted as referring to a painting; P. Rotondi, *Manifestazioni di paganesimo umanistico nella civiltà urbinate del rinascimento*, 1960.

64. V. Cian, 'Pietro Bembo e Isabella d'Este Gonzaga' in *G.S.L.I.*, ix, 1887, p.102.

65. Luzio-Renier, 'La coltura', in *G.S.L.I.*, xxxiii, 1899, pp.48–9, and xxxvi, 1900, p.330.

66. Guarino, letter to Leonello of 5 November 1447, ed. Baxandall, in *J.W.C.I.*, xxviii, 1965, p.202, l.1–3: *industria* should be amended to read *industriae*.

67. Guarino, *loc. cit.*

68. Cartari, *Le imagini con la spositione de i Dei de gli antichi*, 1556, f.xvv–xvir.

69. Theocritus, *Cyclops* (Idyll xi) ll.1 ff. This prologue turns on the theme that the Muses are the only cure of love. Lucian, *Dialogues of the Gods*, xv, Venus and Cupid. This dialogue also explains that Cupid never dares assault Pallas.

70. See Luzio-Renier, 'La coltura', in *G.S.L.I.*, xxxvi, 1900, p.331; cf. also G. Turba, 'Galeotto del Carretto tra Casale e Mantova' in *Rinascimento*, ser.2, xi, 1971, p.110.

71. See Luzio, *I Precettori d'Isabella d'Este*, 1887, pp.55–63; Luzio-Renier, 'La coltura' in *G.S.L.I.*, xxxv, 1900, pp.193–206.

72. Cited by Luzio-Renier, 'La coltura' in *G.S.L.I.*, xxxvii, 1901, p.232.

73. Cian, *art. cit.*, pp.102,99, n.3.

74. Luzio-Renier, 'La coltura' in *G.S.L.I.*, xxxiii, 1899, pp.48–52; for Lorenzo da Pavia see *id.*, *Il lusso* in *Nuova Antologia*, cxlix, 1896, pp.274–8, and the edition of the correspondence between Lorenzo and Isabella published by C. M. Brown (*Isabella d'Este and Lorenzo da Pavia: documents for the history of art and culture in Renaissance Mantua*, 1982).

75. Luzio-Renier, 'La coltura' in *G.S.L.I.*, xxxix, 1902, p.246.

76. Luzio-Renier, 'La coltura' in *G.S.L.I.*, xlii, 1903, pp.87–9,107.

77. For the identification of these compare the scourge held by St Benedict in Mantegna's Santa Giustina altarpiece.

78. White hares and birds gather round the feet of St Benedict in a miniature for the Feast of St Benedict in an Italian

gradual of the second half of the fifteenth century, in the Library of the V. & A. Museum (Reid MS 82). The invention can only be intended to suggest innocence and peace. For a summary with literature of the debate about these animals and their symbolical meaning see Lehmann, *op. cit.*, pp.71–3,167–8.

79. Lehmann, *op. cit.*, pp.165–6.

80. In Plutarch's *Moralia*. The passage is from the introductory paragraph.

81. For this poem, see the reference cited in note 60. Fiera has taken the names of his three Cyclops who prepare Vulcan's vengeful net from Virgil, *Aeneid*, VIII, 424. The translation of the poem given in the text is from the version printed in 1515: in the 1537 version 'Mars' own bed' becomes Mars' lawful bed (*legitimos* is substituted for *proprios*); 'avenging hands against Mars' becomes 'against the *adulterer*' (*moechum* is substituted for *Martem*); '*chaste* bed of Mars' becomes 'bed of our Mars' (*casto* is dropped in favour of *nostri*). I do not see in these changes anything more than clarifications, contrary to Jones (art. cit. note 60). He translates the *forma* of the second line as form, but in Latin *forma* also means beauty, and this is surely the meaning required by court decorum. Any serious suggestion that Isabella had allowed herself to be painted naked would never have been permitted to a court poet, one moreover addressing Isabella herself. The reference to 'thy image' below is not literal, but continues the compliment. It must be remembered that there was serious authority for interpreting the story of Mars and Venus as a warning against adultery. Hence the importance of interpreting the individual figures and symbols of a picture like the *Parnassus* in terms of its general meaning, which is plain enough from the action. Distortion follows from attempts to interpret such pictures by adding together interpretations of single features.

82. Luzio-Renier, 'Niccolò da Correggio' in *G.S.L.I.*, xxii, 1893, pp.69–70. It should be noted that this letter clarifies the context of vying exchanges of complimentary verses in which Fiera's poem was plainly written. It is important not to see such poems as literal *ekphrases*, but as *lusus* – exercises of the fancy suggested by a particular work of art. Thus Fiera's poem refers to three of Vulcan's assistants, Steropes, Brontes and Pyracmon, who are not present in the picture, while Vulcan's action is certainly not that of urging them on to prepare the net which is to be the instrument of his vengeance.

83. For the negotiations with Giovanni Bellini see p.264, n.23. For the *Pallas* see Cat.no.40.

84. For Astraea see Ovid, *Metamorphoses*, I, 89–150; Hyginus, *Poeticon Astronomicon*, II, 25. The phrase *virtutum comites* occurs in the proemium to Spagnoli's *De calamitate temporum*, Book II, as also the theme of *Virtus deserta* and the image of *Pietas* preparing to return to heaven. There is other evidence that Isabella was deeply interested in the choice open to man between virtue and vice, one of the favourite moral themes of the age. In October 1496 her newly appointed preceptor Giovanni Battista Pio of Bologna translated for her into Latin hexameters the *Tabula Cebetis*, 'nella quale se discrive la vita humana et le virtude e vitij' (Luzio, *I Precettori*, 1887, p.27). It is perhaps worth noting that Justice, Fortitude and Temperance also reappear in company in a later painting for the Studiolo, Correggio's *Three Virtues*.

85. For this convention for the figure of Daphne see W. Stechow, *Apollo und Daphne* (Studien der Bibliothek Warburg, 23), 1932, pl.1–13. Stechow identifies the figure (p.20, n.4) as *Virtus deserta*, on the analogy of Mantegna's engraving. While this is always possible, the tree is an olive, not a laurel. The figure is not labelled, as in the engraving or

like the other allegorical personifications in the picture, and to identify the motif as symbolizing the union of learning and chastity is in better opposition to the predominantly erotic imagery of the Vices.

86. For Isabella's eager pursuit of learning see Luzio-Renier, 'La coltura', in *G.S.L.I.*, xxxiii, 1899, pp.5–27. In fact the Greek letters contain a Latin inscription. The Hebrew letters are apparently meaningless, but E. Cohen sees two words representing God in them (*Le Studiolo*, Louvre Cat., p.73, n.151).

87. The reference is in Philostratus' dialogue *Heroica*, ed. Boissonade, 1806, p.25 (*Opera*, ed. Kayser, ii, 1871, p.136, c.I, i). For the *Imagines* of Philostratus see K. Lehmann-Hartleben, 'The *Imagines* of the Elder Philostratus' in *A.B.*, xiciii, 1941, pp.16–44. By December 1515 Isabella had owned for some years a Latin version of Philostratus' *Imagines* which she had caused to be made by Demetrios Moscos, a Greek humanist settled in Mantua, where he taught Greek until 1519 (Luzio-Renier, 'La coltura', in *G.S.L.I.*, 1899, xxxiii, pp.22–3; xlii, 1903, p.77, no.50). Boethius, *De consolatione Philosophiae*, i, prosa III, calls Philosophia 'omnium magistra virtutum'.

88. Truth is the identification adopted by R. Förster in his brilliant study of the iconography of the picture (in *J.P.K.*, xxii, 1901, pp.159–63). Förster was unaware of the source in Philostratus, but based his identification on the inscription on a *cartello* attached to the window of the prison wall behind which Truth is figured as captive in a painting of the *Calumny of Apelles* by a follower of Mantegna, now in the Museum of Nîmes. This picture was published by Förster (in *J.P.K.*, viii, 1887, pp.54–6). The inscription reads *Virtutum Omnium Hic/Vi Retenta Est Mater/O Saeculum Miserum O/Crudele Saeculum*. Another inscription on a *cartello* across the steps leading up by the wall makes it clear that the *Mater omnium virtutum* is here certainly Truth, for it reads *O Me Infelicem Deam Veridicam/ Que Nunquam Nunquam Nunquam/ Aut Turpiter Mea Maxima Cum Infamia/ Ad Aures Principum Misella Acciar*. But Förster failed to note that here the allegory and inscriptions are especially appropriate to the theme of the Calumny of Apelles, in which lies almost bring Apelles to death. It is not safe then to apply the inscription in this picture as a key to Mantegna's inscription. There seems no particular allegorical point in the introduction of Truth into *Pallas expelling the Vices*. Contemporaries, familiar with the concept of the four Cardinal or Moral Virtues, would have divined at once that three of them had taken refuge in heaven from the Vices, while the fourth and most important, Prudentia, had been imprisoned. The description of Chastity in the *Trionfo della Castità* of Isabella's favourite poet Petrarch was interpreted as figuring the four Moral Virtues (cf. e.g. Gesualdo's commentary on the lines beginning 'Honestate, & uergogna a la front'era'). Nevertheless, Förster's interpretation of the figure as Truth has won general acceptance. There may also be a source for the invention in Horace, *Odes*, IV, 9,28: 'paulum sepultae distat inertiae/celata virtus'.

89. Cicero, *De Legibus*, I, 17,47; 22,58. Cicero's remarks are in the context of a discussion of virtue and vice. Battista da Campo Fregoso, *Anteros*, 1496, de viiv–d viiii.

90. Aristotle, *Ethics*, vi, in the original reference, really vii, 10.

91. Seneca, preface to *Declamationes*.

92. Cicero, *Tusculanae Disputationes*, IV, 35,75. In c.7 Cicero lists the components of lust 'ira, excandescentia, odium, inimicitia, discordia, indigentia, desiderium et cetera eiusmodi'.

93. Augustine, *De Civitate Dei*, XIV, 16.

94. *op. cit.*, f.iii r.

95. For Isabella and the *Cárcel de Amor* see Luzio-Renier, 'La coltura' in *G.S.L.I.*, xxxv, 1900, p.244; *G.S.L.I.*, xlii, 1903, p.77, no.43.

96. Spagnoli, *Trophaeum Gonzagae*, Bk. III (ed. of Paris, 1513, iii, f.cvir); *De calamitate temporum*, Bk II, in ed. cit., ff.xliiir–xlivv.

97. Ovid, *Amores*, I, 7–8; *Fasti*, vi, 652; *Tristia*, I, x, 1. It has been suggested that the coral crest probably derives from the description of Pallas in the opening section of Bk VI of Martianus Capella, *De nuptiis Mercurii et Philologiae*. There may also be some inspiration for the figure from Lucian, *Dialogues of the Gods*, xv, Venus and Cupid. Lucian makes Cupid say that 'he fears Pallas, for she is frightful and fierce, and when I approach her with drawn bow, she shakes her crest and terrifies me, and I tremble and my weapons fall from my hands ... She ever looks on me fiercely and with suspicion: so much so, that should I so much as fly past her, with my torch brought close, she at once declares "If you approach me, I swear by my Father, I will transfix you with my spear, or seize you and throw you into Tartarus, and or tear you limb from limb."' But Lucian's description of Pallas's serpent tresses differs from Mantegna's figuration.

98. G. de Tervarent, *Attributs et symboles dans l'art profane*, ii, 1959, 410–11, provides a convenient summary of the figurations of Fortune and her sail and of Venus with a sail in quattrocento art.

99. Spagnoli, *De calamitate temporum*, ed. cit., ff.xxxiv–xxxv. For *Contra Amorem* see ff.xcviv–xcviir.

100. *Anteros*, e ir–iiv.

101. See Cat.nos.193 and 200.

102. Love often appears in English eighteenth-century poetry with azure wings, but I have not been able to trace a classical origin for the figuration.

103. It was Förster (in *J.P.K.*, xxii, p.162) who first identified the figure with the bow and quiver as Diana and the figure with the torch as Chastity, and interpreted their action as pursuit of the Vices. His identification and interpretation have been accepted at least in their general lines (e.g. in Verheyen, 1971, pp.31–5, and Louvre Cat., 1975, p.38). Against the identification it should be noted first that the inscription on the scroll wound round the olive-tree refers to DIVAE COMITES (divine or goddess companions) of the Virtues. If this pair are to be associated with Pallas as divine companions of the Virtues, as Förster supposes, then we should expect all three to be goddesses. But Chastity is not a goddess, and as a virtue is not very aptly termed a 'divine companion' of the other Virtues of Fortitude, Temperance and Justice.

The *Divae Comites*, moreover, are to assist in the act of expelling the Vices. But the figure with bow and arrow simply carries them: she makes no use of them and is unprepared for battle, being barefooted, like Venus. Her action is surely flight, not pursuit: her raised right hand indicates terror and a call for aid to her mistress Venus.

Though Förster recognizes that her companion's attribute is a torch, he makes no attempt to explain why a torch, which lit or unlit is a token of the fires of Love, should be carried by Chastity. No other instance of Chastity with this attribute is known, and for this reason alone Förster's identification is more than dubious, especially as the other attributes and allegorical features of the picture are all perfectly conventional. Again her action is flight, not pursuit, and like her companion, she must be considered a nymph of Venus.

104. Such moustaches appear nowhere else in quattrocento art, except in the Perugino, as far as the author is aware.

105. Aldrovandi, *Ornithologia*, i, ed. of 1646, p.518.

106. *Anteros*, 1496, dviiiiv–eir.

107. *Anteros*, 1496, av*v*.

108. For Saba da Castiglione and Isabella see Luzio, 'Lettere inedite di fra Sabba da Castiglione' in *A.S.L.*, ser.2, iii, 1886, pp.91–112.

109. Saba da Castiglione, *Ricordi ovvero ammaestramenti*, ed. of Milan, 1559, p.82. The quotation from Ovid, and the thought and the imagery of the picture, can also be paralleled in a letter from a religious humanist who was a friend of Mantegna and a member of Mantuan literary circles, Matteo Bosso. Writing in the autumn of 1501 to the novice Giovanni Castrocuccio (Bosso, *Epistvlarum tertia pars*, Kvii,*v*–Kviii,*r*) he says, '*Sunt praeterea & alia presidia contra irrventes libidinis faces et intestini ardoris insertas nobis ac nativas iniurias praeter illa quae modo perstrinximus: quibus qui se tueri cupit: munire in adversum facile poterit. Quo in genere haec omnia sunt, infirmitas, inopia, luctus, criminationes, fatigationes, detrimenta rerum, iniuriae hominum, praepossessionesque laborum, & aduersa reliqua: quorum est plena undique uita. Quae nos cum petunt, incursant, arietant et feriunt: explosa fugit Venus, abuolatque Cupido. Dum igitur vexantur electi, & pugiles Christi homines atterruntur, incommodis exterreri ne debeantur. In praessuris et angustiis uirtus radices altius figit, roboraturque ualidius ac dimissa marcescit, & quid possit ignorat. Vnde qui una manu tam lepide, ac lasciue teneros pinxit amores: [Ouidius] altera idem hoc tutissimum porrexit antidotum Ocia si tollas periere cupidinis arcus. Deque Aegisto dum quaeritur quare sit factus adulter: id adstruitur statim, Desidiosus erat.*' Similarly his letter 93 of 4 April 1502 to Arcuano Buzzacarino: '*haec time iuvenilis aetatis naufragia tibi vehementer, in primis ocium quod cunctarum virtutum continentiae praesertim, atque mundiciae uenenum dici, ac parricidium merito potest, institutum perspicax omne, factumque propositum deservans, atque effeminans. Intendisti nam animum litteris: qua susceptione nikil beatius, atque libero homine dignius.*'

110. Ovid, *Remedia Amoris*, 141–9.

111. Spagnoli, *De calamitate temporum*, in ed.cit., ii, f.xliii–*v*.

112. For this letter see Luzio-Renier in *G.S.L.I.*, xxxv, 1900, pp.215–16. So too on 8 February 1493 Guarino again congratulates Isabella on her eagerness to learn, 'trovandosi al di de hogi poche vostre pare, e forsi niuna in Italia che sia litterata' (Luzio, *I Precettori d'Isabella d'Este*, 1887, pp.21–3). The quotation from Cicero is from *Tusculanae Disputationes*, V, 36,105 (*quid est enim dulcius otio litterato*). That from Seneca is from Epistula 82.

113. Cit. by Luzio-Renier in *G.S.L.I.*, xxxv, 1900, p.223.

114. Alberti, *Della pittura*, ed. Mallé, 1950, pp.104–5. Cat.no.195.

115. Letter to Isabella of 16 October 1506 (Kristeller, 1902, p.584, doc.193).

116. Spagnoli, *ed. cit.*, ii, ff.xcixv–cr.

117. Dione was the mother of Venus (cf. the passage cited from Hedo on p.196). The fount of Libethrus near Magnesia, in Macedonia, was sacred to the Muses, who were sometimes known as the Libethrides.

118. For this picture and its documentation see Cat.no.41.

XII The Paintings in Monochrome

1. Dürer, *Schriftlicher Nachlass*, ed. E. Heidrich, 1910, p.124.

2. The story first appears in Ridolfi, 1648, p.71: '*Raccontasi, ch'essendo venuto in Italia Alberto Durero famoso Pittore, & intagliatore di Stampe, ciò risaputosi da Andrea lo invitò con particolare messo a Mantoua, desiderando riconoscerlo, e trattar seco per l'accutezza del suo ingegno, il che incontrando volontieri Alberto, si pose in viaggio: ma prima, che giongesse a Mantova Andrea morì, di che molto si condolse il Durero; onde soleua dire non essergli accaduta cosa la più trista in sua vita.*' The agreement of dates makes this story at least possible.

3. For this group see Cat.nos.50–7, 141–3.

4. See Cat.nos.92 and 93.

5. Vasari, ii, 1878, p.214. Marc' Antonio Michiel (Anonimo Morelliano) (1884, p.66) says they were 'de chiaro e scuro'.

6. For Pizzolo see Rigoni, 1970, pp.31,43, doc.XII; for the San Francesco scenes and those of the Scuola della Carità see Muraro, in *B.M.*, ci, 1959, pp.89–96; *id.* in *Boll. Mus. Civ. Pad.*, l, 1961, pp.21–66; *id.* in *Da Giotto a Mantegna*, exh.cat. Padua, 1974, pp.67–74.

7. An early example is the composition by Francesco di Giorgio of which a version in terracotta is in the V. & A. Museum (251–1876; *Catalogue of Italian Sculpture*, i, 1964, p.266, No.282).

8. Saba da Castiglione, *Ricordi*, ed. of 1559, Ricordo CIX, p.114.

9. Luzio, *Isabella d'Este e Francesco Gonzaga promessi sposi*, 1908, p.26; Rossi, in *Rivista italiana di numismatica*, i, 1888, pp.28–31; Luzio-Renier, 'Di Pietro Lombardo . . .' in *Archivio storico dell'arte*, i, 1888, pp.433–8; C. Perina in Istituto Carlo d'Arco, *Mantova: Le Arti*, i, 1960, p.562. See Part III, chapter 2 of this last work for a study of sculpture in Mantua during the later fifteenth century.

10. For these see V. & A. Museum, *Catalogue of Italian Sculpture*, *vol. cit.*, pp.353–7, No.380.

11. For this see Cat.no.57.

12. For the relations between the Cornaro and the Bellini as early as 1471 see U. Schmitt, 'Gentile Bellini' in *Dizionario biografico degli italiani*, vii, 1965, p.696. For Francesco Cornaro see Sanuto, *Diarii*, *passim*, especially iii, 86; vii, 74; viii, 250,449–50; ix, 645; xii, 179; xiv, 403; xxiii, 362. Bembo, *Opere*, iii, 1727, p.26 (letter of 14 June 1533), pp.142–3 (letter of vigil of our Lady, August 1525, to Cola Bruno).

13. That Niccolò Bellini, whose existence is argued for by G. Robertson (*Giovanni Bellini*, 1968, p.10, n.5), really did exist is confirmed not only by this reference but by a document of 1511 printed by Luzio-Renier, 'La coltura' in *G.S.L.I.*, xxxvii, 1901, p.214.

14. For the relations between Isabella and Bembo see Cian, 'Pietro Bembo e Isabella d'Este Gonzaga' in *G.S.L.I.*, ix, 1887, pp.92–100; Luzio-Renier, 'La coltura' in *G.S.L.I.*, xxxvii, 1901, pp.201–9.

15. Bembo, in a letter of 11 January 1506 to Isabella (Kristeller, 1902, pp.576–7, doc.173).

16. See Hieronymus Avantius, *Marco Cornelio. S.M. in porticu Cardinali Veronae Episcopatum Ineunti gratulatur*, Venice, 1504 (oration delivered 4 November), f A*v*. '*Nec pro dignitate celebrabimus corneliam progreniem super omnes Europe familias ut asserit Sextus pompeius festus. Antiquissimam nobilissimam & rebus per omnes aetates splendide gestis florentissimam. Ex qua paene infinitos etiam praetereo. Clarus semper erit ille (ut scribit Cicero) Cuius consilio atque uirtute Annibal eatenus bello invictus italia decedere atque in africam redire coactus est. Huius memoriam quum post epulum de maiorum more celebraret Quintus Maximus gratias egit diis immortalibus quod tantus vir in rempublicam romanam potissimum decus nactus fuisset necesse enim fuisse ibi esse imperium terrarum: ubi ille fuisset. Ornatur alter eximia laude gentilis tuus quod duas urbes Romano imperio infestissimas Carthaginem atque Numantiam deleuit. L. Cornelius Nasica ab aevo condito virorum optimus eiudicatur.*'

17. G. Negri (H. Niger), *In funere Francisci Cornelii cardinalis oratio*, 1546; Avantius, *op. cit.*, A iii *v*.

18. Letter of 31 January 1506 from Isabella to Bembo (Kristeller, 1902, p.579, doc.176): abbreviated, for the full text see Cian, in *G.S.L.I.*, ix, 1887, p.107n.).

19. Valerius Maximus, VIII, 15 (*quæ cuique magnifica contigerunt*), 3.

20. Livy, XXIX, 14.

21. Lucretius, *De rerum natura*, II, 600–43.

22. For this see L. Budde & R. Nichols, *Catalogue of the Greek*

and Roman sculpture in the Fitzwilliam Museum, 1964, pp.77–8; M.J. Vermaseren, *Corpus cultus Cybelae Attidisque*, vii, 1977, no.39.

23. Reinach, *Répertoire de reliefs*, iii, p.321.

24. Juvenal, iii, 66, vi, 511–16.

25. cf. W.H. Roscher, *Ausführliches Lexikon der Griechischen und Römischen Mythologie*, II-i, 1890–7, s.v. Kybele, 1647.

XIII Devotional Pictures

1. For the pictures discussed in this chapter see Cat. nos. 35, 42–9. Kristeller, 1902, p.579, no.176. For the plague that raged in Mantua in 1506 see the reference in Luzio-Renier, *Il lusso* in *Nuova Antologia*, cxlviii, 1896, p.309. Cian, in *G.S.L.I.*, ix, 1887, pp.107–9; Luzio, in R. Accademia Virgiliana di Mantova, *Atti e memorie*, n.s.v., 1912, p.89. It began at Carnival time and lasted until September: more than 2000 people in Mantua and its district are said to have died.

2. Kristeller, 1902, p.583, doc.190.

3. STABILE is in evident allusion to the instability of fortune.

4. See Lodovico Dolce, *Trattato delle Gemme*, ed. of 1617, pp.66–7.

5. The presence of the device proves this.

6. Luzio, *Galleria*, 1913, pp.23–4, n.3.

7. See Luzio, in *A.S.L.*, n.s., 1890, p.661; Kristeller, 1902, pp.564–5. doc.149.

8. This is the sense given for *professore* by Florio, *Queen Anna's New World of Words*, 1611, s.v.

9. Kristeller, 1902, p.575, doc.168; for Saba's letter see Luzio in *A.S.L.*, ser.2, iii, 1886, p.106.

10. The letter is printed in Kristeller, 1902, p.577, doc.174, and reproduced in facsimile by Garavaglia, 1967, p.84. It is wrongly endorsed 13 January (for the correct date, established by Brown, see p.444).

11. Kristeller, 1902, pp.580–1, docs.179,180. Rossi, *loc. cit.* in note 12; Luzio, in *Rivista d'Italia*, xii (pl.2), 1909, pp.871–2. For Gian Giacomo Calandra (1488?–1543) see the article by R. Zapperi, in *Dizionario biografico degli italiani*, xvi, 1973, pp.427–30. Gian Giacomo's brother Federico was superintendent of the Gonzaga cannon foundry, and Gian Giacomo was a virtuoso with a taste for literature and art. He invented a technique of bronze founding and was employed by the Gonzaga a number of times in their negotiations with artists. Zapperi's birth date of 1488 for him seems most implausible: D'Arco (ii, pp.45–6) implies one of 1478. For the suspension of all business in Mantua on account of the plague see also note 13 below.

12. For these letters see Rossi, in *Rivista italiana di numismatica*, i, 1888, pp.187–8, 187n.2.

13. Kristeller, 1902, pp.581–2, docs. 181–5. For criticisms of Isabella's part in such transactions see e.g. Luzio, *Il lusso*, *art. cit.*, pp.308 ff. In a letter written to Taddeo Albano on 27 April 1506 she explains that because of the plague she is in the worst possible straits since all the revenues assigned for her maintenance are unpaid on account of it: 'se la peste non fusse sopragionta a Mantova, qual ni ha in tutto levate le entrate dove havimo lo assigno di la provisione nostra, non haveressimo passato il termine . . . Et tanto più quanto che non gli vedimo ordine nin a parechi mesi, perchè dovendo vivere bisogna trovar dinari in prestito et forsi ad interesse.'

14. For the bust identified as Faustina see Levi, *Sculture greche e romane del Palazzo Ducale di Mantova*, 1931, no.130. The identification is questioned by Martindale, 1979, p.140.

15. Kristeller, 1902, p.565, doc.150. For the two miniaturists named Francesco da Castello see the articles by K. Csapodo-Gárdonyi and M. Harrsen in *Dizionario biografico degli italiani*, xxi, 1978, pp.794–6.

16. W. Braghirolli in *Giornale di Erudizione Artistica*, i, 1872, p.202, n.1; L.C. Pélissier, *Louis XII et Ludovic Sforza*, ii, 1896, pp.366,371. See also Cat.no.86.

17. See for both these references Brown, in *B.M.*, cxiv, 1972, p.862, n.5.

18. For Frederick see Luzio, in *A.S.L.*, ser.4, xv, 1911, pp.257–8.

19. Fernández de Oviedo, *Historia general y natural de las Indias*, ed. J. Pérez de Tudela Bueso, i, 1959, p.xxiv.

XIV Mantegna's Technique

1. Kristeller, 1902, p.515, doc.7.

2. For the subject of Mantegna's pigments and varnishes at Mantua see C.M. Brown in *B.M.*, cxi, 1969, pp.538–44. For the Striggi doc. of 1470 see p.541; cf. also *id.*, in *B.M.*, cxiv, 1972, p.862, docs.v–vII.

3. Vasić Vatovec, 1979, pp.302,303.

4. Kristeller, 1902, p.554, doc.121; Brown, *art. cit.*, in *B.M.*, 1969, p.543.

5. Kristeller, 1902, pp.562–3, no.144.

6. For this see the articles cit. under CONDITION in Cat.no.39.

7. Canuti, ii, 1931, p.236, doc.376, letter of 30 June 1505.

8. Luzio, *Galleria*, 1913, p.24 (as 25 October); Brown, *art. cit.*, *B.M.*, 1972, p.862, doc.IV (as 5 October).

9. Puppi, 1972, p.69. Kristeller, 1902, p.525, doc.39; p.534, doc.69.

10. Eastlake, *Materials for a history of oil painting*, ii, 1869, p.253.

11. Canuti, ii, 1931, p.236, docs.377,378.

12. Kristeller, 1902, p.523, doc.33.

13. Kristeller, 1902, p.544, doc.95; p.563, doc.147; Brown, *art. cit.*, *B.M.*, 1969, pp.541–2.

14. Kristeller, 1902, p.574, doc.167. Letter from Isabella to Bentivoglio of 14 December 1504, pub. Luzio, in *Rivista d'Italia*, xii (pt.2) 1909, pp.864–5. Lomazzo, *Idea del tempio della pittura*, 1590, p.49.

15. For the drawings discussed below see the catalogue section on drawings, nos.176–95.

16. Levi, *Le collezioni veneziane d'arte e d'antichità*, i, 1900, pp.xxxv–vi; Mardersteig in *La Bibliofilia*, xli, 1939, p.107.

17. Lomazzo, *op. cit.*, p.17. The first suggestion of such a treatise was made by Moschini (1826, p.47).

18. Published by Moschini (1826, p.49n) from the copy Bettinelli made for the Cavaliere Giovanni de'Lazara.

XV The Engravings

1. S. Fornari da Reggio, *La spositione sopra l'Orlando furioso*, ii, Florence, 1550, p.509; Vasari, 1550, i, pp.512–13; *id.*, 1568, i, p.492 (ed. of 1880, v, p.496). For Campagnola and his letter see pp.16,393.

2. Scardeone, 1560, p.372; Cellini, from the variant introduction as published in C. Milanesi's ed. of the *Trattati*, 1857, p.13. Datable to 1565. Lomazzo, *Idea del tempio della pittura*, 1590, p.56.

3. Kristeller, 1902, p.530, doc.55.

4. Kristeller, 1902, p.531, doc.58, p.534, docs.66,68.

5. Malaguzzi-Valeri, *Notizie di artisti reggiani*, 1892, p.13.

6. Luzio, *Galleria*, 1913, p.22, n.3. For Zanetto Bugatti (working *c.*1458–75) see Malaguzzi-Valeri, *Pittori lombardi del quattrocento*, 1902, pp.125–36, and M.R. Franco Fiorio in *Dizionario biografico degli italiani*, xv, 1972, pp.14–15, s.v. Bugatti.

7. Malaguzzi-Valeri, *Notizie*, cit., pp.13,21.

8. Malaguzzi-Valeri, *Notizie*, cit., pp.13,21.

9. By Kristeller, 1901, pp.382–4.

10. Kristeller, 1902, pp.550–1, docs.112–14. Mantegna uses the term 'quadretino' in both his letters, so they clearly refer to one and the same work.

11. For details of engravings by or after Mantegna see the section on engravings in the Catalogue.

12. These arguments are stated forcibly by Sheehan (in Levenson–Oberhuber–Sheehan, *Early Italian Engravings from the National Gallery of Art*, 1973, pp.170–6). For the drawing attributed to Zoppo see Popham & Pouncey, 1952, p.164, no.263, and L. Armstrong, *The Paintings and Drawings of Marco Zoppo*, 1976, p.416, D.18. The attribution to Zoppo is, however, rejected by Fiocco (in *G.B.A.*, ser.6, xliii, 1954, p.228).

13. For the early building history of Sant' Andrea see E.J. Johnson, *S. Andrea in Mantua*, 1975, pp.8–62.

14. For these and other motifs of the Venetian ornamental vocabulary of the quattrocento see L. Armstrong, *Renaissance miniature paintings and classical imagery: The Master of the Putti and his Venetian Workshop*, 1981.

15. N. Comes (Natale Conti), *Mythologia*, ed. of Frankfurt, 1596, pp.466–7 (Lib. v, c.8).

16. In the sixteenth century this commentary was still attributed to Tzetzes' brother Isaac, to whom the expression *ichthyocentaur* in connection with Triton is credited by Giraldi (*De deis gentium*, 1548; in ed. of 1565, p.148).

XVI Mantegna's Last Years

1. For Suora Theophila see Kristeller, 1902, pp.567–8, doc.155; for Mantegna's will and its codicil, *id.*, pp.570–2, doc.163, and pp.578–9, doc.175; for Mantegna's death see his son Francesco's letter to the Marchese Francesco of 15 September, 1506 (*id.*, p.582, doc.186).

2. See Lazzarini & Moschetti, 1908, pp.69,175, doc.173.

3. Kristeller, 1902, p.533, doc.64. The *Moise ebreo* of this document may also have been a young painter: D'Arco (i, p.45, no.6) records a *Moisé ebreo* of Castellazzo who was a painter and died in October 1526 aged 60 and so was presumably aged about 11 in October 1475. But this is very conjectural.

4. For Carlo see D'Arco, i, pp.46–7, and L. Cogliati Arano, in *Dizionario biografico degli italiani*, xiii, 1971, pp.601–2, s.v. Braccesco, Carlo. Little is known of Mantegna's pupils: the long list compiled by D'Arco (i, pp.45–9) is really a list of painters known to have been his contemporaries in Mantua.

5. Vasari, v, 1880, pp.299–301.

6. Vasari, v, 1880, p.280. For Caroto see M.T. Franco Fiorio, *Giovan Francesco Caroto*, 1971, and especially pp.18–19 for his training.

7. Mantegna's own expression on 14 June 1468 (Kristeller, 1902, p.525).

8. For the dead painter son see p.128. For Bernardino see Selvatico (in Vasari, v, 1849, p.181), who is followed by D'Arco (i, p.47). It is not clear on what the identification rests or whether Mantegna really had a son of this name; a confusion may have arisen from Coddé (*Memorie biografiche degli artefici mantovani*, 1837, p.96), who records a Bernardino Mantegna as a son of Andrea born in 1490, though in fact this Bernardino belonged to a different family (cf. D'Arco, *loc. cit.*, compare *id.*, ii, p.272, no.5). Moreover the date 1493 for Bernardino's death seems to be an arbitrary deduction from the date of publication of Bosso's *Recuperationes Faesulanae*, in which Bosso's letter about Mantegna's dead painter son was first printed.

9. Kristeller, 1902, p.544, docs.97, 98; *id.*, p.556, no.128.

10. Kristeller, 1902, p.567, doc.153; D'Arco, ii, pp.44–5, no.56; p.272.

11. Kristeller, 1902, pp.545–6, doc.102; Scardeone, 1560, p.372.

12. The first mention of this supposition in print appears to be in Zani, *Materiali per servire alla storia dell'origine e de' progressi dell' incisione in rame e in legno*, 1802, pp.236–45, printing *Notizie* about Mantegna and his 'figli pittori Francesco e Lodovico' collected in the 1780s by Pasquale Coddé.

13. Kristeller, 1902, p.546: 'Lodovico servitore di Vostra Sᵃ e mio figliuolo'.

14. Kristeller, 1902, p.558, doc.133; D'Arco, ii, pp.41–2, doc.52; Kristeller, 1902, p.569, doc.158.

15. Kristeller, 1902, p.557, doc.129; p.575, doc.169; Resti-Ferrari, p.274; Kristeller, p.575, doc.170. It is hard to know what charges Lodovico made under cover of religion against the gentlemen of the Marchese's household. Perhaps they were charges of heresy. If so, they may have related to the strange doctrine that found favour in Mantua in 1503–4, when popular preachers claimed that Christ was born of three drops of blood close to the heart of the Virgin, and not in her womb. This heresy had to be suppressed by the Inquisitor Fra Girolamo da Faenza (cf. Donnesmondi, *Istoria ecclesiastica*, ii, 1616, pp.93–4).

16. Reproduced by Luzio, *Galleria*, 1913, pl. facing p.56. See the same plate for a specimen of his elegant signature.

17. Luzio, *Archivio Gonzaga*, ii, 1922, p.160.

18. D'Arco, ii, p.48, no.60; pp.73–5, nos.92–4.

19. Gerola, p.912, doc.13 of 24 April 1488. For the devotion felt to San Bernardino by Francesco and Bernardino Squarcione see Sambin in *Medioevo e rinascimento veneto . . . studi in onore di Lino Lazzarini* (*Medioevo e umanesimo*, 34, 1979), pp.455–6,457–64. Kristeller, 1902, p.584, doc.191.

20. Kristeller, 1902, p.550, doc.111, pp.555–6; *La scienza a corte*, by D. Franchini *et al.*, 1979, p.197.

21. The sonnet is printed by Luzio-Renier, 'La coltura' in *G.S.L.I.*, xxxiv, 1899, p.91, n.4.

22. Kristeller, 1902, p.556, doc.127.

23. Kristeller, 1902, p.584, doc.191; p.580, doc.178; pp.582–3, docs.187,188,189. In 1506 Isabella says of the proposed repairs to the Camera Picta that 'Li figlioli del q. mess. Andrea Mantegna toranno la impresa de raconzare la Camera.' It might be inferred from this that Lodovico was indeed a painter, but as a letter from Francesco (Kristeller, 1902, p.584, doc.191) makes it clear that he alone repaired the Camera, Isabella can only have meant that she gave the *charge* of the repair to Mantegna's sons. Francesco plainly says in his original letter about the Camera that 'ms. Andrea Mantinea o il figliol, la reconcij'.

24. Kristeller, 1902, p.585, no.196.

25. Moschini, 1826, p.59, citing the copy of his will on f.367 of the *Libro Ordinario* of Mantua, and the notice of him as already dead in an entry of 17 June 1510 in the same *Libro* (f.901).

26. D'Arco, ii, p.75, doc.95; p.76, n.9.

27. Kristeller, 1902, p.586, doc.200; pp.586–7, docs.201–2; D'Arco, ii, p.80, no.103. For the exact dates of Lang's visit see Luzio in *A.S.L.*, ser.iv, xviii, 1912, pp.113, 115, cf. also p.118, n.1.

28. D'Arco, ii, p.80, n.104.

29. D'Arco, ii, p.81, n.105 (cf. also Kristeller, 1902, p.587, doc.203).

30. Kristeller, 1902, p.587, doc.204; Moschini, 1826, p.58, citing for the accord of 1517 with Libera the *Libro Ordinario* of Mantua, f.752.

31. D'Arco, ii, p.53, n.4, p.271, n.3,4.

32. Zani, *op. cit.*, p.242. For the façade see Cat.no.58.

33. For the chapel and its documentation see Cat.no.61.

34. E.J. Johnson, *S. Andrea in Mantua*, 1975, p.74, n.45.

35. Kristeller, 1902, p.583, doc.190, p.585, doc.198.

36. Yriarte, 1901, p.146.

37. Zani, *op. cit.*, p.239.

38. There is no mention of the chapel in the codicil to Mantegna's will (Kristeller, 1902, pp.578–9, doc.175), but the augmentation of the endowment and of the bequest for the decoration is mentioned in a letter from Lodovico

Mantegna to the Marchese Francesco of 2 October 1506 (Kristeller, 1902, p.583, doc.190) and is confirmed both by the agreement between Mantegna and the chapel of 11 August 1504 and by Yriarte's documents (see note 36).

39. This is a very vexed question. The tradition goes back in print to Donnesmondi (*Istoria ecclesiastica di Mantova*, ii, 1616, p.47). The attribution was eagerly canvassed in the late eighteenth century by Coddé, by Zani and by Pungileoni, who could trace no documents justifying it. Chronologically the problem is complicated by the lack of documents for the history of the chapel between October 1506 and the completion of its decoration in 1516, as well as by the uncertainty which still attends Correggio's date of birth and his early studies and works. The problem is discussed by C. Gould (*The paintings of Correggio*, 1976, p.29–32) without reaching any definite solution.

40. Judith, 13 ; 23.

41. cf. Tervarent, *Attributs et symboles dans l'art profane*, i, 1958, 109, s.v. *compas*. In my interpretation of the iconography of the chapel I have used the Biblical commentary of Cornelius à Lapide, which conveniently collects authorities.

PLATES

Autograph Paintings and Sculpture

1. The Altar of the Ovetari Chapel, Padua (Cat. no. 1)

2. Left wall of the Ovetari Chapel with frescoes of St James (Cat. no. 1)

3. Right wall of the Ovetari Chapel with frescoes of St Christopher (Cat. no. 1)

4. St Peter. From the ceiling of
the Ovetari Chapel, Padua (Cat. no. 1)

5. St Paul. From the ceiling of the
Ovetari Chapel, Padua (Cat. no. 1)

6. St Christopher. From the ceiling of
the Ovetari Chapel, Padua (Cat. no. 1)

7. Gigantic head of Pizzolo.
Padua, Ovetari Chapel (Cat. no. 1)

8. Gigantic head of Mantegna.
Padua, Ovetari Chapel (Cat. no. 1)

9. Top range of the St James frescoes. Padua, Ovetari Chapel (Cat. no. 1)

10. *The Calling of James and John*. Padua, Ovetari Chapel (Cat. no. 1)

11. *The Preaching of St James*. Padua, Ovetari Chapel (Cat. no. 1)

12. *The Baptism of Hermogenes*. Padua, Ovetari Chapel (Cat. no. 1)

13. *The Trial of St James*. Padua, Ovetari Chapel (Cat. no. 1)

14. *St James on the way to Execution.* Padua, Ovetari Chapel (Cat. no. 1)

15. *The Execution of St James*. Padua, Ovetari Chapel (Cat. no. 1)

16. St James. Detail of Plate 14

17. The executioner. Detail of Plate 15

18. Spectators. Detail of Plate 12

19. Roman soldier. Detail of Plate 13

20. Roman soldiers. Detail of Plate 15

21. *The Assumption.*
Padua, Ovetari Chapel (Cat. no. 1)

22. The Virgin. Detail of Plate 21

23. *The Martyrdom of St Christopher.* Padua, Ovetari Chapel (Cat. no. 1)

24. Head of a guard. Detail of Plate 23

25. Three portrait heads. Detail of Plate 23

26. *The Martyrdom of St Christopher*,
scene 1. Padua, Ovetari Chapel
(Cat. no. 1)

27. *The Martyrdom of St Christopher*.
Copy of Mantegna's fresco. Paris,
Musée Jacquemart-André

28. *The Martyrdom of St Christopher*,
scene 2. Padua, Ovetari Chapel
(Cat. no. 1)

29. *The Martyrdom of St Christopher*.
Copy of Mantegna's fresco. Paris,
Musée Jacquemart-André

30. *The Sacred Monogram held by St Anthony of Padua and San Bernardino*. Before removal. Padua, Museo Antoniano (now in the Presidenza dell'Arca del Santo) (Cat. no. 2)

31. *St Euphemia*. Naples, Museo e Gallerie Nazionali di Capodimonte (Cat. no. 4)
32. *St George*. Venice, Accademia (Cat. no. 8)

33. *The Adoration of the Shepherds.* New York, Metropolitan Museum of Art (Cat. no. 5)

34. *Shepherds and Peasants.* Drawing.
Windsor, Royal Coll. (Cat. no. 5)

35. *Shepherds and Peasants.* Fragment from a version.
Private Coll. (see Cat. no. 5)

36. The Altarpiece of San Zeno. Verona, San Zeno (Cat. no. 9)

37. Virgin and Child. Detail of Plate 36

38. *The Agony in the Garden.* Tours, Musée des Beaux-Arts (Cat. no. 9)

39. St Peter, St Paul, St John the Evangelist and
St Zeno. Detail of Plate 36

40. St Benedict, St Lawrence, St Gregory Nazianzen and
St John the Baptist. Detail of Plate 36

41. *The Resurrection*. Tours, Musée des Beaux-Arts (Cat. no. 9)

42. The Evangelist and mourning women. Detail of Plate III

43. *St Sebastian*. Vienna, Kunsthistorisches Museum (Cat. no. 10)

44. Cloud motif. Detail of Plate 43

45. Landscape. Detail of Plate 43

46. *Portrait of Cardinal Lodovico Trevisan.*
Berlin–Dahlem, Staatliche Museen (Cat. no. 11)

47. *Portrait of Francesco Gonzaga.* Naples, Museo e
Gallerie Nazionali di Capodimonte (Cat. no. 12)

LVDOVICVS MEDIAROTA
PATAVINVS S.R.E.CARDINALIS

49. Coat of arms of Cardinal Trevisan.
Woodcut. From J.P. Thomasinus, *Illustrium
Virorum Elogia*, Padua, 1630

48. LEFT *Lodovico Trevisan.* Engraving after a
portrait by Mantegna. From J.P. Thomasinus,
Illustrium Virorum Elogia, Padua, 1630

50. *The Adoration of the Magi* (after cleaning). Florence, Uffizi (Cat. no. 14)

51. *The Ascension*. Florence, Uffizi (Cat. no. 16)

52. Christ with the Virgin's Soul.
Ferrara, Pinacoteca Nazionale (Cat. no. 17)

53. The Exequies of the Virgin. Madrid, Prado (Cat. no. 18)

54. The ceiling of the Camera Picta. Mantua, Palazzo Ducale (Cat. no. 20)

55. *Julius Caesar*. From the ceiling of the Camera Picta
(Cat. no. 20)

56. *Augustus*. From the ceiling of the Camera Picta
(Cat. no. 20)

57. *Tiberius*. From the ceiling of the Camera Picta
(Cat. no. 20)

58. *Caligula*. From the ceiling of the Camera Picta
(Cat. no. 20)

59. *Claudius.* From the ceiling of the Camera Picta
(Cat. no. 20)

60. *Nero.* From the ceiling of the Camera Picta
(Cat. no. 20)

61. *Galba.* From the ceiling of the Camera Picta
(Cat. no. 20)

62. *Otho.* From the ceiling of the Camera Picta
(Cat. no. 20)

63. *Hercules and Antaeus*. From the ceiling of the
Camera Picta (Cat. no. 20)

64. *Hercules and Cerberus*. From the ceiling of the
Camera Picta (Cat. no. 20)

65. *Hercules and the lion*. From the ceiling of the
Camera Picta (Cat. no. 20)

66. *Hercules and the Hydra*. From the ceiling of the
Camera Picta (Cat. no. 20)

67. *Hercules shooting an arrow*. From the ceiling of the
Camera Picta (Cat. no. 20)

68. *Nessus transfixed by Hercules' arrow*. From the
ceiling of the Camera Picta (Cat. no. 20)

69. *Orpheus playing the lyre*. From the ceiling of the
Camera Picta (Cat. no. 20)

70. *Orpheus in the Underworld*. From the ceiling of the
Camera Picta (Cat. no. 20)

71. *Orpheus clubbed to death*. From the ceiling of the
Camera Picta (Cat. no. 20)

72. *Arion charming a dolphin*. From the ceiling of the
Camera Picta (Cat. no. 20)

73. *Arion rescued by a dolphin*. From the ceiling of the
Camera Picta (Cat. no. 20)

74. *Periander questioning the pirates*. From the ceiling
of the Camera Picta (Cat. no. 20)

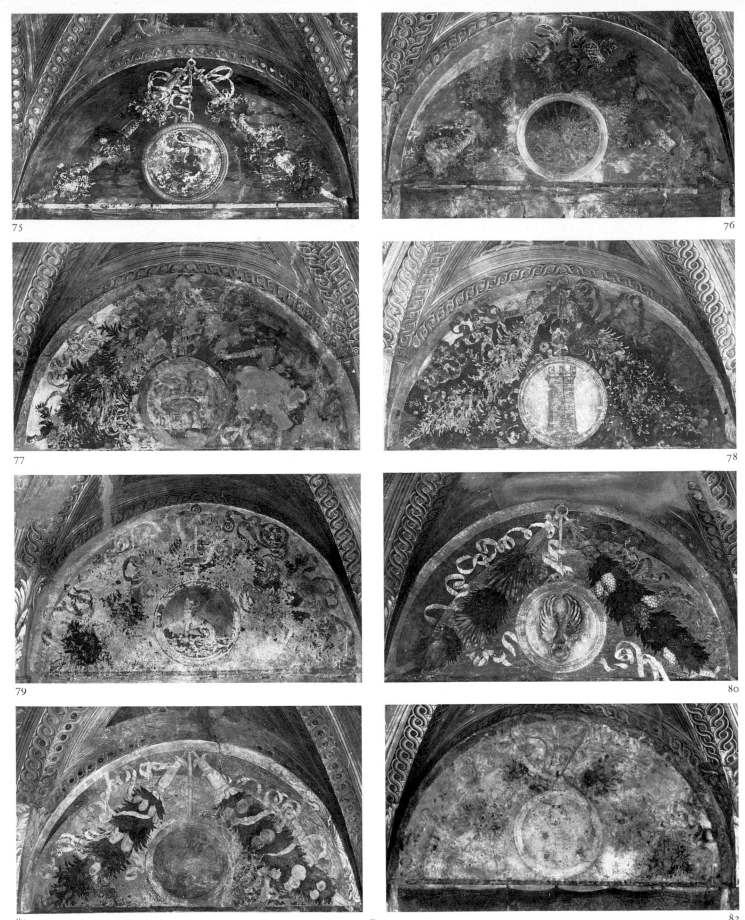

75–82. Gonzaga devices from the lunettes of the Camera Picta (Cat. no. 20). 75. A turtle dove.
76. The radiant sun. 77. Doe gazing at the sun. 78. Battlemented tower. 79. A hound seyant.
80. Two wings expanding from a ring. 81. Dragon. 82. Device illegible.

83a. East and south walls of the Camera Picta (Cat. no. 20)

83b. South wall of the Camera Picta (Cat. no. 20)

84a. Putti holding the inscription (before cleaning). Mantua,
Palazzo Ducale, Camera Picta (Cat. no. 20)

84b. Putti holding the inscription
(after cleaning)

85. West and north walls of the Camera Picta (Cat. no. 20)

86. The outdoor scene of the Camera Picta (after the recent cleaning). Mantua, Palazzo Ducale (Cat. no. 20)

87. The indoor scene of the Camera Picta. Mantua, Palazzo Ducale (Cat. no. 20)

88. Barbara of Brandenburg and her children. Detail of Plate 87

89. Men riding camels. Detail of Plate 86

90. Grooms with mastiffs and a horse. Detail of Plate 86

91. Courtiers and attendants. Detail of Plate 87

92. Unidentified figure. Detail of Plate 87

93. Cardinal Francesco. Detail of Plate 86

94. Rodolfo Gonzaga. Detail of Plate 87

95. Federico Gonzaga. Detail of Plate 86

96. *San Bernardino attended by two angels*. Milan, Brera (Cat. no. 21)

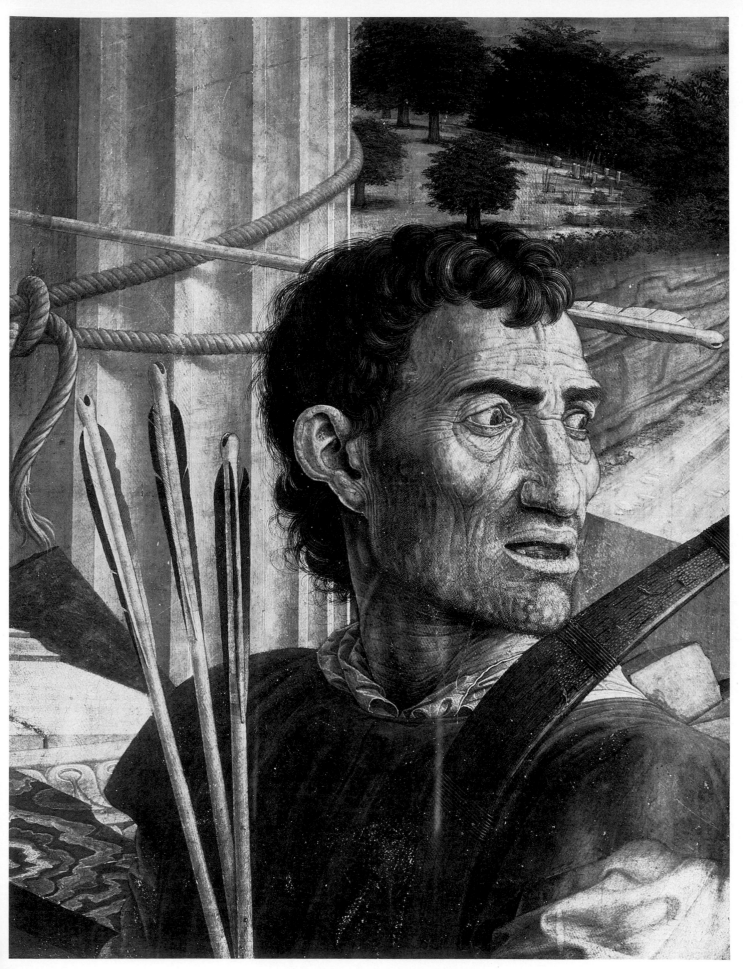

97. Head of an archer. Detail of Plate XI

98. *Virgin and Child*. Milan, Museo Poldi–Pezzoli (Cat. no. 24)

99. *Christ Child Blessing*. Washington, National Gallery of Art, Kress Coll. (Cat. no. 26)

100. *Virgin and Child*. Berlin-Dahlem, Staatliche Museen (Cat. no. 27)

101–9. *The Triumphs of Caesar*. Hampton Court Palace,
Royal Coll. (Cat. no. 28)

101–3. Canvases I, II and III

104–6. Canvases IV, V and VI

107–9. Canvases VII, VIII and IX

110. *The Triumphs of Caesar*. Canvas I. *The Standard-Bearers*. Hampton Court Palace, Royal Coll.
(Cat. no. 28)

111. *The Triumphs of Caesar.* Canvas II. *Bearers of statues of gods, of an image of a captured city, siege engines, inscribed tablets and trophies.* Hampton Court Palace, Royal Coll. (Cat. no. 28)

112. *The Triumphs of Caesar*. Canvas III. *Bearers of military trophies and spoils of silver vessels.*
Hampton Court Palace, Royal Coll. (Cat. no. 28)

113. *The Triumphs of Caesar. Canvas IV. Bearers of golden vessels and a precious marble vase, the sacrificial oxen and trumpeters.* Hampton Court Palace, Royal Coll. (Cat. no. 28)

114. *The Triumphs of Caesar.* Canvas V. *Trumpeters, sacrificial oxen and elephants.*
Hampton Court Palace, Royal Coll. (Cat. no. 28)

115. *The Triumphs of Caesar*. Canvas VI. *Bearers of spoils of golden vessels and bearers of trophies and crowns.* Hampton Court Palace, Royal Coll. (Cat. no. 28)

116. *The Triumphs of Caesar*. Canvas VII. *Captives, buffoons, a soldier and a standard-bearer.*
Hampton Court Palace, Royal Coll. (Cat. no. 28)

117. *The Triumphs of Caesar.* Canvas VIII. *Musicians and standard-bearers.*
Hampton Court Palace, Royal Coll. (Cat. no. 28)

118. *The Triumphs of Caesar*. Canvas IX. *Julius Caesar on his triumphal car.*
Hampton Court Palace, Royal Coll. (Cat. no. 28)

119. *The Triumphs of Caesar*. 'The Senators'. Drawing. Vienna, Albertina

120. *Judith*. Washington, National
Gallery of Art (Cat. no. 30)

121. *Virgin and Child* (*The Madonna delle Cave*).
Florence, Uffizi (Cat. no. 31)

122. *Virgin and Child with St John the Baptist and the Magdalen*. London, National Gallery (Cat. no. 32)

123. *The Redeemer*. Correggio,
Collegio Contarelli (Cat. no. 33)

124. *Pietà (The Man of Sorrows supported by two angels)*.
Copenhagen, Statens Museum for Kunst (Cat. no. 35)

126. *The Descent into Limbo*.
Copy. Bologna, Pinacoteca

125. LEFT *The Descent into Limbo*.
Private Coll. (Cat. no. 34)

127. *Virgin and Child in glory attended by angels and by St John the Baptist, St Gregory the Great, St Benedict and St Jerome*. Milan, Museo del Castello Sforzesco (Cat. no. 37)

128. Lorenzo Costa: *Comus*. Paris, Louvre (Cat. no. 41)

129. Head of St Sebastian. Detail of Plate 130

130. *St Sebastian*. Venice, Galleria della Ca' d'Oro (Cat. no. 42)

131. *The Adoration of the Magi.* Copy of Plate XVI.
Philadelphia Museum of Art, Johnson Art Coll. (see Cat. no. 43)

132. *The Holy Family with the Infant Baptist.*
Dresden, Staatliche Museen (Cat. no. 44)

133. *Virgin and Child with three saints.*
Paris, Musée Jacquemart-André (Cat. no. 45)

134. *Virgin and Child with two saints.*
Verona, Museo di Castelvecchio (Cat. no. 46)

135. *Virgin and Child with the Infant St John the Baptist, St Catherine of Alexandria, and other saints.*
Turin, Galleria Sabauda (Cat. no. 47)

136. *Ecce Homo*. Paris, Musée Jacquemart-André (Cat. no. 48)

137. *The Holy Family with the Infant Baptist.*
London, National Gallery (Cat. no. 49)

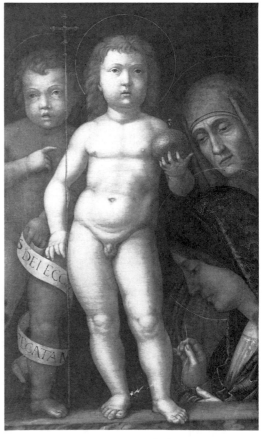

138. *The Holy Family with the Infant Baptist.*
Paris, Petit-Palais (see Cat. no. 49)

139. *Samson and Delilah*. London, National Gallery (Cat. no. 50)

140. *A Sibyl and a Prophet.* Cincinnati Art Museum
(Cat. no. 51)

141. *Judith.* Dublin, National Gallery of Ireland
(Cat. no. 56)

142. *Judith.* Montreal,
Museum of Fine Arts
(Cat. no. 52)

143. *Dido.* Montreal,
Museum of Fine Arts
(Cat. no. 53)

144. *Tuccia*. London,
National Gallery (Cat. no. 54)

145. *Sophonisba*. London,
National Gallery (Cat. no. 55)

146. *The Introduction of the Cult of Cybele at Rome.* London, National Gallery (Cat. no. 57)

147. LEFT Priests and attendants of Cybele bearing her litter. Detail of Plate 146

148. Priests of Cybele bearing her litter. Roman altar. Cambridge, Fitzwilliam Museum

149. Mantegna's house in Mantua

150. Interior courtyard

151. The foundation stone

152. Painted room decoration (detail)

153. Mantegna's Funerary Chapel. Mantua, Sant'Andrea (Cat. no. 58)

154. *The Baptism of Christ* (designed by Mantegna and executed by his son
Francesco Mantegna?). Mantua, Sant'Andrea (Cat. no. 60)

155. *The Family of Christ with the Family of St John Baptist* (probably completed
by Francesco Mantegna). Mantua, Sant'Andrea (Cat. no. 59)

156a. View of upper right wall of the Funerary Chapel showing St Matthew and St Mark. Mantua, Sant'Andrea (Cat. no. 58)

156b. View of upper left wall of the Funerary Chapel showing St Luke and St John. Mantua, Sant'Andrea (Cat. no. 58)

157–63. Details from the Funerary Chapel. After Mantegna? (Cat. no. 58). 157. *Judith.* 158. *Prudence.*
159. *Tobias and the Angel.* 160. Putto with arms of Mantegna. 161. Mantegna's arms. Detail from the *paliotto.*
162. Putto holding arms (of Bellini?). 163. *The Decollation of the Baptist.*

164. Frescoes from the façade of Sant'Andrea. Attributed to Mantegna. a) *The Ascension*
b) *The Holy Family* c) *The Deposition* d) The *sinopia* of *The Deposition* (Cat. no. 58)

Lost or Destroyed Paintings by or with Early Attribution to Mantegna

165. *The Lamentation over the dead Gattamelata*. Drawing. London, Wallace Collection (see Cat. no. 67)

166. After Mantegna: *Lodovico Gonzaga*. Engraving. From Roscio, Mascardi et al., *Ritratti et elogii di capitani illvstri*, Rome, 1646 (see Cat. no. 71)

167. *Design for a statue of Virgil*. Drawing. Paris, Louvre, Cabinet des Dessins (see Cat. no. 85)

Partly Autograph, Studio and Other School Works

168. *Mucius Scaevola*. Munich, Staatliche Graphische Sammlung (Cat. no. 139)

169. *The Judgement of Solomon*. Paris, Louvre (Cat. no. 142)

170. *The Sacrifice of Isaac*. Vienna, Kunsthistorisches Museum (Cat. no. 140)

171. *David holding the head of Goliath*. Vienna, Kunsthistorisches Museum (Cat. no. 141)

172a. After Mantegna: *The Deposition*. San Remo,
Coll. P. Manuel Gismondi (see Cat. no. 91)

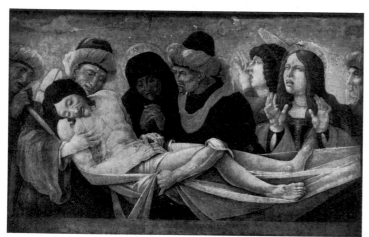

172b. After Mantegna: *The Deposition*. Angri,
Chiesa dell'Annunziata (see Cat. no. 91)

173. *Occasio*. Mantua, Palazzo Ducale (Cat. no. 143)

174. *Holy Family with the Magdalen*. New York,
Metropolitan Museum of Art (Cat. no. 144)

175. *Christ and Simon carrying the Cross*. Verona,
Museo del Castelvecchio (Cat. no. 145)

176. *Christ carrying the Cross.* Oxford, Christ Church (Cat. no. 146)

177. *Holy Family with the Infant Baptist.*
Princeton Art Museum (Cat. no. 147)

178. *Virgin and Child with St Juliana.* Verona,
Museo di Castelvecchio (Cat. no. 148)

Paintings after Mantegna

179. *The Resurrection*. London, National Gallery
(Cat. no. 149)

180. *The Maries at the Sepulchre*. London,
National Gallery (Cat. no. 150)

181. *Noli me Tangere*. London, National Gallery (Cat. no. 151)

182. *Portrait of Francesco Sforza.* Washington,
National Gallery of Art (Cat. no. 152)

183. *Portrait of Rodolfo Gonzaga.* New York,
Metropolitan Museum of Art, Bache Coll. (Cat. no. 154)

184. *Portrait of Lodovico Gonzaga and Barbara of Brandenburg.* Untraced (Cat. no. 153)

185. *The Resurrection*. Bergamo, Accademia Carrara (Cat. no. 155)

186. *Judith with the head of Holofernes*. Washington, National Gallery of Art, Kress Coll. (Cat. no. 156)

Paintings Attributed to Mantegna

187. *St Jerome in the Wilderness*. São Paulo, Museu de Arte (Cat. no. 157)

188. *Virgin and Child*. Boston, Museum of Fine Arts (Cat. no. 158)

189. *St Mark*. Frankfurt, Städelsches Kunstinstitut (Cat. no. 159)

190. Painted frame of the Tomb of Federico Corner. Venice, Santa Maria dei Frari (Cat. no. 160)

191. *Virgin and Child attended by cherubim and angels*. Berlin-Dahlem, Staatliche Museen (Cat. no. 161)

192. *Virgin and Child*. Tulsa, Oklahoma, Philbrook Art Center (Cat. no. 162)

193. *St Jerome in Penitence*. Washington,
National Gallery of Art, Mellon Coll. (Cat. no. 163)

194. *Virgin and Child with St Jerome and St Louis
of Toulouse*. Paris, Musée Jacquemart-André (Cat. no. 164)

195. *Virgin and Child attended by seraphim*. New York,
Metropolitan Museum of Art (Cat. no. 165)

196. *Virgin and Child attended by cherubim*.
Milan, Brera (Cat. no. 166)

197. *Portrait of a Man*. Washington,
National Gallery of Art (Cat. no. 167)

198. *Portrait of a Man*. Milan,
Museo Poldi–Pezzoli (Cat. no. 168)

199. *Virgin and Child*. Untraced. (Cat. no. 169)

200. *Virgin Annunciate*. Formerly, San Diego
Museum of Art (Cat. no. 170)

201. *Crucifixion.*
New York Historical Society (Cat. no. 171)

202. *Sacra Conversazione.* Boston,
Isabella Stewart Gardner Museum (Cat. no. 172)

203. *Virgin and Child.* Untraced (Cat. no. 173)

204. *Virgin giving suck to the Child.* Washington,
National Gallery of Art, Kress Coll. (Cat. no. 174)

Drawings by Mantegna

205. *St James led to Execution*. Drawing. London, British Museum (Cat. no. 176)

206. *Four Saints*. Drawing. Formerly
Chatsworth, Duke of Devonshire Coll. (Cat. no. 177)

207. *St Andrew and two Saints reading books*.
Drawing. Untraced (Cat. no. 178)

208. *Saint reading*. Drawing. London,
British Museum (see Cat. no. 178)

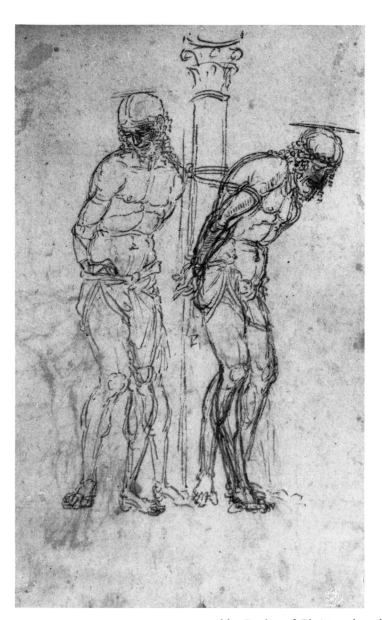

209a and b. *Studies of Christ at the column*. Drawings. a) *Recto* b) *Verso*.
London, Courtauld Institute Gallery (Cat. no. 179)

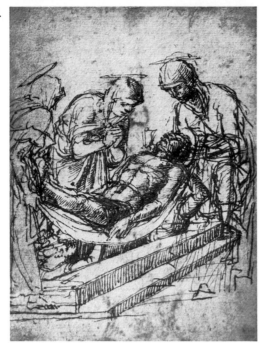

210. *The Entombment.*
Drawing. Brescia,
Pinacoteca Tosio-
Martinengo
(Cat. no. 180)

211. *Hercules and
Antaeus.* Drawing.
Florence, Uffizi
(Cat. no. 183)

212. *Virgin and Child.* Drawing.
Hamburg, Kunsthalle (Cat. no. 181)

213. *Seven Apostles watching the Ascension.* Drawing.
Cambridge, Mass., Fogg Museum of Art (Cat. no. 182)

214. *Five designs for a cross*. Drawing. Frankfurt, Städelsches Kunstinstitut (Cat. no. 184)

215. *A man lying on a slab of stone.* Drawing.
London, British Museum (Cat. no. 185)

216. *Bird on a branch catching a fly.* Drawing.
London, British Museum (Cat. no. 186)

217. *Eagle perched on a branch.* Drawing.
London, British Museum (Cat. no. 187)

218. *Virgin and Child with a seated angel.* Drawing. London, British Museum (Cat. no. 190)

219. *Battle of the Sea-Gods*. Drawing. Chatsworth, Duke of Devonshire Coll. (Cat. no. 189)

220. *A dancing Muse*. Drawing. Munich,
Staatliche Graphische Sammlung (Cat. no. 191)

221. *A dancing Muse*. Drawing.
Berlin, Kupferstichkabinett (Cat. no. 192)

222. *Allegory of Ignorance, Virtus Combusta*. Drawing. London, British Museum (Cat. no. 193)

223. *A man seated between two female figures*. Drawing.
London, British Museum (Cat. no. 194)

224. *The Calumny of Apelles*. Drawing. London, British Museum (Cat. no. 195)

Lost Drawings

225. *The Annunciation*. Tapestry. The Art Institute of Chicago (see Cat. no. 198)

226. *Christ in Limbo*. Drawing. Berlin–Dahlem, Staatliche Museen (see Cat. no. 203)

Engravings by Mantegna

227a and b. *The Entombment.* Engravings. a) First state. Vienna, Albertina. b) Fourth state.
London, British Museum (Cat. no. 205)

228a and b. *The Risen Christ between St Andrew and St Longinus*. Engravings. a) Early impression. New York, Metropolitan Museum of Art. b) Later impression. London, British Museum (Cat. no. 206)

229. *Bacchanal with Silenus*. Engraving. Early state. New York, Metropolitan Museum of Art, Harris Brisbane Dick Fund, 1929 (Cat. no. 208)

230. *Battle of the Sea-Gods*. Engraving. London, British Museum (Cat. no. 210)

231. *Bacchanal with a wine vat*. Engraving. London, British Museum (Cat. no. 209)

232. *Battle of the Sea-Gods*. Engraving. London, British Museum (Cat. no. 211)

Engravings after Mantegna's Designs

233. *The Flagellation*. Engraving.
London, British Museum (Cat. no. 214)

234. *The Descent from the Cross*. Engraving.
London, British Museum (Cat. no. 214)

235a and b. *The Entombment*. Engraving. a) Earlier state with four birds.
b) With three birds. London, British Museum (Cat. no. 215)

236a. *The Descent into Limbo*. Engraving.
London, British Museum (Cat. no. 216)

236b. *The Descent into Limbo*. Drawing.
Paris, Ecole des Beaux-Arts (see Cat. no. 216)

237. *The Adoration of the Magi*. Engraving.
London, British Museum (Cat. no. 217)

238a and b. *Hercules and Antaeus.* Engraving. London, British Museum (Cat. no. 219).
Engraving. Copy by Giovanni Antonio da Brescia. London, British Museum (see Cat. no. 219)

238c. *Hercules and Antaeus.* Engraving. Copy.
London, British Museum (see Cat. no. 219)

239a and b. *Virtus Combusta* and *Virtus Deserta*. Engravings. London, British Museum (Cat. no. 220)

240. *Four Muses dancing*. Engraving. London, British Museum (Cat. no. 221)

241. *Silenus with a group of children*. Engraving. London, British Museum (Cat. no. 222)

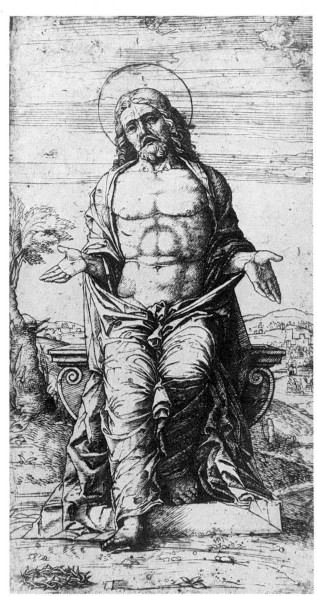

242. *The young prisoner*. Drawing (after engraving?).
London, British Museum (Cat. no. 223)

243. *Pietà (The Man of Sorrows)*. Engraving.
London, British Museum (Cat. no. 224)

244. *Hercules and the Hydra*. Engraving.
London, British Museum (Cat. no. 225)

245. *Holy Family with St Elizabeth and St John*.
Engraving. London, British Museum
(Cat. no. 227)

247. *Hercules and the Hydra*. Engraving.
London, British Museum (Cat. no. 229)

246. LEFT *Judith*. Engraving.
London, British Museum (Cat. no. 228)

Comparative Works

248. Squarcione: *St Jerome with attendant saints*. Padua, Museo Civico

249. Giovanni Bellini: *The Presentation in the Temple.*
Venice, Galleria Querini-Stampalia

250. Squarcione: *Virgin and Child*.
Berlin-Dahlem, Staatliche Museen

251a and b. *The Justice of Trajan*. Cassone panels. Klagenfurt, Landesmuseum

252a and b. *The Triumphs of Petrarch*. From left to right: The Triumph of Fame, Time, Divinity, Love, Chastity and Death. Cassone panels. Colorado, Denver Art Museum, Samuel H. Kress Coll.

253a and b. *The Triumphs of Petrarch*. Cassone panels. Graz, Cathedral

254. *The Entombment*. Miniature after Mantegna. London, Courtauld Institute Gallery, Seilern Coll.
255. *The Dead Christ*. Version of Plate x. Glen Head, N.Y., De Navarro Coll.

256. Lorenzo Costa: *The Triumphs of the Gonzaga*. Prague, National Gallery

257. *Satyrs rebuked for unveiling a sleeping water nymph*. Untraced (see Cat. no. 175)

CATALOGUE

Autograph Paintings and Sculptures

1. FRESCOES OF THE OVETARI CHAPEL, PADUA

PADUA Plates 1–29; Figs 1–3

DESCRIPTION AND CONDITION: The Cappella Ovetari in the right transept of the church of the Eremitani (Augustinian friars) in Padua was destroyed by Allied bombs on 11 March 1944, and of Mantegna's frescoes *The Assumption of the Virgin* and *The Martyrdom of St Christopher*, which had been removed for restoration, alone survive, together with fragments of *The Execution of St James*. The clearest description of the chapel before its destruction is given in Crowe & Cavalcaselle (1912, pp.14–15), and see overleaf, Fig. 18). The chapel consists of a rectangular space entered through an arch and separated by a second arch from a pentagonal tribune or arch. The entrance arch was decorated with a fourteenth-century fresco of *St Christopher* and a Mantegnesque *Pietà* and angels, which were discovered in the course of restoration in the 1920s.

The pointed vault of the main chapel was divided into four compartments, each containing a medallion framed in a garland of leaves and fruit and enclosing an Evangelist. At each of the corners was an angel holding an inscribed scroll and standing on a cloud (a,b,c,d, on plan). On the *right side* were the frescoes of St Christopher (see ICONOGRAPHY; g,h,j,i,x,y on plan). On the *left side* were the frescoes of St James (see ICONOGRAPHY; r,q,s,t,u,v on plan). The frescoes of St James were divided by a framework consisting of a central vertical bar crossed by two horizontal bars, all with richly moulded borders and all decorated except on the central vertical bar with a stem linking bunches of fruit and laurel leaves. Across the pointed arch were suspended two swags of leaves and fruit with two winged putti clambering on them: from the upper transverse bar below were suspended three swags, with two winged putti clasping them at either end, and four others clambering on them towards the centre. In the middle two putti were seated on the central swag, holding a tournament shield bearing the arms of Ovetari quartering those of Capodilista (Ovetari: *gules, a fess argent charged with three stars gules between three morions*

argent; Capodilista: *or, a stag rampant gules with rose*). The shield was also held up by putti standing on a vase-shaped pedestal resting on an acanthus baluster stem. The intersection of the lower horizontal bar and the vertical bar beneath the stem was set with a quatrefoil bearing the bust of a boy turned three-quarters to the right.

The framework of the St Christopher frescoes, though constructed on similar lines and with similar divisions to the framework of the St James frescoes, presented important differences. The topmost section was decorated at the sides, down the central bar, and along the base of the right-hand panel with a plaited stem linking bunches of leaves and fruit which is a variation on the motif decorating the St James framework. The base of the left-hand panel was by contrast decorated with a motif of cornucopiae, ribbons and flowers. The motifs of hanging swags, shield and putti below were, however, a repetition of the same motifs on the opposite wall, but at the sides the frame bent inwards more sharply to fit the vaulting than at the corresponding level opposite. Below, the vertical bar was decorated with a flat strip of banded laurel, with a winged putto clinging to its upper part. The lower horizontal bar was not treated as a decorative frame, but as a moulded cornice, decorated with antique ornament, and the lowest section of the vertical bar was transformed into a fluted Ionic column with a cushion capital, apparently supporting the cornice and scenes above.

The *front face of the apse arch* had a gigantic human head at either side, above the capital of either pier (see ATTRIBUTION). Between, was a monochrome border of a garland of fruit and leaves linking bucranes (f,f,f on plan). The *soffit of the arch* (e on plan) was decorated with fourteen seraphim in red and yellow monochrome with gilt haloes on a blue ground. The *tribune* was pierced by windows in the four lateral sides and by a rosette or a roundel at the top of the central face containing a glass window representing St Christopher. The central face of the pentagon was decorated with *The Assumption of the Virgin* (p on plan). The vault of the apse was a semi-dome, divided into five triangular sections corresponding with the walls of the pentagon beneath. On the four lateral sides, matching the central window, were roundels representing the four Doctors of the Church (l,m,n,o on plan). In the central section was God the Father: to the left St James and St Peter, to the right St Paul and St Christopher (k,k,k,k,k on plan).

The frescoes were already badly damaged by damp by the first half of the nineteenth century (Selvatico, 1849, p.163) and in the early 1880s the *Assumption* and the *Martyrdom of St Christopher* were detached and from 1886 to 1891 were restored by Antonio Bertolli, who mounted them on canvas. They have been recently restored and mounted on new canvas by O. Nonformale. A controversy was started by Fiocco's extraordinary claim (1927,

pp.180,183–4), based on a neo-classical outline engraving executed *c*.1790 by Francesco Novelli after a drawing of the fresco by Luca Brida, that the fresco of the *Assumption* had been arbitrarily lengthened during the nineteenth-century restoration. Conclusively refuted by Moschetti (*op. cit.* below) and Fogolari (*op. cit.* below) the claim was nevertheless repeated by Fiocco (1937, pp.29–30,179), and is accepted by Cipriani (1962, p.53) and Garavaglia (1967, 14M). It is rightly rejected by Tietze-Conrat (1955, p.192) and Camesasca (1964, p.23, by implication).

The altar of the chapel was reconstructed *c*.1710. From the time of Rossetti (1765, p.158) it was observed that it obstructed the view of the tribune. Excavations in 1930 revealed that two tombs dating from the quattrocento and identifiable as those of the founder Antonio degli Ovetari and his wife Imperatrice lay in the floor almost immediately under the tribune arch. Their disposition, with a wide central wall between them, was interpreted, surely correctly (see ICONOGRAPHY), as indicating that the altar steps originally stood between them and that the altar itself was immediately behind them. Accordingly, the altar was moved forward to this position, so removing all obstacles to a view of the fresco of the *Assumption* (see the report by Fogolari, in *Boll. d'A.*, ser.iii,xxvi, 1932–3, pp.433–4; refuting an adverse article by Moschetti, in *Boll. M.C. di P.*, n.s., vi, 1930, pp.1–33).

The frescoes of the chapel are reproduced by V.Moschini, *Gli affreschi del Mantegna agli Eremitani di Padova*, Bergamo, 1944 (black and white), and Fiocco, *Mantegna: La cappella Ovetari nella chiesa degli Eremitani*, Milan, 1947, reproducing photographs taken in March 1944, a few days before the destruction of the frescoes; reprinted with introduction by T. Pignatti, Milan, 1978. Of earlier descriptions those in Crowe and Cavalcaselle (i, 1871, pp.324–40) and Kristeller (1901, pp.61–118) are particularly important, not least for their analyses of Mantegna's technique.

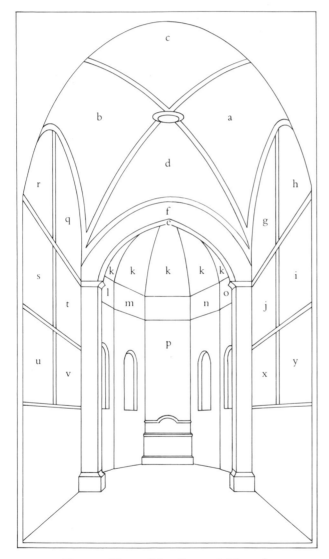

Fig. 18. Plan of the Ovetari Chapel

BRIEF CHRONOLOGY AS ESTABLISHED BY DOCUMENTS

1448, 16 May. Contracts for one half of the frescoes given to Antonio Vivarini and Giovanni d'Alemagna in partnership and for the other half to Niccolò Pizzolo and Andrea Mantegna in partnership.

1448, 8 July. Payment of 12 ducats to Giovanni da Pisa for the altarpiece.

1448, 19 October–1449, 6 June. Pizzolo alone is named in the accounts as receiving payments.

1449, 16 July. Mantegna's first recorded payment for work in the chapel.

1449, 8 July. Giovanni da Pisa's altarpiece almost complete, and has now to be painted and gilded.

1449, 27 September. No work has been done by Pizzolo and Mantegna except in the tribune. Mantegna has painted the three figures of St Peter, St Paul and St Christopher: he is to complete their backgrounds and ornamental borders and leave the rest of the tribune to Pizzolo. Of the six histories of St James, he is to paint five and Pizzolo the sixth: clearly by this date none of them had been begun.

1450, 9 June. Giovanni d'Alemagna has died: it appears that he and Antonio Vivarini had only worked on the vault of the main chapel, which was still unfinished.

1450, 25 August–1451, 19 May. Between these dates 150 ducats are disbursed to Madonna Imperatrice for payments 'to the painters'.

1451, 25 February–1451, 23 October. Payments to Mantegna.

1451, 24 July. First appearance of Bono da Ferrara in the accounts.

1451, 30 July. Last appearance of Bono da Ferrara in the accounts.

1451, 30 October. First and only mention of Ansuino da Forlì in the accounts. Two upper registers of St Christopher frescoes probably complete by this date. Last recorded payment to Mantegna in Ser Campolungo's accounts.

1451, 27 November. Final payment to Antonio Vivarini, signifying completion of work on vault of main chapel.

1451, 22 December. Pizzolo reappears by name in the accounts.

1452, 9 June. Last recorded payment to Pizzolo.

1453, November. Before this date Pizzolo had completed the rest of the decoration of the tribune except for the *Assumption*, some blue backgrounds and some decorative details.

1457, early January. By this date Mantegna has painted the *Assumption*. The histories of St James are also completed.

SUMMARY OF THE DOCUMENTATION: The Cappella Ovetari was founded by Alberto di Bono degli Ovetari, probably in the middle of the fourteenth century. Moschini (1826, pp.36–7) cites a will of 11 November 1372 drawn up 'in loco fratrum Heremitarum in capella ss. Jacobi et Xristophori olim nob. viri Alberti Boni de Ovetariis de Cittadella' which in his day was preserved in the archives of the Leone family, heirs of the Ovetari. This document shows that the trecento dedication of the chapel was to St James Major and to St Christopher. Various trecento tombstones establish that it was the funerary chapel of the Ovetari family. That of its founder, now set in the back wall below the *Assumption*, is inscribed 'Sepulchrum Alberti Boni q̃ Dñi Johãis de Ovetariis de Citadella et suorum heredium. Hic eciam jacet nobilis vir Blaxivs qᵈᵃ Dñi Nicolai de Ovetariis de Citadella q. obiit anno dñi MCCC.LXXXXI die lune XVI Octob' (for this inscription and some notes on Antonio degli Ovetari see Gonzati, *La basilica di S. Antonio da Padova*, i, 1852, p.192).

The frescoed decoration of the chapel was commissioned by Antonio di Biagio degli Ovetari, by a will made on 5 January 1443, in which he bequeathed the chapel to Jacopo Leone. The relevant clause of this reads: 'Item voluit dictus testator quod statim post ejus mortem cum ducatis septingentis aureis, ornari et depingi capella ipsius testatoris cum historiis sanctorum Iacobi et Christophori in Ecclesia Haeremitanorum Paduae, pulchre et condecenter et fieri antea ferrata ita quod sit honorifice ornata et depicta quam citius fieri potest' (first published by Selvatico, 1869, p.153, from the will in the archives of the Leone family).

The will provided for 700 gold ducats to be expended on decorating the chapel with frescoed histories of St James Major and St Christopher and on an iron grille to be set up at its entrance. This provision was to take effect only on the death of the testator. On 22 April 1446 Antonio added a codicil to this will ordering his executors to sell a farm at Valdezoccho, which he had previously bequeathed to his wife, and employ the proceeds 'in ornatu et pictura capelle dicti testatoris modo et forma in testamento contentis' (Kristeller, 1902, p.514, doc.3).

THE EXECUTORS: The heraldic shields on the walls of the frescoes, in which the arms of Ovetari are quartered with those of Capodilista, show that Ovetari's wife, Imperatrice, who subsequently saw to the execution of the frescoes, belonged to the Capodilista family. The marriage was evidently childless: hence perhaps the sums of money lavished on the chapel. The bearings on the shield, not hitherto interpreted, explain why male members of the Capodilista family took a leading part as executors in commissioning and supervising the execution of the frescoes, and also why two members of the Forzatè family, a cognate branch of the Capodilista, appear as executors. The important role played by Francesco Capodilista indicates that he was a close relative, perhaps a nephew, of Imperatrice. The Capodilista were one of the most prominent families of Padua in the fifteenth century (see M. Blason Berton's edition of Giovan Francesco Capodilista's illuminated family chronicle, *De viris illustribus familiae Transelgardorum Forzate et Capitis Listae*, Rome, 1972). Francesco (c.1405–28 March 1460), the son of Giovan Francesco (d. before August 1452), a celebrated jurist, also became a distinguished jurist and from before 1441 lectured in law at the University of Padua. He played a leading role in the life of the city and held many of its offices, and was also a poet in the Petrarchan tradition (for Francesco see L. Trenti in *Dizionario biografico degli italiani*, xviii, 1975, pp.633–5). There is a portrait of him in his father's chronicle (repr. ed. cit., f.34), which also contains a passage (pp.52,72) mentioning that in compiling it c.1436 he had used a chronicle belonging to the brothers Antonio and Niccolò degli Ovetari. In 1440 Francesco accompanied Antonio Borromeo, whose portrait is said to figure in *The Martyrdom of St Christopher*, as his advocate to Florence.

EXECUTION OF THE WILL: The date of Antonio degli Ovetari's death is not recorded. But it occurred before 16 May 1448. On that day Francesco Capodilista, doctor of civil and canon law, who acted as proxy for his father Giovanni Francesco, and Ser Francesco di Maestro Pietro da San Lazaro, acting as executors on behalf of Antonio's widow Imperatrice, and two other executors, Francesco and Antonio Forzatè, drew up an agreement with Maestro Giovanni d'Alemagna and his brother-in-law Maestro Antonio da Murano (Vivarini) to fresco the right-hand wall of the chapel, the main crossing, both sides of the wall above the entrance-arch and the entrance arch itself.

The agreement stipulated that the executors were to hand over the chapel to the painters with its walls roughmortared, its windows finished and the ironwork complete. They were also to erect a wooden partition down its middle at their own expense. The painters on the other hand had to pay for a temporary door and the scaffolding on which they were to work. They were to paint in fresco, not in oils, to use best German blue (azurite) and gold stars on the main vault, and to decorate the bosses. In the histories and figures, wherever blue was used for the garments, they were to employ the best ultramarine blue rather than the cheaper Teutonic blue, 'as was done in the chapel of the Baptistery of Padua', but they were to use Teutonic blue in the ground. Moreover all the colours they used were to be good and suitable 'as approved by a good man'. The work was to be completed by December 1450. In payment the two masters were to receive 350 gold ducats, of which 50 were to be paid to them in advance for their expenses in preparing for the work. The remaining 300 ducats were to be paid in six payments rated according to the work completed or to be completed (contract printed in Lazzarini-Moschetti, xv, 1908, pp.317–19).

A marginal note dated 15 July 1448 records Antonio Vivarini's receipt in his own name and that of Giovanni d'Alemagna, of the payment made to him that day of the promised earnest of 50 gold ducats.

By a second contract, also drawn up on 16 May 1448, the executors hired Niccolò Pizzolo and Andrea Mantegna to paint the other half of the chapel, on the same conditions as those made with Antonio Vivarini and Giovanni d'Alemagna, and for the same sum of 350 ducats. The two painters also contracted to make an altarpiece in relief 'according to the design exhibited before me, the notary, and the witnesses named below and approved by both parties, and I the notary have subscribed my name on the back of this design or picture.' Mantegna was absent from the drawing up of this contract, but his brother Tommaso subscribed to it in his name and acted as his guarantor (Lazzarini-Moschetti, xv, 1908, pp.319–20). On 15 July 1448 Niccolò and Mantegna in their turn acknowledged receipt of 50 gold ducats as an earnest for their work (Lazzarini-Moschetti, xv, 1908, p.320).

The money for the payment of these earnests had been raised on 8 July, only a few days before, by sale of the farm at Valdezoccho which Antonio's codicil had set aside for the purpose (Lazzarini-Moschetti, v, 1908, pp.320–1). The proceeds of the sale, 3800 lire, later, on 7 June 1452, after a new valuation of the farm, reduced to 3262 lire 2 soldi, were left as a deposit in the hands of the purchaser Ser Campolongo di Bartolomeo da Campolongo, who bound himself on the same day to hand them over on demand to Antonio's executors 'ut possint et valeant ipsos denarios dare et numerare magistris pictoribus qui pingunt et pingere debent capellam quondam dicti domini Antonij in ecclesia heremitarum' (Lazzarini-Moschetti, xvi, 1908, pp.68–9). Campolongo's two separate accounts of his disbursements from 8 July 1448 until 28 January 1455 still survive and help to clarify the history of the frescoes (Lazzarini-Moschetti, xvi, 1908, pp.73–4; Rigoni, 1970, pp.43–4). The sum deposited with him was not nearly equivalent, it should be noted, to the 700 gold ducats which Antonio degli Ovetari had reserved for the decoration of the chapel and which formed the basis of the two contracts. Ser Campolongo's first account, from 1448 to 1452, gives a rate of 100 ducats to 570 lire on 8 July 1448 so that the 3800 lire deposited with him were equivalent only to about 660 ducats. On the later valua-

tion of the farm the sum would have been equivalent only to about 572 ducats.

The only detailed specifications for the subjects of the frescoes appear in the contract with Vivarini and Giovanni d'Alemagna. This lays down that the Four Evangelists were to be depicted on the main vault of the chapel on a blue ground decorated with gold stars, and that there was to be 'a solemn history of the Passion of Our Lord Jesus Christ' on the inner wall above the entrance-arch. The entrance-arch itself was to be 'adorned with several figures after the fashion of the cappella maggiore', frescoed by Guariento, and the outer wall was to be painted 'with an honourable ornamental border at the discretion of a worthy man'. Nevertheless, as Paccagnini (1965, p.78) points out, the work to be executed had already been determined, for the payments to be made had evidently been calculated on a basis of fourteen payments to each artist of 25 ducats. These must have been intended to correspond to the fourteen 'histories' or parts into which the work allotted to each artist was divided (as we know from the appraisal made in February 1454 of Pizzolo's work).

On 30 August 1448 Ser Francesco da San Lazaro acknowledged the receipt of 50 gold ducats paid that day from the moneys deposited with Ser Campolongo. Of these 38 were for the iron grille which Antonio degli Ovetari had ordered to be bought for the chapel and which had now been set up. The other 12 had been disbursed on 8 July 1448 to Giovanni da Pisa, described as 'master painter of a certain altarpiece, in execution of the will of the said Messer Antonio' (Lazzarini-Moschetti, xvi, pp.70–1; Rigoni, 1970, p.44). On 19 October 1448 Francesco Capodilista received 71 lire 6 soldi (12½ ducats) from Ser Campolongo, and gave them to Niccolò Pizzolo as a part payment for the painting of the chapel. On 16 December 1448 Messer Antonio Forzatè, Francesco Capodilista and Ser Francesco da San Lazaro received 25 ducats 'to give to the painters' and an extended term was allowed to Ser Campolongo for the next payment, the executors having been allowed one by the painters (Lazzarini-Moschetti, xvi, p.71; Rigoni, 1970, p.44).

Pizzolo alone is recorded by name as receiving payments for the frescoes for some time. On 19 October 1448 he was paid 71 lire 6 soldi (12½ ducats, see above; Lazzarini-Moschetti, xvi, p.71, doc. CI bis, p.73; Rigoni, 1970, p.44), on 26 April 1449 10 ducats (57 lire), on 6 June 1449 2 ducats 1 lire 12 soldi (13 lire). Mantegna first appears in Ser Campolongo's accounts on 16 July 1449, when he was paid 25 ducats, but this was a sum more or less equal to what Pizzolo had already been paid.

On 8 July 1449 Giovanni da Pisa (Rigoni, 1970, p.44) received a further 68 lire 8s (12 ducats) in part payment of the altarpiece he was making. His work must however have been complete, or almost complete for now a quarrel broke out between Pizzolo and Mantegna about their work in the chapel, and in particular over who was to decorate and gild the altarpiece. They took their quarrel to arbitration, committing the settlement of it first to Messer Jacomo Alvarotti, doctor of laws, on 30 July 1449 (Rigoni, p.42) and then to the Venetian nobleman Messer Pietro di Marco Morosini, as their common friend. Morosini gave his decision on 27 September 1449 (Rigoni, 1970, pp.17–20). He had carefully examined their work in the chapel together with experts, conferring more especially with Maestro Francesco Squarcione. He had also conferred with the two contending parties, separately and together. He now made his arbitration. First, in order that Pizzolo and Mantegna might go on working together like good friends in peace and goodwill without further dispute, the work was to be divided between them as follows: Pizzolo alone was to 'make and complete and decorate and gild the altarpiece of the chapel' at his own risk and expense, according to the agreement made with Antonio degli Ovetari's widow Imperatrice, and he alone was to receive payment for it without contradiction from Maestro Andrea 'who was to intermit himself in nothing concerning the altarpiece'. Secondly, Pizzolo alone was to complete the decoration of the tribune above the altar, which the two masters had already commenced. Mantegna was merely to complete the three figures of St Peter, St Paul and St Christopher by painting ornamental borders and other 'necessary things around the bodies of the said saints'. Furthermore, Pizzolo was to paint the right half of the tribune arch without interference from Mantegna, who was to paint the left half. Of the six divisions allotted to the histories of St James, the principal work assigned to the two painters, Pizzolo was to paint only the lowest one beside the inner arch of the chapel towards the altar. These frescoes were to constitute Pizzolo's half of the whole commission, and in consideration of them and of certain other extra contributions to its completion he was to receive 175 ducats, a half-share of the 350 ducats promised by Imperatrice as payment to the two artists.

Mantegna, for his part, as his half-share of the work and as an equivalent to Pizzolo's extra contributions to it, in addition to completing the three figures of saints was to paint the left half of the tribune arch. He was also to paint the five other divisions of the histories, to wit, the three set one above the other on the entrance side of the wall, and the two above the division to be painted by Pizzolo. In addition he was to paint all the ornamental borders between from top to bottom. For this work he was to receive 175 ducats. Moreover, since the two masters had bought many colours and wooden scaffolding at their joint expense, the colours remaining were to be equally divided between the two. The scaffolding on the other hand was to be used in common until the work was finished, and then to be divided between them equally. Furthermore, Pizzolo was to take down the wooden wall they had erected to shut off the tribune from the chapel, either wholly or in part, so as to let through enough light for Mantegna to work by. Finally, since the Ovetari executors had declared that the two masters had already been paid more money than they had done work, Morosini ordered them to give the executors a *fideiussio* (pledge) that they would execute work equivalent to the value of the money they had received. They were also to give a guarantee that the money would be returned if either of them died, and to complete the work by the date of December 1450 already agreed.

Giovanni d'Alemagna and Antonio Vivarini had been working with equal tardiness. Only on 23 July 1449 was a second payment made to them in the shape of 20 ducats received by Giovanni (Rigoni, 1970, p.44). No further

payment to him is recorded and by 9 June 1450 he was dead. A legal document of that date records that Antonio Vivarini and Francesco Capodilista had chosen arbitrators to assess and value the work executed by Antonio and his dead partner. Capodilista had chosen Pizzolo as his arbitrator and Vivarini Francesco Squarcione. In their award the two arbitrators declared that they had divided the work allotted to the two artists into 13½ parts. Of these only 3½ had been completed, or rather would be completed when the main vault was finished as it had been begun. It seems then that only the decoration of the vault, computed as 3½ parts of 13½ parts, had been begun, and for this work when finished a sum of the order of 90 ducats would be due to the two partners, of which they had already received at least 70, and possibly a little more from the 25 ducats disbursed on 16 December 1448. Antonio Vivarini was to finish the vault, and he had presumably completed it by 27 November 1451, when he received a payment of 57 lire (10 ducats), the last recorded to him, from Madonna Imperatrice (Lazzarini-Moschetti, xvi, 1908, pp.71–2; Rigoni, 1970, p.45).

Meanwhile, Imperatrice had received from Ser Campolongo in 1450 and early in 1451 a number of sums of money with which to pay 'the painters' in her chapel, their names unfortunately being unspecified. On 25 August 1450 she received 50 ducats, on 15 October 20 ducats, on 24 December 15 ducats, on 22 February 1451 another 15 ducats, on 19 March 1451 25 ducats and on 19 May 1451 25 ducats, amounting in all to the considerable sum of 150 ducats (Lazzarini-Moschetti, xvi, 1908, pp.73–4; Rigoni, 1970, pp.44–5). Some of this money was in all probability paid out as an earnest in making an agreement with two new masters, Bono da Ferrara and Ansuino da Forlì, to paint the histories of St Christopher. Bono is first named in Ser Campolongo's accounts on 24 July 1451 (Rigoni, 1970, pp.40–5) when he was paid 5 ducats by Francesco Forzatè. On 30 July he was paid another 13 ducats, after which he disappears from the accounts. These sums are much too small to have been an earnest. Ansuino is mentioned only once, as intended for a share with Mantegna of 171 lire (3 ducats) paid on 30 October 1451 to Madonna Imperatrice (Rigoni, 1970, p.45). Again the sum is too small for an earnest. The fresco of *St Christopher bearing Christ* in the left upper register below the lunette was signed OPVS BONI; the adjoining fresco of *St Christopher and the soldiers of the King of Samos* on the right was signed OPVS ANSVINI.

Payments continued to Pizzolo and Mantegna from the late autumn of 1449. On 23 October 1449 (13 October in Lazzarini-Moschetti) Pizzolo was paid 20 ducats, and Puppi (*Eremitani*, 1970, p.80) is surely correct in suggesting that these were his payment for colouring and gilding the altarpiece. On 25 February 1451 Mantegna received 28 lire 10 soldi (5 ducats). On 23 October 1451 he was paid 20 ducats, and a week later, on 30 October, a part-share of the 30 ducats drawn by Madonna Imperatrice to make a payment both to him and to Ansuino. Pizzolo's next payment was made even later, on 22 December 1451, when he received 10 ducats. He got no more money until 9 June 1452, when he was given his last recorded payment of 34 lire 34 soldi (approx. 7 ducats). Between May and November 1453, probably towards the latter end of this period, Pizzolo was assassinated (Rigoni, 1970, pp.44–5; the ducat equivalents in Lazzarini-Moschetti, xvi, 1908, pp.73–4).

His death was followed by the customary assessment and valuation of the work he had accomplished. A dispute over his work in the tribune soon arose between Madonna Imperatrice and Basilio, the *telaruolo* (linen-draper) who had acted as Pizzolo's guarantor and so was liable for completion of the contract. To arbitrate in their dispute the parties had recourse to Francesco Squarcione and Giovanni Storlato. In an award of 6 February 1454 (Rigoni, 1970, pp.20–1) the two masters declared that they had divided all the work, finished and unfinished, allotted to Pizzolo in the tribune into four 'histories' or parts. Over and above these, they affirmed, Pizzolo had executed a figure of 'Christ Blessing', i.e. God the Father. Accordingly they reckoned that this figure was equivalent to the figure of the Virgin of the Assumption which Pizzolo was to have painted on the wall behind the altar 'without understanding also any Apostles for we have as yet no concern with your difference concerning the Apostles'. Basilio was therefore only to pay for the completion of all that still remained to be finished in the four histories, to wit, the blue grounds, the gold diadems, the ornamental *boccatelli* (bosses) on a wooden bar that ran across the arch, some parts of the arch itself, the borders along the bottom of the windows and the rest of the decorative painted panels on the walls beneath. He was not bound to do more than complete this ornamentation of the chapel and could leave the space left for the *Assumption* blank. All in all, they assessed the work completed by Pizzolo as three parts of the four. What remained to be done was the missing fourth part, to wit, the *Assumption*, and the ornamental decorations they had specified. This award was officially ratified by a judge on 21 June 1454 (Rigoni, *loc. cit.*).

The work done by Mantegna in the chapel is partly clarified by evidence given in a case brought to settle a dispute between him and Madonna Imperatrice early in 1457. On 14 February the painter Pietro da Milano gave evidence as one of the three expert arbiters called in to give testimony – the others were Francesco Squarcione and Giovanni Storlato. Pietro testified on behalf of Mantegna that 'a month ago or thereabouts Maestro Andrea . . . took the witness to the chapel of Madonna Imperatrice and showed the witness equally the part belonging to Maestro Niccolò Pizzolo and the part belonging to himself, Maestro Andrea, both which parts were wholly completed. And the said Maestro Andrea also said to the witness that he had finished certain works which had been left unfinished on account of Maestro Niccolò's death, which works were now finished as the witness himself saw . . . Again, he answered that all he, the witness knew, was that he had seen the histories both of the Assumption of the Blessed Virgin, which is behind the altarpiece, and also the history of St James, which histories are splendidly and worthily finished. And the said histories and paintings are by the hand of the said Magister Andrea, as the witness perceived from the paintings themselves. And he said that the witness knew so because he is well acquainted with paintings from the hand of the said Magister Andrea. Nevertheless he did

not see them being painted, but from his long experience in this art of painting he knows the said pictures are from the hand of the said Magister Andrea; inasmuch as among painters it is always well known by whose hand any picture is painted, especially when it is from the hand of some eminent master.'

Pietro was then questioned by the opposing counsel on the interrogatories put forward by Madonna Imperatrice, Mantegna's adverse party. First he admitted, 'that the Apostles of our Lord Jesus Christ, as all say, were in number twelve.' The purpose of this interrogatory appears in Pietro's reply to the next question. 'He answers that in his judgement the whole figures of the twelve apostles could not fittingly be painted entire, in consideration of the smallness of the space, and in consideration too that the said figures are executed with great art. Though it is true that the faces of some other apostles could have been represented behind the backs of the figures which are there, yet in his judgement they could not have been put there fittingly, having regard to the art of perspective.' Finally he testified that 'Maestro Andrea deserved as much for these eight figures, which are excellently posed and with good action, as for twelve figures not entire, for as he said before, twelve entire figures could not have been executed.' His only other evidence was that in the Virgin's cloak ultramarine had been used, and in the ground of the fresco around the Virgin German blue (azurite).

Storlato, who had been to inspect the chapel in company with Squarcione and Pietro da Milano, gave his evidence next day. He too declared that 'they had seen the place where the Assumption was, and in his judgement figures of all twelve apostles could have been put there, but they would have had to have been of smaller size than those that are there now. But in truth, had he wished to make depictions of the size of those that are there, it would not have been possible to make more.' (Rigoni, 1970, pp.21–3.)

For other analyses of these documents see Tietze-Conrat (1955, pp.5–7), Davies (1961, pp.328–9), Paccagnini (in *Mantua*, 1965, pp.75–85, closest and most convincing) and Puppi (in *Eremitani*, 1970, pp.74–7). See also the analysis in Lazzarini-Moschetti (*op. cit.*) who of course did not know of Ser Campolongo's second account.

EARLY LITERATURE: The earliest known description of the chapel occurs in Marc' Antonio Michiel (*Anonimo Morelliano*, ed. Frizzoni, 1884, pp.64–5): '*La cappella a man destra dell' altar maggiore fu dipinta, la faccia sinistra tutta da Andrea Mantegna; la faccia destra la parte di sotto dal ditto, la parte de sora parte da Ansuino da Forli, e parte da Buono Ferrarese, ovver Bolognese: la nostra Donna che va in cielo, con gli Apostoli, driedo l'altar, con le figure in alto sotto la cupola da Niccolò Pizzolo Padoano, con li Evangelisti con li armari in prospettiva. Le figure de terra cotta tutte tonde sopra l'altar de ditta Cappella furono de man de Zuan de Pisa compagno de Donatello, e suo arlevo, che el ditto menò seco a Padova.*' In connection with this see the note on the attribution of the *Assumption* below.

Scardeone (1560, p.373), gives an account of the chapel which records Squarcione's famous criticisms: '*Pinxit postmodum* [after the San Luca altarpiece and the Gattamelata fresco] *sacellum Eremitarum, & primò historiam D.*

Iacobi apostoli incertis coloribus: quam cum Squarzonus eius magister, & pater adoptiuus satis commendasset, & colores damnasset, stomachatus eius verbis Mantinea, sub illa postea pinxit historiam D. Christophori, quae ibidem pingenda restabat: & in ea non amplius imagines a Romanis statuis, ut prius, quas adumbrare tantum licebat, sed a uiuis hominibus traxit: quae quidem uulgo magis approbantur, ac longo interuallo prioribus praeferuntur: quamuis auctor ipse picturas a Romanis imaginibus extractas quam à uiuis corporibus, magis probaret: hac potissimum ratione, quod statuarii & sculptores antiqui de multis corporibus perfectas ipsorum partes sibi eligebant, absque uitio formandas. Sed qui naturam tantum uniuscuiusque uiuentis imitatur, cùm nullum ferè corpus reperiatur, quod uitio careat, necesse sit eos, qui eiusdem naturae imitatores esse uelint, eodem uitio cum ipsa natura peccare.' In his life of Squarcione (p.371) Scardeone adds: *'Hujus imago conspicitur in sacello Eremitarum, ubi Mantinea effinxit ad ejus similitudinem satellitem senem discinctum prominente aqualiculo, viridi indumento vestitum, & hastatam mucronem tenentem.'*

It is more than likely that Scardeone's source for this account of the chapel was a lost letter (see p.20) from Girolamo Campagnola (*c.*1433/5–22) to Leonico Tomeo (d.1531). This was unknown to Vasari in 1550, since he makes no mention in his first edition of Mantegna's relations with Squarcione and refers only briefly and inaccurately to the Eremitani frescoes. It had come to his knowledge by 1568, by which time Vasari had seen the frescoes for himself. His account (1568, pp.488–9) now offers close verbal similarities to Scardeone's, but includes details which indicate an independent source, earlier in date than 1560, and common to both – compare also Vasari's opening paragraph with the related sentences in Scardeone's life of Squarcione (1560, p.371), and Selvatico (1849, p.162, n.4) and the note on portraits (below) for evidence that Vasari was translating from a Latin he did not perfectly understand. This common source can only have been Campagnola, whom Vasari cites a few lines above as his authority for Mantegna's apprenticeship to and adoption by Squarcione. The point is of considerably more than academic interest for it takes the traditions recorded by Scardeone and Vasari of Squarcione's criticisms and Mantegna's portrayal of certain living personages in the frescoes and about their identity back to a Paduan who was the friend and exact contemporary of Mantegna, a member of the same circle, and more than usually well informed. (For Campagnola, who was born in Padua in 1432 or 1435 and died there in 1522 see Safarik, in *Diz. biog.*, xvii, 1974, pp.317–18.) It should be noted that Scardeone (1470–1566) knew him personally (1560, p.244).

Vasari's account of the chapel (ed. Milanesi, iii, pp.387–91) reads: *'. . . e sopra tutto* [Squarcione] *biasimò senza rispetto le pitture che Andrea aveva fatte nella detta cappella di San Cristofano; dicendo che non erano cosa buona, perchè aveva nel farle imitato le cose di marmo antiche, dalle quali non si può imparare la pittura perfettamente; perciocchè i sassi hanno sempre la durezza con esso loro, e non mai quella tenera dolcezza che hanno le carni e le cose naturali, che si piegano e fanno diversi movimenti; aggiugnendo che Andrea arebbe fatto molto meglio quelle figure, e sarebbono state più perfette, se avesse fattole di color di marmo, e non di que' tanti colori; percio-*

cchè non avevano quelle pitture somiglianza di vivi, ma di statue antiche di marmo o d'altre cose simili. Queste cotali reprensioni punsero l'animo d'Andrea: ma dall'altro canto gli furono di molto giovamento; perchè, conoscendo che egli diceva in gran parte il vero, si diede a ritrarre persone vive; e vi fece tanto acquisto, che in una storia che in detta cappella gli restava a fare, mostrò che sapeva non meno cavare il buono delle cose vive e naturali, che di quelle fatte dall'arte. . . Comunque sia, in questa ultima storia, la quale piacque infinitamente, ritrasse Andrea lo Squarcione in una figuraccia corpacciuta, con una lancia e con una spada in mano. Vi ritrasse similmente Noferi di messer Palla Strozzi, fiorentino; messer Girolamo dalla Valle, medico eccellentissimo; messer Bonifazio Fuzimeliga, dottor di leggi; Niccolò orefice di Papa Innocenzio VIII, e Baldassarre da Leccio, suoi amicissimi; i quali tutti fece vestiti l'arme bianche brunite e splendide come le vere sono, e certo con bella maniera. Vi ritrasse anco messer Bonramino cavaliere, e un certo vescovo d'Ungheria, uomo sciocco affatto, il quale andava tutto giorno per Roma vagabondo, e poi la notte si riduceva a dormire come le bestie per le stalle. Vi ritrasse anco Marsilio Pazzo, nella persona del carnefice che taglia la testa a Sant'Iacopo, e similmente se stesso. Insomma, questa opera gli acquistò, per la bontà sua, nome grandissimo.'

In view of Vasari's use of Campagnola, some interest attaches to the tradition he records that the commission was originally awarded to Squarcione (Milanesi, *loc. cit.*).

SEQUENCE OF WORK AND INTERPRETATION OF THE DOCUMENTATION AND LITERATURE: The documents imply, even though they do not state, that the subject-matter of the decoration had already been determined by 16 May 1448, and that the contracts with the four artists were drawn up on the basis of a previous understanding. The altarpiece had already been designed, presumably because Masses were already being sung for Antonio degli Ovetari's soul, and an earnest of 12 ducats for its execution in terracotta was paid to Giovanni da Pisa on 8 July 1448. Giovanni was paid a further 12 ducats on 8 July 1449, and this may be taken as his final payment, since the dispute between Pizzolo and Mantegna resolved by the arbitration of 27 September 1449 turned in part on who was to colour and gild the altarpiece. Clearly there was an agreement by which the two pairs of masters began work on the ceilings of the chapel; hence we find Pizzolo and Mantegna working at first on the ceiling of the tribune, while Giovanni d'Alemagna and Antonio Vivarini began by painting the vault of the main chapel. Most of the work on the main vault was done by Giovanni, since he alone received payment for it before 9 June 1450. After that date it was continued by Vivarini, who completed it by 27 November 1451. Vivarini was to have received a sum of the order of 20 ducats for the finished work; since the last payment to him by name on 27 November 1451 was only of 10 ducats, he had presumably received the other 10 ducats earlier as part of one of the sums of money paid to Madonna Imperatrice in 1450 and early 1451 for the 'painters'.

At first Pizzolo seems to have begun by himself in the tribune. He was paid 12½ ducats on 19 October 1448, corresponding, by Paccagnini's reckoning, to half a section, another 10 ducats on 26 April 1449 and on 6 June 1449 2 ducats 1 lire, corresponding in all to another half section.

Mantegna was paid 25 ducats on 16 July 1449; from the award of 27 September 1449 it is clear that this payment must have been for the nearly completed figures of St Peter, St Paul and St Christopher on the vault of the tribune. But in the award it is expressly stated that the money the two masters had received exceeded the extent of the work they had done. The award left Pizzolo to finish the tribune, and allotted him in addition the right-hand side of the tribune arch and one history of the St James series. Mantegna had not begun any of the five remaining histories of St James, nor the left-hand side of the tribune arch, but was now to begin on them, since Pizzolo was to take down the enclosure that shut off the tribune (and therefore the light) from the rest of the chapel. From the award of 6 February 1454 it seems that originally Mantegna was to have painted the figures of God the Father and St James, and that these were left to Pizzolo as a result of the dispute, thus separating the two artists from each other. Presumably too the 'three and a half parts' of the main vault that Giovanni d'Alemagna had completed before his death had been completed by 27 September 1449 and included the sections adjoining the left wall, since it was now possible for Mantegna to begin work on the histories of St James on that wall.

Pizzolo seems to have continued with some energy, for he was paid 20 ducats (four-fifths of the value of another section) on 23 November. The small payment of 5 ducats made to Mantegna on 25 February 1450 indicates that he had by that date made only a small beginning. Presumably he had only completed two histories of St James or little more by 23 October 1451, when he is next mentioned as receiving a payment, this time of 20 ducats, followed by a further payment of a share of 30 ducats a week later. This calculation is based on the assumption that Madonna Imperatrice spent part of the 150 ducats she drew from Ser Campolongo between 25 August 1450 and 19 May 1451 on commissioning and paying for the four histories of St Christopher on the opposite wall. The fresco of *St Christopher bearing Christ* was executed by Bono da Ferrara who was paid 5 ducats on 24 July 1451 and 13 ducats a week later. At 25 ducats a history, 7 ducats and his expenses still remain to be accounted for from the moneys drawn by Imperatrice. On 6 August Bono was ordered by the Paduan guild of painters not to paint any more in the city without becoming a member of the guild, and it can be assumed that he left the city almost immediately and that his work on the frescoes was finished. Similarly Ansuino da Forlì received a last recorded payment on 30 October 1451 of a share of 30 ducats: again his earlier payments must have been made from Madonna Imperatrice's withdrawals. Since Bono and Ansuino signed the two frescoes on the middle register, the frescoes in the lunette must have been executed earlier (see ATTRIBUTION), and some 50 ducats must be allowed for the price of these.

It is also important to note that the upper portion of the framework of the St Christopher frescoes imitates that of the St James frescoes, though with some variations. In particular the motif of swags, clambering putti and shield bearing arms across the top of the middle register was evidently carefully copied from Mantegna's similar motif on the opposite wall – understandably so, since this decoration gave prominence to the arms of the patrons. Since Bono and Ansuino appear to have been working on their frescoes in the spring and summer of 1451, it seems virtually certain that Mantegna had completed this portion at least of the St James frescoes by early 1451, and possibly before. It will be recalled that the award of 27 September 1449 specifically allotted the borders between the histories of St James to Mantegna. Bono and Ansuino may have worked from drawings by Mantegna, and perhaps even to his instructions (see ATTRIBUTION); their dependence on his art is plainly heavy.

If this argumentation is accepted, then the four upper histories of St James were completed by the end of October 1451. Work was now resumed by Pizzolo, who received 10 ducats on 22 December 1451. Six months later he was given the next and last payment Campolongo records him as receiving of some 7 ducats. Shortly before, on 7 June 1452, the prudent Ser Campolongo, suspecting that the moneys he had paid out were approximating ever more closely to the true value of the property he had purchased, arranged for a survey which reduced its original valuation of 3800 lire (approx. 660 ducats) to 3262 lire 10 soldi (approx. 570 ducats). By this date he had paid out 2963 lire 2 soldi (approx. 520 ducats), leaving a balance of 300 lire (approx. 50 ducats).

In estimating the progress of the work we must take into account payments of 114 lire (20 ducats) made on 13 May 1452 to Messer Bonifacio Frigimelica. This must represent a payment to either Mantegna or Pizzolo or to both. (Paccagnini's claim that this and other payments to representatives of Madonna Imperatrice may be for expenses not connected with the chapel ignores the legal documents of 1448 constituting the purpose of the deposit.) The remaining two payments in the accounts of Ser Campolongo were disbursed on 10 December 1454 (1453 in another entry) and on 28 January 1455 to Magister Giovanni da Verona, who was acting as proctor for Madonna Imperatrice and the executors of her husband's will in June 1454 and February 1457 (Rigoni, 1970, p.21). The first payment was of 129 lire (22 ducats), the second of 100 lire (17½ ducats). These figures, together with the payment of May 1452, would represent a plausible payment to Mantegna for two frescoes. They suggest, however, that the complex possibilities of advances in excess of work done and late payments for completed work must always be taken into account.

Paccagnini has pointed out that the accounts of Ser Campolongo record only what he paid out for the frescoes from the deposit in his hands, not necessarily what was actually paid for them in full. That deposit, always less than the 700 ducats allotted by Antonio Ovetari to his chapel, eventually proved inadequate. However, the documents prove for certain only that the fresco of the *Assumption* was painted by Mantegna between February 1454 and January 1457 and that the frescoes of St James were completed between the same dates. This implies an interval in the completion of the frescoes, and it is noteworthy that the last recorded payment to Mantegna in Ser Campolongo's accounts is dated 30 October 1451, that the last payment they record to Pizzolo was on 9 June 1452, and that Ser Campolongo made no further disbursements with the exception of a minimal sum of 21 soldi until 10 December 1453 (or 1454) and again on 28 January 1455, when he made payments to Giovanni da Verona. On the other hand, we know that Mantegna accepted and completed important commissions for the Santo in 1452 and for Santa Giustina in 1453–4. It seems very probable therefore that he abandoned work on the frescoes in 1452 and only resumed it at the earliest in 1455, and most likely in 1456. Romanini's observation (1965, p.461) that the dispute over the *Assumption* must have arisen shortly after its completion and that Imperatrice would not have waited for two years before taking it to court, seems wholly justified. The documents concerning this dispute also imply that Mantegna only executed the history of St James originally allotted to Pizzolo after Pizzolo's death.

The reasons for this break are to be sought in the near exhaustion of Ser Campolongo's deposit and in Imperatrice's search for more moneys, as well as in possible disputes and disagreements. Since the original deposit proved after the second valuation of the Valdezoccho property in 1452 to be considerably less than 700 ducats, as Paccagnini says, the remainder of the money must have been found from elsewhere. There is no mention in the documents up to the end of 1456 of Mantegna's two frescoes of St Christopher, and Paccagnini's argument from this silence that they were not executed until 1457 or later is therefore irrefutable. Now that both Scardeone's and Vasari's account of the frescoes can be shown to depend on the testimony of Girolamo Campagnola, the tradition that these two frescoes were painted last is seen to rest on a stronger foundation than had been thought and serves to confirm Paccagnini's conclusion.

The old view that they were the last to be executed is also defended by Davies (1961, pp.328–9) and Romanini (1965, pp.449–51), who advance convincing relationships of perspective, construction and style with the San Zeno altarpiece. The opposite thesis, that these two scenes precede the four lower scenes of the St James cycle, first proposed by Eisler (1903, pp.160–3), was advocated independently by Ragghianti ('Casa Vitaliani' in *Cr.d'A.*, ii, 1937, pp.243–50) and is accepted by Rigoni (1948, in 1970, pp.34–5) and Tietze-Conrat (1955, pp.5–7).

ATTRIBUTION: The history of the attribution of the frescoes falls into four periods, that preceding Lazzaretti-Moschini (1908), that from 1908 until Rigoni's first article (1927), that from 1927 until her second article (1948) and that from 1948 onwards. Ridolfi (1648, p.69) copies Vasari's attributions. The local Paduan antiquaries Rossetti (1776, pp.150–5) and Brandolese (1795, pp.216–18) were more critical, in particular Brandolese, who knew Michiel's description of them. They attribute the *Assumption* to Pizzolo, but Brandolese records eighteenth-century opinions that the lunette frescoes of the St James cycle were not by Mantegna and that the lunette frescoes of the St Christopher cycle were not by Ansuino and Bono. These points are still at issue. Selvatico (1849, pp.161–3) assigned the two lunette frescoes of St James to a hand close to Marco Zoppo; Crowe & Cavalcaselle (1871, p.325; 1912, p.30) as designed by Mantegna and coloured by Pizzolo; Thode (1897, p.18) as by Mantegna, but in execution largely by an assistant, perhaps Bernardo

Parentino; Knapp (1910, p.178) as possibly but not certainly youthful works by Mantegna; Venturi (1914, p.65) as by Pizzolo; Fiocco (1926, p.184) also as by Pizzolo, a judgement revised in 1937 (pp.24–5,198) in favour of an attribution to Mantegna, *c.*1449, before any contact with Jacopo Bellini. Longhi (1926, p.136) believes they were designed by Mantegna and executed by Pizzolo; for Tietze-Conrat (1955, p.193), Cipriani (1962, pp.14–15,49), Garavaglia (1967, Nos.14E and F) they are by Mantegna. Camesasca (1964, pp.12–14) also accepts Mantegna's authorship, and dates them after his return from Ferrara. He suggests that the figures of St Peter, St Paul and St Christopher were begun by Pizzolo and completed by Mantegna. The diversity of judgements about these frescoes, certainly authentic early works by Mantegna, owes its origin to the false assumption that the Ovetari frescoes were executed in smooth and rapid succession.

The current attribution of the St Christopher lunette frescoes is to Gerolamo di Giovanni da Camerino (left scene: first proposed by Longhi, 1926, p.136) and to Ansuino (right scene). But Rigoni (1948, reprinted in 1970, p.34) and Castelfranco (1962, pp.31–2) incline to attribute the left scene, on account of its accurate perspective, to Ansuino assisted by Mantegna. There can be no doubt of the attribution to Ansuino of the right scene, and the only real problem is the attribution of the left scene, which is not by Bono, as the change of ornament in the border between it and his signed fresco below clearly indicate.

The fresco of the *Assumption* was first attributed to Mantegna by Woltmann (cf. Cartwright, 1881, p.6) and by Venturi (*Storia*, vii, 3, 1914, pp.79–80). The attribution was clinched by Rigoni's publication of the documents of 1457. The original design by Pizzolo for this fresco certainly included the Apostles, as conventional iconography demanded, and they are mentioned in the arbitration of 6 February 1454 between Madonna Imperatrice and Pizzolo's guarantor Basilio as the subject of a dispute between the two. Fiocco (1959, p.86) suggests that the Virgin and the Apostles were not executed at the same time, but this is most unlikely. Recently L. Grossato (in *Da Giotto al Mantegna*, exh. Padua, Palazzo della Ragione, 1974, No.82) has claimed that the 'sension biancha' of the arbitration of 1454 means 'the Assumption (sension) left white', and implies that a cartoon by Pizzolo was already sketched on the wall. Mantegna, in his view, took this as his guide, and added the Apostles as his own contribution. As we have seen, the documents do not support the second part of this hypothesis. The astonishing spatial conception, with its bold central void and emphasis on the ascent of the Virgin, can only be the invention of Mantegna. That drawings and even a cartoon had been prepared by Pizzolo is, however, highly likely.

J. Fletcher (in *B.M.*, cxxiii, 1981, pp.602–3) points out that Michiel originally gave the *Assumption* to Mantegna, but then crossed out his name, leaving the fresco unattributed, not with an attribution to Pizzolo, as published editions of his text suggest.

The side of the entrance-arch into the apse facing the main chapel was decorated with an antique ornament of bucranes and garlands, with two gigantic heads, in 'stone-colour' according to Kristeller, at the spring of the arch. The interest of this decoration was noted by Kristeller (1901, p.70), who regarded the whole scheme as an attempt at a revival of the antique, the ornamental motifs being the earliest lively re-creation of the antique in the chapel, and the heads an effort to introduce sculptural motifs in imitation of the antique. The heads were cleaned during the restoration of 1930–2, for which see Fogolari (art. cit. in *Boll. d'A.*, ser. iii, xxvi, 1932, pp.433–44), who published the head on the right with an attribution to Mantegna. The heads are plainly portraits, and that on the right was correctly identified by Fiocco (1937, pp.24,198) as a self-portrait by Pizzolo and that on the left as a self-portrait by Mantegna. Fiocco suggested that they were inspired by the heads painted by Uccello round the clock of Santa Maria del Fiore. Tietze-Conrat (1955, p.193) confused the head of Pizzolo with that of Mantegna (cf. Fiocco, pp. cit., pl.18) but accepted the thesis of self-portraiture by Mantegna, and compared the design of an ornamental motif rising from two heads to that of corbels on Venetian Gothic funerary monuments. She dates the decoration to the earliest period of the frescoes. Her confusion between the heads is maintained by Cipriani (1962, p.49), by Camesasca (1964, p.112) who lists the head on the right as a 'supposed self-portrait' with a date *c*.1450, and by Garavaglia (1967, p.89, No.14D).

In fact, as Fiocco correctly saw, it is the head on the left, corresponding to the St James frescoes, that is clearly a self-portrait by Mantegna, resembling in age and features the self-portrait in the *Trial* scene of the frescoes and that in the Berlin *Presentation*. The smoother, tighter handling also suggests that this is a work by Mantegna: the coarser, more realistic strength of the other head is characteristic of Pizzolo. The pair of heads clearly constitute a form of signature, given their pose, which seems to refer to the frescoes on the walls of the tribune. They are therefore likely to have been executed between September 1449, after Morosini's award of the painting of the left half of the tribune arch to Mantegna and of the right half to Pizzolo, and the death of Pizzolo in the middle of 1453. The most plausible date within this bracket is perhaps the second half of 1450 or early in 1451, before the appearance in the chapel of Bono da Ferrara and Ansuino da Forlì.

ICONOGRAPHY

I. General
Only Puppi (*Eremitani*, 1970, pp.73–4) discusses, briefly and inconclusively, the iconography of the chapel. Fiocco (1947) wrongly states that the church was dedicated to St James Major and St Christopher: the church was dedicated to St James Major and St Philip, as the consecration stone of 1435 (Portenari, 1623, p.448) makes clear.

The choice of subjects for the principal frescoes was obviously dictated by the saints to whom the chapel had been dedicated on its foundation, St James Major and St Christopher. These two saints share the same feast day, 25 July, as Fiocco pointed out; they were also appropriate saints for a funerary chapel, since the suffrage of St James Major was invoked for the dying, while St Christopher was much revered as a protector against an evil death, that is, sudden death without time to receive the sacraments. St James was in addition one of the two co-patrons

of the church. Antonio degli Ovetari's personal choice of saintly patrons probably appears most clearly in the altarpiece of the chapel (already designed by 16 May 1448), which shows the Virgin and Child, flanked on the Virgin's right hand by St John the Baptist, St Peter Martyr and St Anthony, and on her left hand by St James Major, St Christopher and St Anthony Abbot. The predella depicts the Adoration of the Magi. Above is a half-length figure of the Blessing Christ of the kind frequent on medieval tombs. His pose of blessing becomes pointless unless it is admitted that the altar originally stood just beyond the tombs of the founders (see DESCRIPTION). Hence the tomb slabs and altar together formed a species of altar tomb, making an ensemble typical of late medieval funeral chapels and funerary devotion.

Mary and the saints are present as intercessors for Antonio's soul, and the Blessing Christ represents the pious hope that it would be admitted into heaven by Christ after judgement. Mary, as mediatrix between man and her Son, appears again in the fresco of the *Assumption* behind the altar. The figure of the God the Father in the vault above is a normal complement of such an Assumption scene. The Apostles Peter and Paul and the two patron saints of the chapel, St Christopher and St James, appear on the vaults beside the Father as mediators in heaven. The Four Evangelists are represented on the main vault and the Four Doctors of the Church, St Ambrose, St Gregory, St Augustine and St Jerome, as the teachers of the Church and therefore of the Christian soul.

There is no trace of the Passion of Christ that was to decorate the inside wall of the arch that opens into the chapel.

II. The Frescoes of St James Major and St Christopher
The principal literary source of these two cycles is generally assumed to have been the *Legenda Aurea* of Jacopo de Voragine. Puppi (*Eremitani*, 1970, p.74) notes that there were various copies of the *Legenda* in the Library of the Eremitani.

Left wall

The Calling of James and John Lunette (left)   Plate 10
Christ, attended by St Peter and St Andrew, calls James and John. In the background their father Zebedee casts his nets in the lake of Galilee (Matthew, 4, 20–2: Mark, 1, 19–20).

The Preaching of St James   Plate 11
The story now follows the *Legenda Aurea*. After Christ's death St James preached the gospel in Spain. Making only nine converts, he left two of them to continue his work and returned with the other seven to Judea. Here a certain magician named Hermogenes in conjunction with the Pharisees sent one of his disciples named Philetus to prove to the Jews that James's preaching was false. Instead James converted Philetus; in revenge Hermogenes cast a spell on him which made him unable to move. But James liberated him by a miracle, whereupon the infuriated Hermogenes summoned up demons and commanded them to bring James and Philetus to him bound. But when the demons came to James in the air, they began to speak with howls: 'O James, have pity on us, for though our time is not yet come, we are burning.' James said to them:

'Wherefore have you come to me?' They then told him that Hermogenes had sent them to take him and Philetus captive, but as they came an angel bound them with fiery chains and greatly tormented them. James then said the angel should free them, but that they must bring Hermogenes to him, bound but unharmed.

The scene represents the opening dialogue with the demons: below are the seven disciples and Philetus, struck with fear and terror, together with a ninth figure.

Knabenshue (1959, p.63) discusses the costume worn by St James.

The Baptism of Hermogenes Plate 12

The demons obey, bring back Hermogenes bound, and ask for licence to torment him. James refuses, and orders Philetus to release him from his bonds. Hermogenes, in gratitude, goes away and brings back all his books of magic for the Apostle to burn. James orders him to cast them into the sea, after which he returns, embraces the Apostle's feet and asks him to receive him. This narrative of the *Legenda Aurea* is conflated by Mantegna into a single scene, in which the Apostle baptizes Hermogenes, whose magic books (*codices*) and scrolls (*volumina*) lie on the pavement before him (there is no direct reference to baptism in the text of the *Legenda* although it is implied). The turbaned figure in the background may be a hostile Pharisee: the man in the right foreground has picked up one of the books of magic and is reading it.

Moschetti (1929–30, pp.238–9) identifies the classical roundel set in the loggia as Antinous bringing a horse to the Emperor Hadrian, and suggests that the closest antique prototype is a relief of this subject in the Museo Maffeiano, Verona. Blum (1936, p.14) rejects this identification and suggests that some Attic tomb relief inspired Mantegna as well as the Verona relief.

The Trial of St James First register (left) Plate 13

Angry at the conversion of Hermogenes, the Jews rebuke James, who converts many of them. The high priest Abiathar rouses the people against him and has him brought before Herod Agrippa, who condemns him to death. The scene expands the very terse narrative of the *Legenda*.

The lower relief on the arch shows two fronting medallions of Emperors, with the inscription T.PVLLIO/T.L.LINI/ IIIIIII VI. ./ALBI. ./. . . ./ S.E. . ./. On the pedestal is the inscription AVG.P. . . ./ROM. . .IO. . ./VMAN. . .P. . Moschetti (1929–30, pp.232–6) showed that the upper inscription copies that on an ancient slab at Monte Buso, near Este (now lost), which was also copied by Giovanni Marcanova and by Jacopo Bellini (Louvre Sketchbook, f.50). Differences between their versions and Mantegna's suggest that he made his copy independently (cf. Tamassia, 1956, pp.222–3). The source of the pedestal inscription has not been traced. Moschetti (*loc. cit.*) identifies the Emperors as Augustus and Vespasian: Blum as Augustus and Nero (1936, pp.13, 34–5) and as derived from Roman coins. Blum suggests that Augustus is shown as a representative of a 'good' Emperor, Nero as that of a 'bad' Emperor, but this seems over-interpretation. The relief of a pagan sacrifice above is an allusion to the Roman custom of offering Christians the choice between sacrificing to the gods and martyrdom (for more complex inter-

pretations see Blum, 1936, p.34 and Knabenshue, 1959, p.67).

The triumphal arch was thought by Eisler (1903, p.169) to have been derived from the Arch of Titus in Rome and by Blum (1936, pp.7–8) from the destroyed Arco dei Gavi in Verona (for this see Anti, 'L'arco dei Gavi a Verona' in *Architettura e arti decorative*, i, 1921, pp.121–39; Avena, *L'Arco dei Gavi ricostruito dal Comune di Verona*, 1932). Knabenshue (1959, p.68) suggests that Mantegna's source was a representation of an arch on the reverse of a Roman coin. His thesis is unconvincing. The arch is undoubtedly an eclectic elaboration from several sources, including the Arco dei Gavi, from which Mantegna quotes an inscription in the following scene, rather than a literal reproduction of a single model.

Herod Agrippa wears a classical costume of Late Imperial type – a *tunica talaris*, over which is a *colobium*. To this is added a scarf. Knabenshue (1959, p.65) acutely suggests that the two figures behind the chair are inspired by an ivory consular diptych, such as that of Magnus (Paris, Cabinet des Médailles). Less convincing is his suggestion that Herod's costume is taken from a diptych of this kind; the view that its sources are eclectic seems more plausible. Knabenshue relates the zoomorphic supports of the *sella curulis* to Donatello's *Madonna and Child* on the altar in the Santo. The figure on the canopy of estate holds an orb and a military standard, and stands on a globe. It is rightly identified by Blum (1936, p.34) as an emblem of Roman rule: Knabenshue (1959, pp.66–7) also attributes an astrological significance to it.

For the armour see Knabenshue's interesting analysis (1959, pp.68–71) and Martindale (1979, pp.130–1).

St James on the way to Execution Bottom register (left) Plate 14

As James is led to execution he cures a paralytic man who is lying in the road. The scribe Josias, who was leading the saint by a rope, throws himself at his feet, asks his forgiveness and begs to be made a Christian.

A related drawing (Plate 205) which, unlike the fresco, includes both the miraculously cured paralytic and Josias, establishes that the kneeling figure is Josias and not, as has been claimed (e.g. by Venturi, *Storia*, vii, 3, 1914, pp.112–17), the paralytic.

On the classical arch behind the group of St James and the paralytic is a relief with a medallion suspended from a palm inscribed L. VITRVVIVS / CERDO ARC / HITETVS. It was already realized by Selvatico (1841, p.17) that this inscription was copied from that on the Arco dei Gavi at Verona (L. VITRVVIVS LL CERDO / ARCHITECTVS) but he observed, correctly, that Mantegna's arch does not reproduce the Arco dei Gavi. From minor differences in transcription Eisler (1903, p.164) argued that the Arco dei Gavi was not directly known to Mantegna. However, Mantegna was artist more even than antiquary (compare the original inscription, repr. by Anti, *op. cit.*, fig.11, which is in two lines on a block of stone). Blum (1936, p.13) points out that the motifs of the sculptured frieze of the arch (a *decursio* of troops, Victory in her car) derive from Roman coins.

The jar and rudder under the medallion inscription are represented in an old copy of the fresco in the Musée Jacquemart André (see below) together with a circle and a palm-tree inscribed *La Vita el fine*. Giehlow (1916, pp.88–9) concluded that Mantegna used symbols as hieroglyphs – the jar symbolizing life, the rudder guidance, the circle eternity and the palm victory. The copyist would have added the inscription to clarify the meaning. Although accepted by Iversen (1961, pp.68–9), this seems an anachronistic interpretation of the relief: more probably the allegorical symbolism was added by the later copyist. The jar is in fact a sacrificial wine-jug (*urceus*). Iversen (*loc. cit.*) suggests as Mantegna's source the well-known antique frieze from San Lorenzo fuori le mura, Rome, which Mantegna certainly knew by *c.*1490. This does show an *urceus*, but no rudder; again Mantegna may have blended his sources to make an original design.

The Execution of St James Bottom register (right)
Plate 15
The executioner prepares to cut off the saint's head by bringing down a mallet on a primitive form of guillotine (*mannaia*). This motif may also be inspired by an antique sacrificial relief (compare Maffei, *Musaeum Veronense*, 1749, lxxv, 2).

The city on the hill represents Jerusalem. Eisler (1903, p.165) points out that the two reliefs on the arch-gateway reproduce a coin of Nero (*annona Augusti et Cereris*), in reverse, first noticed by Portheim (1886, p.275), and a coin of Septimius Severus; Blum (1936, p.14); Tamassia (1956, p.224), who derives the first relief of a trophy between two figures from a coin of Trajan (Cohen, II, no.184).

Right wall (the four upper frescoes not by Mantegna)

St Christopher before the King Lunette (left)
St Christopher, who wishes to serve the mightiest of all masters, has entered the service of one of the world's greatest kings, and asks him why he makes the sign of the cross when the devil is named. The King tells him that he fears the devil, and Christopher resolves to leave him and enter the devil's service.

St Christopher meets the Devil Lunette (right)
St Christopher encounters the devil with his retinue in a great desert, and enters his service.

The scene is wrongly identified by Fiocco (1945).

St Christopher bearing Christ across the river
First register (left)
According to the *Legenda*, on discovering that the devil fears Christ, Christopher quits his service and seeks Christ. He at last finds a hermit who converts him, and when Christopher says he cannot fast or pray, tells him to serve Christ by carrying passengers across a river (scene in right background). Christopher makes a hut by the river, and using a long perch for a staff carries passengers incessantly. At last he carries over a Child, who weighs him down intolerably, and who reveals when on the other side that he is Christ.

St Christopher and the soldiers of the King of Samos in Lycia First register (right)
Christopher goes to Samos in Lycia, and after prayer, receives the gift of preaching in the Lycian tongue. King Dagnus sends 200 soldiers to arrest him: they find him praying for the conversion of the people and are afraid at his giant size. Two hundred more soldiers sent by the King at once begin to pray with Christopher, who rises, asks them why they have come and voluntarily consents to be arrested.

Wrongly identified by Fiocco (1945).

The Martyrdom of St Christopher. Scene 1
Bottom register (left)   Plate 26
Infuriated by Christopher's constancy in refusing to sacrifice to the pagan gods, King Dagnus first orders him to be martyred by fiery pitch, and when this fails to kill him, to be shot to death by arrows. The arrows all remain suspended in the air, but when the King mocks Christopher, believing him dead, one of the arrows comes out of the air, strikes him in the eye and blinds him.

The palace wall is set with an antique relief of two half-busts of a young man and woman, making a pair with the relief set in the façade in the companion fresco. The relief in this fresco is inscribed T. PONENVS / M.F. MARCEL / . . . PATRIS / DIAE / . . . / . . . / HI (?) QVI.VI . . . / III . . . XXXVIII. The antique slab from which this was copied is now untraced, but was seen in the original or in a drawing by Furlanetto in the nineteenth century. The inscription, as reproduced from Furlanetto's papers by Mommsen (*Inscrip.Gall.Cis.pars prior*, p.295, n.2989) reads T PONENVS / M.F. MARCEL / PATRI / IIII XXXVIII. Moschetti (1929–30, pp.229–31) believes that the busts may have been included in the original. Blum (1936, pp.14–15) points out that both reliefs are typical Roman tomb-reliefs and compares them with that of the Opii in the Museo Civico, Padua. A closer comparison is perhaps the tomb slab of C. Fannius (Orsato, 1652, p.53; Furlanetto, 1847, pp.328–9). Compare Tamassia (1956, p.226).

For the ornament on the entablature compare the similar ornaments on the Temple of Hadrian, Ephesus (for this see Foss, *Ephesus after antiquity*, 1979, pp.70–2, with lit.; for a good illustration of a relevant detail see *Vogue*, January 1985, p.124).

The Martyrdom of St Christopher. Scene 2
Bottom register (right)   Plate 28
Next day St Christopher is martyred by beheading as he himself had prophesied after the King had been blinded. Mantegna shows his body being dragged away and his severed head lying on a platter ready for presentation to the King, who has been told by Christopher that if he smears some of his blood on his eye he will recover his sight.

The scene is not a combined one, as claimed by Tietze-Conrat (1954, p.194), except in the sense that a unitary setting has been devised.

The fresco was already badly damaged in 1849 (Selvatico, 1849, p.163) and the composition has to be reconstructed from the copy in the Musée Jacquemart-André (see Plate 29).

For an analysis of the perspective of the Ovetari frescoes see Castelfranco (1962). The antique sources of the frescoes were the subject of a pioneering study by Eisler (1903).

PORTRAITS:
The St Christopher Frescoes
Only Selvatico (1849, pp.164–5n.) has attempted to identify the personages named by Vasari. Since the tradition of their identification goes back to Campagnola, it must

be treated seriously. Squarcione is to be identified as the short, fat man holding a combined axe and lance (Vasari has wrongly translated the Latin *hastata mucro* as lance and sword) in the first scene of St Christopher's martyrdom. The young soldier standing behind him on the left is the young Mantegna. Other personages certainly appear as actors: but the three figures standing on the right are simply portraits: from their costume they probably represent Nofri di Palla Strozzi, Messer Girolamo della Valle and Bonifacio Frigimelica (corrupted by Vasari into Fuzimeliga).

Nofri (Onofrio) di Palla Strozzi (1411–after 1457). The favourite son of Palla Strozzi (1372–1462), the wealthy Florentine banker and famous patron of humanists, who was exiled to Padua from Florence in 1433 with the rest of the Albizzi faction. Onofrio, his youngest son, accompanied him (Litta, iv, Strozzi, tav. ix). He was a banker, and through him payments were made to Donatello for the Gattamelata monument in 1447 (A. Gloria, *Donatello fiorentino e le sue opere mirabili nel Tempio di S. Antonio*, Padua, 1895, p.xix). Strozzi was also a humanist, who took a special interest in geography. On 1 March 1457 Jacopo Antonio Marcello writes to René of Anjou that he has obtained a *mappamondo* for him from Onofrio Strozzi, who lives in Padua and takes particular delight in all liberal studies. It appears that Strozzi was an intimate and special friend, almost a brother, of Marcello, who was one of Mantegna's patrons and the Maecenas in Padua of Janus Pannonius (see Martin, in *Mémoires de la Soc. Nat. des Ant. de France*, ser. 6, ix, 1900, pp.264–5).

Girolamo della Valle. Scardeone (1560, p.239) gives a notice of him. He was a celebrated physician, and also an orator and a poet. One of his poems, *De Passione Christi*, was dedicated to Pietro Donato, the humanist Bishop of Padua. He died at Ravenna while on a mission to Rome for the Venetians 'not without suspicion of poison secretly administered'. Scardeone also records that 'Hujus hominis imago ex uiua oris effigie, manu Andreae Mantineae praestantis pictoris, admodum scitè picta conspicitur in sacello Eremitarum, & facie, & habitu, quo tunc temporis fuerat'. From Zonta & Brotto, it appears that he was the son of Ser Conte delle Valli, notary and citizen of Padua (2185). Girolamo, already a magister, became a doctor of arts on 12 November 1444 (1877). He is recorded as a student of medicine on 7 September 1445 (1970), and obtained his doctorate of medicine on 29 October 1450 (2452). Meanwhile he had been appointed in 1446 to an extraordinary chair in theoretical medicine in the University at a salary of 20 ducats, raised to 40 in 1453. In 1459 he changed to an ordinary chair in practical medicine which he held until his death in 1472 (Facciolati, *Fasti Gymnasii Patavini*, pt.2, 1757, p.127).

Bonifacio Frigimelica (Frizimeliga). A doctor of laws. He appears in Ser Campolongo's account of disbursements for the chapel on 13 May 1452 as receiving 114 lire (20 ducats), probably acting for Madonna Imperatrice (Rigoni, 1970, p.45). He appears twice in the records of Padua University (Zonta & Brotto, 766, 1686), first on 21 March 1430 as a student, and on 2 March 1443 as a law student.

Messer Bonramino cavaliere. The name was correctly interpreted by Selvatico as derived from a Latinized form of Borromeo (at this date the name was sometimes spelt Bonrameo). He can be identified as Messer Antonio, son of the Borromeo who founded the great family bank in Venice and was master of the mint to Francesco II da Carrara. Antonio was a doctor of laws, who lectured in Pavia, a banker in Venice and finally a great proprietor in Padua, where he founded the chapel of the Madonna in the church of S. Maria de' Servi (Litta, iv, Borromeo, tav.1). He was one of the wealthiest and most important of Paduan citizens, rich enough to lend the Comune 15,000 ducats in 1432, while his tax-return of 1444 shows him owning property to the value of 120,541 lire in Padua and its territory (Ventura, 1964, p.74). He is constantly mentioned in contemporary documents as *miles* (i.e. *cavaliere*) and appears several times as a witness at honorific acts of conferring doctorates from 2 December 1433 onwards. On 5 and 6 May 1436 he was present at a particularly splendid act when a doctorate was conferred on a Venier: among the other witnesses were Francesco Capodilista and his father Giovanni Francesco, Palla Strozzi, Lancellotto, a nephew of the King of Cyprus, Jacopo, son and proctor of the Doge Francesco Foscari, and Leonello de Leone (Zonta & Brotto, 969, 1118–19, 1449). He died on 29 December 1459 (Salamonius, *Inscriptiones*, 1701, p.199).

Niccolò. Described by Vasari as goldsmith to Pope Innocent VIII, but Müntz (*Les arts à la cour des Papes Innocent VIII, Alexandre VI, Pie III*, 1898, pp.108–9) says that there is no trace of a goldsmith of this name in the Papal archives. Moschini (1826, p.21) notes a Paduan goldsmith named Niccolò di Battista who was living in 1447 and was the son of a painter. From the documents about Niccolò di Battista published by Sartori it can be deduced that he was born *c*.1415–20. He was known as Niccolò del or dal Papa, and accordingly it seems virtually certain that Vasari found this name and profession recorded in a Latinized form (e.g. *Nicolaus Papae aurifex*) in Campagnola's letter (see above) and assumed that its bearer had been goldsmith to Innocent VIII. Sartori first records Niccolò del Papa as a goldsmith in 1444. In 1449 he is found declaring that he is more than 25 years old. It was he who made the metal Holy Name of Jesus for the fresco of Sant'Antonio and San Bernardino painted by Mantegna above the entrance to the Santo (Cat.no.2, Plate 30) and this, it may be felt, clinches the identification of Vasari's Niccolò with Niccolò del Papa and substantiates the tradition he has transmitted. Later in 1454 Niccolò was commissioned by the Massari dell'Arca of the Santo to mount Donatello's bronze reliefs and bronze figures of the Evangelists on the high altar of the Santo. He never carried out the work, and the Arca was still reclaiming the earnest it had paid him at the time of his death on 5 December 1470 (Sartori, *Documenti per la storia dell'arte a Padova*, 1976, pp.356–9).

Baldassare da Leccio. Presumably a member of the noble Paduan family of De Liccio (Lisio, Licio) cited in Zonta & Brotto (501,840).

Vescovo ungherese. This must be Janus Pannonius (1434–72) who is known to have been in Padua from the autumn of 1454 until late in 1458. The fact that his portrait appears in the frescoes of St Christopher's martyrdom is yet another argument for their late date. See Cat. no.68.

Execution of St James

Marsilio Pazzo. Usually identified as a member of the Pazzi family of Florence, but this cannot be correct, since no Pazzi of this name is listed in Litta. Is there again some confusion due to Vasari's misunderstanding of Campagnola's Latin, as with Niccolò del Papa (see above)? If so, the model may have been a certain Marsilio the madman.

LATER FAME: The perspective of the frescoes was greatly praised by Daniele Barbaro in the manuscript of his *Pratica della Prospettiva*, published 1569 in a shortened version. The manuscript version, as printed by Morelli (*Anonimo Morelliano*, 1800, pp.142–3), reads: '*Più basso ancora è conceduto di fermare il punto nel quadro, come si vede aver fatto l'unico imitator della natura Messere Andrea Mantegna nella città sua di Padova nella chiesa degli Eremitani, che dipingendo quasi al sommo d' una cappella, pose il punto non solamente più basso nel quadro, ma di sotto a quello nel pariete; e per quello che si vede, è posto all'altezza degli occhi de' riguardanti, in modo che di molte figure che sono ivi dipinte alcune non sono perfettamente compiute, per esser ascose dal piano in che fermano le piante; cosa in vero non meno lodevole, che artifiziosa. E quale fu quell'opera del Mantegna, che lodevole ed artifiziosa non fosse? Certo niuna, che io mi creda. E credenza non solamente ne rendono le altre in detto luoco dipinte da lui; ma eziandio il Trionfo di Cesare figurato per lui in Mantova, che per quello che universalmente se ne ragiona, e cosa tanto al vero simile, che si tien per certo che altramente esser non doveva esso Cesare a Roma trionfante. Sì maestrevolmente pose ogni cosa al suo luoco, e talmente esprimendola con le principali linee, che chiaramente si vede che ciascuna figura dimostra far qualche naturale operazione, restando alla destinata distanza considerate.*'

Portenari (1623, p.449) also bears witness to the admiration generally felt for the perspective effects in the frescoes: 'La cappella de gli Ouetarij fabricata per vigore del testamento di Antonio Ouetario fatto l'anno 1443, nella quale sono le laudatissime figure di Andrea Mantegna Padouano pittore rarissimo, & in particolare quel meraviglioso scurzo di S. Christoforo decapitato, che in poco spazio appare di grandezza di gigante.'

VERSIONS AND COPIES: The admiration excited by Mantegna's Ovetari frescoes is also attested by the existence of very early versions and copies. Marc' Antonio Michiel (*Anonimo Morelliano*, 1884, pp.74,226) records in the house of a Paduan cloth merchant 'In casa de M . . . da Stra marcadante de panni. El retratto piccolo della Cappella delli Heremitani dell'opera del Mantegna fu de man de . . .' In 1546 he records in the house of Michiel Contarini by the Misericordia in Venice (as part of the inheritance of Pietro Contarini and Francesco Zeno): 'Vi è un ritratto colorito piccolo della Istoria di San Cristoforo che fece il Mantegna a Padoa in li Eremitani, de man del detto Mantegna, molto bella operetta.'

Selvatico (1849, pp.199–200) suggests that the Da Stra copies or versions may be the set of four small panels which in the eighteenth century belonged to the Scotti family of Padua (Rossetti, 1776, p.346: 'modelli di Andrea Mantegna di que' tanto celebri quadri a fresco, che fece nella famosa Cappella in Chiesa agli Eremitani, essendovi anche una Crocifissione del Signore dello stesso

Mantegna, ch'egli non pose in esecuzione ch'io sappia.' cf. also Moschini *Breve guida . . . di Padova*, 1817, p.98, and G. de' Lazara in a letter of 1809 (Campori, 1866, p.364)). According to Lazara, they represented the two lowest compartments on both sides. By 1849 they had passed from Casa Scotti to the Marchesi Orologio in their palace by the Teatro Nuovo. Three of them are generally identified as the copies attributed to Francesco Benaglio of *St James on the way to Execution* and *The Martyrdom of St Christopher* (both scenes) now in the Musée Jacquemart (1031: tempera on panel, transferred to canvas, 51 × 51 cm except for the panel of St James, 51 × 53 cm). See Crowe & Cavalcaselle (1871, pp.329,336, copies of St James on the way to Execution and of his Martyrdom, still with Marchese Galeazzo Dondi-Orologio). A fourth panel from the same series is in the Schickler collection, Paris.

The Contarini version of *St Christopher* was identified by Selvatico (*loc. cit.*) as the fine copy now in the Galleria Nazionale, Parma (No.437, tempera on paper, 80 × 40 cm: formerly in the collection of Conte Leopoldo Cicognara, Venice; ceded by him to the Galleria in March 1829; for Cicognara, an original study by Mantegna: for Selvatico (1849, p.199), Crowe & Cavalcaselle (1871, p.337) and Ricci (*R. Galleria di Parma*, 1896, pp.48–9) a copy. For its history see G. P. Clerici, in *La Bibliofilia*, xix, 1917–18, pp.97–113. The Jacquemart-André and Paris copies are discussed by Gräff (in *Monatshefte für Kunstwissenschaft*, iii, 1910, pp.107–9). See also p.398.

2. The Sacred Monogram held by St Anthony of Padua and San Bernardino.

Inscribed: IN NOMINE IESV OMNE GENV FLECTATVR CELESTIVM TERRESTRIVM ET INFERNORVM (Philippians, 2, 10). See below. Padua, Santo, Museo Antoniano (now in the Presidenza dell'Arca del Santo, where seen 1984). Fresco, detached. 316 cm. base measurement   Plate 30

CONDITION: Much restored and repainted (see below).

PROVENANCE: See below.

This fresco originally decorated the lunette of the central doorway on the façade of the Santo. The Name of Jesus was executed in gilt metal by the Paduan goldsmith Niccolò del Papa (for whom see p.399) who had a contestation in 1455 with Gregorio Dottori over his dues 'occasione Jesu facti et positi super portam sancti Antonii confessoris.' Dottori claimed that full payment had been completed with 6 *staia* of grain delivered to Niccolò, but Niccolò insisted that this was a payment made before he had incurred the expense of setting it up and of adding certain tubes and a stone behind it amounting to 6 gold ducats and more (ante quam dictus Jesus fuisset insculpitus et positus in muro et pro ponere ipsum in muro inibant expense ducatorum sex auri et ultra in certis canonibus et uno lapide qui ibat post dictum Jesum). The dispute was submitted to arbitration on 22 August. For the relevant documents see Sartori (*Documenti per la storia dell'arte a Padova*, 1976, p.357, s.1455). Later Mantegna painted Niccolò's portrait in his fresco of the martyrdom of St Christopher in the Eremitani (see Cat. 1).

Below the fresco ran an inscription with Mantegna's

signature and the date of completion, 22 July 1452 (see Salamonio, cit. below). According to Gonzati (*La basilica di S. Antonio da Padova*, i, 1852, pp.124–5) this inscription was 'lungo l'imposta' (his plate shows the fresco in position).

The fresco is recorded by Marc' Antonio Michiel (ed. Frizzoni, p.20: 'Sopra la porta maistra della chiesa el S. Francesco e S. Bernardino inchinati, che tengono il *Jesus* in mano furono de man del Mantegna, come appar per la sottoscrizione.'). Gonzati prints a document of 26 November 1610 by which the painter Gasparo Zatton was commissioned to 'rinfrescar il Nome di Gesù e due figure sopra la porta'. Salamonio (*Urbis Patavinae inscriptiones sacrae, et prophanae*, 1701, p.351) records Mantegna's inscription as 'Supra magnum Templi ostium Nomen Iesu exornatum variis picturis hac inscriptione. I. ANDREAS Mantegna optimo favente Numine perfecit. M.CCCC.LII.XI.Ke. Sextil'. By 1776 (Rossetti, pp.35–6) the inscription had been covered up by a *cartello* recording the concession of a perpetual indulgence to the Basilica: and this was still the case in Gonzati's day. The fresco was restored again in 1769 by Francesco Zanoni (Rossetti, *loc. cit.*): the head of San Antonio had already been restored by Pietro Liberi (Fiocco, 1937, p.200).

The verse from Philippians of the inscription was chosen by San Bernardino himself in designing his emblem of the Holy Name: on the tablet displaying the emblem that he used in preaching it was generally inscribed in the outer circle enclosing the letters of the Name of Jesus (Facchinetti, *San Bernardino, mistico sole del secolo xv*, 1933, pp.358–61; Origo, *The World of San Bernardino*, 1964, pp.118,278).

3. Polyptych of St Luke (*Polittico di San Luca*)

Milan, Pinacoteca di Brera, 200 (Malaguzzi-Valeri, 1908, pp.113–14; Modigliani, 1950, pp.42–3).
Tempera on poplar. 230 × 177 cm.   Plate 1

CONDITION: The altarpiece has lost its original frame, and is now shown as a set of separate panels. See below.

PROVENANCE: Painted for the Cappella di San Luca of the church of Santa Giustina, Padua (see below). Recorded by Scardeone (1560, p.372: 'Pinxit & alteram insignem tabulam altaris ad corpus D. Lucae Evangelistae in aede D. Justinae, ubi nomen eius artificiosè comprehenditur'). Cavacius (*Historiarum Coenobii D. Justinae Libri sex*, 1606; 1696, p.227) records that the altarpiece was commissioned by the abbot Mauro dei Folperti of Pavia; 'Extremo vitæ suæ anno produxit claustrum antea inchoatum ... delubrum Sancti Lucæ Evangelistæ vetustate fatiscens, reparavit, aram multis ornamentis extulit, ac tabulam eiusdem locavit Andreae Mantegnae optimo ejus aetatis pictori ...' An inventory of 31 December 1691 (ASP, S. Giustina, busta 82, VI c.277, printed by Sartori, in *Santa Giustina*, 1970, pp.433, 458–9) lists it as one of fifteen altarpieces in the church and as following the altarpiece of the Beata Giacoma da Castelfranco: 'dietro s. Luca d'Andrea Mantegna con 12 figure, in tolla, qual serviva per tabernacolo'. By the second half of the eighteenth century the picture had been moved from the church into the abbot's apartment, where it was seen by Rossetti (1765, p.214; 1776, p.213; 1780, p.217). Later the Abate

Zani claimed that Rossetti had ignored Scardeone's reference to the picture as containing Mantegna's name '*artificiose*' represented, and suggested it must be present as a cipher or in some symbolic fashion. His claim was rebutted by Brandolese (1795, pp.102–3): '*Noi però potemmo mostrare al ben. Editore che quantunque questo cel. quadro sia nella più desiderabile conservazione, tuttavia assolutamente questa marca non si vede più. E da avvertirsi che le figure son colorite in campo d'oro, e dorato è pure l'ornamento del quadro; verisimile la marca sarà stata nel campo oppure nel ornato; e siccome alcuni anni sono fu questa tavola colpita da un fulmine che fece sparire tutto l'oro, e lasciò intatta la pittura, così è verisimile che in quell'incontro sia sparita ancora la marca accennato dallo Scardeone.*' See also Moschini (1826, pp.35–6). Transferred to Brera in 1811.

The altarpiece was commissioned from Mantegna on 10 August 1453 (contract and subsequent documents printed in Kristeller, 1902, p.515). Mantegna undertook to paint all the figures and supply the colours at his own expense, and to paint the ground of the carved ornament of the framework with blue (*azzuro tedesco*). For the painting he was to receive 50 Venetian ducats, 10 to be paid at once as an earnest, 15 when the altarpiece was half-finished, and the remainder on its completion (the decoration of the frame was to be separately valued by a certain Don Antonino). On 11 February 1454 he was paid 10 further ducats, on 18 November 12 more, and he had also received 5 ducats by or on the same day. He now contracted to gild all the part of the frame executed by Maestro Guglielmo that still had to be gilded and to add all other necessary ornaments to the said frame. He was to receive 22 ducats for the work and complete it if possible by Christmas, or at the latest by Easter 1455. The gilding was still in course of completion on 19 February 1455.

For the chapel and shrine of St Luke see *Santa Giustina*, 1970, pp.97–106: for Storlato's frescoes in the chapel Moschetti in *Atti del R. Istituto Veneto di Scienze, Lettere ed Arti*, Anno Accademico 1925–6, lxxxv, pt.2, pp.411–26, and *Santa Giustina*, 1970, pp.169–71. For bequests of money accumulating in 1443 for the chapel see Tonzig, *op. cit.* below, p.300.

Panels of the St Luke Polyptych
Upper row
a) St Daniel of Padua
Panel with pointed arch. 66 × 37 cm.
Daniel can be identified by his youth, his deacon's dress, by the model of Padua that he holds, and by his banner. He was represented with similar attributes by Giusto de' Menabuoi in the late fourteenth century and by Domenico Campagnola in the sixteenth (see Venturi, ix, 3, figs.349,343). According to the legend current in Santa Giustina (see Cavacius, 1606, pp.52–4) the discovery of the saint's body was due to a vision in which he appeared as a deacon to a blind man of Tuscany and ordered him to go to Padua, seek out the oratory of St Prosdocimus (see below) in Santa Giustina and enquire for his, the deacon's, tomb. In return his sight would be restored. The invention of the saint's tomb, inscribed HIC REQUIESCIT CORPUS DANIELIS MARTYRIS ET LEVITAE, is historical, and took place on 26 December 1075. By command of Bishop Ulderico of Padua the body was translated from Santa

Giustina to the new cathedral he was building on 3 January 1076. Representations of St Daniel are local to Padua. For the literature of the saint see Daniele (in Istituto Giovanni XXIII, *Biblioteca Sanctorum*, 1964, s.v.).

b) St Jerome in Penitence
Panel with pointed arch. 66 × 37 cm.

c) Pietà, flanked (*left*) by the Virgin and (*right*) St John lamenting.

d) St Maximus, Bishop of Padua
Panel with pointed arch. 66 × 37 cm.
Generally tentatively identified as St Augustine, this figure represents St Maximus, Bishop of Padua, whose body, together with those of St Felicity of Padua, St Julian of Padua and three Holy Innocents, was discovered in Santa Giustina on 2 August 1052, in consequence of a vision in which an old man commanded the abbot Bernardo to disinter them. Pope Leo IX, who happened to be in Padua on his way to Hungary, immediately canonized Felicity, Julian, the Innocents and Maximus. The iconography seems to derive from the fourteenth-century carved figure of St Prosdocimus on the portal of Santa Giustina (repr. Tonzig, in Padua, Museo Civico, *Bollettino*, xxii, 1929, p.183). According to legend Maximus was the successor of Prosdocimus, whose acts he wrote: in the Middle Ages two sermons were also attributed to him. These writings are represented by his book. For his history see Daniele (in *Bibl. Sanct.*, ix, 1967, pp.62–3).

e) St Julian of Padua
Panel with pointed arch. 66 × 37 cm.
In spite of the impossible attributes of the sword and palm, generally identified as St Sebastian. The figure can be plausibly identified as St Julian of Padua whose body was discovered in a marble coffin, holding the bones of three Holy Innocents, relics Julian had brought back from his repeated pilgrimages to Palestine. Nothing was known of him in medieval or Renaissance Padua save that he was a patrician and flourished well before the sack of the city by Agilulf in AD 606 (Scardeone, 1560, p.105). The sword indicating his noble birth was presumably given him by contagion from St Julian the Hospitaller: the palm indicates his rank as a confessor (for St Julian of Padua see Daniele, in *Bibl. Sanct.*, vi, 1965, 1208–9). He is figured again as a noble youth, but without attributes, in Romanino's altarpiece painted for the high altar of Santa Giustina in 1513 (repr. in *Santa Giustina*, 1970, pp.210 ff., where his identity is established by a companion medallion of the Three Holy Innocents). On Gian Francesco de Surdis' sculptured altar-shrine of San Giuliano of 1561–2 he is shown as a youth in armour with a sword (*Santa Giustina*, 1970, p.229, fig.20).

Lower row
f) St Scolastica or St Felicity of Padua
Panel with pointed arch. 97 × 37 cm.
Generally identified as St Scolastica, sister of St Benedict, who is also represented in Romanino's altarpiece of 1513 (see above). The presence of St Benedict and her appearance among the major saints of the altarpiece perhaps support the identification. However, Scolastica is normally shown as a youthful virgin and there is a possibility that

the figure really represents St Felicity of Padua (see d, above). The inscription on her tomb declared that she had been a nun (*illustris foemina Deo devota sacro velamine dedicata*) and that after serving God day and night she had been received into heaven. Local hagiography developed this into a tradition that she was a nun in Santa Giustina: indeed Ongarello, writing in the sixteenth century, declares she became abbess there (Portenari, 1623, p.416). She had her own feast-day in Santa Giustina until 1810 (for St Felicity see Daniele, in *Bibl. Sanct.*, v, 1964, 604–5).

g) St Prosdocimus
Panel with pointed arch. 97 × 37 cm.
St Prosdocimus, according to legend, was sent by St Peter in AD 46 from Rome to convert Padua. He was a Greek whom Peter had converted at Antioch. He became first Bishop of Padua, and is shown with a pitcher or ewer to symbolize the water of baptism with which he regenerated his converts. Prosdocimus was the guardian of Giustina and brought her up in the Christian faith.

h) St Luke
Panel with pointed top. Cracked right centre.
119 × 61 cm.
The identity of the saint, rather strangely queried by Camesasca (1964, p.106), is confirmed by the contract of 10 August 1453, which specifies 'una so pala da esser mesa a l'Altar de San Luca in la dita Gesia di Santa Justina'.

i) St Benedict
Panel with pointed top. 97 × 37 cm.
The attribute which the saint holds in his right hand has not been correctly identified. It is the bundle of rods which Benedict frequently holds. The thorns emphasize its purpose as a scourge; they echo the penitence of St Jerome above. Benedict appears as the founder of the Benedictine order, to which Santa Giustina belonged.

j) Santa Giustina of Padua, Virgin and Martyr
Panel with pointed top. 97 × 37 cm.
According to legend, Giustina was the daughter of Vitalianus Justinus, King of Padua, who was converted by Prosdocimus to Christianity, together with his wife Prepedigna, and built Santa Sofia, the first Christian church in Padua. Giustina was brought up a Christian by Prosdocimus (see above) and refused to abjure her faith during the first persecution of the Christians in Padua conducted by Maximianus. Accordingly, after arrest and trial she was put to death by the sword. Her body was buried by Prosdocimus in front of his oratory of Santa Maria, later known as that of San Prosdocimus, which became part of the Basilica founded in her honour. St Benedict and Santa Giustina were chosen as their especial patrons by the reformed congregation of Santa Giustina, later known as the Congregatio Cassinense, founded in 1419 by Ludovico Barbo, abbot of Santa Giustina. Her joint role as patron of the congregation with St Benedict explains their juxtaposition on the altarpiece: otherwise as the titular saint of the monastery one would expect to find her in the post of honour occupied by St Scolastica. For Giustina and her cult see Amore & Prevedello (in *Bibl. Sanct.*, vi, 1965, 1345–9).

4. St Euphemia. Inscribed on the arch: SANTA EVFEMIA. Inscribed on the *cartello* in Roman capitals: OPVS ANDREAE

MANTEGNAE / MCCCCLIIII. Naples, Museo e Gallerie Nazionali ·di Capodimonte, Cat.61, inv.83946 (De Rinaldis, *Pinacoteca del Museo Nazionale di Napoli: Catalogo*, 1911, pp.84–6).

Tempera on canvas. 171 × 78 cm.   Plate 31

CONDITION: See Naples, Sopraintendenza alle Gallerie della Campania, *IV Mostra di Restauri*, 1960, p.115. Badly burnt in the late eighteenth century, when the tempera was irremediably darkened. Subsequently the original thin canvas, reduced almost to ashes, was lined and saturated with oil which has made it rigid. Restored *c.*1960, when removal of repaint revealed part of the background of the sky, and of the swag of fruit in the rear, though this last is very faint. The folds of the mantle are lost, and the landscape background dimmed.

PROVENANCE: First recorded in the Museo Borgia, Velletri, a collection formed by Cardinal Stefano Borgia (1731–1804). Acquired from the Museo in 1817. Inventoried by Conte Borgia in 1814 as 'Gran quadro in tela, alto pal. 7 on. 9 sopra pal. 3½. Rappresentante Santa Eufemia col nome del Mantegna che la dipinse nel 1454. Quadro raro illustrato dal dotto Cav D'Agincourt, e fatto incidere, ma danneggiato dal fuoco' (*Documenti inediti per servire alla storia dei Musei d'Italia*, i, 1878, pp.325–6). The reference is to D'Agincourt's celebrated work *Histoire de l'Art par les monuments*, ii, Paris, 1823, p.120; iii, 1828, p.142, pl.cxxxix. As is well known, D'Agincourt's materials and plates were collected in the late eighteenth century. He notes 'Cette peinture est inédite.'

The attribution of the picture to Mantegna and the genuineness of the inscription, attacked by Morelli (1891, p.231), are defended by Kristeller (1901, p.137). The letters take no account of the illusionistic crumplings of the parchment *cartello*, but are simply inscribed over them, with no attempt at additional illusionism (compare also the inscription on the London *Agony in the Garden* where MANTEGNA is not transposed into the genitive).

5. The Adoration of the Shepherds
New York, Metropolitan Museum of Art, 32.130.2.
Tempera, transferred from wood to canvas.
40 × 55.5 cm.   Plate 33; Fig.4

CONDITION: Cut down on left and right (see below).

PROVENANCE: Coll. of A. Rouse Boughton-Knight, Downton Castle, Herefordshire, exh. RA, 1882; engraved in *Magazine of Art*, vi, 1883, p.78; with Duveen (Duveen, 1941, No.75); coll. of Clarence H. Mackay; bought by the Museum, 1932.

This picture has been identified with one recorded in a list compiled in 1588 of paintings set up from 1586 by Bastiano Filippi 'in la capeletta de la Ser^ma Duchessa di ferrara in corte' i.e. of Margherita Gonzaga (see Cat. no.18; cf.Venturi, in *Archivio storico dell'arte*, i, 1888, pp.425–6). These included 'uno Prosepio de Andrea Mantegna' which was placed together with four other paintings not by Mantegna on the door wall of the chapel. On another wall were 'una m^a Morta de m. Andrea Mantegna' and 'uno quadro di messer Andrea Mantenga'. Filippi's adaptations of these pictures to this setting included 'Zunta': stucco-work and oil-colouring; he

began work in 1586. Like Titian's *Bacchus and Ariadne* and other Este pictures this *Presepio* may have passed from the Castello of Ferrara into the hands of the Aldobrandini on the devolution of Ferrara to the church in 1598. A Nativity was inventoried in 1626 among the pictures and works of art belonging to Donna Olimpia Aldobrandini (Della Pergola, 1960, p.428: '23. Uno quadro con la Natività di N.S. di mano di *Andrea Mantegna* del n. 24'). This Aldobrandini picture is probably that which in the late eighteenth century was in Villa Aldobrandini, Rome; brought to England *c.*1800 by Alexander Day, by whom exh. for sale at 20 Lower Brook Street, 1800–1 (Buchanan, *Memoirs of Painting*, ii, 1824, p.6: '12. Andrea Mantegna – The Birth of Christ'). However, Charles I also owned a 'Natevitye of Christ done Andrea Mantenger' (Millar, 1972, p.64: not in Vanderdoort's catalogue, cf. Millar, 1960). This is listed among the pictures which came from Wimbledon (No.66) and were appraised on 8 September 1649: valued at £40, it was sold to Hunt and Bass, merchants, on 1 March 1653 (cf. also Cosnac, p.413). The present painting has also been identified with this picture.

Drawings of motifs from this composition, which evidently made a great impression, are at Windsor (12794, Popham-Wilde, p.174, No.15, fifteenth century) and in the Uffizi. The Uffizi drawing is of the Virgin and Child. The Windsor drawing (Plate 34) is of the group of shepherds and the man and woman behind. It introduces a tree-trunk in the foreground; this feature also appears together with a boy behind the woman in a fragment of a contemporary version of the picture (Plate 35) last recorded in the Martin Le Roy (pseud., i.e. Marquet de Vasselot) Coll., Paris (*Catalogue raisonné de la collection Martin Le Roy*, v, 1909, Leprieur & Pérate, *Peintures*, pp.35–8, pl.ix: repr. in Yriarte, 1901, p.215, wrongly identified). There can be little doubt that the tree-trunk and boy are original features of the composition. The Le Roy picture (tempera on poplar, 25 × 16 cm, lightly painted, worn in places, not retouched) was previously in the Albert Goupil Coll.; its present location is untraced. Leprieur and Pérate assign it to Mantegna's workshop, largely on the ground that Mantegna would not have repeated himself exactly, but praise its quality.

The New York picture was first published in *The Magazine of Art*, v, 1882, p.77 as Mantegna. Schmarsow (in Leipzig, University, *Festschrift zu Ehren des Kunsthistorischen Instituts in Florenz*, 1897, p.135) assigned it to Pizzolo, Yriarte (1901, pp.216–18) to Mantegna. Crowe & Cavalcaselle (1912, p.81n) gave the design to Mantegna, but the execution only in part. Ignored by Thode (1897), Cruttwell (1908) and Knapp (1910), the picture was dismissed by Kristeller (1901, p.453) as by a pupil. Its status as an autograph early work was reaffirmed by Berenson (1932, 1968). Accepted by Fiocco (1937, pp.31,200–1) as executed *c.*1449–52, under the influence, experienced in Ferrara, of Rogier van der Weyden. Cipriani (1962, pp.24–5,54–5) also acknowledges Flemish influence, but dates the picture to the later 1450s; Camesasca (1964, pp.15–16) suggests that it may derive from a lost prototype by Rogier van der Weyden or Dirk Bouts, and dates it to 1449, immediately after Mantegna's return from Ferrara. Garavaglia (1967, No.7) accepts his dating, and suggests a close relationship with the São Paulo *St Jerome*

(Plate 187, Cat.no.157). Rejected by Tietze-Conrat (1955, pp.190–1) as the work of a pupil using Mantegna's drawings. She inclines to accept Offner's verbal dating of c.1460, and his suggestion that the picture is from a predella.

6. The Agony in the Garden
Signed OPVS/ANDREAE/MANTEGNA.
London, National Gallery, 1417 (Davies, 1961, pp.335–8)
Panel 63 × 80 cm. (painted surface)   Plate 11

CONDITION: Excellent. Some damage on Christ's dress: a few small *pentimenti*, e.g. sole of Christ's right foot.

PROVENANCE: First recorded in the Aldobrandini collection, Rome. Possibly mentioned in an Aldobrandini inventory of 1611 (No.18), but certainly a picture listed in the inventory of Olimpia Aldobrandini, taken in 1626 (No.178): 'Un quadro con Christo orante nell'horto con cinque angeli che tengono li misterij della passione con tre discepoli et la turba di mano di Andrea mantegna del No.339.' Listed (under 15 March 1710) in the inventory taken from 18 November 1709 after the death of Principe Giovanni Battista Pamphili Aldobrandini (*Inventarium bonorum repertorum post obitum clar. mem. Principis Johannis Baptiste Pamphilij Aldobrandini*, in Rome, Archivio di Stato, not. Paolo Fazio, No.2661). Described in this inventory as: 'Vn quadro in tauola con Nostro Sig.re che ora nell'Orto con cinque Angeli, che tengono li misteri della Passione con li trè Apostoli, e la turba alto palmi trè di mano d'Andrea Mantegna con corn.e dorata.' Later in the collection of Cardinal Fesch, first in France, then from 1815 in Rome (*Catalogue des tableaux . . . de feu son Eminence le Cardinal Fesch*, 1841, p.61, No.1372); Fesch sale (part iv, 17 March onwards, 1845, p.97, No.687): bt. by Artaria, of Golden Square, London, 1230 scudi. Owned by Farrer. Coll. of W. Coningham by 1845–6 (*Cabinet de l'Amateur*, iv, 1845–6, p.142, in article on Fesch sale). Coningham sales (London, 9 June 1849, lot 58 (bought in); 12 April 1851, lot 57, bt. Chaplin). By 1853 in the coll. of Thomas Baring: exh. Manchester Art Treasures Exhibition, 1857 (*Provisional Catalogue*, No.290; *Definitive Catalogue*, No.98), and at the RA (1870, No.58). Bequeathed by Baring with his other pictures to the Gallery.

This picture has been variously dated. Crowe & Cavalcaselle (1871, pp.141,382; 1912, p.85) identify it as the 'operetta' on which Mantegna was engaged in 1459 for Jacopo Antonio Marcello, an identification accepted by Thode (1898, p.47) and Kristeller (1901, pp.163–7). Knapp (1910, p.100) dated it after 1464, misled according to Tietze-Conrat by the then state of the painting, whose colour-scale was only returned to its original austerity by the restoration of 1939–40. An early date was reproposed by Venturi (1914, pp.134–6, contemporary with the first Eremitani frescoes) and by Berenson (1932, 1968). By contrast Fiocco (1937, pp.44,202) absurdly associates it with Mantegna's Roman period (1488–90) on the ground of its Fesch provenance. Tietze-Conrat (1955, pp.10,185) rather rashly claims that its size precludes its identification with the 1459 'operetta' – the word may merely be used in contradistinction to an altarpiece or other sizeable com-

mission. She dates the picture c.1450 on the basis of parallels between the sleeping Apostles and the top register of the St James frescoes. Meiss (1957, pp.45–6), who is anxious to claim the Marcello 'operetta' as a miniature, also rejects the identification. Various dates in the 1450s are advocated by Arslan (1961, p.169, before 1459, perhaps c.1454), Longhi (1962, pp.18,20, anterior to the San Zeno *Crucifixion*), by Cipriani (1962, pp.25–55, c.1459) and Camesasca (1964, pp.25–6,106, c.1450–5) and Paccagnini (1961, p.21, c.1460, contemporary with the San Zeno altarpiece). Bottari (1961, p.312) argues for a date later than c.1459–60.

Davies (1961, *loc. cit.*) points out that since Mantegna changed his signature to Mantinia c.1470–5 (in fact the change is already documented in June–July 1468, cf. Baschet, 1866, pp.332–3) the presumption is that the picture was executed before that date. Less convincing are his arguments that the design is clearer and the realism more consistent than in the San Zeno *Agony* and that the unusual iconographical feature of the angels bearing the Instruments of the Passion rather than the customary chalice or cross is another indication that it is later in date. Noting that there are nevertheless resemblances between the two pictures, he opts for a date in the early 1460s. In fact the topography of Jerusalem, of the Valley of Jehoshaphat and of Mount Olivet is reproduced with more attempt at accuracy in the San Zeno *Agony* (q.v.) evidently from fuller knowledge. Hence the substitution of the chalice in the same picture is to be regarded as a further piece of exactitude, not as an earlier and therefore less inventive motif. Accordingly Longhi must be correct in dating the present picture before the San Zeno *Agony*, probably in the middle 1450s. This conclusion is also supported by stylistic arguments. In the San Zeno *Agony* the whole composition is more concentrated with less use of extraneous scenery for picturesque effect, while the devices for dividing up the picture and leading the eye are subtler, as is the balance of the different parts.

A drawing in the British Museum (1895–9–15–80, Popham & Pouncey, ii, 1950, p.104, no.167) is a copy of the figures of Judas and the Roman soldiers in this painting. It bears an old attribution to Carpaccio, and Popham and Pouncey think it seems Venetian, and not impossibly by Carpaccio. If so, it would be evidence that the painting was in Venice in the later fifteenth century: it might even suggest that the *Agony* was painted for a Venetian patron.

7. The Presentation in the Temple
Berlin-Dahlem, Staatliche Museen, 29 (Posse, 1909, p.89)
Distemper on fine canvas (*renzo*). Not relined or backed on canvas, but mounted on a wooden frame with a wooden back, an arrangement dating from at least as early as the late eighteenth century and possibly from the early sixteenth (see below).
68.9 × 86.3 cm.   Plate IV

CONDITION: Not good. Giovanni de' Lazara notes in 1803 (see below) that it was not as well preserved as the Ca' d'Oro *St Sebastian*.

PROVENANCE: Acquired with the Solly collection, 1821. On the back is an eighteenth-century oval seal with the arms of Gradenigo surmounted by a coronet. An export seal of the Accademia di Brera, also on the back, indicates that it left Italy between *c*.1815 and 1821.

Recorded by P. Brandolese (1759–1809) of Padua (see Selvatico, 1849, p.190) and by Giovanni de' Lazara (letter of 9 March 1803 giving detailed description in Campori, 1866, pp.351–2) as in Casa dei Gradenigo, Padua. It was sold by the Gradenigo in 1803 (cf. provenance of Cat. no.42) to a person unknown. The Casa dei Gradenigo had descended to this family from Cardinal Pietro Bembo and the picture is therefore usually identified as one described by Marc' Antonio Michiel in Bembo's collection (Morelli, pp.17–18; Frizzoni, p.44: 'El quadro in tavola della Nostra Donna che presenta el puttino alla circoncisione fu de mano del Mantegna, ed è a mezze figure'). The identification goes back to the late eighteenth century (De' Lazara).

A second version of this picture (Plate 249), now universally attributed to Giovanni Bellini, is in the Galleria Querini-Stampalia, Venice, painted on panel and measuring 105 × 80 cm. It repeats the composition of the present picture, with the addition of two figures, a middle-aged woman and a young man to left and right respectively. Because it is painted on panel this picture was identified by Morelli (1880, p.433), Frizzoni (*loc.cit.*) and A. Venturi (1914, p.477) as the Bembo picture and regarded as Mantegna's original. Morelli, who considered all Mantegna's works on canvas to be late, thought the Berlin picture a later autograph version, executed *c*.1490–1500. De Lazara's detailed description of 1803 puts it beyond question that the Gradenigo picture is the same as the Berlin picture; this in turn is a strong presumption in favour of its being the Bembo picture. The likeliest explanation of the discrepancy is that Michiel made an error in his notes: alternatively the picture may always have been, as now and as it was in the late eighteenth century, mounted on canvas stretched over a frame with a wooden back. It is accepted as an autograph original by Selvatico (1849, *loc. cit.*), Crowe & Cavalcaselle (1871, pp.386–7; 1912, pp.88–9), Thode (1898, p.48), Yriarte (1901, pp.191–3), Kristeller (1901, pp.143–5), Knapp (1910, pp.71,174), Berenson (1932; 1968), Fiocco (1937, pp.48–9), Tietze-Conrat (1955, p.179), Paccagnini (1961, p.29), Longhi (1962, pp.18,20), Cipriani (1962, pp.20,57), Camesasca (1964, pp.17,115–16,127–8), Garavaglia (1967, No.38).

There is a division of opinion in the literature about its date. Some students place it in Mantegna's Paduan period; Thode, as *c*.1458–9; Kristeller, as *c*.1456, Knapp, as *c*.1453–4, close to the St Luke polyptych; Tietze-Conrat and Cipriani. Others place it in the 1460s; Crowe & Cavalcaselle, as *c*.1464, contemporary with the Uffizi triptych; Fiocco, *c*.1460, contemporary with the Madrid *Exequies* (Plate 53); Paccagnini, as tentatively *c*.1466, close to the Uffizi *Circumcision*; Longhi (1962, pp.18,20) as *c*.1465, painted at the same time as the Bellini version; Camesasca, as *c*.1465, Garavaglia, as 1465–6. It has generally been assumed that Mantegna designed the composition: Camesasca considers that Bellini was its inventor rather than Mantegna.

All these datings ignore the iconography of the picture. Wolfgang Prinz (in *Berliner-Museen*, xii, 1962, pp.50–4)

has convincingly identified the two figures in the rear as the young Mantegna and his wife Nicolosia Bellini. He argues that their pose to the left, with eyes directed out of the picture, also towards the left, indicates that they are looking at an altar; however, their pose may result from a compositional necessity. He dates the picture *c*.1454, to the time of their marriage (mentioned as taking place or shortly to take place in February 1453) and points out that it is the earliest surviving portrait of an artist and his wife. In fact the theme of the Presentation in the Temple suggests that the picture is a votive one, commemorating the safe birth of the couple's first child, or Nicolosia's happy survival after a difficult delivery. Accordingly the date *c*.1454–5 is the earliest that can be proposed for it.

On this interpretation the Bellini version (for which see Dazzi, in *Arte Veneta*, iii, 1949, pp.153–8, and Dazzi & Merkel, *Catalogo della Pinacoteca della Fondazione Querini Stampalia*, 1979, pp.34–5, no.3) would also be a votive picture, painted to offer the thanks of Giovanni Bellini and his mother and family for Nicolosia's safe delivery. In support of this argument it should be noted that the wife is allotted in both versions the post of honour on the left or dexter side of the picture, and is placed, significantly, behind the Virgin, the patroness of women in childbirth. Pignatti (*Giovanni Bellini*, 1969, No.37) suggests that in the Bellini version the middle-aged woman on the left is Anna, wife of Jacopo Bellini, while the two young men are Giovanni (in front) and his younger brother, Gentile (behind). He regards the Bellini picture as a later copy, executed *c*.1460–5, of the Mantegna (which he dates as no later than 1460).

8. St George

Venice, Gallerie dell'Accademia, 98 (S. Moschini Marconi, *Gallerie dell'Accademia . . . .: opere d'arte dei secolo XIV. e XV*, Rome, 1955, pp.139–40)

Panel 66 × 32 cm.   Plate 32

CONDITION: Restored by Pellicioli in 1933. The colour, in movement, was fixed: some old restorations were removed and replaced by new ones, notably on the saint's right arm, on the corslet and on the dragon's body and muzzle, where the tongue was an addition.

PROVENANCE: Acquired from the Manfrin collection in 1856.

Universally accepted as autograph. The older dating of this picture was in the late 1450s or early 1460s: Selvatico (1849, p.187) as *c*.1461, Crowe & Cavalcaselle (1871, p.387; 1912, pp.89–90) as early 1460s, the type close to that of the St Lawrence of the San Zeno altarpiece. This dating is accepted by Thode (1898, p.54), by Knapp (1910, pp.102,175) as *c*.1462, by Venturi (1914, pp.159–60) and by Arslan (1961, p.166, as contemporary with the San Zeno altarpiece), and is pushed back even farther by Tietze-Conrat (1955, p.199), followed by Cipriani (1962, pp.23,56), to the second half of the 1450s, contemporary with the Ovetari *Execution of St James*. The other view, propounded by Kristeller (1901, pp.225–7), Fiocco (1937, pp.54–5), Paccagnini (1961, p.37), Camesasca (1964, pp.29,108) and Garavaglia (1967, No.41), is that it shows clear reminiscences of works of art in Florence, notably those of Donatello and Andrea del Castagno, and should therefore be dated *c.*1467–8, after Mantegna's return from Florence.

Given the Squarcionesque construction and features, a date *c.*1456–7, perhaps just before the San Zeno altarpiece, is the most plausible.

The view behind shows the city of Selene, in Libya, beneath whose walls, according to the *Legenda Aurea*, St George slew the dragon.

9. ALTARPIECE OF SAN ZENO, VERONA
Plates 36–42, III

For dimensions of the three panels on which the altarpiece is painted see below.

GENERAL CONDITION: *Frame.* A central motif missing from the lunette. *Predella.* The three panels, now in the Louvre and at Tours (see Plates 38, 41 and III) are replaced by copies on canvas. See below.

HISTORY: For the circumstances of the commission and the original setting see text and below. The altarpiece is recorded by Vasari (1550, p.511: 'fece a San Zeno in Verona la tauola dello altar maggiore, de la quale dicono, che e' lauorò per mostra vna figura bellissima, auendo gran volontà di condurre tal lauoro'; 1568, p.489, where this is changed to 'In S. Maria in organo . . . fece la tauola dell'altar maggiore, e similmente quella di s. Zeno'). In the early sixteenth century the altarpiece was taken down from the high altar and set up on four consoles against the rear wall of the apse. It is mentioned by Ridolfi (1648, p.70 'fece . . . vn' altra [tauola] in S. Zeno con più figure de Santi'). The painting is recorded in various local guide-books until the 1790s. In 1797 it was taken by the French to Paris (*Notice des principaux tableaux recueillis en Italie par les Commissaires du gouvernement français*, brumaire an VII, pp.38–41, Nos.25–30), where in 1806 the predella was dis-membered. In 1814 the altarpiece was reclaimed by the Austrian government, largely through the protests of Benedetto del Bene, a *letterato* of Verona, who commis-sioned from Paolino Caliari the copies of the predella which now substitute for the originals. In 1871 it was placed on the south wall of the *cappella maggiore*: it was reset on the high altar in 1935.

TECHNIQUE: Painted on three panels of poplar. On each of these a ground of white priming was first laid. On two of the panels a second layer of priming was then applied with a layer of very thin silk on which the painting itself is executed; on the left-hand panel the silk was laid on a coarse canvas, and the second layer of priming was applied. The silk turns a little over the edges of the panels. *Central Panel.* 212 × 125 cm. The painted area does not continue on the edges covered by the frame and here the white priming is visible. On the right edge are sketches in sepia of architectural details. The figures 1443 are inscribed in black on the lower edge of the carpet, in the right corner (Puppi, 1972, fig.59). On the reverse of the panel, which is left rough, the numbers 64, 44, 44 and 45 are inscribed at the top left; beneath are other lines, apparently carpenter's marks. *Left panel.* 213 × 134 cm. On the extreme right edge of the priming is inscribed in burnt ochre PER TE/PARTE/PORTO. The letters are Roman capitals. On the extreme

left edge, painted in sepia ink, are the letter M and two lines which make an angle. *Right panel.* 213 × 135 cm. Drawn on the extreme right edge in sepia ink are the letter X, a small classical shield, and a piece of framework decorated with leaves. On the extreme left edge are a sketch of the left half of a human body (Da Lisca, 1956, p.230, suggests this is a sketch for the Baptist), a number 9 and other, indecipherable lines. Here, probably because the panel was already evincing a tendency to crack, it was reinforced by wooden pegs (*tasselli a doppia coda di rondine*) and by transverse plug-gings of gesso, glue and hempen thread. It was for this reason that a canvas was laid on this panel (see above). *The frame,* though damaged in places, is almost entirely original. It is executed in soft wood (poplar or lime), covered with a thick priming of gesso and glue, and made up in places where the wood was faulty with a priming of grey stucco. It was then gilded on a ground of reddish-brown bolus. Where the mouldings are formed of two strips of wood, a thin hempen cloth is laid over the join and incorporated with the priming. The scroll ornaments are executed in gesso in relief: the ground of these and the other carved sections is decorated with *azzuro d'Al-lemagna* (azurite). The same blue is used in the four pil-asters of the framework of the predella, but here it is laid on fragments of parchment taken from old registers belonging to San Zeno.

The cornice-shaped base which separates the altarpiece from the predella is not original: executed in pinewood, it seems to have been substituted for an earlier member in the sixteenth century, when the altarpiece was removed (see above) and set on four carved consoles against the rear wall of the apse.

Some portions of the supporting timbers of poplar and pine that strengthened the back still remain. Nailed to the base of the columns is a horizontal panel of pinewood painted on both sides. On the inner side, in exact cor-respondence with the pilasters of the predella, this painted decoration simulates porphyry, resembling the simulated porphyry of the left side of the predella and the simulated marbles of the painting proper. On the outer, eight-pointed stars in blue are figured round the edge. Another piece of pinewood painted to simulate porphyry has also been placed as a reinforcement behind the base. The underside of the base is rough and full of nail-holes, indi-cating that it originally rested on another architectural member.

CONDITION: The original reinforcement of poplar bars behind the panels eventually caused cracking in two of the panels and curving in some of the painted surfaces, and paint began to flake from the areas along the cracks. About 1919 strips of silk were glued over these to prevent the colour from falling, and since earlier restorations and varnishings had darkened the colouring it was decided to have the painting completely restored. The restoration was carried out at Brera and completed in 1935. As far as concerned the painted surface, treatment was limited to bubbled areas, to fixing flaking areas, and to the removal of drops of wax and some of the coat of dirt. The original reinforcement was also removed. See Puppi (1972, pp.12–15), and also for the interesting photo-graphic documentation.

The Agony in the Garden.

Tours, Musée des Beaux-Arts

Egg tempera on a panel laid with fine canvas and *gesso duro* ground (see CONDITION) 71.5 × 94 cm.   Plate 38

CONDITION: Restored before despatch to Tours in 1806. The picture has suffered much from scaling: in 1870 Clément de Ris noted that patches of colour were missing from the centre of the landscape, from the angel's hand, from the rock bottom right and from Christ's robe. Consequently it was transferred by the restorer Cordeil to a backing of fine canvas on a new panel. Treated for scaling in 1954 (Morette, *La connaissance des primitifs par l'étude du bois*, Paris, 1961, p.250; Hoog, in *Archives de l'art français*, ser.4, xxiv, 1969, pp.353–63).

PROVENANCE: From the predella of the San Zeno altarpiece. Despatched to the museum of Tours from the Musée Central, Paris, in February 1806.

The Crucifixion. Inscribed INRI on the titulus of the cross and SPQR on the standard.

Paris, Louvre, No.1373 (Hautecoeur, 1926, p.81).

Panel 67 × 93 cm.   Plate III

PROVENANCE: The central panel of the predella of the altarpiece of San Zeno. Retained at the Louvre after the altarpiece proper was returned to Verona in 1815: the two side panels had already been despatched to Tours.

The composition of this panel is discussed by Meiss ('Jan van Eyck and the Italian Renaissance' in *Venezia e l'Europa: atti del XVIII Congresso Internazionale di Storia dell'Arte*, Venice, 1956, pp.65–7), who terms it an example of the 'plateau' composition found in scenes of the Crucifixion from the fourteenth century. He points out that it is also found in the Netherlands from the 1420s onwards, first of all in works by Van Eyck, and most notably a *Crucifixion* now known only from copies (including an unfinished one in the Museo Civico, Padua) of probably Italian origin (see text, p.26), and a panel of related design in the Accademia, Venice, which Meiss calls Paduan, *c.*1460, and associates with Squarcione and the early Mantegna. He goes on to postulate the influence of this lost *Crucifixion* in the present panel. Although Meiss is aware of the motives of historical and antiquarian exactitude underlying this particular iconography, he does not perhaps give sufficient weight to them and ignores the exceptional feature which is Mantegna's representation of both sides of the 'plateau'.

The Resurrection

Tours, Musée des Beaux-Arts

Tempera on panel 71 × 94 cm.   Plate 41

CONDITION: Restored *c.*1803–6, before despatch to Tours (see below). Treated for scaling in October 1943, December 1946, restored in December 1947 (in the figure of Christ), in June 1954, September 1958, September 1963 (treatment for scaling and some small retouches), and February 1968 (again treatment for scaling and some retouches).

PROVENANCE: From the predella of the San Zeno altarpiece (q.v.). Sent to the museum of Tours from the Musée Central, Paris, in February 1806. See also *lit.cit.* under *The Agony*, CONDITION.

DOCUMENTS: As published by Puppi (1972) except where indicated.

1) *1457, 5 January.* Lodovico Gonzaga to Mantegna. In thanking Mantegna for agreeing to enter his service, the Marchese says, 'to us it seems all the better that you should remove yourself thence as quickly as possible to go to Messer Protonotary [Gregorio Correr] since that district [Padua] is under suspicion of the plague.'

2) *1457, 27 November.* Lodovico Gonzaga to Gregorio Correr. The Marchese has not heard from Mantegna for a long time, he would like to know if he has finished his work for Correr.

3) *1458, 6 January.* Lodovico Gonzaga in answer to a letter of 31 December from Gregorio Correr. Thanks him for a letter enclosed from Mantegna in which the painter says he cannot come to Verona at this time as he had hoped.

4) *1458, 16 April.* Lodovico Gonzaga to Mantegna. Lodovico agrees that Mantegna may wait over a further six months to finish 'quel lavorero del reverendo Messer lo protonotario di Verona' and other business he has in hand.

5) *1459, 2 February.* Lodovico Gonzaga to Gregorio Correr. At Correr's request he is pleased to grant Mantegna two months more in which to complete the altarpiece.

6) *1459, 2 February.* Lodovico Gonzaga to Mantegna. He grants him a further two months in which to complete the altarpiece. Enclosed in the previous letter.

7) *1459, 29 June.* Lodovico Gonzaga to Mantegna. He is pleased to hear that the altarpiece will soon be finished. From those who have spoken to the Protonotario on behalf of the Marchese he understands that Correr would prefer not to have the altarpiece taken to Mantua from Padua, but brought direct to Verona. Accordingly he acquiesces in this arrangement. (The Marchese had evidently hoped to get Mantegna to Mantua by having the nearly finished altarpiece brought there too, so depriving him of all excuse for remaining in Padua.)

8) *1459, 31 July.* The accounts of San Zeno record expenses connected with the stabling of Mantegna's horses in the abbey stable (doc. discovered by Eberhardt and published by Herzner in his review of Puppi, in *A.B.*, lvi, 1974, pp.440–2).

9) *1460, 26 January.* Entry in the account books of San Zeno, recording payments totalling 238 4 6 made from 24 July 1459 until 21 January 1460 in connection with 'la pala conduta da Padoa per l'altar grande di San Zeno', including 15 gold ducats paid in Padua to Mantegna as part of the price for the altarpiece (the document as published by Puppi should be read with the correction published by Herzner: see no.8).

For the ecclesiastical history of San Zeno see Biancolini (*Notizie storiche delle chiese di Verona*, i, 1749, pp.26–100).

For the original setting of the altarpiece see A. da Lisca (*La basilica di San Zenone in Verona*, 1939; 2nd ed., 1956). Puppi (1972) is a monograph, with unpublished documents, on the picture and its background. For a view linking the altarpiece with the choir as part of a unified scheme see Mellini & Quintavalle (1962); for justified criticisms of this scheme see the review of Puppi (1972) by Herzner in *A.B.*, lvi, 1974, pp.440–2. But Herzner's suggestion that the altar was originally topped by an image of God the Father is iconographically absurd.

ICONOGRAPHY: This was first investigated by Hourticq (in *G.B.A.*, ser. 5, vi, 1922, pp.365–75), who links the presence of St Peter and St Paul, St Laurence, St John the Baptist and St John the Evangelist with the Veronese churches of San Giovanni in Fonte, San Lorenzo, Santi Apostoli, San Giovanni in Foro and the Duomo. This explanation is accepted by Puppi (1972, pp.53–4), but it would be interesting to know more of the relics and special feast-days of San Zeno before accepting it as conclusive. See also text, pp.71–2.

PATRON: For Gregorio Correr see the literature cited in text, p.256, note 15. It was Hourticq and Puppi (1972, pp.37, 53) who first pointed out that the figures 1443 inscribed on the carpet correspond to the year when Correr was given San Zeno *in commendam*. Hourticq suggests the inscription may commemorate Correr's gratitude to the Virgin for the gift.

For a related drawing of the four saints in the left panel of the altarpiece and other related drawings see Plates 206, 207, 208; Cat.nos. 177 and 178.

The altarpiece is generally regarded as wholly autograph, except by Tietze-Conrat (1955, pp.191,198), who attributes the *Agony in the Garden* to a pupil using designs by Mantegna and the *Resurrection* to a pupil who may have had only a design by Mantegna for the Christ.

10. St Sebastian. Signed in Greek letters ΤΟ.ΕΡΓΟΝ. ΤΟΥ. ΑΝΔΡΕΟΥ. (rest concealed by stone)

Vienna, Kunsthistorisches Museum, 301 (*Katalog der Gemäldegalerie*, i, 1960, pp.76–7, No.588)

Poplar 68 × 30 cm.   Plates 43, 44, 45

CONDITION: A narrow strip added on either side.

PROVENANCE: Listed in 1659 in the inventory of Archduke Leopold Wilhelm (*Vienna Jahrbuch*, i, 1883, p.cxi: 'No.455. Ein Stückhel von Öhlfarb auf Holcz Scti Sabastiani, gebunden an ein grosse stainene Seülen, mit fünffzehen Pfeyllen, darandert/einer durch den Kopff. In seiner schwartzen Ramen, das innere Leistel geflambt vnd verguldt, die Höche 4 Span, die Braidte 2 Span 2 Finger. Original von Andrea Mantegno [*sic*]').

Universally accepted as autograph (doubted only by Selvatico, 1849, p.203, and Berenson, *Study and Criticism*, 1902, p.97, later withdrawn). Crowe & Cavalcaselle (1871, p.387; 1912, p.90), Thode (1898, p.55) and Venturi (1914, pp.168–72) date it to the early Mantuan years. Kristeller (1901, pp.168–70) as painted in Padua, shortly before Mantegna's departure for Mantua. Knapp (1910, pp.88,175), Fiocco (1937, pp.43–4), Tietze-Conrat (1955, p.200), Paccagnini (1961, p.20) and Cipriani (1962, pp.23–4,57) incline to identify it as the *operetta* on which Mantegna was busy for Jacomo Antonio Marcello in March 1459 and to date it accordingly. For Berenson (1932, 1968) it is early, for Arslan (1961, p.168) *c.*1460–70, for Longhi (1962, p.20) after 1470, for Camesasca (1964, pp.28,37,117) *c.*1470–5, for Garavaglia (1967, No.43) *c.*1470. E. Battisti (in *Arte, pensiero e cultura a Mantova*, 1965, pp.49–52) basing himself on the 'poesia delle rovine' of the painting, which he wrongly considers a late feature, argues for a dating in the 1470s, and suggests the plague of 1474 or preferably of 1478 as its inspiration. The close resemblance between the figure of Sebastian and that of

the good thief in the San Zeno *Crucifixion* indicates a date *c.*1458–9, as does the evident similarity between the architecture and that of the *Circumcision* of *c.*1460–4 (see Plate VI). The liripipe sleeves of the right-hand archer in the background also support this dating (compare R. Levi Pisetsky, *Storia del costume in Italia*, ii, 1964, pp.368,384). The Greek inscription, moreover, finds its natural cultural context in Padua, rather than Mantua.

In the upper left corner a bearded man on a white charger half emerges from a cloud. This motif, which has no iconographical justification in the Legend of St Sebastian, was identified by Kristeller as a representation of Theodoric, King of the Goths, who is shown in a relief on the façade of San Zeno, Verona, executed *c.*1138, as riding a horse given to him by the devil which will lead him to hell in pursuit of a demon stag. The identification is gratuitous: moreover Kristeller misunderstood the inscription on the relief and so misinterpreted the scene. Theodoric was damned in Veronese tradition as an Arian heretic (Da Lisca, *La basilica di San Zeno*, 1941, pp.76–7) and there is no reason why he should appear in a painting of St Sebastian. Janson ('The image made by chance', in *16 Studies*, n.d., pp.65–6) points out that the horseman is not merely in the clouds, but is himself a cloud, and suggests that Mantegna has emphasized an accidental resemblance following a Renaissance concept, already found in Alberti, which makes Nature herself an artist who can produce images in her own works. For a discussion of the problem, see text (p.80).

The Greek inscription is a literal rendering of the traditional Latin formula OPUS ANDREAE M(ANTEGNA). Sebastian was martyred in the Campagna, and the scattered ruins in the background are surely intended to suggest this rather than Rome or Verona, as so often supposed.

11. Portrait of Cardinal Lodovico Trevisan (later known as Mezzarota Scarampo)

Berlin-Dahlem, Staatliche Museen, 9 (Posse, 1909, p.89)

Tempera on poplar 44 × 33 cm.   Plate 46

PROVENANCE: Acquired in 1830 through exchange with Edward Solly. On the back are two official seals, one bearing the Austrian crowned eagle with the initials of the Emperor Francis II and the other that of the Reale Accademia di Brera in Milan, indicating that when licence was granted for the picture's export at some date after 1815 and before 1830, it was in a collection in the Lombardo-Veneto.

The identification of the sitter in the present portrait rests on the existence of an old copy with the arms, name and titles of the Cardinal (untraced). This was in the collection of the Rev. Walter Bromley Davenport (sale Christie's, 12 June 1863, lot 55 'Andrea Mantegna. Portrait of Cardinal Mediarota . . . His name and titles are inscribed . . .', bt. in, £11.6s.; sale Christie's, 6 March 1897, lot 131, 'F. Bonsignori Portrait of a Cardinal. The original of this picture is by Andrea Mantegna and is in the Berlin Gallery', bt. Green, £21). Mezzarota is known to have been a surname given posthumously to the sitter (see below) and accordingly the inscription on the copy can only date at the earliest from the later fifteenth century.

An engraved portrait of the Cardinal (Plate 48) figures in Tommasini (*Illustrium Virorum Elogia*, Padua, 1630, pp.13–18). Tommasini (Thomasinus) states that 'it was most carefully copied from an original delineated in former days in the house of the noble Francesco Leone by the hand of Andrea Mantegna, an excellent painter of Padua of those times' (*Nimirum ea diligentissimè expressa est ad exemplar delineatum olim in aedibus Viri nobilis, Francisci Leonis, manu excellentis illius aevi Pictoris Andreae Mantineæ Patauini*). Tietze-Conrat (1955, p.180) assumes that the Berlin portrait is that mentioned in this passage, and that the engraving was taken from it. But the engraving does not reproduce the Berlin portrait faithfully. The face is shown turned to the right, and is pronouncedly oval in type, and even if this is attributed to reversal and to engraver's licence, there still remains a discrepancy in the costume, since in the engraving the cardinal is shown wearing a robe under a buttoned and hooded gown or coat. The treatment of the hair in the engraving is therefore its closest point of resemblance with the Berlin portrait. Accordingly it is unsafe to assume that the Leone portrait is identifiable with the Berlin portrait, even though in Tommasini's preceding portrait of Cardinal Francesco Zabarella (p.2) the costume is evidently anachronistic and probably to be attributed to the engraver. Here, however, Tommasini seems to have had no original to follow, whereas in the dress of Pietro da Abano (p.20) an authentic contemporary costume is carefully reproduced.

Several alternatives are possible as explanations of the Leone portrait. It may have been a second portrait or part of another composition by Mantegna, perhaps from the same drawing (see below); it may have been an unfaithful copy of the Berlin portrait; or again it may be the Berlin portrait, reversed for Tommasini's engraving and given another costume by a copyist indifferent to accuracy. Strictly construed, Tommasini's Latin can only mean that Mantegna painted the portrait in the house of Francesco Leone; the implication of this is that it was a fresco or part of a fresco. Other portraits of the Cardinal are 1) a medal (Hill p.197, no.756) attributed to Cristoforo di Geremia and generally dated *c*.1461–5 (inscribed on the obverse L. AQVILEGENSIVM. PATRIARCA. ECCLESIAMRESTITVIT and on the reverse ECCLESIARESTITVTA and, in exergue, EXALTO). The features, in profile to the right, are not dissimilar from those of the Berlin portrait; 2) an untraced portrait in the Accademia Delia, founded in 1608 for the *cavalieri* of Padua; the long eulogistic inscription beneath is transcribed by Tommasini (*loc. cit.*). The Accademia Delia was suppressed in 1801 (Checchi, 1961, p.634).

The Cardinal's arms are reproduced by Thomasinus, who says that they were to be seen on the church of S. Lucia (see below) and on the buildings of the hospital of San Francesco (see below) in Padua. His cut shows them in a Mannerist frame, held by two angels (Plate 49). The text explains that this is how Mantegna had painted them on the south wall (p.18) or façade (pp.14, Fff(4)r) of S. Lucia (p.18, 'Adjicitur eiusdem Stemma tale, quale pictum cernitur ab Andreâ Mantineâ in muro Meridionalis [sic] Ecclesiae S. Luciae', cf. also p.Fff(4)r, index of *stemmata*). This painting presumably disappeared when the

façade of S. Lucia was reconstructed in the eighteenth century.

The present portrait has been variously dated: Crowe & Cavalcaselle (1871, pp.386–7; 1912, p.89n., unaware of the identity of sitter) as *c*.1464, Morelli (1880, pp.432–3) as *c*.1460, Thode (1898, pp.39–40) as from the Paduan period, Kristeller (1901, p.170–2) as painted in Padua, and contemporary with the San Zeno altarpiece and the Vienna *St Sebastian* (Plate 43); Knapp (1910, pp.89,175) *c*.1459–60, first datable work of Mantuan period; Venturi (1914, pp.136–8) an early work, *c*.1450–2. Accepting the thesis that it was painted during the Council of Mantua, Berenson (1932, 1968) dates it to 1459, Fiocco (1937, pp.46–7) as painted in Mantua before the closure of the Council in February 1460, Cipriani (1962, pp.27,57) as painted during the Council of Mantua, Camesasca (1964, pp.26,28,115) as painted probably during a brief preliminary sojourn at the Council. Tietze-Conrat (1955, pp.11–12,180), who assumes a Paduan provenance for the picture (see above), argues that it is more likely to have been painted in Padua, but rather inconsistently dates it *c*.1460 while implying that Mantegna was in Mantua in 1459. Her view is adopted by Paccagnini (1961,p.22), as *c*.1459. Meiss (1957, p.19–20) as *c*.1463, Arslan (1961, pp.165–6) as close in date to the Ovetari frescoes. Gilbert (1962, p.9) links it with the San Zeno altarpiece.

All the known events of the Cardinal's life support the thesis that the portrait dates from the Council of Mantua. One of the most prominent and important figures in the Church during the middle of the fifteenth century, he was born in Venice *c*.1401, the son of Maestro Biagio Trevisan, a physician. His mother's name is said to have been Mezzarota, but this name, which he is often given from the late fifteenth and sixteenth centuries onwards, may have taken its origin from his arms (see above). The name Scarampo seems to have been given to him in error after his death because of his protection or semi-adoption of two brothers called Scarampo. The confusion was first cleared up by Paschini (see below). He took a degree in arts and medicine at Padua, and entered the household of the Venetian Cardinal Condulmer, who in 1431 became Pope Eugenius IV. Eugenius made him a cubicularius. In 1434 he accompanied the Pope on his flight to Florence, where he became a friend of Niccolò Niccoli. On 24 October 1435 he was made Bishop of Trau, on 6 August 1437 Archbishop of Florence, on 19 December 1439 Patriarch of Aquileia, and on 11 January 1440 Camerlengo or Treasurer of the Church. An able and strict administrator, he restored the Pope's authority in Rome in 1440, and commanded the Papal contingent at the Battle of Anghiari (29 June 1440). His share in the victory was rewarded by promotion to the Cardinalate on 1 July 1440: his titular church was San Lorenzo in Damaso (for these events see P. Paschini, 'La famiglia di Ludovico cardinal camerlengo' in *Arcadia*, v, 1926; id., 'Da medico a Patriarca d'Aquileia e cardinale di S.R.C.' in *Memorie storiche Forogiuliesi*, xxii, 1927, cit. in A. Alcaro, *Lodovico Scarampo*, Bologna, 1931).

Lodovico played a prominent part in the diplomatic, military and administrative life of the Church until his death 'at the third hour of the night' on 22 March 1465. It is his movements between *c*.1450 and his death that have a bearing on the present portrait. They can be traced with great fullness from the letters printed by G. Caetani, *Epistolarivm Honorati Caetani: lettere familiari del Cardinale Scarampo*, supplemented by references in Eubel, *Hierarchia catholica medii aevi*, ii, 1901, and Pastor, *History of the Popes*, together with scattered references in other sources. The Cardinal was in Rome from 20 January 1450 until late June or early July 1451 but on 26 July 1451 was in Ferrara on his way to Venice. On 24 August he was at Philiberg and on 7 September 1451 at Treviso (for all these dates see Caetani). From Treviso he presumably went to Padua, for on 20 October 1451 he concluded his purchase of the Arena at Padua from Francesco and Gabriele Capodilista, for whose association with the Ovetari frescoes see Cat.no.1 (Urbani di Gheltof, 'La chiesetta dell' Arena in Padova' in *Bollettino di Arti, Industrie e Curiosità Veneziane*, ii, 1878–9, p.71; Prosdocimi, in *Boll. del M.C.P.*, ser.3, viii, 1960, p.6, n.2). On 27 November 1451 he was back in Rome and again active in the Curia (Caetani; Eubel, p.33, no.125). From 1452 onwards he did not stir from Rome, except for an occasional sojourn at Albano (Caetani) until Calixtus III appointed him in 1456 Legate *a latere* and admiral of the fleet which he had built to fight the Turks after the fall of Constantinople. He left Rome for Ostia on 31 May (Pastor, ii, 1897, pp.371 ff) or 11 June 1456 (Eubel, p.34, n.144) and three weeks later set sail for Naples, whence he departed on 6 August for the Eastern Mediterranean. In the successful sea-campaign that followed he made his headquarters at Rhodes where he remained until early in 1459. He entered Rome 'coming from the land of Rhodes', on 8 March 1459 and left immediately to join Pope Pius II and the Curia in Siena, which he reached on 16 March. Here he began once more to participate in the general affairs of the Church (Eubel, p.35, no.167).

He now accompanied the Pope to the Council of Mantua, which he entered in the train of Pius II on 27 May 1459. The Mantuan chronicler Schivenoglia (pp.135,137) describes him as 'de anij 60 et era homo pizolo, negro, peloxo, molto superbo e schuro' and as moving about with a great escort of splendidly mounted horsemen. The Cardinal left Mantua on 8 February 1460 (Schivenoglia, p.144) and went to Modena on his way to Siena, which he had reached on 28 March, and which he left after 15 April for Rome, where he was back on 24 April. In Rome he remained until 1462, when he made a long sojourn in Florence from about May to June 1462 (Rossi, in *Arch. Stor. dell'Arte*, i, 1888, p.409), returning to Rome only on 15 January 1463. He may have visited Padua and Venice in the late months of the year; according to Scardeone he was made a citizen and patrician of Venice in 1462 (Scardeone, 1560, p.130; see also below). He made a second visit to Florence later in 1463, and was in Prato on 19 December, in Florence on 15 February 1464 (Caetani), in Siena on 6 March 1464, in Florence again some days later on his way to Venice and then back in Siena on 10 April on his way to Rome (Eubel, p.37, n.214), where he died less than a year later.

Clearly the Council of Mantua was the sole occasion in the 1450s and the 1460s on which the Cardinal made a prolonged sojourn in North Italy, and therefore the only occasion during which Mantegna can have made a

portrait sketch of him. Although the Cardinal bought a palace in Padua and was known as a protector of Paduans (Scardeone), although too he was on terms of close friendship and alliance with Marchese Lodovico Gonzaga (see e.g. Pastor, *vol. cit.*, pp.540–4; Rossi, *art. cit.*, p.410), on chronological grounds alone he can have little opportunity of seeing anything of Mantegna's work in Padua except for the altarpiece of S. Sofia. Given the Paduan provenance of the portrait therefore, the presumption is that it was executed not to the Cardinal's own commission, but to that of his brother Andrea or more probably of his nephew Francesco Trevisan, to whom the Cardinal gave on 27 December 1462 the splendid palace and gardens he had built on the site of the Arena (Scardeone, 1560, pp.99,131; Prosdocimi, p.6). He had evidently erected this palace as a family palace for his nephew, since he had little personal connection with Padua after *c*.1430.

A plausible reconstruction of the history of the picture is that Mantegna took a sketch from life during a quick visit to Mantua made at some date between 31 July 1459 and 8 February 1460 in order to give the Marchese Lodovico advice about his new chapel. He then painted the portrait in Padua, finishing it before he left to settle in Mantua, in April or at the latest May 1460 (see text p.77). The portrait probably hung in the palace of the Arena (from which, according to Scardeone, Andrea and Francesco Trevisan got the name of Dall'Arena) until Andrea and Francesco had run through the immense fortune bequeathed to them by the Cardinal and Francesco was forced to sell the Arena to Alvise and Giovanni Foscari on 17 June 1472 (Scardeone; Prosdocimi, *loc. cit.*). Afterwards Francesco was forced to beg his living from his kinsfolk and finally died a pauper's death in the hospital of San Francesco, with which his uncle had some association since his arms were painted on its walls, according to Tommasini (see above).

This is the second surviving picture in which Mantegna represents watered silk: it appears earlier in the figure pushed back by the guard in the fresco of *St James on the way to Execution*.

12. Portrait of Francesco Gonzaga

Naples, Museo e Gallerie Nazionali di Capodimonte (De Rinaldis, *Pinacoteca del Museo Nazionale di Napoli: Catalogo*, 1911, pp.86–8)

Oil on panel 25 × 18 cm.   Plate 47

CONDITION: The surface rubbed and worn. A *pentimento* along the line of the chin.

PROVENANCE: In Palazzo Farnese, Rome, before 1760, when despatched to Naples as 'Un quadruccio in tavola pal.1. Un Cardinale giovane. Maniera di Giov. Bellino'.

Traditionally given to Giovanni Bellini or his school, this picture was first attributed to Mantegna by Frizzoni (in *Napoli nobilissima*, iv, 1895, p.24), who identified the sitter as Francesco Gonzaga (1444–83), the second son of Marchese Lodovico, on the grounds of resemblances with the portrait of Francesco in the Camera Picta. The attribution was accepted by Kristeller (1901, pp.173–5), who had already made it independently and dated the picture to Mantegna's early years in Mantua. Accepted as autograph by Knapp (1910, pp.90,175, as 1461), Venturi (1914, p.72),

Berenson (1932, 1968), Fiocco (1937, pp.47, 202–3), Paccagnini (1961, p.28, as *c*.1460–3), Arslan (1969, pp.166–7, *c*.1463, recalls Gentile Bellini), Cipriani (1962, pp.57–8, as *c*.1462), Camesasca (1964, pp.28,115, *c*.1462–3), and Garavaglia (1967, No.31, as *c*.1461). Regarded as a copy or repetition by Tietze-Conrat (1955, pp.20,190, repetition of a large original), Meiss (1957, p.26, as possibly a copy), Gilbert (1962, p.6, mediocre copy of a Mantegna original, a judgement that seems to be based on a misunderstanding of the costume). See also the controversy between Meiss and Gilbert (in *B.M.*, 1962, pp.164–5).

Generally regarded as a portrait of Francesco, except by Fiocco, who suggests it may be his younger brother Lodovico, a suggestion rightly refuted by Paccagnini, Cipriani and Coletti & Camesasca (1959, pp.52–4). The date of 1462 or 1463 proposed by most scholars assumes that the costume is that of a cardinal and that the portrait was painted after Francesco received his cardinal's hat on 18 December 1461 at the youthful age of 16, after which he left for the Curia. The costume is in fact that of a prelate of the Papal Curia (cf. the portrait of Carlo de' Medici, Plate V and the portrait of Lodovico, Francesco's brother, in the outdoor scene of the Camera Picta) and not that of a cardinal, as comparison with e.g. Mantegna's portrait of Cardinal Lodovico Trevisan clearly demonstrates. It must therefore have been painted after Francesco had been appointed a Protonotary Apostolic on 11 February 1454 (Vatican Archives, Reg. Vat. 402 f.37ᵛ, document kindly communicated by Dr D. Chambers; cf. also G. Viviano Marchesi Buonaccorsi, *Antichità ed eccellenza del protonotariato appostolico partecipante*, Faenza, 1751, p.179) and before his promotion to the cardinalate. 1460 or 1461 are therefore the only possible dates for the portrait.

13. THE CHAPEL OF THE CASTELLO DI SAN GIORGIO

The construction of a new chapel was part of Lodovico Gonzaga's transformation of the Castello di San Giorgio, built by Bartolino da Novara in 1395–*c*.1400, from a fortress into a fortress-palace. The chapel was constructed during the late 1450s and was almost complete and ready for decoration by June 1459. Its designer was Mantegna, though the actual builder was a professional architect, in all probability the Marchese's court architect Luca Fancelli. Little is known of its appearance, except that it was small, had a dome without a drum resting directly on four arches, two of them engaged in the walls, and that it bore some resemblance to the Cappella della Vergine Incoronata, adjoining the Duomo, which was erected in 1477–80 (see below). The painted decorations of the chapel were dismantled in the sixteenth century, probably in the 1570s, during the alterations made by Guglielmo Gonzaga, Duke of Mantua, to the Corte Vecchia. Among these was the construction *c*.1563 of a new chapel: Paccagnini (1969, pp.63–4) would prefer to date the dismantling to *c*.1574, when Guglielmo moved from the Corte Nuova to the newly decorated apartments in the Corte Vecchia.

DOCUMENTS:

1) *1480, 19 September* – Petition concerning the Cappella della Vergine Incoronata from the Chapter of the Duomo to Marchese Federico Gonzaga: '*Perchè s'è finito quello poco principio de la fabrica a quella capella di nostra Donna di voti in S. Pedro, secondo il disegno de la bona memoria de lo Illᵐᵒ Signor V°̃ Padre, cioè quelli quattro Archi dove và suso la Cuba sopra l'Altare di nostra Donna . . . Il resta da fare la Cuba. Alcuni dicevano che la staria bene comenzarla a voltar e dargli il tondo immediate e suso questi Archi fatti come sta quella di Castello e far la lanterna cum le finistre in cima . . .*' (D'Arco, ii, pp.14–15).

2) *1459, 4 May*. Lodovico Gonzaga to Mantegna in Padua. He urges Mantegna to come to Mantua at once; he ought to have finished all his other undertakings and the chapel of the Castello is now almost completed. Lodovico is more than certain it will please him since it has been done according to the fashion he has prescribed. The Marchese's wish now is to have it completed as Mantegna wants it to be ('*perché la Capella del Castello è come finita, la qual siamo più che certi ve piacerà per esser facta al modo vostro né voressimo farla compire se non in la forma e modo ordenarite*'. Kristeller, 1902, p.520, doc.19; Vasić Vatovec, 1979, p.180).

3) *1459, 29 June*. Lodovico Gonzaga to Mantegna in Padua. Though pleased to grant him a further delay, he asks him to come over to Mantua for a day from Verona when he takes the San Zeno altarpiece there. Lodovico wants him to inspect the chapel and give him his opinion before anything else is done in it so that the little that is wanting to its completion can be despatched ('*Havemo ben pregato il prefato monsignor e cosi ancor pregiamo vui che quando fareti condure la tavola a Verona el sia contento che per uno zorno veniati qua a nui che cene fariti singulare apiacer che voressimo solamente vedestive questa nostra capella et dicestive il parere vostro prima se gli facia altro aciò che la possiamo far compire che puocho gli resta a fare*'). Kristeller, 1902, p.520, doc.20; Vasić Vatovec, 1979, p.180.

4) *1461, 30 May*. Luca Fancelli to Lodovico Gonzaga. 'We are attending to the windows of the Camarino and to the chapel' (Vasić Vatovec, 1979, p.181).

5) *1462, 22 September*. Lodovico Gonzaga to Alberto Pavesi: 'We desire you to let Andrea Mantegna have six ducats to give to the man who is putting gold on our little chapel.' (ASM, Busta 2888, Copialettere, Libro 46, c.46, published by Brown, 1972, p.861, n.2.)

6) *1466, 9 July*. Platina from Rome to Marchese Lodovico. He offers him an antique alabaster vessel as a present to serve for a holy-water basin in his chapel. ('*Reservavi iamdiu tuo nomine vasculum rotundum ex alabastro, mira arte fabricatum, quae capellae tuae magno erit ad continendam aquam sanctam ornamento; id . . . extra urbem inventum*'). Luzio-Renier, in *G.S.L.I.*, xiii, 1889, p.435.

EARLY REFERENCES: 1) Vasari, 1550, p.509: '*Perche Andrea gli dipinse nel castello di Mantoua nella cappella di quello, vna tauoletta; nella quale con storie di figure non molto grandi, mostrò che meritaua gli onori, che gli erano fatti; perche questa opera è molto stimata fino al presente da tutti i lodati ingegni.*' In 1568 (p.489): '*quel Signore, che sempre stimò assai, e fauorì la virtù d'Andrea, gli fece dipingere nel castello di Mantoa, per la cappelletta una tauoletta, nella quale sono storie di figure non molto grandi, ma bellissime.*'

2) Ridolfi, 1648, p.70: '*Ma inuaghitosi della di lui maniera il Marchese Ludouico Gonzaga . . . lo condusse a*

Mantoua, oue gli dipinse vna tauola per il suo Palagio, che fù rubbata da Tedeschi nel sacco di quella Città l'anno 1630.'

3) Scannelli, 1657, p.271: 'e l'opere migliori, che si possono alla giornata in qualche parte osservare [di] ... Andrea, sono quelle, che dipinse in Mantoa al Marchese Gonzaga, e dicono sia nel Castello, anco al presente nella picciola Chiesa alcune sue pitture.'

RECONSTRUCTION: The information of Ridolfi and Scannelli, when compared with the strictly contemporary documents, is revealed as the merest hearsay. The position with regard to Vasari is more complex, since his is the only known account of the chapel that describes Mantegna's work in it before its presumed date of destruction. Modern scholarship has been inclined to associate with the chapel of the Castello a letter written from Goito on 26 April 1464 in which Mantegna says of certain pictures that he has not yet varnished them since their frames have not yet been gilded and furthermore he does not have with him in Goito the necessary materials. In his opinion, moreover, these should be the last pictures to be put up in the little chapel. It is clear, however (see text, p.86), that these pictures were intended for the chapel of Lodovico Gonzaga's new palace at Goito. The letter therefore cannot be used as evidence for the decoration of the chapel of the Castello. The question now arises as to whether the chapel, which probably was little larger than an oratory, being a private chapel to the Marchese's apartments, was decorated with only one small history on panel, as Vasari says, or whether its walls were set with a series of histories, as those of the chapel at Goito evidently were. The probability is that the decoration was much more ambitious than Vasari implies, since the chapel is cited in Francesco Gonzaga's honorific decree of 1492 as one of the three great works, the others being the Camera Picta and the Triumphs, that Mantegna had executed for his family (Kristeller, 1902, p.551, doc.115). It is a question whether Vasari ever saw the chapel in the Castello, even on his second journey to Mantua in 1565, since he says even less of it in 1568 than in 1550. This suggests the possibility that the chapel had been remodelled and stripped of many of its paintings by Mantegna before 1550.

It is most unlikely that the chapel walls were entirely frescoed, as suggested by Tietze-Conrat (1955, p.13), or that they were a series of framed paintings like those in Mantegna's own funerary chapel (see Cat. nos 58–60), as she also suggests (1955, pp.13,243–4). Accordingly, the reconstruction proposed by Paccagnini (1962; 1979, pp.58–63) is very convincing. On the analogy of the Cappella del Perdono in the Palazzo Ducale, Urbino, he suggests that the walls were set with long vertical panels enclosed in a gilded framework. Some modifications, however, are indicated. The chapel must have had at least one entrance and a sacristy. These may have formed a kind of antechapel, as in the Belvedere of Innocent VIII (see Cat. no.29), or the sacristy may have been a separate room, in which case the walls of the chapel would have been pierced by two entrances. Some solution must also have been found to reconcile the circular form of the arch with the line of the panels: the means employed was presumably a heavy cornice as in the Circumcision (Plate

VI). If so, the lunettes above may well have been frescoed. Paccagnini's scheme has the advantage of reconciling the iconographical disparities among the panels that can conjecturally be associated with the chapel by allowing for the loss of a number of panels that made up the series, among which he would include those recorded in Ferrara in 1586–8 (see Cat. nos. 5 and 18). The altar end of the chapel is likely to have been shaped as a curved niche, rising above the altar, as in the Cappella del Perdono. In this would have been set the Adoration of the Magi (Cat. no.14 below) with two vertical panels to either side. As Kristeller (1901, pp.213–14) had already observed, this is the only plausible explanation of the concave form of this panel, which is possibly cut down at the top as Longhi notes (1962, p.20). Finally, there may be some echo of the chapel's architecture in the Florence Circumcision (see Cat. no.15).

Panels generally associated with the Chapel of the Castello di San Giorgio
'The Florentine Triptych'

This so-called 'triptych' consists of three pictures in the Uffizi (Inv.910, Catalogo generale, 1979, p.364, No. P 993): The Ascension, The Adoration of the Magi and The Circumcision, which have been shown framed together since 1827 (Uffizi archives, Filza 51, n.49). Their history and literature as a group are given first: each panel is then treated singly.

These pictures have often been discussed as if they were intended by the artist to form a single unit, in spite of the disparities in their size and composition. Their early history proves incontrovertibly that their alliance dates only from the nineteenth century.

They are first recorded in the inventory taken in March 1587 of pictures belonging to Don Antonio de' Medici, son of the Grand Duke Francesco I and Bianca Cappello, which were then in the Galleria of the Casino di San Marco, Florence (not the Villa Magia, Pistoia, as Gronau stated in Kunstchronik, no.34, 25 May 1917, col.368, when noting the existence of the 1587 references). The original entries read: 'Vno quadro in asse torto con una offerta di magi e altre figure drentoui disse di mano del mantegna. Ornamento di Noce intag.to tocco d.o alto b l0/2 largo b10 2.

Dua Quadri in tauola con piu figure drentoui uno l'ascensione di Cristo e l'altro la circuncisione ornamento di Noce profilato d.o alti b l0/2 e larghi b2/3 inc.a. (Florence, A.S.F., Guardaroba 136, f.153v–154r) These two entries follow each other, which suggests that the three pictures, though separately framed, were regarded as having an association with each other. They are next listed in the inventory taken in 1621 of the estate of Don Antonio de' Medici (A.S.F, Guardaroba 399, p.252v: '4634 Vn'quadro in asse alquanto concau entroui l'adoratione di magi con ornamento intagliato, et profilato d'oro alto un b.o e3/4 dissero di mano del mantegna. 4635 Due quadri in asse in uno l'ascensione, et nell'altro La circuncisione di N.S.G.C. con ornamenti di noce profilati d'oro Lunghi b.a uno e mezzo, et larghi 2/3 inc.a di mano del Mantegna'). They entered the Florentine Galleria on 24 May 1632. (Inventario di quadri, et altro della Eredità del S.re Antonio Medici che erano al Casino ..., p.57, MS.71, Biblioteca of the Uffizi). Here the Mantegna Adoration is for the first time confused with the Botticelli Adoration from Santa Maria Novella, which also belonged to Don Antonio. They are listed in the inventory of 1635 (Uffizi MS.82, f.112, no.22, the *Ascension* and *Circumcision*, f.113, no.31, the *Adoration*, again attributed to Botticelli), in that of 1704 (p.28, *Circumcision* and *Ascension*, p.113, *Adoration*, again as Botticelli) and in later inventories.

Crowe & Cavalcaselle (1871, pp.385–6; 1912, pp.87–8) connect the triptych with the panels mentioned in Mantegna's letter from Goito of 1464, and relate its style to that of the Ovetari *Assumption*. Thode (1898, pp.51–2) regards it as Mantegna's earliest work for Lodovico, painted in Padua c.1458. Kristeller (1901, pp.213–20) assumes that the triptych dates from Mantegna's earliest years in Mantua and was painted by the artist as an ensemble. Knapp (1910, pp.93–7,175) as painted c.1463–4, most probably for the Castello chapel. Venturi (1914, pp.162–6) as c.1460, associable with the *tavoletta* mentioned by Vasari in the chapel. All relationship with the chapel was denied by Fiocco (1937, pp.51–2), who argued from their long history in Florence that they must have been executed to Medici commission during Mantegna's visit to Florence which he lengthens to two years in 1466–7, especially as Scannelli mentions the paintings of the Mantua chapel in 1657. Tietze-Conrat (1955, pp.12–13, 181–2) also rejects all connection with the chapel. She was the first to point out that the triptych was an artificial ensemble, in that the *Presentation* does not match the other two panels and in that the combination of the three is iconographically arbitrary. Paccagnini (1961, pp.31–3) accepted her arguments about the incoherence of the triptych, but insisted that the panels were part of the decoration of the chapel (see above). The disparateness of the triptych is accepted by all subsequent students and the panels are now exhibited separately.

14. The Adoration of the Magi
Florence, Uffizi
Tempera on panel (concave) 77 × 75 cm. Plate 50; Fig. 5

CONDITION: Two cracks down the centre. A large cigar-shaped loss in the centre left, running from the camel's head to the upper rock.

Kristeller (1901, pp.213–14) points out that the light comes from the front, and diffuses itself to right and left, so that the picture must have been placed in a small space opposite a small window. For Tietze-Conrat (1955, p.182) this is perhaps merely intended as part of a *tour de force* of perspective. See under RECONSTRUCTION above.

A drawing for the central part of the composition is reproduced in an engraving after Mantegna (see Cat. no.217).

15. The Circumcision and Presentation of Christ and the Purification of the Virgin. In the lunettes (left) *The Sacrifice of Abraham* (right) *Moses showing the tablets of the law*
Florence, Uffizi
Tempera on panel 86 × 43 cm. Plate VI

Saxl (in *J.W.C.I.*, ii, 1938–9, p.362) identifies the subject as the *Presentation*, followed rather hastily by Tietze-Conrat (1955, pp.181–2) who claims that the *Sacrifice of Isaac* and *Moses showing the tablets of the Law* are prototypes of the Presentation. In fact the composition conflates the Circumcision of Christ, which took place eight days after his Birth (Luke, 2,21) and his Presentation in the Temple, which according to Luke (2,22–39) took place when the forty days of Mary's 'purification according to the law of Moses were accomplished'. The central motif shows the moment after the priest of the Temple has completed the Circumcision. On the left Joseph holds the two turtle-doves which Mosaic law (Lev. 12,2–8) commanded those women of Israel who had no lamb to bring to the priest, one bird as a burnt-offering and one as a sin-offering, after the forty days of their purification were fulfilled. Behind the Virgin an old woman holds Christ's clothes on her arm and a young woman rests her hand on the head of a child. None of these three figures has a halo, and they cannot be identified as saints (thus Garavaglia, 1967, No.34C, proposes to identify the child as the young Baptist). Their pose indicates that they are merely friends or attendants of the Virgin.

The scene of *Moses showing the tablets of the Law* may be placed above the Virgin to indicate her obedience to the law of Moses, as narrated by Luke. A statue and bust of Moses were already introduced into the Temple by Ambrogio Lorenzetti in his *Presentation* of 1342 (Florence, Uffizi) for just this purpose (see D. C. Short, in *A.B.*, xxviii, 1946, p.28). But more probably this scene and that of the *Sacrifice of Isaac* are present in allusion to the history and typical meaning of the Temple and of the Old Covenant (see text p.92).

For a related drawing in the Kunsthalle, Hamburg, see Cat. no.181. Perogalli & Sandri (*Ville delle province di Cremona e Mantova*, 1973, pp.54,56, n.12) discuss the relationship of the arches in the background with the portico of the courtyard of the Castello di San Giorgio, attributed by Fiocco (1937, pp.107–8) to Luca Fancelli working under the influence or to the design of Mantegna.

16. The Ascension
Florence, Uffizi
Tempera on panel 86 × 54 cm. Plate 51

For a related drawing in the Fogg Art Museum, Cambridge, Mass., see Cat. no.182. A drawing in pen and blue wash of Christ ascending in the Uffizi (1674F) seems to derive from this picture, with variants: it has been ascribed to Mantegna.

17. Christ with the Virgin's Soul
Ferrara, Pinacoteca Nazionale
Tempera on panel 27.5 × 17.5 cm. Plate 52

CONDITION: Much damaged: cut down at sides (see below).

PROVENANCE: Formerly coll. G. Barbacinti, Ferrara; acquired in the second half of the last century by E. Vendeghini.

Attributed to Vittore Carpaccio, until given to Mantegna in 1920 by Longhi. In 1926 (p.137) he published it as by Mantegna, following this in 1934 by his identification of it as the central part of the missing upper section of the Madrid *Exequies of the Virgin* (see below).

18. The Exequies of the Virgin
Madrid, Museo del Prado, 248 (*Catálogo de las pinturas*, 1952, pp.373–4)
Panel 54 × 42 cm. Plate 53

CONDITION: The upper section sawn off, apparently before 1639 (see above, and also entry below).

PROVENANCE: First recorded, with a provenance from Mantua, in the collection of King Charles I c.1639 (Millar, 1960, p.81): 'A mantua peece Done by Andrea Mantenia: Item a little peece of Andrea Mantenia being the dying of our Lady, the Appostles standing aboute with white wax lighted Candles in their hands and in the Landscept where the Towne of Mantua is painted in the water lake, where a Bridg is over the said water towards the Towne, in a little black ebbone woodden frame done upon the wrong lighte.' Miller, 1960, p.209: 'A Peece of Eleaven figures being the Death of our Ladie some Apostles standing by her with Tapers in their handes By Andrea Montania.' Identified at the court of Charles I as a 'fellow peece' with the *Sacra Conversazione* in Boston (Cat. no.172): bought with this picture at the sale of Charles's effects held after his execution in 1649 by act of Parliament. (Millar, 1972, p.266: '169. The death of Mary in water Cullo! £15.') Sold to John Baptist Gaspars, 22 March 1650, for £17. 10s. Sent by Alonso de Cardenas, Spanish ambassador, to King Philip IV of Spain. Spanish royal collections.

The provenance of this picture is discussed by Tietze-Conrat (1955, pp.186–7), who wrongly argued that the picture could not have come from Mantua since neither it nor its 'fellow peece', the Boston *Sacra Conversazione*, were mentioned in Mantuan documents. However, the *Sacra Conversazione* is mentioned in the Mantuan inventory of 1627, and her argument that neither picture came from Mantua cannot be sustained. She preferred to identify both pictures as the 'mᵃ. Morta' and a *quadro* of subject unspecified which were mounted in 1586–8 on the walls of the *cappelletta* (small chapel) of Margherita Gonzaga, last Duchess of Ferrara and daughter of the Duke Guglielmo, who most probably dismantled Mantegna's chapel in the Castello of Mantua. It is in fact not impossible that the present picture was sent off to Ferrara after the dismantling of Mantegna's chapel (see Cat. no.13) and was later returned to Mantua on the devolution of Ferrara in 1598. A. Lazzari (*Le tre ultime duchesse di Ferrara*, 1913, pp.232–3) collects documents of 1584 which show Margherita assembling pictures for the decoration of her chapel. These were to be mounted on its walls in frameworks of her own design. Hence she was greatly concerned with their measurements and with finding pictures of matching size. As her personal property, the pictures of her chapel, or most of them, would certainly have returned with her to Mantua on her final departure from Ferrara in December 1597. She died in Mantua on 6 January 1618, and some of her pictures presumably then returned to her nephew, Duke Ferdinando Gonzaga. Certainly the 1627 inventory of the Galleria of Mantua does list (Luzio, 1913, p.116, No.330) in the *camera* adjoining the *camerino delle dame* 'Tre quadri, in uno dipintovi l'essequie della B.V. ...' (the other two pictures were evidently in no relationship except that of situation). For an alternative possibility see No. 484 'Un quadretto d'asse dipintovi La Madonna morta senza cornici. L12' (Luzio, p.123). The Ferrarese provenance of the upper fragment of *Christ with the Virgin's soul* perhaps supports such a reconstruction. A hypothesis might be that the upper part

of the *Exequies* was cut off when being taken down from the chapel wall, or else was cut off before being mounted on it in 1586–8, to make it match another picture.

The composition was reconstructed by Longhi in 1934, when he showed that the dimensions of the original panel must have been 86 × 42 cm, exactly those of the side panels of the *Ascension* and *Circumcision* from the so-called Florentine triptych (see Plates 51 and VI). He rather rashly deduced that the panel was a rejected element of the triptych, for which one of the other two panels had been substituted. His reconstruction is accepted by Fiocco (1937, pp.48,203), Tietze-Conrat (1955, pp.186–7), Paccagnini (1961, pp.34–5), Cipriani (1962, pp.28,59–60), Camesasca (1964, pp.27,107), Garavaglia (1967, No.34E). These students, with the exception of Fiocco, also accept the connection of the panel with the chapel of the Castello of Mantua. Again Paccagnini's conclusion, that it was part of the series of *tavole* set on the chapel walls (see Cat. no.13), is most persuasive in spite of Longhi's criticisms (1962, p.20).

Kristeller (1981, pp.220–2), followed by Paccagnini (*loc. cit.*) rightly identifies the background as the Ponte di San Giorgio, which crossed the lake to join the Castello di Corte with the borgo di San Giorgio. Fiocco (*loc. cit.*) as Mantua among its lakes; Tietze-Conrat (*loc. cit.*) wrongly calls it a dam between Porta della Pusterla and Ceresea, whose construction she claims as one of Lodovico Gonzaga's greatest achievements: but this seems to be a confusion with his embanking and draining of this part of the banks of the Mincio.

Universally attributed to Mantegna except by A. Venturi (in *L'Arte*, XXVII, 1924, pp.139–40), who gave it in a moment of aberration to Giovanni Bellini. Fiocco claims that the composition derives from the mosaics of the same subject in the Cappella dei Mascoli in San Marco, Venice (see text, p.93) whose design he dates to c.1454 and attributes to Mantegna (1927, pp.228–37).

ICONOGRAPHY: This is discussed by G. Holzherr, *Die Darstellung des Marientodes im Spätmittelalter* (Tübingen thesis), 1971, pp.83–4.

DATING: The thesis that the four panels belonged to the same ensemble and were painted for the chapel of the Castello di S. Giorgio is now generally accepted, as is a dating in the early 1460s. Attempts have been made to date each panel more precisely within the wider bracket of the early 1460s. Arslan (1961, pp.167–8) argues that the chiaroscuro lunettes of the *Circumcision* reflect Mantegna's contacts with Tuscan art in 1466–7 and that the two other panels reflect the antique statuary style of his Paduan works. Longhi (1962, p.20) dates the *Ascension* earliest, perhaps contemporary with the *Exequies*, to which it may have been a companion panel. In his view the *Adoration* is later, while the figures of the *Circumcision* were painted some years before the background, though all three pictures must have been painted before 1470 when their influence can be detected in miniatures executed in Siena by Liberale da Verona (cf. Del Bravo, in *Paragone*, XIII, 1962, No.147, pp.53–60). Camesasca (1964, pp.26–8, 107–8) dates the *Ascension* c.1460, close to the San Zeno altarpiece, the *Exequies* c.1461, the *Adoration* to 1464–6, the *Circumcision* to 1464 (for figures), to *c.*1470 for background. From the documents assembled above it appears that work on the panels is unlikely to have begun much before 1462. See text, pp.86–8, for arguments that it may have been protracted into 1468 or later. Stylistically the *Adoration of the Magi* is earlier than the other panels, in that it still recalls Jacopo Bellini. The refined classicism of the other three panels suggests a dating in the mid-1460s.

19. Portrait of Carlo de' Medici

Florence, Uffizi, Inv. 8540 (*Catalogo generale*, 1979, p.364, No. P994)

Tempera? on panel 40.6 × 29.5 cm.   Plate v

CONDITION : Poor : colour much worn. There are gashes in the area of the neck and upper left cheek.

PROVENANCE : Formerly in Palazzo Pitti, No. 375. First identifiable in Inghirami (*L'Imp. e Reale Palazzo Pitti*, 1828, p.53, No.1) it figures in guide-books to the Pitti as an anonymous portrait of a man until the end of the century. Transferred to the Uffizi in 1925.

Traditionally identified as a portrait of a Gonzaga (exh. as such, Mantua, *Mostra iconografica Gonzaghesca*, 1937, p.15, No.66). In 1912 Schaeffer (in *Monatshefte für Kunstwissenschaft*, v, pp.17–21) identified it as a portrait of Carlo de' Medici (*c.*1430–92), illegitimate son of Cosimo de' Medici. Carlo first held the high curial dignity of Protonotary Apostolic, and later also became Proposto of the Pieve (now Duomo) of Prato, to which dignity he was appointed on 3 August 1460. The costume of the sitter in this portrait is that of a prelate, and the portrait medallion of Carlo on the monument erected to him in the Pieve of Prato to the commission of Duke Cosimo I de' Medici by Vincenzo Danti in 1566 derives from this picture and shows him wearing a similar costume. As a comparison in support of the identification Schaeffer adduced a portrait medallion in a genealogical tree of the Medici engraved *c.*1580 by Martino Rota, and suggests that the present picture may well be that listed in the 1553 inventory of Duke Cosimo I (Conti, *La prima reggia di Cosimo I*, 1893, p.138) as 'uno quadretto pittovi M.̃ Carlo de' Medici proposto di Prato.'

According to Vasari (1872, ii, p.624) Carlo is represented in one of Lippi's frescoes in the choir of the Pieve, executed *c.*1460–4. The features of the sitter disagree, however, with those of the stout priest standing at the foot of St Stephen's bier in the fresco of the *Exequies of St Stephen*, who is traditionally identified as a portrait of Carlo. Accordingly Tietze-Conrat (1955, p.183) suggests that Carlo may be portrayed in the man behind the priest. The features of this figure certainly resemble those of the sitter in the portrait, and the removal of overpaint during a recent cleaning of the fresco has strengthened the likeness. The absence of an authenticated contemporary portrait of Carlo (for whom see Pieraccini, *La stirpe de' Medici*, i, 1947, pp.95–9) is a difficulty in clinching the identification, but the resemblance of the Mantegna and Lippi portraits and the derivation from the Mantegna of Danti's sculptured portrait, first pointed out by E. Borsook (in *Mitt. Flor. Kunst. Inst.*, xix, 1975, p.28, fig.40, pp.56–7), make it virtually certain. It is accepted by K. Langedijk (*De portretten van de Medici*, 1968, p.16), by E. Borsook (*loc. cit.*), and by the compiler.

Given by Crowe & Cavalcaselle (1864, ii, pp.310–11) to Andrea del Castagno. Ignored by Kristeller (1901). The attribution to Mantegna, first suggested by C. Ricci, was rightly sustained by Suida (in *Z.B.K.*, n.s. xvi, 1904–5, p.190) and Berenson (*North Italian Painters*, 1907, p.254). Accepted as autograph by Borenius (in Crowe & Cavalcaselle, 1912, p.97n, as related to the Camera Picta), Venturi (1914, p.172), Berenson (1932, 1968), Fiocco (1937, pp.47,202), Paccagnini (1961, p.39), Gilbert (1962, p.6), Cipriani (1962, pp.29,60), Camesasca (1964, pp.28–9,116) and Garavaglia (1967, No.39). Tietze-Conrat (*loc. cit.*) does not pronounce because of its condition, but of recent scholars Rühmer (1961, p.cv) alone rejects it as too feeble for Mantegna.

Most of those students who give the portrait to Mantegna and accept the identification of the sitter as Carlo de' Medici date the portrait to Mantegna's sojourn in Florence (1466), except for Venturi, who places it *c.*1464, and Fiocco, who places it close to the Trevisan portrait (1459–60). In support of Fiocco's dating is E. Borsook's suggestion that Mantegna and Carlo may have met at the Council of Mantua (May 1459–60), but Mantegna's short visit will hardly have allowed of much acquaintance. In the absence of detailed information about Carlo's movements, the traditional date is here preferred. His costume is that of a Protonotary Apostolic, a dignity which by Papal Bull of 5 September 1463 was perpetually conjoined with that of Proposto of Prato. For his taste as a collector of medals see V. Rossi, 'L'indole e gli studi di Giovanni di Cosimo de' Medici' in *Rendiconti della R. Accademia dei Lincei*, ser. v, ii, 1893 ; for his relationship with Prato see [Baldanzi], *La Cattedrale di Prato*, 1846, pp.169–81.

20. CAMERA PICTA (Camera degli Sposi)

Mantua, Palazzo Ducale

The room is 808 × 808 cm.

Plates 54–95, VII, VIII, IX, Fig. 6

Door wall. *Left compartment.* Coletti & Camesasca identify the horse as of Hungarian breed, and the dogs (1959, p.56) as *alani* (boar-hounds).

Centre compartment. The three hunting-dogs are identified by Coletti & Camesasca (p.56) as *segugi* (blood-hounds). *Above* the door seven winged putti support in the air a gilded tablet, inscribed ILL. LODOVICO II M. M./PRINCIPI OPTIMO AC/FIDE INVICTISSIMO/ET ILL. BARBARAE EIVS/ CONIVGI MVLIERVM GLOR./INCOMPARABILI/SVVS AND- REAS MANTINIA/PATAVVS OPVS HOC TENVE/AD EORV̄ DECVS ABSOLVIT/AN(N)O MCCCCLXXIIII. In the eighteenth century (see Brandolese, *Testimonianze*, 1805, p.13) the date was read by Zani as MCCCCLXXIIII, by Brandolese himself as MCCCCLXXIV, and by a 'diligentissima persona' who took the trouble to compare these two dates with the original as MCCCCLXXXIII. Documents support the reading of MCCCCLXXIIII, which is also that of the tablet as restored (see below).

Right compartment. The paper held by Cardinal Francesco Gonzaga is inscribed *A*(nd)*rea me p*(inxit) (inscription read by Signorini, 1972). The dog behind the Marchese Lodovico is identified by Coletti & Camesasca (1959, p.56) as a Bergamesque shepherd's dog. The presence of portraits of the Emperor Frederick III and Christian II,

King of Denmark, mentioned by Equicola, is confirmed by contemporary documents published by Signorini ('Federico III e Cristiano I nella Camera degli Sposi' in *Mitteilungen des Kunsthistorischen Institutes in Florenz*, xviii, 1974, pp.227–50).

The self-portrait on the pilaster to the right of the doorway in the west wall was discovered and published by Signorini ('L'autoritratto del Mantegna nella Camera degli Sposi' in *Mitteilungen des Kunsthistorischen Institutes in Florenz*, xx, 1976, pp.205–12).

The gateway of the village and that of the city in the background both display panels bearing the Gonzaga arms on the field of four eagles divided by a red cross granted to Gianfrancesco Gonzaga in 1433 by the Emperor Sigismund when he raised Mantua to the rank of an Imperial fief.

Fireplace wall. *Left compartment.* For the dog beneath the Marchese's chair see Signorini ('Two notes from Mantua' in *J.W.C.I.*, xli, 1978, pp.317–20). For the various identifications that have been proposed of personages in this scene and the companion scene see Coletti & Camesasca (1959, pp.51–6). The family group (see doc.4) includes all Lodovico's children with the exception of his daughter Dorotea, who died 19–20 April 1467 (not 1468 as stated by C. Elam, see bibliography at end of entry; cf. Coniglio, 1967, p.75). It omits Federico's wife Margherita and Federico's two little daughters Chiara (b.1464) and her younger sister Maddalena. The females of the family are all omitted in the outdoor scene, which does introduce, however, Federico's two little sons Francesco (b.1466) and Sigismondo (b.1469).

Lunettes. The lunettes above the compartments on all four walls are decorated with pairs of upcurving beribboned swags of fruit and foliage. From the junction of each of these hangs a framed medallion on which is painted a Gonzaga *impresa*. In their poor state of preservation not all of these are legible. The following are those that can be plausibly identified.
Fireplace wall (north wall). *Lunette above window* (Plate 75). Possibly the device of a turtle-dove on a branch with the motto VARI AMOR, or that of a rose-bush with a single flowering rose and the motto *Invenimus inter spinas rosam.* *Last lunette* (Plate 76). A radiant sun, first adopted by Marchese Lodovico after the battle of Caravaggio in 1441, with the motto *Per un dixir* or *disir.*
Wall facing door (east wall). *First lunette* (Plate 77). An animal on a red field with a *cartello* bearing the Gothic letters B. . ./er/crof. Convincingly identified by Coletti & Camesasca (1959, p.59) as the well-known Gonzaga device of a doe gazing at the sun with the German motto *Bider Croft* (against force). *Second lunette* (Plate 78). A pentagonal or hexagonal battlemented tower on a white (perhaps originally red) field.
Wall facing chimney-piece. Lunette over doorway (Plate 79). A dog seyant. Convincingly identified by Coletti & Camesasca (1959, p.59) as the white dog, with collar, lead and muzzle recorded by Equicola (1521, p.xxx) as a device first adopted by Gianfrancesco Gonzaga, father of Lodovico, *c.*1432.
Door wall (west wall). *First lunette* (Plate 80). Two wings expanding from a ring. A Gonzaga device that appears

elsewhere in the Gonzaga palace, both before and after the reign of Marchese Lodovico. *Last lunette* (above the principal figures) (Plate 81). A green winged dragon with twisted tail standing on a yellow rock in a red field. A dragon appears as a Gonzaga device on the marriage *cassoni* of Paola Gonzaga, now in the Cathedral of Graz.

Ceiling. The ceiling is divided into diaper-shaped panels by gilded simulated ribs. The spandrels formed where these panels meet the lunettes are decorated with mythological subjects.

The diaper-panels are distributed as eight smaller diapers round a large central one. The smaller panels each contain a representation of a putto holding up a ribboned wreath of fruit and laurels encircling a medallion containing a bust of a Roman emperor. All the emperors except one are identified by an inscription. Commencing with the first medallion above the fireplace wall, they show the first eight Caesars of the Lives of Suetonius.
1) Julius Caesar (inscribed IVLIVS . CAESAR)
2) Augustus (inscribed OCTAVIANI . AVGVSTVS)
3) Tiberius (inscribed TIBERIVS . CAESAR)
4) Caligula (inscribed CAIVS . G . / IMPER.)
5) Claudius (inscribed . . . VS / CA . . .)
6) Nero (no inscription)
7) Galba (inscribed GALBA / IMPER.)
8) Otho (inscribed OTHO / IMPER . C.)
Above the window on the fireplace side. First spandrel (Plate 69). Orpheus playing the lyre, while a lion, an orange-tree, and two women, one a nymph holding a bow, listen to his music. The scene represents the legend that Orpheus's lyre had power to draw animals and plants. *Second spandrel* (Plate 70). Orpheus in the underworld plays his lyre and charms Cerberus and a guardian of the underworld. *Third spandrel* (Plate 71). Orpheus clubbed to death by the Thessalian women.
Above the wall facing the door (east wall). *First spandrel* (Plate 72). Arion is cast into the water by pirates and charms a dolphin by his music. *Second spandreal* (Plate 73). Arion is rescued by a dolphin. *Third spandrel* (Plate 74). Periander, tyrant of Corinth, questions two of the pirates, who are brought before him for judgement.
Above the wall facing the fireplace wall (south wall). *First spandrel* (left) (Plate 67). Hercules shooting an arrow. This scene is continuous to that in the second spandrel. *Second spandrel* (Plate 68). Nessus transfixed by the arrow of Hercules as he carries off Deianira. *Third spandrel* (Plate 65). Hercules fighting with the Nemean lion.
Above the door wall (west wall). *First spandrel* (left) (Plate 66). Badly preserved, but probably Hercules and the Hydra. *Second spandrel* (Plate 63). Hercules and Antaeus. *Third spandrel* (Plate 64). Hercules victor over Cerberus.

DOCUMENTS : These are published most fully by Signorini and by Brown (1972, with corrections in *B.M.*, cxv, 1973).
1) *1465, 26 April.* Lodovico Gonzaga to Carlo de Magni, ordering him to obtain immediately two cart-loads of fresh, sound lime (*calcina di scalia*) and send it to the Marchese, taking care it is not spoilt on the journey as it is required for painting 'la camera nostra de castello' (Brown, p.862).
2) *1465, 16 June.* Date painted as a simulated *graffito* on

the left side of the window embrasure in the north wall of the room (*1465.d.16.iunii*).

3) *1468, 19 July*. Lodovico Gonzaga to his factors, ordering them to obtain 6 *pesi* of linseed oil, well-sieved and clean, and consign it to Mantegna for mixing with the colours he is using in painting 'la camera nostra ... in castello' (Brown, p.862).

4) *1470, 10 April*. Pietro da Pusterla and Tommaso da Bologna, ambassadors of the Duke of Milan, are taken by Lodovico to see '*una camera fa depingere, dove è retracta al naturale soa signoria, madonna Barbara sua consorte, domino Federico e tuti l'altri figlioli et figliole; et parlando de queste figure ne fece venire le figliole tutte due, cioè madonna Paula minore et madonna Barbara maiore, quale ad nui, per quello ne intendiamo, è parsa una bella e gentile madonna et de bono aere et bono mainere.*' Published by A. Tissoni Benvenuti, 'Un nuovo documento sulla "Camera degli Sposi" del Mantegna' in *Italia medioevale e umanistica*, xxiv, 1982, pp.357–60.

5) *1470, 22 October*. Lodovico Gonzaga to Zaccaria Saggi in Milan. In answer to a request for a Crucifixion to be painted by Mantegna for Alessandro Sforza, Lodovico regrest 'that Andrea is a man so made that it is years now since he began painting our *camera* and the half of it is not yet finished, and it is not possible to give him ever so little interruption without his prolonging the work for months and years.' The letter closes with a lament that Lodovico never expects to see the work finished (Brown, p.862).

6) *1471, 5 October*. Lodovico Gonzaga to his factors, ordering them to deliver 3 *pesi* of oil of nuts (*olio di noce*) to Mantegna for his work on the *camera* (Brown, p.862).

7) *1474, 1 March*. Lodovico Gonzaga to Giovanni de' Strigi in Venice, ordering him to send two *migliara* of beaten gold for *la camera nostra de castello*, since 'we should like to see Andrea Mantegna finish it, at any rate by the time the Serene King of Denmark has returned here on his journey back' (Brown, p.862).

8) *1474, 17 March*. Same to same. Repeats the order to purchase and despatch the gold as quickly as possible (Brown, p.862).

9) *1474, 23 March*. Same to same. Orders him to buy a pound of azurite (*azurino de Alemagna bono*) for the *camera*: says he has received one *migliaro* of gold and would like the other as soon as possible (Brown, p.862).

10) *1474, 23 June*. Lodovico Gonzaga to Luca Fancelli, saying that the pavement under the *lectera* (settle) in the *camera* should be of the same pattern as the pavement of the rest of the room (Brown, p.862).

11) *1474, 20 August*. Same to same. Concerning the stones that are to be brought for the capitals of the pilasters in the *camera* (Brown, p.862).

12) From letters of 26 November, 30 November and 4 December 1475 between Lodovico Gonzaga and Zaccaria Saggi, concerning the portraits of the Emperor Frederick III and King Christian of Denmark in the outdoor scene it is plain that the *camera* was by that date fully finished (Signorini, 'Federico III e Cristiano I nella Camera degli Sposi del Mantegna' in *Mitteilungen des Kunsthistorischen Institutes in Florenz*, xviii, 1974, pp.227–50, especially pp.230–2).

EARLY REFERENCES: 1) Antonio Crema, *Cronaca*, 1486, MS Biblioteca Guastalla, 'la archetipa camera del castello di Mantova, picta per Mes. Andrea Mantinea, el primo homo de li disegni over picture che se retrova in tutta la machina mondiale' (*cit.* D'Arco, ii, p.27, n.i; Kristeller, 1902, p.491, No.8).

2) Mario Equicola, *Cronaca di Mantova*, 1521, sig. S6: '[*Lodovico*] *Recepi magnificentissimamente Federico terzo Imperadore in Mantua il quale per honorare la nobilita di gonzaga diede per consorte a Federico del signor Ludouico predicto primo genito Margarita di Bauera sua parente ... Honoro Anchora grandemente Re di Dacia, luno & laltro di Mano di Mantegna retracto di naturale si uedeno in la camera depincta del Castello di Mantua le pincture dela quale son tali che ben representano del auctore la excellentia, qual fu dicto Andrea Mantegna primo excitatore a nostri tempi dela pictura, per ho dal dicto Marchese tenuto in gran pregio.*' (*Dell' istoria di Mantova*, 1608, ed. B. Osanna, p.187: '[*Lodovico*] *Riceuè magnificentissimamente Federico terzo Imperadore in Mantoua ... Honorò ancora il Re di Dacia. L'uno, & l'altro di questi si vede ritratto di naturale per mano di Andrea Mantegna, nella camera dipinta del Castello di Mantova, le pitture della quale sono tali, che ben rappresentano l'eccellenza dell' autore, qual fù detto Mantegna, primo eccitatore a' nostri tempi della pittura, & però dal detto Marchese tenuto in gran pregio.*')

3) Vasari, 1550, pp.509–10: '*vna camera con vna volta lauorata in fresco; doue sono dentro molte figure, che scortano al disotto in su, molto lodate certamente, & da lui benissimo considerate: Et ancora ch' egli auesse il modo del panneggiar suo crudetto, & sottile, & la maniera alquanto secca: e' ui sono però cose con molto artificio, & con molta bontà da lui lauorate & ben condotte.*'

EARLY LITERATURE: Mentioned by Carlo Ridolfi in 1648 (p.70, 'vna camera detta degli Sposi'). It is this reference that consecrated the name of Camera degli Sposi. Cadioli (*Descrizione delle pitture, sculture ed architetture, che si osservano nella Città di Mantova*, 1763, pp.34–5) attributes the oculus 'per la sua maggior morbidezza' to Correggio (cf. Cat. no.58) and says the Camera was 'malconcia assaissimo, ed in gran parte disfigurata'. Antoldi (*Guida pel forestiere ... nella città di Mantova*, 2nd ed., 1817, pp.38–9; id., *Descrizione del Regio Cesareo Palazzo di Mantova*, 1815, pp.26–7, same text in both), draws attention largely to the inscription and oculus. Susani (*Nuovo prospetto ... di Mantova*, 1818, pp.33–4) also draws attention to the scenes on the walls and the portraits of the Caesars. The Camera was however, generally ignored by seventeenth- and eighteenth-century travellers: in Mantua itself there was a revival of admiration for it in the eighteenth century and in 1790 the two wall scenes were given as a subject to the art students of the city to draw in a competition for scholarships to study in Rome (Moschini, 1826, pp.41–2).

CONDITION: For the complex history of the techniques, restoration and condition of the Camera see above all Coletti and Camesasca (1959, pp.65–71), supplemented by Paccagnini ('Appunti sulla tecnica della "Camera Picta" di Andrea Mantegna' in *Scritti di storia dell'arte in onore di Mario Salmi*, ii, 1962, pp.395–403).

The Camera was already in need of some repairs in the autumn of 1506, when a serious possibility arose that Julius II might come to visit Mantua and be lodged there.

In obedience to her husband's commands, Isabella d'Este undertook to have it restored. The work was to have been done by Francesco Bonsignori, on account of Mantegna's death on 13 September. But by 24 September Mantegna's sons had agreed to undertake it and the repairs were actually done by Francesco Mantegna, who began them in October (D'Arco, ii, pp.67–71, Nos.83,84,85,87; cf. also Ferrato, *Alcune lettere di principesse di Casa Gonzaga*, 1879, pp.3–4).

Too much is made in Mantuan tradition of the effects of the Sack of Mantua in 1630: steady neglect and the lapse of Mantua in 1707 to the Emperor, which reduced the Palazzo Ducale to a set of government offices, were far more certainly responsible for the poor state into which the Camera had fallen by 1763 (cf. Cadioli, above). About 1790 the Austrian government employed Martin Knoller (1725–1804), its court painter in Milan, to make restorations in the Palazzo Ducale. According to Intra, a late nineteenth-century local historian of Mantua, Knoller restored only some passages in the right-hand compartment of the outdoor scene. Other restorations were undertaken by Luigi Salatelli.

The French and Austrian troops quartered in the Palazzo during the Napoleonic wars left inscriptions scratched on the wall (cf. Coletti & Camesasca, fig.92). Serious restoration began in 1876, under pressure from Morelli: Cavenaghi cleaned away Knoller's restorations and attended to the entire outdoor scene, while in 1876 Gaetano Bianchi restored patches of the fireplace wall (for these restorations see Intra, 'La reggia mantovana' in *A.S.L.*, vi, 1879, pp.295–6). A further experimental attempt at restoration was made from October 1893 to the end of 1894 by Bigoni and Centenari, but in 1895 the work was classed as completed, as the Camera now appeared to be safeguarded from damp.

About 1927 it was decided to attempt the restoration of the other two walls, from which Mantegna's feigned hangings had almost vanished, and of the lunettes, but these restorations, undertaken by A. Raffaldini, were abandoned after a short time. Meanwhile a ministerial commission recommended that action should be taken to remedy damp in the fireplace wall, which was believed to be responsible for its serious condition (Coletti & Camesasca, fig.84). A second commission set up in 1931 recommended different treatment, based on a thorough technical examination in which the restorer Mauro Pellicioli came to the conclusion that Mantegna painted the door wall in true fresco, but had executed the fireplace wall, the lunettes and the garland framing the oculus *a secco*. Pellicioli then proceeded to restore the Camera between 1938 and 1941, removing the stucco applied by previous restorers as a base for their infilling, fixing the *intonaco*, and filling in the gaps with an *intonaco* whose basis was marble dust. The paintings were then cleaned; after cleaning, the damaged areas were toned or filled in with fresco or oil colours. The two walls decorated with hangings, which required heavy restoration, since so little was left of the decoration, were washed and the original ornament was as far as possible reconstructed. A new restoration was begun by the Istituto Centrale del Restauro in September 1974, and is not yet finished. So far the two left-hand compartments of the outdoor scene have been cleaned. In the course of cleaning it has become plain that the lunettes above these compartments underwent a thorough restoration at some early date: the blue of their ground is now greenish, in contrast with the blue below.

In 1962 Paccagnini took further Kristeller's observation of 1901 (pp.263–4) that the paintings were not executed in true fresco, but using a thick substance laid over a hard *intonaco*, and smoothed over to produce a ground much less porous than the ground of true fresco. As a result the colour was not absorbed by the ground, but remained a separate layer, and subsequently flaked. It was maintained, however, by others that the right-hand compartment of the outdoor scene, in which the joined sections of fresco are visible (see below), was executed in true fresco, the reason being that Mantegna was under pressure to finish the work quickly (cf. C. Elam, 1981–2, p.121). Recent investigations in connection with the latest restoration confirm that this wall and the ceiling are executed in true fresco.

In its present condition the *dado* is in a poor state, either ruined or repainted. The *pilasters* are heavily restored, much of their gold ground having fallen and been replaced in yellow.

At the end of the nineteenth century the *scene on the fireplace wall*, as can be seen from a photograph taken *c*.1893 by Naja of Venice (repr. Coletti & Camesasca, fig. 84; Paccagnini, fig.1), was in the words of Kristeller (1901, p.263), 'a mere ruin'. In addition there are three serious cracks. One runs down from the spandrel and lunette above the curtain, along its edge, and through the figure of the messenger. Another runs from the hands to the feet of the Marchese and a third along the right border of the wall (Coletti & Camesasca, figs. 89, 84, 88). There are losses in the face of the dwarf, and losses in the legs of the figures in the right compartment (fig. 88). Sky much darkened.

On the *south wall* facing the outdoor scene traces of the original hangings remain only in the middle of the first set and the upper zone of the third. The decoration on the *west wall*, facing the fireplace wall, is largely modern: only some traces of the original gold remain. The Gonzaga arms held by putti over the doorway are painted on a replastered area: they are not by Mantegna.

On the *wall with the outdoor scene* much of the paint on the extreme left is gone, entailing the loss of almost all the drawn-back curtain and of a figure, whose pointing hand alone remains. There are extensive restorations in this compartment, especially in its lower half. In the next compartment the faces of the two servants are in part a restoration on a new *intonaco*. Of the putti holding the inscription only the two on the top right are still in part original: in the others the surface is heavily patched. Coletti & Camesasca suggest an early date, perhaps even 1506, for this restoration. The inscription is heavily repainted (but its form is attested by early sources, e.g. P. Brandolese, *Testimonianze intorno alla patavinità di Andrea Mantegna*, 1805, p.13, though with some uncertainty about the reading of the date, as noted above). In the original inscription the N of *Incomparabili* was the wrong way round. The date was moved by Pellicioli (see below) from its original position on the left to one in the centre.

In the right compartment a crack runs down from the top of the tree right through the Cardinal's face (Coletti & Camesasca, figs. 86–7). There are losses in the dress of the Marchese, of the Cardinal, of the young Lodovico and of Federico (see Coletti & Camesasca, fig. 85), and along all the lower part, including some of the dado. In this compartment the joints of the plaster as it was laid on in sections for painting are visible: eleven of these sections correspond to the heads of the figures, while some thirty others can be counted in the rest of the compartment, making a total of from forty to forty-three sections. Coletti & Camesasca (p.71, fig.66) note that this number need not correspond to the number of days it took Mantegna to paint the compartment: these may have amounted to no more than twenty. In the dress of the young Lodovico there is a trace of a *pentimento*. It should be noted that in 1475 the Marchese Lodovico could envisage the scraping out of a head and the insertion of another as a possibility (cf. his letter of 30 November 1475, pub. Signorini, in *Mitteilungen K.I.F.*, xviii, 1974, p.232).

On the *ceiling* there are signs of flaking, especially in the garland. The scene in the spandrel tentatively identified as Hercules and the Hydra (see above) is largely gone. The medallions of Claudius and Nero are in a bad state: those of Octavian and Nero are much repainted, and the hair of Galba is also repainted. Almost all the inscriptions on the medallions of the Emperors are heavily restored.

ICONOGRAPHICAL INTERPRETATIONS: In spite of Kristeller's recognition (1901, pp.243,253) that these two scenes were ideal, not historical, attempts have been made to discern historical events in them. That the subject-matter of the scenes is essentially a family group portrait of Lodovico and Barbara and of the sons and daughters who were still living with them in 1469–70 is now at last unequivocally established by the letter recently published by A. Tissoni Benvenuti (see doc. 4). Before Signorini's discovery that the Camera was begun in 1465, the established interpretation of the open-air scene in the Camera was that it represented the Marchese Lodovico meeting Cardinal Francesco Gonzaga on his return from Rome to Mantua in 1472 (cf. e.g. Coletti & Camesasca, 1959, pp.49–51). This thesis, first advanced by Crowe & Cavalcaselle (1871, pp.390–4), rests on a passage describing the meeting by the contemporary Mantuan chronicler Schivenoglia (p.170). Signorini and Brown would argue that 1472 is too late for the scene, and Signorini prefers the alternative thesis that identifies it as a representation of another scene, also described by Schivenoglia (pp.147–8). This was the meeting on 1 January 1462 between Francesco, who had just been made a cardinal, and his father Lodovico. Camesasca (1959, p.50) has nevertheless adduced very strong arguments, based on the age of the protagonists, for rejecting this interpretation. See text p.111.

OTHER BIBLIOGRAPHY: The study of the Camera was greatly advanced by the articles of Brown and Signorini (cit. above, 1972, 1974, 1976, 1978). Signorini's views can now be studied in his extended work on the *Camera, Opvs hoc tenve. La Camera Dipinta di Andrea Mantegna: lettura storica iconografica iconologica*, 1985, which appeared after this book had gone to press. This should be used with what was previously the standard monograph on the Camera, L. Coletti & E. Camesasca (*La Camera degli Sposi del Mantegna a Mantova*, Milan, 1959), beautifully illustrated and well documented. Of other studies those of Crowe and Cavalcaselle (1871, i, pp.390–4) and Kristeller (1901, pp.235–66) are important for their historical and critical acuteness. Garavaglia (1967, pp.100–8) gives a catalogue raisonné of the room and its principal features: this should be used in conjunction with C. Elam, in *Splendours of the Gonzaga*, exh. cat., V. & A. Museum, 1981–2, pp.118–21, No.29).

21. San Bernardino attended by two angels. Inscribed on a medallion on the keystone of the arch: LAVS / DEO; on the frieze of the cornice HVIVS LINGVA SALVS HOMINVM (This man's tongue was men's salvation). On the *cartello* a date which now reads as 1460 (see below).
Milan, Pinacoteca di Brera
Canvas (two longitudinal pieces sewn down the middle)
220 × 385 cm.   Plate 96

CONDITION: Very poor. The date on the much-damaged *cartello* is in its present state a later addition: it is placed too irrationally on the *cartello*, slightly to centre left, to bear any relation to a genuine original inscription. For eighteenth-century evidence as to the true reading of the date, see below.

PROVENANCE: From San Francesco, Mantua (see below). One of the paintings taken by the French from the church, which had been suppressed in 1782. Deposited by them in Palazzo Gonzaga, and consigned on 30 April 1811 to Milan: received in Brera that May (Matteucci, *Le chiese artistiche del Mantovano*, 1902, p.177).

The picture was formerly the altarpiece of the now destroyed Chapel of San Bernardino in San Francesco. Cadioli (1763, p.60) gave it to a pupil of Mantegna: 'Le pitture poi dell'altare di S. Bernardino sono di mano d'uno degli scolari di Mantegna.' Attributed in the later eighteenth century to Mantegna himself, first by Volta, who in a MS note to Cadioli's guide (1763) wrote: 'Il quadro poi dell'altare di S. Bernardino è opera del Mantegna, essendovi sotto la cornice segnato l'anno 1469.' It is not clear if this reference is to the *cartello*, which was already abraded by 1838 (see *Guida per l'I.R. Pinacoteca di Brera*, p.35, No. 111, which says that Mantegna's name was once inscribed on it: 'eravi il nome dell' Autore, ora perduto: vi si legge però la data del 1460'). The attribution to Mantegna was adopted in 1795 by Bettinelli, who mentions a magpie as a feature of the picture (D'Arco, ii, pp.228–9).

The picture's poor condition has greatly influenced modern judgements. Ignored by Crowe & Cavalcaselle (1871, 1912), Kristeller (1901) and Knapp (1910), it is given by Venturi (1914, p.458), Tietze-Conrat (1955, p.189) and Cipriani (1962, p.81) to a follower. Tietze-Conrat explicitly rejects any connection even with Mantegna's workshop. On the other hand for Berenson (1932, 1968) it is a workshop picture. Fiocco (1937, pp.55,204–5) is the only scholar to regard it as fully autograph, but Ragghianti (1962, p.27) emphasizes its Mantegnesque quality and Longhi (1962, p.16) and Camesasca (1964, pp.28,34,116) argue strongly that the picture is a beautiful invention and in part an autograph work by Mantegna. This view has much to commend it, if we allow for the intervention of assistants (see text, p.110). The present date on the *cartello* is read as 1469 by Fiocco and Berenson (tentatively), but is rightly dismissed as a later addition by Tietze-Conrat (see above). Camesasca dates the picture to the 1460s. Elements in the design related to the Camera Picta suggest that the 1469 seen by late eighteenth-century antiquaries on the picture is a correct record of its date.

All previous writers discuss this enormous altarpiece without reference to its provenance. According to Donnesmondi (i, 1612, p.386) the chapel of San Bernardino was refounded in 1450, the year of his canonization, by the Marchese Lodovico Gonzaga. According to Marani (1961, p.34, n.48) it was originally dedicated to St Anthony of Padua. The founding of the chapel, also known as the Cappella dei Signori, was connected with the completion of San Francesco, which was extended by the addition of a choir, cupola and side-naves in the mid-fifteenth century. The work was evidently completed by 2 December 1459, when the church was solemnly consecrated in the presence of Pope Pius II (Intra, *Mantova ne' suoi monumenti*, 1883, p.94). Various paintings in San Francesco have also been associated with Mantegna's school (cf. Kristeller, 1901, p.456; Matteucci, 1902, *loc. cit.*; Luzio & Paribeni, 1940, p.45; and Perina, 1962, pp.321–7). Perina's attempt to associate the present picture with the fresco of the *Virgin in glory* formerly in the apse of the *cappella maggiore* of San Francesco as the work of a single follower of Mantegna is unconvincing. Matteucci claims this fresco was executed in 1516, but in any case it cannot have been painted before 1487, when the *cappella maggiore* was constructed (Donnesmondi, i, 1616, p.70; Marani, 1961, pp.95–7, 115, n.164).

The altarpiece clearly represents a commission by Lodovico Gonzaga, as might be expected from the family cult of San Bernardino, who came to preach at Mantua in 1420 at the invitation of Paola Malatesta, wife of Giovanni Francesco Gonzaga and Lodovico's mother (Donnesmondi, *loc. cit.* and pp.364–5). San Francesco was moreover the funeral church of the Gonzaga and Lodovico was buried in the chapel of San Bernardino at his own request.

22. St Sebastian

Paris, Louvre, cat. 1373A (Hautecoeur, 1926, pp.82–4)
Canvas 257 × 142 cm.   Plates 97, XI; Fig. 7

PROVENANCE: For early history see below. Recorded in the late seventeenth and eighteenth centuries as hanging in the Sainte-Chapelle, Aigueperse, Auvergne (Audigier, *Histoire d'Auvergne*, C.17, Paris, Bibliothèque Nationale, fonds-français 11478, pt.3, p.56: 'Aigueperse. La Sainte-Chapelle où est représenté Saint Sébastien, qui charme tous ceux qui ont du goust pour la peinture'; Piganiol de la Force, *Nouvelle description de la France*, v, Paris, 1718, pp.517–18; Dulaure, *Description des principaux lieux de la France*, pt.V, Paris, 1788, p.101). After the Revolution the painting was transferred to an altar in one of the chapels of the apse of the collegiate church of Notre Dame, Aigueperse, where it was noted in the Guide Richard (various eds.), by François Lenormant (in *Athenaeum*

français, 22 July 1854, p.686) and by E. Montégut (*En Bourbonnais et en Forez*, 1881, p.123). Exh. with an attribution to Mantegna at Clermont-Ferrand, May–June 1863, No.417. First published as a Mantegna by Mantz (in *G.B.A.*, ser.2, xxxiv, 1886, pp.375–87). Acquired from the municipality of Aigueperse by the Louvre in June 1910.

Vimont's fundamental article on the provenance of the picture (in *Revue d'Auvergne*, 1887, pp.237–46) has been neglected in the literature. It is generally agreed that the *St Sebastian* reached Aigueperse in the Auvergne through the connection between the Bourbon-Montpensier family and the Gonzaga established by the marriage on 26 February 1481 between Chiara Gonzaga (b.1 July 1464), daughter of the Marchese Federico, and Gilbert de Bourbon, Comte de Montpensier and Dauphin of Auvergne. Negotiations for this match began in June 1480. Gilbert de Montpensier followed Charles VIII on his Italian expedition in 1494, was made Viceroy of Naples and died at Pozzuoli on 5 October 1496. Chiara Gonzaga died on 2 June 1503 (Moréri, *Grand Dictionnaire*, s.v., Bourbon-Montpensier). A medal of her in French costume, with an inscription which indicates that it was executed after her marriage, is attributed to the Mantuan medallist Melioli (Foville, in *G.B.A.*, Ser.3, xxxix, 1908, pp.391–3: Hill, No.200, pl.37). Chiara Gonzaga left Mantua for France in June 1481 (Coniglio, 1967, p.100), but was there in December and January 1486 on a visit to her family (Luzio & Renier, 1893, pp.7–8) and made a number of later visits to Mantua, where she eventually ended her life (see e.g. Luzio, in *A.S.L.*, ser.2, vii, 1890, p.646).

The Sainte-Chapelle of Aigueperse, founded in 1475 by Louis I de Bourbon-Montpensier (d.May 1486), father of Gilbert (the Papal bull authorizing its foundation as a collegiate church is dated 9 Kal Novembris 1475), adjoined his castle of Aigueperse, which was still in course of construction in 1485: this was destroyed after an agreement between Gilbert de Montpensier and the municipality of Aigueperse of 7 March 1486 by which Gilbert undertook to build only a house with towers instead (Tardieu, *Grand Dictionnaire historique du Puy-de-Dôme*, 1877, pp.61–4). This house and its contents were destroyed by a fire in 1574 and only the Sainte-Chapelle escaped destruction. For this reason, and because it is not listed in the inventory of the château taken on 18 November 1507, Vimont argued plausibly that the *St Sebastian* must have hung in the Sainte-Chapelle from a very early date. In fact the inventory (for which see Le Roux de Lincy, in Société des Bibliophiles Français, *Mélanges de Littérature et d'Histoire*, 1850, pp.112–30, and J. M. de la Mvre, *Histoire des dvcs de Bourbon*, ii, 1868, pp.502–7n, cf. also pp.480 ff. for much interesting information about Gilbert and the Montpensier family) lists no pictures, but only tapestries (these do not include one of St Sebastian, as Vimont claims). The *Nativity* of Benedetto Ghirlandaio, which also hung in the Sainte-Chapelle, was painted for Gilbert de Montpensier in 1489 (Reinach, in *Bulletin Archéologique*, 1918, pp.201–7).

Universally accepted as autograph. Opinion is divided between those who date it to the 1450s, either as an early work, contemporary with the *St Euphemia* of 1454 (Kristeller, 1901, pp.138–43) or as a close to the San Zeno altarpiece (Fiocco, 1937, p.43) and those who date it *c*.1470–80, on the ground of analogies with the Camera Picta (Thode, 1898, pp.110–11; Knapp, 1910, p.174, contradicting p.74; Borenius, in Crowe & Cavalcaselle, 1912, p.97; Tietze-Conrat, 1955, pp.27, 195; Cipriani, 1962, pp.29, 64–5; Camesasca, 1964, pp.28, 118; Garavaglia, 1967, No.56). Battisti (in *Arte, Pensiero, e Cultura a Mantova*, 1965, p.52) dates it *c*.1489, rightly connecting it with the Aigueperse Sainte-Chapelle. The association, even if it does not date the picture tightly, nevertheless excludes a Paduan origin and a dating in the 1450s. Rather than a wedding-present, which, as Kristeller argues, so huge a picture is unlikely to have been, it should be regarded as an altarpiece specially commissioned by or for the Montpensiers after Chiara's marriage. Stylistically it differs from the pictures Mantegna painted after his return from Rome, and the most likely bracket for it is therefore 1481–8. Within this span, a date *c*.1482–5 is perhaps most plausible, since Mantegna was busy with the *Triumphs* by 1486. It accords well with the style of the picture, which is intermediate between that of the Camera Picta and that of the *Triumphs*.

Borenius and Cust (in *B.M.*, xvii, 1910, pp.213–14) publish a picture of *St Sebastian* in the English royal collections (acquired in 1847 as a Mantegna) which they attribute to Parentino and which clearly derives important features from Mantegna's picture. It has recently been shown by C. Brown (in *L'Arte*, vi, 1969, pp.152–64; *id*. and A. M. Lorenzoni, in Mantua, Accademia Virgiliana, *Atti e Memorie*, ser.2, xli, 1973, p.119) that Parentino was in Mantua between 1484 and 1486. If this picture is by Parentino, then his residence in Mantua fixes an approximate date for the completion of Mantegna's painting. There seems in fact to be little doubt about the attribution, which is accepted by Shearman (Royal Collection, *Early Italian Pictures*, 1983, pp.182–3).

There is a close replica of the composition on canvas in the church of the former Chartreuse of Sainte-Croix-en-Jarez (Loire). Attention was first drawn to this in 1886 (R. Ville, in *Chronique des arts et de la curiosité*, 27 November 1886, pp.290–1; cf. also *Revue du Lyonnais*, ii, 1886, p.466; *id*., iii, 1887, p.151; A. Vachez, in *Mémoires de la Société Nationale des Antiquaires de France*, ser.6, viii, 1899, pp.235–6). In 1887 the painter Léon Bonnat and Tausia, Conservateur des Peintures at the Louvre, went to inspect the picture, and dismissed it as a late sixteenth-century copy of the Aigueperse painting. Most probably it was a gift of Jean II, Seigneur of Saint-Chamond from 1487 to 1534. He was in the service of Anne of Brittany, whose daughter Suzanne married in 1505 Charles, son of Gilbert de Montpensier and Chiara, and he also took part in the French campaigns in Italy. Alternatively it may have been given by Jean's brother Théodore (before 1471–d.1527), a powerful ecclesiastic who was a friend of Pico della Mirandola (for these two brothers see Condamin, *Histoire de Saint-Chamond*, 1890, pp.158–61, 166–87). According to an early eighteenth-century source, they both contributed to the embellishment of the old Church of the Chartreuse of Sainte-Croix.

For an enquiry into the symbolism of the picture see the unconvincing article by M. Levi d'Ancona ('Il Mantegna e la simbologia: il S. Sebastiano del Louvre e quello della Ca d'Oro' in *Commentari*, xxiii, 1972, pp.44–52) and a more suggestive study by J. G. Caldwell, in *J.W.C.I.*, xxxvi, 1973, pp.373–7.

23. Lamentation over the Dead Christ

Milan, Pinacoteca di Brera, 199 (Malaguzzi-Valeri, 1908, pp.112–13; Modigliani, 1966, pp.42–3)

Tempera on canvas 68 × 81 cm.   Plate x

CONDITION: Very worn in parts.

PROVENANCE: See below. Acquired by the Accademia di Belle Arti from the heirs of the painter Giuseppe Bossi in 1824. Engraved in 1809 when in Bossi's possession by Scotto. Bossi bought the picture in Rome, presumably in 1806, having become aware of its existence, *c*.1802 (see *Lettere di Giuseppe Bossi ad Antonio Canova*, Padua, 1839, pp.26–7, letter from Bossi in Milan to Canova in Rome dated 17 December 1806: 'Ecco il momento i cui tu puoi favorirmi col farmi avere il mio desiderato Mantegna. Fallo portare in una cassetta, e se credi possa giungere intatto, lasciaci anche quel cristallo, il cui colore giova a quel dipinto ... Per tal mezzo ... io avrò questa desiderata anticaglia, che sospiro invano da quattro anni.' A letter from same to same of 21 March 1807 reports 'Il quadretto è arrivato in ottimo stato').

This celebrated composition was admired from the first and the history of its various versions is complicated. 'Un Cristo in scurto' (a foreshortened Christ) is listed among the pictures by Mantegna which were in his house at his death in a letter of 2 October 1506 written by his son Lodovico to the Marchese Francesco (Kristeller, 1902, p.583, doc.190). It is mentioned again in a letter of 12 November 1507 from Lodovico Mantegna to Isabella d'Este (Kristeller, 1902, p.585, doc.198, incompletely published by Zani, 1802, Gaye, iii, p.564 and D'Arco, ii, p.74) in which Lodovico says 'quello Christo in scurto' had been taken together with the Cornaro *Cult of Cybele* (Cat. no.57) by Cardinal Sigismondo Gonzaga, who had promised Lodovico in return 100 ducats, to be paid at the rate of 5 ducats weekly. It is mentioned yet again on 28 October 1531 in a letter from Ippolito Calandra to Duke Federigo referring to the preparation of apartments in the Castello for the new Duchess Margherita Paleologa: 'Nel camerino dove alogierà la Ill.ma Signora Duchessa vi è da metere se'l pare a V.Ex., forse da sei quadri ... come quello quadro che fece el Mantegna de quello Christo ch'è in scurto' (published by Luzio in *Archivio Storico dell'Arte*, i, 1888, p.184). It is last mentioned in Mantua in 1627 as in the Camerino delle Dame of the Palazzo Ducale: 'un quadro dipinto: N.S. deposto sopra il sepolcro in scurzo con cornici fregiate d'oro di mano del Mantegna – L.90.(47).' (D'Arco, ii, p.161; Luzio, 1913, p.115, no. 318.)

VERSIONS: This Mantua picture was almost certainly Mantegna's original. It is usually, but wrongly regarded as identical with one recorded in the inventory of Cardinal Mazarin, taken in 1661. '*Deux autres tableaux faicts par Andréa Mantegna, sur thoille, l'un représentant Nostre-Seigneur qui porte sa croix au Calvaire, et plusieurs diverses figures; et l'autre Nostre Seigneur mort à la renverse en racourcy et plusieurs autres figures au naturel, chacun hault de deux pieds dix poulces et large de deux pieds quatre poulces, garnis chacun de leurs bordures de bois doré, prisez ensemble la somme de mil livres, cy . . . 1000 L.T.'* The dimensions of these pictures and their joint valuation indicate that they were a pair: moreover their format was a vertical oblong, not a horizontal oblong like the Brera picture (Cosnac, *Les richesses du Palais Mazarin*, 1884, p.302, no.997). The painting of the Dead Christ must however be that referred to by Félibien (*Entretiens*, i, 1669, p.169): *'Aussi [Mantegna] s'attachoit–il beaucoup à finir ce qu'il faisoit, & sur tout à mettre exactement tous les corps en perspective. Vous avez pû voir au Palais Mazarin un Christ mort qui paroist couché de son long, & que l'on voit racourci depuis le dessous des pieds jusqu'au haut de la teste.'* This reference indicates that the principal composition was the same as that of the Brera picture. By an extraordinary confusion, which appears to date back to D'Arco (ii, p.70), Félibien's reference to the Palais Mazarin, erected by the Cardinal for himself in Paris, is invariably in the modern literature construed as meaning Palazzo Mazzarini in Rome.

Mazarin's pictures were perhaps the two which were listed by the Cardinal's agent Bordeaux among the pictures that had belonged to Charles I which were up for sale at Somerset House in May 1650: '157 un homme portant un croix, par Mantegne' valued at £40 and '160 Un Jesus-Christ mort, par le mesme [i.e. Mantegna]' valued at £30 (Cosnac, *op. cit.*, p.416). These are also listed in Millar, 1972, p.195, No.157 (of the pictures at Hampton Court), 'Christ Carrying ye Cross: by Andrea Mantenger,' sold to John Jackson, a lawyer, on 23 October 1651 and valued at £40; *loc. cit.*, No.160 (of the same group): 'A Christ dead: done by Andrea Mantenger,' valued at £30 and sold to Edmund Harrison, Embroiderer in the Wardrobe, on 23 October 1651. Bordeaux is known to have bought two Mantegnas from a private person in London for the Cardinal in 1654 (Cosnac, *op. cit.*, pp.59,207,208,243). In any case one of the pictures belonging to Charles I was perhaps a picture listed in the Mantua inventory of 1627 (Luzio, 1913, p.95, no.77: 'Un quadro con N.S. in scurzo deposto di croce con le Marie'). It is true that on 17 October 1627 Daniel Nys noted this picture as one of those on the agreed list which had not yet been sent to him from Mantua (Luzio, p.147). It is not certain whether it was found and sent on at this time (cf. Luzio, p.153, letter from Nys of 13 December), but it may well have been sold in the later dealings. For a Mantegnesque composition of *Christ carrying the Cross* see Cat. nos. 145 and 146; Plates 175 and 176.

A version on panel was in the collection of Donna Olimpia Aldobrandini by 1626 (Della Pergola, 'Gli inventari Aldobrandini' in *Arte antica e moderna*, 1960, p.433). The inventory reads: '132. Un quadro con Christo in scorto in una tavola morto con doi donne che piangono di mano di Andrea Mantegna del n.260.' Della Pergola (p.442) notes that the medium is different from the Brera picture. Olimpia Aldobrandini married in 1647 as her second husband Prince Camillo Pamphili, nephew of Pope Innocent X, and it can therefore be assumed that the Aldobrandini picture was that offered for sale to Louis XIV by Camillo Pamphili in September 1665, when it was seen by Bernini with other pictures offered to Louis XIV by Pamphili (Rose, *Tagebuch des Herrn von Chantelou über die Reise des Cavaliere Bernini nach Frankreich*, 1919, pp.263 ff: not in French eds.).

Neither the Mazarin nor the Pamphili picture was acquired by Louis XIV (see Bailly, *Inventaire des tableaux du Roy rédigé en 1709 et 1710*, ed. Engerand, 1899). A version in which Nicodemus, St John, and a third male saint are added to the three Maries was advertised in Padua, Palazzo della Ragione, *Da Giotto a Mantegna*, exh. cat., 1974, at end, with a provenance from a Roman collection (canvas, 76 × 192 cm).

Yet another version is recorded in the De Navarro Collection, Glen Head, N.Y. (linen mounted on canvas, 63.7 × 75.7 cm.; cut at either side: much damaged). This was with the Jacob M. Heimann Gallery, New York, in 1941. It has the same composition as the Brera version but omits the figures and the jar of unguent (Plate 255). Published by H. Tietze (in *A.A.*, xxix, 1941, pp.51–6) as the original of the other versions and as the picture mentioned in the early documents, the Brera version being a sweetened copy, painted either by Mantegna or his assistants. Tietze-Conrat (1955, p.192) regards it as a *modello* executed *c*.1466 from which Mantegna painted enriched versions. The attribution to Mantegna is rejected by Paccagnini (1961, p.63), Arslan (1961, p.170, old copy by a Lombard Mannerist from the ambience of Figino), Longhi (1962, p.20, a miserable copy made perhaps a century later), Cipriani (1962, pp.43,68, a too faithful copy), Camesasca (1964, p.111, late sixteenth century), Garavaglia (1967, No.58, as generally rejected).

Camesasca notes that a version in oil passed through a Milan saleroom in 1963 as by an Italian master of the second half of the quattrocento: he dates it as no earlier than the late sixteenth century.

DATING: The Brera version is universally accepted as autograph, but with no unanimity as to date. The earliest opinion, that of Crowe & Cavalcaselle (1871, pp.394–5; 1912, p.96), places it shortly after the completion of the Camera Picta. This dating is advocated by Longhi (1962, pp.20–1) and even more strongly by Camesasca (1964, pp.40–1,110–11), who rejects the common argument that its tragic sentiment implies a late date, relates the interest in foreshortening to the figures on the ceiling of the Camera Picta, and dates it as begun between 1478 and 1485, perhaps completed before *c*.1480, certainly no later than the 1490s. For Kristeller (1901, pp.230–4) and Bercken (1927, p.129) it can only be understood as a preparatory exercise for the ceiling of the Camera, and Bercken dates it *c*.1464. Yriarte (1901, pp.240–2) is unique in suggesting it may date from the Paduan years. A date in Mantegna's last years was first advocated by Thode (1897, pp.114–15) and is accepted by Knapp (1910, p.115, after 1501), Venturi (1914, pp.228–9), Berenson (1932, 1968), Fiocco (1937, pp.74–5,209), Paccagnini (1961, pp.62–3) and Cipriani (1962, pp.42–3,68). In publishing the Glen Head version H. Tietze dated the composition to the middle or third quarter of the fifteenth century, claiming that in 1500 foreshortening had become a secondary branch of art. Tietze-Conrat (1955, p.188) admitted the Brera picture as an autograph version of the

Glen Head *modello* (see above), a late date being indicated by its delicate colour scale.

Fiocco had been among the first to find the mourners a disturbing element: they were condemned as later additions by Rathe (*Die Ausdruckfunktion extrem verkürzter Figuren*, 1938, p.13), and Tietze-Conrat. This view is adopted by Arslan (1961, pp.169–70), who argues that the original work consisted only of the Dead Christ, perhaps executed *c.*1470, to which the mourners were added later than the 1480s. Cipriani rejects the view that the mourners are a later addition: Camesasca still regards them as such. There can be no question that the mourners belong to the composition as first conceived, since the theme of the picture is the conventional one of the Lamentation over the dead Christ. It is the composition and treatment that are of extreme originality. Mantegna's style assumes generalized, idealizing ennoblement of treatment in the 1480s; no surviving late work includes the figures treated with an uncompromising realism, sometimes exaggerated to a point of grotesqueness recalling German fifteenth-century art, that recur in Mantegna's work before this date. The watered silk of the pink pillow is, by contrast, a regular feature of Mantegna's later pictures. The severe plainness of realism in the *Lamentation*, in combination with the larger figure-style, delicate, subdued scale of colour and the watered-silk pillow, suggest that the most plausible date for it is in the late 1480s or early 1490s. Mantegna may have intended the picture for his own private devotion: certainly its unorthodoxy of composition and treatment and low colouring would not have commended it to the average fifteenth-century patron.

24. Virgin and Child

Milan, Museo Poldi-Pezzoli (Russoli, 1955, pp.184–5: Natale, 1982, p.113, no.98)

Tempera on canvas 43 × 45 cm.   Plate 98

CONDITION: Restored *c.*1860 by G. Molteni. Much abraded and retouched.

PROVENANCE: Sold to Poldi-Pezzoli by G. Morelli *c.*1856.

Universally accepted as autograph, but with an even wider range of dates than usual. It was originally placed by Morelli (1890, p.360) and Thode (1897, p.112) as a late work (last decade of Mantegna's life), a dating accepted by Venturi (1914, p.242, *c.*1500), and reproposed by Longhi (1962, pp.19,20). Kristeller (1901, pp.129–32) by contrast dated it in the early 1460s, followed by Knapp (1910, p.92) and Fiocco (1937, p.49), while Paccagnini (1961, p.26) places it close to the San Zeno altarpiece and the Vienna *St Sebastian*. Arslan (1961, p.163), Tietze-Conrat (1955, pp.20,189) and Cipriani (1962, p.67) advance it to *c.*1485, a late date also being advocated by Longhi (1962, p.20), while Camesasca (1964, pp.37,119) puts it *c.*1475 and Garavaglia (1967, No.44) *c.*1470. Russoli (*loc. cit.*) does not pronounce: Natale accepts a date in the late quattrocento.

An influence from Lippi has often been postulated, surely wrongly. The picture is closely related in conception and treatment to Mantegna's other late Madonnas, and the use of a watered stuff for the Virgin's cloak, in which it also resembles them, is another indication of a late date for it, probably *c.*1485–95.

A slightly smaller version belongs to Prof. T. Spano of Venice.

The iconography of the Virgin with the sleeping Child was studied in relation to this picture by A. Alisi, *Andrea Mantegna e il tema della Dolce Madre*, 1931. It seems to have originated in Venice in the late fourteenth or early fifteenth century (G. Firestone, 'The sleeping Christ-Child in Italian Renaissance representations of the Madonna' in *Marsyas*, ii, 1942, pp.43–62). Miss Firestone does not cite some of the paintings discussed by Alisi, whose study she seems not to have known, and would like to regard all representations of the sleeping Christ Child as prefigurements of his Passion. This is certainly too rigid an interpretation of the motif, proceeding from too great an emphasis on Christ and too small an emphasis on Mary, though it would certainly account for the pensiveness of Mantegna's Virgin and the picture's sombre background. Almost always, in both altarpieces and Madonnas representing the theme, the Virgin is shown praying to the Child, and the invention was certainly in origin a variation on the theme of the Virgin as a human mother adoring the divine Child. Mantegna's *Madonna* shares with two pictures by Cosmé Tura, one in the National Gallery, London, and one in the Accademia, Venice, the distinction of a more intimate and domestic treatment. The sentiment of Tura's Venice *Madonna*, as noted by Alisi, is expressed in its verse inscription: SVIGLIA EL TVO FIGLO DOLCE MADRE PIA / PER FAR IN FIN FELICE L'ANIM / A MIA. That of his London *Madonna*, which originates from the Roverella altarpiece, has been clarified by Davies's discoveries about the original reading of its inscription (1961, pp.513–16). This too appealed to the Virgin to awaken her Child in order to admit the souls of the Roverella to Paradise. In Mantegna's picture the Virgin is not awakening the Child, but rather supporting him protectively as he sleeps. Its iconography, then, seems rather to emphasize the Virgin's power as an intercessor through the more usual appeal to her protective motherhood.

25. Virgin and Child

Bergamo, Accademia Carrara, no. 484 (170)

Canvas 43 × 31 cm.   Plate xv

CONDITION: Thinly painted. The surface is worn, especially on the Child's face and arm. Damaged on head-dress (above the left lock of hair), on the collar and just above the fold on the left shoulder.

PROVENANCE: Bequest of Conte Carlo Marenzi, 1851.
Universally accepted as autograph. There is no agreement as to date. A late date is proposed by Crowe and Cavalcaselle (1871, p.408; 1912, p.109, shortly after 1492), by Morelli (1890, p.360; 1891, p.227, in the 1490s), Thode (1897, p.112, last decade of Mantegna's life), by Venturi (1914, p.228, as *c.*1497), by Longhi (1962, pp.19,20, partly on grounds of thin tempera technique), and by Cipriani (1962, p.69). Kristeller (1901, pp.129–32), Knapp (1910, pp.99,175), Fiocco (1937, p.49), Paccagnini (1961, p.27) and Gilbert (1962, p.6) date it to the early Mantuan years, *c.*1463–4. Tietze-Conrat (1955, pp.20,179) pushes it back to a date shortly before Mantegna's move to Mantua, while Arslan (1961, p.163) terms it a youthful work.

Camesasca (1964, pp.37,120) dates it c.1480 at the earliest, Garavaglia (1967, No.45) c.1470. There can be no doubt that this beautiful picture is a late work, dating from the bracket 1485–95. This conclusion is dictated by the conception and treatment, as of a coloured bas-relief, which relate it to Mantegna's other late Madonnas, though in its contained naturalism it seems earlier than his compositions of the Holy Family.

26. Christ Child Blessing

Washington, National Gallery of Art (1146), Kress Coll. 1563 (Shapley, 1968, p.25; 1979, pp.298–9)
Thinly painted on unprepared canvas 70.3 × 35 cm.
Plate 99

CONDITION: Abraded and darkened.

PROVENANCE: First recorded in the Cook Collection, Richmond (Borenius, Catalogue, i, 1913, p.153, no.128). Later with Contini Bonacossi, Florence; acquired from him by Kress in 1948.

Tentatively identified by Tietze-Conrat (1955, p.201) with a painting of this subject attributed to Mantegna in an inventory taken c.1728 of paintings belonging to the Gonzaga di Novellara (Campori, p.642: 'Un puttino vestito, alto on. 20, largo 10. del Mantegna . . . dob.14'). She regards it as an example of the kind of picture which was sent as a New Year's gift (cf. Cat. no.33).

Kristeller (1901, p.455) and Knapp (1910, p.158) attribute it to a Veronese follower; Borenius (1913, loc. cit.) as school of Mantegna. Affirmed as autograph by Berenson (1932, 1968) and accepted by Fiocco (1937, pp.67–8,205), Tietze-Conrat (1955, p.201), Longhi (MS opinion cit. Shapley), Cipriani (1962, p.52), Camesasca (1964, pp.37,119), Garavaglia (1967, No.37) and Fredericksen and Zeri (1972). There is no agreement about its date. Longhi, followed by Cipriani, dates it to the Paduan period, Garavaglia c.1465, Camesasca c.1475–80, Shapley as probably 1480–90, Fiocco to the early 1490s after Mantegna's return from Rome. The resemblance between the Child and the Child in the Poldi-Pezzoli Madonna suggests a date in the bracket 1485–95.

27. Virgin and Child. In a frame (from another picture?) inscribed below AVE MARIA: GRACIA, and painted above with a God the Father in glory (sixteenth century in date)

Berlin-Dahlem, Staatliche Museen, S5 (Posse, 1909, p.88)
Tempera on canvas 42 × 32 cm.
Plate 100

CONDITION: Old relining. A pentimento to the left of the head? Much damaged bottom right and left, and in the background and on the drapery, and much repainted, except in the Virgin's face and the Child.

PROVENANCE: Coll. Conte della Porta, Vicenza (according to some sources, coll. Conte Trissino, Vicenza); with a London dealer: James Simon coll. c.1897; exhibited by him Berlin, Kunstgeschichtliche Gesellschaft, Austellung von Kunstwerken des Mittelalters und der Renaissance aus Berliner Privatbesitz, 20 May–3 July 1898 (commem. vol., 1899, p.43).

Universally accepted as autograph, but with no agreement as to date. For some critics Donatello's evident influence makes it early; Knapp (1910, p.77) as 1454; Tietze-

Conrat (1955, pp.20,179) as Paduan period; Arslan (1962, p.163) 1454 or before. For Berenson (1932, 1968) and Longhi (1962, pp.19,20) late. For Fiocco (1937, p.49) from the early Mantuan years; for Cipriani (1962, pp.26,58) c.1459–60. Paccagnini (1961, p.30), followed by Gilbert (1962, p.6), argues that the softer pictorial treatment indicates a date contemporary with or shortly after Mantegna's Tuscan journey of 1466. Camesasca (1964, pp.37,119) as probably later than 1475; Garavaglia (1967, No.54) as c.1475. The Child is close in type to those of the Washington Christ Child Blessing and of the Poldi-Pezzoli Madonna, but the Virgin's robe, with its low-cut neck, indicates a later date, as does her ringleted hair-style. Probably c.1490–5.

28. THE TRIUMPHS OF CAESAR

Hampton Court Palace, Royal Coll. (now exhibited in The Orangery)   Plates 101–119; Fig. 9

MEDIUM: The nine canvases are painted in tempera on a thin gesso priming over a 'twilled' linen canvas. Each canvas consists of three vertical strips, two broad and one narrow, sewn together (for a detailed analysis see Martindale, 1979, pp.125–6).

CONDITION: From the late seventeenth century the Triumphs have been radically restored a number of times. Perry Walton, Keeper of the King's Pictures, restored and relined three of the canvases between December 1690 and July 1693. The work of restoration then passed to Louis Laguerre, who was paid for it in 1701 and 1702. His hand is still conspicuous in the most heavily restored canvases. Laguerre's treatment seems to have included relining the remainder of the canvases. Further restoration work was carried out on four of the canvases by Joseph Goupy in 1717. Their condition gave rise to grave concern in the nineteenth century, but it was decided that they were too fragile for serious restoration to be attempted. Roger Fry had begun restoring the first canvas with a view to fixing the paint with cellulose in 1910, apparently unsuccessfully. In 1931–4 Kennedy North was employed to treat the pictures. He fixed the paint by loading the paint surface with paraffin wax and relined them. North's restoration, though it arrested flaking, was crude. A new restoration was begun by Mr John Brealey in 1962 and completed in 1974. One canvas, No. VII (The Captives), was not treated, since tests showed that scarcely any original paint was left beneath the restoration. The principle followed by Brealey was to reveal Mantegna's original paint, except where scientific examination again showed that little or nothing of the original was left beneath. (For an account of the successive vicissitudes of the pictures and detailed notes on their present condition see Martindale, 1979, Introduction by A. Blunt, pp.109–22, 126–8.) For condition of individual paintings see the entries below. As stressed by Martindale, the tonality of the paintings, even where Mantegna's original surface has been revealed, is now too bold owing to the loss of Mantegna's glazes over the body colour.

I. The Standard-Bearers

266 × 278 cm.   Plate 110

CONDITION: Poor. Face of soldier carrying the female goddess with cornucopia a modern restoration: much of the rest of the figures and drapery are restorations by Laguerre. Mantegna's hand is apparent in parts of the dress of the Moor and the soldier on the right (Martindale, 1979, pp.133–4).

II. Bearers of statues of gods, of an image of a captured city, siege engines, inscribed tablets and trophies
266 × 278 cm. Plate 111

CONDITION: Comparatively well preserved. The figure on the right carrying a female statue largely by Laguerre, otherwise the painting is almost entirely the work of Mantegna, though the surface is now rather worn (Martindale, 1979, p.138).

INSCRIPTIONS: A tablet is inscribed: IMP. IVLIO CAESARI / OB GALLIAM DEVICT. / MILITARI POTENCIA / TRIVMPHVS / DECRETVS INVIDIA / SPRETA SVPERATAQ.

On a second tablet is a second inscription, partly concealed by the first: MORA / RES ET / O . . . ARI / AN M VE / RIA MQ / O.N. R.A

III. Bearers of military trophies and spoils of silver vessels
268 × 278 cm. Plate 112

CONDITION: Not well preserved. The drapery and faces of the principal figures are largely restorations by Laguerre: only the face in profile on the extreme left has elements by Mantegna (Martindale, 1979, p.141). By contrast some details of the trophies well preserved.

In the drawing in the Albertina, Vienna (see below) the left car is inscribed: PONTIFEX M. IMP (*Pontifex Maximus, Imperator*) / DANT / IIII.V / TR / NIVM.

In the same drawing the chest is inscribed: QVESTRI (? for *equestri*)

IV. Bearers of golden vessels and a precious marble vase, the sacrificial oxen and trumpeters
266 (varying to 268) × 278 (varying to 279) cm. Plate 113

CONDITION: Well preserved: the only canvas to retain the sky as painted by Mantegna more or less undamaged. The figure on the extreme left largely restored by Laguerre: the face of the bearer next to this figure retouched, as is the hillside. The lettering a later restoration, but preserving the original inscriptions (Martindale, 1979, p.145).

To one of the trumpets is attached a pennon inscribed SPQR DIVO IVLIO CAESARI D.P.P.P. On another pennon is the inscription SPQR IVLIVS CAESAR P.M. Both these inscriptions are attested by Schraderus in 1592 (see below).

In the Vienna painted copy (see below) the standard behind the ferculum is inscribed DIVO / CESAR / PATER / PATRI / E.

V. Trumpeters, sacrificial oxen and elephants
267 × 277 cm. Plate 114

CONDITION: Well preserved: some water staining which may be of an early date, since it lies beneath the retouching (Martindale, 1979, p.147).

VI. Bearers of spoils of golden vessels and bearers of trophies and crowns
268 × 278 cm. Plate 115

CONDITION: Well preserved except in the sky and at the right-hand end of the aqueduct, with the spectators who stand on it. Otherwise largely by Mantegna, with much survival of detail, e.g. in trees top left (Martindale, 1979, pp.149–50).

VII. Captives, buffoons, a soldier and a standard-bearer
Plate 116

No measurements of original size possible as Kennedy North folded forward the edges of his new canvas in his rebacking of 1931–4 (see above)

CONDITION: Already 'much spoyled' in the seventeenth century: entirely repainted by Laguerre, but following Mantegna's original work (Martindale, 1979, pp.152, 111).

The *tabula ansata* is inscribed SPQR LIBERATORI VRBIS. This inscription is attested by Schraderus in 1592 (see below).

VIII. Musicians and standard-bearers
268 × 278 cm. Plate 117

CONDITION: Almost entirely overpainted by Laguerre: only the crowned busts still contain original detail (Martindale, 1979, p.156).

The banner with Romulus and Remus is inscribed SPQR.

IX. Julius Caesar on his triumphal car
268 × 279 cm. Plate 118

CONDITION: Poorly preserved in general. Caesar's chariot much damaged: Caesar's head largely a restoration. The foliage on the left a restoration by Laguerre: that behind the arch is by Mantegna (Martindale, 1979, p. 157).

The standards are hung with inscribed tablets. These read:
1) VENI VIDI VICI (Martindale, *op. cit.*, p.157, 'substantial remnants of autograph Mantegna lettering').
2) [SP?] QR / [   ] CLEMENTISSIMO / PRINCIPI IN B.G.P. ARM. V. / CIV. P. AF. VICTOR DEDIC / NVMINI [   ] MAIESTATIQ

In the Vienna painted copy (see below) this inscription reads:
[   ] QR / [   ] CLEMENTISSIMO / PRINCIPI C. IN. B.G.P. ARM. V / CN GR R AF VICTOR DEDIC / NVMINI [   ] MAIESTATIQ.

On the Bowhill tapestry after this canvas (see below) the two middle lines read: PRINCIPI C IN BGP ARM V / CIV GR R A F VICTOR DEDIC

A possible interpretation of these lines might be: *Senatus populusque Romanus [Caesari] Clementissimo Principi in Bello Gallico parta armis victoria Civili Pontico Africano victor dedicavit numini [Romano] Maiestatique.*
3) S.. / NO.R.. / M . . . (on tablet behind Caesar).
4) SPQR / DIC (*Senatus populusque Romanus / Dictatori*) (on the banner).
5) GAL   D / PRO   DED / RIM (on circular tablet behind Caesar).

There are records of other inscriptions on this canvas. Over the arch behind the Bowhill tapestry records CAIVS MCF / CO V PFTR / PIQ TRI. The Vienna painted copy is inscribed here: CAIVS MCF / CCVII PRT / FRG. Martindale (1979, pp.176–7) expands these inscriptions to read CAIVS MARIVS CAII FILIVS CONSVL VII PRAETOR TRIBVNVS PLEBISQUE [AVGVR] TRIBVNVS [MILITARIS]. He points out that this reading must be correct since the inscription is that found in the *Sylloge Signoriliana*, a fourteenth-century collection of inscriptions which was much copied in the fifteenth century. At that date the inscription was believed to have come from an arch at Rimini.

Schraderus (1592, see below) clearly copied the inscriptions on the *Triumphs*, beginning with this canvas and working forwards to the first. It is therefore virtually certain that the inscription which he records and which is so crucial for the iconography of the *Triumphs* appeared on this canvas. It reads: *D. Iulij Caesaris, ob invidiam constanter superatam & hostes fortiter deuictos, duplex victoria: VENI, VIDI, VICI.*

DOCUMENTS: 1) 1486, 26 August. Silvestro Calandra to Marchese Francesco. 'This day Duke Ercole d'Este after dinner entered a boat for a pleasure jaunt on the lake . . . We disembarked at the Porto de Corte to go and see the Triumphs of Caesar which Mantegna is painting which pleased him greatly' (*per andare a vedere li Triomphi di Cesare che dipinge el Mantegna, li quali molto li piaqueno*) (Kristeller, 1902, p.544, doc.96; Luzio & Paribeni, 1940, p.7; Martindale, 1979, p.181, doc.1).

From June 1488 to September 1490 Mantegna was in Rome.

2) 1489, 31 January. Mantegna in Rome to Marchese Francesco in Mantua. 'I recommend my Triumphs to Your Excellency: if any repairs are made to the windows, let them not be spoiled, for in truth I am not ashamed to have painted them and I still have hopes of painting others if it please God and Your Lordship' (D'Arco, ii, p.20; Kristeller, 1902, p.546, doc.102).

3) 1489, 23 February. Marchese Francesco in Mantua to Mantegna in Rome. Francesco would be pleased if Mantegna could expedite the Pope's commissions, for he will remember that he has works entrusted to him by the Marchese to finish here in Mantua, most especially the *Triumphs*, which, as he says, are an excellent work and one the Marchese would be very glad to see complete (*di qua anche haueti de lopere nostre ad finire, et maxime li triumphi: quali, come vui diceti, e cosa digna et nui voluntieri li vederressimo finiti*). Good order has been taken that they be well preserved, because if for Mantegna they are the works of his hand and talent, Francesco is no less proud of having them in his house where they will also be a record of Mantegna's loyalty and art (Kristeller, 1902, p.546, doc.103; Martindale, 1979, p.181, doc.3).

4) 1491, 16 July. Bernardo Ghisolfo to Marchese Francesco. Work has begun on the loggia and *solaro* at Marmirolo. Francesco Mantegna and Tondo Tondi will begin work together on the triumphs and think it best to paint them on canvas as Messer Andrea Mantegna has done, and they say that by doing so they will work more quickly and the canvases will be more beautiful and more durable, and in this every expert in this art agrees with them (Kristeller, 1902, p.550, doc.111; Martindale, 1979, p.182, doc.4).

Two letters of 1507 exchanged between Gian Francesco Vigilio and the Marchese Francesco (printed in Luzio & Paribeni, 1940, pp.16–17) evidently refer to these *Trionfi* at Marmirolo and not to Mantegna's, as is sometimes wrongly assumed. From Ulisse Aldrovandi's description of Mantua of c.1580 (printed in *La Scienza a Corte: collezionismo eclettico natura e immagine a Mantova fra*

Rinascimento e Manierismo, by A. Zanca and others, Rome, 1979, pp.194, 237) it appears that they depicted the *Triumphs of Alexander*: 'in loco nuncupato Marmirolo . . . Aula magna depicta cum historia triumphi Alexandri Magni ab Ecc.ti Mantegna.'

5) 1492, 15 February. The preamble to Francesco's deed granting land at Borgoforte mentions among Mantegna's works which have deserved reward 'the triumph of Julius Caesar, which he is now painting for us with figures that are almost alive and near breathing, inasmuch as the action seems to be happening rather than to be represented' (*que modo Iulij Caesaris triumphum prope vivis et spirantibus adhuc imaginibus nobis pingit adeo ut nec repraesentari sed fieri res videatur*) (Kristeller, 1902, p.551, doc.115; Martindale, 1979, p.182, doc.6).

This is the last known reference to the *Triumphs* as still in course of execution.

6) 1492, 10 December. Antimaco writes to Isabella d'Este from Mantua that 'everything beautiful in the town is being shown to the [Venetian] ambassador: he has already seen the *spalliera*, the *Camera depincta*, the little chapel [*capeletta*] and the things of Messer Andrea Mantegna, viz. the triumphs and his other delightful works.' (Martindale, 1979, p.182, doc.6.)

7) 1494, 2 March. Isabella d'Este in Mantua to Marchese Francesco. Giovanni di Pierfrancesco de' Medici came here this morning to dine, and she has lodged him in the palace. After dinner he came to visit her: she caressed him greatly and showed him the Camera and the Triumphs (Luzio & Renier, 1893, p.69n; Kristeller, 1902, p.554, doc.123; Martindale, 1979, p.182, doc.9).

8) 1497, 14 January. Fedele da Forlì in Mantua to Marchese Francesco. He is busy with preparations for the feast. Would it not be better to cover the courtyard of the palace with a wooden ceiling rather than with the canvas one which Lodovico Gonzaga proposes. Since Francesco intends to exhibit the Triumphs and many other precious ornaments among the decorations, if it were to rain they would be at risk (Luzio & Paribeni, 1940, p.10; Martindale, 1979, p.183, doc.12).

9) 1501, 13 February. Sigismondo Cantelmo in Mantua to Ercole d'Este in Ferrara. One of the sides of the temporary theatre erected by the Marchese and Marchesa for the acting of classical comedies was decorated with the six paintings of the Triumph of Caesar by the hand of the unique Mantegna (*Una delle bande era ornata delle sei quadri del Cesareo triumpho per man del singulare Mantengha*) (Campori, *Lettere artistiche inedite*, 1866, p.5; Luzio & Paribeni, 1940, pp.12–15, better transcription). From the context it appears that the side ornamented with the *Triumphs* was one of the long sides decorated with eight blind arches in which the *Triumphs* were hung.

UNCERTAIN REFERENCES: Two letters of 1494 from Teofilo Collenuccio to Marchese Francesco describing the decoration of a '*palazzina vostra*' (Kristeller, 1902, pp.555, docs.124, 125) and mentioning two *Triumphs* (*li doj Triomphi*) are wrongly associated by Kristeller (1901, p.290), followed by other scholars, with the Gonzaga palace in Mantua and with Mantegna's *Triumphs*. Expressions in the two letters make it clear that they refer to a small palace outside Mantua. Mantegna painted a picture expressly for this '*palazzina*': this work, it is again clear from the letters, was a single independent composition (see Cat. no.83). That the *palazzina* was probably Gonzaga seems to be confirmed by a letter of 14 February 1503 to the Marchese Francesco from Giovanni Maria Turotto in Gonzaga concerning 'li tellari de li triumphi . . . che sono qua' (Martindale, 1979, p.183, doc.15; cf. also doc.16). For other *trionfi* by Francesco Mantegna and Tondo Tondi at Marmirolo see above: these were evidently movable, as were those at Gonzaga, since there was question of bringing them in to Mantua as theatre decorations in 1506 (Martindale, 1979, p.184, doc.20).

1) 1505, 11 January. Il Milanese writes to the Marchese Francesco suggesting that in order to decorate the palace for a play the canvases (*telari*) at Gonzaga should be sent for and also Mantegna should be asked for his (*chel se dimandino li soi al mantegna*). Printed by Martindale (1979, pp.33, 184) who rightly points out that it is uncertain whether the *Triumphs of Caesar* are meant.

2) 1506, 31 December. The Marchese Francesco, writing from Gonzaga about the decorations for a play, says that the 'triumphs at Mantua' can be used (Martindale, 1979, p.184).

3) 1507, 20 May. Fra Mariano da Gonzaga, writing from Rome to the Marchese Francesco, asks him to commend him 'to the triumphs likewise of Andrea Mantegna', and especially to 'the little picture (*quadretto*) opposite us when we sat at the play' (Martindale, 1979, p.184).

EARLY DESCRIPTIONS AND REFERENCES:

I. *Before removal to Palazzo San Sebastiano*

1) Pomponius Gauricus, *De sculptura*, 1504 (colophon dated 25 December, text composed in 1503), 1969 ed., p.101. With reference to Giulio Campagnola's copies after Mantegna, Gauricus writes, 'Laudatur Iulius noster quod Palladiam illam Mantenii nostri turbam, Caesareosque triumphos tam bellissime sit imitatus.'

Campagnola's skill in copying Mantegna while yet a boy of about thirteen is lauded in a letter of octavo. Kal decembris (24 November) 1495 by Matteo Bosso, *Epistolae*, Mantua, 1498, No.86, f.h.viv: 'Quid quod stilo atque peniculo claros ita aemulatur pictores: ut uix ulla uel Mantineae uel Bellini imago tam porro sit elegans: quam si in mentem induxerit atque contenderit non examussim effingat, & propius aequet.'

II. *After removal to Palazzo San Sebastiano*

1) 1512, 11 December. Marchese Francesco writes from Mantua to the Archdeacon of Mantua that he has given a solemn feast to Francesco Sforza, Duke of Milan, and to his gentlemen 'in la sala di triumphi di Cesar qui a. s.to sebastiano' (Martindale, p.184, doc.22A).

2) 1515, 3 November. Letter from Amicoma della Torre to Federico Gonzaga describing a visit by the Venetian ambassadors to Palazzo San Sebastiano where they particularly admired 'li Triumphi di messer Andrea mantinea . . .' (Martindale, p.183, doc.23).

3) 1515, 6 November. The above is confirmed by a letter from Piero Soranzo to Marco Contarini (in Sanuto, *Diarii*, xxi, 1887, col.279) recording that 'intrati nel palazo, era adornato con bellissime depenture da la spaliera in su forte bellissime di man dil Mantegna.'

4) *Novella trentesima* 'Diversi detti salsi de la viziosa e lorda vita d'un archidiacono mantovano' in Matteo Bandello, *Le novelle*, ed. G. Brognoligo, i, 1928, pp.412–19. The story

reflects Bandello's experiences during his service at the court of Mantua from 1515 to 1522. 'Fu domandato dapoi fuor di camera e andò in sala ove sono dipinti i divini trionfi di Giulio Cesare imperadore di mano d'Andrea Mantegna, con tanti altri bellissimi quadri di pittura eccelentissima.'

6) Mario Equicola, *Chronica di Mantva*, 10 July 1521, f. V7 (1608 edn, p.212). '*Vedemo . . . Nel ultima Parte dela cita, propinquo alla chiesa di san sebastiano palazo superbissimo edificio & bello, per securamente collocare in una salla ad solo questo effecto fabricata, lo triumpho de. C. Iulio Cesare fatiga de molti anni di misser Andrea Mantegna. parea dicto triumpho trunco & mutilato per non ui essere quella pompa che sequir solea il triumphante. Mancauanoui li spectatori, al che prouede Francesco prudentemente chiamando alla sua liberalita Lorenzo costa; homo non solamente in pictura excellentissimo, ma amabile & honorato cortegiano. Questo, oltra le altre laudate opere, con ingegno, arte, & scientia, de dicta bellissima sala il capo & fine adorna.*'

7) Sebastiano Serlio, *Libro Quarto di Architettura*, Venice, 1537, cap. X. '*e in questo fu molto aveduto, e ricco di giudicio messer Andrea Mantegna ne i triomphi di Cesare, ch'ei fece in Mantoua al liberalissimo Marchese Francesco Gonzaga: ne la quale opera per esser i piedi de le figure superiori a la veduta nostra non si vede pianura alcuna, ma le figure (come ho detto) posano sopra una linea, ma tanto bene accomodate che fanno l'ufficio suo mirabilmente. e certo questa pittura di che io parlo è da esser celebrata, e tenuta in pregio grande: ne la qual si vede profondità del disegno, la prospettiva artificiosa, la inventione mirabile, la innata discretione nel componimento de le figure, e la diligentia estrema nel finire.*'

8) Vasari, 1550, p.510: '*. . . al detto Marchese [Lodovico] per memoria dell' vno & dell' altro nel palazzo di San Sebastiano in Mantoua dipinse il triomfo di Cesare, intorno a vna sala, cosa di suo la migliore ch'e facesse gia mai. Quiui con ordine bellissimo situò nel trionfo la bellezza & l'ornamento del carro: colui che vitupera il trionfante, i parenti, i profumi, gli incensi, i sacrifizii & i sacerdoti i prigioni & le prede fatte per gli soldati, & l'ordinanza della squadre, & tutte le spoglie & le vittorie: & le citta & le rocche in vari carri contrafece con vna infinita di Trofei in su le aste, & varie armi per intesta & per indosso, acconciature, ornamenti & vasi infiniti; & tra le moltitudine de gli spettatori, vna donna che ha per la mano vn' putto che essendoseli fitto vna spina in vn piede, lo mostra alla madre & piagne, cosa bellissima & naturale. Et certo che in tutta questa opera pose il Mantegna gran diligenzia & fatica non punto piccola; non guardando ne a tempo ne a industria nel lauorare.*' 1568, p.490, as above, with some change of words and addition of two details, viz. 'il tori pel sacrificio coronati', 'i Liofanti'. Then continues: '*Costui, come potrei hauer accennato altroue hebbe in questa historia vna bella, e buona auertenza, che hauendo situato il piano doue posauano le figure, piu alto, che la ueduta, dell' occhio, fermò i piedi dinanzi in sul primo profilo, e linea del piano, facendo sfuggire gl' altri piu adentro di mano, in mano, & perder della veduta de piedi, & gamba, quanto richiedeua la ragione della veduta, & cosi delle spoglie, vasi, & altri istrumenti, & ornamenti: fece veder sola la parte di sotto, & perder quella di sopra, come di ragione di prospettiua si conueniua di fare.*'

9) Simone Fornari da Reggio, *La Spositione sopra l'Orlando Furioso*, ii, Florence, 1550, p.509: '*Fra l'altre sue molte dipinture è molto lodato quella, che egli nel palazzo di San*

Sebastiano in Mantova ripresentando il triompho di Cesare dipinse.'

10) Scardeone, 1560, pp.372–3. *'Pinxit autem ibi [at Mantua] triumphos Caesaris in septem tabulis arte stupenda, & admirabili judicio, et alias laudatissimas tabellas aeneas, incisas formis ad effingendos Romanos triumphos.'*

11) Vasari, 1568, p.424, records in his life of Lorenzo Costa: *'Dipinse ancora nella sala grande, dove hoggi sono i trionfi di mano del Mantegna, due quadri, cioè in ciascuna testa uno.'*

12) Ulisse Aldrovandi, c.1580. In his *Itineraria Mantuae*, Aldrovandi describes a visit to the 'Praetorium famosi artificis Andreae Mantengae picturis decoratum in quo cernuntur eius septem tabulae peramplae in quibus Caesaris dictatoris triumphus gallicus arte tam excellenti depictus est ut celeberrima Italiae pictorum tabulae illae referantur' (*La scienza a corte: collezionismo eclettico natura e immagine a Mantova fra Rinascimento e Manierismo*, by A. Zanca and others, 1979, p.237, doc.60).

13) Blaise de Vigenère, *La somptueuse et magnifique entrée du . . . Roy Henry III . . . en la cité de Mantoue*, Paris, 1576, p.21 (describing the visit of Henri III of France to Mantua in 1574): *'Or tout ioignant cette porte de la Pisterle, y a un fort beau palais appellé sainct Sebastian, ouquel dans une salle ou gallerie haulte se voient douze tableaux des triomphes de Cesar, faicts de la main du bon maistre André Mantegne, qu'on tient pour le plus beau et accomply chef d'oeuvre de platte peincture qui soit pour le iordhuy en toute la terre, de sorte qu'ayant l'ouvrier laisse tout expres quelque chose à parachever en l'un des chevaux qui tient le char triomphal, il ne s'est onques depuis trouvé homme qui ait osé entreprendre d'y mettre la main pour le parfaire.'*

14) Raffaelle Toscano, *L'edificatione di Mantova*, 1587, p.27.

> *Di figure diuerse, adorne, e belle*
> *Quest' el palazzo in bell' ordin distinto*
> *Doue son sette Tauole, & in quelle*
> *Il trionfo di cesare è dipinto*
> *Con magistero tal, chel grande Apelle*
> *Ne resta, e Zeusi superato, e uinto . . .*

15) L. Schraderus, *Monvmentorvm Italiae quae hoc nostro saeculo & a Christianis posita sunt libri qvatvor*, Helmstadt, 1592, p.335. 'Praetorium nobilissimis picturis And: Mantognae decoratum est, & extant in illo tabulae VII. quibus triumphus Caesaris excellentissima arte est expressus.' Schraderus also gives a copy of the inscriptions (p.343): 'In Palatio DVCIS.

AD DEPICTVM IVLII CAESARIS TRIVMPHVM

D. Iulij Caesaris, ob inuidiam constanter superatam, & hostes fortiter deuictos, duplex victoria: VENI, VIDI, VICI

    SPQR Liberatori vrbis   SPQR. Iulius Caesar P.M.
    SPQR Iulio Caesari dict.   PPP

Imperatori Iulio Caesari ob Galliam deuictam militari potentia triumphus decretus, inuidia spreta superataque.

16) Hentzner, *Itinerarivm*, 1612, p.388, describing a visit in April 1600: 'Praetorium Andreae Mantengae famosi artificis nobilissimis picturis decoratum; in quo cernuntur septem eius tabulae peramplae, in quibus Caesaris Dictatoris Triumphus Gallicus arte tam excellenti depictus est, ut inter celeberrima praeclarissimaque summorum pictorum opera merito censeri queat' (compare Aldrovandi, No. 12, above).

PATRON AND CIRCUMSTANCES OF THE COMMISSION: According to Sebastiano Serlio (1538) and Andrea Andreani (1599), the *Triumphs of Caesar* were commissioned by Francesco Gonzaga who succeeded as Marchese in July 1484. Recently Martindale (1979, pp.42–6) has argued that they were commissioned by his grandfather the Marchese Lodovico c.1474–8. Vasari (1550) certainly says this, but his evidence on the point is not reliable: thus he also says they were painted for Lodovico (d.1478) to decorate Palazzo San Sebastiano, which was only begun after 1502. Most probably he made a slip of the pen: Francesco Gonzaga himself speaks of them as *'opere nostre'* that remain to be finished in his letter of 23 February 1489 to Mantegna in Rome (Kristeller, 1902, p.546). Martindale supports his argument by claiming that the first canvases of the *Triumphs* are contemporary with the two panels in Klagenfurt (see text, p.131) decorated with reliefs of the *Justice of Trajan* (Plates 251a and b), which can be dated c.1476–7 because they originate from two wedding *cassoni* made for Barbara Gonzaga on the occasion of her marriage in 1477 with Leonhard, Count of Görz. These undoubtedly derive from designs by Mantegna, but in conception and style they belong to an earlier phase of his art and bear no relation to the advanced style of the *Triumphs*.

Martindale's argument that only Lodovico possessed 'the cultural interests and classical attainments' to commission the *Triumphs*, while Francesco was comparatively unlettered cannot be sustained. In fact (see text, p.142) Triumphs were among Francesco's favourite themes for paintings. Moreover, it is now known that the *Triumphs* painted on canvas for the decoration of Marmirolo depicted the triumphs of Alexander. As this series was conceived only in 1491, there can be no doubt that it was commissioned by the Marchese Francesco. It cannot reasonably be argued that the degree of culture required to commission triumphs of Caesar exceeds that required to commission triumphs of Alexander. Besides the examples cited in the text, Francesco's *camarino* at Gonzaga was decorated with two *trionfi* which were ready for hanging in 1494 (Martindale, 1979, p.183). Furthermore, in 1492 Bonsignori was busy painting for Francesco a *Trionfo de la Fama* which included a portrait of the Marchese's great-grandfather Giovanfrancesco (see Martindale, 1979, p.182) and probably of other Gonzaga as well.

DATING AND LOCATION: Martindale (1979, pp.42–6, 75–91) advances the inception of the *Triumphs* to c.1474–8, in order to fit his theory that they were commissioned by Lodovico Gonzaga. This date is too early (see above) and the true date is probably shortly after Mantegna's letter to Lorenzo de' Medici of 26 August 1484 (Kristeller, 1902, p.542, No.88), in which he is still doubtful of patronage from the newly succeeded Francesco. Martindale also argues (*op. cit.*, p.43) that each of the canvases would have taken Mantegna about a year to paint, on the analogy of the *Madonna della Vittoria* (see Cat. no.36). This was begun and completed within the ten months from 30 August 1495 to 6 July 1496 and is smaller than the individual canvases of the *Triumphs*. However, it is by no means certain that Mantegna spent the whole of these ten months designing and painting the *Madonna della Vittoria*. We know that the subject-matter of the

Madonna underwent fresh modification after 30 August 1495 and that the picture was probably not actually designed or begun before November 1495, and probably even later. A speedier rate of working is therefore virtually certain. We should remember that between June 1488 and January 1490 Mantegna not only evolved designs for the decoration of the entire Belvedere chapel (see Cat. no.29) but largely completed the work, though it included four major figure-compositions, in at least two of which the figures were life-size, and several smaller histories together with figures of saints and Virtues and many ornamental motifs. It is equally difficult to accept Martindale's time-scheme for the *Triumphs*. He argues that they were begun *c.*1474, that six canvases were completed by the time of the death of Marchese Federigo in 1484, that the tonality of canvases IV and V indicates a later dating for them, perhaps *c.*1484–8, and that Canvases VI and VII were executed after Mantegna's return from Rome in September 1490.

It has been shown above that the *Triumphs* were begun under the Marchese Francesco, *c.*1484–5. Some of them were certainly completed by June 1488, otherwise Mantegna's letter of 31 January 1489 asking the Marchese to take care of the *Triumphs* and saying that he still hopes to paint others is meaningless. Mantegna was still working on the series in February 1492. By 2 March 1494, however, they were being shown to Giovanni de' Medici as a finished work (Kristeller, 1902, p.551, doc.115; Martindale, 1979, p.182, doc.9: summarized as Documents 6 and 7 above).

As regards the original number of canvases contemplated see the text (pp.148–9) for arguments that they were to have been ten in all, but that the series was left unfinished, as indeed Equicola (1521) testifies. Martindale (1979, pp.64–5,86) argues for more. The problem of the original extent of the series is linked to the problem of the setting for which it was originally designed. No document has yet appeared which unequivocally records either the setting for which they were first intended or the room or place in the Castello or elsewhere in the Gonzaga Corte in which they were housed before seven of them were installed *c.*1507 in Palazzo San Sebastiano (see below). Paccagnini (*Il Palazzo Ducale di Mantova*, 1969, pp.86–9), who believes that the *Triumphs* were to have been eleven in all, argues that they were designed for the great *sala* of the Castello. The *sala* was illuminated by three windows overlooking the courtyard of the Castello, and Paccagnini suggests that the *Triumphs* were hung around the other three walls, above the door level, and so at about six feet above the ground. This height would correspond to the viewpoint above eye-level assumed in the compositions. But his suggested number of eleven canvases would involve an asymmetrical disposition of the *Triumphs* around the walls of the *sala* and is therefore unacceptable. Martindale (1979, pp.34–42) argues that the *Triumphs* were intended to decorate the corridor or gallery known as the *Corridoio del Passerino* in the Palazzo della Corte. This corridor, however, was divided up in the fourteenth century into small rooms and is not known to have been reopened before the creation of the Appartamento della Guastalla in the seventeenth century. Martindale (1979, pp.35n,95n) has shown that the *sala*

of the Castello was often decorated with a *spalliera* that was exhibited to distinguished visitors at their own request. This *spalliera*, contrary to the usual assumption, was certainly a hanging of some sort, for a letter of 1 September 1492 (Luzio, 1913, p.25, n.1) says that it will be shown '*destesa*' (spread out). Evidently it was not kept permanently on view, since it had to be brought out, unrolled and hung up for inspection. The presumption is, then, that it was a rich and valuable textile hanging, not a leather hanging, as is generally believed. The term *spalliera* is used in the fifteenth-century documents which mention it in connection with the *sala*, as opposed to the term *tapezarie* (tapestries) used for the hangings of other rooms. This usage indicates that it rose only to shoulder height, which is the literal connotation of the term *spalliera*. Presumably then it served as a textile dado, of the sort often simulated in fifteenth-century painting, which was hung up around the lower part of the walls of the *sala* on special occasions. In considering the potential relationship of the *spalliera* and the *Triumphs* it should be born in mind that later in Palazzo San Sebastiano the *Triumphs* were mounted 'above the *spalliera* (*da la spaliera in su*, see DESCRIPTION II, 3). The first mention of the *spalliera* is in the same letter of 24 August 1486 in which Silvestro Calandra tells the Marchese Francesco that Ercole d'Este, after seeing it, dined, then went boating on the lake, but, feeling indisposed, came back to land and went to see the *Triumphs* Mantegna was painting. The association of his inspection of the *spalliera* and the *Triumphs* may not be fortuitous. It could well be that having seen a rich hanging purchased to decorate the lower part of the walls of the *sala*, he went on to see the canvases proposed for its decoration above. See text (pp.149–50).

Martindale (1979, pp.35, 128–9) has claimed that the nine canvases we have fall into groups of three, the first three forming one group, the next a second, and the last three a third, and that 'some more substantial interruption occurred after every third painting.' Correctly, however, he makes the reservation that Canvas VII forms an acknowledged dissonance in the composition of its group, raising the question of whether one or more canvases were originally to have been added to the nine. It was Kristeller (1901, p.283) who first suggested that the canvases were intended to be mounted on a single long wall, and Martindale (1979, pp.34–42) buttresses this argument, which supports his hypothesis about the original location of the *Triumphs*, by the observation that the light 'though almost frontal, has a slight bias towards the spectator's left.'

The drawing for the 'Senators' (see Plate 119) can be cited as evidence for the incompleteness of the *Triumphs* as we have them, as can the signs that Mantegna never quite finished one of the last three canvases (No. VII), to be taken with the testimony of Blaise de Vigenère (see above) that already in the sixteenth century visitors were told that Mantegna had not finished No. IX. We have no evidence for the internal dating of the sequence, and Martindale (1979, pp.66, 129–30, 147) points to inconsistencies in the treatment of the landscape in Canvases IV and V and Canvases VIII and IX which suggest that these never received their final touches. A plausible hypothesis might be that the first six *Triumphs* were painted between *c*.1485 and June 1488, before Mantegna's journey to Rome, and the last three between September 1490 and December 1492, after his return to Mantua, and that work on these three was abandoned before they were quite finished, i.e. rather abruptly.

The proposal of M. Vickers (in *B.M.*, cxx, 1978, pp.365–71) to associate the *Battle of the Sea-Gods* and the *Bacchanals* with the scheme of the *Triumphs*, made on the ground that these engravings record lost large-scale compositions, is rightly refuted by C. Hope and E. McGrath and by Martindale (in *B.M.*, *vol. cit.*, pp.603, 675). See also Martindale, 1979, p.42, n.6.

LATER HISTORY: This too is far from simple, although some facts are clear. Francesco Gonzaga decided to transfer the *Triumphs* to his new palace of San Sebastiano, also known as Palazzo della Pusterla (for this see Marani, 1961, pp.184–5, 192–3). They are known to have been installed in the Sala Grande, on the first floor of the palace, by 1512 (see DESCRIPTION II, 1). This room, according to Equicola, was specially built to give them safe housing. The building of the palace was nearing completion in 1506, and a letter of 5 November 1506 tells Francesco, who pressed on the work with great energy, that 'De le casa tuta e fenita de soto e se comencio a lavorar di sopra ala sala' (Martindale, 1979, p.93). The decoration of the palace was also well under way by 24 September 1506, when Isabella d'Este wrote to her husband: 'Sono stata ad vedere gli allogiamenti novi de Sancto Sebastiano, che sono molto belli et quelle picture compareno mirabilmente' (D'Arco, ii, p.68; Kristeller, 1902, p.583, doc.189), and Lorenzo Costa was working there in April 1507 (Venturi, 'Lorenzo Costa' in *Archivio storico dell' arte*, i, 1888, pp.251–2). An unsigned letter of 17 April 1506 to the Marchese Francesco, then in Venice, speaks of 'pilasters for the canvases of Messer Andrea'. One of these pilasters was already gilt, one was ready to be inlaid, two were nearly finished and two were roughed out. The master who was making them could not promise when he would finish them, but would finish them quickly. According to Yriarte (*Cosmopolis*, v, 1897, p.746) they were designed by Francesco Mantegna (he cites, but does not print, a document which he claimed showed this).

D'Arco (ii, p.64) associates these pilasters with the *Triumphs* as a commission for their framework. In this he is almost certainly correct, both because six pilasters in the Lombard-Venetian style of *c*.1500 are shown on one of the sheets of Andrea Andreani's set of woodcuts of Mantegna's *Triumphs*, made in 1598 and published in 1599, and because of one other significant fact. There is a disparity between the six pilasters specified and the number of the *Triumphs*, which would have required eight had all nine canvases been transferred to San Sebastiano. But there is concordant testimony from five sixteenth-century authors that only seven of them were to be seen in San Sebastiano. Accordingly Equicola's testimony of 1521 that the *sala* was specially constructed to house the *Triumphs* should be carefully interpreted, as Francesco evidently selected only seven of them. They must have been set in a framework of pilasters, most probably on a long wall above a dado, as suggested by Martindale (1979, p.95).

Among the canvases installed in the *sala* were certainly Nos. I. *The Standard-Bearers*, II. *Bearers of statues . . .*, IV. *Bearers of golden vessels . . .*, VII. *Captives,* and IX. *Julius Caesar*, since the inscriptions on these are recorded by Schraderus in 1592 (see DESCRIPTION II, 15). According to Equicola, as we have seen, it was Francesco's intention to employ Lorenzo Costa to complete the sequence of the *Triumphs* with the procession that followed Caesar and the spectators. In fact he commissioned from Costa a painting 'a guazzo' (tempera, so as to match Mantegna's), evidently huge, of many naked men lighting fires and sacrificing to Hercules, with his own life-size portrait and life-size portraits of his three sons, Federigo, Ercole and Ferrante. This is now lost, but must have been painted at least two or three years after the birth of Ferrante in 1506, and before Francesco's death in 1519. A second painting by Costa, in oil, signed and dated 1522, which is the same height and twice the length of the *Triumph* canvases, depicts Federico Gonzaga holding the *bastone* of Captain-General of the Church, an appointment he received in 1520–1 (Prague, National Gallery, see Plate 256). Martindale rightly points out that this picture seems ingeniously devised to represent Equicola's 'pompa che sequir solea il triumphante'. The lost painting by Costa may therefore have been intended, among other meanings, to represent spectators of the triumph, and so would have opened the sequence, as Costa's later painting would have closed it. These pictures by Costa are known to have been set at the head and foot of the room, that is, on its shorter walls (Vasari, 1568, p.424).

On this reconstruction, only seven of the original *Triumphs* were taken to San Sebastiano, and these were selected so as to leave room for the first and last scenes which would open and close the series in a manner more historically accurate and with more explicit laudation of the Gonzaga than Mantegna's original conception. It will be noted that the canvases still remained nine in all, a fact which tends to confirm the hypothesis advanced above that nine was always the total number executed of the series. The two not moved to the *sala* at San Sebastiano presumably were housed elsewhere in the Gonzaga palaces or at San Sebastiano itself. Vigenère, it is true, mentions twelve paintings, but this figure probably comprises all the paintings, including those by Costa, that Henri III and his suite saw in the *sala*.

By 1626 the seven *Triumphs* together with the pictures by Costa had been brought back to the Palazzo Ducale. The inventory of January 1627 (D'Arco, p.158; Luzio, 1913, p.105) lists nine *Triumphs* as in the Galleria della Mostra: '213. Nove quadri grandi dipintovi li trionfi di Cesare, di mano del Mantegna, stimati scudi 150 l'uno, L.8100.' In the autumn of 1627 Vincenzo II installed them in a special apartment, and excluded them from the sale of the Mantua pictures to Charles I. However, Vincenzo's successor, Carlo I, sold them in 1629 to Daniel Nys of Venice, who had acted as the King's agent in the earlier sale (Luzio, 1913, pp.75–8, 147, 159–67). The exact date at which they reached England is unknown. They were hung at Hampton Court where they were listed in the Parliamentary inventory of October 1649 as for sale at a valuation of £1000. They were, however, reserved from sale (Millar, 1972, pp.186, xx), and have remained at Hampton Court ever since (for their vicissitudes see Law, *Mantegna's Triumph of Julius Caesar*, 1921, and Martindale, 1979, pp.109–22).

SOURCES: 1) *Literary*. Of ancient authors, Mantegna can be shown to have used, directly or indirectly, Livy, Appian (triumph of Scipio Africanus in *Romaica*, viii, trans. Pier Candido Decembrio in 1453, printed in Latin, Venice, 1477), Josephus, *The Jewish Wars*, VIII, c.36 (printed in Latin, Rome, 1475), Suetonius (see below; printed Rome, 1470) and Plutarch. In the fifteenth century three important discussions of Roman triumphs, collecting references from ancient authors, were compiled. One of these, Giovanni Marcanova's *De dignitatibus Romanorum triumpho et rebus bellicis*, is now lost, but must have been written before 1465 (Martindale, 1979, pp.51, 58, n.2). Its loss is to be deplored, given its author's possible relationship with Mantegna. The others are Flavio Biondo's *Roma triumphans*, composed in 1457–9, and printed in 1472 (at Mantua?), and Valturio's *De re militari*, composed in 1460, printed at Verona in the original Latin in 1472 and again in Italian and Latin in 1483. The references in Josephus, Appian and Suetonius are tabulated by Martindale (1979, pp.178–80).

2) *Visual*. There has been much discussion of these: for an able summary see Martindale (1979, pp.68–73). See also LITERATURE below.

ICONOGRAPHY: Caesar triumphed for the first time as dictator in 45 BC. He held four triumphs after defeating the younger Scipios in Africa, all in the same month, but on separate days, and a fifth after his victory over the younger Pompeys in Spain. The first four triumphs celebrated his victory in the Gallic wars, his victory in the Alexandrian campaign, his victory over Pharnaces, King of Pontus, and his victory over the younger Scipios and King Juba in Africa. There has been some disagreement over which and how many of these triumphs are represented in Mantegna's paintings. Tamassia ('Visioni di antichità nell' opera del Mantegna' in *Rendiconti della P. Accademia Romana di Archeologia*, ser.3, xxviii, 1955–6, p.243) suggests that the *Triumphs* represent all five of Caesar's triumphs. This view is rejected by Martindale (1979, pp.17, 58), who claims however that they represent only the first and, according to Suetonius, the most magnificent of these triumphs, the Gallic triumph. It is universally agreed that Mantegna used Suetonius as his historical source for Caesar's triumphs since it is Suetonius alone who records that Caesar used elephants in the Gallic triumph, and also that the *titulus* VENI, VIDI, VICI was carried in the Pontic triumph. The passage (*Divus Iulius*, 37) runs: '*Confectis bellis quinquiens triumphavit, post devictum Scipionem quater eodem mense, sed interiectis diebus, et rursus semel post superatos Pompei liberos. Primum et excellentissimum triumphum egit Gallicum, sequentem Alexandrinum, deinde Ponticum, huic proximum Africanum, novissimum Hispaniensem, diverso quemque apparatu et instrumento. Gallici triumphi die Velabrum praetervehens paene curru excussus est, axe diffracto, ascenditque Capitolium ad lumina, quadraginta elephantis dextra atque sinistra lychnuchos gestantibus. Pontico triumpho inter pompae fercula trium verborum praetulit titulum veni, vidi, vici non acta belli significantem, sicut ceteris, sed celeriter confecti notam.*'

Clearly the first part of the procession up to VIII represents the Gallic triumph as is indicated by the inscription on II. On VIII a smaller procession is opened by an Asiatic musician and on IX a man appears bearing the *titulus* VENI VIDI VICI. This second part must therefore represent the Pontic triumph. Hence the *Triumphs* are a conflation of the Gallic and Pontic triumphs, which are in fact the only two about which Suetonius gives historical details. This interpretation is supported by the inscription recorded in Schraderus (1592) but which has now disappeared: 'D. Iulii Caesaris, ob invidiam constanter superatam & hostes fortiter devictos, duplex victoria': followed by VENI, VIDI, VICI. The *duplex victoria* (double victory) can only refer to the Gallic and Pontic triumphs. It may also be that these two triumphs were chosen as the only two not contaminated by civil war: however, the absolute certainty of the exclusion of the others cannot be established, for if they are alluded to in the long inscription of Canvas IX (see entry above), then clearly the *Triumphs* represent all five of Caesar's actual triumphs, but allusively rather than literally. Only the Gallic and Pontic triumphs are shown reasonably fully, and Mantegna must have selected these two as the most picturesque and exotic, the least liable to create confusion between soldiers and captives and the only two for which authentic historical information was available, and built up the other motifs from details drawn from Plutarch's description of the triumph of Aemilius Paulus and Appian's description of the triumph of Scipio Africanus, probably as interpreted by Flavio Biondo and Valturio.

LITERATURE: The sources, literary and visual, of the *Triumphs* are discussed by Portheim (in *Rep. f. K.*, ix, 1886, pp.266–80, fundamental); Giehlow (in *Vienna Jahrbuch*, xxxii, 1915, pp.88–94, introduces Valturio); Wiesbach (*Trionfi*, 1919, pp.41–8); Blum (1936, pp.68–86); Luzio & Paribeni (1940); Tamassia (1956, pp.244–9). The composition of the reliefs is discussed with his usual eloquent acumen by Kristeller (1901, pp.283–97): less interesting are the observations of Fiocco (1937, pp.60–3) and Tietze-Conrat (1955, pp.21–3, 183–4). An attempt by Waterhouse (in *B.M.*, lxiv, 1934, pp.103–7) to rearrange the traditional order of the pictures is conjectural and unconvincing. The *Triumphs* have recently been accorded a full study by Martindale (1979): especially worthy of note is his investigation of Mantegna's literary and visual sources (pp.56–74).

COPIES: Because of the damage and heavy restoration endured by the *Triumphs*, early copies, whether paintings, engravings or drawings, have some importance. Problems also arise concerning the status of the engravings and drawings.

1) *Early references*. The *Triumphs* immediately became famous. They were copied between 1497 and 1503 by Giulio Campagnola, and by 1509–10 copies were sculptured on one of the façades of the Château de Gaillon. Weiss (see Cat. no.87) notes that these must have derived from drawings of the originals. The Venetian collector Gabriele Vendramin (d.1547) owned a book of drawings which included the *Triumphs* (inventory of 1567–9, pub. Ravà, in *Nuovo Archivio Veneto*, n.s. xxxix, 1920, p.175: 'Un altro libro longo coverto di cuoro rosso de 37 carte

computado li Trionfi del Mantegna dissegnade a mano.').
2) *Painted copies.* A number of these were executed in Mantua by Lodovico Dondi in the early seventeenth century. Five from one set (corresponding to Nos. II, IV, VI, VII, IX) signed and dated 1602 by Dondi are in the Alte Pinakotek, Munich (copper, 19 × 18 cm.: Martindale, 1979, pp.103–4, figs.98–102). Another set commissioned from Dondi by Duke Vincenzo I was paid for in 1614 (Luzio, 1913, p.105). Four copies from a set by an anonymous hand (ex Galleria Spannochi, Siena) are in the Pinacoteca, Siena (oil on copper, 21 × 19 cm., corresponding to Nos. I, II, IV, V; Martindale, 1979, p.103, figs.104–7). A set executed in grisaille on paper on canvas (38 × 38 cm.), from the collection of Archduke Leopold Wilhelm, governor of the Low Countries from 1646 to 1656, is in the Kunsthistorisches Museum, Vienna (Martindale, 1979, p.104, figs.78–86). These copies have been attributed to the painter Bernardo Malpizio and linked with Andreani's woodcuts of 1598–9 which have some association with Malpizio (Portheim, 'Andrea Mantegna's Triumph Cäsar's' in *Repertorium für Kunstwissenschaft*, ix, 1886, pp.279–80; Martindale, 1979, pp.104–6) with which they share a number of differences from the other copies (but see Martindale's tabulation of the variations from the originals among the copies, p.107).

On the sale of the *Triumphs*, Daniel Nys undertook to replace them with a set of full-scale copies, to be executed in Venice (Luzio, 1913, p.157). Two full-scale copies with a provenance from the Manin Coll., Venice, were in the Cernazai sale (Udine, 24–31 October 1900) but are now untraced (Martindale, 1979, p.103). A series of copies in fresco was discovered during the demolition of a Mantuan palace (Via Mazzini, 16) in 1926, restored and transferred to the Palazzo Ducale (Luzio & Paribeni, 1940, pp.31–9, repr. pls.x–xvi; Martindale, 1979, pp.104–6, figs.108–16). Their date has been disputed. That now inscribed on them reads MDCLXXIII. Luzio claimed that this date had been painted over an earlier date, which he read as MDCXXVIII or MDLXXVIII. Luzio, who believed the series had been commissioned by Monsignor Tullio Petrozzani, a sixteenth-century dignitary of the Gonzaga court, to whom the palace had belonged, preferred the earlier date (1578). Fiocco (in *Boll. M.C.P.*, 1939–40, pp.186 ff) favoured the reading 1628, while Paccagnini (1961, p.47) unequivocally preferred to read 1674 (sic 1673?). Martindale inclines to think they were painted before the originals left Mantua in 1629. Free copies of three of the *Triumphs* were also made by Rubens (Rooses, iii, p.208, Nos.715–17).

Copies of single canvases. 1) Formerly in the Northwick Coll. (Waagen, iii, 1854, p.201, as by a Venetian artist; Northwick sale, Thirlestane House, Cheltenham, 26 July and days following, 1859, lot 1575; Crowe & Cavalcaselle, 1871, p.416). 2) Brescia, Pinacoteca Tosio e Martinengo (*Catalogo*, 1927, No.25 (131): oil on panel, 18.5 × 19.5 cm., attributed to a sixteenth-century Mantuan artist). Copy of No. VII (*The Captives*).

Other copies recorded in documents. 1) Mantuan inventory of January 1627 (Luzio, 1913, pp.105,119): 'Nella Galaria della Mostra . . . 232. Un quadro copiato il trionfo di Cesare. L. 120 . . . Nella stanza detta la libraria . . . 399. Sedici quadertini sopra il rame, copiati li trionfi di Cesare,

con cornici fregiate d'oro, L. 192.' (Perhaps the series executed by Dondi in 1614? see above.); 2) Gonzaga di Novellara inventory of drawings *c.*1728 (Campori, 1870, p.645): 'Un trionfo in acquerello, alto on. 14 e largo 8., del *Mantegna*. dob. 5.'

3) *Engravings.* According to Scardeone (see above), besides painting the *Triumphs of Caesar* Mantegna engraved 'other greatly admired brazen tablets, engraved with contours to represent the Roman triumphs'. Scardeone seems to imply that these were different works from the *Triumphs of Caesar*. According to Vasari (1568, ii, p.491) Mantegna engraved the *Triumphs* himself (*fra l'altre cose fece i suoi trionfi*). Neither of the two known early engravings after the *Triumphs* which are attributed to Mantegna's school reproduces the finished compositions, and since the late nineteenth century it has been recognized that they were probably made after drawings by Mantegna. Hind (p.23) suggests that the incompleteness of the set makes it probable that they were not engraved under Mantegna's own direction, but by pirate engravers who contrived to get hold of some of his designs. The two engravings are of the *Elephants* (fifth scene: Hind, 14; for an early copy see Hind, 14a) and of the *Soldiers carrying trophies* (sixth scene: Hind, 15; for two early copies see Hind, 15a and b, the latter in reverse). Another Mantegnesque engraving (Hind, 16) reproduces a composition usually called *The Senators*, which seems in fact to show senators (first two files) followed by scribes (next three files) and shield-bearing soldiers, together with a boy (*puer*) between the files of senators and scribes. According to Valturio (*De re militari*, XII, 4; ed. of 1472, pp.356–7), the senate preceded the triumphal car: here they are introduced behind it. The rest of the scene illustrates Appian's description of the triumph of Scipio Africanus (in the translation of Piero Candido Decembrio: '*Vehebantur et cum eo pueri, virginesque . . . demum qui exercitum secuti fuerant scriptores: ministri: scutiferive*').

4) *Drawings.* For clarity these are arranged in the order of the canvases to which they relate.

Canvas I. Trumpeters and banner-carriers. Paris, Louvre, coll. Edmond de Rothschild, 775 DR, 26.5 × 26 cm., pen and brown ink. Identified by Kristeller (1901, p.441) as a copy after the original. Martindale (1979, p.163, fig.51) considers it an autograph study, on the ground of the tentative nature of some features and revisions in others. He also emphasizes the importance of the pilaster profiles outlined to the right and left as evidence of an architectural setting. Unique to this drawing, these seem to differ slightly in design: such differences, taken with the sketch-like modifications present in the drawing, lend support to his contention that this may be an original *modello* by Mantegna, and not a study made with a view to installing the *Triumphs* in Palazzo San Sebastiano. But the hatched background should be noted.

Canvas III. Trophies of arms and booty. Vienna, Albertina, No.2584, 26 × 26.1 cm., inscribed on margin at bottom 'Andrea Mantegna'. For Waagen (cit. Wickhoff, below) a copy of a Mantegna engraving: for Wickhoff (in *Vienna Jahrbuch*, xii, 1891, p.ccv, No.SL9) a copy of the Andreani woodcut. Martindale (1979, pp.78,164, No.53) argues that it is a copy of a preliminary study by Mantegna. Again, the hatched background should be noted.

Canvas V. The Elephants. Paris, private coll., 25.1 × 26 cm., brown ink, pen and wash. Published by Martindale (1979, p.164) as rather better than the engraving of this subject (Hind, 14, see above); in view of lines suggesting tracing on the surface, he suggests that it is the drawing made for the engraving. Other, derivative drawings in Boston, Isabella Stewart Gardner Museum; Haarlem, Teyler Coll., B12(8); Milan, Ambrosiana.

Canvas VI. Soldiers carrying trophies. Dublin, National Gallery of Ireland, Inv. No.2187, 26 × 26 cm., pen and brown ink. Published by Martindale (1979, p.166) as a copy of Mantegna's preliminary study rather than of the engraving of this canvas.

Canvas VII. The Captives. Chantilly, Musée Condé, Inv. Ecole Italienne, II, 33, 27 × 27 cm., pen and brown ink. Kristeller (1901, p.278, fig.10) believed this to be a good old copy and the only drawing related to Mantegna's original sketches for the *Triumph*. For Martindale (1979, p.165) also a good copy of Mantegna's original.

Canvas IX. The Triumphal Car. London, British Museum, 1895–9–15–773, 26.2 × 27.3 cm., pen, brown ink and red chalk, washed with brown, yellow, green, and heights red with white. For Popham & Pouncey (1950, p.105, No.169) an old and feeble copy presumably preserving one of Mantegna's first ideas. For Martindale (1979, pp.164–5, No.54) also an unfinished copy of a preliminary study.

The Senators (see also engravings above). Vienna, Albertina, Inv. No.2585, 25 × 26.8 cm., pen and brown ink. For Wickhoff (*Vienna Jahrbuch*, xiii, 1891, pp.ccv, cclii, No.SL10) a copy of the engraving. For Martindale (1979, pp.165–6) of better quality than the engraving, by an artist of some talent.

RELATION OF DRAWINGS AND ENGRAVINGS TO THE TRIUMPHS: There is general agreement that the surviving early drawings and engravings connected with the *Triumphs* derive from Mantegna's original sketches and designs, rather than from the completed paintings. Martindale (1979, p.77) points out that technical examination of Mantegna's surviving paint has revealed no *pentimenti* of importance, and rightly concludes that Mantegna must have worked from a series of carefully prepared *modelli*. He also points out that the surviving early drawings and engravings are virtually of the same dimensions, 26–27 cm. × 26–27 cm. He deduces that this is an indication of the existence of fairly finished studies, which were fitted into a model of the setting for which the *Triumphs* were intended. This last conclusion is plausible but speculative: but his general conclusion, that almost all the drawings and engravings are copies made for practice or for illicit publication, seems unchallengeable. They are important as evidence for the evolution of the final design, rather than for the original appearance of the finished works.

EARLY TAPESTRIES: A Tournai tapestry of *c.*1520–30 derives from the engravings of the *Elephants* and *Soldiers carrying trophies* (E. J. Kalf, 'Prenten naar Andrea Mantegna in verband gebracht met een Wandtapijt' in *Bulletin van het Rijksmuseum*, xxiii, 1975, pp.166–72). Three tapestries from a series woven at Mortlake after the *Triumphs*, probably in the last quarter of the seventeenth century, survive at Bowhill House, Scotland (Coll. Duke of Buccleuch): for these and other references to Mortlake tapestries after the *Triumphs* see Martindale (1979, p.110).

29. THE BELVEDERE CHAPEL

The villa of Belvedere (for which see Ackerman, *The Cortile del Belvedere*, Rome, 1954; Redig de Campos, *I palazzi vaticani*, 1967, pp.70–8) was built as a summer retreat by Pope Innocent VIII (Giovanni Battista Cibo, elected 29 August 1484–d.25 July 1492). The vineyard on which it was built was paid for on 6 April 1485, and the structure was completed in 1487. According to Vasari, the architect was Antonio Pollaiuolo, but at most he gave a design, and the building was erected by the builder and architect Jacopo Cristoforo da Pietrasanta. The decoration of the secular apartments was entrusted to Pinturicchio, probably in 1487, and Mantegna was called to decorate the chapel and sacristy.

DOCUMENTS: 1) *1488, 24 April*. Mantegna to the Marchese Francesco. The Marchese had promised to speed him on his way as soon as Messer Antonio Socaciano arrived from Venice: Messer Antonio has just come, and Mantegna eagerly solicits licence to depart since the task he has undertaken can only bring the Marchese honour (Braghirolli, in *Giornale di erudizione artistica*, i, 1872, p.201; Kristeller, 1902, p.545, doc.100).

2) *1488, 2 or 10 June*. A letter from Francesco Gonzaga Marquis of Mantua in answer to one from Pope Innocent VIII, despatching Mantegna to the Pope to serve him as requested and asking that he may be allowed to return when his work is finished (Gaye, iii, p.561; D'Arco, ii, p.19; Kristeller, 1902, p.545, doc.101).

3) *1489, 31 January*. Mantegna to Francesco Gonzaga. He is working hard for the Pope, but would prefer to be at home in Mantua. The Pope gives him only money enough for his food. Can the Marchese obtain benefices for his son Lodovico to the value of 200 ducats in Mantua or its territory: Mantegna would rather pawn all he has than ask the Pope for a penny, but if Innocent were to provide Lodovico with a benefice, he would accept it. But he prays for the Marchese's interposition, since it is so difficult to obtain benefices (D'Arco, ii, p.20; Kristeller, 1902, pp.545–6, doc.102).

4) *1489, 23 February*. Francesco Gonzaga to Mantegna in answer to the preceding. Francesco is pleased Mantegna is serving the Pope, but wishes the work he is doing in Rome could be finished expeditiously, since he has left other works to be finished in Mantua. If Lodovico can obtain benefices in his domains to the value of 200 ducats, the Marchese will be pleased (D'Arco, ii, pp.20–1; Kristeller, 1902, p.546, doc.103).

5) *1489, 15 June*. Mantegna to Francesco Gonzaga. Congratulates him on his courtesy and liberality to Djem, brother of the Sultan. Mantegna is in high favour with the Pope and all the Apostolic palace, but receives nothing save his expenses. Not daring to ask for a recompense, however small, he begs the Marchese to remember his old servant and to maintain him in the provision he has so long received from Casa Gonzaga, otherwise he will be in short straits if he gets no money in Mantua any more

than in Rome. 'Lopera è grande a un huomo solo che vogli hauer honore maxime ad Roma dove sonno tanti juditii dihomini da bene; Et cossì come li barbari el primo ha el palio ad me bisogna hauerlo in ultimo se addio piacerà.' Djem is in Rome and 'spesse fiate vien amanzare quì in palazo novo dove io depingo'. Mantegna will send the Marchese a drawing of him when ever he can catch him in the same pose for long enough: but the Turk's eyes are as restless as a lover's and Mantegna cannot fix him in his memory (D'Arco, ii, pp.21–2; Kristeller, 1902, pp.546–7, doc.104).

6) *1489, 16 December*. Francesco Gonzaga to Mantegna. Francesco understands Mantegna's task in Rome is now nearly finished and that he has completed its more important and remarkable parts ('Andrea crediamo che lopera laqual vui faceti a la Sta di N.S. sia proxima ala fine et che habiate perfecto le cose più digne e de magior importantia'). On 16 February next Francesco is to be married to Isabella d'Este, and would like Mantegna back in Mantua to help in devising some of the ceremonies. He is therefore to take an early opportunity of finding the Pope in a good mood and request licence to depart and return to Mantua, and the sooner the better. Francesco is writing to the Pope to make the same request and promising that Mantegna can return later to Rome if necessary (D'Arco, ii, pp.22–3; Kristeller, 1902, p.548, doc.106).

7) *1489, 16 December*. Francesco Gonzaga to Pope Innocent VIII. Letter to request Mantegna's return, as above. 'Si non perfecerit que a Sanctitate vestra demandata fuerunt, parum superesse existimo.' (D'Arco, ii, p.23; Kristeller, 1902, p.548, doc.105.)

8) *1490, 1 January*. Mantegna to Francesco Gonzaga. Mantegna is greatly distressed that he will not be able to come to Francesco's wedding, but he has been very ill, and his illness has left him with certain pains and swellings in the leg, and he can neither ride nor even move without danger of a relapse (D'Arco, ii, p.23; Kristeller, 1902, p.549, doc.108).

9) *1490, 1 January*. Innocent VIII to Francesco Gonzaga. Confirms that he would gladly have given Mantegna licence to return, had it not been for his sickness. In this winter weather Mantegna would be in danger of his life if he were to make the journey to Mantua (D'Arco, ii, pp.24–5; Kristeller, 1902, p.548, doc.107).

10) *1490, 6 September*. Innocent VIII to Francesco Gonzaga. A brief accompanying Mantegna on his return expressing the Pope's satisfaction with the perfection of Mantegna's work for him (D'Arco, ii, p.24; Kristeller, 1902, p.549, doc.109).

Pastor (English ed., v, 1901, p.326) wrongly associates a letter of 25 February 1484 from Bishop Lodovico Gonzaga in Mantua to Cardinal Giuliano della Rovere in Rome with the commission for the chapel, an error copied by later writers. A document purporting to be a Papal payment to Mantegna for work in the chapel and dated 15 September 1486 published by Federici (in *Archivio della Soc. Romana di Storia P.*, xxx, 1907, p.490) is a palpable forgery, as Federici himself seems to have suspected.

EARLY REFERENCES: 1) Paulus Cortesius, *De cardinalatu*, 1510, f.87: '*Atque etiam maxime apparet in acuta dicacitate sal cum per dissimulationem non intelligendi cogitatae dicacitati,*

praeter expectationem respondetur, quale illud fuit Innocentii. VII (sic) hominis patientis & lenti, sed callida comitate blandi. Nam cum sacellum in suburbano palatino Picturis ornare decreuisset Andreamque Mantegnem, qui tum maxime frugi ac uerecundus naturae imitator in pingendo putaretur, sponte conductum adhibuisset atque is cum primo quoque tempore ad eum uenisset, bienniique prope spatium pinxisset, nec assem quidem ab eo accepisset, statuissetque pro eo quod erat ingeniosus & pictor, aliqua ei interpunctione salis tenacem remunerandi procrastinationem exprobrare, simulachrum muliebri specie adultaque aetate inchoasse dicitur, quod cum Innocentius aspexisset, quaesissetque ex eo quaenam esset illa tam decursa aetate anus, Atque is ingratitudinem esse respondisset, commode inquit prope posset patientia pingi.'

This is clearly an early version of the famous story in Vasari (1550, pp.511–12) in which the figure painted by Mantegna is said to have been a Virtue and to have been called Discretion by the artist in answer to the Pope's enquiry. In Cortesius the story has much more point. Since Paolo Cortese (1465–1510) became an apostolic scriptor in 1481 and was later a Papal secretary and protonotary he should be regarded as a well-informed source. His statements about the length of Mantegna's stay in Rome and the Pope's failure to pay the artist or to make him any present or reward are borne out by the contemporary documents and there is no good reason for doubting the essential truth of the story as he gives it. He composed *De cardinalatu* in the last years of his life, and probably wrote the anecdote in its present form after 1507. Scardeone (1560, p.372) also gives a version of the story, in which the Vices are added to the Virtues: '*Romam quoque aliquando ab Innocentio VII (sic) Pont. Max. accitus, augustissimum delubrum in palatio Vaticano depinxit: ubi quum aliquod sacerdotium dari uni ex filijs suis in retributionem diu frustraque sperasset, jussus aliquando à Pontifice ut pingeret septem uitia capitalia, de industria fecit, ut uacaret locus, in quo appinxit ingratitudinem. Interrogatus autem a Pontifice, cur quum septem sint tantum uitia, octauum sic iniussus addiderit? Respondit, quum locus uacaret, quia ego nullum uitium existimaui scelestius ingratitudine, eam ipsam uacuo spacio cum alijs septem peccatis iure apponendam esse putaui. At Pontifex calliditate pictoris agnita, dissimulans, subrisit, dicens: Rectè tu sane. Sed quoniam ex hoc latere octo uitia apparent, quamuis septem tantum sint: ita quoque è regione in altero latere septem illis uirtutibus octauam appinges patientiam, quae non infimum sanè locum inter uirtutes tenet, quamvis cum illis septem uirtutibus non connumeretur, sicut nec ingratitudo cum septem peccatis. Cognovit Mantinea vir astutus callidam imposturam Pontificis & dissimulans id nosse dictum, sicut & ille factum, & dolens se esse pari astutia, & non ut optabat, liberali quapiam gratia compensatum: peraegrè tamen tanto Pontifici paruit. Atqui tandem peracto opere, bona spe frustratus, subtristis, Roma relicta, Mantuam . . . reversus est.*'

2) Raffaelle Maffei Volaterranus, *Commentarii Vrbani*, Rome, 1506, lib. xxi, f. cccr: '*Andreas Mantenga Mantuanus aedes quas Belvedere cognominant in Vaticano ab Innocentio VIII. adibitus ornauit miro tenuitatis opere.*'

3) Battista Fiera, *De Ivsticia pingenda*, 1515 (ed. J. Wardrop, London, 1957). This dialogue between Mantegna and Momus is set in Rome, and its theme is the depiction of a figure of Justice, which Mantegna has been commissioned to paint by the Pope 'sic iussit qui omnia potest'

(*ed. cit.*, p.18). As suggested by Wardrop, presumably the dialogue was inspired by Mantegna's decoration of the chapel, which included a figure of Justice, and it may record an actual moment in its execution.

4) On 29 March 1496, Francesco Gonzaga, on his way to Naples, halted in Rome and was received with honours by Pope Alexander VI. 'Doppo pranzo andosene a la vigna del Papa et vide le picture del Mantegna' (Luzio, 'Isabella d'Este e i Borgia' in *A.S.L.*, ser. v, xli, 1912, p.488).

5) Simone Fornari, *La Spositione sopra l'Orlando Furioso*, ii, Florence, 1550, p.509: 'Fu da Innocentio VIII chiamato a Roma, dove egli con molta diligentia lavorò una cappella minutissimamente.'

6) Fuseli, who saw the frescoes while living in Rome from 1776 to 1778, says that they had 'freshness, freedom and imitation' (*Lectures on Painting*, 1830, p.55).

7) Claude-Henri Watelet (1718−86). 'Il [Mantegna] peignit à Rome une petite chapelle du Belvedere avec un soin qui approche cet ouvrage de la miniature' (in Watelet, *Dictionnaire des Arts*, vi, 1792, p.157).

The chapel was destroyed under Pope Pius VI in 1780. Its measurements are established by Pietrangeli (see below) as 3.20 × 3.50 m. Adjoining it was a sacristy.

RECONSTRUCTION: The principal sources for the chapel and its adjoining sacristy are the descriptions of Agostino Taja (composed *c.*1712, published in his *Descrizione del Palazzo Apostolico Vaticano*, 1750, pp.401−7) and of Giovanni Pietro Chattard (*Nuova descrizione del Vaticano*, iii, 1767, pp.140−4). These were reprinted by Müntz (in *Arch. S.A.*, ii, 1889, pp.481−3). Three modern reconstructions have been attempted, by Frizzoni ('Il Mantegna a Roma' in *Rass. d'A.*, xvii, 1917, pp.195−201); Sandström, 'The programme for the decoration of the Belvedere of Innocent VIII' in *Konsthistorisk Tidskrift*, xxviii, 1959, pp.35−75; Pietrangeli, 'Mantegna in Vaticano' in *L'Urbe*, xxiv, 1961, No.6, pp.95−103. See text, pp.154−7, for discussion. A recent essay is E. Pogány-Balás, 'On the problems of Mantegna's destroyed fresco in Rome representing the "Baptism of Christ",' in her *Influence of Rome's antique monumental sculptures . . .*, 1980, pp.58−65).

A drawing in the Uffizi (334E) of a man pulling on a stocking is traditionally called a copy of Mantegna and may reproduce the motif so much admired by Vasari in the *Baptism of Christ*.

30. Judith

Washington, National Gallery of Art (Widener Coll.).
F. R. Shapley, *Catalogue of the Italian Paintings*, i, 1979, pp.296−7, no.638
Wood 30.5 × 18 cm.   Plate 120
Inscribed on a gesso surface on the back of the panel: AN: MANTEGNA

PROVENANCE: Sometimes identified as 'the little Judith of Raphael' exchanged in the early 1620s by Charles I 'when you were Prince' (i.e. before 1624), for a Bellini and Parmigianino belonging to the Steward of his Household, William Herbert, 3rd Earl of Pembroke, who died in April 1630 (Millar, 1960, p.15, No.15; see also p.81, No.26, where the Judith is described as 'beeing a little intire figure': variant, M. S. Ash 1514, f.102 '. . . halff so

big as te liff, s.t.'. Recorded at Wilton House, Wiltshire, in 1751 (R. Cowdry, *A description of the pictures . . .*, 1751, p.74, as in the Corner-Room: 'JUDITH putting *Holofernes*'s Head into a Scrip, which is held open by her Maid. 5. By Mantegna'). By 1776 moved into the Colonnade-Room (*A new description . . .*, 1776, p.106). Seen by Waagen (iii, 1854, p.151), where the suggestion of its identity with the Charles I *Judith* is first made. For the history of the Wilton collection, which suggests that the identification may be dubious, see the introduction in Lord Pembroke (*A catalogue of the paintings and drawings in the collection at Wilton House*, 1968). Sold Sotheby's 5−10 July, 1917; Carl W. Hamilton, N.Y.; with Duveen's 1920; bt. Joseph E. Widener; Widener Coll. in National Gallery, 1942. For details of exhibitions see Shapley, *loc. cit.*

The close relationship of the composition to the Dublin *Judith* (Cat. no.56) is generally recognized. The traditional attribution to Mantegna, maintained by Passavant and Waagen, was first disputed by Crowe & Cavalcaselle (1871, p.404, n.2; 1912, p.105n) who dismissed the picture as a Flemish sixteenth-century copy, probably after an engraving. An unfavourable judgement was also advanced by Berenson (1901, pp.97−8, by an imitator) and Kristeller (1901, pp.375n, 453, feeble work by an imitator). For Yriarte (1901, p.208) it is autograph. In 1907 (p.255) and in 1918 (*A. in A.*, pp.127−8) Berenson reclassed the picture as an autograph Mantegna, an opinion in which Venturi (1914, p.247) also concurred. Rejected by R. Schwabe (in *B.M.*, xxiii, 1918, pp.215−16, by an imitator) and by Tietze-Conrat (1955, pp.201, 245, invention by Mantegna or his circle, perhaps a copy after Mantegna by a sixteenth-century amateur) and doubtfully accepted by Fiocco (1937, p.68, coloured variant of Dublin *Judith*). The picture has been more or less unanimously accepted as autograph in recent years (Cipriani, 1962, pp.28−9,64; Camesasca, 1964, pp.37,46−7; Garavaglia, 1967, No.74; Fredericksen & Zeri, 1972). The dates assigned to it vary from *c.*1495 (Berenson), *c.*1475 (Camesasca), 1490 (Garavaglia) and Cipriani's wavering dating of either *c.*1464 or *c.*1488, given analogies with both the Florence triptych (Cat. nos. 14−16) and the *Madonna delle Cave* (Plate 121). Certainly an autograph work of *c.*1490.

Yriarte notes the existence of a version on copper in the Czartoriski Museum, Cracow (now Museum Narodoseje, inv. no.XII-331; 38.5 × 24.5 cm.). This dates from the seventeenth century: F. R. Shapley (*loc. cit.*) regards it as a close repetition.

31. Virgin and Child (*Madonna delle Cave*)

Florence, Uffizi (Inv.1348, *Catalogo generale*, 1979, p.365)
Tempera on panel 32 × 29.6 cm.   Plate 121; Fig. 10

CONDITION: Good.

PROVENANCE: First recorded by Vasari (1568, p.497) as in the collection of Principe (later Grand Duke) Francesco de' Medici: '*Mentre, che Andrea stette a lauorare in Roma . . . dipinse, in vn quadretto piccolo, vna N. Donna col Figliuolo in collo, che dorme, e nel campo, che è vna montagna, fece, dentro a certe grotte alcuni scarpellini, che cauano pietre per diuersi lauori, tanto sottilmente, & con tanta pacienza, che non par possibile che con vna sottil punta di pennello si possa far tanto bene. Il qual quadro è hoggi appresso lo Illustrissimo*

S. Don Francesco Medici, Principe di Fiorenza, il quale lo tiene fra le sue cose carissime.' The first inventory of the Florentine Galleria in which the picture is recorded is that of 1704 (Uffizi MS, f.138, No.1128: *'Un simile [quadrettino] in tauola alto b½, largo s.7.4.: dipintoui di maniera antica la Madonna SS.ᵐᵃ uestita di rosso, con manto turchino, con Giesù bambino nudo in collo, con ueduta di una grotta, e paese in lontananza, con molte figurine, che alcuni lauorano di piche, con adornam:ᵗᵒ di albero tinto di nero marizzato di giallo.'*

Vasari dates this picture to the Roman sojourn of Mantegna, in 1488–90. The fact that the Child is awake and not, as in his description, sleeping is rightly credited by Knapp (1910, pp.175–6) to a slip of Vasari's pen. Vasari's dating was accepted by Crowe and Cavalcaselle (1871, pp.402–3; 1912, p.104), Thode (1897, pp.85–7) and Yriarte (1901, p.238). Kristeller (1901, pp.227–30) proposed a dating *c*.1468, after the Tuscan visit, and this is re-argued by Paccagnini (1961, p.38) both claiming stylistic relationship to the Venice *St George*. Knapp (1910, p.104) and Fiocco (1937, p.53) misinterpret the Medici provenance as evidence that the picture was painted during Mantegna's sojourn of 1466 in Tuscany. It is not mentioned in Lorenzo de' Medici's inventory of 1492, which perhaps also disposes of Tietze-Conrat's tentative attempt (1955, p.182) to identify it as the *operetta* Mantegna promised Lorenzo in a letter of 26 August 1484. Meiss (in *Venezia e l'Europa: atti del XVIII Congresso Internazionale di Storia dell'Arte*, Venice, 1956, p.65) dates it in the 1450s, apparently because of his wish to associate what he terms the 'plateau' composition with the influence of Van Eyck. Recent opinion favours the traditional dating. Arslan (1961, p.170) as *c*.1490; Longhi (1962, p.20) thinks it may well be *c*.1488–90; Cipriani (1962, pp.40,66–7) and Camesasca (1964, pp.38,110) as 1488–90, Garavaglia (1967, No.68) as 1489. The latest date of all is proposed by Venturi (1914, p.242), who places it *c*.1500. The picture is more or less contemporary with the National Gallery *Virgin and Child with St John the Baptist and the Magdalen*, universally accepted as a late work, where the grape-purple colour of the lining of the Virgin's cloak recurs in the Magdalen's dress. It is, however, probably a little earlier: Vasari's statement that it was painted during Mantegna's Roman sojourn may therefore be correct.

The landscape and figures are interpreted realistically by Kristeller, who identifies the rock as a special form of volcanic basalt, rare in Italy, but found at Monte Bolca, near Ronca, between Vicenza and Verona, and by Fiocco, for whom the quarries are a souvenir of Carrara. It is interpreted symbolically by Hartt (in *G.B.A.*, ser.6, xl, 1952, pp.329–42). He rightly identifies the column and the sarcophagus as symbols of the Passion, but his attempts to read the other elements of the landscape symbolically (the mountain is the mountain of Daniel 2, 34 ff; the wheatfield is a eucharistic symbol; the shepherds figure Christ the Good Shepherd, the stone on which the Virgin sits is the threshing-floor of Daniel etc. etc.) have not won acceptance. Equally implausible is his attempt to identify the mountain as a Gonzaga *impresa*. The mount on which the Virgin is seated is that of Golgotha, and the mount behind is that of the sepulchre, which is already being shaped.

32. Virgin and Child with St John the Baptist and the Magdalen

Inscribed on the outside of the scroll round the Baptist's staff: (ec)CE AG(nus Dei ec)CE (qui tollit pec) CATA M(vndi) and on the inside of the first fold: *Andreas Mantinia C.P.F.*

London, National Gallery, 274 (Davies, 1961, pp.329–30). Canvas 136 × 114 cm. (picture surface). Edged with a red-spotted black band, so that the total painted surface measures 139 × 116.5 cm. Plate 122

CONDITION: Exceptionally good; some losses on Virgin's chin and neck: some rubbing, e.g. on right side of Magdalen's hair, and canopy. *Pentimento* on Baptist's left shoulder. Cut down: the speckled edge is what remains of a marble window, originally touching the top of the canopy, which was represented as behind and cut off by it. This window is partly overpainted, partly overcleaned: it seems that the outer edges of the canvas have all been cut except possibly that on the left. Cleaned in 1957.

PROVENANCE: First recorded in the printed literature in 1795 as in Palazzo Andreani (Adriani), Milan (C. Bianconi, *Nuova guida di Milano*, Milan, 1795, p.119: 'Degno è di grande ammirazione un bellissimo Quadro del Mantegna, che rappresenta la Vergine col Bambino in grembo avente a fianchi S. Giovanni Battista, e S. Maria Maddalena'). Engraved as in the collection of Mario Andreani by Zanconi and Carpani (*Raccolta delle migliori dipinture*, 1839, No.8). According to Pirovano (*Milano nuovamente descritta*, 1822, p.256) still in Palazzo Andreani. This palace (now known as Palazzo Sormani) was originally Palazzo Monti (for this see Bascapé, *I palazzi della vecchia Milano*, Milan, 1945, pp.327–34). It was built by Cardinal Cesare Monti, Archbishop of Milan from 1632 (in residence from 1635) until his death in 1650. He was a collector of pictures (see Nicodemi, in *Rass. d'A.*, xiv, 1914, pp.279–88). Borroni, *Forastiere in Milano*, i, 1808, p.49, was the first to record or claim that the picture had originally belonged to Monti before descending to his ultimate heirs, the Andreani (who were also collectors of pictures). Since the site of Palazzo Monti was not acquired until *c*.1635–50, the tradition, first recorded in the National Gallery *Catalogue*, ed. of 1859, p.137, that it was placed in the private chapel of the palace in 1610 cannot be correct. It seems, however, that it was later the altarpiece of the chapel until removed into the apartments by the Andreani. Later in the collection of Giacomo Mellerio (1777–1847), statesman, philanthropist and man of taste (Bascapé, *op. cit.*, pp.38–42, 76–7), in Palazzo Mellerio. Sold by Mellerio's heir, Conte Cavazzi della Somaglia, to the dealer Baslini in 1855: sold by Baslini to Roverselli, from whom acquired by the Gallery in 1855.

Accepted by Selvatico (1849, pp.188–9), Crowe & Cavalcaselle (1871, p.411; 1912, p.112, but see below), Kristeller (1901, pp.320–1, 442, No.28), Knapp (1910, p.114), Venturi (1914, pp.226–8), Berenson (1932, 1968), Tietze-Conrat (1955, p.185), Davies (1961, *loc. cit*), Cipriani (1962, pp.38,69) and Garavaglia (1967, No.102) as autograph. But some of these critics find fault with the picture – Selvatico criticizes it for pallid colour, Crowe & Cavalcaselle for the proportions of the figures, Tietze-

Conrat for the poor invention and dry brushwork. Accordingly Crowe & Cavalcaselle (1871, p.482; 1912, p.189) proposed to attribute the execution to Caroto, and Fiocco (1937, p.72), who finds it dry and schematic, suggested some workshop assistance. The picture is unjustly dismissed by Camesasca (1964, p.43) as largely a workshop production.

Universally regarded as a late work painted either c.1495–7, close to the Trivulzio Madonna and the *Madonna della Vittoria* (Kristeller, Thode, Venturi, Fiocco, Cipriani) or c.1500 (Knapp, Tietze-Conrat, Berenson, Garavaglia). The Child closely resembles the Child in the Santa Maria della Vittoria altarpiece – indeed it seems to be the same figure in reverse and with the *déhanchement* rather more emphasized, while the loose free hair of the two saints is close in treatment to that of St Michael and St George in the same picture. The C.P. of the signature was interpreted by Selvatico as *Civis Patavinus*, but Brandolese (*Testimonianze intorno alla Patavinità di Andrea Mantegna*, Padua, 1805, p.12) and Davies are surely correct in interpreting it as *Comes Palatinus*. It is a curious fact that Mantegna is known to have used the title *Comes Palatinus* only in the Belvedere chapel, on the Correggio *Redeemer* (dated 1493), and on this picture which is perhaps a reason for dating it slightly before the Santa Maria della Vittoria altarpiece. He is referred to as 'Miles et Comes Dominus Andreas Mantegna' in the contract of sale of 1492 for his house in Padua. Mantegna's use of the title also suggests then that the picture was painted in Rome or shortly after his return. In any case a date c.1490–5 seems preferable.

An engraving after a drawing of the Holy Family by Mantegna (Cat. no.227; Plate 245) shows a very similar composition.

33. The Redeemer.

Inscribed on the book: EGO SVM: NOLITE TIMERE (Luke, 24, 36). Inscribed on left side: MOMORDITE VOS MET IPSOS ANTE EFFIGIEM VVLTVS MEI. Inscribed along the bottom ... IA P.C. D D MCCCCLXXXXIII $-\frac{\mathrm{D}}{\mathrm{V}}$. J.A.

Correggio, Congregazione di Carità (exh. Museo Civico) Tempera on canvas 55 × 43 cm.   Plate 123

CONDITION: Restored c.1958 by Renato Pasqui, when it was noted that too vigorous earlier restorations had deprived the tempera of its tone and relief. Accordingly Pasqui confined himself to removing those earlier restorations whose character had altered and to toning in these passages with the rest (Quintavalle, *Ritrovamenti e restauri*, exh. cat., Modena, 1959, pp.16–17, No.7). See also below.

PROVENANCE: Identified by A. O. Quintavalle (*Mostra del Correggio*, Parma, 1935, pp.22–4, No.17) as a painting of this subject commissioned from Mantegna and sent to Correggio in 1493 (source of information not stated). According to A. Ghidini (in *Il Palazzo dei Principi in Correggio*, n.d. (c.1977), p.97) the painting was originally part of the collections of the Counts of Correggio. When the city was forfeited in 1630 by Principe Siro da Correggio and his palace was occupied and sacked by the Imperial troops, the picture was rescued by the Contarelli family of Correggio. The last descendant of the Contarelli

bequeathed it in the mid-nineteenth century to the Congregazione di Carità of Correggio. The Congregazione sold it c.1915 for a derisory sum to the Marchese Matteo Campori of Modena, whereupon it was published as a Mantegna by Frizzoni (see below). After a lawsuit the picture was returned to the Congregazione and is now housed in the Museo Civico of Correggio.

First published as a Mantegna (see above) by Frizzoni ('Un dipinto inedito di Andrea Mantegna' in *L'Arte*, xix, 1916, pp.65–9, repr. before and after restoration). Rightly accepted as an autograph work by Venturi (*Correggio*, 1926, p.14), Fiocco (1937, pp.76,210), Paccagnini (1961, p.48), Rühmer (1961, p.cv), Gilbert (1962, p.9, as probably by Mantegna), Cipriani (1962, p.67) Camesasca (1964, pp.40,122), Garavaglia (1967, No.83), Berenson (1968, ignored 1932). Tietze-Conrat (1955, p.181), who had not seen the picture, is alone in rejecting it.

The *Redeemer* is important for the study of Mantegna in that, apart from the *Triumphs*, on which he worked over a period of nearly a decade, it is the first dated painting by him to survive from his later decades. It serves as an anchor for a number of pictures conceived in a similar spirit, and which show similar features, e.g. costumes in watered silk and a black or near-black background, among them the Brera *Dead Christ*, the Poldi-Pezzoli *Madonna* and the Bergamo *Madonna*.

The partly missing inscription along the bottom should be read *A? Mantinia Palatinus Comes dono dedit 1493 die 5 Januarii*.

34. The Descent into Limbo

Private coll.
Panel 38.6 × 42 cm.   Plate 125

PROVENANCE: First certainly recorded in the collection of Sir Stephen Courtauld, Taynuilt, Argyll, by whom it was exhibited at the Winter Exhibition of the Burlington Fine Arts Club, 1934–5, No.23. Sold as property of the Trustees of a deceased Estate at Sotheby's, 11 July 1973, lot 10, bt. Colnaghi, £490,000.

Mantegna was working on a picture of the *Descent into Limbo* for the Marchese Lodovico in June 1468 (see Cat. no.70). On stylistic grounds this work cannot be identified as the present picture, but is presumably that whose composition is recorded in an engraving and other versions (see Cat. nos. 203, 216; Plates 226, 236a). A small picture of the same subject attributed to Mantegna was recorded in 1709 in the collection of Ferdinando Carlo, last Duke of Mantua (see Cat. no.137): its dimensions and medium broadly correspond. The Duke's pictures were later sold in Venice. Hence it is possible that this picture remained in a Venetian collection and was subsequently acquired by Conte Jacopo Durazzo of Genoa, Imperial Ambassador in Venice from c.1774 until his death. Durazzo was commissioned in 1774 by Albert of Saxe-Teschen, founder of the Albertina, to form a collection of engravings for him, and subsequently formed a second collection for himself. His interest in engraving and its history probably explains his interest in Mantegna (Benincasa, *Descrizione della raccolta di stampe di S.E. Il Sig. Conte Jacopo Durazzo, Patrizio Genovese*, Parma, 1784). After his death in 1795 the picture passed to his heirs in Genoa. It is mentioned in two letters written in January 1797 from Venice by the engraver Francesco Novelli to the Abate Mauro Boni (Campori, *Lettere artistiche inedite*, Modena, 1866, p.325: 'ci assicura che ebbe una maniera più secca il quadro che hanno S.Eᶜ Durazzi cioè il Limbo che come ella ben vede non è della sua più bella maniera'; p.327, 'a dir il vero siamo certi che ebbe una maniera ne' suoi principj assai secca . . . ciò ci assicura anche il quadro del Limbo che tengono li Durazzi a Genova, che come ella ben vede è molto lontano dal suo ultimo bel stile.' Jacopo's collections were subsequently dispersed in the nineteenth century.

The composition is known in other versions. One, formerly in the collection of the Conti Valier at Asolo *c.*1937 (panel, 71 × 55 cm.), was later on the art market in New York. It is said to have been seen in the Valier collection by Canova. Fiocco (1937, p.77, fig.159) classes it as one of his putative group of late works left unfinished in the studio, and attributes the landscape to Correggio. Tietze-Conrat (1955, pp.197–8) accepts a late date for the invention. Elam, in V. & A., *Splendours of the Gonzaga*, p.17, as *c.*1468. Cipriani (1962, p.79) also considers the invention Mantegnesque, but thinks the execution of the Valier picture is not by Mantegna and the ex-Courtauld picture a replica. Garavaglia (1967, No.34) thinks the ex-Courtauld version the better. All students rightly consider a third version (Plate 126) in the Pinacoteca of Bologna (formerly Zambeccari coll.: Crowe & Cavalcaselle, i, 1871, p.415, n.5) as an inferior work. There can be no doubt that the ex-Courtauld version is Mantegna's original, and its probable provenance from the ducal collections of Mantua lends support to this view. The composition was engraved at least four times in the eighteenth century (Hind, 1948, p.19, No.9), once with the initials of Mantegna and the date 1492. Whether or not this records an authentic date, in style the picture is closely related to the National Gallery *Virgin and Child with St John the Baptist and the Magdalen* (Cat. no.32; Plate 122) and like it must date from the early 1490s. A drawing in the Berlin Kupferstichkabinett of the Christ (see Cat. no.203) is rightly associated with the picture by Mezzetti (in Paccagnini, 1961, p.169, No.124): but she, like Degenhart (1958, p.24) and Mohle (in *Z.f.K.*, xxii, 1959, pp.169–70), regards it as a faithful copy, of excellent quality, rather than as an original.

35. Pietà (The Man of Sorrows, supported by two angels). Inscribed ANDREAS MANTINIA on the right of the sarcophagus base.

Copenhagen, Statens Museum for Kunst No. Rm.Sp.No.69 (*Catalogue of old foreign paintings*, 1951, pp.181–2, no.416). For studies with excellent surveys of previous literature see Moltesen, in Copenhagen, *Kunstmuseets Aarsskrift*, xi–xii, 1926, pp.88–116, and H. Olsen, *Italian paintings and sculpture in Denmark*, 1961, pp.23–4,73).
Tempera on panel 78 × 48 cm.   Plate 124

CONDITION: The hand of the angel on the right and the leg of the angel on the left restored: otherwise the condition is good.

PROVENANCE: First recorded in the collection of Cardinal Silvio Valenti Gonzaga (1690–1756), of the family of the Marchesi Valenti, Mantua. His sale (Amsterdam, 18 May 1763): bt. for the royal Danish collection. For the Cardinal and his collection see Olsen, 'Et malet Galleri of Pannoni; Kardinal Silvio Valenti Gonzaga Samling' in *Kunstmuseets Aasskrift 1951*, 1952, pp.90–103). Listed in a *Verseichnis* made in 1763 (No.5) of the royal Danish pictures (MS in Library of Statens Museum for Kunst), where the stone of the sarcophagus is identified as 'jaspis', and the landscape as a view of Mantua.

Sometimes identified with a picture of the same format listed in the Mantua inventory of 1627 (see Cat. no.105).

Now universally accepted as by Mantegna, though doubts were once expressed by Portheim (in *J.P.K.*, vii, 1886, p.224) and Vollmer (in *Monatshefte für Kunstwissenschaft*, ii, 1909, p.550). Its provenance from the collection of Cardinal Valenti, secretary of state to Pope Benedict XIV, has long been considered a good reason for dating this picture to Mantegna's Roman sojourn of 1488–90 (Crowe & Cavalcaselle, 1871, p.403; 1912, pp.104–5; Thode, 1897, pp.87–8; Fiocco, 1937, pp.70–1, 208; Camesasca, 1964, pp.38,120; Garavaglia, 1967, No.69). The Cardinal's Mantuan origin and Gonzaga connections make this argument untenable. Kristeller (1901, pp.327–30) and Knapp (1910, pp.105,176) date it *c.*1500. Venturi (1914, pp.216–19) places it *c.*1490–5, contemporary with the Venice *St Sebastian*. Tietze-Conrat (1955, pp.180–1) considers that its pathos and drapery style suggest a date *c.*1495–1500, followed by Cipriani (1962, pp.40–1, 70). The general style is that of Mantegna's last decade, but the aerial perspective of the landscape makes its only other appearance in the *Parnassus* (1496–7). The type of Christ recalls the St John of the Santa Maria in Organo altarpiece (1497), while his parted lips find a parellel in the parted lips of Francesco Gonzaga in the Santa Maria della Vittoria altarpiece (1495–6). On stylistic grounds a date of *c.*1495–7 is by far the most plausible for this remarkable picture.

36. The Madonna della Vittoria. The Virgin and Child, attended by St Michael, St George, St Andrew, St Longinus, St Elizabeth and The Infant Baptist, blessing Marchese Francesco Gonzaga.

Inscribed on the medallion in the centre of the Virgin's footstool: REGINA / CELI LET. / ALᴸELVIA. Inscribed on the banner of the Infant Baptist: ECCE / AGNVS / DEI ECCE / Q(*vi*) TOLL / IT P(*eccata*). M(*vndi*).
Paris, Musée du Louvre, 1374 (Hautecoeur, 1926, p.84).
Canvas 280 × 166 cm.   Plate XIV; Fig. 11

PROVENANCE: For the circumstances of the commission see text. Preserved in Santa Maria della Vittoria, Mantua, until 1797. Its frame is described by Bettinelli, 1774, p.37: '. . . sopra il quadro *Victoriae memor* in memoria della battaglia del Taro del 1495. La cornice pure ad intaglio elegante di quel tempo in circa, nel quale si legge F.S.C. in più luoghi, e due mani sorgenti di mezzo a due ale (emblema da spiegarsi)'; p.136: 'Quanto a intagli in legno noterò solo la vaga, e nobil cornice del quadro del Mantegna nella Chiesa della Vittoria.' The altarpiece was greatly admired in the eighteenth century and was lavishly praised by Lanzi (*Storia pittorica della Italia*, ii, ed. Capucci, 1970, p.188), largely for qualities such as *pastosità* of paint that were not generally associated with the *stile secco* of Mantegna. Significantly he remarks: 'a me pare quasi l'ultimo passo dell' arte prima di giungere alla perfezione che acquistò da Leonardo.' In February 1797 the altarpiece was removed by Thouin and Wicar, the French Republican commissaries in Italy 'pour les sciences et les arts', and sent to Paris. After the fall of Napoleon it was not returned, in spite of the insistence of the Mantuan Podestà Marchese di Bagno, because it hung in the royal apartments at the Tuileries and the Austrian government were reluctant to embarrass the French king by demanding its return.

Portioli noted in 1882–3 (see below) that the church, long secularized, still contained remains of paintings 'che secondo gli avanzi, che ebbi a vedere alcuni anni sono conviene credere che siano state disegnate dal Mantegna stesso, ed eseguite sotto la di lui direzione.'

For the history of this famous painting see A. Portioli ('La vera storia di un dipinto celebre' in *Giornale di erudizione artistica*, ii, 1873, pp.145–58; *id.*, 'La chiesa e la Madonna della Vittoria di A. Mantegna in Mantova' in *Atti e memorie della R. Accademia Virgiliana di Mantova*, 1882–3, pp.55–79, also in *A.S.L.*, x, 1883, pp.447–73) and A. Luzio ('La Madonna della Vittoria del Mantegna' in *Emporium*, 1899, pp.358–74). It is essential to consult all three articles.

The inscriptions recorded by Bettinelli (see above) on the frame are to be interpreted as *Victoriae memor Franciscus sacravit* (Francesco, in grateful memory of his victory, dedicated [me]).

The picture is discussed in the text. The erroneous identification of St Elizabeth as a portrait of Isabella d'Este originates with Lanzi (*loc. cit.*).

A copy in white on sheets of paper mounted on canvas and coloured dark brown (273 × 166 cm.) was exhibited as a tracing of the altarpiece in the Galleria of Mantua from 1850 to 1915. Subsequently placed in store, it was rediscovered in the Castello and published by L. Ozzola (in *Civiltà*, i, 1942, pp.67–74) as an original cartoon by Mantegna. Tietze-Conrat (1955, pp.25, 206–7) declared it a *spolvero* or tracing from the original cartoon made by a pupil for transfer to the canvas. It was rightly dismissed as a copy by Fiocco (in *Riv. d'A.*, xxxiv, 1942, pp.99–102, and in *B.M.*, xci, 1949, pp.213–14), who identified it as a late eighteenth-century tracing of the altarpiece made before its despatch to Paris in 1797 which is mentioned by Portioli (cf. *A.S.L., vol. cit.*, p.473). The neoclassical linear style of the drawing is unmistakable, and Fiocco's opinion was subsequently vindicated after a technical examination and on stylistic grounds by Paccagnini ('Sul disegno della "Madonna della Vittoria" nel Palazzo Ducale di Mantova' in *Boll. d'A.*, ser.iv, xli, 1956, pp.177–82). Paccagnini showed that the maker of the tracing was probably the Antonio Ruggieri who made a drawing of the composition in 1797 which was subsequently engraved by F. Novelli in 1804. Paccagnini suggested that certain resemblances between the Mantuan drawing and the engraving indicate that either it or a reduced copy of it was used by Novelli. In fact Moschini (1826, p.44) records that the commission for the drawing was given to Ruggieri by the Cavaliere Giovanni de' Lazara of Padua, who subsequently commissioned the engraving

from Novelli, and dedicated it to Bettinelli with an inscription composed by Lanzi. This is confirmed by letters from Lazara to G. M. Sasso of December 1801 and June 1802 (Campori, *Lettere artistiche inedite*, 1866, pp.344–6). These reveal that Ruggieri's copy of his original prize drawing, 'still preserved in the Accademia of Mantua', was indeed of smaller size and was commissioned from him by Lazara through Bettinelli; Lazara now promised to send it to Sasso to be engraved for his proposed history of the Venetian school if Sasso would undertake to give the work of engraving to Francesco Novelli.

37. Virgin and Child in glory attended by three music-making angels and by St John the Baptist, St Gregory the Great, St Benedict and St Jerome (*Madonna Trivulzio*). Behind the Baptist a scroll winding round the trunk of a lemon tree is inscribed: HIC VENIT IN TES / TIMONIVM VT / TESTIMONIV(m) PE / RHIBERET DE LVMI / NE M (John, 1, 7) and in larger capitals below T / MVND. On a document held by one of the singing angels is the signature *A. Mantinia pi / an. gracie / 1495: 15 / augusti*. St Gregory's cope is inscribed Sc MATHE / APOSTOLV and SAN / APO.
Milan, Museo del Castello Sforzesco
Tempera, thinly painted on three pieces of canvas stitched longitudinally, 287 × 214 cm. Plate 127

CONDITION: Poor. Recently cleaned and restored.

PROVENANCE: From Santa Maria in Organo, Verona; sold to Pertusati in Milan; Milan, Galleria Trivulzio; acquired by the Museo in 1935. For fuller details see below.

The vicissitudes of this altarpiece were clarified by Gerola (*Le antiche pale di S. Maria in Organo di Verona*, 1913, pp.19–20). Vasari records it as on the high altar of Santa Maria in Organo (1550, p.510: 'Fece ancora in Verona nella chiesa di Santa Maria in Organo a Frati di Monte Oliveto la tauola dell' altar maggiore; la quale ancora oggi è tenuta cosa lodatissima'; 1568, p.489: 'In s. Maria in organo a i frati di Monte Oliveto fece la tauola dell' altar maggiore, che è bellissima'). The picture is also mentioned by Ridolfi (1648, p.70: 'In Santa Maria in Organo fece vna tauola con Maria Vergine posta tra due Santi, & à piedi stanno tre Angeletti, che suonano, e cantano'). This seems to be the origin of the confusion between Mantegna's altarpiece and one by Girolamo da' Libri which is first found in Dal Pozzo (1718, pp.246–7: 'Nella terza [cappella] de' Bonalini hora de Conti dal Pozzo la Madonna sedente col Bambino in seno con S. Bartolamio, e S. Zeno, e di sotto tre Angeli che suonano, e cantano d'Andrea Mantego [sic] secondo alcuni: Ma il Vasari la dice di Girolamo da i Libri'). Dal Pozzo also adds an additional confusion for he says that the old altarpiece of the high altar was 'la Pala con la Madonna in mezo a S. Benedetto, e S. Monica di Girolamo dai Libri.' But he does record that the altarpiece of the high altar was removed in 1714, when Baroque renovation of the church began. Mantegna's altarpiece was sold before 1779, since its purchase by Pertusati was recorded by the painter G. B. Cignaroli (d.1770) in his annotated copy of Dal Pozzo (printed by Biadego, in Venice, R. Dep. di Storia Patria, *Miscellanea*, xi, 1890, p.41, note to passage on altarpiece of high altar: 'Questa Pala e stata venduta al sig. Pertusatti'). It is also mentioned by S. Dalla Rosa (*Catastico delle pitture e sculture di Verona*, 1804, MS1008 of Biblioteca Comunale, Verona, p.156). The picture was seen in the Trivulzio collection by P. Juan Andrés in 1791 (*Cartas familiares*, iv, Madrid, 1793, p.140): '*un corredor ó pasillo, es una pequeña galeria, donde hay un quadro grande de Manteña, que lleve la data* anno graciae 1497 15 Augusti, *y aunque excelente por la grandiosidad de las figuras, y la viveza de los colores, no llega en mi concepto de mucho al de la Virgen de la Victoria que tenemos en Mantua ... y que aunque trabajado despues de este, que es del año de 1495, es sin embargo mas duro, y falto del empasto y de la morbidez que se echa de ver en algunas figuras de este.*'

For the relationship of the church and picture see text (p.184). St Benedict is present as the patron saint of the Benedictine order, St Gregory as one of its glories – he is shown in the white Olivetan habit. Both these saints were represented several times in the other altarpieces of the church (cf. Dal Pozzo, *loc. cit.*). For the presence of St John Baptist see below. The Virgin is shown partly as a *Vergine Assunta*: this is because the church is dedicated to the Assumption of the Virgin. Gerola notes that the date of the signature, 15 August 1497, is precisely the date of the festival of the Assumption of the Virgin.

The picture was commissioned under the rule of Fra Francesco da Lisca of Verona, abbot of Santa Maria from 1495 to 1499. The documents concerning it in the *Libro di spese* of the monastery run from 8 October 1496 to 22 December 1496 (pub. Milanesi, in Vasari, iii, 1878, p.393n; Kristeller, 1902, pp.562–3, doc.144). In documents of 10 November and 22 December 1496 Fra Giovanni da Verona, the famous wood-carver and *intarsia* worker, appears as the intermediary between the convent and Mantegna, going from Verona to Mantua, where the picture was being painted (for Fra Giovanni see P. Lugano, in *Bull. senese di storia patria*, xii, 1905, pp.135–228; see p.139 for the popularity of the name Giovanni with Veronese who took the Olivetan habit). It is known that the sacristy and campanile of Santa Maria in Organo were designed by Fra Giovanni and begun on 2 July and 7 August 1495 respectively, and it must have been he who drew or carved the model of the church used by Mantegna. The sacristy was not completed until 1505 and the campanile until 1533, and Mellini and Quintavalle (1962, p.19) emphasize the interest of the model as indicating the original design for the entire reconstruction, which was later modified in the sixteenth century. The frame for the altarpiece was carved in 1496–7 by the Veronese sculptor Gregorio Mazzola (information communicated by P. Brugnoli to Puppi, 1972, p.43).

For Santa Maria in Organo see Biancolini (*Notizie storiche delle chiese di Verona*, i, Verona, 1749, pp.287–318); P. Vesentini (*La chiesa di S. Maria in Organo*, Verona, 1954).

As the Baptist's inscription is from John 1, 7, the T/MVND at the end may be from verse 9 (*erat lux vera, quae illuminat omnem hominem venientem in hunc mundum*).

For some notes on Mantegna's influence on late fifteenth- and early sixteenth-century Veronese painters see Del Bravo (*Liberale da Verona*, 1967, pp. 29–30).

38. Mantegna and the Studiolo of Isabella d'Este

Two paintings certainly executed for the Studiolo of Isabella d'Este by Mantegna survive, the *Parnassus* (Plate XII) and *Pallas expelling the Vices* (Plate XIII). A painting of *Comus* was begun by him, and copied and finished after his death by Lorenzo Costa (Plate 128). Two other pictures by him 'feigned as of bronze' were also installed in the Studiolo, probably by 1523, certainly by 1542, and may have been executed for it as early as 1492 (see Cat. nos. 92 and 93).

For the origin and vicissitudes of the Studiolo see Gerola, 'Trasmigrazioni e vicende dei Camerini di Isabella d'Este' in *Atti e memorie dell'R. Accademia Virgiliana*, xxi, 1929, pp.253–90, and E. Verheyen, *The paintings in the Studiolo of Isabella d'Este at Mantua*, 1971. An exhibition catalogue (Soprintendenza per i Beni Artistici e Storici per le Provincie di Mantova, Cremona e Brescia, *Gli Studioli di Isabella d'Este; documenti, vicende, restauri*, Mantua, Archivio di Stato, Mantua, 1977) admirably summarizes the known history and documentation of the Studiolo and the collections it housed. See also the catalogue of the Louvre exhibition, *Le Studiolo d'Isabelle d'Este*, ed. S. Béguin, 1975.

Mantegna was asked by Isabella to paint a picture for the Studiolo by the first days of March 1492, for on 4 March Isabella's secretary Silvestro Calandra wrote to her that he was 'pressing Andrea Mantegna so that when the Studio is finished he too will not fail her for his part' (*solicitando Andrea Mantegna che, quando [lo Studiolo] serrà finito, anchor lui dal canto suo non li manchi*) Gerola (*op. cit.*, pp.255 n2, 256 n2, from AG,F,II,8).

Verheyen (p.10) claims that this commission had no connection with the *Parnassus* or the *Pallas* and that it refers to some other picture. He believes that Isabella's first intention was probably to hang the studio with portraits of her friends and relations, according to a contemporary usage attested at Pesaro (see Cat. no.77) and in a more elaborate form at Urbino. In his view this first scheme did not take effect beyond a portrait of Isabella del Balzo, Countess of Acerra (see text, p.188). But it is also possible that one or both of the two small paintings 'feigned as of bronze' were painted at this time. In July 1494 the floor of the Studiolo was paved with tiles decorated with Gonzaga *imprese*, but Verheyen thinks that it was not until a visit to Ferrara in the spring of 1495 that Isabella conceived the idea of more elaborate decorations in the form of paintings. On 1 May 1495 her secretary Capilupo sent her a drawing with exact measurements of the *camerino*: as Verheyen points out, this must have been done so that Isabella could discuss her projects with advisers, possibly artists, at the Ferrarese court. In May 1496 she ordered white Carrara marble to make frameworks for the door and window of the *camerino*, and hired a painter from Padua named Bernardino to repaint the room. Bernardino probably painted a blue ceiling centring on a Gonzaga device: traces of such a ceiling still remain in the *grotta* below. Bernardino began work in September 1496.

Whatever Isabella's earlier projects, Mantegna probably only actually began work on a major painting for the Studiolo when she made up her mind to have her *camerino* redecorated. The actual commission was probably given, as Verheyen and Brown (1969, p.541) suggest, in the winter of 1496.

DOCUMENTS: 1) *1496, December.* Visit to Mantua of Lorenzo da Pavia, a famous maker of musical instruments from Venice (Brown, *loc. cit.*).

2) *1497, 6 June.* Isabella d'Este in Mantua to Lorenzo da Pavia in Venice. We remind you to send the varnish for varnishing the picture of Messer Andrea Mantinea as you promised both him and me. Use all diligence to see that it is good, and advise us of the cost, when we shall send you the money (A.S., Busta 2992, Copialettere, Libro 8, p.76; cit. by Brown, 1969, p.542; *id.*, 1982, p.44).

3) *1497, 14 June.* Same to same. Mantegna has received the varnish, which pleases him greatly, but there is not enough. Could Lorenzo send twice as much again, as quickly as possible, for Mantegna has now begun to varnish the picture (A.S., Copialettere, cit., p.81, in Brown, *loc. cit.*).

4) *1497, 3 July.* Alberto da Bologna in Mantua to Isabella d'Este in Ferrara. Work goes on in her *studio*, and on her return Isabella will find the framework (*piedistalli*) made and set up above Mantegna's painting and perhaps its gilding all finished (Kristeller, 1902, p.563, doc.164).

5) *1501, 25 June.* Michele Vianello in Venice to Isabella d'Este in Mantua. Giovanni Bellini is anxious to serve the Marchesa by painting a picture for her studio, but most unwilling to paint the *historia* she has given him for a subject. He knows how good her judgement of pictures is and his work will have to stand comparison with that work of M. Andrea, and he says that he can do nothing that will be any good with her *historia (ma de quel istoria li a data V.S. non si poria dire quanto la fa mal volentieri, per che sa il giudizio di V.S. poi va al paragone di quel opera de M. Andrea).* Accordingly if the Marchesa will allow him to choose his own subject she will be better served. (Braghirolli, in *Archivio Veneto*, xiii, 1877, p.377.)

6) *1502, 13 July.* Isabella d'Este in Mantua to Lorenzo da Pavia in Venice. He is to send as much varnish to varnish Mantegna's picture as he sent for the other one, and it is to be of the same excellence (A.S., Busta 2993, Copialettere, Libro 13, p.94; Brown, 1982, p.66).

7) *1502, 30 July.* Isabella acknowledges receipt of the varnish (A.S., Busta cit., Copialettere, Libro 14, p.2: Brown, *loc. cit.*; 1982, p.67).

8) *1502, 22 November.* Isabella d'Este in Mantua to Vincenzo Bolzani in Florence. A letter in the series concerning the negotiations with Perugino for a painting for the Studiolo, which began on 15 September 1502. She is certain Perugino will not wish his paintings to be of less excellence than fame reports, especially as they will be in comparison with the paintings of Mantegna (*maxime andando al paragone de li quadri del Mantegna*) (Canuti, *Il Perugino*, ii, Siena, 1931, p.210).

9) *1504, 12 January.* Isabella d'Este in Mantua to Pietro Perugino in Florence. She sends him the height of the biggest figure in Mantegna's paintings, with which his own figures should be in proportion (Canuti, *vol. cit.*, p.217, no.329).

10) *1504, 12 January.* Isabella d'Este in Mantua to Angelo del Tovaglia in Florence. She is sending the size of the figures Perugino is to paint, so that he can proportion them to match those of the paintings already in the Studiolo, in reply to a request from both of them (sent to her on 10 December 1503). She would have sent it earlier, but has not been able to obtain it before now from Mantegna (Canuti, *vol. cit.*, pp.216–17, no.328. This letter accompanied No.9).

11) *1504, 10 November.* Isabella d'Este in Mantua to Paride da Ceresara. She does not know who is the more disgusted by the delays of painters, she who sees her *camerino* not yet finished, or Paride, who has to make a new invention every day (*M. Paris. Non sapemo chi habbi in maggior fastidio la longhezza de li pictori, o nui che non vediamo finito el nostro Camarino, o vui che ogni dì havete ad fare nove inventione*) (Canuti, *vol. cit.*, p.223).

12) *1504, 1 December.* Antonio Galeazzo Bentivoglio to Isabella d'Este. He has spoken to Costa and told him that Messer Andrea's painting (*quadro*) appeared to be lustred, or varnished, which made him marvel, it being on canvas. Isabella must let Bentivoglio know whether it is lustred, and if so, with what lustre, or else whether it is varnished or not (Luzio, in *Emporium*, xi, 1900, pp.358–9).

13) *1505, 30 June.* Isabella d'Este in Mantua to Perugino in Florence. The picture has arrived safe and sound, and pleases her because it is well designed and well coloured, but it would have been more to your honour and our satisfaction had it been finished more highly, since it has to hang beside those of Mantegna, which are *netti* (sharp and well finished) to a supreme degree. She regrets that Perugino was dissuaded by Lorenzo from colouring it in oils (Canuti, *vol. cit.*, p.236).

14) *1505, 10 August.* Perugino in Florence to Isabella d'Este in Mantua. He is sorry he was not told the method of colouring adopted by Mantegna, because it would have been easier for him to colour the picture in oils than in glue tempera, and the work would have been more delicate with a more delicate ground underneath (Canuti, *vol. cit.*, p.236).

Kristeller (1901, pp.348–59) recognized that none of these documents proved that the *Parnassus* was the first picture executed by Mantegna for the Studiolo, but assumes that it must have been the first by reason of its style and its superiority to the *Pallas*. Verheyen (1972, p.14), who seems to be unaware of docs. 6 and 7, wrongly claims that the two pictures were executed at a very short interval from each other, on the strength of the measurements of a *spalliera* of *verdura minuta* which the Marchesa ordered for her studio on 4 December 1497. He argues that its measurements were fixed to allow space for two pictures, but the *spalliera* was surely intended for the lower, not the upper part of the wall. In any case the documents published by Brown are conclusive: see in addition the text (p.192) for a further argument. Verheyen is anxious to make the pictures roughly contemporary in date in order to bolster his conclusions about their iconography. A possibility which both Verheyen and Brown neglect is that Isabella originally intended the *istoria* she commissioned from Bellini in late February or March 1501 as a pair to her first picture from Mantegna. She had in fact begun a first negotiation for it in November 1496, and followed this overture to Bellini with another to Perugino in April 1497 (Verheyen, p.15). Realizing that Bellini was going to fail her, probably by March 1502, she may have turned to Mantegna; only a few days after she can have received Mantegna's second picture she cancelled her commission to Bellini and asked for the return of her earnest of 25 ducats (letters of 10 and 15 September 1502, printed by Braghirolli, in *Archivio Veneto*, xiii, 1877, p.379).

The *Pallas* must be the *Palladiam turbam* which in 1503 Pomponius Gauricus records Giulio Campagnola as having copied from Mantegna (see p.427). It is plain from a letter of 10 September 1497, in which his brother-in-law attempts to procure a place for him in the Marchese's household, that at this date Campagnola had not yet been to Mantua (published by Luzio, in *Archivio storico dell'arte*, i, 1888, pp.184–5).

ORIGINAL SETTING: Attempts have been made to reconstruct their original arrangement in the Studiolo of the Castello by Gerola (pp.279–80) and by Verheyen. Although many of their conclusions differ, both agree that since the light of the *Parnassus* comes from the left, it must have been placed on the right-hand long wall of the Studiolo close to the window, which was in the narrow east wall of the room. Similarly the *Pallas*, which is lit from the right, must have been placed in the corresponding position on the left-hand wall. Verheyen (p.19) assumes that there was room for only five paintings in the Studiolo; Gerola places one of the two small 'feigned bronze' pictures by Mantegna of the 1542 inventory on the east wall, next to the window, the other on whichever of the two long walls was not pierced by a doorway (situation unknown). But see two letters of March 1501 and January 1503 from Isabella about doorways that faced each other in her *camerino* (Rossi, in *Rivista italiana di numismatica*, i, 1888, pp.176–7).

ICONOGRAPHICAL STUDIES: Attempts to elucidate and interpret the pictures have been made by Förster ('Studien zu Mantegna und dem Bildern im Studier zimmer der Isabella Gonzaga' in *J.P.K.*, xxii, 1901, pp.154–80); Wind, *Bellini's Feast of the Gods*, 1948; Gombrich, 'An interpretation of Mantegna's Parnassus' in *J.W.C.I.*, xxvi, 1963, pp.196–8; Verheyen, *op. cit.*; P. W. Lehmann, 'The sources and meaning of Mantegna's *Parnassus*' in P. W. Lehmann & K. Lehmann, *Samothracian Reflections: Aspects of the revival of the antique*, 1973, pp.59–178; M. A. Debout, 'La réprésentation des Vices par Mantegna: l'hermaphrodite à tête de singe' in *Revue du Louvre*, xxv, 1975, pp.227–9; M. Vickers, 'The Source of the Mars in Mantegna's "Parnassus"' in *B.M.*, cxx, 1978, pp.151–2. Förster remains the fundamental study: there are valuable single observations in Gombrich, P. Lehmann and M. A. Debout.

39. Parnassus

Paris, Musée du Louvre, Inv. INV 370

Egg tempera on fine canvas 150 × 192 cm.   Plate XII

CONDITION: Accounts of the condition of this picture have been published in recent years by Mme Hours, in *Revue du Louvre*, xix, 1969, pp.39–42, and in *Le Studiolo*, 1975, pp.57–8, 78n., 282. In her later analysis, she notes that the condition of the picture is less good than she originally thought. On relining in the seventeenth century, a strip of 11 cm. was added along the top and other strips of about 2 cm. added to the sides. There are *pentimenti* in the faces of some of the Muses, especially in the face

in profile of the Muse in yellow: there are *pentimenti* too in the garden hedge in front of the rock. A microscopic analysis (by J. P. Rioux & E. Martin in *Le Studiolo*, 1975, p.60) has revealed a number of repaints in oil: Mme Hours notes that these are especially heavy in the landscape. The colours used are of the finest quality. The ground is a thin layer of gesso laid on with glue.

PROVENANCE: Executed for the *camerino* of Isabella d'Este in the Castello of Mantua (see above). In 1522 Isabella moved into the Corte Vecchia, or old Palazzo Gonzaga, which was not yet conjoined with the Castello, where from 1515 she had had re-created the suite of *camerini* usually known as her Studiolo. These were near completion in 1522, and in November that year a project for removing and remounting the pictures which decorated her old *camerino* was under discussion (Gerola, *op. cit.*, pp.269 ff). Work appears to have been completed by 1525. The *Parnassus* is recorded in the inventory of the Studiolo taken in 1542 (Luzio, 1908, p.423) as 'nel studio che è in Corte vecchia appresso la Grotta'. It followed Costa's *Allegory of the Court of Isabella* and Perugino's *Combat of Love and Chastity*. The entry reads '*E più un altro quadro di pittura appresso el sopra scritto nella medema facciata di mano del già m. Andrea Mantegna nel quale è dipinto un Marte una Venere che stanno in piacere con un Vulcano et un Orpheo che suona, con nove nimphe che ballano.*'

The principal pictures of the Studiolo seem to have been disposed of during the 1620s. On 24 April 1627 Nys, Charles I's agent, offered to accept a lot of paintings at valuation '*con patto che mi sia dato ancora il ballo del Mantegna e quadro del Costa vecchio della Grota*'. On 1 May, acknowledging a reply of 27 April, he says, '*vedo che non besogna pensare alli duo quadri della Grota, cioè il Ballo del Mantegna et quello del Costa*' (Luzio, 1913, p.141). Luzio (1913, pp.300–11) thinks that he was refused because the five main Studiolo pictures had already been given to Cardinal de Richelieu as part of presents of paintings made to him by the Mantuan court during the years 1624–9.

Richelieu installed them in the now destroyed Château de Richelieu, begun in 1632, where they were again placed in a cabinet setting, in the room called the Cabinet du Roy, in the upper division of the panelling, between the cornice and the ceiling. The paintings had been sent to the Château de Richelieu by late 1636 or early 1637 for they were seen at that date in the Cabinet du Roy by Gaspard d'Albi when he presented Poussin's *Bacchanals* to Richelieu (*Le Studiolo*, 1975, pp.61, 78 n.288). They are described in the rare guide-book of Vignier, *Le chasteav de Richelieu*, Saumur, 1676, pp.61–8: '*Le Cabinet du Roy. Il est d'une figure presque quarrée, ayant six toises dans un sens & un peu plus de cinq dans un autre. Son Lambris regne depuis le Parquet jusqu'au Plat-fonds de la hauteur de quinze à seize pieds . . . Depuis la Corniche du Lambris jusqu'au haut du Plat-fonds un compartiment doré d'or bruni renferme des Tableaux admirables, tant des anciens Mâitres que des modernes. Celuy qui est au dessus de la Porte est d'André Mantegne, représentant une* MINERVE *qui chasse les Vices d'un lieu délicieux.*

    La vice & la vertu ne s'accordent jamais
    Il faut que l'un des deux céde à l'autre la place:
       Aussi Minerve chasse
    Ce monstreux Tyran de ce charmant Palais.

A coté de ce Tableau à main droite en entrant, il y en a aussi un autre d'André Manteigne dont on ne sçait point le sujet. . . . Comus le Tableau qui le suit [i.e. Perugino's Combat of Love and Chastity] paroît une Isle consacrée à Vénus. On y voit un Mont couvert de Myrtes & de quelques Cyprés, & sur le devant du Tableau Vénus conduisant un Amour qui porte en ses mains des couronnes de myrthe; En suite l'on y voit quelques Faunes, qui s'amusent à faire des guirlandes pour couronner leurs Amantes, dont quelques unes semblent endormies, pendant que des Poëtes méslez avec des femmes joüent de divers instrumens. A l'emboucheure de cette Isle se voit une manière d'Arc triomphal, au devant duquel il y a un Mercure qui en défend l'entrée à la DISCORDE, *à la* FRAVDE & *à* l'ENVIE. *C'est encore un ouvrage de Lorenzo Costa peintre Ferrarois très-estimé.*

> *Sans doute c'est encor icy l'Isle charmante,*
> *Où d'une âme reconnoissante*
> *Paphé fit à Venus un Temple glorieux;*
> *Mais afin d'y passer joyeusement la vie,*
> *Mercure avec un fouët chasse loin de ces lieux*
> *La Discorde, la Fraude, & la jalouse Envie.'*

The pictures were still in the Cabinet in September 1800, when the commissaries of the French government noted them: '*Dans le cabinet du Roi, nous eûmes la satisfaction de trouver, encastrés dans la boiserie, deux très-beaux tableaux de Mantegne, bien conservés; ces deux tableaux, peints sur toile, ont 5 p. 1° de haut, sur 5 p. 7° de large. L'un représente le Parnasse et Apollon qui fait danser les Muses au son de sa Lyre: l'autre, Minerve chassant les vices, deux compositions d'un goût exquis . . .*' As a result of their report, the French government acquired the two Mantegnas, the two Costas and the Perugino, and removed them in 1801 to the Musée Central des Arts, Paris. The two Mantegnas were later exhibited at the Musée Napoléon (Bonnaffé, *Recherches sur les collections des Richelieu*, 1883, pp.34,108–11).

For two preliminary drawings for the *Parnassus* see Cat. nos. 191 and 192; Plates 220 and 221.

A number of scholars consider features of the picture untypical of Mantegna. Crowe & Cavalcaselle (i, 1871, p.409) believe that the 'gayer tints' indicate the collaboration of Bonsignori. Rühmer (1961, p.cvi) considers the background untypical of Mantegna, and suggests it may be by a painter from the circle of Garofalo. Verheyen (1971, p.35 n) rightly rejects this view. A comparison for the background is found in the Copenhagen *Pietà* (Cat. no.35; Plate 124).

Mantegna drew heavily on antique sources for his figures. His borrowings are discussed by Blum (1936, pp.98–105), Picard (in *Rev. Arch.*, ser.6, xxxix, 1952, pp.124–8) and P. Lehmann (in *Rev. Arch.*, n.s., 1968, pp.197–214). Against the earlier view that Mantegna derived the group of the Muses from the Borghese Dancers in the Louvre, P. Lehmann claims that it derives from a drawing by Ciriaco d'Ancona, now known only in copies, of a frieze from Samothrace (formerly Louvre: now on permanent loan to the Samothrace Museum).

40. Pallas expelling the Vices

There are a number of inscriptions. That on the scroll attached to the tree reads: AGITE PELLITE SEDIBVS NOSTRIS/FOEDA HAEC VICIORV̄ MONSTRA/VIRTVTVM

COELITVS ADNOS/REDV̄TIVM/DIVAE COMITES. A responding inscription appears on a white banderole above the natural aperture in the wall on the right: ET MIHI VIRTVTV̄ MATRI/SVCCVRRITE DIVI. On the left bank of the pool is the inscription OTIA SI TOLLAS/PERIERE/CVPIDINIS ARCVS (Ovid, *Remedia Amoris*, 139). Some of the figures wear inscribed attributes. (*Right*) Avarice has a white bandeau inscribed AVARICIA; Ingratitude wears one inscribed INGRATITVDO. The golden coronet of Ignorance is inscribed INIORANCIA. (*Left*) Idleness is labelled OTIVM, Sloth INERTIA. The hermaphrodite monkey-headed monster wears a scrolling white band around its left arm inscribed IMMORTALE ODIVM/FRAVS ET MALITIAE. From cords tied round its body are suspended inscribed labels and bags. The two labels top left are inscribed in Greek; one has been read by J. Bousquet as Ζελσ (for the Greek Ζῆλοσ=jealousy). The pendant bag on the right is inscribed SEMINA. On the opposite side is a bag inscribed MALA, while the bag over the thigh below is inscribed PEIORA and the pendant bag swinging out to the left is inscribed PESSIMA. Over the bottom of the belly are two white labels inscribed (*left*) SVSPICIO, (*right*) in Greek, as yet undeciphered. (For a discussion of this last figure and its inscriptions see M. A. Debout, in *Revue du Louvre*, xxv, 1975, pp.227–9. She quotes J. Bousquet's opinion that the Roman capitals are patterned on Hadrianic models, while the Greek imitates Byzantine tenth- and eleventh-century models.) The spelling of INIORANCIA for IGNORANTIA is either due to restoration or is a practical illustration of the vice.

Paris, Musée du Louvre. Inv. INV 371

159 × 192 cm.   Plate XIII

Executed in a mixed technique: most of the picture is in egg tempera, but Mantegna has used a little oil in the blues. Over some of the areas in blue he has superimposed a layer of egg tempera, probably to modify the effect of the oil. The colours used are of the finest quality. The ground is a thin layer of gesso, laid on with glue.

CONDITION: Like the *Parnassus*, enlarged by a strip measuring 11 cm. along the top, and by strips measuring 2 cm. at the sides.

PROVENANCE: Recorded in the inventory of the Studiolo taken in 1542 (Luzio, 1908, pp.423–4) as on the left of the entrance to the 'studio che è in Corte vecchia appresso la Grotta'. The entry reads: 'E più un quadro di pittura posto al lato sinistro dell'entrata della Grotta, di mano di Andrea Mantegna, nel quale è dipinto la vertù che scaccia li vitii, fra li quali èvi l'ocio condotto dalla inercia et l'ignorantia portata dalla ingratitudine et avaritia.' Luzio (1913, pp.300–1) suggests that the picture was given to Cardinal de Richelieu as part of presents of paintings made during the years 1624–9. For its later history see Cat. no.39.

41. Comus

Paris, Musée du Louvre, Inv. INV 256

Egg tempera on a thin ground of gesso; the blues, as in the *Parnassus*, executed in oil of nuts. 152.5 × 238.5 cm.

           Plate 128

CONDITION: The condition of this painting is crucial to the question of its authorship (see entry below). The picture has been relined, and is in a poor state of preservation. It is thinly painted, with cracks in the ground and numerous paint losses. Some slight *pentimenti*, notably to the right of Comus. The surface much repainted in oil (*Le Studiolo*, 1975, pp.59,61).

A painting of Comus begun by Mantegna for Isabella d'Este is mentioned in documents of 1506.

DOCUMENTS: 1) *1506, 13 July*. Mantegna to Isabella d'Este. Although he is not yet completely recovered from his illness, he has been using such little genius as God has given him in the Marchesa's service and has almost finished designing Her Excellency's *historia* of Comus and will go on with it insofar as his *fantasia* shall aid him (*ho quaxi finito di dessignare la instoria de Comos de Vostra Ex. quale andarò seguitando quanto la fantasia me adiuterà*). For this letter and its correct dating see Brown (in *Revue du Louvre*, 1969, p.38, n.25). It was mistakenly dated to January by Kristeller.

2) *1506, 14 July*. Isabella d'Este to Gian Giacomo Calandra. On his visit to Mantegna he is to say how pleased she is that he has nearly finished the design of the history of Comus he is executing for her and if she does not give him money it is because she is in difficulties (*Apresso gli dirai che havimo havuto gran piacere che lhabbi como finito il dessigno de la Historia de Comos chel ni fa*) (Verheyen, 1972, p.20n).

3) *1506, 15 July*. Gian Giacomo Calandra to Isabella d'Este. He has been to visit Mantegna and has desired to see the picture. On it are designed these figures: the god Comus, two Venuses, one clothed, the other naked, two Amores, Janus with Envy in his arms, pushing her out, Mercury and three other figures turned to flight by Mercury. Some other figures are still wanting but the design of these ones is most beautiful. (*Jo ho voluto vedere la tabula: in la quale sono dissegnate queste figure, il dio Como, due Veneri une vestita, laltra nuda, dui amori, Iano cum la Invidia in braccio suspingendola fuori, Mercurio: e tre altre figure volte in fuga da esso Mercurio: gli ne manchano anchora alcune altre, ma il disegno di queste è belissimo.*) (Kristeller, 1902, p.580, doc.180.)

4) *1506, 7 August*. Isabella d'Este to Mantegna. She regrets she cannot take on herself a liability for 27 ducats more than the 100 she has already accepted as a debt to be discharged by her to Mantegna's creditor Bosio in payment of the *Faustina*. She is too short of money, otherwise she would willingly disburse them as an earnest for the picture he is to paint for her and to suit his convenience (*per darvi ara dil quadro ni havete a fare*) (Kristeller, 1902, p.582, doc.185).

5) *1506, 20 September*. Lodovico da Campo San Piero in Mantua to Francesco II Gonzaga. After Mantegna's death on 13 September Isabella and Cardinal Sigismondo have taken the few things he had and divided them between themselves (Brown, 1974, p.103).

A painting of *Comus* was executed for the Studiolo of Isabella by Lorenzo Costa and is listed in an inventory of 1542 (Luzio, 1908, p.423) as in the 'studio che è in Corte Vecchia', to the left of the window: 'E più un altro quadro a man sinistra della finestra di mano di m. Lorenzo Costa in lo qual è dipinto un archo triomphale et molte figure che fanno una musica con una fabula di Leda.' The date

when the commission was given to Costa has not been discovered. Gerola ('Trasmigrazioni' cit. in Cat. no.38, p.257) says Costa was given the commission in 1509, but Verheyen (p.19) claims that it must have been painted after January 1511. Kristeller (1901, pp.358–60), followed by all subsequent writers (including Varese, *Lorenzo Costa*, 1967, pp.74–5) except Lauts, deduces from Calandra's description that Isabella had taken the canvas (if this is the correct interpretation of Calandra's *tabula*) on which Mantegna had sketched out a number of the figures and later handed it over to Costa for completion. Lauts (*Isabella d'Este*, 1952, p.182) suggests that Costa was given the same *invenzione* and painted an entirely new picture. The problem is discussed in two important articles by C. Brown and Mme. Hours (*Revue du Louvre*, xix, 1969, pp.31–42). After an X-ray examination of the *Comus* in 1964, Mme Hours concluded that so far as X-ray examination is concerned, the pictorial preparation and facture must be entirely by Costa. She accepted, however, that the main lines of the composition are by Mantegna, and there is no real incompatibility between her position and that of Brown, who rightly emphasizes that Mantegna can only have had time to sketch figures on the canvas, as Calandra's description implies. Verheyen (1972, pp.46–9) postulates that Costa merely copied Mantegna's design, completing it where it was unfinished with figures of his own, and suggests that the resultant composition may be a rearrangement of Mantegna's, rather than a re-creation of it. He also argues (pp.19–20) that Mantegna's picture was not originally intended for the Studiolo. This last claim is implausible.

The Louvre has now re-examined the picture (*Le Studiolo*, 1975, p.31) and formed the opinion that the picture was begun by Mantegna. Nevertheless in the same work (p.59) Mme Hours restates her belief that X-rays of the picture show no evidence of Mantegna's hand, and that if he began it, his contribution must have been limited to a light preliminary sketch in a medium lacking in density. The evidence of style suggests that the figures of Comus, Venus and Amor on the left, those of Leda, Bacchus and a nymph in the foreground and those of Janus, Mercury and the Vices on the right were designed by Mantegna. Some of the other figures may have been executed on indications left by him on the original canvas, but in large part their realization, as well as that of the landscape, must be the work of Costa. See text, pp.208–9, where the author argues, like Verheyen, that the picture must be in part a copy of Mantegna's composition, if there is really no evidence of underdrawing by Mantegna, and that Costa copied Mantegna's figures on to a new canvas.

42. St Sebastian. On the ledge to the right is a burning white candle on a brown base, with a scroll winding round it inscribed: NIL NISI DIVINVM STABILE / EST CAETERA FVMVS.
Venice, Galleria della Ca' d'Oro, Dono Franchetti, no.140
Canvas 210 × 91 cm.   Plates 129, 130

CONDITION: In 1884 (see PROVENANCE) described by Frizzoni as 'sensibilmente manomesso dal ristauro'. The surface is worn, and there are areas of repaint on the chest, loincloth, right leg and right arm. A *pentimento* along the lines of the legs and arms shows that the figure was originally a little more to the left.

PROVENANCE: First recorded by Marc'Antonio Michiel in the house of Pietro Bembo, Padua (1884, pp.50–1: 'El San Sebastiano saettato alla colonna più del naturale, sopra una tela, fu de mano del Mantegna'). Seen in Casa Gradenigo, Padua, in March 1803 by Giovanni de' Lazara (Campori, 1866, p.351: '. . . ho riveduto i giorni scorsi con sempre nuovo piacere il sorprendente S. Sebastiano del nostro inarrivabile Mantegna di casa Gradenigo'). According to Selvatico (Sopra un dipinto di Andrea Mantegna nella Galleria Scarpa alla Motta di Friuli, Padua, 1839; reprinted in Scritti d'Arte, 1859, pp.40–4; see also 1849, pp.194–5) it remained in the possession of Bembo's descendants until 1807, when sold by one of them, Signora Cornelia Gradenigo, to the celebrated anatomist and surgeon Antonio Scarpa (1752–1832), professor at Pavia. Bequeathed by Scarpa to his brothers, who resided at Motta di Friuli. Sold by the Scarpa family to Barone Giorgio Franchetti, of Venice, by whom bequeathed to the Ca' d'Oro (Fogolari, Nebbia, Moschini, La R. Galleria Giorgio Franchetti alla Ca' d'Oro, 1929, pp.23–4,34,38,113).

Selvatico (see above) was the first to propose the generally accepted identification of this picture with a St Sebastian mentioned in Lodovico Mantegna's letter of 2 October 1506 to Francesco Gonzaga as still remaining in the studio and as having been intended by his father for Lodovico Gonzaga, Bishop of Mantua, for certain unspecified reasons (Kristeller, 1902, pp.583–4, doc.190: 'Deinde gliè un San Sebastiano il quale nostro padre voleva fossi di monsignor vescovo di Mantua per alcune cose che intenderà poi V. Ill.S. le quali seriano troppo prolixe da scrivere'). Cardinal Sigismondo Gonzaga laid an embargo immediately after Mantegna's death on any picture leaving the studio, but it does not appear from Lodovico's letter that he actually wished to purchase this picture, as he certainly wished to purchase the Dead Christ (Cat. no.23) and the Corner Cult of Cybele (Cat. no.57). There is of course no proof that this St Sebastian of 1506 must be the same as the present picture. From a letter of 28 October 1506 (Brown, 1974, p.103) we know that the Marchese Francesco forbade anything to be given to Lodovico Gonzaga.

There are two widely held divergent opinions about the dating of the present picture. The first regards it as one of Mantegna's latest works (Crowe & Cavalcaselle, 1871, p.409; 1912, pp.110–11; Morelli, 1890, p.360; 1891, p.229; Thode, 1897, p.110; Kristeller, 1901, pp.330–1, 442 as 1497; Knapp, pp.122,176–7; Fiocco, 1937, p.75; Paccagnini, 1961, p.64; Cipriani, 1962, pp.41,70; E. Battisti in 1965, p.51, associating it with the plague of 1506). The second dates it c.1490, close to the Triumphs (Venturi, 1914, p.216; Tietze-Conrat, 1955, pp.27,199, an ambiguously expressed opinion; Arslan, 1961, pp.168–9, close also to Judith of 1491; Camesasca, pp.40–1,121, begun c.1480, and completed c.1490; Garaviglia, 1967, No.73). Camesasca, developing a suggestion of Kristeller, also claims that the picture was abandoned by Mantegna c.1490, and gone over almost entirely after his death, perhaps by one of his sons, and that the drapery was enlarged over the crutch as a result of a second posthu-

mous intervention. The features closely resemble in treatment those of St Michael in the Madonna della Vittoria (1496), and a late dating is also supported by the advanced conception of the nude with its emphasis on the ideal and the heroic. A date c.1504–6 seems plausible on stylistic and historical grounds (see below).

If this is the picture left in Mantegna's studio at his death, then the presumption is that he painted it of his own volition for himself, since Francesco's words 'il quale . . . voleva fossi di monsignor vescovo di Mantua' imply that he made a verbal gift or bequest of it to Lodovico Gonzaga before his death. They do not imply, as suggested by Kristeller, that the picture was commissioned by Lodovico Gonzaga. The device of the candle and motto, with its lesson of the vanity of all wordly things, which melt away and vanish in smoke like a candle, compared with divine things, which alone are stable and lasting, seems to be Mantegna's own invention. It expresses a mood of profound disillusionment with this life that corresponds best with the financial troubles and losses of his latest years. To St Sebastian, popular as he was as a protector against the ever-recurrent plague, Mantegna seems to have had a special devotion.

For an enquiry into the symbolism of the picture see a most unconvincing article by M. Levi d'Ancona ('Il Mantegna e la simbologia: il S. Sebastiano del Louvre e quello della Ca' d'Oro' in Commentari, xxiii, 1972, pp.44–52).

43. The Adoration of the Magi

J. Paul Getty Museum, Malibu
Oil and tempera mixed on fine canvas 54.5 × 71 cm.

Plate XVI

CONDITION: Paint surface rather worn.

PROVENANCE: Coll. Louisa Lady Ashburton, by whom exh. London, RA, 1871, No.287, and London, New Gallery, Exhibition of Venetian Art, 1894–5, No.22, as Mantegna. Coll. Marquis of Northampton. Exh. London, RA, Exhibition of Italian Art (Balniel & Clark, Commem. Catalogue, 1931, p.63, No.184; London, Victoria & Albert Museum, Splendours of the Gonzaga, 1981–2, p.122, No.32). Sold Christie's 18 April 1985, lot 16, with full lit.

Generally regarded as the best surviving example of a much-copied composition, but with no agreement as to whether it is autograph. Yriarte (1901, pp.211–12), Kristeller (1901, pp.143,145–6, 438–9), Berenson (1901, pp.95–6; 1932, 1968) and Tietze-Conrat (1955, p.192, with reserve except for the invention) assign it to Mantegna himself. Knapp (1910, pp.123,177) gives it emphatically to the workshop, as does Ragghianti (1962, p.39). For Venturi (1914, p.476) it is by Francesco Mantegna, an attribution also proposed by Cipriani (1962, p.82). Fiocco (1937, p.68) finds that workshop intervention cannot be excluded, while Camesasca (1964, p.128) simply lists it as close to Mantegna's last works. Garaviglia (1967, No.106) as generally rejected. When shown at the Splendours of the Gonzaga exhibition held at the V. & A. Museum in 1981–2 its autograph status became patent, and it was correctly catalogued by C. Elam (exh. cat., p.122, No.32) as a late work, *c.*1500–5. In colouring it is close to the altarpiece of Mantegna's chapel, while the revival of the window-frame finds a parallel in the *St Sebastian* of the Ca' d'Oro.

A late date is proposed by all students, even by Kristeller, who compares it with the Berlin *Presentation* but believes it to repeat at a later date types evolved during the Paduan period (he lists it by a slip under 1454 on p.438). The bowl is of interest as an early representation of Chinese porcelain: the Christie sale catalogue notes that it may however be early Persian ware. The cataloguer also suggests that the censer held by Melchior is Turkish Tombak ware, and that the agate bowl or cup held by Balthasar may be Persian.

A close copy (Pl.131) is in the Johnson Coll., Philadelphia Museum of Arts (canvas, 61 × 68 cm., provenance unrecorded, in Johnson Coll. by 1902). Perkins (in *Rass. d'A.*, v, 1905, p.135) lists it as a contemporary copy; Berenson (1907, p.255) as autograph; *id.* (*Johnson Cat.*, i, 1913, pp.135–6) as a studio copy; Venturi (1914, p.476), probably by Francesco Mantegna; Tietze-Conrat (1955, p.197), a copy; Sweeny (*Johnson Cat.*, 1966, p.47, No.213) a copy. Other versions by various artists are noted by Kristeller (p.439): 1) Berlin, Museum, no.22 (attrib. Francesco da Santa Croce, destroyed 1945); 2) London, C. Butler coll. (see Cat. No.165), as ascribed to Giovanni Bellini or Previtali; 3) Verona, Museo di Castelvecchio, as ascribed to Catena; 4) Venice, Galleria Querini-Stampalia, as ascribed to Francesco da Santa Croce (Dazzi & Merkel, *Catalogo*, 1979, p.43, no.17). Larger than the original and with additional figures. 5) Leningrad, Hermitage, as ascribed to Francesco da Santa Croce. 6) Coll. Binetti (sale, Rome, Sangiorgi, 1892, lot 149, repr.; 7) Treviso, private coll., Virgin and Child only, copied into a *Virgin and Child with Sts Joseph and Catherine.*

Berenson (1901, *loc. cit.*) also notes as versions of the *Virgin and Child* two Madonnas exh. at the New Gallery in 1894 (see PROVENANCE), one, unidentifiable in catalogue, ascribed to Bonsignori and No.12 (C. Butler coll.), assigned by him to Francesco da Santa Croce.

Tietze-Conrat (*loc. cit.*) notes a version on panel with an additional figure on either side in the J. Murnaghan coll., Dublin.

A *Head of a Negro* (Milan, private coll., canvas, 39 × 28 cm) published in *L'Arte* (n.s. xii, December 1941, appendix) as by Mantegna is regarded by Cipriani as a copy of the Negro king in the Ashburton picture. More plausible is Tietze-Conrat's view (p.190) that it is a fragment from a Mantegnesque *Adoration of the Magi*.

The early history of the Castle Ashby *Adoration* has not been established, but the Mantuan inventory of 1627 lists in the first cupboard to the left on entering the 'stanza detta la libraria' a small painting of the *Adoration of the Magi*: '358. Un quadretto dipintovi N.S. ch'è visitato dai Maghi con cornice nera' (Luzio, 1913, p.118). See also Cat. no.115.

44. Holy Family with the Infant Baptist
Dresden, Staatliche Museen, N.G.-W.E.2 (Jahnig, *Die Romanischen Länder*, 1929, p.24, No.51)
Tempera on canvas 75.5 × 61.5 cm.   Plate 132; Fig. 14
CONDITION: Good.

PROVENANCE: Purchased in Venice by Sir Charles Eastlake in October 1854 from the painter Natale Schiavoni (1777–1858), together with five other pictures. Exh. by Lady Eastlake at the RA, 1870, No.56. Sold by her through the dealer L. Gruner to Dresden in 1876 for 40,000 marks (see Lady Eastlake, *Journals and Correspondence*, ii, 1895, p.20; Robertson, *Sir Charles Eastlake and the Victorian Art World*, 1978, p.281, no.34).

Universally accepted as autograph (Waagen, iv, 1857, pp.113–14; Crowe & Cavalcaselle, i, 1871, pp.399–400, 1912, pp.101–2; Morelli, 1880, p.166, 1894, p.229; Thode, 1897, p.74; Kristeller, 1901, pp.322–4, 442; Knapp, 1910, p.112; Berenson, 1932, 1968; Fiocco, 1937, p.70; Tietze-Conrat, 1955, pp.26, 181, probably; Paccagnini, 1961, p.50; Cipriani, 1962, pp.42, 69; Camesasca, 1964, pp.123–4; Garavaglia, 1967, No.84). Waagen dated it 'to his ripest time', as not earlier than 1500. Crowe & Cavalcaselle propose to identify it as the Ferrara *Madonna* (Cat. no.76) and date it accordingly, followed by Thode, who would also accept an earlier dating. A late dating is proposed by all other students: Kristeller and Venturi, as *c.*1496–7, contemporary with the *Madonna della Vittoria*; Knapp, *c.*1498–9; Paccagnini, *c.*1491, related to the Brera *Madonna with Cherubim* (Cat. No.166); Cipriani, early 1500s; Camesasca, 1495–1500; Garavaglia, 1495. Tietze-Conrat relates the Christ Child to that of the *Madonna della Vittoria*; Venturi and Cipriani see the influence of Leonardo.

There is no agreement as to the identity of the two saints, except that they are members of the Holy Family. Crowe & Cavalcaselle identified them as Joseph and Anna; Waagen, Thode and Kristeller as Joseph and Elizabeth. Fiocco points out that Mantegna invariably represents Joseph as bearded and proposed either Joachim and Anna, the Virgin's parents, or Elizabeth and Zacharias, the Baptist's parents.

Often identified as the Giunti Madonna (Cat. no.124), an identification first proposed by Eastlake (Waagen, *loc. cit.*).

45. Virgin and Child with three saints
Paris, Musée Jacquemart-André (*Catalogue*, 1933, p.146, No.1041)
Tempera on canvas (? transferred from panel)
57 × 42 cm.   Plate 133

CONDITION: Very rubbed and worn. Crowe & Cavalcaselle (1871, pp.399–400) record that it was inscribed 'ANDREAS MANTEN'.

PROVENANCE: Coll. of Frédéric Reiset (d.1879), Paris; coll. of Vicomte de Tauzia; coll. of M. Rumford, Paris, from whom acquired in 1890.

Regarded by Crowe & Cavalcaselle (1871, *loc. cit.*; 1912, p.101) as an autograph work of *c.*1485, possibly the Ferrara *Madonna* (see Cat. no.76). Also accepted as autograph by Morelli (1891, p.230). Assigned by Venturi (1914, p.472) to an anonymous Veronese hand who also painted the *Virgin and Child* in Verona (Cat. no.46), an attribution accepted by Paccagnini (1961, p.51). For Berenson (1932, 1968) either a late ruined original or a workshop piece. For Fiocco (1937, pp.76, 209) a late autograph; Tietze-Conrat (1955, p.196) by a follower; Cipriani (1962, p.82) among attributed works, with the rider that its condition does not permit a sure judgement; Garavaglia (1967, No.100), partly autograph, *c.*1500.

Usually described as a Virgin and Child with three saints. The bearded and haloed figure must be St Joseph; the others cannot be identified.

46. Virgin and Child with two saints
Verona, Museo di Castelvecchio
Canvas 76 × 55.5 cm.　　　　　　　　　Plate 134

CONDITION: Ruined: badly restored *c.*1900: restored *c.*1946, with some improvement in its condition. Damaged on left side.

PROVENANCE: First recorded in the Bernasconi coll., Verona. This picture has been identified by some students with a Madonna recorded in the Spedale degli Incurabili, Venice (see Cat. no.144).

As is generally acknowledged its condition makes assessment of this picture difficult. For Morelli (1890, p.360; 1891, p.226) an autograph work. Attributed to the school or workshop of Mantegna by Thode (1897, p.74) and Yriarte (1901, p.248, as derived from a Mantegna composition). For Kristeller (1901, pp.324,442, No.30) a doubtful work, if by Mantegna painted *c.*1497–1505. Assigned by Knapp (1910, pp.160,179) tentatively to Bonsignori: the invention is close to Mantegna, but the handling is Veronese. For Venturi (1914, p.472) by the anonymous Veronese hand who also painted the Jacquemart-André *Virgin and Child* (Cat. no.45). Fiocco (1937, pp.69, 207) resolutely affirms that it is not Veronese, but a late autograph work: this is also the verdict of Cipriani (1962, p.70). Tietze-Conrat (1955, p.200) assigns it to a follower, possibly Bonsignori, and describes it as a version of the Dresden *Madonna*, a judgement accepted by Berenson (1968), who earlier (1932) had classed it as a ruined autograph. Paccagnini (1961, p.51) thinks that the attribution to Mantegna himself is plausible, that the picture is of higher quality than the Jacquemart-André picture and related to the Turin *Virgin and Saints* (Cat. no.47, Plate 135). Garavaglia (1967, No.103), as autograph.

In spite of all it has suffered, clearly a late autograph work, like the other comparable pictures of this type. The types of the Virgin and Child are related to those of the altarpieces of Santa Maria della Vittoria and Santa Maria in Organo, and Kristeller's dating of *c.*1497–1505 is therefore the most plausible. The bright colouring also agrees with this late dating.

The subject of the picture is usually identified as the Holy Family and a female saint. The green book held by the male saint is not an attribute of St Joseph, and this identification is therefore doubtful. The drapery of this figure may have been finished by an inferior hand.

47. Virgin and Child with the Infant St John the Baptist, St Catherine of Alexandria, and other saints
Turin, Galleria Sabauda, 164 (Gabrielli, *Maestri italiani*, 1971, p.166)
Tempera on panel 61.5 × 87.5 cm.　　　　Plate 135

CONDITION: Surface worn. Partly ruined by a fire in the

nineteenth century: much restored (completely so on upper left) and repainted.

PROVENANCE: Formerly in Palazzo Reale, Turin.

Its condition makes judgement of this picture very difficult. The more unfavourable view, that it is a workshop piece (Thode, 1897, p.74; Kristeller, 1901, pp.324–5, 442, No.31; Venturi, 1914, pp.484–8; Tietze-Conrat, 1955, p.198), finds its most extreme expression in Knapp (1910, pp.161, 180), who assigns it to a Mantegna imitator. Crowe & Cavalcaselle (1871, pp.417, 482; 1912, p.118n, p.189) seem to regard it as possibly by Mantegna, later as a work partly executed on his design by Caroto. Morelli (1890, p.360; 1891, p.226) stoutly maintained its status as an autograph work, while Yriarte (1901, p.247) thought it an autograph work of middling quality. It is also regarded as autograph by Fiocco (1937, pp.69, 207) and Cipriani (1962, p.68) and initially (1932) by Berenson, who later (1968) classed it as either a ruined or a studio work. Bottari (1961, p.312) doubts it and Gilbert (1962, p.6) seems to reject it as 'empty'. Recent opinion has steered a middle course, attributing the design and part of the execution to Mantegna, with additions by an assistant (Paccagnini, 1961, p.49; Ragghianti, 1962, p.26; Camesasca, 1964, pp.41, 123). Unanimously dated late (*c.*1493 by Camesasca, 1495 by Garavaglia, 1967, No.88). Its condition makes a firm assessment impossible.

The saint on the extreme right is St Catherine of Alexandria. The woman in matron's costume behind her is probably St Elizabeth: next to her is a bearded male figure who from what can be seen of his costume is most probably a saint, perhaps her husband, Zacharias. The other female saint has no identifying attribute; the bearded male saint on the left, reading a book, cannot be certainly identified: his action suggests that he is not St Joseph.

48. Ecce Homo.
Christ is held by two Jews, one of whom wears a paper cap bearing a cursive Greek inscription. A youthful figure behind to the right wears a similar inscribed cap. A fourth head of a Jew appears in profile behind on the left. Above are labels inscribed (*left*) CRVCIFIGE EVM / TOLLE EVM / CRVCIFIGE CRVC and (*right*) CRVCIFIGE EVM / CRVCIFIGE TOLLE / EV(m) CRVCIFIGE (conflated from Luke 23:18,21).
Paris, Musée Jacquemart-André (*Catalogue*, 1933, p.147, No.1045)
Tempera on canvas 54 × 42 cm.　　　　　Plate 136

PROVENANCE: Acquired from Bardini, Florence, in 1891. Previously in a Milanese collection.

Yriarte (1901, p.235) hesitated to pronounce on this picture because of its condition, but regarded it as very possibly by Mantegna. Kristeller (1901, p.454) calls it a schoolwork, close to Liberale da Verona; Venturi (1914, pp.262, 482) assigns it to Francesco Mantegna. Berenson (1932, 1968) and Tietze-Conrat (1955, p.196) call it a shop-work, while Fiocco (1937, p.76) regards it as autograph. Recent criticism tends to follow the lead of Cipriani (1962, p.82), who catalogues it among attributed works, but with the rider that its quality is high and its manner very close to Mantegna's latest manner (Camesasca, 1964, p.128; Garavaglia, 1967, No.92). A late date is universally proposed. A design of great distinction, and certainly a late work, *c*.1500, by Mantegna, as its austere colour, with the only strong accent the Jew's yellow turban, confirms. For the window-frame and black ground compare the Correggio *Redeemer*.

The Mantua inventory of 1627 includes (Luzio, 1913, p.117, no.338), 'Un quadro dipintovi N.S. *Ecce uomo* con la corda al collo con cornice di violino. L.36.'

For notes on the iconography of the present picture see Hartt (in *G.B.A.*, ser.6, xl, 1952, p.332). The lettering (Roman and pseudo-Syriac) seems by the same hand as that in the *Pallas*.

49. Holy Family with the Infant Baptist
London, National Gallery, 5641 (Davies, 1961, pp.338–9)
Canvas 71 × 50.5 cm.   Plate 137

CONDITION: Seriously damaged by rubbing and flaking. When engraved by C. Canella, *c*.1820–40 (repr. Richter, *The Mond Collection*, i, 1910, pp.255–67, pl.L), the Virgin was shown holding an olive-branch in her right hand and her left hand clasped her right above the wrist. Restored between 1885 and 1891 by Cavenaghi who stripped it and reconstructed the olive-branch as a book. Cleaned in 1946/8 when these later additions were removed, and the book was restored as the fold of the Virgin's mantle. Davies notes that no evidence has been found in Mantegna's paint to justify either olive-branch or book.

PROVENANCE: Coll. of Cav. Andrea Monga (1794–1861), Verona, by 1856; acquired from the Monga coll. in 1885 by J. P. Richter, and in his collection at Florence until 1891, when sold by him to Dr Ludwig Mond; Mond Bequest, 1924; entered the Gallery, 1946.

Acquired by Richter and later published by him (*The Mond Collection*, i, 1910, pp.255–67) as by Mantegna. Accepted as an autograph work by Morelli (letter to Richter of 17 March 1887 in Morelli & Richter, *Italienische Malerei der Renaissance im Briefwechsel . . .*, I. and G. Richter, eds., 1960, pp.502–3). Almost universally accepted as an autograph Mantegna, dating from the 1490s (Thode, 1897, p.74; Berenson, 1901, pp.96–7, 1968; Yriarte, 1901, pp.214–15; Kristeller, 1901, pp.326–7, 442; Knapp, 1910, p.106, *c*.1490; Venturi, 1914, pp.224–5; Fiocco, 1937, p.70; Tietze-Conrat, 1955, p.185, with reserves about condition; Davies, 1961, *loc. cit.*; Paccagnini, 1961, p.65, *c*.1497; Cipriani, 1962, pp.42, 69–70; Camesasca, 1964, p.43). Garavaglia (1967, No.85), who dates it *c*.1495, is unique in postulating extensive workshop intervention.

A version of the composition (Plate 138) in the Petit-Palais, Paris (canvas, 72.5 × 45 cm.) was formerly in the Couvreur coll. (sale, Paris, 27 November 1875, lot 52), the Dollfus coll. (sale, Paris, 1–2 April 1912, lot 71), an anonymous coll. (sale, Paris, no details) and another anonymous coll. (sale, Paris, 23 November 1927, lot 30). Davies suggests it may be identical with the picture seen by Mündler in August 1856 in Palazzo Marescalchi, Bologna. In this St Joseph is replaced by St Elizabeth, the Virgin is unquestionably mending her cloak – with a gold needle and thread – and the oval well is replaced by a straight stone ledge.

The iconography of the picture has been much dis-cussed. Kristeller emphasized the originality of the invention, noting that before Mantegna representations of the Infant Christ as Imperator Mundi (cf. also Plate 99) appear only in German art. In fact the invention represents a combination of figures and motifs arranged to illustrate the symbolic themes of the Virgin's humility, and of Christ's humility in consenting to be born, though Lord of the world, of a Virgin's womb. Cameron Taylor (in Richter, *Mond Collection, loc. cit.*) rightly saw the subject as a very literal figuration of Isaiah's famous prophecy of Christ (7:14): *Ecce Virgo concipiet et pariet filium, et vocabitur nomen eius Emmanuel*. Emanuel signifies God with us, and by the Fathers was regarded as an expression of the mystery of the Incarnation. In later verses (9:6) Isaiah says *Parvulus enim natus est nobis et filius datus est nobis, et factus est principatus super humerum eius*. That these words were in the mind of the inventor of the picture is confirmed by the inscription ECCE AGNVS DEI on the Baptist's scroll, which here alludes to Christ as a sacrifice for man's redemption. For Isaiah (53:7) later declares of Christ's offer of himself for our salvation in his Passion: *et quasi agnus coram tondente se obmutescet et non aperiet os suum*.

The parapet within which the Virgin sits is undoubtedly oval, and was accordingly identified by Cameron Taylor (see J. P. Richter, 1910, *loc. cit.*) as the *fons signatus* (fountain sealed) of the *Song of Solomon* (4:12). This became a popular symbol of the Virgin's sealed womb of which Christ was born from *c*.1480 onwards. As an analogy Cameron Taylor cited a French fifteenth-century miniature illustrating a poem on the Virgin as the *puteus aquarum viventium* (fount of living waters) (Paris, Bibl. Nat., MS français 145) in which the infant Christ stands on the parapet of a circular well, supported by the Virgin, who stands on that of a square well. This interpretation is generally accepted, though Davies (1961, p.338) queries whether Mantegna would have suspended the Virgin in the well. Such a doubt does not allow for the symbolic, rather than realistic, visual thinking that underlies the picture: compare the unreality of the figures in relation to their setting of the Santa Maria in Organo altarpiece. Fry (in *B.M.*, viii, 1905, p.92) rightly links the motif of the well with the cult of the Immaculate Conception.

Loss and restoration have obliterated the action of the Virgin, which has been much questioned. She is shown sewing in the Petit-Palais version, and Kurz (in Davies, *loc. cit.*) pointed out that sewing was arguably her original action in this picture. That she is showing her great humility by mending her own clothes with a needle is confirmed, as Kurz suggests, by G. F. Caroto's *Madonna*, dated 1501, now in Modena, in which she performs the very same action (for this picture see M. T. Franco Fiorio, *Giovan Francesco Caroto*, 1971, pp.85–6, fig.1). Caroto was a pupil of Mantegna, and this *Madonna* is his earliest known work, painted under Mantegna's strong influence. Given that the iconographical motif of the Virgin sewing is so rare – it appears again in pictures known to the compiler only in a Cariani of *c*.1524–8 (Rome, Palazzo Barberini, exh. RA, 1983, *The Genius of Venice*, pp.165–6, no.31) – Caroto's motif must have been suggested by Mantegna's painting, for which 1501 is therefore a *terminus ante quem*.

There may also be an allusion to the Virgin as *ancilla Domini* (the Lord's handmaiden) in her act of mending, since mending was a task performed by maids. In the Petit-Palais version St Elizabeth replaces St Joseph, and Christ and the Baptist stand on a parapet. If this change figures the motif of *hortus conclusus* rather than the more mystical *fons signatus*, there is nevertheless no significant alteration of the composition's symbolic meaning. The scroll held by the Baptist is inscribed (Agnu)S / DEI ECCE / (qui tollis) PECATA M(undi). It too seems a work of quality and was perhaps painted *c.*1497–1500 by Mantegna himself, though its condition makes it difficult to be certain whether it is not simply a fine studio picture.

The iconographical invention is so singular that it must have been devised by some devotee of the Virgin. Although admired in Mantua and Verona for some years, it was to have no lasting success because of its peculiarity. In the London picture Mantegna has expressed the theme of humility with disconcertingly monumental majesty of figure-style.

A dating *c.*1497–1500 is highly plausible.

50. Samson and Delilah.
On the tree in Roman capitals is the hexameter inscription: FOEMINA / DIABOLO TRIBVS / ASSIBVS EST / MALA PEIOR (a bad woman is threepence worse than the Devil).
London, National Gallery, 1145 (Davies, 1961, pp.334–5)
Linen, in monochrome 47 × 37 cm. (excluding a black band about ½ cm. wide all round, parts of which have been trimmed) Plate 139

CONDITION: On the whole good, but rubbed in parts. Many very small losses, some apparently under old retouches.

PROVENANCE: First recorded in the Sunderland sale (Christie's, 15 June 1883, lot 82), in the collection known as the Sunderland Drawings. Some or all of these drawings were bought before 1728 by the Procuratore Zaccaria Sagredo of Venice from Bartolommeo Buonfiglioli at Bologna: coll. Consul Joseph Smith by 1761; bought in 1763 by Consul John Udny and brought to England, where acquired by the Duke of Marlborough and placed in the library at Blenheim. It is not certain whether this is also the history of the present picture.

Except by Knapp (1910, p.126), who considers it a workshop piece, universally accepted as an autograph Mantegna (Thode, 1897, p.109; Kristeller, 1901, pp.369,443, as the finest of the small monochromes; Venturi, 1914, p.242; Berenson, 1932,1968; Fiocco, 1937, p.68; Tietze-Conrat, 1955, pp.184–5; Davies, 1961, *loc. cit.*; Paccagnini, 1961, p.69; Gilbert, 1962, p.6; Cipriani, 1962, pp.40,71; Camesasca, 1964, pp.44,111; Garavaglia, 1967, No.95). From Tietze-Conrat onwards it has been accepted as the touchstone by which to assess the quality of the other monochromes. Universally regarded as late. For Kristeller, *c.*1505–6, for Venturi, *c.*1500, for Tietze-Conrat and Garavaglia, *c.*1495, Camesasca would prefer a year or two before 1495; Cipriani dates it to the Roman sojourn of 1488–90. Davies inclines to think that the present picture, the Dublin *Judith* (Cat. no.56), the Paris *Solomon* (Cat. no.142) and the Vienna *David* (Cat. no.141) and *The Sacrifice of Isaac* (Cat. no.140) belong to a single series. This is implausible.

The scene is from Judges 16:18–20, but it is Delilah who cuts Samson's hair in Mantegna's picture, not a barber. Tietze-Conrat points out that the inscription is a proverbial saying found at least as early as the fourteenth century (Adolphi *Fabula ix*, in Leyserus, *Historia Poetarum et Poematum Medii Aevi*, 1741, p.2028; *El Conde Lucanor*, ed. Knust, p.387).

51. A Sibyl and a Prophet
Cincinnati Art Museum, 27.406 (Mary M. Emery Coll.)
Oil on canvas 58 × 48 cm. Plate 140

CONDITION: Various small areas of repaint, mostly along centre top to bottom. The edges, previously folded back, were flattened in 1972. The left edge certainly approximates to the original, though it could be that the composition continued a further ¾ in. more: it is less certain that the present top, bottom and right edges are so nearly original. On turning back the painting on the edges was found to be of pinkish tone: the present brown effect of the canvas is probably due to its heavy varnish.

PROVENANCE: Coll. Duke of Buccleuch, Montague House, London; exh. by him RA, 1872; with Duveen's (Duveen, 1941, No.76); Mary M. Emery Coll., Cincinnati.

On the back is an old (seventeenth-century?) inscription: 'No.290. DIANDREA. MANTENGNA.'

Classed as a school-work painted from Mantegna's design and under his supervision by Kristeller (1901, pp.373,444) and Venturi (1914, p.262), but otherwise universally accepted as autograph (Yriarte, 1901, pp.212–14; Knapp, 1910, p.118; Berenson, 1932, 1968; Fiocco, 1937, p.68; Tietze-Conrat, 1955, p.180, at least the invention; Cipriani, 1962, pp.34–5, 65; Garavaglia, 1967, No.99; Fredericksen & Zeri, 1972). Cipriani prefers a date *c.*1485, immediately before the *Triumphs*, but the general view is rightly that this is a very late work (Knapp, as *c.*1495; Garavaglia, *c.*1500). Tietze-Conrat points out that it was intended for a high position, given the perspective and the foreshortened bodies.

The old identification of the subject was Tarquin and a Sibyl, though Kristeller and Knapp both suggested a Sibyl and a Prophet. In 1953 Landsberger (in *Cincinnati Art Museum Bull.*, December 1952, pp.123–4) argued that the male figure does not wear a crown or any other feature of royal dress, such as Tarquin might be expected to wear, and suggested that the scene represented is that in Esther 4, where Mordecai appears before the palace gateway of Ahasuerus to bewail the edict that all the Jews are to be killed on a certain day. The action of the picture in which the female figure points to a text on the roll does not correspond to this scene as described in Esther (in which moreover Esther and Mordecai communicate through messengers). Nor is Mordecai shown in sackcloth and ashes, as the text requires. However, Landsberger is probably correct in identifying the scroll as a copy of a Jewish Purim scroll on which the Book of Esther is inscribed: certainly the text is intended to simulate Hebrew. His identification of the scene is accepted by Réau (*Iconographie de l'art chrétien*, ii, I, 1956, p.338), but Wind (*Michelangelo's Prophets and Sibyls*, 1960, pp.60–1) develops Kristeller and Knapp's suggestion and identifies the subject as a Sibyl expounding holy writ to a prophet, in the compiler's view, correctly.

52. Judith

Montreal, Museum of Fine Arts, No.103 (Steegman, *Catalogue*, 1960, p.86)

Varnish-glazed tempera on linen: bronze-toned grisaille (*finto di bronzo*?) 64 × 30 cm.   Plate 142

PROVENANCE: R. A. Markham coll. John E. Taylor coll., London; sale, Christie's, 5 July 1912, lot 26 (bt. Agnew, with Plate 143, £1627 10s.). Purchased by Montreal, 1920. See entry below. A pair to *Dido*.

53. Dido

Montreal, Museum of Fine Arts, No.104 (Steegman, Catalogue, 1960, p.86)

Varnish-glazed tempera on linen. Bronze-toned grisaille (*finto di bronzo*?) 64 × 30 cm.   Plate 143

PROVENANCE: R. A. Markham coll., John E. Taylor coll., London; sale, Christie's, 5 July 1912, lot 26 (bt. Agnew, with Plate 142, £1627 10s.). Purchased by Montreal, 1920. See entry below. A pair to *Judith*.

Yriarte (1901, pp.209–11), Fiocco (1937, p.68) and Cipriani (1962, p.71) regard these two pictures as autograph. They have been more generally attributed to the workshop or to an accomplished follower (Berenson, 1901, pp.98–9, and 1968; Kristeller, 1901, pp.372–3; Cruttwell, 1908, p.101; Knapp, 1910, p.127; Venturi, 1914, p.248; Schwabe, in *B.M.*, xxxiii, 1918, p.215, pl.2; Paccagnini, 1961, p.74; Garavaglia, 1967, Nos.76–7). Tietze-Conrat (1955, p.190) accepts neither invention nor execution as Mantegna's work. This seems particularly unfair to the *Dido*, an invention of great distinction. Generally dated late; Paccagnini even suggests 1516, arguing that they are by a hand which painted some of the frescoed decorations of Mantegna's funerary chapel. Paccagnini also notes that Dido's head recalls that of the antique bust of Faustina which was traditionally thought to have been Mantegna's (see text, p.224–5).

It is possible that these two pictures have a Mantuan provenance. The sale of Count Schulenburg of Zell (London, Christie's, 12–13 April 1775, second day, lot 17) included 'Mantegna. Four paintings, imitations of basso-relievo'. According to the sale catalogue, the principal part of the collection was purchased 'from out of that celebrated cabinet of the *Duke of Mantua*' by Field-Marshal Matthias-Johann von Schulenburg (1661–d. Verona, 1747), who was generalissimo of the Venetian troops. As he only took service with Venice in 1715, he must have made his purchases some years after the death of Ferdinando Carlo, last Duke of Mantua, in 1708. But the 1709 inventory of the Duke's pictures does include 'Quattro quadri (2 × 4 [*quarte*]) l'uno rappresenta chiari e scuri, la Bella Judith et altre figure di mano del Mantegna' (Luzio, pp.84–6, 316–18). The *quarta* equals a modern *spanna*, according to Luzio, so the dimensions correspond. The equivalent is 32 × 64 cm. See also Cat. no.138.

54. Tuccia

London, National Gallery 1125a (Davies, 1961, p.340)

Poplar 72.5 × 23 cm. (painted surface)   Plate 144

CONDITION: Painted up to the edges, and probably cut down a little at the sides and top. Otherwise well preserved.

A pair to *Sophonisba* (Plate 145). The identification of the subject is due to Kristeller (see below).

55. Sophonisba

London, National Gallery, 1125b (Davies, 1961, pp.340–1)

Wood 72.5 × 23 cm. (including an addition of 3 cm. on the right and of 1 cm. at the top. The paint continues up to the original edges. As now exhibited, the painting seems narrower than the *Tuccia* because of the conceal-ment of the repainted areas).   Plate 145

CONDITION: Less well preserved than the companion picture of *Tuccia* (Cat no.54)

PROVENANCE: *Tuccia* and *Sophonisba* are first recorded in the Duke of Hamilton's coll., as in the boudoir of the new state-rooms of Hamilton Palace, by Waagen (iii, 1854, pp.304–5: 'Andrea Mantegna – 2 and 3. Summer and Autumn; two small figures of masterly execution in chiaroscuro. They . . . belong . . . decidedly to the latest and maturest time of the master'). Previously in Beck-ford's coll.? Bought by the Gallery at the Hamilton sale (24 June 1882, lot 398).

Tietze-Conrat (1955, p.186) suggests that these two pictures may possibly have been included in the sale of Count Schulenburg of Zell (see Cat. no.53), but this is unlikely, since the four Schulenburg pictures probably comprised Cat. nos. 52 and 53 and seem to have been of a size. Tietze-Conrat wrongly refers to this sale as the Bertels sale, which took place five days before.

Tuccia and Sophonisba are heroines of Chastity: their popularity in fifteenth-century Italy was probably due to the mention of them in Petrarch's *Trionfi*, Sophonisba in the *Trionfo dell'Amore*, Tuccia in the *Trionfo della Castità*.

The earlier identification of these pictures as *Spring* and *Summer* was corrected by Kristeller (1901, pp.372,444). It is generally assumed that they were intended as com-panion pictures, though Davies and Camesasca are not sure. Longhi (opinion in Shapley, 1968, p.42) proposes to associate these pictures with the London *Cybele* and the Washington *Scipio* as part of the Cornaro commission (Cat. no.57), followed by Braham (*B.M.*, cxv, 1973, p.458).

Crowe and Cavalcaselle (1871, p.395; 1912, pp.96–7) class them as autograph, c.1475. Dismissed by Morelli (1891, p.230) and Frizzoni (*Arte italiana del Rinascimento*, 1891, p.299) as fakes, but technical examination has con-firmed their genuineness (see Davies). Although Thode (1897, p.106) regarded them as autograph, in spite of some carelessness of drawing, earlier opinion on the whole regarded them as school-works (Berenson, 1901, pp.96–9; Kristeller, *loc. cit.*; Cruttwell, 1908, p.101; Knapp, 1910, p.125). Berenson (1932, 1968) later classed them as partly autograph, but Tietze-Conrat (1955, p.186) still considers them shop-work, and Davies catalogues them as by a follower. Recent opinion, following Venturi (1914, p.248), rightly regards them as autograph works of high quality (Cipriani, 1962, pp.39–40, 71; Camesasca, 1964, pp.44,126; Garavaglia, 1967, Nos.97–8; A. Smith, *Andrea Mantegna and Giovanni Bellini*, 1975, p.47).

56. Judith

Dublin, National Gallery of Ireland, 442

Tempera on linen, mounted on millboard, 46 × 36 cm.

Plate 141

CONDITION: A crease runs across the middle. Some spots rubbed.

PROVENANCE: Bought in Italy by the Hon. Lewis Strange Wingfield (1842–91), traveller, author and artist; coll. of John Malcolm of Poltalloch; with Colnaghi's, from whom purchased by the Gallery, 1896.

Published by Yriarte (1901, p.205) and Berenson (1901, p.97; 1902, pp.57–8) as autograph. For Kristeller (1901, pp.373,444) a school-work of good quality, for Knapp (1910, p.124) and Venturi (1914, p.244) a workshop picture. Reaffirmed by Schwabe (in *B.M.*, xxxiii, 1927, p.215), Berenson (1932, 1968) and Fiocco (1937, p.68) as a late autograph work, but Tietze-Conrat (1955, p.181) accepts only the invention as Mantegna's and finds weaknesses of execution. Some small intervention by the workshop is postulated by Paccagnini (1961, p.73), Camesasca (1964, pp.44,47,122) and Garavaglia (1967, No.75); for Cipriani (1962, p.80) a workshop picture. Certainly a late autograph work, as Gilbert (1962, p.6) claims.

Davies (1961, p.334) suggests, implausibly, that it possibly formed part of the same series as the Paris *Judgement of Solomon*, and the Vienna *David* and *Isaac*.

57. The Introduction of the Cult of Cybele at Rome

The two tombs on the left beside the paved way are inscribed: (*left-hand tomb*) P. SCYPIONIS / EX HYPANENSI (*or* IENSI?) / BELLO / RELIQVIAE (*right-hand tomb*) S.P.Q.R. / C N SCYPIO / NI CORNELI / VS F.P. (*filius posuit*)

The centre of the ledge is inscribed: S HOSPES NVMINIS IDAEI C. The three central words of this inscription are taken from Juvenal, III, 138.

London, National Gallery, 902 (Davies, 1961, pp.330–3)

Canvas 73 × 268 cm. (exposed surface); 75 × 271 cm. (canvas)

Plates 146, 147; Fig. 13

CONDITION: The bottom and left sides are true edges. The top edge was folded over, in places almost to 1.2 cm. of the painted surface, but since this edge is ragged and in places there is no fold, the loss (if any) cannot be great. About 1.2 cm. height regained in 1976–8 (see below). The right side was folded back over the whole depth of the stretcher (to a little over 3 cm.) and ends in a clean cut: again nearly 5 cm. regained in 1976–8. A triangle (exposed h. 20.5 cm., w. 15 cm.) inserted in the bottom right corner is also painted over the edge of the stretcher, but its execution appears not to be contemporary. The insertion may have been necessary because the stuff on which the picture is executed was already strained before painting (see Davies).

Much damage, especially in the figure of the priest on the extreme left, the shoulder of the man walking before the litter, the drapery and hands of the stooping woman, the legs and right arm of the drummer-boy.

A few *pentimenti*: thus the priest on the left appears not to have been given a mitre at first. The inscriptions on the tombs retouched.

Cleaning (1976–8) revealed that the background is divided into two marble panels, one of fiery red to the left, one of yellowish colour on the right. The line of division between them descends on to the head of the principal figure of the waiting group, indicating that he is Publius Scipio.

PROVENANCE: Engraved before 1815 by Francesco Novelli (1764–1836). Recorded by Moschini (*Guida per la città di Venezia*, II-i, Venice, 1815, p.237) in Palazzo Corner, later Mocenigo di San Polo, in Campo di San Polo, Venice: '*Presso i signori di questo palazzo si custodisce una scelta raccolta di quadri di ottimi maestri. Particolarmente vi si ammira un fregio che i giudici più intelligenti riconoscono per fattura di Andrea Mantegna, e che come tale si offerse a stampa dal nostro Francesco Novelli.*' Sold between 1815 and 1835 to Antonio Sanquirico (Selvatico, in Vasari, 1849, p.196: '*La terza opera rimasta nello studio di Andrea quando morì, fu un Trionfo di Scipione, che fino a pochi anni sono vedevasi a Venezia conservatissimo in casa Cornaro, poi Mocenigo a San Polo. Questa tela, ch'è senza dubbio uno della più belle tempere a chiaroscuro che mai eseguisse il Mantegna, fu venduta per pochi denari dagli ignoranti possessori al signor Sanquirico*'). In the recent restoration seals (probably nineteenth-century) of the Mocenigo family were found on the back of the stretcher. By 1835 in the coll. of George Vivian, who lent it to the British Institution both that year (No.157) and in 1844 (No.77), and to the Manchester Art Treasures Exhibition in 1857 (*Provisional Catalogue*, No.289; *Definitive Catalogue*, No.102) and to the RA in 1871 (No.274). Purchased from Captain Ralph Vivian by the Gallery, 1873.

DOCUMENTS: These are published by D'Arco, Luzio and Brown (in *B.M.*, cxvi, 1974, pp.101–3).

1) *1505, 15 March.* Letter from Verona from Cardinal Marco Cornaro to Francesco Gonzaga. His brother Messer Francesco desires to obtain a certain work from the hands of Mantegna. Accordingly the Cardinal has despatched the bearer, Niccolò Bellini, who is Mantegna's brother-in-law and a familiar of the Cardinal (i.e. a member of his household), to ask for Francesco's permission to employ his court painter, and to beg him to commission Mantegna to undertake the work for his brother (Brown, pp.102–3, No.1).

2) *1506, 1 January.* Letter from Venice from Pietro Bembo to Isabella d'Este. Francesco Cornaro is Bembo's near kinsman and intimate friend. Some time ago he agreed with Mantegna to paint him some canvases (*telari*) for the price of 150 ducats, and gave him 25 as an earnest, having previously sent him the necessary measurements and given Mantegna opportunity to consider the work that would be required. Now Mantegna is refusing to execute the paintings at the price stipulated and is asking for much more money, since the work is greater than he thought. Francesco is naturally surprised and indignant, especially as he has a letter from Mantegna agreeing to the terms. Bembo asks Isabella to persuade Mantegna to abide by his agreement and to make a beginning on the paintings (*dar principio alla tolta impresa delle sue pitture*). If when they are finished Isabella thinks them worth more than the original price, Francesco will gladly pay the difference. In return for Isabella's help he will serve her in Venice by expediting Giovanni Bellini in his work for her, since

he has great influence with the master (D'Arco, ii, pp.57–8; Kristeller, 1902, pp.576–7, doc.173).

3) *1506, 31 January.* Isabella d'Este to Bembo. Mantegna has been very ill of late, and very near to death, and though better now, is not in a fit state to be spoken to about paintings or anything else, except his health. But when he is better, Messer Francesco Cornaro will find that no interposition could have been more effective than that of Bembo, as Isabella will prove (Kristeller, 1902, p.579, doc.176).

4) *1506, 23 September.* Letter from Francesco Gonzaga in Gubbio to Cardinal Sigismondo Gonzaga. Nothing is to be sold or even removed from Mantegna's house until Francesco's return, whether pictures, antiquities or rarities (Brown, p.103).

5) *1506, 2 October.* Lodovico Mantegna to Francesco II Gonzaga. One of the two pictures left by his father of which he wishes to dispose in order to carry out his bequests is 'quella opra di Scipion Cornelio principiata già a nome di mess. Francesco Cornaro.' Since Cardinal Sigismondo Gonzaga wants both this and the *Dead Christ*, Lodovico asks Francesco to write to him with permission to take and pay for them (D'Arco, ii, p.70; Kristeller, 1902, p.583, doc.190).

6) *1506, 28 October.* Letter from Castello San Pietro from Francesco Gonzaga to Lodovico Mantegna. The Cardinal may have whatever he wants (Brown, p.103).

7) *1506, 18 November.* Letter from Bologna from Cardinal Marco Cornaro to Francesco Gonzaga. Asks for 'quello quadro Cornelio de mano del quondam Miser Andrea Mantegna' and for the other things he has requested from the Marquis. He is sending the bearer to collect them to prevent any accident. Written with his own hand (Brown, p.103).

8) *1506, 26 November.* Letter from Francesco Mantegna to Francesco Gonzaga. He has returned all the canvases that were prepared for the paintings ordered by the Cornari (*tutte le tele parechiate per dipingere a li Cornari*). The one which is finished (*quella chè finita*) he had sent, as Francesco knows, to Cardinal Sigismondo simply for him to look at again, but the Cardinal has kept it and refuses to return it. Francesco had hoped to keep the picture as part of his share in the division of Mantegna's inheritance, both in memory of his father and to make studies from it (*per haver dove studiare*). The Cornari are entitled only to the earnest of 25 ducats, which he is willing to repay. He begs the Marquis to let him have this canvas which is the only one of his father's paintings remaining to him (D'Arco, ii, p.72; Kristeller, 1902, p.585, doc.196).

9) *1506, 29 November.* Letter from Francesco Gonzaga to Cardinal Marco Cornaro. One of his first acts on returning home has been to enquire about the picture of Scipio begun by Mantegna (*intendere dil quadro di Cornelio, principiato per il quondam Messer Andrea Mantegna*). He finds it is in the hands of his brother Cardinal Sigismondo, who is greatly attached to it, but to please his brother and Cardinal Cornaro is willing to resign it to the latter as a gift. But since it is a notable work (*per essere cosa assai degna*), he wishes to present it in person to Cardinal Cornaro on his way to Rome (Brown, p.103).

10) *1507, 23 January.* Letter from Bologna from Cardinal Marco Cornaro to Francesco Gonzaga. He has been to salute Cardinal Sigismondo Gonzaga, who has presented him with Mantegna's picture according to promise. The gift is most acceptable '*per esser cossa digna et excellente, provenuta di mano di homo famoso et primario a li tempi nostri ne' l'arte de la pictura*' (Brown, p.103).

11) *1507, 12 November.* Letter from Lodovico Mantegna to Isabella d'Este. Lodovico tells Isabella that Cardinal Sigismondo took the four pictures his father was painting for the Cornari and the *Dead Christ* and offered in return 100 ducats, to be paid in weekly payments of 5 ducats. He has however not received all the money, and is still owed 25 ducats. He needs the money to pay for his father's exequies and for mourning and to satisfy debts (Kristeller, 1902, pp.585–6, doc.198).

For this picture see the text (pp.214 ff.). Its iconography is discussed by A. Braham (in *B.M.*, cxv, 1973, pp.457–63), who accepts the identification of the youthful figure ecstatically kneeling in greeting as Claudia Quinta, which was first advanced by E. T. Cook in *A popular handbook to the National Gallery*, 1888, i, p.184. For the story of Claudia Quinta see Ovid, *Fasti*, iv, 143–306, and Livy, xxix, 14. The clearly depicted Adam's apple on the throat makes this identification impossible, as Alistair Smith was the first to point out (verbally to the author). For the *Continence of Scipio* by Giovanni Bellini (74.8 × 356.2 cm.), almost certainly a pendant to the present composition executed on a canvas handed over to Bellini after Mantegna's death, see Shapley (1979, pp.52–4, No.1090). This is inscribed TVRPIVS/IMPER/VENERE/Q.A. MIS AI which can be plausibly interpreted as *Turpius Imperatori Venere Quam a Misericordia Adfectari* (it is more disgraceful for a general to be moved by lust than by mercy) – for another interpretation by Panofsky see Shapley (*op. cit.*). The identification of the so-called Claudia Quinta as a male figure disposes of the association often attempted on grounds of a common theme of female chastity between the London and Washington pictures and the London *Tuccia* and *Sophonisba* (Cat.nos.54 and 55; Plates 144 and 145). On the other hand *The Continence of Scipio* and the *Cult of Cybele* share a common literary source in Valerius Maximus (IV, iii, 1, *Continence*; VIII, xv, 3, *Reception*).

The insertion in the bottom right-hand corner of a triangular piece of canvas painted with a laurel is unexplained. The SC of the inscription, in larger letters, was probably suggestd by the many Roman coins and medals on which this formula appears.

58. MANTEGNA'S FUNERARY CHAPEL IN SANT' ANDREA, MANTUA

Below the frescoed figure of Judith is the date MDXVI

Plates 153–164; Fig. 17

DOCUMENTS: 1) *1504, 1 March.* In his will of this date Mantegna orders his body to be buried in or in front of the chapel of San Giovanni Battista in Sant'Andrea, under a marble slab with an inscription recording his name and surname. His exequies are to be celebrated honourably, and Mass is to be said for his soul on the 7th and 30th day of every month and on his anniversary in the said church of Sant'Andrea. To the chapel he bequeaths 100 ducats, either in money or in a property of the same value yielding an annual revenue of 5 ducats: in return the priests of Sant'Andrea are to celebrate three anniversaries, one for himself, one for the souls of his father and mother, and one for the souls of his dead wife Nicolosia and of his kin. His sons and heirs were to expend 50 ducats on the erection of an altar, on a missal, chalice, cope and the other things required by a priest for celebrating Mass. They were also to expend another 50 ducats in decorating the chapel with pictures and other ornaments as they thought fitting, and to do so within a year of Mantegna's death (D'Arco, ii, pp.50–3; Kristeller, 1902, pp.570–2).

2) *1504, 11 August.* The chapel of San Giovanni Battista in Sant'Andrea was formally granted to Mantegna by the college of canons, chaplains and clergy on 11 August 1504, after the artist had petitioned their Primicerio, the Protonotary Lodovico, successfully for it (act printed by Gaye, iii, 1840, pp.565–8; D'Arco, ii, pp.54–5; Kristeller, 1902, pp.573–4, doc.166). The grant sets forth that Mantegna had now for some years desired to make choice of a chapel to decorate and endow as a funerary chapel for himself and his family. The endowment would be of at least 100 ducats. His especial preference was for the chapel of San Giovanni Battista, which was the first on the left at the entrance of the church and had as yet been granted to no one. At the present moment this chapel was simply a structure of rough brick, with no adornment of colours. Accordingly, informed of their Primicerio's assent, the clergy of Sant'Andrea now gladly granted him this chapel to decorate and endow, with the faculty of building a tomb in it and the right of burying corpses in the chapel whenever he and his descendants should wish. In addition Mantegna sought the exclusive grant of a plot of empty soil, measuring some 12 *braccia* wide by 20 *braccia* long, which lay behind the chapel, in order to prevent anyone else from obstructing the entrance of light into the chapel by building on it. He wished to enclose the plot in a wall and build a low cell on it beneath the window-level of the chapel. In this cell, now that he was broken with age, it was his intention to pass some hours for his recreation, warming himself with a small fire in winter, and making a little garden in the middle of the plot for his pleasure. This concession the clergy of Sant'Andrea were also pleased to make him, following the lead of the Primicerio. Accordingly they granted the plot to him and to his heirs in perpetuity, on condition Mantegna made a door in the wall to which he and his heirs and one of the church officers should each hold a key and on condition that preachers in the church might be allowed from time to time to use the cell for their rest and recreation.

3) *1506, 2 October.* Letter from Lodovico Mantegna to Francesco Gonzaga. Among the pictures left in Mantegna's estate are 'gli duj quadri che vanno ala sua capela'. Lodovico also mentions that he and Francesco intend to carry out their father's bequest of 100 ducats for the decoration of his chapel 'in ornarla in termine di uno anno, la qual cosa parendone iusta et honesta voressimo mandare ad executione.' Unless they can get the money for two pictures that Cardinal Sigismondo wants they cannot satisfy his creditors nor finish his chapel (*nè finire la capella sua*) (D'Arco, ii, pp.70–1; Kristeller, 1902, p.583, doc.190).

EARLY REFERENCES AND DESCRIPTIONS: 1) Scardeone (1560, p.372): 'sepultus est humi in phano divi Andreae, ubi aeneum capitis ejus simulacrum visitur, quod sibi suis conflaverat manibus, cum hoc disticho ibidem inciso: ESSE PAREM HVNC NORIS SI NON PRAEPONIS APELLI / AENEA MANTINIAE QVI SIMVLACHRA VIDES.'

2) Vasari (1550, p.512, simple mention of burial in S. Andrea, with epigram; 1568, p.487, woodcut after bronze head of Mantegna in chapel, p.497, repetition of 1550 passage).

3) Donnesmondi, ii, 1616, pp.47–8: '*E prima dalla sinistra parte ci si appresenta la capella del Mantigna, in cui vedesi una Madonna co'l puttino, con San Giuseppe, San Giouan Battista, Zaccaria, e Lisabetta intorno, opra dello stesso Mantigna singolarissima, e più delicata del solito; Iui anco dipinse Antonio da Correggio ne gli angoli della cuba i quattro Euangelisti, e sopra la finestra dell' altare alcuni Angioli di chiaro scuro, che sostengono vn scudetto, riceuendo il lume dal di sotto in sù, che paiono appunto di rilieuo. E in questa capella sepolto il detto Mantigna Cittadino Mantouano, communemente istimato Prencipe de' Pittori di suo tempo: onde iui nel muro è vna testa grande di bronzo, che al naturale lo rappresenta, con questi due versi sotto* [epigram above].'

4) Ridolfi, 1648, p.71: '*hauendosi Andrea eretta vna Cappella in Sant' Andrea, vi dipinse etiandio nello Altare la Vergine Santissima, Sant' Anna, e San Gioachino, e'l pargoletto Battista, che si abbraccia con Giesù parimente fanciullo, & i Santi Gioseppe, e Zaccheria, con l'incensiere in mano: feceui ancora à fresco da vna parte il battesimo di Christo, gli Euangelisti, e le armi Mantegna tenute da bambini.*'

5) Cadioli, 1763, pp.53–4: '*. . . la picciola cappella di S. Giovambatista, di cui fu proprietario il nostro Andrea Mantegna. Vi dipinse però il quadro dell' altare, in cui veggonsi effigiati la Madonna, S. Anna, S. Giovacchino, il pargoletto Battista, che abbracciasi col Bambino Gesù, ed i Santi Giuseppe, e Zaccaria, ed è pur di suo mano il quadro laterale di essa cappella, esprimente il Battesimo di Gesucristo, amministratogli dal Battista . . . E la bella testa di bronzo al naturale, che in questo lato vedete, ella è sua effigie . . . Li quattro Evangelisti, che son ne' pennachj della cupoletta di questa cappella, sono, come le pitture dell' atrio, di man del Correggio: e v' erano anche diversi Angioli a chiaroscuro sopra la finestra dell' altare, cui convenne di ceder campo alla finestra medesima, che non ha guari volle ingrandirsi, tutti opera del medesimo autore . . .*'

6) Zani, *Materiali per servire alla storia dell'origine e de' progressi dell'incisione . . .*, Parma, 1802, p.242, reproduces a passage from a letter sent to him by Bianconi: '*Che poi il Vestibolo della Chiesa di S. Andrea di Mantova . . . sia dipinto da Francesco Mantegna, si deduce chiarissimamente con tutta sicurezza da una lettera dello stesso Francesco alla Marchesa* [Isabella] *. . . nella quale dice che non può per allora servire sua Excellentia di certe commissioni dategli, perchè già promesso ai Preti di S. Andrea non solo di finire la Cappella della sua casa lasciata imperfetta dal Padre; ma il Vestibolo ancora della loro Chiesa.*'

7) Coddé (in Pungileoni, *Memorie istoriche di Antonio Allegri detto il Correggio*, iii, 1821, pp.2–3) mentions the altarpiece of the Holy Family as recently spoiled by crude varnish.

CONDITION: Intra (*La basilica di S. Andrea in Mantova*, 1882, p.9n; also in *Archivio Storico Lombardo*, ix, 1882, pp.289–303) records that the frescoes on the ceiling, previously covered with whitewash, were restored by B. Bosio of Mantua in 1875.

59. The Family of Christ with the Family of St John the Baptist

Mantua, Sant'Andrea, Chapel of San Giovanni Battista
Canvas 40 × 169 cm.　　　　　　　　　　　Plate 155

CONDITION: Restored c.1800.

St Joseph, on the left, wears a hat whose band is inscribed with Hebrew letters. On the right are St Elizabeth and St Zacharias: Tietze-Conrat (1955, p.188) points out that Zacharias, whose identity has been questioned (but see REFS. 3 and 4 above), carries his usual attribute of a censer (he was offering incense on the altar in the Temple when Gabriel revealed that his barren wife would bear a son who would be the precursor of the Messiah, Luke 1:13). The ultimate source of the scene is the narrative in the *Meditations* of the Pseudo-Bonaventura (cap.xi), which tells how the Holy Family rested in the house of Zacharias and Elizabeth on their return from the Flight into Egypt. The iconography of this picture, originally the altarpiece of the chapel, is explained by the chapel's dedication to St John the Baptist.

60. The Baptism of Christ

Mantua, Sant'Andrea, Chapel of San Giovanni Battista
Canvas 228 × 175 cm.　　　　　　　　　　Plate 154

The document cited above in the quotation from Zani (Cat. no.58, REF.6) has escaped all attention, though its existence was noted in 1802. Of the pictorial decorations of the chapel, only the *Holy Family* is known to have been attributed to Mantegna's own hand as early as 1616. Donnesmondi's attribution of the frescoes of the *Four Evangelists* and angels to Correggio led to a long controversy in the eighteenth and nineteenth centuries which is still not satisfactorily settled (see Gould, *The paintings of Correggio*, 1976, pp.29–32). The attribution of the *Baptism* to Mantegna is attested from 1648. In the nineteenth century D'Arco (i, 1857, pp.47,49–50) accepted that the two pictures were those mentioned in Lodovico Mantegna's letter of 1506, but gave the *Baptism* to Lodovico and Francesco Mantegna, retaining an attribution to the failing Mantegna for the *Holy Family*. Crowe & Cavalcaselle (1871, pp.416–18; 1912, pp.118–19) gave both pictures to pupils, in the case of the *Baptism* perhaps Francesco Mantegna, who may also have executed the *Evangelists*. Morelli, by contrast, insisted that both were autograph works (1880, p.166; 1891, p.227). Thode (1897, p.125) thinks both pictures were begun by Mantegna, but completed by Francesco. Yriarte (1901, pp.162–3,168) accepts the *Holy Family* as by Mantegna, but gives the *Baptism* to Francesco. Kristeller (1901, pp.331–3) thinks the *Holy Family* mainly but not entirely by Mantegna, and gives the execution of the *Baptism* wholly to a pupil – perhaps Antonio de Pavia. Knapp (1910, pp.65–9) gives the *Holy Family* to Mantegna, the *Baptism* and the *Evangelists* to a pupil working after a sketch by Mantegna. For Venturi (1914, pp.248–52) the frescoes and the two pictures were at best only designed by Mantegna: he suggests that Correggio may have finished the *Holy Family*. Berenson (1932; 1968, p.240) regards the *Holy Family* as autograph, the *Baptism* as a studio work, and the frescoes as after a design by Mantegna. Fiocco (1937, pp.64,76) believes the *Holy Family* is largely by Mantegna and the *Baptism* only

his invention. Tietze-Conrat (1955, p.188) accepts the *Holy Family* as by Mantegna, but will not credit him with so much as the invention of the *Baptism*. For Paccagnini (1961, pp.76–7) the *Holy Family* was designed and partly executed by Mantegna, and perhaps finished by Correggio, to whom he assigns the *Evangelists*, while the *Baptism* has little connection with Mantegna's late style and was perhaps executed c.1514–16 by Francesco Mantegna. Cipriani (1962, p.80) rejects both pictures, but thinks the *Holy Family* may be by Francesco. Camesasca (1964, pp.42,124) in much the closest analysis of the *Holy Family* considers the Virgin, Child, St Joseph and St Elizabeth as autograph, but that the last two figures were gone over by another hand, and that the rest of the picture was completed in oil by another hand. In the *Baptism* only the idea may be Mantegna's. Garavaglia, 1967, Nos.111–12. The heads of Joseph and Zacharias were certainly completed by another hand in the present compiler's view, while the execution of the *Baptism* must also be by another hand.

CONCLUSION: The pictorial decoration of the chapel was begun by Mantegna, who roughed out and executed, at least in part, the *Holy Family* and the underdrawing of the *Baptism* for the chapel. These were probably finished by Francesco Mantegna, more heavily in the case of the *Baptism*. The fresco decoration was also executed by Francesco Mantegna, and was completed in 1516, certainly after considerable interruption. The designs to which Francesco worked were most likely not his own, but Mantegna's. For a description and analysis see text, pp.248ff.

61. FRESCOES ON THE FAÇADE OF SANT'ANDREA

　　　　　　　　　　　　　　　　Plates 164a, b, c, d

Portico. These consisted of compositions representing the *Ascension, St Andrew and St Longinus*, the *Deposition* and the *Holy Family*. They are described by Donnesmondi in 1616 (*Historia ecclesiastica*, ii, p.49) with an attribution to Correggio, working in the manner of Mantegna: '*Sotto la loggia auanti la Chiesa sono due figure, vna di Sant'Andrea, é l'altra di San Longino, con l'Ascensione di Christo sopra la porta, e i dodeci Apostoli intorno, di mano d'Antonio da Correggio, ne i primi tempi, ch'egli imitaua il Mantegna. Nel scender la scalinata sotto il portico, è vna Madonna col puttino, fatta dall'istesso con maniera più morbida, e delicata. Nella testada dell'istessa loggia, à rimpetto di questa Madonna, vi dipinse l'istesso nostro Signore nella sepoltura, ma in altra più bella maniera delle precedenti.*' The frescoes are again described by Cadioli (1763, p.49): '*Entrando nell' atrio, ecco a prima giunta darci all' occhio li due accenati Santi Andrea, e Longino, uno per parte della porta mastra, e varie altre figure d'Appostoli dall' un lato, e dall' altro della finestra, ch'è sopra la porta stessa; le quali stanno in atto di riguardare la figura del Redentore salire al Cielo, che v'è anch' ella dipinta superiormente alla sovrapposta cornice: e v'ha pure una Pietà in alto sul muro in capo all' atrio, ed un' altra Madonna col Bambino, alla medesima altezza, dalla parte opposta, che viene a riuscire sopra l'ingresso della scala, per cui discendesi al portico de' mercanti.*' Cadioli maintains the attribution to Correggio, and notes that the frescoes were much damaged. In 1830–4 (Matteucci, p.146) the three tondi of the *Ascension, Deposition* and *Holy Family* were covered up, while the frescoes of

St Andrew, St Longinus and of the Apostles were destroyed. The three tondi were recovered in 1915 and published by Pacchioni (in *Boll. d'A.*, x, 1916, pp.147–64) who gave the *Ascension* to a follower of Mantegna and the other two tondi to Correggio. Pacchioni notes the influence of Mantegna on them, but dismisses any likelihood of his authorship, on grounds of their inferior quality. Before the Mantegna exhibition of 1961 (Paccagnini, 1961, pp.55–9) the three frescoes and their *sinopie* were detached and exhibited. Paccagnini gave the *Ascension* to Mantegna himself, perhaps with an assistant, and reaffirmed the attribution to Correggio of the other two. The attribution to Mantegna himself of the *Ascension* and its *sinopia* (both diam. 245 cm.) was immediately rejected by Longhi (1962, pp.15–16), but accepted by Arslan (1961, pp.170–1, the *sinopia*), by Gilbert (1962, p.9, wrongly dated 1488; reaffirmed by him in opposition to Meiss in *B.M.*, civ, 1962, pp.164–5), and by Rühmer (1961, p.cv, as by a follower of Mantegna – the *Ascension* only). Camesasca (1964, pp.38, 120) thinks that Mantegna may have given the designs for all three tondi, since there is some evidence that the frescoes of the *Deposition* and *Ascension* were painted over earlier works. Also accepted by Berenson (1968). All this literature and discussion ignores a letter from Francesco Mantegna to Isabella d'Este written after 1506 (see Cat. no.58, doc.6, quoted from Zani, 1802, p.242) in which he excuses himself from executing certain commissions for her because he has promised the priests of Sant'Andrea to paint their vestibule. However, the Correggesque character of the *Deposition* and *Holy Family* is marked.

Façade. A frescoed tondo of St Andrew and St Longinus attributed to Mantegna was first recorded on the façade of Sant'Andrea by Cadioli (1763, p.49): 'Li due Santi Andrea Appostolo, e Longino Martire, dipinti a fresco sopra la più eminente parte della descritta facciata, oggimai logori, e quasi guasti del tutto, sono del Mantegna.' Little was left by the time of Susani (1818, pp.114–15): 'l'esterna facciata ... in mezzo alla quale verso la sommità esiste l'avanzo di una grande medaglia dipinto a fresco per mano di Andrea Mantegna rappresentante Sant'Andrea Appostolo e il martire S. Longino, delle quali due figure rimangono ora appena le teste.' Detached before the Mantegna exhibition of 1961 (for lit. see above), when the date MCCCCLXXXVIII was found inscribed beneath it. Published by Paccagnini (1961, pp.54–5) as an autograph Mantegna, an attribution accepted by Camesasca for the design alone, but rejected by Arslan.

Perina (1961, pp.281–4) regards all the façade frescoes as part of a single programme executed by Mantegna and his assistants in 1488, the date inscribed under the tondo of St Andrew and Longinus, the *Deposition* and *Holy Family* having been reworked later by Correggio. It should be noted that in the second half of 1488 Mantegna was in Rome. The *Ascension* and the lost *St Andrea and St Longinus* to either side of the doorway formed according to Cadioli a linked composition together with the Apostles: the *Ascension* is the most Mantegnesque of all the surviving *tondi*, and may well have been executed about 1488. The engraving of *The Risen Christ between*

St Andrew and St Longinus (Plates 228a and b) suggests that Mantegna had some involvement with designs for the decoration of the façade of Sant'Andrea, but a sure judgement of the surviving fragments is made impossible by their condition (see Cat.no.206). They are at present (1985) stored in Mantegna's chapel.

62. Bust of Andrea Mantegna

Mantua, Sant'Andrea, Chapel of San Giovanni Battista
Bronze bust set on a medallion of porphyry inset in a moulded frame of Istrian stone
H. of bust 47 cm. Diam. of medallion 70 cm. Frontispiece
The bust is set on the left return wall of the entrance, above a tablet inscribed with an elegiac distich: ESSE PAREM / HVNC NORIS / SI NON PREPO / NIS APELLI / AENEA M(an)TINIAE / QVI SIMVLACHRA / VIDES
It was taken by the French in 1797 and returned to Sant' Andrea *c*.1814–16

EARLY REFERENCES: The first printed reference to the bust occurs in Scardeone (1560, p.372): 'sepultus est humi in phano diui Andreae, ubi aeneum capitis eius simulachrum visitur, quod sibi suis conflauerat manibus, cum hoc disticho ibidem inciso [as above].' Donnesmondi, ii, 1616, p.47: 'iui nel muro è una testa grande di bronzo, che al naturale lo rappresenta, con questi due versi sotto ... [as above].' Amadei, ii, p.440: 'In memoria di un così rinomato pittore, il Marchese gli fece ergere, nella piccola cappella ... un busto di bronzo, colla testa cinta d'alloro, ed invece delle due pupille degli occhi vi fece incastrar due diamanti ...' The bust is mentioned in local guidebooks (Cadioli, 1763, p.54; Susani, 1818, p.117; *id.*, 1829, p.51; *id.*, 1831, p.117) and was often commented on by travellers. It also attracted the attention of connoisseurs and historians of art (e.g. Bettinelli, *Delle lettere e delle arti mantovane*, 1774, pp.38,144; Moschini, 1826, p.55).

Although Scardeone states unequivocally that Mantegna cast the bust himself, by the early nineteenth century there was a tradition in Mantua that it was the work of the medallist Sperandio ([D'Arco], *Monumenti di Pittura e Scultura trascelti in Mantova*, 1827, pp.7–8; D'Arco, i, pp.73–4). The attribution was upheld by D'Arco, and found its way into Perkins (*Les sculpteurs italiens*, ii, 1869, pp.260–1), who admired it as perhaps the finest bust of modern times. The attribution was queried by Fabriczy (in *Arch. Stor. dell'Arte*, i, 1888, pp.428–9), who pointed out that as Sperandio died *c*.1500, he was unlikely to have executed the bust, which Fabriczy believed to be posthumous, and suggested an attribution to the medallist Bartolomneo Melioli (d.1514), who was master of the Mantuan mint from *c*.1492 until his death. Simultaneously Rossi (in *Rivista italiana di numismatica*, i, 1888, pp.453–4; v, 1892, p.483) proposed a tentative attribution to the goldsmith Gian Marco Cavalli (*c*.1454–*c*.1508), who appears as a witness together with the stonecutter Zaccaria di Giovanni di Santo Columbano to the deed consigning the chapel in Sant'Andrea to Mantegna (for Cavalli see Norris, in *Dizionario biografico degli italiani*, xxii, 1979, pp.734–5). In fact Cavalli had been associated with Mantegna from at least as early as February 1483, when he contracted to make goldsmiths' work for the Marchese Federico after Mantegna's designs.

As a result of this suggestion Bode (in *J.P.K.*, x, 1889, pp.211–16; xi, 1890, pp.56–9) also ascribed to Cavalli the very similar bust of the poet Battista Spagnoli (d.1516), now in the Berlin Museum, whose ground is now lost but which was of porphyry and Istrian stone, evidently in imitation of Mantegna's roundel. Documents concerning a tomb for Spagnoli are printed incompletely by Bode (*art. cit., J.P.K.*, 1890) and more fully by Luzio-Renier (*La coltura* in *G.S.L.I.*, xxxiv, 1899, pp.63–6). From these it appears that Spagnoli's brother Tolomeo, the Marchese Francesco's powerful secretary, ordered an expensive marble tomb from a Milanese sculptor, who on 21 July 1517 received an earnest of 100 gold scudi. By 18 April 1518 the base of the tomb had been cut, and in June 1519 Tolomeo Spagnoli requested permission to have 'una statua di bronzo di esso m^{ro} Battista', which he intended to have put 'sopra la sepoltura' cast by the founders of the Gonzaga cannon-foundry. Permission was granted that same day. It is quite clear from the tenor of these documents that what Tolomeo commissioned was not the Berlin medallion, as is always supposed, but a monumental tomb, with base, sarcophagus (*conca*) and a bronze effigy to be laid on the sarcophagus. Tolomeo, however, was a scoundrel, and on the exposure of his rogueries after the death late that same June of his protector the Marchese Francesco, he was obliged to flee from Mantua, so arresting work on the monument. The Spagnoli medallion cannot therefore be dated to 1519; presumably it was commissioned later by some of the poet's admirers to commemorate him in the church of Santa Maria delle Grazie from which it is said to originate. Radcliffe's argument, therefore, that it cannot be the work of Cavalli, who was dead by 1519, is even more irrefutable than he realized (see *Splendours of the Gonzaga*, V. & A. Museum, 1981–2, exh. cat., pp.121–2, No.30).

There seems no good reason to contest the earliest attribution of Mantegna's head to Mantegna himself, as recorded by Scardeone in 1560. The case for his authorship is argued by Camesasca (1964, pp.49–50), and Middeldorf (in *Apollo*, cvii, 1978, p.314) who considers the head to be plainly the work of an amateur sculptor. The attribution is accepted by Radcliffe. The design of the whole must also be by Mantegna, but the actual cutting of the porphyry ground and Istrian stone frame must have been done by a stone-cutter.

The general consensus as to the date of the bust is *c.*1480 (Tietze-Conrat, 1955, p.248) or 1480–90 (Camesasca, *loc. cit.*; Garavaglia, 1967, p.125). Fiocco (1937, p.103) dates it as a very late work, possibly Mantegna's last.

Much literature has clustered round Mantegna's putative activity as a sculptor, none of it convincing. We may cite for their tendency to enlarge his sculptural *oeuvre* Fiocco (1937, pp.95–103); *id.*, 'A. Mantegna scultore' in *Rivista d'Arte*, xxii, pp.220–8; Paccagnini, 'Il Mantegna e la plastica dell' Italia' in *Boll. d'A.*, ser.4, xlvi, 1961, pp.65–100.

See text (pp.130–2) for Mantegna as a sculptor and for the head.

Lost or Destroyed Paintings by or with Early Attribution to Mantegna

63. Altarpiece of Santa Sofia

In 1447–8 Mantegna painted the altarpiece of the high altar of the ancient church of S. Sofia, Padua, which had been restored *c.*1400 (see Canella, 'Santa Sofia' in *Padova*, ix, February 1935, pp.60–1; for the church see also C. Bellinati & others, *La chiesa di Santa Sofia in Padova*, 1982). Scardeone (1560, p.372) records the altarpiece and the dated inscription on it: 'Pinxit Mantinea Patavii penè puer, in aede S. Sophiae icona Mariae virginis, ubi legitur: *Andreas Mantegna Pat. an. septem & decem natus, sua manu pinxit, M.CCCC.XLVIII.*' In 1568 Vasari (p.488), perhaps copying Campagnola (see p.393) says: 'Poi dunque che ebbe fatta Andrea allora che non aveva più che 17 anni, la tauola dell'altar maggiore di s. Sofia di Padoa, la quale pare fatta da un vecchio ben pratico e non da un giovanetto . . .' The altarpiece was mentioned in 1583 by the painter L. Maganza (Magagnò), who was also a poet in the Paduan dialect, in *La Qvarta Parte delle Rime*, Venice, 1583, f.66r:

> *E chi uorà guardare*
> *Su l'altar grande de Santa Sophia,*
> *Sotto a i pie d'una Verghene Maria,*
> *Questa no xe bosia,*

El verà scritto, che quel Barba Andrea
Mantegna, ieri Pauan, e si n' haea
Vint' agni, che'l fasea
Si belle impenzaure . . .

Maganza implies that the inscription was under the Virgin's feet, and gives Mantegna's age as 20 when he painted it (probably as a round figure).

The altarpiece was painted for a certain Maestro Bartolommeo di Gregorio, a master baker, the same who had already commissioned in 1429–30 a *Pietà* of carved and painted stone from the sculptor Egidio da Wiener-Neustadt for an altar in the same church of Santa Sofia (Rigoni, 1970, p.58). Information about Bartolommeo was collected by Moschetti (in *Boll. M.C. di P.*, xiv, 1911, pp.83–4). His father Gregorio was granted in 1404 four houses in the contrada San Biagio by the prior of Santa Sofia. These he sold to his son Bartolommeo in 1428–9. Bartolommeo's bakery, rented from Santa Sofia, was also in the contrada San Biagio. It appears that he had no children by his wife Caterina, whom he married in 1429, for on his death, which probably took place in 1447, he left as his heirs the Confraternity of St Anthony of Padua. On 20 December 1447, at the petition of the *guardiano* of the Confraternity, the crier (*praeco*) of the Podestà of Padua notified Mantegna, who is termed *Magister Andreas pictor*, 'that he was to complete the altarpiece he was executing and is bound to execute for the said late Maestro Bartolommeo within the term he is bound to execute it, otherwise the said confraternity, if the picture is not completed within the said term, purposes that the said Magister Andrea shall return the money he has received and that it will have no more wish for the altarpiece' (Rigoni, 1970, p.58n). The picture had been completed by 16 October 1448, when Mantegna, who had already been paid 40 ducats by Bartolommeo, was paid another 32 lire 16 soldi (approx 5½ ducats) due to him for 'some other images and other works on the said altarpiece, above and beyond what he was bound'. The sum was paid him by the draper and wool-merchant Ser Bernardo di Olzinate, out of his own money, but as a member of the Confraternity and in its behalf (Lazzarini-Moschetti, 1908, xv, pp.137–8,297–8, doc.lxv). Lazzarini-Moschetti (*loc. cit.*) note that Squarcione received only 30 ducats for the Lazara altarpiece in 1449.

The altarpiece probably owed its removal and ultimate disappearance to the Benedictine nuns who were given Santa Sofia in 1578, and who remodelled the church, substituting a new high altar in rich Late Mannerist style. Selvatico (1849, p.160n.) notes that the altarpiece is mentioned in a late seventeenth-century *Descrizione delle pubbliche pitture di Padova*, an anonymous MS that had belonged to the Abbate Jacopo Morelli (1745–1819).

64. Double Portrait of Leonello d'Este and Folco da Villafora.

Ferrara, 1449

On 23 May 1449 the accounts of the Ferrarese court record a payment to Maestro Bonzani (Bongianni), a painter, for a panel ready prepared and framed. On one side of this Maestro Andrea da Padoa was to paint a portrait of the Marchese Leonello d'Este, on the other side one of Leonello's Camerlengo and friend, Folco da Villafora. The relevant document was published by A. Venturi (in *Rivista storica italiana*, i, 1884, pp.606–7) from the Archivio di Stato, Modena (*Memoriale*, 1449), and reads: '*Antonio de Rainaldo per conto de so officio de dare adi xxiij de magio L. una soldi oto marchesini per lui a m° Bonzani depintore per lo prexio de uno quadro lungo incastrado e incornisado e terzessado e rassado da tuti dui i lati lo quale fiece tore lo Illustrissimo nostro. S. per farse retrare dal naturale a m° Andrea da Padoa dipintore da uno lato dal altro lato folcho da villafora come appare per Bolletino de mano de Guglielmo fussaro. – L 1. s. viiij. d.*

It is clear from the term '*quadro lungo*' that the portrait was of the tall, narrow, vertical type we know from a number of surviving portraits of this period, e.g. Pisanello's portrait of Leonello in the Accademia Carrara, Bergamo. The Marchese's portrait would have been on the front face, and that of Folco on the reverse. Folco, who belonged to one of the greatest and most powerful families of Ferrara, received lavish gifts from Leonello: rich clothes, a splendid apartment in the Castello, the palace which is now the Seminario of Ferrara, and in 1447 the lordship and palace of Savonuzzo. Leonello also gave him a gold ring inscribed with his own name (Venturi, *loc. cit.*; Pasini Frassoni, *Dizionario storico-araldico dell' antico ducato di Ferrara*, 1914, p.610).

Maestro Andrea da Padoa was identified by Venturi (*doc. cit.*) as Mantegna. The identification was also proposed by Campori ('I Pittori degli Estensi' in *Atti e memorie delle RR. Deputazioni di Storia Patria per le provincie modenesi e parmensi*, ser. 3, iii – 2, 1886, p.537) and is generally received (cf. also Puppi, 1972, pp.41,48, n.52).

The picture is perhaps that recorded in an Este inventory of 1494 (Campori, 1870, p.30): 'Due teste retracte dal naturale cum la cornise dorate, dove è la faza del S^re Leonello.' These seem, however, to have been two portraits independently framed.

65. Portrait of a Nun

A set of 47 sonnets in MS Estense III. D.22 in the Biblioteca Estense, Modena, by a poet named Ulisse, includes one celebrating a portrait of a nun painted by Mantegna.

Ulixes. pro Andrea mantegna pictore. dicto
squarzono. pro quadam monialj.

Quando fortuna e il ben disposto cielo
sciolse dal proprio nido alle salse onde
quel spirto divo, in chui natura infonde
virtu, che vince ognaltro col penelo.

Duno angelico volto soto un velo
che per stupore ogni anima confonde
el gia fu cinto de le sacre fronde
che di giove non teme alcun suo telo.

La mano industriosa et l'alto ingegno
limagine, raccolta nel concepto
scolpì in pictura propria viva et vera.

Non pigli adunque la sua mente a sdegno
sio desidero per qualunque affeco
eterna far la sua memoria in terra.

The sonnet was first published by Quadrio (*Della Storia e della Ragione d'ogni poesia*, vii, 1739–49, p.101) and republished by A. Venturi (in *Der Kunstfreund*, No. xix,

1855, pp.290–1). Among the other sonnets are two in praise of Jacopo Bellini, one celebrating his triumph in painting the portrait of the Marchese Leonello d'Este better and more quickly than Pisanello. The second sonnet must have been written in or shortly before August 1441. The writer of these sonnets is generally identified as Ulisse Aleotti (d.1488), a Venetian notary employed in the Doge's chancery from 1421 onwards. In 1447 he was at Padua, probably in the suite of one of the Venetian Rettori. Mantegna and Squarcione chose him as one of two arbitrators in a dispute settled on 26 January 1448, as is known from the voiding of the compromise by the Corte Maggiore of Venice on 2 January 1455/6. (For Aleotti see F. Stefani, in *Archivio veneto*, xxix, 1885, pp.191–2; F. Rizzi, in *Dizionario biografico degli italiani*, ii, 1960, p.155.)

The portrait must have been painted before 1460, when Mantegna settled in Mantua, but as Venturi (*Storia*, vii, 3, 1914, pp.21–2) points out, the words '*dal proprio nido alle salse onde*' indicate that it was executed in Venice, during a visit from Mantegna, and not in Padua. A date *c*.1452–3, when Mantegna was preparing for marriage with Nicolosia Bellini, is perhaps plausible.

66. St Benedict
Padua, San Benedetto-Novello

The Anonimo Morelliano (1800, p.24; 1844, p.67) records in this church: '*El S. Benedetto in tela in Coro fu de mano del Mantegna.*'

The monastery of San Benedetto-Novello (for which see Portenari, 1623, pp.442–4; Universo, in Bellinati & Puppi, eds., *Padova, basiliche e chiese*, ii, 1975, pp.307–8) was handed over in 1442 by its abbot *in commendam*, Francesco dal Legname, to Benedictine monks of the Olivetan order. The commission for the picture of St Benedict can probably be linked to a redecoration of the church under their auspices: it was presumably painted during the 1450s. The first abbot of the new monastery was Ognibene Savonarola, who was a kinsman of Mantegna's neighbours in the contrada di S. Lucia.

67. Frescoes in Palazzo Gattamelata, Padua

A painting by Mantegna of the *Lamentation of the People over the dead Gattamelata* is mentioned by Paolo Giovio (Jovius) in his eulogy of the celebrated *condottiere* Erasmo da Narni, better known as Gattamelata, which was composed in 1524. The passage is found in an epigraph which appears under Gattemelata's portrait in only one edition of his *Elogia virorum bellica virtute illustrium*, that of Basle 1561 (not traced, quoted from Tietze-Conrat, *op. cit.* below) and reads: '... La cui morte onoro il senato/ E piu il pennel del Mantegna/ Coloritore del pianto e della/ Consternazione del popolo.'

Scardeone (1560, p.372) also records that Mantegna painted a chamber in 'an ancient house over the arch near Santa Lucia with the history of Gattamelata' (*Pinxit thalamum vetustae domus super fornicem prope D. Luciam cum historia Gattamelatae*). According to Ridolfi (1648, p.69), probably translating Scardeone, 'Colorì poi a fresco vna stanza nella Casa vecchia appresso Santa Lucia con historie di Gattamelata, chiaro capitano de' suoi tempi.' The frescoes were destroyed in a fire on 5 November 1760

(Rossetti, 1765, p.228: 'Vicino a questa Chiesa (di S. Lucia) nella Casa al volto detto della Malvasia, v'era una stanza tutta dipinta a fresco, con alcune azioni di Gattamelata di *Andrea Mantegna*, della quale parla il Ridolfi ... e lo Scardeone ... che per fatale incendio seguito a 5. Novembre 1760 affatto è perita.'

The house can be identified from these references as the twelfth-century palace known as the Casa di Ezzelino il Balbo (for which see Gallimberti, *Il volto di Padova*, 1968, pp.157–8, and Puppi & Zuliani, eds., *Padova: case e palazzi*, 1977, pp.24,311, cf. also pp.164–5). Unfortunately the history of the house's ownership is poorly recorded, but the presence of the frescoes suggests that in the mid-fifteenth century it belonged to Gattamelata's widow, Giacoma della Leonessa (d.1466), or else was leased by her (in 1457 she bought the newly constructed palace built by the notary Pietro Marcato, which on 2 October 1459 she gave to her natural granddaughter Caterina (for whom see below).

The composition of the fresco described by Giovio appears to be recorded in two early drawings and an engraving. 1) Drawing 1 (Plate 165), now in the Wallace Collection, usually ascribed to Antonio Pollaiuolo, though either as much reworked or as a poor copy of a lost original. It represents a lamentation over the body of a young man, which is laid out on a table on the shroud in which it is to be wrapped. It is first recorded in the Praun collection of Nuremberg, whose drawings were purchased in Italy, mostly at Bologna, between 1600 and 1615 by Paul von Praun (Murr, *Description du Cabinet de Monsieur Paul de Praun*, 1797, pp.37,46: '3. La mort d'Erasme de Narni, surnommé *Gattamelata*, célèbre Général Vénitien (mort en 1440) pleuré par le peuple; fait à la plume, et lavé en bistre'). The drawing was engraved in reverse by J.T. Prestel of Frankfurt in 1777 with a French inscription identifying the subject as in Murr's catalogue. There can be little doubt that both Prestel and Murr record an earlier identification of the subject, perhaps inscribed on an old mount. 2) Drawing 2, a poor copy, cut on both sides, of the Praun drawing, formerly in a private collection in Munich. Published by Courajod, in *L'Art*, xix, 1879, pp.163–4. 3) The engraving (Bartsch, ix, p.130, no.30) by AC, usually identified as Alaert Claesz of Utrecht, exists in impressions dated 1555. It reproduces the composition in reverse from the drawing and in an architectural setting.

Tietze-Conrat (in *B.M.*, lxvii, 1935, pp.217–19) showed that the resemblances between the engraving and the Wallace drawing prove them to derive from a finished work, which she considers is more faithfully reproduced in the engraving. She also clarified the identity of the young man whose death is lamented. This is Gianantonio (b.*c*.1427), the only son of Gattamelata by his wife Giacoma della Leonessa. He died of a head wound at some date in 1457, certainly before 25 April, when his mother made a will in which he is mentioned as dead (Eroli, *Erasmo Gattamelata da Narni, suoi monumenti e sua famiglia*, 1876, p.366). At that date his mother Giacoma had obtained permission to erect a funerary chapel in Sant'Antonio, dedicated to St Anthony of Padua and San Bernardino, to hold the bodies of her husband and son. Their tombs were probably completed by 17 February

1458, certainly by 23 May 1459 (see Lazzarini, in *Il Santo*, iv, 1931–2, pp.228–33). The verse epitaph on the tomb of Gianantonio was composed by the humanist Galeotto Marzio (see Cat. no. 68) also from Narni, like Gattamelata (Gonzati, *La basilica di S. Antonio di Padova*, ii, 1853, p.134).

Tietze-Conrat assumed that the chamber was decorated with only one fresco, the *Lamentation*, and supposed that this was painted as 'an overmantel' (see also 1955, p.246). But from the descriptions in Scardeone and Rossetti it is clear that the entire chamber was frescoed and that there were several histories. If the association between the composition recorded in the drawings and engraving and the decoration of the chamber in the Casa di Ezzelino is a real one, we can suppose that the frescoes represented incidents in the life of Gattamelata (d.1441) and his son Gianantonio, who was also a *condottiere*. It would follow that they were commissioned by Giacoma della Leonessa to record the brief glories of the family, raised to feudal splendour by the elder Gattamelata, born the son of a baker in a small Umbrian town, and extinguished by the untimely death of Gianantonio, its sole male heir. Giacoma was sole heir to her son, who died intestate. She is known to have been linked by close ties of friendship with Mantegna's patron, Jacopo Antonio Marcello, for on 2 October 1459 in a codicil to her will she declares that he has negotiated on her behalf a betrothal between Caterina, the natural daughter of Gianantonio, then aged three, and Francesco di Antonio Dotto of Padua (Eroli, p.371). A second link between Mantegna and Giacoma can be found in Galeotto Marzio da Narni, whom Mantegna painted with Janus Pannonius in a double portrait of 1458 (see Cat. no. 68).

If this reconstruction of events is correct, the frescoes would have been commissioned during 1457 and would have been one of the engagements that delayed Mantegna in Padua until 1460. The authorship of the Wallace Collection drawing has not been clarified. Panofsky (*Albrecht Dürer*, ii, 1943, p.96) rejected an attribution to Mantegna, certainly correctly, for its style is very different from his, but much less plausibly denied all connection between it and the Gattamelata frescoes, preferring to identify it as a subject from Virgil (*Aeneid*, XI, 29–35), the lamentation over the dead Pallas. This is far-fetched, and ignores the early evidence of Giovio that Mantegna did indeed paint a popular lamentation ovet Gattamelata, with the figures distraught with mourning. Sabatini (*Antonio e Pietro Pollaiolo*, 1944, p.90) suggests that the drawing is a copy of the Pollaiuolo cartoon which belonged to Squarcione (see p.19). Alternatively it may be a Paduan or Venetian drawing after Mantegna's original fresco, since the Gattamelata frescoes enjoyed some fame in the fifteenth and sixteenth centuries. It should be noted that there are similar compositions in Jacopo Bellini's sketchbooks. The Pollaiuolesque features of the drawing might then be due to the influence of Squarcione's cartoon.

68. Double Portrait of Janus Pannonius and Galeotto Marzio da Narni

Painted in 1458

This painting, now lost, is known from the laudatory elegy by Janus Pannonius, printed in his *Poemata*, i,

Utrecht, 1784, pp.276–9, from a Corvine manuscript. The poem is dated 1458 in its title.

Laus Andreae Mantegnae, Pictoris Patavini.
A. MCCCC LVIII.
ELEGIA. II.

Qualem Pellaeo fidum cum rege sodalem
   Pinxit Apelleae, gratia mira, manus;
Talis cum Iano tabula Galeottus in una,
   Spirat inabruptae nodus amicitiae.
Quas, Mantegna, igitur tanto pro munere grates,
   Quasve canet laudes, nostra Thalia, tibi?
Tu facis ut nostri vivant in secula vultus,
   Quamvis amborum corpora terra tegat.
Tu facis, immensus cum nos disterminet orbis,
   Alter in alterius possit ut esse sinu.
Nam quantum a veris distant haec ora figuris?
   Quid, nisi vox istis desit imaginibus?
Non adeo similes speculi nos lumina reddunt,
   Nec certans puro splendida lympha vitro.
Tam bene respondet paribus distantia membris,
   Singula tam proprio ducta colore nitent.
Num te Mercurius divina stirpe creavit?
   Num tibi lac, quamvis virgo, Minerva dedit?
Nobilis ingenio est, et nobilis arte vetustas,
   Ingenio veteres vincis, et arte, viros.
Edere tu possis spumas ex ore fluentes,
   Tu Veneris Coae perficere effigiem.
Nec Natura valet quicquam producere rerum,
   Non valeant digiti quod simulare tui.
Postremo, tam tu picturae gloria prima es,
   Quam tuus historiae gloria prima Titus.
Ergo operum cultu terras cum impleveris omnes,
   Sparseris et toto nomen in orbe tuum;
Ilicet, accitus superas transibis ad arces,
   Qua patet astriferae, lactea zona, viae;
Scilicet ut vasti pingas pallatia coeli,
   Stellarum flammis sint variata licet.
Cum coelum ornaris, coelum, tibi praemia, fiet,
   Pictorum et, magno sub Iove, Numen eris.
Nec tamen his fratres cedent pietate poëtae,
   Sed tibi post Musas proxima sacra ferent.
Nos duo praesertim; quorum tua dextera formas
   Perpetua nosci posteritate facit.
Interea haec gratam testentur carmina mentem,
   Vilior his Arabi turis acervus erit.

It reads in translation:
'As the hand of Apelles with its wondrous grace painted the Pellaean king [Alexander] with his faithful companion, so Galeotto breathes with Janus in one picture, a knot of unbroken friendship. What thanks then shall our Thalia sing to thee, Mantegna, for such a gift, what praises? Thou makest our faces to live for centuries, though the earth cover the bodies of us both. Thou makest the one able to lie in the other's bosom, whenever a wide world shall separate us. For in what do these faces differ from our true shapes? Surely these images want but a voice? The mirror's light does not reflect us as faithfully or glittering water that rivals pure glass, so well does the proportion answer to each member, so clearly does each single thing glow, portrayed in its own proper colour. Say, did Mercury give thee birth and an origin divine,

did Minerva, though a virgin, give thee milk? Renowned for genius, renowned too for art is antiquity, yet thou surpassest the ancients in genius and art. Thou couldst represent foam flowing from a mouth, or the form of the Venus of Cos. Neither can Nature produce aught that thy fingers cannot simulate. Lastly, thou art as much the prime glory of painting as thy Titus [Livy] is the prime glory of history. Accordingly when thou hast filled all lands with the adornment of thy works and hast spread thy name over all the world, thou shalt be summoned hence and pass upwards to the towers of heaven, where the star-bearing ways expand a milky girdle, so that thou mayest paint the palaces of vasty heaven, varied though they be with the flames of stars. When thou hast ornamented heaven, heaven shall become thy reward, and thou shalt be the god of painters, under great Jove. Yet neither shall their brethren the poets yield to them in piety, but shall bring thee thy next offerings after the Muses. We two especially, whose forms thy right hand causes to be known to an eternal posterity. Meanwhile let these verses testify to our grateful mind: a heap of Arabian incense is not of so great price.'

Janus Pannonius, the celebrated Hungarian humanist and poet, was born on 29 August 1434 near Zagreb. In the spring of 1447 he was sent to the school of Guarino of Verona in Ferrara and remained there until he was 24. Here he met and became the intimate friend and room-companion of another pupil at the school, Galeotto Marzio (Martius). Born at Narni c.1428, of an ancient family, Marzio was to become a famous humanist and philosopher. In 1450 he left Ferrara, and later that same year was teaching at Padua where he also studied medicine. In the autumn of 1454 Janus also transferred to Padua, where he studied and wrote poetry until 1458, when he obtained his degree and left for Hungary, after visiting Rome and Florence. He is the Hungarian Bishop traditionally said to have been portrayed by Mantegna in the Ovetari frescoes (see p.399) for in 1459 he was made Bishop of Quinquecclesie (Pècs). In 1461 Marzio went to visit him in Buda. He returned to Hungary in 1465 and was with Janus in 1472 when the conspiracy he had organized against Matthias Corvinus was crushed and Pannonius himself died near Zagreb on his flight into Italy. Marzio, after an eventful life, died c.1497 and was buried at Montagnana, in the territory of Padua (Huszti, *Janus Pannonius*, 1931; G. Martius, *De egregie, sapienter, iocose dictis ac factis Regis Mathiae*, ed. L. Juhasz, 1934).

For a more or less contemporary miniature-portrait of Janus Pannonius see the title-page of an MS of Plautus executed for his uncle Johannes Vitéz, Bishop of Varadin and later Archbishop of Gran (c.1400–72), c.1459 in Ferrara (for this see *Matthias Corvinus und die Renaissance in Ungarn 1458–1521*, exh. cat., Schallaburg, May–November 1982, p.156, no.34, cf. also pp.138–9, no.11, p.143, no.15. The MS is now in Vienna, Nationalbibliothek, Cod. 111). Mantegna's lost portrait is discussed by J. Balogh ('Ritratti ungheresi dipinti dal Mantegna' in *Szazadok*, 1927), Bettini & Puppi (1970, pp.89–90), Margolin (in Budapest, *Acta Litteraria*, xiv, 1972, pp.341–51), Balogh (in *Janus Pannonius, Tanulmanyok*, ed. Kordos & Kovacs, 1975, pp.83–92; *Matthias Corvinus*, exh. cat. cit., pp.155–6).

Sambucus (cit. Huszti, p.359) says Janus was of a 'rather thin and small habit of body, with a liberal and open countenance, and a rather square neck'.

69. Designs for decorations at Cavriana

The Gonzaga palace, now Villa Siliprandi, at Cavriana, near Mantua, passed in 1441 after the death of Marchese Gianfrancesco to his younger son Giovanni Lucido, on whose death in 1448 it passed to the Marchese Lodovico (Litta, *Gonzaga*, tav.3; Bertolotti, *I comuni e le parrochie della provincia mantovana*, 1893, p.57). It was important as a fortified post on the confines of Mantua and Brescia. The Marchese Lodovico began work on remodelling it in 1461 (Marani, 1961, p.61, with references to documents in the Archivio di Stato; Schivenoglia, p.146: 'Nota che del sopra scripto ano 1461 el signor mes. Lodovigo fe fare over refare la rocha de Chavriana over le fe chomenzare con molte personij tutij Vilanij de Mantoa'; Vasić Vatoveć, 1979, pp.248–52). The work seems to have been entrusted at first to Giovanni da Padova. From 1462 Luca Fancelli was also involved and it was he who charged Samuele da Tradate, a painter, son of the sculptor Jacopino da Tradate and one of Mantegna's companions on the famous excursion to Lake Garda of 1464, with the decoration of the state-chambers. In October 1462 (cf. letters cit. by Vasić Vatoveć, pp.251,256, n.17) Samuele was commissioned to paint the ceiling of a chamber at Cavriana to designs by Mantegna.

DOCUMENTS: 1) *1463, 19 February*. Vicario of Cavriana to Marchese Lodovico. Maestro Samuele is working hard (Luzio, 1913, p.22).
2) *1463, 17 March*. Same to same. Samuele is hard at work. The ceiling is not yet finished (Luzio, *loc. cit.*).
3) *1464, 7 March*. Mantegna to Marchese Lodovico from Goito. During the last few days Samuele has come to Goito from Cavriana bringing the measurements of the four walls of the *camera*. Since Mantegna does not yet know what the Marchese's intentions are, he has done nothing so far and awaits Lodovico's commands. It would be better if he adjust the designs on the spot; in the meantime he prays the Marchese to come to his help with money, of which he stands in great need (Mantua, cited by Baschet, 1866, p.330; pub. in full by Kristeller, 1902, p.522, doc.31).
4) *1464, 12 March*. Letter from Marchese Lodovico to Mantegna in answer to the above. He asks him to wait till his return from Belgioioso so that they can decide on the subject of the decorations (cit. by Baschet, 1866, pp.329–30).
5) *1464, 12 March*. Giovanni Cattaneo of Cavriana to Marchese Lodovico from Cavriana. Samuele has finished the ceiling of the *camera*, as His Excellency must already know, and Cattaneo now begs the Marchese to send Samuele Mantegna's designs, so that he may get on with the work. At present he is putting gesso on the doorway and windows of the *camera* (quoted in part by Baschet, *loc. cit.*, in full by Kristeller, 1902, p.523, doc.32).

Luzio (*loc. cit.*), who does not cite his source, says that the decorated chambers of Cavriana included a *stanza d'Ercole* and a *stanza del Sole*. See Kristeller (1901, pp.209–10) and Marani (*loc. cit.* and p.153, n.17). For the subsequent vicissitudes of the palace see Perogalli & Sandri, *Ville delle province di Cremona e Mantua*, 1973, pp.267–8.

70. The Descent into Limbo

In a letter of 28 June 1468 to the Marchese Lodovico Mantegna reports that he has begun a painting on panel of 'the history of Limbo' ('*O principiato el quadro dove fo la instoria del limbo chome mi a comandato la I.S. vostra. Vero e che io o avuto el dito quadro Cioe el ligname molto tardi et questo E stato per la molta pegricia di Vicencio marangone o di altri che nogli a data el lignamo. Inzegneromi a mia possanaie di farlo piacere ala I.S. vostra.*' (Printed by Baschet, 1866, p.332; Kristeller, 1902, p.525, doc.39; repr. in facsimile in Luzio, 1913, p.56 (Pl.facing).) Identified by C. Elam as Cat. no. 34 (q.v.).

71. Two Portraits

On 2 August 1471 the Marchese Lodovico wrote from Gonzaga to Mantegna, telling him that the painter Zanetto da Milano, who was then at Gonzaga, wished to go on to Mantua in order to see Mantegna's works. Mantegna has already asked to come out to Gonzaga to show the Marchese 'those two portraits' (*quelli due retracti*). It would be a good idea if he were to come out next day and bring the portraits with him: then Zanetto could go back with him to Mantua (Baschet, 1866, p.333; Kristeller, 1902, p.527, doc.44). See text, p.86.

These portraits are sometimes identified as portraits of Lodovico and Barbara of Brandenburg. What is certainly a lost portrait of the Marchese Lodovico by Mantegna is engraved (probably in reverse) in Roscio, Mascardi and others, *Ritratti et elogii di capitani illvstri* (Filippo de' Rossi, Rome, 1646, p.152). It shows him wearing a *berretta capitanesca*, and a breastplate over a coat of mail (Plate 166). In conception it is very close to the portrait of Carlo de' Medici, painted in the 1460s, and must also be very close in date. For a similar lost portrait of Francesco Sforza known from a copy see Cat. no. 152; given the close resemblance of the hat and armour worn by Sforza, these may have been companion portraits.

72. Commission for Portraits

A letter of 6 July 1477 from Mantegna in Mantua to Marchese Lodovico is written in response to a demand for certain portraits to be painted. As they are wanted so quickly, he would like to know the size, and whether they are to be simply drawings or are to be painted in colour on canvas or on panel. If the Marchese wants to send them a long distance he can paint them on very thin canvas so that they can be wrapped round a stick. Moreover, as the Marchese well knows, it is impossible to paint life-like portraits without being able to see the sitters; and their Excellencies are out of Mantua. He will do as they think fit: meanwhile he will wait to hear from them and to receive small panels or canvases on which to begin the portrait. (*. . . aviso la Ex.^cia vostra chome volendo far queli ritrati, non intendo, volendoli la S. vostra si presto, in che modo habia a fare, o solamente disegnati o colorite in tavola o in tela e de che statura. Se la S. vostra li volesse mandare lontano se possono (?) farli suso tela sotile per poterli avoltare suso un bastonzelo. Anchora chome sa la Ex.^cia vostra non si può far*

bene dal naturale chi nona comodita di vedere. Le Ex.^cia Vostre sono fuora de la tera, mi govenero come parera a quele, aspetaro de intendere et di avere o tavolete oli telariti ch'io posa dare principio aditi ritrati.) Published by Braghirolli, in *Giornale di erudizione artistica*, i, 1872, p.196; Kristeller, 1902, p.534, doc.69. Braghirolli proposes the natural interpretation of this letter, that it refers to portraits of Lodovico and Barbara of Brandenburg. See Cat. no. 71.

73. Commission for a picture for Bona of Savoy, Dowager Duchess of Milan

On 9 June 1480 Bona of Savoy wrote in the name of her eleven-year-old son Giovanni Galeazzo Sforza, Duke of Milan, to the Marchese Federico, sending him 'certain drawings for a picture' and asking him to have it painted by 'your D. Andrea Mantegna, the famous painter' (*li certi designi de penture quali pregamo che vi piacia farli retrare per el vostro D. Andrese Mantegha pentore celebre*': first published by Motta, in *Archivio storico lombardo* (n.s.3), xxii, 1895, p.421). On 20 June the Marchese Federico, in a famous letter of reply to the Duchess, say that he has received the sketch and pressed '*Andrea Mantegna mio pictore*' very hard to put it into elegant form. But Mantegna has told him that the work is better suited to a miniaturist, since he is not used to painting small figures. He would rather paint a Madonna or something else about a *braccio* or a *braccio* and a half high with the good leave and pleasure of the Duchess. If Federico knew how to get the Duchess's request fulfilled, he would set about satisfying it with all speed, but commonly such excellent masters have something fantastic in their natures, and one must make do with what one can get from them ('*ma communemente questi magistri excelenti hanno del fantasticho e da loro convien tuore quello che se po havere*'). Accordingly, should the Duchess not be served as speedily as she wishes, Federico begs her to excuse him (Kristeller, 1902, p.538, docs. 78,79).

74. The Badia Madonna

Vasari (1550, p.510) records that above the door of the library in the Badia of Fiesole was a half-length Virgin and Child by Mantegna: 'Alla badia di Fiesole fuor di Fiorenza al monastero de canonici regolari è vn quadro d'vna meza Nostra donna sopra la porta della libraria, con diligenza lauorato da lui.' In 1568 (p.489) he writes: '*stando in Verona lauorò, e mandò in diversi luoghi, e n' hebbe vno Abbate della Badia suo amico, e parente, vn quadro nel quale è vna N. Donna dal mezzo in su, con figliuolo in collo, & alcune teste d'Angeli, che cantano fatti con grazia mirabile. Il qual quadro è hoggi nella libreria di quel luogo, e fu tenuta allora, e sempre poi come cosa rara.*' Borghini (1584, p.356) merely copies Vasari, but Bottari, his editor of 1730 (p.289, n.3), notes, 'Questo quadro è stato levato di quella libreria, e del monastero ancora.'

See text, p.128 for the probable association of this Madonna with Mantegna's friend, Matteo Bosso. See also Cat. no. 166.

75. Decoration of a Chamber for Marchese Federico

A letter of 25 February 1484 from Bishop Lodovico Gonzaga to Giovanni della Rovere (c.1457–1501), Prefetto di Roma, transmits Mantegna's regrets that he can-not paint a picture for Giovanni because by the end of this summer he has to finish the decoration of a chamber he has already begun for the Marchese. He is afraid that he will not have enough time, especially as the Marchese is pressing for the work's completion since he wants to move into the rooms ('*per havere ad finire per tutta questa estate una camera ad lo Ill. S. Marchese . . . alla quale ha già dato principio e dubitando che lo tempo abbia ad mancharli, et instando lo prelibato signor Marchese la expeditione per volere S. Signoria andare ad habitarli, allega essere talmente impossibile . . .*). Printed by Baschet (1866, p.481; Kristeller, 1902, pp.541–2, doc.87).

76. Virgin and Child with other figures
Ferrara; painted for Eleanora d'Aragona, Duchess of Ferrara

According to Braghirolli (1872, p.199), this picture was begun in 1484, then interrupted, and only finally completed in November 1495. He does not cite documents to substantiate these statements and none has been unearthed as yet. Although Brown (1969, p.541, n.7) points out that these dates probably represent the results of careful research, nevertheless there remains a very serious possibility that the 9 of 1495 is a misprint for 8, given that Eleanora d'Aragona (for whom see L. Chiappini, *Eleanora d'Aragona*, 1956) died on 11 October 1493. Moreover Braghirolli cites as his authority Baschet (1866, pp.481–2), who assumes that the picture was completed in December 1485, since he was unaware of Document 6 below. Six letters concerning the commission are known (Kristeller, 1902, pp.543–4, docs. 90–5).

DOCUMENTS: 1) *1485, 6 November*. Marchese Francesco Gonzaga to Eleanora d'Aragona. He understands the Duchess wishes to have a certain picture by Mantegna of the Madonna and some other figures which is as yet not completely finished (*uno certo quadro de la madonna cum alcune altre figure non in tutto finite de mano de Andrea mantinia*). Accordingly he has commanded Mantegna to finish it with all due pains, and he hopes when it is completed either to send it on shortly or to bring it with him on his forthcoming visit to the Duchess.
2) *1485, 6 November*. Francesco Gonzaga to Mantegna. The Marchese sends on the Duchess's letter and commands Mantegna to use all his diligence in finishing the picture as quickly as possible and to employ his genius on it, so as to give every satisfaction to the Duchess, whom the Marchese is very anxious to please.
3) *1485, 10 November*. Eleanora, Duchess of Ferrara, to Francesco Gonzaga. She thanks him for the letter in which he informs her that he has ordered Mantegna to finish her picture. She is even more grateful for the news that he is to bring it with him on his forthcoming visit.
4) *1485, 14 November*. Francesco Gonzaga to Mantegna. By the previous letter he had commanded Mantegna to finish a picture of the Madonna and some other figures (*uno quadro de la Madonna cum alcune altre figure*), which the Duchess of Ferrara has requested. Since he has not heard that Mantegna has put his hand to the work, he now repeats his command to him to finish it as quickly as possible.

5) *1485, 12 December*. Francesco Gonzaga to Mantegna. A reminder to Mantegna to use expedition and finish the picture he has begun for the Duchess with all diligence: the Marchese wishes to give it to her as a New Year's gift. In return Mantegna will find the Marchese generous in his gift to him.
6) *1485, 15 December*. Francesco Gonzaga to Mantegna. He is certain Mantegna will use such diligence in finishing the picture that he will do the Marchese honour and bring no small glory to himself. Lodovico da Bologna is about to go to Venice: if Mantegna has not already spoken to him about the varnish he wants, let him do so at once and Lodovico will bring him the varnish so that there may be no delay on this account.

The tenor of the correspondence suggests that the picture was commissioned by Eleanora d'Aragona, and after some delay was nearly finished by 6 November 1485, when Francesco Gonzaga was asked by her to press the master to complete it quickly. The picture was nearly ready to receive the last varnish by 15 December and was presumably completed by New Year's Day, 1486. It has been variously identified as the Brera Madonna (Cat. no. 166), as a picture listed in the 1493 inventory of the Guardaroba Estense (Cat. no. 79) and as the Dresden *Holy Family* (Cat. no. 44).

77. Portrait of Maddalena Gonzaga
Pesaro, Library of the Castello

The inventory taken on 21 October 1500 of the library of Giovanni Sforza (1466–1510), Lord of Pesaro, records among other portraits in this room one in profile of Maddalena Gonzaga by Mantegna: 'La testa del Ill. M. Magdalena de ma del Mantegna in profillo' (pub. Vernarecci, 'La libreria di Giovanni Sforza Signore di Pesaro' in *Archivio storico per le Marche e per l'Umbria*, iii, 1886, p.522). Maddalena Gonzaga, born on 10 July 1472, was betrothed to Giovanni Sforza on 9 September 1486, and was married on 28 October 1489 in Pesaro, where she died in childbirth on 8 August 1490 (Luzio & Renier, *Mantova e Urbino*, 1893, pp.5,8,48,54 n.5). The portrait must therefore have been painted either during the negotiations for the marriage, at the time of the betrothal or during the three years of the engagement. Very probably a record of it survives in Melioli's medals of Maddalena (Hill, pp.48–9, Nos. 197–8, pl.36) which were presumably executed after September 1486, since their inscriptions seem to allude to plighted troth. The portrait was presumably lost in the fire that destroyed the Sforza library at Pesaro in 1514.

78. Judith
Florence, Palazzo Medici

The inventory taken in 1492, after the death of Lorenzo de' Medici, lists as in the Scrittoio of Palazzo Medici 'Una tavoletta in una cassetta dipintovi su una Giuditta chon la testa d'Oloferno e una serva, opera d'Andrea Squarcione' (Müntz, *Les collections des Médicis*, 1888, p.78). The Scrittoio contained the jewels, gems and other precious objects of the Medici, and since this small panel was kept in a casket we can deduce that it was a highly finished work of the type intended for close inspection in the hand and designed to be treated as a precious work of art. It precedes in the inventory two pictures of the same sort by Jan van Eyck and Petrus Christus; before them comes an ivory diptych, after them an ivory chessboard. The name given to Mantegna might suggest that the compilers noted the authorship from an inscription on the painting, which could indicate a work of the 1450s or 1460s, when Mantegna was still known by this name of Andrea Squarcione. But on 2 March 1480/1 Lorenzo de' Medici wrote to Mantegna thanking him for the gift of a painting which may well have been the *Judith* of the 1492 inventory (Del Piazzo, *Protocolli del carteggio di Lorenzo il Magnifico*, 1956, p.136: 'Marzo 1480 et 1481. A dì 2 . . . A Andrea Mantinia, dipintore a Mantova; lettera grata per la dipintura et opera sua mandata, ringraziandolo, etc.').

79. Virgin and Child with Seraphim
Ferrara

Listed in the 1493 inventory of the Guardaroba Estense (Campori, 1870, p.1): 'Uno quadro de legno depincto cum nostra dona et il figliolo cum serafini de mano del sopradicto Mantegna.' The next entry, invariably ignored, records a copy of it executed by a Modenese artist: 'un altro quadro retracto del sop. ° di mano di uno modenese.' Mantegna's original is generally identified as the *Virgin and Child* painted for Eleanora of Aragon, Duchess of Ferrara (see Cat. no. 76). See also Cat.no.166.

80. The Three Maries
Ferrara

Listed in the 1493 inventory of the Guardaroba Estense (Campori, 1870, p.1): 'Uno quadro di legno depincto cum le marie di mano di Andrea Mantegna.' Presumably a painting of the Three Maries at the Sepulchre: for a treatment of this subject by Mantegna see Plate 180 (copy of a lost picture).

81. Portrait of Isabella d'Este

Late in 1492 or early in 1493 at the request of her kinswoman Isabella del Balzo, Countess of Acerra, later Queen of Naples, Isabella ordered Mantegna to paint her portrait. On 12 January 1493 she wrote to Jacopo d'Atri that she was hastening on the portrait so as to send it after him to Naples where he was to present it to the Countess. In exchange she asked for the Countess's own portrait. On 2 April she begs the Countess by letter to send her one on panel, since those she has just received on paper and in wax are not very like, promising her own portrait, as the Countess had requested. On 20 April, she repeats her thanks in a second letter to the Countess for the portraits already received, but regrets that she cannot send her own portrait after all for the moment since Mantegna has done it so badly that it is not in the least like her (*perche el pictore ne ha tanto malfacta, che non ha alcuna de le nostre simiglie*). She is now sending for another painter from outside Mantua who is said to imitate nature well: this, as appears from a letter of 13 January 1494 accompanying the gift of the portrait, was Giovanni Santi, court painter to the Duchess of Urbino (Luzio, in *Emporium*, xi, 1900, pp.347–8; Kristeller, 1902, pp.553–4, docs. 118–20,122).

82. A Pavilion decorated by Mantegna
Ferrara

According to R. Bacchelli (*La congiura di Don Giulio d'Este*, Milan, 1943, pp.129,165) the *Memoriale* of Francesco Mazzoni, *cancelliere* of the Conte Albertino Boschetti (begun on 10 March 1492 and preserved in the Archivio Boschetti, San Cesario) records that in 1494 Ercole d'Este, Duke of Ferrara, sent as a present to King Charles VIII of France, during his invasion of Italy, a '*padiglione*' painted by Andrea Mantegna.

83. Unknown subject

A painting by Mantegna of an unknown subject is mentioned in letters from Teofilo Collenuccio to the Marchese Francesco of 7 April 1494, written from Gonzaga. Collenuccio reports that Francesco's *camerino* has been carpeted, but that Mantegna's painting (*quadro*) is not hung up because Ghisolfo has not yet come out from Mantua with its *cantinelle* (frame). A second letter of the same date from the same to the same reports that it is now hung up in its gilded frame (Kristeller, 1902, p.555, docs.124–5; Martindale, 1979, p.183, docs.10–11).

84. The Virgin

An epigram by Panfilo Sasso praises a Virgin painted by Mantegna: 'Admiratur Ingenium Andreae Mantegnae Pictoris Eximii/ Arte novus mira vivum me pinxit Apelles/ Aspice divinum Pygmalionis opus/ Igneus excelsis in me si spiritus astris/ Descendat: natum virgo iterum pariam.' (He admires the genius of the excellent painter Andrea Mantegna. 'The modern Apelles painted me with wondrous art: behold the divine work of this Pygmalion. If a fiery spirit were to descend into me from the stars, again I should give virgin birth to a son.')

This epigram was first printed in 1499 at Brescia in Sasso's *Liber Primus Epigrammatum*. It has not been noticed since Zani (*Enciclopedia metodico critico ragionata delle belle arti*, pt. I, xii, 1822, p.329).

85. Project for a statue of Virgil

For Isabella d'Este's project of erecting a statue to Virgil, conceived early in 1499, see text, p.189. The design was to be executed by Mantegna, and the great Neapolitan humanist Pontano was consulted as to its form and costume. Baschet (1866, pp.486–90) associated a drawing (Plate 167) of a statue of Virgil in the His de la Salle collection (now Louvre, Cabinet des Dessins, R.F.439) with this project and attributed it to Mantegna. The drawing (33.9 × 21.4 cm) is cut to a gable shape at the top: the lower part of the pedestal and putti pricked for transfer. The inscription reads: P. VERGILII/MARONIS A/AETERNAE SVI MEMORI/AE IMAGO. The attribution was rightly questioned by Kristeller (1901, p.403), who pointed out that the drawing has been reworked; he is followed by Fiocco (1937, p.84), Tietze-Conrat (1955, p.207), Paccagnini (1961, p.171) and Martineau (in V. & A. Museum, exh. cat., *Splendours of the Gonzaga*, 1981–2, p.152, No. 92). Nevertheless the possibility that this drawing is a copy of a design by Mantegna cannot be discounted: it must certainly have some association with Isabella's project. The likeness of Virgil as envisaged by Battista

Fiera (see text) is probably recorded in the terracotta bust of the poet which he commissioned and set up in 1514 on the Arco Fiera (now in the Palazzo Ducale, Mantua; for this see Portioli, *op. cit.*, Paccagnini, 1961, p.154, repr., and *Splendours of the Gonzaga*, 1981–2, pp.155–6, Nos.98–100).

86. Altarpiece presented to Cardinal Georges d'Amboise

On 19 November 1499, in order to ingratiate himself with Cardinal d'Amboise (see Cat.no.87) the Marchese Francesco sent him a present of an altarpiece by Mantegna (L.G. Pélissier, *Louis XII et Ludovic Sforza*, ii, 1896, p.366).

87. Devotional painting for Cardinal Georges d'Amboise

The known documents concerning this are published by Pélissier, 'Les amies de Ludovic Sforza' in *Revue historique*, xlviii, pt. 1, 1892, pp.57–8, n.3.

DOCUMENTS: 1) *1499, 26 October*. Gemetto de Nessonis from Milan to Isabella d'Este in Mantua. Gemetto has visited the Cardinal of Rouen, who has promised to serve the Marchesa. He is building a little chapel and has been told that Isabella has the first painter in the world; he would pay anything to have something from his hand. Gemetto thinks Isabella would do well to try every means to get something from Mantegna and present it when Monsignore comes or when she thinks best ('*Ozi ma butato certi botoni como fa far una capelletta e che ge stato detto che la S.V. a el primo pittore del mondo, e che pagaria ogni gran cossa a aver qualche cossa del suo. Per ho mi par che la S.V. dè cerchar ogni modo e via a aver qualche cossa de messer Andrea e presentarlo a la venuta de Monsignore o quanto parera a la V.S.*' Mantua, Arch. Gonzaga, Exliv, 3, 1499, no. 1634). 2) *1499, 4 November*. Same to same. The Cardinal thanks her a thousand times and is better pleased to have a devotional picture by Mantegna than to gain two thousand ducats. He is to give me a drawing of what he wants; Gemetto will forward this to Isabella, who must ask the Cardinal for anything she wants of him ('*Mons. de Rohan regracia la S.V. per mille volte e a più caro d'aver una sua devotione de Mantegna che de guadagnar doi millia ducati, e me debe dar el dessegno de quello chel vole, poi le mandaro a la S.V., e se quella vol cosa alcuna da lui le debia comandare*' (*id. ib.*).

Given the great political importance of the Cardinal, it is virtually certain that this picture was painted. Indeed Luzio (in *Archivio storico lombardo*, ser 3, xv, 1901, p.155) claims that it was a St John with a portrait of the Cardinal and his arms, but he wrongly cites as his source Pélissier, and treats doc. 2 as a letter of thanks for this picture. Possibly he has amalgamated discoveries of his own with those of Pélissier. The chapel for which the picture was intended can be identified as either the chapel or the private oratory that Georges d'Amboise erected as part of his extensive reconstruction of the archiepiscopal palace of Rouen. Payments for the chapel are recorded from 28 February 1495 to 29 September 1499 and for the oratory from 30 September 1497 until 29 September 1499 (Jouen, *Comptes, devis et inventaires du manoir archiépiscopal de Rouen*, 1908, pp.xxii–xxiv,393–6, plan facing p.400), but may have

continued to be made later since the building accounts for the following years are not specific. A number of paintings are listed in the undated rough inventory of the Cardinal's furnishings in the palace (published by Deville, *Comptes... de Gaillon*, 1850, pp.486–99), including a *Pietà* by Perugino in the Cardinal's chamber. The chapel contained several pictures, mostly small, and it would be unwise to assume that the Cardinal commissioned an altarpiece (cf. also Cat. no. 86 for an altarpiece by Mantegna presented to him in November 1499). One wall of the courtyard of the château of Gaillon, which was built by the Cardinal from 1502, was ornamented by 1509–10 with reliefs of the triumphs of Caesar after Mantegna. (Jacopo d'Atri to Isabella d'Este, ed. Weiss, in *J.W.C.I.*, xvi, 1953, p.7: 'In el quadro dal lato de la prima porta gli è sculpito tutto il triumpho de Iulio Cesare, ne la forma ch'el famoso Mantinia lo depinse, de non troppo grande figura ma ben e con bona gratia intagliato.') Weiss suggests implausibly that the Cardinal's devotional picture was intended for Gaillon.

88. Triumphs of Petrarch

The letter of 13 February 1501 from Sigismondo Cantelmo to Duke Ercole d'Este (see Cat.no.28) describing the temporary theatre erected in Mantua which was decorated along one side with six canvases from the *Triumphs of Caesar* also says that the front of the stage was decorated with the *Triumphs of Petrarch*, again painted by Mantegna: 'Dintorno alla scena al frontespitio da Basso erano li triumphi del petrarcha ancor loro penti per man del p.to Mantengha...' Attempts have sometimes been made to link these with six panels of the *Triumphs of Petrarch*, formerly in the Alte Pinakotek, now in the Kress Collection (K10–15; see for their history and literature Shapley, *Paintings from the Samuel H. Kress Collection, Italian Schools XV–XVI Century*, 1968, pp.27–8, then shown in Denver Museum, Colorado). Shapley attributes them to a follower of Mantegna and suggests that they may be imitations of the Mantegna *Triumphs* described in 1501. Their style and costume belong to the 1450s and 1460s and imitate Mantegna's Paduan manner: it is therefore most unlikely that they copy Mantegna's Mantuan *Triumphs of Petrarch*, even allowing for old-fashioned style in a *cassone* painter. For the Mantegnesque ivory carvings of the *Triumphs of Petrarch* on two chests in Graz see Plates 253a and b and text p.131.

89. Painting for Louis de la Trémoille, Vicomte de Thouars, Prince de Talmont

During the negotiations with Louis XII of France that preceded and followed his conquest of Milan (1500) Francesco Gonzaga had occasion to use the influence at court of Louis de la Trémoille (1460–1525), general of the French army in Italy, whom his agent, Jacopo d'Atri, describes in a letter of 27 June 1500 as 'il più fidelle e sincero amico che habiamo' (Pélissier, *Louis XII et Ludovic Sforza*, ii, 1896, p.373n).

On 16 August 1502 Francesco told Angelo Ghivizzano in a letter that he was about to despatch a painting for La Trémoille, and was using particular care because the picture was one of the finest Mantegna had ever painted (published by Brown, in *B.M.*, cxiv, 1972, p.862 n.5:

'Dirai che li mandaremo . . . il quadro de Monsignore de la Tremoglia, non ni parendo mandarlo per altro per essere una de le più belle cose che mai habbi facto Messer Andrea Mantinea:').

90. Atalanta and Hippomenes

A painting of this subject by Mantegna is praised in a poem by the humanist Domizio Falcone of Mantua (d.1505), an intimate friend of Castiglione. The two were shown panting in the race, Atalanta, bare-armed, her tunic pulled up, its folds blowing back and her hair streaming in the breeze, halting lest she overtake Hippomenes, while he turns back his head to gaze at her in astonishment (Vat.lat.2836, f.7, discovered by E. Battisti, printed by E. Faccioli, in Istituto Carlo d'Arco, *Mantova: Le Lettere*, ii, 1962, p.382). Although Falcone's date of birth is undiscovered, the poem can be dated to *c.*1490–1505.

The subject of Atalanta and Hippomenes was probably made the theme of this painting because Petrarch mentions their story in his *Trionfo d'Amore* (capitolo 2).

91. Pietà
Naples, San Domenico

Pietro Summonte (1453–1526) writing in 1524 to Marc' Antonio Michiel on art in Naples records an altarpiece of the *Pietà* by Mantegna in San Domenico (Nicolini, *L'arte napoletana del rinascimento e la lettera di Pietro Summonte a Marcantonio Michiel*, 1925, p.164: 'In Santo Dominico una cona, dove è Nostro Signore levato dalla croce e posto in un lenzolo, di mano del Mantegna, al quale, come sapete miglior di noialtri, è tenuta assai la pictura, poiché da lui cominciò ad rinovarsi la antiquità, ad cui successe il vostro Ioan Bellino.' The picture is untraced and Nicolini (pp.255–7) suggests that a *Pietà* by Orazio Borgianni in San Domenico might be a copy of it. This claim is rightly rejected by Bologna (*Opere d'arte nel salernitano*, 1955, p.47, and in *Paragone*, No.75, vii, 1956, pp.56–61), who points out that the so-called Borgianni is a copy of a well-known picture in the Galleria Spada. Bologna argues that the lost composition is reflected in two pictures, a *Deposition* (Plate 172b) which is part of a polyptych in the church of the Annunziata, Angri, between Naples and Salerno, painted *c.*1515 by a South Italian artist, and a *Deposition* (Plate 172a) belonging to Avv. P. Manuel Gismondi of San Remo, attributed by Bologna to a South Italian artist working in the first half of the seventeenth century. The relationship between the composition and the Castle Ashby *Adoration* (Plate XVI) is striking, and tends to confirm his claim. If so, the lost original would have been painted *c.*1500.

92. Unidentified subject

The inventory of the Studiolo of Isabella d'Este taken in 1542 records a painting 'feigning bronze', with four figures as set above the entrance door of the 'studio che è in Corte Vecchia'. The entry reads: 'E più un quadro finto di brongio sopra alla detta porta di mano di m. Andrea Mantegna con quattro figure dentro' (Luzio, 1908, p.423).

Zimmermann suggested that Cat.no.175 might be this picture, but see this entry.

93. Unidentified subject

The inventory of the Studiolo of 1542 records a second picture 'feigning bronze' which was set over the door that led from the 'studio che è in Corte Vecchia' into the Grotta. The entry reads: 'E più un altro quadro finto di brongio, posto sopra alla porta nell'entrare nella Grotta di man del detto Mantegna, in lo quale è dipinto una nave di mare con alcune figure dentro e una che casca nell'acqua' (Luzio, 1908, p.423). The subject may have been Arion whose story is an *exemplum* of the power of music.

94. Christ and the Samaritan woman

In a letter of 10 November 1549 from Verona Timoteo de' Giusti asks Cardinal Ercole Gonzaga for a copy of a picture by Mantegna of this subject (Kristeller, 1901, p.448, communicated by Luzio).

95. David

Among the pictures left by Gabriele Vendramin of Venice in 1547 (see Ravà, in *Nuovo Archivio Veneto*, n.s.xxxix, 1920, p.170) was 'Una toleta con un re David depinto de man de Andrea Montagna (*sic*)'.

96. Portrait of Matthias Corvinus, King of Hungary
Como, Museo Gioviano

First recorded in the collection of portraits of Paulo Giovio (Jovius). Said by him to be by Mantegna, and to have borne a close likeness to an equestrian portrait of Corvinus (b.*c.*1440; reigned 1458–90) painted in the Campo de' Fiori, Rome. Engraved in Jovius, *Elogia virorum bellica virtute illustrium veris imaginibus supposita, quae apud Musæum spectantur*, Florence, 1551, p.159); 'Effigies eius armata equestris, luculentissimè depicta Romae in Campo Florae, contra Podium cubiculi mei in angulo Laurentianae domus spectatur, ad quam arridet altera persimilis Andreae Mantiniæ manu picta, quae in Musaeo nostro conspicitur' (wrongly interpreted by Kristeller, p.450, as meaning that the equestrian portrait was also by Mantegna).

The portrait is now lost, but a sixteenth-century copy (Uffizi 675) survives among the series of copies of the Gioviano portraits executed by Cristofano Allori for Cosimo I de' Medici (Rovelli, *L'opera storica ed artistica di Paolo Giovio*, 1928, p.169, no.58). Judging by the copy, Giovio's attribution must be regarded as optimistic. Rovelli (p.142) notes that some Hungarian portraits were obtained by Giovio from a Hungarian named Tomasso Nadasto.

97. A Christ
Bologna, Casa Lodi

The Bolognese painter Pietro Lamo records in 1560 a Christ by Mantegna in Casa Lodi, Bologna (Lamo, *Graticola di Bologna*, 1844, p.30: 'in Casa delodo un cristo de ma del Mantegna.'). Casa Lodi was in Galliera, and by 1844 had passed to the Zacconi, according to Lamo's editor.

98. Works in Verona

Vasari (1568, p.489) records that Mantegna painted in Verona 'vna tauola per l'altare di s. Christofano, e di s.

Antonio. Et al canto della piazza della Puglia fece alcune figure.' These works have never been identified.

99. Judith

On one of his visits to Italy during the late sixteenth century the Spanish painter Pablo de Céspedes saw a painting of *Judith* by Mantegna in the house in Rome of Alessandro de' Medici (1535–1605), later Pope Leo XI. He describes it in the fragments of his *Discurso de la comparación de la antigua y moderna pintura y escultura* of 1604 (ed. Sánchez Cantón, *Fuentes literarias para la historia del arte español*, ii, 1933, p.15: '. . . *yo vi de su mano* [de Mantegna] *una tablita al temple en casa del señor Alexandro de Medicis, que despues fué cardenal y arzobispo de Florencia: contenía a Judit que se disponía a cortar la cabeza al capitan de los asirios, y su sierva vieja, y él durmiendo debaxo del pabellón: cierto cosa divina: ella atendía al favor del cielo con resolucion de tan gran hazaña. Tenia una veste lucida, como dice Plinio, de azul ultramarino, tan delgada y linuosa, que aunque se hiciera con agua sola, no se pudiera reducir a mayor fineza, mostrando todos los perfiles del desnudo con gracia maravillosa. La vieja atenta a abrir su talega, vestida como lo requería su edad y oficio, y el pabellon atornasolado de una seda, que los italianos llaman tabi, que casi imita nuestro gorgoran, tan propio que parecía verdadero. Era de aquella fineza esta pintura que en sí tenía la manera buena al temple sobre talla, muy semejante en la hermosura del colorido a la buena iluminación y casi de las postreras obras del temple que hasta entonces se había usado, porque poco despues se inventó la manera al olio, y dexáronla los más de los pintores que se siguieron. Era de tanto primor esta manera al temple, de tanta limpieza y polideza, que Miguel Angel Buonarota viendo que en su tiempo se dexaba, y se aplicaban a la manera del olio, me dicen que el buen viejo casi llorando decía que era muerta la pintura.*' Céspedes says that he saw the picture in Alessandro's house before he became Archbishop of Florence (1574) and a Cardinal (1583) so presumably his description dates from some time in the years 1569–73 when Alessandro had already begun his fifteen years' residence in Rome as ambassador from Cosimo I to the Pope (Pastor, *History of the Popes*, xxv, 1937, pp.18–20: for his interest in art see pp.22–3).

Unlike the other known *Judith* compositions by Mantegna, this scene appears to have shown Judith about to slay Holofernes, rather than handing his head to Abra.

100. The Baptism, Death, Resurrection and Ascension of Christ
Florence, Casino de San Marco

Four small pictures on panel of these subjects were among the pictures belonging to Don Antonio de' Medici inventoried in March 1587 in the Galleria of the Casino di San Marco (see Cat.no.13). The inventory entries read: 'Tre quadretti in asse del mantegni di piu figure della passione alti b º/2 larghi b º/4 ornamento di noce profilata dº./Vno quadro simile a detti entroui una resurretione' (ASF Guardaroba 136, f.157v). These are presumably identical with four pictures inventoried among Don Antonio's estate in 1621 (ASF Guardaroba 399, f.274r: 'Quattro quadretti in asse entroui in uno il Battesimo, la morte la Resurrettione, et ascensione di N S con ornamenti tocchi d'oro alti bª ½inc.ª.').

101. Judith
Florence, Casino di San Marco

A small picture of Judith by Mantegna was also inventoried among the pictures of Don Antonio de' Medici (see Cat.no.100) in March 1587 as in the Galleria of the Casino di San Marco: 'Vno Quadretto di una Giuditta del mantegni ornamento di legno tinto profilato d.º alta b ²/3 larga b º/2' (ASF, Guardaroba 136, f.158r).

102. A woman carrying a basin with three heads

A list of the pictures in the Rocca of Colorno belonging to Contessa Barbara Sanseverino drawn up on 16 June 1612 prior to their confiscation by Ranuccio I Farnese lists '16º Un quadro di una donna con un bacile con tre teste sopra, guazzo di man del Mantegna' (G. Bertini, *La Quadreria Farnesiana e i quadri confiscati nel 1612 ai feudatari parmensi*, Parma, 1977, p.31).

103. The Three Graces, with a view of Mantua

An inventory of the pictures belonging to the Conte Annibale Chieppio of Mantua, taken on 29 April 1623, lists a 'quadro di mano del Mantegna con sopra le Tre Gratie e Mantova vecchia incornisato di noce con due perfili d'oro' (Archivio D'Arco-Chieppio, busta 52, cit. C. Perina in Istituto Carlo d'Arco, *Mantova: Le Arti*, ii, 1961, p.297, n.48).

104. St Jerome

In the Mantuan inventory of 1627 a head of St Jerome is listed in the antechamber to the Appartamento Nuovo of Duke Ferdinando: 'Un quadro dipintovi una testa di S. Geronimo con cornici bianche di mano del Mantegna. L.60' (D'Arco, ii, p.160; Luzio, 1913, p.113, no.297).

105. The Resurrection

The Mantuan inventory of 1627 lists a vertical picture of this subject on panel in the Appartamento Nuovo of Duke Ferdinando 'under the clock' (D'Arco, ii, p.165; Luzio, 1913, p.129, no.586: 'Un quadro longo dipintovi N.S. quando resusitò, sopra l'asse, opera del Mantegna. L.90'). See Cat.no.35.

106. The Woman taken in Adultery

The Mantuan inventory of 1627 lists as hanging in the '*passettino piccolo*' of the Appartamento Nuovo of Ferdinando 'under the clock' a picture on canvas of this subject, with quarter-length figures: 'Un quadro sopra tella dipintovi N.S. et l'adultera con un puoco di busto senza cornice di mano del Mantegna, L.72' (D'Arco, p.166; Luzio, 1913, p.131, no.621). Subsequently in the collection of Charles I.

The pictures of Charles I which came from Whitehall and were inventoried at Somerset House in September 1649 included: '7. Christ & ye Adulteresse, done by Andre Mangengr.' Sold to the painter De Critz on 23 October 1651. Valued at £10 (O. Millar, *The inventories and valuations of the King's Goods 1649–1651*, Walpole Society, 43rd Volume, 1972, p.298). The 1627 description suggests a composition of the type of the Castle Ashby *Adoration of the Magi* (Plate XVI).

107. Christ carrying the Cross

The Mantuan inventory of 1627 lists in the 'coridore longo che passa da S. Barbara in Castello' a half-length of this subject: 'Un quadro con N.S. che porta la croce, mezza figura, oppera di Mantegna, con ornamento fregiato d'oro. L.90' (D'Arco, ii, p.156; Luzio, 1913, p.97, no.118). Later in the collection of Charles I: included among the pictures sold after his execution, as: '157. Christ Carrying ye Cross: by Andrea Manteger.' Sold to Jackson on 23 October 1651. Valued at £40 (O. Millar, *The inventories and valuations of the King's Goods 1649–1651*, Walpole Society, 43rd Volume, 1972, p.195). See Cat.no.146.

108. Tobias

The Mantuan inventory of 1627 lists in a cupboard on the right at the head of the library a picture of Tobias as one of four 'quadri lavorati a guazzo con cornici nere fregiate d'oro, L.240' (D'Arco, ii, p.164; Luzio, 1913, p.124, no.509).

109. Esther

The Mantuan inventory of 1627 lists a picture of Esther as one of four 'lavorati a guazzo' (see Cat.no.108).

110. Abraham

The Mantuan inventory of 1627 lists a picture of Abraham as one of four 'lavorati a guazzo' (see Cat.no.108). See also Cat.no. 140.

111. Moses

The Mantuan inventory of 1627 lists a picture of Moses as one of four 'lavorati a guazzo' (see Cat.no.108).

112. David and Goliath

The Mantuan inventory of 1627 lists in the second left-hand cupboard of the library a small picture of David and Goliath (Luzio, 1913, p.119, no. 381: 'un quadretto fatto di chiaro in scuro dipintovi David che ha tagliato la testa a Golia, di mano del Mantegna con cornici di noce, L.60'). See Cat.no.141.

113. Lamentation over the Dead Christ

The collection of Roberto Canonici (d.1638) of Ferrara, entailed on his family by a will of 1627 and a codicil of 1631, contained a picture of this subject signed by Mantegna (Campori, 1870, p.117). This picture was seen by Crowe & Cavalcaselle (i, 1871, p.212) in the house of Conte G.B. Canonici of Ferrara: they assigned it to Carpaccio or his school, or else to Michele da Verona. Subsequently it was acquired by the Kaiser Friedrich Museum, Berlin, and firmly given to Carpaccio by Bode (in *J.P.K.*, xxvi, 1905, pp.145–7) and Molmenti & Ludwig (*The life and works of Vittorio Carpaccio*, 1907, pp.218–19). Crowe & Cavalcaselle had already noted that the signature was forged; they record that it was on the side of the tomb and read 'Andreas Mantinea f.'. The appearance of a forged signature by Mantegna which can be dated before c.1632 is a warning to treat attributions to the artist made even in the sixteenth century with caution.

A similar form of Mantegna's name reappears in a false early signature on at least one other picture (see Cat.no.172).

114. Dead Christ

The collection of Roberto Canonici (see Cat.no.113) included a picture of this subject. '*Un Christo morto di Andrea Mantegna, posto sopra a una sedia appresso a una fabrica rovinata, che è in un paese dove sono alcuni animali, et uccelli, et duoi vecchi lo stano mirando che sono sentati, e sono più nudi che vestiti, ha la cornice d'oro, e negra; scudi cento cinquanta.*' (Campori, 1870, p.117.)

115. The Nativity

The pictures of Charles I, sold after his execution, included: '(66) The Natevitye of Christ done by Andrea Mantenger.' Sold to Hunt and Bass on 1 March 1653: valued at £40 (O. Millar, *The inventories and valuations of the King's Goods 1649–1651*, Walpole Society, 43rd volume, 1972, p.64). Is this the Castle Ashby *Adoration* (see Cat.no.43)? If so, it may be a picture listed in the Mantua inventory of 1627.

116. The Ascension

The pictures of Charles I, sold after his execution, included: '(70) The Assention of Christ done by Andrea Manteng^r. a mantue preece.' Sold to Murray on 23 October 1651; valued at £2.10s. (O. Millar, *The inventories and valuations of the King's Goods 1649–1651*, Walpole Society, 43rd Volume, 1972, p.64).

117. A group singing

The pictures of Charles I, sold after his execution, included: '159. A company of Fellows, singing: by And^r Mantenger.' Sold to Jackson on 23 October 1651. Valued at £60 (O. Millar, *The inventories and valuations of the King's Goods 1649–1651*, Walpole Society, 43rd Volume, 1972, p.195).

118. The Dead Christ

The pictures of Charles I, sold after his execution, included: '160. A Christ dead: done by Andrea Mantenger.' Sold to Harrison on 23 October 1651. Valued at £30 (O. Millar, *The inventories and valuations of the King's Goods 1649–1651*, Walpole Society, 43rd Volume, 1972, p.195).

119. A head

A picture of an ideal head was listed in the inventory taken c.1640 of the collection of Paolo Coccapani (1584–1650), Bishop of Reggio: '131. Una testa di maniera di mano del Mantegna' (Campori, 1870, p.149).

120. A head

A second picture of an ideal head, described as of a man and attributed to Mantegna, was listed in the Coccapani collection c.1640 (see Cat.no.119): '159. Una testa di maniera di mano del Mantegna, è un huomo' (Campori, 1870, p.151).

121. Judith

John Evelyn (*Diary*, ed. De Beer, ii, 1955, p.113) notes that on 1 March 1644 he saw 'A Judith of Mantegnia's' in the Paris hôtel of Roger de Plessis de Liancourt, duc de la Roche-Guyon (1598–1674).

122. Fresco in Verona

According to Ridolfi (1648, p.70) Mantegna painted in Verona 'sopra la piazza del Lago vna facciata a fresco'.

123. Christ's Charge to the Apostles
Padua, Scuola dello Spirito Santo

According to Ridolfi (1648, p.70) Mantegna painted this subject in the Scuola dello Spirito Santo: 'Nello Spirito Santo dipinse il Salvatore, che manda gli Apostoli à predicare per il Mondo.' This must be an error, as Rossetti (1795, pp.262–3) points out, since the confraternity and Scuola dello Spirito Santo were only founded in 1575–6 (Portenari, 1623, p.496).

124. Virgin and Child with St John the Baptist and two other saints

Ridolfi (1648, p.72) records in the collection of Bernardo Giunti in Venice 'vna Madonna col bambino in seno, e due Santi à lato con San Giouanni in mezze figure delle eccellenti opere sue'. For Giunti, who married in 1599 and was a descendant of the famous Florentine printers, his father being Tommaso, see Savini-Branca (1964, pp.221–3).

125. Virgin and Child

Ridolfi (1648, p.72) lists 'vna picciola Madonna pure à chiaroscuro' as in the collection of Jacopo Pighetti of Venice. This picture is listed in Pighetti's inventory of 2 January 1647 as 'Una Madonina de chiaro scuro' (Savini-Branca, 1964, p.122).

126. Portrait of a Jurisconsult

A portrait of a jurisconsult attributed to Mantegna was listed in the collection of Giovanni Pietro Curtoni (d.1656) of Verona. In 1668 this collection was acquired by Alessandro II Pico, Duke of Mirandola: it was later dispersed in Bologna together with the rest of the Pico gallery in the early eighteenth century (Campori, 1870, p.196: 'Andrea Mantegna, Un ritratto di Iuris consulto'). A possible identification of this picture is the Poldi–Pezzoli portrait (Cat.no.168).

127. Unknown subject

In the Muselli collection, Verona, in 1662 was a work attributed to Mantegna. It is not clear from the entry whether it was a portrait or a drawing: 'In un Camerino il ritratto di *Paolo* di sua mano, del *Parmigiano*, diversi ritratti e figurini del *Parmigiano* et altri disegni del medesimo, uno del *Mantegna*' (Campori, 1870, p.192).

128. Unknown subjects

According to Martinioni (in Sansovino, *Venetia città nobilissima*, ed. of 1663, p.377) Barone Ottavio de Tassis, General of the Imperial posts in Venice, had 'molte, &

esquisite pitture di Paris Bordone, di Andrea Mantegna, del Tintoretto, e d'altri insigni Pittori'.

129. The Flight into Egypt

The inventory of Carlo II, Duke of Mantua, taken on 10 November 1665, lists a small panel of this subject in a *camerino* of the Palazzo Ducale: 'Uno piccolo [quadro] sopra l'asse con sopra N.S. che và in Egitto: originale di Andrea Mantegna' (D'Arco, ii, p.183; *Fonti per la storia della pittura, iv, Serie Documentaria: Lettere e altri documenti intorno alla Storia della Pittura. Raccolte di quadri a Mantova nel sei – settecento*, 1976, p.44).

130. Portrait of a Woman

A small portrait on panel of a woman with lowered eyes, wearing a circlet of pearls round her forehead, is first recorded in the inventory of Cardinal Antonio Barberini, taken in 1644, without an attribution (M. Aronberg Lavin, *Seventeenth-Century Barberini Documents and Inventories of Art*, 1975, p.170, No.314). By the time of his posthumous inventory, taken in 1671, it had acquired an attribution to Mantegna: 'Un quadretto in Tavola d Una Testa d Una Donna con gl' occhi bassi, et un cerchio di perle nella fronte di mano d'Andrea Mantegna alto un palmo inc.a con Cornice di Ebano' (Lavin, *op. cit.*, p.301, No.194; p.339, No.78). Bequeathed to Cardinal Francesco Barberini, it later passed to Prince Urbano Barberini and was appraised for him by Maratta c.1686 as by Titian (Lavin, p.422, No.24; see the editor's note for eccentricities of attribution in this list).

131. Unidentified subject

The inventory taken c.1680 of the Palazzo del Giardino, Parma, lists among the Farnese collection: 'Un quadro alto br. 1 on. 4 e largo on. 11. Un signore con candela in mano che salisce una scala, presso del quale altre figure, di Andrea Mantegna' (Campori, 1870, p.285).

132. Susanna and the Elders

The Farnese inventory of c.1680 (see Cat.no.131) also lists: 'Un quadro alto br.1 on. 6 e largo br.1. on 3 e ½, in tela sopra tavola. Abbozzo con donna, si dice Susanna, con due vecchi, tutto guasto. Si dice del Mantegna' (Campori, 1870, p.303).

133. Melancholy

The inventory taken in 1685 of the collection of Principe Cesare Ignazio d'Este of Modena (see Campori, 1870, p.328), lists: 'Un quadro su l'ascia di mano del Mantegna con 16 fanciulli, che suonano e ballano, sopra scrittovi *Malancolia*, con cornice dorata alta on. 14, larga on. 20½' (Campori, 1870, p.328). This lost picture has attracted special attention from German scholars because of a conjectured influence on Dürer's engraving of *Melancholia*. Klibansky, Saxl and Panofsky (*Saturn and Melancholy*, 1964, pp.307,384) regard it as the earliest known 'symbolic' representation of Melancholy. They suggest with great plausibility that it is copied in a picture by Cranach of 1533 (pl.130, formerly Volz coll., The Hague, perhaps cut down) which shows fifteen putti making music and dancing and is inscribed MELANCHOLIA. They suggest that Mantegna, in showing sixteen putti, probably had in mind the ancient statue of the Nile, recorded by Pliny (XXXVI, 58) with 'sixteen children playing about it'. Giehlow (1903, p.40) long ago observed that the music and dancing were symbols of two amusements which were recommended as antidotes to Melancholy. Judging from the Cranach picture, Mantegna's lost original was a work of the early 1490s related to the Studiolo pictures. Dürer's knowledge of it seems to be confirmed by his drawing L623 (Tietze & Tietze-Conrat, *Kritisches Verzeichnis der Werke A. Dürers*, 1, 1928, p.21), which shows six dancing and music-making putti, and is signed and dated 1495 (Moscow, Coll. Sidorow, pub. in *J.P.K.,* xlviii, 1927, pp.221–3, by Sidorow, who first connected it with the Mantegna picture). Tietze-Conrat, 1955, p.247.

134. The Life, Miracles and Martyrdom of St Sebastian

The inventory of Queen Christina of Sweden taken *c.*1689 lists seven panels of these subjects attributed to Mantegna: 'Sette tavole in piedi con la vita, miracoli e martirio di San Bastiano ben dipinte e conservate, con figure poco minori di due p.^mi, architetture e paesi rispettivamente, del Mantegna, tutti eguali di misura, alte p.^mi tre ed un quarto e larghe p.^mi dui, ed un q.^to con cornici compagne liscie dorate alla romana' (Campori, 1870, p.358).

135. A Portrait

An inventory taken *c.*1706 of Ferdinando Carlo, last Duke of Mantua, lists a portrait on panel attributed to

Mantegna, valued at 20 *doppie* (D'Arco, ii, p.188; cf. *Fonti*, cit.cat.no.129, p.52). It measured a Mantuan *braccio* (64 cm).

136. The Virgin giving suck to the Child

An inventory taken *c.*1706 of Ferdinando Carlo, last Duke of Mantua, lists a panel of this subject in the Duke's own chamber: 'Uno [quadro] lungo mezzo braccio con la B.V. che allatta il puttino dipinto sull'asse dal Mantegna' (D'Arco, ii, p.189; cf. also *Fonti*, cit.cat.no.129, p.54, different order of words).

137. Christ's Descent into Limbo

The inventory taken *c.*1706 of Ferdinando Carlo, last Duke of Mantua, lists a very small picture of this subject (less than a *braccio*) in one of the two antechambers of the Palazzo. 'Uno [quadrettino] più picolo di G.C. che và al limbo fatto dal Mantegna' (D'Arco, ii, p.189; *Fonti*, cit. cat.no.129, p.51). In another inventory of 1709 published by Luzio (1913, p.317): 'Il limbo del Montagna [*sic*] in tavola ($2\frac{1}{2} \times 3$ [quarte]).' Its dimensions were thus roughly 40×48 cm. (cf. *Fonti*, cit.cat.no.129, pp.49, 56).

138. Judith and three other Pictures

An inventory taken in 1709 of the pictures belonging to Ferdinando Carlo, last Duke of Mantua, lists: 'Quattro quadri (2×4 [quarte] l'uno) rappresenta chiari e scuri, la Bella Judith et altre figure di mano del Mantegna' (Luzio, 1913, p.318). These pictures measured therefore about 45.5×91 cm.

Partly Autograph, Studio and Other School Works

139. Mucius Scaevola

Munich, Staatliche Graphisches Sammlung
Canvas 40.8×34cm.   Plate 168

CONDITION: Cut down on left.

PROVENANCE: Collection of Sir Thomas Lawrence.

A small picture by Mantegna of this subject, and in this technique, was noted by Marc'Antonio Michiel *c.*1528 in the house of the collector Francesco Zio (Giglio)

(Frizzoni, p.179: 'El quadretto de Muzio Scevola, che brusa la mano propria, finto de bronzo, fu de mano de Andrea Mantegna'; see Frizzoni's remarks, pp.176–8, for the correct dating of this note, wrongly headed 1512 in the manuscript in a later hand). Crowe & Cavalcaselle (1871, p.417) suggest that the Zio picture may be the *Mucius Scaevola* by an anonymous artist that belonged to Charles I, but this was on panel (Vanderdoort, 1757, p.67, no.7). The brownish dark grey, with bright lights, and clear brown ground of the present picture perhaps support its identification with the Zio picture described as 'finto di bronzo'.

The present version is autograph for Morelli (1891, p.233), Berenson (1932, 1968) and Cruttwell (1908, p.88), but is rejected by Kristeller (1901, pp.371, 443) as doubtfully authentic, and if so, entirely by pupils after a design by Mantegna. Also rejected by Tietze-Conrat (1955, p.190), who regards it, followed by Cipriani (1962, p.83), as a Venetian copy of an invention by Mantegna. This is by no means implausible. Also a copy for Gilbert (1962, p.6). For Knapp (1910, p.129) and Paccagnini (1961, p.72) a school work. Since Fiocco (1937, p.68) opinion has generally postulated partial workshop intervention (Camesasca, 1964, pp.44,124; Garavaglia, 1967, No.78). Universally regarded as a late work from the 1490s or early 1500s.

Fiocco and Tietze-Conrat point out that the composition has been cut on the left and the latter suggested, unconvincingly, that the missing portion is perhaps to be identified as a drawing inventoried in the collection of the Gonzaga di Novellara in 1770 (Campori, 1870, p.673: 'Andrea Mantegna Mantovano. Signore sedente in trono, con persone dai lati che lo corteggiano: disegno acquerellato e lumeggiato').

140. The Sacrifice of Isaac

Vienna, Kunsthistorisches Museum, 1842 (Oberhammer, *Katalog der Gemäldegalerie*, i, 1960, p.77, No.590)
Linen 48.5 × 36.5cm.   Plate 170

PROVENANCE: See *David holding the head of Goliath*, Cat.no.141.

141. David holding the head of Goliath

Vienna, Kunsthistorisches Museum, 1965 (Oberhammer, *Katalog der Gemäldegalerie*, i, 1960, p.77, No.589)
Linen 48.5 × 36cm.   Plate 171

PROVENANCE: Listed in 1659 in the inventory of the Archduke Leopold Wilhelm of Austria (1614–62) as framed together with the *Sacrifice of Isaac*: '408 und 409 Zwey Stückhel einer Grössen von Öhlfarb auff Leinwandt grau in grau, das erste di Opfferung Abrahams, vndt das andere der David mit des Holofernis Kopff in der linckhen Hand. In einer schwartz glatten Ramen, hoch 2 Span 8 finger vndt braidt 2 Span 8 Finger. Von Mantegna Original' (*Vienna Jahrbuch*, i, 1883, p.cviii).

Kristeller (in *Vienna Jahrbuch*, 1912, p.42) suggested that the *David* is probably the picture of this subject attributed to Mantegna listed in the 1627 inventory of Palazzo Ducale, Mantua (see Cat.no.112). He also drew attention to another, unattributed picture of the same subject in the same technique listed in the 1627 inventory in the Appartamento Nuovo of Duke Ferdinand 'under the clock' (D'Arco, ii, p.165; Luzio, 1913, p.129, no.582 'un quadretto sopra la tella di chiaro fatto in scuro David che ha tagliato la testa a Golia con cornici. L.24'). The present pictures of *David* and the *Sacrifice of Isaac* are generally identified as two of a series of four kept in the right-hand cupboard (*armadio a mano destra*) of the *Stanza detta la Libreria* (D'Arco, ii, p.164; Luzio, 1913, p.124, no.509:4 [quadri] lavorati a guazzo di mano di Andrea Mantegna,

in uno Tobia, nel 2° Ester, nel 3° Abram e nel 4° Moise – L.240', but *David* is not present in this set. These entries in the 1627 inventory prove the existence of pictures of these two subjects in this technique in early seventeenth-century Mantua which were attributed to Mantegna.

Published by Kristeller (in 1912, *op. cit.*) as autograph, a judgement maintained by Berenson. Fiocco (1937, p.68) postulated workshop intervention, and they are assigned preponderantly or entirely to the workshop by Oberhammer (1960, *loc. cit.*), Paccagnini (1961, p.70, with the reserve that the *Sacrifice* is partly by Mantegna), and by Gilbert (1962, p.6), Cipriani (1962, p.83), Camesasca (1964, p.44) and Garavaglia (1967, Nos.79–80). Tietze-Conrat (1955, pp.200–1, with wrong provenance) dismisses them as coarse paintings based on Mantegna's designs. Paccagnini and Gilbert correctly note that the *Sacrifice* is of finer quality than the *David*.

142. The Judgement of Solomon. The throne has a pseudo-Hebrew inscription in a medallion.

Paris, Musée du Louvre
Canvas. Grey, on ground of pinkish marble. 46.5 × 37cm.
                                                  Plate 169

CONDITION: Abraded, with losses bottom left.

PROVENANCE: Not recorded.

Tietze-Conrat (1955, p.194) suggests that this picture may be the painting of this subject in a similar technique recorded *c*.1640 in the collection of Paolo Coccapani (1584–1650), Bishop of Reggio (Campori, 1870, p.148: 'No.96. Il Giudicio di Salomone fatto a guazzo di mano di Andrea Mantegna'). Coccapani also owned a drawing of the same subject attributed to Mantegna (Campori, 1870, p.154: 'La sentenza di Salomone del Mantegna bello D.15').

Autograph for Morelli (1891, p.233), Thode (1897, p.109) and Berenson (1932, 1968, after an initial hesitation in 1901), but for other critics wholly or partly a shopwork at best. Kristeller (1901, pp.370–1, 443) gives it to the workshop; Knapp (1910, p.128) to the school. Fiocco (1937, p.68) as Mantegna, but with school intervention. Tietze-Conrat (1955, p.194) gives the design to Mantegna, the execution to the workshop; Paccagnini (1961, p.71) and Camesasca (1964, pp.44, 125) agree, but think some details, e.g. the figure of Solomon, suggest Mantegna's own hand, an opinion accepted by Garavaglia (1967, No.86) and the compiler. For Gilbert (1962, p.6) close to Mantegna but not necessarily by him; for Cipriani (1962, p.84) a dubious attribution. Datable *c*.1500–6.

Kristeller (1901, p.453) notes a much-damaged fresco of this subject with life-size figures by a pupil of Mantegna 'in the second house of the Piazza S. Andrea on the Piazza d'Erbe of Mantua'.

143. Occasio

Mantua, Palazzo Ducale (formerly Museo, No.17)
Fresco, transferred to canvas. 168 × 146cm.   Plate 173

CONDITION: Much restored.

PROVENANCE: From Palazzo Biondi, Mantua.

Warburg (*Gesammelte Schriften*, i, 1932, p.51) was the first to relate the invention of this picture to an epigram by

Ausonius (XII, *In simulachrum Occasionis et Poenitentiae*). Occasio (Opportunity) standing on a ball, with winged feet, and her hair concealing her face, corresponds exactly to the description in the poem. The other figure of the poem is Penitence, who remains after Opportunity has passed by and been missed. Warburg thought the picture a literal figuration of the epigram, and that the young matron standing on a square pedestal was Penitence. This is also the explanation preferred by Tervarent (*Attributs et symboles dans l'art profane*, ii, 1959, p.266). Doren (*Fortuna im Mittelalter und in der Renaissance*, 1922–3, p.136) surmised that she represented Sapientia. Wittkower (in *J.W.C.I.*, i, 1937–8, pp.318–19) prefers to call the figure of Occasio Chance and identifies the matron as Virtus, who stands on a square, and therefore stable, base. He interprets the fresco as meaning that Virtus-Constantia should be opposed to the whims of Chance. There can be no doubt that the figure of Occasio represents the tempting but dangerous opportunities with which Fortune seeks to deceive the rashness of youth. The inspiration of the other female figure is not the epigram by Ausonius, but the personification of Vera Eruditio (True Learning) in the *Tabula Cebetis* (xviii–xix). A woman in late middle age, it is she, not her daughter Virtus, as Wittkower implies, who is described as standing on a square and immovable rock, signifying that the road leading to her is firm and sure and offers certain rewards in contrast with Fortune's rolling globe, signifying the inconstancy of her gifts. The composition therefore combines two classical figurations, known to the Renaissance purely from literary sources. Together they signify that youth, so easily deceived by the delusive charms of Fortune and her tempting opportunities, can be preserved by the prudent restraint of True Learning and the lessons of wisdom she teaches.

Originally set on the canopy of the chimney-piece in Palazzo Biondi, Mantua. Palazzo Biondi, now Cavriani, is a medieval building in the street formerly known as Via Salita. Formerly a Gonzaga palace, it was decorated according to tradition by Mantegna and Giulio Romano. The fresco was first noted by Kristeller (1901, p.457), who assigned it to a pupil, possibly Antonio da Pavia. Fiocco (1937, pp.75–6) as a late work close to the London *Cybele*, finished by a pupil; Tietze-Conrat (1955, p.188) as school of Mantegna; Paccagnini (1961, p.75, No.54) as an invention of Mantegna executed by a pupil; Cipriani (1962, p.80) as by a follower; Garavaglia (1967, No.87) as designed and partly executed by Mantegna. Certainly by a follower, given its coarseness of execution, though the invention may well be Mantegna's, probably following the indications of a humanist pedagogue.

144. Holy Family with the Magdalen
New York, Metropolitan Museum of Art, Altman Coll., No.14.4.0.643 (Wehle, 1940, pp.127–8)
Oil on canvas 57.1 × 45.4cm.   Plate 174

PROVENANCE: Coll. of Pietro d'Aiuti, Munich and Naples; with Dowdeswell, London, from whom bought 1903, by Eduard Weber, Hamburg; Weber sale (Berlin, Lepke, 20–2 February 1912, lot 20); with Duveen's (Duveen, 1941, No.78); acquired 1913 by Benjamin Altman, New York.

A picture of this subject by Mantegna is recorded in the church of the Spedale degli Incurabili, Venice, founded in 1522 (Boschini, *Le ricche minere della pittvra veneziana*, 1674, Dorsoduro, p.21: 'In Sacrestia la Beata Vergine, con il Bambino, S. Gioseffo, e Maria Maddalena, è opera vnica in Venezia di Andrea Mantegna'; A.M. Zanetti, *Descrizione di tutte le pubbliche pitture della Città di Venezia*, 1733, p.330: 'Nella sagristia evvi un quadretto di mezze figure con la Madonna; opera unica in pubblico di Andrea Mantegna'; A.M. Zanetti, *Della pittura veneziana*, Venice, 1771, p.72: '*Altro non trovasi in Venezia della sua mano, che un quadro che sta nella Chiesa degl'Incurabili, in sagristia, con la Madonna, S. Giuseppe, e Santa Maria Maddalena. Chi conosce il merito del Mantegna per le altre opere sue sa ritrovar sempre l'autore istesso; ma chi dovesse conoscerlo per questa sola, non ne potrebbe formare una giusta idea.*' This picture cannot have been painted for the Incurabili but must have been acquired for it at a later date.

Attributed to Mantegna by Bode (in *Kunstchronik*, xv, 1904, p.134) as *c*.1495 and by Woermann (*Wissenschaftlich. Verzeichnis der älteren Gemälde der Galerie Weber*, 1907, p.21, No.20, as comparable to the Dresden *Holy Family* and painted between 1495–1500). It was accepted by S. de Ricci (in *Les Arts*, xi, 1912, p.14), who identified it as the Boschini picture, but rejected by Knapp (1910, pp.162,180) as by an imitator of Mantegna: for him the type of the Child is not Mantegnesque. Venturi (1914, pp.262,483) as Francesco Mantegna. Accepted as an autograph late work by Monod (in *G.B.A.*, ser. 5, viii, 1923, pp.185–6), Berenson (1932,1968), Fiocco (1937, pp.69–70), Wehle (1940, *loc. cit.*) and Fredericksen & Zeri (1972). Tietze-Conrat (1955, p.191) assigns it to a later artist under the influence of Mantegna, while Cipriani (1962, p.81) catalogues it among attributed works, Camesasca (1964, p.128) as close to the autograph late works and Garavaglia (1967, No.105) as probably by Francesco Mantegna. Possibly one of the pictures by a pupil which according to Vasari (see text, p.244) Mantegna allowed to pass for his in his old age.

145. Christ and Simon carrying the Cross
Verona, Museo di Castelvecchio
Canvas 52 × 65cm.   Plate 175

CONDITION: Much damaged and altered by poor restoration.

PROVENANCE: First recorded in the collection of the Conti Morando di Rizzoni: Coll. Dr Cesare Bernasconi.

The earlier attribution to Francesco Mantegna is tentatively advocated by Crowe & Cavalcaselle (1871, p.418; 1912, p.119). Kristeller (1901, p.453) gives it to a pupil: for Berenson (1932,1968) late, either a copy or a ruined work. Fiocco (1937, pp.75–6,209–10), who also notes the poor condition, but classes it among the works left in Mantegna's studio at his death, attributes at least the design to him, and finds it much superior to the Oxford version of the same theme (Cat. no.146; Plate 176). Tietze-Conrat (1955, p.200) withholds judgement in view of the poor condition, but thinks it closest to the Copenhagen *Christ* (Cat. no.35; Plate 124). Cipriani (p.83) places it among attributed works and Garavaglia (1967, No.70) does not pronounce an account of its condition.

Paccagnini (1961, p.52) considers that the prototype of the composition must be by Mantegna, but revives the old attribution to Francesco Mantegna, with a dating of c.1514–16. For Gilbert (1962, p.9) a late shopwork. The foreshortening of the face in three-quarter profile is not very successful, and the dramatic highlighting in white on the nose, under the eyes, on the eyebrows and forehead is applied with crude emphasis. The type of all three heads is too small and mean for Mantegna and the simulated wooden frame is untypical of him, but there is some understanding of his system of bas-relief composition, delicate colouring, and gradation of light and shade. The picture is clearly by an artist trained in Mantegna's studio and in his late style and it is quite likely that he should be identified as Francesco Mantegna.

146. Christ carrying the Cross

Oxford, Christ Church, 74 (Byam Shaw, *Paintings by Old Masters at Christ Church Oxford*, 1967, p.65)
Canvas, backed with another canvas, 63 × 77.8cm.

Plate 176

CONDITION: Cleaned by J.C. Deliso, 1964. A strip about 38 mm. high at the top is a later addition. Large hole in left hand of Roman soldier right: local restoration in face of Christ and in draperies, where rubbed surface showed red bolus ground obtrusively.

PROVENANCE: Bequeathed to Christ Church by General Guise, 1765.

Crowe and Cavalcaselle (1871, p.418; 1912, p.119) suggest this picture may be one recorded in the 1627 inventory of Palazzo Ducale, Mantua. This was later in the collection of Charles I (see Cat.no.107).

Given by Crowe and Cavalcaselle to Francesco Mantegna, by Kristeller (1901, p.453) tentatively to a Veronese pupil, by Berenson (1932, p.370) to Jacopo da Montagnana, by Fiocco (1937, pp.209–10) to the workshop as a poor piece close to the Jacquemart-André *Ecce Homo*, by Garavaglia (1967, No.71) also to the workshop. Byam Shaw (1967, *loc. cit.*) concurs, but defends the pic-

ture as a good quality work close to such late autograph Mantegnas as the Copenhagen *Pietà* and the Venice *St Sebastian*. The type of the Jews on the left is close to those of the *Ecce Homo* (Plate 136) and the painting may well be a copy of a lost original by Mantegna, dating from his last years, c.1500.

147. Holy Family with the Infant Baptist

Princeton Art Museum, Cannon Coll., No.35.53
Canvas 50.8 × 40.6cm.   Plate 177

CONDITION: The figures of St Joseph and the Infant Baptist painted out by a nineteenth-century restorer: the figure of the Baptist uncovered by a partial restoration c.1940, the figure of St Joseph left concealed (see Mather, in *A. in A.*, xxxi, 1943, pp.21–6). The picture probably lacks a left-hand section with another figure.

J.P. Richter (MS catalogue of the Cannon Coll., 1926, No. 41) classes it as school of Mantegna. After partial cleaning, published in 1943 by Mather (see above) as very probably a late autograph Mantegna. The attribution has rightly not found favour, and the picture is either given to the school or to a close follower of Mantegna (Tietze-Conrat, 1955, p.197; Garavaglia, 1967, No.107; Berenson, 1968) or classed as a copy (Fredericksen & Zeri, 1972).

148. Virgin and Child with St Juliana

Verona, Museo di Castelvecchio
Tempera on canvas 75 × 55cm.   Plate 178

CONDITION: Very poor.

PROVENANCE: Formerly in the Monga Coll., Verona.

Classed by Berenson (1932, 1968) as a copy, and by Fiocco (1937, pp.69,207) as a crude workshop picture by a Veronese artist perhaps using drawings by Mantegna. Cipriani (1962, p.84) and Garavaglia (1967, No.101) consider it a poor workshop picture. A crude copy or adaptation of a picture by Mantegna; probably executed during the decade 1500–10, judging from the square neckline of St Juliana's costume.

Paintings after Mantegna

149. The Resurrection

London, National Gallery, 1106 (Davies, 1961, pp.341–2)
Panel 42.5 × 31cm. (painted surface)   Plate 179

CONDITION: Good, though some faces rubbed.

PROVENANCE: From Palazzo Capponi, Florence. Acquired with Cat. no.150 by the Rev. John Sanford in 1832. As below until Coningham sale (1849, lot 39), bt. Webb; perhaps G.H. Morland sale, 9 May 1863 (lot 117), bt. Herrmann; His de la Salle, Paris: his sale, London, 27 November 1880 (lot 93), bt. Danlos; purchased by the Gallery from A. W. Thibaudeau, 1881. See Cat.no.151.

150. The Maries at the Sepulchre
London, National Gallery, 1381 (Davies, 1961, p.342)
Panel 42.5 × 31cm. (painted surface)   Plate 180
CONDITION: Good.

PROVENANCE: From Palazzo Capponi, Florence. Acquired with Cat. no.149 by the Rev. John Sanford in 1832. Catalogue (for sale), 1838 (No.22); not included in his sale, 1839 (for Sanford and his coll. see Nicolson, in *B.M.*, xcvii, 1955, pp.207–14); W. Coningham sale (9 June 1849, lot 40, as ex-Sanford coll.); bt. Farrer: Lord Taunton coll. (exh. British Institution, 1860, No.4): Lady Taunton (exh. RA, 1870, No.143). Bequeathed by Lady Taunton to the National Gallery. See Cat.no.151.

151. Noli Me Tangere
London, National Gallery, 639 (Davies, 1961, p.341)
Panel 42.5 × 31cm. (painted surface)   Plate 181
CONDITION: Good.

PROVENANCE: Sale of Francis Duroveray, London, 2 March 1850 (lot 238), bt. Nieuwenhuys. Bought with E. Beaucousin coll., Paris, 1860.

These three panels (Plates 179,180,181), evidently part of a series, were attributed by Yriarte (1901, pp.203–5) to Francesco Mantegna. Kristeller (1901, p.455) gave them to a good pupil of Mantegna's first period, presumably having seen, correctly, that the style they represent is that of the late 1450s. Fiocco (1937, pp.69–70) rejects the attribution to Francesco Mantegna, and suggests one to Carlo Crivelli. The three have been disregarded in the literature of Mantegna since Davies (1961, *loc. cit.*) classed them as possibly the work of a late imitator of Mantegna. Technical examination carried out by the National Gallery in 1982 shows that they must date from no later than the first half of the sixteenth century. See text (p.87) where it is argued that they are copies of paintings executed by Mantegna early in the 1460s, probably for a Gonzaga chapel.

152. Portrait of Francesco Sforza. Inscribed AN.
MANTINIA/PINX. ANNO/M.CCCC/LV
Washington, National Gallery of Art, No.600 (Shapley, 1979, pp.75–7)
Panel 72 × 62cm.   Plate 182

CONDITION: Possibly restored between 1889 and 1898, removing notably a floral design above the imitation Cufic of the armour's border. Restored again *c.*1945.

PROVENANCE: Galleria Sciarra Colonna, Rome (published by L. Vicchi, *Dieci quadri della Galleria Sciarra*, Rome, 1889, pl.1). Acquired by Widener in 1898: presented to the National Gallery in 1942.

Identified by Morelli (1891, pp.165–6) as a portrait of a Gonzaga, probably Lodovico. He condemned the signature as forged and attributed the picture to Bonsignori. This judgement was generally accepted until F. Shapley published the picture (in *A.Q.*, viii, 1945, pp.25–39). She correctly identified the sitter as Francesco Sforza

(1401–65) and attributed the picture to Mantegna or alternatively to Bonsignori copying Mantegna. Tietze-Conrat (1955, p.202) accepts a derivation from an original painted *c.*1459, at the Council of Mantua, and thinks it close to the Mezzarota portrait. Cipriani (1962, p.84) thinks it may be a copy by Bonsignori from an original by Mantegna of later date than the 1455 of the inscription. Berenson (1968, p.242), who earlier rejected the inscription as forged, also lists it as a copy of Mantegna. In her latest study of the picture (1979, *loc. cit.*) Mrs Shapley strongly affirms an attribution to Bonsignori.

The present portrait perhaps originates from a series of portraits of *condottieri* on the lines of those executed for the Castello of Ghedi *c.*1505 (Brescia, Pinacoteca Tosio-Martinengo, variously attributed). The inscription is self-evidently a later addition, though perhaps made well before 1671 (see below), just as spurious signatures were added at an early date to other paintings it was desired to pass off as Mantegnas (compare Cat.no.113 and 172). Apart from its manner of placing, the form of Mantegna's name is one not attested until 1468 (see Cat.no.6). He seems in fact to have signed as Mantegna throughout the 1450s, and his signature in the known certainly authentic instances after 1448 until *c.*1468 takes the form OPUS ANDREAE MANTEGNA.

As F. R. Shapley and Tietze-Conrat recognized, this portrait must be after a lost original by Mantegna. The date 1455 which Mrs Shapley, misled by the inscription, assigned to that original is stylistically some ten years too early, and Bock (in *Z. für Kunstgeschichte*, xx, 1957, p.197) is surely correct in attributing the picture to the years when Mantegna was working on the Camera Picta. The original may have been executed for Lodovico Gonzaga as the portrait of a friend and ally; it need not necessarily antedate Sforza's death on 8 March 1465. The present picture may be the portrait attributed to Andrea Mantegna which in 1671 was listed in the inventory of the collections of Cardinal Antonio Barberini taken after his death: 'Un ritratto d'Un huomo Armato con Berrettone rosso in Capo di Andrea Mantegna' (M. A. Lavin, *Seventeenth-Century Barberini Documents and Inventories of Art*, 1975, p.298). This picture passed to Cardinal Francesco Barberini (Lavin, pp.336,338, No.59) and then to Cardinal Carlo Barberini. A further inventory taken in 1692–1704 lists it as 'Un' altro [ritratto] di un huomo armato in Tavola con beretta rossa in Tela [*sic*] da tre p. mi' (Lavin, p.442). The measurement of *c.*68cm. given by this entry corresponds with those of the present picture. Alternatively the Barberini picture may be the lost portrait of Lodovico Gonzaga engraved for a book published in Rome in 1646 (see Cat.no.71), which may have been a companion portrait to that of Francesco – the armour and hat are closely similar.

153. Portraits of Lodovico Gonzaga and Barbara of Brandenburg
Untraced
Panel 70 × 102cm.   Plate 184

These are first certainly recorded in the late eighteenth century, when they were in a Venetian collection (letter of Gio. Maria Sasso to Giovanni de' Lazara, *cit.* Selvatico, 1849, pp.193–4). Selvatico, who wrongly says they are mentioned by Ridolfi, also records their sale to the Duke of Hamilton, and that they were poorly engraved in the late eighteenth century (for this engraving see Borenius, *Four early Italian engravers*, 1923, p.51). Waagen (iii, 1854, p.298) records them in the Hamilton Palace coll. as 'Portrait of a gentleman and his wife. Animatedly conceived and very warmly coloured, but not refined enough for this great master.' Later in the Cernuschi coll. (sale, Paris, 25 May 1900, lot 53, sold 12.800 frs, as tentatively by Mantegna). According to photographs in the Kunsthistorisches Institut, Florence (177078, from Bild Archiv, Cologne, 87420, and 70007) the picture passed through a Lempertz sale in Cologne and was also with Fiorentini, Venice. Lodovico is described in the Cernuschi sale catalogue as wearing a red hat and a doublet of cloth of gold, embroidered in black, and red sleeves lined with gold. Barbara wore a dress of embroidered cloth of gold and a white head-dress. On the column dividing them is a shield with their arms. The shape of the shield suggests that the picture is a sixteenth-century copy after earlier originals. Tietze-Conrat (1955, p.197) points out that the portrait of Barbara is derived from the Camera Picta, while that of Lodovico shows him as a younger man than in the Camera Picta, and rightly suggests that the picture combines two unrelated prototypes. That of Lodovico must have been painted *c*.1460, soon after Mantegna's arrival in Mantua.

Since these portraits form one panel, they cannot be the portraits of the 'Duke and Duchess of Mantua' attributed to Mantegna which were in the collection of the painter Niccolò Renieri. This was put up for disposal by lottery on 4 December 1666 in Venice (Savini-Branca, 1964, p.104, No.G62: 'Vn Quadro mano d'Andrea Mantegna, oue è dipinto il Duca di Mantoua fatto in tauola al naturale alto quarte 4. e vn terzo, largo 3. e vn terzo. Vn altro Quadro compagna della medesima mano, oue è dipinto la Duchessa sua Moglie, con Cornice compagna'). See also Segarizzi (in *Nuovo Archivio Veneto*, n.s., xxviii, 1914, p.186).

A commission for two portraits, possibly of Lodovico and Barbara, to be painted by Mantegna, is attested by a letter of 6 July 1477 (see Cat.no.72, cf. also 71).

154. Portrait of Rodolfo Gonzaga
New York, Metropolitan Museum of Art (Bache Coll.)
Panel 10.7 × 8.2cm.   Plate 183

PROVENANCE: An unnamed Italian family: with Kleinberger; Jules S. Bache Coll. (*Catalogue*, 1929, No.11; 1944, p.11).

This portrait was first attributed to Mantegna by Berenson (1932; 1968). It is rejected by Fiocco (1937, pp.47–8,203) as Mantegnesque but too weak for the master himself, and by Tietze-Conrat (1955, pp.191–2), who suggests that it derives from an original of Mantegna of *c*.1475 (see below), and that the colouring indicates a Venetian copyist, e.g. Michiel Contarini. Also rejected by Cipriani (1962, pp.83–4) and Garavaglia (1967, No.53).

Originally identified as a portrait of Marchese Francesco Gonzaga, an identification rightly questioned by Fiocco. The correct identification of the sitter as Rodolfo Gonzaga (1451–95), his younger brother, was made by Tietze-Conrat on the basis of a sixteenth-century portrait in the Ambras collection, Vienna (Kenner, in *Vienna Jahrbuch*, xvii–l, 1896, p.225, No.105), which is inscribed with Rodolfo's name and derives, as Kenner points out, from an original by Mantegna. Kenner, followed by Tietze-Conrat, dates the original *c*.1475. The pose of the Ambras picture with the hand pressed to the heart suggests a marriage or betrothal portrait, and a date in the later 1470s, before Rodolfo's marriage on 1 January 1481 to Antonia Malatesta, is therefore probable. The prototype of the present picture may date from the late 1460s or the 1470s and was certainly by Mantegna.

155. The Resurrection
Bergamo, Accademia Carrara, No.714 (F. Rossi, *Accademia Carrara, Bergamo: catalogo dei dipinti*, 1979, p.46)
Tempera on panel 48 × 37cm.   Plate 185

CONDITION: Completed on the left by a narrow painted strip.

PROVENANCE: Coll. Guglielmo Lochis (cf. Lochis, *La Pinacoteca e la Villa Lochis . . . presso Bergamo*, 1858, p.82, no.clxiii, as by Mantegna). His bequest, 1859.

Dismissed by Fiocco (1937, pp.70, 227) as a poor work, not attributable to Francesco Mantegna, but from Mantegna's workshop. A replica of the composition, attributed to Mocetto, is in the Museo Civico, Padua. The composition certainly derives from one by Mantegna presumably dating from *c*.1491, since the summit of the mountain is cut off in the same fashion as the mountain of the *Madonna della Cave* (Plate 121).

156. Judith with the head of Holofernes
Washington, National Gallery of Art (289), Kress Coll. 325 (Shapley, 1968, pp.25–6; Shapley, 1979, pp.299–300)
Paper on canvas (technical examination has shown that the paper is of fifteenth century date) 34.7 × 20.2cm.
                                                     Plate 186

CONDITION: Good.

PROVENANCE: With Contini Bonacossi, Florence. Acquired by Kress, 1935.

Mantegna is known to have treated the popular subject of Judith in compositions of this type a number of times (see e.g. Plates 120,141,142,157,246). He was certainly producing them by 1491. Two drawings of this subject in the Chatsworth Coll., probably copies, are inscribed with signatures and the dates 1472 and 1486 (Kristeller, 1901, p.458). Another drawing is in the Boymans-van Beuningen Museum, Rotterdam (Koenigs Collection). A similar composition is recorded in reverse in two engravings by Girolamo Mocetto (Hind, 10), and another in two engravings by Zoan Andrea (Hind, 5,5a).

Although F. R. Shapley cites various verbal opinions in favour of the present drawing as an original by Mantegna, she is surely right in attributing it with Tietze-Conrat (1955, p.208) to a follower. It suggests a fairly careful, close copy of an original by Mantegna of the years 1490–1506.

Paintings Attributed to the Young Mantegna

157. St Jerome in the Wilderness
São Paulo, Museu de Arte
Panel 48 × 37cm. Plate 187

CONDITION: Restored top left corner.

PROVENANCE: First recorded in Christie's sale (20 November 1936, lot 97, anonymous property, bt. Betts, £4410). Collection of Prince Paul of Yugoslavia, London (by 1938).

Published by Borenius (in *B.M.*, lxxii, 1938, pp.105–6) as an autograph early work, close to the Ovetari frescoes. The attribution is contested by Fiocco (1937, pp.76–7), who assigns it to Marco Zoppo, *c.*1470, under the influence of Mantegna and Giambellino, and by Tietze-Conrat (1955, p.197, from a photograph). It is reaffirmed by Berenson (1952,1968) and accepted by Bottari (1961, p.312, with reserves), Longhi (1962, p.16), Cipriani (1962, p.57, as dating from the later 1450s), and Camesasca (1964, pp.14–15,35,106, as painted *c.*1449–50, after Mantegna's return from Ferrara and as showing the influence of Rogier van der Weyden and Piero della Francesca), and Garavaglia (1967, No.6). Not attributable to Mantegna since neither in sentiment, nor in colour, nor in its rather nervous line is it close to Mantegna's early works, but certainly the work of an artist with a Paduan–Venetian formation.

158. Virgin and Child
Boston, Museum of Fine Arts, 33.682 (*Bulletin*, xxii, 1934, pp.20–4)
Tempera on panel 48 × 35cm. Plate 188

CONDITION: Good. Cleaned, 1933, by Moroni, Milan. Restorations in Virgin's mantle and elsewhere.

PROVENANCE: Coll. Ferdinand von Quast (1807–77), Radensleben, Ruppin, Brandenburg (*Die Kunstdenkmäler der Provinz Brandenburg*, I, 3, 1914, p.197).

Already associated with Mantegna's school in the Von Quast coll., the picture was acquired by Boston as an autograph early work of *c.*1454, on the opinion of Fiocco published in 1937 (pp.32,201, as influenced by Jacopo Bellini). Rightly rejected by Suida (1946, p.61, as from the workshop), by Tietze-Conrat (1955, p.180, as by an early follower) and by Cipriani (1962, p.80, as close to such imitators of Mantegna as Lazzaro Bastiani). Classed by Garavaglia (1967, No.4) and Berenson (1968) as a copy.

159. St Mark. Inscribed on the *cartello* INCLITA MAGNANIMI VE . . ./ EVANGELISTA PAX TIBI . . ./ ANDREAE MANTEGNAE . . ./O . . . LABOR
Frankfurt, Städelsches Kunstinstitut, No.18 (Weizsäcker, *Catalog*, 1900, p.40, as Bonsignori)
Canvas 82 × 63.7cm. Plate 189

PROVENANCE: Acquired in 1867 at the Paris sale (Pillet, 3–6 June 1867) of the Marqués de Salamanca (*Catalogue des tableaux anciens . . . composant la galerie de M. le Mis de Salamanca*, Paris, 1867, p.43, No.58, as Mantegna, bt. Kaulbacher of Frankfurt, 6600 frs.). The sale catalogue notes: 'Au bas du tableau, un cartel portant une inscription en partie effacée, et la signature du maitre: ANDREAE MONTEGNAE LABOR.' The collection of the Marqués was largely formed in Madrid: the sale catalogue gives the earlier provenance of the picture as the 'galerie du comte d'Uceda'.

The attribution of this striking picture and the authenticity of the inscription have been much discussed. Morelli (1891, pp.166n,23) rejected the inscription as a fraudulent addition and gave the picture to Francesco del Cossa. Later it was attributed by the Gallery to Bonsignori, and by Knapp (1910, pp.163,180) tentatively to Marco Zoppo. It was reclaimed for Mantegna as an early autograph work by Berenson (1932,1968). Fiocco (1937, pp.28–9,199) after an initial tentative attribution to Niccolò Pizzolo (1927, p.149) held that resemblances to the Ovetari *Assumption* (then recently documented as by Mantegna) justify the ascription. He accepts the genuineness of the inscription and dates the picture *c.*1449. The attribution to Mantegna and an early dating are reaffirmed by Suida (1946, pp.57–8), Ragghianti (1962, p.40), Longhi (1962, p.16), and Camesasca (1964, pp.15,113, after return from Ferrara, or perhaps even before). Tietze-Conrat (1955, p.183) violently disagrees, and assigns the picture to an artist having nothing in common with Mantegna except a Paduan training. L. Moretti (in *Paragone*, ix, 1958, no.99, pp.60–3) proposes an attribution to the miniaturist Leonardo Bellini. Cipriani (1962, pp.80–1) is divided between Fiocco's first ascription to Pizzolo and the early Mantegna, but catalogues it among attributed works. Garavaglia (1967, No.12) as Mantegna. The inscription, with its use of LABOR for OPVS is suspect, all the more because in its use of a genitive form MANTEGNAE it differs from the inscription on Cat.no.6. Stylistically the picture is certainly Squarcionesque, but the type of the saint is not idealized enough for the early Mantegna. The jewelled robe is also uncharacteristic, as is the treatment of the halo.

160. Painted frame of the tomb of Federico Corner

Venice, Santa Maria dei Frari, Cappella Corner   Plate 190

CONDITION: Much restored.

The tomb of Federico Corner (d.c.1385) is in the chapel of San Marco, which was founded in 1417 by his grandson Giovanni (Sansovino, 1663, pp.188,197; Paoletti, pp.185,200). The frescoed frame, which had been removed, was cleaned and replaced above the monument c.1920. It consists of two medallions of Roman emperors and four putti, forming an integral part of the monument, which is by a sculptor Sansovino calls 'Jacomo Padovano'. The monument is in an advanced Renaissance style and must date from many decades later than the foundation of the chapel, which is in fact known to have been still unfinished and without priests in 1473. Accordingly the suggestion of Fogolari (*Chiese veneziane: i Frari e i SS. Giovanni e Paolo*, Milan, 1931, p.facing tav.12) that the monument dates like the stained glass and the Vivarini altarpiece from 1474 has everything, including style, to recommend it.

The fresco was attributed to Mantegna by Fiocco (1927, pp.241–4; *Dedalo*, vii, 1927, pp.535–44; 1937, pp.39–40,180), who dated the monument c.1450, and suggested that the painted decoration was executed in 1454 [*sic*] when Mantegna married Nicolosia Bellini. Accepted by Berenson (1932,1968, as a largely autograph early work), the fresco is rejected by Longhi (1934, p.512), Tietze-Conrat (1955, pp.9, 199–200) and Cipriani (1962, p.84). Otherwise passed over in the recent literature, except for a mention by Garavaglia (1967, No.21). The dating of the monument carries with it that of the fresco: just as the monument cannot be by an immediate follower of Donatello, so the fresco cannot be by Mantegna.

Tietze-Conrat points out that the single well-preserved emperor derives from a Carrara medal (Hill, pl.I, No.2), inspired by a coin of Vitellius.

161. Virgin and Child, attended by cherubim and angels holding the Instruments of the Passion

Berlin-Dahlem, Staatliche Museen, 27 (Posse, 1909, p.88)
Tempera on poplar 79 × 67cm.   Plate 191

PROVENANCE: Acquired with the Solly coll., 1821.

The traditional ascription to Mantegna, accepted by Crowe and Cavalcaselle (1871, pp.340n,386–7, as c.1464), was first questioned by Morelli (1893, p.230), who substituted an attribution to Bartolommeo Vivarini (accepted by Van Marle, xviii, 1936, pp.94–6, and Pallucchini, *I Vivarini*, 1962, pp.39–41). The picture has also been attributed to Lazzaro Bastiani by Collobi (in *Cr. d'A.*, iv–v, 1939–40, p.38), Longhi (1962, p.17) and Cipriani (1962, p.79) and Camesasca (1964, p.127). The attribution of this hard, poor picture to Mantegna is quite untenable, but it continues to figure in the literature of the artist, though generally unfavourably: Thode (1897, pp.34,46, as an early autograph work); Kristeller (1901, pp.120–2, also as an early autograph work, perhaps preceding the Ovetari frescoes); Knapp (1910, pp.157,179,

not by Mantegna, from his school); Fiocco (1937, p.201, a late caricature of the Butler Madonna in New York [Plate 195 q.v.] by a mediocre Paduan artist); Richter (1939, pp.63–4, a studio version dating from 1470s, based on a lost original also copied by Giovanni Bellini in the Correr Madonna and the Trivulzio Madonna); Tietze-Conrat (1955, pp.179,191, not by Mantegna); Ragghianti (1962, p.40, derived from the same cartoon as the Tulsa Madonna, Plate 192 q.v.); Garavaglia (1967, No.20) as generally rejected; Berenson (1968, copy of the Tulsa Madonna).

162. Virgin and Child. On the base are two shields of arms (unidentified).

Tulsa, Okla., Philbrook Art Center (3370). On loan from Kress Foundation K1653 (Shapley, 1968, pp.26–7)
Panel 67.8 × 49.5cm.   Plate 192

CONDITION: Abraded all over.

PROVENANCE: First recorded in Padua, coll. Barbieri family (probably by descent from Giuseppe Barbieri, a nineteenth-century Paduan collector recorded by Selvatico, 1849, p.185); coll. Dr Fusaro, Padua; coll. Prince Jérôme Napoléon, Paris (sale, Christie's 9–11 May 1872, no.311, as Mantegna, bt. Graves); coll. Charles Butler (exh. RA, 1880, no.220, 1894, no.148, as Mantegna; sale Christie's, 25 May 1911, lot 49); coll. Leopold Hirsch (sale Christie's 11 May 1934, lot 115, bt. Collings); Wildenstein's, London and N.Y.; Kress acquisition, 1949.

Published by Crowe & Cavalcaselle (1871, p.340n; 1912, p.43) as more plausibly by Mantegna than any of the other pictures then attributed to him in Paduan private collections, but as so badly rubbed that the wood was bare in many places. They noted the relationship with the *Virgin and Child* in a painted frame in Berlin (Cat. no.161) with which the picture has since frequently been associated in the literature. Republished by Richter (1939, pp.63–5) as the latest of Mantegna's Madonnas, completed by Bonsignori c.1490 after Mantegna had outlined the whole and painted the Child and the medallion. Of modern critics only Berenson (1946, MS opinion, cit. Shapley,1968) claims it as an autograph Mantegna. Shapley, who notes that the unsatisfactory condition makes dating hazardous, gives it to a follower of Mantegna. See Cat.no.161.

163. St Jerome in Penitence

Washington, National Gallery of Art, 32 (Shapley, 1979, p.348, no.32)
Panel 80 × 55cm.   Plate 193

PROVENANCE: Coll. Arthur Sulley, London; with Duveen's (Duveen, 1941, No.74); coll. Otto H. Kahn, New York, by 1927, sold 1936 to A.W. Mellon; Mellon coll., 1937.

Published as Mantegna's earliest surviving work by L. Venturi ('Un'opera inedita di Andrea Mantegna' in *L'Arte*, xxx, 1927, pp.31–3) and accepted by Berenson (1932,1968, as early) and by Fiocco (1937, pp.25,198, as autograph, c.1449, contemporary with the upper frescoes of St James in the Ovetari Chapel). Rejected by Longhi (1934, p.512), by Tietze-Conrat (1955, p.202, as by a distinguished hand, perhaps a Ferrarese influenced by Squarcione) and by Ragghianti (1962, pp.39–40, as not even by a Ferrarese, perhaps by a miniaturist). Cipriani (1962, p.83) among attributed works. Recatalogued by F.R. Shapley (*loc. cit.*) as Paduan–Ferrarese school, with a variety of suggested names.

164. Virgin and Child with St Jerome and St Louis of Toulouse

Paris, Musée Jacquemart-André (*Catalogue*, 1933, pp.141–2, No.1020)

Tempera on panel 67 × 43cm.   Plate 194

CONDITION: Much repainted.

PROVENANCE: Acquired from Guggenheim, Venice, 1887. This is clearly the picture listed in 1814 in the Lechi collection, Brescia, as a Mantegna (Lechi, 1968, p.118, No.29; pp.179–88, No.82, dimensions, medium and description correspond perfectly). Bought for the Lechi coll. in Milan; sold at some date after 1866.

For Yriarte (1901, p.235), the intact portions suggest Mantegna, for A. Venturi (1914, pp.262,488) a workshop picture. Promoted to an autograph work by Berenson (1932,1968) and Fiocco (1937, p.30, as *c.*1452, contemporary with the Santo fresco). Later opinion has downgraded it: for Tietze-Conrat (1955, p.196) not even a workshop picture; catalogued by Cipriani (1962, p.82) among attributed pictures and rejected by Bottari (1961, p.312) and by Gilbert (1962, p.6, as an inferior work). A second view attributes the invention to Mantegna, the execution to another hand: thus Paccagnini (1961, p.24) as by a pupil influenced by Gentile Bellini; Arslan (1961, p.165) as reflecting Mantegna's early style, but from coarsenesses of treatment clearly finished or copied by a follower; Rühmer (1961, p.cv) as by the same hand as the Turin *Holy Family* (q.v.); Longhi (1962, p.20) as executed by Giovanni Bellini; Ragghianti (1962, p.26) as by a painter under the influence of Giovanni Bellini. Is this striking painting an early Giovanni Bellini?

165. Virgin and Child attended by seraphim (The Butler Madonna)

New York, Metropolitan Museum of Art, no.32.100.97 (Wehle, 1940, pp.128–9). Friedsam Bequest, 1931

Tempera on an arched panel. The cherubim executed in simulated gold. 43.7 × 28.6cm.   Plate 195

PROVENANCE: Sometimes confused with the Madonna at Tulsa formerly in the Barbieri, Fusaro and Butler colls. (see Cat.no.162). First recorded in the coll. of J. Stirling Dyce, London; coll. Charles Butler, London; Basle, private coll., *c.*1927; coll. M. Friedsam, N.Y.

Yriarte (1901, p.209) and Kristeller (1901, pp.123,437) were the first to recognize a relationship between this picture and the Madonna in Berlin (Cat.no.161). Yriarte gave it to Mantegna himself, as did Kristeller, though with some hesitation because of its condition. Knapp (1910, pp.158,79) as by an imitator of Mantegna. Called autograph by Berenson (Friedsam cat.p.77; 1932,1968, as an autograph early work). Accepted as autograph by Fiocco (1937, pp.32,201), who dates it *c.*1454, at the moment of Mantegna's marriage, which explains the influence of Jacopo Bellini, and regards the Berlin version as a poor copy. Richter (in *Apollo*, xxix, 1939, p.63) regards it as perhaps the earliest of Mantegna's surviving Madonnas and dates it to the early 1450s. Catalogued in 1940 by Wehle as workshop, but reclaimed as autograph by Suida (1946, p.61), a view affirmed by Arslan (1961, p.165, as executed when in contact with Jacopo Bellini), by Gilbert (1962, pp.6–9, face damaged and repainted, but associable with the St Luke polyptych, the angels by the workshop), by Cipriani (1962, pp.52–3, as *c.*1454), by Longhi (1962, p.17) and by Camesasca (1964, pp.16–17 as early in the 1450s). Camesasca argues that it derives from a prototype by Giovanni Bellini, from which a Madonna in Berlin (Cat. no.161) also derives. For Paccagnini (1961, p.23) possibly a work produced by Mantegna and Giovanni Bellini in close collaboration. See also Garavaglia (1962, No.19). The relationship with the Berlin Madonna is denied by Ragghianti (1962, p.40). Tietze-Conrat (1955, p.191) regards the invention as derived from some important model, but rightly thinks the execution does not justify an attribution to the young Mantegna.

Other Paintings Attributed to Mantegna

166. Virgin and Child attended by cherubim

Milan, Pinacoteca di Brera, 198 (Malaguzzi-Valeri, 1908, pp.111–12; Modigliani, 1966, p.41)

Poplar 70 × 88cm.   Plate 196

CONDITION: Much repainted until restored in 1885 by Cavenaghi (compare the reproductions on the plate in *L'Arte*, January 1886, pp.161–7). A crack runs right down the centre left. The Child is restored on the right thigh.

PROVENANCE: On the back is the inscription: 'No. 8° Sᵃ Mᵃ Maggiore' (see below). First recorded in Santa Maria Maggiore, Venice (F. Sansovino, 1663, p.270: 'Molti altri quadri si veggono appoggiati alle colonne, & attaccati in altri luoghi della Chiesa, vno de'quali è di Giovanni Bellino dove è dipinta nostra Donna'). Mentioned by A. M. Zanetti, again with an attribution to Bellini (*Descrizione di tutte le pubbliche pitture della città di Venezia*, 1733, p.364: 'Sopra le colonne vi sono diversi quadri posticcj . . . Una Madonna in tavola con diversi Cherubini, opera preziosa di Gian Bellino. Un'altra quasi simile del Conegliano'). Listed as a work of supreme merit among the pictures selected by Pietro Edwards, Delegato della Corona, for despatch to Milan under the government of Eugène de Beauharnais (Malamani, *Memorie del Conte Leopoldo Cicognara*, ii, 1888, p.371: 'S. Maria Maggiore: Gio. Bellino: B.V. col bambino, e molti Cherubini; in tavola; preziosa pittura, pregiudicata nel bambino da una candela'). Transferred to Brera in 1808 by the Intendenza Generale dei Beni della Corona, Milan: to this transfer the inscription on the back presumably refers.

Until the cleaning of 1885, attributed to Bellini. The attribution to Mantegna was made after the restoration by Cavenaghi and made a sensation (see e.g. Frizzoni, in *Z.B.K.*, xxi, 1885–6, pp.100–3). Thode (1897, p.57) identified it as the Madonna painted for Matteo Bosso (see Cat.no.74) and dated it accordingly to 1466–7, during Mantegna's visit to Florence. Subsequently it has generally been identified as the Madonna begun in 1485 for Eleanora d'Aragona, Duchess of Ferrara, which in turn is usually identified with the Madonna attended by seraphim listed in a Ferrarese inventory of 1493 (see Cat.nos. 76 and 79). Identification and date were proposed by Frizzoni (*loc. cit.*) and are accepted by Kristeller (1901, pp.306–8), Knapp (1910, pp.107,176), Fiocco (1937, pp.68–9), Tietze-Conrat (1955, pp.188–9), Paccagnini (1961, p.44) and Berenson (1968 only). Longhi (1962, p.20), who thinks the picture cut down, will only accept that an advanced date of this kind is plausible; Cipriani (1962, pp.37,67), who emphasizes the Bellinesque design, rejects the identification with the 1485 Madonna but regards it as the Madonna of the Ferrarese inventory, with a date *c*.1492. Camesasca (1964, pp.17–18,123) rightly points out that it differs from Mantegna's other pictures, and is inclined to attribute it to Giovanni Bellini, citing Middeldorf's (verbal) opinion in support. He dates the picture *c*.1480–5. The attribution to Mantegna is very doubtful. It is difficult to reconcile its style with his work in the 1480s and 1490s.

167. Portrait of a Man

Washington, National Gallery of Art, 1088 – Kress 1709 (Shapley, 1968, p.25: *id.*, 1979, pp.297–8)
Transferred from wood to canvas (before 1940) and later (1950) to masonite 24.3 × 19.1cm.   Plate 197

CONDITION: Fair. Background abraded: restoration due to vertical split through face. Meiss (1957, p.88, n.1) suggests that the picture has been cut down with the loss of a parapet at the base.

PROVENANCE: Gaál, Balatonföldvar, Hungary (before 1906): coll. of Dr Ludwig Keleman, Budapest, until 1929.

With Jacques Seligmann, New York (shown by them at various exhs., 1939–49, details in Shapley). Acquired by Kress in 1950.

First attributed to Mantegna by Suida (in Vienna, *c*.1926) and later published by him as an autograph Mantegna (1946, p.63). Accepted as autograph by Tietze-Conrat (1955, p.201), Cipriani (1962, pp.29,60, close in date to the Camera Picta), Camesasca (1964, pp.37,118, close in date to the fresco of the court in the Camera), Garavaglia (1967, No.42, as *c*.1470), Shapley (1968, *loc. cit.*; 1979, *loc. cit.*, though with some reserve, as *c*.1460), Berenson (1968). Meiss (1957, pp.26,88n.41) hesitates on account of the picture's condition; Fredericksen and Zeri (1972) also rightly treat the attribution with some reserve. Tietze-Conrat rejects an untenable attempt made by Frankfurter ('Masterpieces of Art', N.Y. World's Fair, May–October 1939, no.233) to identify the sitter as Janus Pannonius.

168. Portrait of a Man

Milan, Museo Poldi-Pezzoli, No.627 (Russoli, 1955, pp.185–6; Natale, 1982, p.112, No.97)
Panel 33 × 25cm.   Plate 198

CONDITION: Restored by Cavenaghi *c*.1900, and by Brambilla Borcilon 1974. Much abraded, but executed in pigments of high quality (the background painted with lapis lazuli).

PROVENANCE: Unrecorded. According to Borenius (in Crowe & Cavalcaselle, 1912, p.111) possibly a portrait belonging in 1871 to Bertini, Milan; then attributed to Tura. See also Cat. no.126.

Mantegnesque features in this portrait, which has also been called Ferrarese, were first recognized by Berenson (*Venetian Painters*, 1894, p.90), who gave it to Francesco Bonsignori. The attribution to Mantegna himself was advanced by Suida (1946, pp.64–5, closely connected with the Washington portrait of a man, Cat. no.167), and is accepted by Longhi (1962, p.21) and Camesasca (1964, pp.28,116, autograph work of high quality, tentatively datable *c*.1465). Russoli (1955, *loc. cit.*) and Paccagnini (1961, p.111) regard it as close to Mantegna, but more probably by Bonsignori; Berenson (1968) also lists it as by a close follower. Natale (*loc. cit.*) re-argues the attribution to Mantegna, with supporting opinions. Rejected as not weighty enough by Tietze-Conrat (1955, pp.189–90); catalogued by Cipriani (1962, p.81) among attributed pictures. Research into the costume might clarify the origins of this fine portrait, which appears to date from the middle of the century. The treatment of the salient veins of the forehead and of the ear has no parallel in Mantegna's work, and the whole lacks Mantegna's strength of conception and execution.

169. Virgin and Child. Inscribed on the ledge: OPVS ANDREAE MANTEGNAE.

Untraced
Tempera on canvas (*rensa*) 43 × 34cm.   Plate 199

CONDITION: Reproduced before cleaning by Fiocco (*B.M.*, 1949, p.213).

PROVENANCE: Basle, private coll. In 1953 on the art-market. According to Fiocco, formerly in 'an ancient palazzo of Mantua'.

Published by Fiocco (*op. cit.*) and dated by him to Mantegna's Paduan period (*c.*1452–4). Rejected by Tietze-Conrat (1955, p.179) as derived from Mantegna, by Cipriani (1962, p.79) and Garavaglia (1967, No.3). Berenson (1968) as possibly a copy.

170. Virgin Annunciate.
Inscribed on the ledge: ANDREAS PAT. On the reading desk is the inscription AVE MARIA.

Formerly San Diego, California, Fine Arts Gallery (*Catalogue*, 1947, p.37). Acquired by gift, 1946

Linseed oil on fine canvas (according to other sources, tempera) 65.5 × 57cm.   Plate 200

CONDITION: Said to be not finished, especially in the right background.

PROVENANCE: Gianna Cavallari, Padua; Prince Trivulzio, Milan; 1946 in a private coll., New York.

Attributed to Mantegna in earlier MS opinions by Venturi (1935), Fiocco (1936), Gronau and Morassi (1936) and Suida (1936). Published by Suida (1946, pp.61–2) as *c.*1460, close to the San Zeno Madonna. Accepted by Fiocco (1949, p.214), but rejected by Tietze-Conrat (1955, p.197, as a portrait of a female saint, possibly by Antonio da Pavia), by Cipriani (1962, p.84), and by Garavaglia (1967, No.30). The background is derived from that of the Venice *St George*: the 1947 San Diego *Catalogue* also refers it to a drawing in the sketchbook of Jacopo Bellini. Tietze-Conrat rightly observes that the form of the signature is unacceptable.

171. Crucifixion
New York Historical Society, Gallery of Art (*Catalogue*, 1915, p.63)

Canvas 83.5 × 58.2cm.   Plate 201

The inscription on the *cartello* now lost.

PROVENANCE: Bryan Bequest, 1867.

Acquired with an attribution to Mantegna, which was rejected by Berenson (in *G.B.A.*, ser.3, xv, 1896, p.198) in favour of one to Jacopo da Montagnana. Reattributed to Mantegna by Suida (1946, pp.58–61) as rather later than the San Zeno *Crucifixion*, by which it is influenced. Rejected by Tietze-Conrat (1955, p.192), who assigns it to a Paduan or Veronese painter influenced by Mantegna working in the late fifteenth century, by Cipriani (1962, p.84), who discounts Mantegna's influence, and Garavaglia (1967, No.24). Tietze-Conrat suggests it may be identical with a Crucifixion seen by Selvatico (1849, pp.187–8) years before in the hands of Beltrami, a picture dealer and restorer of Cremona, and described by him as 'una tavoletta con figure alte appena un piede, ma d'una espressione tenerissima'.

172. Sacra Conversazione (*Virgo inter virgines*).
Inscribed on the face of the rock a little to the right in the near foreground: ANDREVS MANTINA (the MA in monogram)

Boston, Isabella Stewart Gardner Museum, P15 S5 (Hendy, 1931, pp.228–31; 1974, pp.153–6)

Tempera on light hardwood 53.5 × 42.8cm.   Plate 202

CONDITION: Cleaned in 1951, when its appearance was greatly altered. Enlargements were removed from all four sides: overpainting removed to reveal a worn condition, with severe abrasions. The restoration also disclosed brilliant colouring and delicately fine painting, and the scene of the Death of St Peter Martyr, previously painted out. The signature, believed by Fiocco and Berenson to be a later addition, remained unaffected by the cleaning (full details in Hendy). But see below.

PROVENANCE: Listed in 1627, without an attribution to Mantegna, among the pictures in the Camera dei Cani of Palazzo Ducale, Mantua (D'Arco, ii, p.165; Luzio, 1913, p.129, No.580: 'Un quadretto d'asse dipintovi con la B.V. con il puttino et S. Giovanni et sei sante che la circonda assisa in tera L.36'). Sold to Charles I in or before 1632: recorded in Charles I's inventory *c.*1639 by Vanderdoort with an attribution to Mantegna (Millar, 1960, p.82: '[33] Item another as aforesaid fellow peece of Andreo Mantenia alsoe in the like ebbone Joyned in another woodden frame where our Lady Christ and St John and Six other woemen Sᵗˢ sitting by and in the Lanskipp a Sᵗ Christopher Carring Christ over the water, alsoe another Sᵗ being Sᵗ George on horse back running with a Speare to kill the Dragon, and alsoe on high upon the rock a Sᵗ ffranncis, and Sᵗ Jerrom, and a Sᵗ Dominica painted upon the right Light' (in the margin: 'A mantua peece Done by Andrea Mantenia'). Millar, 1960, p.209: '[37] A peece of or Ladie, Christ, Sᵗ John, and sixe Saincts kneeling by them. By Andrea Montania.' Identified at the court of Charles as a 'fellow peece' of Mantegna's *Exequies of the Virgin*, now in Madrid (Cat. no.18 q.v.). Sold together with this picture in the sale of Charles's effects held by act of Parliament after his execution (Millar, 1972, p.266, No.170 (of pictures at St James's Palace): 'Mary and divers Sᵗˢ [valued] at £15'). Probably sold to John Baptist Caspars, 26 March 1650, for £17. Sent by the Spanish ambassador Alonso de Cardenas to King Philip IV of Spain: Spanish royal collection until 1856, when presented by Queen Maria Cristina to her daughter Maria on her marriage to Principe Filippo del Drago (see *Almanach de Gotha*, 1888, p.282). Bought by Mrs Gardner from Principe del Drago in October 1899 through Richard Norton in Rome.

The composition with six female saints seated on the ground in an open landscape around the Virgin seems to derive from a Flemish prototype (compare the left wing of the diptych of Jean du Celier, by Memling, now in the Louvre). Hendy claims that it is possibly the first Italian instance of a *Sacra Conversazione* of this Netherlandish type. The attribution and date have been much disputed. For Berenson (1932,1968) it is largely autograph, for Longhi (1934, p.511; 1962, p.62), Fiocco (1937, pp.70–1) and Hendy (1974, *loc. cit.*) wholly so. For Tietze-Conrat (1955, p.180), who wrongly identifies it as one of the pictures attributed to Mantegna mounted in the chapel of the Duchess of Ferrara in 1586–8 (see Cat.nos. 5 and 18) it is by a minor Ferrarese artist working *c.*1480. Ragghianti (1961, p.40) sees the landscape and some of the figures as in precise relationship to the mature Mantegna, but an echo of Ercole Roberti in the rocks and some other figures. Cipriani (1962, p.79) and Garavaglia (1967, No.34) as doubtful, Camesasca (1964, p.128) as closest to Mantegna of all doubtful works. Fredericksen & Zeri (1972) as a school-work, perhaps rightly.

The dates assigned to it range from c.1460 (Hendy), c.1480–90 (Longhi, 1934), c.1480 (Tietze-Conrat), much later than 1480 (Cipriani), c.1490–5 (Fiocco), among latest works (Longhi, 1962). S. Newton (in Hendy) dates the costume of the saints c.1497–1500, which indeed is the most plausible date for the picture. It is composed of Mantegnesque motifs, to which a spurious signature has been added by an early hand, rather as one was added before 1632 to Cat.no.113 (q.v.), in order to pass it off as an original work by Mantegna.

173. Virgin and Child
Untraced
Oil on panel 87.6 × 76.3cm.   Plate 203

CONDITION: Formerly much repainted: cleaning c.1932 revealed that it is unfinished. Fry (see below) reproduced it before and after cleaning.

PROVENANCE: With Podio, Bologna; with Agnew's, London: Coll. W.U. Goodbody, Invergarry, Scotland.

Published by Fry (in *B.M.*, lxii, 1933, pp.53–4) as by Mantegna, painted c.1470, given that the medium is oil. Fry recognized that the picture reproduces, with slight modifications, the Donatello composition known as the *Verona Madonna* from the best-known version of it, a terracotta relief from Verona now in the Metropolitan Museum. Though emphasizing the picture's unfinished state Fry admitted the feebleness of the vase and parapet and attributed these to a pupil. Accepted by Fiocco (1937, pp.69,207) who compares it with the Brera *Madonna* (Cat. no.166) for its treatment of a sculptural theme, and, with reserve, by Camesasca (1964, p.128). Rightly rejected by Tietze-Conrat (1955, p.184), who points to weaknesses in the adaptation from Donatello and considers it too close to the original to be by Mantegna and without typological analogy with his other works. Also rejected by Cipriani (1962, pp.79–80) as untypical of Mantegna. Garavaglia (1967, No.9). A curious iconographical feature is the bush in the vase.

174. Virgin giving suck to the Child
Washington, National Gallery of Art (377). Kress Coll. 483 (Shapley, 1968, p.26; Shapley, 1979, pp.300–1)
Canvas 56 × 41cm.   Plate 204

CONDITION: Good, but some restorations.

PROVENANCE: First recorded in the coll. of James Hugh Smith-Barry (1748–?) of Marbury Hall, Cheshire. Coll. of Lord Barrymore (Smith-Barry). Exh. London, Grafton Galleries, *National Loan Exhibition*, 1909–10, No.88 (Cook & Brockwell, *Catalogue*, 1909, p.135, as School of Mantegna). Arthur Hugh Smith-Barry, Lord Barrymore, Marbury Hall, Northwich, Cheshire (sale Sotheby's, London, 21 June 1933, No.89, as Mantegna). With Duveen, New York (*Duveen Pictures in Private Collections of America*, 1941, No.79, as Mantegna). Acquired by Kress, 1937.

A picture of this subject, attributed to Mantegna, is recorded in the inventory taken c.1706 of the Galleria of Ferdinando Carlo, last Duke of Mantua (D'Arco, ii, p.189: 'Uno [quadro] lungo mezzo braccio con la B.V.

che allatta il puttino dipinto sull' asse dal Mantegna'). Neither medium nor dimensions correspond with the present picture. According to Ormerod (*History of . . . Chester*, 1882 ed., i, p.635) Smith-Barry's pictures and antique statues were chiefly collected at Rome. The present picture is not identifiable in the 1819 printed catalogue of Marbury Hall, but it may be suspected that Smith-Barry acquired it as a Correggio.

Traditionally (?) ascribed to Mantegna: attributed by Kristeller (1901, p.455) to a sixteenth-century Veronese artist. Demoted in 1909 to School of Mantegna (see above). Attributed in 1930 by Ricci (*Correggio*, pp.23,149) to Correggio, and in 1937 by Fiocco (pp.78,210) to the late Mantegna. Richter (in *Apollo*, xxix, 1939, p.63) and Suida (in *Pantheon*, xxvi, 1940, p.276) accept the attribution to Mantegna, but later opinion has not settled in favour of either artist. Tietze-Conrat (1955, pp.201–2) assigns it to a follower of Mantegna, perhaps one of his sons. Berenson (1968) hesitantly as a late Mantegna. Shapley (1968, *loc. cit.*) as from the circle of Correggio, perhaps Mantegna, an attribution later modified (1979, *loc. cit.*) to circle of Mantegna. Garavaglia (1967, No.104) and Fredericksen & Zeri (1972) as attributed to Mantegna or Correggio. Painted by an artist under the influence of Mantegna, but the type of the Virgin and the treatment of light and shade oppose an attribution to the artist himself. Neither costume nor ornamented haloes can be paralleled in his late works, with which this picture must be more or less contemporary.

175. Satyrs rebuked for unveiling a sleeping water nymph
Canvas relined 26 × 33cm.
Neptune
Canvas relined 33 × 13.8cm.
Mars
Canvas relined 33 × 13.8cm.
Untraced

These three monochrome panels, in an unnamed private collection, were published by Zimmermann (in *Pantheon*, xxiii, 1965, pp.17–21) as works of Mantegna's last decade. The attribution is rejected by Garavaglia (1967, Nos.108–10). They appear to be motifs of the same composition as a painting which was first published in 1862 by G.B. Sezanne (*Belle Arti. Illustrazione artistico-storica di una pittura classica di Giulio Pippi detto Giulio Romano*, Florence, 1862, with a line-engraving). This composition (see Plate 257, canvas, 36 × 56cm.) contained urns dedicated to Virgil (left) and Battista Spagnoli (right) and must have been painted after Spagnoli's death in 1516, probably by Leonbruno. It was subsequently in the Rey-Spitzer coll., Paris, and later in the Bourgeois sale (Cologne, 27–9 October 1904, lot 49, as by Mantegna). It was published with an attribution to Leonbruno by A. Venturi (in *L'Arte*, vii, 1904, p.393) and Gamba (in *Rass d'A.*, vi, 1906, pp.91–2). The *Mars* reproduces a motif from Cat.no.194; the old woman recalls such Mantegnesque figures as Invidia in the *Battle of the Sea-Gods*. The compiler has not seen these paintings and so cannot judge of their relationship to the picture attributed to Leonbruno. No provenance for them is given by Zimmermann.

Sezanne gives no details of the history of his picture.

Drawings by Mantegna

176. St James led to Execution
London, British Museum, 1976-6-16-1
Pen and brown ink, on paper lightly stained brown
15.5 × 23.4cm.   Plate 205
PROVENANCE: Spencer Coll.; Sir Thomas Lawrence;
John Malcolm; A. E. Gathorne Hardy.

Unanimously agreed to be closely related to the fresco
of the same subject in the Ovetari Chapel, the drawing
is a key piece in the long controversy as to whether certain
drawings are to be assigned to Mantegna or to Giovanni
Bellini (see below). The traditional ascription to
Mantegna is accepted by Kristeller (1901, p.101–2),
Knapp (1910, p.xx), Clark (in *B.M.*, lvi, pp.182–3),
Muchall-Viebroock (1942, pp.73–5) and Tietze-Conrat
(1955, p.204, noting the existence of a copy in the
Louvre). Doubt about the attribution was first expressed
by Colvin (in *Vasari Society*, i, 1905–6, p.20), and was
strengthened when the links between the style of the
drawing and a group attributed to Bellini by Morelli
(1890, pp.355–6, including Cat.nos.180 [Plate 210] and
177 [Plate 206]) were perceived. Fiocco (in *L'Arte*, n.s.
iv, 1933, pp.185–94; *Arte Veneta*, iii, 1949, pp.40–54)
assigned it to Giovanni Bellini, copying an original study
by Mantegna. This is also the opinion of Mezzetti (1961,
p.174). The attribution to Mantegna was reaffirmed by
Wilde (*Seilern Catalogue: Addenda*, 1969, p.39), who
adduced the iconography (though he misread the scene)
as his chief argument for claiming it as a preparatory
study. The drawing adheres in fact more closely than the
fresco to the *Legenda Aurea*, but in itself this does not dispose of the stylistic problem.

The vibrant, sketchy style of this drawing and others
in the group differs from Mantegna's drawing style as seen
in later drawings. The gap between the two styles is
chronologically disturbingly small – the present drawing
dates from *c*.1455 at the earliest, and Plate 206 Cat.no.177)
must date from *c*.1456 again at the earliest, while the
drawings associable with the Cappella di San Giorgio date
from *c*.1462–4. The only explanation that reconciles them
is that advanced by Wilde, who sees the group as representing drawings made during Mantegna's initial stages of
creation (see his comment on Cat.no.177).

The attribution of these drawings as between Mantegna
and Bellini is a celebrated crux of connoisseurship. Some
of them have been attributed to both artists by various
scholars since the 1890s (cf. Morelli, i, 1892–3, p.271; D.
von Hadeln, 1925, pp.16, 46–52, 1935; Clarke, 1930,
pp.182–7, 1935; H. & E. Tietze-Conrat, 1944, pp.73–94;
Robertson, 1968, pp.21–8). It cannot be said that any
unanimity has been achieved. The most recent corpus of
Mantegna's drawings has been assembled by Byam Shaw

(in Istituto Alinari, *Biblioteca di disegni*, iii, 1978). In the
present writer's view, a drawing such as the *St James led
to Execution* is presumptively Mantegna's because it shows
in the treatment of the lower members his unique perspective. The other early drawings assembled here are
included as putatively by Mantegna.

177. Four Saints (St Peter, St Paul, St John the Evangelist and St Zeno)
Formerly Chatsworth, Duke of Devonshire Coll.
Pen and brown ink 19.5 × 13.2 cm.   Plate 206
PROVENANCE: William Cavendish, 2nd Duke of Devon-
shire, as Perino del Vaga. Chatsworth drawings sale
(Christie's, 3 July 1984, lot 26).

It is generally agreed that this drawing is closely connected
with the left-hand panel of the San Zeno altarpiece (Plate
36). The framing pilasters appear to either side, but the
poses and disposition of the figures in the pictorial space
differ. St Peter holds only a book, so does St Paul: both
saints look inwards, not outwards at the spectator. San
Zeno is shown in a frontal pose, not looking inwards and
not with a crozier, as in the picture. The drawing must
therefore be either a preliminary design for the picture
or a copy of one. A drawing of St Peter in the Ambrosiana
shows this figure as in the present drawing (first noted
by Pouncey). As with Cat.nos.176,178,179,180, there is
no agreement as to whether the Chatsworth drawing is
by Mantegna. Morelli (1890, p.356) attributed it to Bellini, followed by Venturi (*Studi dal vero*, 1927, p.226), Fiocco (in *L'Arte*, n.s. iv, 1933, p.192) and Mezzetti (1961,
p.173, as *c*.1461–4). Kristeller (1901, p.153n) regards it as
a copy after the painting, followed by Tietze-Conrat
(1955, p.200). Wilde (in *Seilern Catalogue: Addenda*, 1969,
pp.39–40) reargued the attribution to Mantegna, claiming
it to be an original *modello*, carefully prepared for submission to the patron. For him it supplies a link between
Cat.no.176 (St James) and Mantegna's later drawings.

178. St Andrew and two Saints reading books
Untraced
Pen and brown ink on pink-washed paper 17.9 × 19.3 cm.
                                                            Plate 207
PROVENANCE: E. Prideaux Coll. (L.888): anonymous
sale, Christie's, 7 July 1959, lot 70 (bt. Hatvany,
14,800gns): Hatvany sale, Christie's, 24 June 1980, lot 3.

On its emergence in 1959, attributed by Popham to Giovanni Bellini, like the rest of a small group of such drawings which include the *Study of a Saint reading* (No.1895-9-
15-780) in the British Museum (Popham & Pouncey,
No.11) and a sheet with studies of St John Baptist and

other saints formerly in the Koenigs Coll. which may be a copy of a Mantegna. The attribution of the British Museum drawing of a *Saint reading* (Plate 208) to Mantegna was made by Tietze-Conrat (1955, p.205) and is accepted by Degenhart & Schmidt (*Corpus der Italienischen Zeichnungen*, ii, 1968, p.363, n.13) and Byam Shaw ('Mantegna' in *Biblioteca di Disegni*, iii, 1979).

If the present drawing is by Mantegna, the free grouping of the saints and their careful variety of pose argues for a date contemporary with the San Zeno altarpiece (*c.*1456–9). The foreshortened feet seen *di sotto in sù* and the cornice seem to suggest a work intended to be seen slightly above eye-level, and therefore a fresco rather than an altarpiece. This *di sotto in sù* foreshortening is a feature in favour of the attribution to Mantegna.

179. Studies of Christ at the column (*recto* and *verso*)
London, Courtauld Institute Gallery, formerly Count Antoine Seilern, 56 Princes Gate, London SW7
(*Catalogue: Italian Paintings & Drawings, Addenda*, 1969, No.345, pp.37–41, with full literature)
Pen and ink 23.4 × 14.4cm.   Plates 209a and b
The studies on the *verso* were first uncovered in 1958 after removal of a sheet of paper pasted over them.

PROVENANCE: Coll. John Skippe; Edward Holland; Rayner-Wood; E.H. Martin sale, Christie's, 20–21 November 1958, No.36.

Published by Russell (in *Vasari Society*, ser.2, pt.xi, 1930, p.7, No.3) as a Bellini, an attribution reargued by Hadeln (in *B.M.*, lxi, 1932, p.230). Subsequently Clark (in *B.M.*, lvi, 1930, p.187) claimed that the studies on the *recto* must be for a composition of the *Flagellation* by Mantegna recorded in two engravings (see Cat.no.213). This is one of the drawings whose attribution has been shifted between Bellini and Mantegna. Wilde (in *Seilern Catalogue, Addenda*, 1969, *loc. cit.*) points out that the uncovering of the studies on the *verso* confirms Mantegna's authorship. He rightly considers that the composition reflected in the two engravings was a painting rather than a drawing, and notes that the most finished study of Christ in the present drawing is the same size as the figure of Christ in the engraving, a correspondence which to him suggests that the painting was of roughly the same dimensions (*c.*46 × 31cm.). He considers the studies on the *verso* were made before those on the *recto*, and dates the whole drawing to *c.*1460, transitional between the St Christopher frescoes in the Ovetari Chapel and the predella of the San Zeno altarpiece and the panels now in Florence and Madrid probably originating from the Cappella di San Giorgio. If Wilde is correct in attributing this and the previous nos. to Mantegna, and the existence of four separate studies on this sheet is a very strong argument in favour of his case, then it is tempting to associate these designs, with their Corinthian columns recalling the architecture of the *Circumcision* (Cat.no.15) and their elongated, graceful figures, as studies of one of the lost panels painted in the early 1460s for the Cappella di San Giorgio, or for a chapel in one of the other Gonzaga palaces.

Kristeller (1901, p.448) lists as a lost 'picture' by Mantegna a *Flagellation* published by Erman, 'Sur la Princesse Barbe de Brandebourg' in Berlin, *Mémoires de*

l'Académie Royale des Sciences et Belles-Lettres ... 1803, 1805, Classe des Belles-Lettres, pp.17–25. On consulting this article it appears that the work in question was a painting in enamel of the Flagellation in a frame of gold filigree work. This object was presented on 23 May 1803 to Queen Louise of Prussia, together with a manuscript giving its history, by the Abbate Conte d'Ayala, a Sicilian ex-Jesuit, who had been minister of the Republic of Ragusa at the court of Vienna for some fifteen to twenty years.

According to the manuscript the enamel was painted by Mantegna, and given by him to the Marchesa Barbara of Brandenburg who mounted it in an 'altar' of gold filigree worked with her own hands. This story seems to have arisen from the letters B.F. impressed on a piece of red wax on the back of the enamelled picture, which were interpreted as *Barbara Fecit*. Barbara in turn gave the work to the nuns of San Paolo in Mantua, and it was the privilege of the abbesses of this convent to keep it in their chamber. When San Paolo was suppressed by the Emperor Joseph II, the last abbess took the enamel away with her and gave it before her death to a friend who in turn presented it as a souvenir to the Abbate d'Ayala.

The technique of painted enamel at once excludes Mantegna's authorship, but its use together with that of gold filigree suggests a Venetian work, perhaps after Mantegna. D'Arco (ii, p.171) and Crowe & Cavalcaselle (1871, ii, p.417) also list it as a painting by Mantegna.

180. The Entombment
Brescia, Pinacoteca Tosio-Martinengo
Pen 13 × 9.5cm.   Plate 210

Like Cat.nos.176–9, disputed between Mantegna and Bellini. Assigned to Bellini by Morelli (1890, p.355), Hadeln (in *B.M.*, lxi, 1932, p.230) and Fiocco (in *L'Arte*, n.s. iv, 1933, p.192). Reattributed to Mantegna by Longhi (1927, p.137), Clark (in *B.M.*, lxi, 1930, p.187, later retracted), Tietze-Conrat (1955, p.203) and Wilde (in *Seilern Catalogue: Corrigenda and Addenda*, 1971, p.45). Hadeln and Wilde draw attention to the iconographical originality of the drawing: the two Maries hold the shroud, while the body is supported by two men inside the tomb. Wilde, who dates it shortly after 1464, accepts Clark's view that it is a 'first idea' for the central group of Mantegna's engraving of this subject (see Cat.no.205), so disregarding the complex relationship between Mantegna's designs and the engravings by or after him.

181. Virgin and Child
Hamburg, Kunsthalle, No.21263
Silverpoint, heightened with white, on grey-green paper 28.2 × 9.8cm.   Plate 212

PROVENANCE: Bequest of E. Harzen, 1863.

First ascribed to Mantegna by Koopmann (in *J.P.K.*, xii, 1891, p.41). Published by Pauli (Prestel-Gesellschaft XIII: *Zeichnungen alter Meister in der Kunsthalle zu Hamburg: Italiener*, 1927, No.1) as an autograph study for the Virgin and Child in the Uffizi *Circumcision* (Cat.no.15). The ascription is rejected by Fiocco (1937, p.85) and Tietze-Conrat (1955, p.205) as a *simile* drawing like the closely related drawing in the Fogg (Cat.no.182), but their arguments are ably refuted by Mezzetti (1961, p.166). Also accepted as autograph by Popham (1930, no.153) and Clark (1931, No.755). Clearly, like the Fogg study, a highly finished preparatory *modello*.

182. Seven Apostles watching the Ascension.
Inscribed (lower right) *Mantegna* in an eighteenth-century hand.
Cambridge, Mass., Fogg Museum of Art, 1926.42.1
Brush (faded) heightened with white, on grey-green paper 29 × 21.8cm. Plate 213

PROVENANCE: Erizzo-Moscardo Coll.?; Luigi Grassi; gift of Mrs Jesse J. Strauss to Fogg Museum.

Identified by Mongan & Sachs (1940, pp.18–19, No.25) as an autograph study for the Uffizi painting of this subject (Cat.no.16), an attribution first tentatively advanced by Popham (in *O.M.D.*, vi, 1932, p.62) on the basis of a photograph. Rejected by Fiocco (1937, p.85) and emphatically by Tietze-Conrat (1955, p.203), who points out that it corresponds exactly with the picture and claims that it is a *simile* drawing, that is, made in the workshop as a record of the composition for further use. The relationship between the Hamburg *Virgin* (Cat.no.181) and the present drawing, first recognized by Popham, was for her a supporting proof of this view, since she believed the Uffizi *Circumcision*, whose Virgin is the subject of the Hamburg drawing, to be later in date than the *Ascension*. This argument loses its substance if it is accepted that these two pictures are from the Cappella di San Giorgio. Mezzetti (1961, p.166) argues convincingly that this and comparable drawings by Mantegna should not be regarded as first thoughts, set down in summary incisive lines, but as monochrome *modelli* immediately preparatory to the finished painting. The existence of such drawings by Mantegna can in fact also be surmised from the Mantegnesque engravings which clearly reproduce others of the kind now lost, as well as from the instances (Cat.nos.191,192,221) in which both a preparatory drawing of great elaboration and an engraving survive.

183. Hercules and Antaeus
Florence, Uffizi, 1682 F
Brown wash, with white heightening: some outlining in pen: the stream executed in blue. Recently laid down on paper 26.4 × 16.4cm. Plate 211

Published by Mezzetti (1958) as an autograph drawing. She identifies it as the design for the closely similar motif of *Hercules and Antaeus* on the ceiling of the Camera Picta, but on grounds of style prefers a dating in the late Paduan period. The date *c*.1465–8 seems more plausible. The group, as observed by Mezzetti, clearly derives from an antique prototype: possibly this is a medal of Hadrian which was known to the Renaissance (repr. by Du Choul, *Discours de la religion des anciens Romains*, Lyons, ed. of 1567, p.190).

184. Five designs for a cross
1) The Pietà 2) The Pelican in her Piety 3) The Virgin mourning 4) St John the Evangelist 5) The Virgin in prayer.
Frankfurt, Städelsches Kunstinstitut
Pen and ink. Each 8.7 × 8.5cm. Plate 214

These small designs were first published by Clark (*Old Master Drawings*, iv, March 1930, pp.60–2, pl.58), who identified them correctly as designs for the 'niellated plaques on the arms of a Cross' (in fact, for the ends and centre knop). He attributed them to Mantegna, with a tentative dating *c*.1465–70, as having something in common with the San Zeno predella panels, but rather later in date. The attribution is questioned by Tietze-Conrat (1955, p.204), who thinks their minuteness of execution incompatible with Mantegna's known dislike to painting small figures (see Cat.no.73). She wrongly thinks that the designs may be intended for a book cover, but correctly assigns them a later date than Clark. A date in the 1480s seems most probable. The drawings are plainly not the work of a goldsmith, but of an artist making designs for a goldsmith (see text, p.133). The Mantegnesque character of these drawings is self-evident, not least in the figure of the Virgin, recalling in a later form the Virgin of the Ovetari *Assumption*, and the precision with which the framework is imitated and the ground is shaded seems typical of Mantegna. All in all, the compiler feels that Clark's attribution is not unjustified.

185. A man lying on a slab of stone
London, British Museum, 1860-16-63 (Popham & Pouncey, 1950, p.94, No.155)
Pen and brown ink over traces of black chalk, 16.3 × 14cm. (with strips at top and bottom, 20.3mm. high) Plate 215

PROVENANCE: Coll. William Young Ottley; Sir Thomas Lawrence (L.2445); S. Woodburn (sale, Christie's, 6 June 1860, lot 545).

Engraved as by Mantegna in Ottley, *The Italian Schools of Design*, 1823, p.16. Accepted as autograph by Selvatico (1849, p.207), Morelli (1891, p.233), Thode (1897, p.115, fig.101), Kristeller (1901, pp.405,445), Berenson (1902, p.50), Cruttwell (1908, p.108), Fiocco (1937, p.81), Muchall-Viebroock (1942, p.77), Popham & Pouncey (1950, *loc. cit.*), Tietze-Conrat (1955, p.205). Accepted only hesitantly by Knapp (1910, p.li).

Identified by Thode as a study for or variant of the Brera *Dead Christ* (Plate x), a thesis rejected by Muchall-Viebroock, and by Popham & Pouncey, who point out that the man is trying to raise himself and that the pose suggests knowledge of an antique *Dying Gaul*. Given the stone slab and shroud the motif seems appropriate to a subject like Christ restoring the son of the widow of Nain to life, or more probably, the Raising of Lazarus. The anatomy of the torso is closely related to that of the Aigueperse *St Sebastian* and that of the *Dead Christ*. Probably datable to the early 1480s, a date also supported by the hair-style. Kristeller relates the technique to that of Mantegna's engravings, notably the *Bacchanal with a wine vat* (Cat.no.209).

186. Bird on a branch catching a fly
London, British Museum, 1946-7-13-7 (Popham & Pouncey, 1950, p.99, No.166)
Pen and brown ink, 12.8 × 8.8cm. (corners cut) Plate 216

PROVENANCE: J. Richardson sen. (L.2183); Sir Thomas Lawrence (L.2445); S. Woodburn (sale, Christie's, 6 June 1860, lot 552); Sir Thomas Phillips; T. Fitzroy Fenwick.

Attributed to Mantegna by Richardson (d.1745). Accepted by Fiocco (1937, p.85), Popham & Pouncey (1950, *loc. cit.*) and Tietze-Conrat (1955, p.205). A pendant to Cat.no.187.

187. Eagle perched on a branch
London, British Museum
Pen and brown ink, 10.4 × 11.5cm.   Plate 217

PROVENANCE: J. Richardson sen.; A. Dyce; J.C. Robinson; Hon. A.E. Gathorne-Hardy (*Catalogue of Drawings*, 1902, No.37). Sold Gathorne-Hardy sale (Sotheby's, 28 April 1976, lot 7).

A pendant to Cat.no.186, also from the Richardson coll. The old ascription to Mantegna, reproposed by Ricketts (*Vasari Society*, iii, 1907–8, No.6), is accepted by Popham (*O.M.D.*, vii, 1932–3, pp.40–1), Fiocco (1937, p.85), Tietze-Conrat (1955, p.204) and Mezzetti (1958, pp.240,241–2, n.15; and in Paccagnini, 1961, p.165). An antique origin for the motifs of the Gathorne-Hardy drawing was suggested by Ricketts; Mezzetti points out that they derive from a Roman imperial relief of a type represented in the Uffizi (Manouelli, *Galleria degli Uffizi: le sculture*, i, 1958, No.1, probably discovered in 1568). She notes that the motifs recur on the main doorway of Sant' Andrea in Mantua, executed in the late fifteenth century (*c.*1488?) by the Mantuan sculptors Antonio and Paolo Mola; and concludes that the drawings are sketches made for a scheme of sculptural decoration. The differences between these two drawings and the others generally accepted as by Mantegna lead her to propose an early date for them, contemporary with the Ovetari frescoes. This seems unacceptable, if only because the drawings seem to have been made for some work of decorative art, and a dating to the Mantuan period is therefore more plausible.

188. Judith.
Signed and dated in a marginal inscription whose letters are alternately vertical and horizontal: ANDREAS MANTINIA MCCCCLXXXXI: FEBR (a number giving the day may be missing between the year and month)
Florence, Uffizi, Gabinetto dei Disegni, No.404 E (A. Forlani Tempesti & A.M. Petrioli Tofani, *I grandi disegni italiani degli Uffizi*, 1974, cat.no.18)
Pen, brown wash, with some heightening in white. Paper much yellowed. 38.8 × 25.8cm.   Fig. 15

PROVENANCE: Recorded in Florence, MS Inventario, ii, 1793, n.14.

Accepted as autograph by Selvatico (1849, p.174, n.1), Morelli (1891, p.233), Thode (1897, pp.99–100), Kristeller (1901, p.375), Berenson (1902, pp.50,56–7), Knapp (1910, pp.xliii, lii), Fiocco (1937, p.81) and Tietze-Conrat (1955, p.204).

This drawing, which was in the Uffizi by the later eighteenth century (cf. also Selvatico, *loc. cit.*), is generally identified with a drawing owned by Vasari (1568, p.491): '*Nel nostro libro è in vn mezzo foglio reale vn disegno di mano d'Andrea finito di chiaro scuro, nel quale è vna Iudith, che mette nella tasca d'una sua schiaua Mora la testa d'Oloferne, fatto d'un chiaro scuro non piu usato, hauendo egli lasciato il foglio biancho, che serue per il lume della biacca tanto nettamente,*

che vi si veggiono i capegli sfilati, e l'altre sottigliezze, non meno che se fussero stati con molta diligenza fatti dal pennello. Onde si puo in vn certo modo chiamar questo piu tosto opera colorita, che carta disegnata.' The dimensions correspond to the dimensions of Vasari's drawing, but not the technique. Berenson (1902) evaded the difficulty by claiming the white heightening as a late addition. Tietze-Conrat rightly rejects this explanation, and notes that the drawing (now mounted on card) lacks the characteristic mount usually found on drawings from Vasari's *Libro*. This exceptional drawing is an early example of a presentation drawing intended as a finished work in itself.

189. Battle of the Sea-Gods
Chatsworth, Duke of Devonshire Coll., No.897
Pen and ink, 26 × 38.2cm.   Plate 219

PROVENANCE: Coll. of N.A. Flinck (1646–1723); W. Cavendish, 2nd Duke of Devonshire.

Until recently this drawing was generally accepted as a finished drawing for the left half of Mantegna's engraving of this subject (see Cat.no.210). In favour of this view are Kristeller (1901, p.404), Berenson (1901, pp.253–4), Fiocco (1937, p.81), Muchall-Viebroock (1942, pp.76–7), Hind (1948, p.15) and Tietze-Conrat (1955, p.204). Knapp (1910, pp.liii,xlix) was the first to classify it as a copy, and his view has recently been re-argued by Mezzetti (1958, p.240; 1961, p.170), who considers it a close copy of the engraving by an artist, perhaps of Venetian origin, of the circle of Mantegna. The composition is datable before 1494.

190. Virgin and Child with a seated angel
London, British Museum, 1858-7-24-3 (Popham & Pouncey, 1950, p.99, No.159)
Pen and light brown ink, 19.7 × 14cm.   Plate 218

PROVENANCE: Count Nils Barck (L.1959); Tiffin.

Accepted as autograph by Morelli (1891, p.233), Kristeller (1901, pp.404–5, 444), Berenson (1902, pp.52–4), Knapp (1910, pp.xlv, liii), Fiocco (1937, p.81), Muchall-Viebroock (1942, pp.75–6), Popham & Pouncey (1950, *loc. cit.*), Tietze-Conrat (1955, p.205) and Mezzetti (1958, pp.240, 241, n.12).

Clearly a study for an altarpiece. There is no agreement about its date. For Kristeller, contemporary with the Camera Picta; for Muchall-Viebroock an early work; for Berenson, Mantegna's earliest surviving drawing dating from his middle period, an opinion shared by Tietze-Conrat, who reacts against the dating close to the *Madonna della Vittoria* proposed by Knapp, Fiocco, Popham & Pouncey, and Mezzetti. The Virgin's robe, with its sleeves slashed underneath, and the angel's sleeve, held by double armlets, are details of costume that favour a dating in the 1490s (cf. the Dresden *Madonna* and the Cincinnati *Sybil and Prophet*) and the type of the child also supports a late dating. Possibly a rejected design for the *Madonna della Vittoria*, given the attitude of the Child.

191. A dancing Muse
Munich, Staatliche Graphische Sammlung, No.3066
Pen and brown wash, heightened with white (the contours partly pricked for a *spolvero* transfer)

Mounted at a later date on a sheet of paper: the remounting has produced a distortion of twenty degrees in the figure. 52 × 29cm. (irregularly cut)   Plate 220

PROVENANCE: Mannheimer Sammlung (in the Electoral Cabinet by 1780).

A study for the similar figure in the *Parnassus*. Dismissed as a workshop copy by Morelli (1880, p.103) and Kristeller (1901, p.443), it was vindicated as an autograph original by Berenson (1901, p.253), Popham (1931, no.155) and Clark (in *B.M.*, lvi, 1950, p.187), but was again demoted to the rank of copy by Fiocco (1937, p.85) and Tietze-Conrat (1955, p.207). It was reclaimed as autograph by Degenhart (1958, p.23), who points out that it is the same size as the figure in the painting, and identifies it as a *spolvero* drawing (one whose outlines were traced on a drawing for transfer by forcing white powder through holes pricked in the contours of the original sketch and subsequently used for transferring the motif to the picture by the same process). Accepted as autograph by Möhle (1959, p.169) and Mezzetti (1961, p.167). See also Cat. no.192.

192. A dancing Muse

Berlin, Kupferstichkabinett, No.5058
Pen and wash, heightened with white. The paper enlarged on all four sides and the hands and feet completed by another hand. Retouched in lower part. 45.7 × 31.1cm.
                                                                          Plate 221

PROVENANCE: A. von Beckerath Coll., Berlin.

For Kristeller (1901, p.443) a copy. The dimensions correspond to those of the corresponding Muse in the *Parnassus*, and Degenhart (1958, p.24) identifies this drawing as a *spolvero* like the Munich drawing of another Muse in the same picture (Cat. no.191; Plate 220). He assumes that both were made from a full-sized sketch of the entire composition and then worked up for eventual transfer to the picture. Accepted by Möhle (1959, p.169) and Mezzetti (1961, p.168).

193. Allegory of Ignorance. Inscribed VIRTVS COMBVSTA below the burning laurel in the bottom right corner, across the join, and AM in monogram in the bottom left corner, entirely on the attached strip.

London, British Museum, Pp.1–23 (Popham & Pouncey, 1950, pp.95–7, No.157)
Pen and ink and point of brush on a brown ground, heightened with white: the background black over red. The blind woman and one of the sphinxes shaded with red; the rubies in the crown of Ignorance, the fire on the right and the blindfold woman's scarf coloured red. The satyr and blindfold man unfinished. 28.7 × 44.3cm. (including a strip of some 13mm. added or reattached to the lower edge).   Plate 222

PROVENANCE: Förster (see below) plausibly identifies this drawing as part of a drawing by Mantegna described in 1549 by Michel Angelo Biondo (*Della nobilissima pittura*, Venice, 1549, p.18: 'disopra una carta dipinse Mercurio con Madonna Ignorantia sopra una tella, il quale parea che strascinasse la detta Ignorantia di sotto con gran copia di altri ignoranti di varie scientie ed arti.' Venice, Casa

Giovanelli (in later eighteenth century, cf. Selvatico, 1849, pp.206–7); bt. from Giovanelli coll. by John Strange (d.1799), British Resident in Venice 1773–88: Strange sale, Christie's, 24 March 1800, lot 105; coll. of C. T. Metz (by whom engraved in 1798): Metz sale (T. Philips, 6 May 1801, lot 92); Payne Knight Bequest, 1824.

The traditional ascription to Mantegna is accepted by Waagen (i, 1854, p.227), Thode (1897, p.106), Kristeller (1901, pp.374–5, 444), Berenson (1902, pp.50, 60–1), Knapp (1910, p.xliv), Fiocco (1937, p.80), Muchall-Viebroock (1942, pp.77–8), Popham & Pouncey (1950, *loc. cit.*) and Tietze-Conrat (1955, pp.205–6). There is general agreement that this is a late work, of *c.*1490–1506.

The composition was engraved with a lower half (see Cat. no.220) representing a pit or dungeon heaped pell-mell with the bodies of those who have tumbled into it. On the right a man struggles up, extending both hands to Mercury, who grasps his right hand to pull him out. On the left is the figure of a nymph, partly metamorphosed into a laurel-tree, with a *cartello* inscribed VIRTVS DESERTA attached to the trunk. Around the tree are piled fragments of columns and slabs, one inscribed VIRTVTI/S.A.I.

Explanations of the iconography are attempted by Förster (in *J.P.K.*, xxii, 1901, pp.78–87, fundamental), Popham & Pouncey (1950, *loc. cit.*), D. & E. Panofsky (*Pandora's Box*, 1956, pp.44–8), Battisti (1965, pp.33–6) and Dwyer (in *Marsyas*, xv, 1970–1, pp.58–62).

MOTIFS AND SOURCES: *Upper scene.* The fat crowned woman seated on a globe also appears in *Pallas expelling the Vices* and in *The Calumny of Apelles* where she is labelled *Ignorantia*. Since she holds a rudder, an attribute of Fortune, to whom the attribute of a ball also belongs, Förster concluded that she represents *Fortuna-Ignorantia*, in other words Ignorance in the guise of Fortune. The figure should perhaps be explained in a rather different fashion. That Ignorance is represented as Fortune crowned and enthroned on the globe signifies that she is its queen, and an arbitrary and capricious one. Förster rightly explains the sphinxes, which recall the sphinx-shaped arms of antique thrones, as emblems of Ignorance. As classical sources he cites the *Tabula Cebetis* (c.7,8, Fortune, a woman mad and blind, seated on a round stone, signifying her inconstancy) and Dio Chrysostom (X, *De servis*, 32; Loeb. ed., pp.441–2), and for a Renaissance parallel an emblem of Alciati (ed. of Lyons, 1551, p.202) in which the candid virginal face, feathers and lion's paws of the sphinx are the disguise assumed by Ignorance, since some owe their ignorance to their frivolity, some to the lure of pleasure and some to pride of heart. The two attendants of *Ignorantia* are identified by Förster as *Adulatio* (wrongly, for Lust), a young woman holding two torches and blindfold, and *Avaritia*, the old woman with a leathern bag. Two other leather bags lie in front of the globe: on the right a fire consumes a laurel, the tree of Apollo and therefore of *Virtù* (virtuous knowledge, hence the inscription VIRTVS COMBVSTA). *Lower scene.* Mercury is the god of the arts, of ingenuity, and of eloquence: he is rightly explained by Förster as a symbol of the cultivation of our faculties in virtuous exercises. Virtue, by which Mantegna means both virtue in the moral and *virtù* in the Renaissance sense, is represented as Daphne half-changed into a laurel-tree, at once the tree of Apollo and, as Daphne, a symbol of chastity. The broken stones or columns among which she grows deserted are probably intended to suggest a shrine or temple to Virtue, fallen through neglect. The inscription on one of them is interpreted by Förster as VIRTVTI . SEMPER . ADVERSATVR . IGNORANTIA, a proverbial phrase twice used by Mantegna in letters of 31 January 1489 (D'Arco, ii, p.20) and 28 November 1491 (Braghirolli, p.204) to the Marchese Francesco Gonzaga.

MEANING: The general meaning of the allegory is that Ignorance, attended by her handmaids, Lust and Avarice, rules the world contemptuously and destroys the virtuous arts (*virtù*). The upper scene is an allegorical illustration of her rule, and shows the consequences of it. A blind, naked girl raises her right arm to retain her poise, encouraged by a young man with ass's ears to take a step that will inevitably lead her to fall into the pit below. It is difficult to be certain whether the young man is a seducer, satirically represented, or an allegorical figure. The ass's ears are most probably an emblem of folly, or there may be some allusion to Midas or to Ptolemy as depicted in the *Calumny of Apelles*, or to the ears of a satyr. The loathsome demon satyr is a personification of sexual lust: his bagpipe deafens her ears to any warning. Thus chastity is overthrown through wilful blindness and folly. Behind is a male figure, blindfold within a hood, with a stick and a guide-dog. Förster aptly cites the famous Gospel verse, *Numquid potest caecus caecum ducere? Nonne ambo in foveam cadunt?* (Luke 6:39, 'Can the blind lead the blind? Shall they not both fall into the pit?').

The lower scene shows the plight of the ignorant, who lie tumbled in a helpless heap in the pit of a dungeon whose door is tightly barred against them. Virtue, aptly represented by a symbol figuring both chastity and *virtù*, stands neglected, in her fallen shrine. Only one of the ignorant strives to escape from the pit, assisted by Mercury, that is, with the aid of the good and ingenious arts. Popham & Pouncey point out that the substitution of laurel leaves for wings on Mercury's feet emphasizes the association of virtue and the arts. Förster suggests as the inspiration of the allegory a passage in Galen's treatise of exhortation to study the arts (*Protreptikos*, c.iii, ff.) in which Mercury is said to have been represented combating Fortune in many ancient pictures and statues.

The allegorical theme is so closely allied to the theme of the Studiolo that it is tempting to wonder if this is not a composition originally designed for it and later abandoned (or perhaps represented in one of the unidentified pictures listed in the 1542 inventory of the Studiolo). Yet against this view is the repetition of motifs from *Pallas expelling the Vices*: their presence suggests that it is perhaps rather a variation executed on the theme.

The figure of *Ignorantia*, with rudder but without globe, is copied in a painting by Leonbruno (now in the Brera) which also copies motifs from *Pallas expelling the Vices* and incorporates them into a composition inspired by the *Calumny of Apelles* to illustrate Fortune's capricious rule of the world (for this see Gamba, in *Rass. d'A.*, vi, 1906, pp.92–3).

194. A man seated between two female figures

London, British Museum, 1861-8-10-2 (Popham & Pouncey, 1950, pp.94–5, No.156)

Pen and brown ink and brown wash, with touches of white heightening. The man shaded in brick-pink: the woman to right in blue. Right arm and bow of the woman to left executed on a separate piece of paper, carefully attached. Watermark of a cockatrice (like Briquet, No.2653): a fragment of the same watermark on the attached piece. 36.4 × 31.7cm. Plate 223

CONDITION: Small areas made up near right edge.

PROVENANCE: John Strange coll. (probably his sale, part of the same lot as Cat.no.193, which was sold as one of two drawings by Mantegna); C.M. Metz, by whom engraved; his sale (T. Philips, 6 May 1801, lot 91, with provenance from Strange coll.); J. Heywood Hawkins: Colnaghi.

The traditional ascription to Mantegna is accepted by Morelli (1891, p.233), Thode (1897, p.106), Kristeller (1901, pp.374, 444), Berenson (1902, pp.50, 59–60), Cruttwell (1908, p.106), Knapp (1910, p.xlvii), Fiocco (1937, p.80), Muchall-Viebroock (1942, p.78), Popham & Pouncey (1950, *loc. cit.*), Tietze-Conrat (1955, p.206).

Universally regarded as a late work. Berenson and Popham & Pouncey relate it to the *Parnassus* of 1497, and regard it as close in handling to the *Judith* of 1491: Berenson prefers a date shortly before, Tietze-Conrat one contemporary with the Studiolo paintings. The type of the male figure, thin-shanked with strong torso, is also found in the Baptist of the London National Gallery altarpiece (Plate 122). A date in the early 1490s is plausible: a similar composition, of Mars enthroned between Neptune and Ceres, decorates Caesar's triumphal car in the last canvas of the *Triumphs* (Plate 118).

The figures were identified as 'perhaps the Judgment of Hercules' in the Philips sale cat., as Mars, Diana and another goddess by Thode, and as Mars, Diana and Venus by Kristeller. Popham & Pouncey also identify the man as Mars, though rightly noting the sceptre as an unusual attribute, and the woman on the left as Diana. They are doubtful about the identification of the woman on the right as Venus, and suggest that if the curving object above her left shoulder is a rainbow, she may be Iris, in spite of the absence of wings. Tietze-Conrat considers the subject allegorical rather than mythological. Given the sceptre, Mars seems a dubious identification.

The figure on the left is adapted in a drawing in Mantegnesque style inscribed IFT (in a later hand?) in the V. & A. Museum (Dyce 148, 28 × 21.6cm.; Ward-Jackson, *Italian Drawings*, i, 1979, pp.18–20, no.12 repr.), where two Cupids are added and the figure is identified in an inscription as Venus. The male figure is copied in a picture by Leonbruno formerly in the Rey-Spitzer coll. (repr. *Rass. d'A.*, vi, 1906, p.91). For this composition see Cat.no.175, where he holds a lance and is certainly Mars.

195. The Calumny of Apelles

London, British Museum, 1860-6-16-85 (Popham & Pouncey, 1950, pp.97–9, No.159)

Pen and three shades of brown, with occasional touches

of white. Watermark apparently a crown (Popham & Pouncey compare Briquet, No.4744). 20.7 × 38cm.

Plate 224

PROVENANCE: Copied by Rembrandt (copy also in B.M.); coll. S. Van der Schelling, Amsterdam; brought with Rembrandt copy to England *c.*1718; coll. J. Barnard, London (sale, Greenwood, 16 February 1787, lot 88, bt. West); coll. Sir Thomas Lawrence (L.2445); coll. W. Esdaile; coll. S. Woodburn (sale, Christie's, 7 June 1860, lot 763). For full provenance see Popham & Pouncey, *loc. cit.*

The youthful Ptolemy, with ass's ears, is seated left, attended right by a slender woman, labelled *Sospicione*, and left by a stout crowned woman, labelled *Ignorantia*. He extends his hand to a man, labelled *ĩvidia*, who leads forward a crowned woman, holding a lighted torch in her right hand and with her left dragging along a young girl whose hands are upraised in prayer. She is labelled *Calumnia/d'apelle*: the girl is labelled *Inocentia*. Attending her are two young women, labelled *deceptione* and *insidia*. Behind an old woman, labelled *penitentia*, turns with clasped hands to the upward pointing figure of *Verita*.

Possibly a drawing for an engraving. Engraved by Girolamo Mocetto (B. xiii, p.113,10) with an added background of the Campo di San Zanipolo. Accepted as autograph by Förster (in *J.P.K.*, viii, 1887, pp.46–8), Morelli (1891, p.233), Muchall-Viebroock (1942, p.76), Popham & Pouncey (1950, *loc. cit.*, as *c.*1504–6), Tietze-Conrat (1955, p.206). The attribution to a pupil, proposed by Kristeller (1901, p.461), is accepted by Berenson (1902, p.50, by exclusion) and Fiocco (1937, p.85). Mezzetti (1958) also expresses doubt. Clearly a late work, of *c.*1495–1506, closest to *Pallas expelling the Vices*, but perhaps a little later.

The sources and iconography are carefully studied by Förster (*loc. cit.*) and Popham & Pouncey (*loc. cit.*). The subject (for which see also Giglioli, in *Rass. d'A.*, xx, 1920, pp.173–82) derives from a famous description of the Calumny of Apelles in Lucian's *De Calumnia*, a dialogue which was rendered into Latin and Italian several times during the fifteenth century. The passage concerning Apelles' picture was also rendered in Latin and Italian by Alberti in his *De Pictura*. In Lucian the king sits on the right: Mantegna has reversed the scene, but this also occurs in other treatments of the subject (for this see Förster). He has also named *deceptione* the figure who is usually named *fraude*, and has labelled the victim *Inocentia*, a name not found in any of the known Latin or Italian versions of Lucian. Too much significance should not be attached to these variations. Popham & Pouncey wrongly identify the figure of *invidia* as a woman: his costume and hairstyle are those of a man, as demanded by the text. His ears are not ass's ears, as they also claim, but fox or vulpine ears. See also Cat.no.193.

Lost Drawings

196. Drawing of the Gonzaga arms

On 7 August 1460 Zaccaria Saggio wrote from Mantua to Marchese Lodovico to say among other things that he has sent 'the arms executed by Andrea Mantegna' (*quel arma fata per Andrea Mantegna*). Published by Kristeller (1902, p.521, doc.22). It seems probable that this was a drawing of the Gonzaga arms made for use on tapestry or some other decorative object. Compare the documents referring to payments made in 1420 by Giovanni Francesco Gonzaga to the painter Giovanni Corradi for six sheets of parchment painted with the Gonzaga arms and foliage which were intended for the tapestry weaver Niccolò da Francia (Braghirolli, in *Atti e memorie della R. Accademia Virgiliana di Mantova*, 1879–80, pp.10–11).

197. Design for a tapestry or tapestries

On 5 December 1465, Galbridio, a member of the Marchese Lodovico's household, reminded him to send his *tapezziere* Maffeo and Giovanni de Strigii to buy the silk for the *apparamento* designed by Andrea Mantegna (Ve aricordo de mandare Mafii tapeciro chomo Johan de Strigii a Venesia per comperare la sida per quelo apparamento che Andreia Mantegna a fato el designo). Published by Braghirolli, 'Sulle manifatture di arazzi in Mantova' in *Atti e memorie della R. Accademia Virgiliana di Mantova*, 1879–80, p.19; Kristeller, 1902, p.524, doc.35). *Apparamento* could refer to a single tapestry, but is more likely to refer to a set of tapestries or bed-hangings.

Tapestries after designs by Mantegna belonging to the Gonzaga are mentioned as celebrated in a letter of 27 December 1519 by Marc' Antonio Michiel, describing the Pope's exhibition in Rome of seven of the eight Raphael tapestries for St Peter's: 'che furono giudicati la più bella cosa, che sia stata fatta in eo genere a nostri giorni, benche fussino celebri li razzi di Papa Giulio de l'anticamera, li razzi del Marchese di Mantova del disegno del Mantegna.' Michiel's words seem to refer to tapestries executed after designs made late in Mantegna's career, rather than to these early tapestries. See also Cat.no.198.

198. Design for tapestry of Indian birds

On 11 July 1469 Marchese Lodovico wrote from Goito to Mantegna asking him to make drawings of an Indian cock and hen from those in the palace garden at Mantua. He was to send the drawings to Goito, since the Marchese wished them to be included in one of his tapestries. (*Dilecte noster. Nui voressemo, che vedestive ad ogni modo de ritrarne due galine de India del naturale uno maschio et una femina et mandarle qua retracte, per che le voressimo per metter suxo la tapezzeria nostra: potereti veder le nostre che sono ne lo zardino li a Mantua. Godii xi Julii 1469.* Printed by Baschet, 1866, p.333; Kristeller, 1902, p.526, doc.42.) See text, p.103.

For a Gonzaga tapestry of the Annunciation, apparently after a design by Mantegna, now in the Art Institute, Chicago (Ryerson Coll.) see text p.133 and Plate 225.

199. Designs for plate for Marchese Federico

On 12 February 1483 Lancilotto degli Andreasi wrote from Mantua to the Marchese Federico saying that he had concluded a bargain with the goldsmith Giovanni Francesco Cavalli concerning new pieces of plate to be made from certain old pots (*ole*) and also concerning the jugs (*bocali*) designed by Andrea Mantegna. A second letter of 17 February 1483 asks for instructions as to the shape of the vessels that are to be made, namely whether they should be in the form of the old pots or in the form designed by Andrea Mantegna. If they are to be made according to Mantegna's design, Lancilotto would like to know if they are to be of greater or less weight than the old pots. Cavalli has bound himself not to charge for the fashion if his work does not please the Marchese, and a certain Tommaso has given a promise on his behalf that the work will be well done. In addition Lancilotto sends the design Mantegna has made of the flask so that the Marchese can judge of its shape before the work is begun (Kristeller, 1902, p.541, docs.84,85).

200. Fame

An inventory of the drawings of Alfonso d'Este, later Duke of Modena (1591–1644), taken in the second decade of the seventeenth century lists: 'La Fama di penna d'And.ª Mantegna.' Alfonso's drawings were bequeathed by him in 1629 to his son Obizzo, later Bishop of Modena (Campori, 1870, p.56). A drawing of the same subject was in the Canonici coll. (see Cat.no.201).

201. Fame

A drawing of this subject attributed to Mantegna was in the Canonici coll. in 1632 (see Cat.no.113): 'La fama di Andrea Mantegna' (Campori, 1870, p.126).

202. Three drawings

Listed *c.*1640 in the Coccapani coll. (see Cat.nos.199, 120), with no indication of subject: 'Tre disegni d'Andrea Mantegna di poco valore. D.i.' (Campori, 1870, p.159).

203. Christ in Limbo

Ridolfi (1648, p.72) records as in the collection of Padre Anselmo Oliva of Brescia, an Inquisitor in Venice, 'Vn gentilissimo disegno à chiaro scuro di Christo, che libera i Santi Padri dal Limbo'. Usually identified as the drawing (Plate 226), now in the Staatliche Museen, Berlin, which is generally regarded as a fine copy of the Christ in the *Descent into Limbo* now in a private collection (see Cat.no.34).

204. A drawing

What was possibly a drawing by Mantegna, subject unspecified, is listed in 1662 in the collection of the Muselli family of Verona, as in a *camerino* of the palace. The Muselli drawings were sold in the first half of the eighteenth century to Crozat (Campori, 1870, p.192: 'uno [disegno] del Mantegna'). See Cat.no.127.

Engravings by Mantegna

For the documentation of the engravings of Mantegna and a study of this subject see text, Chapter XV.

From the earlier lists of engravings assembled by Bartsch (*Peintre-Graveur*, xiii, 1811, pp.222–43) and Passavant (*Peintre-Graveur*, v, 1864, pp.73–9), Kristeller (1901, pp.384–7) chose only seven which he was prepared to accept as engravings designed and executed by Mantegna himself. His classification is generally received and corresponds, with only one exception, to the list given by Vasari. That Mantegna executed engravings with his own hand was challenged by Tietze-Conrat in 1943 (*G.B.A.*, ser.6, xiv, pp.375–81; 1955, pp.241–2): her arguments have not won acceptance, but her case that the engravings attributed to his own hand are works executed by professional engravers working in his shop and under his close supervision has not been answered.

As always for early Italian engravings, it is essential to consult the entries and discussions concerning Mantegna's œuvre and that of his followers and copyists in A.M. Hind, *Early Italian Engraving*, 1938–48, ii, 1948, *Known masters other than Florentine monogrammists and anonymous,* cited as Hind below. The best recent general discussion of Mantegna's engravings is in J.A. Levenson, K. Oberhuber, J.L. Sheehan, *Early Italian Engravings from the National Gallery of Art*, exh.cat., National Gallery of Art, Washington, 1973, pp.165–232. See also D. Alston, C. Bowman, D. Landau, *Prints by Mantegna and his school*, Christ Church Picture Gallery, Oxford, 1979.

205. The Entombment

Inscribed on the front of the tomb: HVMANI/GENERIS/REDEMPTO/RI.

B. xiii, 229, 3. *c*.33.2 × 46.8cm.

1st state Plate 227a; 4th state Plate 227b

Dated by Kristeller (1901, pp.399–400) among Mantegna's very late works. Hind (1948, pp.6,10–12, No.2) by contrast dates the design *c*.1450–9, contemporary with the San Zeno altarpiece, though the actual plate may have been engraved later, perhaps as late as the 1490s. Tietze-Conrat (1955, p.242) also dates the engraving to the 1490s, but regards the design as only a few years earlier, contemporary with the *Triumphs*. Mezzetti (1961, p.195, No.143) claims that the first design seems to date from before 1478, since the group of three holy women is copied in a drawing which has been attributed to Marco Zoppo, who died in that year (Popham & Pouncey, 1950, p.164, No.263). The engraving itself she considers a late work. Levenson–Oberhuber–Sheehan (1973, pp.170–5, No.70) relate the style to the pictures associable with the Cappella di San Giorgio (Cat.nos.13–18) and date it to the 1460s. The borrowings that have been cited in the *Pietà* by Agostino dei Fonduli of Padua in San Satiro, Milan (contracted for in 1483: gesture with which woman holds head of the Virgin) and in a *Deposition* in S. Maria del Castello, Viadana (gesture of upflung hands) attributed to the same sculptor (for whom see M. Bandirali, in *Arte Lombarda*, iii, 1958, pp.29–44) are adduced to support a dating in the early 1480s for some features, but it should be noted that the St John has a close parallel in the *Crucifixion* of the San Zeno predella. Since the Entombment is a subject Mantegna must have been called on to design several times, it is a fair question whether the composition of the engraving is not simply a late version of the theme incorporating inventions from earlier designs. The argument advanced by Levenson–Oberhuber–Sheehan, that the tonal technique used in it must antedate such stronger, more boldly plastic engravings as the *Bacchanals* and the *Battle of the Sea-Gods*, can therefore only affect its dating relative to those other engravings. A date *c*.1488–90 seems most plausible. The dramatic aggressiveness, mannered drapery and the classicism of the composition differ from the statuesque emotion and comparative realism of Mantegna's earlier style and are more easily associable with Mantegna's late works. We may note too that the form of the rock of the sepulchre is close to that of the *Madonna delle Cave* in Florence (*c*.1490) while the type of Christ is close to the Copenhagen *Pietà* of the mid-1490s. Again the representation of the summit of the rock as cut-off is a device found only in the 1490s, in the *Madonna delle Cave*, while the landscape recalls that of the Copenhagen *Pietà*.

Levenson–Oberhuber–Sheehan note that the inclusion of the Entombment and the group of the fainting Virgin

in a single composition is an iconography of Florentine origin. The engraving was copied in reverse by a more or less contemporary engraver (Bartsch, xiii, 296, a: Hind, 2a), possibly Zoan Andrea. The vertiginous perspective of the landscape background, falling away from the hillside, not as is usual rising behind it, has not received its due, nor the dramatic chiaroscuro.

206. The Risen Christ between St Andrew and St Longinus

B. xxiii, 231, 6. 39.2 × 32.5cm.   Plates 228a and b

Dated by Kristeller (1901, pp.399–402) in the later 1490s, after the four mythological prints. For Hind (1948, pp.6,16–17, No.7) *c*.1500; Tietze-Conrat (1955, p.242) as from the early 1490s; Mezzetti (1961, p.199, No.148) as executed after 1488 because of the presumed relationship with the frescoes now detached from the façade of Sant' Andrea (see Cat.no.61), and probably during the 1490s. A date in the late 1480s or 1490s is supported by the thin shanks and strong torso of the figures, a characteristic of Mantegna's late works (compare e.g. Plate 122). Levenson–Oberhuber–Sheehan (1973, pp.178–9, No.72) argue unconvincingly for a date *c*.1472, relating the engraving to the inception of Sant' Andrea (see below).

The specifically Mantuan iconography of the image has always been recognized. St Andrew and St Longinus were the patrons of Mantua, and an association between the engraving and the church of Sant' Andrea, begun on 12 June 1472, was already postulated by Kristeller, who suggested that the original design may have been intended for a group of statues to be set on the high altar of the church. Tietze-Conrat was rightly of the opinion that it is more likely to have been a design for a fresco above a door, and Mezzetti later connected it with the *sinopia* for the recently discovered fresco of the *Ascension* in the atrium, claiming the figures of the saints probably derive from the lost figures of St Andrew and St Longinus which are known to have flanked the *Ascension*. Certainly the design is at least as likely to be linked with the completion *c*.1488 of the façade (see Cat.no.61) as with the inception of the church, with which Levenson–Oberhuber–Sheehan connect it. They also reject any relationship between the print and the fresco of the *Ascension*. See text, p.239 where it is argued that the original drawing may represent a rejected design for a fresco to decorate the façade of Sant' Andrea.

207. Virgin of Humility 1st state: without haloes. 2nd state: haloes added.

B. xiii, 232, 8. 34.5 × 26.8cm.   Fig.16

Kristeller (1901, pp.392–3) concludes that since the earlier impressions lack the haloes the engraving must be from a study of mother and child for a Madonna rather than from a finished work. He dates it *c*.1480–90, contemporary with the *Triumphs*, and considers it Mantegna's earliest engraving. Hind (1948, pp.6,10, No.1) thinks that the design dates from *c*.1450–5, even if the plate was engraved much later. Tietze-Conrat (1955, p.242) dates it *c*.1490 (see below) while Mezzetti (1961, pp.193–4, No.142) dates it *c*.1466. Levenson–Oberhuber–Sheehan (1973, p.194, No.77) class it as one of Mantegna's most mature engravings, executed during his later career. Tietze-Conrat's attempt to connect it with Mantegna's letter of 21 December 1491 (see Cat. no.212) has not met with acceptance, on the ground that the *quadretino* it mentions was not certainly a Madonna. A derivation dated 1491 in the form of an altarpiece by the Maestro LX (also attributed to Zenale) is in the Louvre. To be dated before 1491, probably in the late 1480s. From a drawing: compare the Uffizi drawing of *Judith* of 1491 (Fig.16). The motif of the *Virgin of Humility* recurs in the Poldi-Pezzoli *Virgin and Child* (Plate 98).

208. Bacchanal with Silenus

B. xiii, 240, 20. *c*.33.5 × 45.4cm.   Plate 229

Generally regarded as the left-hand section to the *Bacchanal with a wine vat* (Plate 231): Hind (1948, p.12, No.3) suggests that it was probably engraved on the same plate. It illustrates a further episode of the triumph of Bacchus in the crowning of Silenus and the rout of his drunken train. The moral intention of the pair is certainly to condemn, in elegant classical style, the vice of drunkenness and its consequences.

    Levenson–Oberhuber–Sheehan (1973, p.186, No.74) date it slightly later than the companion print, surely implausibly. Other bibliography and dating as for Cat.no.209. Copied by Dürer in 1494.

209. Bacchanal with a wine vat

B. xiii, 240, 19. *c*.33.5 × 45.4cm.   Plate 231

Generally regarded as the right-hand section of a composition of which the *Bacchanal with Silenus* (Cat. no.208) is the left-hand section: the composition is however discontinuous. Dated by Kristeller (1901, pp.393–9) as contemporary with the other three mythological engravings and therefore executed at the same time as the *Triumphs*, and before 1494, when two of the four (see Cat.nos.208,211) were copied by Dürer. Hind accepts his view (1948, pp.6,13–14, No.4), and dates it *c*.1490. Tietze-Conrat (1955, p.243) dates the invention of all four mythological prints *c*.1465–70; Mezzetti (1961, pp.196–7, Nos.144–7) accepts this dating. Levenson–Oberhuber–Sheehan (1973, pp.182–5, No.73) regard this as the earliest of the four prints and date it *c*.1475, shortly after the completion of the Camera Picta. A date in the later 1480s or early 1490s seems plausible. It must date from before 1494, when the companion print was copied by Dürer.

    The subject is the triumph of Bacchus over the senses. The antique visual sources used by Mantegna in the two *Bacchanals* are discussed by Blum (1936, pp.90–4) and Simon (1971, pp.26–32). Kristeller suggested that all four mythological engravings may derive from designs for wall-decorations in a Gonzaga country villa. Tietze-Conrat, accepting this suggestion, postulated that the gap between the two halves was calculated to allow for the interruption of a door or window. But the theory that the four designs were for frescoes is implausible, especially if it is accepted that their meaning is a moralizing one. Motifs from them were, however, later adapted for decorative friezes, both in fresco and in terracotta (cf. e.g. Kristeller, 1901, p.394n). Battisti (1965, pp.25–31) wrongly translates *Ithyphallus* in a poem by Battista Fiera as Bacchus, instead of correctly as Priapus, and misleadingly dates the engravings to the 1460s in consequence

of this mistranslation. More plausible is his claim that a passage from Calpurnius Siculus, *Eclogue* X, 39–65, may have helped to inspire Mantegna.

210. Battle of the Sea-Gods

B. xiii, 239, 18. *c*.34 × 44.5cm.   Plate 230

Left section of a composition of which Cat. no.211 is the right section.

The scraggy figure of Envy holds a tablet inscribed INVID with other markings beneath. These have been read as letters (Zani, 1802, p.140), as 1461 by Petrucci (in *Dedalo*, xi, 1930–1, pp.416–18), as XCIII (for 1493) by Hind, as a transcription into Greek or Hebrew of *Invidia* by Tietze-Conrat, as Erys (Fury) by Battisti (1965, p.31). To the right can be seen the tail of the sea-centaur in the left of the companion plate. For a related drawing see Cat. no.189; Plate 219.

211. Battle of the Sea-Gods

B. xiii, 239, 17. 33 × 44.7cm.   Plate 232

Right-hand section of Cat. no.210.

These two engravings must have been made before 1494, when the left-hand section was copied by Dürer. Kristeller (1901, pp.393–7) thought they formed part of the same series as Mantegna's other two mythological engravings and therefore dated them as contemporary with the *Triumphs*, *c*.1484–94. For Hind (1948, pp.6,15–16, Nos.5–6) *c*.1490. Tietze-Conrat (1955, pp.242–3) relates them to the *Orpheus* of the Camera Picta and dates the design to *c*.1465–70, the engraving to before 1494. Mezzetti (1961, pp.196–7) accepts this relationship and dating. Levenson–Oberhuber–Sheehan (1973, pp.188–93, Nos.75,76) rightly deny that the four mythological engravings were conceived as a series and date the *Battles* later than the *Bacchanals* as probably in the second half of the 1480s, contemporary with the *Triumphs*.

    The antique visual sources of the engravings are discussed among others by Blum (1936, pp.89–90), Eichler (in *Festschrift Karl M. Swoboda*, 1959, pp.91–5) and P. Bober (in *Essays in Memory of Karl Lehmann*, 1964, pp.43–8). P. Bober has shown convincingly that Mantegna's principal antique source was a mutilated (and now fragmentary) antique sarcophagus relief representing a marine thiasus about the chariot of Neptune, which is now built into the frieze of the garden façade of the Villa Medici, Rome. This relief, known to the Renaissance in completer form, was very popular in the quattrocento and cinquecento, and drawings of it, either from the original or copied from other drawings, were evidently common in artists' pattern-books in North and Central Italy. The popularity of the relief explains why it appears in a Paduan miniature executed in a copy of a printed edition of Petrarch, published in 1472 (Bonicatti, in *Rivista d'Arte*, xxxii, 1957, pp.143–6; Meiss, 1957, p.63), and in a miniature in a manuscript of Pliny's *Historia Naturalis* (Biblioteca Nazionale, Turin, Membr. sec. xv [1,22–3], f.54) which has been dated 1460–70 (Bovero, in *B.M.*, xcix, 1957, pp.261–5, fig.12) or shortly after 1470 (Salmi, in *Arte Veneta*, viii, 1954, pp.134–5). There is no need therefore to assume with Bovero that Mantegna's engraving derives from this miniature or that the engraving influenced the miniature as claimed by Mezzetti (1961, p.191).

The iconography of the engravings was first seriously discussed by Förster (in *J.P.K.*, xxiii, 1902, pp.205–14), who associated it with the description of the Ichthyophagi in the *Bibliotheca* of Diodorus Siculus (iii, 15–17), whose first five books were translated into Latin by Poggio Bracciolini *c.*1447–55, first printed at Bologna in 1472, and had been reprinted a number of times by 1493. The relationship is rightly denied by Tietze-Conrat. Simon (1971, pp.32–8) implausibly associates the scene with Virgil's storm in *Aeneid*, I, 82ff. The general view that the scenes illustrate strife excited by envy must however be correct: for observations on the theme of envy in Mantegna's thought see Battisti (1965, pp.33–8). See text, pp.240–1, for the visual conception of the scene as a mock-tourney.

An attempt to trace a source for the figure of Invidia in Breydenbach's *Opusculum Sanctarum peregrinationum*, published at Mainz in February 1486, is made by Vickers, 'The sources of Invidia in Mantegna's *Battle of the Sea Gods*' in *Apollo*, n.s. cvi, 1977, pp.270–3, and is unconvincing. Another article by the same author on possible sources for these engravings, the *Triumphs* and the *Bacchanals* (in *B.M.*, cxviii, 1976, pp.824–34) has been shown to rest on a misconception (cf. Martindale, 1979, p.74). Very convincing, by contrast, is his suggestion (in *G.B.A.*, ser.6, ci, 1983, pp.97–101) that the figure of Neptune is derived from the Felix Gem, now in the Ashmolean Museum, which has been shown by Brown (Vickers, *op. cit.*, pp.102–4) to have belonged to Cardinal Francesco Gonzaga.

Unidentified Engraving by Mantegna

212. A small engraving, probably a Madonna

On 7 December 1491 Silvestro Calandra wrote to the Marchese Francesco Gonzaga to tell him that he has had a ring and case fitted to the little *quadretino* by Andrea Mantegna, which the Marchese left in his care, so that it can safely be carried. In accordance with his commands, he is despatching it by courier. A letter of 21 December 1491 from Mantegna reveals that the Marchese had made a present to someone of this '*quadretino*'; he now sends

him a second, since the plates for making others still remain to him by the grace of the glorious Virgin Mary, from whom he has ever obtained more graces than he has deserved (*Jo ue ne mando un altro Rimanendomi pero le stampe da farne deli altri per Gracia di la Gloriosa Vergine Maria dalla quale sempre ho obtenuto molte più gratie chio nono meritato*). Published by Braghirolli (in *Giornale di erudizione artistica*, i, 1872, pp.204–5; Kristeller, 1902, p.551, doc.114).

Engravings after Mantegna's Designs

From the episode of Simone di Ardizone (see pp.235–8) we know that already in 1475 Mantegna was interested in employing a professional engraver to reproduce his compositions. Some twenty engravings survive that are certainly after drawings or paintings by him: indeed Hind attributes some of them to Mantegna's own hand. The following is a list of those accepted by modern scholarship as executed more or less directly after Mantegna's designs.

213. The Flagellation of Christ i) with the pavement

unfinished. The seated soldier on the left is wrongly identified as Pilate by Levenson–Oberhuber–Sheehan (1973, p.205, no.78); ii) with a landscape. The pavement is repla-

ced by a rocky ledge and a landscape background, suggesting that the composition was re-engraved with the addition of these features, probably *c.*1480–90. B. xiii, 227, 1. Hind, Nos.8 and 9. 40 × 31.1cm. (with the pavement; Plate 233); 46.7 × 36cm. (with landscape). See Cat. no.216.

214. The Descent from the Cross B. xiii, 230, 4. Hind,
10. 49.9 × 23.7cm. Plate 234. See Cat. no.216.

215. The Entombment i) with four birds; Plate 235a
ii) with three birds; Plate 235b. Levenson–Oberhuber–Sheehan (1973, p.206, No.79) regard the version with four

birds as the original engraving after Mantegna and the state with three birds as a copy. B. xiii, 228, 2. Hind, 11. 45.8 × 35cm. See Cat. no.216.

216. The Descent into Limbo B. xiii, 230, 5. Hind, 9. 44.6 × 34.7cm. Plate 236a. Probably unfinished. A related drawing is in the Ecole des Beaux-Arts, Paris (Plate 236b).

These four prints are generally assumed to form a series, engraved by a single hand at about the same date, but there must be some doubt as regards version (i) of the *Flagellation*. There is universal agreement that the designs must date from an earlier period than the engravings. The *Flagellation* is so closely linked to the Ovetari frescoes in spatial conception, in the types and in the scaling of the figures that it must date from the 1450s or early 1460s. A preparatory study for the composition is in the collection of Count Seilern (see Cat. no.179). All scholars agree, however, that this study is not for a finished drawing for the engraving, but for a painting. But it is unfortunate that the suggestion, first advanced by Wilde (in *Seilern Catalogue Addenda*, 1969, p.37) that these four engravings reproduce paintings rather than drawings by Mantegna has won general acceptance. Tietze-Conrat (1943 and 1955, pp.243–4) suggested that the *Descent from the Cross*, the *Entombment* and the *Descent into Limbo* reproduce lost compositions executed by Mantegna in the 1460s for the Cappella di San Giorgio. This is plausible for the *Descent* and the *Entombment*, which are strikingly close in style to the Uffizi *Adoration*. The *Descent into Limbo* may well be related to the picture of this subject Mantegna promised to execute for the Marchese Lodovico in 1468 (see Cat.no.70); in turn this would support the suggestion that this painting was intended for the Cappella (see text, p.87). See Cat. no.179 for the *Flagellation*.

217. The Adoration of the Magi B. xiii, 233, 9. Hind, 13. 38.8(r.) − 39(l.) × 28.3cm. Unfinished? or simply Mantegna's original faithfully reproduced? It has always been recognized that it reproduces the principal motif of the Florence *Adoration* (see Plate 50), executed in the early 1460s, probably for the Cappella di San Giorgio. Plate 237.

218. The Triumphs of Caesar For engravings after the *Triumphs* see Cat.no.28.

219. Hercules and Antaeus B. xiii, 237, 16. Hind, 17. About 34.5 × 25cm. Plate 238a. Inscribed in the alternately vertical and horizontal lettering which is an idiosyncrasy of Mantegna: DIVO HERCVLI INVICTO. Copied by Giovanni Antonio da Brescia (Plate 238b).

For designs by Mantegna on the theme of Hercules made in 1463 for Cavriana and c.1465 for the Camera Picta see Cat.nos.69 and 20. Mezzetti (1958, pp.235–6, and 1961, p.202) rightly points out that this composition differs from the Uffizi drawing of this subject (Cat.no.183, Plate 211) and suggests that the plastic solidity and statuesque poses of the figures indicate a fuller knowledge of the antique that Mantegna can only have obtained during his sojourn in Rome (1488–90). She derives the figure of Hercules from an antique group of this subject now

in Palazzo Pitti (see her article for an interesting collection of fifteenth- and early sixteenth-century versions of the theme). The style of the design as reflected in the engraving suggests a dating in the 1490s. A drawing in the British Museum is rightly identified by Popham & Pouncey (1950, p.102, No.162) as a version of Mantegna's original design rather than a copy or preliminary study. B. xiii, 202, 1. (Hind 18) is another version of the theme (Plate 238c).

220. Virtvs Combusta B. xiii, 303, 16 and 17. Hind, 22. Upper half, about 29.8 × 43.4cm. Plate 239a. Lower half, 29.9 × 43.6cm. Plate 239b. For a discussion of this print see Cat.no.193.

221. Four Muses dancing B. xiii, 305, 18. Hind, 21. 25–26 × 34–35cm. Plate 240. Based in reverse on the famous group of the Muses in the *Parnassus* (Plate XII). The variations in the poses and views of the figures indicate that the engraving is based on a preliminary study and not on the picture itself. Presumably the group was completed by a right-hand section, now lost. See Cat.nos. 191 and 192. The print is generally attributed to Zoan Andrea (Hind, 1948, p.27, No.21; Levenson–Oberhuber–Sheehan, 1973, p.228, No.85).

222. Silenus with a group of children B. xiii, 327, 17. Hind, 24. About 17.3 × 25.5cm. Plate 241. Another engraving (Hind, 1948, p.29, 24a) shows the same composition in reverse. Hind relates the composition to a school of Mantegna drawing at Chatsworth of the *Triumph of Silenus*.

223. The young prisoner Hind, 25. 20.2 × 13.2cm. Plate 242. Unique impression in Rothschild coll. There are two drawings of the same subject, one in the Rennes museum (20 × 15cm.: *Catalogue*, 1876, 28e cadre, No.1, as by Mantegna), the other in the Albertina, Vienna (18.9 × 13cm.: pen, washed in light red; pricked for transfer). The Albertina drawing is inscribed *Iulio Campagnoli apelli pinx*: a later hand has added a landscape and the inscription *sic mea vota*. The subject was engraved again c.1566–80 by Adamo Sculptor (B. xv, 428, 103) with the inscription *servus eo laetior quo patientior*; this version is closer to the Rennes drawing than to the present engraving. Hind (1948, p.30) was inclined to attribute the Rennes drawing to Mantegna himself. The subject is presumably a youth who is a prisoner under the yoke of love. The design must date from the 1490s or early 1500s.

224. Pietà (The Man of Sorrows) B. xiii, 232, 7. Hind, 26. 20.7 × 11.1cm. Plate 243. The engraving itself must date, as Hind points out, from c.1520. It reproduces with variations and omissions Mantegna's picture of this subject in Copenhagen and is probably based on his original design for it. The same drawing, according to Hind (p.63, No.4), probably served Zoan Andrea for his engraving of the composition, in which the two angels of the picture are retained. See Cat.no.35.

225. Hercules and the Hydra B. xiii, 237, 15. Hind, 27. 14.3 × 11.1cm. Plate 244. Inscribed in Mantegnesque alternately vertical and horizontal lettering DIVO HERCVLI INVICTO. Borenius (*Four early Italian engravers*, 1923, p.50) rightly relates the figure to that of Vulcan in the Parnassus: the original design presumably dates from *c.*1495–1500.

226. Hercules and the Nemean Lion B. xiii, 323, 11. Hind, 2. *c.*28.2 × 25.3cm. Inscribed in Mantegnesque alternately vertical and horizontal lettering DIVO HERCVLI INVICTO. Engraved by Giovanni Antonio da Brescia. Hind suggests that he may have used a drawing (composition in reverse to the print) in Christ Church, Oxford, which he believes to derive from a design by Mantegna.

227. Holy Family with St Elizabeth and St John B. xiii, 320, 5. Hind, p.38, No.4. 30.1 × 25.7cm. Plate 245. Leverson–Oberhuber–Sheehan (1973, p.240, No.89) suggest that this engraving, attributed by them to Giovanni Antonio da Brescia, reproduces a design by Mantegna for a picture of the Holy Family such as that in Dresden (Cat.no.44). More probably the design was for an altarpiece (compare Cat.no.32, Plate 122): it can be dated *c.*1495.

228. Judith B. xiii, 295, 1. Hind, 5. 31.7 × 22.6cm. Plate 246. Inscribed . DIVA ./. IVDIT . Signed .Z.A. (Zoan Andrea). Hind attributes the plate to Zoan Andrea, and points out that it must date from after 1497, since it is engraved over Zoan Andrea's copy of Dürer's *St Jerome* of *c.*1497 (cf. Hind, p.68, No.20). Kristeller (1901, p.375n) and Hind relate the composition to two drawings ascribed to Mantegna (one inscribed ANDREAS MANTINIA MCCCC LXXII.IV) at Chatsworth. The original design was clearly related to Cat. nos. 120 and 141 (q.v.).

229. Hercules and the Hydra B. xiii, 324, 12. Hind, 20. Plate 247. Inscribed DIVO HERCVLI INVIC / TO in Mantegnesque alternately vertical and horizontal lettering (in reverse). Signed I.F.T. A pen drawing in the British Museum (Popham & Pouncey, i, 1950, No.163) is inscribed *Mantegna*; for Hind this is an early copy of the print, for Popham & Pouncey, the engraver's drawing, and therefore by the I.F.T. who signs the print (presumably a Giovanni Francesco from some place beginning with T, e.g. Treviso). Popham & Pouncey prefer to identify the subject as a faun and a snake, as the pointed ears are those of a faun, the figure is beardless and there is no lion-skin. The figure in *Hercules and the Hydra* also has faun-like ears and no lion-skin, but is bearded. It seems that a faun was drawn in the original, but taken for Hercules by the engraver who perhaps copied the inscription from another source. Original *c.*1495.

Mantegna and Book-Illumination

Mantegna's Paduan patron Jacopo Antonio Marcello (1398–after 1461) was long known to have been in close relations with King René of Anjou, both as a supporter of the Angevin cause in Italy and as a sharer of the King's scientific and humanist tastes (for Marcello see E. Cicogna, *Della famiglia Marcello*, 1841, pp.18–19; Lecoy de la Marche, *Le roi René*, ii, 1875, i, pp.273, 279, 533, 536, ii, pp.180–2, 194; Martin, 'Sur un portrait de Jacques-Antoine Marcello' in *Mémoires de la Société des Antiquaires de France*, ser. 6, ix, 1900, pp.229–67; Meiss, *Andrea Mantegna as Illuminator*, 1957, *passim*).

Meiss (*op. cit.*) set out to prove that two illuminated MSS, known to have been sent as gifts by Marcello to France in the 1450s, were illuminated in part by Mantegna and his workshop. The first of these is a Latin life and passion of St Maurice with Latin verses composed by Marcello himself (Paris, Bibliothèque de l'Arsenal, MS 940; 39ff; 18.7 × 13cm.). This was commissioned by Marcello for presentation to the Ordre du Croissant, founded by René on 11 August 1448, to which Marcello was admitted, together with Francesco Sforza, on 26 August 1449, receiving a copy of its ceremonial and constitutions in the following year. In return for his admission to the Order, at whose chapters he could naturally not be present in person, he despatched this manuscript history and celebration of the Order's patron saint to Angers in June 1453 as a complimentary gift.

Meiss gave six of the lesser miniatures to a Lombard illuminator, but attributed two of the four full-page miniatures, the *Chapter of the Order of the Crescent* (f.C v) and a half-length portrait in right profile of Marcello himself (f.38v) to Mantegna. The other two full-page miniatures, of St Maurice (f.34 v) and of an elephant bearing a tower symbolizing Venice (f.39), he gave to Mantegna and assistants, along with some of the decorated initials (ff.1,8).

The second manuscript is Albi, Bibliothèque Roche-gude, MS 4 (389 ff.: 37 × 25cm.). It contains Strabo's *Geographia*, in the Latin translation made by Guarino of Verona. As Guarino's autograph MS of this translation

(now Oxford, Bodleian, Cod. Canon. Lat.301) was completed by him on 13 July 1458, and then given by him to his patron Marcello, the Albi manuscript, commissioned by Marcello for presentation to René, must have been executed after this date and presumably before 13 September 1459, the date of Marcello's prefatory letter of presentation to René. It contains two full-page miniatures – Guarino presenting his translation to Marcello (f.3 v) and Marcello presenting the manuscript to René (f.4.) – and these are attributed by Meiss to the workshop of Mantegna, sixteen of the initials (Books II to XVI) being given to Mantegna himself. Meiss also suggests that this manuscript was the *operetta* undertaken for Marcello which brought further delay in the first half of 1459 to Mantegna's departure for Mantua.

The attribution was immediately refuted in a review by Fiocco (in *Paragone*, ix, no.99, March 1958, pp.55–8), who suggested the name of Leonardo Bellini, a kinsman of Jacopo, for the St Maurice miniatures, and that of Marco Zoppo for the Strabo miniatures, this last an attribution that has found no favour. His review is followed by an essay on Leonardo Bellini by L. Moretti (pp.59–66), who also preferred a Venetian origin for the St Maurice miniatures and rejected one to Mantegna. M. Levi d'Ancona ('Postille a Girolamo da Cremona' in *Studi . . . in onore di Tommaso de Marinis*, iii, 1964, pp.53–4) proposes an attribution to Girolamo da Cremona. Robertson (*Giovanni Bellini*, 1968, pp.17–21) considers the St Maurice miniatures 'the works of a major artist', and suggests they may possibly be early works by Giovanni Bellini. Mantegna is known to have declared in 1480 (Kristeller, 1902, p.538, doc.79) that he was unused to painting small figures, and that a work Bona of Savoy, Duchess of Milan, wished him to execute for her would be better suited to a miniature-painter ('seria opera più presto da miniatore'). Bellini on the other hand certainly executed one portrait in a manuscript in the 1480s (Robertson, *op. cit.*, p.20). G. Mariani Canova (*La miniatura veneta del rinascimento, 1450–1500*, 1969, pp.2, 14–18, 141, cat.1, pp.142–3, cat.2) gives the St Maurice manuscript to an anonymous Venetian master influenced by Jacopo Bellini, and the Strabo to a Paduan master under strong Ferrarese influence. She wholly rejects any association of Mantegna with miniature-painting. For another discussion see Alexander (*Italian Renaissance Illuminations*, 1977, pp.55–9). In the compiler's view the attribution to Mantegna of any of the miniatures in these two manuscripts is not sustainable. The figure-style of the scenes is too frail and the settings, though influenced in the case of the St Maurice manuscript by Albertian perspective, are too insubstantially conceived and too atmospheric and impressionistic in treatment. Their interest for the student of Mantegna is that they illuminate the advanced artistic taste of his patron Marcello. Some association with the Bellini is likely for the St Maurice manuscript.

The influence of Mantegna on North Italian miniaturists was certainly strong (see p.87 for copies of his Mantuan paintings, p.225 for a request by a miniaturist for a work from his hand). Levi d'Ancona (*op. cit.*, pp.54–5) publishes with an attribution of some of its miniatures to Girolamo da Cremona an *Antiphonary* (London, Society of Antiquaries) whose miniatures were already attributed to Andrea and Francesco Mantegna in the sixteenth century. That of f.19 (repr. Levi d'Ancona) is a close derivation from the Ovetari *Martyrdom of St Christopher*. It must be one of the earliest imitations of this composition, and perhaps was executed *c.*1458–62. A miniature in the Cleveland Museum, attributed to Mantegna on acquisition (Milliken, 'The Pietà by Andrea Mantegna' in *Bulletin of the Cleveland Museum*, xxxix, 1952, pp.172ff) is rightly identified in Levenson–Oberhuber–Sheehan (1973, p.206) as a copy of the engraving of the *Entombment with Four Birds* (Plate 235a). This powerful influence should be attributed to Mantegna's paintings and engravings: that he worked as an illuminator seems disproved by his disavowal of 1480.

Abbreviations

of titles referred to in the Notes and Catalogue

A. in A.   *Art in America*, 1913–

A.B.   *Art Bulletin (Bulletin of the College Art Association)*, 1913–18, 1919–

Anonimo Morelliano, 1800   J. Morelli ed., *Notizia d'opere di disegno nella prima metà del secolo XVI esistenti in Padova Cremona Milano Pavia Bergamo Crema e Venezia scritta da anonimo di quel tempo (i.e. Marc' Antonio Michiel)*, Bassano, 1800.

Anonimo Morelliano, 1884   G. Frizzoni ed., *Notizia d'opere di disegno pubblicata e illustrata da D. Jacopo Morelli, seconda edizione . . .*, Bologna, 1884.

Arch. S.A.   *Archivio storico dell'arte*, 1889–

Armstrong   Lilian Armstrong, *The Paintings and Drawings of Marco Zoppo*, N.Y. & London, 1976.

A.S.L.   *Archivio storico lombardo*, 1874–

Battisti, 1965   E. Battisti, 'Il Mantegna e la letteratura classica', in *Arte, pensiero e cultura a Mantova nel primo Rinascimento in rapporto con la Toscana e con il Veneto, Atti del VI Convegno Internazionale di Studi sul Rinascimento*, Florence, 1965, pp. 23–56.

Berenson, 1901   B. Berenson, *The Study and Criticism of Italian Art*, London, 1901

Berenson, 1902   B. Berenson, *The Study and Criticism of Italian Art. Second series*, London, 1902.

Bettinelli, 1774   S. Bettinelli, *Delle lettere e delle arti mantovane*, Mantua, 1774.

Blum, 1936   I. Blum, *Andrea Mantegna und die Antike*, Strasbourg, 1936.

B.M.   *The Burlington Magazine*, 1903–

Boll. d'A.   *Bollettino d'Arte*, 1907–

Boll. M.C.di P.   *Bollettino del Museo Civico di Padova*, 1898–

Bottari, 1961   S. Bottari, 'Le mostre del Mantegna e del Crivelli', in *Arte Veneta*, xv, 1961, pp. 312–15.

Braghirolli, 1872   W. Braghirolli, 'Alcuni documenti inediti relativi ad Andrea Mantegna', in *Giornale di Erudizione Artistica*, i, 1872, pp. 194–207.

Brandolese, 1795   *Pitture, sculture, architetture ed altre cose notabili di Padova nuovamente descritte*, Padua, 1795.

Brown, 1972   C. M. Brown, 'New documents for Andrea Mantegna's Camera degli Sposi', in *B.M.*, cxiv, 1972, pp. 861–3.

Castelfranco, 1962   G. Castelfranco, 'Note su Andrea Mantegna', in *Boll. d'A.*, xlvii, 1962, pp. 23–39.

Camesasca, 1964   E. Camesasca, *Mantegna*, Milan, 1964.

Campori, 1866   G. Campori, *Lettere artistiche inedite*, Modena, 1866.

Campori, 1870   G. Campori, *Raccolta di cataloghi ed inventarii inediti*, Modena, 1870.

Cipriani, 1962   R. Cipriani, *Tutta la pittura del Mantegna*, Milan, 1962.

Coletti & Camesasca, 1959   L. Coletti, *La Camera degli Sposi del Mantegna a Mantova. Testo di L. Coletti, con un appendice di Ettore Camesasca. Milan, 1959.

Cr. d'A.   *Critica d'Arte*, 1935–42, 1949–

Dal Pozzo, 1718   Bartolommeo dal Pozzo, *Le vite de' pittori, de gli scultori, et architecti veronesi*, Verona, 1718.

D'Arco, 1857   Carlo D'Arco, *Delle arti e degli artefici di Mantova*, 2 vols, Mantua, 1857.

Degenhart, 1958   B. Degenhart in Halm, Degenhart & Wegner, *Hundert Meister Zeichnungen aus der Staatlichen Graphischen Sammlungen, München*, Munich, 1958.

Diz. biog.   *Dizionario biografico degli italiani*,

Duveen, 1941
pub. Istituto della Enciclopedia Italiana, Rome, 1960–
Duveen Bros, New York, *Duveen pictures in public collections of America*, New York, 1941.

Eisler, 1903
R. Eisler, 'Mantegnas frühe Werke und die römische Antike', in *Monatshefte über Kunst und Kunstwissenschaft*, iii, 1903, pp. 159–69.

Eremitani, 1970
S. Bettini & L. Puppi, *La Chiesa degli Eremitani di Padova*, Vicenza, 1970.

Fiocco, 1927
G. Fiocco, *L'arte di Andrea Mantegna*, Bologna, 1927.

Fiocco, 1937
G. Fiocco, *Mantegna*, Milan, 1937.

Fiocco, 1949
G. Fiocco, 'Two unknown paintings by Andrea Mantegna', in *B.M.*, xci, 1949, pp. 213–14.

Garavaglia, 1967
L'opera completa del Mantegna. Presentazione di M. Bellonci; apparati critici e filologici di N. Garavaglia. Milan, 1967. (Other editions have introductions by other authors.)

G.B.A
Gazette des Beaux-Arts, 1859–

Giehlow, 1915
K. Giehlow, 'Die Hieroglyphenkunde des Humanismus in der Allegorie der Renaissance . . .' in *J.P.K.* (Vienna Jahrbuch), xxxii, 1915, pp. 1–231.

Gilbert, 1962
C. Gilbert, 'The Mantegna Exhibition' in *B.M.*, civ, 1962, pp. 5–9.

G.S.L.I.
Giornale storico della letteratura italiana, 1893–

Hendy, 1974
P. Hendy, *European and American paintings in the Isabella Stewart Gardner Museum*, Boston, 1974.

Holzherr
Gertrud Holzherr, *Die Darstellung des Marientodes im Spätmittelalter*, Tübingen, 1971.

J.P.K.
Jahrbuch (der K.) preussischen Kunstsammlungen, 1880–

J.W.C.I.
Journal of the Warburg and Courtauld Institutes, 1937–

Knabenshue, 1959
P. D. Knabenshue, 'Ancient and mediaeval elements in Mantegna's *Trial of St. James*', in *A.B.*, xlii, 1959, pp. 59–73.

Longhi, 1926
R. Longhi, 'Lettere pittoriche. Roberto Longhi a Giuseppe Fiocco', in *Vita artistica*, i, 1926, pp. 127–39.

Longhi, 1934
R. Longhi, 'Risarcimento di un Mantegna', in *Pan: rassegna di lettere, arte e musica*, ii, no. 3, March 1934, pp. 503–12.

Luzio, 1908
A. Luzio, 'Isabella D'Este e il Sacco di Roma', in *Archivio storico lombardo*, ser. 4, x (anno xxxv), 1908, pp. 5ff, especially for section vi, 'L'inventario della Grotta d'Isabella D'Este', pp. 413–25.

Luzio & Paribeni, 1940
Reale Accademia d'Italia, *Il trionfo di Cesare di Andrea Mantegna*. A cura di A. Luzio e di R. Paribeni. Rome, 1940.

Marani, 1961
E. Marani, 'Architettura', in Istituto Carlo d'Arco, *Mantova: Le Arti*, ii, *Dall'inizio del secolo xv alla metà del xvi*, 1961.

Mantua, 1965
Arte, pensiero e cultura a Mantova nel primo rinascimento in rapporto con la Toscana e con il Veneto. Atti del VI Convegno Internazionale di Studi sul Rinascimento, Florence, 1965.

Mellini & Quintavalle, 1962
G. L. Mellini & A. C. Quintavalle, 'In margine alla Mostra del Mantegna', in *Critica d'Arte*, ix, No. 4, 1962, pp. 1–20.

Mezzetti, 1958
A. Mezzetti, 'Un "Ercole e Anteo" del Mantegna', in *Boll. d'Arte*, ser.4, xliii, 1958, pp. 232–44.

Michiel, Marc' Antonio, see Anonimo Morelliano

Millar, 1960
O. Millar, *Abraham Van Der Doort's Catalogue of the Collections of Charles I*. Edited with an introduction by O. M. London, 1960 (The thirty-seventh volume of the Walpole Society).

Millar, 1972
The inventories and valuations of the King's goods, 1649–1651, ed. by O. Millar, 1972 (The forty-third volume of the Walpole Society).

Moschetti, 1929–30
A. Moschetti, 'Le iscrizioni lapidarie romane negli affreschi del Mantegna agli Eremitani', in *Atti del R. Istituto Veneto di Scienze, Lettere ed Arti*, lxxxix-2, 1929–30, pp. 227–39.

Moschini, 1826
G. A. Moschini, *Della origine e delle vicende della pittura in Padova*, Padua, 1826.

Moschini, 1944
Vittorio Moschini, *Gli affreschi del Mantegna agli Eremitani di Padova*, Bergamo, 1944.

Paccagnini, 1969
G. Paccagnini, *Il Palazzo ducale di Mantova*, Turin, 1969.

Pallucchini, 1956
R. Pallucchini, *La pittura veneta del quattrocento*, Bologna, 1956.

Portenari, 1623
A. Portenari, *Della felicità di Padova*, Padua, 1623.

Portheim, 1886
F. Portheim, 'Andrea Mantegnas Triumph Cäsars', in *Repertorium für Kunstwissenschaft*, ix, 1886, pp. 266–80.

Posse, 1909
Königliche Museen zu Berlin. *Die Gemäldegalerie des Kaiser-Friedrich-Museums: Vollständiges beschreibender Katalog . . . bearbeitet von Hans Posse. Erste Abteilung, Die Romanischen Länder*, Berlin, 1909.

Puppi, 1972
L. Puppi, *Il trittico di Andrea Mantegna per la Basilica di San Zeno Maggiore in Verona*, Verona, 1972.

Puppi, 1975
L. Puppi, 'Andrea Mantegna: alcune note e postille', in *Antichità viva*, xiv, 1975, pp. 3–11.

Ridolfi, 1648
Carlo Ridolfi, *Le meraviglie dell'arte, Ouero le vite de gli'illvstri pittori veneti, e dello stato*, Venice, 1648.

Romanini, 1965
A. M. Romanini, 'L'itinerario del Mantegna e il 'primo' rinascimento padano-veneto', in

Arte in Europa: scritti di storia dell'arte in onore di Eduardo Arslan, i, Pavia, 1965–6, pp. 437–64.

Rossetti, 1765   G. B. Rossetti, *Descrizione delle pitture, sculture, et architetture di Padova,* Padua, 1765.

Rossetti, 1776   *Descrizione delle pitture, sculture ed architetture di Padova,* Padua, 2nd ed., 1776.

Rossetti, 1780   3rd ed. of above.

Rühmer, 1961   Review by E. Rühmer of Mantegna exhibition, Mantua, in *Pantheon,* xix, 1961, pp. cii–cvi.

Santa Giustina, 1970   P. L. Zovatto, N. Ivanoff, G. Bresciani Alvarez, D. Rup. Pepi O.S.B., P. Ant. Sartori, *La Basilica di Santa Giustina: arte e storia,* Padua, 1970.

Sartori, 1976   P. Antonio Sartori, *Documenti per la storia dell'arte a Padova,* ed. C. Fillarini, Vicenza, 1976.

Savini-Branca, 1964   S. Savini-Branca, *Il collezionismo veneziano nel '600,* Padua, 1964.

Scardeone, 1560   Bernardino Scardeone, *De Antiqvitate Vrbis Patavii, & claris ciuibus Patauinis libri tres,* Basle, 1560.

Signorini, 1985   *Opus hoc tenve: la Camera Dipinta di Andrea Mantegna, lettura storica, iconografica iconologica,* Mantua, 1985.

Simon, 1971   E. Simon, 'Dürer und Mantegna 1494', in *Anzeiger des Germanischen Nationalmuseums,* 1971–2, pp.26–32.

Suida, 1946   W. Suida, 'Mantegna and Melozzo', in *A. in A.,* xxxiv, pp. 57–72.

Tamassia, 1956   A. M. Tamassia, 'Visioni di antichità nell'opera del Mantegna', in *Pontificia Accademia Romana di Archeologia,* ser. 3, xxviii, 1956, pp. 213–49.

Testi   Laudedeo Testi, *La storia della pittura veneziana,* Bergamo, 2 vols, 1909–15.

Thode, 1897   H. Thode, *Mantegna,* Bielefeld & Leipzig, 1897.

Ventura, 1964   A. Ventura, *Nobiltà e popolo nella società veneta del '400 e '500,* Bari, 1964.

Venturi, 1914   A. Venturi, *Storia dell'arte italiana,* vii, *La pittura del quattrocento,* iii, 1914.

Weiss, 1958   R. Weiss, *Un umanista veneziano: Papa Paolo II,* Venice-Rome, 1958.

Zani, 1802   P. Zani, *Materiali per servire alla storia dell'origine e de' progressi dell'incisione in rame e in legno,* Parma, 1802.

Z.B.K.   *Zeitschrift für bildende Kunst,* 1866–1932.

Zonta & Brotto, 1922   G. Zonta & G. Brotto, *Acta graduum academicorum Gymnasii Patavini ab anno MCCCCVI ad annvm MCCCCL,* Padua, 1922.

Select Bibliography

MANTEGNA

Documents
Only books and articles containing documents referring to a number of aspects of Mantegna's life are included here.

G. A. MOSCHINI, *Della origine e delle vicende della pittura in Padova*, Padua, 1826

C. D'ARCO, *Delle arti e degli artefici di Mantova: notizie*, Mantua, 1857–(9)

A. BASCHET, 'Recherches de documents d'art et d'histoire dans les archives de Mantoue. Documents sur Mantegna' in *Gazette des Beaux-Arts*, xx, 1866, pp.318–39

W. BRAGHIROLLI, 'Alcuni documenti inediti relativi ad Andrea Mantegna' in *Giornale di Erudizione Artistica*, i, 1872, pp.194–207

P. KRISTELLER (see below) published invaluable appendices of documents in the two editions of his great book (1901, 1902). That in the German edition (1902) is much fuller. Kristeller collected much of the previously published material, but it is still indispensable to consult the works listed above

V. LAZZARINI AND A. MOSCHETTI, 'Documenti relativi alla pittura padovana' in *Archivio Veneto*, n.s., xv, 1908, pp.72–190,249–321; xvi, 1908, pp.68–102 (also as separate work, Venice, 1908, reprinted by Forni, Sala Bolognese, 1974, ed. Muraro)

G. GEROLA, 'Nuovi documenti mantovani sul Mantegna' in *Atti del Reale Istituto Veneto di Scienze, Lettere ed Arti*, lxviii, pt.2, 1908–9, pp.905–15

A. LUZIO, *La Galleria dei Gonzaga venduta all'Inghilterra nel 1627–28*, Milan, 1913

E. RIGONI, 'Nuovi documenti sul Mantegna' in *Atti del Reale Istituto Veneto di Scienze, Lettere ed Arti*, lxxxvii, pt.2, 1928, pp.1178–9 (reprinted in 1970 vol.: see under Padua)

M. D. RESTI-FERRARI, 'Aggiunta al Codice diplomatico mantegnesco del Kristeller' in Mantua, Accademia Virgiliana, *Atti e memorie*, xix–xx, 1929, pp.263–80

G. FIOCCO, 'Regesto' in his *Mantegna*, 1937 (refers to a number of documents in the archives of Padua), pp.150–73

C. M. BROWN, 'New documents concerning Andrea Mantegna' in *Burlington Magazine*, cxi, 1969, pp.538–44

C. M. BROWN, 'New documents for Andrea Mantegna's Camera degli Sposi' in *Burlington Magazine*, cxiv, 1972, pp.861–3

C. M. BROWN, 'Gleanings from the Gonzaga documents in Mantua – Gian Cristoforo Romano and Andrea Mantegna' in *Mitteilungen des Kunsthistorischen Institutes in Florenz*, xvii, 1973, pp.153–9

L. PUPPI, 'Nuovi documenti (e una postilla) per gli anni padovani del Mantegna' in *Antichità viva*, xiv, 1975, pp.3–11

A. SARTORI, *Documenti per la storia dell'arte a Padova*, ed. C. Fillerni, Vicenza, 1976

A. MARTINDALE, *The Triumphs of Caesar*, London, 1979 (for appendix of documents)

Primary Sources
The earliest notes on Mantegna's works we possess are those made by Marc'Antonio Michiel. They were published by Jacopo Morelli in *Notizia d'opera di disegno nella prima metà del secolo XVI* (Venice, 1800; new ed. by Frizzoni in 1884 as the Anonimo Morelliano). Mantegna figures in the dialogue *De Ivsticia pingenda* by the Mantuan humanist and physician Battista Fiera, first published in his *Hymni divini* (Mantua, 1515) and edited with a translation and notes by J. Wardrop, London, 1957. The earliest known life of Mantegna was published by Vasari, in the first edition of his *Le Vite de più eccellenti architetti, pittori et scultori italiani* (i, 1550, pp.508–13). A second, independent short biography by the Paduan antiquary and local historian, Bernardino Scardeone, was published in 1560 in his *De antiquitate urbis Patavii et claris civibus Patavinis* (Basle, pp.371–3). Comparison between it and the revised and enlarged version of Mantegna's life which Vasari published in his second edition (1568, i, pp.487–92) shows that

both took material almost verbatim from the account of Mantegna given by the artist's Paduan friend and contemporary Girolamo Campagnola the Elder (*c*.1433/5 – 1522) in his lost Latin letter to the philosopher N. Leonico Tomeo concerning the artists of Padua (see pp.16, 393). The woodcut portrait of Mantegna in this edition of Vasari is taken from the bronze bust in Sant'Andrea, Mantua.

Many contemporary and early references to Mantegna are collected by Kristeller in the appendices to the two editions of his monumental work on the artist (1901,1902, see below). Others are noted in the course of the present book.

Early Literature

The life in Carlo Ridolfi, *Le meraviglie dell'arte, Ouero le vite de gli'illvstri pittori veneti, e dello stato* (Venice, 1648, pp.63–73) is chiefly of value for its references to work by or attributed to Mantegna. His portrait also is taken from Mantegna's bust, with a knight's chain added. Mantegna preserved a conventional reputation as a great artist, but there was little real interest in his work in the Baroque age, except for the *Triumphs*. Neither Mantua nor Padua produced significant studies of their own artistic history in the later seventeenth or early eighteenth century. The first important Mantuan study of Mantegna was produced by the Abbate Severio Bettinelli (1718–1808) in his *Delle lettere e delle arti mantovane* (1774), a general survey of Mantua's contributions to culture. About the same time Paduan antiquaries also began more serious investigation into their city's artistic traditions, and the Cavaliere Giovanni de' Lazara (1744–1833) even commissioned the Venetian engraver Francesco Novelli to engrave Mantegna's principal works for a publication which never appeared. A controversy between Mantua and Padua for the honour of having given birth to Mantegna was successfully terminated in favour of Padua by Pietro Brandolese's *Testimonianze intorno alla patavinità di Andrea Mantegna* (Padua, 1805).

The interest of eighteenth-century antiquaries and collectors in Mantegna's prints as *incunabula* of the genre was considerable, and they also collected his pictures as illustrations of the history of painting. As a painter, however, he was first restored to significance in the history of Italian, as opposed to North Italian, art by the encomiums of Luigi Lanzi, in his *Storia pittorica della Italia* (1809). The diffusion of Mantegna's reputation north of the Alps, especially in Germany, owed much to Goethe's brilliant descriptions of the Ovetari frescoes in his *Italienische Reise* (1816–17) and his later essay on the *Triumphs*.

The serious investigation of Mantegna's life dates from the Abbate Giannantonio Moschini, *Della origine e delle vicende della pittura in Padova* (1826), still indispensable as a source. The art-historical study of his work really begins with the Marchese Pietro Selvatico (1803–80) of Padua, who edited his life and compiled an account of his works for the first Milanesi edition of Vasari (v, Florence, 1849, pp.157–241: reprinted in the second, iii, 1878, pp.383–459). Undoubtedly the major contribution of nineteenth-century scholarship to the study of Mantegna was made by Crowe and Cavalcaselle in their *History of Painting in North Italy* (London, 1871). Their chapters on Mantegna

(i, pp.214–419) survey his life and work with their usual thoroughness of physical examination, acumen of perception and command of source-material. They also contain an admirable critical census of works by or attributed to Mantegna, still useful to consult for the additions which unscrupulous forgery or hopeful enthusiasm had assembled by the middle of the century around the genuine corpus, and which their sharp judgement did much to shear away. Morelli's application of his method to the *oeuvre* of Mantegna (*Die Galerien zu München und Dresden*, Leipzig, 1891, pp.225–34) suffers from his belief that all the early works were executed on panel and all the late ones on canvas. Meanwhile archival investigation began unearthing many new and significant documents concerning the artist (see above), culminating in the researches of Alessandro Luzio in Mantua and Vittorio Lazzarini in Padua.

General Monographs

The first separate study of Mantegna in English, Julia Cartwright's *Mantegna and Francia*, appeared as late as 1881.

The first scholarly art-historical monograph is that of H. Thode, *Mantegna*, Bielefeld & Leipzig, 1897.

In 1901 appeared the first edition, in London and in English translation, of Paul Kristeller's *Andrea Mantegna*, followed by a second German edition, published in Berlin in 1902. In spite of inevitable errors, notably of dating, that time has shown up, this great book remains the one indispensable work on the artist, and is a model of perceptiveness and thoroughness. Kristeller did not attempt a full catalogue raisonné of Mantegna's works, compiling what are essentially annotated lists of works by or attributed to the artist and of lost works.

The following are the principal monographs on Mantegna, which for one reason or another should still be consulted:

C. YRIARTE, *Mantegna, sa vie – sa maison – son tombeau – son oeuvre dans les musées et les collections*, Paris, 1901 (1900)

F. KNAPP, *Andrea Mantegna: des Meisters Gemälde und Kupferstiche*, Stuttgart, 1910 (in series *Klassiker der Kunst*)

G. FIOCCO, *L'arte di Andrea Mantegna*, Bologna, 1927 (2nd ed. Venice, 1959)

G. FIOCCO, *Mantegna*, Milan, 1937

E. TIETZE-CONRAT, *Mantegna: paintings, drawings, engravings: complete edition*, London, 1955. An introductory essay, followed by the first attempt at a proper catalogue raisonné of Mantegna's works, a task in which the author has been followed only by R. Cipriani and N. Garavaglia (see below)

G. PACCAGNINI (with A. Mezzetti and M. Figlioli), *Andrea Mantegna*, Mantua, 1961 (Catalogue of the exhibition of Mantegna and his circle held at Mantua in 1961)

R. CIPRIANI, *Tutta la pittura del Mantegna*, Milan, 1962 (3rd ed.)

E. CAMESASCA, *Mantegna*, Milan, 1964

N. GARAVAGLIA, *L'opera completa del Mantegna*, Milan, 1967 (with introductions by different authors in its Italian, French and English editions)

In addition the study of Mantegna in A. VENTURI, *La pittura del quattrocento*, iii, 1914 (vol. vii of his *Storia dell'arte italiana*) and BERENSON's lists should be consulted.

Other General Monographs and Studies
Those starred are of greater importance.

G. J. WAAGEN, *Über Leben, Wirken und Werke der Maler Andrea Mantegna und Luca Signorelli* in *Historisches Taschenbuch*, s.3,i,1850

A. F. G. A. WOLTMANN, *Andrea Mantegna*, 1878, in *Kunst und Künstler des Mittelalters*, Abt. 2,1, n.51

M. CRUTTWELL, *Andrea Mantegna*, London, 1902 (reissued 1908)

A. BLUM, *Mantegna: biographie critique*, Paris, 1911

G. PACCHIONI, *Andrea Mantegna (Piccola collezione d'arte)*, Florence, 1921

U. OJETTI, *Andrea Mantegna: discorso tenuto nel Palazzo ducale di Mantova . . . nel quinto centenario della morte dell' artista*, Rome, 1931

A. NEPPI, *Mantegna*, (Profili) Rome, 1934

W. G. CONSTABLE, *Mantegna and humanism in fifteenth century Italy*, Newcastle, 1937 (*William Henry Chorlton Memorial Lectures*, 18)

W. BOECK, *Mantegna. Der Meister der oberitalienischen Frührenaissance*, Burg b. M., 1942

R. WILENSKI, *Mantegna and the Paduan School*, London, 1947 (Faber Gallery)

P. D'ANCONA, *Mantegna*, Milan, 1956

A. KUTAL, *Andrea Mantegna*, Prague, 1958 (*Nové prameny*, sv21)

★ G. PACCAGNINI, *Andrea Mantegna*, Milan, 1961

P. HETHERINGTON, *Andrea Mantegna* (*Masters*, no.33), London, 1964

★ A. SMITH, *Andrea Mantegna and Giovanni Bellini* (London, National Gallery, Themes and Painters, 12), London, 1975

Special Studies and Periodical Literature
The studies listed here cover broader aspects of Mantegna's art: for the bibliography of single works see the entries in the catalogue.

a) *Books*

V. FAGGIOTTO, *Mantegna a Padova. Suoi dipinti nel convento di S. Agostino*, Padua, 1887

H. G. BEYEN, *Andrea Mantegna en de verovering der ruimte in de schilderkunst*, The Hague, 1931

I. BLUM, *Andrea Mantegna und die Antike*, Strasburg, 1936

M. MEISS, *Andrea Mantegna as illuminator: an episode in Renaissance art, humanism and diplomacy*, Glückstadt, 1957

W. PAATZ, *Giorgione in Wetteifer mit Mantegna*, 1959 (Abhandlungen der Heidelberger Akademie der Wissenschaften, Phil.-Hist. Klasse, 1959, Abh.3)

A. MARTINDALE, *The Triumphs of Caesar*, London, 1979 (added here for its coverage of other aspects of Mantegna's art)

b) *Articles*

R. EISLER, 'Mantegna's frühe Werke und die römische Antike' in *Monatsberichte über Kunst und Kunstwissenschaft*, iii, 1903, pp.159–69

W. SUIDA, 'Mantegna and Melozzo' in *Art in America*, xxxiv, 1946, pp.57–72

A. M. TAMASSIA, 'Visioni di antichità nell'opera del Mantegna' in *Pontificia Accademia Romana di Archeologia*, ser.3, xxviii, 1956, pp.213–49

O. KURZ, 'Sannazaro e Mantegna' in *Studi in onore di Riccardo Filangieri*, ii, Naples, 1959, pp.277–83

A. M. ROMANINI, 'L'itinerario del Mantegna e il "primo" rinascimento padano-veneto' in *Arte in Europa: scritti di storia dell'arte in onore di Eduardo Arslan*, i, Pavia, 1965–6, pp.437–64

C. GILBERT, 'The Mantegna Exhibition' in *Burlington Magazine*, civ, 1962, pp.5–9

E. RÜHMER, Review of the Mantegna Exhibition held at Mantua in 1961, in *Pantheon*, xix, 1961, pp.cii–cvi

S. BOTTARI, 'Le mostre del Mantegna e del Crivelli' in *Arte Veneta*, xv, 1961, pp.312–15

G. CASTELFRANCO, 'Note su Andrea Mantegna' in *Bolletino d'Arte*, xlvii, 1962, pp.23–39

G. L. MELLINI AND A. QUINTAVALLE, 'In margine alla mostra del Mantegna' in *Critica d'Arte*, ix, no.4, 1962, pp.1–20

M. MURARO, 'Mantegna e Alberti' in *Arte, pensiero e cultura a Mantova nel primo Rinascimento*, Florence, 1965 (see Mantua, below), pp.103–32

E. BATTISTI, 'Il Mantegna e la letteratura classica' in *Arte, pensiero e cultura a Mantova nel primo Rinascimento in rapporto con la Toscana e con il Veneto (Atti del VI Convegno Internazionale di Studi sul Rinascimento)*, Florence, 1965, pp.23–56

E. POGÁNY-BALÁS, 'Prototypes in Mantegna's engravings', chapter ii of her *Influence of Rome's antique monumental sculptures on the great masters of the Renaissance*, 1980, pp.48–57

C. ROMANO, 'Verso la maniera moderna: da Mantegna a Raffaello' in Einaudi, *Storia dell'arte italiana*, Parte Seconda, ed. F. Zeri, ii, 1981, pp.5–85

PADUA

There is a vast local literature of Padua. For the history and cultural life of the city in the fifteenth century see:

M. SAVONAROLA, *Libellus de magnificis ornamentis regie civitatis Padue*, ed. Segarizzi, 1902 (R.I.S. xxxiv)

B. SCARDEONE, *De antiquitate urbis Patavii et claris civibus Patavinis libri tres*, Basle, 1560

There is no full modern study of the city in the fifteenth century.

For documents and studies of artistic life in fifteenth-century Padua, in addition to Lazzarini and Moschetti (cit. DOCUMENTS above) see also:

E. RIGONI, *L'arte rinascimentale in Padova: studi e documenti*, Padua, 1970 (the collected edition of the author's fundamental documentary studies originally published as articles in journals)

A. SARTORI, *Documenti per la storia dell'arte a Padova*, ed. C. Fillerni, Vicenza, 1976

For the city's churches and monuments see:

C. BELLINATI AND L. PUPPI, *Padova: basiliche e chiese*, Padua, 1975

L. PUPPI AND F. ZULIANI, *Padova: case e palazzi*, Padua, 1977

To the art of the city in the fourteenth and fifteenth centuries the best introductions, with much bibliographical information, are the catalogues of two exhibitions held in the Palazzo della Ragione, Padua. These are:

Da Giotto al Mantegna, Padua, 1974

Dopo Mantegna: arte a Padova e nel territorio nei secoli xv e xvi, Padua, 1976

MANTUA

The most useful early local history is the vast eighteenth-century compilation of AMADEI, *Cronaca universale della città di Mantova*, published in five vols., Mantua, 1954–7.

For ecclesiastical history see I. DONNESMONDI, *Dell' istoria ecclesiastica di Mantova*, Mantua, 1612–16 (facsimile reprint 1977).

For modern, scholarly accounts of the history, culture and art of the city see MANTUA: Istituto Carlo d'Arco per la storia di Mantova, *Mantova: la storia, le lettere, le arti*, Mantua, 1958–65 (by various authors). These volumes contain much original research and admirable bibliographical documentation.

For early Renaissance culture in Mantua see also Florence: Istituto Nazionale di Studi sul Rinascimento, *Arte, pensiero e cultura a Mantova nel primo Rinascimento in rapporto con la Toscana e con il Veneto*, Atti del VI Convegno internazionale di Studi sul Rinascimento (27 September–1 October 1961), Florence, 1965.

For the medieval and Renaissance topography of the city the fundamental work is still S. DAVARI, *Notizie storiche topografiche della città di Mantova nei secoli xiii. xiv. e xv.*, Mantua, 1903 (enlarged reprint of studies originally published in the *Archivio Storico Lombardo*, 1897). This should be supplemented and corrected from the articles on the topography of Mantua published by E. MARANI as 'Vie e piazze di Mantova – analisi di un centro storico' in successive numbers of the periodical *Civiltà Mantovana*, from no.1, 1966 –.

Of importance for Mantegna is G. PACCAGNINI, *Il Palazzo ducale di Mantova*, Turin, 1969.

For the building activities of Alberti and Fancelli in Mantua see:

E. J. JOHNSON, *S. Andrea in Mantua: the building history*, Pennsylvania, 1975

A. SALZONA, *Mantova città dell'Alberti: il San Sebastiano: tomba, tempio, cosmo*, Parma, 1979 (with valuable appendix of documents)

C. VASIĆ VATOVEĆ, *Luca Fancelli architetto: epistolario gonzaghesco*, Florence, 1979 (an important collection of documents concerning the building projects of Mantegna's Gonzaga patrons)

THE GONZAGA

For a published repertoire of the Archivio Gonzaga, Mantua, see *L'Archivio Gonzaga di Mantova*, ed. P. Torelli & A. Luzio, 1920–2.

The most useful modern history of the family is G. CONIGLIO, *I Gonzaga*, Milan, 1967 (with bibliography).

Its ramifications are still most easily traced in well-documented genealogies of the Gonzaga published in P. LITTA, *Famiglie celebri italiane*, iv, Milan, 1835.

See also:

Rome, Accademia Nazionale dei Lincei, and Mantua, Accademia Virgiliana, *Mantova e i Gonzaga nella civiltà del Rinascimento: atti del Convegno . . .*, Mantua, 1977

G. AMADEI AND E. MARANI, *I Gonzaga a Mantova*, Milan, 1975, an account of the Gonzaga in terms of their patronage

D. K. CHAMBERS AND J. MARTINEAU, eds., *Splendours of the Gonzaga*. exh. cat., London, Victoria and Albert Museum, 1981

For the Marchese Lodovico Gonzaga and his son Federico the fundamental contemporary narrative source is A. SCHIVENOGLIA, *Cronaca di Mantova dal 1445 al 1484*, of which one version was published by C. d'Arco in J. MUELLER, *Raccolta di cronisti e documenti storici lombardi inediti*, ii, Milan, 1856, pp.119–94.

For the Marchese Francesco Gonzaga a contemporary narrative source is J. PROBO D'ATRI, *Croniche del Marchese di Mantova* (pub. in *Archivio storico lombardo*, vi, 1879, pp.38–68, 333–66, 500–13).

For the Gonzaga as patrons of humanism see LUZIO-RENIER, 'I Filelfo e l'umanismo alla corte dei Gonzaga' in *G.S.L.I.*, xvi, 1890, pp.119–217.

ISABELLA D'ESTE

There are two principal full-length biographies:

J. CARTWRIGHT, *Isabella d'Este, Marchioness of Mantua*. London, 1903 (often reprinted)

J. LAUTS, *Isabella d'Este, Fürstin der Renaissance, 1474–1539*, Hamburg, 1952

Both depend largely on the studies of A. LUZIO and G. RENIER which are fundamental for our knowledge of Isabella. Those especially relevant to this book are:

'Delle relazioni d'Isabella d'Este Gonzaga con Ludovico e Beatrice Sforza' in *Archivio storico lombardo*, xxvii, 1890, pp.74–119, 346–99, 619–74

Mantova e Urbino. Isabella d'Este ed Elisabetta Gonzaga nelle relazioni familiari e nelle vicende politiche, Turin, 1893

'Niccolò da Correggio' in *Giornale storico della letteratura italiana*, xxi, 1893, pp.205–64, xxii, 1893, pp.65–119

'Il lusso di Isabella d'Este Marchesa di Mantova' in *Nuova Antologia*, cxlvii, 1896, pp.441–69; 'Il guardaroba', cxlviii, 1896, pp.294–324; 'Gioelli e gemme'; cxlix, 1896, pp.261–86, 666–88, 'L'arredo degli appartamenti'

(A. Luzio solus) 'Isabella d'Este e la Corte Sforzesca' in *Archivio storico lombardo*, xv, 1901, pp.145–76

La coltura e le relazioni letterarie d'Isabella d'Este, Turin, 1903. (A rare publication collecting articles originally published in the *Giornale storico della letteratura italiana* from 1899–1903, as follows: LUZIO-RENIER, 'La coltura e la relazioni letterarie di Isabella d'Este Gonzaga' in *G.S.L.I.*, xxxiii, 1899, pp.1–62 (La coltura); xxxiv, 1899, 'Le relazioni litterarie. I. Gruppo mantovano', pp. 1–97; xxxv, 1900, 'II. Gruppo ferrarese', pp.193–257; xxxvi, 1900, 'III. Gruppo lombardo', pp.325–49; xxxvii, 1901, 'IV. Gruppo Veneto', pp.201–45; xxxviii, 1901, 'V. Gruppo emiliano', pp.41–70; xxxix, 1902, 'VI. Gruppo dell'Italia centrale', pp.193–251; xl, 1902, 'VII. Gruppo meridionale', pp.289–333; xlii, 1903, 'Appendici', pp.75–111.

For Isabella's artistic patronage the recent studies of C. M. BROWN are also fundamental (for the literature of the Studiolo see *Catalogue*).

'"Una testa di Platone Antica con la punta dil naso di cera": unpublished negotiations between Isabella d'Este and Niccolò and Giovanni Bellini' in *Art Bulletin*, li, 1969, pp.372–7

'"Lo insaciabile desiderio nostro di cose antique": new documents for Isabella d'Este's collection of antiquities' in *Cultural Aspects of the Italian Renaissance: essays in honour of Paul Oskar Kristeller*, Manchester, 1976

'The Grotta of Isabella d'Este' in *Gazette des Beaux-Arts*, ser.6, lxxxix, 1977, pp.155–71; xci, 1978, pp.72–82

C.M. BROWN with A.M. LORENZONI, 'Isabella d'Este e Giorgio Brognolo nell' anno 1496' in *Atti e memorie dell'Accademia Virgiliana*, n.s. xli, 1973, pp.97–122

C.M. BROWN with A.M. LORENZONI, *Isabella d'Este and Lorenzo da Pavia: documents for the history of art and culture in Renaissance Mantua* (Travaux d'Humanisme et Renaissance, 189), Geneva, 1982

Index of Locations of Works Illustrated

Index of Names